A Companion to Contemporary British and Irish Poetry, 1960–2015

Blackwell Companions to Literature and Culture

This series offers comprehensive, newly written surveys of key periods and movements and certain major authors, in English literary culture and history. Extensive volumes provide new perspectives and positions on contexts and on canonical and post-canonical texts, orientating the beginning student in new fields of study and providing the experienced undergraduate and new graduate with current and new directions, as pioneered and developed by leading scholars in the field.

Published Recently

78. *A Companion to American Literary Studies*	Edited by Caroline F. Levander and Robert S. Levine
79. *A New Companion to the Gothic*	Edited by David Punter
80. *A Companion to the American Novel*	Edited by Alfred Bendixen
81. *A Companion to Literature, Film, and Adaptation*	Edited by Deborah Cartmell
82. *A Companion to George Eliot*	Edited by Amanda Anderson and Harry E. Shaw
83. *A Companion to Creative Writing*	Edited by Graeme Harper
84. *A Companion to British Literature, 4 volumes*	Edited by Robert DeMaria, Jr., Heesok Chang, and Samantha Zacher
85. *A Companion to American Gothic*	Edited by Charles L. Crow
86. *A Companion to Translation Studies*	Edited by Sandra Bermann and Catherine Porter
87. *A New Companion to Victorian Literature and Culture*	Edited by Herbert F. Tucker
88. *A Companion to Modernist Poetry*	Edited by David E. Chinitz and Gail McDonald
89. *A Companion to J. R. R. Tolkien*	Edited by Stuart D. Lee
90. *A Companion to the English Novel*	Edited by Stephen Arata, Madigan Haley, J. Paul Hunter, and Jennifer Wicke
91. *A Companion to the Harlem Renaissance*	Edited by Cherene Sherrard-Johnson
92. *A Companion to Modern Chinese Literature*	Edited by Yingjin Zhang
93. *A New Companion to Digital Humanities*	Edited by Susan Schreibman, Ray Siemens, and John Unsworth
94. *A Companion to Virginia Woolf*	Edited by Jessica Berman
95. *A New Companion to Milton*	Edited by Thomas Corns
96. *A Companion to the Brontës*	Edited by Diane Long Hoeveler and Deborah Denenholz Morse
97. *A Feminist Companion to Shakespeare, Second Edition*	Edited by Dympna Callaghan
98. *A New Companion to Renaissance Drama*	Edited by Arthur F. Kinney and Thomas Hopper
99. *A Companion to Literary Theory*	Edited by David Richter
100. *A Companion to Literary Biography*	Edited by Richard Bradford
101. *A New Companion to Chaucer*	Edited by Peter Brown
102. *A Companion to the History of the Book, Second Edition*	Edited by Simon Eliot and Jonathan Rose
103. *A Companion to Contemporary British and Irish Poetry, 1960–2015*	Edited by Wolfgang Görtschacher and David Malcolm

A COMPANION TO

CONTEMPORARY BRITISH AND IRISH POETRY, 1960–2015

EDITED BY
WOLFGANG GÖRTSCHACHER AND
DAVID MALCOLM

WILEY Blackwell

This edition first published 2021
© 2021 John Wiley & Sons Ltd

All rights reserved. No part of this publication may be reproduced, stored in a retrieval system, or transmitted, in any form or by any means, electronic, mechanical, photocopying, recording, or otherwise, except as permitted by law. Advice on how to obtain permission to reuse material from this title is available at http://www.wiley.com/go/permissions.

The right of Wolfgang Görtschacher and David Malcolm to be identified as the authors of the editorial material in this work has been asserted in accordance with law.

Registered Offices
John Wiley & Sons, Inc., 111 River Street, Hoboken, NJ 07030, USA
John Wiley & Sons Ltd, The Atrium, Southern Gate, Chichester, West Sussex, PO19 8SQ, UK

Editorial Office
The Atrium, Southern Gate, Chichester, West Sussex, PO19 8SQ, UK
For details of our global editorial offices, customer services, and more information about Wiley products, visit us at www.wiley.com.

Wiley also publishes its books in a variety of electronic formats and by print-on-demand. Some content that appears in standard print versions of this book may not be available in other formats.

Limit of Liability/Disclaimer of Warranty
While the publisher and authors have used their best efforts in preparing this work, they make no representations or warranties with respect to the accuracy or completeness of the contents of this work and specifically disclaim all warranties, including without limitation any implied warranties of merchantability or fitness for a particular purpose. No warranty may be created or extended by sales representatives, written sales materials, or promotional statements for this work. The fact that an organization, website, or product is referred to in this work as a citation and/or potential source of further information does not mean that the publisher and authors endorse the information or services the organization, website, or product may provide or recommendations it may make. This work is sold with the understanding that the publisher is not engaged in rendering professional services. The advice and strategies contained herein may not be suitable for your situation. You should consult with a specialist where appropriate. Further, readers should be aware that websites listed in this work may have changed or disappeared between when this work was written and when it is read. Neither the publisher nor authors shall be liable for any loss of profit or any other commercial damages, including but not limited to special, incidental, consequential, or other damages.

Library of Congress Cataloging-in-Publication Data

Names: Görtschacher, Wolfgang, 1960– editor. | Malcolm, David, 1952– editor.
Title: A companion to contemporary British and Irish poetry, 1960–2015 / edited by Wolfgang Görtschacher, David Malcolm.
Description: Hoboken, NJ : Wiley-Blackwell, 2021. | Series: Blackwell companions to literature and culture ; 103 | Includes bibliographical references and index.
Identifiers: LCCN 2020013124 (print) | LCCN 2020013125 (ebook) | ISBN 9781118843208 (cloth) | ISBN 9781118843246 (adobe pdf) | ISBN 9781118843253 (epub)
Subjects: LCSH: English poetry–20th century–History and criticism. | English poetry–21st century–History and criticism. | Irish poetry–20th century–History and criticism. | Irish poetry–21st century–History and criticism.
Classification: LCC PR611 .C65 2020 (print) | LCC PR611 (ebook) | DDC 821/.91409–dc23
LC record available at https://lccn.loc.gov/2020013124
LC ebook record available at https://lccn.loc.gov/2020013125

Cover Design: Wiley
Cover Image: Courtesy of Lothar Ponhold

Set in 10.5/13pt Garamond by SPi Global, Pondicherry, India
Printed and bound by CPI Group (UK) Ltd, Croydon, CR0 4YY

10 9 8 7 6 5 4 3 2 1

Contents

Notes on Contributors ix
Preface xvii

Section 1 Introduction—1960–2015: A Brief Overview of the Verse 1

1   Introduction—1960–2015: A Brief Overview of the Verse 3
    Wolfgang Görtschacher and David Malcolm

Section 2 Contexts, Forms, Topics, and Movements 29

a. Institutions, Histories, Receptions

1   Some Institutions of the British and Irish (Sub)Fields of Poetry:
    Little Magazines, Publishers, Prizes, and Poetry in Translation 31
    Wolfgang Görtschacher

2   Anthologies: Distortions and Corrections, Poetries, and Voices 63
    David Kennedy

3   Minding the Trench: The Reception of British and Irish Poetry
    in America, 1960–2015 71
    Daniel Bourne

4   Readers: Who Reads Modern Poetry? 87
    Juha Virtanen

b. Genre, Kind, Technique

1   Manifestos and Poetics/Poets on Writing 97
    Daniel Weston

2   The Genres of Contemporary British and Irish Poetry 107
    Gareth Farmer

3	The Elegy *Stephen Regan*	119
4	The Sonnet *David Fuller*	129
5	Free Verse and Open Form *Lacy Rumsey*	143
6	Satire *David Wheatley*	159
7	The Traditional Short Lyric Poem in Britain and Ireland, 1960–2015 *Tim Liardet and Jennifer Militello*	169
8	(Post)Modern Lyric Poetry *Alex Pestell*	179
9	The Long Poem After Pound *Will May*	191

c. *Groupings, Themes*

1	Generations *Robert Hampson*	201
2	The Movement *David Malcolm*	213
3	The Liverpool Poets *Ludmiła Gruszewska-Blaim*	223
4	The British Poetry Revival 1960–1978 *Robert Sheppard*	235
5	Poets of Ulster *Martin Ryle*	245
6	The Martian School: Toward a Poetics of Wonder *Małgorzata Grzegorzewska*	255
7	Linguistically Innovative Poetry in the 1980s and 1990s *Scott Thurston*	263
8	Concrete and Performance Poetry *Jerzy Jarniewicz*	273
9	Performances of Technology as Compositional Practice in British and Irish Contemporary Poetry *John Sparrow*	283
10	"Here to Stay": Black British Poetry and the Post-WWII United Kingdom *Bartosz Wójcik*	305

11	Anglo-Jewish Poetry *David Malcolm*	319
12	Gay and Lesbian Poetry *Prudence Chamberlain*	329
13	Women Poets in the British Isles *Marc Porée*	339
14	Irish Women Poets *Monika Szuba*	349
15	Religious Poetry, 1960–2015 *Hugh Dunkerley*	359
16	Love Poetry *Eleanor Spencer*	371
17	Political Poetry *Ian C. Davidson and Jo Lindsay Walton*	381
18	Radical Landscape Poetry in Scotland *Alan Riach*	393
19	*Coincidentia Oppositorum*: Myth in Contemporary Poetry *Erik Martiny*	403
d.	The Past and Other Countries	
1	History and Poetry *Jerzy Jarniewicz*	417
2	British and Irish Poets Abroad/in Exile *Glyn Pursglove*	427
Section 3	**Poets and Poems: Canon, Off-Canon, Non-Canon**	**441**
1	John Agard *Ralf Hertel*	443
2	Eavan Boland *Peter Hühn*	453
3	Paul Durcan *Jessika Köhler*	461
4	James Fenton *David Malcolm*	473
5	Bill Griffiths *Ian C. Davidson*	485
6	Excluding Visions of Life in Poems by Thom Gunn *Tomasz Wiśniewski*	501

7	"Now Put It Together": Lee Harwood and the Gentle Art of Collage *Robert Sheppard*	511
8	Listening to Words and Silence: The Poetry of Elizabeth Jennings *Jean Ward*	523
9	"Forever in Excess": Barry MacSweeney, Consumerism, and Popular Culture *Paul Batchelor*	535
10	When Understanding Breaks in Waves: Voices and Messages in Edwin Morgan's Poetry *Monika Kocot*	549
11	Grace Nichols *Pilar Sánchez Calle*	561
12	F. T. Prince *Will May*	573
13	Kathleen Raine *Glyn Pursglove*	583
14	"Everything Except Justice Is An Impertinence": The Poetry of Peter Riley *Peter Hughes*	595
15	Anne Stevenson *Eleanor Spencer*	607
16	Paula Meehan—Vocal Cartographies: Public and Private *Wolfgang Görtschacher*	619
Index		629

Notes on Contributors

Paul Batchelor is an associate professor of English literature and creative writing at Durham University. He wrote his PhD on Barry MacSweeney's poetry at Newcastle University, and edited *Reading Barry MacSweeney* (NCLA/Bloodaxe, 2013). His poetry collections are *The Sinking Road* (Bloodaxe, 2008) and *The Love Darg* (Clutag, 2014). He reviews for the *Times Literary Supplement*.

Daniel Bourne is a poet, translator of poetry from Polish, editor, and professor of English and environmental studies at The College of Wooster in Wooster, Ohio, where he has taught creative writing and poetry since 1988. He attended Indiana University (Bloomington), where he received his Bachelor of Arts in comparative literature and history in 1979, and a Master of Fine Arts in creative writing in 1987. He was a Fulbright fellow in Poland between 1985 and 1987. Bourne is an editor and founder of the *Artful Dodge* literary magazine.

Prudence Chamberlain is a lecturer in creative writing at Royal Holloway, University of London. She is the author of *The Feminist Fourth Wave: Affective Temporality* (Palgrave Macmillan, 2017) and the coauthor of *House of Mouse* (KFS, 2016). Her poetry reviews have featured in *Poetry Review*, *Hix Eros*, and *Shearsman Magazine*, and her critical writing on feminism in both *Gender and Education* (2016) and *Social Movement Studies* (2014).

Ian C. Davidson is a poet and a critic. His recent poetry publications include *Gateshead and Back* (Crater, 2017), *On the Way to Work* (Shearsman, 2017), *In Agitation* (KFS, 2014), and *The Tyne and Wear Poems* (Red Squirrel, 2014). He edited the special Bill Griffiths issue for the *Journal of British and Irish Innovative Poetry*, and has published extensively on space and poetry and poetics. His recent critical work has examined relationships between mobility and writing in the work of Diane di Prima, George and Mary Oppen, Philip K. Dick, and Patrick Hamilton. After living in Wales for most of his life, he moved to Newcastle upon Tyne and then Dublin, where he works in UCD as professor of English, Drama and Film.

Hugh Dunkerley is reader in creative writing and contemporary poetry at the University of Chichester in the United Kingdom, where he runs the MA in creative writing. He is a critic and poet. His most recent poetry collections are *Hare* (2010) and *Kin* (both Cinnamon Press 2019).

Gareth Farmer is a lecturer in modern and contemporary literature at the University of Bedfordshire, United Kingdom. He is the coeditor of the open access *Journal of British and Irish Innovative Poetry*.

David Fuller is emeritus professor of English and former chairman of the Department of English Studies at the University of Durham. From 2002 to 2007, he was also the university's public orator. He has held a University of Durham Sir Derman Christopherson fellowship, and fellowships at the Huntington Library, the Centre for Reformation and Renaissance Studies of the University of Toronto, and the Yale Center for British Art. He is the author of *Blake's Heroic Argument* (Croom Helm, 1988), *James Joyce's "Ulysses"* (Harvester, 1992), *Signs of Grace* (with David Brown, Cassell, 1995), and essays on a wide range of poetry, drama, and novels from Medieval to Modern, including work on Chaucer, Spenser, Marlowe, Shakespeare, Ben Jonson, Blake, Shelley, Keats, T. S. Eliot, William Empson, and the theory and practice of criticism.

Wolfgang Görtschacher, senior assistant professor at the University of Salzburg, is the author of *Little Magazine Profiles: The Little Magazines in Great Britain, 1939–1993* (1993) and *Contemporary Views on the Little Magazine Scene* (2000), owner-director of the small press Poetry Salzburg, editor of the little magazine *Poetry Salzburg Review*, coeditor of the academic journal *Moderne Sprachen*, and the President of AAUTE (Austrian Association of University Teachers of English). He (co)edited *So Also Ist Das/So That's What It's Like: Eine zweisprachige Anthologie britischer Gegenwartslyrik* (2002), *Raw Amber: An Anthology of Contemporary Lithuanian Poetry* (2002), *The Romantic Imagination: A William Oxley Casebook* (2005), *Fiction and Literary Prizes in Great Britain* (2006), *Ovid's "Metamorphoses" in English Poetry* (2009), *Mozart in Anglophone Cultures* (2009), and *Sound Is/As Sense* (2016, with David Malcolm).

Ludmiła Gruszewska-Blaim is associate professor of English and American literature at the University of Gdańsk. She specializes in cultural semiotics, (post)modernist poetics, and utopian studies. She is the author and (co)editor of books on twentieth- and twenty-first century literature and cinema. Her book publications on poetry include *Visions and Re-visions in T. S. Eliot's Poetry* (1996; in Polish); *Essays on Modern British and Irish Poetry* (2005; coedited with David Malcolm); *Here/Now—Then/There: Traditions, Memory, Innovation in Modern British and Irish Poetry* (2011; coedited with David Malcolm).

Małgorzata Grzegorzewska is a professor in the Institute of English Studies at the University of Warsaw. Her principal research interests lie in Shakespeare studies, Renaissance poetry, and the interrelations of drama, verse, and metaphysical and theological concerns.

Robert Hampson is professor of modern literature at Royal Holloway, University of London. During the 1970s, he coedited the poetry magazine *Alembic*. He coedited *New British Poetries: The Scope of the Possible* (Manchester UP, 1993); *Frank O'Hara Now* (Liverpool UP, 2010); *Clasp: Late Modernist Poetry in London in the 1970s* (Shearsman Books, 2016); and *The Salt Companion to Allen Fisher* (with cris cheek, Shearsman Books, 2019). His collection of poems, *Reworked Disasters* (KFS, 2013), was long-listed for the Forward Prize.

Ralf Hertel is a professor of English literature at the University of Trier, Germany. He is the author of *Making Sense: Sense Perception in the British Novel of the 1980s and 1990s* (Brill Rodopi, 2005) and coeditor of *Performing National Identity: Anglo-Italian Cultural Transactions* (with Manfred Pfister, Brill, 2008) and *On John Berger: Telling Stories* (with David Malcolm, Brill Rodopi, 2015).

Peter Hughes is a poet, painter, and the founding editor of Oystercatcher Press. He was born in Oxford in 1956, based in Italy for many years, and now lives on the Norfolk coast. He is the author of over a dozen books of poetry, which include *Nistanimera*, *The Sardine Tree*, *The Summer of Agios Dimitrios*, *Behoven*, and *The Pistol Tree Poems*. Nathan Thompson has described the latter as "flickering, intense, innovative and utterly mesmerizing."

Peter Hühn was for many years a professor of British studies at the University of Hamburg. His principal interests include: English poetry of the sixteenth and seventeenth centuries, Modernism, Yeats, and contemporary poetry. He has also worked extensively in the field of narratology. His current research projects include: concepts of plot in the British and American crime novel of the eighteenth and nineteenth centuries and, in particular, the popular genre in the twentieth century; contemporary British and Irish poetry, postmodernist tendencies. A recent publication is *Facing Loss and Death: Narrative and Eventfulness in Lyric Poetry* (De Gruyter, 2016).

Jerzy Jarniewicz is a Polish poet, translator, and literary critic, who lectures in English at the University of Łódź. He has published 12 volumes of poetry, 13 critical books on contemporary Irish, British, and American literature and has written extensively for various journals, including *Poetry Review*, *Irish Review*, and *Cambridge Review*. He is the editor of the literary monthly *Literatura na Świecie* (Warsaw) and has translated the work of many novelists and poets, including James Joyce, John Banville, Seamus Heaney, Raymond Carver, Philip Roth, and Edmund White. His most recent works include two anthologies: *Sześć Poetek Irlandzkich – Six Irish Women Poets* (Biuro Literackie, 2012) and *Poetki z Wysp – Women Poets from Britain* (Biuro Literackie, 2015), which he selected and translated.

David Kennedy was senior lecturer in English and creative writing at the University of Hull, United Kingdom. He researched modern and contemporary poetry in English with special interests in elegy, ekphrasis, and experimental writing. He published articles in *English*, *Irish Studies Review*, and *Textual Practice*. He is the author of *Necessary Steps: Poetry, Elegy, Walking, Spirit* (Shearsman Books, 2007) and *The Ekphrastic Encounter* *in Contemporary British Poetry and Elsewhere* (Ashgate, 2012), and he is the coauthor of *Women's Experimental Poetry in Britain 1970–2010: Body, Time and Locale* (Liverpool UP, 2013). David Kennedy died in 2017.

Monika Kocot is assistant professor in the Department of British Literature and Culture at the University of Łódź, Poland. Her academic interests include: contemporary Scottish poetry, Native American prose and poetry, literary theory, literary criticism, and translation. She is the author of *Playing Games of Sense in Edwin Morgan's Writing* (Peter Lang, 2016) and coeditor of *Języki (pop)kultury w literaturze, mediach i filmie* (Wydawnictwo Uniwersytetu Łódzkiego, 2015). She is a member of the Association for Cultural Studies, the Association for Scottish Literary Studies, and the Polish Cognitive Linguistics Association. She is the President of the K. K. Baczyński Literary Society.

Jessika Köhler is a lecturer in English literature, specializing in Irish studies, at the University of Hamburg and the Leuphana University of Lüneburg. She is currently researching space and place in contemporary Irish poetry.

Tim Liardet is a professor of poetry at Bath Spa University, England, and a Poetry Book Society selector. Twice shortlisted for the T. S. Eliot Prize, for *The World Before Snow* (Carcanet) in 2015 and *The Blood Choir* (Seren) in 2006, Tim Liardet has produced 10 collections of poetry to date. He has also been long-listed for the Whitbread Poetry Prize, and has received several Poetry Book Society Recommendations, a Poetry Book Society Pamphlet Choice, an Arts Council England Writer's Award, a Society of Authors Award, and a Hawthornden fellowship. His most recent collection is *Arcimboldo's Bulldog: New and Selected Poems* (Carcanet, 2018).

Jo Lindsay Walton took his Master's degree in social and political theory at Birkbeck, and is completing a PhD in creative writing at Northumbria University on finance and speculative fiction. His publications include the novel *Invocation* (Critical Documents, 2013). He coedits the poetry reviews journal *Hix Eros* and the poetry micropress Sad Press.

David Malcolm is a professor of English at SWPS University of Humanities and Social Sciences in Warsaw. He previously taught for twenty-eight years at the University of Gdańsk. He has published extensively on British and Irish fiction and poetry. His translations of Polish and German literature have been published in Europe, the UK, and the USA. He is co-organizer of the *Between.Pomiędzy* Festival of Literature and Theatre which has been held annually in Sopot, Poland, since 2010.

Erik Martiny has taught Anglophone literature, art, and film in Cork, Aix-en-Provence, Saint-Germain-en-Laye, and Paris. He currently teaches preparatory school students at the Lycée Henri-IV in Paris. His work has focused on literature and the visual arts. His articles appear in the *TLS*, *The London Magazine*, *The Wallace Stevens Journal*, and *The Cambridge Quarterly*. His book on the poetics of filiation, *Intertextualité et filiation paternelle* *dans la poésie anglophone*, was published in 2008. He has also written on the connections between film and fiction, having edited a volume of essays, *Lolita: From Nabokov to Kubrick and Lyne* (Editions Sedes, 2009). He also edited *A Companion to Poetic Genre*. His debut novel *The Pleasures of Queueing* (Mastodon Publishing) came out in 2018.

Will May is a senior lecturer in English at the University of Southampton. He is the author of *Stevie Smith and Authorship* (OUP, 2010) and *Postwar Literature: 1950–1990* (Longman, 2010), and editor of *The Collected Poems and Drawings of Stevie Smith* (Faber, 2015) and the essay collection *Reading F. T. Prince* (Liverpool UP, 2015). He is currently writing a history of whimsy in Anglo-American poetry.

Jennifer Militello has produced three collections of poetry with Tupelo Press, *A Camouflage of Specimens and Garments* (2016), *Body Thesaurus* (2013), named a finalist for the Alice Fay di Castagnola Award by Marilyn Hacker, and *Flinch of Song* (2009), winner of the Tupelo Press First Book Award, as well as the chapbook *Anchor Chain, Open Sail* (Finishing Line, 2006). Her poems have appeared in *American Poetry Review*, *The New Republic*, and *The Paris Review*. She teaches in the MFA program at New England College.

Alex Pestell's study *Geoffrey Hill: The Drama of Reason* was published by Peter Lang in 2016. He has edited John Wilkinson's *Schedule of Unrest: Selected Poems* (Salt, 2014) and written on Pound, Williams, Bunting, and Zukofsky. He lives in Berlin.

Marc Porée is professor of English literature at the École Normale Supérieure in Paris (PSL). As a romanticist, he has published numerous articles and chapters on the major Romantic poets. He also writes on British contemporary fiction and/or poetry and translates from English into French (Lord Byron, Joseph Conrad, Thomas de Quincey, Ann Radcliffe, R. L. Stevenson), chiefly for Gallimard. He occasionally contributes to the online review *En Attendant Nadeau*.

Glyn Pursglove retired from his position as a reader in English at Swansea University in 2015. He has published many books and articles on English poetry from the seventeenth century to the present. His most recent book was *Oro Español: Traducciones Inglesas de Poesía Española de los Siglos Diecisés y Diecisiete* (Ediciones Universidad de Valladolid, 2014).

Stephen Regan is professor of English at Durham University, where he is also the Director of the Centre for Poetry and Poetics. He is the author of two books on Philip Larkin, and he has written extensively on the work of W. B. Yeats, Seamus Heaney, and other Irish poets. His essays on modern poetry have appeared in *The Cambridge History of English Poetry* (2010), *The Cambridge Companion to Twentieth-Century English Poetry* (2008), and *The Oxford Handbook of Modern Irish Poetry* (2012). He is editor of *Irish Writing: An Anthology of Irish Literature in English 1789–1939* (Oxford UP, 2004), and also edited the new Oxford World's Classics edition of George Moore's *Esther Waters* (Oxford UP, 2012).

Alan Riach is professor of Scottish literature at Glasgow University, general editor of the collected works of Hugh MacDiarmid, author of *Representing Scotland in Literature, Popular Culture and Iconography* (2004) and coauthor of *Arts of Resistance: Poets, Portraits and Landscapes of Modern Scotland* (2009), described by the *Times Literary Supplement* as "a landmark book," *Arts of Independence: The Cultural Argument and Why It Matters Most* (2014), and *Arts and the Nation* (2017). His books of poems include *Homecoming* (2009) and *The Winter Book* (both Luath Press, 2017).

Lacy Rumsey is associate professor of English at the École Normale Supérieure de Lyon. He has published extensively on British and American poetry, with a particular focus on rhythm. Recent essays include a reassessment of the free-verse prosody of Walt Whitman's *Leaves of Grass*, an analysis of the meters of Louis MacNeice's *The Burning Perch*, and studies of contemporary British poets R. F. Langley and Jeff Hilson. He is currently completing a book on the prosody of free verse.

Martin Ryle is emeritus reader in English at the University of Sussex. His research interests include twentieth-century Irish writing in English, and he has published articles on Paul Muldoon, John McGahern, and Derek Mahon. He is a member of the editorial advisory board of *Green Letters*.

Pilar Sánchez Calle is senior lecturer of English and American Literature at the University of Jaén, Spain. Her research focuses on contemporary English and North American literature, with special emphasis on the representation of gender, identity, and exile. Some of her publications include "No City of God: Urban Images in the Fiction of Nella Larsen and Jessie Fauset," "Private Dreams, Public Realities: An Analysis of Female Characters in Ronald Firbank's *The Flower Beneath the Foot*," and "The Artist as a Mongrel Girl: Mina Loy's *Anglo-Mongrels and the Rose*."

Robert Sheppard's two main literary critical works are *The Poetry of Saying* (Liverpool UP, 2005) and *The Meaning of Form in Contemporary Innovative Poetry* (Palgrave, 2016), though he has written a monograph on Iain Sinclair and edited a companion to the work of Lee Harwood. His poetry is partly collected in *Complete Twentieth Century Blues* (Salt, 2008) and selected in *History or Sleep* (2015), from Shearsman, who publish other works, including the collaboratively written volume of fictional poetry, *Twitters for a Lark: Poetry of the European Union of Imaginary Authors* (2017). He lives and writes in Liverpool, United Kingdom, and is emeritus professor of poetry and poetics at Edge Hill University.

John Sparrow is a poet and digital artist. He is interested in materiality and the use of forms as rhetorical devices, particularly as they relate to live performance, modular and reflexive writing, and generative texts. He likes to explore texts whose compositions are affected by external influences, and allow for chance and random processes to infiltrate the writing process. He is currently completing a PhD in generative digital poetics. He lives in Phoenix, Arizona, with his wife and cats.

Eleanor Spencer teaches in the Department of English Studies at Durham University, where she is also Vice Principal and senior tutor at St. Chad's College. She was previously a Frank Knox Memorial fellow at Harvard University, and is the editor of the *New Casebooks on American Poetry since 1945* (Palgrave Macmillan, 2017).

Monika Szuba is lecturer in English literature at the University of Gdańsk, Poland. Her research, which mainly focuses on twentieth and twenty-first century poetry, is informed by environmental humanities and phenomenological perspectives. She is the editor of *Boundless Scotland: Space in Scottish Fiction* (University of Gdańsk Press, 2015) and coeditor, with Julian Wolfreys, of *The Poetics of Space and Place in Scottish Literature* (Palgrave, 2019). She is the author of *Contemporary Scottish Poetry and the Natural World: Burnside, Jamie, Robertson and White* (Edinburgh UP, 2020).

Scott Thurston is reader in English and creative writing at the University of Salford. A poet and critic, he has written several volumes of poetry and published widely on innovative writing. He edited *The Salt Companion to Geraldine Monk* (2007) and compiled a book of interviews with innovative poets called *Talking Poetics* (Shearsman Books, 2011). Thurston also coedits the *Journal of British and Irish Innovative Poetry* and co-organizes The Other Room poetry reading series in Manchester.

Juha Virtanen is lecturer in contemporary literature at the University of Kent. His monograph, *Poetry and Performance During the British Poetry Revival 1960–1980: Event and Effect*, was published by Palgrave Macmillan in 2017. His own poetry publications include *Back Channel Apraxia* (Contraband, 2014) and *–LAND* (Oystercatcher Press, 2016). He coedits *DATABLEED* together with Eleanor Perry.

Jean Ward is an associate professor at the Institute of English and American Studies of Gdańsk University, Poland. She specializes in religious poetry, is the author of *Christian Poetry in the Post-Christian Day: Geoffrey Hill, R. S. Thomas, Elizabeth Jennings* (Peter Lang, 2009), has contributed to collections of critical essays both in English and in Polish, on Jennings's poetics and her relationship with other poets, including George Herbert, G. M. Hopkins, T. S. Eliot, and David Jones.

Daniel Weston is senior lecturer of English literature at the University of Greenwich. His monograph, *Contemporary Literary Landscapes: The Poetics of Experience*, was published by Ashgate in 2017. He has published work on modern and contemporary poetry, prose fiction, and non-fiction, with particular emphasis on literary geographies and place writing.

David Wheatley is a reader in English and creative writing at the University of Aberdeen. He is the author of six collections of poetry, including *The President of Planet Earth* (Carcanet, 2017), and the author of the critical study *Contemporary British Poetry* (Palgrave, 2014). He has also edited the poetry of James Clarence Mangan (2003) and of Samuel Beckett (2009), for Gallery Press and Faber and Faber, respectively.

Tomasz Wiśniewski was for several years the Deputy Director for Research in the Institute of English and American Studies at the University of Gdańsk. He is a cofounder of the Between.Pomiędzy Festival, and the founder of the Beckett Research Group in Gdańsk. He has published *Complicite, Theatre and Aesthetics* (Palgrave Macmillan, 2016), and a monograph on Samuel Beckett (Universitas, 2006). He is a member of the editorial board of the global portal *The Theatre Times* and the literary quarterly *Tekstualia*.

Bartosz Wójcik is a translator, literary critic, and cultural manager. He has published scholarly papers on the works of, among others, Patience Agbabi, Jean Binta Breeze, Linton Kwesi Johnson, Kei Miller, Mutabaruka, Michael Smith, and Derek Walcott. He is the author of *Afro-Caribbean Poetry in English: Cultural Traditions* (Peter Lang, 2015) and works at the Centre for the Meeting of Cultures in Lublin, Poland (spotkaniakultur.com).

Preface

With such a long, multi-authored book on such a complex and provocative subject, editors of necessity feel that the reader deserves a few words of explanation before he/she starts to read it.

In our choice of topics and poets, we have been guided by what we felt to be important and useful. We are well aware that another two editors would have approached the field quite differently. We have aimed to open up contemporary British and Irish poetry to a variety of readers in order to give them some sense of the richness of individual poets, genres, forms, techniques, traditions, concerns, and institutions that make up these two distinct but interrelated poetries.

We have encouraged the authors of the essays in this volume to shape their contributions as they thought best. As readers of poetry, we have a fondness, *inter alia*, for technical analysis of rhythm, meter, and sound. Not all the authors share this interest to the same degree, although all their analyses and interpretations are well-grounded in the textual material of the poetry they discuss. Such diversity is as it should be. Further, we have allowed authors a latitude in the length of their essays. Some contributions are more concise than others. However, we insisted that the extent of the longer essays be justified in terms of the complexity and interest of the subjects that they address. Further, several essays are provocative and do not bow to established pieties. Again, surely, this is as it should be.

The volume has been several years in preparation. As a result, while we have tried to make sure it is as up-to-date as possible, some poets in the meantime may have published additional poems, and commentators published new studies. But this is an inevitable part of discourse in modern and contemporary literary studies.

Readers will be struck by the absence of separate essays on some well-known and outstanding poets. Philip Larkin, Ted Hughes, Seamus Heaney, Tony Harrison, and Geoffrey Hill are obvious examples, as is Carol Ann Duffy. We felt that the world did not need another separate essay on Larkin or Heaney, for instance. But a glance at the list of contents and the index to this volume will show that such celebrated poets (eximious within an extravagance of writers) appear continually throughout the volume in discussions of wider issues. In the essays on individual writers, we have chosen poets who deserve greater individual prominence than they have achieved hitherto, or writers who are emerging as major poetic voices.

From a personal perspective, we note with sadness the death of one of our contributors, the gifted poet and critic David Kennedy. In addition, we thank D. M. de Silva for his advice. We also thank the editorial team at Wiley-Blackwell for their patience and support.

Wolfgang Görtschacher
David Malcolm

SECTION 1
Introduction—1960–2015: A Brief Overview of the Verse

1.1
Introduction—1960–2015: A Brief Overview of the Verse

Wolfgang Görtschacher and David Malcolm

Introduction

The story is a well-known one, and this volume presents it in individual essays. The Movement. Alvarez's *The New Poetry*. The Liverpool poets. The Northern Irish. The British Poetry Revival. The Martians. Linguistically innovative poetry. Black British poetry. Women's poetry. Gay and lesbian voices. The abiding forces of regional poetry. American models. The stars: Philip Larkin, Ted Hughes, Seamus Heaney, Geoffrey Hill, Tony Harrison, Paul Muldoon, and Carol Ann Duffy.

It occurred to us that we could retell that story here. But it had been told so often, and is told, we believe—with much else besides (thematic and genre- and technique-centered essays, essays on writers within and without any obviously stellar grouping)—in the span of pieces contained in this volume. We felt we should do something different.

Our premises are twofold. First, the best and fullest engagement with poetry is an engagement, above all, with individual poems. Second—and this is, to a degree, a corollary of the first premise—this engagement involves an analysis and interpretation of what we would call technique, that is, the formal properties of a piece of verse. These properties include line length, stress placement, meter, and a panoply of phonological features (rhyme and other sound effects). These we conceive to be integral to the meaning of a poem, as much as—and in conjunction with—thematic reference and imbrication in the historical and social contexts. These premises have guided the organization of the introduction.

A Companion to Contemporary British and Irish Poetry, 1960–2015, First Edition.
Edited by Wolfgang Görtschacher and David Malcolm.
© 2021 John Wiley & Sons Ltd. Published 2021 by John Wiley & Sons Ltd.

It consists of three parts. In the first, we suggest that a great deal of modern criticism of poetry does everything in its power to avoid speaking about technical aspects of any piece or body of verse. We are not sure why, except that it is probably easier to maunder on impressionistically about the topics of a piece of verse as Fiona Sampson does than to sit down and actually analyze a poem. We contend, however, that if you do not analyze and interpret technique, you are at best only doing half your job. Thus, the second part of this opening chapter contains brief analyses of 20 poems of substance from the period embraced by this collection. Restrictions of available space limit how much we can do in any analysis. We have adopted a minimum technique of analysis, which has the merit of being accessible. We hope readers can see the general principles underlying our approach. We contend that this set of analyses offers some interesting insights into how British and Irish poetries are configured in the second half of the twentieth century and at the beginning of the twenty-first century. Our discussions perhaps allow a slightly different—and complementary—story to the traditional one. It certainly brings with it some unexpected juxtapositions. Thus, third, we offer some general remarks on British and Irish poetry in the period.

1.

It is, of course, very difficult to prove an absence.[1] However, let us suggest that although the contemporary discussion of contemporary poetry is complex and valuable, there is a tendency to avoid the technical. There is a disposition among commentators to talk of the contextual and the thematic, but not what one might call the formal or the technical aspects of poetry. Let us present some examples.

Here Martin Booth writes about Thom Gunn's poetry in *British Poetry 1964 to 1984* (1985).

> Gunn wrote with an urgency that was appropriate to the times. This gained him few readers. What got him far more and was to extend his reputation were his poems that were about matters close to the common heart. Lorry drivers, "rockers" in leather jackets, Elvis Presley, death and, in more recent books, homosexuality and drugs. (226–227)

The topical focus (a correct one, surely, let it be noted) is evident here, as it is in Michael Schmidt's earlier *A Reader's Guide to Fifty Modern British Poets* (1979), in a comment on Roy Fuller's poetry.

> His landscape is finally not Africa but suburbia where, as in the war poems, and sometimes with equal power, he celebrates arrivals, departures, the long ennui. (250)

Here, however, justice compels one to note that Schmidt, elsewhere in this important study, alludes, if fleetingly, to formal aspects of texts. For example, he writes of Fuller's defense of "threatened forms and values" (245), and of Gunn's use of "strict form and literary idiom," in contradistinction to his (Gunn's) poems' subject matters (378). One should also note Schmidt's ringing assertion in *Reading Modern Poetry* (1989):

> The abiding meaning of any poem is a function of technical properties —whether deliberately or accidentally achieved – which give it life beyond its occasion and its "ideas." (56)

While the point could scarcely be made better, one is compelled to note that a lot of Schmidt's practice in his books is not much guided by it, at least not thoroughly or consistently.

Chapter 4 of David Kennedy's insightful and important book *New Relations: The Refashioning of British Poetry, 1980–1994* (1996) deals, at least in part, with Peter Reading's engagement with meter and form (120–153), but such a technique-oriented approach is not typical of the study. More representative is his Chapter 5, entitled "The Noise of Science," which focuses on poets' engagement with scientific subjects and scientific lexis (which can be seen as part of a formal concern) (153–184). A representative quotation from Keith Tuma's *Fishing by Obstinate Isles: Modern and Postmodern British Poetry and American Readers* (1998) is the following on Peter Riley's work. "The ontological concerns of Riley's poems," Tuma writes, "might call for glosses from any number of modern philosophers," such as Heidegger and Merleau-Ponty (219). It is not our intent to suggest that such a perspective is wrong, but to note that it certainly does not seem to see the formal or technical properties of Riley's verse as meaning-bearing or integral to any analysis or interpretation—or at least, not in any explicit manner.

The topical focus of much commentary on contemporary poetry is also apparent in Fiona Sampson's study *Beyond the Lyric: A Map of Contemporary British Poetry* (2012). For example, she writes the following about Carol Ann Duffy's poem "Prayer":

> "Prayer" […] offers a redemptive view of the suburbs. It suggests that their particular vision of the quotidian, evoked as a child practicing scales and the shipping forecast of the radio, could offer transcendence. (123)

It would be hard to tell from this (and this passage is representative of the way Sampson discusses verse) whether the critic is dealing with a poem, an essay, or a short story (one only knows it is not a novel because the title is not in italics). Even when there is an acknowledgement that form is important, the reference is superficial. The following is a comment on the poet Ahren Warner. He is,

> on the page at least, a brainy flâneur who seems to have emerged fully formed. Already fascinated by, and thinking through, broken poetic forms and continental philosophy when he was still in his teens, Warner is no scholarly postmodernist mumbling to himself. His is an engaged, boulevardier's voice. He may allude to philosophers and their ideas but […] does so simply because this material is within range of a well-stocked mind. His light touch with such material can be deliciously witty. (206–207)

What are these "broken poetic forms," one wants to ask? One notes no mention of the substance of verse here—line length, line breaks, rhythm, meter, and sound. What is the use of this impressionistic insubstantiality? Such comments as mentioned earlier are more disappointing because Sampson insists that her book is concerned with the "craft" that "poem-making largely involves" (280–281). It is not clear where the author deals with "craft" as we would understand the term. In justice, it has to be said that elsewhere Sampson does concern herself with something like "craft." For example, in the special numbers of *Agenda* (Spring/Summer 2011) devoted to John Burnside's poetry, she does discuss rhythmic aspects of his verse, along with sentence length, stanza and line breaks, and phonological aspects of his texts (115–118). However, the conclusions she draws from such analysis are impressionistic and subjective, and opaque. Burnside's poetry has "an accelerated, slippery tunefulness" (114), and he belongs to a "school of expanded lyricists" (119). It is very hard to know what Sampson means by either comment.

There is no excuse for such ignoring of the technical. A wide range of approaches to formal and technical aspects of verse is available to the contemporary commentator. Indeed, some have been available for a long time. Geoffrey Leech's great *A Linguistic Guide to English Poetry* (1969) is still very helpful in any discussion of poetry. Marina Tarlinskaja's *English Verse: Theory and History* dates from 1976. The first edition of Harvey Gross's and Robert McDowell's fine *Sound and Form in Modern Poetry* appeared in 1964 (the second edition dates from 1996). The following is just a selection of more recent texts that seem particularly useful in the matter of analysis and interpretation of poetry:

> Derek Attridge, *Poetic Rhythm* (1995)
> Philip Hobsbaum, *Metre, Rhythm and Verse Form* (1996)
> David Baker, ed., *Meter in English: A Critical Engagement* (1996)
> Timothy Steele, *All the Fun's in How You Say a Thing* (1999)
> Nigel Fabb and Morris Halle, *Meter in Poetry: A New Theory* (2008)
> Martin Duffell, *A New History of English Metre* (2008)
> Christoph Küper, ed., *Current Trends in Metrical Analysis* (2011)

Not all of these are easy books to read, nor are the systems of analysis they propose entirely (or at all) compatible with each other. But they are there, and they propose ways of analyzing verse that pay due attention to the specifics of the poetic text. Gross and McDowell (1996) lay down the challenge to those who would talk about poetry:

> We venture that rhythmic structure neither ornaments conceptual meaning nor provides a sensuous element extraneous to meaning: prosody is a symbolic structure like metaphor and carries its own weight of meaning. (2–3)

> Our view is that meter, and prosody in general, is itself meaning. Rhythm is neither outside a poem's meaning nor an ornament to it. (10)

In his essay "A Return to Form" (2008), Derek Attridge notes what he sees as a return to formal concerns in literary studies, after a dominance of (useful and illuminating) historical and culture-focused approaches to literature over the preceding 30 years. "Since 2005," he writes, "the signs of a revitalization of formal study have multiplied" (565). Attridge has reservations about some recent returns to form (for example, those undertaken by Terry Eagleton, Tom Paulin, and Helen Vendler), on the grounds of lack of consistency and accuracy. But he welcomes a concern with technique, indeed, a concern with form, a renewed attention to the "formal analysis" (573) that is the poem. He argues that such an approach is ethically appropriate, but is also accurate, grounded, and appropriate in literary studies. One should note that Attridge is certainly not arguing for a disregard of topic or reference to extratextual context. He is, however, urging that a good reading is one that also considers textual configurations, shapings, and substances. Such an interest in technique and form is also illustrated by Angela Leighton's illuminating *On Form: Poetry, Aestheticism, and the Legacy of a Word* (2007), which charts some of the vicissitudes of formalist and neoformalist approaches to the literary text.

2.

Here are analyses of 20 poems that we feel to be of substance from the period 1960 through 2015. The poems are discussed in chronological order. They are poems by well-known and less well-known poets.

Philip Larkin, "An Arundel Tomb" (1964) (Larkin 1964, 45–46)

The title of this poem is immediately striking. Why the indefinite article? Is it one tomb among many? Are there other examples of such tombs, with the meanings added by the poem? Further, the title refers to a documented monument, and the text itself offers an accurate description of it, except for the assertion that "little dogs" lie at the feet of the couple. A dog lies at the feet of the woman, a lion at the feet of the man.

The subject matter is clearly and rationally set forth over seven stanzas of the same length: the tomb is described (stanzas 1 and 2); the speaker's response and direct reflection are given (stanzas 2–5); general reflection on time, change, and endurance follows (stanzas 6–7). An act of observation and reflection on the part of the speaker is recorded, but that act is consistently impersonal (line 8: "the eye"; line 11: "one sees"; line 42: "us"). Order and consistency are embodied in technical aspects of the text. Each stanza contains six lines. All lines are eight syllables in length. The rhyme scheme is largely consistent (abbcac). Iambs and diambs dominate in the poem. All such features are appropriate in a text that celebrates traditional married love, unity in death, and the survival of a feudal and aristocratic past.

However, this poem is also a technically disordered piece. For example, while iambs and diambs dominate stanza 1, several other feet are prominent (amphibrachs and amphimacers). Lines 5 and 6 both end in four beat feet that can only be construed as diambs with some difficulty, and are best understood as fourth paeons (xxx/). In addition, foot divisions are uncertain at the ends of lines 2, 3, and 4. Are these amphimacers or in line 2 a single-stress foot followed by an iamb, and in lines 3 and 4 trochees followed by single-stressed feet? In a poem about unity, isolated single stresses carry a contestatory semantic weight, while in a poem about tradition and order, metrical irresolution is surely disruptive. In fact, several lines can only be scanned as iambic if the reader places the values of the metronome over natural speech, for example, stanza 3, line 5 and stanza 7, line 5. Further, the first lines of stanzas 6 and 7 both contain metrically monstrous feet: "at their identity" (xxx/xx) and "has transfigured them into" (xx/xxxx)—although other scansions are possible.

Further disorder can be seen in phonological patterning, which in this poem is always local, and in a rhyme scheme that does fracture on occasion, for example, the anisobaric rhymes in lines 10 and 12, and in lines 14 and 15. This is particularly clear in the last, seemingly triumphant stanza: lines 37 and 41 ("into / true") and lines 38 and 39 ("fidelity / to be"). It is surely important that the concluding "love" does not actually rhyme fully with the preceding "prove." In addition, in a poem celebrating unity, the persistent recurrence of enjambment (11 examples, plus the radical enjambment between stanzas 4 and 5) must disturb. One can also notice a further degree of uncertainty in the poem's puns: inter alia "proper habits" (line 3), "faithfulness in effigy" (line 14), and "blazon" (line 40). Paronomasia disrupts as much as enjambment: things are not what they seem.

Attention to technique reveals a much more ambiguous poem than a superficial reading brings. "Untruth" and disorder become as important as the survival of tradition and "love." What appears as a celebration of tradition becomes something much more questioning and fragmentary. Are there other such monuments, English history incarnate, seemingly solid and unambiguous, that reveal themselves as complex and ambiguous?

Lee Harwood, "The Sinking Colony" (1968–1969) (Harwood 2004, 153–155)

Ambiguity in history is central to Harwood's poem. Title and epigraph enact the equivoque of the rest of the poem. What is the sinking colony? Is the end and insubstantial nature of empire announced by it? Why is the epigraph a quotation from a translation of André Gide's *Les Faux-monnayeurs*? Is the factitious nature of any account signaled from the very start?

The poem itself is a designedly broken thing, the meaning of which—apart from brokenness—must remain unclear. It is divided into six sections. Sections 1, 2, 3, and 5 are in prose, without any obvious phonological or rhythmic patterning. A majority of sentences are without terminal punctuation (12 out of 21). Section 2 also contains three lines of broken verse (six noncohesive phrases, with a space between each of the first pair and the second pair). Section 4 consists of verse, but the lines are irregular in length (from 14 to 4 syllables) and in numbers of main stresses per line (from 7 to 2). It is very hard to see any traditional metrical patterning. The same is the case with the verse in section 6.

The speaker in the six sections is unstable: an "I" and a "we." Although all sections have narrative elements, there is no coherent narrative over the whole poem, and any narrative in any single section is elliptical and incomplete. Section 1 is set in British India. Section 2 refers to mountains and foothills, but whether these are those of section 1 is not clear. Similarly, the rains mentioned in section 3 may or may not be Indian rains. Are mansion, crops, and rain in section 4 those of earlier sections? Are they Indian or English? Old or modern? Section 5 shifts unambiguously to another part of the Empire, to Canada, and to another kind of weather. Section 6 with its violence may follow on from section 5, although one cannot be sure. The gate recurs here, although it is hard to see why there is a gate in a Canadian clearing.

However, there are elements of coherence in the text. The verse is not quite as disordered as it seems. The last four lines of section 4 contain two quasi-end rhymes ("alternating / skipping," "days / face"), and other lines end in echoes ("grounds / storms," "machinery / dry"). The same intermittent semi-rhyme is notable in section 6: ("shot / knots / padlock," "all this / in this"). A certain framework is offered by the recurrent motifs of rain, gate, crops, and mansion. Action, too, occurs in central parts of the British Empire (India and Canada). Two expeditions are referred to, in sections 1 and 5.

Nonetheless, it must be acknowledged that fragmentariness and a concomitant obscurity mark the poem. History (events, accounts) is a matter of incomplete and inconclusive narratives, impressions (section 4), and reflections (section 3). Unease is recurrent: the speaker in section 1 has limited possibilities; the speaker in section 2 is "unnerved"; section 3 is entitled "The ache?"; there is a "sigh" and "pain" in section 4; there is violence and "little comfort" in section 6. There are hints of coherence (mentioned earlier), but mostly "There were complexities" (section 3) and, as the speaker has it in section 5, "I cannot work it out." Empire—England?—is fragmented; the colonial power is sinking.

Seamus Heaney, "Requiem for the Croppies" (1966) (Heaney 1990, 12)

The title of the poem unambiguously announces a defiance of empire, and goes on to offer precisely what the title announces—a laudatory dirge for Irish rebels. Strikingly, this threnody for insurrection is enacted within a metropolitan and traditional English-language genre, for the requiem is a sonnet, albeit one that deviates from traditional established models.

Such deviation occurs on several levels. This sonnet is a narrative sonnet, not a lyric expression of feeling. The speaker is plural, not the traditional singular one. Subject matter does not quite fit the traditional octave/sestet division. Lines 1–4 form a focused quatrain, but the next subject (the Croppies' tactics) runs from line 5 to line 9. The remaining five lines are, thus, a decapitated sestet. Lines are mostly 10 syllables long, although six lines are longer, and lines 9, 10, 11, and 14 are considerably longer. The numbers of main stresses per line are also variable (from three to six), and the last line can legitimately be read as having between four and six main stresses. The poem certainly has iambic elements, and anywhere between six and eight feet can be scanned as iambs or diambs. But six, and possibly seven, feet are trochees or ditrochees. There are several rather long feet: for example, "through reins and rider" (line 7) should probably be scanned x/x/x; "cattle into infantry" (line 8)—/xxx/xx; and "in our broken wave" (line 12)—xx/x/. Six lines end in an unstressed syllable.

Rhyme is disruptive. The rhyme scheme template itself—abab cdcd efe efe—is not that of an established sonnet template. Further, 6 out of 14 lines end in a questionable rhyme: "barley / country" (1, 3), "infantry / day" (6, 8), "cannon / thrown / coffin" (9, 11, 13), and "conclave / wave / grave" (10, 12, 14). In this last sequence, "wave / grave" is a full rhyme, but "conclave" rhymes anisobarically with both.

The poem is an elegy for rebellion and a smack in the face to established authority. The sonnet tradition (high status, metropolitan, relatively rigid) is appropriated and undermined, perhaps by a folk tradition with its narrative celebration of outlaws and rebels and its freedom with rhyme. Like Harwood, and not like Larkin, Heaney is unambiguous about empire and history.

Ted Hughes, "Crow Tyrannosaurus" (1974) (Hughes 1974, 13–14)

Like all the texts in *Crow*, this poem has a savage subject matter, the slaughter-permeated pulse of "Creation." Crow is a brutish part of this, an avian tyrannosaurus rex. The text is appropriately marked by a violent irregularity. Line length varies—from 3 syllables to 13. The numbers of main stresses per line vary greatly too—from one to five—although, in fact, lines with similar numbers of stresses do cluster in places: for example, in stanza 6 where three-stress lines enclose a two-stress one. There is no rhyme, and no metrical regularity. Indeed, beyond noting the numbers of main stresses per line and their variability, there is probably no point in attempting a traditional metrical analysis of the poem. Stanzas 8 and 9 are set out to emphasize fracture. Fixed form has been rejected. It seems a "shapeless cry" (line 12).

But, for all that, there is a surprising degree of regularity in the text. All the first seven stanzas have four lines, and stanzas 8–10 can be seen as retaining something of a four-based shape: stanzas 8 and 9 together make up four lines, and stanza 10 consists of four phrasal units set out separately. Although the text does not rhyme, there is at least local phonological orchestration. Note the recurrence of /k/ sounds in stanza 1, and of /d/ and /b/ sounds in stanza 4. Note, too, the recurrence of related vowel sounds—/æ/, /ɛː/, /ɪ/, and /iː/—in the last line in stanza 2. There is extensive lexical repetition—"sorrow," "body," "weeping," "Alas," "grubs," "stabbed." There is certainly syntactic parallelism: for example, stanzas 2 and 3. Stanza 7 adopts a parallel "And" structure. Stanzas 8 and 9 are syntactically parallel, and also repeat the same lexis ("weeping" and "stabbed"). Further, order is created by the marked presence of homeoteleuton in the poem: "ing" endings are everywhere in the text, and stanza 10 comes near to rhyming with its repeated "ness" suffix.

The logical coherence and cohesion of the poem is also an orderly element in it. Stanza 1 introduces creation and Crow. Stanzas 2–5 show animal life and human life as death-bringing. In stanza 6, Crow reflects on all the elements mentioned earlier. Stanza 7 begins with a contradictory "But," and stanza 10 opens with a consequential "Thus."

The shapeless "blort" (line 16) that the poem seems at first sight, and, at a certain level, is, is modified by a strong ordering and coherence, by kinds of traditional shaping. The echoes of biblical free verse also give the text a somewhat ordered and traditional quality. But it is the order of savagery, the coherence of stabbing. However, the tensions in the poem's technique might alert the reader to the irony in the text's title. A crow is not a tyrannosaurus. Hyperbole is at play here (as it is in so many of Hughes's beast poems).

Geoffrey Hill, "Mercian Hymns XXV" (1971) (Hill 2006, 85)

Mercian Hymns consists of 30 short prose poems. They center on the person and deeds of the historical, but almost legendary, Anglo-Saxon king Offa, on the childhood of the modern speaker, and on the experiences of his relatives in the semi-industrial past. These are connected by motifs of digging and lost and recovered artifacts, by physical history, by memory, and by cruelty and suffering. Hymn xxv contains no reference to Offa, but it belongs wholly within the collection because it involves a recovery of the fragmented past.

The poem is neatly ordered into an opening and a closing stanza (which are precisely the same text), which bracket two stanzas amplifying the material in the first and last. The opening and closing stanzas have a liturgical and solemn, declamatory quality: "I speak this in memory." It has an appropriate formality of lexis—"childhood and prime womanhood"—although this is, to some extent, offset by the dialect (but also archaic) word "darg." It is also spoken in the present, in memory of the speaker's grandmother, and by someone who is able to brood on Ruskin's *Fors Clavigera* (although the letters therein were directed to working men).

The two central stanzas expand on the "nailer's darg" mentioned in lines 1 and 4. Although the grandmother is not directly present, the "nailshop" is, with its smell and its dust. The workshop is strangely static; in view are the effects of labor, oddly pretty ("damson-bloom") and fatal and terrible ("hare-lipped by the searing wire"). An elliptical narrative is embedded in these stanzas, implying an accident during work there. One assumes the grandmother is involved, most likely as someone attempting to care for a mutilated family member or fellow worker. The "posthumous clamour" suggests a fatal accident. As in the enfolding stanzas, language is mixed: "back of the cottage" is informal and regional; "posthumous clamour" is formal and Latinate. Ruskin, too—and hence an educated and metropolitan world—is present in the "quick forge" in stanza 3.

As with all the hymns, stanzas are interwoven by patterns of phonology: /m/ and /s/ sounds in stanzas 1 and 4, /s/ structures stanzas 2 and 3 also, as do a harsh /k/ and softer /d/, /t/, and /eɪ / in "cradle a face hare-lipped."

The point of the text is to revise a metropolitan and intellectual (if well-meaning) view of the world of manual labor. "Darg" is a harsh word for unremitting work. In a miracle of elliptical coherence, Hill brings together the present and the past, and an intellectual world and a world of labor. The hidden savagery of a West Midlands (Offa's kingdom lay there), small-scale, semi-industrial nailshop is linked to the cruelties of an Anglo-Saxon kingdom. Both must be excavated. Memory and artifact are similarly fragments of a vital but vanished past. There is a stubborn insistence on their value. All this is woven together by recurrent motif and a web of sound effects.

John Montague, "The Rough Field" (1972) (Montague 1989, 12–13)

The third section of Chapter 1 of *The Rough Field* ("Between small whin-tough fields") begins with a marginal note (as many sections of the collection do). The prose paratext contextualizes the account of the speaker's grandfather that follows, and gives the poem a rooting in a documented history and reality. It consists of three verse paragraphs of approximately the same length, organized in a perspicuous manner. First, there is a situation, captured in a daguerreotype of the speaker's grandparents; second, there is the origin of that situation, a post-Famine Ireland in which some Catholics achieve some measure of advancement. Third, the poem shifts to 60 years later, the dispersal of the patriarchal Montague's family and the changes that time has wrought on his farm.

The text is on the border of speech and verse. Lines are of a wide variety of lengths. A line is usually made of a coherent phrase (there are only 6 examples of enjambment in the poem's 43 lines). There is a relaxed rhythmic patterning, for most lines have three or four main stresses, and even the two broken lines at the paragraph breaks, when taken together, follow this pattern. Three lines are more densely stressed with five main stresses: line 16, emphasizing post-Famine mobility; line 20, embodying that mobility; and line 36, pointing to the endurance of agriculture despite the decline of the Montague farmhouse. The same kind of unobtrusive patterning can be seen in phonological aspects of the text: paragraphs 1 and 3 are governed by /s/ sounds, and even in the much less phonologically organized second paragraph, lines 16–18 are woven with /r/ sounds, and lines 19 and 20 with /p/ sounds, while /s/ runs through the paragraph up to line 24. Lines 25–29 (semantically and historically crucial) evade the prevailing /s/ patterning of the rest of the text.

The poem does drift into rhyme of sorts on occasion: lines 26 and 29—"Puritan / gentleman"; lines 30 and 31—"broken / Brooklyn"; and lines 42 and 43—"stove / stone." Such rhymes have an ironizing effect: "rustic gentleman" is nearly an oxymoron, even without the odd rhyme; pride is brought low and broken in Brooklyn; the assonance of "stove / stone" makes clear the point about the reduction of the heroic past. Similarly, the poem slips from a prosaic literalness in the double meanings of "spirit" (line 11)—vitality and alcohol; "conceit" (line 16)—arrogance and a cunning image; and "Tagues" (line 25)—both a family name and an abusive term for Catholics. But these slippages are rare. The poem says precisely what it means on the surface. It offers an account of a patriarch, his personal rise in the context of social change, a decline brought by time, and the endurance of agriculture ("Dagda's cauldron" [line 41]) that outlasts human transience. The poem is a personal account and a broader social and historical account, seen within a context of a continuance of older ways of cultivation and planting.

Jenny Joseph, "Warning" (1974) (Joseph 1992, 42)

The title of this very popular poem (according to a BBC poll in 1996) is paradoxically threatening. It points to a future of bad behavior and imperiling of social norms. However, it must—like much of the poem—be seen as ironic and humorous. The speaker's misconduct will scarcely shift the social order.

The poem is lucid in its organization. In the first stanza, the speaker indicates the forms her delinquencies will take. Stanza 1 brings in the addressee, or at least a more general "you," suggesting how one could further behave badly. But stanza 3 sets out all the conforming things that "we" all must do now. The last stanza, however, briefly suggests that the malfeasance could start now, for the sake of practice. This semantic lucidity is coupled with a rhetoric of syntactic parallelism that shapes the first three stanzas: "I shall," "you can," and "now we must." Stanza 4 breaks the pattern: it asks the only question in the poem, and has no syntactic parallelism. However, it does neatly tie the poem up by its echoing of the first words of the poem in "When," "I am," and "old."

The regularity and coherent organization of the poem are further marked rhythmically. Iambic feet clearly dominate the piece, clustering especially in stanza three, that is, in the stanza that is about the force of norms. Although there is a variation in line length—from 4 to 14 syllables—most lines vary only from 11 to 13 syllables. With very few exceptions, lines have four to five main stresses. This cohesive regularity is challenged in places, however. Amphibrachs (x/x) are scattered throughout the text, and several feet of four to five syllables (long by English versification norms) can be identified. In addition, 10 out of 22 lines end in an unstressed syllable. All this makes the poem less controlled and coherent, and perhaps less decisive and certain. But predominantly, this is a poem about disorderly behavior that is extremely orderly, and that within very traditional parameters of rhetoric and rhythm. Just as the speaker's proposed misdeeds are ultimately quite modest in their scope (and are proposed, not implemented), so the text remains within the traditional parameters of a well-made and lucid piece of verse. Its challenges to the social and cultural order are finally, at best, comic.

Anne Stevenson, "A Love Letter: Ruth Arbeiter to Major Paul Maxwell" (from Correspondences *{1974}) (Stevenson 2005, 237–238)*

Although this text is part of a longer sequence of poems, it is relatively free-standing, and can be read on its own. It would be a shame not to discuss it, as it is a fine and moving love lyric. The title, in keeping with the convention of *Correspondences: A Family History in Letters*, presents the piece as a letter (and, in fact, the poem is so laid out), but it is, of course, not a letter, strictly speaking, but a poem. However, the opening, "Dearest," and the closing, "Ruth," along with place and date do give it the appearance of a letter. The body of the text is, however, a five-stanza love poem, from a married woman to her absent lover. The piece is an extraordinary mixture of the quotidian and the ecstatic. When thinking of her lover, the speaker (writer) enters rapturous states of consciousness (a "brighter isolate planet" [line 3], "these incredible perspectives / openings entirely ours" [lines 45 and 46]), which are contrasted with worlds of children, husband, and chores. These dizzying and electric moments and spaces are, indeed, embedded in a context of others and duty. But the speaker seems so entwined in the everyday that there is no escape. She abides in a "damaging anguish" attenuated by memories, visions, intuitions.

The piece is relatively disorderly, as one might expect with such unassuaged and incurable mental pain. The five stanzas are of varying lengths (as paragraphs of a letter might be). Lines, too, vary in length—from 13 or 14 syllables to 4 or 5. Numbers of main stresses per line are also variable, from 2 or 3 through 5 or 6. There are no obvious rhymes. Enjambment is rife—for example, lines 7–9, 16–19, 21–23, 30, 31, 33, 34, 37, and 38. Only the relatively hopeless last stanza is devoid of them.

But there is phonological patterning, although it is of an astringent sort. Thus, there are hints of end rhyme: in stanza 1, "continually" (which occurs twice) and "unexpectedly," "live / love," and "eat / articulate"; in stanza 2, "home / them," and "habit of / pain of"; in stanza 3, "ago / shadow," "distance / intensity / miss," and "stone / sun"; in stanza 5, "say / continually," "children / friends," and "perspectives / numbness." But these are at best hints, half echoes, and far from full rhymes. There is some local alliteration: /d/ in lines 10, 11, and 16–19; /k/ in lines 25 and 26; /s/ in lines 26–34; and /tʃ/ in lines 43 and 44. The most marked patterning device is the prevalence of lines that end on an unstressed syllable: in stanza 1, lines 1, 2, and 6–9; in stanza 2, lines 2, 6 (perhaps), and 7–10; in stanza 3, lines 2, 4–7, 10, and 12; in stanza 4, lines 1–4 and 5–7; and in stanza 5, lines 4–7. That makes 30 lines out of a 48-line poem.

The function of all the preceding is surely to create an intensely moving but peculiarly astringent and hopeless love poem. The emotion is there in the lexis and in the technical disorder, but rhyme is weak and dissonant (if it is there at all, as more than a shadow of rhyme), and the unstressed line endings conjure a tentativeness, a longing that will not be satisfied ever (as we know from the rest of the sequence it was not).

Tony Harrison, "Turns" (1978) (Harrison 1984, 149)

"Turns" has 16 lines, but is usually seen as a species of deviant sonnet. It certainly maintains a fundamentally iambic, 10-syllable line throughout. It also has a variation on the complex rhyme scheme one associates with the sonnet. The paradox in the choice of genre—as in the case of Heaney's "Requiem for the Croppies"—lies in the way in which a traditional and established form is used to attack and subvert traditional and established order.

On the one hand, the text is marked by extreme regularity and in accord with tradition. Iambic feet (including diambs and even a triamb ["in purple Indian ink"]) dominate the poem. Lines are of a consistent 10-syllable length, although line 2 has 12 syllables (and is an alexandrine), and line 7 has 9 syllables. There is a rhyme scheme, and it is, to a degree, regular. The first four lines run abab; lines 9–12 are effe; and lines 13–16 are ghgh. Deviance occurs to some extent in the second quatrain, which is not, in fact, a quatrain, but two pairs of rhyming lines attached to other sections. Thus, lines 5 and 6 set up a cd pattern that is taken up in lines 7 and 8, but the rhyming lines are separated by a section break, enacting a break between son and father, which is far from absolute.

Despite its closely ordered echoes of the sonnet, the poem is riven by technical tensions (and, thus, enacts its subject matter of generational and social strain). There is very little phonological patterning in the poem (no sonic regularity), except in the conclusive and rhetorically powerful last two lines, with their resounding /b/, /s/, and /k/ sounds. The lines may almost all have 10 syllables, but stress placement is not regular and is often unresolved. For example, line 1 can have five or six main stresses, depending on a choice to accent "more" and "class." Line 10 must surely have seven main stresses, including the irreducible "H A H" of the father's initials, which must be scanned /// (a molossus). In line 8, there is a tension between a metronomic scansion and one more in accord with natural speech; it could be seen as consisting of a single main stress followed by five iambic feet, or as /x/|x/|x/x|/// (although even other scansions are possible). Line 14 is barely iambic and could be scanned in at least two ways: /x/|x/|x/xx|x/ or ///|x/|//x|//. This irresolution contests orderliness and control. Linguistically, the formal sonnet is permeated by informal lexis: "so folk might think" (line 11), "nowt" (line 13), "trap" (line 14), and "busk" (especially as a transitive verb) (line 15).

Finally, too, it must be stressed that this is a 16-line sonnet, and by definition deviant and contestatory. It enacts a defiance of tradition and established order, while practicing tradition and order, and employing them for its dissenting purposes.

Fleur Adcock, "The Ex-Queen Among the Astronomers" (1979)
(Adcock 1996, 1742–1743)

The title of the poem proclaims the opposition that structures it. The poem invents its own myth with figures of male astronomers on one side and the raging, disruptive ex-queen on the other. The poem's organization of its subject matter expresses this juxtaposition clearly. Stanzas 1–3 present the astronomers—male, using devices to view the universe, diminishing it as they scrutinize it. Stanzas 4 and 5 present the banished ex-queen, dangerous, constrained by the past, embittered, out for some kind of vengeance. Stanzas 6–8 present her actions as she sexually distracts or intrudes upon the astronomers' sleep and minds.

However, strangely for a poem about disorderly conduct, this text is marked by extreme regularity. Apart from lines 14, 26, and 27, every line has eight syllables. Further, lines with four main stresses predominate, although there are almost as many that are really three-main-stress lines, but which—for reasons indicated in the following text—could be read as four-main-stress lines. In fact, the poem is not quite as regular in this respect as it might seem at first. Three lines (3, 13, and 25) clearly have five main stresses. Phonology, however, is very consistent: /s/—sometimes modulated to /ʃ/ and /z/—run throughout the whole text. Rhyme is very regular—abca—although one might note that this is not a usual iambic tetrameter rhyme scheme (abab, abcb, or abba might be more readily expected). Rhythmic regularity is very clear in the text too. Almost all lines can be scanned as iambic tetrameters.

However, disorder creeps into the text, as the ex-queen invades the astronomers' bodies and minds. Enjambment is present throughout—lines 2–3, 3–4, 9–10, 15–16 (perhaps), 21–22, 23–24, 25–26, 26–27, and 29–30 (that is 18 lines out of 32). Further, while it is possible to read almost all lines as iambic tetrameters, to do so frequently requires placing main stresses on unaccented syllables in words (for example, "telescopes"—/x/x—line 7) or function words (for example, "of" in line 4, or "when" in line 8). Such metronomic readings (which the text encourages) are countered by different scansions. For example, one can read line 5—"They calculate, adjust, record"—as x/x/x/x/, but that is a mechanical scansion, and the line should probably be x/xx|x/|x/. The same tension can be observed in many lines. Metronomic order is queried by a more natural placement of stresses. Indeed, there are also several manifestly non-iambic lines—for example, line 6—"watch transits, measure distances"—which must be scanned //x|/x|/xx. Lines 24, 26, and 27 are similar in this respect.

Thus, a male order is questioned thematically, and an iambic order is challenged in rhythm and meter. However, the orderliness of the poem is assertive, and thematically one must ask what the ex-queen actually changes with her wild sexual swishing among the astronomers. She is still exiled, they go back to diminishing the stars, and the iambic metronome keeps ticking away.

Linton Kwesi Johnson, "Inglan Is a Bitch" (1980) (Johnson 1991, 13–14)

The contestation of tradition and authority noted in poems discussed earlier meets the reader (or listener) full in the face in Johnson's poem. It is a radically disruptive piece of work (as befits its speaker, his situation, and his view of the world).

This is most obviously manifested in language. The poem is in Jamaican patois, and the deviance from standard English is flaunted at almost every level: orthography (England becomes "Inglan"), phonology (the underground is rendered as "andahgroun"), and grammatical structure ("do not get fi know" [do not get to know] is not a recognized structure in standard English, although something similar exists in other English insular dialects). These examples are drawn from the first stanza. The language of the whole poem is thus (it is interesting to note that the poem shows no lexical deviance from standard English—unlike Hill's and Harrison's work).

Contestation of tradition is also present in the poem's status as a piece meant for oral delivery and public performance. In respect of poems discussed earlier, Heaney, Hughes, and Harrison are known as charismatic and powerful readers of their verse, but most encounters with their work are visual rather than aural. Johnson's poem is also a printed text, but its existence as a sung version with music (on the record *Bass Culture* [1980]) and its identification as dub poetry, which is often accompanied by music, place it within a different order of orality. Its public and performance aspect is apparent in its refrain (half the poem) and in its constant repetitions (for example, "well mi duh day wok an' mi duh nite wok / mi duh clean wok an' mi duh dutty wok" [stanza 9]), both well-attested features of oral narrative and lyric production. A surprising feature of the readily available recordings of Johnson's own performances of the poem is his relaxed, slow, benign, almost weary manner of rendition, which adds a level of meaning to the text, a gentle rhythmic quality that one might not expect.

The text plays fast and loose with established poetic tradition, too, in its freedom with rhyme. Although four stanzas rhyme aabb, there is a variety of rhyme schemes—aaaa (stanza 1), aabb- (stanza 5), -a-a (stanza 7). Indeed, sometimes repetition is used instead of rhyme— for example, "Inglan is a bitch" in several versions of the refrain, and the first two lines of stanza 9 ("nite wok / dutty wok"). Some line endings that are presented as rhymes would not count as such in much poetry—for example, stanza 12, "escapin it / fram it." At one point, the poem slips into an irresistible internal near-rhyme—stanza 11, "faktri / Brackly / crackry." Surprisingly, line length is not extremely variable. The lines of the refrain are shorter than those in the rest of the text, but they are consistently so. The line length is reasonably regular, certainly within individual stanzas, and usually fluctuates only between 8 and 10 syllables, although there are much longer lines (for example, the last line in stanza 9, or the second line in stanza 11). Main stress placement again shows some variation, but is not nearly as disordered as, for example, Hughes's "Crow Tyrannosaurus." A majority of lines have three main stresses, although there are lines that rise to five stresses (stanza 13, last two lines, or stanza 9, first two lines). The poem's status as a piece for oral performance complicates the issue of stress placement, as this is a feature (among others) that can vary radically even among the renditions of the same performer.

All these technical features are aspects of the poem's whole contestatory purport: it is the voice of the West Indian working-class diaspora, a marginalized voice of a marginalized community, insisting here on being listened to and taking its place in the literary world. Stanzas 11 to 13 enunciate part of the world of someone from this community—15 years of work in a factory, pushed out on public relief at 55—although, in fact, such experience is not limited to workers of West Indian heritage in Britain.

Yet, this text is not without its traditional and established qualities. There is a long tradition in English of public verse drawing on the experiences of working-class and marginalized groups. The ballad-like beginning of stanza 1 ("w'en mi jus' come to Landan toun") echoes a host of working-class and, for example, Irish pieces about emigration to the big city. English poetry also has a strong tradition of political verse, and at least some of that rendered in nonstandard language. John Davidson's "Thirty Bob a Week" (1894) and Hamish Henderson's "Freedom Come All Ye" (1960) are examples that spring readily to mind. As we have pointed out in the earlier text, main stress placement is not very variable, especially in the refrain. The poem's rhymes are mostly full, although the last line in several versions of the refrain ("fram it") is not, and nor are the rhymes in lines 3 and 4 of stanza 5 ("meet / sleep"). But despite these mainstream orderly aspects of the poem, it is still a rebarbative, contestatory piece, rattling at the doors of English literature (which has, of course, opened those doors to it in the subsequent 50 years).

Hilary Davies, "The Ophthalmologist" (1987/1991) (Davies 1991, 14)

The title of the text points to an everyday figure and, indeed, the subject matter is a visit to an eye doctor to be fitted for new lenses. The poem is divided into two unequal sections: one of 21 lines presents the ophthalmologist's room, work, and accouterments; a second of 11 lines presents the (presumably female) speaker's response to his ministrations. However, the poem renders the quotidian sinister by its emphasis on the power of the eye doctor, his intrusiveness ("his gentle fingers / That play around my head more intimately / Than most men's should do" [ll. 5–7]), the shadowy ambience of his room (as opposed to the "greening" [l. 29] of the world beyond), the odd attractiveness of his instruments, and the seeming impossibility of exit at the end. Indeed, the whole visit is overlaid with mythic overtones—the devilish suggestion (he shows her "All the kingdoms"—compare Matthew 4.8 and Luke 4.5), and also the way in which the underground capture of the speaker reflects the myth of Hades and Proserpina (the speaker's inability to return from the shadows to a green world is telling).

This sinister and mythological transformation of the everyday is embodied in highly accessible verse. It is free verse without rhyme, with only local sound effects, in no fixed form, and with no fixed line length. There is little enjambment; a line is usually a complete sense unit. It is a poem—at a certain level—passing itself off as a piece of everyday speech. The language is neither unduly formal nor informal, but of an educated neutrality. The language, too, is mostly literal, although it does become nonliteral at times, for example, lines 16–21, line 26, and the powerful concluding lines 31 and 32, in which the doctor/devil/lord of the underworld reveals his lures, "The honey of his systems underground." The everyday visit, in its relatively everyday language, in its accessible verse, is transmogrified into the minacious and improper.

Robert Sheppard, "Fucking Time: Six Songs for the Earl of Rochester" (Dated 1992) (Sheppard 2004, 24–27)

This appears to be, on one level, a quite Rochesterian piece—it is lewd throughout—and, on another, not at all, for it seems quite disorderly—an antithesis to Rochester's polished pentameters. Ambiguity is embedded in the title. The songs for Rochester do not look Rochesterian or like songs. The first part of the title is triply ambiguous: "fucking time" means time for fucking; it means contemptible and vexatious time; and it means that this poem is messing about with, screwing over, kicking the butt of time.

Although the sequence as a whole is made up of the same number of stanzas with the same number of lines, the layout of the piece is nontraditional and certainly non-Rochesterian. Lines are centered. Although there is a degree of similarity, lines are of substantially varied lengths and have varied numbers of principal stresses. There is much enjambment—for example, of the 12 lines of the first song, 7 run on, including the lines that end and begin all the stanzas (apart from line 1, that is). There is little rhyme, apart from that in stanza 1 in poem 6. Song 2 has metaleptic deletions. Nothing could be more different from Rochester's neoclassical technique.

But the subject matter is overtly Rochesterian, revolving around sex, physicality, disease, corruption, the bestial, and use of the body and others for advancement and sordid delectation. Even the fountains piss (song 2, line 1). There is much of dildoes, dog turds, and restless mares (song 3). Indeed, there is a kind of deviant ordering to the poem. The presence of local alliterations and consonance is unignorable. Most lines only vary between two and three main stresses. Forty five of the sequence's 72 lines end in unstressed syllables; trochees occur in 34 lines. The alliteration is part of Rochester's patterning in his verse, but the profoundly non-iambic rhythm is not. This poem is at once a telling *hommage* to the great seventeenth-century libertine poet, and yet a piece couched in a modern, innovatory idiom, yet with its own sly and disruptive patterning.

Val Warner, "England, Our England" (From Tooting Idyll {1998}) (Warner 1998, 37)

The poem is made up of the address of a homosexual lover to his partner, in which he reflects on and faces up to the outbreak of war in 1939. The title, seemingly propagandistic, is not, in fact, so. The speaker's and his partner's England is a gay one, criminalized, despised. It mutates sadly into a homophobic "England, their England" in line 12.

The organization of the subject matter is complex. In lines 1–4, the speaker wishes simply to live and die in the moment. Lines 4–7 offer the addressee's vision of appropriate conduct: to make a last stand in hell's mouth. Lines 8–10 offer a conditional "If," in which no one goes to war. In lines 10–12, England is seen as a garden facing destruction, but in lines 12–14, this England is seen, correctly, as a place that imprisons homosexuals. Lines 14–17 offer at best a limited resolution: the addressee will side with the "workers," who spit at gay men.

The poem presents movements of thought and feeling, which interweave. Different subjects melt into each other in the same line. There is much enjambment. Stanza length is irregular. One has a clear sense of a mind coping with personal, historical, and national complexities.

This sense of a mind speaking to itself is marked in the informal lexis and syntax (see ll. 1–2; note the recurrent ellipsis points, as the speaker pauses). This sense is augmented by a lack of rhyme, although all lines but line 4 have 10 syllables and four or five main stresses. Stanzas, too, are of irregular lengths, thus suggesting natural, formally unconstrained reflection. There are patterns of alliteration, to be sure (/h/ in lines 1 and 2, /l/ in lines 13–16), but these are local, and suggest intensity rather than technical shaping. One striking feature of the poem, which surely bears semantic weight, is the presence of compound lexis: "live-long," "mayfly-like" (which is doubly compounded), "blue-sky," "last-stand," "wheelchair," "twilight," "speedwell," and "birthright." Here, the whole subject of the poem—are we together, are we together with the country that disowns us?—is foregrounded. Various kinds of history (national, personal, sexually oriented) come together in a carefully realized enactment of uncertainty.

David Constantine, "Visiting" (2002) (Constantine 2004, 305)

The title points to an everyday experience and one that is a mainstay of lyric verse—a visit to a place associated with the speaker's past, in this case, a childhood garden seen from an adult perspective (ll. 5–8). However, this experience—often disturbing enough in itself—is turned into something sinister, sorrowful, and macabre.

The text is divided into three sections (of eight lines, six lines, and two lines). The first section is an account of a visit to a garden known from childhood and of the speaker's (who is not present as a personal pronoun here) response to change. The second section reveals that there are ghosts within the garden, and in it the speaker (now an "I") considers how he might wait to encounter them, perhaps until death, the "time of the naked soul" (line 11). The final two lines form a most ambiguous conclusion. The ghosts are thin, but the "I" is infinitely thin. Is the speaker a ghost forever banned from return, from reunion with the others whom he seeks to embrace?

The shift from the quotidian to the metaphysical, from the everyday to myth is embodied in a linguistic movement. The "old way in" becomes a "locus" (line 3). The visitor becomes "naked somnambule" (no article). The garden has "iron gates" and a "pit-bull" (line 4), dark lexis that contrasts with memories of pleasure in a suburban garden ("cricket," "bonfire," "snowman" [line 7]). The garden is utterly de-suburbanized and estranged in the "bars" (line 12), "the foul dog" (line 13), and the insubstantial "multitude" who throng it (line 13). The garden becomes the underworld, guarded by Cerberus, haunted by the untouchable shades.

Indeed, the whole poem is marked by unsettling movement on various other levels too. On the level of form or genre, one must ask whether this is any kind of sonnet. The main body of the poem is divided into an octave and a sestet. The final couplet pushes one to wonder if it is a 16-line sonnet. There is certainly a rhyme scheme, but it is fragmented and odd. There is no space to go into this here in detail, but a poem that rhymes "somnambule / pitbull" (ll. 3–4), or "there" (l. 6) with "enter" (in the distant line 11), is advertising its fragmentary inconclusiveness. The final line endings "I" and "infinity" court rhyme without achieving it. Line length is similarly disorderly: sections 1 and 2 have lines from 8 to 12 syllables in length; the final couplet is made up of a six-syllable line and a 10-syllable line.

Rhythmically, the text is certainly marked by a recurrent caesura, although it divides each line nonsymmetrically. It is certainly not an iambic poem. Line 12 is the only clear example of a predominantly iambic line. While there are usually four to five main stresses in lines (although not in line 9, nor in lines 15 and 16), the poem is about as hard to scan as one of Thomas Hardy's elegiac pieces (on which it is surely modeled).

The poem enacts an unsettling move from commonplace to mythic. An uneasy, hopeless experience is embodied in a deviant sonnet with deviant rhymes. It ends on a sinister ambiguity. Who is the ghost?

Paul Muldoon, "Moy Sand and Gravel" (2002) (Muldoon 2002, 8)

Despite its business-like, seemingly *realia*-based title—Moy is a documented place, there is a River Blackwater, and it is certainly credible that the town has a gravel-and-sand business and an Olympic Cinema—this poem is an ellipsis, a puzzle, a riddle. The reader is invited to ask what the hidden narrative might be that connects a film, its stars, and two industrial washing towers. The text does not offer much help.

The language is neutral to informal ("smackety-smack" [line 5]). The references are to popular entertainment of an unspecified period and to the local. Technically, the poem seems—and is—hugely disordered. It is made up of one long quasi-sentence, which is not really a grammatically acceptable sentence, lacking as it does a subject and main verb. Who comes out of the cinema? Who is taken aback? When? Under what circumstances? Line length varies wildly—from 6 to 17 syllables. Lines have three to five main stresses and no clear metrical patterning.

But there are intricate symmetries. There are two six-line stanzas. There is a complicated rhyme scheme (abacad ebeced), but it is symmetrical, and it has full rhymes. There is clear phonological patterning—for example, /t/ sounds in lines 1–3, /s/ sounds in lines 4–6, and the /t/, /w/, and /l/ sounds that run through lines 7–12. There is internal rhyme in line 10: "dredged / Blackwater's bed." Alliteration occurs symmetrically: "smackety-smack" (line 5) and "load by load" (line 11). Of course, there are two film stars and two cleaning towers.

Thus, the poem establishes a riddle and a disorder, but suggests a pattern behind the elisions. The reader is left with much freedom, but must try to make the connections (as in a traditional riddle poem). Perhaps it is thus. In the Olympic Cinema (surely a place for the gods, unconstrained by mortal issues), there is popular, romantic, glamorous love.

Outside, there is the Blackwater and the attempt to make something clean. Surely, a sexual subject matter underlies the text. On the one hand, there is the cinema's illusion; on the other, there is the reality of an irredeemable defilement. But the poem is so—fruitfully—ambiguous that other readings can also convince.

Jackie Kay, From The Adoption Papers *(1991) (Chapter 3 "The Waiting Lists"— "I Thought I'd Hid Everything") (Kay 2007, 20–21)*

This poem tells an anecdote clearly and captures a historical moment with accuracy and benignity. It is written in a relaxed free verse, with line length (from 11 to 3 syllables) and numbers of main stresses per line (from one to five) aiming to give the sense of a voice recounting an incident. One's sense of a voice talking naturally to someone is reinforced by a lack of metrical patterning (although three iambic trimeters—lines 13, 26, and 44—do occur). The three-line stanzas do not serve any purpose other than to break up the narrative into smaller and more accessible units. One wonders, indeed, if the poem would lose anything substantial if it were written out as prose.

The voice is that of a woman who is being assessed by a child adoption agency for a baby that she desperately wants, although it transpires that she values a political honesty too. The woman is Scottish, and the language has several markers of standard spoken (and sometimes written) Scots—"hid" (line 1), "widnae wan" (line 2), "she's no be" (line 5), "willnae" (line 18), "times" (line 35). The reader is made privy to an account by a woman, a Scottish woman, delivered in an accessible and informal manner. The account is humorous. The woman conceals all (or almost all) the objects that will identify her as a communist. The copies of *The Daily Worker* and the Paul Robeson poster are hidden away, and so on. The historical and national moment—this must be sometime in the 1950s in Scotland—is captured through artifacts. The narrative ends happily. The assessor, a woman too, turns out to be for peace, and not averse to the speaker's aversion to nuclear weapons. A clear, accessible, and instructive story is told, as a prelude to the darker complexities of the rest of *The Adoption Papers*.

Carol Ann Duffy, "Adultery" (1993) (Duffy 2004, 116–117)

The title is unassuaged, unsoftened. It is impossible to break up the 11 stanzas into smaller thematic units. The poem is an emotional cascade uttered by a (probably) female speaker. Is it addressed to anyone? A "you" is mentioned throughout the poem, but it is better to recognize this as a piece of self-address, rather than as address to another.

The poem seems utterly disordered. There is no rhyme. Line length is extremely variable—from 5 to 15 syllables. Numbers of main stresses per line are also variable—between three and five in most cases, although line 2 has two or three, and line 32 has seven. Indeed, it is difficult to see any regular pattern of stresses and feet in the whole poem. Single-stress feet and four- or even five-syllable feet occur frequently. For example, line 33—"in a marital bed, the tarnished spoon of your body"—appears to be patterned, thus: xx/xx/|x/x/|xx/x. This is a typical line scansion in the poem. Main stresses cluster—for example, in lines 4 and 5, in line 12, and in line 20. There is much enjambment—lines 2, 3, 6, 7, 15, 16, 25, 26, 29, 30, 41, 42, 43, and 44, and the radical interstanzaic enjambments of lines 8, 9, 12, 13, 20, and 21.

The abrasive and disjointed quality of the above is augmented by aspects of the language. Imperatives organize the text: "Wear" (line 1), "Suck" (line 13), "Do it do it do it" (line 17), "So write" (line 37). Fragments are rife: for example, "A sick, green tint" (line 4), "Sweet darkness / in the afternoon" (ll. 17–18), "Then, selfish autobiographical sleep…" (ll. 32–34), "And all / for the same thing twice" (ll. 41–42). Syntax breaks down: "up against a wall, faster" (l. 15). Punctuation goes by the board at times: "Do it do it do it" (l. 17). Questions do not have question marks—lines 28 and 43. Repetitions give a raw intensity to the text: "Do it do it do it" (l. 17), "all for the same thing twice. And all / for the same thing twice" (ll. 41–42), and "Fuck. Fuck" (l. 43).

Part of the text's disturbing quality lies in its conjunction of the literal and the figurative—simile/metaphor/metonymy. Indeed, this juxtaposition structures the poem. For example, in stanza 1, "dark glasses" (literal) join with looking "as though through a bruise" (simile). The gloves and hands of stanza 2 (literal) meet with the speaker's sense of being "naked under your clothes all day / slim with deceit" (metaphor) in stanza 3. The "telltale clock" (metonymy) morphs into the adulteress's excited face on a bed sheet (literal) in stanzas 5 and 6. And so on. This intense and powerful poem pushes constantly at the containing forces of verse, of language constraints, and of consistency (literal or nonliteral) to produce something very like a dramatic monolog of a speaker who is shaken and disturbed by the joys and terrors of her actions.

Mimi Khalvati, "Ghazal: The Servant" (2007) (Khalvati 2011, 21)

This poem announces its extraterritorial quality from the start. It is a ghazal, a Middle-Eastern and Asian form (although it has been practiced in English). The text is addressed to "Ma'mad" (the informal Persian for Mohammed). The speaker refers to herself (such reference is traditional in a ghazal) as "Maryam." The speaker is in some distress. There is a curfew. There is blood on the streets. The addressee is delayed. Children are missing. But this is a highly elliptical poem. The context and its outcome are unknown. This fragmentary quality contrasts with the text's extreme regularity. Each of the five stanzas has two lines followed by a refrain. Two eight-syllable lines are followed by a four-syllable one. Only lines 4, 10, and 14 deviate, and then only by one (possibly elided) syllable. Main stress placement is regular, and follows a 4-4-2 pattern. The refrain recurs. Rhymes are regular and predominantly full—"grows / flows / blows / throws / goes"—although there is deviancy in some rhymes—"rose" and "so," and "flame" and "time." Also "child" in stanza 5 lacks any rhyming word, and the refrain's "rain" matches nothing in the poem.

The poem aims at a non-English experience—revolution, repression, danger—and does so through a relatively unfamiliar fixed form. The poem's sinister quality lies in its fragmentary quality, and in its not quite complete regularity. Although it is an exotic piece, it echoes traditional English ballads and folk songs, and the use of those traditional forms by Wordsworth, Stevie Smith, and James Fenton. Its focus on uncertainty, danger, and betrayal is not, of course, exotic, but is part of universal human experience. The ghazal invokes the ballad, and all that ballads are about.

D. S. Marriott, "The Wreck of the Mendi" (2008) (Marriott 2008, 98–101)

The poem uses the traditional genre of the elegy to mourn the 616 Black South African soldiers drowned when their ship sank in the English Channel in 1917. The poem's epigraph is a dedication to these soldiers, and it and the text proper refer to the documented circumstances of the sinking and the deaths. The subject matter is presented in three sections: sections I and II offer complementary narrative accounts of the sinking and the conduct of the soldiers as they meet death; section III views the event from the speaker's present, looks at the result of the disaster, and ends in a (traditional) memorial for those lost at sea. Each section begins with a long sentence, stretching over several three-line stanzas, followed by shorter ones.

The speaker of the poem is unnamed, and, indeed (unlike the speaker in Hopkins's "The Wreck of the Deutschland"—to which the poem's title and subject matter clearly refer), makes no appearance within the poem. Unlike Hopkins's text, too, the poem is written in what is effectively free verse. The three-line stanzas have lines of quite substantially varying lengths. Main stresses, too, vary, although only from two to four. The piece is unrhymed. Relatively short lines allow a focus on the constituent phrases of the text, for example, in the second stanza of section II: "the hull breached, overrun / men in the wrack / gasping in a peopled darkness." This appears to be the only function of such division.

However, the poem is marked by a far from prosaic linguistic strategy. There is a degree of lexical and consequently semantic mystery to the text. For example, "instress" is used twice (in I.5 and II.8), but not in any sense that Hopkins would recognize. Equally unusual is the use of the word "burls" (a burl is a growth on a tree with a deformed grain) in II.1. ("Burl" occurs in a similar metaphorical sense in "The Wreck of the Deutschland.") The word "reeved" (twined, twisted) is used in II.7—and it is used in "The Wreck of the Deutschland" too. The word "tain" (a French word—not strictly an English one—for the silvering used on mirrors) occurs in II.5, along with "dredges" as a plural noun (this last is very obscure, unless the meaning of a mixture of grains, like the mixture of the South African dead, is being activated).

Further, there is a marked degree of opacity of reference in many phrases. It is very hard to gloss I.9. The relevance of the phrase "less the lash" in II.1 is not clear. (Is it a reference to slavery or indentured labor, but, if so, why is it here? Is it a reference to Hopkins's verse?) It is difficult to paraphrase II.7 and II.8. While the general import of III.1 can be intuited—the "black load-bearers" are the dead—but who is the "him" that they carry? One certainly must work to unpick the complexities of III.5—the "unaccounted-for blood," prayers silvering the "dredges." However, this is not incompetence, but an essay at a vatic dignity—and one that recalls Hopkins's verbal strategy in "The Wreck of the Deutschland." The substantially forgotten, marginalized Black soldiers (abandoned to their fate by the vessel that sank the Mendi) are recalled into a dignified mystery. Introductory sentences are suitably grand, references are to a canonical English poem, and the dead are reshaped in numinous mystery. They are themselves, South Africans of many peoples, who meet a cruel end nobly, but the poem's ending locates them as some of the British maritime war dead who "have no grave but the sea" (quoting from the Tower Hill Memorial). They are at once marginal to and yet assimilated to and instated in a national memory.

3.

In this section, we wish to set out certain regularities and shared features of the texts discussed earlier. As always with such a proceeding, the question must arise as to whether these regularities have been generated only by the *corpus* of texts chosen, or whether they are of general application. Finally, we believe that the reader must decide. It is for her or him to disprove or endorse the account given here. It should also be stressed that these categories are not exclusive, and that poems not mentioned as part of one category could in some cases readily be included in another.

Very general categories can be observed. First, there are texts in which an interplay of order and disorder is constitutive of the poem's meaning. In general and beyond this *corpus*, a balance between order and disorder is apparent in many poems (although by no means all), but in some poems the concatenation of ordering and disordering devices is particularly prominent. From our *corpus*, we would include: Larkin's "An Arundel Tomb," Harwood's "The Sinking Colony," Heaney's "Requiem for the Croppies," Stevenson's "A Love Letter," Harrison's "Turns," Adcock's "The Ex-Queen Among the Astronomers," Sheppard's "Fucking Time," Muldoon's "Moy Sand and Gravel," Khalvati's "Ghazal: The Servant," and Marriott's "The Wreck of the Mendi." Second, there are texts that (although this is a matter of interpretative balance) directly and relatively unambiguously present and enact their meanings.[2] Here, we would include the analyzed poems by Harwood, Heaney, Montague, Joseph, Johnson, Davies, Warner, Kay, and Duffy. Marginal cases might be the poems by Stevenson and Duffy. Joseph's "Warning" is a difficult case. On one level, it is what it says it is—a warning to respectable society—but that social order will scarcely be shaken by the threatened behavior. Third, we observe a group of poems that are marked by self-undermining and irony. This includes the pieces by Larkin, Hughes, Joseph (probably), and Adcock.

A secondary level of categorization can be observed in several poems. First, a varying engagement with varying traditions is apparent. The tradition is social in poems by Larkin, Heaney, Harrison, Johnson, and Marriott. There is clearly an antiestablishment and antimetropolitan tenor to all these texts, apart from Larkin's, although an aristocratic and established order is slyly undermined in that text. The engagement with tradition is literary (although that is not without social implications) in texts by Heaney, Harrison, Johnson, Muldoon, Sheppard, Khalvati, and Marriott. It is more exclusively social in Larkin's "An Arundel Tomb." Second, fragments and ellipses organize texts by Harwood, Hill, Constantine, Muldoon, and Khalvati. Third, the demotic voice is apparent in several texts: in those by Hill, Harrison, Johnson, Warner, Kay, Duffy, and Marriott. These demotic voices have different implications and resonances (English varieties, Scots, Black English), but they do have a commonality that jars metropolitan linguistic norms. Fourth, mythological transformation of the everyday is present in a small number of poems: Davies's "The Ophthalmologist," Constantine's "Visiting," and Adcock's "The Ex-Queen Among the Astronomers." The degree to which Hughes's "Crow Tyrannosaurus" is a mythologization of the commonplace is open to discussion. It is our impression that the mythologizing category is underrepresented in our *corpus* (as is demonstrated by several essays in this volume). Fifth, women's voices (although far from unambiguous ones) are present in texts by women poets: Joseph, Stevenson, Adcock, Davies, Kay, and Duffy. It is interesting to note that Val Warner's poem does not focus on women's experience, although other poems in *Tooting Idyll* do.

Finally, two thematic focuses of poems in the *corpus* deserve to be stressed. First, the motif of impotence is rife among these texts: the figures on Larkin's tomb; Crow who is not a tyrannosaurus rex, but only a crow; Joseph's prefigured old lady, whose misdemeanors are limited in impact; Johnson's put-upon immigrant; Davies's entranced and entrapped visitor to the eye doctor; Constantine's wretched revenant; Adcock's bitter ex-queen; Warner's musing gay speaker; and Khalvati's concerned voice. This motif can be contrasted with the more active figures in Kay's text (though the speaker is still dependent on the inspector's goodwill), in Heaney's rebels (though they are defeated), in Montague's socially mobile farmer (though it all comes to naught in the end), and in Hughes's murderous Crow (though he is still just a megalomaniac crow). Second, history permeates many of the poems discussed. This is, above all, the matter of England and of Ireland, but our hypothesis is that a concern with history (both broadly and restrictively conceived) runs through much British and Irish poetry of the last 60 years. Such a concern is apparent in Larkin's, Harwood's, Heaney's, Harrison's, Hill's, Montague's, Johnson's, Warner's, Kay's, and Marriott's verses, in which grand events are interwoven with local and personal histories. If we interpret the term history even more broadly, other texts (for example, all the texts by women writers) could be included in this grouping.

So let this be our story about British and Irish poetry since 1960: technically complex in its working of order and disorder; engaged, often in a disruptive and ironic fashion, with literary and social traditions; offering demotic and marginalized voices and focuses; permeated by motifs of impotence; and fascinated with history.

But these are generalities. The engagement with the individual text and collection, and their attentive reading (on several levels), is the thing.

Notes

1 A version of the opening section of this introduction appeared in Wolfgang Görtschacher and David Malcolm, eds., *Sound Is/As Sense: Essays on Modern British and Irish Poetry*, vol. 6 (Gdańsk: University of Gdańsk Press, 2016), 9–13.

2 We are aware that such a statement sounds paradoxical. Of course, all poems (all texts) mean what they say and say what they mean, in as much as the interaction of subject and technique is the meaning. However, some poems seem to complicate their ultimate meanings much more than others, and the interplay of a manifest meaning and a latent one is what the poem says and does. Other poems do this to a markedly lesser extent.

References

Adcock, Fleur (1996). "The Ex-Queen Among the Astronomers." In: *The Norton Anthology of Poetry*, 4e (eds. Margaret Ferguson, Mary Jo Salter and Jon Stallworthy), 1742–1743. New York/London: W. W. Norton.

Attridge, Derek (1995). *Poetic Rhythm: An Introduction*. Cambridge et al: Cambridge University Press.

Attridge, Derek (2008). "A Return to Form." *Textual Practice*, 22 (3): 563–575.

Baker, David (ed.) (1996). *Meter in English: A Critical Engagement*. Fayetteville, AR: University of Arkansas.

Booth, Martin (1985). *British Poetry, 1964 to 1984: Driving through the Barricades*. London/Boston/Melbourne/Henley: Routledge/Kegan Paul.

Constantine, David (2004). *Collected Poems*. Tarset: Bloodaxe.

Davies, Hilary (1991). *The Shanghai Owner of the Bonsai Shop*. London: Enitharmon Press.

Duffell, Martin J. (2008). *A New History of English Meter*, Studies in Linguistics 5. London: Legenda and Maney Publishing.

Duffy, Carol Ann (2004). *New Selected Poems*. London et al: Picador.

Fabb, Nigel and Halle, Morris (2008). *Meter in Poetry: A New Theory*. Cambridge: Cambridge University Press.

Gross, Harvey and McDowell, Robert (1996). *Sound and Form in Modern Poetry*, 2nd ed. Ann Arbor: University of Michigan Press.

Harrison, Tony (1984). *Selected Poems*. Harmondsworth, London: Penguin.

Harwood, Lee (2004). *Collected Poems*. Exeter: Shearsman.

Heaney, Seamus (1990). *New Selected Poems, 1966–1987*. London: Faber and Faber.

Hill, Geoffrey (2006). *Selected Poems*. London: Harmondsworth.

Hobsbawm, Philip (1996). *Metre, Rhythm and Verse Form*. London/New York: Routledge.

Hughes, Ted (1974). *Crow: From the Life and Songs of the Crow*. London: Faber and Faber.

Johnson, Linton Kwesi (1991). *Tings an Times: Selected Poems*. Newcastle upon Tyne: Bloodaxe.

Joseph, Jenny (1992). *Selected Poems*. Newcastle upon Tyne: Bloodaxe.

Kay, Jackie (2007). *Darling: New and Selected Poems*. Tarset: Bloodaxe.

Kennedy, David (1996). *New Relations: The Refashioning of British Poetry, 1980–1994*. Bridgend, Wales: Seren – Poetry Wales Press.

Khalvati, Mimi (2011). *Child: New and Selected Poems, 1991–2011*. Manchester: Carcanet.

Küper, Christoph (ed.) (2011). *Current Trends in Metrical Analysis*. Frankfurt: Peter Lang.

Larkin, Philip (1964). *The Whitsun Weddings*. London: Faber and Faber.

Leighton, Angela (2007). *On Form: Poetry, Aestheticism, and the Legacy of a Word*. Oxford: Oxford University Press.

Marriott, D. S. (2008). *Hoodoo Voodoo*. Exeter: Shearsman.

Montague, John (1989). *The Rough Field*. Oldcastle, County Meath: The Gallery Press.

Muldoon, Paul (2002). *Moy Sand and Gravel*. London: Faber and Faber.

Sampson, Fiona (2011). "The Expanded Lyric: John Burnside and the Challenge to British Tradition." In: *Dwelling Places: An Appreciation of John Burnside*. *Agenda*, 45.4/46.1 (Spring/Summer), 112–121.

Sampson, Fiona (2012). *Beyond the Lyric: A Map of Contemporary British Poetry*. London: Chatto and Windus.

Schmidt, Michael (1979). *A Reader's Guide to Fifty Modern British Poets*. London/New York: Heinemann/Barnes and Noble.

Schmidt, Michael (1989). *Reading Modern Poetry*. London/New York: Routledge.

Sheppard, Robert (2004). *Tin Pan Arcadia: Those Twentieth Century Blues*. Cambridge: Salt.

Steele, Timothy (1999). *All the Fun's in How You Say a Thing*. Athens, OH: Ohio University Press.

Stevenson, Anne (2005). *Poems 1955–2005*. Tarset: Bloodaxe.

Tuma, Keith (1998). *Fishing by Obstinate Isles: Postmodern British Poetry and American Readers*. Evanston: Northwestern University Press.

Warner, Val (1998). *Tooting Idyll*. Manchester: Carcanet.

SECTION 2
Contexts, Forms, Topics, and Movements

Section 2a. Institutions, Histories, Receptions

2a.1
Some Institutions of the British and Irish (Sub)Fields of Poetry: Little Magazines, Publishers, Prizes, and Poetry in Translation

Wolfgang Görtschacher

Introduction

Any analysis of the institutions at work in the field of British and Irish poetry (original and translated), which allows itself to be seduced by the attractions of comprehensiveness and representative quality, must be doomed to failure. The extent and degree of detail called for would involve the writer in a project of encyclopedic dimensions, such as could provide occupation for an army of academics and experts for whole years to come. Consequently, the account offered here of the fields and subfields of British and Irish poetry, while it certainly does not ignore what is characteristic and tries to be as complete as possible, does not make the mistake of sanctifying as "representative" any and every feature that can be identified, discussed, and documented; working within limits, it tries to achieve a consistent and coherent picture; it looks at various institutions like the "little magazines," poetry publishing in general, the system of awards and prizes meant to encourage poetry, and tries to describe the character of their operation and effects on British and Irish poetry, including, as an integral aspect, the translated poetry published in Britain and Ireland. My selection of institutions (and the picture I have produced) must be to a degree subjective, but I have

A Companion to Contemporary British and Irish Poetry, 1960–2015, First Edition.
Edited by Wolfgang Görtschacher and David Malcolm.
© 2021 John Wiley & Sons Ltd. Published 2021 by John Wiley & Sons Ltd.

worked on the basis of criteria that would be generally recognized and am convinced that I have focused on factors and elements of crucial importance to the production of poetry in Britain and Ireland. What is perhaps important that I think I have introduced the reader to a landscape of poetry well worth knowing: pulsing with life, maintaining itself with resource amid the usual discouragements and high hopes, and characterized by an interesting variety of magazines, publishers, policies of publishing, as well as theories and trends in the practice of poetry.

The Little Magazines

> Testing one's work out in magazines and journals can be disconcerting & painful, especially if the pieces sometimes don't come off. (And don't I know it!) But I think it, really, [is] the tough & only school. (Causley 1984)

The *Oxford English Dictionary* (OED) defines a little magazine as "a periodical directed at a readership with serious literary, artistic, or other intellectual interests, usually having a small circulation and considered to appeal to a minority." Richard Price, Head of Modern British Collections at the British Library, stresses their association with "ideas of marginality: political radicalism, support for one minority or another, support for the art form of poetry itself (conceived as a Cinderella art), and for various kinds of aesthetic extremes" and adds to that their noncommercial nature (Price 2013, 178). In his contribution to the *Small Press Yearbook 1994*, Geoffrey Soar highlights various aspects, but maintains with a saddening cogency that "[t]heir 'littleness' relates to their usually small print runs, their lack of financial profitability, and their tendency (by no means invariable) to exist rather briefly" (Soar 1993, 24).

In December 1964, the Library Committee at University College London (UCL), where Soar was responsible for the English library, took an important decision to subscribe to all little magazines published in the UK. However, as the UCL Library Committee soon realized that the small presses were inseparable from the small magazines, they began to buy their publications too and thus founded the Poetry Store Collection. Right from the start, Soar also began to organize exhibitions, which were accompanied by the publication of catalogs (UCL Library 1966, 1970–1971, 1977, 1982, 1992, 1994). To celebrate 25 years of the Little Magazines Collection, he launched, together with David Miller, an exhibition at the Royal Festival Hall in late 1990 entitled "Little Magazines and How They Got That Way." In the following year, the exhibition moved to Durham University Library and the Flaxman Gallery, Staffordshire Polytechnic, at Stoke-on-Trent. Advised by Stuart Montgomery (Fulcrum Press), Bob Cobbing (*And*, Writers Forum), and Lee Harwood (*Tzarad*), Soar managed to collect "some 3000 magazine titles and 6000 small-press publications" (Soar 1993, 25) by 1990. At present, the Little Magazines Collection subscribes to around 200 magazines and has a collection of 3500 titles, while the Poetry Store Collection contains over 7000 titles (UCL Website 2019).

Its American counterpart, on a more international and larger scale, is the Little Magazine Collection at the Department of Special Collections, Memorial Library, University of Wisconsin–Madison. It holds approximately 7000 English-language literary magazines published in the United States, Great Britain, Canada, Australia, and New Zealand, and maintains about 1200 subscriptions. The American definition agrees with Soar's as far as the "noncommercial" aspect of the publication is concerned. In addition, little magazines are seen as "avant-garde in nature" and "often associated with significant literary, cultural, and artistic movements," which is why they have been "especially influential in the historical development of modern and experimental poetry." An important component of little magazines on both sides of the Atlantic is the publication of interviews with authors and artists, which provide "valuable insights into their creative processes and the context of their works." Since 1975, the librarians at the Department of Special Collections have indexed the interviews in yearly files and published them as a section in *Serials Review* (Digital Collections, University of Wisconsin–Madison Libraries 2019).

Histories and bibliographies of British and Irish poetry magazines published between 1960 and 2019 have not been numerous. Remembering my commitment to modesty of scale, I shall refer interested readers to only the most important studies before I offer some insights into the current situation of print and online magazines. The first important publication is the *Comprehensive Index to English-Language Little Magazines, 1890–1970*, eight volumes edited by Marion Sader and published in 1976, which indexed only 100 titles but "brought together British and American titles for the first time and listed reviews and illustrators along with the primary literature" (Reilly 1985, 5). Only very rarely are editors of British and Irish little magazines interested in compiling and publishing an index relating to the writers and work they have published. Glyn Pursglove, reviews editor of *Acumen* magazine, regularly compiles an author index of every 10 issues, which is published at the back of the tenth or eleventh issue. Andreas Schachermayr is the compiler of author indexes for *Ore Magazine* (1954–1995), *The Poet's Voice* (second series, 1994–2000), and, together with Tom Clyde, for Nos. 100–107 of *HU*, published as a 22-page booklet in 1999 and posted free with issue 107. Already 4 years earlier, an author index to issues 1–99 had been issued as a separate paperback. Issues 1–21 of *Poetry Ireland Review* were indexed by Richard Hayes; the index was first published as a contribution to *PIR* 36 (1992) and as a booklet in 1993.

Other publication types to celebrate the history or longevity of a little magazine are festschrifts or "best-of" anthologies or a compound publication that incorporates both genres. The University of Salzburg Press backlist contains various books celebrating little magazines. In 1989, James Hogg commissioned Fred Beake, founder-editor of *The Poet's Voice*, to compile an anthology from the issues of his magazine, which was published as *A Mingling of Streams*. This valuable publication, including poems by regular contributors, extracts from Beake's editorials, and a checklist, inaugurated Hogg's attempt to save little magazines from being consigned to oblivion. The second volume in this series, published 4 years later, was devoted to a selection of poetry from *Stride*'s 33 issues, entitled *Ladder to the Next Floor*, which also included essays and notes on the magazine as well as a checklist. *Salute to "Outposts"* (1994), celebrating the magazine's fiftieth anniversary, contains essays, an interview with editor Roland John, poetic appreciations, photographs, and an anthology of poems published in the magazine. The series was continued in 1997 with *Veins of Gold: Ore, 1954–1995*. This 250-page volume offers 100 poems, five commissioned essays on the magazine's history, an interview with editor Eric Ratcliffe, many photographs, and the aforementioned bibliography.

Only a very small number of editors have taken the initiative to edit and publish volumes celebrating their magazine's history, either as a special issue or as a separate publication. *PN Review* 100, subtitled "A Calendar of Modern Poetry," an adaptation of the title of Edgell Rickword's monthly of the 1920s (*The Calendar of Modern Letters*, March 1925–July 1927), is a fascinating example of the former category, because editor Michael Schmidt asked 80 poets, his regular contributors, to edit the issue, selecting a clutch of poems, or extracts from longer poems, to characterize their work. In addition, Schmidt opened up the doors of his archive of letters to the public, commissioning Mark Fisher to edit *Letters to an Editor*, which covers 20 years of Carcanet and *PN Review*'s history from 1969 to 1989.

Valuable examples of the separate-publication category are *Poetry Wales 25 Years*, edited by Cary Archard and published in 1990, and *Agenda—An Anthology: The First Four Decades 1959–1993*, published by Carcanet Press in 1994. While Archard tried—with hindsight—to chart a history of *Poetry Wales* by arranging the material chronologically, William Cookson's aim was "to gather a collection of good poems, and essays about poetry, that can be enjoyed as a book in its own right. I've prepared it as if I were editing a bumper issue of *Agenda* out of an unusually rich welter of submissions—not surprising after thirty-five years!" (Cookson 1994, xiii).

What Richard Hayes said about his work of indexing *Poetry Ireland Review* can be transferred to the process of compiling such anthologies, in particular collections of material from defunct magazines, which permits one to re-encounter the known magazine at a different level. One views and examines a certain number of issues of the magazine in question

> holistically, [in order to receive] a macroscopic view of the magazine, permitting one to watch its development from above, a development invisible for the reader following the magazine from issue to issue, with an eye too close to the action. In a way, the process of compiling an index offers the possibility of a new way of reading a little magazine, an *unnatural* way of reading, at odds with the rhythm of the magazine's production and transferred from one social and cultural context to another. (Hayes 1992, 53)

This review of the magazine works by way of a disruptive reading, which in turn can reveal processes by which the magazine developed as well as central questions and editorial concerns. An awareness of such possibilities clearly influenced editors Sasha Dugdale and David and Helen Constantine when they set out to arrange *Centres of Cataclysm*, an anthology, thematically arranged, celebrating 50 years of *Modern Poetry in Translation*.

"Best-of" approaches were applied by both Sean McMahon for *Great Irish Writing: The Best from The Bell*, edited more than 20 years after the publication of the last issue, and Gerald Dawe and Jonathan Williams for *Krino, 1986–1996: An Anthology of Modern Irish Writing*, which appeared the same year that the farewell issue had left the magazine's headquarters in Co. Galway. In addition, the *Krino* anthology offered an index as an appendix. Edited by Neil

Pattison, Reitha Pattison, and Luke Roberts, *Certain Prose of The English Intelligencer* contains a selection, chronologically arranged, of prose from the poetry worksheet, which was privately circulated from January 1966 to April 1968. These publications may be categorized as rescue operations, saving the spirit, tone, and strength, and above all much of what their editors considered the most important material published in their respective magazines, because without them these texts would not be easily accessible for the reading public, stored away in archives and basements of a small number of specialist libraries.

On the occasion of the centenary of the Poetry Society and its magazine *Poetry Review* in 2009, Fiona Sampson, its editor at the time, put together a substantial best-of anthology: *A Century of Poetry Review*. Sampson admits in her introduction that "this anthology represents not necessarily the most important British poetry of the last hundred years, but rather *what has been seen* as most important" (Sampson 2009, xv). Instead of dividing up the magazine's history into periods of editorial tenure, Sampson offers a conservative, rather uninspired decade-by-decade approach, implying that the history of poetry is shaped by decades rather than other criteria. The editorship best represented in the anthology is the one held by Peter Forbes (1987–2002), hailed by Sampson as the magazine's "greatest period of editorial transparency [and] perfectly reflect[ing] a zeitgeist" (Sampson 2009, xxi). One third of the anthology's pages reflect Forbes's aims, which he also outlined in 1987, in a private letter to me, as "to present the best of modern poetry in English in a context of poetry's relationship to the other arts and to the wider world of politics, science." This aim was apparent in theme issues devoted to travel, the other arts, science, and politics. There was also a good deal of prose—interviews, essays, polemics, and reviews—and the poets featured belonged, as he said, "to no dominant clique [with] a good proportion [of] fairly new writers." Poems by Primo Levi, Joseph Brodsky, John Ashbery, Aimé Césaire, C. K. Williams, Les Murray, among others, as well as essays by Derek Walcott on "The Poet in the Theatre" and Miroslav Holub on "Poetry Against Absurdity" testify to Forbes's international outlook.

At least twice in the magazine's history the editorship has been outspokenly pro-avant-garde; first under Eric Mottram (1971–1977) and then under the dual aegis of David Herd and Robert Potts (2002–2005). Although Mottram published work by more than 120 poets, only five poets (Ian Hamilton Finlay, Frances Horovitz, Basil Bunting, Lawrence Ferlinghetti, and Allen Ginsberg) gained admittance to the anthology. Sampson describes the editorial policy of Potts and Herd as "anti-poetry-lite, criticism-led [...] unafraid of seriousness and risk" (Sampson 2009, xxi–xxii), but only two poems of their editorship were admitted. One of the most impressive areas of this anthology is its prose, which includes extracts from interviews by writers such as W. S. Graham, Ian Hamilton, and Douglas Dunn. In addition, there are critical essays by Lascelles Abercrombie, Norman MacCaig, Derek Stanford, Tom Paulin, and, of course, Philip Larkin's notorious essay on Sylvia Plath entitled "Horror Poet." Finally, there are the extracts from the manifestos of Marinetti, Pound, Don Paterson, and John Kinsella.

One wonders why the Poetry Society did not consider a two-volume publication, one devoted to poetry, the other to prose, as a more appropriate celebration of its house journal's century. Another option that might have resulted in a more satisfactory work would have been the commissioning of an editorial team, each editor being assigned a certain period of the magazine's history. This observation leads me to my last point of criticism: the desirability of a division into editorial periods that should have been introduced by policy statements extracted from editorials.[1]

Critical studies of individual little magazines are very rare. Some examples stick out: in 2016, Gerry Cambridge published *The Dark Horse: The Making of a Little Magazine*, a fascinating analysis and retrospective account of the first two decades of Scotland's transatlantic poetry magazine (Cambridge 2016, 11), which published issue 41 in September 2019. The core of Bruce Wilkinson's *Hidden Culture, Forgotten History* is a critical study and contextualization of the little magazine *Move*, edited by Jim Burns from Preston between December 1964 and April 1968, and *Poetmeat*, a Blackburn-based magazine run by David Cunliffe, Tina Morris, and Kirby Congdon from 1963 to 1967 (Wilkinson 2017). Anne Mulhall's important essay on *Cyphers*, established in 1975 by Leland Bardwell, Pearse Hutchinson, Eiléan Ní Chuilleanáin, and Macdara Woods, is a model of its kind. Its author contextualizes *Cyphers* in relation to *Poetry Ireland Review* and argues that the magazine has offered "an alternative gloss on the interrelations of literature and the 'home land', mapping (or recovering) an unofficial geography of the place of that home spatially and historically" (Mulhall 2007, 206).

For a history of the British and Irish little magazines up to the late 1990s, I refer interested readers to my own two monographs: *Little Magazine Profiles* (1993) and *Contemporary Views on the Little Magazine Scene* (2000), which among other things describe the scene and situation of little magazines, on the eve, as it were, of that phenomenon of decline at the turn of the millennium, when a number of magazines ceased publication. David Miller and Richard Price recorded only 18 new magazines in 1999 and 14 new titles for 2000, which led to "significant deficits in net new titles—when 'deaths' exceed 'births' (10 and 8, respectively)" (Miller/Price 2006, 228). *Light's List 2003* mentions 425 titles that were still published in the previous year, 275 magazines were listed in *Poetry Writers' Yearbook 2007*, and 133 magazines had entries in *The Writer's Handbook 2009*, a figure that declined to 127 titles a year later; for 2011, 126 magazines were registered. The subject index of the very unreliable *Writers' & Artists' Yearbook 2019* only refers to 61 magazines (Harris 2018). The National Poetry Library has 150 entries for print and online magazines, including *Planet: The Welsh Internationalist* and the *TLS*, which publish a maximum of half a dozen poems per issue, if that. The Scottish Poetry Library currently subscribes to 88 magazines (Scottish Poetry Library 2018).

There is perhaps consolation to be found in the knowledge that, despite these figures and the impression they give that, in comparison to previous decades, the number of little magazines is in sharp decline, the number of long-lived poetry magazines has never been greater at any time since 1945. This may be regarded as more claim than fact and a wishful reading of the entrails. Statistics, too, are more than apt to lend themselves to congenial interpretations. Nevertheless, the figures are there, available for study and interpretation, and it is not too much to expect that a sound and disciplined scholarship is capable of approaching them without bias and drawing the right conclusions. The roll-call, which follows, of the names of magazines, enjoying a degree of prestige, and which have also weathered the storms of at least two decades—and/or have published more than 50 issues—is certainly impressive. It comprises a number of names the reader will recognize and though by no means complete indicates a condition of considerable vitality: *Acumen, Agenda, Ambit, Blithe Spirit, Cyphers, The Dark Horse, Dream Catcher, Envoi, The Frogmore Papers, The Interpreter's House, Iota Poetry, The London Magazine, Magma, Modern Poetry in Translation, Mslexia, New Welsh Review, The North, Obsessed with Pipework, Orbis, Oxford Poetry, Pennine Platform, PN Review, Poetry Ireland Review, Poetry London, Poetry Review, Poetry Salzburg Review, Poetry Scotland, Poetry Wales, The Rialto, Shearsman, Smoke, The Stinging Fly, Stand, Tears in the Fence, Under the Radar,* and *Wasafiri.*

The 2002 flier of the UK Little Magazines Project, set up at Nottingham Trent University's English and Media Studies Department in October 1998, is, accordingly, justified in starting off with the following premise:

> The enduring and continuing importance of little magazines is unquestionable. Apart from publishing many of the major literary figures of the twentieth century [...] before they were acceptable to mainstream publishers, they have also been fundamental to the genesis, growth and dissemination of literary and artistic movements [...]. Importantly, they have also provided a space for the work of many poets, writers and artists who have not been a part of any movement or group, and who remain resistant to categorization. (Ellis/Lucas/Smith/Miller 2002)

This thesis still holds true at a time when hypertext and multimedia options on the Internet are expanding and an increasing number of computer-literate poets have emerged writing on and for the computer or website, making use of the exciting potential of the web. All this activity acknowledged, Hamilton-Emery's dystopia envisaging the extinction of print magazines—"Print magazines are finished"—has fortunately proved to be a vision too pessimistic. However, when he argued a decade ago—"Poetry magazines will move online. There will be more of them. They will increasingly network with each other" (Hamilton-Emery 2010, 18)—he foresaw not a disaster but a development that editors avail themselves of in a great variety of ways. *The High Window* is an online quarterly review of poetry, launched in 2016 and coedited for the first 12 issues by David Cooke and Anthony Costello. Since 2018, Cooke has edited another 6 issues until summer 2020. A model issue contains a substantial selection of new poems from more than 30 poets, a featured American poet, a translation section with a national focus (Catalan, Polish, Franco-Canadian, French, Italian, Japanese, Kazahk, Spanish, and classical Greek and Latin poetry), a featured UK poet, a resident artist, and detailed and in-depth reviews. The website also contains a page with weekly posts that supplement the quarterly journal. Cooke also runs The High Window Press, which aims at publishing four volumes of poetry a year to coincide with the four quarterly issues of the magazine. Founded in 2015, it has published books by established poets such as Patricia McCarthy, Anthony Howell, and Wendy Klein as well as debut collections, for example, most recently, by Tim O'Leary (Cooke 2019).

A very different format is represented by *Ink Sweat & Tears*, a webzine based in the UK, which was founded by Charles Christian in 2007 as "a platform for new poetry and short prose, and experimental work in digital media." Its current editor, the poet and visual artist Helen Ivory, "publishes and reviews poetry, prose, prose-poetry, word & image pieces and everything in between. Our tastes are eclectic and magpie-like and we aim to publish something new every day" (*Ink Sweat & Tears* 2019).

When *Agenda*'s founding editor William Cookson died in early 2003, Patricia McCarthy, who had coedited the magazine with Cookson for 4 years, found it relatively easy—with a certain amount of very welcome financial support from public and private funding organizations—to continue the publication of the magazine, indeed, producing bumper special issues on—for example—Derek Walcott, Cookson, and on Irish poetry with a special focus on John Montague. Cookson had edited the magazine for 44 years "with a complete self-confidence in his own judgement" (Gowrie 2003, 29). However, Gowrie deplored the fact that the Arts Council had ended its support after 27 years and that he had failed to make them reverse their decision. With the special memorial issue for Cookson, McCarthy launched *Agenda* Broadsheets for young poets, which were included free to subscribers in each issue of the magazine and are now available online from their website. Two years later McCarthy had once again acquired an Arts Council England grant. She continued *Agenda*'s tradition of publishing special issues, either on poets long associated with the magazine (C. H. Sisson, Geoffrey Hill, and T. S. Eliot) or on themes (lauds, exiles, scentings, family histories, new generation poets, and the power of poetry). Two recent theme issues commemorate the Great War—Requiem: The Great War; 1918. They "seek to demonstrate how, deep in our psyches, that supposed 'war to end all wars' lives on today" (McCarthy 2018, 5). The demonstration is achieved through war poems by Michael Longley, Hilary Davies, Alison Brackenbury, and William Bedford; poems in translation by Anna Akhmatova, Guillaume Apollinaire, and Pierre Jean Jouve; and essays on David Jones, Ivor Gurney, as well as French, German, Italian, and Russian poetry of the Great War. The variety of nations, times, and genres ensures the reader "a universal overview [...] of the poetic output [...], and [...] a balanced outlook" (McCarthy 2014, 7). McCarthy always publishes supplements to issues online as pdf files on the magazine's website—of poems and paintings, of essays and reviews, of translations. General interest essays, audio recordings, and the broadsheets for young poets and artists are also available online and free of charge.

The Manchester-based *PN Review*, operating since autumn 1973 under the editorship of Michael Schmidt, is indispensable reading for poets, academics, or anyone interested in what is going on in the world of poetry. Many features make *PNR* remarkable, particularly its essays on poetics, its thought-provoking editorials; some readers, however, might find challenging Schmidt's interest in the longer poem and poem sequences and its international outlook, which also includes certain American poets. Schmidt's approach differs from that of the previous editors in that *PNR* is both a print and an online magazine. A 1-year individual subscription for £39.90 includes six issues of the print magazine and unlimited access to the archive, while a print and digital subscription for UK institutions costs £149.

Poetry Translation

The Translators Association (TA), set up in 1958 to provide literary translators with an effective means of protecting their interests and sharing their concerns, has suggested "a rate for poetry of £1.10 per line, with a minimum of £35 per poem" (Translators Association 2018), although they wisely add that "members are advised to take a case by case approach as rates for poetry vary," which implies that poetry translators usually receive payment well below the suggested rates. Across the Atlantic, the 2017 Authors Guild Survey of Literary Translators' Working Conditions, which collected information from 205 translators on payment, royalties, copyright, and various other aspects of the literary translation profession, shows that 65% of literary translators earn less than $20,000 per year and only about 7% earn 100% of their income from translation work. The authors of the survey draw the straightforward conclusion that "a large number of US translators are being paid rates that make it difficult, if not impossible, to earn a living." Even more worrying is that 41% of the translators report that "payment of their fee has sometimes depended on the publisher receiving a grant." (The Authors Guild 2017) Whether similar figures also apply to the current situation of British and Irish translators is a subject about which one can only speculate.

For some translators, the prizes awarded for their work, though very few in number, offer at least the occasional possibility of supplementing a meager income. The Society of Authors lists on its website 10 translation prizes worth £15,000, which are awarded in mid-February of the year following publication, the majority of them for "full length [...] works of literary merit and general interest" translated from a given language into English. The prizes are awarded annually, biennially, or every 3 years, in recognition of outstanding translations from works in Arabic, Dutch, French, German, Italian, Spanish, and Swedish. One of them is the TA First Translation Prize, an annual £2,000 prize shared between the translator and his or her editor. It was established in 2017, endowed by Daniel Hahn, with support from the British Council, "for a debut literary translation into English published in the UK," and like all British poetry prizes is administered within the terms of a closed-shop policy (The Society of Authors, 2019), meaning that only books first published in Great Britain are eligible. However, the likelihood of a translator of poetry winning such a prize is small. The awards usually go to prose works; indeed, among the 14 prize winners of 2017 and 2018, one finds with—or without—surprise not one translator of a collection of poetry. An important award, exclusively for translators of poetry, is the Popescu European Poetry Translation Prize, which is worth £1,000 and was launched in 1983. It is awarded biennially by The Poetry Society for a volume of poetry translated from a European language into English.

Launched in 2010 by the London Book Fair, the Literary Translation Centre is an important institution that is made up of 10 partner organizations: Arts Council England Literature Department, the British Centre for Literary Translation, the British Council Literature Department, the Calouste Gulbenkian Foundation, the English PEN's Writers in Translation programme, Free Word, Literature Across Frontiers, the Translators Association (Society of Authors), the Wales Literature Exchange, and Words Without Borders. The ultimate aim of the Literary Translation Centre is to "enable publishers and translators to come together, network and attend a variety of seminars on literary translation to further this art throughout the UK and abroad." One of the programs, PEN Translates, launched in 2012 with financial support from Arts Council England, encourages UK publishers to publish more books from other languages. Up to 75% of the translation costs are funded; if a publisher's annual turnover is less than £500,000, there is the possibility that up to 100% of the translation costs will be covered. This measure has been effective in so far as it has encouraged more publishers, big and small, to consider publications of translated poetry.

The most important publishers of poetry in translation are three of the "Big Five"—Bloodaxe, Carcanet, and Faber. However, two publishers specializing in poetry translation are more prominent—Arc Publications and Seagull Books, based in Kolkata, India, but with a registered division in London. The symbolic capital of Arc Publications—accumulated prestige, recognition, and respect, as Pierre Bourdieu defines it in *Language and Symbolic Power* (1991)—is widely accepted. In particular, the program "Poetry in Translation," which encompasses no fewer than five series—Visible Poets, Arc Translations, Arc Classic Translations, New Voices From Europe and Beyond, and Anthologies in Translation—has been eminently successful. The appointment of Jean Boase-Beier as series editor of "Visible Poets" in 2000 was an especially fortunate move. Boase-Beier conceived "Visible Poets" as a series of bilingual books with a preface by the translator and an introductory essay by an eminent scholar. As Professor of Literature and Translation at the University of East Anglia, where she established and ran the MA in Literary Translation until her retirement in 2015, she also edits the "Arc Translations" and "Arc Classic Translations" series. The shortlist of the 2015 Popescu European Poetry Translation Prize serves as a good example of Arc's prestige: among the six shortlisted books were three Arc titles, translations from French, German, and Polish, and the winner came from among them: Iain Galbraith for his translation of Jan Wagner's collection *Self-Portrait with a Swarm of Bees*.

Little magazines often publish translations, either in a regular section, as is the case in *Acumen*, *Poetry Salzburg Review*, *Shearsman*, and *The High Window*, or as separate issues. The latter case is best represented by *Agenda*—under William Cookson's editorship there were several special issues published: on German poetry (1994), Spanish poetry (1997), and Greek poetry (1999). In 1997, there was also a special issue devoted to Michael Hamburger's translations and his own poetry. The current editor Patricia McCarthy has been responsible for the publication of issues on modern Turkish poetry (2001/2002), translation as metamorphosis, and Rainer Maria Rilke. In terms of translations, the most important magazine, however, has been *Modern Poetry in Translation (MPT)*. Ted Hughes's brainchild, launched together with Daniel Weissbort in 1965, was intended as "a cumulative and accumulating index of contemporary writing" (Weissbort 2004). No magazine has been more concerned with the theory and practice of translation or more devoted to introducing to English readers poets from many cultures who would not be known without translation. *MPT* 21 and 22 (both 2003), the last two issues under Weissbort's editorship, highlighted once again the magazine's initial aim "to provide a platform for the poetry of the first post-War generation of Eastern European poets." Weissbort's penultimate issue is a potpourri of all the objectives the editors had pursued over the years, including features of two contributors of long standing—Michael Hamburger and James Kirkup—with, more surprisingly perhaps for the general reader, a long section devoted to Hughes's unpublished translations in order "to draw attention [...] to his importance as a translator himself of poetry and of poetic drama." Weissbort followed up his intentions with regard to Hughes by editing a book of the poet's *Selected Translations* (2006). As part of the same program, he also published a monograph, *Ted Hughes and Translation* (2011), and a number of essays in poetry magazines and academic journals. For Weissbort, the magazine's ultimate achievement under his and Hughes's editorship was that it "help[ed] to make English readers, and English poets, see poetry as the very opposite of parochial, even if it was so intimately bound up with language. This paradox, the paradox in fact of poetry translation, remains a productive one" (Weissbort 2004).

When David and Helen Constantine took over the editorship of *MPT* with No. 23 in 2004, the new editors "felt the same urgency of the project, the same spirit, in very different times." The editorial policy of their 9 years was shaped by three premises. The first was that "poetry matters: because it tells the truth in mendacious times and because that truth, through the forms and rhythms of poetry, excites in people under whatever repressive and demanding structures the demand for greater freedom," which they shared with the founding editors. Their second premise was that "translation matters: because it brings valuable things from abroad into our home country." Premise number three related to their interpretation of the word *modern* in the magazine's title, which they understood to mean "any new and lively version of any poetry of any age. So translation crosses frontiers of both space and time" (David and Helen Constantine 2016, 20). When Sasha Dugdale was appointed as new editor in 2013, not only did the magazine's shape and design change but also its frequency and editorial policy. Dugdale started to publish three issues per year, with each issue offering a focus section. She started off with predominantly European foci (Dutch, Romanian, and Polish) and managed to get the respective national literature organizations on board to make a financial contribution. Later issues of her 4-year period contained sections that represented the magazine's global approach toward poetry in translation, ranging from Brazilian and Uruguayan poetries to Iranian and Korean ones. Other sections focused on African, Indian, and Arabic languages and the poetry produced in them. With the current editor Clare Pollard, who took over in 2018, *MPT* seems to have moved into a more politically engaged and more intriguing period. She introduced the editorial to her first issue, entitled "Profound Pyromania," with a quotation from "Manifesto for Ultratranslation," published by Antena, a language justice and experimentation collaborative founded by Jen Hofer and John Pluecker: "Who we choose to translate is political. How we choose to translate is political" (Pollard 2018). Her first four issues have contained sections on Caribbean and Hungarian poetry as well as work by LGBTQ+ authors. In what she calls her Brexit issue, Pollard argues that "[i]f Brexit has posed the question of who we are, we must listen for answers in all of our languages," which is why she has collected "translations from Welsh, Scottish Gaelic, Cornish, Irish, Anglo-Saxon, Arabic, Polish, Turkish and British Sign Language (BSL), and poems drawing on Jamaican Patois, Scots, Ulster Scots, Shetlandic, Spanish, Angloromani, Black Country Dialect, Portuguese and the fabulous Inklisch of Sophie Herxheimer's Grandmother" (Pollard 2019).

Right from its start, *MPT* has always been financially supported by the Arts Council England. For the 3-year financial period 2012–2015, the magazine received £117,500, a grant that was increased to £120,000 for the years 2015–2018.

A rival in the field of poetry translation seems to have emerged with *Asymptote*, an online magazine that was launched by its editor Lee Yew Leong in January 2011 as "a reaction to the literary parochialism [he] experienced living in Singapore back then" and with the mission "to unlock the literary treasures of the world." The decision to publish it online "stems from [the editors'] commitment to social justice. Providing free access to the world's literature – for everyone, regardless of geography, language or class – is emboldened by an online platform" (Leong n.d.). In its 34 issues published up to now (August 2019), the magazine "has featured work from 121 countries and 103 languages, all never-before-published poetry, fiction, nonfiction, drama, and interviews" (Leong 2019). According to its founding editor, the editorial team "operate[s] differently from other translation journals in that [they] don't just sit back and wait for translations to come to [them. They] actually identify the good work from writers [that have not yet been introduced to the English speaking world] and actively seek out translators to help to translate the work for [them]" (Habash 2011). In 2015, the magazine won London Book Fair's International Literary Translation Initiative Award and also became a founding member of *The Guardian*'s Books Network with "Translation Tuesdays," a weekly showcase of new literary translations that was published until 2017.

Another issue in this context is the question: how well known and widely published are British and Irish poets in translation? While this would be the subject for a separate encyclopedic study, I shall briefly comment on translations into German, as this is the field I am most familiar with. (See also Romer 2013 on British poetry translated into a variety of European languages.) One important series of German publications, Edition Lyrik Kabinett, is run by Hanser Verlag and comprises collections by John Burnside, Lavinia Greenlaw, Michael Longley, Geoffrey Hill, Robin Robertson, and Derek Walcott. Fischer Verlag, another prestigious German press, published a volume of Alice Oswald's poetry in 2018, translated by Melanie Walz and Iain Galbraith.

As for the series, Poets Laureate: how many of their collections are available in German translation? Just one each: Jan Wagner translated for Berlin Verlag Simon Armitage's *Zoom!* (2011). Carol Ann Duffy's sole publication *Die Bauchrednerpuppe* (1996) appeared in Margitt Lehbert's translation more than 20 years ago under the imprint of the Residenz Verlag. Under her own imprint, Edition Rugerup, Lehbert has published one volume each of Derek Mahon, John Montague, Gabriel Rosenstock, Iain Crichton Smith, and Robin Fulton.

With regard to Nobel Laureate, Seamus Heaney, the situation is scarcely better. Under Michael Krüger's directorship until 2013, Hanser Press published three collections of Heaney's poetry, one volume of Selected Poems, and a translation of *The Government of the Tongue*. For Fischer Verlag, Krüger edited a volume of Selected Poems from 1965 to 2006, entitled *Die Amsel von Glanmore* and published in 2011. The obvious question is why are only very few collections of Heaney's one dozen poetry books available in German translation?

A very different case is that of Michael Hamburger: together with Ted Hughes, he is probably the most widely translated British poet into German. Fifteen volumes of Hamburger's poetry were published by Literarisches Colloquium Berlin, Hanser, Droschl, and Folio. The last issued seven collections, six of them translated by Peter Waterhouse. This track record of Hamburger's poetry in German translations, largely due to the close relationship that Hamburger and Waterhouse enjoyed for many years, has led some critics to the conclusion that Hamburger is better known as poet in German-speaking countries than in Britain (Hamburger 1998, 31–32). In a 1998 interview with Peter Dale, Hamburger acknowledges "the very generous reception given to my work in Germany, where there are two book-length studies of it and a miscellany of essays by various critics, as well as many more serious and searching reviews of it in the general press – Swiss and Austrian also – than in Britain or in America" (Hamburger 1998, 34; Romer 2013, 553). A more recent case is Kate Tempest: from her five collections of poetry that she has published until 2018, three of them are already available in German translation, all published by Suhrkamp Verlag.

The latest, more wide-ranging (bilingual) anthology of British and Irish poetry was published by Haymon Verlag in 2002 as *So also ist das/So That's What It's Like*, edited by Ludwig Laher and myself. It comprises work by 28 British and Irish poets, translated by Austrian poets and graduates of my own "Literary Translation" course, taught at the University of Salzburg. Iain Galbraith edited a volume of Scottish poetry since 1900, *Beredter Norden. Schottische Lyrik seit 1900*, that was published by Lehbert's Edition Rugerup in 2011.

It is a rather unsatisfactory résumé. British and Irish poetry is, with very few exceptions, more or less unknown in any breadth or depth in the German-speaking countries. (One wonders whether the situation is substantially different in other European countries, or, indeed, elsewhere in the world.) The lamentable and arbitrary situation can only change if national organizations, such as Arts Council England, the British Council, the Publishers Association, the "Big Five" of British publishers, Literature Ireland (formerly known as Ireland Literature Exchange), Wales Literature Exchange, the Scottish Poetry Library, and Literature Across Frontiers increase their efforts and programs to support interested translators and publishers, and, thus, raise the profile of British and Irish poetry on the German book market (as well as on others). A model for such an initiative could be TOLEDO, a program of the Robert Bosch Stiftung and the Deutscher Übersetzerfonds. In 2019, it launched JUNIVERS, a program geared toward the needs and desires of poetry translators, with the ultimate aim of finding new translators and new languages for German poets. For six days in June, 18 translators, arriving at the Literarisches Colloquium Berlin from countries such as Brazil, India, Poland, Italy, Argentina, and Greece, among many others, participated in a collective translation workshop and cooperated with guests such as Thilo Krause, winner of the Peter Huchel Prize, with a number of local poets, and also myself, conducting a workshop on translating the Austrian poet Erich Fried. Such an initiative will hopefully result in many more books of German poets in a wide variety of languages. British cultural administrators might take note.

The Poetry Presses

In 1992, Nigel Wheale defined small presses as "one, or rarely more than two individuals, who, usually in their spare time and at their own expense, write or edit poetry, print and bind it more or less competently, and circulate it, almost invariably at a loss, or at best only barely covering their costs" (Wheale 1992, 9). They usually publish collections by individual poets and are often run alongside a little magazine. According to Wheale, print-runs range from 200 to 500 copies, rarely sell well or out, are not stocked by bookshops, and their "working life [...] is normally quite short because the activity occurs at the margins of viability, and they routinely succumb to accumulated pressures of debt and/or despair in equal measures" (Wheale 1992, 9). Some of the characteristics in this definition are valid for quite a number of the small presses publishing during the British Poetry Revival between 1960 and 1975, but, I would argue, it was already outdated in the 1980s, let alone in the early 1990s. Peter Forbes, at the time editor of *Poetry Review*, and Jonathan Barker, Literature Officer at the British Council, argue in their joint essay "Poetry Publishing Today" that "some of the subsidized small presses [...] now constitute the main outlet for poetry book publication, and match the majors in attractive production, prestige, and often in marketing flair." The "big league," comprising Bloodaxe, Carcanet, Peterloo, Anvil, Seren, Enitharmon, and Littlewoood Arc, "are more prolific than the majors" (Forbes/Barker 1992, 236). The essay by Forbes and Barker offers a substantial list of 52 poetry book publishers for Great Britain and Ireland (Forbes/Barker 1992, 237–238).

Half a decade later, Peter Finch described poetry as "a minority art made consumer friendly" that is "[b]right, visible, fashionable" (Finch 1996, 116), and Michael Horowitz put forward the thesis that "[h]appily, the *arriviste* atmosphere of ten to fifteen years ago when seven per cent or so of English poets and literary careerists controlled at least 84 per cent of the publishing, taste-making, grant-and-prize and allied opportunities for poets, is on the wane across Britain" (quoted in Finch 1996, 116). Despite an astounding list of 320 poetry presses—an increase of more than 600% in 4 years—and "this undoubted success" (Finch 1996, 117), Finch warns of "cracks" that can already be seen. In particular, he detects a "quietly indecisive" attitude among the mainstream commercial publishers, reports of the small presses' concern that more unsold copies than expected had been returned by bookshops, and finally offers his feeling that "the boom if not quite bust is certainly on the point of turn" (Finch 1996, 117).

Despite a slight increase in the number of poetry presses to 326 in 1997, Finch continued his warnings that "[i]n the rush to mount the bandwagon publishers are now putting out far too many books and as a consequence reviewers are increasingly ignoring them" (Finch 1997, 108). Although Finch notices great successes such as *Poems on the Underground*, he raises doubts about poetry that is seen as "a kind of spectator sport" (Finch 1997, 107) and "a branch of the entertainment industry" (Finch 1997, 108). To support his argument, Finch refers to the survey *Public Attitudes to Poetry* (1995), commissioned by the Arts Council England: the majority of the population has a problem with poetry's image ("out-of-touch, gloomy, irrelevant, effeminate, high-brow and elitist"; Finch 1997, 108), there are not enough readers, and those who read do not read enough.

At the turn of the millennium, the situation of the poetry publishing industry changed completely. Despite Oxford University Press's abandoning its poetry list, two and half thousand volumes of verse were published in 1999 (Finch 2000, 112). The list of poetry presses supplementing Finch's essay only comprises 106 entries, which means that within 4 years more than 200 publishers stopped operations. They range from commercial publishers such as Faber & Faber, Cape, Chatto & Windus to "specialists," headed by Carcanet and Bloodaxe, and small presses, Finch's third category, such as Rockingham Press, Redbeck, and Words Worth. Despite these figures, Finch's résumé of the situation is, very surprisingly if compared to 4 years ago, almost enthusiastic: "Never before have new poets been faced with so many publishing opportunities. And if there is any criticism then this is it. Too many books jamming the market" (Finch 2000, 123).

Seven years later, in 2007, the list of UK and Irish publishers showed an impressive figure of 200 entries, while by 2009 the number of poetry presses had decreased enormously to only 122 operators, a decline that continued in 2010 (116 presses), and more or less stopped when *The Writers' Handbook 2011* listed 112 businesses. The *Writers' & Artists' Yearbook 2019* should only be mentioned in passing, as it is perfectly unreliable. Its listings seem to have been produced with the intention of entertaining: the publishers-of-poetry list comprises only 37 presses, including one—Hippopotamus Press—which has not published a single collection since 2002, the year Roland John launched David Clarke's *Touching on Love*. In his essay, Neil Astley only refers to 27 poetry presses, rather like a list of friends collected from his mobile phone that are invited to his very exclusive party (Astley 2018, 366).

In contrast to these figures, the British and Irish poetry scene is populated by poetry presses, which publish an impressive number of single-author collections, single-poet pamphlets, and anthologies. Today's situation is similar to the one in the mid-1990s as Finch described it: poets producing work of a certain quality will almost always find their way into print. Not every poet will perhaps find a home at the headquarters of "The Big Six"—Bloodaxe Books, Jonathan Cape, Carcanet, Chatto & Windus, Faber & Faber, and Picador (Astley 2018, 366)—but many small presses and their staff are prepared to offer high-quality support during the production process and often better and more personal mentoring with regard to publicity, distribution, and royalties. As Matthew Sperling has argued, "most new small-press volumes are now only a Paypal transaction away. Poetry readings are no longer the preserve of the locals and regulars in obscure pub back rooms, but are advertised, digested, and sometimes broadcast on blogs, newsfeeds, and other social networking technologies" (Sperling 2013, 196–197).

When studying the poetry presses in operation since 1960, one may consider the question of whether, compared to trade publishers in other fields, there are, on the British and Irish poetry scene, publishers who may be regarded as "big." In this context, it is of paramount importance to analyze the financial situation of the presses, in particular how taxpayers' money has been distributed among them. Starting in the mid-1990s—according to the published lists, the heyday of British and Irish poetry presses—one among many reasons why six publishers felt, and still feel, they are "biggish" when compared to fellow competitors could perhaps be found in *The Arts Council of England Annual Report 1994–1995*. It records the following grants and guarantees for the time period April 1, 1994, to March 31, 1995: Anvil Press Poetry received £61,600 and Carcanet £67,800 with an additional grant, for *PN Review*, of £17,580. The sense of conscious bigness is self-explanatory when one compares these figures with grants allocated under the headings "Small Presses": Enitharmon Press £200, Peterloo Poets £325, Dangeroo Press £350. Under the heading "Translations," Dedalus received £11,915, and Bloodaxe Books £2,290.

A decade later, in the year 2006, an Arts Council initiative involving a new client hit the headlines of newspapers and trade journals: Salt Publishing was awarded £185,000 of investment spread over the next 3 years. According to Salt's press release, also posted on the

BRITISH-IRISH-POETS discussion list, three ACE senior managers—John Hampson, Senior Strategy Officer, David Gilbert, former Managing Director of Waterstone's, and Gary McKeone, outgoing Director of Literature—had struck a deal with Chris and Jennifer Hamilton-Emery. In the official phrasing of the report: they "consulted with Salt to help build a business plan which will see the company become one of the largest independent poetry and short story publishers in the UK" (Hamilton-Emery 2006). This sounded like—and was, indeed, no less than—a bid for a takeover of the UK poetry scene. Until then, Salt could offer only a rather modest list of successes, among them a shortlisting for the 2005 Jerwood Aldeburgh First Collection Prize. However, they had launched four international series: in 2000 Salt Modern Poets followed by Salt Companions to Poetry (2001), Salt Modern Poets in Translation (2004), and Salt Studies in Contemporary Poetry (2003): all of which constituted a very ambitious program codesigned by John Kinsella, located in Perth and editor of the biannual magazine *Salt* (14 issues, 1990–2004), and Chris Hamilton-Emery, who at the time had published two collections with Barque (2000) and Arc (2002), having also been Press Production Director at Cambridge University Press for 8 years until 2002. The two poet-editors were joined in the undertaking by Hamilton-Emery's wife Jennifer, a senior manager in the National Health Service, Linda Bennett, a former director of Waterstone's, and John Skelton, former Managing Director of Open University Press. This line-up of expertise, the international outlook of the publishing program, and the well-structured approach of four series must have been very persuasive. In 2005, Chris Hamilton-Emery offered a résumé of the first 6 years: "This year we began stocking up our new distributors in Australia and selling ebooks, and from those first four titles in 2000, we now publish around forty books a year across three continents and have grown from £8,000 to an £80,000 business" (Hamilton-Emery 2005, 166–167). However, the ambition of developing "an international profile as a highly-innovative publisher of a broad poetry and literature list" (Hamilton-Emery 2006) was never fulfilled. The adjective *broad* is in sharp contrast to Hamilton-Emery's "alternative vision" set out in his contribution to *PN Review*, which was to

> give everyone in the UK the chance of accessing a poetry which is intellectually ambitious, which transcends national boundaries and pastoral, which takes risks in reinventing the world, rather than describing it. A poetry interested in diversity, theory, and life as it *can* be lived, rather than life as we have it. I want a literature of aspiration and innovation. (Hamilton-Emery 2005, 9)

This "vision" gives the impression that the selection of writers, published by Salt from 2007 to 2013, and the poetics they represent(ed) was far too narrow to attract enough reviews, readers, and sales. Salt published 80 titles per year during the period of the 3-year grant. Together with Shearsman—Tony Frazer received an ACE grant of £17,500 over a 3-year period (2005–2007) and published 39 books in 2007, 63 titles in 2009, and another 54 books in 2010—they flooded the poetry scene and gave the impression that the great majority of poetry books came from one or other of the two presses from 2007 to 2010. After their "Just One Book" campaign launched in May 2009, when they asked people to involve themselves in the project by buying just one book, Hamilton-Emery declared in August 2009: "The flaw in the programme was that we based it on title count. We scaled up our publishing operations and when the funding stopped we were actually left in a very exposed position. [...] With the benefit of hindsight if we'd really thought it through we would have managed the cash differently – we'd have been less expansive and had a look at building our cash reserves" (Flood, 2009). Barely 4 years later, Salt dropped their single-author collections, as their sales had declined by a quarter in 2012 and total sales halved in the years 2008–2012. "It's simply not viable to continue doing them unfunded," Hamilton-Emery admitted, "we have tried to commit to single-author collections by funding them ourselves, but as they have become increasingly unprofitable, we can't sustain it" (Flood 2013). In 2018, when Salt relaunched their Modern Poets list, Hamilton-Emery started to commission single-author collections once again, also inviting unsolicited British submissions: "Identity in publishing is important, perhaps critical in building your business, you can't understand Salt without its poetry, the building blocks of its success." When defining his aims for the list, Hamilton-Emery seems to have learnt his lesson. Although he wants "to provide opportunities for debuts [... and] take risks," his focus is now "on the individual talents rather than any given poetics" (Hamilton-Emery 2018). However, *The Bookseller's* recent article on "High Returns and Slow Sales Hit Salt with £15,000 Shortfall," and Jennifer Hamilton-Emery's announcement that they "need to recapitalise the business," followed by the already (in)famous appeal to "our loyal readers to buy a book and help us climb out of the hole" (Chandler 2019) make the situation sound like *Groundhog Day*.

Let us now compare Salt's approach and dealings with Andy Croft's Smokestack Books imprint, which was modeled on the American Curbstone Press, the French publisher Le Temps des Cerises, and Fore Publications in the UK. It was launched in 2004, helped by an initial ACE grant of £20,480, with a clearly defined aim: "I wanted to make an intervention on a larger stage and on a more professional scale, combining poets of local, regional, national, and international reputation" (Croft 2019a). Although this policy statement sounds rather broad in its scope, the term *intervention* carries definitely political connotations, implying for Croft "contributions to a conversation about a particular issue" by "oppositional, dissident, unfashionable and radical poets" (Croft 2019b, 33). The list of titles, meant as specific interventions, is long and impressive: Mayakovsky's epic poem *Lenin* (the centenary of 1917), *Crisis*, an anthology edited by Dinos Siotis (the Greek economic and political crisis), *A Rose Loupt Oot*, edited by David Betteridge (the fortieth anniversary of the Upper Clyde Shipbuilders [UCS] work-in), and Amir Darwish's *Dear Refugee* and *Don't Forget the Couscous* (the Syrian refugee crisis). Tom Wintringham's *We're Going On!* marks the seventieth anniversary of the beginning of the Spanish Civil War and David Cain's *Truth Street* the thirtieth anniversary of the Hillsborough disaster. *New Boots and Pantisocracies*, edited by W. N. Herbert and Andy Jackson, relates to the first 100,days of the Cameron government, while two sequences occupy themselves with Brexit—John Gohorry's *Squeak, Budgie!* and Martin Rowson's *Pastrami Faced Racist*. In response to the rise of neo-Fascism and anti-Semitism in Europe, Croft published András Mezei's *Christmas in Auschwitz* and Guus Luijters's *Song of Stars*, as well as the anthology *Survivors: Hungarian Jewish Poets of the Holocaust*, edited by Thomas Ország-Land. Finally, a percentage of the sales of *A Blade of Grass: New Palestinian Poetry*, edited by Naomi Foyle, is donated by Croft to help finance the legal fees of Ashraf Fayadh and Dareen Tatour, Palestinian poets imprisoned in Saudi Arabia and in Israel on charges relating to their poetry (Croft 2019a, b, 33). Croft wants to "keep open a space for what is left of the socialist and communist poetic traditions in the twenty-first century," which also means "publishing books that otherwise would be unlikely to appear in print," and, when referring to the press's international focus, "putting into English poets whose work is either unavailable or unknown in the UK" (Croft 2019b, 33).

Although Smokestack only received another five ACE grants (2006/7: £26,125; 2008/9: £17,891; 2010: £6,200; 2011: £8,300; 2012: £6,200; Croft 2019c), Croft has managed to publish more than 160 books since 2004. The lack of continuous financial support meant that Croft could no longer pay his authors a nominal fee of £500 after the final ACE grant in 2011. However, he also felt "a kind of liberation. I suddenly had much greater control over the budget, which was no longer dependent on funding decisions made elsewhere. And I don't have to justify my editorial decisions to anyone" (Croft 2019a). In 2018, Croft published 15 titles and the press, as Croft admits, "is pretty well self-financing [...]. So, as long as I never pay myself anything for running Smokestack it breaks even" (Croft 2019a). This situation may change because of very recent developments. Much to Croft's own surprise, one of his interventions—David Cain's *Truth Street*—was shortlisted in the 2019 Forward Best First Collection category and featured by *The Guardian*, a first for a Smokestack title (Croft 2019a,b, 33, Flood 2019). Croft was not overwhelmed, roundly declaring: "Of course the only reason that *The Guardian* are interested in *Truth Street* is that it has been shortlisted for one of the little Forward prizes. They rang me up to ask for a review copy when the shortlist was published, despite the fact that I had sent them a review copy several months earlier when the book came out" (Croft 2019d). As for the shortlisting itself, one of the reasons for it may have been the jury's sensitivity to the political dimension of things. Andrew McMillan, one of the jurors, declared that "a lot of these collections, especially from newer poets, are really getting down in the mud and wrestling with the intricacies and difficulties of our new political situation" (Flood 2019). McMillan's observation coincides with a trend that Donna Ferguson had, almost rhapsodically, described in *The Guardian* as a "passion for politics, particularly among teenagers and young millennials, [that] is fueling a dramatic growth in the popularity of poetry" (Ferguson 2019). Under these new circumstances, Croft may reconsider his plans to close Smokestack in 2021.

British and Irish Poetry Prizes

> In a way, it is unfortunate that we have to have a prize culture at all. But we do have to have it. Because we do, unfortunately, have to make a fuss to draw people's attention to the better work that's being produced. (Burnside 2016, 17)

Prizes have become a normal part of any moderately successful literary career. When a poet makes a submission of new poems these days, it has, accordingly, become part of the procedure to give the covering letter or email the character of a bio/bibliographical note. In it, quite understandably, the poet points out that he or she has won a poetry prize, even if it is a prize too obscure to have been heard of. In fact, many poets, almost like accountants, keep lists of even every shortlisting in poetry competitions or awards. The entries in the "Notes on Contributors" sections of any poetry magazine are quite illuminating in this respect. In the "Some Contributors" section of *PN Review* 221 (2015), Kathleen Bell, a poet from the East Midlands, draws attention to the shortlisting of her chapbook *at the memory exchange* (Oystercatcher Press) for the 2014 Saboteur Awards. The Italian poet Pierluigi Cappello needs to inform readers of the magazine that "[a]mong his awards are a Montale Europa Prize (2004), the Bagutta Opera Prima Prize (2007), and the prestigious [sic!] Viareggio-Rèpaci Prize (2010)" (87). The American poet Marilyn Hacker received the "PEN Award for Poetry in Translation in 2009, the PEN / Voelcker Award for her own work in 2010, and the Prix Argana from the Beit-as-Sh'ir / House of Poetry (Morocco) in 2011" (87). Mimi Khalvati, we are told, received a Poetry Book Society Recommendation and a Poetry Book Society Special Commendation. Maitreyabandhu, a poet from Henley-in-Arden, Warwickshire, who was ordained into the Triratna Buddhist Order in 1990, "has won the Keats-Shelley Prize, the Basil Bunting Award, and the Geoffrey Dearmer Prize," and his first collection is a Poetry Book Society Recommendation. And, finally, the poet and critic Neil Powell published *Benjamin Britten: A Life for Music*, which was Biography of the Year at the 2013 East Anglian Book Awards. One is reminded of James F. English's book *The Economy of Prestige* subtitled *Prizes, Awards, and the Circulation of Cultural Value*, published in 2005. The opening chapter is called "Prize Frenzy" and takes for its epigraph the verdict of the Dodo in *Alice's Adventures in Wonderland*: "Everybody has won, and all must have prizes." The British literary world—its poetry scene in particular—seems to operate on the same principle.

As early as 1989, Margaret Drabble had reflected on the literary prize system and the steady increase in the number of prizes, arguing that "poets more than any other category of writer need prizes and bursaries to keep aloft" (Drabble 1989, 251). Kathryn Gray in 2015 admits that prizes can be regarded as "a welcome opportunity to financially reward the purveyors of an art form who typically went largely unremunerated for their efforts" (Gray 2015, 8), but reminds "the children of prize culture" (Gray 2015, 8), whom she defines, appropriately, as "those of us in the mainstream," that "the pragmatism of consensus" among the judging panels "limits individual passions in favour of general acceptance" (Gray 2015, 9). Gray regards this phenomenon as "profoundly unhealthy" (Gray 2015, 11) for new poets, "who should still be thinking of their art in terms of play and exploration" (Gray 2015, 11). Instead, many of them are focused from the start on the prize culture and cultivate "the kind of work that is well received," which may lead to what Gray calls "the problem of homogeneity" (Gray 2015, 12).

John Burnside, who received both the T. S. Eliot Prize and the Forward Prize in 2012 and was a member of the Man Booker Prize jury in 2015, is, though aware of the problems, inclined, understandably, to emphasize the importance of literary prizes:

> There is the Martin Scorsese case, the most disturbing thing, when someone goes through years of missing prizes, not being entirely forgotten, for some reason, and that's sad when that happens because prizes do matter, they make a difference. They make a difference to sales, make a difference to publicity. And nobody in their right mind would say, "Oh, I only write for myself.

I don't care if 12 people read my book or 12,000." You'd much rather 12,000 people, because you're trying to communicate something as well. You may take great pleasure in the process of making these things as well, but you do want to show it to people and say, do you feel that way about it? So they do matter a lot. And, of course, you can't get into a situation like you have with children, "Everyone gets a prize." It's difficult. The only time it bothers me is when I'm quite convinced that the prize was awarded for non-literary reasons. (Burnside 2016, 16)

Perhaps everyone's having to get a prize is the reason for the confusion of their numbers. If we start out by consulting Wikipedia, the page for "List of poetry awards" offers 21 entries for the United Kingdom ("List of Poetry Awards: United Kingdom" 2019) with only two for Ireland. ("List of Poetry Awards: Ireland" 2019) However, the Wikipedia page for "British poetry awards," ("British Poetry Awards" 2019) which obviously leaves out the Irish Republic, lists 31 poetry prizes for Britain alone. Writers' handbooks usually list more than 200 literary prizes for Great Britain and Ireland, the majority of them being awarded for new novels, with just around 10% awarded in the field of poetry. When I scanned the "Prizes" section of *The Writer's Handbook 2010* (Turner 2009) for poetry prizes and awards and, in addition, consulted the relevant index entry, the figure I arrived at was 35 for Great Britain and Ireland. The *Writers' & Artists' Yearbook 2019* has 40 entries for poetry in its "Prizes and Awards" subject index, including listings for Arts Council England and its Irish equivalent An Chomhairle Ealaíon. The two national organizations deserve their listings in the index, because they offer financial support for awards or administer them. Through the Grants for the Arts Libraries fund (which became Arts Council National Lottery Project Grants from March 2018 onward), Arts Council England supported the Society of Authors Translation Prizes in March 2018 with £6,767 and the Somerset Young Poets Competition 2018 with £7,500 (Arts Council England, 2018). Their Irish counterpart announced in December 2018 a new award in memory of Anthony Cronin. Applications were invited from mid-career writers in the English or Irish language who work in any form. The primary purpose of the new award is "to enable the writer to undertake travel or a residency abroad" in order to conduct research for a new work. Its ultimate aim, however, is to help writers "build the international dimension" of their career. The total maximum amount that may be awarded is €13,000, which is made up of €10,000 for living and writing and €3,000 for travel expenses (The Arts Council/An Chomhairle Ealaíon 2019, 2–3).

In the chapter "Platforms and Performances" of his book *The Cambridge Introduction to British Poetry, 1945–2010*, Eric Falci places the proliferation of poetry prizes in the 1990s, in particular in the context of "newly established writing programs and workshops." The consequence of this development was that "more poets took up teaching positions at colleges and universities," which led to the institutionalization of poetry "as a craft and *product*" (emphasis added) in higher education (Falci 2015, 181). At the time several programs, including Poems on the Underground (1986), National Poetry Day (1994), and Poetry on the Buses (1998), were launched. These gave contemporary poetry a public presence and increased its profile considerably. The two Nobel Prizes for Derek Walcott in 1992 and Seamus Heaney in 1995 cemented trends indicative of postwar British poetry more broadly, [...] saying nearly as much about the advance of Caribbean and Northern Irish poetry and the reorientation of British poetry in the previous several decades as they did about the achievements of each poet individually. (Falci 2015, 181)

The most notable or noticeable instances of the so-called proliferation of poetry prizes in the early 1990s are two major awards: the Forward Prizes (established in 1991) and the T. S. Eliot Prize (inaugurated in 1993), which started to offer significant cash rewards and, for a while, televised award ceremonies.

The *Writers' & Artists' Yearbook 1992* seems to confirm Falci's thesis: it lists 21 British and Irish prizes and awards for which collections of poetry could be submitted. Nevertheless, it must not be forgotten that even if poetry was not categorically excluded in the statements of eligibility, the great majority of literary prizes was never or hardly ever awarded to poets. An award illustrative of this propensity and also one of the most prominent on the 1992 list is *The Mail on Sunday*–John Llewellyn Rhys Prize, inaugurated as early as 1942 by Jane Oliver in memory of her husband John Llewellyn Rhys, a young writer killed on 5 August 1940 while serving as a bomber pilot in the Royal Air Force. It became part of the proliferation phenomenon when in 1987 *The Mail on Sunday* became its sponsor and the prize money was substantially increased: the winner received £5,000 and the runners-up £500 each. This went on until 2003 when the BookTrust, in its own definition "the largest reading charity in the UK," became its administrator, after which, in 2011, the UK's second oldest literary award was suspended. Awarded annually for the best work of literature as opposed to a particular form or genre—the eligibility was very liberal and extended to fiction, nonfiction, poetry, and drama—it was in fact only very rarely awarded to a poet. An examination of the list of winners demonstrates that the "liberal" approach is, generally speaking, to the detriment of poetry. In fact, *The Mail on Sunday*–John Llewellyn Rhys Prize was only once in its history awarded to a poet, that is, in 1984 to Andrew Motion for his collection *Dangerous Play: Poems, 1974–1984* (Salamander Press/Penguin). This distinction, I would like to argue, may in part be owing to Motion's very prominent standing as a poet-cum-academic-cum-critic. He had held, and was still holding, influential positions in the literary business, from 1976 to 1980, teaching English at the University of Hull, and editing *Poetry Review* from 1980 to 1982, the magazine of the Poetry Society. Finally, from 1982 to 1989, he was Editorial Director and Poetry Editor at Chatto & Windus. Don't get me wrong: if, within the context of the literary awards system, I also pay some attention to the background of prize-winning poets, I am not "simply railing against the whole machinery of literary awards, the mainstream publishing establishment, and its tight reviewing network" (Falci 2015, 208). I merely think it important to take this "machinery" apart, look at the pieces and develop an understanding of how it all works, because "[f]ocusing on the prize-winning volumes from the past ten or fifteen years does not produce a capacious enough picture of twenty-first-century British poetry" (Falci 2015, 208).

Among the awards listed in the *Writers' & Artists' Yearbook 1992*, more favorable to poetry are the Whitbread Literary Awards, whose administration actually introduced the poetry category in 1985 to remedy a deficit; until then the four prize categories had been First Novel,

Novel, Children's Book, and Biography. Most satisfyingly, the winner of the inaugural award was Douglas Dunn with his famous collection *Elegies* (Faber & Faber), a moving account of his wife's death. Subsequent winners up to 1992 were Peter Reading, Seamus Heaney, Peter Porter, Michael Donaghy, Paul Durcan, Michael Longley, and Tony Harrison, at the time and, even more so in retrospect, a prestigious and high-quality list of British and Irish poets. The winner of each category received £2,000 and the overall winner for the Whitbread Book of the Year obtained £20,500 on top of the Nomination Award. When in 2006, Costa Coffee, a subsidiary of Whitbread, took over sponsorship of the awards, the total prize fund was increased to £60,000. Since then each of the category winners receives £5,000 and the overall winner a further £30,000. The terms of eligibility are defined as follows:

> Books must be submitted directly by publishers, not by authors. Authors of submitted books must have been resident in the United Kingdom or Ireland for over six months of each of the previous three years (although UK or Irish nationality is not essential). Books must have been first published in the UK or Ireland between 1 November of the previous year and 31 October of the current year. Books previously published elsewhere are not eligible.

The jury for each category consists of three judges: usually, an author, a bookseller, and a journalist, who select a shortlist of four collections from which they proceed to choose the winner. The Costa Book of the Year is selected by a panel of nine judges, which includes five authors, one from each of the five categories; the Costa Chairman; and "three other people in the public eye who love reading." In an interview for *Poetry Salzburg Review*, Burnside, who was the author judge for the poetry category in 2013, points out some of the problems of the Costa Book Awards and critiques them:

> I very passionately went in to try to get the poetry book to win, but the others ... they liked the poetry book, but they felt that it wasn't as substantial a piece of literary work as a novel. I don't know why people think that [laughs]. That's the view. And also you have the arguments that come and say – we are talking to a wider public, we are trying to get people to read. If you're going to give them something which is going to mystify them ... The poetry that I was fighting for was Michael Symmons Roberts's book *Drysalter* (2013), which I think with a bit of application anybody could read, with a bit of work. But there's that perception which is basically if you ask them to do much work, too much work, it will be off-putting. They have to work their way towards that kind of book, which sometimes means that that kind of book doesn't get a prize. But he [i.e. Michael Symmons Roberts] has won prizes, the Forward Prize and the Whitbread Prize, and was on the shortlist of the T. S. Eliot Prize in 2013, and that's good. (Burnside 2016, 15–16)

Along with Burnside the jury for the poetry category included Olivia Cole, a journalist and winner of the 2003 Eric Gregory Award, who had published a first collection of poetry, and Daniel Eltringham, whose PhD at Birkbeck, University of London, is on Wordsworth and Prynne, and who has published on R. F. Langley, Peter Riley, and Sean Bonney, and is also the coeditor of the excellent online poetry journal *The Literateur*. Considering Cole's and Eltringham's expertise in poetry, it is not surprising that Burnside reached a unanimous decision with them in favor of Michael Symmons Roberts's collection. In addition to the prejudice, vexing to Burnside, that a collection of poetry "wasn't as substantial a piece of literary work as a novel" there is the problem presented by the jury's brief itself, which, Burnside points out, requires them "to select well-written, enjoyable books that they would strongly recommend anyone to read" (Costa Book Awards 2019). This practically rules out the choice of a volume of adventurous and innovative verse. Both these aspects are reflected in the composition of the jury for the Costa Book of the Year. It was chaired by Rose Tremain, the author of 14 novels and five collections of short stories, who taught Creative Writing at the University of East Anglia and was its chancellor. The "three other people in the public eye who love reading" were: Natascha McElhone, British stage, screen, and television actress; Richard Osman, a BBC and Channel 4 presenter, producer, and director; and Sharleen Spiteri, songwriter and lead singer of the Glasgow-based rock band Texas. The authors from the juries of the other four categories were Matt Cain (First Novel), Gerard Woodward (Novel), Anne de Courcy (Biography), and Emma Kennedy (Children's Book). When one studies the personal websites of the jury members and other sources relating to them, it is, admittedly, almost always difficult to assess whether or not there is a potential interest, let alone expertise, in regard to poetry. However, in order to avoid mere speculation, let us continue considering the personal literary background of each figure from the jury. It can be assumed that Sharleen Spiteri as a songwriter may have a certain perhaps debatable predilection for poetry. Woodward, who is both a poet and a novelist—he has published six collections of poetry, six novels, and two collections of short stories—won an Eric Gregory Award for poets under 30 (1989), and for his first collection of poetry, *Householder*, the Somerset Maugham Award (1991). As all the other jury members have a personal background in prose and fiction, one can certainly understand Burnside's difficulties, and eventual failure, in persuading his fellow adjudicators to vote for the poetry book.

In the abovementioned interview, Burnside mentions awards that he seems to hold in higher regard than the Costa: the Forward Prizes and the T. S. Eliot Prize. The Forward Prizes were set up in 1992 by William Sieghart, an entrepreneur and publisher, who also founded National Poetry Day in 1994—a day of celebration of verse on the first Thursday in October—and, 1 year later, the Forward Arts Foundation, a charity that administers both poetry projects. Its mission is threefold: "to deepen appreciation of poetry's value; to celebrate excellence in poetry; to increase poetry's audience" (Forward Arts Foundation 2019). For Sieghart, "[p]oetry is a magnificent companion in this busy modern world, often giving us a vocabulary for emotions we cannot express" (Treneman 1997). The Forward Prizes are awarded in three categories: Best Collection, Best First Collection, and Best Single Poem. For the twenty-fifth anniversary in 2016, the value of the Forward Prize for Best Collection was increased to £15,000, while each of the shortlisted poets was awarded £1,000. The winner of the Best First Collection received £5,000 and the poet of the Best Single Poem could cash a check worth £1,000. Since 2013, the Forward Prizes have been presented live on stage, a special event at the Royal Festival Hall in London's Southbank Centre in late October, after readings from the shortlisted collections. In contrast to the Costa Book Awards, the judging panel includes only poets and poetry editors. The 2016 panel was chaired by Malika Booker, writer and spoken word artist, and included the poets George Szirtes and Liz Berry, the singer/songwriter Tracey Thorn, as well as Don Share, editor of *Poetry Magazine*. The shortlist of each category consisted of five nominations. The really surprising aspect of the three shortlists was the omission of publications from some established publishers, for example, Faber & Faber and Chatto & Windus (an imprint of Random House). A close consideration of the poets on the three shortlists left me not just surprised but positively—in both senses of the word—puzzled: there was a striking absence, perhaps with the exception of Alice Oswald, of the so-called "big names." I could only agree with Malika Booker, chair of the judges, when she asserted, admittedly going a little over the top (which, no doubt, appealed to the press):

> In this 25th year of the Forward prizes, I feel we're seeing a complete resurgence and a breaking down of barriers within and around poetry. Just look at the shortlist: there are eleven women and the multiplicity of voices is testimony to the fact that the poetry published here now feels totally global. These collections and works represent the very best of contemporary poetry. Fresh, vibrant and full of new insights and challenging ideas, each demands attention and we're all daunted by the prospect of choosing our winners. (Bainbridge 2016)

The shortlist of Best Collection was headed by Trinidad-born Vahni Capildeo (Carcanet Press), who was to receive the prize, and Choman Hardi (Bloodaxe Books)—born in Sulaymaniyah, Kurdistan, she lived in Iraq and Iran before seeking asylum in the UK in 1993. Their poems deal with migration, protest, and polylingualism, some of today's big issues. Alice Oswald (Cape Poetry) and Denise Riley (Picador Poetry) are poets who could not be more different in terms of their publishing careers. Oswald published her first collection, *The Thing in the Gap-Stone Stile*, with Oxford University Press in 1996. She received immediate and prestigious recognition, winning the Best First Collection category of the Forward Prizes. In November 1998, Oxford University Press infamously announced the closing down of its poetry list, which meant the loss of their chief avenue of publication to some 50 poets, including D. J. Enright, Sean O'Brien, Craig Raine, and Peter Porter (Glaister 1999). This is the reason why Oswald published her second collection, *Dart*, with Faber & Faber, for which she received the T. S. Eliot Prize. Oswald stayed with the London publisher until 2011, when she entrusted to them her sixth collection, *Memorial*—which was shortlisted, again, for the T. S. Eliot Prize. However, Oswald withdrew her collection from the shortlist in December 2011, because she took issue with the fact that the Poetry Book Society, the administrator of the prize, had signed a 3-year sponsorship deal with Aurum, an investment company managing hedge funds (Flood 2011; Waters 2011). One could suppose that the step caused some friction with her publisher; which could not have been abated when she gave her next collection, *Falling Awake* (2016), to Cape Poetry, an imprint of Penguin Random House's Vintage Books. In contrast to Oswald, Denise Riley stepped into the poetry pool at the other end and with less of a splash. She published with a small imprint. Her *Selected Poems* was brought out by Ken Edwards's Reality Street in 2000. Her shortlisted collection, *Say Something Back*, was her first collection with Picador, an imprint of Pan Macmillan owned by the privately held Georg von Holtzbrinck Publishing Group that is based in Stuttgart. With Ian Duhig's *The Blind Roadmaker*, Picador had a second collection on the shortlist.

The second award that Burnside mentions is the T. S. Eliot Prize, which was inaugurated in 1993, celebrating the Poetry Book Society's fortieth anniversary and in honor of its founder. It is "awarded annually to the author of the best new collection of poetry published in the UK and Ireland." (TSEliot.com 2019). In 2016, following the closing down of the Poetry Book Society, the T. S. Eliot Foundation, which was set up in 2012 following the death of Valerie Eliot to promote the poet's work and legacy, took over the running of the prize. The Foundation increased the value of the prize: the winner receives £20,000 and each of the shortlisted poets £1,500. A shortlist of 10 books was announced in October and the Shortlist Readings took place on January 15, 2017, in the Southbank Centre's Royal Festival Hall. The winner, Jacob Polley for his collection *Jackself* (Picador), was announced at an award ceremony the next day (January 16, 2017), where Polley and the shortlisted poets were presented with their checks (Poetry Book Society n.d.). A close study and analysis of the winners from 2006 until 2018 gives the impression of monotony and predictability; it could be argued that a desirable momentum of surprise has been missing as regards the publishers of the winning poets. In the past decade, Faber & Faber published the winning poet four times: Heaney in 2006, Walcott in 2010, Olds in 2012, and Hannah Sullivan in 2018. Cape came up trumps on three occasions: Burnside in 2011, Olds in 2012, Ocean Vuong in 2017; Bloodaxe twice with Hadfield in 2008 and Gross in 2009, while Picador (O'Brien in 2007) and Carcanet (Morrissey in 2013) could celebrate only one poet each from their list. In this context, Eric Falci rightly observes that "one aspect of the ecosystem of contemporary British poetry is the enduring importance of a very small number of London-based imprints whose slim volumes dominate the prize circuit and reviews pages" (Falci 2015, 209). For David Wheatley, "prizes occupy the threshold between the trading floor of reviews, group membership and public visibility, and the unknown territory of the literary afterlife. Reputation is not double-entry book-keeping, and no amount of entries in the first column can guarantee a healthy surplus in the second." He calls prizes "racing tips, punts on posterity," which are "heavily prone to error" (Wheatley 2015, 163). Already in 2002, Michael Schmidt had warned that "[p]oetry prizes are now the vehicle of literary reception. Control the prizes, and you control the culture of reception" (Schmidt 2002, 1). He arrived at this conclusion after reading Bookworm in *Private Eye* (26 July–8 August 2002) who analyzed the Forward Prize and its judges:

> This year's judges include two poets published by Picador (Sean O'Brien and Michael Donaghy), who have shortlisted two other Picador poets (Peter Porter and Paul Farley) for the £10,000 top prize. Last year's judging panel also included two Picador poets – Donaghy (again) and Peter Porter.
>
> Last year Porter gave the main prize to Sean O'Brien. What's the betting O'Brien won't give it back to his mentor, enabling both to pocket ten grand? Or will their protégé Paul Farley be the one to take the loot this time round?
>
> Last year the £5,000 prize for "best first collection" went to another Picador poet, John Stammers (a product of Donaghy's poetry workshops), and the £1,000 "best single poem" prize was given to Ian Duhig for a poem – you guessed it – from his forthcoming Picador collection. The same poem earlier won Duhig the £5,000 top prize in the Poetry Society's

national poetry competition, judged by a three-man panel including his mate Don Paterson, the foul-mouthed Scottish bard who also happens to be the poetry editor at, er, Picador.

This year's five-poet Forward shortlist includes two other chums, David Harsent and John Fuller (winner of the Forward prize in 1996, when one of the judges was again Sean O'Brien). And Sean O'Brazen was one of three judges of the 1997 T. S. Eliot prize (worth £5,000), which was awarded to ... his own editor, Don Paterson.

Duhig, Donaghy, O'Brien, Harsent and Paterson all have the same agent, TriplePA, aka Gerry Wardle – who just happens to be Sean O'Brien's partner. And Donaghy, Duhig, Farley, Fuller, Harsent, Paterson and Porter have all received fulsome write-ups from the *Sunday Times*'s main poetry critic, one Sean O'Brien. (Bookworm 2002, 25; also cf. Stone 2016)

In a 2014 blog post, Fiona Moore analyzed the shortlists, from 2004 to 2013, of the T. S. Eliot Prize and the Forward Prize for Best Collection, counted the publishers of the shortlisted books, and compared them with the judges' and the Poetry Book Society selectors' publishers. All the winning collections were published by one of the "Big Five": Bloodaxe, Cape, Carcanet, Faber, and Picador. When she added to the "Big Five" other big publishers (e.g., Seren, Chatto, Gallery Press), only 2% of the shortlisted books came from small publishers. The Forward Prize percentage at 14 was slightly better. Ninety-three percent of the Eliot Prize judges and three out of every four Forward judges were published by one of the "Big Five." Even currently speaking, in 2018 and 2019, the situation has not changed a bit: two Bloodaxe titles and one each from Faber, Cape, and Carcanet are on the 2019 Forward Best Collection shortlist. The three judges who are also poets are Tara Bergin (Carcanet), Andrew McMillan (Cape), and Carol Rumens (Seren/Blooadaxe). The 2018 T. S. Eliot shortlist comprised four books from Faber, two from Penguin, and one each from Bloodaxe, Carcanet, Picador, and, finally, from the small press Happen*Stance*. The jury was chaired by Sinéad Morrissey (Carcanet), the other two jurors were Daljit Nagra (Faber) and Clare Pollard (Bloodaxe).

The prize system is not simply to be characterized as big handouts serving the interests of "big" publishers though. One of the most prestigious awards has, in fact, little to offer in the way of prize money. The Geoffrey Faber Memorial Prize, at its initiation in 1963 was worth just £1,000, then increased to the not exactly princely sum of £1,500 in 2014. It has, however, a list of winners who make up a who's who of contemporary poetry: among them are Seamus Heaney (1968), Geoffrey Hill (1970), Douglas Dunn (1976), Paul Muldoon (1982, 1992), John Burnside (1994), and Alice Oswald (2006). This impressive line of tradition was maintained when its administration celebrated the fiftieth anniversary of the award in 2014, with the judges Julia Copus, Ruth Padel, and Max Porter giving the prize to two joint-winner collections: *Bright Travellers* (Jonathan Cape) by Fiona Benson and *Black Country* (Chatto & Windus) by Liz Berry. The terms of eligibility of the prize, it must be added, preserve it from narrowness; it varies the category of its recipients by alternately recognizing a volume of poetry or of fiction by a citizen of the UK, Ireland, or the Commonwealth under the age of 40, that last condition saving it from being permanently committed to established authors. A final important aspect: the judges are not inevitably and a priori Faber authors, but are nominated afresh every year by the editors of newspapers and magazines.

The guidelines defining the rules and conditions of entry usually contain the stereotype requirement "first published in the UK or the Republic of Ireland." The T. S. Eliot Foundation administering the T. S. Eliot Prize, famously described by Andrew Motion as "the prize most poets want to win," concedes simultaneous publication in another country within 1 year. The Forward Arts Foundation defines the eligibility of entries for their three poetry categories in almost identical terms. The Costa Book Awards differ from the previously mentioned awards only in that the author must have been resident in the UK or Ireland for at least 6 months per year in the preceding 3 years. Even the Michael Marks Awards for poetry pamphlets, established in 2009, confine entry to UK publications. By recognizing the enormous contribution that small presses and little magazines make to the poetry world, this award is very welcome. Previous winners—among them the Crater Press, Oystercatcher Press, Happen*Stance*, smith|doorstop, Flarestack Poets, Rack Press, Mariscat Press, The Emma Press, and Guillemot Press—have more than deserved the award. However, the parochial policy of the institutions administering these awards is reminiscent of mercantilism, perhaps all the more understandable in the wake of Brexit, but unthinkable for the German-language poetry scene.

The majority of the Irish poetry awards contrast pleasantly with their British counterparts at least with regard to the lack of complication in the situation. The Patrick Kavanagh Award, one of the most prestigious poetry prizes in Ireland, is simply confined to poets born in Ireland, or of Irish nationality, or long-term residents of Ireland. It is awarded for a first unpublished collection and the winner receives €1000. The sole adjudicator is Brian Lynch, poet, novelist, and president of the society (the Patrick Kavanagh Society n.d.). Similarly, the Poetry Now Award is presented for the best single volume of poetry by an Irish poet.[2] Two prestigious poetry prizes are awarded annually at the Mountains to Sea dlr Book Festival and are administered by Dún Laoghaire–Rathdown County Council—the *Irish Times* Poetry Now Award and the Shine/Strong Poetry Award. The latter is presented annually to the author of the best first collection of poems published by an Irish poet in the previous year. As Poetry Salzburg had published Jim Maguire's first collection *Music Field* in June 2013, the administrators were contacted so as to establish whether the poet's eligibility was somehow nullified by the possible ineligibility of his European publisher. It had not been specified in their Publishers Guidelines whether or not a publisher had to be operative in the Republic. The reply received the very next day confirmed that the sole condition was that the author had to be an Irish citizen or resident in Ireland for the past 5 years and that there was no need for the publisher to be operative in the Republic. Jim Maguire's collection was shortlisted and he was invited, together with four other shortlisted poets, to give a reading in the new Central Library and Cultural Centre in Dún Laoghaire. Although he did not win the award, it was, in his own words, "a thrill" for him to participate in such a prize reading.

Summing up, one might remark that the administrators of UK poetry prizes should devise and implement a code of practice. Joey Connelly quite rightly asks: "Why not require declarations of interest, both of the judges involved in the shortlisting process, and of those selecting the panels of judges? Why not lay bare the process by which these judges are chosen, and the shortlists assembled?" (Connelly 2014, 126). Moore suggests "a wider range of judges, such as magazine editors, small-press-published poets, reviewers (the latter are often poets too)" (Moore 2014). In a reply to Moore's post, Norbert Hirschhorn suggests as a possible code of conduct the Council of Literary Magazines and Presses (CLMP) Contest Code of Ethics. For a more global outlook, one could recommend that the Irish stipulations for eligibility might be studied and also implemented.

Notes

1 For a critical evaluation of *Poetry Review*, see also Price 2013, 181–182.
2 See Thomas McCarthy (2015, 520–521) for an account of the importance of receiving the Patrick Kavanagh Award. However, McCarthy arrives at the following summation:

> One's personal poetry, the fruit of one's temperament, is an unassailable realm. Its success or failure has hardly anything to do with anyone else in the deepest sense. There is, of course, the *post facto* politics of published texts, the world of reviews and awards, yet this world is but a distant rumbe of thunder barely audible in the realm where poems get written. So often one meets very new poets who are obsessed with the "politics" of poetry and its trivia: they make the heart sink because you feel that they may never arrive at that point of repose where their deepest work will get written. The place where poems get made is much quieter than the place of fame. (526)

References

Arts Council England (2018). "Grants for the Arts Awards Made Between 01 January 2018–31 January 2018". www.artscouncil.org.uk/grants-arts-0#section-1 (accessed 19 August 2019).

Astley, Neil (2018). "Getting Your Poetry Out There." In: *Writers' & Artists' Yearbook 2019* (ed. Joanne Harris), 362–367. London et al.: Bloomsbury.

Bainbridge, Ashton (2016). "Forward Prizes for Poetry Shortlists Announced" (13 June). https://fmcm.co.uk/news/2016/6/13/forward-prizes-for-poetry-shortlists-announced (accessed 9 August 2019).

Bookworm (2002) "Poets Cornered". *Private Eye*, No. 1059 (26 July – 8 August), 25.

"British Poetry Awards" (2019). Wikipedia. https://en.wikipedia.org/wiki/Category:British_poetry_awards (accessed 19 August 2019).

Burnside, John (2016). "'… really interesting stuff happens on the borderlines'. Interview with Wolfgang Görtschacher and David Malcolm." *Poetry Salzburg Review* 29: 7–18.

Cambridge, Gerry (2016). *'The Dark Horse': The Making of a Little Magazine*. Fife: HappenStance.

Causley, Charles (1984). Email to R.G. Bishop (10 September).

Chandler, Mark (2019). "High Returns and Slow Sales Hit Salt with £15,000 Shortfall". *The Bookseller* (1 August)". https://www.thebookseller.com/news/salt-asks-readers-help-after-difficult-years-trading-1048871 (accessed 20 August 2019).

Clyde, Tom and Andreas, Schachermayr (1999). *HU: An Author Index to Issues 100–107*. Greyabbey: HU Publications.

Connelly, Joey (2014). "The Glittering Prizes." *The Poetry Review* 104 (2): 123–126.

Constantine, David and Constantine, Helen (2016). "Introduction." In: *Centres of Cataclysm. Celebrating Fifty Years of Modern Poetry in Translation* (eds. Sasha Dugdale, David Constantine and Helen Constantine), 20–21. Hexham: Bloodaxe.

Cooke, David (2019). "Submissions". *The High Window*. https://thehighwindowpress.com/submissions (accessed 20 August 2019).

Cookson, William (1994). "Introduction." In: *Agenda: An Anthology: The First Four Decades 1959–1993*, xiii–xxvi. Manchester: Carcanet Press.

Costa Book Awards (2019). "FAQs: Costa Book Awards – How Do the Costa Book Awards Work?" www.costa.co.uk/faqs/#costa_book_awards (accessed 24 August 2019).

Croft, Andy (2019a). Unpublished Interview with Wolfgang Görtschacher.

Croft, Andy (2019b). "Stripped Naked by the Flames." *PN Review* 45 (5): 31–33.

Croft, Andy (2019c). Email to the author (28 August).

Croft, Andy (2019d). Email to the author. (29 August).

Digital Collections, University of Wisconsin-Madison Libraries (2019). "Little Magazine Interview Index". http://digital.library.wisc.edu/1711.dl/LittleMagInt (accessed 20 August 2019).

Drabble, Margaret (1989). "Pleasure and Prestige: A Writer Reflects on the Prize System." In: *British Book News*, 250–251.

Ellis, R.J., John Lucas, Stan Smith, and David Miller (2002). *Little Magazines*. The Nottingham Trent University.

English, James F. (2005). *The Economy of Prestige: Prizes, Awards, and the Circulation of Cultural Value*. Cambridge, Mass; London: Harvard UP.

Falci, Eric (2015). *The Cambridge Introduction to British Poetry, 1945–2010*. Cambridge: CUP.

Ferguson, Donna (2019). "Poetry Sales Soar as Political Millennials Search for Clarity". *The Guardian* (21 January). https://www.theguardian.com/books/2019/jan/21/poetry-sales-soar-as-political-millennials-search-for-clarity (accessed 24 August 2019).

Finch, Peter (1996). "Poetry Matters." In: *The Writer's Handbook 1997* (ed. Barry Turner), 116–135. London: Macmillan.

Finch, Peter (1997). "Poetry – All the Same Thing?" In: *The Writer's Handbook 1998* (ed. Barry Turner), 107–129. London: Macmillan.

Finch, Peter (2000). "Poetry as Ordinary Life." In: *The Writer's Handbook 2001* (ed. Barry Turner), 112–137. London: Macmillan.

Flood, Alison (2009). "ACE in a Hole". *The Bookseller* (20 August). https://www.thebookseller.com/feature/ace-hole# (accessed 20 August 2019).

Flood, Alison (2011). "Alice Oswald Withdraws from TS Eliot Prize in Protest at Sponsor Aurum". *The Guardian* (6 December). https://www.theguardian.com/books/2011/dec/06/alice-oswald-withdraws-ts-eliot-prize (accessed 24 August 2019)

Flood, Alison (2013). "Salt Abandons Single-Author Collections Amid Poetry Market Slump". *The Guardian* (24 May). https://www.theguardian.com/books/2013/may/24/salt-poetry-market-slump (accessed 24 August 2019).

Flood, Alison (2019). "Hillborough Survivors' Words Shortlisted for Forward Poetry Prize". *The Guardian* (22 May). https://www.theguardian.com/books/2019/may/22/hillsborough-survivors-words-forward-poetry-prize-shortlist-truth-street-david-cain (accessed 20 August 2019).

Forbes, Peter (1987). Letter to Wolfgang Görtschacher. N.dat.

Forbes, Peter and Barker, Jonathan. "Poetry Publishing Today." In: *Writers' & Artists' Yearbook 1992*, 231–245. London: A & C Black.

Forward Arts Foundation (2019). "About Us". http://www.forwardartsfoundation.org/about-us (accessed 20 August 2019).

Glaister, Dan (1999). "Minister Steps into Oxford Poetry List Row". *The Guardian* (4 February).

https://www.theguardian.com/uk/1999/feb/04/danglaister (accessed 24 August 2019).

Görtschacher, Wolfgang (1993). *Little Magazine Profiles: The Little Magazines in Great Britain 1939–1993*. Salzburg Studies in English Literature: Poetic Drama & Poetic Theory 77: 6. Salzburg: University of Salzburg.

Görtschacher, Wolfgang (2000). *Contemporary Views on the Little Magazine Scene*. Salzburg: Poetry Salzburg.

Gowrie, Earl of (2003). "Address." *Agenda* 39 (4): 29–31.

Gray, Kathryn (2015). "'To Tell Your Name the Livelong Day': The Paradox of the Poetry Prize." *The Dark Horse* 35: 8–14.

Habash, Gabe (2011). "Young Journal *Asymptote* Takes Literature All Over the World". *Publishers Weekly* (29 September). https://www.publishersweekly.com/pw/by-topic/digital/content-and-e-books/article/48772-asymptote-takes-literature-all-over-the-world.html (accessed 24 August 2019).

Hamburger, Michael (1998). *Michael Hamburger in Conversation with Peter Dale*. London: Between the Lines.

Hamilton-Emery, Chris (2005). "Outtakes and Upsurges: Starting Salt Publishing." *PN Review* 32 (2): 8–9.

Hamilton-Emery, Chris (2006). "Salt Publishing Awarded £185K Investment from Grants for the Arts". BRITISH-IRISH-POETS Archives (20 October). www.jiscmail.ac.uk/cgi-bin/webadmin?A2=ind06&L=BRITISH-IRISH-POETS&D=0&P=1045335 (accessed 20 August 2019).

Hamilton-Emery, Chris (2010). "Poetic Visibility and Relevance at the End of the Noughties." In: *The Writer's Handbook 2011* (ed. Barry Turner), 12–19. Basingstoke: Macmillan.

Hamilton-Emery, Chris (2018). "A Certain Vocation: Relaunching the Salt Modern Poets List". https://www.saltpublishing.com/blogs/news/a-certain-vocation (accessed 20 August 2019).

Harris, Joanna (2018). *The Writers' & Artists' Yearbook 2019*. London et al.: Bloomsbury.

Hayes, Richard (1992). "*Poetry Ireland Review*, Issues 1–21: A Re-View." *Poetry Ireland Review* 36: 53–66.

Ink Sweat & Tears (2019). "About *IS&T*". www.inksweatandtears.co.uk/pages/?page_id=2 (accessed 20 August 2019).

Leong, Lee Yew (2019). "About". *Asymptote*. https://www.asymptotejournal.com/about (accessed 24 August 2019).

Leong, Lee Yew (n.d.). "Lee Yew Leong on *Asymptote*". Poetry Society of America. https://www.poetrysociety.org/psa/poetry/crossroads/site_visits/Asymptote (accessed 24 August 2019).

"List of Poetry Awards: Ireland". (2019). Wikipedia. https://en.wikipedia.org/wiki/List_of_poetry_awards#Ireland (accessed 19 August 2019).

"List of Poetry Awards: United Kingdom". 2019 Wikipedia. https://en.wikipedia.org/wiki/List_of_poetry_awards#United_Kingdom (accessed 19 August 2019).

McCarthy, Patricia (2014). "Introduction." *Agenda* 48 (3–4): 7–8.

McCarthy, Patricia (2018). "Introduction." *Agenda* 52 (1–2): 5–7.

McCarthy, Thomas (2015). "Poetry and the Memory of Fame." *Poetry* 206 (5): 517–526.

Miller, David and Price, Richard (2006). *British Poetry Magazines 1914–2000. A History and Bibliography of 'Little Magazines'*. London: The British Library; New Castle, DE: Oak Knoll Press.

Moore, Fiona (2014). "Poetry Prizes: The Elephant on Stage". *Displacement Poetry* (14 January). http://displacement-poetry.blogspot.com/2014/01/poetry-prizes-elephant-on-stage.html?spref=fb (accessed 20 August 2019).

Mulhall, Anne (2007). "Forms of Exile: Reading *Cyphers*." *Irish University Review* 37 (1): 206–229.

Patrick Kavanagh Society (n.d.). "The Patrick Kavanagh Poetry Award 2016". https://patrick-kavanaghcountry.com/wp-content/uploads/2016/04/Rules-Patrick-Kavanagh-Poetry-Award-2016.pdf (accessed 24 August 2019).

Poetry Book Society (n.d.). "The T. S. Eliot Prize 2016: More about the Prize".

Pollard, Clare (2018). "Editorial: Profound Pyromania". *Modern Poetry in Translation*, 1. http://modernpoetryintranslation.com/editorial/editorial-profound-pyromania (accessed 24 August 2019).

Pollard, Clare (2019). "Editorial: Our Small Universe". *Modern Poetry in Translation*, 1. http://modernpoetryintranslation.com/editorial/editorial-our-small-universe (accessed 24 August 2019).

Price, Richard (2013). "CAT-Scanning the Little Magazine." In: *The Oxford Handbook of Contemporary British and Irish Poetry* (ed. Peter Robinson), 173–190. Oxford: Oxford University Press.

Reilly, Deborah (1985). "Little Magazine Interview Index: At a Glance." *Serials Review* 11: 5–19.

Romer, Stephen (2013). "European Affinities." In: *The Oxford Handbook of Contemporary British and Irish Poetry* (ed. Peter Robinson), 538–557. Oxford: Oxford University Press.

Sader, Marion (ed.) (1976. Series One) 8 vols. *Comprehensive Index to English-Language Little Magazines, 1890–1970*. Millwood, NY: Kraus-Thomson.

Sampson, Fiona (ed.) (2009). "Introduction: *For God's Sake, Do Something!*" In: *A Century of 'Poetry Review'*, xi–xxiv. Manchester/London: Carcanet: Poetry Review, 2009.

Schachermayr, Andreas (1997). "*Ore* 1954–1995: A Bibliography." In: *Veins of Gold: Ore 1954–1995* (eds. Eric Ratcliffe and Wolfgang Görtschacher), 169–248. Salzburg Studies in English Literature: Poetic Drama & Poetic Theory 105. Salzburg et al, University of Salzburg.

Schmidt, Michael (2002). "Editorial." *PN Review* 29 (1): 1–2.

Scottish Poetry Library (2018). "Live Magazines List November 2018". www.scottishpoetrylibrary.org.uk/wp-content/uploads/2018/12/Live-magazines-list-November-2018.pdf (accessed 20 August 2019).

Soar, Geoffrey (1993). "The Little Magazines Archive." In: *Small Press Yearbook 1994* (ed. John Nicholson), 24–25. London: The Small Press Group.

Sperling, Matthew (2013). "Books and the Market: Trade Publishers, State Subsidies, and Small Presses." In: *The Oxford Handbook of Contemporary British and Irish Poetry* (ed. Peter Robinson), 191–212. Oxford: Oxford University Press.

Stone, Jon (2016). "Poets Can't Do Anything Right. And Maybe That's Their Own Fault" (12 February). http://sidekickbooks.com/booklab/2016/02/poets-cant-do-anything-right-and-maybe-thats-their-own-fault.html (accessed 20 August 2019).

The Arts Council/An Chomhairle Ealaíon (2019). Anthony Cronin Award 2019: Guidelines for Applicants. http://www.artscouncil.ie/uploadedFiles/Main_Site/Content/Funds/ACronin_Guidelines2019_EN.pdf (accessed 20 August 2019).

The Authors Guild (2017). "2017 Authors Guild Survey of Literary Translators' Working Conditions: A Summary". https://www.authorsguild.org/wp-content/uploads/2017/12/2017-Authors-Guild-Survey-of-Literary-Translators-Working-Conditions.pdf (accessed 20 August 2019).

The Society of Authors (2019). "Translation Prizes". https://www.societyofauthors.org/Prizes/Translation-Prizes (accessed 20 August 2019).

Translators Association (2018). "Co-Chairs' Report for the AGM 2018". https://www.societyofauthors.org/SOA/MediaLibrary/SOAWebsite/Committees/AGM-Co-Chairs-report-2018_3.pdf (accessed 20 August 2019).

Treneman, Ann (1997). "Media Families: 11. The Siegharts". *The Independent* (28 April). https://www.independent.co.uk/news/media/media-families-11-the-siegharts-1269776.html (accessed 24 August 2019)

TSEliot.com (2019). "About the T. S. Eliot Prize". https://tseliot.com/prize/about-the-t-s-eliot-prize (accessed 20 August 2019).

Turner, Barry (ed.) (2009). *The Writer's Handbook 2010*. Basingstoke: Macmillan.

UCL Website (2019). "Little Magazines, Alternative Press & Poetry Store Collections". www.ucl.ac.uk/library/special-collections/a-z/little-mags (accessed 20 August 2019).

Waters, Florence (2011). "Poet Withdraws from TS Eliot Prize over Sponsorship". *The Telegraph* (6 December). www.telegraph.co.uk/culture/books/booknews/8938343/Poet-withdraws-from-TS-Eliot-prize-over-sponsorship.html (accessed 24 August 2019).

Weissbort, Daniel (2004). "Email-Interview on *Modern Poetry in Translation*". Conducted by Wolfgang Görtschacher. Unpublished. (7 July).

Wheale, Nigel (1992). "Uttering Poetry: Small-Press Publication." In: *Poets on Writing. Language, Discourse, Society* (ed. Denise Riley), 9–20. London: Palgrave Macmillan.

Wheatley, David (2015). *Contemporary British Poetry*. London: Palgrave.

Wilkinson, Bruce (2017). *Hidden Culture, Forgotten History. A Northern Poetic Underground and Its Contercultural Impact*. N.p. Penniless Press.

2a.2
Anthologies: Distortions and Corrections, Poetries, and Voices

David Kennedy

Anthologies of British mainstream poetry have tended to generate considerable controversy. This is because they are not really concerned with poetry per se but with poetry as a mirror of the nation and its moral life. The convergence of nation, morality, and poetry dates from Robert Conquest's *New Lines* (1956). Conquest argued that the anthology's nine poets represented "a genuine and healthy poetry of the new period" and "a new and healthy general standpoint." His narrative of recovery from recent sickness was reinforced by references to "corruption," "a debilitating theory," and "a condition," and by dismissals of poetry dominated by "the Id," "unconscious commands," "sentimentalism," "unpleasant exhibitionism," and "sentimentality." These generalized terms stood in for any detailed esthetic argument because, as Conquest was forced to admit, the *New Lines* poets shared "little more than a negative determination to avoid bad principles." At the same time, the poetry's "empirical [...] attitude" was "a part of the general intellectual ambience (in so far as that is not blind or retrogressive) of our time." "Ambience" is another generalized word that echoes Conquest's use of "atmosphere" (three times), "moods," and "mood." The implication is that if you have to ask for clearer definitions then you are part of the problem.

Conquest's introduction established some important aspects of mainstream poetry anthologies. First, there is a dismissal of the recent past and a hailing of the present as a site of changes, shifts, trends, or emergent groupings. Second, there is the editor presenting a generalized account of insider knowledge. Finally, this generalization removes the burden of having to justify the selection as a unified whole. This pattern was largely reproduced in

A Companion to Contemporary British and Irish Poetry, 1960–2015, First Edition.
Edited by Wolfgang Görtschacher and David Malcolm.
© 2021 John Wiley & Sons Ltd. Published 2021 by John Wiley & Sons Ltd.

subsequent anthologies but with greater focus on history and politics. For *The New Poetry* (1962), Al Alvarez redefined the restraint of Conquest's poets as "the gentility principle" and demanded that poets wake up to history and engage with "the forces of disintegration." Blake Morrison and Andrew Motion's *The Penguin Book of Contemporary British Poetry* (1982) dismissed "The implication of *The New Poetry* that a correlation necessarily exists between gravity of subject and quality of achievement" (13). They argued that poetry had not developed in that direction and offered Seamus Heaney as their exemplary poet: someone whose work derived from "The Movement virtues of common sense, craftsmanship, and explication" (16) but had developed into oblique, refracting fiction-making. And just as Conquest had buttressed his argument with a lengthy quotation from Coleridge, so Morrison and Motion did the same with Keats.

The 1993 Bloodaxe anthology I coedited with Michael Hulse and David Morley originally had the working title of *Eighties/Nineties* but ended up borrowing Alvarez's title to justify its argument for significant change. The introduction was a naively pluralist, pro-postmodernist, anti-Thatcher polemic that offered rather overdetermined arguments about the extent to which the poetry it collected challenged the age. One other notable feature of these anthologies is the contracting or expanding movement they enact: Conquest (9 poets), Alvarez (28 poets), Morrison/Motion (20 poets), Hulse/Kennedy/Morley (55 poets). It is clear that the Conquest and Morrison/Motion anthologies reflect periods of cultural and political isolationism, conservatism, and cynicism about or exhaustion with ideas of community and the collective. Alvarez's anthology is very much of the 1960s while the Hulse/Kennedy/Morley *New Poetry*'s celebration of diversity was a rejection of Thatcherism's antisociety, a celebration that, with hindsight, looks increasingly like a cover for the impossibility of drawing any meaningful sketch of the contemporary scene. Indeed, where Conquest and Alvarez were able to construct reasonably coherent arguments about the poetry they anthologized, Morrison and Motion and Hulse/Kennedy/Morley seemed to struggle to accommodate the diversity of the contemporary scene. For example, the inclusion of Douglas Dunn, Tony Harrison, and Seamus Heaney by Morrison and Motion spoke to an important trend in postwar British poetry in which the marginal starts to become central. However, such poetry is at a considerable distance from, say, the sophisticated fabulism of James Fenton, and Fenton, in turn, seems equally distant from the exuberant "Martianism" of Craig Raine, which now reads like the ultimate in a post-postwar consensus poetics.

This is the cultural history into which the 2009 anthology *Voice Recognition* sought to write itself. Such writing into history was quite self-conscious, as James Byrne and Clare Pollard invoke Alvarez's anthology to argue that "Technique is not enough. Talent must be fuelled by the experience of a life outside of the poems" (13). Poetry that is the "mere recounting of anecdotes or minor stagings of epiphany" (13) must make way for poetry that registers "the creative stimuli that can be found through travel, translation or through a broad appreciation of visual art" (13) and "a wide appreciation of the 'confessional' American poets" (14). Previous anthologies have often found themselves arguing for shifts that are already over. This was true of Morrison/Motion and the Bloodaxe *New Poetry*. *Voice Recognition* described a recognizable contemporary scene. Unlike its predecessors, *Voice Recognition* did not have a title that refers to poetry. This was reflected in the poetry world that the introduction sketched, a world that was predominantly performance-driven. It was also reflected in a sentence that would have been impossible a few years before: Jay Bernard "is a DJ for the Poetry Society and podcasts regularly" (19).

Voice Recognition thanks "faculty from many universities who provided recommendations." This acknowledgment reflects the fact that none of the poets had published a full-length collection and many of them had undertaken some form of graduate studies. At the same time, the editors could not decide what they thought about creative writing and the academy. They tell us that "Almost every university going seems to have a poetry course, which is frequently backed by renowned faculty" (11). The sentence starts by sounding a note of exhaustion that seems to promise disapproval and yet suddenly swerves into a kind of awkward reverence.

Byrne and Pollard continue to tell us that MAs in Creative Writing "can encourage conformities of style" and "many of the same-sounding, low-stake, well-mannered (but going nowhere) poems we read whilst putting together this anthology were from poets who had recently come along the MA conveyor-belt" (12). The idea that British MA programs are collectively teaching a latter-day version of the well-made poem is bizarre. One suspects that this was *Voice Recognition*'s own version of attacking the recent past as many MAs are overseen or taught by poets who came to prominence in the 1980s and 1990s. As David Cameron remarked to Tony Blair in his first House of Commons speech as Tory leader (07.12.05), "you were the future once."

Blair and Cameron are not as remote from this anthology as one might think. A group of poets whose reference points are from an anthology that is nearly 50 years old, Rilke, Pound, and American confessional poets, and whose work represents (incredibly) "after years of other regions being prominent [...] a real shift back to the capital" (11), has an odd sense of poetry, history, politics, and just about everything else. What they have, in fact, is a gap, and it is a gap they share despite *Voice Recognition*'s representing three distinct generations: b.1988–1991, b.1984–1986, and b.1977–1982. This gap is the result of having grown up through the Blair era. Thatcher's infamous assertion that "there is no such thing as society, only individual men and women and their families" was rewritten by New Labour in a variety of ways. One version might be, say, "there is no such thing as ideology, only things that work and things that don't." But to deny society or ideology or nation is to remove any way of defining the self and the result is that your only reference point is yourself and your convictions. This explains the feeling throughout the introduction of the editors struggling to define their poets *against* anything. Indeed, the "recognition" in the anthology's title is highly significant because previous mainstream anthologies clearly had been matters of definition. The cultural moment that James Byrne and Clare Pollard describe was, in contrast, dehistoricized and depoliticized. Or, as Ahren Warner puts it in "Epistle," "there are no signs of our times" (161). The present is unreadable without a sense of the very recent past.

What is most surprising in the context of a generation-defining anthology is the number of voices that seem to lack confidence or seem to revel in an inability to communicate. The speaker of Heather Phillipson's "Crossing the Col d'Aubisque" finds that "The Smiths are in synch / with what I don't express" (128). The speaker of Jay Bernard's "109" tells us "I don't know if I can talk" (25) and the mother in Emily Berry's "The Mother's Tale" "won't share a drop of emotion" (31). All this has the curious effect of suggesting that the mainstay of mainstream poetry, the personal lyric, is largely inoperative.

By contrast, the few poets who seem genuinely interested in doing something with form, language, and voice—Siddartha Bose, Mark Leech, Toby Martinez de las Rivas, Sophie Robinson, and Ahren Warner—catch the reader's attention with an often quite pronounced sense of provisionality and unpredictability. The opening of Sophie Robinson's "unspeakable" is a good example: "Your name swallows my lips & / the backward downward rage of all / girls knocking through me" (142). These poets have visibly and audibly thought about what is involved in the act of reading and how different types of text produce different reading styles. Their poems repay re-reading because there is much less sense of their colluding with the usual readers of poetry. Crucially, the work of these poets converges with what the mainstream dismisses as *avant-garde* or experimental poetry.

The poetry collected in *Voice Recognition* seems largely unaware of and unconcerned with what has dominated British mainstream poetry since about 1950: anxieties about class, region, gender, and race. Byrne and Pollard are the first anthology editors to show no interest in poetry as a mirror of the nation. In this, of course, they only reflect the attitudes of their chosen poets. But it makes *Voice Recognition* an early monument to a postnational poetry. The editors and their poets have removed one of poetry's principle claims for recognition: its ability to offer unique insights into the relationships between private and public and between self and nation that define us all.

Anthologies, then, tell us particular types of story about poetry and its relationship to the world. As is apparent from the discussion in the preceding text, the story has often little to do with the poetry itself. Chris Jones has written that Alvarez's "essay, 'The New Poetry, or Beyond the Gentility Principle,' has focused people's minds on what anthologies are for: what is each anthology's brief and purpose? Anthologists return again and again to its arguments, assimilating and reacting against its abiding concerns, and from it create new narratives of contemporary literature" (Jones 2014, 2). With the exception of *Voice Recognition*, the anthologies discussed so far can be said to perform what Robert Hewison has identified in postwar British culture as "negative feedback" with the recent past (1987, 300).

The idea of negative feedback provides a story arc in which anthologies of mainstream poetry can, for the most part, be readily located. It is much harder to do this with anthologies of writing from the parallel tradition of experimental poetries. The period under discussion in this companion has seen a number of significant anthologies of such writing. *The New British Poetry 1968–1988* (1988) embraces the diversity of contemporary poetry. It has four editors who managed a section each: women's poetry, Black British poetry, poetry of the British Poetry Revival, and some younger poets. It collects 85 poets and includes poets as disparate as Eavan Boland and Linton Kwesi Johnson. By contrast, Iain Sinclair's *Conductors of Chaos* (1999) emphasizes the outsider and underground nature of experimental poetries and portrays a scene of "remote, alienated, fractured" work written by "apes from the attic" (xvii). It collects 36 poets and seeks to rehabilitate five older poets: J. F. Hendry, W. S. Graham, David Jones, David Gascoyne, and Nicholas Moore.

Other notable anthologies include: Paul Green's *Ten British Poets* (1993); John Matthias's *Twenty Three Modern British Poets* (1971); *A Various Art* by Andrew Crozier and Tim Longville (1987), which gathers J. H. Prynne and 16 other poets associated with *Grosseteste Review* and Ferry Press; *Other: British and Irish Poetry since 1970* (1999) by Richard Caddel and Peter Quartermain; and Nicholas Johnson's *Foil: Defining Poetry 1985–2000* (2000). For the most part, such anthologies have defined themselves against the dominant mainstream poetic. Sinclair mocks the Poetry Society's "New Generation Poets" promotion of the mid-1990s. Crozier and Longville assert that "the poets who altered taste in the 1950s did so by means of a common rhetoric that foreclosed the possibilities of poetic language within its own devices" (12). Similarly, Caddel and Quartermain write that "One purpose of this anthology is [...] to uncover what the forces surrounding The Movement and its successors have helped to bury" (xxii).

The most recent anthology of experimental writing, Nathan Hamilton's *Dear World & Everyone in It: New Poetry in the UK* (2013), departs from this model. It registers important changes in the first decade of the twenty-first century. The book is notable for its methods of selection and composition. An initial group of poets chosen by the editor were then asked to make their own selection. The second group then repeated the process. The result is an anthology of 74 poets and the effect is something like a collage. Much of the work in *Dear World* is interested in formal experiment. The introduction comprises small episodes of prose. The tone of these appears more or less random and entirely personal to the editor until two and a half pages in when a formal proposition is made about poetics, discussing "product" and "process," and then dismissed in the final sentence of that section.

Hamilton values the poets in *Dear World* . . . for two reasons. First, because they construct a linguistic stance against the world. Second, because they seem to be politically angry. There is a struggle going on somewhere and they feel obliged to comment on it. This makes the anthology reminiscent of *Conductors of Chaos* (1999). Hamilton's introduction, like Sinclair's, writes back to the poets. His style is deliberately disorientating and it soon becomes apparent that he is attempting a history of views of poetry in the contemporary period.

Hamilton's concern is that public discussion of contemporary poetry is increasingly difficult. He is very astute in his connection of experimental poetry with the aims and methods of conceptual art while recognizing that the experimental poem is less commodifiable than the material products of fine art. It is here that the problem of public visibility, media relevance, inclusiveness, or lack of representation may lie. Of course, a significant part of the project of experimental poetry is to be resistant to easy commodification. Such concern with the public profile of poetry can be traced through other experimental anthologies of the period.

The introduction to *Other: British and Irish Poetry since 1970* expresses an anxiety about the dominance of a monolithic, centralized culture, which has enabled mainstream poetry to be both highly assertive in its public profile and suppressive of alternatives. What concerns the editors of *Other* and similar anthologies is the ease with which mainstream poetry has turned itself into a national narrative. The question of what national narrative experimental poetry tells remains moot. Editors of experimental poetry anthologies are also concerned about the way that the mainstream poem remains so closely identified with the

Movement poem and its alleged gentility. A national poetry narrative that is largely founded upon genteel anecdote might be expected to be enfeebled and vulnerable, but, in fact, it turns out to be a surprisingly flexible instrument that continues to find an audience. By contrast, experimental poetry with its concern with serious issues and with reinventing poetic language remains largely ignored.

The anthologizing of innovative work remains, then, largely a question of placing such work against the mainstream. *Out of Everywhere: Linguistically Innovative Poetry by Women in North America & the UK* (1996), edited by Maggie O'Sullivan, collects 30 poets with clearly constituted author identities and distinctive poetics. The introduction states that the title of the collection refers specifically to the exclusion of these poets and their writings from the places of cultural reception, and it argues that this is a matter of gender politics. This implies that experimental poetry by women is doubly devalued.

The editor of *Sixty Women Poets* (1993) describes her poets as having been constrained for too long. Anthologies in the period under discussion in this *Companion* have been involved in a cultural power struggle, so much so that a review of the Bloodaxe anthology *The New Poetry* (1993) was entitled "Jihad." Anthologies express wider sets of cultural tensions, which involve negative feedback with the recent past. They are moves in a continuing struggle, markers that are thrown down as challenges to a sometimes barely visible enemy. It is also worth noting that there is a real danger of anthologies misrepresenting the poets they collect. The work of anthologies becomes a matter of distorted history.

A desire to correct the exclusions of distorted histories underwrites the large number of women's poetry anthologies that have appeared since 1960. The earliest of these are passionately feminist: *Cutlasses and Earrings* (1977) by Michèle Roberts and Michelene Wandor, *Licking the Bed Clean* (1978) by Alison Fell et al., and Lilian Mohin's *One Foot on the Mountain: An Anthology of British Feminist Poetry 1969–1979* (1979), which contain mainstream and experimental poetries. Mohin's anthology collects 55 poets born between 1929 and 1955. Mohin identifies "the primary quality" of the poems as "one of redefinition [and] contributions to the long task of renaming the world and our place in it" (Mohin 1979, 5). Other notable postwar anthologies include: Carol Rumens's *Making for the Open: The Chatto Book of Post-Feminist Poetry 1964–1984* (1985) and *New Women Poets* (1990); Fleur Adcock's *The Faber Book of 20th Century Women's Poetry* (1987); Linda France's *Sixty Women Poets* (1993); Maura Dooley's *Making for Planet Alice: New Women Poets* (1997); Jeni Couzyn's *The Bloodaxe Book of Contemporary Women Poets: Eleven British Writers* (1998); Deryn Rees-Jones's *Modern Women Poets* (2005); and Carrie Etter's *Infinite Difference: Other Poetries by UK Women Poets* (2010), which concentrates on experimental poetry.

The feminism of the late 1970s proved hard to sustain—Rumens's 1985 subtitle is a telling one—and Vicki Bertram notes Adcock's antipathy to feminist poetry (see Bertram 1996, 269–273). In place of explicit feminism, new vocabularies of valuation have emerged. For Linda France, women's poetry "often has a wild quality" (1993, 17), while for Jeni Couzyn it reflects "the depth and range of female consciousness" and is "angry, powerful, hurt, tender, and defiant" (1998, 16, 18). Carol Rumens asserts that "any amassing of women's voices will necessarily amount to a fairly radical critique of current society." The poetry in her 1990 anthology is "funny, sexy, witty, rebellious and, perhaps, heartfelt" (1990, 12), uses "eclectic" (1990, 13) forms, and is written by poets who "are behaving more like novelists these days" (1990, 15). Deryn Rees-Jones, surveying a century of women's poetry, notes tendencies toward "the monologue, the surreal, the use of myth and fairytale" (2005, 20) and "a poetics of witness" (2005, 21) and identifies a desire to avoid "excessive femininity" (2005, 22).

Finally, we should not forget anthologies such as E. A. Markham's *Hinterland: Caribbean Poetry from the West Indies and Britain* (1989), Donny O'Rourke's *Dream State: The New Scottish Poets* (2001), and *The Bloodaxe Book of Modern Welsh Poetry* (2003) by Menna Elfyn and John Rowlands. These books remind us that postwar British poetry must be understood as a sometimes bewildering plurality of poetries and voices.

Some 50 years ago, the American critic Randall Jarrell wrote that he was living in the age of anthologies. His comment seems even more pertinent today. For while the era of anthologies that define a cultural moment is probably passing away, recent years have seen the rise of commercial anthologies such as *The Nation's Favourite Poems* or *Essential Poems (To Fall in Love With)*. There are anthologies to help with bereavement and even with depression. Robert Potts, a former editor of *Poetry Review*, calls these "the poetry anthology as lifestyle accessory" (Potts 2003). This does not bode well for the anthology as portal to the exciting and mysterious unknown.

References

Adcock, Fleur (ed.) (1987). *The Faber Book of Twentieth-Century Women's Poetry*. London: Faber.

Allnutt, Gillian, D'Aguiar, Fred, Edwards, Ken, and Mottram, Eric (eds.) (1988). *The New British Poetry 1968–88*. London: Paladin.

Alvarez, Al (ed.) (1962). *The New Poetry*. Harmondsworth: Penguin.

Bertram, Vicki (1996). "Postfeminist Poetry?: 'One More Word for Balls'." In: *Contemporary British Poetry: Essays in Theory and Criticism* (eds. James Acheson and Romana Huk), 269–292. Albany: State University of New York Press.

Byrne, James and Pollard, Clare (eds.) (2009). *Voice Recognition: 21 Poets for the 21st Century*. Tarset: Bloodaxe Books.

Caddel, Richard and Quartermain, Peter (eds.) (1999). *Other: British and Irish Poetry since 1970*. Hanover and London: Wesleyan University Press.

Conquest, Robert (ed.) (1956). *New Lines*. Basingstoke: Macmillan.

Couzyn, Jeni (ed.) (1998). *The Bloodaxe Book of Contemporary Women Poets: Eleven British Writers*. Newcastle-upon-Tyne: Bloodaxe.

Crozier, Andrew and Longville, Tim (eds.) (1987). *A Various Art*. Manchester: Carcanet.

Dooley, Maura (ed.) (1997). *Making for Planet Alice: New Women Poets*. Newcastle-upon-Tyne: Bloodaxe.

Elfyn, Menna and Rowlands, John (eds.) (2003). *The Bloodaxe Book of Modern Welsh Poetry*. Tarset: Bloodaxe.

Etter, Carrie (ed.) (2010). *Infinite Difference: Other Poetries by UK Women Poets*. Exeter: Shearsman Books.

Fell, Alison, Pixner, Stef, Reid, Tina et al. (eds.) (1978). *Licking the Bed Clean: Five Feminist Poets*. London: Teeth Imprints.

France, Linda (ed.) (1993). *Sixty Women Poets*. Newcastle-upon-Tyne: Bloodaxe.

Green, Paul (ed.) (1993). *Ten British Poets*. Cambridge: Spectacular Diseases.

Hamilton, Nathan (ed.) (2013). *Dear World & Everyone in It*. Tarset: Bloodaxe.

Hewison, Robert (1987). *Too Much: Art and Society in the Sixties 1960–75*. London: Methuen.

Hulse, Michael, Kennedy, David, and Morley, David (eds.) (1993). *The New Poetry*. Newcastle-upon-Tyne: Bloodaxe.

Johnson, Nicholas (ed.) (2000). *Foil: Defining Poetry 1985–2000*. Buckfastleigh: Etruscan Books.

Jones, Chris (2014). "The New, New, New Poetry: A Consumer's Guide". Paper presented at 'Anthologies Symposium', Sheffield.

Markham, E.A. (ed.) (1989). *Hinterland: Caribbean Poetry from the West Indies and Britain*. Tarset: Bloodaxe.

Matthias, John (ed.) (1971). *Twenty-Three British Poets*. Athens: Ohio University Press.

Mohin, Lilian (ed.) (1979). *One Foot on the Mountain: An Anthology of British Feminist Poetry 1969–1979*. London: Onlywomen Press.

Morrison, Blake and Motion, Andrew (eds.) (1982). *The Penguin Book of Contemporary British Poetry*. Harmondsworth: Penguin.

O'Rourke, Donny (ed.) (2001). *Dream State: The New Scottish Poets*. Edinburgh: Polygon.

O'Sullivan, Maggie (ed.) (1996). *Out of Everywhere: Linguistically Innovative Poetry by Women in North America & the UK*. London: Reality Street.

Potts, Robert (2003). "Death by a Thousand Anthologies". *The Guardian* (6 December). https://www.theguardian.com/books/2003/dec/06/featuresreviews.guardianreview13 (accessed 14 August 2016).

Rees-Jones, Deryn (ed.) (2005). *Modern Women Poets*. Tarset: Bloodaxe.

Roberts, Michèle and Wandor, Michelene (eds.) (1977). *Cutlasses and Earrings*. London: Playbooks.

Rumens, Carol (ed.) (1985). *Making for the Open: The Chatto Book of Post-Feminist Poetry 1964–1984*. London: Chatto and Windus.

Rumens, Carol (ed.) (1990). *New Women Poets*. Bloodaxe: Newcastle-upon-Tyne.

Sinclair, Iain (ed.) (1999). *Conductors of Chaos*. London: Picador.

2a.3
Minding the Trench: The Reception of British and Irish Poetry in America, 1960–2015

Daniel Bourne

Perhaps not everyone remembers the old adage (at times attributed to George Bernard Shaw from the eastern side of the Atlantic, and at others to H. L. Mencken from the western) that "England and America are two countries separated by a common language." It is an observation that lingers, however, not just in the minds of those bemused by differences in American and British idioms, but also those who consider the existence of some sort of Mid-Atlantic trench between the poetry written on the American shore as opposed to the British.

In his essay, "Poetic Modernism and the Oceanic Divide,"[1] a review of the 2004 anthology *New British Poetry* edited by British poet Don Paterson and Serbian-born American poet Charles Simic, American poet Kevin Clark again raises the question of the existence of such a divide, though noticing the distortions involved in using such a broad categorical brush stroke: "Like cartoons masquerading as reality, the stereotypes are obvious: Contemporary British poets remain rhyming automatons and Americans are still bellowing their free verse yawps" (Clark 2004, 1). He reports that there has been a tendency for American practitioners as well as critics of poetry to claim "that British verse was long ago marked by its staid traditions of form and voice and that American verse has been characterized by its compulsions toward a roughhewn originality" (2). More convincing to Clark appears to be the differing historical dynamics of the two traditions—that is, the way that the two poetries might have different thematic concerns and different ways of wrestling with these concerns. In this

---

A Companion to Contemporary British and Irish Poetry, 1960–2015, First Edition.
Edited by Wolfgang Görtschacher and David Malcolm.
© 2021 John Wiley & Sons Ltd. Published 2021 by John Wiley & Sons Ltd.

regard, Clark finds himself for the most part in agreement "with those who think that British writers have been molded in good part by considerations of class and American writers by ideals that favor the Emersonian individual" (2).

Of course, the perception of this supposed divide dovetails with the chronic spat within American poetry circles themselves, involving what Robert Lowell during his acceptance speech for the 1960 National Book Award for his collection *Life Studies* famously characterized as the divide between "a cooked and a raw" (Lowell 1960), crystallizing the sometimes sharp and sometimes blurred boundaries between poets (and readers of poetry) who expected new American verse to be wrought in the fixed forms of the past and those who proclaimed this new poetry should be "free" to do whatever it wanted. In this schema, the bards and blokes writing in fixed verse in England are very much the cooked, while the poets of America have thrown off the yoke of imperial form and are now the proud pioneers of a wild and wide-open poetry befitting a wild, wide-open land.

Again, the supposed spat is imbued with stereotype; yet, it would also be amiss not to recognize the presence of this sometimes unsettled sea of mistrust and misreading, of controversies over differing conventions and intentions. Above all, there continues to exist a discussion *about* this barrier, and one that has broken down only rarely (and notably) in the examples of just a few poets. At the same time, however, the main observation has to be that despite possible differences of ear and thematic concern, individual British and Irish poets have still continued to land in America with great impact. In fact, to a large degree the genuinely significant influence of British and Irish poetry in America since 1960 is not connected to any similarity of school or movement. There has been no "invasion" akin to Beatlemania c. 1964. Instead, this story has been one of individuals. And, within this story, no character looms larger than Irish poet Seamus Heaney. Also of particular note are British poets Philip Larkin and Ted Hughes as well as Irish poets Paul Muldoon and Eavan Boland. Moreover, both Muldoon and Boland exhibit an instant complication to the supposed Atlantic divide in that both poets came to make their homes at least part of the year within the United States.

Earlier, there was also the interesting case of Denise Levertov, born in Essex in 1923, who moved to the United States at the age of 24, and who by the 1960s had emerged as one of the central figures in American poetry. Connected with the Black Mountain School—Charles Olson, Robert Duncan, Ed Dorn, Robert Creeley, etc.—she ended up fashioning one of the key conceptual components of late twentieth-century American free verse: the notion of organic form. Almost the entirety of Levertov's poetry after her arrival in America was issued by New Directions, a publisher as central to the American literary landscape as the Mississippi River is to the country itself. How can we even conceive of poetry in America toward the end of the twentieth century without thinking of her? And what about W. H. Auden, who was still writing poems after 1960, though his most significant work was behind him? Here, there is even some temporal fuzziness, in that even if we grant Auden's most influential poems were written in an earlier era, a wider reception in America awaited him because of the inclusion of his landmark poem "Musée des Beaux Arts" in the 1976 David Bowie star vehicle film *The Man Who Fell to Earth*, which exposed this poem to an audience beyond the usual poetry crowd.

When Seamus Heaney (1939–2013) died in the summer of 2013, his obituary in *The New York Times* referred to a 1995 review in *Publishers Weekly* stating that Heaney "has an aura, if not a star power, shared by few contemporary poets" (Fox 2013). Here, the reviewer was not singling Heaney out against a backdrop of other UK poetic imports, but was comparing him to all living poets, American or otherwise. In 2008, the year before Heaney celebrated his seventieth birthday, two-thirds of the poetry collections sold in the United Kingdom were written by him ("Heaney," Poetry Foundation 2015e), and, in the United States, his literary presence has been almost equally remarkable.

Born on April 13, 1939, in County Derry, Northern Ireland, Heaney published his first major book of poetry *Death of a Naturalist* (Faber & Faber) in 1966. Awarded the Nobel Prize for Literature in 1995, his other collections include *Door into the Dark* (1969), *Wintering Out* (1972), *Stations* (1975), *North* (1975), *Field Work* (1979), *Station Island* (1984), *The Haw Lantern* (1987), *The Cure at Troy* (1990, a play in verse), *Seeing Things* (1991), *The Spirit Level* (1996), *Electric Light* (2001), and *District and Circle* (2006). Two earlier collected works, both published by Faber & Faber, were *Selected Poems 1965–1975* (1980) and *New Selected Poems 1966–1987* (1990). *Opened Ground: Selected Poems, 1966–1996*, published in the United States by Farrar, Straus and Giroux in 1998, was even on the list of *The New York Times'* "Notable Books of the Year." In 2010, his last collection of poetry, *Human Chain*, was also published in an American edition by Farrar, Straus and Giroux. Not only his poetry, but Heaney himself was also present in America throughout much of his later writing life. Among other contacts, he was Boylston Professor of Rhetoric and Oratory at Harvard University from 1985 to 1997 and Ralph Waldo Emerson Poet in Residence at Harvard from 1998 to 2006. Earlier, he had been a guest lecturer at the University of California, Berkeley.

In America, however, Heaney is no less "Irish." The Poetry Foundation's webpage on Heaney even mentions that in large part the poet's impressive "popularity stems from his subject matter—modern Northern Ireland, its farms and cities beset with civil strife, its natural culture and language overrun by English rule" ("Heaney," Poetry Foundation 2015e). Yet, Heaney's reach cannot be reduced only to a convenient *cause célèbre*, a function of Northern Ireland and "the Troubles" being perpetually in the news in the decades toward the end of the twentieth century. Heaney's work goes beyond the documentary and the topical. Instead, Heaney's treatment of this painful period of Protestant/Catholic conflict in his native land is perhaps as complex as the background issues and events themselves. Moreover, his complicated positioning of himself and his poetry vis-à-vis such subject matter has perhaps become a source of admiration among American poets and poetry readers, in that his bearing witness to these troubles is expressed in narrative and metaphor rather than doctrinaire statement. The very approach to poetry that might make him seem detached and esthetically anesthetized by some readers directly connected to the conflict might in fact make him seem more honest and genuine by poets and readers who mistrust yoking poetry to politics.

Within Heaney's prolific and influential oeuvre, it is his "bog poems," especially, that have captured attention; for example, "The Tollund Man" from *Wintering Out* or "Bog Queen" and "The Grauballe Man" from *North*. Rather than being an escape into archeological romanticism, however, these poems engage in an intense dialogue with the troubled Irish present. Referring in an interview with *The Paris Review* to an essay by American poet Robert Pinsky about the responsibility of the poet involving a *response* or *answer* to the surrounding world, Heaney asserts:

> I see the Bog Poems in Pinsky's terms as an answer. [...] Not quite an equivalent for what was happening, more an attempt to rhyme the contemporary with the archaic. "The Tollund Man," for example, is the first of the Bog Poems I wrote. Essentially, it is a prayer that the bodies of people killed in various actions and atrocities in modern Ireland, in the teens and twenties of the century as well as in the more recent past, a prayer that something would come of them, some kind of new peace or resolution. In the understanding of his Iron Age contemporaries, the sacrificed body of Tollund Man germinated into spring, so the poem wants a similar flowering to come from the violence in the present. Of course it recognizes that this probably won't happen, but the middle section of the poem is still a prayer that it should. The Bog Poems were defenses against the encroachment of the times, I suppose. (Heaney and Cole 1997)

In this "attempt to rhyme the contemporary with the archaic," there is an endeavor to find historical resonance, to avoid the shrill or anemic rhetorical frequencies of overt *littérature engagée*. But there is also a recognition of the anxiety Heaney feels at his own passivity as well as his desire to bear witness, as we can see from his comments about another bog poem, "Punishment:"

> But there was always a real personal involvement [...]. "Punishment," for example [is] a poem about standing by as the IRA tar and feather these young women in Ulster. But it's also about standing by as the British torture people in barracks and interrogation centers in Belfast. About standing between those two forms of affront. So there's that element of self-accusation, which makes the poem personal in a fairly acute way. Its concerns are immediate and contemporary, but for some reason I couldn't bring army barracks or police barracks or Bogside street life into the language and topography of the poem. I found it more convincing to write about the bodies in the bog and the vision of Iron Age punishment. Pressure seemed to drain away from the writing if I shifted my focus from those images. (Heaney and Cole 1997)

This displacement, of course, might have an analog in American literature in the way that Arthur Miller situated his play *The Crucible* in the literal witch hunt of 1690s Salem in order to attack the metaphorical Communist witch hunt taking place in 1950s McCarthyite America. Through this displacement, there comes an anchoring of the present conflict in a longer tradition, a way of recognizing its tangled and complex longevity in human conduct. But there is also a type of pressure put upon the contemporary thinker to use knowledge of this history as a tool of illumination to avoid the ongoing trap of inaction in the face of atrocity.

Likewise in poems such as "Bog Queen" we see Heaney articulating another mutual permeation of one thing with another that is more ontological than temporal, where the boundaries of sentience and death themselves become blurred:

>   through my fabrics and skins
>   the seeps of winter
>   digested me,
>   the illiterate roots
>
>   pondered and died
>   in the cavings
>   of stomach and socket.
>   I lay waiting
>
>   on the gravel bottom,
>   my brain darkening,
>   a jaw of spawn
>   fermenting underground
>
>   dreams of Baltic amber.
>   (Heaney 1998, 108, ll. 9-21)

Here, the body in death constitutes another type of life, the queen's "fabrics and skins (l. 9)" becoming a permeable membrane to "the seeps of winter (l. 10)" absorbing her body into its own greater organism. But even while the brain is "darkening" (l. 18) there is still a bubbling of consciousness, a dream of light: the glint of the Baltic amber that may be adorning her—or perhaps, rather, she herself is the beginning point for the formation of future jewels. And, in the same way, the imagery of this poem—so similar to the "deep imagery" of a James Wright or Galway Kinnell—exists both as finely focused description as well as part of a metaphorically constructed field of meaning; the language remains both concrete and metaphysical at the same time.

Besides Heaney's panoramic yet seamless vision—able to connect past and present, local and universal, sentient and inanimate—is his remarkable voice itself, as sophisticated as it is accessible. American poet Brad Leithauser, reviewing Heaney's 2006 volume *District and Circle* for *The New York Times*, describes how Heaney's voice still "carries the authenticity and believability of the plainspoken—even though (herein his magic) his words are anything but plainspoken. His stanzas are dense echo chambers of contending nuances and ricocheting sounds. And his is the gift of saying something extraordinary while, line by line, conveying a sense that this is something an ordinary person might actually say" (Leithauser 2006). In fact, in the opening to the title poem of Seamus Heaney's 1979 collection *Field Work*, we can see the poet's mouth as well as eye at work, the scene's clarity perhaps whetted rather than merely adorned by the steady play of alliterative [w] sounds:

>   Where the sally tree went pale in every breeze,
>   where the perfect eye of the nesting blackbird watched,
>   where one fern was always green
>
>   I was standing watching you
>   take the pad from the gatehouse at the crossing
>   and reach to lift a white wash off the whins.
>   (Heaney 1998, 170, I. ll. 1-6)

Anchored in place (another element that makes him almost automatically tap into an American audience, despite the fact that he might write about Northern Ireland rather than a James Wright Ohio or a Richard Hugo Montana), as well as attuned to local speech (in the same way that William Carlos Williams aimed to emulate the "brown bricks of American speech"), Heaney's work can indeed be appreciated in America on an anthropological level, a description of the "works and days" of the people populating his world from childhood onward. But there is much more here at work: a scaffolding built so squarely in the ground can hope to climb the higher. The title *Field Work* itself bespeaks the upper reaches of Heaney's poetic sweep. Not only does the phrase refer to the quotidian notion of agricultural work conducted in the field—planting and spading and herding and so on—but also the idea of field work in the sense of scientific investigation, in the sense of Heaney being a full-fledged practitioner of his art immersed in the past and influential in the future of poetry on both sides of the Atlantic. Perhaps it is worth noting that in a short essay published by the online news magazine *The Daily Beast*, former U.S. Poet Laureate Natasha Trethewey even claims that Heaney's collection *North* inspired her own poetic investigation into her "South" in her 2007 Pulitzer Prize winning collection *Native Guard*:

> I'd been reading *North* while working on a book of my own, turning again and again to that title poem. In it I found one of the things to which I am most drawn in Heaney's great body of work: that Heraclitus's axiom is as true now as ever—"Geography *is* fate"—and that answering the call of our particular geographies and their attendant histories is a noble undertaking: a necessary one. [...] In grappling with the difficult history and hardships of his homeland, Heaney's work [...] showed me, too, a way into my own work, the calling to make sense of my South with its terrible beauty, its violent and troubled past. (Trethewey 2013)

Besides Heaney from Northern Ireland, two poets from England who have garnered widespread attention are Philip Larkin (1922–1985), born in the city of Coventry, and Ted Hughes (1930–1998), born in the town of Mytholmroyd in West Yorkshire. In fact, these two British poets have perhaps made the leap into American poetry to the point that their work would be equally well known as just about any American-born practitioner of poetry in the latter half of the twentieth century. Kevin Clark, too, notes (wryly) these two British poets' exceptionality for American readers in a remark about their absence: "Now that Larkin and Hughes are dead, most of us may have assumed that British poets have returned to laboring in neat little fields circumscribed by fourteen rhyming lines and 140 syllables. Of course, we're wrong." (Clark, *Georgia* 2005, 403)

Along with the American poetry scene's supposed re-infatuation with form in the 1980s, a movement often referred to as New Formalism, came an acute appreciation of the librarian poet Philip Larkin, who himself earlier had been associated with The Movement, a poetic trend arising in England in the 1950s that was roughly akin to later New Formalism in America. Known for its emotional reserve, its tendency to find its subject matter in a very unromantic present day, and its interest in writing in fixed, traditional form, its practitioners included Larkin, Kingsley Amis (1922–1995), Donald Davie (1922–1995), and Thom Gunn (1929–2004), all of whom continued to write into the last decades of the twentieth century and to be read beyond. Larkin's *High Windows* (1974), his last book of poetry issued before his death in 1985 and readily available on both sides of the Atlantic after its issue in paperback in 1979, has become especially emblematic of the power of Larkin's poetry to combine austerity and form with a strong, hard-chiseled voice. Albeit that his poems were written in form, they also partook of the American ear's need for an authentic voice, a "tweaked" vernacular capable of being both plainspoken and pointed. It was a poetry poised on the tight rope between formal surety and thematic surprise, between the compression of language and an open classicism of tone embodied in the image of "high windows" themselves. The result was a quiet ferocity conveyed to the reader despite the proverbial stiff upper lip of form and tone. Here are the first two stanzas as well as the last in the collection's title poem:

> When I see a couple of kids
> And guess he's fucking her and she's
> Taking pills or wearing a diaphragm,
> I know this is paradise
>
> Everyone old has dreamed of all their lives—
> Bonds and gestures pushed to one side
> Like an outdated combine harvester,
> And everyone young going down the long slide
>
> ....
>
> Rather than words comes the thought of high windows:
> The sun-comprehending glass,
> And beyond it, the deep blue air, that shows
> Nothing, and is nowhere, and is endless.
>   (Larkin 1974, 17, ll. 1-8, 17-20)

Though he may be thought cynical and anti-emotional, through his precise craft he is still able to trace the twisting pathways of the human mind, its sudden shifts in focus and awareness. For example, note in how at the end of the first stanza of the poem the way in which a seemingly personal voyeuristic exaltation on the part of the poet in the sexual lives of others modulates in the first line of the ensuing stanza to a broader statement about the persona's awareness of everyone's progression toward death, even the "young going down the long slide" (l. 8) toward a mechanized grim reaper that is itself "outdated" (l. 7). Then, at the very end of the poem, "[r]ather than words comes the thought of high windows" (l. 17), the infinite nothingness beyond. (Also, dare I say, the combine image itself might be more accessible to American than to British readers.)

As in the case of Seamus Heaney, American poets writing in praise of Larkin have been wont to praise his accessibility. For example, in *New Criterion*, X. J. Kennedy praises Larkin's work by calling it "a poetry from which even people who distrust poetry, most people, can take comfort and delight" (Kennedy 1986, 16). Similarly, another American poet, Alan Shapiro, remarks on Larkin as being "a poet of great and complex feeling" endowing "the most commonplace objects and occasions with a chilling poignancy, [measuring] daily life with all its tedium and narrowness against the possibilities of feeling" (Shapiro 1989). But the cross-Atlantic admiration was not reciprocal. As reported in the Poetry Foundation's online biography, Larkin "distrusted travel abroad and professed ignorance of foreign literature, including most modern American poetry" ("Larkin," Poetry Foundation 2015d). Even more impressive is a possible disconnect between Larkin and the American poetry world in his attempt "to avoid the clichés of his own culture, such as the tendency to read portent into an artist's childhood" ("Larkin," Poetry Foundation 2015d), thus avoiding a source of personal mythology widely popular among American as well as British poets.

By contrast, the attraction of Ted Hughes seems to hinge on a poetry afroth with violence and metaphor. Moreover, not only did Hughes write poetry for children, but his work often seemed to pulsate with a child-like attention to and acceptance of the world in a manner devoid of the easy answers of society or religion, a world where when Little Red Riding Hood gets eaten, she stays eaten. His animal poems both evoked the frissons of a Darwinistic survival of the fittest and a wonder at the ways that beauty went hand in hand with violence, which evidenced itself in the vibrant imagery and torqued rhythms of the poetry itself. Of especial interest have been his "Crow" poems. This is the beginning of "Two Legends":

> Black was the without eye
> Black the within tongue
> Black was the heart
> Black the liver, black the lungs
> Unable to suck in light
> (Hughes 1971, 1, ll. 1-5)

In the beginning was crow and the crow was with crow.... Both creation and anticreation myths, the texts have an almost black hole density to their poetic language. In general, Hughes's work seems anchored in the world of field and pasture, of beast and bird, in a way that made his poems readable within a literary tradition profoundly impacted by Henry David Thoreau and other American nature writers. Of course, Hughes's many years spent in America as well as his complicated marriage with American poet Sylvia Plath have contributed over the years to his high-profile presence on this side of the Atlantic, though not necessarily to the benefit of his reputation as a poet. Indeed, the *succès de scandale* that affected Hughes because of his widely suggested blame for Plath's death and early silencing of her work might have put brackets around his poetic reputation in unfair ways.

Nonetheless, in terms of both praise and criticism of his work, American readers have seemed overall to treat him as one of their own, or, at the very least, to point out the differences between him and other English poets. For example, writing in *Salmagundi*, M. L. Rosenthal asserted not just Hughes's value to American readers, but that he might even be more appreciated here than in his homeland:

> Hughes's work ... is of the same order as some of the most interesting American work of the age. It represents a formal ordering of a kind that the best American poetry has been after for a long time but that British critical hostility has made it difficult for English poets to pursue. Such a triumph is always internationally significant, and the explosive violence in Hughes's poetry seems especially expressive to Americans at this moment. (Rosenthal 1973, 61)

Over the decades, Hughes's work has indeed appeared from major publishing houses as well as in literary journals in the United States. For example, several of his Crow poems (appearing in *Crow: From the Life and Songs of the Crow*, Harper and Row 1971) were originally published in *The New Yorker* (in fact, earlier, Hughes had published poetry in such well-known American journals as *The Atlantic*, *The Nation*, *Harper's Magazine*, and *Poetry*). As a publicity blurb on the back of the first American edition of the book, no less a poet than Anne Sexton proclaimed: "let all the poets of the world bow down their heads in admiration and awe" (Hughes 1971, back cover). The second blurb, from critic Jack Kroll, is in fact a quotation from his review of the slim volume in *Newsweek* (indeed, the very fact that a collection of poetry would be reviewed in *Newsweek* was no mean event) that once again strikes the chord of accessibility and outreach: "One of those rare books of poetry that have the public impact of a major novel or a piece of super-journalism." Then the reviewer goes on to evoke its elemental, virtually primeval force: "If our own organs—our brains, blood hearts—could speak, this would be their language" (Kroll 1971, 114). But these prehistoric cave paintings in Hughes's own mind were not the subject of universal praise by American poem-makers. Robert Pinsky wrote in *The New York Times Book Review* of Hughes's collection: "...for some readers the violence may be justified by deeper rewards; but as for me, I can't find anything under all that ketchup except baloney" (Pinsky 1977, 4–5).

From the generation of Irish poets, after Heaney at least two writers stand out: Paul Muldoon (born 1951) and Eavan Boland (1944–2020). Muldoon, of course, is not only a well-known poet in America, but, as current poetry editor of *The New Yorker,* wields additional influence as a gatekeeper within the American poetic scene. A Roman Catholic born in Northern Ireland, Muldoon's work is anchored in place as is Heaney's, but is nonetheless substantially compact in its referential and associational density. As such, Muldoon's work is perhaps not as accessible to a wider audience as was Heaney's, but is still extremely valued within the poetry world itself. Writing of Muldoon's collection *Moy Sand and Gravel*, which won the 2003 Pulitzer Prize for Poetry, Peter Davison (a prominent American poet who was, moreover, poetry editor for *The Atlantic* over a span of 30 years) noted how the book "shimmers with play, the play of mind, the play of recondite information over ordinary experience, the play of observation and sensuous detail, of motion upon custom, of Irish and English languages and landscapes, of meter and rhyme. Sure enough, everything Muldoon thinks of makes him think of something else, and poem after poem takes the form of linked association." (Davison 2002)

Eavan Boland's relationship to her native Ireland is not only complicated, but might in fact be at least partially responsible for "bringing" her to America. Born in Dublin in 1944 and the daughter of a diplomat, Boland spent much of her childhood living in London, though returning to Ireland for college, where her earliest collections appeared. Starting with the collection *Introducing Eavan Boland*, published by Ontario Review Press in 1981, her work also came to be published on this side of the Atlantic. Until her death, Boland split her time between her native city of Dublin and California, where since 1996 she has been a professor and director of the creative writing program at Stanford University. But it is both Boland's presence as a woman Irish poet as well as her insistence on a more complete and authentic portraiture of women's experience and cultural significance in her poetry that has most markedly defined not just her presence in contemporary Irish poetry but her expanding role among American readers. Although hardly to be reduced to the status of a poetic refugee because of her residency and poetic activity in the United States, in the following interview with the readers of the American literary journal *Smartish Pace*, Boland herself notes the cultural claustrophobia she felt in her homeland:

> I began to write in an Ireland where the word "woman" and the word "poet" seemed to be in some sort of magnetic opposition to each other. Ireland was a country with a compelling past, and the word "woman" invoked all kinds of images of communality which were thought to be contrary to the life of anarchic individualism invoked by the word "poet." I found that a difficult and resistant atmosphere in which to write. I wanted to put the life I lived into the poem I wrote. And the life I lived was a woman's life. And I couldn't accept the possibility that the life of the woman would not, or could not, be named in the poetry of my own nation. (Smartish Pace 2015)

Her endeavor to put the life she lived into her poems resulted in a poetry that was indeed too large to be contained by one country. The Poetry Foundation webpage on Boland notes that her fifth collection, *In Her Own Image* (1980), though published in Dublin, "brought Boland international recognition and acclaim. Exploring topics such as domestic violence, anorexia, infanticide and cancer, the book also announced Boland's on-going concern with inaccurate and muffled portrayals of women in Irish literature and society." ("Boland," Poetry Foundation 2015b)

Within the United States, many of Boland's collections were published by Norton, and, in general, Boland emerged as an iconic presence not just in terms of her subject matter but also her intense and well-gathered style. Writing in *The Southern Review*, Kate Daniels starts off her essay "Ireland's Best" by declaring:

> If one were to compose a scale of oppositions upon which to consider contemporary poetry by Irish women [...] Boland [...] would appear at one end, and Medbh McGuckian [...] at the other. Although their work is fundamentally different—Boland the mistress of a highly cadenced, formalistic verse that favors "a lyric speech, a civil tone" (to use her own words), and McGuckian the wielder of nonlinear, surrealistic pieces—both women share a preoccupation with the liberation of Irish poetry from the historical grip of male readers and writers. (Daniels 1999, 387)

Later in her essay, Daniels argues that both of these women poets might find a receptive audience in the United States because of the similarity of their struggles with that of Adrienne Rich, that their "plaints are recognizable versions of [Rich's] dilemma [...] as a young American poet struggling to emerge from the grip of New Criticism." (387). But thematic similarities can beget boredom as well as receptivity, not to mention gender-connected blind spots, and Daniels, interestingly, also reports of some of her own male colleagues' resistance to Boland. According to them, she is "flat." Nonetheless, writes Daniels, Boland "is one of the most celebrated poets writing today [...]. If her voice is flat, it is the flatness of authority—no nonsense, take-no-prisoners. It is a voice that must be reckoned with" (390).

Of course, there are many other poets worthy of mention. Three books of the aforementioned Irish poet Medbh McGuckian (born 1950) have even been published in America by Wake Forest University Press: *Captain Lavender* (1995), *Shemailer* (1998), and *The Currach Requires No Harbours* (2010). Her work, involving a multilayered exploration of women's consciousness, has been said to be "reminiscent of Rainer Maria Rilke in its emotional scope and John Ashbery in its creation of rich interior landscapes" ("McGuckian," Poetry Foundation 2015c).

Among poets on the other side of the Irish Sea, Carol Ann Duffy (born 1955) has certainly garnered attention in America. Britain's current Poet Laureate, Duffy is not just the first woman, but also the first open member of the LGBTQ community to achieve this recognition. Her poetry is so powerful because it conveys emotional immediacy with historical resonance in a way that constantly blends the personal with the political, and it is no surprise that it has gained an appreciation in America. Kevin Clark admires her offering "a feminist consciousness willing to reexamine itself while ultimately reaffirming itself." (Clark 2005, 405) Writing in *The Antioch Review* of Duffy's *The World's Wife* (1999), Jane Satterfield (born in England but raised in America) has noted Duffy's "masterful subversions of myth and history" in these poems written from the perspective of women connected with various fictional as well as historical male figures of cultural note (Satterfield 2001, 124).

Anne Stevenson (born 1933) too is a "bi-Atlantic" poet in that she was born in England, but raised in the United States from the time she was 6 months old until she graduated—in 1954—with a BA in Music and Literature from the University of Michigan, where she studied with the poet Donald Hall ("Stevenson," Poetry Foundation 2015a). She then moved to England where she has lived for most of her adult life, though returning to Ann Arbor in 1960–1961 to complete an MA in English Literature. Over the years, however, her poetic presence on this side of the Atlantic has certainly remained. *Living in America*, her first collection, was published in Michigan by Generation Press in 1965. Several of her collections have also been published in both London and New York by Oxford University Press, including *Travelling Behind Glass: Selected Poems, 1963–1973* (1974), *Enough of Green* (1977), *Minute by Glass Minute* (1982), and *Four and a Half Dancing Men* (1993). A *Selected Poems*, edited and introduced by the former Poet Laureate Andrew Motion, appeared from the Library of America in 2008. Besides such wide publication, Stevenson has also garnered such awards as the Lannan Lifetime Achievement Award, the Neglected Masters Award from the Poetry Foundation of America, and the Aiken Taylor Award for Modern American Poetry from the University of the South—all in 2007—and, in 2008, an honorary Doctorate of Humane Letters from the University of Michigan.

Suffering from a hereditary condition that robbed much of her hearing by the age of 30, Stevenson has nonetheless become known as a poet attentive to sound—of language as well as of music. According to Emily Grosholz in *The Hudson Review*, "Many of Anne Stevenson's best poems reflect on the action of poetry and music on time" (Grosholz 2009, 406–407). There is, though, evidence of some dissonance between her work and at least a few American readers, not so much in subject matter, but in "poetic ear." Writing in a review of Stevenson's *Poems 1955–2005* (Dufour Editions) in *Poetry*, D. H. Tracy, despite a considerable amount of admiration, nonetheless finds her at times awkward:

She has something of Bishop's patrician sequencing of observation and, less reliably, Plath's way of pogo-sticking from word to word. More socially constituted than either of these poets, she possesses a charity that neither of them had, and suffers from an excess of consciousness that neither of them had either. I say "suffers" because the excess often manifests itself as literary mannerism or a chattiness of tone that does not entrain itself to the formal or dramatic requirements of the poem. Her challenge, generally speaking, is disciplining this excess. (Tracy 2006, 169)

Also important to mention is Jon Silkin (1930–1997), a poet noted for long lines as well as historical witness, especially that involving the literature of World War I. Not only was he well known in America as a poet, but so was his literary magazine *Stand*. A representative appreciation of Silkin's poetry can be glimpsed in the 1970 inaugural issue of *The Iowa Review*, where Merle E. Brown describes his poetry as "many tongued, speaking with more than one voice even when containing only one person [...]. Each creature and each voice [reverberating] with a representativeness beyond itself; if the society of a poem seems small, intimate, and personal at first, upon repeated reading its range widens and implicates a community, a nation, a world [...]" (Brown 1970, 115).

Evidence of yet other interesting poets in the past half-century or so from Ireland or England receiving notice in America can be gleaned from such prominent sources as the *Norton Anthology of Modern and Contemporary Poetry Volume II*. Here we can encounter the work of additional Irish poets such as Thomas Kinsella (born 1928), Michael Longley (born 1939), and Derek Mahon (1941–2020). Other English writers include Kingsley Amis (1922–1995), Donald Davie (1922–1995), Charles Tomlinson (1927–2015), Thom Gunn (1929–2004), Geoffrey Hill (1932–2016), Tony Harrison (born 1937), Craig Raine (born 1944), and Grace Nichols (born 1950). In the case of Nichols, who was born in Guyana in 1950 but eventually settled in England in 1977, we see not just an example of a Black British poet's work being presented in America, but also the addition of postcolonial complexity in that some Anglophone poets from the British Commonwealth may see themselves as being both part of and beyond British poetry.

Another interesting anthology, *New Poets of England and America*, edited by prominent American poets Donald Hall, Robert Pack, and Louis Simpson, was first published in 1957, but continued to be reprinted in America long after 1960. Beyond the familiar names of Amis, Davie, Gunn, and Hill were poets Charles Causley (1917–2003), Michael Hamburger (1924–2007)—whose work as a translator from German was much widely recognized in America than was his own poetry—John Heath-Stubbs (1918–2006), John Holloway (1920–1999), Jon Manchip White (1924–2013), and a lone female representative, Elizabeth Jennings (1926–2001). Meanwhile, an important conduit for Irish poets was *The Faber Book of Contemporary Irish Poetry* (Faber & Faber 1986), edited by Paul Muldoon. Still available in both hard and paperback, this anthology starts with the death of Yeats in 1939 and offers such additional Irish voices as poet and prose writer Patrick Kavanagh (1904–1967), Louis MacNeice (1907–1963), John Montague (1929–2016), Paul Durcan (born 1944), Tom Paulin (born 1949), and, again, a lone female representative within the group, Medbh McGuckian (born 1950).

In this same period, publishing houses such as Bloodaxe Books were also extremely important as transatlantic bridges, known for printing the work of American poets in Great Britain as well as bringing British poetry to American readers. One example is *The Bloodaxe Book of Contemporary Women Poets: Eleven British Poets* (Bloodaxe Books, 1985), which along with the more familiar work of Sylvia Plath and Denise Levertov also offered such women poets as Stevie Smith (1902–1971), Kathleen Raine (1908–2003), Elizabeth Jennings (1926–2001), Elaine Feinstein (1930–2019), Ruth Fainlight (born 1931), Jenny Joseph (1932–2018), Anne Stevenson, Fleur Adcock (born 1934), and Jeni Couzyn (born 1942), who also edited the anthology. Couzyn—as was the case with Stevenson and Nichols—is not just "English." Born in South Africa, she moved to Great Britain in her twenties. Ruth Fainlight, too, was born in the United States, but has made England as well as Spain and France her home.

Certainly, British and Irish poets made their mark on the pages of American literary journals as well. Indeed, it is no surprise that given the centrality of literary magazines in creating the richness and diversity of twentieth- and twenty-first-century American literature—as William Carlos Williams attested, "Without it, I myself would have been early silenced" (Williams 1951, 266)—the field is so vast and multivaried that a separate essay would be needed for a discussion of the appearance of British and Irish poets in the many scores of literary journals being published throughout the United States from 1960 to 2010, with poets both widely known and relatively obscure showing up in particular literary journals. But there are at least two examples of special issues on British literature worth mentioning. One would be the Great Britain special issue of *Atlanta Review 4.2* (Spring/Summer 1988), a 90-page section guest-edited by N. S. Thompson. Two years earlier, *New Orleans Review* also published a British issue (22.2, 1996). Moreover, starting publication in 1966 in England under the editorship of George Cairncross, the journal *Bogg* (whose esthetic seemed much more inclined to the "raw" than the "cooked" side of Lowell's poetic divide) continued to espouse a special interest in British writing even after it moved with its subsequent, American-born editor John Elsberg to the United States in 1980, where it continued publishing until Elsberg's death in 2012 (Darlington 2014). It is also interesting to note that one year earlier, in 2011, an online literary journal, *Antiphon*, started publication, characterized itself as "providing a showcase for the best in contemporary British and international poetry." Edited in England, it is nonetheless present to American readers, appearing in the *Poets & Writers* (pw.org) database of literary magazines, and showing evidence of a continued transatlantic conversation still being conducted within literary journals in online and in hard-copy incarnations. It should be noted, though, that no American literary journal in terms of poetry has ever come close to matching the presence on both sides of the Pond of *Granta,* which, devoting itself to the genres of fiction and nonfiction, at the height of its popularity in the mid-1990s could count its U.S. circulation at 47,000, though with a figure slumping to around 12,000 by 2007 (Garfield 2007).

But back to anthologies, the 976-page edition of *Anthology of Twentieth-Century British and Irish Poetry* (Oxford University Press, 2001), edited by American literary critic Keith Tuma, offers several new poets to American readers. Even such an expansive treatment does not prevent esthetic blind spots, however. Kevin Clark notes that, in terms of current poets, Tuma's selections "highlighting contemporary practitioners of more experimental work" point in a completely different direction than the formalist choices made by Don Paterson and Charles Simic in Graywolf Press's *New British Poetry* (2004), and that "[e]ach anthologist could have borrowed happily from the other's esthetic" (Clark 2005, 407). At the same time, Clark not only identifies a number of newer voices in *New British Poetry*, but also discusses why their work might connect with American readers, regardless of the presence of fixed or more open form. The poets he discusses range from the more familiar— Carol Ann Duffy, Sean O'Brien, John Burnside, Simon Armitage, Jackie Kay, and former UK Poet Laureate Andrew Motion—to other less well-known figures, such as Mark Ford, Lavinia Greenlaw, Jo Shapcott, W. N. Herbert, Alan Jenkins, John Wilkinson, Robert Sheppard, Glyn Maxwell, Robin Robertson, Ruth Padel, and Fred D'Aguiar.

In fact, the reader could do worse in embarking on a look at the issue of British poetry in America than by reading Clark's incisive review of *New British Poetry*. Although I am not so inclined as Clark to bemoan the influence of James Wright (408) on recent American poetry (which of course might be more of an in-house American debate than an issue germane to a comparative regard of American as opposed to British or Irish poetry), Clark usefully offers some specific comparison points between practitioners of both sides of the "divide," noting, for example, some degree of formal eclecticism: "While [co-editor] Paterson's Brits are clearly much more concerned with form, some of his contributors arrange free verse in elaborate stanzas completely familiar to readers of contemporary American poetry. [Some poets even] alternate between formal poems and free verse: reminiscent of [Galway] Kinnell" (408–409). Clark also articulates several commonalities involving both poetic conventions as well as concerns, especially the challenge of navigating one's place between the old and the new:

> Like American poets, our British counterparts seem at home with the first person singular. Some are as concerned with consciousness and conscience as we are. Like many of our poets, some of these Brits wish to reorder imagination so that they may apprehend the changing world. Still, too many seem trapped by the expectations of a critical heritage that is uncomfortable with the new. (409)

The problem with this comment, though, is that it might also describe a number of other national poetries as well. Again, what is most fascinating here is that with British and American poetry it is the ongoing discussion of possible poetic divergence that seems more significant than any particular difference per se.

Ultimately, I imagine that this difference will be connected with the growing importance of a poetry of identity within American literature, something that involves sexual identity as much as ethnic or national identity. Many are the vectors that bring a poet to the page, and I imagine that not so much sorting out poets according to these avenues, but employing an increased awareness of the dynamics between poet, poem, and community (however defined) in illuminating our reading will continue to hold sway. Not so much taxonomy, but *cultural terroir*. Moreover, these categories will continue to be increasingly complicated. How to differentiate between American and British poetry when it is harder to homogenize one poetic tradition or the other into one current, one flavor? Within

America, many poets and readers of poetry might be much more concerned with the dynamics between American poetry written in Spanish and Hispanic American poets writing in English. A striking example of such a confluence occurs with the poet Juan Felipe Herrera (born 1948), U.S. Poet Laureate from 2015 to 2017, who has published his work in both English and Spanish, often in bilingual editions. We indeed have not just bilingual poets, but poems, as in the work of Lorna Dee Cervantes (born 1954), whose linguistic hybridity involves a reclamation of her lingual-cultural heritage, since speaking Spanish was forbidden to her during her childhood (Ramazani et al. 2003, 1010).

This is not to say that British or Irish poetry will be reduced in significance, but that the dynamics between poet, poem, and reader might be refracted by matters of place and cultural background in ways that are more case specific than patterned in any discernable way.

In the end, and to echo a decidedly American voice, Henry David Thoreau, it might not be where a poet comes from that matters as much as the way in which she makes an honest account of her life—or resonates with her various backgrounds—that will make this or that poet worth reading, whether the poet might derive from Kent, Ohio, or Kent, England, from Belfast, Northern Ireland or Belfast, Maine.

Acknowledgment

The author thanks Ransom Patterson for his bibliographical assistance as well as Kevin Clark and David Wiesenberg for their helpful consultations.

Note

1 Please note that this essay references one of two versions of Clark's review, one available at the Digital Commons website at California Polytechnic State University (Clark 2004) and one appearing in *The Georgia Review* (Clark *Georgia* 2005).

References

Brown, Merle E. (1970). "On Jon Silkin's 'Amana Grass'." *The Iowa Review* 1: 115–125.

Clark, Kevin (2004). "Poetic Modernism and the Oceanic Divide". Review of *New British Poetry* (ed. Simic and Patterson). California Polytechnic State University. http://digitalcommons.calpoly.edu/cgi/viewcontent.cgi?article=1014&context=engl_fac (accessed 6 May 2020).

Clark, Kevin (2005). "Poetic Modernism and the Oceanic Divide". Review of *New British Poetry* (ed. Simic and Patterson). *The Georgia Review*, 59.2: 403–409.

Daniels, Kate (1999). "Ireland's Best." *The Southern Review* 35: 387–393.

Darlington, Andrew (2014). "'BOGG': History Of An Irreverent Poetry Magazine". *Eight Miles Higher*. andrew-darlington.blogspot.com/2014/05/bogg-history-of-irreverent-poetry.html (accessed 17 August 2017).

Davison, Peter (2002). "Darkness at Muldoon". Review of *Moy Sand and Gravel* (ed. P. Muldoon).

New York Times (13 October). http://www.nytimes.com/2002/10/13/books/darkness-at-muldoon.html (accessed 26 January 2015).

Fox, Margalit (2013). "Seamus Heaney, Irish Poet of Soil and Strife, Dies at 74". *New York Times* (30 August). http://www.nytimes.com/2013/08/31/arts/seamus-heaney-acclaimed-irish-poet-dies-at-74.html?pagewanted=all (accessed 22 January 2015).

Garfield, Simon (2007). "How Granta Conquered the World". *The Observer*, Guardian News and Media (30 December). http://www.theguardian.com/books/2007/dec/30/culture.features (accessed 6 May 2020).

Grosholz, Emily (2009). "Compacting Time: Anne Stevenson's Poems of Memory." *The Hudson Review* 62 (3): 405–416.

Heaney, Seamus (1998). *Opened Ground: Poems 1966–1996*. New York: Farrar, Straus and Giroux.

Heaney, Seamus and Cole, Henri (1997). "Seamus Heaney, The Art of Poetry No. 75". *The Paris Review* 144. http://www.theparisreview.org/interviews/1217/the-art-of-poetry-no-75-seamus-heaney (accessed 26 January 2015).

Hughes, Ted (1971). *Crow: From the Life and Songs of the Crow*. New York: Harper and Row.

Kennedy, X. J. (1986). "Larkin's Voice." *New Criterion* 4: 16–17.

Kroll, Jack (1971). "The Tree and the Bird." Review of *Crow: From the Life and Songs of the Crow*. *Newsweek* (12 April): 114.

Larkin, Philip (1974). *High Windows*. New York: Farrar, Straus and Giroux.

Leithauser, Brad (2006). "Wild Irish". Review of *District and Circle* (ed. S. Heaney). *New York Times* (16 July) Sunday Book Review. http://www.nytimes.com/2006/07/16/books/review/16leithouser.html (accessed 6 May 2020).

Lowell, Robert (1960). Acceptance Speech of Robert Lowell, Author of *Life Studies*. *National Book Committee Quarterly*, 4: 7.

Muldoon, Paul (ed.) (1986). *The Faber Book of Contemporary Irish Poetry*. London: Faber & Faber.

Pinsky, Robert (1977). Review of *Gamete*, by Ted Hughes and *Collected Poems* (ed. D. Abse). *The New York Times Book Review* (25 December), 137.

Ramazani, Jahan, Ellmann, Richard, and O'Clair, Robert (eds.) (2003. Volume 2 of). *The Norton Anthology of Modern and Contemporary Poetry*. New York: W.W. Norton & Company.

Rosenthal, M. L. (1973). "Some thoughts on American poetry today." *Salmagundi* 22–23: 57–70.

Satterfield, Jane (2001). Review of *The World's Wife*, by Carole Ann Duffy. *The Antioch Review*, 59.1: 123–124.

Shapiro, Alan (1989). "Celebrating Philip Larkin, Visionary of the Everyday". Review of *Collected Poems* (ed. P. Larkin). *Chicago Tribune* (26 April) http://articles.chicagotribune.com/1989-04-16/entertainment/8904040789_1_philip-larkin-collected-poems-visionary (accessed 27 January 2015).

Smartish Pace (2015). "Q&A with Eavan Boland". http://www.smartishpace.com/pqa/eavan_boland (accessed 26 January 2015).

The Poetry Foundation (2015a). "Anne Stevenson". http://www.poetryfoundation.org/bio/anne-stevenson (accessed 26 January 2015).

The Poetry Foundation (2015b). "Eavan Boland". http://www.poetryfoundation.org/bio/eavan-boland (accessed 26 January 2015).

The Poetry Foundation (2015c). "Mebdh McGuckian". http://www.poetryfoundation.org/bio/medbh-mcguckian (accessed 26 January 2015).

The Poetry Foundation (2015d). "Philip Larkin". http://www.poetryfoundation.org/bio/philip-larkin (accessed 19 January 2015).

The Poetry Foundation (2015e). "Seamus Heaney". http://www.poetryfoundation.org/bio/seamus-heaney (accessed 26 January 2015).

Tracy, D. H. (2006). "Review of *Poems 1955–2005*" (ed. A. Stevenson). *Poetry*, 188.2: 169–170.

Trethewey, Natasha (2013). "How Seamus Heaney Influenced Poet Laureate Natasha Trethewey". *The Daily Beast* (3 September). http://www.thedailybeast.com/articles/2013/09/03/how-seamus-heaney-influenced-poet-laureate-natasha-trethewey.html (accessed 2 December 2014).

Williams, William Carlos (1951). *The Autobiography of William Carlos Williams*. New York: Random House.

2a.4
Readers: Who Reads Modern Poetry?

Juha Virtanen

In an already infamous episode of contemporary British and Irish poetry, the presenter and journalist Jeremy Paxman was appointed as one of the judges for the Forward Prize in 2014. The appointment was not controversial in itself. Instead, comments made by Paxman during the judging process raised a series of objections from a number of poets on social media. Poetry, Paxman argued, had "connived at its own irrelevance"; poets were only interested in speaking to "other poets" and reluctant to engage with "ordinary people." What was needed, the presenter suggested, was an "inquisition" where poets would account for the creative and technical decisions they had undertaken while writing their work (Flood 2014). Certain reports of Paxman's speech also featured statistics from the online sales analysis service Nielsen BookScan, which depicted a decline in the sales of poetry publications, from £8.4 million in 2009 to £7.8 million in 2013 (Flood 2014). Moreover, as these statistics encapsulated the overall sales of poetry in UK-based bookshops, the readership for *contemporary* poetry was potentially even smaller than these figures indicate: an Arts Council report on the state of poetry in 2000 concluded that only around 3% of collections sold were written by contemporary writers, and some 67% of this already small percentage pertained to books by a single author (Bridgewood and Hampson 2000, 1). In light of these statistics, one might conclude that Paxman's comments were not entirely unfounded. And yet, in 2012, the poet and critic Robert Sheppard noted that innovative British and Irish poetry was "living through a golden age" (Loydell and Sheppard 2012). A year earlier, Andrew Duncan claimed that the quality of poetry emerging from centers such as London was reaching "a historic peak" (Duncan 2011).

A Companion to Contemporary British and Irish Poetry, 1960–2015, First Edition.
Edited by Wolfgang Görtschacher and David Malcolm.
© 2021 John Wiley & Sons Ltd. Published 2021 by John Wiley & Sons Ltd.

As these figures and observations are all relatively contemporaneous with each other, they pose a conundrum: how can an art form experience a golden age or a historic peak and simultaneously connive at its own irrelevance? Who reads modern poetry? In this chapter, I will endeavor to propose possible answers to these problematic questions. First, I will provide a very brief overview of how these issues have developed from the 1960s to the present day; second, I will outline how these debates are addressed in current scholarship; and, finally, I will suggest some further developments that could contribute toward offering a more comprehensive representation of the readership for modern British and Irish poetry.

In some respects, the objections and controversy around Paxman's comments are surprising, as his sentiments are hardly novel. In 1964, Adrian Mitchell opened his first collection, *Poems*, with an epigraph where he argued that "[m]ost people ignore most poetry because most poetry ignores most people" (Mitchell 1964, n.p.). Here, the underlying claim poses a similar conception of poetry as an elitist praxis that is only interested in communicating with a coterie of like-minded practitioners, which consequently disregards a considerable proportion of the general public. However, Mitchell's repetition of "most" is notable, as it relates this issue of coteries to questions of class. The poetry that ignores most people was—in Mitchell's view at the time—written predominately by "male, middle-class, and university-educated poets," whose intellectualism and academicism ultimately alienated the wider public (Mitchell n.d.).

Although these social characteristics apply equally to both high modernists such as Pound and Eliot and the Movement poets of the 1950s, it is curious that the latter group generally receives greater public acknowledgment than the more experimental works of poets belonging to what some have called "the parallel tradition" (Edwards 2000, 34). Indeed, the Movement's poetics cohere well with a common understanding of what poetry *is*: empirical statements "about the non-verbal external world" (Forrest-Thompson 1978, xi), related through narratively and syntactically coherent, pristine, and closed verses.[1] For instance, in reading Larkin's "As Bad as a Mile," we can—with relative ease—visualize the scene where the apple core misses the basket, and understand the situation as a humorous representation of everyday failures (Larkin 1964, 32). In other words, the poem appears to be accessible, and its accessibility relies on a deliberate limitation of its poetic interactions.[2] However, if we examine a poem such as J. H. Prynne's "The Glacial Question, Unsolved," we are met with a complex mapping of geographical and geological questions that draw upon a series of scholarly references (Prynne 2005, 65–67). In order to understand the poem, we might have to track down Prynne's resources, and work out their implications within the text; at the very least, the poem requires multiple readings. These challenges *are* a pleasure, but the pleasure they provide differs greatly from the experience of reading Larkin's poem. As such, poems where the syntactical elements draw upon "notions of discontinuity and indeterminacy" (Sheppard 2005, 3)—or where the poet deploys complex, specialist vocabulary and concepts from scientific or philosophical discourses, as Prynne does—are frequently regarded as inaccessible, overtly academic, and intellectually elitist.

As reductive as these binary oppositions inevitably are, the history of modern British and Irish poetry offers many examples of such acrimonious factionalisms in terms of its audience. During Eric Mottram's editorship of *Poetry Review* in the 1970s, the editor's commitment to experimental work provoked "puzzlement, outrage, and eventual rejection" (Barry 2006, 152) among the magazine's readers.³ The middle-class, suburban subscribers felt alienated by the apparent difficulty and the profanities of these poems, and dismissed them as dull pieces of infantilism (Barry 2006, 153–154). In other cases, poets themselves have seemingly fetishized the lack of wider readership. Iain Sinclair, for instance, makes frequent references to poetry belonging in exile among ephemeral publications that are difficult to obtain without a "team of private detectives" (Sinclair 1996, xiv). To elaborate, these statements represent a poetic sociality that is mistrustful of a public taste for easy pleasure, and instead regards fellow practitioners as a more receptive audience. While certain recent scholarly works and anthologies have sought to problematize the dichotomous taxonomies of the "mainstream" and the "*avant-garde*," the present panorama still relies upon these cultural stereotypes.⁴ The accessible, more widely read poems are deemed to soothe, console, and pacify "our sharpest experiences of grief and loss and bewilderment" (Goode 2011, iii), while more experimental works go unread because they are seen as acts of self-absorbed obscurantism that disparages readers who are unable to understand it.⁵

Despite this brief overview, a clear narrative begins to emerge. Although the audiences of modern poetry as a whole are significantly smaller than those of novels or films, the internal divisions within this readership limit its public presence even further. While some "mainstream" poets may enjoy comparatively wider acclaim, the readers of experimental poems are supposedly limited to other poets, academics, and university students. A huge swathe of British and Irish poetry is in other words deemed too difficult for reading.

However, I think the assumptions of such narratives should be contested, and recent critical works offer some valuable alternatives to these conceptions of modern readership. In *Aesthetic Theory*, Adorno argues that modern artworks that seem incomprehensible appear as such because they transgress the common practices of (cultural) capitalism. Consequently, the most prominent detractors of these artworks reject them simply on the bases of crude assumptions. As he elaborates on this suggestion, Adorno offers a useful characterization that is applicable to the perceived notions of inaccessibility in modern poetry:

> The non-specialist will no more understand the most recent developments in nuclear physics than the lay person will straightaway grasp extremely complex [modern art]. Whereas, however, the incomprehensibility of physics is accepted [...] modern art's incomprehensibility is branded as schizoid arbitrariness, even though [it] gives way to experience no less than does the scientifically obscure. (Adorno 2013, 320)

This argument is quite similar to Robert Sheppard's view that no poem is more accessible than any other "since all poems are social facts open to social comprehension" and completion (Sheppard 2005, 7). In other words, Sheppard regards poetry as an unfinished task that requires a committed readerly engagement. A poem reveals certain facets of itself while concealing others, thus rendering the reader's task into a continual process of interpretation (Sheppard 2011, 7). To some degree, such views are perhaps indebted to "the convergence of text and reader" (Iser 2008, 295) in reader-response theory—not to mention the tenets of poststructuralist literary analysis—but similar conceptions seem frequent in contemporary criticism. Peter Middleton, for example, has developed a nuanced account of a poem's "long biography," in which the act of reading does not *fulfill* the poetic text; rather, it enacts the poem's continuance in time, which can also manifest itself through publications, performances, reviews, and criticism (Middleton 2005, 23–24).

The perspectives from Adorno, Sheppard, and Middleton all involve a reconfiguration of accessibility. The poem is no longer accessible because it has limited itself to expressing a coherent, empirical situation; rather, the poem's accessibility relies upon an invitation for the reader to participate in the continued production of its meaning. This position is also explicitly present in the poetics of several modern poets. For instance, Allen Fisher sees poetry as a process of constellated possibilities and readerly interactions:

> where meaning is apparent, that meaning changes in relation to the meaning another may give it, or in relation to living after the first realisation of the meaning. And the meaning may take on a multiplicity that is summated or left impossible and so forth. (Fisher 1999, 7)

It should be noted that Fisher does not limit this process of mutable meanings to the act of reading. In fact, his subsequent theorizations also place the poet in a similar position of openness, contingency, and vulnerability. The poem is not a closed unit of autonomous meaning, but simply a "confident approach" that—despite its "lack of solutions"—offers possible proposals about the issues that it examines (Fisher 2007, 11). In other words, Fisher's poetry develops an arena in which both the poet and the reader can collaborate in the assemblage of various interpretations.

Fisher's attention to process and "confidence in lack" help to clarify the experience of reading his early tour de force *Place*. Toward the end of the first book of this project, Fisher includes a section that describes his visit to Dove Cottage, which ends with a peculiar aside that resembles stage directions: "(at this point a reshowing / involved with XIX)" (Fisher 2016, 107). Turning back to the poem in question, its relationship to Wordsworth's cottage seems oblique and—at first—incomprehensible. The text is simply comprised of a short archeological note:

> a Neanderthal skull with a hole in its base
> artificially enlarged
> was found within a circle of stones on the "floor"
> in Monte Circeo, Italy
>
> (Fisher 2016, 68)

However, the poem that follows the visit to Dove Cottage features an encounter with a sheep's skull—with its flesh eaten and lower jaw missing—on top of Threlkeld Knotts. As such, the earlier aside directs the reader to regard the Neanderthal skull as a prefiguration of the sheep's remains in the subsequent poem. In effect, these two fragments integrate each other: Threlkeld Knotts merges with Monte Circeo, and the two skulls blend together. A further degree of resonance between the two poems also emerges via Fisher's archeological resources. After the skull in Monte Circeo was first discovered in 1939, anthropologists proposed that it was a relic of a ritualistic murder involving decapitation and cannibalism (Blanc 1961, 119–136).[6] Thus, the consumed flesh on the sheep's skull potentially reflects a continued sense of brutality that relates to Fisher's overarching anger at London's political superstructures, which have enacted an uneven distribution of opportunity and justice since antiquity. By inviting readers to consider the parallels between these two separate fragments, Fisher encourages a re-evaluation of their individual significations, as well as their relationship to *Place* as a whole.

This brief example in other words demonstrates that Fisher's poetry—which is both syntactically discontinuous and immersed with various ranges of specialist knowledge—is not invested in an inaccessible, incomprehensible obscurantism or elitist derision. Rather, it openly invites its readers to participate in the production of its social comprehensions and completions. Because it openly shows its processes and interconnections, any reader who is willing to engage with the pleasures and complexities of Fisher's work can follow and interrogate its proposals without insurmountable prerequisites of specialist knowledge.

Thus, by contesting the assumptions that underlie the dismissive claims about the inaccessibility of modern poetry, we can begin to map out a more productive understanding of who reads it. At the very least, my preceding discussions have tried to demonstrate *how* modern poetry might be read. But are these notions of readership ideal or actual? Do such readers actually exist?

While poetry's audiences are undeniably smaller than those of other art forms, I would also suggest that the image of decline that emerged in conjunction with Paxman's comments does not paint an accurate portrait. My own experience of attending poetry readings certainly gives some credence to the historic "golden age" depicted by Sheppard and Duncan: Xing the Line, organized by Jeff Hilson in London, and Hi Zero, organized by Joe Luna in Brighton, have on many occasions attracted audiences of around 80–100 people.[7] Moreover, the sales figures I quoted at the beginning of this chapter are based on aggregated "retail sales information from {…} bookshops" (Nielsen BookScan n.d.), and contemporary poetry is not often distributed through such channels. For instance, Shearsman Books, an independent publisher of poetry, consistently sold approximately 10,000 units per year between 2011 and 2014. Each year, over a third of these sales were generated through print-on-demand purchases—the printing technology where a copy is only printed when an order is received. In addition, a considerable number of units are also sold to the poets themselves, who would then resell these copies during readings and other public events. By way of comparison, while both of these sales categories are annually in the thousands, Shearsman's direct sales to retailers usually amount to around 200–400 copies per year (Tony Frazer, email to author, October 2, 2014).[8] A similar situation applied to Ken Edwards's now-retired Reality Street. While the press's annual output between 2011 and 2014 was fairly modest (comprising around four books per year), their sales were consistently robust. Each publication received an average sale of around 200 copies, and the press's most popular volumes tended to sell in the thousands. Moreover, through Reality Street's supporter scheme subscriptions, each book benefited from guaranteed sales of approximately 70–120 copies. As with Shearsman, only a small fraction of these units were sold through bookshops; the majority of Reality Street's sales took place online, either directly via the publisher's website, or through Amazon (Ken Edwards, email to author, October 2, 2014).[9] Furthermore, these are only two indicative examples. Publications from small presses such as The 87 Press, Distance No Object, Contraband, Materials, Oystercatcher, and Veer Books are most readily available directly from their respective websites.

If we add online platforms such as those available from Pamenar Press and *DATABLEED* into these considerations, the channels through which modern poetry can find its readers grow increasingly nebulous and complex. Statistics that focus solely on sales from bookshops therefore offer an incomplete representation of the readership for modern British and Irish poetry. Of course, the poets and publishers I have discussed in this chapter might be wary of conceptualizing their work in terms of retailed units—and rightly so. Such discourses would, inevitably, violate the processual emphases of their respective poetics by turning these publications into marketable products. However, I have offered these examples as my concluding remarks in order to dispel the dismissive misconceptions of an art form that has connived at its own irrelevance. Despite the figures that accompanied Paxman's comments in 2014, subsequent years have begun to tell a different story: in 2015, poetry book sales in the United Kingdom reached an all-time high of £8.8m, and in October 2016, they were set to surpass £10m; commentators attributed this upward trend to the emergence of energetic and innovative young writers, as well as the growing presence of experimental and radical work by BAME (Black, Asian, minority, ethnic) poets (Cowdrey 2016). A committed and dedicated readership of modern poetry clearly exists, and it evinces no signs of decline.

Notes

1 A more detailed account of the Movement poets and their poetics can be found in, for example, Sheppard (2005, 20–34).
2 A more thorough discussion of these readerly practices is available in, for example, Middleton (2005, 1–24).
3 Mottram's commitment to the "parallel tradition"—and his distaste for the "mainstream"—of poetry is discernible in both his essays and his comments in interviews. See, for example, Mottram (1993, 15–50) and Mottram (2000, 48–94).
4 Examples of studies and anthologies that have tried to complicate the perceived divisions between the "mainstream" and the "*avant-garde*" include Barry (2000), Barry (2006), and Hamilton (2013).
5 As a case in point, Don Paterson's introduction to *New British Poetry* claimed that experimental poets were "capable of nothing more than monotone angst […] and a kind of joyless wordplay" (Paterson and Simic 2004, xxxii). As Andrea Brady puts it, this was "so fanatical a diagnosis that all readers might as well ignore it" (Brady 2004, 397).
6 This claim was contested in the 1980s. However, at the time when Fisher was writing *Place,* the cannibalistic ritual was the leading theory about the skull found at Mt. Circeo.
7 More discussion on Xing the Line can be found in Hilson (2012). Archived information about events organized by Luna and Careless is available in Hi Zero (n.d.).
8 The full figures are:
  2013–2014: 9,629 of which print-on-demand sales: 3,590; sales to authors: 3,033; sales to wholesalers: 1,149; direct sales to retailers: 330; SPD [Small Press Distribution] 887.

2012–2013: 10,425 of which p-o-d: 3,976; authors: 3,324; wholesalers 1,137; retail direct: 183; SPD 811.

2011–2012: 10,490 of which p-o-d: 3,977; authors: 2,986; wholesalers: 940; retail direct: 261; SPD 1,374. 2010–2011: 9,838 of which p-o-d: 4,257; authors: 2,917; wholesalers: 441; retail direct: 330; SPD 1,085 (Tony Frazer, email to author, October 2, 2014).

9 In 2016, Edwards decided to cease production of new titles, although "all remaining titles will be kept in print as long as possible" (Edwards n.d.).

References

Adorno, Theodore (2013). *Aesthetic Theory*. London: Bloomsbury Academic.

Barry, Peter (2000). *Contemporary British Poetry and the City*. Manchester: Manchester University Press.

Barry, Peter (2006). *Poetry Wars: British Poetry of the 1970s and the Battle of Earls Court*. Cambridge: Salt Publishing.

Blanc, Alberto C. (1961). "Some evidence for the ideologies early man." In: *Social Life of Early Man* (ed. Sherwood Larned Washburn), 119–136. Chicago: Aldine.

Brady, Andrea (2004). "'Meagrely Provided': a response to Don Paterson." *Chicago Review* 49–50 (3–4/1): 396–402.

Bridgewood, Ann and Hampson, John (eds.) (2000). *Rhyme and Reason: Developing Contemporary Poetry*. Great Britain: Arts Council England.

Cowdrey, Katherine (2016). "Poetry Market Celebrates National Poetry Day with Highest Sales Ever." *The Bookseller* (5 October). http://www.thebookseller.com/news/poetry-market-celebrates-national-poetry-day-highest-sales-ever-405931 (accessed 6 May 2020).

Duncan, Andrew (2011). "Irrepressible Creativity of the London Scene." *Angel Exhaust* (28 March). http://angelexhaust.blogspot.co.uk/2011_03_01_archive.html (accessed 6 May 2020).

Edwards, Ken (2000). "The Two Poetries." *Angelaki* 3 (1): 25–36.

Edwards, Ken (n.d.) "The History of Reality Street." www.realitystreet.co.uk/about-us.php (accessed 21 August 2017).

Fisher, Allen (1999). *The Topological Shovel: Four Essays*. Ontario: The Gig.

Fisher, Allen (2007). *Confidence in Lack*. London: Writers Forum.

Fisher, Allen (2016). *Place*, 2e. Hastings: Reality Street.

Flood, Alison (2014). "Jeremy Paxman Says Poets Must Start Engaging with Ordinary People." *The Guardian* (1 June). http://www.theguardian.com/media/2014/jun/01/jeremy-paxman-poets-engage-ordinary-people-forward-prize (accessed 6 May 2020).

Forrest-Thompson, Veronica (1978). *Poetic Artifice*. Manchester: Manchester University Press.

Goode, Chris (ed.) (2011). *Better than Language: An Anthology of New Modernist Poetries*. Eastbourne: Ganzfeld Press.

Hamilton, Nathan (ed.) (2013). *Dear World & Everyone in It: New Poetry in the UK*. Wiltshire: Bloodaxe Books.

Hilson, Jeff (2012). "Maintenant #92 – Jeff Hilson: An interview with Jeff Hilson by S. J. Fowler." *3:AM Magazine* (22 April). http://www.3ammagazine.com/3am/maintenant-92-jeff-hilson (accessed 6 May 2020).

Hi Zero (n.d.). "Hi Zero: Poetry Readings and Publications out of Brighton, UK." http://hizeroreadings.tumblr.com (accessed 21 August 2017).

Iser, Wolfgang (2008). "The Reading Process: a Phenomenological Approach." In: *Modern Criticism and Theory: A Reader* (eds. David Lodge and Nigel Wood), 294–310. London: Pearson Longman.

Larkin, Philip (1964). *The Whitsun Weddings*. London: Faber & Faber.

Loydell, Rupert, and Sheppard, Robert (2012). "Even the Bad Times are Good." *Stride Magazine* (20 January). www.stridemagazine.co.uk/Stride%20mag%202012/Jan%202012/rupertandrobertint.htm (accessed 6 May 2020).

Middleton, Peter (2005). *Distant Reading: Performance, Readership, and Consumption in Contemporary Poetry*. Tuscaloosa: University of Alabama Press.

Mitchell, Adrian (1964). *Poems*. London: Jonathan Cape.

Mitchell, Adrian (n.d.) "Adrian Mitchell Interview." *The Poetry Archive*. http://www.poetryarchive.org/interview/adrian-mitchell-interview (accessed 21 August 2017)

Mottram, Eric (1993). "The British Poetry Revival." In: *New British Poetries: The Scope of the Possible* (eds. Robert Hampson and Peter Barry), 15–50. Manchester: Manchester University Press.

Mottram, Eric (2000). "Our education is political: Interview with Wolfgang Görtschacher." In: *Contemporary Views on the Little Magazine Scene* (ed. Wolfgang Görtschacher), 48–94. Salzburg et al: Poetry Salzburg.

Nielsen BookScan (n.d.) "Measuring and analyzing sales around the world." www.nielsenbookscan.co.uk/controller.php?page=48 (accessed 21 August 2017).

Paterson, Don and Simic, Charles (eds.) (2004). *New British Poetry*. Minneapolis: Graywolf Press.

Prynne, J. H. (2005). *Poems*. Wiltshire: Bloodaxe Books.

Sheppard, Robert (2005). *The Poetry of Saying: British Poetry and Its Discontents 1950–2000*. Liverpool: University of Liverpool Press.

Sheppard, Robert (2011). *When Bad Times Made for Good Poetry: Episodes in the History of the Poetics of Innovation*. Exeter: Shearsman.

Sinclair, Iain (ed.) (1996). *Conductors of Chaos*. Great Britain: Picador.

Section 2b. Genre, Kind, Technique

2b.1
Manifestos and Poetics/Poets on Writing

Daniel Weston

A survey of poetry manifestos needs to start by establishing the role that this kind of document plays in the period under consideration and historically. I will start to map out this role and these trajectories from an example. Andrew Motion was one of 30 contemporary poets commissioned to write a brief statement for a collection published in 2000. Motion's statement is paradigmatic of many poets' hesitation. He perceives a disparity between poetry and manifestos: "Poetry manifestos invariably say 'yes' and 'no', but poetry itself 'maybe' and 'perhaps'." The "peculiar kind of intelligence" possessed by poetry is "not inevitably the intelligence of analysis and exegesis, but the intelligence of feeling things upon our pulses." Thus, "poetry is hindered as well as helped by manifestos" (2000, 233). Similar views had been expressed by, for example, James Fenton in his "The Manifesto against Manifestos" (1983, 12–16), and by Derek Walcott: "manifestos create a kind of poetry that really isn't poetry at all – it's really a rhythmical manifesto" (2000, 170). In one sense, Motion's point is beyond debate: the declarative form and often insistent tone of the manifesto necessarily do violence to the subtleties of poetry in setting out precepts. And yet, Motion's position demands scrutiny. The description of things *felt* "upon our pulses," emotional experience, as the matter of poetry reveals a romantic inheritance still dominant in mainstream poetry today. It is to be expected that the then Poet Laureate, now *Sir* Andrew, should take up this stance. The manifesto more commonly announces a revolutionary or strongly reforming program of change. In the twentieth century, it is primarily associated with modernists "making it new," and, after mid-century, with neo-modernist groups who work in this tradition. The message and the medium are related: those with an iconoclast's sense of poetic tradition write "manifestos" more often than those minded otherwise. For this reason, a brief but broadly representative survey of poets' views needs to take account of a wider sample of "statements." Before arriving at the post-1960 period, it is necessary to describe the romantic and modernist poles between which modern debate has shuttled. Though the mainstream/experimental divide that this leads to has oriented much discussion of contemporary poetry, it is not always helpful. It is nonetheless a more apparent fault line in manifestos than in poetry itself. For this reason, I begin with the historical debate that informs and perpetuates it, before turning toward the issues on which there is more consensus. In short, academic categorizations by a Manichean division are overstated, but they offer a useful starting point.

I begin with the romantic idea of poetry's purpose and then chart modernist challenges to it that inform poetics across the whole of the twentieth century. Motion's description of poetry's "intelligence of feeling things upon our pulses" (reporting interior experiences, emotional and bodily) bears a strong trace of Wordsworth's famous declaration that "poetry is the spontaneous overflow of powerful feelings: it takes its origin from emotion recollected in tranquillity" (1984, 611). For Wordsworth, the poet's contemplative reflection on his/her own experiences allows him/her to compose poems whose power derives from their offering distillations of the powerful feelings attached to those experiences. The reader, it is supposed, experiences similar feelings and responds to the poet's skill in expressing this shared response to the world in his/her skillful use of language and form. Thus, lyric poetry is essentially a communicative act of identification. Keats's pithier formulation expresses the same: "Poetry [...] should strike the reader as a wording of his own highest thoughts, and appear almost a remembrance" (1947, 108).

These powerful formulae, dominant through the nineteenth century, are strongly challenged at the advent of modernism. Writing in 1911, T. E. Hulme declares his objection to "the sloppiness [of romanticism] which doesn't consider a poem is a poem unless it is moaning or whining about something or other." His polemic zeros in on the terms in which Wordsworth had conceived poetry's function: "Verse to them always means a bringing in of some of the emotions that are grouped round the word infinite." Castigating the expression of feeling, Hulme hails a new era: "I prophesy that a period of dry, hard, classical verse is coming," for which "the great aim is accurate, precise and definite description" (2012, 2062–2063). Ezra Pound's 1918 prediction is similar: twentieth-century poetry will "move against poppycock, it will be harder and saner, [...] austere, direct, free from emotional slither" (1954, 13). The different kind of poetry that Pound envisages is apparent in the manifestos for Imagism written with F. S. Flint. The first principle of this movement is "direct treatment of the 'thing' whether subjective or objective," signifying an attack on Wordsworth's conjoining of experience and emotion (1972, 129). T. S. Eliot, the modernist responding most directly to Wordsworth, avers that "emotion recollected in tranquillity" is "an inexact formula." For Eliot, the business of the poet "is neither emotion, nor recollection, nor, without distortion of meaning, tranquillity. It is a concentration, and a new thing resulting from the concentration, of a very great number of experiences [...] which does not happen consciously or of deliberation." Consequently, "poetry is not a turning loose of emotion, but an escape from emotion; it is not the expression of personality, but an escape from personality" (1953, 29/30). The result is "difficult" poetry: "The poet must become more and more comprehensive, more allusive, more indirect, in order to force, to dislocate if necessary, language into his meaning" (119). If, in romantic thought, the poem is a transparent medium of felt communication, then modernist ideas draw attention to the opacity of language and favor a poetics of impersonality.

It is important to state that the modernist takeover was not complete and that the subsequent period has seen an unresolved debate between these two traditions. Scholarly discourse, with its propensity to periodize, has characterized each decade with a few key figures and the styles they work in—the high modernism of Pound and Eliot in the 1920s, political poetry and Auden in the 1930s, Dylan Thomas and new romantic verse in the 1940s, a return to plain speaking with the Movement in the 1950s—and to chart an oscillation. However, each of the "schools" is not, in reality, confined within these temporal limits. Rather, a continual back and forth operates between a mainstream coming down from a postromantic lineage on the one hand, and a neomodernist experimentalism on the other. This dispute is defining, but in the period that this book covers most poets inhabit the gray area between. Sampling statements reveals that not all poets see themselves in one camp or the other: many attempt to balance or combine the two approaches.

Seamus Heaney is a modern poet taking up romantic poetics, and one of the most explicit in linking his view of poetry's task to Wordsworth's. His essay "Feeling into Words" (1974) takes its lead (and its title) from Wordsworth. Heaney's emphasis on the importance of "[f]inding a voice," meaning "that you can get your own feel into your own words and that your words have the feeling of you about them," is clearly related to the personal expression at the heart of Wordsworth's theory of poetry (1980, 43). Heaney draws a distinction between "craft" and "technique." The former, learnt initially from others' verse, is "the skill of making"; whereas the latter

> involves not only a poet's way with words, his management of metre, rhythm and verbal texture; it involves also a definition of his stance towards life, a definition of his own reality. It involves the discovery of ways to go out of his normal cognitive bounds and raid the inarticulate: a dynamic alertness that mediates between the origins of feeling in memory and experience and the formal ploys that express these in a work of art. (47)

Heaney expresses the transmission of Wordsworthian ideas but he also demonstrates the repackaging of them and the lineage they pass through. Heaney's phrasing, gesturing toward the unconscious and psychoanalysis, translates "emotion" into a specifically twentieth-century terminology. Though Heaney rebuffs Eliot's poetics of impersonality, he also echoes Eliot's idea of craft. In the inclusion of craft, he moves away from the romantic idea of the inspired poet creating *ex nihilo* (which comes more from Coleridge, in his poems devoted to the imagination, than Wordsworth). Auden—who emphasizes craftsmanship and observes that "every poet [...] requires a training in the poetic use of language" with which he/she might act on "a crowd of recollected occasions of feeling"—is also an influence here (1963, 61). Most important for Heaney, after Wordsworth himself, is W. B. Yeats who he quotes in his explanation of technique. For Yeats, "a poet writes always of his personal life" by projecting his concerns through adopting "masks." By this method, the poet becomes "more type than man, more passion than type" (1997, 379). From these influences, Heaney finds craft and technique to be related but awards primacy to the latter.

Heaney is one of a triad of now canonical writers who follow romantic leads in focusing on poetry's ability to recuperate experience and feeling. The other two are Ted Hughes and Philip Larkin. Hughes's "Words and Experience" (1967) at first stresses the separation of the two titular items—"our experience of life" is embedded in us "quite a long way from the world of words"—before turning to the process of giving expression: "Words are tools, learned late and laboriously and easily forgotten, with which we try to give some part of our experience a more or less permanent shape outside ourselves" (1967, 119). Hughes shares with Heaney a vision of poetry reaching what is deeply felt but inarticulate. Hughes's description gives the process a more elemental than unconscious sense: "[t]he struggle truly to possess his own experience, [...] to regain his genuine self, has been man's principal occupation, whenever he could find leisure for it"; and to do this men "have invented art—music, painting, dancing, sculpture, and the activity that includes all of these, which is poetry" (124). In this long view, poetry is a primal, almost sacred act. The poet thus accrues cultural capital when capturing experience is a fundamental human activity from prehistory onward.

Larkin's figuration of the same process is much more prosaic than Hughes's (in keeping with the radical differences between their poetries), but it comes to something similar. Larkin "write[s] poems to preserve things I have seen / thought / felt (if I may so indicate a composite and complex experience) both for myself and for others, though I feel that my prime responsibility is to the experience itself, which I am trying to keep from oblivion for its own sake." Like Hughes, Larkin sees this as a universal practice: "the impulse to preserve lies at the bottom of all art" (1983b, 79). The terminology of preservation is also employed by Thom Gunn when he suggests that the impetus for poetry comes from wanting to "preserve [people] on paper in the best way I knew, [...] getting my feeling for them into my description of them" (1982, 152). For Larkin, like Keats, the recreation of emotion in the reader is the important communicative point: the poet "construct[s] a verbal device that will reproduce this emotional concept in anyone who cares to read it, anywhere, anytime" (1983a, 80). Constructing a poem might involve both craft and technique as Heaney would define them, and Larkin's poetry has an equally distinctive voice as Heaney's, but here *universal* recognition is important. The implied poetics of Larkin's position is one that might downplay the specific details of the poet's life in order to represent widely applicable experiences that the reader will recognize. More recently, David Constantine has similarly observed that poetry "puts us in living touch with our shared realities" (2000, 226). Clearly there is variety here—Heaney, Hughes, and Larkin have their own particular takes on this set of concerns—but there is nonetheless a discernible shared romantic inheritance across these stalwarts of mainstream poetry. Their statements are all concerned to describe the ways in which poetry expresses felt experiences and perceive this to be its primary function.

The alternative, modernist inheritance that intercepts this romantic lineage is less straightforward to chart when the focus is specifically British and Irish poetry. The North

American poetry scene has played a large part in transmitting the modernist esthetic through the mid-twentieth century and beyond. The association of experimentation with North America and England with its opposite was firm enough for Amiri Baraka (previously known as LeRoi Jones) to declare in 1960 that "[a]ccentual verse, the regular metric of rumbling iambics, is dry as slivers of sand. Nothing happens in that frame anymore. We can get nothing from England" (1960, 425). William Carlos Williams, influenced by Pound and in turn extremely influential for those who followed him on both sides of the Atlantic, elaborates alternative positions for poetry. He draws a likeness between the ways in which our lives "have lost all that in the past we had to measure them by," and the way "our verses, of which our poems are made, are left without any metrical construction of which we can speak." From this position, Williams incites his contemporaries: "We must invent new modes to take the place of those which are worn out" (1954, 337–339). In practice, Williams calls for poets to pay less attention to the profundity of what is said, and more how it is said:

> Most poems I see today are concerned with what they are *saying*, how profound they have been given to be. So true is this that those who write them have forgotten to make poems at all of them. Thank God we're not musicians, with our lack of structural invention we'd be ashamed to look ourselves in the face otherwise. (338)

This, then, is the classic mid-century American modernist call for more attention to formal invention, though Williams is not throwing out content but rebalancing it with mode and measure. The same is true of Charles Olson's famous manifesto, "Projective Verse" (1950). Olson, leader of the experimental Black Mountain poets and theorist of open field poetics, avers that "[v]erse now" must "catch up and put into itself certain laws and possibilities of the breath, of the breathing of the man who writes as well as of his listenings" (1997, 239). Like Williams, Olson indicates that this attention to formal considerations is not separate from poetry's subject, for "FORM IS NEVER MORE THAN AN EXTENSION OF CONTENT," with the corollary that "right form, in any given poem, is the only and exclusively possible extension of content under hand" (1997, 40).

It is with lines of thinking that the modernist-inspired British Poetry Revival of the 1960s and 1970s sought to pollinate domestic poetry. Eric Mottram, whose poetry was influenced by the cut-up and collage techniques of Black Mountain and Beat experimenters, took on the editorship of *Poetry Review* in 1971. In this post, he published the work of the American avant-garde and set up Poetry Information—a series of weekly colloquies on contemporary American, French, and East European poetries (Institute of Contemporary Arts, April–July 1971)—with the aim, he wrote to Robert Duncan, of "counter[ing] establishment biases here, and ignorance about major poetry in the States" (Evans and Zamir 2007, 35). Alongside cultivating international awareness, the British Poetry Revival also sought out neglected British modernist figures (David Jones, Hugh MacDiarmid, Basil Bunting), often themselves in dialogue with North American figures. Bunting, friend of Pound and Louis Zukofsky, has been extremely influential since his "rediscovery" (after decades in obscurity) by Tom Pickard and other young poets in the

1960s. Bunting's *Briggflatts* (1965) provided a model poem—Poundian in scope, drawing on sonata form, and Wordsworthian in theme—and "The Poet's Point of View" (1966) is a short but powerful manifesto.

Here, Bunting shifts the terms in which poetry is discussed away from the mainstream's single-minded and limiting fascination (as he saw it) with formulating meaning out of recuperated experience:

> Poetry, like music, is to be heard. It deals in sound – long sounds and short sounds, heavy beats and light beats, the tone relations of vowels, the relations of consonants to one another which are like instrumental colour in music. Poetry lies dead on the page, until some voice brings it to life, just as music, on the stave, is no more than instructions to the player. [...] Poetry must be read aloud. (2000, 80)

Bunting clearly shares common ground with Olson. The latter is concerned with composition according to the breath, and the former with the conveyance of the aural qualities that this method creates. Both then influence more recent statements, such as Glyn Maxwell's: "to read the true poem, the surviving poem, aloud is to express the very shape of a self, to sound it. Poetry is decoration of the breath with the stirrings of the mind" (2000, 256). Like heard poetry, concrete poetry—"not a visual but a silent poetry"—pioneered by Ian Hamilton Finlay over the same period also prioritizes form over content (2012, 135). There, the importance conferred upon the arrangement of words on the page draws readers away from jumping to content and instead emphasizes the crucial roles played by formal characteristics.

Despite the obvious dispute with the mainstream, there is nonetheless a common desire to communicate here. In Olson's declaration that "[a] poem is energy transferred from where the poet got it [...], by way of the poem itself to, all the way over to, the reader," there is some similarity to Larkin's desire to reproduce an emotional concept in his reader, though in different terms and by different means (240). Likewise, Bunting argues about terminology and method, but also envisions making his audience *feel* when he writes that poetry "is seeking to make not meaning, but beauty; or if you insist on misusing words, its 'meaning' is of another kind, and lies in the relation to one another of lines and patterns of sound, perhaps harmonious, perhaps contrasting and clashing, which the hearer feels rather than understands" (42). Certainly, what is communicated is altered, and the act of communication is more complex, but modernists' statements certainly undermine the caricature of the avant-garde as willful obfuscators. Denise Levertov brings much of this together. A British poet who has spent her adult life in America and has been involved with Black Mountain and Objectivist schools, she observes that "content determines form, and yet that content is discovered only *in* form" (1960, 411). This balancing could be said to express something similar to Heaney's craft and technique.

Along with the issue of communication goes the question of audience. Notwithstanding differences, both mainstream and experimental poets often make a claim for the same popular audience. Given Larkin's desire for his poems to reproduce an emotional concept in a reader "anywhere, anytime," it is unsurprising that he values a popular, nonspecialist audience highly: "poetry, like all art, is inextricably bound up with giving pleasure, and if a poet loses his pleasure-seeking audience he has lost the only audience worth having, for which the dutiful mob that signs on every September is no substitute" (81–82). Such attacks on the academy are widespread and particularly prevalent in poets who address issues of class. Tony Harrison describes his writing as a "quest for a public poetry," and prefers "the idea of men speaking to men to a man speaking to god, or even worse to Oxford's anointed" (1991, 9). For Simon Armitage, this is a politicized issue: "The appropriation of poetry by the literati can be quite properly compared with the enclosure of common land in England, the Highland Clearances and the hijacking of ancient medicine by Western science" (2000, 254). For Eavan Boland, the fault lies as much with the modernists. She proposes that "20th century poetry took a wrong turning." Before this period, "the dialect of poetic Romanticism could honour the powerful vernacular of popular joy and memory." Modernism remade the poem *and* the reader, and this meant "cutting the reader off from the old popular expectations of the poem and the historic popular audience. [...] It meant, above all, compelling the reader [...] to sacrifice an ancient and communal contract between poet and audience [...]. A centuries-old, bright partnership between poet and reader has been injured" (2000, 215–217).

While this may be true of the high modernism of Pound and Eliot, it is not always true of later modernists. Bunting is scathing in his attack on the "the worst, most insidious charlatans [who] fill chairs and fellowships in universities, write for the weeklies or work for the BBC or the British Council or some other asylum for obsequious idlers." Their analysis, he contends, will distract readers from "hear[ing] the meaning, which is the sound" (43). According to Tom Leonard, "the trouble lies in the notion that poetry has to be 'taught' in the first place, and that there is a professional caste of people best equipped so to do." The result is that "Literature shrinks to Teachable Literature. [...] In fact the spread of education as a right to the mass of people has paradoxically led to the deprivation, from them, of much they once held to be valid literature" (1989, xvii–xix). Opposing this tendency, Leonard's own poetry mobilizes experimental technique to capture Glaswegian dialect. Late modernism is not the preserve of scholars—its practitioners wish to reach the same popular audience as their more traditional counterparts.

A related issue is that of the social function of poetry, its ability and/or duty to address public themes. There is clearly a weighty inheritance here. Earlier twentieth-century pronouncements, such as Louis MacNeice's that the poet "is not the loudspeaker of society, but something much more like its still, small voice" (1987, 98), register in more contemporary articulations, such as Levertov's observation that "[i]nsofar as poetry has a social function it is to awaken sleepers by other means than shock" (412). From the 1970s, Northern Irish poets have been particularly exercised by this question: in the context of the Troubles, they have come under pressure to make political comment in their poetry. Heaney explains that he aspires to write poetry that is socially responsible *and* creatively free:

> Poetry cannot afford to lose its fundamentally self-delighting inventiveness, its joy in being a process of language as well as a representation of things in the world. [...] Which is to say that its power as a mode of redress in the first sense – as agent for proclaiming and correcting

injustices — is being appealed to constantly. But in discharging this function, poets are in danger of slighting another imperative, namely, to redress poetry *as* poetry, to set it up as its own category, an eminence established and a pressure exercised by distinctly linguistic means. (1995, 5–6)

Poetry, he argues, ought to take up an ethical stance but also needs to maintain its autonomy: concentrating on ethics risks overlooking esthetics. Heaney presumably thinks the opposite is true as well, but it may be important that he does not actually say as much. Responding to Heaney's division, Douglas Dunn undermines the distinction, resolving the tension: "in answering to the topical or immediate as well as the timeless, a poet might be doing nothing more or less than being faithful to the impulses of experience." This is possible because poetry "exists in a lived vernacular crossed with the discoveries of a vivid observation and imagination" (2000, 163–166). Anne Stevenson resolves the impasse with a paradox: "the ideal poem of the [21st] century will [...] be written by a very rare person — a poet who is in thrall to nothing but poetry's weird tyranny and ungovernable need to exist" (2000, 183). Unsurprisingly, most poets tend to think of poetry as being in thrall to poetry itself first and foremost. It is on this point that there is perhaps most of a consensus.

References

Armitage, Simon (2000). "Re-Writing the Good Book." In: *Strong Words: Modern Poets on Modern Poetry* (eds. W.N. Herbert and Matthew Hollis), 252–255. Newcastle: Bloodaxe.

Auden, W. H. (1963). *The Dyer's Hand and Other Essays*. London: Faber and Faber.

Boland, Eavan (2000). "The Wrong Way." In: *Strong Words*, pp. 215–218.

Bunting, Basil (2000). "The Poet's Point of View." In: *Strong Words*, pp. 80–82.

Constantine, David (2000). "Common and Peculiar". In: *Strong Words*, pp. 226–228.

Dunn, Douglas (2000). "A Difficult, Simple Art". In: *Strong Words*, pp. 163–166.

Eliot, T. S. (1953). *Selected Prose* (ed. John Hayward). London: Penguin.

Evans, Amy and Zamir, Shamoon (eds.) (2007). *The Unruly Garden: Robert Duncan and Eric Mottram, Letters and Essays*. Bern, Switzerland: Peter Lang.

Fenton, James (1983). The Manifesto against Manifestos. *Poetry Review* 73 (3): 12–16.

Finlay, Ian Hamilton (2012). "Concrete, fauve, suprematist, sequential and kinetic poems." In: *Selections* (ed. Alec Finlay), 135. Berkeley, CA: University of California Press.

Flint, F. S. (1972). "Imagisme." In: *Imagist Poetry* (ed. Peter Jones), 129–130. London: Penguin.

Gunn, Thom (1982). *The Occasions of Poetry: Essays in Criticism and Autobiography*. London/Boston: Faber and Faber.

Harrison, Tony (1991). "Poetry is all I write." In: *Tony Harrison, Bloodaxe Critical Anthologies*, 1e, vol. 9 (ed. Neil Astley). Newcastle: Bloodaxe.

Heaney, Seamus (1980). *Preoccupations: Selected Prose 1968–1978*. London/Boston: Faber and Faber.

Heaney, Seamus (1995). "The Redress of Poetry." In: *The Redress of Poetry: Oxford Lectures*, 1–16. London/Boston: Faber and Faber.

Hughes, Ted (1967). *Poetry in the Making*. London/Boston: Faber and Faber.

Hulme, T. E. (2012). "Romanticism and Classicism." In: *The Norton Anthology of English Literature*, Volume F: The Twentieth Century and After, 9e (eds. Jahan Ramazani and Jon Stallworthy), 2059–2064. London: Norton.

Jones, LeRoi (Amiri Baraka) (1960). "How You Sound?" In: *The New American Poetry 1945-1960* (ed. Donald Allen), 424–425. New York/London: Grove/Evergreen Books.

Keats, John (1947). *The Letters of John Keats* (ed. Maurice Buxton Forman). London: Oxford University Press.

Larkin, Philip (1983a). "The Pleasure Principle." In: *Required Writing: Miscellaneous Pieces 1955–1982*, 80–82. London/Boston: Faber and Faber.

Larkin, Philip (1983b). "Statement." In: *Required Writing: Miscellaneous Pieces 1955–1982*, 79. London/Boston: Faber and Faber.

Leonard, Tom (ed.) (1989). "Introduction." In: *Radical Renfrew*, xvii–xix. Edinburgh: Canongate.

Levertov, Denise (1960). "I Believe Poets Are Instruments." In: *The New American Poetry 1945–1960*, pp. 411–412.

MacNeice, Louis (1987). "A Statement." In: *Selected Literary Criticism*, vol. 98 (ed. Alan Heuser). Oxford: Clarendon.

Maxwell, Glyn (2000). "Strictures." In: *Strong Words*, pp. 256–258.

Motion, Andrew (2000). "Yes and No." In: *Strong Words*, p. 233.

Olson, Charles (1997). "Projective Verse." In: *Collected Prose* (eds. Donald Allen and Benjamin Friedlander), 239–249. Berkeley, CA, et al: University of California Press.

Pound, Ezra (1954). *Literary Essays* (ed. T. S. Eliot). London/Boston: Faber and Faber.

Stevenson, Anne (2000). "A Few Words for the New Century." In: *Strong Words*, pp. 181–183.

Walcott, Derek (2000). "In Conversation." In: *Strong Words*, pp. 167–171.

Williams, William Carlos (1954). *Selected Essays of William Carlos Williams*. New York: Random House.

Wordsworth, William (1984). *The Major Works* (ed. Stephen Gill). Oxford: Oxford University Press.

Yeats, W. B. (1997). *The Major Works* (ed. Edward Larissy). Oxford: Oxford University Press.

2b.2
The Genres of Contemporary British and Irish Poetry

Gareth Farmer

Caroline Bergvall, "In Situ" (Sinclair 1996, 5–10; 7)

Introduction

What is this text we see before us? This might be a play where two "Kissers" give instructions or narrate their actions during an aerobic sex scene. But, how will the actors perform the "((("? Perhaps the brackets act as instructions to pause, like musical notation; or perhaps the punctuation is a mimetic representation of the rhythms of a sex act. But, if punctuation is mimetically representing action, then this text is one requiring reading on the page to interpret it as such. While the opening section describes action, the end of the main section is more conceptual, involving a reflection on how "perception" can be "cultivated by unexpected finds." Our perception of the p of textual expressivity is certainly cultivated when experiencing this text. The typographic oddities here are "unexpected," as are the small, italicized notes to the right of the page, which contribute to the text's self-reflective tone. But even these complicate things and we notice that, minus the date, the second is a slightly differently arranged version of the first, with "suddenly" curiously emphasized despite its subordination in parenthesis. *Suddenly*, nothing becomes clear. This writer, we feel, is taking a theme of *"the question of / writing*," as she puts it, to its extreme. This is a text in which an ostensible erotic act is interrupted by all sorts of textual play, self-reflection, and typographic expressivity; it is awkward and disturbing and almost impossible to satisfactorily interpret, let alone categorize.

Caroline Bergvall's poem, "In Situ," appears in Iain Sinclair's 1996 anthology, *Conductors of Chaos*. Bergvall is certainly the conductor of a textual chaos, and the name of the anthology very deliberately situates itself (and the poems therein) as representative of poets who court linguistic disorder. Formally, then, Bergvall's poem announces itself as experimentally extreme and willfully challenging. Indeed, as Sinclair (1996, xvii) concedes, many of the poems he selects are difficult: "The work I value is that which seems most remote, alienated, fractured. I don't claim to understand it but I like having it around." Anticipating a reader's incomprehension, Sinclair continues:

> If these things are "difficult," they have earned that right. Why should they be easy? Why should they not reflect some measure of the complexity of the climate in which they exist? Why should we not be prepared to make an effort, to break sweat, in hope of high return? There's no key, no Masonic password; take the sequences gently, a line at a time. Treat the page as a block, sound it for submerged sonic effects. Suspend conditioned reflexes.

Sinclair favors difficulties and ones representative of social, cultural, and political complexes. A reader should expect to make an effort, not to simply passively consume. Sinclair's comments provide an interpretive context for Bergvall's poem: we must be patient, "[s]uspend conditioned reflexes," and interpret "a line at a time." *Conductors of Chaos* perhaps defines a type of genre that we might call complex, difficult, or conditioned reflex suspending. There *are* ways of containing "In Situ": its subject might make it erotica; it displays aspects of concrete or visual poetry; its multiple registers and typographic excesses are modernist, while its self-reflection and irony make it postmodern. In the end though, despite all these designations, the poem defeats only the most general of categories.

"In Situ" illustrates the difficulty of classification and the fact that genre may be unable to account for the styles of particular poems.

The most interesting contemporary poetry is awkward to classify; indeed, its awkwardness is often produced by its esthetic, cultural, and political aims. Alongside an examination of attempts to designate genres in contemporary British and Irish poetry, this chapter will also assess why certain poems resist classification. A consideration of genre theory in relation to recent debates surrounding the lyric will be followed by a sketch of what I shall call two *"Urtext-species"* of contemporary poetry. With the help of a recent study of contemporary British poetry by Fiona Sampson (2012), the last, brief section of this chapter will sketch and test some possible subspecies of contemporary poetry. As Neil Corcoran (2007, 2) observes, attempting to get to grips with genres is part of the "persistent inquiry—on what is sometimes still virtually a field of battle—into the applicability of the terms "modern," "Modernist," and "postmodern" as ways of understanding the poetry of the twentieth [and twenty-first] centur[ies]."

Genre

Ralph Cohen (2014, 53) observes that "[t]he term *genre* is relatively recent in critical discourse." Genre has only been described as such since the nineteenth century. Prior to that, as Cohen writes, "the terms used for it were 'kinds' or 'species'." He continues:

> Genre has its source in the Latin *genus* which refers in some cases to "kind" or "sort" or "class" or "species." [...] Its root terms are *genre, gignere* – to beget and (in the passive) to be born.

Genus mutated into genre via classifications of sorts and species. The organic roots, as it were, of *genre* are germane to this current chapter that contends that many genres in contemporary British and Irish poetry are hybrids, mostly sharing a similar *genus*, but which split off into *species*. Summarizing the various theories of the development of lyric as a genre in the introduction to the section on "Genre Theory" in their *The Lyric Theory Reader*, Virginia Jackson and Yopie Prins (2014, 14) register the inherent binary conflict in genre theory of the lyric between considerations of "whether the lyric is historically contingent and ephemeral or is dependent on norms and structures continuous across periods and cultures." In order to define a specific genre of poetry, we need to consider whether we approach particular genres as having developed out of specific historical conditions and being subject to a whole range of cultural, social, and political developments, or whether we define specific genres structurally, by identifying formal features marking these genres as distinct.

A comparison of essays in *The Lyric Theory Reader* illustrates the clash between the contingent and the structural in genre theory. Cohen's conclusions, for example, are revised and refined by Jonathan Culler (2014) in a piece entitled "Lyric, History, and Genre." Noting an element of defeatism toward the empirical classification of ahistorical characteristics of certain genres in Cohen's arguments, Culler uses the example of the lyric to show that identifying continuities in genres can be useful (he cites "apostrophe" as characterizing lyric's uniqueness). However, while Cohen and Culler differ in their relative emphasis on history and empirical classification, both describe the development of genres as an organic production of species or subgenres. "Even for Aristotle," Cohen contends, "generic markers are not absolute; they indicate stages through which genre passes." He continues:

> A genre does not exist independently; it arises to compete or to contrast with other genres, to complement, augment, interrelate with other genres. Genres do not exist by themselves; they are named and placed within hierarchies or systems of genres, and each is defined with reference to the system and its members. (55)

Cohen's model is one of organic and competitive development as well as cross-fertilization and hybridity; all characteristics comprising poetry in Britain and Ireland over the last 60 years. Culler (2014, 66) defends a more structuralist position, but nevertheless also presents a dynamic model of genre:

> A claim about a generic model is not as assertion about some property that all works that might be attached to this genre possesses. It is a claim about fundamental structures that may be at work even when not manifest, a claim which directs attention to certain aspects of a work, which mark a tradition and evolution, that is to say, dimensions of transformation.

Generic models and writing about genres relate to the task of capturing "fundamental structures" even as they mutate and transform. "[C]ertain aspects of the work" will mark it out as representative of a particular genre, but a critic must be aware of the processes of evolution (and thereby the transformations and shifts of species) at work. As Culler continues: "A test of generic categories is how far they help relate a work to others and activate aspects of works that make them rich, dynamic and revealing" (66). Genres of poetry, or *species* as I wish to call them, interrelate and reveal aspects of each other. Identifying genres is difficult, as individual works must inform any definition of genre or species. Yet, identification of "generic categories" will inevitably occlude the specificity of particular poetries, as well as exclude many others. Hence, the word *species* will be used here to capture the dynamism and change of poetic *genera* that both Cohen and Culler are eager to acknowledge. Thus, positioning itself between the categorizing instinct of poetics and historical and contingent acknowledgments of literary history, the rest of this chapter will examine the evolution of certain species of contemporary British and Irish poetry.

Urtext-Species of Contemporary British and Irish Poetry

Since 1960, poetry anthologies have abounded, accumulating like a series of reactions and counteractions in a petri dish, with each editor staking a claim to different histories. Robert Conquest's hugely successful anthology *New Lines* (1956) set the tone for the rest of the century. It solidified the reputations of Movement poets such as Elizabeth Jennings and Philip Larkin; it led to the persistence of what Robert Sheppard (2005, 20) has dubbed the "Movement Orthodoxy" in contemporary poetry; it has been a touchstone for other anthologies since its publication, and sympathy with, or rejection of, its poets continues to be a badge of identification. There are many surveys of contemporary British and Irish poetry outlining the intricacies and specifics of contemporary anthologies. Notable among these are: Peter Childs, *The Twentieth Century in Poetry: A Critical Survey* (1999); John Goodby, *Irish Poetry since 1950* John Goodby, *Irish Poetry Since 1950* (2000); Robert Sheppard, *The Poetry of Saying: British Poetry and Its Discontents* (2005); Fiona Sampson, *Beyond the Lyric: A Map of Contemporary British Poetry* (2012); and David Wheatley, *Contemporary British Poetry* (2015). Each of these surveys offers rich summaries of the editorial positioning of specific anthologies: Alfred Alvarez's reaction to the "gentility" of *New Lines*, with his *The New Poetry* (1962); The attempt of Blake Morrison and Andrew Motion to consolidate a new generation of poets after the Movement in *The Penguin Book of Contemporary British Poetry* (1982); Iain Sinclair's answer to this latter with a collection of marginalized poets in *Conductors of Chaos* (1996); the collection of radical poets in *The New British Poetry 1968–1988*, edited by Gillian Allnutt, Fred D'Aguiar, Ken Edwards, and Eric Mottram; and Keith Tuma's attempt to show an American readership that more innovative poetry was being written in Britain and Ireland in his *Anthology of Twentieth-Century British and Irish Poetry* (2001). Anthologies are a weapon of choice in what Corcoran (2007, 2) calls the "field of battle" over what constitutes representative contemporary British and Irish poetry. And the disputes continue in a recent argument between the poet and academician Andrea Brady and Don Paterson, one of the editors of an anthology designed for the American market called *New British Poetry* (2004).

Paterson's introduction to *New British Poetry* contains a bad-tempered attack on what he calls "the Postmoderns" whose work he considers "incomprehensible" (xxix), and who apparently produce poems with "*a special category of difficulty whose sensible interpretation or interpretations cannot be confirmed*" (xxix—emphasis in the original). Their "monotone angst," "effete and etiolated aestheticism," and "joyless wordplay" (xxxii) offer Paterson little pleasure. His attack is also a defense of "Mainstream" poets who, in contrast to the Postmoderns, "still sell poetry to a general readership" (xxv), write "honest" (xxx) poetry of "*real* originality*" (xxxi—emphasis in the original), "are engaged in an open, complex and ongoing dialogue with the whole of the English tradition" (xxxi), and do not "engage with the false and very un-British paradigm of artistic progress" (xxiv) as the Postmoderns do. Paterson's introduction demonstrates an extreme anxiety tied up with a defense of one's poetic tribe against the apparent encroachment of un-*real* poets and poetries. In a letter of response published in *Chicago Review*, Brady (2004) outlines the contradictions in what she describes as Paterson's "most hateful digression on experimental poetry recently bundled into print" (396) and the "violence of its assault on all nonconformist practices" (402). Paterson's attack on "Postmoderns," his defense of the "Mainstream," and Brady's searing response exemplify the ongoing disputes between mainstream and marginal or experimental poetries. Hence, Sheppard (2005, 27) (a "Postmodern") offers these unattractive descriptions of Movement poetry:

The Movement favoured a poetry of closure, narrative coherence and grammatical and syntactic cohesion: a poetry of "backgrounded" form rather than a poetry of foregrounded artifice. Its emphasis on the demotic, upon "tone" and upon speaking voice, posited the existence of a stable ego, an author-subject, as the unifying principle of the poem; its rhetoric operated at a social level.

Many of the poems in Paterson's anthology—those of Gillian Allnutt, Simon Armitage, Carol Ann Duffy, and Lavinia Greenlaw, for example—exhibit such traits. Paterson's own poem in the anthology, "Imperial" (161), is a case in point. A single voice describes the sticky and jaw-tiring seduction of what we assume to be a man of a woman. The poem opens with the casual but daring question: *"Is it normal to get this wet? Baby, I'm frightened"* (l. 1) with the next line observing, "I covered her mouth with my own" (l. 2). Simple, if disturbingly predatory, language overlays an iambic trot toward an inevitable consummation: "we gave ourselves up, one to the other / like prisoners over a bridge" (ll. 7–8). The poem ends with a jaunty joke: "the night we lay down on the flag of surrender / and woke on the flag of Japan" (ll. 11–12). The end rhymes of "surrender" with "tender" and "Japan" with "plan"—in the first and second lines respectively—are designed to produce a triumphant finale confirming the speaker's (and poet's) wit and ingenuity. It is an uncomfortable poem of poetic and physical domination. "Imperial" also exploits a reader's possible expectation that Paterson may have broader cultural or political points, but then undermines this hope with the bathos and irony of neat end rhymes and a crumpled flag. Paterson produces a little, well-made poem: it is syntactically coherent, it deftly inhabits iambic meter, and is spoken from a confident (and creepy) singular perspective.

By contrast, Sheppard prefers what might be called open poems, with disruptive grammar and syntax; poems which exhibit or foreground their artifice and materiality. What Sheppard (2005, 142) later describes as "linguistically innovative poetry" also usually questions the stability of a unified speaking voice as well as subjectivity and identity. For example, Brady's (2005, 54) "Saw Fit" takes as its subject Lynndie England, a US soldier involved in the torture and humiliation of Iraqi prisoners in Abu Ghraib. "Saw Fit" ventriloquizes a number of conflicting viewpoints, dramatized through the paratactic arrangement of a range of discourses:

> Gitmo in legal twilight, red and green hazard
>   net the sea
> scape beyond enduring
> freedom, the nightly movie. Montage of flag,
> soldier, airplane. Get more for your
> money with American
> express more blood from your nipples (ll. 1–7)

There are several voices here–from advertising and politics, as well as contemporary argot—all jostling, none of which takes precedence. The artifice of the poem is foregrounded: enjambment, for example, is deliberately jarring, with single words interrupted to become phrases offering abrupt shifts of meaning. "American / express" becomes "express more blood" in a charged and brutal textual environment designed to shock. Unlike Paterson's Japanese flag, glimpses of American and British flags fracture and flex across the whole of the poem and form part of a strategically arranged montage, which the arrangement of lines reflects and which evokes the crude assemblages of tortured prisoners and props photographed by soldiers such as Lynndie England to take away as trophies. Paterson's perspective is fixed on his sexual conquest; Brady's mutates, shifts, and challenges. Brady's response to Paterson's introduction to this volume illustrates, therefore, that there are two dominant *Urtext-species* in contemporary poetry, which act as framing contexts for many other species. These I shall call without apology: the *orthodox* and the *innovative*. As should be clear, Paterson favors and represents the orthodox; Brady, on the other hand, is of the innovative camp. Each flies a flag for very different poetic practices.

Species of *Orthodox* and *Innovative* Contemporary British and Irish Poetry

Many of the species that Sampson (2012) outlines in her *Beyond the Lyric: A Map of Contemporary British Poetry* can be grouped under what Sheppard refers to as poetries of the "Movement Orthodoxy." Sampson describes, for example: "The Plain Dealers," octogenarian poets such as Dannie Abse and Elaine Feinstein who "use familiar, lived-in language" (13); "The Dandies," poets of plain speak but who have a little more "linguistic fancy dress" (36), as she puts it; and "The Oxford Elegists," poets such as Andrew Motion and John Fuller who produce a tone of high culture as well as an emotional register of "truth, decency and restraint" (58). Sampson's list of "Movement orthodoxies" is completed with "The new formalists" who write poetry, so she argues, which is "almost [the] complete opposite of today's widely published poetry of inertia." Sampson's term, "inertia," describes a kind of "notebook" poetry written by poets who "don't accept that making a poem involves transformational effort" (227). As a reaction to the abundance of such poetry, Sampson argues, "today, exploring and reviving strict form, Ciaran Carson, Mimi Khalvati and Don Paterson are leading the new formalism" (228). The new formalism uses traditional poetic meter as part of what appears to be a reactionary poetic practice and which results in poems such as "Imperial."

Related to Sampson's designation of "notebook" poetry, as well as the type of light, metrical and rhyming verse often produced by progenitors of species in the "Movement Orthodoxy" is a pervasive form of contemporary light verse. A good deal of Carol Ann Duffy's poetry (our current Poet Laureate) falls into this category. Hence, the opening of Duffy's poem, "Prayer" (Paterson and Simic 2004, 51):

> Some days, although we cannot pray, a prayer
> utters itself. So, a woman will lift
> her head from the sieve of her hands and stare
> at the minims sung by a tree, a sudden gift. (ll. 1–4)

The "sudden gift" of the metaphor at the end of the stanza offers a little, darkening twist for a reader, but the rest of the poem relies on its unassuming language and its simple, poignant scene to evoke a reader's sympathy. As Wheatley (2015, 88) has observed, there is only a little skip from poems like "Prayer" to "poetry of light entertainment in the tradition of [John] Betjeman and Pam Ayers." Paterson's description of the poetry market in his introduction to *New British Poetry* illustrates his alignment of "Mainstream" verse with the values of market capitalism, namely: products should be easily accessible and consumable and the quantity of their consumption determines their value. In *The Political Unconscious*, Frederic Jameson (1983, 93) notes how once dominant genres, "along with so many other institutions and traditional practices, fall [...] casualty to the gradual penetration of the market system and money economy." As a consequence, poetries courting simplicity and ease and evoking ideologies of common feeling are liable to be easily reified into products. This, in turn, often makes them indistinguishable from species of light verse: they frequently use the same formal devices and register as what might be called "ad-verse," that type of whimsical poetry used in adverts to sell fast food.

While Sampson draws on an admirably wide field of poetic practice in her book, innovative poets are under-represented. However, her category of the "Exploded Lyric" does try to account for types of poetry which, Sampson argues, is characterized by "an implicit, and sometimes an explicit, critique of most mainstream poetics" (258). Sampson's descriptions of the poetry published by presses such as Equipage, Reality Street, and Shearsman resemble Paterson's in that she views it as reactive and negative. Sampson and Paterson do not see the point in this poetry. Indeed, this may be because their conception of poetry's function is contrary to the aims of those poets they seek to marginalize. While Sampson and Paterson seem to advocate safe, transparent, and unchallenging poetries, much of the work they either ignore or denigrate is motivated by the aim to fold into its formal practices a critique of contemporary poetics as well as social and political conditions. Such critique results in the kind of poetry Sinclair advocates and describes in the preceding text. As Redell Olsen (2007, 43) suggests of orthodox verse, "lyric sensibilities and commitment to normative syntax do not allow for the kind of radical questioning of the limits of representation itself which are key features" of linguistically innovative or experimental artworks. Poets writing innovative poetry very often have, as Olsen goes on to argue, "different priorities than those of the dominant market forces." In other words, they resist the reification of their artworks into easily consumable commodities.

Sampson registers this resistance as a constituent part of innovative poetry when she observes that it might be considered as "*practice*, [and] one whose poetics may exist more in the process than the product" (271—emphasis in the original). In his puckish, freewheeling, and awkward introduction to his edited collection of innovative poetry, *Dear World and Everyone in It*, Nathan Hamilton (2013, 17) remarks that, "The Editor had the idea that some new terms were needed." While he does not acknowledge Sampson as a source of his "new terms," he continues (using her exact terms): "So, let's say there are two general modes of U.K. and U.S. poetry: 'Product' and 'Process'." After a lengthy paragraph outlining the distinctions between the two types of poetry (which mirror those I have suggested between orthodox and innovative), Hamilton gets impatient:

But "Product" and "Process" represent the modern creep of business and corporate language and ideology into all areas of thought and work – dismiss them from your mind entirely. (18)

Hamilton's intervention in his own argument captures the spirit and anxieties of many of the poets and poems represented in his volume. Classification and the use of "corporate" terms freighted with the ideology of the marketplace are to be avoided and outflanked wherever they are detected. And, like Bergvall's poem which begins this chapter, many of the poems Hamilton collects resist ease of classification, consumption, and interpretation. Hence, Hamilton publishes a sequence of poems called "Who Not to Speak To" by Marianne Morris, which offers visually arresting commentaries, interventions, musings, and reflections on contemporary culture and politics as well as on the act of writing itself (I quote from Morris's original publication):

> SUCH PASSIONS ABOUND
>   in the CYPBERSPHERE!
>
> On the Have Your Say website,
> Pitt-Palin Pacified Rice Thatcher's
> **face** is *embroiled* in a **botox debate**
> about one hundred and sixty four people **having**
> **a debate** about the Have Your stick insect
>
> Say
>
>   talentless, jealous, single women and haters are
> *embroiled* in a **patriotic debate**
>
> about themselves
>   a digital mirror sputters
>   the lines rage aimless
>   the passion is aimless.
>   (Morris 2009, 4, ll. 1–14)

The poem is striking, with visual properties designed to evoke the type of affective reaction and sensationalism of newspaper headlines and clickable, online advertorials. Morris mimics media conventions, for example, the way in which TV collapses the high and low debate into sensationalized formulas ready to be wheeled out at any time. There is a "botox debate" but also a "debate about" "having / a debate" as well as a debate "about themselves," with the repetition replicating the formulaic production of vacant debate and implying a concomitant hollowing out of our engagement of such; we consume debates regardless of their content. But, Morris is not writing from a secure position of privilege; she is complicit in, and part of, the processes she describes. Hence, the poem turns on itself toward the end, registering an enervation around the futility of rage. This deflation is mirrored, like the "digital mirror" sputtering, in the "aimless" placement of lines (just as the emboldened, italicized, and enlarged words appear arbitrary). Poetic production falters after such energetic inhabitation of media modes as well as parodic critique of such; it is a poetics which exhausts itself.

Comprising a range of discourses and poetic techniques, "Who Not to Speak To" is difficult to classify as representative of any one genre or species. Corcoran (2007, 4) suggests that this unclassifiability might be a particular feature of contemporary poetic practice. He notes, for example, how many of the essays in *The Cambridge Companion to Twentieth-Century English Poetry* contain a preponderance of words relating to contradiction, such as "division," "difference," and "discrepancy," and acknowledges that many poems of the past half century "appear to speak against themselves, to engage in sometimes fraught dialogues of the self with the self, or of the poem *with its own origins, traditions and generic characterisations*" (my emphasis). These poems, Corcoran argues, "become the scenes of anxieties, tensions, distresses, uncertainties, contentions, and mobilities." It is the mobility and protean nature of innovative or experimental poetry that makes it difficult to classify; only a term such as *Urtext-species* will do. Innovative poetry questions the whole enterprise of genre classification; critiquing classification is its default imperative. In "History and Genre," Cohen (2014, 53) suggests that "genre concepts in theory and practice arise, change, and decline for historical reasons." Since the 1960s, the Western world has experienced the unprecedented and largely unchecked exponential growth of global market capitalism. Since the 1960s, innovative and experimental poets have used poetry and poetic form to think through a whole range of theoretical, cultural, social, and political issues. In innovative poetry, then, self-consciousness is part of a critique of common assumptions about language and the stable self against a background of consumer capitalism. Good contemporary poetry will have a sophisticated understanding of its complicity in a late capitalist world of rampant consumption and competitiveness and will offer a reader glimpses of an awareness of such, as well as imaginative alternatives. As Corcoran (2007, 5) puts it: "Modern poetry, it seems, is nowhere more characteristic of itself than when anxiously but scrupulously doubting itself." And perhaps this doubt, and this evasion of becoming a product, works against the very act of literary classification.

References

Allnutt, Gillian, D'Aguiar, Fred, Edwards, Ken, and Mottram, Eric (eds.) (1988). *The New British Poetry*. London: Paladin.

Alvarez, Alfred (ed.) (1962). *The New Poetry*. London: Penguin.

Brady, Andrea (2004). "'Meagrely Provided': A Response to Don Paterson." *Chicago Review*, 49 (3–4): 396–402.

Brady, Andrea (2005). *Embrace*. Glasgow: Object Permanence.

Childs, Peter (1999). *The Twentieth Century in Poetry: A Critical Survey*. London: Routledge.

Cohen, Ralph (2014). "History and Genre" [1986]. In: *The Lyric Theory Reader: A Critical Anthology* (eds. Virginia Jackson and Yopie Prins), 53–63. Baltimore: Johns Hopkins University Press.

Corcoran, Neil (ed.) (2007). *The Cambridge Companion to Twentieth-Century English Poetry*. Cambridge: Cambridge University Press.

Culler, Jonathan (2014). "Lyric, History, and Genre" [2009]. In: *The Lyric Theory Reader: A Critical Anthology* (eds. Virginia Jackson and Yopie Prins), 63–77. Baltimore: Johns Hopkins University Press.

Goodby, John (2000). *Irish Poetry since 1950: From Stillness into History*. Manchester: Manchester University Press.

Hamilton, Nathan (ed.) (2013). *Dear World and Everyone in It: New Poetry in the UK*. Northumberland: Bloodaxe.

Jackson, Virginia and Prins, Yopie (eds.) (2014). *The Lyric Theory Reader: A Critical Anthology*. Baltimore: Johns Hopkins University Press.

Jameson, Frederic (1983). *The Political Unconscious: Narrative as a Socially Symbolic Act*. London: Routledge.

Morris, Marianne (2009). *Who Not To Speak To*. manemo. https://issuu.com/mannemo/docs/who_not_to_speak_to (accessed 23 February 2018).

Morrison, Blake and Motion, Andrew (eds.) (1982). *The Penguin Book of Contemporary British Poetry*. London: Penguin.

Olsen, Redell (2007). "Postmodern Poetry in Britain." In: *The Cambridge Companion to Twentieth-Century English Poetry* (ed. Neil Corcoran), 42–55. Cambridge: Cambridge University Press.

Paterson, Don and Simic, Charles (2004). *New British Poetry*. Saint Paul, MN: Graywolf Press.

Sampson, Fiona (2012). *Beyond the Lyric: A Map of Contemporary British Poetry*. London: Chatto and Windus.

Sheppard, Robert (2005). *The Poetry of Saying: British Poetry and Its Discontents 1950-2000*. Liverpool: Liverpool University Press.

Sinclair, Iain (ed.) (1996). *Conductors of Chaos*. London: Picador.

Tuma, Keith (ed.) (2001). *Anthology of Twentieth-Century British and Irish Poetry*. Oxford: Oxford University Press.

Wheatley, David (2015). *Contemporary British Poetry*. London: Palgrave.

2b.3
The Elegy

Stephen Regan

The Elegy

In the summer of 1969, The Rolling Stones held a memorial tribute in Hyde Park, London, for their erstwhile guitarist, Brian Jones, who had died in July that year. Addressing an audience of over half a million people, Mick Jagger expressed the fundamental difficulty that faces any aspiring elegist: "I don't know how to do this thing, but I'm going to try" (*Observer*, 6 July 1969). He then recited some of the most memorable and stirring lines from Shelley's "Adonais": "Peace, peace! he is not dead, he doth not sleep– / He hath awaken'd from the dream of life" (Shelley 2003, 541; XXXIX, l. 1). Hundreds of white butterflies were released into the air. The occasion is worth noting because it demonstrates a familiar shift in elegiac art from the confession of inadequacy to the invocation of time-honored rituals and conventions. What occurred in Hyde Park in 1969 is all the more pertinent, given that the decade has often been characterized by its denial or suppression of grief. The 1960s are frequently associated with hedonism, with sexual and political emancipation, and with release from theological and metaphysical shackles. Looking back over half a century, we can see that beneath the apparent existential freedoms of our time there has been a deeply felt public need for sustaining rituals of mourning and a persistent readiness to draw upon the consoling powers of art and song in the face of loss.

In recent times, and especially since 1960, the tendency of the elegy to question its own verbal adequacy and its own ethical, compensatory value has intensified. Even so, the urge to confront the mystery of death and to make the dead live again, if only in the precincts

---

A Companion to Contemporary British and Irish Poetry, 1960–2015, First Edition.
Edited by Wolfgang Görtschacher and David Malcolm.
© 2021 John Wiley & Sons Ltd. Published 2021 by John Wiley & Sons Ltd.

of poetry, has not diminished. American poets such as Robert Lowell, John Berryman, and Sylvia Plath are renowned for the violence and aggression with which they have written about the dead, disrupting traditional codes of mourning in the process. By contrast, a good deal of British and Irish poetry of the postwar period seems less given to violation and more evidently marked by irony and circumspection in its elegiac procedures. This is a poetry that reveals a "principled distrust of the imagination" and a sensitive awareness of "the aggrandizements, covert indulgences, and specious claims which it may incite" (Ricks 1984, 285). Christopher Ricks is writing here about the work of Geoffrey Hill, but his comments have a particular relevance to the poetry of mourning, as they help to explain why Hill's "September Song" has come to be seen as a paradigmatic postwar elegy.

The title "September Song" seems innocuous enough, until we glance at the unnerving dedication: "*born 19.6.32 – deported 24.9.42.*" Even before the stark revelation of death, the poem's ironic drift carries us from deportation to genocide: "As estimated, you died" (l. 4). That simple half line conveys the chilling precision of Nazi planning in the concentration camps, as well as the impossible task of numbering the dead, but it also points to the poem's own confounded attempts to gauge what might be an appropriate response. More candidly and explicitly than in earlier elegies, the speaker of the poem reproaches himself for what must look like a self-interested appropriation of another's suffering:

> (I have made
> an elegy for myself it
> is true)
> (ll. 8–10)

Hill's admission acknowledges the extent to which an elegy is always to some extent a reflection on the writer's own mortality (and here the victim's date of birth is close enough to the writer's own for this to be an acute concern), but the uncertain line-break holds out the possibility that the elegy is nevertheless true. The poem resolutely resists the conventional elegiac ideal of seasonal return and renewal. The implied harvest in "September fattens on vines" (l. 11) only conjures up, by way of contrast, grotesque images of starvation, just as the smoke of "harmless fires" (l. 13) inevitably recalls more perilous flames. The ironic promise of peace and plenty turns the poem toward its final act of self-chastisement. There is no resurrection or renewal here, no likelihood of imaginative indulgence: "This is plenty. This is more than enough" (Hill 2006, 30, l. 14). Intensely preoccupied with making sense of history and tradition, Hill would come to regard the elegiac tenor in his work as unavoidable, while also seeking to resist it. The title of his first major book of poems, *For the Unfallen* (1959), gestures toward the living, as well as the dead, subtly implicating modern warfare in the distant battles of history. His "Requiem for the Plantagenet Kings" provides a potent model for a contemporary elegiac art that mourns the losses of its own century within a long historical perspective. As Henry Hart notes, "Elegies were a natural choice for a poet whose meditations struggled to make the past present" (Hart 1986, 16), but he shows convincingly how much of Hill's work in the genre is iconoclastic and ironic.

A contrast might be drawn here with Basil Bunting, whose work after 1960 is similarly rooted in history, but far less vexed by its own elegiac tendencies. *Briggflatts* (1966), inspired by Bunting's visits to the Quaker hamlet of that name, is strongly autobiographical, but also deeply elegiac, a work of mourning for a lost love, a lost way of life, and an entire region. The mood of elegy derives in part from the death of the poet's son in 1952, and from the sorrowful notes of "A Song for Rustam," written in 1964 at a time when Bunting was preparing himself for the composition of his major work. In that mournful song, Bunting complies with convention by confessing the inadequacy of his artistic resources: "Words slung to the gale / stammer and fail" (Bunting 2000, 197, ll. 19–20). In *Briggflatts*, he would reassert the struggle with words, but retain the brisk couplet: "Pens are too light. / Take a chisel to write" (I. 116–117). He would also retain the lilting [l] and the long vowel [a:] at the end of a verse line or section: "furrows fill with may / paving the slowworm's way" (I. 12–13). The slowworm amid the blossom is an emblem of encroaching death, and like the mason's mallet timed "to a lark's twitter" (I. 15) it serves as a powerful elegiac motif in the sonata-like structure of the poem (Bunting 2000, 61–63). As Bunting anticipated, *Briggflatts* would become "a great hymn to death," embracing a culture shaped by St. Cuthbert's love of creation, as much as by its violent Viking inheritance (Burton 2013, 358). The poem's coda asserts its own artistic originality, while keeping open an imaginative connection with the elysian fields of pastoral tradition: "A strong song tows / us [...] / to fields we do not know." (Bunting 2000, 81, ll. 1–4)

Ten years after writing *Briggflatts*, Bunting composed "At Briggflatts Meetinghouse," an elegiac meditation on final things, but also a celebratory ode in praise of the transient beauties of nature: "Look how clouds dance / under the wind's wing, and leaves / delight in transience" (Bunting 2000, 145, ll. 10–12). Bunting's own death, another decade on, prompted an elegiac tribute from Tom Pickard, who had been so instrumental in encouraging the writing of *Briggflatts*. "Spring Tide" observes the seasonal movements of traditional elegiac poetry, but it pushes back against the usual symbolic associations of spring. Noting, in its dedication, the birth of Basil Bunting in spring 1900 and his death in spring 1985, the poem records the political struggle of the preceding year and the breaking of the Miners' Strike by the Thatcher government. Where it finds some brief transcendence is in the delicate image of kites and the child repeating the word as *keats*, a poetic felicity that justifies the Keatsian beauty of "rainbow-winged mosquitoes / stringed against the cockney clouds." The poem is insistent, though, on its northern heritage and its unillusioned view of a world of struggle. It returns us to the North Sea and a dark horizon, and it closes with a subdued and somber waking: "You, the dark spring tide / and the spring / were gone" (Pickard 2014, 103–104; 3. 18–20).

Tony Harrison came into Bunting's orbit in Newcastle in the late 1960s, but it was the poems recalling his Leeds childhood and the death of his parents that established his reputation in the 1970s and 1980s. Initiating an elegiac sequence that would never be completed, Harrison purposefully titled one collection of poems *From the School of Eloquence* (1978) and another *Continuous* (1981). These are hurt and hurtful poems, in which Harrison's grief swells into anger at the divisive effects of education and social class that had already separated him from his family. In fractured, nonconforming sonnets of 16 lines, he plays out a bitter drama between working-class solidarity and self-improvement, repeatedly sticking the boot into his own educated sensibility. The grim pun in "Book Ends" prepares us for a stark confrontation between learning and loss, with the image of book ends cleverly suggesting both separation and togetherness in the relationship between father and son. The poem is all the more affecting for its casual opening, imbued with the cadences of conversational speech: "Baked the day she suddenly dropped dead / we chew it slowly that last apple pie." (I. 1–2) The syntactical inversion is rhythmically true, but it also cunningly allows the attention to focus on the familiarity of the domestic setting, eventually letting the opening word "Baked" explode in the final word "books": "what's still between's / not the thirty or so years, but books, books, books" (I. 15–16). The uncomfortable contraction of "us" and "is" in the penultimate line is a telling instance of Harrison's insistent disruption of conventional lyric smoothness in his sonnets. Sometimes, a single isolated line of rough-hewn iambic pentameter is just as effective: "Your life's all shattered into smithereens" (Harrison 1987, 126, I. 13). Harrison's distinctive achievement as an elegist is in combining an educated knowledge of convention that goes back to the classics with a working-class struggle for articulacy. As he tries to devise an inscription for the mother's gravestone, he imagines his father quipping: *"You're supposed to be the bright boy at description / and you can't tell them what the fuck to put!"* (II. 11–12). In other ways, though, Harrison's dilemma is that of any other elegist: "I've got to find the right words on my own" (Harrison 1987, 127, II. 13).

Harrison's father is mourned in several elegiac sonnets, including "Marked with D," which powerfully invokes the language of prayer ("Our Father") to recall the daily bread of the baker, while (again with a grim pun) denying either resurrection or social advancement to "The baker's man that no-one will see rise / and England made to feel like some dull oaf" (Harrison 1987, 155, ll. 13–14). In "Continuous," father and son find common ground for once in a shared love of gangster films—"James Cagney was the one up both our streets." (l. 1)—though that admission is prompted by a rueful comparison of the cremation service with a day out at the cinema (Harrison 1987, 143). The desecrated graves of Harrison's parents in a Leeds cemetery are the focal point of his controversial and confrontational *v.* (1985), which in the style of Thomas Gray's *Elegy Written in a Country Churchyard* (1751) contemplates the changing social order and ends with the poet's own epitaph. Written in the aftermath of the Miners' Strike of 1984–1985, *v.* is one of the great elegiac works of the postwar years, despairingly pitting the depleted pastoral resources of apple and hawthorn against the violence of the times, and finding solace only in song. "A Kumquat for John Keats" (1981) deserves its place among the best of English bitter-sweet self-elegies, while "The Heartless Art" (1985) shows Harrison at his most skeptical and self-reproachful, penning an elegy for a friend and neighbor in America and opportunistically storing up the name Seth to rhyme eventually with death.

Don Paterson, who has acknowledged Harrison's influence on his own hard-hitting and wryly self-questioning poems, is keenly aware that seeking a rhyme for death might seem heartlessly detached or dubiously self-serving. In "Phantom," his seven-part elegy for Michael Donaghy, his willingness to confront these moral and esthetic scruples underwrites the risk he takes in composing a poetic conversation with the spirit of his friend and fellow poet. The closing section draws on Dante's encounters with the dead, but it also vividly recreates the voice of Donaghy and emulates his style.

> *I knew the game was up for me the day*
> *I stood before my father's corpse and thought*
> *If I can't get a poem out of this…*
> *Did you think any differently with mine?*
> (Paterson 2012, 167, Section VII, ll. 47–50)

The interrogation here is skillfully done, with Paterson allowing his doubts about the legitimacy of elegy to surface through Donaghy's own misgivings about the genre in his poem "The Excuse." The metapoetic dimension of "Phantom" does not diminish the emotional power of its intimate address. Paterson works toward the final confrontation with his dead friend in a speculative mode, delicately approaching it through the image of the skull in Francisco de Zurbarán's painting, "St Francis in Meditation" (1639), until the skull becomes his own.

Paul Farley, a close contemporary of Paterson and Donaghy, shows superbly well how a modern elegy might position itself between heaven and earth, reaching out for transcendence while fearing a fall to the ground. "Laws of Gravity" is an elegy for his father, a Liverpool window cleaner, in which the ladder functions as a metaphysical conceit. Like Harrison, Farley uses the language of his father's occupation to denote the struggles and aspirations of working-class life, while also marking his distance from them. The son fondly imagines that the father had sublime visions at the top of the ladder and that his ledger book contained a kind of poetry, so that their "stories overlap" (Farley 1998, 8, l. 56), but a shared fear of failing and falling is what most obviously persists. Even as it seeks to elevate the father, the elegy senses the laws of gravity and notes how its own verse "descends the page" (l. 67). The poem's precarious balancing act is movingly summed up in the son's closing homage to his father: "I'll hold the foot for you" (l. 67). If the elegiac poetry of the past 50 or so years has sometimes questioned its own procedures and doubted its own consolatory powers, it has nevertheless sought to extend and modify, rather than simply reject, the well-established conventions of the genre.

As the work of Douglas Dunn amply testifies, the contemporary elegy has also shown a remarkable trust in lyric forms, including the sonnet, and lyric devices of rhyme and meter. Dunn's *Elegies* (1985) is dedicated to his wife, the artist and curator, Lesley Balfour Dunn, who died in 1981. Like Thomas Hardy's "Poems of 1912–13," these conjugal elegies recall the blissful days of early love and grieve over missed opportunities, but they do so without bitterness or blame. At the same time as acknowledging the painful emptiness of the present, they tenderly evoke the pleasures and privileges of the past. The opening poem, with its allusions to Katherine Mansfield's short story "Bliss," establishes a voice that is candid and confiding, seeking consolation and continuity in memories of a shared artistic and literary life: "I flick / Through all our years, my love, and I love you still" (Dunn 1985, 9, ll. 11–12). The sonnets in *Elegies* keep alive a dedication to art and beauty in the face of death, though the decorative mobiles of aeroplanes and birds in "A Silver Air Force" and "Sandra's Mobile" are delicate and fragile. "The Kaleidoscope" rehearses familiar elegiac conventions, but these are modestly confined to ordinary domestic rituals and settings. There is a subdued urge for transcendence in the opening infinitive, "To climb these stairs" (l. 1), with the speaker offering himself consoling fictions that he "[m]ight find" (l. 5) his wife alive again. The sonnet risks sentimentality in closing with a rhyming couplet, but the rhythm is skillfully measured and controlled: "Grief wrongs us so. I stand, and wait, and cry / For the absurd forgiveness, not knowing why" (ll. 13–14). For all its epistemological uncertainty, the poem cannot refrain from summoning a theological vocabulary of "prayer and hope" (l. 8). In many contemporary elegies, a residual religious imagery seems to reassert itself in the absence of any other sustaining scheme of belief, and here the speaker of the poem notes how domestic objects and situations are transformed by grief into a sacramental offering and communion: "My hands become a tray / Offering me, my flesh, my soul, my skin" (Dunn 1985, 20, ll. 11–12).

Vestiges of sacredness inform Andrew Motion's early elegies for his mother, who had a riding accident when he was 17 and died in hospital after remaining in a coma for nearly 10 years. "In the Attic" invests the mother's clothes with "patterns of memory // a green holiday, a red christening" (ll. 12–13), and the speaker kneels in that "upstairs" place, trying to relive the time she wore them. The attic dust takes on symbolic meaning as the poem contemplates the mother's "unfinished lives" (Motion 1978, 52, l. 14). The language of prayer and religious ritual also shapes "The Legacy," which opens with scattered ashes and presents the poet at his mother's desk, "watching the lamp resurrect / her glistening lives" (ll. 5–6). The poem reflects on immortality as "light" (l. 8), as many earlier elegies have done, but here the word has suggestions of insubstantiality as well. Where the poem can more readily discern an idea of immortality is in the act of writing, with poetry as a kind of legacy, "transcribing itself for ever" (Motion 1978, 58, l. 15). The transcription of loss has, in fact, been an enduring quality of Motion's work since *The Pleasure Steamers* (1978), with his poetry showing an acute sensitivity in the way that it inhabits the lives and afterlives of others, whether it be Anne Frank (in "Anne Frank Huis") or Harry Patch, one of the last survivors of the First World War (in "The Death of Harry Patch"). Among his finest elegies, "Fresh Water" draws powerfully on the river symbolism of traditional elegiac verse to mourn the death of a friend, Ruth Haddon, in the Marchioness riverboat disaster on the Thames in 1989. The death of the poet's father in 2006 prompted new ways of exploring absence and preserving the illusion of presence. "All Possibilities" subtly fuses memory and miracle: "My dead father, who never knew what hit him / is taking his evening walk through the village" (Motion 2009, 56, ll. 1–2). "The Mower" gives a new twist to the archetypal image of death by recalling childhood memories of grass cutting. The speaker imagines his father coming back after death, "but cutting clean through me then vanishing for good" (Motion 2009, 58, l. 52). Motion extends the pastoral resources of the elegy without any straining for effect. "The Gardener," an elegy for Lieutenant Mark Evison who was killed in Afghanistan in 2009, commemorates a soldier who liked "lending a hand" (l. 5) in the garden and watching the popular TV show, *Gardeners' World* (Motion 2015, 112). The typography of the poem, with its irregular lineation, catches the speech of the soldier's mother, while his death is foreshadowed in the compost heaps and the cherry tree of the garden.

Seasonal and pastoral motifs have a powerful presence in the poetry of Anne Stevenson, whose sequence of "Sonnets for Five Seasons" mourns the death of her father, Charles Leslie Stevenson, in 1979. The tightly compressed form of the sonnet is used inventively to explore a protracted winter and an anxious spring. A numbing grief gives way to modest hope in nature's restorative patterns, but the elegy cannot altogether abandon its vestigial theological vocabulary: "Birches knelt under ice. Roads forgot / their way in aisles of frost. There were no petals" ("The Circle." Stevenson 2005, 373, ll. 10–11). In the later "Elegy" for her father, a shared love of music ensures his continuing presence: "his audible image returns to my humming ears" (179, l. 54). The death of Frances Horovitz, whose own *Elegy* for her father was published as a pamphlet in 1976, sent Stevenson back to the pastoral mode and the lyrical ballad in "Willow Song." Horovitz (also the subject of Gillian Clarke's elegy "The Hare") is the inspiration behind "The Fiction-Makers," and she is one of a number of poets celebrated and mourned in *A Lament for the Makers* (2006), Stevenson's Dantesque dream vision, written after the death of Peter Redgrove and dedicated to Philip Hobsbaum.

Ted Hughes is the subject of Stevenson's "Invocation and Interruption," and her skills in poetic dialogue are evident again in her dream encounter with "the man in black feathers" in *A Lament for the Makers* (Stevenson 2006). Hughes had himself set new standards for the elegy, with early poems such as "Griefs for Dead Soldiers" and "Six Young Men" mourning England's war dead, and later poems such as "Remains of Elmet" and "Mill Ruins" mourning the casualties of history and the passing of a whole way of life in rural West Yorkshire. *Moortown* (1979), originally titled *Moortown Elegies*, was dedicated to the memory of Jack Orchard (Hughes's father-in-law) and includes "The Day He Died," one of the most compelling reworkings of pastoral convention in postwar poetry. Hughes draws on the familiar idea that nature itself mourns the loss of a loved one ("The bright fields look dazed," l. 14), but he also offers a new take on the idea of managing the land: "From now on the land / Will have to manage without him" (Hughes 2003, 533, ll. 21–22). *Birthday Letters*, published just a few months before Hughes's death in October 1998, is a powerful elegiac collection of poems, primarily addressed to Sylvia Plath. "Daffodils," a reworking of an earlier poem of that title, suggests the extent to which the book is also a revision of himself and his relationship with Plath. The poem opens in a casually colloquial style—"Remember how we picked the daffodils?" (l. 1)—but it acquires a metaphysical charge reminiscent of seventeenth-century poetry, closing with the painful conceit of the scissors, a wedding present used to cut the flowers, somewhere in the earth, "Sinking deeper / Through the sod – an anchor, a cross of rust" (Hughes 2003, 1125–1126, ll. 64–65).

A close attachment to the land ensures that Seamus Heaney, like Hughes, is always at ease with the conventions of pastoral elegy. *Death of a Naturalist* (1966) mourns his own loss of childhood innocence while acknowledging (in "Requiem for the Croppies") a long history of sacrifice in the struggle for Irish freedom. Versions of the pastoral are given a powerful elegiac function in *Field Work* (1979), especially in "The Strand at Lough Beg" (in memory of his second cousin Colum McCartney, the victim of a random sectarian assassination), and "Casualty" (for a fisherman, Louis McNeill, "blown to bits" in a pub bombing [Heaney 1998, 155], l. 38). Remarkably, Heaney has McCartney's shade reprimand him in the title poem of the penitential *Station Island* for having "saccharined" his death with "morning dew" (Heaney 1998, 261, Section 8, l. 76). Heaney's family elegies, including the early "Mid-Term Break" (for his infant brother), "Clearances" (a sonnet sequence for his mother), and "Uncoupled" (for his cattle-farmer father), are among some of the most poignant and deeply moving poems of loss in the English language. A strong sense of his own approaching death gives the family poems in *Human Chain*, his final collection, an extraordinary tenderness and intimacy.

Michael Longley has likewise established his reputation as a writer who shaped the Troubles elegy with moving and memorable poems of loss, including "Wounds," "Wreaths," and "The Ice-Cream Man," while also revealing his powers as a love poet and a nature poet. Longley's elegies for the victims of sectarian violence are models of ethical and esthetic restraint, chastened by his acknowledgment in "Kindertotenlieder" that "[t]here can be no songs for dead children" (Longley 2006, 61, l. 1). His scrupulous art conditions his later poems of loss for friends and fellow poets in *Snow Water* (2004) and *A Hundred Doors* (2011), and also tempers his candid self-elegies in these books, as he ponders his own mortality amid the changing landscapes of his beloved Co. Mayo. Longley's close contemporary Derek Mahon sedulously avoided any explicit elegiac response to the Troubles, though his best-known poem, "A Disused Shed in Co. Wexford," can justly claim its place as a poem of mourning that eloquently speaks for the victims of war and political oppression. Its epigraph is taken from Giorgos Seferis: "Let them not forget us, the weak souls among the asphodels" (Mahon 1979, 79). Mahon's suave, ironic style recalls that of Louis MacNeice, to whom he pays tribute in a finely measured elegy, "In Carrowdore Churchyard."

Paul Muldoon has written some of the most bewildering, experimental elegies of the past few decades: "Incantata" (for the artist Mary Farl Powers), "Yarrow" (for his mother, Bridget Regan), "Turkey Buzzards" (for his sister Maureen), and "Sillyhow Stride" (for Warren Zevon). Muldoon's style is densely allusive, cryptic, and digressive. It flouts traditional elegiac codes and conventions, but it is also strangely consoling, with its occasional intimacies being all the more effective for being unexpected, and its formal intricacies of rhyme and rhythm offering steadiness in the face of futility. "Cuthbert and the Otters" was commissioned for Durham Book Festival in the summer of 2013 and modulated into an elegy for Seamus Heaney later that year. The otter, an emblem for both saint and poet, appears magically in the funeral procession at Bellaghy (recalling the carrying of Cuthbert by his fellow monks), but much is concentrated in a single line paying homage to the translator of *Beowulf*: "I cannot thole the thought of Seamus Heaney dead" (Muldoon 2015, 4, l. 21). In sharp contrast to Muldoon's prolonged meditation, Ciaran Carson's "In Memory" takes just a single well-shaped sentence to record the life of the naturalist who peered into wells and to note how, after his death, "that unfathomable / darkness / echoes / still" (Carson 2014, 21, ll. 16–19).

To mourn the loss of a great writer is one of the motivating impulses that has shaped the tradition of the English elegy from "Lycidas" onward. It helps to explain the persistence and prestige of the elegy, and it takes us to the core of the genre, which has always been, to some extent, about the continuing vitality of the imagination in the face of darkness and about the need of the living to carry on. If the contemporary elegy has sometimes appeared skeptical and anticonsolatory, it has also been remarkably resilient as a form, registering and responding to changing ideas of death and the afterlife in our own time. Very likely, poets will continue to be drawn to the elegy, satisfying a hunger in themselves "to be more serious" and validating their own belief in poetry as a form of survival, "If only that so many dead lie round" ("Church Going." Larkin 2012, 37, ll. 60–61).

REFERENCES

Bunting, Basil (2000). *Complete Poems*. Newcastle: Bloodaxe.

Burton, Richard (2013). *A Strong Song Tows Us: The Life of Basil Bunting*. Oxford: Infinite Ideas.

Carson, Ciaran (2014). *From Elsewhere*. Oldcastle: Gallery Press.

Clarke, Gillian (1997). *Collected Poems*. Manchester: Carcanet.

Dunn, Douglas (1985). *Elegies*. London: Faber.

Farley, Paul (1998). *The Boy from the Chemist is Here to See You*. London: Picador.

Harrison, Tony (1987). *Selected Poems*. London: Penguin.

Hart, Henry (1986). *The Poetry of Geoffrey Hill*. Carbondale: Southern Illinois University Press.

Heaney, Seamus (1998). *Opened Ground: Poems 1966–1996*. London: Faber.

Hill, Geoffrey (2006). *Selected Poems*. London: Penguin.

Hughes, Ted (2003). *Collected Poems*. London: Faber.

Larkin, Philip (2012). *The Complete Poems* (ed. Archie Burnett). London: Faber.

Longley, Michael (2006). *Collected Poems*. London: Jonathan Cape.

Mahon, Derek (1979). *Poems 1962–1978*. Oxford: Oxford University Press.

Motion, Andrew (1978). *The Pleasure Steamers*. Manchester: Carcanet.

Motion, Andrew (2009). *The Cinder Path*. London: Faber.

Motion, Andrew (2015). *Peace Talks*. London: Faber.

Muldoon, Paul (2015). *One Thousand Things Worth Knowing*. London: Faber.

Paterson, Don (2012). *Selected Poems*. London: Faber.

Pickard, Tom (2014). *Hoyoot: Collected Poems and Songs*. Carcanet: Manchester.

Ricks, Christopher (1984). *The Force of Poetry*. Oxford: Oxford University Press.

Shelley, Percy Bysshe (2003). *The Major Works* (eds. Zachary Leader and Michael O'Neill). Oxford: Oxford University Press.

Stevenson, Anne (2005). *Poems 1955–2005*. Tarset: Bloodaxe.

Stevenson, Anne (2006). *A Lament for the Makers*. Thame: Clutag.

2b.4
The Sonnet

David Fuller

If the sonnet ceased to exist, it would be immediately reinvented: its use by so many poets, in such different cultural situations, for such various subjects, is evidence that the form corresponds to a basic human expressive need. This is the view of Don Paterson, who, perhaps more than any contemporary poet, has been little short of obsessed with the sonnet. He has included sonnets in each of his five books of original poems, most recently *40 Sonnets* (2015). His books also include *Orpheus* (2006), versions of Rilke's *Die Sonette an Orpheus*, an anthology, *101 Sonnets: From Shakespeare to Heaney* (1999), and a commentary on Shakespeare's sequence, *Reading Shakespeare's Sonnets* (2010). He has written sonnets in a great variety of forms—rhymed and unrhymed, Italian (conventionally with separate octave and sestet, rhymed, with variations, abba abba/cde cde), and English (four quatrains and a couplet: abab cdcd efef gg). Like other contemporary poets, he has also written sonnets in his own invented versions and extensions—highly various explorations of sonnet form that do not admit of representative illustration. "Archaic Torso of Apollo (after Rilke)" (Paterson 1997) shows one characteristic vein, and some representative issues about sonnet form.

> You'll never know that terrific head,
> or feel those eyeballs ripen on you –
> yet something here keeps you in view,
> as if his look had sunk inside
>
> and still blazed on. Or the double axe
> of the breast couldn't blind you, nor that grin

> flash along the crease of the loins
> down to the low centre of his sex.
>
> Or else he'd sit, headless and halved,
> his shoulders falling to thin air –
> not shiver like the pelt of a wolf
>
> or burst from his angles like a star:
> for there is nowhere to hide, nothing here
> that does not see you. *Now change your life.*

The focus is finally the injunction implicit in the sculpture—that it should both emerge and amaze. It emerges from all that is implied about what has been lost in what remains—the meaning imagined in the absent eyes from the sexual intensity present in the loins. Also what is implied about the viewer: no modern life will live up to those implications. That intensity is in part created by the poem's music of structure: the pressure in "or ... Or ... nor ... Or ... or"; the syntax that rhyme and sense seem to have concluded ("head ... inside") but that bursts beyond the quatrain, "and still blazed on"; the urgency of the four-beat line (not Rilke's), shorter than is usual for the form; the emphasis added by alliteration. This is the sound of sense deployed through one version of sonnet structure—emphatic, pressing forward, at one with the poem's violent imagery: the blinding "axe / of the breast," a weapon connected by rhyme with the focus of all this intensity, the "centre of his sex"; the "shiver" and "burst," connecting wild nature (wolf) and release into the cosmos (star) with what flashes along the loins; the final rhythms, emphatically crowding stresses toward the accusatory injunction:

>   /   /
> nothing here
> /   /   /   /   /
> that does not see you. *Now change your life.*

What does this show about the sonnet? That it is an especially "musical" form—not only because of its demanding rhyme patterns, but because of the "music" of its structure. Sonnet structure can be used for very different kinds of argument, but in the Italian sonnet especially there is a tendency to bring together the balance, complementarity, and antithesis that are basic components of musical form—simple binary (AB: octave, sestet); simple ternary (ABA: statement, related alternative, restatement), which is the origin of sonata form (exposition, development, recapitulation). In the sonnet, anything comparable to this can take highly varied forms. It may lead to closure (the final couplet of the English or Shakespearean form); it may lead to nonclosure (the argument of the sestet counterpoised to that of the octave without resolving their difference). It may be that the sonnet's mode of complementarity (ternary form's restatement, sonata form's recapitulation) is the poem as a whole: the reader's reflection on the implications of octave and sestet taken together. In each case there is a pattern of argument, recognizable as pattern irrespective of how its logic is worked out. Or there may be in the sonnet structural relationships analogous to those of musical forms, which are seen on the page and heard in the ear as structure as well as a sequence of specific relationships. The more developed musical forms may correspond to the kind of sonnet in which the "but" implied by the sestet break and turn in argument carries the implication not "entirely on the contrary," but a milder "however," leading to (perhaps implied) synthesis. Even when—as frequently with the contemporary sonnet—there is no rhyme, this music of architecture is still often present. The ways in which pattern is fulfilled differently in poetry and music arise from the difference that poetry is music + content, while the "content" of music is to an even higher degree its form. Paterson articulates this kind of feeling about the importance of structure per se in arguing that the sonnet corresponds (roughly) to the proportions of the "golden section" (Paterson 1999b, xvii–xxi). While it may be that often none of these arguments works quite precisely, they all point in the same direction: the sonnet offers a satisfaction at the level of formal structure corresponding to something fundamental in human feeling.

As "Archaic Torso of Apollo" shows, emphasis on the importance of music to meaning is not to be mistaken for a view of poetry as pure (verbal) music, an "art for art's sake" esthetic. With poetry "the tingle-test is inapplicable" (Paterson 1997, "Prologue," p. 1)—repudiating the account of A. E. Housman, who recognized poetry by symptoms of its effects: the skin bristles, the spine shivers. On this view, Housman is rejected as ultrapatrician esthete. Paterson spells out his expectation of poetry's moral engagements in his book of versions of the Spanish Modernist Antonio Machado, *The Eyes*.

> Machado's singerless song offers us the chance to make a quiet return to a poetry, if not of moral exhortation, then one of moral instruction; a function contemporary poetry seems to have forgotten it ever performed. (Paterson 1999a, Afterword, p. 59)

Similarly in "Prologue": "A poem is a little church, remember / you, its congregation, I, its cantor." The poet is a singer in a traditional, stylized, and impersonal mode ("cantor"); the poem's "congregation"—its readers—are not passive recipients but active participants in creating meaning; and with the sonnet, part of that meaning arises from its structural music.

Paterson is a musician, a jazz composer and performer. For Anne Stevenson, too, trained as a classical cellist and pianist, the music of sonnet form is an important part of meaning; but the sound of Stevenson can be quite different, here also in an Italian sonnet, "The Circle," the last in a group of "Sonnets for Five Seasons" on the death of her father (Stevenson 2005, 371–373).

> It is imagination's white face remembers
> snow, its shape, a fluted shell on shoot
> or flower, its weight, the permanence of winter
> pitched against the sun's absolute root.
>
> All March is shambles, shards. Yet no amber
> chestnut, Indian, burnished by its tent
> cuts to a deeper centre or keeps summer
> safer in its sleep. Ghosts be content.

> You died in March when white air hurt the maples.
> Birches knelt under ice. Roads forgot
> their way in isles of frost. There were no petals.
>
> Face, white face, you are snow in the green hills.
> High stones complete your circle where trees start.
> Granite and ice are colours of the heart.

After four sonnets playing as many variations on the form—Italian ("Stasis") and English ("Complaint"); the octave–sestet break displaced ("This House") or run through ("Between")—"The Circle" returns to a near-classic form of the Italian sonnet, with divisions clearly marked: abab/abab/cdc/cdd. All the usual musics of poetry are here: as well as the demanding Italian scheme of end-rhyme, elegantly unforced, there is, in abundance, alliteration, assonance, internal rhyme ("centre ... summer"), and internal parallelism ("its shape ... its weight"). Syntax marks form: decisive brevity for beginnings (l. 5) and endings (ll. 8, 11); to make conclusion conclusive, the grammar that in each previous unit runs through line-endings finally coincides with the lineation; and the poem, circling back to the seasonal beginning of the sequence (winter), also completes its own internal circle ("white face ... snow"). Beautiful and signifying sounds, more marked for being drained of color. In "Granite and ice"—the solid and the solidified—the reader may hear Virginia Woolf's archetypes of the literary imagination, "granite and rainbow" (1958), a gamut of permanence and evanescence. A purging of variety for the eye (no amber, no petals; snow, ice, frost, white) contrasts with the variously harmonizing and expressive variety for the ear.

These are two substantially different poems, but both Italian sonnets, and both showing the sonnet more than alive and well in the late twentieth century.

This might not have been expected. While sonnets have been written in almost every period since the form was introduced into English poetry in the sixteenth century, the great Modernists found no use for it. The repudiation of William Carlos Williams was the most extreme (the sonnet "does not liberate the intelligence but stultifies it": 1974, 17)—but this is no surprise. Williams, making his "reply to Greek and Latin with the bare hands" (1963, 2), found no use for any traditional forms. But even Ezra Pound, who revived and revitalized every ancient form he could discover, thought the sonnet a positive cause of dullness: its lack of metrical variation (line length) indicated, he thought, precisely the opposite of what is, in fact, found in Paterson and Stevenson, a damaging divorce between poetry and music (Pound 1951, 157, 14). While the Modernists condemned or ignored the sonnet, however, and though there are still circles in which the sonnet seems "defunct ... a kind of cultural impossibility" (Jeff Hilson, in Paul Muldoon, Meg Tyler, Jeff Hilson, and Peter Howarth, "Contemporary Poets and the Sonnet," in Cousins and Howarth, 2011, 13), poets beginning to write around the mid-century had begun to see a revival. Could the form live? Could it again accommodate a contemporary voice? W. H. Auden showed that it could. Having experimented with a sequence of polished but not especially characteristic love sonnets ("Turn not towards me lest I turn to you"), Auden produced two ambitious and highly characteristic sequences using the sonnet as a vehicle for political and cultural analysis. "In Time of War" (1939, later retitled "Sonnets from China") offered a view of the present in the context of an account of a whole phase of Western civilization. "The Quest" (1940), an equally ambitious 20-sonnet coda to *New Year Letter*—Existentialist and Freudian, vernacular and oracular—Auden described as reflecting eclectically on features common to fairy tales, quest myths, boys' adventure stories, and detective novels. It is indicative that one of the most important and experimental contemporary writers of sonnets, Paul Muldoon, should cite Auden on the enabling nature of form: "those who confine themselves to free verse because they imagine that strict forms must of necessity lead to dishonesty do not understand the nature of art, how little the conscious artist can do and what large and mysterious beauties are the gift of language, tradition, and pure accident" (in Cousins and Howarth, 2011, 10). With Auden's sequences the sonnet was rehabilitated with entire contemporaneity.

While Auden experimented with varying traditional forms, his younger American contemporaries—Robert Lowell, John Berryman, Ted Berrigan—offered later twentieth-century British and Irish poets models of experiment with the sonnet in different directions. In the last decade of his writing, Lowell became positively obsessed with the form, experimenting with it in four collections, beginning with the largely free-verse sonnets of *Notebook 1967–1968*. As the titles of subsequent books indicate (*History, For Lizzie and Harriet* [Lowell's second wife and their daughter]), for Lowell the form could accommodate an immense range of material, public and private—some of it so intimate that publication was a subject of controversy. Seamus Heaney learned from this. Is the modern taste for the democratic-demotic at odds (he asked) with the traditional form; or is the unrhymed, loose sonnet an ideal vehicle for the modern impulse "to cage the minute"? Is a pleasure in the "high rhetorical modes of poetry" at odds with this; or can the attempt to seize the moment and the pleasures of conscious art (form, rhetoric) coincide (Heaney 1980, "Full Face: Robert Lowell," 221–224)?

In *Berryman's Sonnets* (1967), John Berryman offered a different model. This 115-poem sequence is on the traditional sonnet subject of obsessive, illicit, and partly thwarted love. The backgrounds in Petrarch and Sidney are written in, including an Astrophil-type attempt at objective presentation of the self-persona ("Berryman's sonnets," as though the speaker is an alter ego), and the form is Italian in rhyme scheme and octave–sestet division, albeit qualified by colloquial diction and syntax that mitigate to the ear the formality evident to the eye. British and Irish poets attending to American avant-garde writing would also have noticed a contrary example, the *The Sonnets* of Ted Berrigan (1964, 1966; expanded 1982), in its final form a sequence of 88 numbered poems (with lacunae and extras), with a submerged and fragmentary narrative of loves and friendships and a variety of counter-cultural engagements (in music, film, reading). The experiments are those of the period (Burroughs and cut-ups, for example); and though there are references to a "method," this is distinctly uncodified. A sonnet composed of the opening lines of 14 earlier sonnets (XXX), a sonnet consisting of a patterned reordering of another (XV/LIX): these are among the more orderly examples of fragmentary repetitions recontextualized, the same and changed. Despite invocations of European admirations and predecessors more recent than Berryman's (Rimbaud, Apollinaire), the overriding aim and method is Whitmanic—to register an idiosyncratic human presence in its apparent randomness.

One major voice that hardly fits these currents of the age, to which he is a critical outsider, is that of Geoffrey Hill, whose sonnet sequences include "Funeral Music," "Lachrimae," and "An Apology for the Revival of Christian Architecture in England." "Lachrimae, or seven tears figured in seven passionate pavans" (1978, 15–21), its title from the lutenist-composer John Dowland, its epigraph from the Catholic martyr and poet Robert Southwell, and its final poem a free translation from the Spanish Baroque (Lope de Vega), is not attempting anything with the bare hands. The perspective is that of a religious observer trained in Ignatian spiritual disciplines, analyst rather than participant—though recognizing that finally observation and analysis can only be valid on the basis of participation. While the sequence both intimates and postpones the possibility of spiritual renewal in a contemporary context, there is no simple contrast of spiritually coherent past and present of secularized skepticism. Forms of difficulty mutate; difficulty is permanent. Similarly with sonnet form: Hill recalls but also draws back from Auden on disciplines as enabling, citing "that strange relationship with form and language in which you partly guide them, and they partly guide you" (Hill 1980, 213). The more strict the form, the stronger its guidance, or the more agonistic the wrestling—and the form here is strict, the Italian sonnet, with octave–sestet division marked, and rhyme scheme mitigated only by an acceptance of half-rhyme.

"An Apology for the Revival of Christian Architecture in England" (1978, 22–34) uses the same demanding Italian form, though with more variation in rhyme patterns. It, too, shows Hill attracted to subjects that present themselves as ambiguous, for which the sonnet, with its "turn" implying the expectation of an alternative viewpoint, is a naturally expressive structure. The poems make full use of this: celebration of the relation of Gothic architecture and cultivated landscape to religious and social institutions, developed slowly and in response to local circumstances, is juxtaposed with critique of the costs, from suppression of disruptive erotic feeling to oppression of English laborers and colonial (Indian) peasants. The degree of critique is open to question: how far Hill is analyzing the nostalgia he presents, how far he is implicated in its pleasures, depends on a nice estimate of a range of contrary indications, and possibly where a reader starts from culturally and politically. Hill invokes Milton's view of poetry, as more "simple, sensuous and passionate" than philosophy (sonnet 6). Sensuous and passionate the poems are, but their beauty of sound and shape—some of the most formalized sonnet structures in modern poetry—can be lost in an obliquity of compression that sometimes puzzles even sympathetic commentators.

Perhaps the most successful of Hill's sonnet sequences is "Funeral Music" (1968, 23–32), a less ostentatiously formal unrhymed sequence on three men executed during the English civil wars of the later fifteenth century. "Funeral Music: an essay," printed with the poems (1968, 67–68), describes Hill's fundamental attitude to his subjects—"admiration and skepticism": his three men are Jekylls and Hydes, divided between intellectual interests and engagement in the violence of their age. The essay also describes the kind of style Hill was attempting: "a florid grim music broken by grunts and shrieks," a mixture of the disciplined and ascetic with a mode that is again more sensual. This is poetry as Auden saw it, "the clear expression of mixed feelings" (1941, 119), or, as Hill himself describes it, "making [...] poetry out of one's mixed feelings of attraction and repulsion" (Haffenden

1981, 76–99 [91]). The sonnets' symmetries do not here correspond to the usual structures of the form, but they reflect the balanced octave–sestet antithesis in varied points of view (engaged in conflict; detached in contemplation), mixture of voices (combative, meditative), and shifts of register. Each offers a disciplined cameo. "We meditate / A [...] mystery" (Sonnet 2): "we" includes the reader, "mystery" the speaker's semi-incomprehensible present, an imagined future (enmities reconciled), and an actual past, battles remembered as real and surreal. Mind and soul antitheses are balanced in a free version of the octave–sestet pattern (Sonnet 4): the soul is perhaps immortal, a belief needed to construct a tolerable view of the world (seeing the horrors of history as having some meaning); the intellect has properties ascribed in Christianity to God, a "heathen" belief that would also make life tolerable. "My little son [...]" (Sonnet 6) similarly adapts an octave–sestet division: a father participates through his son in the innocent vision of childhood, which is related to the primal innocence of humankind before the Fall; experience takes over with opposite possible consequences. In a conclusion in which little is concluded, sonnet shapeliness itself is eloquent. A poised drawing together (Sonnet 8) both uses and cuts across sonnet form with an affirmative-questioning indirectness: the "octave" through negatives ("not as [...] but as"); the "sestet" on the edge of finding no meaning ("If it is [...] or / If it is not"). Finally, the situations are generalized by a pained question about purpose and value that any reader, deflected from fullness of being by contingency, and from freedom of choice by historical forces, might share:

> Then tell me, love,
> How that might comfort us – or anyone
> Dragged half-unnerved out of this worldly place,
> Crying to the end, "I have not finished."

Disorder leading to anarchy, in the individual and in society, is exemplified by the horrors of a bloody civil war. How the order elicited or imposed by the sonnet form interacts with that is not easy to say: there is both containment and intensification.

The form that for Hill suits poised ambivalence, in *The School of Eloquence* Tony Harrison employs for engaged polemic. Begun in the mid-1970s, and by the *Collected Poems* (2007) developed to three extended sequences, *The School of Eloquence* takes its title from a code name for the suppressed working-class radical organization of the French Revolution period, the London Corresponding Society (LCS). Harrison is a voice of the LCS in Margaret Thatcher's Britain. The sonnets are Meredithean, with 16 lines (on the model of *Modern Love*, 1862), the Shakespearean structure of three rhyming quatrains (in various patterns) followed by a final quatrain often organized so as to give an extra emphasis to endings (ghgh). Harrison's fundamental subjects are oppression and exploitation, with an emphasis on language and class, making inventive use of his Leeds working-class accent and regional dialect ("my own voice ... the language that I spoke at home": "Them & {uz} II," 134) to clash expectations of formal tradition with the voice of an outsider. "National Trust" (2007, 131) exemplifies the method with typical wit and passion. Unlike Hill's interacting complementarities, Harrison's binaries are unequivocal: gentlemen (oppressing, exploiting) and men (oppressed, exploited).

The expanded sonnet form expresses an overflowing of rage at injustice, for which a final couplet is not enough. The command of language in fiercely pointed puns is a political weapon: inarticulacy is oppressed; language is power. The gentlemen plumbing the literal depth of a mine shaft are plumbing moral depths to which they were blinded by class. And while there may be subtleties to dwell on, there is also a straightforward meaning that is not in doubt: the nation trusted in a racket organized for the advantage of the few and exploitation of the many. A form with elite associations is taken over for anti-elite purposes: ambivalent meditation is replaced by straightforward polemic. The art of the sonnet is fiercely deployed in Paterson's "forgotten" function of poetry, moral instruction.

Seamus Heaney's likewise politically engaged but more quietly probing voice also found in the sonnet a major form. There are important individual poems which use the taut structure for an artistic or political manifesto, but by implication, obliquely not polemically (from "The Forge," "Requiem for the Croppies," "The Seed Cutters," and the double sonnet, "Act of Union," to "A Shiver" or "Out of Shot"; 1998, 19, 22, 95, 127; 2006, 5, 15). And, beginning with "Glanmore Sonnets" and "Clearances," there are several sequences ("Glanmore Revisited," "Sonnets from Hellas," "District and Circle," "The Tollund Man in Springtime"; 1991, 33–39; 2001, 38–43; 2006, 17–19, 55–57). More relaxed and expansive, through grouped and interacting cameos, these deal with issues and values central to Heaney's recurrent concerns.

"What is my apology for poetry?" "Glanmore Sonnets" (1979, 33–42), partly about the nature and value of poetry, addresses the question that Sonnet 9 of the sequence asks. Poetry reveals what is both "marvellous / And actual" (39). Writing within a traditional formal structure, the poet is nevertheless a conduit of the natural world: one function of poetry is revelation (actual), but of what is otherwise unnoticed, unseen (and so marvelous). "Opened ground" (33, 34; Heaney later used this as the title of collected poems; Heaney 1998)—the plowed field, nature prepared by art—is analogous to the poem. The "twig-combing breeze [...] is cadences" (35); the call of the cuckoo is iambic (x/); nature prompts; the poet transcribes and transforms. Even with a (mutably) set form, finding the precise shape is discovering what is in the material waiting to be revealed, analogous to the action of the sculptor's chisel in the marble (34). In discussing a poem's coming into being, Heaney distinguished between technique and craft ("Feeling into Words," 2002, 19). The poet is attentive, like the water-diviner (technique): attuned to what is present in the world or the word, albeit (as a later sonnet has it) for ordinary perceptions "out of shot"; and (craft) the poet uses the form, here of the English and the Italian sonnet, but in a flexible and undemonstrative way, with an art that conceals art and is based in nature. Glanmore is a "hedge-school" (34), an education outside the formal education system. Heaney invokes Wordsworth: he is learning from nature and from childhood memories, with which he connects through the language (dialect, colloquialisms) he knew as a child (Sonnet 5). The musical terms of the shipping forecast, the exotic names of trawlers (Sonnet 7), were an education preparing for "Words entering almost the sense of touch" (34). But while Heaney's subject in these sonnets is, in part, the art and craft of writing, based in receptivity to nature, it is also love—though not in the sonnet tradition of yearnings illicit and unconsummated. Wyatt and Sidney, the literary courtship of Shakespeare's Lorenzo and Jessica, and the legendary adultery of Diarmuid and Gráinne are invoked; but it is married love that these sonnets celebrate, erotically charged ("birchwood in lightning" [40]), but also sacred (Sonnet 10).

The sequence "Clearances" (1987, 24–32), dedicated to Heaney's mother and written shortly after her death, is also made up of love poems of a kind, but again unusually for the sonnet form, love poems of a son for his mother. The dedication repeats the analogy of the sculptor's chisel seeking the form present in the marble, but in domestic mode: "She taught me [...] / How easily the biggest coal block split / If you got the grain and hammer angled right" (24). Reflecting on his mother's life can help him to hear in experiences forms and meanings. Reflection begins with snapshots of family history—keynotes of a tribal context in a long-ago Protestant-to-Catholic marriage; visiting grandparents with mother, ill-at-ease with alien domestic *mores*; a childhood memory of domestic intimacy: each of these in an octave, with death-related reflections in the sestet. Heaney catches the transient moment; what in another culture might be seen for its power of epitome as "a genre piece" (Sonnet 1)—"out to tea" (Sonnet 2), "Sunday morning peeling potatoes" (Sonnet 3), "bringing in the washing" (Sonnet 5)—retains its feeling of the ordinary with a conversational tone (half-rhymes muted by run-on syntax colloquially cutting across the shapes of form), but intensifies that by verbal music supported by the discipline of sonnet structure. It is a mixture Heaney heard in Lowell, though executed in his own characteristic voice. A sonnet on difficulties of communication caused by differences of education is ironically marked by verbal skill—"governed my tongue" (28; reverted to less educated speech) is the opposite of Heaney's "government of the tongue" skill as a writer (1988). Lawrence is invoked for the submerged sexual element in mother–son relations, but "close [...] by holding back" (29) is the keynote of this intimacy. The sequence ends with two magnificent poems of general reflection on death: how the living become guardians of the continued life of the dead in those who loved them (Sonnet 7). And finally the painful paradox of death as an absence so complete that it is the presence of a space that can never be either filled or forgotten: "a space / Utterly empty, utterly a source"; "A soul ramifying and forever / Silent, beyond silence listened for" (32). That is the common human experience: the poet does, as the dedication proposes, listen to the experiences the dead gave and find their meanings.

This is the traditional form, used as the vehicle of a fundamental transhistorical experience—feelings about the death of a parent—modified to accommodate a contemporary voice. Paul Muldoon puts the sonnet form to new uses, tonally and in other ways. "October 1950" (2001, 76), a sonnet on the poet's conception, which humorously recalls the most famous of literary conceptions (Tristram Shandy's), and, despite odd line lengths, colloquial diction ("my father's cock," "Fuck the Pope"), humorous half-rhymes (Pope/pub), and chatty parallelisms ("Whatever it is" beginning octave, sestet, and last line), has an emphatically classic formal structure of octave (quatrains: abab cdcd) and sestet (tercets: efg egf). Similarly with "Why Brownlee Left" (2001, 84), a title apparently offering an explanation for a poem recording only a mystery: form—a humorous pattern of rhymes and half-rhymes (abacdebc efdfgg), some emphatic (went/content), some only just plausible (farmhouse/famous; foot to/future)—establishes the quirky teasing tone which is its meaning. And there is much comparable zany inventiveness throughout Muldoon's early volumes, as in "Wystan" ("7, Middagh Street"; 2001, 175), an upside-down sonnet (sestet, octave) with typical Muldoon just-about rhymes (coast/metamorphosed).

The principle of formal zaniness has been extended to sequences, as in "The More a Man Has the More a Man Wants" (2001, 127–147). A fragmentary narrative in connectable cameos of an on-the-run gangster-terrorist figure in 49 (7 × 7, but unnumbered) stanzas each of 14 lines, this is a sonnet sequence of sorts—albeit scarcely recognizable as using sonnet form, especially when each line is just one word (46), with "him- / self" divided to make up the 14—though this hammers home the numerology (14 × 7 × 7), which is tossed away by a final isolated "Huh." "The Bangle (Slight Return)" (2001, 458–476) plays a similar trick with the form in reverse: a sequence of 30 numbered sonnets with an outer garment of ostentatious formality (octave two quatrains, sestet two tercets), this clashes figures of classical epic with "skinnymalinks" and "jackaroos" over three narrative areas: Virgil and *The Aeneid*; a journey (imaginary) made by Muldoon *père* ("da") in Australia; Muldoon himself in a Paris restaurant, ordering, fantasizing about other diners, and struggling to pay his bill—with confusions including "errata" reported (uncorrected) in earlier poems of the sequence. Fiction under control (Virgil directing the action of his epic), fiction out of control (confused with history: da in Oz), and life out of control (Muldoon in Paris)—and though the sonnet form may be felt as asserting order, an alternative form of the control that has apparently been lost, this too unravels in the uncorrected errata. In all this, there is a general sense that the sonnet can be made to fizz postmodernly. While Heaney and others (following Lowell) freed up the sonnet form by breaking down traditional regularities, Muldoon (reversing this) has built it up again, in new directions with new disciplines, partly invented, and often very demanding.

Muldoon puts these experiments and disciplines to their most ambitious use in the sequence "Horse Latitudes" (2006a, 3–21). The title refers to subtropical desert regions, including Nashville, Tennessee and Iraq. Muldoon is in one, thinking about the other. All 19 poems have titles of battles beginning with "B" (but not Baghdad, a conscious gap), all (obviously punning on the title) notable for the participation of horses or mules. Various British attempts to subdue colonies (America, India, Ireland) are implicitly paralleled with the 2003 US-led invasion of Iraq. Politics intersects with the personal—the agenda of the Bush presidency in the Iraq War (in this account, oil-based) with the battle with cancer of a lover called "Carlotta," with interventions from her grandfather, who muted mules for the Italian army in World War II. The battles named sometimes take over their poem, are sometimes juxtaposed with the situation of the lovers in Nashville, but more often their significance is left for the reader to elicit. In the partly invented form (abcd dcbe eff abc), close rhymes (dd ee ff) indicate that, for those with ears to hear, there are others (the rhymes of lines 2–4 repeated reversed in lines 5–7 draw together the quatrains of the octave; the rhymes of lines 1–3 repeated in lines 12–14 draw together the octave and sestet). Technically it is a *tour de force*, typical of a poet whose experiments with haiku ("instant messages"— texts), villanelle, pantoum, sestina, terza rima, and ghazal indicate a pleasure in formal disciplines. The formal discipline clashes against various kinds of free-wheeling verbal play (puns, etymologies, urban demotic). The demanding structure prompts or enables some of this play, most obviously in rhyme. It is a brilliance of verbal surface that can be found in equal measure (and not only by different readers) fascinating and irritating. The play of wit brings serious subjects (war, cancer) into uncertain perspectives, but these are not, as with Hill, subjects that are inherently ambiguous. Muldoon's methods of reading poetry as evinced by his *The End of the Poem* (2006b) imply that the limits to interpretation may be anywhere an engaged and inventive reader chooses—that is, virtually without end. How imaginative meditation might apply this to the verbal pyrotechnics of "Horse Latitudes," so as to elicit meaningful relations between the Second Iraq War, culturally and historically various battles beginning with "B," and the personal narrative of Carlotta, her illness, and her grandfather, is an open question.

There are many other poets writing in Britain and Ireland in this period whose sonnets might be discussed. These include poets already established by 1960 and continuing to write thereafter, such as: Patrick Kavanagh (*Come Dance with Kitty Stobling*, 1960, contains his most famous sonnets); Edwin Morgan in "Glasgow Sonnets," witty Petrarchan cameos of the city (*From Glasgow to Saturn*, 1973); Peter Scupham in "The Hinterland" (1977), 15 sonnets formally interlinked, each beginning with the last line of the previous poem (in the manner of Donne's "La Corona"); and Roy Fuller in two extended sequences, *Subsequent to Summer* (1985) and *Available for Dreams* (1989). The list also includes contemporaries of Hill, Heaney, and Harrison, such as: Michael Longley (whose main work lies in other forms, but whose "Ceasefire" is one of the most cited sonnets of the Northern Ireland Troubles; 1998, 118); Brendan Kennelly, whose *Cromwell* (1987) is a nonchronological dream-and-nightmare narrative, mainly in sonnets; or, for humorous parodies of the love sonnet, Wendy Cope in the cliché-ridden persona of Jason Strugnell (*Making Cocoa for Kingsley Amis*, 1986). George Szirtes is the author of several sequences, including those collected in *Portrait of My Father in an English Landscape* (1998) and *The Budapest File* (2000, "The Lost Scouts"). Carol Rumens's sequence in the persona of Sylvia Plath, "Letters Back," is a kind of literary criticism, giving views on errors of interpretation, especially the psychoanalytic (*Hex*, 2002). David Constantine's *A Poetry Primer* (2004) consists of Meredithian sonnets, taking a wry view of some basic terms of poetry criticism. Leontia Flynn (*Drives*, 2008) writes sonnets with more virtuosity, verve, and variety than several paragraphs could summarize.

An alternative tradition, attending more to Ted Berrigan than Robert Lowell, and including Tom Raworth, Peter Riley, and Alan Halsey, alongside American avant-garde writers such as Kathleen Fraser and Rachel Blau DuPlessis, can be sampled in the anthology edited by Jeff Hilson (2008). Though there are notable exceptions (some represented in the Reality Street collection), the form has been used less by women poets in the context of post-1960s feminism, which may reflect its historic association in love poetry with a male voice that places women in a position of admiration for qualities now often regarded as repressive. If so, the American Marilyn Hacker's *Love, Death, and the Changing of the Seasons* (1986), a narrative mainly in Petrarchan sonnets about love between an older and a younger woman, with references to the Shakespeare sequence on a similar older man/youth situation, might have begun to reclaim centers of form and emotional content for a female perspective.

Finally, two poets who have developed through new routes the music of sonnet structure on which Don Paterson and Anne Stevenson insist. Ciaran Carson's *The Twelfth of Never* is an ambitious sequence of 77 fundamentally Italian sonnets in rhymed alexandrines, a phantasmagoric and at times exuberantly manic mixture of history, myth, and folklore, in a range of settings from Ireland to Japan, "where everything is metaphor and simile" (1999, 13). A similar range in historical periods, from the Napoleonic Wars to the Northern Ireland Troubles, is framed by 1798 (the Irish Rebellion) and 1998 (the Good Friday Agreement ending the Troubles). If the outline of a "yet-to-be republic" (47) emerges from this, as the title indicates, it exists only in a postulated future. The rumbustious tone, developed from Carson's demotic free versions of sonnets by Baudelaire, Mallarmé, and Rimbaud (*The Alexandrine Plan*, 1998), also draws into the sonnet's high culture associations Carson's flute-playing engagement with Irish folk song, and pleasure in "dancing jigs and reels to McNamara's band" (78).

Similarly experimental is *For All We Know*, more obviously a narrative in sonnets, dialogues between two lovers, who meet in 1970s Belfast and variously travel to post-1968 Paris and pre-1990 GDR Dresden. The sequence is both formalized and fragmentary: in two parts, each of 35 sonnets (some double or quadruple) in unrhymed fourteen-syllable lines, each with a parallel of the same title in the same sequence in the two parts. The relation of the parallels, however, is often tangential, and a central analogy for the structure is the musical form of fugue which, like the sonnet, is a disciplined form susceptible of almost infinite variation (imitation, augmentation, diminution, inversion), different voices using in varied forms the same basic materials, "continuously shifting [...] fragments that remain [...] perpetually unfinished" (epigraph). A basic subject of *For All We Know* is the fluidity of identity in relation to personal, cultural, and political circumstances. Narrative variation need not be an index of untruth, since all memory is recreation ("The lie is memorized, the truth is remembered," claims a former *Stasi* agent [Carson 1998, 30]). Similarly with variation of language between parallel poems or repeated motifs, there is "the interminable wrestle with words and meanings"—quoted from T. S. Eliot, in three forms (Carson 1998, 28, 77), none quite Eliot's. The sonnet, traditionally used for a poetic narrative of love, is reworked as a form for fragmentary narrative with polyphonic interactive echoes.

Alice Oswald, notable for her interest in orality and realization of poetry in the living voice (*Memorial*, 2011, recreating material from Homeric epic), has experimented not with sequences, but with the audible shape of the individual poem. Like Don Paterson, with his analogy of the golden section, she sees the form as related to a fundamental structure of human experience, "like an in-breath and an out-breath" (2005b). "Owl" (2005a, 6) is characteristic, an upside down sonnet (sestet/octave), with only the octave rhyming, and syntax and typography grouped in counterpoint to rhyme and the main break in sense, between response to and interpretation of the bird's call. The poem opens up a possibility of imaginative participation in an animal awareness not apprehensible to humans, from which is derived a sense of presence that makes the natural world seem more real. Imaginative quasi-religious attention to nature is typical, with structural and rhetorical music freer than the classic shapes of sonnet form, but not less evident. The reader who follows Oswald's preference for reading aloud, dwelling in the sounds of phrase, line, syntactic unit, and overall structure, will recognize that what emerges from this music is central to the poem's meaning. Typography is used to imply a structure of sound (line length, syntax, rhythm, spacing, punctuation). In the manner of Hopkins's sonnets about the natural world, the sound of words is crucial to realizing the *haecceitas* (this-ness) of the unique; an adjustment, even dislocation of perception partly by the implied orality. Where Heaney has "words entering almost the sense of touch" ("Glanmore Sonnets" 2; 1997, 34), Oswald requires, as with the Homeric rhapsode, the physicality of the speaking-singing voice. It is indicative that she is uneasy about printing poems because she finds that readers so often fail to voice the aural qualities crucial to their expressivity implied by their printed forms. Yet her sonnets often leave creative space for the reader—to make sense of open images, fluid and unpunctuated syntax, and irregular structural groupings. More than many mainstream British poets, Oswald experiments with freedoms derived ultimately from American poetry—from Williams and Olson—which can be traced back to the fundamental orality of Homer and composition on the breath, the arc of sound that readers who read only with the eyes, not with the ears, fail to hear from the page. She does this, however, without abandoning the disciplines of English form and meter fundamental to the tensions that create a singing line. It is an interest "in how you can (re)create an oral tradition within a literary tradition" (2005b).

Whether analogous to the golden section, the in-breath and the out-breath, the complementarity and antithesis which are basic components of musical form, or some yet-to-be-recognized fundamental shape of human need; Shakespearean, Petrarchan, rhymed, unrhymed, in sequences themed and narrative; from poised ambivalence to engaged polemic to postmodern pyrotechnics; avoided by the Modernists, revived by Auden, remodeled by free-wheeling Americans—the sonnet has been reinvented. The paradox that Heaney heard in Lowell, the form that might both capture the evanescent moment in the democratic-demotic and retain its historic contact with conscious art and the high rhetorical modes, has been and continues to be exploited variously for both extremes of that gamut, and for much else in between.

References

Auden, W.H. (1941). *New Year Letter*. London: Faber.

Berrigan, Ted (1982). *The Sonnets*. New York: United Artists.

Berryman, John (1967). *Berryman's Sonnets*. New York: Farrar, Straus and Giroux.

Carson, Ciaran (1998). *The Alexandrine Plan*. Oldcastle: Gallery.

Carson, Ciaran (1999). *The Twelfth of Never*. London: Picador.

Carson, Ciaran (2008). *For All We Know*. Oldcastle: Gallery.

Constantine, David (2004). *A Poetry Primer*. Birmingham: Delos Press.

Cope, Wendy (1986). *Making Cocoa for Kingsley Amis*. London: Faber.

Cousins, A.D. and Howarth, Peter (eds.) (2011). *The Cambridge Companion to the Sonnet*. Cambridge: Cambridge University Press.

Flynn, Leontia (2008). *Drives*. London: Cape.

Fuller, Roy (1985). *Subsequent to Summer*. Edinburgh: Salamander.

Fuller, Roy (1989). *Available for Dreams*. London: Collins Harvill.

Hacker, Marilyn (1986). *Love, Death and the Changing of the Seasons*. New York: Arbor House.

Haffenden, John (ed.) (1981). *Viewpoints: Poets in Conversation*. London: Faber.

Harrison, Tony (2007). *Collected Poems*. London: Viking.

Heaney, Seamus (1979). *Field Work*. London: Faber.

Heaney, Seamus (1980). *Preoccupations: Selected Prose 1968–1978*. London: Faber.

Heaney, Seamus (1991). *Seeing Things*. London: Faber.

Heaney, Seamus (1987). *The Haw Lantern*. London: Faber.

Heaney, Seamus (1988). *The Government of the Tongue: The 1986 T. S. Eliot Memorial Lectures*. London: Faber.

Heaney, Seamus (1998). *Opened Ground: Poems 1966–1996*. London: Faber.

Heaney, Seamus (2001). *Electric Light*. London: Faber.

Heaney, Seamus (2002). *Finders Keepers: Selected Prose 1971–2001*. London: Faber.

Heaney, Seamus (2006). *District and Circle*. London: Faber.

Hill, Geoffrey (1968). *King Log*. London: André Deutsch.

Hill, Geoffrey (1978). *Tenebrae*. London: André Deutsch.

Hill, Geoffrey (1980). "Under Judgement," interview with B. Morrison, *The New Statesman* (8 February), pp. 212–214.

Hilson, Jeff (ed.) (2008). *The Reality Street Book of Sonnets*. Hastings: Reality Street Editions.

Kavanagh, Patrick (1960). *Come Dance with Kitty Stobling and Other Poems*. London: Longmans.

Kennelly, Brendan (1987). *Cromwell*. Bloodaxe: Newcastle upon Tyne.

Longley, Michael (1998). *Selected Poems*. London: Cape.

Lowell, Robert (1970). *Notebook*. London: Faber.

Lowell, Robert (1973a). *History*. London: Faber.

Lowell, Robert (1973b). *For Lizzie and Harriet*. London: Faber.

Meredith, George (1862). *Modern Love and Poems of the English Roadside, with Poems and Ballads*. London: Chapman and Hall.

Morgan, Edwin (1973). *From Glasgow to Saturn*. Cheadle: Carcanet.

Muldoon, Paul (2001). *Poems 1968-1998*. London: Faber.

Muldoon, Paul (2006a). *Horse Latitudes*. London: Faber.

Muldoon, Paul (2006b). *The End of the Poem*. London: Faber.

Oswald, Alice (1997). *The Thing in the Gap-Stone Stile*. London: Faber.

Oswald, Alice (2005a). *Woods etc.* London: Faber.

Oswald, Alice (2005b). Interview with Janet Phillips. *Poetry News*, summer. http://www.poetrysoc.com/content/publications/poetrynews/pn2005 (accessed 6 May 2020).

Oswald, Alice (2011). *Memorial. An Excavation of the Iliad*. London: Faber.

Paterson, Don (1997). *God's Gift to Women*. London: Faber.

Paterson, Don (1999a). *The Eyes: A Version of Antonio Machado*. London: Faber.

Paterson, Don (1999b). *101 Sonnets: From Shakespeare to Heaney*. London: Faber.

Paterson, Don (2015). *40 Sonnets*. London: Faber.

Pound, Ezra (1951). *An ABC of Reading*. London: Faber.

Rumens, Carol (2002). *Hex*. Tarset: Bloodaxe.

Scupham, Peter (1977). *The Hinterland*. Oxford: Oxford University Press.

Stevenson, Anne (2005). *Poems 1955-2005*. Tarset: Bloodaxe.

Szirtes, George (1998). *Portrait of My Father in an English Landscape*. Oxford: Oxford University Press.

Szirtes, George (2000). *The Budapest File*. Newcastle upon Tyne: Bloodaxe.

Williams, William Carlos (1963). *Paterson*. New York: New Directions.

Williams, William Carlos (1974). *The Embodiment of Knowledge* (ed. Ron Loewinsohn). New York: New Directions.

Woolf, Virginia (1958). *Granite and Rainbow: Essays*. London: Hogarth Press.

2b.5
Free Verse and Open Form

Lacy Rumsey

Introduction

In the period since 1960, and indeed ever since the great Modernist experiments of the 1910s, a high proportion of poetry published in Britain and Ireland has eschewed regular metrical form. Readers do not respond to lines such as the following with the descriptive categories learnt from poems of earlier centuries: the specific acts of formal recognition implied by labels such as *ballad stanza* or *iambic pentameter* will not be elicited by such varied, unpredictable pieces of language:

> Bartending is a branch
> of show business. Your bartender
> can flirt as heavy as he wants
> without danger of being
> taken for real, thanks
> to the wide spread
> of wood between
> him and the customer. [...]
> (Thom Gunn, "Classics,"
> Gunn 2000, 66, ll. 1–8)

A Companion to Contemporary British and Irish Poetry, 1960–2015, First Edition.
Edited by Wolfgang Görtschacher and David Malcolm.
© 2021 John Wiley & Sons Ltd. Published 2021 by John Wiley & Sons Ltd.

```
                    nailed Eagles    beryl    alter vasish
                        Owls, Blood-bed
                    Bird-gear           turbulent
                    Ruled
                    it,

                    Raven
                        blue acquiescing tar
                                            thread
                    the.air.it.will.be.tinned.
                                            pull —
                        feather against call —
```
(Maggie O'Sullivan, "Hill Figures" (1993),
O'Sullivan 1996, 70–71; 70, ll. 1–11)

Not only do the passages by Gunn (1929–2004) and O'Sullivan (born 1951) lack any regular meter—that is, a meter that recurs in each line, or in some other predictable pattern—but they also operate almost wholly without metrical language.

Metrical language, as theorized in the "beat prosody" developed since the 1980s by Derek Attridge, is "language written in such a way as to make possible the experience of beats [...]. We say that a stretch of language has beats when, on hearing it or reading it aloud, we sense an impulse to move at regularly occurring places—to bring down the hand, to nod the head, to tap the foot" (Attridge 1995, 9). A line such as the following:

The sea comes in like nothing but the sea,
(Glyn Maxwell, "The Sea Comes in Like Nothing but the Sea," Maxwell 2002, 1, l. 1)

will be experienced as a five-beat metrical line—specifically, as an iambic pentameter by any reader familiar with the rhythms of metrical poetry in English. It can be scanned, using the methods of beat prosody, as follows:

```
x   /   x   \   x   /   x   x   x   /
The sea comes in like nothing but the sea,¹
```

The / mark represents a prominent (stressed) syllable, the x mark a nonprominent one; \ indicates an intermediate degree of stress. When a syllable is experienced as giving rise to a beat, the scansion mark associated with it is underlined, as in this scansion.

Although this line will probably be read with only three prominent (stressed) syllables, plus one intermediate stress, five rhythmic pulses—beats—will nonetheless be experienced: the reader who taps a rhythm as she or he reads will find herself or himself tapping on *but* despite its not being pronounced with any particular prominence. Beats are cognitive and perceptual phenomena that respond to the prominence patterns and the timing of speech. It is largely because readers experience Maxwell's line (and the others in his poem) as a sequence of five such beats that they can identify it as an instance of iambic pentameter—even if they would not themselves analyze it in such terms.

In metrical poetry in English, with the arguable exception of syllabic and quantitative meters, every line is experienced as a sequence of metrical beats. This returning rhythmic pulse helps to connect poetry to music, and indeed to other rhythmic experiences such as dance; its continued power largely explains the persistence of metrical poetry even in an age that has largely abandoned meter. In the extracts by Gunn and O'Sullivan, on the other hand, whole passages of the poem are experienced as beat-free. Beats may be present intermittently: in the O'Sullivan poem, for example, one might want to perform the strikingly punctuated sequence "the.air.it.will.be.tinned." (l. 9) as a staccato six-beat, while, in reading the Gunn aloud, the sequence "the wide spread / of wood between / him and the customer" (ll. 6–8) may fall into a five-beat pattern, with beats associated with the syllables "wide," "spread," "wood," "him," and "cust-." Yet such sporadic sequences of beats by no means dominate our experience of these poems. If poetry such as this is to affect us—to move us, to excite us, to give shape and dynamism to our experience of the time that we devote to the poem—then it must do so, at least in part, by other means.

Preliminary Questions

The earliest poetry in English in whose rhythm it was widely recognized by the poet's contemporaries that a fundamental shift away from meter had taken place was Walt Whitman's *Leaves of Grass* (1855), but it was not until the early twentieth century that an agreed terminology for such a mode of poetry began to fall into place. In the early decades of the twentieth century, the French term *vers libre* and the English *free verse* were in competition (Hartman 1980, 10); unsurprisingly, the English term came to dominate. Written in lines—a consideration which distinguishes free verse from prose poetry, and which for many critics (e.g., Ramsey 1968, 106) has made the line the crucial component of free-verse form—the free-verse poem in English became, in the first half of the twentieth century, a powerful instrument in the hands of American and British poets such as T. S. Eliot, William Carlos Williams, and D. H. Lawrence. In consequence, the term *free verse* became a relatively uncontroversial one—debatable as to its precise definition, but widely accepted as necessary.[2]

In the second half of the twentieth century, other terms became popular, and one of them—*open form*—has displaced *free verse* to a certain extent in critical discussions of British poetry (e.g., Brinton 2009, 26). Theorists of open form—among whom the most influential was the American poet Charles Olson, in particular in his essay "Projective Verse" (1950)—note that poetic form can have powerful links not only to speech, but also to an ambitious use of the printed page, allowing poetry to be printed in varied and even multidirectional ways such that the line seems less crucial, or less reliable, as a basic unit of form. In recent years, the term *free verse* has come to seem to some readers (e.g., Perloff 1998) to be associated with an outdated or relatively orthodox poetics; this may be seen as rather a paradoxical development, given early free-verse writers' status as "verse revolutionaries" (Carr 2009), but it is, of course, in the nature of literary history for formal developments—or, at the very least, the names given to such developments—to dislodge each other over time.

This chapter does not seek to offer a precise boundary between free verse and open form. Although the open-form poem may look more formally various than the free-verse one, both terms are defined in an essentially negative way, and the choice between them is often made more on criteria of a poet's (or a critic's) wider allegiances and alignments than on technical grounds. Instead, one can simply note the existence of this terminological difficulty—or richness of terminological choice!—and also that of a third term, *non-metrical poetry*, which is often favored by prosodists, and which can be safely used in relation to both free verse and open form.

The period since 1960 has, in the UK and Ireland, been one of significant achievement in non-metrical poetry. Although one of the most popular and technically brilliant of English poets of the period, Philip Larkin (1922–1985), published almost exclusively in meter, he was very much an exception. Basil Bunting (1900–1985) and W. H. Auden (1907–1973), major figures of the previous generation, continued to produce substantial non-metrical work, while, among poets who came to significant prominence in the period, Seamus Heaney (1939–2013), Geoffrey Hill (1932–2016), and J. H. Prynne (born 1936) are at ease in both metrical and non-metrical forms, though by no means all in the same proportions. Heaney wrote primarily in meter, with a period of non-metrical writing in the 1970s; Prynne writes primarily in non-meter, though making powerful recourse to an intermittent metricality; Hill was deeply engaged with both. There is a wide range of other significant and interesting poets worked or work either both in metrical and non-metrical forms, or predominantly in the latter—among these, one might cite Stevie Smith, R. F. Thomas, Edwin Morgan, Roy Fisher, Eavan Boland, Tom Leonard, Barry MacSweeney, Grace Nichols, Paul Muldoon, Geraldine Monk, Jackie Kay, Kathleen Jamie, Simon Armitage, and Keston Sutherland.

No single approach to these different poets' use of form will suffice, for, in the words of Eleanor Berry's very helpful study "The Free Verse Spectrum," "free verse practice is […] a multidimensional array" (Berry 1997, 895). Berry postulates five dimensions or axes along which free-verse poems may be placed: line length (shorter or longer); line integrity (primarily defined by the extent to which a poem makes use of run-on lines); line grouping; sensory basis of the form (aural, visual, or both); and relation of form to meaning (organic—that is, with the progression of a poem's form appearing to depend on the progression of its meaning—or abstract) (882). Even if one disagrees with certain aspects of this list—for example, its lack of any specific allusion to rhythm and meter—it is invaluable in directing our attention to some of the most important aspects of free-verse form, and in emphasizing that form's potentially plural basis.

There can be no attempt in this brief chapter to offer a comprehensive taxonomy of recent British and Irish poetry along these multiple lines. What follows is, instead, a consideration of how *two* important aspects of the formal potential implicit in free verse and open-form poetry can be put to use. The first is its potential for setting up patterns of *alignment and disalignment*, notably of syntax and line, syntax and stanza, rhythm and line, line and page margin, and, more diffusely, in the relationship between canonical models of what poems can look like on the one hand and the actual layout of a poem on the page on the other. The second is its potential for unusual *rhythmicity*, since readers of poetry, including free verse, may be presumed to expect, accept, and respond to rhythmic patterning more marked than that which is found in non-poetic uses of language.

Patterns of (Dis)alignment

In considering free-verse and open-form poets' handling of alignment and disalignment, a useful sense of the range of possibilities can be gained by comparing work by two very different poets, Ted Hughes (1930–1998) and Tom Raworth (1938–2017).

Hughes's "The 59th Bear" comes from *Birthday Letters* (1998), the poetic sequence that he devoted to his first wife, the American poet and fiction writer Sylvia Plath, who committed suicide in 1963. It shares its title with a short story written by Plath in 1959 ("The Fifty-Ninth Bear"), a story that, like the poem, turns on an event that took place during Plath's and Hughes's visit to the Yellowstone National Park that year: as they slept at a campsite, a bear attacked their parked car, tearing out a window to eat the biscuits and oranges that were within (Hughes 2007, 150–151). Plath's story, which describes a husband and wife rather like Hughes and herself, ends with the bear not just attacking the car, but also killing the husband (Plath 1979, 105). Hughes's poem reflects both on the couple's visit to Yellowstone, and on what Plath made of it in her story.

The poem begins as follows:

> We counted bears – as if all we wanted
> Were more bears. Yellowstone
> Folded us into its robe, its tepees
> Of mountain and conifer.
> Mislaid Red Indian Mickey Mouse America
> Pointered us from campground to campground –
> We were two of many. And it was as novel-astonishing
> To you as to me. Paradise, we saw,
> Was where wild bears ate from the hands of children.
> ("The 59th Bear," Hughes 1998, 89–95; 89, ll. 1–9)

The lineation here plays several different roles. It is almost—but not quite—entirely enjambed, with line-breaks frequently interrupting the sentence in a "hard" way, that is, at a point where the syntax would not naturally provoke an intonational break: for example, between a verb and its direct object (l. 1), between the subject of a verb and the verb (l. 2), or between a noun or adjective and the prepositional phrase that modifies it (l. 3, l. 7). Likewise, full stops are more frequently located within the lines (l. 2, l. 7, l. 8) than at their end (l. 4, l. 9).

The effect of this is triple. At a very local level, the enjambments permit a certain rhetorical reinforcement of particular effects: thus, in the phrase "Yellowstone / Folded us into its robe," the way in which the line-break is enclosed within the sentence may be taken as emblematic of the way in which the couple are enclosed within their environment; a reader who responds to such an effect may feel that the enjambment is offering him or her a more powerful (because more concrete) experience of the "fold[ing]" described in the line than the meaning of the words alone can evoke. More diffusely, the regular enjambments create opportunities for the reader to infer that there is something more complex or sophisticated occurring in this text than a simple sequence of reminiscences; as the syntax is repeatedly cut across, the disalignment between sentence and line creates a distancing effect, with potential for a dramatizing or ironizing of the statements being made. Readers who find a rather wry or ironic tone to these lines are very likely to be responding to this diffuse effect of the lineation, without necessarily realizing it. In turn, this sense of irony creates room for a complex response to the clauses and phrases that are *not* enjambed, or that are enjambed less challengingly:

> Mislaid Red Indian Mickey Mouse America
> Pointered us from campground to campground – (ll. 5–6)

There is a syntactic break after "campground –," while what follows "America" can be considered a "soft" enjambment, since, in everyday speech, lengthy noun phrases are frequently followed by an intonation-group boundary. The two lines recount a certain voluntary obedience to the traditional tourist experience, and the relative alignment of syntax and line is one index of that obedience; it helps to create a delicate balance between obedience and deflating irony, the irony being made present by the piled-up and capitalized modifiers of "Red Indian Mickey Mouse America" and the mock docility of the verb "[p]ointered," a verb that suggests touristy passivity while at the same time functioning as an index of poetic activity, since, absent from the *Oxford English Dictionary* (OED), it is apparently a neologism coined by Hughes. Had the previous lines not been so heavily enjambed, this moment of line–syntax alignment would have been trivial. That it is no more than a moment is demonstrated by the line that follows, whose internal full stop and enjambment after "we saw" again put disalignment to work in the service of irony and distance.

At the end of this long poem, reflecting on how Plath "[t]ransformed our dud scenario into a fiction," and did so (though this is not stated in the poem) by imagining his (or his avatar's) being killed by the bear, Hughes again uses lineation to subtle tonal effect.

>   At that time
> I had not understood
> How the death hurtling to and fro
> Inside your head, had to alight somewhere
> And again somewhere, and had to be kept moving.
> And had to be rested
> Temporarily somewhere.
> ("The 59th Bear," Hughes 1998, 94–95, closing lines)

The content of the lines is clearly more emotionally stark than that of the poem's opening, suggesting that the imagined death within Plath's story is a manifestation of death's sustained and destructive presence in her consciousness; an anticipation, or perhaps a warding-off, of her final self-destruction. This emotional charge combines with a subtly different use of patterns of alignment and disalignment to produce a very different set of effects. The lines are enjambed, but less challengingly so, in terms of the conflict with syntax, than in the poem's opening: the line-breaks tend to fall at phrasal boundaries, and the lines so run on can in many cases be read in the first instance as complete clauses ("I had not understood"; "the death [...] had to alight somewhere").

This greater "softness" of the enjambments, in the context of a strong emotional charge, makes them feel much less witty and self-distancing than the earlier examples: instead, they assume a primarily mimetic role, imitating the sense of ceaseless, nervous motion that the poem assigns to Plath. The two final lines, shorter, ending on a full stop, and making use of a "soft" enjambment between them, seem much more aligned—and of course, since they come at the poem's end, much more closural—than those that immediately precede them. The effect is not the ironic obedience seen earlier, but rather something like a mournful taking stock of the resting-places that are constituted by the end of a poem, and the end of a life.

Hughes's poem shows how free verse can use patterns of alignment and disalignment—here, of lineation and syntax—to create powerful effects, both at a very local level—adding richness or concreteness to a particular word, phrase, or image—and more diffusely. Effects such as these are not inherent in the various techniques used, but emerge from their interplay with different poems', and different passages', meanings. In open-form poetry, disalignment has the potential to be more various, since, while "The 59th Bear" basically respects the canonical shape of a poem—its left-hand margin is only once departed from—poems by open-form writers such as Lee Harwood, Maggie O'Sullivan, or Harriet Tarlo are more various in their use of page layout, and indeed in other markers of traditional poetic shape, such as punctuation and capitalization.

An important, though relatively restrained example of this is provided by Tom Raworth's "You Were Wearing Blue," from his first collection, *The Relation Ship* (1966).

>   the explosions are nearer this evening
>   the last train leaves for the south
>   at six   tomorrow
>   the announcements will be in a different language
>
>   i chew the end of a match
>   the tips of my finger and thumb are sticky
>
>   i will wait at the station and you
>   will send a note, i
>   will read it
>   it will be raining
>
>   our shadows in the electric light
>
>   when i was eight they taught me *real*
>   writing
>   to join up the letters
>
>   listen you said i
>   preferred to look
>   at the sea   everything stops there at strange angles
>
>   only the boats spoil it
>   making you focus further
>   ("You Were Wearing Blue" (complete), Raworth 2003, 5–6)

The disalignments here are more pervasive than in the Hughes poem: the text is arrayed in varied and unpredictable ways, including departures from the left-hand margin and mid-line tab stops as well as hard enjambments between subject and verb ("i / preferred") and adjective and noun ("*real* / writing"). All of these work against any sense of the poem's being aligned with a predetermined, line-by-line, fixed-margin shape; at the same time, the absence of capital letters and most punctuation weakens the sense of its material's being arrayed in accordance with the canons of English sentence construction, while the absence of obvious discursive links between stanzas, which each describe a single episode, image, or situation, weakens—though it does not destroy—any hypothesis that they may be collectively aligned with a coherent sequence of thought. As with the Hughes poem, the primary effect of these disalignments is to help the reader to locate and respond to a sensibility or tone: here, one of fantasy, reverie, sporadic excitement, and an acceptance of discontinuity.

If patterns of alignment and disalignment play a diffuse but vital role in creating the sensibility of "You Were Wearing Blue," they, also, as in the Hughes poem, have smaller-scale effects. Some are similar to those seen in "The 59th Bear," notably the greater alignment of line and phrase in the poem's final lines, which plays a closural role. Others are very different. The absence of punctuation, in particular, creates many moments of insoluble ambiguity. For example, the lines

> listen you said i
> preferred to look (ll. 15–16)

can be interpreted in at least four different ways ("Listen," you said. I preferred to look ...; "Listen," you said, "I preferred to look ..."; Listen, you said "I preferred to look ..."; Listen, you said [that] I preferred to look ...). Though some will seem more probable than others, there is no way of choosing between them with any certainty. In the same way, readers will be unable to determine how the poem's rather glamorous references to correspondence, rendezvous, and flight relate to its evocations of past and present time; refusing the orthodoxies of "*real*" writing," the poem self-consciously refuses "to join up the letters"—the missives which its characters exchange, and the typographical signs which, were they to be lined up in conventional fashion, might make everything clear at last. Such ambiguities are Romantic ones, encouraging, in their insolubility, a spirit of acceptance and play which one might relate to a Keatsian "negative capability" or Wordsworthian "wise passiveness": refusing to reach for certainty, the poem prefers the sensuous effects of a plunge into the sea's immensity over any attempt to "focus." Raworth's use of collage-like juxtapositions, a mode of (dis)alignment that was crucial to both modernist poetry and 1960s popular culture, constructs a contemporary formal equivalent for such preferences.

Rhythmicity, Metricality, Meter

Assessing the relationship of free verse to rhythmicity inevitably entails a consideration of its relationship to poetic meter, which is the strongest and most organized variety of rhythmicity in language. This relationship is a vexed and controversial one: for some critics, who draw on an understanding of free verse set out in an influential essay of 1917 by T. S. Eliot, free verse is "haunted" by meter, and, at its best, is always close to it (Eliot 1975); for others, such an approach denies free verse the right to attempt something genuinely new, and free of meter (e.g., Holder 1995). It may be useful to note that this debate can be defused somewhat by a familiarity with those recent approaches to meter that define it, as we have seen, in terms of sequences of metrical beats, and not through the canonical labels of foot-scansion—useful though these may continue to be in certain contexts. As phoneticians have shown (e.g., Couper-Kuhlen 1993), everyday spoken English moves in and out of sequences of beats very readily; it should be uncontroversial to propose that free verse might seek to make use of, and control, that movement.

Paradoxically, it may be poets otherwise associated with meter who have worked hardest to detach their free verse from it. In some of Seamus Heaney's poems of the first half of the 1970s, for example, not only are the familiar meters avoided, but the language is organized in such a way that readers are very unlikely to experience any sustained sequence of beats.

> As if he had been poured
> in tar, he lies
> on a pillow of turf
> and seems to weep
>
> the black river of himself.
> The grain of his wrists
> is like bog oak,
> the ball of his heel
>
> like a basalt egg.
>   ("The Grauballe Man,"
>   Heaney 1998, 115–16;
>   115, ll. 1–9)

"The Grauballe Man," from Heaney's 1975 volume *North*, offers, instead of beats, a rhythm based in the prominence patterns of the different intonation groups into which the sentences will fall when read aloud. For example, the three prominences of:

```
            x   /
           he lies
  x   x   /   x   x     /
  on  a  pillow of     turf
```

echo those of

```
  x  /  x   x    x      /
  As if he  had been poured
  x   /
  in tar
```

The echo is reinforced by alliteration, the second and third prominences in both phrases beginning with [p] and [t], respectively. Likewise, the syntactic parallelism of the poem's second sentence—the repeated pattern "The [...] of [...] [is] like [...]," strengthened by alliteration in [b] and [g]—is given rhythmic reinforcement by the fact that three of the sentence's four noun groups include two prominences:

```
x   /    x  x   /
the grain of his wrists

x   /    x  x   /
the ball of his heel

x  / x   /
a basalt egg
```

That these prominence patterns do not coalesce into sequences of metrical beats is due to a combination of factors, all related to Heaney's very close control of his material: the brevity of the lines; the irregularity of their stress patterns; the almost systematic use of enjambment; and the careful diction, which encourages readers to prefer a slow, deliberate reading style to one which would play down irregularity in search of a strong rhythm; the lines' consonantal density may have a similar influence on reading style.

Such an avoidance of metricality and meter may form part of Heaney's ethical positioning in these poems of violence. "The Grauballe Man" ends with simple, irregular forms:

```
x    x   /  xx    /
with the actual weight

x   /   / x   / x
of each hooded victim,

    /    x    /
slashed and dumped.
```
(Heaney 1998, 116, ll. 46–48)

The starkness of these lines is clear if we compare them to a hypothetical metrical version, in which a more regular stress pattern, and an avoidance of enjambment, leading to stronger parallelism between lines, would encourage the reader to find a pattern of beats throughout:

```
x   ∕   xx    ∕
with actual weight,

x   ∕  x   ∕  x
of hooded victims,

    ∕   x    ∕
slashed and dumped
```

The sonorous quality of these last, invented lines is significantly less varied, and more obvious, than that of the lines which Heaney actually wrote. Avoiding making meter of the words "slashed and dumped" may constitute a way for the poet to avoid deploying too neat a flourish, too easy a rhetoric, in his confrontation with the suffering of others.

If Heaney's poem prefers to avoid metricality and meter, much other free verse engages very creatively with these stronger and more regular rhythms. At times, this engagement leads to the presence within a free-verse poem of instances of, or allusions to, a recognizable poetic meter. Several of the poems in J. H. Prynne's *The White Stones* (1969), for example, end with single five-beat lines that have a close relationship to iambic pentameter.

```
                    [...] the action of month and
    hour is warm with cinnamon & clear water,
    the first slopes rise gently at our feet.
    ("Crown," Prynne 2015, 116–17; 117, ll. 44–46)
```

Its proximity to pentameter imparts a sense of climax to the final line of "Crown," and reinforces its quiet lyricism.

```
         x   /    /   \    /   x x  x   /
         the first slopes rise gently at our feet.
```

Although a reading of free verse for meter can sometimes, as here, be productive, it can also degenerate into the kind of hunt that constructs what it thinks it finds, and that—to return to the debate alluded to earlier—underplays the specifically *non*-metrical nature of the medium.

Rather than "Lo! A tetrameter!," a more helpful approach to free verse rhythm is often, therefore, one that looks, not for meters, but for *metrical language*—which is to say, as noted earlier, for stretches of language that give rise to the experience of beats. We hear beats in iambic pentameter, but we also hear them in the sporadic rhythmicity of everyday speech.

```
         \       / \     x  /  xx  /   x
         There's no point in arguing really.
         (Couper-Kuhlen 1993, 93; scansion symbols adapted)
```

This utterance, from a telephone phone-in analyzed by the phonetician Elizabeth Couper-Kuhlen, can usefully be considered as a three-beat sequence—an example of what, to use the terminology of beat prosody, I am calling *metrical language* or simply *metricality*. However, only in certain contexts (ones in which poetic meter was felt as a contextual or organizing presence) would it be worth considering it an example of a poetic *meter* such as trimeter. If we examine free verse and open-form poetry in a spirit similar to that with which we might approach everyday speech, with an ear for metricality and not simply meter, a rich, non-normative (or, more accurately, less normative) account of its rhythms may emerge.

Metricality of the simplest kind is present in the reading of the Maggie O'Sullivan extract suggested earlier:

```
              / /   /   /    / /
              the.air.it.will.be.tinned.
```

The six-beat rhythm emerges from one possible performance of the phrase, a reading that has interpreted the phrase's being set off as a single line and unusually punctuated as encouragements to imbue it with a strong sense of rhythm.[4] Such a rhythm is an example of metricality, but there is little point in considering it meter—unless one feels that this deliberately blunt rhythm offers an ironic allusion to the English alexandrine or hexameter, which there is little clear reason to do. By contrast, such an allusion may well be present in the opening line of "A misremembered lyric" (1993) by Denise Riley (born 1948), which is also likely to give rise to six beats:

> A misremembered lyric: a soft catch of its song
> (Riley 2000, 51, l. 1)

Metricality in Riley's poems is typically loaded with connotation, and this line is no exception. Its rhythm is not quite that of an alexandrine, since the mid-line pause is too strong for the line to hang together as a single metrical sequence, given the lack of any contextual push to metricality. Rather than hearing it as a coherent six-beat line, we are perhaps more likely to hear it as two three-beat half lines, which we can notate thus:

```
[x  /  x /  x      / x] [x  /    /    x  x   /  ]
 A misremembered lyric: a  soft catch of its song
```

Coming close to meter proper, the rhythm helps the line to function as an imperfect echo or memory of poetic beauty, one of the many voices by which Riley's poem is inhabited.

Such interplays with meaning, and with meter, represent some of the ways in which free-verse poets have created complexity through the intermittent use of metrical language. Another technique consists in the running-on of metrical sequences across line boundaries—a combination of rhythmicity and disalignment that is inaccessible to metrical verse. For example, when, in "Cook Ting" (2002), by R. F. Langley (1938–2011), metricality emerges strongly and surprisingly after a dozen lines of straightforward free verse, it does so in a way that a rapid or silent reading might well not pick up on:

> [...] The cliff is history. You
> throw yourself in where the fish are
> thickest. Take hold of a word and
> turn it on. Tourbillion. A blade
> is so sharp it can dance round
> the joint. Silvery energies
> answer the point. The carcase of
> an ox flops open. [...]
> (Langley 2015, 79–80;
> 79, ll. 12–19)

The poet is not exactly concealing his metricality; although the four-beat sequences contained in this passage snake over the line-ends, the pattern that they make is emphasized by rhyme. In what follows, only the four metrical sequences, whose beginnings and ends are marked by square brackets, are scanned:

```
                                              [ x
         [. . .]    The cliff is history.  You
            /   x   x   /   x     x   /   x
         throw yourself in where the fish are
            /  x  ]    [\   /   x  x  /   x
         thickest.  Take hold of a word and
            /  x  / ]                [x   /
         turn it on.  Tourbillion.  A blade
          x  \   /    x  x    /    x
         is so sharp it can dance round
           x  /  ]   [/   x x / x   x
         the joint.  Silvery energies
          /  x    x  /    ]
         answer the point.  The carcase of

         an ox flops open.
```

At this point in Langley's poem, three situations or narratives seem to be associated in overlay with its imagery: a cook cuts up an ox, seagulls dive for sprats, and a poet chooses his words. The effect of the meter, and indeed the rhyme, is one of deliberate and exuberant excess; an implicit celebration of the poet's (and the cook's, and the natural world's) ability to offer more than is required by mere necessity.[5]

A less assertive but more sustained interplay of metricality and free-verse line can be found in Geoffrey Hill's "The Jumping Boy" (2006). The character of the title, who has a "plebeian bullet head" and, "at home on the king's highway," is watched by a girl as he jumps, may be understood to be located in a childhood memory, or in a picture. The poem seeks to transmit a sense of the "serious joy" that the boy has in jumping, and also of the mixed feelings—admiration and loss—of the older poet, looking on, or back. It is composed of four numbered free-verse sections of diminishing length, and makes use of highly patterned—but unobtrusive—formal devices, among which is an intermittent metricality.

The poem begins with a series of three-beat sequences, which gradually become more complex (that is, with more uneven prominence patterns) as the first section proceeds, before petering out:

```
              [/    x   x   /  x    / ]  [ x  /
              Here is the jumping boy, the boy

                x   /    x x   /  ]
              who jumps as I speak.

              [x  x  x   /   x   x   /    /   x ]
              He is at home on the king's highway,
```

```
      [x  /   x    x  /   / ]  [x    /
      in call of the tall house, its blind
      /  x /  ]
      gable end, the trees — I know this place.
              ("The Jumping Boy," Hill 2006, 7–8; 7, ll. 1–5)⁶
```

Thereafter, though non-metricality is predominant, passages of metrical language recur at key structural points in the poem, such as the five-beat sequence that begins its second section:

```
      [x   /    x \     x  x   /  xx
      He leaps because he has serious
      /  x  /  x]
      joy in leaping.
                                    (ll. 12–13)
```

and the three-beat sequence that closes the poem, echoing its opening, and creating a sense of return:

```
                                  [ x  /  /  /
      Jump away, jumping boy; the boy I was
        \      / ]
      shouts go.
                              (Hill 2006, 8, ll. 26–27)
```

Metricality is by no means the only formal device used in the poem, which at perhaps its most memorable point turns, instead, to a very delicate use of a pattern of disalignment:

>   [...] He is winning
>   a momentous and just war
>   with gravity.
>   (Hill 2006, 7, ll. 20–22)

The diminishing line length and above all the enjambments, which offer freedom from the strict observance of lineation, combine beautifully with the meaning of the words to give a sense of lightness, of a form that is throwing off constraints. Such effects, whose symbolic potential is evident in this context, are likely to help Hill's readers feel that the "war / with gravity" is pleasurably, if momentarily, being won.

It must be acknowledged that a significant proportion of the free verse written between 1960 and 2015 was less formally accomplished than the examples discussed here. Much of the poetry of the period (as of other periods) offers the reader satisfactions that draw more or less exclusively on poetry's potential to offer a privileged arena in which to pursue communication, or conceptual experiment, with the form in which this activity is couched, be it metrical or free, acting primarily as a frame. Formal devices such as those deployed by

Hill, Hughes, Prynne, or Riley, which bring esthetic pleasure, dynamism, rhetorical power, and a sense of craft to the experience of the poems in which they are deployed, show how such a conception of poetry underestimates the complex pleasures that the art can offer. Despite the common conception of free-verse and open-form poetry as less "formal" than metrical verse, the work discussed in this chapter demonstrates as creative and powerful an engagement with the linguistic material of poetry as can be found anywhere.

Notes

1 The scansion marks used here are those of Attridge 1995, which are well suited to the scansion of free verse. Other works by Attridge feature a different series of marks, though the principles that govern them are identical. The use of a fixed-width font such as Courier permits the scansion marks to be placed in exactly the right positions.

2 Probably the best account of the history of free verse in English is provided by Beyers 2001. Other significant studies are Hartman 1980, Kirby-Smith 1996, and Cooper 1998.

3 "You Were Wearing Blue" is © The Estate of Tom Raworth, and is reprinted with the permission of Carcanet Press Limited, Manchester, UK.

4 The performance of non-metrical poetry can be difficult to predict on the basis of the written text alone. The poet herself, in a recording made at SUNY Buffalo in 1993, reads the line differently: http://writing.upenn.edu/pennsound/x/OSullivan.php.

5 Cook Ting (or Cook Ding) appears in one of the major texts of Taoism, the Zhuangzi or Chuang Tzu. Cutting up an ox with perfect rhythm, guided only by his sense of the Way, Ting functions as an exemplary figure.

6 "The Jumping Boy" is © The Literary Estate of Sir Geoffrey Hill, and is quoted with its permission.

References

Attridge, Derek (1995). *Poetic Rhythm: An Introduction*. Cambridge: Cambridge University Press.

Berry, Eleanor (1997). "The Free Verse Spectrum." *College English* 59: 873–897.

Beyers, Chris (2001). *A History of Free Verse*. Fayetteville: University Arkansas Press.

Brinton, Ian (2009). *Contemporary Poetry: Poets and Poetry since 1990*. Cambridge: Cambridge University Press.

Carr, Helen (2009). *The Verse Revolutionaries: Ezra Pound, H.D. and the Imagists*. London: Cape.

Cooper, G. Burns (1998). *Mysterious Music: Rhythm and Free Verse*. Stanford: Stanford University Press.

Couper-Kuhlen, Elizabeth (1993). *English Speech Rhythm: Form and Function in Everyday Verbal Interaction*. Amsterdam: Benjamins.

Eliot, T. S. (1975). ""Reflections on Vers Libre" (1917)." In: *Selected Prose of T. S. Eliot* (ed. Frank Kermode), 31–36. London: Faber.

Gunn, Thom (2000). *Boss Cupid*. London: Faber.

Hartman, Charles O. (1980). *Free Verse: An Essay in Prosody*. Princeton: Princeton University Press.

Heaney, Seamus (1998). *Opened Ground: Poems 1966–1996*. London: Faber.

Hill, Geoffrey (2006). *Without Title*. London: Penguin.

Holder, Alan (1995). *Rethinking Meter: A New Approach to the Verse Line*. Lewisburg: Bucknell University Press.

Hughes, Ted (1998). *Birthday Letters*. London: Faber.

Hughes, Ted (2007). *Letters of Ted Hughes* (ed. Christopher Reid). London: Faber.

Kirby-Smith, H.T. (1996). *The Origins of Free Verse*. Ann Arbor: University Michigan Press.

Langley, R.F. (2015). *Complete Poems* (ed. Jeremy Noel-Tod). Manchester: Carcanet.

Maxwell, Glyn (2002). *The Nerve*. London: Picador.

Olson, Charles (1997). ""Projective Verse" (1950)." In: *Collected Prose* (eds. Donald Allen and Benjamin Friedlander), 239–249. Berkeley: University California Press.

O'Sullivan, Maggie (ed.) (1996). *Out of Everywhere: Linguistically Innovative Poetry by Women in North America & the UK*. London: Reality Street.

Perloff, Marjorie (1998). "After Free Verse." In: *Close Listening: Poetry and the Performed Word* (ed. Charles Bernstein), 86–110. New York: Oxford University Press.

Plath, Sylvia (1979). "The Fifty-Ninth Bear". In: *Johnny Panic and the Bible of Dreams*, 2e, 94–105. London: Faber.

Prynne, J. H. (2015). *Poems*. Hexham: Bloodaxe.

Ramsey, Paul (1968). "Free Verse: Some Steps Toward Definition." *Studies in Philology* 45: 98–108.

Raworth, Tom (2003). *Collected Poems*. Manchester: Carcanet.

Riley, Denise (2000). *Selected Poems*. London: Reality Street.

2b.6
Satire

David Wheatley

The origins of postwar satire can be traced to the fallout from Modernism and the 1920s. Reviewing Hugh Walker's *English Satire and Satirists* in 1925, T. S. Eliot wrote: "there is no more difficult subject to treat in such a scheme than the subject of satire. For it has not – as has the drama, for instance – any definite technique" (Eliot 1925). Often, he finds, writers of great satire have not devoted themselves primarily to the genre. The greatest satirist of all, Jonathan Swift, did not establish his style in easily imitable ways, but reacted to convention (social and literary) in line with his inner turmoil, thus "fulfilling that destiny of his nature which slowly and inevitably led to madness." Eliot had experienced his share of turmoil during the composition of *The Waste Land*, and made efforts thereafter to purge the more unruly elements of his sensibility; by 1928 he was pronouncing himself "Classicist in literature, royalist in politics, and Anglo-Catholic in religion" (Eliot 1970, 1). Also during this period, he attempted and abandoned a satirical poem, *Coriolan*, completing only two short sections. A reader with much to say on Eliot's creative evolution during these years, Geoffrey Hill, comments on this dereliction several times in his critical prose. "To have abandoned *Coriolan* and to have completed [the Christian verse drama] *The Rock* instead is indicative of a savage defeat," he writes in "A Postscript to Modernist Poetics" (Hill 2008, 579). Shakespeare's *Coriolanus* was a favorite of Eliot's, and in his poem he sketches a figure who shares with its tragic hero an ambition for public office but also a fundamental unfitness for office. The passing parade of worldly glory is heavily deprecated before the final lines dismiss the unfortunate hero: "We demand a committee, a representative committee, a committee of investigation / RESIGN RESIGN RESIGN" (Eliot 1985, 143).

A Companion to Contemporary British and Irish Poetry, 1960–2015, First Edition.
Edited by Wolfgang Görtschacher and David Malcolm.
© 2021 John Wiley & Sons Ltd. Published 2021 by John Wiley & Sons Ltd.

As Hill suggests, *The Rock* is paltry fare by comparison, but Eliot's previous experiences with satire had not always gone smoothly. Introducing his *Oxford Book of Modern Verse* in 1936, W. B. Yeats dismissed Eliot as a shallow social commentator, "working without apparent imagination" and writing of "men and women that get out of bed or into it from mere habit" (Yeats 1936, xxi). If any grandeur attached to Eliot's pessimistic vision, Yeats was blind to it, in much the same way that he failed to find any merit in the lacerating satire of Wilfred Owen's war poetry. Where Eliot led, however, exchanging *The Waste Land* and *Coriolan* for *The Rock* and *Four Quartets*, British poetry followed, and between Eliot's satirical retreat and Auden's departure to the United States, the postwar period in British poetry was a less than golden age for the vigorous social engagement that makes for good satire. The advent of the Movement in the 1950s produced its share of middlebrow social comedy—Kingsley Amis's "Something Nasty in the Bookshop," Philip Larkin's "Fiction and the Reading Public," D. J. Enright's "Since Then"—but it was not until the radical social change of the 1960s that satire regained the prominence in British poetry it had enjoyed in the 1930s. In June 1965, the "First International Poetry Incarnation" was staged at the Albert Hall in London amid a climate of radical excitement, as captured in Michael Horovitz's 1969 anthology *Children of Albion: Poetry of the "Underground" in Britain*. In his satirical anthem "To Whom It May Concern," Adrian Mitchell puts the rhythms of popular song to hard-hitting use.

> Every time I shut my eyes all I see is flames.
> Made a marble phone book, carved all the names
> So coat my eyes with butter
> Fill my ears with silver
> Stick my legs in plaster
> Tell me lies about Vietnam.
>   (Horovitz 1969, 221, ll. 10–15)

The combination of musicality and menace is Audenesque, as is the poem's desire to maintain a certain level of whimsy in its descriptions of the horrors of Vietnam. Another 1960s anthology, Al Alvarez's *The New Poetry* (1962), had inveighed against the "gentility principle" of British verse, but here was a poetry determinedly internationalist in focus and recognizably of the Left. As an anthology piece, "To Whom It May Concern" speaks for mid-1960s optimism, confident of its ability to face down the horrors of contemporary politics. Yet not all contemporary satirists wrote with such confidence. One poet from Alvarez's anthology, the Australian Peter Porter, affected the voice of the malcontent in "John Marston Advises Anger," seeing in swinging London an orgy of *nouveau riche* vulgarity.

> It's a Condé Nast world and so Marston's was.
> His had a real gibbet – our death's out of sight.
> The same thin richness of these worlds remains –
> The flesh-packed jeans, the car-stung appetite
> Volley on his stage, the cage of discontent.
>   (Alvarez 1966, 168–169, ll. 28–32)

The Elizabethan satirist Marston was a misanthrope, for whom sexual license was an index of social decay. The contrast with Mitchell illustrates a basic division in satire, between optimists and pessimists, reformers and scourges of society. The abolition of the death penalty in the United Kingdom in 1965 might seem like a moment of social progress, but Porter's persona sees only the dissembling of an unaltered cruelty and violence. Social injustice and consumer capitalism remain the forces they always were, trapping us in our "cage of discontent."

Another aspect of the split I am proposing involves performance. Eight thousand people attended the Albert Hall reading of 1965, cementing the association between protest poetry and public performance, while Porter speaks in the voice of the disaffected highbrow, consoling himself among his cultural fragments but issuing no populist calls to arms. In another poem anthologized by Alvarez, "Annotations of Auschwitz," Porter taps the extremist subject matter familiar from the American confessional poets of the time. The Movement poets did not write about Auschwitz, and while Adrian Mitchell throws off British reserve with glee, Porter's approach is more problematic. Of a trip on the Underground, Porter's speaker observes: "[…] I am not a Jew, / But scratches web the ceiling of the train," (Alvarez 1966, 170–171; 170, III ll. 4–5) and passing a restaurant he imagines its display of roast chickens as a poultry holocaust: "This, say the chickens, is their Auschwitz, / And all poultry eaters are psychopaths" (Alvarez 1966, 170–171; 171, VII ll. 3–4). Reminders of the Holocaust on the London Tube could be a measure of the speaker's moral sensitivity or a satire on the excesses of confessionalism, if we see the speaker as appropriating the Holocaust with no supporting context (Plath's Holocaust poems "Daddy" and "Lady Lazarus" having already come in for this accusation). Equally, the closing image of the martyred chickens might imply indignation at the casual violence of the carnivore worldview, but this is hardly borne out by the rest of the poem. Rather, what Porter is doing is catching himself in the moment of finding esthetic opportunities in violent subject matter ("[…] Such death, says the painter, / Is worthwhile – it makes a colour never known," Alvarez 1966, 170–171; 171, VI ll. 3–4), and turning the indignation back on himself.

Another poet of the mid-1960s moment is Christopher Logue. He pioneered the poster poem, and sold over 10 000 copies of his poem "I Shall Vote Labour." Harold Wilson became Prime Minister in 1964 after 13 years of patrician Conservative rule, but rather than cheer-lead for the new political mood, Logue engaged in satire that was by turns louche ("I shall vote Labour because if I do not vote Labour / my balls will drop off") and darkly pessimistic ("I shall vote Labour because / deep in my heart / I am a Conservative," Logue 1996, 42–43, ll. 30–32). Logue wrote for *Private Eye*, the satirical magazine founded in 1961. Despite its attacks on the British political establishment, many of its writers were products of the British public school system, often lending its humor the quality of an upper-class in-joke. The mass media furnished Logue with abundant material, often involving sex, violence, and the clamorous voices of the socially marginalized. Mock tabloid headlines (prefiguring the work of Peter Reading) vainly attempt to hold all this chaos together:

> SPORTS-HERO SWALLOWS OIL SLICK
> FAMOUS IDIOT JOINS CABINET
> BIG RISE FOR SECRET POLICE
> FIJI VANISHES
> (Logue 1996, 95, ll. 37–40)

Like Porter, Logue maintains a dual focus: on the seediness of his material, but also on our reactions to it, which he manipulates with pantomimic gusto. The poet places himself in a symbiotic relationship with the spirit of the times, a strategy not without risks—his treatment of sexual violence, for instance, may strike contemporary readers as tritely sensationalist. There is something cartoonish in Logue's work, but this quality is also what distinguishes the versions of Homer he began to produce at the same time and which became his life's work. For all its transient subject matter, satire forms a bridge from the contemporary to the world of classical antiquity (here again, Logue shows affinities with Peter Reading).

Another aspect of modern poetic satire is the question of race and gender. Even at the height of the 1960s, the scale of unquestioned bias in British poetry was extreme: all 24 of the British writers featured in *The New Poetry* are white men. Where satire is concerned, Geoffrey Grigson's *The Oxford Book of Satirical Verse* (1986) features 14 poets born in the twentieth century, only two of whom are women (Phyllis McGinley and Stevie Smith). Faced with such conformity, the Montserratian E. A. Markham was driven to experiment with personae, publishing books as the fictional Antiguan poet Paul St Vincent and as white feminist Sally Goodman. Other writers simply fell by the wayside. The relaxed social mores of the 1960s induce much disapproval of sexually unembarrassed young women in Peter Porter's Marston, but a real-life sexually liberated female 1960s satirist, Rosemary Tonks, found herself written out of literary history for almost 40 years. Tonks published two collections, *Notes on Cafés and Bedrooms* (1963) and *Iliad of Broken Sentences* (1967), before suffering a mental breakdown in the 1970s, after which she blocked republication of her work. Her poems are potent satires of the seedy underbelly of 1960s London, but also function, with their French symbolist quality, as ripostes to the Anglo-Saxon lyric mode.

> O she who would paper her lamp with my wings!
> That hour when all the Earth is drinking the
> Blue drop of thunder; and in
> Dark debris as of a magician's room, my beast
> A scented breathing
> To the East.
> ("Running Away," Tonks 2014,
> 42, ll. 54–59)

As the 1960s ended, British poetry entered a transitional phase. The radical Eric Mottram became editor of *Poetry Review*, triggering infighting at the Poetry Society with his enthusiasm for Black Mountain poetry and its English counterparts. As recorded in Peter Barry's study *Poetry Wars*, the atmosphere was bleak and divisive (Barry 2006). One poet at least, Roy Fisher, put this *Kulturkampf* to satirical use in poems such as "On the Neglect of Figure Composition." Fisher paints a conflict between "Zoggists," devoted to "His Late / Majesty King Zog of Albania," and "Iannists," whose spiritual leader is revealed as a polytechnic lecturer in the Midlands (Fisher 2005, 148). The poem follows the warped logic of a *Monty Python* sketch while making a serious point about the perceived opacity of poetry in a mass culture losing all connection with that art form. Poetry and its audience are recurring themes in Fisher, as in "Paraphrases," in which the poet is pestered by the inane requests of a student writing a thesis on him. Movement populism invested heavily in poetry as the province of the common reader rather than the academic specialist, but Fisher depicts the ways in which the poem has become an object of generalized commodification and administration. In his later poem "The Poetry Promise" (2000), Fisher speaks the language of consumer guarantees ("Equalising Opportunities," "Developing Access," "Observing Guidelines")—terminology that has become the norm in the academy and arts administration, but which we normally see as inimical to the language of poetry. Fisher's vocabulary makes a satirical point about the place of poetry in our culture, and its ability to confront directly the language of administration; it is also very funny.

The major British verse satirist of the late twentieth century is arguably Peter Reading, who emerged in the 1970s, and whose work exploits and embodies a host of contradictions. Among the angriest of political poets, he is simultaneously a radical quietist, never happier than when bird-watching or meditating on Propertius or Li Po. Despite his political indignation, he is conspicuously short of any interest in causality, preferring to reduce his opponents to caricatures and indulge in scatological humor and crass anathemas. He is the subject of an admiring chapter in Tom Paulin's *Minotaur: Poetry and the Nation State* (Paulin 1992, 285–294), which attempts to recruit him to Paulin's postcolonial radicalism, but Reading's true political colors may be closer to Tory anarchism. Reading appears to share with Winston Churchill the belief that democracy is the worst kind of government, except for all the others: sequences such as *5x5x5x5x5* give voice to a Hogarthian gallery of rogues, eccentrics, and grotesques, leading only to confusion and anarchy, but unable to impose any controlling voice of sanity. Like many other satirists, Reading sometimes finds it expedient to use a persona version of himself in his poems, though when "Peter Reading" intervenes Pirandello-like in the world of *5x5x5x5x5* (killing off one of its characters), the maneuver is more laughable than cruel. The use of "Peter Reading" allows for a satirical heightening of his *saeva indignatio* but also, as in "Fiction," for postmodernist games with authenticity and narration, though Reading is a sterner moralist than the epithet "postmodernist" normally allows. More so than any of the other writers considered so far, however, Reading is a satirist in everything he writes. His Tory anarchism finds expression in his forms too: Reading makes frequent use of classical syllabic meters but delights in wild collages too, interleaving his work with mocked-up classified documents from nuclear power plants, humorous headlines from tabloid newspapers, and other comic effects, such as deliberately broken and faded type. The collection *Ob.* (1999) is a good example of late-period Reading, featuring a death mask of the poet on its cover and using the Reading persona to drive its multipurpose defeatism. In a period when many poets have taken refuge in the academy, Reading (describing a disastrous attempt to do likewise) finds rich pickings in the world of institutional creative writing.

> Possibly I may find time to peruse your
> puerile outpourings
> (I don't remember your name);
> more likely, though, I shall not.
> (Reading 2003, 57, ll. 1–4)

I began by noting Geoffrey Hill's disapproval of T. S. Eliot's abandoning of his satirical poem *Coriolan*. The satirical element has never been lacking in Hill's work, but the late period inaugurated by *Canaan* (1996) has been particularly rich in stinging social commentary. Its poems were composed in the dying days of John Major's administration, with its high-profile scandals and sleaze. Memory forms an important site of resistance in Hill's work to cultural amnesia in a nation "with so many memorials but no memory," as Hill put it in another work of the 1990s, *The Triumph of Love* (Hill 1998, 40). His response to a parliamentary cash-for-questions scandal sends Hill back to the age of Marvell and Milton, not in a spirit of uncritical nostalgia, but the better to hold the present to historical account. Contemporary narratives of tradition may be no better than fig-leaves for plutocratic banditry; "To the High Court of Parliament" compares self-serving politicians to feasting rats ("[...] the slither-frisk / to lordship of a kind / as rats to a bird-table," Hill 1996, ll. 1, 2–4). Addressing England directly in the poem's final stanzas, Hill references the scandal in which Dame Shirley Porter, then Conservative leader of Westminster City Council, sold cemeteries and other land in Central London to property developers for 85 pence. England is now "of genius / the eidolon:"

> privatize to the dead
> her memory:
>   let her wounds weep
> into the lens of oblivion.
> (Hill 1996, 1, ll. 9–12)

Hill's Conservatives are not interested in conserving anything, only in profiteering and in the evisceration of history. An "eidolon" is an apparition or double, and in offering himself as a conscience of the nation, Hill is aware that he may be speaking for a double of contemporary Britain, one whose existence has dwindled to a wraith.

"Eidolon" is not a word we would expect to find in a poem by Adrian Mitchell, and the scholarly dimension of Hill's work has proved a stumbling block to some readers, who see in it only obscurantism and reactionary politics (cf. Paulin 1992). The satirists considered in this chapter have fashioned their work from variously high- and low-cultural material, and Hill is no exception; the life of his satire is in the interplay between these extremes. While the rhetoric in *Canaan* might seem "a bit 'high'," in the words of *Mercian Hymns* (Hill 2006, 69), its political indignation is deep-felt and radical. The cover of *Speech! Speech!* (1999) shows a Daumier print of a grinning music-hall audience, and this volume and *The Triumph of Love* (1998) make extensive use of heckling as a satiric device. In his mimicry of comedians such as Ken Dodd and Frankie Howerd, Hill demonstrates the dialogic aspect of his writing, setting himself up for repeated comic pratfalls. It would be misguided, however, to argue that a few deflationary remarks in square brackets are enough to convert Hill's poems into sites of polyphonic freedom. The anger of *The Triumph of Love* has a muttering, paranoid quality reminiscent of Browning's "Soliloquy of the Spanish Cloister": could the "speaker" and the "editor" be aspects of the same, tortured voice? The original title of Eliot's *The Waste Land* was *He Do the Police in Different Voices*, a reference to a Dickens character with a gift for mimicry; the central character in the poem, Tiresias, is described as "uniting all the rest" (Eliot 1985, 82), but suffers persecution from the gods for his omniscience. When Hill's satirical voice appears to claim prophetic authority, it does so in full and painful knowledge of how ridiculous it must appear to the objects of its heckling. There is menace in the crowd's reaction too. The epigraph to *The Triumph of Love* is from Nehemiah, and finds the prophet angrily rejecting the crowd ("And I sent messengers unto them, saying, I am doing a great worke, so that I can not come down," Hill 1998). If he is distrustful, it is for a good reason: his enemies are plotting to kill him.

As Oxford Professor of Poetry, Hill took satirical pot-shots at the Poet Laureate, Carol Ann Duffy, whose concept of satire differs substantially from his. Duffy's work has verged on satire in collections such as *The World's Wife*, in which she rewrites fairy tales with a feminist twist, but Hill finds in her poetry an insufficiently critical relationship to language. Who would not wish that plain English alone, as employed by Duffy, was sufficient to meet the complexities of the contemporary world? Hill, though, has grave doubts that this is the case, and disputes her claims to work in plain English: "this is not democratic English but cast-off bits of oligarchical commodity English" (Flood 2012). For a contemporary satirist, the available linguistic registers far exceed Duffy's plain English and Hill's more recondite vocabulary.

Much contemporary English floats on a sea of mindless advertising, spam email, and tabloid journalism, and a poetic satire which did not harness this opportunity would be failing in its duty. One younger poet who has addressed this condition is Sam Riviere, whose work cultivates a glittering and affectless surface, seemingly at odds with any emotional engagement. In *81 Austerities* (2012), Riviere applies the language of advertising to poetry, in lyrics saturated in literary in-jokes and careerist self-consciousness. Thus, "Crisis Poem" begins:

> In 3 years I have been "awarded"
> £48,000 by various funding bodies
> councils and publishing houses
> for my contributions to the art
> (Riviere 2012, 3, ll. 1–4)

For young poets today, a self-promoting online presence has become professionally *de rigueur*, but Riviere's language would normally be reserved for a grant application or a CV, not the poem itself. Is the poem hoping to trade its show of credentials for increased readerly respect? The slippage between speaker and author was lost on one reviewer, who took Riviere's poems entirely at face value: "Some will love it, others may call it superficial and repetitive, or say he's using social networking to push his poetry" (Padel 2012). The feedback loop of postmodern irony extends to include our responses to the poem, which will always run the risk of being an extension of the joke. In enjoying poems about this phenomenon are we achieving satirical distance from, or merely perpetuating modern narcissism by other means? *81 Austerities* ends with a set of notes on its poems, passing lightly ironized judgment on its themes of atrocity and pornography ("not sure how this works – I imagine it is arbitrary," Riviere 2012, 111), but indicating no way out. Riviere's second collection, *Kim Kardashian's Marriage* (2015), is no less anaerobic in its poker-faced dissection of celebrity culture.

Satire thrives on ambiguous perspectives and mixed messages, ingratiating itself with its readers one moment and sinking its fangs into them the next. I began with the suggestion that contemporary satire was born in the fallout from Modernism, but in one major contemporary poet at least, Tom Raworth, the modernist tradition has reconnected vigorously with a vein of broad satiric humor. "80 percent prefer chips to poetry," he announces in his one-line poem "Chips" (Raworth 2010, 72). The general reader remains indifferent to poetry at large, modernist or otherwise, but where lies the art's salvation? Rather than nurse his wounded pride, Raworth writes carefree formal poems satirizing formal poems ("I could go on like this all day / Ti-tum ti-tum and doodly-ay"), and, in "Listen Up," a doggerel satire on the theme of war.

> God's on our side, he's white and Yankee
> he'd drop the bombs, he'd drink a tank: we
> know he's stronger than their Allah
> as is our righteousness and valor!
> We'll clip Mohammed's ears and pecker
> And then move on to napalm Mecca.
> (Raworth 2010, 46, ll. 25–30)

This is best described as a fine poem doing an excellent job of pretending to be a terrible poem. With its swipes at Western imperialism, its politics are hard-hitting, but it lands its punches with no less force on the self-deluding satire that fancies rhyming couplets are any defense against a line of tanks. Finally, in its humorous openness to being entirely misconstrued (he said what about Arabs?), the poem fulfills the first and most enduring duty of satire—to jab a challenging forefinger squarely in the chests of its readers, leaving us by turns arraigned, disoriented, and amused, or quite possibly all three at once.

References

Alvarez, A. (ed.) (1966). *The New Poetry*. Revised edition. London: Penguin.

Barry, Peter (2006). *Poetry Wars: British Poetry of the 1970s and the Battle of Earls Court*. Cambridge: Salt Publishing.

Eliot, T. S. (1970). *For Lancelot Andrews*. London: Faber and Faber.

Eliot, T. S. (1985). *Collected Poems 1909–1962*. London: Faber and Faber.

Eliot, T. S. (1925). Review of Hugh Walker, *English Satire and Satirists*, "Then and Now, 1925." *Times Literary Supplement* (10 December), 854.

Fisher, Roy (2005). *The Long and the Short of It: Poems 1995–2005*. Tarset: Bloodaxe.

Flood, Alison (2012). "Carol Ann Duffy is 'Wrong' about Poetry, Says Geoffrey Hill." *The Guardian* (31 January). https://www.theguardian.com/books/2012/jan/31/carol-ann-duffy-oxford-professory-poetry (accessed 24 August 2019).

Hill, Geoffrey (1996). *Canaan*. London: Penguin.

Hill, Geoffrey (1998). *The Triumph of Love*. Boston: Houghton Mifflin.

Hill, Geoffrey (2006). *Selected Poems*. London: Penguin.

Hill, Geoffrey (2008). *Collected Critical Writings*. Oxford: Oxford University Press.

Horovitz, Michael (ed.) (1969). *Children of Albion: Poetry of the "Underground" in Britain*. London: Penguin.

Logue, Christopher (1996). *Selected Poems*. London: Faber and Faber.

Padel, Ruth (2012). Review of Sam Riviere, *81 Austerities*. *The Guardian* (3 August). https://www.theguardian.com/books/2012/aug/03/81-austerities-sam-riviere-review (accessed 24 August 2019).

Paulin, Tom (1992). *Minotaur: Poetry and the Nation State*. London: Faber and Faber.

Raworth, Tom (2010). *Windmills in Flame: Old and New Poems*. Manchester: Carcanet.

Reading, Peter (2003). *Collected Poems, 3: Poems 1997–2003*. Tarset: Bloodaxe.

Riviere, Sam (2012). *81 Austerities*. London: Faber and Faber.

Tonks, Rosemary (2014). *Bedouin of the London Evening: Collected Poems & Selected Prose*. Tarset: Bloodaxe.

Yeats, W. B. (ed.) (1936). *The Oxford Book of Modern Verse 1892–1935*. Oxford: Clarendon Press.

2b.7
The Traditional Short Lyric Poem in Britain and Ireland, 1960–2015

Tim Liardet and Jennifer Militello

It was either during a radio interview or one of his public readings that Seamus Heaney—one of the greatest of all stimulators of poetic discourse—said something along the lines of truthfulness in lyric poetry becoming recognizable as a "ring of truth" within the medium itself. Keats would nod in approval. So would Shelley. So would Emily Dickinson. And perhaps this "ring of truth" is the criterion of exactly what a lyric poem *is*. Some linguistic organism that is kept helplessly, inevitably *true*. In possession of this particular arcane quality: the burning core of the real.

Any attempt to provide a detailed history of the short lyric would automatically lead to dilution and the merest scratching of a deceptive thin ice. When attempting something as slippery as locating the landmarks of the lyric poem in Britain and Ireland between 1960 and 2010, the priority seems to be the consideration of poets during these years who in some dramatic sense *fed* the lyric form. Who in some sense nurtured, even *updated* it, edged it toward evolution, brought the poetic dialogue happening between writers of the lyric to a landing on a continent it had never formerly seen. Who in some sense augmented the form and made it sing or speak in a new and unignorable way. If a form is not made new in this way, made to speak to the age in which it is expected to survive, it will perish and fall into desuetude. The lyric's once thriving, though tiny, metropolis might become its own Gunkanjima, ruined by neglect. Part of a poet's responsibility, arguably again, might be to protect such forms, as a necessary territory or habitat, to encourage them to adapt and to retain a sense of vital relevance.

A Companion to Contemporary British and Irish Poetry, 1960–2015, First Edition.
Edited by Wolfgang Görtschacher and David Malcolm.
© 2021 John Wiley & Sons Ltd. Published 2021 by John Wiley & Sons Ltd.

The safest definition of the traditional lyric is a poem that is supposedly susceptible of being sung; it could be set to the accompaniment of a musical instrument. It is also a poem that expresses intense personal emotion. The lyric abandons the narrative or allows the narrative to be constructed through the language, rather than vice versa. If narrative poetry story-tells, the lyric *sings*. The sonnet is the acme of the tradition, the most compressed and complex form existing in the English language, the form that has cramped, and then created space for, the artistic elbows of poets for many centuries; that continues to force even the most accomplished neophytes to suffer the indignities of disfigured diction, to speak like a faux Keats. Catullus and Horace, to put it another way, are still posing dilemmas for contemporary poets. When the lyric is attempted, in whatever form, some sort of epistemological line falls into place, which links the contemporary poet with Petrarch, Shakespeare, Spenser, Milton, Burns, Blake, Wordsworth, Keats, Shelley, Hugo, Goethe, and Dickinson. Each of these poets had to figure out, or perhaps reinvent, exactly what needed to be done with the lyric tradition. The best of them—Dickinson—transformed it forever. The least of them fed it scraps. At its best, the lyric poem is about torque and held power. About compression. It is language placed under pressure by urgency. It has the emotional landscape at its center. The great lyric poem is direct. It slices through the hide of linguistic flatness to the oxygenated muscle of the heart.

Born an American, a former student of Lowell, and categorized as a Confessional poet, Sylvia Plath entered the British lyric tradition on a slight skew. She published her first collection *The Colossus and Other Poems* in 1960, and her further collections appeared posthumously in 1965, 1968, 1971, 1981, and 1985. Plath belongs, among other things, to the school of word choice bred by Dickinson and Hopkins and marked by the understanding that stirring rich language into the pot substantially sweetens the broth. The lyric was also the perfect lair for constructing an obsessive mythology of self. But what she contributed possibly more than any other poet to the lyric tradition is the exploded lyric. "Daddy," "Lady Lazarus," and "Morning Song" are examples of this. The first of these poems contains 16 unrhymed cinquains, the second almost 30 unrhymed tercets, and the third 6 unrhymed tercets. In all three, each stanza is a lyric poem in its own right, full of a kind of gravid energy. Each poem is its own tower, built of these blocks. This lyric quality—an explosion in infinite slow motion—the way in which images and clauses get larger, are magnified—is undoubtedly Plath's greatest contribution to the history of the lyric. In the title poem from *Ariel*, she evoked the "substanceless blue" which was her chosen place,

> Stasis in darkness.
> Then the substanceless blue
> Pour of tor and distances
>
> [...]
> And I
> Am the arrow,
>
> The dew that flies
> Suicidal, at one with the drive
> Into the red
>
> Eye, the cauldron of morning.
> (Plath 1966, 36–37, ll. 1–3, 26–31)

In Plath's hands, the short lyric was amplified, moving away from a still center in order to expand upon and enlarge the burn of her inventive ring of truth.

In the poems of Ted Hughes, on the other hand, it became thigh-length waders, patches on a coat. It became a kind of shamanistic condescension. Though on balance he may be regarded as having always been too busy constructing the grand narrative of his own epic universe, often, especially in his later work procuring a leggy, even shambolic, species of free verse, he was nonetheless, at times, a fine practitioner of powerfully original lyric poems, especially in his earlier years. Here he is writing in *Lupercal,* in a poem entitled "The Good Life," right at the beginning of our period, in 1960:

> Nothing of profit to be got
> So poor-bare to wind and to rain,
> His spirit gone to patch his boot,
> The hermit returned to the world again.
> (Hughes 1960, 36, ll. 1–4)

Though pedestrian compared with Plath's imagistic force, Hughes has compressed an unwieldy energy into 16 lines; as if, at first reading, there were insufficient room for such unwieldiness to breathe. Hughes shed his formal corsetry as he got older, when his poetry vanished into litany and the search for the active verb. But either side of 1960, it could be argued, he still clutched his formal reins to write lyrics like this. Characteristic of Hughes, however, is the way in which this almost-sonnet, whose volta sets off with the ninth line, sabotages the traditional lyric while simultaneously reinvigorating it. "The Good Life" shuns any Keatsian idea of beauty, preferring the clearly deliberate grammatical ugliness of the opening line, moving closer and closer to the folk-song rhythms espoused by Robert Graves. It is the Hughesian lyric *par excellence,* big-boned and linguistically bloody, shouldering its way into view in its essentially pre-Feminist understanding. When its West Yorkshire vowels mulch with soft Massachusetts inflection, it reads almost like a parody of the lyric quatrain.

In the hands of Philip Larkin—his ungainly left always at war with his gainly right—the short lyric became the hot potato subsequent poets would either catch or fumble. And many *would* fumble it. He was the lyric master with whom whole generations of poets had to make their peace. Larkin published *The Whitsun Weddings* four years into our period. "The Importance of Elsewhere," "As Bad as a Mile," "A Study of Reading Habits," "Nothing to be Said," "First Sight," "Ignorance," to name but a few, show all he had learned from Yeats about the short lyric. In *The North Ship,* published in 1945, Yeats, it felt, had all but shouldered Larkin out of sight. By 1964, however, Larkin had incorporated his Yeatsian echolalia and was sounding strongly like himself, setting off the train of lyric influence that many subsequent poets would flourish upon or fall foul of. Between 1964 and 1974, Larkin was systematically turning himself into the evil/kindly stepfather of the English lyric tradition. The shabby postwar Englishman spoke in a shabby postwar way. By 1974, and the publication of *High Windows*, he had developed the short lyric to such an extent that it could comfortably accommodate the nihils of his own existence and distil the gimmick of a theatrical misanthropy.

His development of the quatrain waded deep into twentieth century, downbeat phonetics, and it is fitting that the uncharacteristically loosest version of this form is used to effect the conclusion of this masterly book, its devastating vision of a godless, deserted universe:

> [...] And immediately

Rather than words comes the thought of high windows:

> The sun-comprehending glass,
> And beyond it, the deep blue air, that shows
> Nothing, and is nowhere, and is endless.
> (Larkin 1974, 16, ll. 16–20)

In the hands of Medbh McGuckian, the short lyric became as much a political as an esthetic vehicle of expression. She received the lyric tradition, by inventing her own lyric; she received it and rotated it and deepened it in the vortex of her own sexual politics and awareness of the constrictions of gender. Her first collection—*The Flower Master*—was published half way into our period, in 1982. She consistently showed herself to be one of the most original lyric poets to have emerged during these 50 years. It is generally considered that her work is enigmatic, an enigma cultivated by a mysterious syntax which belongs wholly to her: "I gaze into the sealed eyes of my mother / Seen, not visited, not forgotten" (McGuckian 1982, 36, ll. 7–8), she writes in "She Wears the Sky." This poem, like so much of her work, is like a wavering of sunlight cast into shadowed water, suggestive of sunken shapes, bicycles, or ships, but never quite elucidating the bottom of the pond. By 1984, in *Venus and the Rain*, her lyrics had become compellingly suggestive in their use of metaphor, far-reaching in implication. "From the Dressing-Room" is a first-rate example of what McGuckian does with the short lyric, often "American" in its line-breaking, rich in tone, and never far from its own Feminist source. It is sonnet-like, but not a sonnet. It is controlled and tight, but also loose:

> Oh there
> Are moments when you think you can
> Give notice in a jolly, wifely tone,
> Tossing off a very last and sunsettey
> Letter of farewell, with strict injunctions
> To be careful to procure his own lodgings,
> That my good little room is lockable,
> But shivery, I recover at the mere
> Sight of him propping up my pillow.
> (McGuckian 1984, 26, ll. 17–25)

The range of this poem is remarkable. It moves by degrees between the confessional and the postcolonial, the intensely personal to the arc where it bisects a wider history. "From the Dressing Room," like so many of McGuckian's poems, uses the lyric to push language to its limits, always expecting more of it. The use of "staving in" (l. 2), "springless" (l. 15), and "sunsettey" (l. 20) are characteristic McGuckian tropes. The rich opulent language is inseparable from the poem's overall intent, as it allows McGuckian's particularly imagistic construction of each moment to resonate beneath the surface of what is actually said. As is the case with Hughes's poems, the larger political landscape has been shrunk to fit and become situational. The effect of that is a lyric bursting with emotion but spoken in quietude. In terms of linguistic precision, the poem is reminiscent of a Vermeer interior. The volta "I can take anything now…" (l. 13) sets the two quasi-sonnet halves against one each other, like millstones softly grinding her phonetics into meaning.

The short lyric reached its highest point in Britain and Ireland during this period in the hands of Seamus Heaney. The publication of *The Haw Lantern,* in 1987, was its high-water mark. This collection saw his own lyric gift at its very peak. It appeared three years after *Station Island*, an overplump collection weighed down by the deadening effects of political obligation. *The Haw Lantern* returned Heaney to what he was best at: the pellucid short lyric. It reminded us Heaney was the most *physical* of poets who lived in a physicalist universe. The tactility of his sensual world-view arose from every word he wrote in this book: "Scuts of froth swirled from the discharge pipe" ("The Milk Factory," 33, l. 1); "When the inner palm of water found my palm" ("A Postcard from Iceland," 37, l. 9); "I had a vision … Of turned-up faces where the tree had stood" ("The Wishing Tree," 36, ll. 7-9). The culmination of this is the sonnet sequence *Clearances*, which is the book's center of gravity.

In the book's title poem, almost everything that was said in *Station Island* is distilled into no more than 150 words of "The Haw Lantern":

> […]
> and you flinch before its bonded pith and stone,
> its blood-prick that you wish would test and clear you,
> its pecked-at ripeness that scans you, then moves on.
> (Heaney 1987, 7, ll. 12–14)

The breath-to-Diogenes metaphor is masterly, the lantern the very thing that Diogenes carried in broad daylight, looking for an honest man. The poem is set in Diogenes's large ceramic jar, in which the old philosopher slept. As Heaney sonnets go, it is even looser than usual, thereby deliberately signaling its refusal to be a sonnet Petrarch might recognize. True, it does have a quintet and an octave of sorts, but its "pentameter" is lackadaisical and only intermittently iambic. There is not one example of pure rhyme. The poem is its own slightly scruffy miracle and shuns the chance to incarnate the form to which it implicitly alludes, and fails, therefore, in and of itself, to live up to Diogenes's test, who judged always what was done in action rather than in theory. The Anglo-Saxon monosyllables are like ripe fruit. Could this be one of the greatest lyric poems Heaney wrote? It carries all the Heaney hallmarks, the prolonged vowels, the deft and subtle intermingling of clauses framed in the familiar gentleness of tone.

The lyric needed to meet with a language more demotic, more streetwise, less "poetic," and to catch up with the wider implications of British class. This kind of new synthesis was achieved by Don Paterson. In his hands, the short lyric was put to work stirring, and blowing upon, his own dialectical soup. With the publication of his first collection, *Nil Nil,* in 1993, he rose rapidly to the forefront of British poetry. From the outset, his work was characterized by a formal probity adjusted to facilitate a heady mix of intellectually sophisticated language and a self-consciously rougher colloquy. He moved, in his early work, between streetwise knowing what's-what to the working class boy who got education and wanted to let the world know he had. His principal vehicle was the sonnet, brought alive by a post-Rimbaudian sensibility and vocabulary which fizzes. A particularly good example of this is "Obeah":

> My life became one long apostrophe—
> muttering the three ur-syllables of her name,
> doodling her initials to a cryptogram.
> Chain-smoking and the 'slavery of tea and coffee'
> left me light enough to forge her succubus
> tooth by tooth, the tiny hands and feet,
> the calves like folded wings...On one such night
> I got up and hit out west, passing her house;
>
> bumped up on the kerb, cars sat in line
> like after-hour drinkers elbowed at the bar,
> hushed as the stranger walks in off the moor—
> their premonitory stare, blank as a mirror.
> I saw the dawn scried in each polished screen,
> The gibbeted mascots as I drew in closer.
> (Paterson 1993, 12, ll. 1–14)

In 2006, Paterson breathed new life into Rilke's *Die Sonette an Orpheus*, translating into his own versions the 55 sonnets that comprised the sequence. It was a *tour de force*, part faithful to the original, part adding new contemporary pizzazz. His greatest achievement was to remind us that the sonnet, in particular, continued to have a primary role in the development of the lyric.

If Paterson bedded the lyric poem down in the world, it still needed new blood, new exceptional talent to foster it. It needed experimentation. It needed to adjust to the forces of the shifting milieus that would shape it. In the hands of Glyn Maxwell it acquired a wholly new sound and a sense that it was brought into the world without forceps. Maxwell's lyric signature became the use of big bold rhymes and half rhymes, simultaneously submerged and softened by the subtlest forms of enjambment. There is always a sense when reading a Maxwell lyric poem that you have never quite heard its very particular music before and that, despite its often complex structure, the poem arrived in the world with a certain consummate ease. Rhyme is used as a metaphor for thought, the way it loops and progresses, as it did *The Breakage*, published in 1998, when considering the Arctic explorer, in "Edward Wilson":

> A dream of English watercolourists
> all spreads out on the hills: the sky is blue.
> No breeze, nothing creative, not the least
> exploratory dab. Then the same view
>
> clouds and differs [...]
> (Maxwell 1998, 33, ll. 1–5)

In Kathleen Jamie's poems, the short lyric line was stripped of all adornment. The sonnet got skinny, got spare, dressed down, plain even, shedding adjectives as quickly as it shed its rhyme schemes. This was the lyric poem on crash diet, trying to adjust itself to the equally spare realities of the Scottish landscape. In "Swallows," published in *The Tree House* in 2004, it is the birds themselves which supply what a rhyme scheme withholds:

> I wish my whole battened
> heart were a property
> like this, with swallows
> in every room—so at ease
>
> they twitter and preen
> from the picture frames
> like an audience in the gods
> before an opera
>
> and in the mornings
> wheel above my bed
> in a mockery of pity
> before winging it
>
> up the stairwell
> to stream into light.
> (Jamie 2004, 18, ll. 1–14)

In the hands of Gwyneth Lewis, a student of Joseph Brodsky, the lyric impulse found its vaudeville; it was given improvisation, wit, and turned into the right sort of lean burn engine that could power a whole book. Her *Parables and Faxes,* published in 1995, was another high water mark of the British lyric. The book was a lyric tap dance, a juggle, a high-wire act of formal dexterity. The dust was blown off the oldest and most recalcitrant of lyric forms. In the ensuing 75 odd pages, the heroic couplet, sonnet, quatrain, villanelle, and terza rima made their appearances like characters in her formal dramatis personae. Lyric forms were tamed, used for ventriloquy. Rhyme was revitalized and reinvented, driving the poems from page to page. Almost every line in the book sings to another line, never so effectively as in "A Soviet Waiter":

> Convenience is my currency,
> discomfort my stock-in-trade.
> When grown men start to beg for food
> I know I've got it made.
>
> (Lewis 1995, 28, ll. 13–16)

Larkin's hot potato was thrown from poet to poet, botched and mishandled, dropped, picked up bruised. So was Plath's steaming, dented thurible. Between 1960 and 2010, the lyric was fostered and loved, abused, changed forever, honored, and obeyed. Thom Gunn upheld, and chiseled at, its oldest traditions. It would be impossible to look at this period without mentioning his exemplary *oeuvre* of lyric poems. Powerfully influenced by Shakespeare, coexisting with Hughes, and shadowing his vision of a violent universe with his own sort of urban violence, he extended the limits of the lyric, made it new and vibrant; his attempts at free verse, however, finally threw into sharp relief what might have been a chronic dependence on rhyme. Indeed, the lyric tradition needed its esthetic caretakers, which it did, it found them in Elizabeth Jennings and Ruth Pitter. Jennings developed a lyric line that found its source in Donne, perhaps, and spoke in many registers. Ruth Pitter continued to write highly traditional lyric poems, which could have been written a hundred, possibly two hundred, three hundred years earlier. In tone, tempo, and subject matter, they seemed to belong to another, less anguished, less secular age.

Michael Longley rivaled Heaney during this period, writing crystalline lyric poems, which seemed to get shorter and shorter and become more gem-like the shorter they became. Paul Muldoon, by midway through our period, had told us all about his Irish childhood, distilled into perhaps the most original and freest of lyrics, glued by the most inventive species of assonance yet invented by a poet, most notably, perhaps, in *Mules, Why Brownlee Left*, and *The Annals of Chile*. In *Night Photograph*, in 1993, Lavinia Greenlaw developed her own version of the short lyric line in poems like "Beyond Gravity." In *Rembrandt Would Have Loved You*, in 1998, Ruth Padel wrote "Icicles Round a Tree in Dumfriesshire." This extended and highly celebrated poem was remarkable for its 10 asymmetrical stanzas, each of which was its own lyric poem of immense intensity, and the poem itself an exploded lyric:

> A suspended gleam-on-the-edge,
> As if sky might tear any minute. Or not for ever for long. Those icicles
> Won't be surprise any more. The little snapped threads
> Blew away. Glamour left that hill in Dumfries.
> The sculptor went off with his black equipment.
> Adzes, twine, leather gloves.
>
> (Padel 1998, 2, ll. 71–76)

Peter Porter, the Australian poet who had lived in England since 1951, and published here between 1961 and 2010, heard homophony like no one else has before or since and elevated it into a phonic unity, creating a new language of which rhyme was a natural characteristic, placed at the service of his lyric forms. One of his principal achievements was to resuscitate rhyme—to make it not merely a way of structuring a poem's esthetic space, within which each word softly finds its mate without disfiguring the diction, but a means of expanding the rhyme lexicon itself. The structural and ornamental devices of verbal configuration in his finest lyric poems are brought into play in the least obtrusive way possible and a good example of this would be "Late Lines" from *Max is Missing*, 2001, winner of the Forward Prize for Best Collection:

> Miscellanies as far afield as Tottel
> Asserting death's the answer to life's quiz
> And Philip Larkin with the second bottle
> Pouring, saying, 'This is all there is'—
> (Porter 2001, 9, ll. 1–4)

There were highly significant lyrics written during this period in Ireland by Vona Groarke, Maurice Riordan, Ciaran Carson, Tom Paulin, Sinéad Morrissey, Katie Donovan, and Tom French; in England, Scotland, and Wales by David Harsent, Sean O'Brien, Alan Jenkins, Hugo Williams, Pascale Petit, Robin Robertson, John Burnside, Robert Crawford, Paul Farley, Deryn Rees-Jones, John Fuller, Simon Armitage, Sarah Maguire, Vicki Feaver, Carol Ann Duffy, Michael Symmons Roberts, and Charles Tomlinson, to name but a few very important names. Of all these poets, Geoffrey Hill arguably did most for the evolution of the short traditional lyric. Indeed, he did with it what only he could do: first he honored it by writing poems that were as technically flawless as those written by Donne and Marvell. Then, he developed it, then he reconstructed, then revolutionized it. In *Mercian Hymns*, in 1971—which some argue was his pinnacle of poetic achievement—his lyric excellence finally struck its counterpoints in prose, and he invented a new kind of lyric, the lyric prose-poem, no better epitomized than in "XI":

> The strange church smelled a bit 'high', of censers
>   and polish. The strange curate was just as ap-
>   propriate: he took off into the marriage-service.
> No one cared to challenge that gambit
>   (Hill 1971, no page numbers
>   in this volume, ll. 1–4)

In the latter years of this period, in the poems of a wide range of richly gifted young poets the lyric found dynamic release: it was fed into a crucible of new and eclectic possibility. Notable among these poets were Andrew McMillan, Emily Berry and Sarah Howe. McMillan's 2015 collection *Physical*, a study of male friendship and homoerotic love, was hugely influential in its raw but exquisitely-built lyrics, nodding to the tutelage of Thom Gunn. Also in 2015, Sarah Howe's *Loop of Jade*, combining a scholarly inscrutability with incisive language and imagery informed by her dual Anglo-Chinese heritage, in the opinion of many reviewers, redefined the modern lyric. In "Crossing from Guangdong," the second poem from this collection, Howe showed how her version of the lyric was mysterious, if not abstruse, though always rendered with exactitude: "[…] I watch the sun come up / through tinted plexiglass. I try to sleep / but my eyes snag on every flitting, tubular tree, / their sword-like leaves […]" (Howe 2015, 10, ll. 17-20)

The experimental euphonies of a highly energised new wave of black and minority ethnic poets, writing against systemic exclusion, in the five years before 2015, was gathering force. Their versions of the lyric were utterly distinctive, brilliant, often allegorical. Notable among these poets were Kei Miller, Raymond Antrobus, Vahni Capildeo, Jay Bernard, Malika Booker, and Kayo Chingyoni, to name but a few. In a thrilling update of the lyric line, in 2013, in "Status," from his collection *Shapes & Disfigurements of Raymond Antrobus*, Antrobus mixed grief, memory and the protocols of social media with a new electrified colloquy:

> Maybe you change your profile picture,
> upload one of you in your dad's arms as a white cotton baby,
> where his face is a bright heart
>   smiling into your black newborn eyes.
>   (Antrobus 2013, 16, ll. 4–8)

Where will the lyric of Britain and Ireland go from here? One might imagine it spinning in a universe of its own making, reinventing an array of experiences and emotions through language and breath. Its musical, emotional dialogue has been enriched and changed; the way that the tradition has been individually understood has defined what the lyric became and literary history, as we know, has a way of elongating its own game of Chinese whispers. The lyric has been raveled and unraveled, stitched and sewn, molded, melted, gold-plated, bronzed, and what is to come will be woven of the past scraps of what has been done. However, its shape might be remade and resung, it is very much alive and will continue to invigorate our language, will speak truths made of water, of wind, of air and earth, older than stone.

References

Antrobus, Raymond (2013). *Shapes & Disfigurements of Raymond Antrobus*. Portishead: Burning Eye.

Greenlaw, Lavinia (1993). *Night Photograph*. London: Faber and Faber.

Heaney, Seamus (1987). *The Haw Lantern*. London: Faber & Faber.

Hill, Geoffrey (1971). *Mercian Hymns*. London: Andre Deutsch.

Howe, Sarah (2015). *Loop of Jade*. London: Chatto & Windus.

Hughes, Ted (1960). *Lupercal*. London: Faber and Faber.

Jamie, Kathleen (2004). *The Tree House*. London: Picador.

Larkin, Philip (1974). *High Windows*. London: Faber and Faber.

Lewis, Gwyneth (1995). *Parables and Faxes*. Newcastle: Bloodaxe.

Maxwell, Glyn (1998). *The Breakage*. London: Faber and Faber.

McGuckian, Medbh (1982). *The Flower Master*. Oxford: Oxford University Press.

McGuckian, Medbh (1984). *Venus and the Rain*. Oxford: Oxford University Press.

McMillan, Andrew (2015). *Physical*. London: Cape Poetry.

Padel, Ruth (1998). *Rembrandt Would Have Loved You*. London: Chatto and Windus.

Paterson, Don (1993). *Nil-Nil*. London: Faber and Faber, London.

Plath, Sylvia (1966). *Ariel*. London: Faber and Faber.

Porter, Peter (2001). *Max Is Missing*. London: Picador.

2b.8
(Post)Modern Lyric Poetry

Alex Pestell

The history of British and Irish poetry written in the wake of modernism is a history of American influence. It is almost impossible to imagine the major movements, presses, readings, small groupings, and anthologies without at the same time thinking of the American poets whose work crossed the Atlantic in haphazard and unpredictable ways, bringing modernism back to islands from which it seemed to have been driven. This chapter is focused on the lyric, but postwar lyric poetry on these islands is freighted with an ambition borrowed from the encyclopedic epics of the United States; indeed in some cases considered here lyric is positively saturated with the weight of responsibility suggested by Ezra Pound's notion that an epic is "a poem including history" (Pound 1968, 86). The idea of the lyric as Horatian *otium* is discarded; to seek a retreat from history's incursions viewed as a quixotic absurdity. In one sense, the subject of the lyric is overdetermined with overlapping contexts, making intention a figment, binding song to noise, eviscerating the repertory of verse forms. But simultaneously this sense of an evaporating agency, which can at times result in a liberating abdication of conventional forms of self-expression, can at others apply such pressure to the "I" of the lyric that it acquires a density—an unfamiliar density, to be sure—that no amount of textual play can eradicate.

But reading a poem, any poem, from this multifarious grouping of postwar practices immediately puts such equivocations in doubt. We might begin with John James (1939–2018), a Welsh poet whose debt to American writers—in particular Frank O'Hara and the New York School—is manifest. "A Theory of Poetry" adopts O'Hara's transference of painterly surfaces to the page:

> it's very important
> to make your lines
> bands of alternating colour
> running from one side to the other
>
> these will bind
> your poem together
> like an egg
> & make it exist
>   (James 2002, 133–138; 135,
>   ll. 1–8)

But, as the second-person pronoun that runs through this poem suggests, James is far from abandoning the fiction of intimate communication that underwrites so much lyric. Like O'Hara, James contains multitudes. In contrast to the poem mentioned earlier, in a text like "Inaugural Address," the "bands of colour" do indeed stretch from side to side, allowing little room for an "I" to operate (the only "I" in the poem is the Rastafarian "I & I," now reduced to an abbreviation for "Industrial Investment" [158, l. 24]).

> Good-bye Auschwitz Hello Angkor Vat Pol
> Pot Napoleon III Pinochet Pinocchio of Chairman Hua
> Haussmann Mussolini Sant'Elia The God
> Father of High Tech & he with no lustre on his
> bite in the echo chain of Sardis the thatcher the carter
> Teheran the Arc of the Shah
> The Biggest McDonald's Advertisement In The World
>   (James 2002, 181–185; 185, ll. 62–68)

In fact, it is difficult to come to a synoptic view of the fate of the lyric subject in this period, simply because, while one influential agglomeration of theories from 1960 on centered around the extinction of the subject as signifier, writers varied in their allegiance to this new order. Proximity to the academy was one factor in the degree to which they identified with this theory-vanguard, though even the most embedded poets differed significantly in their approaches. Class was another factor, but not in a way that would allow us to make a simple equation between radical politics and an esthetics of devastated grammar. Some "I"s are more equal than others, and a poem could be the means by which a subaltern "I" might be winched onto the landscape.

> right inuff
> ma language is disgraceful
>
> ma maw tellt mi
> ma teacher tellt mi [...]
> sum wee smout thit thoat ah hudny read chomsky tellt mi
> a calvinist communist thit thoat ah wuz revisionist tellt mi
>
> po-faced literati grimly kerryin thi burden a thi past tellt mi
> po-faced literati grimly kerryin thi burden a thi future tellt mi
>   ("Right Inuff," Leonard 1995, 120, ll. 1–4, 10–13)

For Tom Leonard (1944–2018), the author of this poem, dialect poetry is a response to a class-system which operates through a normalized model of speech. What is at stake in his use of dialect is not national but class status. As Derrick McClure argues, Leonard's poem is not written in a Scots that could form the basis of a national literature (as, for example, Hugh MacDiarmid's might have done) (McClure 2000, 172–174). Instead, it is deliberately "thi langwij a thi guhtr," a basilect that often comes across as helplessly blunt as well as alive in a way that "official" dialects are not. Leonard's work acknowledges that poetry is instrumentalized as a class signifier: "The 'beauty' of a lot of English poetry [...] for many, is that the softness of its vowel-enunciation reinforces their class status in society as the possessors of a desirable mode of speaking" (Leonard 1995, 65). If certain forms of speech are viewed as the property of a class of people whose interests are antagonistic to the writer, it is no surprise that Leonard ends up looking elsewhere, specifically to the United States, for other models. If the pattern of "received pronunciation" (RP) was instantiated as a marker of validity, Leonard writes, what he receives from William Carlos Williams is a kind of writing for which language is not an instrument of possession. Instead, Williams's poetics was an incitement to treat "the medium of poetry, language, as an object in itself" (Leonard 1995, 96).

It would be hard to find a greater concentration of RP accents than at the University of Cambridge, but this was the setting in which another major transference took place of poetic energy from language as an instrument of possession to language as self-reflexive medium, and again under American auspices. Under the guidance of writers such as Andrew Crozier (1943–2008), Elaine Feinstein (1930–2019), R. F. Langley (1938–2011), J. H. Prynne (b. 1936), and Peter Riley (b. 1940), an Olsonian poetics of history, geography, and anthropology was elaborated through the 1960s, and would go on to have a major effect upon subsequent developments in British and Irish poetry. "I didn't start writing," admitted Langley in an interview, "until I found out about American poetry. [...] It was really Olson who convinced me that I might write something myself" (quoted in Brinton 2005, 65). In fact, the poets comprising the so-called "Cambridge School" were not solely academics, and not solely based in the environs of Cambridge. Although Crozier, for example, began his career as a teaching fellow at Cambridge, his subsequent travels in the United States and appointments to lectureships at the universities of Essex, Keele, and Sussex in the United Kingdom were instrumental in bringing American modernist and avant-garde poetry to a British readership. The poets involved in this loose grouping used the little magazine as a way, less to broadcast their influence, than to form debates over poetry and poetics: *The English Intelligencer* of Crozier and Riley, *Grosseteste Review* of John Riley and Tim Longville, and Crozier's *The Park* all contributed to the debate in the late 1960s.

What was it about Olson that provoked this explosion of activity in the late 1960s and early 1970s? It might be helpful to consider what Olson did *not* represent. In a retrospective essay entitled "Thrills and Frills: Poetry as Figures of Empirical Lyricism," Crozier considered what was held to be the canonical British poetry in the 1950s, 1960s, and 1970s. Crozier argued that canonical poetry (embodied in the work of the Movement poets, especially those collected in Robert Conquest's *New Lines* {1956}) tends "to apprehend or, at least, allude to the discrete"—whether a work of art, an exotic location, or an isolated experience (Crozier 1983, 204). The authors considered in Crozier's essay (especially Philip Larkin) use these discrete phenomena as occasions for their own authoritative utterances, rather than grounds for the communication of a shared intelligence of the world. Given this pervasive skepticism, which entails a distance between the writer and the occasion of their poem, regular meter is employed to lend the text the support it needs by reference to a tradition of writing which modernism had supposedly interrupted, to the detriment of subsequent poetry. Lastly, Crozier ties the cultural and social positions defended by the Movement poets to "a new kind of literary professionalism, utilizing the cultural prestige of poetry to diversify into new markets – universities, the media, the secondary education syllabus" (Crozier 1983, 209). This is not a manifestation of mere personal ambition, though: Crozier finds that the Movement poets are promulgating an ideal of "social normality," predicated on intellect and empiricism (Crozier 1983, 212).

Olson and the American poets connected with Black Mountain provided a model that stood in polar opposition to the Movement. For these poets, modernism was not a tasteless interruption, but a vital repository of forms and techniques apposite to the experiences of late capitalism. Unlike the Movement poets, abstract thinking was not viewed with suspicion, and large timescales provided a background to audacious connections between disparate phenomena and modes of apprehension. Furthermore, emotions were not viewed as an embarrassing contamination of the poem's sterile ground; as Charles Altieri puts it, the Black Mountain poets "shift[ed] the basic unit of poetic intelligence from concerns for aesthetic complexity to concerns for emotional intensity and speculative scope" (Altieri 1984, 39; quoted in Mellors 2005, 96). Olson's work chimed with an exploratory tendency among the poets loosely affiliated to Cambridge in the late 1960s, and indeed friendships were struck up across the Atlantic between Olson, Ed Dorn in the United States, and Prynne and Tom Raworth in the United Kingdom, as well as between John Ashbery and Lee Harwood. (For more on these friendships, see Neil Pattison's introduction to Pattison et al. 2014, iv–vii.)

Olson's "projectivist verse" enjoins, among other things, a dual attention: to the syllable and to the object under regard in the poem. A poetry of process distinguishes projectivist poetry from the Movement poets' stability and distance: the process being that wherein the largest claims upon the poet's attention come to define the most microscopic details of prosody, voice, and breath. In Prynne's early volume *The White Stones* (1969), this resulted in a poetry that bore some resemblances to the scope, rhetoric, and ambitions of Olson's work. But Prynne's poems of the later 1960s and early 1970s begin to move away from Olson's calm epochal grasp, toward a poetry that is both startlingly free of recognizable convention and yet bound, with a daunting insouciance, to the fiction of its own conventions.

> As through its lentil abscess
> sun tempers the fad in leaf-fall
> by stunned silica the pass
>
> is concessionary until soldered
> across the output, you see
> what it takes; if at all
>   (*Down Where Changed*,
> Prynne 2005, 298, ll. 90–95)

If there is a syllabic intelligence at work here, it is difficult to discern an object or set of phenomena to which it is being applied in a projectivist sense. Meter is not obviously organized according to any principle of incremental perception. Instead it rushes breathlessly on past the expected pause between "stunned silica" and "the pass," and halts willfully with a semicolon to separate two clauses which *sound* as if they ought to make sense together: "what it takes; if at all." These feints are all the more unnerving in that they occur in a context which seems entirely certain of its logic. One could perhaps see how the sun could be said to possess, or *be*, a "lentil abscess," especially if we find the root "lens" in lentil. "Abscess" sounds catastrophic, but again etymology leads us to "withdrawal" or "absence," giving the sun a disturbingly intimate and simultaneously almost mythical resonance. But what is "the fad" and how does it sit in "leaf-fall"; more importantly, to what can we ascribe the authoritative tone with which the poem presumes to be able to identify and, presumably, denounce "fads"? One possible reading might take its cue from Andrew Duncan's observation that Prynne's worldview shifts from the idealistic, or future-oriented, to the pragmatic, as a political tactic ("This shift of attention between long timescales and short is important for Prynne") (Duncan 2003, 123). So the promise of the enlightening long-view embedded in such geological words as "lentil," "silica," "the pass," is swiftly truncated: "lentil" by "abscess," "silica" by "stunned," and the quick reversal into "the pass," and this last by its sudden metamorphosis into molten solder on a circuit board. We are here far from a postmodern absence of authority: this is more like a late-modernist investigation of the grounds of authority.

The mainstream "canon" examined in Crozier's essay was, he says, "largely made up of males," and this is one respect in which little difference is discernible between the canonical and the marginal streams of production (for a recent overview of poetry by women in Britain, see Kennedy and Kennedy 2013). Among the overlapping circles that spun eccentrically from Cambridge, few women have made impressions in histories of the poetry of the period, with second-wave feminism's theoretical achievements garnering far more attention, even to this day. Veronica Forrest-Thomson (1947–1975)—a student of Prynne—wrote elegant, cerebral poems partly in response to her reading in French structuralism; her life and writing were cut short at a tragically young age. Her contemporary Anna Mendelssohn (1948–2009), who also wrote as Grace Lake, could only tangentially be named a Cambridge poet (having studied there in 1985 after spending some time in prison for her association with the anarchist group The Angry Brigade). Mendelssohn's work contains moments of direct confessional crammed next to a late modernist autonomy wary of its status, and a political commitment that seeks the subterranean power-lines between status and confession:

> his trombone and our voices sliding along parallels. without encapsulation
> she won herself an education. ranting and raving the whole while
> about how long it was taking me to read a page, a paragraph, a sentence,
> a word! and that's what I was left with. a letter. [...]
>
> unable not to listen, tied up by devastation, in
> a landscape blown west, a concordat over gravestones
> the minimum of civilisation. compelled to be mutually destroyed
> for a mother's transcendence, at the station master's suggestion.
>   ("Half," Lake 1993, n.p., ll. 1–4, 32–35)

Denise Riley, also born in 1948, is also wary of the "station master's suggestion[s]"; yet her writing frequently finds its addressee and adversary in language, in poems that (like her theoretical work) discover identities to have been instantiated in patterns of speech that pre-exist self-consciousness.

The predominance of men in the poetic landscape of the 1960s to the 1980s was not unique to Cambridge. As Robert Sheppard points out, "When Maggie O'Sullivan [...] edited *Out of Everywhere: Linguistically Innovative Poetry by Women in North America & the UK* in 1996, she could only find nine British poets to join the 21 from across the Atlantic" (Sheppard 2005, 162. The book's sequel, recently published, contains a higher proportion of British and Irish poets [see Critchley 2015]). An influential writer herself, O'Sullivan (b. 1951) writes poems that could with partial truth be described as late modernist, in that their puns, portmanteau words, and focus on the non-semantic in language recall the sensuous wordplay of late Joyce or even early Beckett. In fact, her lineage is more European than Irish, with Beuys, Heidegger, and Schwitters as presiding spirits, and her work displays a concern with the materials of art and their performance that separates it from the work emanating from (a symbolic) Cambridge "school."

> Billow churn, jazzy curve. Bee zen. of Glovewort.
> Utter Glaze. fridge roseflocking mutagenic. fridge Acanthus, lash prim thistle twist of pure nutmace, low flambé lead split: erosion. But child, Bead & reel, yellowed air soft mightily, i bleed & soak, pooling olive, prolonging sund sund sundering.
> ("A Natural History in 3 Incomplete Parts," O'Sullivan 2006, 77, ll. 18–19)

Sound's materiality is figured as a "mutagenic" process, in which the noise of words is disarticulated and reconfigured as vocables attracted to each other via family relations—assonance, conceptual recognition, rhythmic mirroring. Capitals, underlines, and punctuation do not conform to syntactic norms, leaving them resembling residual icons, dislodged in the course of the poem's "jazzy curve." Language is subjected to a "low flambe lead split," an "erosion" which leaves spiky vegetation ("Acanthus," "thistle," "nutmace") to flourish in the sundered surface of the text.

O'Sullivan is part of a London grouping—in overviews such as the present chapter the suggestion of affiliation is a useful fiction—which is often contrasted with the Cambridge grouping already considered. As one critic puts it, the London scene is characterized by an "investment in performance and cross artform collaborations," while the Cambridge poet allegedly has a higher "regard for the artifactual status of the poem as a resolved and 'finished' object" (Tuma 1998, 203–204). Poets associated with the London-based Writers Forum, such as Bob Cobbing and Eric Mottram, took the page less as foil for the metrical arrangement of words than as a stage for mixed-media language-based events, edging away from the lyric and toward a concrete poetry, which, in the words of Mottram, "abjures the grip of sentence as a main basis of design" (Mottram 2005, 9). For Mottram—who coined the term "British Poetry Revival" to designate the concentration of experimental poetic activity in Britain from the 1960s onward—the Americans provided the cue to experiment with form, teaching British poets that "Poetic space need not be rigidly enclosed or shaped under hard linear dimensions, restricted to traditional sentence logic and grammatical usage" (Mottram 1993, 27). London poets were markedly more sympathetic to contemporary developments in American poetry in the 1970s, particularly the Language poets, for whom "traditional sentence logic and grammatical usage" were malign markers of an authoritarianism analogous to political oppression.

Such analogies have been viewed with suspicion by a group of poets loosely connected to one another by affiliations with Cambridge, in particular with J. H. Prynne. Rod Mengham (b. 1953), a poet and academic who studied under Prynne, wrote that Language poetry "is inspired by the conviction that reference in language is linked to commodity fetishism" (Mengham 1989, 118). To put it crudely, by foregrounding the means by which language is produced, the Language poets put the reader on an equal footing with the author, producing a space in which meanings are no longer dictated by the whims of a privileged figure of authority. But for Mengham, as for his contemporaries D. S. Marriott (b. 1963) and John Wilkinson (b. 1953), the parallelism between linguistic and political signifier is not sufficiently demonstrated, nor is the corollary that (in the words of Marriott) Language poetry's "indetermination is [...] enabling as a non-commodified basis for communication" (Marriott 1995, 78). It seemed as if this "indetermination" could only capitulate to a commodified language that was in fact far more agile, easily able to co-opt the use of non-referential language into its circuit. Not only that, but (as Prynne argued in his "Letter to Steve McCaffery") if we are in the business of making analogies:

> Isn't the supermarket the correct analogy, where the consumer is generically trained to value a freedom of choice precisely fetishised by the brand alternatives of late capitalism, the wonderfully smart play of vacuity by which the reader of the labels can rustle up preference, advice, loyalty, thrift.
>
> (Prynne 2000, 41–42)

In an irony which many critiques of the movement have since echoed, the freedom of choice offered by Language poetry's decentered syntax is about as empowering as our "freedom" to pick commodities from supermarket shelves.

Indeed, looking at the history of the lyric in our period, especially in its relationship to modernism, the wish to abolish stable connections between language and identity appears peculiarly perverse. In her essay "Delusions of Whiteness in the Avant-Garde," Cathy Park Hong quotes James Baldwin on the "conditions forged in history" which black people are forced to confront and to alter (Hong 2016). Given these historical conditions, in which identities are inescapably involved and entailed, the supposedly revolutionary notion that "renouncing subject and voice is anti-authoritarian" (Hong's characterization of the *avant-garde*'s delusion) seems quixotic at best, damaging at worst. She is talking about the contemporary *avant-garde*, but she also finds that the history of modernism in the twentieth century is tainted by the assumptions that motivate this delusion. If modernism is associated with difficulty, formalism, and intellectualism, any poetry that seeks to manifest the politics of identity—of race, class, or gender—risks accusations of simplicity and sentimentalism. Historians of modernism have consequently enshrined writers—usually men, almost always white—whose position in society means that these questions never arise. This situation is worse in the United Kingdom than in the America Hong's essay addresses, and has continued into the poetries avowedly stemming from modernism: it would be difficult to find more than one person of color on the lists of the majority of small presses operating since the 1960s.

To the extent that the study of modernism is implicated in modernism's development as a period marker, this essay cannot avoid partaking in the same delusion of whiteness, and this delusion cannot be ruptured by a cursory conspectus of some falsely monolithic BAME (black, Asian and minority ethnic) tradition in British writing. Modernism has influenced some writers more than others, and in oblique ways: for Edward Kamau Brathwaite (1930–2020), whose verse trilogy *The Arrivants* (1973) was a key text in the emerging literature of the British Caribbean diaspora, T. S. Eliot is an important reference point (Brathwaite 1984, 30–31). Anthony Joseph's (b. 1966) poetry, by contrast, owes more to Dada and surrealism, as well as (in his poetic "novel" *The African Origins of UFOs* [2006]) a kind of afrofuturism that connects with a tradition of musical experiment going back to the 1950s, though Joseph's self-described influences include a host of literary and musical modernists.

> My influences – some cubist poetry, William Carlos Williams, Pound, the Beats, Ginsberg, Black Mountain, Wilson Harris, Monk, Bukowski, Baraka, Dorothea Brande, Negritude, and then I discovered surrealism.
>
> (Quoted in Arana and Ramey 2004, 124)

D. S. Marriott, already mentioned earlier, is a poet and academic who wrote his doctoral dissertation on the poetry of J. H. Prynne; his poetry explores black history, among other things, through an impacted, allusive rhetoric that is by turns literary, anecdotal, and political. Readers will find many more poets of color writing from Britain in our period, but they will have to look beyond most of the anthologies and presses that occupy even the margins of the culture (Marriott's publication by Salt and Shearsman is the exception that proves the rule). Sandeep Parmar's excellent article "Not a British Subject: Race and Poetry in the UK" deals in greater detail with this "absence of poets of colour in the 'British avant-garde'," with particular reference to Marriott's work (Parmar 2015).

Modernist-inflected poetry in Britain and Ireland from the late 1990s to 2015 has been characterized by many as a kind of Renaissance, with small presses, readings, and journals proliferating at a rate to rival the 1960s. Only a few poets can be gestured at here. Peter Manson (b. 1969) is a poet whose journal *Object Permanence* (in Manson's words "a magazine of experimental / modernist poetry"), run with Robin Purves, was crucial to introducing a wealth of experimental poetry to Scotland.[1] Manson is perhaps best known for his long poem *Adjunct: an Undigest*, a compilation of mathematically arranged found material, hilariously recomposing news items, death notices, and journal entries (Manson 2009). Manson and Purves published (and Manson was published by) two poets, Keston Sutherland (b. 1976) and Andrea Brady (b. 1974), whose Barque Press has become an important repository of politically engaged poetry. Both editors studied at Cambridge, with Prynne, and their poetry combines the erudition and formal innovativeness of the Cambridge tradition (if such can be said to exist) with a political urgency.

> Gitmo in legal twilight, red and green hazard
> net the sea
> scape beyond enduring
> freedom, the nightly movie. Montage of flag,
> soldier, airplane.
> ("Saw Fit," Brady 2013, 58, ll. 1–5)

In this poem, the political enters through channels more available to a first reading than some of Brady's other texts. It handles various aspects of the detention of prisoners in Operation Enduring Freedom, which at the time of the poem's first publication (2004) had been underway for 3 years and was to endure another ten. It begins with a series of curt substantive clauses that decry the disregard for international law that characterized the treatment of prisoners in the Guantanamo Bay detention camp, before going on to complicate this by narrowing its focus on Lynndie England, one of several US soldiers court-martialed for her abuse of prisoners in the Abu Ghraib prison in Baghdad. As the poem proceeds, what Brady describes as "suddenly-historical actors"[2] such as England are located on a series of much larger planes constituted by politics, geography, and the spectacular aspect of non-historical actors' (i.e., we readers') relationship to historical events.

Work done by Sutherland at the University of Sussex has helped to make Brighton another (southern English) focal point of experimental or modernist poetry, with many new poets emerging from the area, including Verity Spott (b. 1987) and Timothy Thornton (b. 1986). Poets in London, including Ulli Freer (b. 1947), Sean Bonney (1969–2019), Jeff Hilson (b. 1966), and Frances Kruk (b. 1981), show continuity with preceding generations. Mixed-media, concrete and sound poetry arguably play a greater role in the work of contemporary London poets than those in, say, Cambridge, Bristol, or Brighton. Bonney's *Baudelaire in English* (2008), for example, is a type-written poem sequence layering words upon words at angles producing verbal markings of varying densities (Bonney 2008). Jeff Hilson has redefined the sonnet through the entwining of song-like lyric and found language, mixed with an oblique surrealism recalling Gertrude Stein (see, for example, Hilson 2010). In Ireland, under the direction of poet Trevor Joyce, Cork plays host to the annual SoundEye Festival of the Arts of the Word, which stages work by a huge variety of poets in the modernist tradition, and which again—as its name suggests—includes poetry that reaches beyond the page to performance, video and sound poetry. The list goes on: the online archive of poetry readings and documents, *Archive of the Now* (founded by Andrea Brady), has recordings of hundreds of poets from the United Kingdom.[3] In part because of the Internet, British and Irish poets are now becoming better known in the United States, teaching, getting published, and getting written about in American journals, presses, and universities. As the internecine squabbles of the earlier generations of the avant-garde fade away, the first two decades of the twenty-first century have seen the resurgence of an overwhelming interest in the possibilities and problems of the lyric on the part of poets in Britain and Ireland. Space does not permit the more detailed overview that these poets deserve, but readers interested in more recent poetry should seek out the work of Nat Raha, Jennifer Cooke, Danny Hayward, Marianne Morris, Sarah Hayden, Luke Roberts, Francesca Lisette, Reitha Pattison, Richard Parker, Amy De'Ath, and Sam Walton, among many others.

Notes

1 https://petermanson.wordpress.com/object-permanance
2 www.argotistonline.co.uk/Brady%20interview.htm
3 http://www.archiveofthenow.com

References

Altieri, Charles (1984). *Self and Sensibility in Contemporary American Poetry*. Cambridge: Cambridge University Press.

Arana, R. Victoria and Ramey, Lauri (2004). *Black British Writing*. London: Palgrave Macmillan.

Bonney, Sean (2008). *Baudelaire in English*. London: Veer Books.

Brady, Andrea (2013). *Cut from the Rushes*. Hastings: Reality Street Editions.

Brathwaite, Edward Kamau (1984). *History of the Voice: The Development of Nation Language in Anglophone Caribbean Poetry*. London: New Beacon Books.

Brinton, I. (2005). "Black Mountain in England (1)." *PN Review* 31 (3): 65–68.

Critchley, Emily (ed.) (2015). *Out of Everywhere 2: Linguistically Innovative Poetry by Women in North America & the UK*. Hastings: Reality Street.

Crozier, Andrew (1983). "Thrills and frills: poetry as figures of empirical lyricism." In: *Society and Literature 1945–1970* (ed. Alan Sinfield), 199–233. London: Methuen.

Duncan, Andrew (2003). *The Failure of Conservatism in Modern British Poetry*. Cambridge: Salt.

Hilson, Jeff (2010). *In the Assarts*. London: Veer Books.

Hong, Cathy Park (2016). "Delusions of whiteness in the Avant-Garde." *Lana Turner Journal* Accessed January 31. http://www.lanaturnerjournal.com/7/delusions-of-whiteness-in-the-avant-garde.

James, John (2002). *Collected Poems*. Applecross, Cambridge: Salt.

Kennedy, David and Kennedy, Christine (2013). *Women's Experimental Poetry in Britain 1970-2010: Body, Time & Locale*. Liverpool: Liverpool University Press.

Lake, Grace (1993). *Viola Tricolor*. Cambridge: Equipage.

Leonard, Tom (1995). *Intimate Voices: Selected Work 1965–1983*. London: Vintage.

Manson, Peter (2009). *Adjunct: An Undigest*. Cambridge: Barque Press.

Marriott, D. S. (1995). "Signs Taken for Signifiers: Language Writing, Fetishism and Disavowal." *fragmente* 6: 73–83.

McClure, J. Derrick (2000). *Language, Poetry, and Nationhood: Scots as a Poetic Language from 1878 to the Present*. East Linton: Tuckwell Press.

Mellors, Anthony (2005). *Late Modernist Poetics: From Pound to Prynne*. Manchester: Manchester University Press.

Mengham, Rod (1989). "Review [untitled] of writing by Clark Coolidge, Steve McCaffery, Charles Bernstein, and Barrett Watten." *Textual Practice* 3 (1): 115–124.

Mottram, Eric (1993). "The British Poetry Revival, 1960–75." In: *New British Poetries: The Scope of the Possible* (eds. Robert Hampson and Peter Barry), 15–50. Manchester: Manchester University Press.

Mottram, Eric (2005). *Towards Design in Poetry*. London: Veer Books.

O'Sullivan, Maggie (2006). *Body of Work*. Hastings: Reality Street Editions.

Parmar, Sandeep. (2015). "Not a British Subject: Race and Poetry in the UK." *The Los Angeles Review of Books* (6 December). https://lareviewofbooks.org/essay/not-a-british-subject-race-and-poetry-in-the-uk (accessed 6 May 2020).

Pattison, Neil, Pattison, Reitha, and Roberts, Luke (eds.) (2014). *Certain Prose of the English Intelligencer*, 2e. Cambridge: Mountain Press.

Pound, Ezra (1968). *Literary Essays of Ezra Pound* (ed. T.S. Eliot). New York: New Directions.

Prynne, J. H. (1969). *The White Stones*. Lincoln: Grosseteste Press.

Prynne, J. H. (2000). "A Letter to Steve McCaffery." *The Gig* 7: 40–46.

Prynne, J. H. (2005). *Poems*. Fremantle, AU and Northumberland, UK: Fremantle Arts Centre Press and Bloodaxe.

Sheppard, Robert (2005). *The Poetry of Saying: British Poetry and Its Discontents 1950–2000*. Liverpool: Liverpool University Press.

Tuma, Keith (1998). *Fishing by Obstinate Isles: Modern and Postmodern British Poetry and American Readers*, Avant-Garde and Modernism Studies. Evanston, Ill: Northwestern University Press.

2b.9
The Long Poem After Pound

Will May

Introduction

How long is a long poem? Edgar Allen Poe quipped that verse long enough to be a long poem was too long to be a poem. While his neat inversion is distinctive, its fallible logic is shared by less scornful definitions of the form, too. Critical accounts of the long poem tend to underline their own provisional quality, and the ludicrous nature of the genre they attempt to define. "Long" is a "rational but helpless qualification" notes Jarvis (2010, 609); when reading Ezra Pound's *The Cantos*, the word "poem" is put under pressure too. The long poem might include sections of prose, music manuscript, hieroglyphics, calligraphy, or woodcuts. It might be unfinished, and published in fragments, like David Jones's unnamed long poem that begins with *The Anathemata* (1952) and continues in *The Sleeping Lord and Other Fragments* (1974), or it may take the form of several linked poems in one volume, like Brendan Kennelly's *The Book of Judas* (1991). It may stray close to fiction, as in Anne Carson's novel-in-verse *Autobiography of Red* (1998), or set up shop nearer the contemporary art gallery, like Maggie O'Sullivan's postmodern elegy *Murmur* (2011), which uses paper crenellations, crayon drawings, and stitchwork to achieve many of its poetic effects. The modern poem is often associated with linguistic play and postmodern difficulty, as studies by Kinney (1992) and McHale (2004) suggest, yet some of the most notable long poems by British and Irish writers in the last 50 years have been works commissioned by national broadcasters for primetime television. The commercial successes of recent works by Simon Armitage, Tony Harrison, and Kate Tempest challenge our sense of the form, too: long

---

A Companion to Contemporary British and Irish Poetry, 1960–2015, First Edition.
Edited by Wolfgang Görtschacher and David Malcolm.
© 2021 John Wiley & Sons Ltd. Published 2021 by John Wiley & Sons Ltd.

poems do not tend to profit from summary, but they have not tended to make a profit, either. As DuPlessis (2008) notes, our messy definitions of the long poem echo "the endless cultural acts of the long poem itself: creolized, inclusive, errant, omnivorous, palimpsestic, and overwritten with more writing." The long poem can inspire copious exegesis and commentary, but, like Pound himself, it sits awkwardly in modern poetic history.

Pound's Impasse? Bunting, Jones, Hill

From 1960 to 1972, Pound's late cantos were appearing in various periodicals: as Bush (1999) notes, the editorial decision to "complete" the poem with the later drafts and fragments won Pound new readers among the experimental writers of the 1960s; perhaps, after all, Pound's work might form "a bridge over worlds" (Pound 1994, 802). *The Cantos* suggested both a possibility and an impasse, as Basil Bunting's shoulder-shrugging poetic tribute concedes. His wry "On The Fly-Leaf of Pound's Cantos" (1945) begins with dumbstruck monosyllables: "There are the Alps. What is there to say about them?" (Bunting 2000, 132). Yet the poem does find other things to say about them, not least in suggesting their influence will be felt in unexpected ways: "Who knows what the ice will have scraped on the rock it is smoothing?" (Bunting 2000, 132). The question suggests a kind of rewriting, as Pound's monumental achievement is slowly reshaped over time. The question is tellingly echoed in Bunting's own *Briggflatts* (1965): "Who cares to remember a name cut in ice / or be remembered?" (Bunting 2000, 66). Even as the poem alludes to Pound's mountain range, it erases his name. The poem comes across a "peak unscaleable," recalling a nameless man who once "traversed limestone to gabbro" with "file sharp" (Bunting 2000, 72), but, if that hero might be Pound, it finds distinct ways to better his dimly remembered feat. Bunting takes the glacial shift of Pound's Alps and chisels out a new language, packed tight in ice and rock:

> Heat and hammer
> draw out a bar.
> Wheel and water
> grind an edge.
> (Bunting 2000, 68)

Here, making is a process of refining rather than building, chiseling rather than constructing. *Briggflatts* looks for "shapes to carve and discard," knowing that "brief words are hard to find" (Bunting 2000, 64). The verse's tendency to concentration and condensation suggests another way out of Pound's impasse. It rewrites the long poem's purpose from one of journeying to one of making: the poem is centered in the North of England, and takes its name from a Quaker meeting house near Sedbergh in Cumbria. It allows other kinds of meetings, too, combining free verse with rhymed couplets.

Bunting's critical prose aligns Pound less with the modern voice than a longer tradition of wayward makers. He compares Pound to Spenser rather than himself:

each planned a very long poem which was to mirror the world, and neither planned it thoroughly enough, so that as time went on and their interests changed, the original plan had to be distorted to make room for new ideas, so that the form is not easily grasped and the poem looks to impatient readers as though it were shapeless. (Docherty 1999, 51)

It is a defense of modernist difficulty, and of the poem that cannot be read in one sitting, but it is also a way of distancing *The Cantos* from his own work, which is determined to find the best shape for the best words in the best order. The poem is in five parts, moving from the 13-line stanzas of part one to more irregular patterns. The epigraph of *Briggflatts* calls the poem an autobiography, but it is one more attentive to the shape of the work than the life.

Reviewing a new translation of *The Song of Roland* in 1937, David Jones marveled at its "aboriginal validity" that derives "from the bowels" (Jones 1978, 99). His own version of the long poem is ancestral, mythic, and bodily, perhaps appropriately for an artist and writer whose first professional encounter with a long poem was creating the copper-plate engravings for a 1929 edition of Coleridge's *The Rime of the Ancient Mariner*. "The Tribune's Visitation," one of the poems from *The Sleeping Lords and Other Fragments* (1974) invokes "the April mocked man" who is "crowned and cloaked" (Jones 1992, 197), as if Chaucer and T. S. Eliot were battling it out for supremacy, and the incomplete cycle ends with a vision of a sterile world waiting for the return of a king:

> Does the land wait the sleeping lord
> or is the wasted land
> that very lord who sleeps?
> (Jones 1992, 230)

Yet Jones avoids the shadow of Eliot and Pound by looking further back into history. His preface to *The Anathemata* begins with a quotation: "I have made a heap of all that I could find" (Jones 1952, 9). Yet it comes from Nennius, Roman historian of Britain, rather than a modernist precursor. Jones also rejects the simultaneity of Eliot's critical vision; introducing his own poem as "necessarily insular" and contingent upon the poet being "a Londoner, of Welsh and English parentage, of Protestant upbringing, of Catholic subscription" (Jones 1952, 11). Like Bunting, who anchors his long poem to a particular locale, Jones does not take on the role of the omnipresent orator.

These gestures offer a more provisional version of the long poem than *The Waste Land*: a subtitle calls *The Anathemata* "fragments of an attempted writing." The preface notes the poem is an offering which "has no plan, or at least is not planned," and "has themes and a theme"; like a meandering conversation between friends, it moves by association: "you won't make much sense of one bit unless you read the lot" he insists (Jones 1952, 33). Jones's authorial voice is at once serious and provisional, a contradiction which is only heightened with the publication of *The Sleeping Lord and Other Fragments* (1974), where the flyleaf alone tells us that these unfinished poems together with *The Anathemata* "build a new long work which has a strange and unique unity of the imagination."

The difficulty of Jones's allusive work is often countered by its sound: he notes *The Anathemata* is a poem to be read aloud with "deliberation" (Jones 1952, 35); "The Sleeping Lord" is "essentially a piece for the ear rather than the eye" (Jones 1974, 70). Yet the sounds of these poems, as he admits, may also be obscure to readers unfamiliar with Welsh and "The Sleeping Lord" is given a series of phonetic footnotes. Like Bunting's *Briggflatts*, Jones gives us a way of reading his work not through its genre but through its figuration. His poems are full of images of fragments, chewings, offcuts, and debris, "selected boles, *orneus,* assembled and tied with iron" (Jones 1952, 177). Their mode is often interrogative, as if Joyce's "Ithaca" were recast as a poetic drama. We are offered a series of competing definitions for what we are reading within the poem itself. The conclusion of *The Anathemata* finds Jones's singular voice sounding over the towering hills of Pound and Eliot:

> Of which cry?
> His, by whom all oreogenesis is
>   his hill-cry who cries from his own *oreosi*.
> *Ante colles* he is and
>   before the fleeting hills
> in changing order stood.
>
> (Jones 1952, 233)

Like Bunting, Jones wrests the long poem away from Pound and Eliot by claiming a distinct vernacular topography, taking in the "carboniferous vaultings" of the Gower (Jones 1974, 71) in his account of Lord Llywelyn, Prince of Wales. Alongside the "domestic litter and man-squalor" of his poetic landscape, the reader is drawn repeatedly to the "flint-worked ivory" and the "sea-shell trinkets" (Jones 1974, 71); nature and man have an affinity in their making.

Another kind of archaeological process is at work in Geoffrey Hill, whose prose sequence *Mercian Hymns* (1971) haunts the Welsh border, and whose long poems explore a series of other divisions, or fine lines; between integrity and sincerity, construction and deconstruction, obscurity and commitment, the portentous and the parodic. For many readers of modern poetry, Hill has offered a just reply to his "outclassed forefathers" (Hill 1971, XXIX); literary history might place David Jones before Hill rather than after Pound, as the "*ante colles*" conclusion to Jones's poem suggests. Hill's essay on Pound's "Envoi" (1919) wonders how questions of voice and identity might be mitigated by the long poetic sequence: the lyric I becomes relational, and contingent (Hill 2008). Yet if the form might rescue the lyric I from the dangers of the confessional, its scale presents other challenges: as Hill's own work acknowledges, contemporary literary culture makes deliberate difficulty a calculated risk:

> Erudition. Pain. Light. Imagine it great
> unavoidable work; although: heroic
> verse a non-starter, says PEOPLE. Some believe
> we over-employ our gifts.
>
> (Hill, 2000, 1)

The temptations of a long poem might be "unavoidable" for a poet but, unavoidably, it requires a concomitant effort from its reader. The words chiseled by Bunting and sounded out by Jones are mined by Hill both as defense and exploration of his craft. Etymology, rather than form or landscape, becomes his archaeological object. In *The Triumph of Love* (1998), Hill reminds us that obnoxious used to mean "easily wounded" (Hill 1998, 81), and his work can be as pugnacious about the demands it makes on the reader as Jones is apologetic. Yet we are always reminded that getting from beginning to end will be harder for the poet than the reader:

> *Vergine bella*, now I am half-way
> and lost – need I say – in this maze of my own
> devising. I would go back and start
> again; or not start at all, which might
> be wiser. No. Delete the last four words.
> (Hill 1998, 39)

This *cri de coeur*, which comes halfway through *The Triumph of Love* (1998), seems to be an admission of authorial anxiety common to the contemporary long poem. James Merrill's epic *The Changing Light at Sandover* (1982) begins with the bard's confessional for not writing a confessional poem: he errs by undertaking the work in its present form, admitting a novel or a newspaper article would be the best way of reaching a large audience in a short time. Yet Hill's plea is more knowing than generic. After all, Dante's *Inferno* begins with a man who has wondered into darkness halfway through his life; he is lost before the poem's epic labyrinth has even begun, we might say. Hill grafts spiritual and formal uncertainty together. The passage also stands unblinking in the face of the contemporary long poem's other gnawing tension: the bardic oratory of its ancestry against the commercial insignificance of a printed page of poetry. The poem's outcry is rhetorical—the phrase "need I say" is put under particular pressure by Hill—yet the insinuation of verbal excess, of weaving a maze that befuddles its subject rather than occupying them, is cut short by the instruction to "delete the last four words." Here Hill plays both Eliot and Pound, the creator and the reviser. He asserts a new confidence in the poem's right to be, but in a gesture of revision that removes words rather than adding them. Is a long poem lost or rescued by being abridged?

News to Me: Harrison, Armitage, Tempest

"PEOPLE," as Hill calls the public, tend to be left out from histories of the modern long poem. The "Very Long Poem" (which Peter Middleton helpfully shortens to VLP) might have once kept "warriors occupied during the feasting" (Middleton 2010), but it is assumed that contemporary readers are likely to find them "arcane" (Boland 1995, xi). To write a long poem is to commit a sort of transgression, but to avoid writing one for commercial reasons is no better. For W. H. Auden, it would only acknowledge poetic form itself as "market-made / a commodity / Whose value varies," and the poet themselves as "a vendor who has / To obey his buyer" (Auden 1976, 474). Yet in a curious twist to this conundrum, some of the most widely read and heard long poems of the past 50 years have found large readerships across different media, often coming to the attentions of television audiences presumably too distracted to read long poems.

Tony Harrison's *V* (1985), a Marxist elegy in a Leeds city churchyard, was adapted for television in 1987. The autobiographical poem takes in the National Front and the graffiti that covers the tombstones of his family plot. It is also a kind of catechism, as Harrison's imagined National Front vandal appears to him in the graveyard, berating him for his learning and profession—*"it's not poetry we need in this class war"* (Harrison 2007, 273). The mining industry leaves its marks all over the topography of this poem; the graves tilt from subsidence, perched on a hill made unstable from a coal seam. Yet if the setting suggests elegy, the poem's preoccupation with audience, form, and language makes it explicitly a long poem. It is a poem which rakes over "all the versuses of life" (Harrison 2007, 266): black and white, communism and fascism, Hindu and Sikh, male and female; yet it knows that poetic verses cannot assimilate these differences. Instead, it worries that there may be altogether too many verses; the skinhead vandal in the graveyard speaks in part for Harrison when he roars that "poet" is a dirtier four-letter word than most of the expletives sprayed throughout the graveyard. Perhaps the most striking versus in the poem is the length of the work itself (122 quatrains) against the four-letter concision of graffiti. The skinhead is given no public voice, so takes a gravestone as the page on which to make his words visible; the poet is afforded all the trappings of cultural prestige, but wonders how large his audience might really be.

The poem follows the speaker back to his comfortable home, where he listens to Alban Berg's opera *Lulu* on his stereo with his girlfriend. Yet this world of high culture is no longer separate from the rubbish-strewn graveyard and social unease; soon, the television news flickers into view:

> As the coal with reddish dust cools in the grate
> on the late-night national news we see
> police v. pickets at a coke-plant gate,
> old violence and old disunity.
>
> (Harrison 2007, 277)

The miners' strikes that frame the evening news in 1984 must have some relationship to the long poem *v.* which is broadcast on national television in 1987, but whereas the media become part of the texture of the contemporary long poem, the poem has no role to play in the news. The long poem's chosen locale, the graveyard, might tell us something about its supposed audience. The derelict tombstones are abandoned, as families move on from Leeds in search of "fuller lives" (Harrison 2007, 267) and the long poem, too, might feel its audience dwindling. It's a poem that begins by imagining the next millennium, and tells the 3000-year story of coal, but, all the same, it wonders how long mere words might last.

Simon Armitage's 1000-line poem *Killing Time* (1999) effects a similar combination of contemporary news bulletin and social comment. Commissioned for broadcast on New Year's Day 2000, the poem sews together the Columbine school massacre, surveillance culture, reality television, operation Desert Storm, and reckless New Year hedonism. As in Harrison's poem, there is an implied comparison between the work itself and other, apparently more transitory forms of writing. The narrator is drawn to sandwriting in Scarborough which declares that *"Jesus is Lord,"* but a few days later it has been washed away to "lard, lurid, blurred" (Armitage, 21). Similarly, the Audenesque speaker casts a cynical eye over a world glued to screens: the poem's opening envoy to a Muse is to a television which can only be fed on a diet of news. Even Chaucer is now "at his laptop, / auto-checking his screenplay proposal for spelling and style" (Armitage, 39). The millennial setting and the poem's length suggest a link between time and form, yet telling that, for all the poem's description of premillennial tension, the moment of reaching 2000 comes as a disappointment.

Millennium jitters in December 1999 become the model for how we experience the long poem: "this is the month when hours in the day are short, when the last and final word / comes only minutes after the first" (Armitage, 6). The long build-up in the long poem—some 2000 years—is a moment of bathos: so many are "determined to opt out" and head for spots "at grid references / where nothing really matters," that the earth's most distinctive millennial sound is "a silence so profound it figures on the Richter scale" (Armitage, 46). The poem's title gestures toward apocalypse or the decided date of a psychopath for a serial shooting, but it also suggests blank space, and the need to fill in time. The slow wait for the millennium is also the patient ear, straining to catch the final word of the poem. The poem's last announcement—the "and, finally" of the newscast—is that in a Yorkshire village "nothing happened at all" (Armitage, 52), but the police are responding by installing security cameras. The suspicious eye is likely to catch nothing worth seeing.

Thirteen years into the new millennium, Kate Tempest's long poem *Brand New Ancients* (2013) takes in some similar sights to Armitage. No panoramic vision of Britain is complete without a vision of Simon Cowell grandstanding on *X Factor*, for example; the poem has a keen eye for the ways contemporary culture has exhausted its faith in heroism. Yet, unlike Armitage, Tempest makes her poem a plea for readers and listeners to find new gods in everyday life. Even Cowell's waspish tongue might be the stuff of epic, as she imagines a future lay by troubadours which will sing "the Deeds of Simon" (Tempest 2013, 2). Although, like *The Waste Land*, the poem turns to myth to tell the story of modern London and, in particular, two families and their slow descent into desperation, its gaze is panoramic, and its oratory optimistic.

The poem's own genesis also suggests new avenues for the contemporary long poem. It began its life as a commission from the Battersea Arts Centre, where it was performed over a live score composed by Nell Catchpole. Tempest built up her wide following performing at poetry slams. Like Jones or Bunting before her, she puts sound at the center of the long poem, but, unlike her predecessors, she has found a way to make audiences attend to those sounds. The poem was awarded the 2013 Ted Hughes Prize for innovation in poetry. In fact, Tempest was reviving a much earlier version of the long poem, a form which, despite the narrative apologies of its own practitioners, has found brave new worlds on the other side of Pound's intimidating Alps.

References

Armitage, Simon (1999). *Killing Time*. London: Faber.

Auden, Wystan Hugh. (1976). "The age of anxiety." In: *Collected Poems* (ed. Edward Mendelsohn), 447–536. London: Faber.

Boland, Eavan (1995). *Object Lessons: The Life of the Poet and the Woman in our Time*. Manchester: Carcanet.

Bunting, Basil (2000). *Complete Poems*. Newcastle: Bloodaxe.

Bush, Ronald (1999). "Late Cantos LXII-CXVII." In: *The Cambridge Companion to Ezra Pound* (ed. Ira N. Nadel), 109–138. Cambridge: Cambridge University Press.

Docherty, Jennifer (ed.) (1999). *Basil Bunting on Poetry*. Baltimore: John Hopkins University Press.

DuPlessis, Rachel Blau (2008). "Considering the Long Poem: Genre Problems." *Readings*. www.bbk.ac.uk/readings/issues/issue4/duplessis_on_Consideringthelongpoemgenreproblems (accessed 15 Decembers 2018).

Harrison, Tony (1985). *V*. Newcastle upon Tyne: Bloodaxe.

Harrison, Tony (2007). *Collected Poems*. London: Viking.

Hill, Geoffrey (1971). *Mercian Hymns*. London: Andre Deutsch.

Hill, Geoffrey (1998). *The Triumph of Love*. Harmondsworth: Penguin.

Hill, Geoffrey (2008). "Envoi (1919)." In: *Collected Critical Writings* (ed. Kenneth Haynes), 243–264. Oxford: Oxford University Press.

Jarvis, Simon (2010). "The Melodics of Long Poems." *Textual Practice* 24 (4): 607–621. https://doi.org/10.1080/0950236.

Jones, David (1952). *The Anathemata*. London: Faber.

Jones, David (1974). *The Sleeping Lord and Other Fragments*. London: Faber.

Jones, David (1978). "The Roland Epic and Ourselves." In: *The Dying Gaul* (ed. David Jones). London: Faber.

Jones, David (1992). *Selected Works of David Jones*. Cardiff: University of Wales Press.

Kinney, Clare Regan (1992). *Strategies of Poetic Narrative*. Cambridge: Cambridge University Press.

McHale, Brian (2004). *The Obligation Toward the Difficult Whole*. Tuscaloosa: University of Alabama Press.

Merrill, James (1982). *The Changing Light at Sandover*. New York: Random House.

Middleton, Peter. (2010). "The Longing of the Long Poem." *Jacket* 4. http://jacketmagazine.com/40/middleton-long-poem.shtml (accessed 15 December 2018).

O'Sullivan, Maggie (2011). *Murmur*. London: Veer Books.

Pound, Ezra (1994). *The Cantos of Ezra Pound*. London: Faber.

Tempest, Kate (2013). *Brand New Ancients*. London: Picador.

Section 2c. Groupings, Themes

2c.1
Generations

Robert Hampson

And the years pass until one generation dies / and their knowledge with them
("One, two, three." Harwood 2004, 199–201; 201, ll. 56–57)

The category of "generations" was forcibly levered into the public discourse of poetry in 1993 and 1994 by the campaign to promote the "New Generation Poets." The campaign was initiated by three poetry publishers, supported by the Poetry Society and *Poetry Review*, and promoted by the PR company Colman Getty. The publishers were Bill Swainson (Harvill), Christopher Reid (Faber), and Robert Robinson (Secker, shortly to be Cape). The Steering Group included Jacqueline Simms, Poetry Editor at Oxford University Press. The campaign was, as Stan Smith puts it, a "concerted and successful media drive" (Smith 2007, 194) with television, radio, and print media appearances; group readings; and displays in bookshops and libraries. *The Observer* published a poem a week, and Radio 1 FM agreed to promote the poets in its search for "the new rock 'n roll." The campaign was even given an international reach—including the United States and the West Indies—through support from the British Council. (To be more accurate, the campaign opportunistically appropriated two events already arranged by the British Council: Simon Armitage's US tour and Glyn Maxwell's visit to the West Indies.) The promotion was very successful: it produced, Smith suggests, a rise in audience numbers for readings by the selected poets and an increase in sales of poetry books for the publishers involved, but it was also the first time a poetry movement had been "constructed by a committee" (2007, 195).

The Special Issue of *Poetry Review*, produced to "celebrate" the "New Generation Poets" contained work by each of the poets, a brief profile of each poet, and supporting

---

A Companion to Contemporary British and Irish Poetry, 1960–2015, First Edition.
Edited by Wolfgang Görtschacher and David Malcolm.
© 2021 John Wiley & Sons Ltd. Published 2021 by John Wiley & Sons Ltd.

material—including a whole-page "Calendar of Events" listing the "New Generation" nationwide poetry readings for May (*Poetry Review*, 84.1, Spring 1994). The stated criteria for inclusion as a "New Generation" poet were: (i) being under the age of 40, and (ii) being a UK citizen "or normally resident in the UK." Apart from Pauline Stainer (born in 1941 and over 40) and Susan Wicks (born in 1947), most of the poets included were born between 1954 and 1963. Given this range, Smith suggested, "the concept of a generation had become somewhat factitious" (2007, 195). Nevertheless, he claims, this group had a certain homogeneity: as a whole they might be described as "Thatcher's children, products of the entrepreneurial get-rich-quick culture of the 1980s" (201).

The *Poetry Review* introductory essay by Peter Forbes, "Talking About the New Generation," by echoing *The Who*'s "Talking about My Generation," suggests an implicit contrast with the generation that came of age in the 1960s, while the explicit generational contrast is with a group of poets from "ten years" earlier (Andrew Motion, Blake Morrison, James Fenton, Paul Muldoon, Christopher Reid, and Craig Raine), clearly harking back to the Motion/Morrison *Penguin Book of Contemporary British Poetry* (1982), in which all these featured. Nevertheless, Forbes noticeably finds it difficult to define how this new group actually constitutes "a generation." He begins by talking about "the journalistic clichés of the new pluralism, regionalism, and the rise of the working-class voice," but has to admit these are not represented in this collection. There are "no performance poets, no Afro-Caribbean poets," and he falls back on claiming that these anthologized poets represent "true plurality" through their "wilful individuality" (Forbes 1994, 4). As Smith suggests, "The New Generation hype itself reproduces the public relations ethos of the 1980s" (Smith 2007, 201). It is certainly hard to escape the feeling that this "generation" has about as much authenticity as a Pop Idol boy band.

There were precedents for this idea of a poetic "generation." In his *Autobiographies*, W. B. Yeats had tried to mythologize the poets of the Rhymers' Club (Lionel Johnson, Ernest Dowson, Arthur Symons, John Davidson, and others) by calling them the "Tragic Generation" (Yeats 1926, 343–430). Through the epigraph to his novel *The Sun Also Rises*, Hemingway had popularized the idea of the "Lost Generation" as a term used to refer to his generation of post-World-War-1 American writers—or, more precisely, his 1920s circle of American expatriates in Paris that included Gertrude Stein and F. Scott Fitzgerald (Hemingway 1927). Samuel Hynes introduced the idea of a "generation" into more recent poetry criticism in his ground-breaking study *The Auden Generation* (1976), a chronological account of Auden, Spender, Isherwood, Day-Lewis, and their contemporaries through the 1930s. Hynes's Preface begins: "This book is about the making of a literary generation – the young English writers of the 1930s" (Hynes 1976, 9). Hynes then defines this "generation" more precisely: "the men and women born in England between 1900 and the First World War, who came of age in the twenties and lived through their early maturity during the Depression" (9). Hynes further argues that a generation is "people of roughly the same age in roughly the same place," who are constituted as a generation through "consciousness of unique shared experience" (17). That "consciousness" is not fixed, but develops "as circumstances change" (17). In the case of this generation of writers *entre deux guerres*, their initial sense of separateness arises from missing combat experience in the First World War and from the removal, by the War, of their fathers, older siblings, and school seniors. Their generational consciousness developed subsequently through their responses to the economic and political crises of the 1930s. For Hynes, it is not simply a matter of "shared experience," however, but also of sharing experiences at a particular stage in their individual development that creates the consciousness of a generation. There is also an acknowledged limiting factor in Hynes's account of a specifically *literary* generation: as he notes, he focuses on the "middle-class members of the generation" (10). Accordingly, the "Auden Generation" is educated at public schools and Oxbridge, and is entirely male. In this, Hynes was describing a phenomenon which Donald Davie had recently begun to attack. In his essay "The Varsity Match," Davie had criticized the Oxbridge domination of English literary culture, which meant that "for the last fifty years each new generation of English poets [...] was formed or fomented or dreamed up by lively undergraduates at Oxford" and then "picked up its Cambridge recruits [...] only afterwards and incidentally" (Davie 1973, 73).

Smith (2007) takes a more psychological approach to the idea of generations. He argues that, throughout the twentieth century, from the modernist revolution engineered by Ezra Pound, every poetic movement found its primary identity precisely through an "Oedipal revolt against the discursive self-image of its predecessor" (159). The clearest example, in modern times, was the Movement's systematic disparagement of not only Romanticism and modernism, but the political poetry of the 1930s, the surrealists and the New Apocalyptics—and, above all, Dylan Thomas (Morrison 1980, 25, 91–92, 133–134, 145–191, 202–203). In the period since World War II, this Oedipal conflict between generations can be traced through a succession of anthologies, which each strove to replace an older generation of writers. Thus, Robert Conquest begins the Introduction to his *New Lines* anthology (1956), which introduced the Movement, with an account of how "a group of poets" emerged in the late 1920s who turned out to be "the typical poets of the 1930s" and how another group of writers "with quite different attitudes" began to emerge at the end of the 1930s "who were to dominate the 1940s" (Conquest 1956, xi). The logic is clear: since the 1950s is approaching its end, it is clearly time to identify the group who will dominate the next decade. Each of these earlier groups was presented to the public by an anthology, and "no anthology of this sort has appeared in this country for more than ten years" (xi). In addition to the passage of time, Conquest also suggests that "a general tendency has once again set in" (xi), which one might take as the marker of a new generation. But he goes further than just identifying a new generation with a new outlook (and this is where the Oedipal element comes in): he attacks "the corruption which has affected the general attitude to poetry in the last decade" (xii), and describes the new group presented in the anthology as representing "the restoration of a sound and fruitful attitude to poetry" (xiv), based on "a rational structure and comprehensible language" (xv). Conquest was promoting Kingsley Amis, Philip Larkin, D. J. Enright, and others as an antidote to Dylan Thomas and the poetry represented by the *New Apocalypse* anthology, which embodied what he saw as an overemphasis on the unconscious (xi) and what he termed the "debilitating theory that poetry *must* be metaphorical" (xii). At the same time, he was also critical of poetry that, as he saw it, submitted to "great systems of theoretical constructs" (xv) or more recent work, like William Empson's, that betrayed "a tendency to over-intellectualise" (xvi). Instead, Conquest advocated a low-key empiricism. As Enright puts it, in his deliberately buttoned-down, brief elegy "On the Death of a Child," "The big words fail to fit. Like giant boxes / Round small bodies" (Conquest 1956, 57, ll. 8–9). Or as Donald Davie asserted, in his poem "Remembering the Thirties," "The Anschluss, Guernica – all the names / At which those poets thrilled, or were afraid / For me mean schools and schoolmasters and games" (Conquest 1956, 71, ll. 13–15), and so, instead of an emotional engagement with big themes, "A neutral tone is nowadays preferred" (Conquest 1956, 72, l. 41).

In the next decade, following the same pattern, Al Alvarez's *The New Poetry* (1962) explicitly aimed to present the work of "a new generation of poets": "British poets who began to come into their own in the fifties" (Alvarez 1962, 24, 15). In his influential introductory essay, "Beyond the Gentility Principle," Alvarez attacks the poetry published in Conquest's *New Lines* as "academic-administrative verse, polite, knowledgeable, efficient, polished" (19). To make his point, he constructs a poem by sampling eight of the nine poets in Conquest's anthology in order to show the similarity "in the quality of both the language and the experience" of the anthologized poems, which he labels a "unity of flatness" (204). Against this, he argues the need for a "new seriousness" in poetry (24), which he defines as "the poet's ability and willingness to face the full range of his experience with his full intelligence" (24). His gatekeepers, the older American poets Robert Lowell and John Berryman, provide the touchstones for this "new seriousness," but the anthology as a whole effectively consolidates Conquest's program. Alvarez includes some of the same poets (Larkin, Enright, Gunn, Davie) in his "personal anthology" (15), but he extends the range a little by showing an openness to Scottish poets (Norman MacCaig and Iain Crichton Smith), poets engaged with a wider European culture (Michael Hamburger and Christopher Middleton), and slightly younger poets (Ted Hughes, Peter Redgrove, Geoffrey Hill) with a different agenda. Nevertheless, *The New Poetry* is effectively a repackaging of Conquest's generational grouping rather than a post-*New Lines* "new generation."

Twenty years later, Blake Morrison and Andrew Motion edited *The Penguin Book of Contemporary British Poetry* (1982), which explicitly claimed to introduce a new generation of poets. In the Preface, the editors note that they have deliberately excluded poets who appeared in the Alvarez anthology, and they argue, in the Introduction, that a number of English poets "all under forty" have emerged with a different esthetic, involving "greater imaginative freedom and linguistic daring than the previous poetic generation" and "a degree of ludic and literary self-consciousness reminiscent of modernism" (Morrison and Motion 1982, 12). The anthology accordingly includes the "Martians" Craig Raine and Christopher Reid and playful poets like Paul Muldoon, but also Seamus Heaney, the Scottish social realist Douglas Dunn, and the Northern Irish poets, Derek Mahon, Michael Longley, Medbh McGuckian, who do not seem to fit this rubric. This Oedipal gesture of a break from the past is also repeated in *The New Poetry* (1993), edited by Michael Hulse, David Kennedy, and David Morley. Their Preface claims that the anthology represents "a distinctive new generation of poets" (Hulse, Kennedy, and Morley 1993, 14) writing in the 1980s and early 1990s, and, accordingly, they explicitly exclude poets who appeared in the Morrison/Motion anthology. Apart from Pauline Stainer again, the poets in this collection were born between 1944 and 1964 (David Morley), with the majority born between 1944 and 1956. The Introduction begins by asserting a change in values in the 1980s and presents the poetry in the anthology as a response to that: "The new poetry emphasises accessibility, democracy and responsiveness, humour and seriousness [...]" (Hulse et al. 1993, 16). Given the range covered by "humour and seriousness," it is hard to see how these are distinctive markers of a generation.

That reference to poets "under forty" in the Morrison/Motion Introduction was a sign of things to come (Morrison and Motion 1982, 14). More recent anthologies such as *Voice Recognition: 21 Poets for the 21st Century* (2009), for example, emphasize their focus on "young poets" and "poets under 35" (Byrne and Pollard 2009, 10, 13). Thus, Nathan Hamilton's *Dear World & Everyone In It* (2013) similarly focusses on "young poets in the UK" and describes its "guideline age" as "under 35" (Hamilton 2013, 29). Indeed, Hamilton's introductory essay is aggressively ageist. According to Hamilton: "Young Poets" complain that "Old Editors" choose boring poems to win poetry competitions; old "tutors" do not "get" the Young Poets' work; and some "Young Poets" were excluded on the grounds that they "seem to write to appeal to Old Poets" (Hamilton 2013, 17, 16). In their Introduction to *Voice Recognition*, Byrne and Pollard justify their emphasis on young poets by rightly seeing the present moment as a time when "the presence of young poets is beginning to revitalise the scene" (Byrne and Pollard 2009, 10). However, they then conjure up a time when poetry "belonged to older writers," when "being a poet was uncool," and a poetry reading meant "warm white wine in a pokey bookshop or plodding recitals in a half-empty village hall" (Byrne and Pollard 2009, 10)—a mythic and very partial vision that has more in common with John Major's evocation of spinsters on bicycles riding to evensong than with the sociology of poetry readings. This description hardly fits with the youthful Liverpool poetry scene of the 1960s, the Morden Tower readings organized by Tom and Connie Pickard in the same period, the New Departures events organized by Michael Horovitz, or later reading series like the London SubVoicive series or the Cambridge Conference of Contemporary Poetry. With scarcely more accuracy, they mention the increased support for young writers: Foyle Young Poets of the Year Award, the Eric Gregory Award, the Michael Marks Awards for Poetry Pamphlets, as well as spoken-word events and the reading series Openned at The Foundry (curated by Alex Davies and Steve Willey between 2006 and 2009) (Byrne and Pollard 2009, 11). The Foyle's Award (which began in 2000) is for poets between the ages of 11 and 17, but the Eric Gregory Awards, which support younger writers, have been running since 1960, and the Michael Marks Awards (which began in 2009) are not specifically for young poets. The Openned reading series did find a new young audience for poetry, but it included older and younger poets as readers.

The really significant difference between this generation and earlier ones is the growth of Creative Writing programs within the UK university sector. One anxiety connected to this, as the editors of both these anthologies suggest, is the overproduction of merely competent poetry. Thus, the editors of *Voice Recognition* make very clear that theirs is not an anthology of Creative Writing "workshop poems." They mention the large number of proficient poets, producing "same-sounding, low-stake, well-mannered (but going nowhere) poems" (Byrne and Pollard 2009, 12) whom they rejected. Nevertheless, about a third of the poets anthologized acknowledge coming through Creative Writing programs: Emily Berry, Sarah Jackson,

Sandeep Parmar, Kate Potts, Sophie Robinson, and Jack Underwood. (Hamilton's 74 poets include a higher proportion of contributors who have come through such programs.) Clearly, Creative Writing programs can also nurture original voices. The other marker for this generation, according to Byrne and Pollard, is the credit crunch and its exposure of the corporate values of the last decade (Byrne and Pollard 2009, 11), but it is less clear how this is evidenced in the writing included in the anthology. For Hamilton, what distinguishes this generation of "Young Poets" is that they are "less likely than previously to be concerned with the construction of a coherent assertive character / persona or self with reference to a presumed world of common knowledge" (Hamilton 2013, 23), where it sounds as if his target is the Movement poets Alvarez criticized in the introduction to his 1962 anthology. Contrary to what Hamilton suggests, there is a substantial body of twentieth-century poetry written without "the construction of a coherent assertive character / persona" and without the assumption of a "world of common knowledge." From Ezra Pound, T. S. Eliot, Gertrude Stein, and Mina Loy through the Objectivists, the New York School, and the Language Poets—and their British equivalents from David Jones through to contemporary poets such as Denise Riley, Allen Fisher, J. H. Prynne—there is a well-established tradition of poetry operating precisely within these terms. In his eagerness to set up a generational conflict and to promote newness, Hamilton ignores those aspects of the past which do not suit his argument.

The editors of *Voice Recognition* are rightly very conscious of their editorial predecessors: they explicitly cite Alvarez's *The New Poetry* as a major influence (Byrne and Pollard 2009, 13). They also show their awareness of the generational discourse of the New Generation and the Next Generation, a promotion launched by the Poetry Book Society (PBS) in 2004 to celebrate the tenth anniversary of the New Generation. This was repeated in 2014 as "a prestigious accolade announced only once every ten years" (Poetry Book Society 2014). The initial New Generation promotion has now become a new tradition. According to the PBS website, "20 poets are chosen only once every ten years and expected to dominate the poetry landscape of the coming decade" (Poetry Book Society 2014). In line with Conquest's *New Lines* Introduction, the implication is that a "generation" is 10 years: the accolade brings with it the prospect of 10 years' "domination," but it also implies built-in obsolescence. This is not so much Oedipal conflict, as that business of Fraser's sacrificial priest-kings or the seven Athenian youths and seven Athenian maidens sent to feed the minotaur. In other respects, however, the notion of a generation is much less clear in this decadal celebration of "New Generations." The 20 poets for 2014 (who included Jen Hadfield, Helen Mort, Kei Miller, and Daljit Nagra) ranged in age from Kate Tempest (27) to Annie Freud (66). Although it is difficult to see them as a coherent cohort, the age range is explicable by the criteria: the promotion is described as recognizing "emerging poets who published their first collection in the last ten years" (Poetry Book Society 2014). In 2014, the collections represented included three each from Cape, Faber, Bloodaxe, and Carcanet, and two each from Picador and Salt, which seems a suspiciously neat distribution. The panel of judges included Robert Crawford from the New Generation Poets and Clare Pollard and Paul Farley from the 2004 Next Generation, and the project again had the support of the Arts Council and the British Council. The idea of a "generation" clearly works well for promoting poetry, but this is a different concept of a "generation" from the birth-cohorts we have seen so far in other groupings.

Another anthology from 2014, Karen McCarthy Woolf's *Ten: The New Wave*, offers an interesting variation on this pattern. Like *Voice Recognition* and *Dear World & Everyone In It*, *Ten* anthologizes the work of younger poets. In her Introduction, McCarthy Woolf describes the poets of her "new wave" as "for the most part, although not exclusively, under 30" (McCarthy Woolf 2014, 17). (The biodata for the 10 poets included is rather coy about date of birth—perhaps to play down the relevance of age to this anthology.) McCarthy Woolf follows this with the explicit claim that these poets occupy "a different generational space to their predecessors" (McCarthy Woolf 2014, 17). She notes Hamilton's ascription, in his Introduction to *Dear World*, of "a capacity for formal experiment, linguistic drama and 'ironisation'" as characteristic of poets of this generation. However, she follows Roddy Lumsden, in his Introduction to *Identity Parade: New British and Irish Poets* (Lumsden 2010), in "resisting the temptation to look for 'connections between the writings of those in a generation' instead identifying a culture of 'pluralism'" (McCarthy Woolf 2014, 16). Like Forbes, in *Poetry Review*, she links this pluralism to "a confidence to pursue idiosyncratic avenues" (McCarthy Woolf 2014, 16). As Nathalie Teitler puts it, in her Preface, this is "the authentic diversity that comes from people expressing their own individuality" (Teitler 2014, 14).

However, Woolf's anthology is striking in a number of ways. First, there is the "geographic diversity" of her poets: Warsan Shire was born in Kenya; Eileen Pun in New York; Sarah Howe in Hong Kong; Inua Ellams in Nigeria; Kayo Chingonyi in Zambia. The other poets, born in the United Kingdom, come from a range of ethnic backgrounds. This might seem to complicate the idea of a coherent generation, but what they all have in common (as McCarthy Woolf argues) is their "rootedness in contemporary Britain" (McCarthy Woolf 2014, 16). What is also striking is their relationship to their "predecessors." In her Preface, Teitler notes that *Ten: The New Wave* is the successor to *Ten: New Poets* (Bloodaxe 2010), edited by Bernardine Evaristo and Daljit Nagra (Evaristo and Nagra 2010). She concedes that, after only 4 years, it might seem premature to describe these poets as a "new wave." She explains this by reference to a longer history of Black and Asian poetry in the United Kingdom and the "decades of hard work by BME (Black ethnic minority) poets building supportive networks" (Teiler 2014, 12–13). She cites Evaristo's "Afro-Style School" set up at Spread the Word in 1995, although she could have taken the history back to earlier groups of Black writers in the 1960s and 1970s or Ravinder Randhawa's Asian Women Writers' Workshop of the 1980s. She focusses, in particular, on Evaristo's development program for Black and Asian poets, The Complete Works, which was also rolled out through Spread the Word. The Complete Works provides poets with a "space for discussion of race / identity / different cultural approaches" (Teitler 2014, 13), and it is the institutional history of The Complete Works that justifies the anthology's subtitle "The New Wave." *Ten: New Poets* represented the work of the first group of poets included in this program; *Ten: The New Wave* represents the second group of poets to pass through the scheme. As McCarthy Woolf, who was part of the first Complete Works cohort, puts it: "This is a new generation not only in terms of age but also because many were discovered, nurtured and informally mentored by their predecessors" (McCarthy Woolf 2014, 13). This relationship between "generations" is also reflected in the anthology, where each new poet is introduced by an older mentor.

The Morrison/Motion anthology not only marked a break from its precursor. It also notoriously began with the assertion that, during much of the 1960s and 1970s, "very little – in England at any rate – seemed to be happening" (Morrison and Motion 1982, 11). Two other anthologies, *A Various Art* (1987) and *The New British Poetry, 1968–1988* (1988), served to disprove this—and also open another perspective on the question of poetic generations. This question is best approached through the Hulse/Kennedy/Morley Introduction, which, in its reflection on the past, confines itself to a single gnomic reference to "the excesses of the 1960s" (Hulse et al. 1993, 26). This presumably refers to the rise of poetry readings and the impact of Beat poetry during this period. Michael Horovitz and Pete Brown toured the country during the 1960s with their poetry and jazz performances, "Live New Departures"; the International Poetry Incarnation, organized in response to Ginsberg's presence in London, filled the Albert Hall in June 1965; and the Liverpool Poets had a popular audience and published a best-selling collection, *The Mersey Sound* (Henri, McGough, and Patten 1967). Michael Horovitz's *The Children of Albion* (1969) provides a useful starting point. Despite the generational claim implicit in its title—which is encouraged by the cover image of a naked young man, a detail taken from Blake's "Albion Rose"—Horovitz does not once use the word "generation" in his lengthy "Afterwords" (Horovitz 1969, 316–377). Although we have been encouraged to think of a 1960s "generation," the children of the Welfare State coming of age in the late 1960s, most of the poets in the anthology were born in the 1930s and early 1940s, with two born in the 1920s. The subtitle ("Poetry of the 'Underground' in Britain") affirms that the anthologized poets represented the counterculture of the 1960s, but, despite the foregrounding of William Blake and the references to Allen Ginsberg and Gregory Corso, poets in the collection were not simply followers of the Beats: the poetics represented parallel the range of poetries in the "other" tradition as represented in Donald Allen's 1960 anthology, *The New American Poetry* (Allen 1960, xi). Thus, Adrian Henri (who had entertained Ginsberg in Liverpool in 1965) is omitted as a "pop artiste" (Horovitz 1969, 328), while non-Beat poets such as Andrew Crozier, Paul Evans, Roy Fisher, Lee Harwood, Edwin Morgan, Tom Raworth, and Carlyle Reedy are included.

Two other anthologies help to clarify the picture. The Introduction to *A Various Art* (1987), edited by Andrew Crozier and Tim Longville, begins by presenting its contents as representing what the editors think of as the most valuable work produced by "a generation of English poets now entering its maturity" (Crozier 1987, 11). These are not young poets selected for their promise, but mature poets who "began to publish in the 1960s," such as Anthony Barnett, Veronica Forrest-Thomson, Doug Oliver, J. H. Prynne, and Peter Riley (Crozier 1987, 11). Beginning to publish in the 1960s is their generational mark: it indicates both a "time-span" and "a formative moment" (Crozier 1987, 13). The editors, however, consciously eschew the "reference of national representation" asserted by the various "polemical anthologies" that have appeared since the 1950s, which have also asserted "their contemporary novelty of style and taste" (Crozier 1987, 11). Instead, Crozier makes clear that this is a personal choice, and, indeed, apart from Iain Sinclair, all the poets in the anthology are published by Ferry Press, Grosseteste Press, and/or Street Editions. In this context, the notion of "generation" becomes complicated. Having noted the university education of most of the contributors, Crozier observes: "Their social formation, in other words, had much in common with that of the poets who generated and were the beneficiaries of the shift in taste in the 1950s" (Crozier 1987, 11). However, although they share a common "social formation" with the Movement poets, they do not share a common poetics: "the poets who altered taste in the 1950s did so by means of a common rhetoric that foreclosed the possibilities of poetic language" and narrowed "conceptions of the scope and character of poetic discourse" Crozier 1987, (12). In addition, the "redefinition of taste in the 1950s" and the accompanying "wholesale rewriting" of the history of modern poetry (Crozier 1987, 12) left the *various art* poets facing "a depthless version of the past" (Crozier 1987, 12). With the ground cut from beneath their feet in this way, their recourse was to "postwar American poetry, and the tradition that lay behind it," that of Pound and Williams. Although there is a clear rejection of the "shift of taste" engineered in the 1950s, this is not articulated as generational conflict. Instead, the way forward for a poetry of "commitment to the discovery of meaning and form in language itself" (Crozier 1987, 14) is through the discovery of a workable "tradition" (Crozier 1987, 12)—a term not found in the anthologies discussed so far.

The issue is further clarified by *The New British Poetry*, whose title clearly echoes that of Donald Allen's influential American anthology from 1960. Allen's Preface begins by describing the years since the end of the Second World War as "a singularly rich period" for American poetry. Allen then outlines three generations of poets who are all active in this period. The "older generation" of Pound, William Carlos Williams, Hilda Doolittle (H.D.), E.E. Cummings, Marianne Moore, and Wallace Stevens, who have produced their "finest achievements" since 1945; a "second generation, who emerged in the thirties and forties" and have now "achieved their maturity" (Elizabeth Bishop, Edwin Denby, Robert Lowell, Kenneth Rexroth, and Louis Zukofsky); and a third generation of "younger poets," who have emerged more recently (Allen 1960, xi). These younger poets follow "the practice and precepts" of Pound and Williams, and have "built on their achievements and gone on to evolve new conceptions of the poem"; they have "created their own tradition" (Allen 1960, xi). This is a more generous sense of a poetic career as a life's work rather than the commercial "generational" model of 10 years' dominance and then being obsolete. It is also a more generous model of intergenerational relations: not conflict, but mutual respect. In his introduction to his section of *The New British Poetry*, Eric Mottram describes it as containing the work of "poets who began writing in the British Poetry Revival of the 1960s and 1970s" (Mottram 1988, 131). There is no mention of "generations" and no hint of Oedipal intergenerational conflict. Mottram writes: "For those who began writing in the sixties, the senior figures were Hugh MacDiarmid, Basil Bunting, and David Jones" (Mottram 1988, 131). What is invoked, instead, as in Allen's Preface, is a modernist tradition and a common, intergenerational enterprise of exploration "in language and form" (Mottram 1988, 132). This is reflected in his selection of poets, which ranges in age from Bob Cobbing (1920), Asa Benveniste (1925), and Gael Turnbull (1928) through to Denise Riley and Barry MacSweeney (both 1948).

Ken Edwards begins the introduction to his section, "Some Younger Poets," by referring to "a whole new generation of young British poets who began publishing their poetry in the 70s" (Edwards 1988, 265), but again this is not a "new generation" defining itself against the old. (Edwards's "Some Younger Poets" includes poets such as Peter Finch and Ulli Freer, both born in 1947, who are actually older than the youngest poets in Mottram's section.) Like Crozier, Edwards describes the "cultural vacuum" created by the "dominance of the Movement poets" and their "suppression of parts of English poetry's past" (Edwards 1988, 267). Like Crozier too, he describes the subsequent search for a tradition: "Many of the poets at the younger end of this selection have *started* by discovering the work of Prynne, Mottram, Raworth, Harwood, Cobbing, or Roy Fisher, only then proceeding backward through these to Pound, Williams, Olson, Ashbery, or O'Hara, and then perhaps on to the current work being done in America or Europe" (Edwards 1988, 267). Interestingly, where the "polemical anthologies" insist on generations replacing each other, the radical poetries of this period are concerned with locating themselves within a tradition of innovation. Thus, a later anthology, *Floating Capital: New Poets from London* (1991), which sets out to register new poets who had emerged in London in the previous decade, begins with work by Bob Cobbing and Allen Fisher "as an acknowledgement of their various and substantial productions before the period covered by the anthology and their importance, in a variety of ways, for many of the writers" in the anthology (Clarke and Sheppard 1991, 122). In the same spirit, the editors begin the Afterword with praise for the two previous anthologies in the field: *A Various Art* and *The New British Poetry* (Clarke and Sheppard 1991, 121). And this relationship worked both ways: Cobbing, through his Writers Forum workshop, collaborated with younger poets such as Bill Griffiths and Laurence Upton. Indeed, 1930s' poets such as Basil Bunting and Carl Rakosi returned to writing as a result of contact with these younger poets: Bunting through his association with Tom Pickard and Barry MacSweeney; Rakosi through correspondence with Andrew Crozier.

As the title suggests, *Atlantic Drift* (2017) is primarily concerned with transatlantic contacts and conversations. Indeed, this is where Robert Sheppard begins his part of the Introduction. He begins by looking back to earlier generations of British poets: to Denise Levertov moving to the US to become a major American poet, to Lee Harwood as an honorary member of the New York School; and to Tom Raworth as a precursor to Language Poetry (Byrne and Sheppard 2017, 9). He invokes Olsen's "Projective Verse" essay as an example of a poetic manifesto, and then he introduces Jerome Rothenberg. He cites approvingly Rothenberg's attempt "to create a new and coherent poetics for our time" (Rothenberg 1981, 3). This immediately raises the questions which "time" and who "we" are. In fact, the citing of Rothenberg (and the inclusion of Rothenberg in the anthology) is a sign of the editors' generous transgenerational approach. The twenty-four poets (from the UK, US, Canada, and Ireland) included in the anthology are not just geographically dispersed, they also cover a range of ages from Rothenberg (born 1931) and Rosmarie Waldrop (born 1935) to younger poets (Sophie Collins, S.J. Fowler, Chris McCabe, and Valzhyna Mort). Although it does not make the claim, this anthology is, implicitly, engaged in the construction of a workable tradition.

In the Introduction to *Voice Recognition*, Byrne and Pollard ask the question: "What makes young poets writing early in this century different from previous generations?" (Byrne and Pollard 2009, 13). However, the prior question to ask is "what is meant by the term 'generation'"? In his classic essay "The Problem of Generations," first published in 1927, Karl Mannheim addresses this question directly. He points out that a generation is not "a concrete group in the sense of a community" (*Gemeinschaft*), where the individuals are united "through naturally developed or consciously willed ties" (Mannheim 1952, 288, 289). Rather, it is a matter of "common location in the social and historical process," which limits individuals "to a specific range of potential experience" and predisposes them "for a certain characteristic mode of thought and experience" (Mannheim 1952, 291). For Mannheim, a generation becomes "an actuality" "only where a concrete bond is created between members of a generation by their being exposed to the social and intellectual symptoms of a process of dynamic destabilization" (Mannheim 1952, 303). There is, he writes, "a certain affinity in the way in which all move with and are formed by their common experiences" (Mannheim 1952, 306). Hynes was clearly drawing on Mannheim for his understanding of the "Auden Generation," but subsequent promoters of "generations" have not had this theoretical rigor.

Mannheim notes, however, that the fact that "people are born at the same time" is not enough to create "a generation": "mere chronological contemporaneity cannot of itself produce a common generation location" (Mannheim 1952, 297). Keith Tuma's exemplary *Anthology of Twentieth-Century British and Irish Poetry* (Tuma 2001) makes this clear: with Basil Bunting (1900) next to Stevie Smith (1902) and Bob Cobbing (1920) juxtaposed to Phillip Larkin (1922). Accordingly, Mannheim suggests that members of the same generation can form separate "generation units" within it (Mannheim 1952, 304), although he adds that "antagonistic generation units" (Mannheim 1952, 306) still constitute "an 'actual' generation" precisely because they are oriented toward each other, even though only in the sense of fighting one another (Mannheim 1952, 307). Jane Pilcher notes that subsequent contributors to generational analysis have argued that the way in which Mannheim uses "generation" is really in the sense of "cohort," and that "generation" and "cohort" should be de-synonymized by confining the former to the parent–child relationship (Pilcher 1994, 483). Certainly, "generation" has a clear meaning in this kinship context, but, once outside the clarity of generational succession within a line of familial descents, we are faced with "the boundary problem of where to delineate social generations in the 'seamless continuum of daily births'" (Pilcher 1994, 487): even if cohorts are defined as "the aggregate of individuals who experienced the same event within the same time interval" (Ryder 1965, 854), who decides which event to choose to define the cohort, which cohort constitutes a "social generation," and how long a "generation" lasts? For the "Auden Generation," there were, at least, clear temporal markers, as Hynes suggests, but over the last 70 years (or, at least since the period of anti-Vietnam War protests in the 1960s and until, perhaps, the millennials with their shared experience of austerity, debt, and diminished prospects as the legacy of 2008), it is hard to argue that there have been distinctive social generations with a self-conscious sense of shared collective subjectivity, although there have been various journalistic (and political) attempts to promote such groupings. As for the length of a "generation," Mannheim notes the suggestion that a generation lasted for about 30 years: "during the first thirty years of life people are still learning," individual creativeness begins at 30, and "at 60 a man quits public life" (Mannheim 1952, 278). The implication is that the important period of creative life is between 30 and 60. As we have seen, poetry anthologies and poetry promotions have brought the generational span down to a decade. By the same process, they have also reduced the period of active creative life to 10 years: once you are over 35, you are no longer of interest. Given the fuzziness of the concept (and the alternative model of intergenerational association), perhaps it is time to question the heuristic usefulness of "generations" in relation to poetry.

References

Allen, Donald Merriam (ed.) (1960). *The New American Poetry*. New York/London: Grove Press/Evergreen Press.

Alvarez, Al (ed.) (1962). *The New Poetry*. Harmondsworth: Penguin Books.

Byrne, James and Pollard, Clare (eds.) (2009). "Introduction." In: *Voice Recognition: 21 Poets for the 21st Century*, 10–17. Tarset: Bloodaxe Books.

Byrne, James and Sheppard, Robert (eds.) (2017). "Introduction." In: *Atlantic Drift: An Anthology of Poetry and Poetics*, 9–14. Todmorden: Arc.

Clarke, Adrian and Sheppard, Robert (1991). *Floating Capital: New Poets from London*. Elmwood, CT: Potes & Poets Press.

Conquest, Robert (ed.) (1956) 1967. *New Lines*. London: Macmillan.

Crozier, Andrew (1987). "Introduction." In: *A Various Art* (eds. Andrew Crozier and Tim Longville), 11–14. London: Paladin.

Davie, Donald (1973). "The varsity match." *Poetry Nation* 2: 72–80.

Edwards, Ken (1988). "Some Younger Poets." In: *The New British Poetry* (eds. Gillian Allnutt, Fred D'Aguiar, Ken Edwards and Eric Mottram), 265–270. London: Paladin.

Evaristo, Bernardine and Nagra, Daljit (eds.) (2010). *Ten: New Poets*. Hexham: Bloodaxe.

Forbes, Peter (1994). "Talking About the New Generation." *Poetry Review* 84 (1): 4–6.

Hamilton, Nathan (ed.) (2013). *Dear World & Everyone In It: New Poetry in the UK*. Tarset: Bloodaxe.

Harwood, Lee (2004). *Collected Poems, 1964–2004*. Bristol: Shearsman Books.

Hemingway, Ernest (1927). *The Sun Also Rises*. London: Jonathan Cape.

Henri, Adrian, McGough, Roger, and Patten, Brian (1967). *The Mersey Sound*. Harmondsworth: Penguin.

Horovitz, Michael (1969). *Children of Albion: Poetry of the "Underground" in Britain*. Harmondsworth: Penguin.

Hulse, Michael, Kennedy, David, and Morley, David (eds.) (1993). *The New Poetry*. Newcastle: Bloodaxe Books.

Hynes, Samuel (1976). *The Auden Generation: Literature and Politics in England in the 1930s*. London: Bodley Head.

Lumsden, Roddy (ed.) (2010). *Identity Parade: New British and Irish Poets*. Hexham: Bloodaxe.

Mannheim, Karl (1927) 1952. "The Problem of Generations." In: *Essays on the Sociology of Knowledge* (ed. Paul Kecskemeti), 276–320. London: Routledge & Kegan Paul.

McCarthy Woolf, Karen (ed.) (2014). "A True Fellowship." In: *Ten: The New Wave*, 15–20. Hexham: Bloodaxe.

Morrison, Blake (1980). *The Movement: English Poetry and Fiction of the 1950s*. London: Methuen.

Morrison, Blake and Motion, Andrew (eds.) (1982). *The Penguin Book of Contemporary British Poetry*. Harmondsworth: Penguin Books.

Mottram, Eric (1988). "A Treacherous Assault on British Poetry." In: *New British Poetry* (eds. Gillian Allnutt, Fred D'Aguiar, Ken Edwards and Eric Mottram), 131–133. London: Paladin.

Pilcher, Jane (1994). "Mannheim's sociology of generations: an undervalued legacy." *British Journal of Sociology* 45 (3): 481–495.

Poetry Book Society (2014). "Next Generation Poets." http://poetrybooks.co.uk/projects/51 (accessed 6 May 2020).

Rothenberg, Jerome (1981). *Pre-Faces and Other Writings*. New York: New Directions.

Ryder, Norman B. (1965). "The cohort in the study of social change." *American Sociological Review* 30: 843–861.

Smith, Stan (2007). *Poetry and Displacement*. Liverpool: Liverpool University Press.

Teitler, Nathalie (2014). "Preface." In: *Ten: the New Wave* (ed. Karen McCarthy Woolf), 11–14. Hexham: Bloodaxe.

Tuma, Keith (ed.) (2001). *Anthology of Twentieth-Century British and Irish Poetry*. New York: Oxford University Press.

Yeats, William Butler (1926). *Autobiographies*. London: Macmillan.

2c.2
The Movement

David Malcolm

Introduction

People do say some very bad things about the Movement. As Stephen Burt puts it, since the name became current in the mid-1950s, "The Movement as a set of poets, of poems, or of ideas, has been described, attacked, belittled, and occasionally admired ever since" (2009, 33). One should note that any admiration, in Burt's view, has been occasional. Blake Morrison quotes Edna Longley's comment from the early 1970s: "the Movement may be succeeding the Georgians as everyone's favorite Aunt Sally" (1980, 7).

The negative comments on the Movement have three focuses: doubt as to whether the Movement actually existed as a coherent grouping of poets and other writers; accusations of thematic limitation; and accusations of technical impoverishment.

Doubt

As Patrick Deane points out, there have long been critical worries as to how to define the Movement in a coherent and cohesive way. He quotes Ian Hamilton's insistence that the whole thing was a "P.R. job" generated by the editors of *The Spectator* (Deane 2016, 25). Morrison lists the assertions of Jeff Nuttall, Howard Sergeant, and Christopher Logue that the Movement was something of a "gigantic confidence trick" (1980, 3). J. D. Scott's famous (and originally anonymous) puff in *The Spectator* in August 1954 has a fine rhetorical swing

---

A Companion to Contemporary British and Irish Poetry, 1960–2015, First Edition.
Edited by Wolfgang Görtschacher and David Malcolm.
© 2021 John Wiley & Sons Ltd. Published 2021 by John Wiley & Sons Ltd.

to it, but is short on specifics (Scott 1954, 260–261; Morrison 1980, 2; Deane 2016, 26). Certainly the writers involved in the Movement are disparate. Deane writes of a "heterodox, piebald, and loose literary association" (2016, 25). Burt notes that Donald Davie, Philip Larkin, and Thom Gunn insist that they did not share very much with the other writers with whom they were identified (2009, 33). Morrison confirms this, pointing to Kingsley Amis's, Elizabeth Jennings's, and even Robert Conquest's unease at a group identification (1980, 4–5; see also Gunn's comments quoted in Morrison 1980, 41). So, when we talk about the Movement, we may well be speaking about, at best, a press-generated category, and, at worst, a phantom (although phantoms may, of course, produce important effects in the literary world and in literary history).

Thematic Limitation

With regard to this focus, the comments are mostly coherent and very hostile. Three major and connected accusations are leveled at Movement poets (and Movement writers in general, although most of the fusillades are directed at the poets). First, Movement poets are insular and parochial. Deane (in propria persona) writes of the "quietly proud insularity" of the *New Lines* anthology (2016, 32). In the journal *Essays in Criticism* in 1957, Charles Tomlinson writes of Larkin's "intense parochialism," and of the Movement's being marked by "a self-congratulatory provincialism" (quoted in Ludwig 1995, 56). Peter Barry and Robert Hampson write of a parochial turn in British poetry, of which the Movement is a major part (1993, 2–3). Burt notes that critics have described the Movement as "a 'provincial middle-class' revolt against self-conscious sophistication" (2009, 37).

Second, Movement poets are "middlebrow." Tomlinson's 1957 savaging is entitled "The Middlebrow Muse" (Tomlinson 1957; Ludwig 1995, 56). Burt sees Movement poets as writers "who in some ways aimed low" (2009, 33). Robert Hewison notes their eschewing of "any appeal to Mandarin taste" (1981, 114). Morrison, however, sees them writing for "an academic elite" (1980, 129, 117), although by the standards of some that might, indeed, count as middlebrow.

Third, Movement poets are genteel. This is the substance of Al Alvarez's celebrated engagement with the Movement in the "inflammatory introduction" to his influential anthology *The New Poetry* (1962) (Alvarez 1967, 17). The rhetorical *tour de force* of this introduction has had a great effect on how the Movement is understood more than 50 years later. The Movement disdains "wild, loose emotion," Alvarez claims (1967, 23). It is "academic-administrative verse, polite, knowledgeable, efficient, polished, and, in its quiet way, even intelligent" (1967, 23). There is no facing up to "the more uncompromising forces at work in our time," although, in any case, D. H. Lawrence is the only English writer who does so (1967, 26). The cause of this avoidance is "middle-class gentility" (26). The Movement, in particular, and English writing, in general, need to "drop the pretence that life, give or take a few social distinctions, is the same as ever, that gentility, decency and all the other social totems will eventually muddle through" (27–28). Although it will not ensure good work, the poet, Alvarez more than implies, must "walk naked" through the horrors and the revelations of the twentieth century (29), and the Movement poets do not do that. At much the same time as Alvarez and in a more balanced manner, G. S. Fraser confirms this view. "There is a sense in which both the virtues and the vices of the academic mind – precision and balance on the one hand, caginess and a muffled (or muffed) awareness of the world on the other – were the virtues and vices of Movement poetry" (Fraser 1970, 348). Alvarez's accusations have stuck. Stated or unstated, they underlie much more recent commentary on the Movement and on postwar British poetry in general (Gioia 2003, ix–xii).

Technical Impoverishment

Movement poems are technically inhibited and unambitious. Burt writes that the *New Lines* poets "prized clarity and technical facility," which seems to be code for choosing traditional and undemanding verse forms (2009, 33). Alvarez emphasizes D. J. Enright's difference from other *New Lines* poets "since he rarely sticks to the metrical norms on which the rest insist" (1967, 24). Scott's editorial in *The Spectator* speaks of the Movement's "goodbye to the Little Magazine and 'experimental writing'" (quoted Morrison 1980, 2). Fraser writes of Movement poems being "addressed to an ideal 'plain reader'" (1970, 347), presumably one who appreciates recognized forms and rhythms. This view has endured. In the Introduction to *The Penguin Book of Contemporary British Poetry* (1982), Blake Morrison and Andrew Motion write of the "Movement virtues of commonsense, craftsmanship, and explication" (16).

These accusations are all related. A presumed middlebrow, genteel, middle-class reader will enjoy the thematically and technically attenuated pabulum offered by the Movement. In justice, one must note that Conquest in his introduction to *New Lines* encourages such a view. The new poetry is wary of mysticism; it is "empirical"; it refuses "to abandon a rational structure and comprehensible language"; its practitioners demonstrate "a negative determination to avoid bad principles"; and "the central tradition of all English poetry, classical or romantic" is to be espoused (Conquest 1956, xv). The general view set out in the earlier text has now become consensus. Despite Stephen Regan's persuasive relation of Larkin's deployment of Modernist interests and techniques in his poems, including poems from the *New Lines* anthology (2007, 147–158), the modesty of the Movement's thematic and technical ambitions has been endorsed in much criticism. Fraser writes: "I suppose the broadly accepted picture of their poetry as restrained, lucid, concerned with teasing out clearly small or at least manageable moral problems, rather insular, traditionally formal [...] keeping its emotions well under control, given to distancing and irony, is a true picture" (1970, 249). Vincent Sherry describes the standard view of the Movement in similar terms: its "poets, formally conservative and reactionary, battle the (putative) excesses of an energy they do not own, in particular the experimental and convention-dismaying verve of American modernists and postmodernists" (1994, 577–578). This, Sherry insists, is a "caricature," but an enduring and very powerful one. It is reproduced by Gary Day in 1997, who writes of the Movement, "Its restricted subject matter, empirical character, disciplined construction and chaste diction represented a poetic timidity, inviting charges of philistinism and provincialism" (2).

Despite or, really, because of this, critics claim that the Movement has prospered, endured, and its influence can be felt in British poetry over the last 50–60 years. It is argued that it has achieved a wide, if middlebrow (whatever that means) readership. Deane writes of their "rather inexplicable success and influence" (2016, 26; see also 32, 36). Day and Docherty see Alvarez's *The New Poetry* as really just a Movement anthology (1997, 2), while Eric Mottram clearly considers that the opposition to his British Poetry Revival lies in entrenched post-Movement attitudes (1993, 15–50). Morrison and Motion even suggest that through Philip Hobsbaum's influence, Movement values may have impinged on the work of the Northern Irish poets of the 1960s and 1970s (1982, 16). With regard to such enduring influence and popularity, one must, however, note that Amis, Enright, and John Wain all worried about becoming too popular and having too wide a readership (Morrison 1980, 111). One must also note that the only edition of the *New Lines* anthology that is readily available for purchase by an interested reader is a first edition.

2

One of the major problems in discussing the Movement is to know what and whom to discuss. Is it only the nine poets included in *New Lines*? Is it only the work in *New Lines* or all or part of their subsequent work? Should one consider all the intellectual, personal, and political transformations and vagaries of Movement writers (however so defined) over several decades? Can one include prose writers among the personnel? Can other writers who identify themselves with or who somehow can be identified with the presumed values of the Movement be discussed? Such problems vex Morrison. If the Movement is a "sensibility" (as he suggests it is), can anyone writing within such a "sensibility" be fair game for inclusion (1980, 8–9)?

It strikes me in reviewing the secondary material on the Movement that no one has ever done a perhaps reductive, but rather obvious thing. That is to focus exclusively on the poems included in the *New Lines* anthology. The Movement sensu *largo* has been discussed fully by Morrison (1980). The Movement sensu stricto, taken to be the poems printed in *New Lines*, has not. Deane warns that "it was – and remains – difficult to hear what they [Movement poets] might have had to say, left to themselves [...]" (2016, 29). In what follows, I wish to try to do so.

3

I argue that most commentary on the Movement is not only very hostile, but is—if one adopts my particular purview—wrong.[1] The accusations against the Movement (for that is what they are) can be grouped into two categories, one broad and thematic, the other narrower and technical. The thematic accusation is that of limitation, insularity, gentility, and dodging the fierce and the dark. The technical accusation is that Movement poems lack variety and interest.

The Parochial Genteel

Abroad

It is striking how many of the poems in *New Lines* are about non-British places. Such poems are: Jennings's "Afternoon in Florence" (1), "Florence: Design for a City" (4–5), and "Piazza San Marco" (6–7); Gunn's "Lerici" (31) and "On the Move" (31–33) (this has to be set in North America—"The blue jay" is unknown in Europe (line 1), in stanza 3 "whereabouts" (line 18) rhymes with "routes," (line 24) as in US English (line 18, 24), and in any case the poem ends with the paratext "California"); Enright's "Evening in the Khamsin" (53–54), "Baie des Anges, Nice" (54–56), "The Laughing Hyena, by Hokusai" (56–57), "Mid-Mediterranean: September Evening" (58), "Latin Festival" (59) (in which abroad is explicitly contrasted with England), "Lost, Stolen or Strayed" (59–60), and "The Wondering Scholar" (62–63); Conquest's "Nantucket" (74), "In the Rhodope" (76–77), "Dédée d'Anvers" (77–78), and "Near Jakobselv" (80–81). That is almost one out of every five poems in the collection (16 of 77). It should be stressed that these settings are not superficial or matters of local color merely. Jennings's Italian poems are engagements with the observed world; Gunn's California is very American; Enright is interested in his Japanese locales; Conquest's "Nantucket" really is a response to the US Atlantic coast. On a simple level, *New Lines* looks less insular than they say.

Death

The poets in *New Lines* cannot be accused of dodging this central existential issue. Poems about death include Holloway's "Epitaph for a Man" (9–10), "Elegy for an Estrangement" (11–14) (I cannot see a genteel muffing of the topic in, for example, the last stanza, which ends with a dark six-stress line, "Streets of an endless town. Night falls in rain"), and "The Shell" (15). They also include Gunn's "Lerici" (31) and "The Inherited Estate" (40–42) (which last, if not directly about death, certainly about ruin). Enright's "Evening in the Khamsin" (53–54), "The Laughing Hyena, by Hokusai" (56–57), and "On the Death of a Child" (57) also belong in this thematic category, as does Davie's celebrated poem on transience "Remembering the 'Thirties" (70–72).

Vatic Madness and the Dark

When Alvarez suggests that Movement poets do not walk naked through the unhinged horrors of their times, he is wrong. The awful forces, the dark powers are constantly embodied, courted, certainly not ignored, though maybe sometimes overcome in *New Lines* poems. Conquest may have disliked a 1940s surrender to "the Id" (1956, xi), but he did choose a lot of poems with a lot of "Id" in them. "Something of me is out in the dark landscape," Jennings writes in "In the Night" (7–8; 7, l. 6). That dark landscape and its denizens bleed into many of the poems in the collection. One has to be selective to miss it. Holloway's "all the fabulous / Things of the moon's dark side" in "Warning to a Guest" (16–17; 17, ll. 31–32) is relevant here, as are the injunctions to "Shun the black puddles" (l. 6) and "Yet shun that dark foreshore" (l. 18). His "Toper's Poem" (14–15) gives a voice to the deranged.

Gunn's "Merlin in the Cave: He Speculates without a Book" (34–37) enacts a remarkable intensity of feeling and an extreme existential state ("The Rock. The space, too narrow for a hand" [34, l. 8]). Amis's "Here Is Where" (47–48) is scarcely on an even keel. "Scream the place down *here*, / There's nobody *there*" (48, ll. 17–18). There is "Something Nasty in the Bookshop" (46–47). Enright's "The Laughing Hyena, by Hokusai" (56–57) courts the hideous, but "Lost, Stolen or Strayed" (59–60) transforms A. A. Milne's childhood verse (not without its own darkness) into a wild, oriental night in *la boue* ("The last sour jerk of energy that slaps back the rising stairs" [60, l. 9]). "Whom I have knives for could begin with you" begins Davie's "Too Late for Satire" (68–69). "The effect remains, as ever, gaunt and fierce," declares the speaker in his "Limited Achievement" (69, l. 12). Conquest's "Epistemology of Poetry" (73–74), despite its coldly intellectual title and calming conclusion, circles round "dark, wide pupils" (73, l. 14), declares "Now darkness falls" (73, l. 17), and knows "the rash / Disruption of the lightning flash" (74, ll. 19–20). The speaker in his "Nantucket" (74–75) invokes Melville and his whalers ("the boldest men on earth" [74, l. 13]) and ("the demon seas / Of his heart" [74, ll. 14–15]), and the voice in "Anthéor" (75–76) notes how "the hot stars crackle / In a sky of ice" (75, ll. 23–24).

By what overheated standard is any of this an over-refined avoidance of the disturbed and disturbing?

Language

In keeping with this last aspect of *New Lines* verse, the language of its poems is much more diverse and demotic than Alvarez declares it to be ("academic-administrative verse, polite, knowledgeable, efficient, polished" [1967, 23]). The words are much fiercer than Alvarez acknowledges—see the earlier text. Lexis is, certainly, often sophisticated (although what is wrong with that, per se?). See, for example, the rather formal and elegant opening of Jennings's "Afternoon in Florence" (1), "This afternoon disturbs within the mind / No other afternoon, is out of time" (ll. 1–2), or "Light detains no prisoner here at all / In brick or stone but sends a freedom out" (ll. 6–7). Or see, for example, the formal and erudite beginning of Davie's "Remembering the 'Thirties" (70–71): "Hearing one saga, we enact the next. / We please our elders when we sit enthralled" (ll. 1–2). Many other examples could easily be generated. But note, too, the forceful demotic of so many *New Lines* poems. Note the informal slippage of Holloway's "Epitaph for a Man" (9–10): "It took in all the lot" (70, l. 9). Remember Larkin's "Someone would know: I don't" ("Church Going" [20–23, l. 12]) and "'Oh well, / I suppose it's not the place's fault,' I said" ("I Remember, I Remember" [22–23; 20, ll. 34–35]). One could also point to Amis's "our stuff / Can get by without it" ("Something Nasty in the Bookshop" [46–47; 47, ll. 25–26]) and, indeed, the entirety of "The Voice of Authority" (49–50)—"You get a move on, see, do what I say" (49, l. 2). "Then have we missed the bus?" asks the speaker in Enright's "Waiting for the Bus" (53, l. 10), and "To blame is lame" argues the voice in Davie's "Too Late for Satire" (68–69; 69, l. 19). Wain concludes "Minutes of the Last Meeting" (84–85) with the informal, but nonetheless existentially perceptive, "Because the bloody things were always bills" (85, l.19). Again, many other examples of linguistic informality (that is disruptive of gentility, surely) can be generated. *New Lines* courts "this fluency / of drabness in stumbling anyday speech" (Wain's "Who Speaks My Language?" (III) [86–87; 86, ll. 6–7]) as much as linguistic formality and sophistication.

Matters of Substance

Fraser's suggestion that Movement poets are "concerned with teasing out clearly small or at least manageable moral problems" (1970, 249) is misleading. They take on serious issues and in a serious fashion. I have already noted an engagement with death and the darkly deranged in the earlier text. But there are other matters in *New Lines*. For example, note Jennings's focus on problems of perception in "Afternoon in Florence" (1), "Identity" (2–3), "A Way of Looking" (6), and "In the Night" (7–8). I fail to see how the philosophical issues considered by the figures in Holloway's "Elegy for an Estrangement" (11–14) are minor. History and its disruptions are close to several poems in *New Lines*. It is central to Jennings's "Not in the Guide-Books" (5–6)—"For one grown tired of histories" (6, l. 14) the place evoked is a good one. The understatement in Enright's "The Interpreters" (60–62)—"the lot of a sizeable part of a sizeable nation" (61, l. 10)—makes the listing of history's vileness even more forceful. Davie's "Rejoinder to a Critic" (67) and "Remembering the 'Thirties" (70–72) are surely extraordinarily complex and intelligent treatments of the weight of their times. Like Conquest's "Nantucket" (74), they are brilliant historical poems.

There is a strong autothematic element in many *New Lines* poems (*pace* J. D. Scott [1954, 260–261]), which is not a nugatory topic. One might not agree with what the speaker in Amis's "Something Nasty in the Bookshop" (46–47) is saying—although what he says is imbued with ambiguities—but he is certainly addressing a topic of some urgency, at least to writers and readers. Surely, Davie's "The Fountain" (65) is a very intelligent and engaged consideration of art's role in things—"We ask of fountains only that they play" (l. 18). "A Head Painted by Daniel O'Neill" (66–67) reprises Keats's concerns in "Ode on a Grecian Urn" and Yeats's "Sailing to Byzantium." A focus on art and its relations with life is there, too, in Conquest's "Epistemology of Poetry" (73–74) and "Anthéor" (75–76). Again, there are other examples. The issue here is not whether these poems deal with serious subjects well (although I believe they do), but that they do take on matters of substance.

The Technically Timid

As I have shown in the earlier text, the charge of lack of technical ambition, a drab traditionality, a prosy lucidity, is frequently leveled against Movement poetry. As with accusations of thematic limitation, I find this charge to be unsubstantiated in the *New Lines* collection. The poems in *New Lines* do not look like Modernist verse or later twentieth-century experimental poetry, but they do show considerable technical variety and craft (which are surely not to be rejected out of hand as dull). Line length varies substantially throughout the collection, as do number of stresses per line. It is not all iambic pentameters and tetrameters and ballad stanzas. Holloway's "Elegy for an Estrangement" (11–14) is a long semi-narrative poem with a very complex and odd rhyme scheme. Davie deploys unrhymed 10-syllable lines in "The Fountain" (65) and "A Head Painted by Daniel O'Neill" (66–67). In "Nantucket" (74), Conquest uses 10-syllable lines mostly, but they are unrhymed and line length is flexible in places (ll. 1, 15–19). It is not free verse, but it is blank verse. Several of Enright's poems have long unrhymed lines: "Evening in the Khamsin" (53–54), "Baie des Anges, Nice" (54–56), "The Laughing Hyena, by Hokusai" (56–57).

Poets' deployment of half-rhyme in *New Lines* is particularly widespread and interesting. Let us take as an example the last stanza of Jennings's "Not in the Guide-Books" (5–6).

> Yet good, a place like this,
> For one grown tired of histories
> To shape a human myth,
> A story but for his
> Delight, where he might make the place
> His own success
> Building what no one else has bothered with –
> A simple life or death.
> (6, ll. 13–20)

If we ignore the rhythmic and accentual variety of these lines (which is substantial and semantically loaded), we can see that the rhymes offered are disturbingly off the true. The first four lines of this stanza bring together "this / histories / myth / his," which chime but do not rhyme. The rhyming in the last four lines is equally odd. Does "place" chime with "success"? Does "with" rhyme with "death"? Do these rhymes hark back in a slant echo to the rhymes of the first four lines? As with regard to so many *New Lines* poems, to belittle the ambiguities and disturbances of this craft as a simple, explicatory technique is deeply misleading. This brief analysis of an aspect of an extract from one poem suggests that there are complexities galore in the rest of the collection.

They can say all the bad things they like about the Movement. With regard to the *New Lines* collection, they are wrong.

Note

1 I wish it to be clear that I am taking no position with regard to the 1950s or subsequent political, social, or cultural attitudes expressed by various *New Lines* poets. That is a legitimate subject for discussion, but it is not mine.

References

Alvarez, Al (1967). "The New Poetry, or Beyond the Gentility Principle." In: *The New Poetry* (ed. A. Alvarez), 21–32. Harmondsworth: Penguin.

Barry, Peter and Hampson, Robert (1993). "The Scope of the Possible." In: *New British Poetries: The Scope of the Possible* (eds. Robert Hampson and Peter Barry), 1–11. Manchester/New York: Manchester University Press.

Burt, Stephen (2009). "The Movement and the Mainstream." In: *Postwar British and Irish Poetry* (eds. Nigel Alderman and C.D. Blanton), 32–50. Malden, MA/Oxford: Wiley-Blackwell.

Conquest, Robert (1956). "Introduction." In: *New Lines: An Anthology* (ed. Robert Conquest), xi–xviii. London: Macmillan.

Day, Gary (1997). "Introduction: Poetry, Politics and Tradition." In: *British Poetry from the 1950s to the 1990s: Politics and Art* (eds. Gary Day and Brian Docherty), 1–22. Basingstoke: Macmillan.

Deane, Patrick (2016). "The Movement: Poetry and the Reading Public." In: *The Cambridge Companion to British Poetry, 1945–2000*, 25–38. Cambridge: Cambridge University Press.

Fraser, G.S. (1970). *The Modern Writer and His World*. Harmondsworth: Penguin.

Gioia, Dana (2003). *Barrier of a Common Language: An American Looks at Contemporary British Poetry*. Ann Arbor: University of Michigan Press.

Hewison, Robert (1981). *In Anger: British Culture in the Cold War, 1945–1960*. New York: Oxford University Press.

Ludwig, Hans-Werner (1995). "Province and Metropolis, Centre and Periphery: Some Critical Terms Re-Examined." In: *Poetry in the British Isles: Non-Metropolitan Perspectives* (eds. Hans-Werner Ludwig and Lothar Fietz), 47–69. Cardiff: University of Wales Press.

Morrison, Blake (1980). *The Movement: English Poetry and Fiction of the 1950s*. Oxford: Oxford University Press.

Morrison, Blake and Motion, Andrew (1982). "Inroduction." In: *The Penguin Book of Contemporary British Poetry* (eds. Blake Morrison and Andrew Motion), 11–20. London: Penguin.

Mottram, Eric (1993). "The British Poetry Revival, 1960–1975." In: *New British Poetries: The Scope of the Possible* (eds. Robert Hampson and Peter Barry), 15–50. Manchester and New York: Manchester University Press.

Regan, Stephen (2007). "Philip Larkin: A Late Modern Poet." In: *The Cambridge Companion to Twentieth-Century English Poetry* (ed. Neil Corcoran), 147–158. Cambridge: Cambridge University Press.

Scott, J. D. (Anon.) (1954). "Poets of the Fifties." *Spectator* (27 August), 260–261.

Sherry, Vincent (1994). "Poetry in England, 1945–1990." In: *The Columbia History of British Poetry* (eds. Carl Woodring and James Shapiro), 577–604. New York: Columbia University Press.

Tomlinson, Charles (1957). "The Middlebrow Muse." *Essays in Criticism*, 7: 208–217.

2c.3
The Liverpool Poets

Ludmiła Gruszewska-Blaim

The Liverpool Poets: Spacing *The Mersey Sound*, 3rd Edition

In the early 1960s, voice in British poetry, so far modulated by the neutral tonality of the Movement, gained an overtly personal dimension and, as a result, a more literal meaning. Responding, among others, to the American jazz-and-poetry revival, and the free verse poetry of Allen Ginsberg, the major figure of the Beat Generation, the British poetic scene changed its orientation. Like jazz played in backstreet clubs and coffee shops at that time, poetry—now purportedly construing the poet's own life and speaking in his/her own voice—slipped into spontaneous, improvised forms. The British counterculture made it "a performance instrument of communal gathering, and (often) the voice of political protest" (Sheppard 2005, 40). The sound of poetry, accompanied by chanting, electric guitars, drums, etc., was no longer metaphoric, caged on the page, and appreciated only by connoisseurs. The desire of all to revive the stagnant channels of poetic communication by pushing out the boundaries of poetry, searching "for voices in the demotic and vernacular" (Wade 2001b, 18), and incorporating other arts to help it speak louder gave new strength to the poetic word, intentionally muffled by the previous post-Second World War decade. Due to an explosion of poetry readings, launched by Michael Horovitz's Live New Departures, the supposedly real voice of poetry started to resound where few had ever heard it before. This explosion of poetry into a performing art in the 1960s had also other consequences, as it "produced a wide number of poets who wrote primarily for the reading circuit or to be heard and seen rather than simply read on the page" (Booth 1985, 112). Poetry writing became an activity for the

---

A Companion to Contemporary British and Irish Poetry, 1960–2015, First Edition.
Edited by Wolfgang Görtschacher and David Malcolm.
© 2021 John Wiley & Sons Ltd. Published 2021 by John Wiley & Sons Ltd.

people and by the people with a less pronounced demand for sophistication and high artistic quality. "My whole poetics," asserted Adrian Henri, "had been formed from the concept (ultimately derived from Williams, Olson, and the Black Mountain poets) of writing for, and in, one's own voice" ("A City of Poems" 1996, 37).

The Liverpool Scene

The Liverpool "beat sound" (or "the Mersey sound") of the 1960s, popularized, on the one hand, by The Beatles as well as by numerous less famous Merseysiders—rock 'n' roll groups greatly influenced by American rhythm and blues artists (Stakes 2001, 164)—and, on the other, by poets experimenting with ways of putting the mundane and the marginal into formally and stylistically accessible verse performed live, became a most important marker of the British wave of counterculture and democratization of art. Adrian Mitchell's famous diagnostic concerning general disregard for poetry—"Most people ignore most poetry because most poetry ignores most people" (1964, 8)—seemed to have been taken seriously into consideration by many of his contemporaries, who decided to compete for a wider audience by addressing it directly. Very young and/or poorly educated people became a natural target and ideal addressees. Living relatively far from the cultural and political centers and acquainted with tabloids and music halls rather than literary classics and opera houses, they flooded pubs and clubs where budding poets read their accessible poetry at jazz concerts. "In the hands of writers such as [Pete] Brown and Henri, jazz-with-poetry mutated gradually into rock-with-poetry as, toward the mid-1960s, the musical style of the day was changing" (Townsend 2001, 172). Adrian Henri, Roger McGough, and Brian Patten—active participants and/or committee members in the Mersey Arts Festival since 1962—were well acquainted with non-establishment forms of artistic creativity, which contested purist divisions into poetry, music, painting, and acting. In their performances that both inspired and were inspired by poetry they created, all arts were by some means present, enhancing an artistic effect. Phil Bowen's description of the "route" taken by one of their most successful achievements, McGough's poem *Summer With Monika*, aptly reflects the nature of sound they helped to popularize: "With its lightness of touch, colour and irreverence adroitly juxtaposing universal irony with the failure of urban domestic love, *Summer With Monika* seemed to catch the mood of the times perfectly. Eventually published in 1967, also an L.P. which guitarist Andy Roberts (who collaborated on the album) felt never got due recognition, it later became a stage play directed by Mel Smith. It was later re-issued featuring illustrations by Peter Blake /.../. More recently it was re-mastered as a C.D. and latterly adapted by McGough as a radio play. The title was taken from a film poster outside Hope Hall / ... /." (Bowen 2008, 51)

Attempting to cajole the public with poems whose immediacy, at least superficially, was on a level with that of rock 'n' roll lyrics, Henri, McGough, and Patten adopted the point of view of a person from the neighborhood who, like the great majority, queues in a fish-and-chip shop in the afternoon, makes love in his rented flat in the evening, listens to Andy Williams or The Beatles at midnight, sees the pretty young girl off to the door at dawn, and gets on the bus early in the morning to muse about the bomb and the end of the world. Under the influence of French Symbolists, Baudelaire and Rimbaud, Apollinaire, San Francisco's Beat scene and Ginsberg, The Beatles, and others, the Liverpool Poets constructed a unique register and voice that were found congenial by their fans. They "listened, learnt, and led" (Mitchell, quoted in Bowen 2008, 3), and their poetics "stitched into the physical, social and cultural context of 'Liverpool,' understood as a geographical location as well as a social construct and a cultural identity" (Gräbner 2016, 71) refreshed the stale atmosphere of old-style poetry readings. Since what the audience demanded from its performing poets in 1967 was "parody of the language of its elders" (Lindop 1972, 105), flouting traditional decorum seemed a must. As Stephen Wade observes, "Liverpool gave poetry in general a sense of the centrality of the art to the popular spirit. Its writers made poetry as important as the strongest emotions. The poems contained in the Liverpool anthologies also demonstrated that there was no subject beyond the scope of poetry" (2001a, xvii). Thus, Ginsberg's declaration that Liverpool had become "at the present moment the center of the consciousness of the human universe" (quoted in Lucie-Smith 1967, 15) surprised and/or angered only those who never ventured beyond the literary canon.

The name Liverpool Poets was coined by Edward Lucie-Smith who, in 1967, published *The Liverpool Scene: Recorded Live Along the Mersey Beat*, an anthology of urban oral culture of the Sixties. Apart from Henri, McGough, and Patten, who judging by various introductions to the period, seem to have appropriated the name, the anthology also featured other Liverpool poets, such as Pete Brown, Mike Evans, and Heather Holden. The publication of *The Mersey Sound* as No. 10 of the prestigious *Penguin Modern Poets* series in 1967, and two other collections in the same year, tied Henri, McGough, and Patten—then relatively unknown performing poets representing the pop poetry movement of the Sixties—into a closely cooperating and extremely successful group that lasted till 1976, when Patten's collection *Vanishing Trick* set an entirely different tone. "The label [Liverpool Poets]," Linda Cookson maintains, "has perhaps brought rather more disadvantages than advantages over the years" (1997, 13). An automatic, cultural association with the 1960s formed in the minds of their readers ("flower power, drug culture, 'free love', and so on" (Cookson 1997, 13)) has never freed the poets from the constraints of the chronotope marked by counterculture, despite the maturation of their talents. Their popularity among the young, mainly rock 'n' roll fans, was scorned by academic critics and more traditionally serious poets, like Douglas Dunn who reproached the Liverpool trio for "subordinating craft to effect" (in *Encounter* quoted in Bowen 2008, 2). However, the three Mersey poets "revelled in being lowbrow, interpreting this as a new kind of writing rather than something determinedly anti-aesthetic" (Wade 2001b, 10).

As their biographers and critics often emphasize, unlike many other casual poetic groups, Henri, McGough, and Patten were well acquainted with each other, "held similar political and social views, were mutually influenced and shared common beliefs regarding direction and audience" (Bowen 2008, 2). By 1967, the trio had participated in multiple poetic ventures, for example, the Sampson & Barlow's readings. Their genuine interest in their real-life audience made them focus most of all on the effect that a poem might produce—"on what a poem did rather than what it was" (Bowen 2008, 2), which is not to say, however, that their poetry was as straightforward or excessively emotional as many critics suggested. The accusation of "[s]entimentality, coarseness of texture, carelessness with details" (Lucie-Smith 1967, 12), highlighted by critics who deemed performance poetry a gimmick, clashes with the fact that over one million copies of *The Mersey Sound* have been sold ever since its publication in 1967. As Henri remarked in an interview: "Talking about performance poetry, in my terms, is a false dichotomy because I see reading the poem out loud and reading the poem on the page as two aspects of the poem's life" (Side 2019).

Penguin Modern Poets 10—The Mersey Sound

Despite marked differences in contents and composition, four editions of *The Mersey Sound* and several additional printings that followed the original, two "revised and expanded" and one restored editions (1967, 1974, 1983, 2007), are often referred to as if they basically constituted the same collection. However, the exultant spontaneity, if not irreverence, characterizing the initial selection and sequence of texts, reflecting the performative rather than manipulative nature of Henri's, McGough's, and Patten's poetry, gradually gave way to a more writerly attitude of the authors to their volume and was, in time, noticeably reduced. In the 1974 and 1983 editions, they not only replaced some of the poems with their more topical equivalents ("The Last Residents," for example, added to the third edition may be read as a response to political events in Eastern Europe), but also eliminated texts (e.g., "Why Patriots Are a Bit Nuts in the Head") deemed "primitive" in attitudes and reasoning (Lindop 1972, 102). In each of the two revised editions, in other words, the Liverpool Poets decided to discard outdated or artistically weaker poems, publishing in their place more appealing works. The alterations they made might also result from a more obvious reason: as performance poets, they needed change, and the editions of their collection provided an opportunity to diversify and modulate their sounds. The 1983 edition may be, therefore, regarded as their third and final attempt to update their printing performance. The latest "Restored 50th Anniversary Edition" that simply replays the original sound, published 40 years after the first publication of *The Mersey Sound* and 7 years after death of Adrian Henri, is more a tribute to their life work than a subsequent stage in the career of the three poets from Liverpool.

Introducing The Mersey Sound, *3rd Edition*

With the Mersey beat shaping their voices and the city of Liverpool influencing their imagery, Henri, McGough, and Patten depict in the three editions of *The Mersey Sound* a universe of the mind shaped in the Sixties. Personal and rebellious undertones heard in their printed and recorded "songs" work in unison with numerous references to pop-songs and pop-culture. As Andrew Duncan notices, "The pop style became big business when Penguin put out *The Mersey Sound*" (2003, 98), and the style involved "direct address;

simplified structures; the replacement of argument by an assumed trust in the poet's character [...]; frequently, an apocalyptic view of world affairs [...]; the claim that political decisions are utterly simple and that the authorities who make things complicated are simply deluded" (2003, 97). Both a dreamy and down-to-earth atmosphere of urban life on the margins is another important characteristic of the pop style, which rendered everyday experience into ordinary people's art. Programmatically subversive, provincial, and democratic, *The Mersey Sound* keeps its distance from all acknowledged centers—political, social, cultural, and artistic—building up a Liverpudlian galactic with tabloid news, pop-songs, obscure street names, rented rooms, and leisure time. The modest poetic galactic succeeds in preserving "the sense of Liverpool as a frontier city, a wild location of forgotten industrialism that was post-boom and embedded in old-fashioned Labour values" (Wade 2001b, 17). And yet, although focused on the banks of the Mersey and the Sixties (see Henri's "Mrs Albion You've Got a Lovely Daughter"), the artistic vision of the Liverpool Poets unexpectedly expands beyond temporal and spatial limits reaching out to other planets or to Wordsworth's daffodils (see Henri's "Galactic Lovepoem" and "The New, Fast, Automatic Daffodils").

It can be argued that the framing poems of *The Mersey Sound*, 3rd edition—Henri's surrealist, anti-Movement opening manifesto "Tonight at Noon" and Patten's dystopic vision of the future in the closing poem of the collection "The Last Residents"—adequately unmask and round up the Liverpool poets' subversive frames of mind and may serve as good examples of the poetics that the Liverpool Poets ultimately subscribed to.

"Tonight at Noon," based on the reverse logic and imagery of the negative, borrows its title from a 1964 album by jazz bassist and composer Charles Mingus, to whom the poem is dedicated. Following, perhaps, the advice offered by the Liverpool R&B band Clayton Squares (also mentioned in his dedication), Henri gives free rein to imagination in his opening poem. Conjuring up the simultaneously nocturnal and midday cityscape as the context for pigeons hunting "cats through city backyards" (l. 11) and white Americans demonstrating "for equal rights / in front of the Black House," (ll. 16–17), he shows that the shape of poetic reality can be free of constant conjunction, even if there are multiple references to the current situation.

Paradoxically, Henri's subversive, poetic negative turning black into white, and vice versa, seems to appeal to the reader's sense of justice and wishful thinking. Most of us wish we could live in a world in which the superpowers declare peace on each other, instead of war, and where unemployment is unknown, for "There's jobs for everyone and nobody wants them" (l. 24). However, Henri's revolution does not stop at that; it goes deeper, into the surreal, inverting the course of history and natural order, seemingly to redress old wrongs: "Hitler will tell us to fight on the beaches and on the landing fields / [...] and Nelson will not only get his eye back but his arm as well" (ll. 12, 14). The readers' growing uncertainty as to how they should react to the alternative reality where "the leaves fall upwards to the trees" (l. 9), the Monster creates Dr Frankenstein, and the dead "bury the living" (l. 28) is happily resolved in the punch line, which provides the motivation. One is expected to breathe with a sigh of relief, for the stakes are not really high: "Tonight at Noon" turns out to be a love song written in the metaphysical poetry mode.

> In forgotten graveyards everywhere the dead will quietly
> Bury the living
> And
> You will tell me you love me
> Tonight at noon.
>
> (ll. 27–29)

The subtle rhetoric of Henri's poem apparently serves a personal purpose. By inviting his readers to accept the fair causes and effects of his revolution, the poet expects them to overlook the fact that his reticent paramour ("you") is manipulated into saying what he wants her to say. Kidnapped from everyday reality and projected into a reverse world of his own making, his significant other is artfully denied freedom of speech.

"The Last Residents" by Patten, the final poem of the collection, is radically different in its scope: what it depicts is not a cagey, topsy-turvy, private world built to "make love, not war," but a spacey, dystopian world of recurrent revolutions that "resolve nothing" (l. 19)—a world inhabited by generations of unsuccessful fellow-poets from the East and the West. The vision of the wasteland, in Patten's poem, written into the cycles of both nature and culture, takes us from Siberia and its snows of yesterday ("Would Russia have changed much? / The snows melted in Siberia?" [ll. 6–7]) to London of the years to come and its "plagued allotments" (l. 22), frequented by the city's last residents, "crying / With disbelief and absurd astonishment" (ll. 23–24). In Patten's poem, the revolutionary notes are played through historical references: Mayakovsky, whose name is the opening keyword of the poem, and Russia with its snow-covered Siberia take us back in time to the beginning of the twentieth century and the rise of the Soviet Union. The reader's thoughts go off into the gloomy future of another futile, revolutionary effort, when the poet from "The Last Residents" reports that in Western Europe, "more subtly now / Are the prisons fed, the warrants issued" (ll. 14–15). Like Mayakovsky before him, "Half-crazy with sorrow," with his "soul finally shipwrecked" (l. 2), he sits watching history repeat itself.

If viewed as utterances entering into a poetic dialog, "Tonight at Noon" and "The Last Residents" do not constitute a buoyant exchange. Henri's revolution that starts with restoring peace and justice, in time attempts to change the laws of nature, and finally entraps the individual within the discourse of the other, may still be construed as playful. But that cannot be said about Patten's grim vision of revolutionary turmoil revealing "The outcome as inevitable" (l. 17) and implicating East and West as potentially dystopic regions.

The Mersey Sound: *Adrian Henri*

The first 25 poems of the volume written by Adrian Henri thrust the reader into a dreamy, here and there surrealist, or clearly Gothicized, world of peripheral spaces and inordinate/uncanny emotions.

> Without you ghost ferries would cross the Mersey manned by skeleton crews…
> Without you white birds would wrench themselves free from my paintings and fly off dripping blood into the night
>
> ("Without You," ll. 3, 9)

> You make me feel like
> something from beyond the grave
> baby
> ("Car Crash Blues or Old Adrian
> Henri's Interminable Talking
> Surrealistic Blues," ll. 11–13)

The poetic trajectory that the poet draws in his songs runs beyond the official centers, that is, along the banks of the River Mersey, through small towns like Bebington, across Liverpool city gardens, right into suburban bedrooms, where "The daughters of Albion / ... / sleep in the dinnertime sunlight with old men" ("Mrs Albion You've Got a Lovely Daughter," ll. 9, 12), or the basements of the popular Liverpool nightclubs, The Cavern and The Sink. The poet's midnight wandering takes him "down muddy lanes," across "city squares in winter rain," through "darkened hallways" into "deserted alleyways" and other out of the way spaces ("In the Midnight Hour"). He seems so fond of marginal places that when he looks for an objective correlative of love, his imagination immediately conjures "the back of vans" ("Love Is," l. 1), or fish-and-chip shops ("Love is fish and chips on winter night," l. 5), rather than a more picturesque, Eliotesque "hyacinth garden." Even in his tribute to T. S. Eliot ("a mock-Eliot sort of thing," as he would call "Poem in Memoriam T. S. Eliot" [see Bateman's interview with Henri—Bateman 2001, 81]), he prefers unpoetic Manchester Piccadilly Gardens or Canning St ("And you 'familiar compound spirit' moving silently down Canning St in a night of rain and fog," l. 24) to other, more symbolically potent spaces. However, as David Bateman rightly observes, Henri's "poetry creates a Liverpool that is both ordinary and magical" (2001, 73), everyday and uncanny—Liverpool where the risen dead join the crowd of ordinary people ("The Entry of Christ into Liverpool").

Henri's nocturnal world of reverse logic and wishful thinking ("Tonight at Noon," "In the Midnight Hour," "Nightsong"), where time can flow backward, has its fragile axis—it spins around "you," or so it seems in several poems, where "you" becomes a direct addressee: 'I tell you baby I almost cried" ("Adrian Henri's Talking After Christmas Blues," l. 34). Her (the "you" is female) presence or absence is said to condition not only the poet's well-being, but also his whole poetic universe, as without her "there would be / no landscapes / ... / no / night / no morning" ("Without You," ll. 29–30, 32–33). Although it is her presence, the poet suggests, that makes the world run and adds color and flavor to its minute components ("Without you they'd forget to put the salt in every packet of crisps," l. 2), in the poetic reality he constructs, for example, in the anaphoric "Without you," the woman is a pawn made to stay or leave by the power of his imagination. Built of essentially unpoetic phenomena, "the smell of the East Lancs Road" (l. 2), "stillborn poems [...] wrapped in brown paper" (l. 5), "plastic flowers" (l. 7), "green apples" (l. 10), "curry powder" (l. 22), and "the Sunday Times colour supplement" (l. 14), the world "Without You" is simultaneously constructed and in the very same line, or the following one, annihilated by the poet's negative thought, which step by step erases every element of the imagined reality, till there is nothing left, apart from *lack* expressed in the anaphoric phrase "Without you." It is behind this phrase, present also in the paratext—the title of the poem—that we can find the figure who creates and, for the time being, upholds the world *for* "you" and *without* "you." Except for "Love from Arthur Rainbow," in which a girl's feelings are depicted ("And he'll find another lover / And she'll sit at home and cry," ll. 19–20), the significant female other (Henri's poems are either directly or indirectly dedicated to his wife and lovers) is a pretext—one of the many—for Henri the poet "to paint." In other words, his creative drive seems more intense than what one can expect from a poet in love: it evidently surpasses the limitations of one-to-one relationship reflected in a portrait. The poet openly admits that when he feels like painting, he wants to paint as many as "50 life-sized nudes of Marianne Faithfull," countless "Welsh maids," and "beautiful girls with dark blond hair" ("I Want to Paint," ll. 10, 12, 15). Also, to satisfy his burning desire for painting, his picture must be "as big as Piccadilly" (l. 14).

The poet in Henri's songs is all the time on the move into various, previously unpenetrated territories and temporal niches: the world "Without You," the future without himself ("Adrian Henri's Last Will and Testament"), the slim bodies of giggling schoolgirls in brown uniforms, cinematic Gotham City ("Batpoem"), or an apocalyptic reality where "General Howard J. Sherman has just pressed the button that killed 200 million people" ("Bomb Commercials").

The transgressive character of Henri's poetic utterance reveals itself in register as well as imagery. He interweaves freely diverse tones, playing—often simultaneously—on popular culture rhythms, themes, and motifs ("Batpoem"), as well as those borrowed from the classics. Thus, Georg Friedrich Händel's musical drama *Semele* is echoed in "Where'er You Walk," whereas *Judas Maccabaeus* inspires "See The Conkering Heroine Come." Henri's transgressions concern, among others, the bounds of decency and the rules of decorum. Gazing under a blue skirt or right through a "pink nylon seethrough bra" (l. 5) ("*City* Part Three"), he finds his "hands under your dress finding you suddenly needing me" ("Spring Song for Mary"). On a different note, his surreal picture of chip-shop crime uses a large dose of black humor impelled by a ghastly visual component: "2 chip-shop proprietors were today accused of selling human ears fried in batter. One of them said 'We believe there is room for innovation in the trade'" ("The New 'Our Times'," V). Summing up Henri's poetics, Bateman asserts: "Besides the sheer visual quality of his poetry and the pop-art use of commercial everyday objects, there is his Warholian wholesale appropriation of styles and even texts presented as new poems; the constant use of collage techniques; and in relation to Kaprow, the constant overlapping of poetry with other arts" (2001, 77).

Henri's poetry, albeit openly personal, that is, adopting a perspective of the concrete individual, who happens to be a poet, a painter, and a lover, does not entirely shun important sociopolitical issues. In "Liverpool Poems," he composes a "prayer from the painter to all capitalists," asking the latter: "Open your wallets and repeat after me / 'HELP YOURSELF!'" (ll. 5, 6–7). However, unlike in McGough or Patten, in most poems by Henri included in *The Mersey Sound* collection, issues such as war, starvation, and nuclear threat are introduced as if incidentally, as if they were by-products of a thoroughly tabloidized culture that would know how to commodify anything, even the entry of Christ into the city. In "The Entry of Christ into Liverpool," "[t]he sonic, visual, and tactile environment is revealed gradually evoking the pace of the speaker and the listener's traversal of the city" (Gräbner 2016, 72). Drowning the momentous event from the New Testament in various cacophonic sounds, countless "posters / signs / gleaming salads / COLMANS MUSTARD / J. Ensor, Fabriqueur de Masques / HAIL JESUS, KING OF THE JEWS / ... / GUIN / GUINN / GUINNESS IS" ("The Entry of

Christ into Liverpool"), the poet reconstructs the postmodern heterarchy responsible for the playful mixing of all codes. It is only in the closing poem of his section, "Spring Song for Mary," that the reader can find a series of unsettling questions—one of them, "Can my poems become food for the starving of Africa and Asia?" (l. 90) being an acute reminder of the limited scope of poetic creative power in the face of an increasing political threat.

The Mersey Sound: *Roger McGough*

McGough's poetry provides a relatively richer palette of sociopolitical issues, which involve eccentricities, male chauvinism, schizophrenia, post-traumatic stress disorder, physical disabilities, mutilation, coma, celibacy, prostitution, wars, nuclear weapon, aging, terminal illness, and death. Each of the poems that tackle one of the abovementioned subjects has its own, subversive, political agenda. McGough's poetry, "fiercely loco-specific," depicting the city that "does contain / … / disturbing elements: for instance, there are portrayals of meaningless violence in his work" (Barry 2001, 19, 23), is not nice and easy. It is harsh and, as such, it successfully alerts its readers to all kinds of dangers and misfortunes they can face in the contemporary world. As much as the thematic weightiness of works such as "Let Me Die a Youngman's Death" or "Head Injury" may affect our reception of McGough's selection, it is, however, the presumably lighter theme of male–female relationships developing in time that functions as the binding agent of his verse in *The Mersey Sound* collection.

Ironic and often dispassionate in tone, most love songs by McGough unveil a tough, male-dominated reality, hardly resembling the arty dreamland or trap-world depicted in Henri's poetry. Already "Comeclose and Sleepnow," laconically grasping the atmosphere of a young girl's defloration, establishes a discernable, emotional, and intellectual distance between the girl and her lover, who, unlike her, knows it all. The ironic distance only becomes more prominent in the next three poems: "Aren't We All" that depicts a casual sex scene with a plain beauty ("Penny for her thoughts / Probably not worth it," ll. 4–5); "A Lot of Water Has Flown under Your Bridge" that points out the girl's promiscuity; and finally, "My cat and i"—a short, playful poem that, through the cat's presence, graciously satirizes the role of women in the poet's life. As the speaker in the poem unsubtly implies, females seem fairly useful at night but become mildly redundant in the morning. However, once we reach "You and Your Strange Ways" and "What You Are," the initially irreverent tone is replaced with curiosity and fascination—an excerpt from *"Summer with Monika"* constitutes a peculiar rounding up. The poet's memories of the summer "lovesongs" ("we made lovesongs with our bodies / i became the words / and she put me to music," ll. 49–51), followed by the description of a honeymoon, and then the first quiet disappointments of the married couple, draw a temporal axis along which his life with Monika is lived. Their love song, first made with their bodies, is sung again—this time with the foreknowledge he lacked in the summer which brought them together and the words he has managed to find and address to his reader. Hopes for a happy ending are dispelled almost from a start by the much too obvious allusion to Ingmar Bergman's 1953 film of the same title.

McGough's poetic universe is limited to some concrete, not particularly impressive spots: the bedroom where the poet and his casual partner make love ("Room's in a mess / And this one's left her clothes allover the place" ["Aren't We All?," ll. 20–21]); the sitting-room where uncle Tom "would scan / the ceiling nervously" for snipers ("Snipers," ll. 11–12); the bus where "the littleman with the hunchbackedback" offers "his seat to the blindlady" ("The Icingbus," ll. 1–2, ll. 4–5); or the road where "The oldman in the cripplechair," hit by "the lethallorry," dies in an accident – "in transit through the air" ("The Fallen Birdman," l. 4, l. 2). All the places McGough makes us see or hear or smell are almost tangible, due to specific, physical characteristics that make them part of consensual reality, for example, a distinct smell of vinegar. As most locations he thus depicts either resemble the spots one passes on the way to a more important destination or serve as objective correlatives of emotions and desires that the poet wants us to (re)construct, they remain irrevocably marginal. Thus, for example, in "Vinegar" he conjures up a fish-and-chip shop, with a priest queuing and smelling, like his Lord on the cross, the vinegar, to express his passing desire for sharing his life with someone on a more regular basis.

Even in his two mock-apocalyptic poems, "Icarus Allsorts" and "At Lunchtime," in which the horizon radically widens, eventually embracing the whole globe, the particular places he focuses on by no means assume grandiose proportions. On the contrary, even at the edge of time and history, the world, according to McGough, will look no better. Unheroic urban scenery, involving little shops, offices, parlors, or "the crowded commuter bus bringing people into the city for work each day, a social space of unusual intimacy in which strangers sit in close and frequent proximity to each other, but remain strangers" (Barry 2001, 24), is all we can expect. When the lethal "mushrooms," in "Icarus Allsorts," rise over the USA and Europe, reaching Buckingham Palace, the Queen and her family go about trivial daily activities, counting money and "Eating bread and honey" (l. 25).

The Mersey Sound: *Brian Patten*

The spaces Patten meanders among are first introduced in the formula put forward in the title of the poem opening his section of *The Mersey Sound* collection: "Somewhere Between Heaven and Woolworths, A Song." Indeed, almost all songs by Patten depict the in-between spaces, suspended between ontologically different realities and evoked to cope with the sensations or memories that escape the empirical dimension of here and now. From typical sights, firmly anchored in the reality of the late 1950s and early 1960s world ("Among the couples on the stairs, // [...] / A girl dressed in denim / With boys dressed in lies." ["Somewhere Between Heaven and Woolworths, A Song," ll. 12, 15–16]), the poet smoothly moves on to the intangible world from behind the mirror—"the forests" one builds daydreaming ("Something That Was Not There Before," "In a New Kind of Dawn").

Patten's speaker, like many other figures he introduces, lives, as it were, in parallel realities. On the one hand, he roams quite ordinary places—the places he notices only because they are marked by either eye-catching or worrisome occurrences, for example, a playground where a seven-year-old child holding a machine gun tries to hide ("Little Johnny's Confession"); or busy roads spotted with "gleaming green sportscars, / riveted with steel" ("A Green Sportscar," ll. 2–3); or rooms full of people endlessly revolving on hard carpets ("Doubt Shall Not Make an

End of You"); or a party venue where "among the woodbines and Guinness stains" late night intercourse takes place ("Party Piece," III, l. 15); or an opera house with "quietly expensive boxes," unexpectedly visited by a timid bird who sings on the stage ("Interruption at the Opera House," l. 2); or the beach with a couple moving slowly in the company of a sandcrab sniffing the salt wind ("Seascape"). On the other hand, along these most reassuring spots modeled on consensual reality, we encounter a room with "tattymemories," "whispering / 'I'm not around you I'm in you all my walls are in you'" ("Room," ll. 4, 36–37); an apartment, where the speaker brings to life multiple generations of long-deceased inhabitants from the past ("After Breakfast"); or a woodshed hosting a green, damp, small dragon which "is out of place here / and is quite silent" ("A Small Dragon," ll. 11–12). This mysterious other world—"a place without names" (l. 21)—appears also in Patten's love songs, in which he instructs his lover: "Feel nothing separate then, / we have translated each other into light / and into love go streaming" ("Doubt Shall Not Make an End of You," ll. 22–24). In his universe suspended "Somewhere Between Heaven and Woolworths," Patten's poet keeps on "Travelling Between Places," glad that he is "Leaving nothing and nothing ahead" ("Travelling Between Places," l. 1). He also travels in time to the celluloid world of his heroic teens, where he can find his old companions polished off by Mr Old Age: Batman, Superman, Zorro, and others ("Where Are You Now, Batman?").

Like some of the poems by McGough and Henri, Patten's "Come into the City, Maud" also becomes a poetic intertextual palimpsest—this time of Tennyson's garden and the contemporary city, "Where the flowers are too quickly picked / And the days are butchered as if they were enemies" (ll. 26–27). In comparison to the two other authors in the collection, Patten tends to make more metapoetic observations. In a lengthy "Prosepoem towards a Definition of Itself," he presents a set of rules for writing. His rule No. 1 demands from poetry and poets a certain degree of exhibitionism and directness: "When in public poetry should take off its clothes and wave to the nearest person in sight." However, the preference for a shabby attire and trivialities—simple form and content—does not make poetry part of the mundane and the unremarkable. To Patten, "Poetry is… / the astronaut stepping for the first time into liquid space." Despite appearances, he intimates, poetry always searches for new terrains, where it finds "among the heart's trash nothing but revelations."

Conclusion

The 2007 "Restored 50th Anniversary Edition" of *The Mersey Sound*, which returns to the roots and atmosphere of the Sixties by copying the original 1967 collection, is, in a sense, an untypical, for fully repetitive, ending to the three Liverpool poets' everchanging stage and publishing "performance." However, as Patten implies in "The Last Residents," watching history and revolution repeat themselves is not an exceptional experience, the only difference being that the unlucky read the proclamation of martial law and the lucky the restored editions of the poetic word.

The Mersey Sound, the bestselling poetry anthology and most appreciated record of its era, is considered the beginning of three long-lasting careers. In 2002, Henri, McGough, and Patten were granted the Freedom of the City of Liverpool, an honorary title that officially sanctioned their "exceptional services" rendered to the city and the nation. They became "persons of distinction" 18 years after the title was given to the members of The Beatles. They are believed to have paved the way for later performance poets.

References

Barry, Peter (2001). "The Hard Lyric: Re-Registering Liverpool Poetry." In: *Gladsongs and Gatherings: Poetry and its Social Context in Liverpool since the 1960s* (ed. Stephen Wade), 19–41. Liverpool: Liverpool University Press.

Bateman, David (2001). "Adrian Henri: Singer of Meat and Flowers." In: *Gladsongs and Gatherings: Poetry and its Social Context in Liverpool since the 1960s* (ed. Stephen Wade), 73–102. Liverpool: Liverpool University Press.

Booth, Martin (1985). *British Poetry 1964 to 1982: Driving through the Barricades*. London: Routledge & Kegan Paul.

Bowen, Phil (2008). *A Gallery to Play to: The Story of the Mersey Poets*, 2e. Liverpool: Liverpool University Press.

Cookson, Linda (1997). *Brian Patten*. Plymouth: Northcote House Publishers Ltd.

Duncan, Andrew (2003). *The Failure of Conservatism in Modern British Poetry*. Cambridge/Applecross: Salt Publishing.

Gräbner, Cornelia (2016). "Poetry and Performance: The Mersey Poets, The International Poetry Incarnation and Performance Poetry." In: *The Cambridge Companion to British Poetry 1945–2010* (ed. Edward Larrissy), 68–81. Cambridge: Cambridge University Press.

Henri, Adrian (1996). "A City of Poems." In: *Liverpool Accents: Seven Poets and a City* (ed. Peter Robinson), 35–38. Liverpool: Liverpool University Press.

Henri, Adrian, McGough, Roger, and Patten, Brian (1967). *Penguin Modern Poets 10 – The Mersey Sound*, 1e. Penguin.

Henri, Adrian, McGough, Roger, and Patten, Brian (1974). *Penguin Modern Poets 10 – The Mersey Sound*, 2e. Penguin Books (revised and expanded).

Henri, Adrian, McGough, Roger, and Patten, Brian (1983). *The Mersey Sound*: Revised Edition, 3e. Penguin Books.

Henri, Adrian, McGough, Roger, and Patten, Brian (2007). *The Mersey Sound: Restored 50th Anniversary Edition*, Penguin Modern Classics. UK: Penguin Classics.

Lindop, Grevel (1972). "Poetry, Rhetoric and the Mass Audience: The Case of the Liverpool Poets." In: *British Poetry Since 1960: A Critical Survey* (eds. Michael Schmidt and Grevel Lindop), 92–106. Oxford: Carcanet Press.

Lucie-Smith, Edward (ed.) (1967). *The Liverpool Scene*. London: Donald Carroll.

Mitchell, Adrian (1964). "Preface." In: *Poems*, 8. London: Jonathan Cape.

Robinson, Peter (ed.) (1996). *Liverpool Accents: Seven Poets and a City*. Liverpool: Liverpool University Press.

Sheppard, Robert (2005). *The Poetry of Saying: British Poetry and Its Discontents 1950–2000*. Liverpool: Liverpool University Press.

Side, Jeffrey (2019). "Adrian Henri Interview." *Argotist Online*. http://www.argotistonline.co.uk/Henri%20 interview.htm; (accessed 5 January 2019).

Stakes, Richard (2001). "These Boys: The Rise of Mersey Beat." In: *Gladsongs and Gatherings: Poetry and its Social Context in Liverpool since the 1960s* (ed. Stephen Wade), 157–167. Liverpool: Liverpool University Press.

Townsend, Pete (2001). "Jazz Scene, Liverpool Scene: The Early 1960s." In: *Gladsongs and Gatherings: Poetry and its Social Context in Liverpool since the 1960s* (ed. Stephen Wade), 168–176. Liverpool: Liverpool University Press.

Wade, Stephen (ed.) (2001a). "Introduction." In: *Gladsongs and Gatherings: Poetry and its Social Context in Liverpool since the 1960s*, ix–xixi. Liverpool: Liverpool University Press.

Wade, Stephen (ed.) (2001b). "The Arrival of McGough." In: *Gladsongs and Gatherings: Poetry and its Social Context in Liverpool since the 1960s*, 7–18. Liverpool: Liverpool University Press.

2c.4
The British Poetry Revival 1960–1978

Robert Sheppard

The British Poetry Revival is less of a school, with shared stylistic characteristics or a unitary poetics, than a general movement of esthetic tendencies and non-native affiliations, aligned with publication networks, poetry reading events, and coalesced in varying degrees with a politics of the "Underground," at least at its inception. It may be seen as opposed to the poetics of narrative cohesion, thematic unity, and metrical conformity, as well as the delimited social perspectives, of Movement poetry of the 1950s and 1960s, but its practitioners and advocates, like that of Blake's revolutionary figure Los, in his epic "Jerusalem – The Emanation of the Giant Albion," tended not to "reason & compare"; their business was to "create" a new poetry and the provisional institutions that sustained it (Blake 1972, 644). With growing confidence, they turned away from official channels of publication and validation. Their work ranged from the international experimental concrete poetry of London-based Bob Cobbing to the local pop-art-inspired happenings and music and poetry performances of Liverpool's Adrian Henri; from the fragmented surrealist lyricism of Lee Harwood in the 1960s, which owed both to Parisian and New York modernism and postmodernism, to the home-grown Anglo-Saxon vocabulary and metrical borrowings of Bill Griffiths in the 1970s; from the increasingly impacted discourse of J. H. Prynne, which derived in part from his personal association with Charles Olson, to the loco-specific work of Allen Fisher, whose open structures and egalitarian politics equally derived from a reading of Olson's projective and proprioceptive poetics. They were—and remained—distressingly male.

A Companion to Contemporary British and Irish Poetry, 1960–2015, First Edition.
Edited by Wolfgang Görtschacher and David Malcolm.
© 2021 John Wiley & Sons Ltd. Published 2021 by John Wiley & Sons Ltd.

"The British poetry revival has been long on the way but slow under its own steam," wrote poets Dave Cunliffe and Tina Morris in their introduction to an anthology edition of their seminal poetry magazine *Poetmeat* in 1964, thus using the term for the first time (Cunliffe and Morris 1965, 3). That their piece was entitled "The New British Poetry" is appropriate, since it clearly alluded to, and suggested, an equivalence with an anthology influential on most of the poets of the Revival, *The New American Poetry*, edited by Donald Allen in 1960, which included Beat, New York, and Black Mountain poets, along with excerpts from free verse poetics (Allen 1960). In 1988, the Paladin anthology *The New British Poetry* echoed these titles, suggesting the longevity of both the work of the British Poetry Revival and of the transatlantic influence.

Eric Mottram edited a section of *The New British Poetry*, which included most of the writers named above, supplementing them with poets such as Thomas A. Clark, Andrew Crozier, Roy Fisher, Barry MacSweeney, Jeff Nuttall, Tom Pickard, and Tom Raworth (Allnut et al. 1988). He had earlier entitled a 1974 essay "The British Poetry Revival: 1960–1974" (Mottram 1974). This was revised for Robert Hampson's and Peter Barry's 1993 edited critical volume tellingly called *New British Poetries*—a long-overdue critical survey of this work—which revises the dates of the Revival to "1960–1975," despite the fact that many of the writers and cultural figures were, and are, still active, such as John James, Wendy Mulford, Colin Simms, Denise Riley, and Iain Sinclair. Mottram's essay is uneven and combines rant against the mainstream with detailed "poetry information" about the writing and organizing of dozens of poets, but the weight of evidence does prove, as Mottram's fellow-editor of *The New British Poetry*, Ken Edwards, puts it, that the British Poetry Revival denoted "an exciting growth and flowering that encompasses an immense variety of forms and procedures" (Edwards 1979, 9). Mottram presents this formal variety as poetics:

> Poetic space need not be rigidly enclosed or shaped under hard linear dimensions, restricted to traditional sentence logic and grammatical usage. The completion of a poem could include a reader's consciousness. The poet's meeting a reader in a formative process need not be dependent on a straight-jacketing notation and the eyes following print on a silent page. A poem need not illustrate dogmas but can enact with gestures flexible enough to hold potentiality as well as ascertained experience and prior formed knowledge. A poem could be a proposition of energies that suggested their sources and need not terminate them in insistent limits. Instead of being marketed as a consumerist item, a poem could be part of the world of physics and philosophy in interaction, requiring an attention beyond instant recognition and reaction. Instead of being an item in a school of rhetoric, a poem could have a variety of articulations, continuity and discontinuity, sentence and parataxis, and an awareness of the imaginative possibilities of relationships between particle, measure, line and paragraph, between existent and new forms.... The poets of the Revival understood the risks of ambitious form and multiple experience.
> (Mottram 1993, 27–28)

While the potshots at the mainstream are reductive (what poet "illustrates dogma"?), the insistence upon deliquescent form at the level of syntax encompasses both the processual stretches of Raworth's short-lined improvisations (Raworth 1974) or the disjunctive articulation of a Prynne lyric (Prynne 1975, 1979); the role of the reader in the different lacunary practices of Harwood (Harwood 1970, 1975) or early Allen Fisher (Fisher 1976, Fisher 1978); the enacting of experience across syntax and line as in the fragmented conversation poems of John James (James 1983) or the tight meditative quatrains of Clark (Clark 1981); the use of complex ideas from science and technology, and the sense of producing a discourse equivalent to those specialisms, in Allen Fisher or Prynne. These all demonstrate different ways of partaking of formal experimentation and expanded content as identified by Mottram. The apprehension of rhythm as an articulation of the total text as in Iain Sinclair's book-length psychogeographical investigations (such as *Lud Heat* 1975) contrasts with Barry MacSweeney's discrete series in *Odes* (1978). Mottram distils many kinds of free verse, processual, objectivist, and projectivist, and precisely defines the formal innovations open to poets of the Cambridge grouping around Prynne, the overlapping London groups, the Durham–Newcastle Objectivist cluster, or any other grouping (or non-grouping) in their active, particular (and under-recorded) locations, from Glasgow to Worcester.

The publishing history of the Revival stretches back to the 1950s, with the emergence of Gael Turnbull's Migrant Press, which provided a springboard for Roy Fisher and Turnbull. While the American free verse tradition is undeniable as a precedent, the literary experimentation of the 1940s, whose major figures, W. S. Graham and Dylan Thomas, as well as neglected poets such as Nicholas Moore and J. F. Hendry, along with Modernist survivors, such as David Jones (whose mythic method derives from high modernism), Basil Bunting (from the Pound/Objectivist grouping), and David Gascoyne (from the Surrealist and European modernist tradition), in short, those who experienced the eclipse of their careers under the Movement orthodoxy, were valuable precursors to the Revival, with their esthetic ambition. Most notable was Bunting, whose 1965 masterpiece *Briggflatts* was nurtured in the youthful Newcastle poetry scene of Pickard, MacSweeney, and others. Turnbull published an impressive list of booklets between 1957 and the mid-1960s, including Bunting's earlier poem, *The Spoils* (1965), in association with Morden Tower bookshop and reading space in Newcastle, as well as books by American Black Mountain poets Robert Creeley and Edward Dorn, Ian Hamilton Finlay's pre-concrete poetry collection, *The Dancers Inherit the Party* (1960), and Turnbull's own impressive improvisation *Twenty Words, Twenty Days* (1966), the title of which describes its time-based constraint and the lexical nature of its starting material. Turnbull said: "I was wanting [...] to create a 'context' that was not narrowly 'national' and in which I felt I might be able to exist as a writer myself" (Pattison et al. 2012, xv). However, the most important Migrant book was the publication in 1961 of Roy Fisher's pamphlet *City*, whose 300 copies (quite a long print-run for the time) were probably distributed by Turnbull in his usual casual way. A handbill inserted into an edition of *Migrant* magazine apprised its readers that it would be mailed to interested parties free. *City* comprises of tightly written prose passages evoking the unnamed Birmingham as hallucinatory, while more personal and perceptual lyrics are woven between them, thus establishing the hero, not as a modernist *flâneur*, but as a petrified recipient of the city's transformative gifts, threatening and liberating by turns.

"By 1964, a lot was happening," noted Turnbull (Pattison et al. 2012, xv). Another term, "Underground," was by this time often used both of poetry and magazines (as of film and later music) and appears in the subtitle of the only popular anthology before *The New British Poetry* to collect this work: Michael Horovitz's Penguin volume *Children of Albion: Poetry of the "Underground" in Britain* (1969). Cunliffe and Morris are both published there, as are Roy Fisher and Harwood, as well as less mature work by John James and Crozier, along with some survivors from pre-Movement days such as Paul Potts, and the intermedia artist Carlyle Reedy (one of the few women in this gathering). One could object to the political implications of subversion in the term "Underground," but poet Jeff Nuttall—in his spirited insider account of those years, *Bomb Culture*—nicely catches the edge of existential threat that underlined creativity: "To a certain degree the Underground happened everywhere spontaneously. It was simply what you did in the H-bomb world if you were, by nature, creative and concerned for humanity as a whole" (Nuttall 1970, 160). Yet that knowledge was often occluded. "When Cobbing, [Keith] Musgrove, [John] Rowan and I were putting on our shows in hired rooms, exclaiming our poetry in public parks, swinging the duplicator handle throughout the long Saturday afternoons of 1963 we had no idea that the same thing was happening all over the world," Nuttall notes, expressing not only solidarity with other named poets (from Cobbing's Writers Forum workshop and press grouping) but also astonishment at the simultaneity of the counterculture (Nuttall 1970, 161). Early contacts by Turnbull with the American avant-garde of Objectivism—Louis Zukofsky visited England in the 1950s—and by others, such as Raworth, who edited *Outburst* magazine, with members of the Beat generation, the Black Mountain constellation, and the New York School, meant there were growing antecedents and encouragements for the 1960s avant-garde. Harwood, translator of Tzara, rediscovered Dada and Surrealism—he knew nothing of the effaced activities of Gascoyne in the 1930s—while others, like *Children of Albion* editor Horovitz and Nuttall himself, reinterpreted Rexrothian poetry and jazz performances, and post-Dada happenings. At its most public, 7000 representatives of the "underground" swelled the Albert Hall for a celebrated and representative poetry reading in June 1965, at which British poets Horovitz, Pete Brown, and Spike Hawkins read alongside American guests Harry Fainlight and Allen Ginsberg (who recited "The Change"). Nuttall recollects: "All our separate audiences had come to one place at the same time, to witness an atmosphere of pot, impromptu solo acid dances, of incredible barbaric colour, of face and body painting, of flowers and flowers and flowers, of a common dreaminess in which all was permissive and benign" (Nuttall 1970, 182–183). It is interesting to compare this effusion to Ginsberg's letter to a friend: "There were too many bad poets at Albert Hall, too many goofs who didn't trust their own poetry, too many superficial bards who read tinkley jazzy beatnik style poems, too many men of letters who read weak pompous or silly poems written in archaic metres [...]. The concentration & intensity of prophesy were absent except in a few instances." Ginsberg does not exempt himself: "I read quite poorly and hysterically" (Miles 2003, 61). The reading was a missed opportunity, since the principal Revival poets were absent from the podium; many were present in the audience.

Although specialist bookshops such as Better Books in London and Unicorn in Brighton stocked the new poetry, dissemination of the work (worldwide as well as nationally) was largely furnished by the postal services. In contrast to the head-counting activities in the Albert Hall (and in retreat from its theatricality), the story of *The English Intelligencer* is instructive about a quieter revolution, which continued throughout our period and beyond. A privately distributed poetry and discussion sheet, it was issued to a fluctuating mailing list of around 30 in 1966–1968, edited by poets Peter Riley and Crozier, with Prynne's assistance. The lists indicate that it went to the Cambridge School but also to Harwood, Paul Green, Pickard, Roy Fisher, Wendy Mulford, Elaine Feinstein (the oldest), MacSweeney (the youngest), and the Liverpool poets. It was the nearest thing to a contemporary e-discussion list (and it utilized the same office duplicator technology that Cobbing had adapted). Simon Perril describes the open exchange of *The English Intelligencer* as "the constitution of trust through the establishment of a 'community of risk'" (Perril 2000, 197). However, when Harwood pleaded for critique of his contributed poems, he received none; there was little discussion of poetics (as a writerly speculative discourse) though there was angst about being derivative of Americans (a suggestion of Turnbull). "Everybody is trying hard to cover up the fact that they're wet through with Mid-Atlantic spray," MacSweeney puts it (Pattison et al. 2012, 140). He is as fierce as Ginsberg as he attacks the "Liverpool poets" and "all jazz-poets" as "the main bad craftsmen, unpoets" (Pattison et al. 2012, 31). More positively, the worksheet published Olsonian considerations of long human histories, by Peter Riley (Pattison et al. 2012, 47–73), in what may be notes for his *Excavations* (2004), and by Prynne, in the famous "A Note on Metal" (Pattison et al. 2012, 104–109), which re-appeared in his important volume *The White Stones* (1969).

The English Intelligencer advertised the Sparty Lea poetry meeting of 1967, which shows (retrospectively) that many of the most vital elements of the poetics were happening far from the supposedly "swinging" countercultural centers, as Cambridge poets Prynne and Peter Riley confronted other readers of the worksheet in person, like John James (from Wales and Bristol) and Newcastle's Pickard, for days of drink and discussion, which cemented poetic friendships and animosities for decades, and which were recorded in a published collage of responses. Between and beyond Better Books in London, run by Cobbing and Harwood at different times, and Caius College, Cambridge, the institutional base of Prynne, and Essex University where Americans Dorn and Ted Berrigan influenced lecturers like Douglas Oliver and students like Ralph Hawkins, magazines proliferated and contacts multiplied. Internationally, the concrete poetry movement influenced many, most notably Cobbing. The ownership of printing technology, the development of performance venues, fed into a practice within which Cobbing was a unique concrete poet, producing visual work for the page that he would then perform as sound poetry scores, often with others, such as Annea Lockwood in the 1960s or Clive Fencott in the 1970s. His *ABC in Sound* (1965/2015), which was broadcast as a vocal piece by the BBC with effects by its Radiophonic Workshop in 1966, is also his first sustained book.

Cobbing's Writers Forum workshop and press are important institutions for the Revival's work, but his organizing of the important Association of Little Presses from 1966 until 1985, a self-help organization for those involved in independent publishing, assisted many publisher-poets. Founder members included both large and small presses, for example, Stuart Montgomery's Fulcrum (which published Roy Fisher and Harwood in hardback) and Writers Forum itself (which published experimentalists such as Dom Sylvester Houédard and Lawrence Upton, as well as Cobbing's own work, as inexpensive pamphlets). Annual General Meetings (AGM) held discussions on practical matters, such as grant aid; at the 1968 meeting there were 14 members, but this doubled within a year, and growth continued throughout the 1970s. Underground magazines, known again as little magazines, were drawn to regular deadlines, standardized formats, and quality production values. The spontaneity of these gift economy anti-commodities was affected in the process but the sense of poetic community, of the type described by Perril, strengthened.

Ambition was brewing in another forum. Mottram, an academic working in the field of American studies at King's College, London, did much to introduce innovative work by American writers, such as Ginsberg, Olson, and Burroughs, to Britain, and, largely outside the academy, to propagate the British work of Harwood, Allen Fisher, and MacSweeney, among others. It was inevitable that both Cobbing and Mottram—one as organizer, the other as editor—should have become involved in the entryist takeover of the Poetry Society, which gained quite an amount of press coverage in the early 1970s, when a group of poets and activists were elected onto its General Council, which housed the National Poetry Centre at a crumbling premises in Earls Court, London, funded by the Arts Council. The radicals set up a series of readings and lectures, opened a print shop for poets, and turned *Poetry Review*, a veteran but mainstream magazine, over to Mottram, eventually printing the editions themselves in Cobbing's print room. They also hosted the important *Poetry Information* reviews magazine. At its best, the new Poetry Society actively supported the writing and publishing of Revival work; but it was incautious in its advance.

The takeover angered disgruntled members of the General Council and the Arts Council, headed by Charles Osborne, commissioned the Witt Report that Osborne hoped (or ensured) would guarantee Arts Council scrutiny and a measure of "control," relatively mild instruments of accountability by today's standards. The report was rejected as interference at a meeting in March 1977; an avalanche of resignations triggered by chairman Nuttall precipitated a mass walk-out. "What the Arts Council's investigating team had failed to achieve in months I accomplished in seconds," boasted Osborne, knowing the radicals were now silenced and de-housed (Barry 2006, 99).

Allen Fisher wrote of the 1980s as "a period of entrenchment and awe [...] speaking in a considerably small room," which suggests that the sense of thwarted ambition or even defeat was genuine and lasting (particularly in London) (Fisher 1985, 163). The former underground poetry went underground in a real sense, and is seldom mentioned in literary histories of the 1970s, as though the radical 1960s had truly been buried. But activity and self-sufficiency continued nationwide; ambitious innovative poetry was being written and disseminated, at readings from Durham to Cardiff, from The Trent Bookshop in Nottingham to Ultima Thule in Newcastle, and at consolidating centers, such as Cambridge, where, through festivals and the magazine *Perfect Bound*, the 1970s generation of Cambridge writers, such as Denise Riley and John Wilkinson, was launched, poets particularly alive to the invasion of continental feminist and literary theory, which they integrated into their poetics (as in Riley's *Marxism for Infants* (1977) and Wilkinson's *Clinical Notes* (1980)). Poets nationally and internationally continued (and continue) to be published by the little presses that remain a vital part of this history, as do readings (which often escape record and analysis).

In the late 1980s, the Carcanet anthology *A Various Art* and the Paladin anthology *The New British Poetry* (the latter launched alongside sizeable mid-career volumes of selected poems by

Harwood and Raworth) bore testimony to this continued poetic development, with the emergence into maturity of writers who had first appeared in the 1970s. *A Various Art*, edited by Andrew Crozier and Tim Longville, constellated its work around Prynne, and collected work published by Ferry Press and Grosseteste Press in particular, including John Riley (proprietor of the latter press with Longville) (Crozier and Longville 1987). The extraordinary "The Veil Poem" (1972) by Crozier (the publisher of Ferry Press), a serial meditation on process and reality that melds Olsonian proprioception with a native Romanticism, demonstrates his early mastery. The death of Veronica Forrest-Thomson in 1976 robbed the anthology (and the wider Revival) of its most subtle poet-critic, and her selection is elegiac, despite the vitality of her poetic theory, which shifted utopianism into poetic artifice itself: "It is only through artifice," she asserts, "that poetry can challenge our ordinary linguistic orderings of the world, make us question the way in which we make sense of things, and induce us to consider its alternative linguistic orders as a new way of seeing the world" (Forrest-Thomson 1978, xi). Processes of what she dubs "naturalization" may be *suspended* to enable this challenge, and "good" naturalization is a reading that accounts for poetic devices, that reads the discourse *through* them; her *Poetic Artifice* (1978) is a good guide to reading the dense lyricism of Prynne, Crozier, and other Revival poets whose work foregrounds artifice, as it also informs the poetics of later linguistically innovative poets.

When Bill Griffiths met Cobbing—both poets anthologized by Mottram in *The New British Poetry*—he recognized a pragmatic and philosophic matching between his poetic artifice and pamphlet form, both in his mentor's work and in his own emerging practice: he "appears to have used the possibilities—advantages—of short-run mimeo as part of his process of composition, as part of his active poetics, his making of forms," comments Alan Halsey (2010, 41). From hand-stitched to hand-colored editions, Griffiths explored modes of making small press books as anti-commodities, while presenting a dense poetry that easily combined translations of Boethius with homages to common vegetables, although exploring the limits of legality and the horrors of incarceration remained his central theme, as in *Cycles* (1976), a partial exploration of his biker days. In contrast to this uniqueness, Allen Fisher's *Place* (2005) exemplified, formally speaking, a method of connecting and juxtaposing materials that became one of the privileged styles of the Revival in the 1970s: the field of patterned energies, with nodes, or notes, of facts disposed upon the page in a primarily spatial disposition, "precisely scored gaps for taking breath," in Sinclair's words, a mode loosely derived from Olson's poetics, as well as nodding toward the ideogrammic method of juxtaposition of Pound's *The Cantos* (Sinclair 2013, 8). Other examples, Sinclair's *Suicide Bridge* (1979) and Harwood's "The Long Black Veil: a notebook" (1970–1972), carry the added heteroglossic dimension of prose passages. Mottram's advocacy of "open field" metrics was formally important, but his keynote paper for the Polytechnic of Central London conference "Inheritance Landscape Location: Data for British Poetry 1977" was premised upon the primacy of the recognition that "a poet works at the intersection of his time and his place," and it grouped many of these 1970s writers (Mottram 1977, 85). This piece was a continuation of Mottram's 1974 "The British Poetry Revival" (and similarly is one of the rare academic surveys of its era), but its focus on geographical and psychogeographical material is more specialized. As in Sinclair's later work, the charting of continuities is furthered by walking out into the culture and gathering what "poetry information" one can.

The British Poetry Revival is only a chapter in a continuing critical story of formally investigative poetries, yet it is a crucial one for establishing the necessitous pattern of alternative institutions for supporting the work (the small presses and magazines being the most obvious), the ever-fading but not expired utopianism that yet tints its background (which I have muted in favor of the literary), and, overwhelmingly, for what Mottram called its "risks of ambitious form and multiple experience" (Mottram 1993, 27–28).

References

Allen, Donald (ed.) (1960). *The New American Poetry 1945–1960*. New York: Grove Press.

Allnut, Gillian, D'Aguiar, Fred, Edwards, Ken, and Mottram, Eric (eds.) (1988). *The New British Poetry 1968–88*. London: Paladin.

Barry, Peter (2006). *Poetry Wars*. Cambridge: Salt.

Blake, William (1972). *The Complete Poems* (ed. W.H. Stevenson). London: Longman.

Clark, Thomas A. (1981). *Sixteen Sonnets*. Nailsworth: Moschatel Press.

Cobbing, Bob (1965/2015). *ABC in Sound*. London: Veer Books.

Crozier, Andrew and Longville, Tim (eds.) (1987). *A Various Art*. Manchester: Carcanet.

Cunliffe, Dave and Morris, Tina (1965). "The New British Poetry." *Poetmeat* 8: 3.

Edwards, Ken (1979). "Reviews." *Reality Studios* 2 (1): 9.

Fisher, Allen (1976). *Place I-XXXVII*. Carrboro: Truck Press.

Fisher, Allen (1978). *Apocalyptic Sonnets*. Durham: Pig Press.

Fisher, Allen (1985). *Necessary Business*. London: Spanner.

Forrest-Thomson, Veronica (1978). *Poetic Artifice*. Manchester: Manchester University Press.

Griffiths, Bill (1976). *Cycles*. London: Pirate Press and Writers Forum.

Halsey, Alan (2010). "Abysses & Quick Vicissitudes: Some Notes on the Mimeo Editions of Bill Griffiths." *Mimeo Mimeo* 4: 41–50.

Harwood, Lee (1970). *The Sinking Colony*. London: Fulcrum Press.

Harwood, Lee (1975). "The Long Black Veil." In: *HMS Little Fox*, 5–34. London: Oasis Books.

Horovitz, Michael (ed.) (1969). *Children of Albion: Poetry of the "Underground" in Britain*. Harmondsworth: Penguin.

James, John (1983). *Berlin Return*. Matlock, London/Liverpool: Grosseteste Press/Ferry Press/Délires.

MacSweeney, Barry (1978). *Odes*. London: Trigram Press.

Miles, Barry (2003). *Inside the Sixties*. London: Pimlico.

Mottram, Eric (1974). "The British Poetry Revival 1960–1974." In: *Modern Poetry Conference, 1974*, 86–117. London: Polytechnic of Central London.

Mottram, Eric (1977). "Inheritance Landscape Location: Data for British Poetry 1977." In: *PCL British Poetry Conference – June 1977* (ed. Paul Evans), 85–101. London: Polytechnic of Central London.

Mottram, Eric (1993). "The British Poetry Revival, 1960–75." In: *New British Poetries* (eds. Robert Hampson and Peter Barry), 15–50. Manchester: Manchester University Press.

Nuttall, Jeff (1970). *Bomb Culture*. London: Paladin.

Pattison, Neil, Pattison, Reitha, and Roberts, Luke (2012). *Certain Prose of the English Intelligencer*. Cambridge: Mountain Press.

Perril, Simon (2000). "Trappings of the Hart: Reader and the Ballad of *The English Intelligencer*." *The Gig* (4/5 November) ("The Poetry of Peter Riley"): 196–218.

Prynne, J. H. (1969). *The White Stones*. Lincoln: Grosseteste Press.

Prynne, J. H. (1975). *High Pink on Chrome*. Cambridge: privately printed (distributed through London: Ferry Press).

Prynne, J. H. (1979). *Down Where Changed*. London: Ferry Press.

Raworth, Tom (1974). *Ace*. London: Goliard Press.

Riley, Denise (1977). *Marxism for Infants*. Cambridge: Street Editions.

Sinclair, Iain (1975). *Lud Heat*. London: Albion Village Press.

Sinclair, Iain (1979). *Suicide Bridge*. London: Albion Village Press.

Sinclair, Iain (2013). *American Smoke*. London: Hamish Hamilton.

Wilkinson, John (1980). *Clinical Notes*. Liverpool: Délires.

2c.5
Poets of Ulster

Martin Ryle

Introduction

The term "Ulster" denotes the nine counties forming the most northerly of Ireland's four provinces, but is also used—although "Northern Ireland" is generally preferred—to refer to the six counties remaining within the United Kingdom under the 1921 Treaty that established what is now the Republic of Ireland. Most members of the Northern Catholic community favor Irish national unity, but the Protestant majority there proclaims allegiance to the British Crown. This division underlay three decades of civil strife, euphemistically called "the Troubles," which began in 1969 and claimed the lives of more than 3500 people, mostly unarmed civilians. Over half of those who died were killed by the Provisional IRA and other nationalist paramilitary groups; the others were victims of Loyalist paramilitaries and state security services.

These statistics are given in *Bear in Mind These Dead*, a memorial volume by Irish journalist Susan McKay (2008). McKay's title is a phrase from "Neither an Elegy nor a Manifesto" by the Belfast-born poet John Hewitt (reprinted in Hewitt 2007, 92–94). Other Ulster poets she mentions include Seamus Heaney, Michael Longley, and Tom Paulin. The Northern Irish poets who began writing during the Troubles are published in England or in the Irish Republic; their work belongs to English-language poetry at large. But they share a formative background in Ulster, in a time when poetry found itself called upon to bear witness to the experience of violence.

A Companion to Contemporary British and Irish Poetry, 1960–2015, First Edition.
Edited by Wolfgang Görtschacher and David Malcolm.
© 2021 John Wiley & Sons Ltd. Published 2021 by John Wiley & Sons Ltd.

Ulster Poetry in the Early 1960s

The leading Ulster poet at the start of our period was Louis MacNeice (1907–1963). Born in Belfast, MacNeice was educated and spent most of his life in England, and is often discussed (with W. H. Auden and others) as one of the group of left-wing writers who came to prominence there in the 1930s. His work includes several poems about Ireland, sometimes expressing disaffection and disillusion. "Valediction" (MacNeice 1987, 52–54) reflects on memories of Belfast ("my mother-city") and on the beauty of the Irish landscape

> when sun quilts the valley and quick
> Winging shadows of white clouds pass
> Over the long hills like a fiddle's phrase.

But the poet, alienated by the cultivation of national and sectarian feeling ("each new fantasy of badge and gun"), determines to acquire a detached attitude like that of a "holiday visitor." Several of MacNeice's Ulster successors have valued his capacity to cast an ironic light on emotion even while acknowledging its power. Derek Mahon's "In Carrowdore Churchyard" (Mahon 2011, 19) pays tribute to that complex vision, with its sense of "fragile ... ambiguity" and its power of "keeping the colours new."

Other Ulster poets already published in the early 1960s include Patrick Kavanagh (1904–1967), W. R. Rodgers (1909–1969), and John Hewitt (1907–1987). John Montague (1929–2016), also in print then, continued to bring out new work until his recent death. Kavanagh was brought up on a farm in County Monaghan, and his commitment to making poetry from incidents of rural life has been shared by many later Ulster poets. The verbal exuberance of Rodgers's verse is now generally regarded as damagingly whimsical. Hewitt has been a weightier presence; a substantial selection of his verse was published on the twentieth anniversary of his death (Hewitt 2007). His evocations of place as the ground of identity anticipate a central theme of his successors' work. "Footing Turf" (Hewitt 2007, 59) illustrates the Ulster inflection he brings to pastoral verse. Working on the bog "on high Barard, the hip / of that long mountain, Trostan," the poet looks down from his remote vantage point, damp with mist and drizzle, to fields at the sea's edge where "the day-long sun shone on the haymakers."

These established poets were joined in the years after MacNeice's death by a group of young writers first published between the mid-1960s and 1980. All are English-language poets, although several employ Irish phrases and have translated poems from Irish. They include James Simmons (1933–2001), Seamus Heaney (1939–2013), Michael Longley (born 1939), Derek Mahon (1941–2020), Ciaran Carson (1948–2019), Tom Paulin (born 1949), Medbh McGuckian (born 1950), and Paul Muldoon (born 1951), all of whom have collections or substantial selections of work currently in print, as do MacNeice, Hewitt, and Montague (for biographical sketches, see Welch 2003). Simmons, who became as well-known for writing and performing songs as for his verse, is probably the least read today.

These writers all at some time lived, studied, or worked in Belfast, and they are linked by ties of mentorship, dialogue, and friendship. Heaney and Longley were members of the

Belfast Group established at Queen's University in 1963 by the English writer Philip Hobsbaum, which brought poets and critics together in a much-valued nonsectarian forum. The Belfast Festival Committee published pamphlets by Heaney, Longley, and Mahon in 1965 and 1966 (see Brearton 2003). In the 1970s, Heaney taught Muldoon and McGuckian at Queen's University (Wills 1993, 15). Today, McGuckian teaches in the Seamus Heaney Centre for Poetry at Queen's University, where Carson holds the Chair of Poetry. Her younger fellow-poet Sinéad Morrissey was a Reader in Creative Writing at Queen's University until February 2017 when she took up her role as Professor of Creative Writing at the University of Newcastle.

Heaney, Mahon, and Muldoon, who have enjoyed international reputations and careers, eventually settled outside Northern Ireland, as did Paulin. But the poets of what is sometimes called the "Ulster Renaissance" have continued to dedicate poems—and volumes—to one another, in a conversation that spans five decades. "Art and Reality," in Mahon's *New Collected Poems* (Mahon 2011, 357), is written in memory of Simmons: "Who would have thought you'd be the first / to quit the uproar of life's feast?" In September 2013, Muldoon spoke at the funeral service held in Dublin for Seamus Heaney.

Heaney, Montague, and Longley

"Personal Helicon," in Heaney's first collection *Death of a Naturalist* (1966), records how as a child the poet was drawn to wells, "the trapped sky, the smells / Of waterweed, fungus and dank moss" (reprinted in Heaney 1990, 9). Rural places in his work are scenes of enchantment and emblems of continuity. Other early poems of retrospect such as "Digging" and "Follower" (Heaney 1990, 1, 6) present Heaney as grounded in place and answerable—across a growing divide—to those who have shared it with him. In the later sonnet sequence "Clearances," he recalls peeling potatoes with his mother: the subsequent separation of mother and child, "never closer the whole rest of our lives," prompts rueful meditation (Heaney 1987, 27). The hope of keeping in touch with his community of origin, and with unspecialized readers generally, is reflected in Heaney's preference for directly intelligible speech and familiar verse forms.

Accountability and allegiance begin with family and birthplace, but extend beyond them. Heaney's work after 1969 became increasingly concerned with how to respond to violence. Some poems suggest an identification with the nationalist cause: these include "Requiem for the Croppies" (Heaney 1969, 24) and "Wolfe Tone" (Heaney 1987, 44), commemorating the 1798 uprising. More usually, Heaney expresses a sense of being both implicated in and alienated from the violence around him, as in "Punishment," from *North* (1975) (reprinted in Heaney 1990, 71). Inspired by the Jutland bog-burials, where archaeologists had unearthed remains of sacrificial victims, the poem depicts the uncannily preserved body of a young woman hanged for adultery. The scene shifts to contemporary Ulster, where the victim is "cauled in tar," a punishment inflicted on women from the nationalist community who went out with British soldiers. The last stanza shows the poet appalled by and complicit in what has been done, one who

> would connive
> in civilized outrage
> yet understand the exact
> and tribal, intimate revenge.

Heaney's public poems have evoked strong, and divergent, critical responses, for example in celebrated essays by Edna Longley and David Lloyd (Longley 1996; Lloyd 1993). Whatever view was taken, his work became an indispensable point of reference for anyone concerned with Irish writing and politics during the Troubles. Heaney's last sustained meditation on these matters is the sequence "Station Island" (Heaney 1984, 61–94), in which a series of ghostly encounters brings the poet into conversation with figures from his past and the past of Irish literature. In the final poem, James Joyce appears, advising Heaney to renounce public political argument: "it's time to swim // out on your own and fill the element / with signatures on your own frequency." Many of the best poems Heaney went on to publish follow that advice. Places no longer root him to the ground; they take him to the border between this world and what lies beyond it, as when he evokes, in the 1991 volume *Seeing Things* (dedicated to Mahon), "the visible sea at a distance from the shore / Or beyond the anchoring grounds" (Heaney 1991, 107).

Heaney's poetic voice sustains a level seriousness, concealing rather than displaying its artifice. It aims to keep poetry in direct touch with other kinds of speech, public and personal. Less ironic than Mahon, never teasingly difficult like McGuckian, Muldoon, or Carson, Heaney's closer affinities are with Hewitt, Montague, and Longley. Hewitt is more defiantly plain-speaking, and relies more often on strongly marked iambic meters; his lines have less fluency, and less authority, than the best of Heaney's. "Footing Turf" (quoted in the earlier text) nonetheless puts one in mind of Heaney in the link it establishes between labor, place, and vision.

Similar topics recur in John Montague's *oeuvre*. Places may be evoked for their communitarian political meanings, as in "A Lost Tradition" (Montague 2012, 47) where "the whole landscape" is presented as "a manuscript / We had lost the skill to read," a palimpsest that, once interpreted, would reveal the dispossession of the Gaelic Irish in the seventeenth-century colonization of Ulster. Obscure rural lives and histories, emblems of a resilient tradition, are also the ground of individual identity. In "First Landscape, First Death" (Montague 2012, 466), Montague pays Wordsworthian tribute to the "remote country hiding place… / which gave me gentle nourishment." This double power of place is his most resonant theme, but his *New Collected Poems* (2012) include other modes of memoir and autobiography, as well as evocations of rural France and America and meditations on war and violence.

Michael Longley's work at the Arts Council of Northern Ireland as Combined Arts Director for literature and the traditional arts (1970–1991) and as Professor of Poetry for Ireland from 2007 to 2010 has given him an important role in Ulster culture. His 1973 volume *An Exploded View* was dedicated to Mahon, Heaney, and Simmons, and he co-edited Hewitt's posthumous *Selected Poems*. The two concluding pieces in Longley's 2006 *Collected Poems*, "The Leveret" and "The Wren" (Longley 2006, 327, 328), illustrate his emotional delicacy and empathetic, closely observed response to nature. They celebrate his grandsons' first visits to the Longleys' house at Carrigskeewaun in Mayo and their encounters with birds, small mammals, and plants: wheatear, tufted duck, leveret, shrew, scabious, fuchsia. Here and in Longley's recent *Angel Hill* (2017), as so often in Ulster poetry, rural place frames family tradition: the making of intimate memory can be contrasted to the public violence registered in other poems.

Longley, who in 2017 received the PEN Pinter Prize, has addressed public matters eloquently through his versions of Greek and Latin poetry. Like Heaney and Muldoon, he finds counterparts there for Irish experiences of seafaring and return, war and commemoration. "Ceasefire" (1995: reprinted in Longley 2006, 225) marks, like Hewitt's "Neither an Elegy nor a Manifesto," a moment when the poet's voice can express a collective mood. Written as the 1994 IRA ceasefire was being negotiated, it shows Priam and Achilles, warring kings in the *Iliad*, as archetypes of the warrior finding courage to forego revenge. "I get down on my knees" (says Priam) "and do what must be done / And kiss Achilles's hand, the killer of my son."

Mahon and McGuckian

In the work of Derek Mahon, places more often engender a sense of exile than of belonging. "A Garage in Co. Cork" (Mahon 2011, 121) evokes an abandoned petrol station, like "a frontier store in an old western / [with] nothing behind it but thin air." The family who ran it must have moved abroad: "Where did they go? South Boston? Cricklewood?" On the Ulster coast at Portrush, the poet watches the Chinese restaurateur gazing across the border into Donegal and "dreaming of home" ("The Chinese Restaurant in Portrush," Mahon 2011, 89). Exile, the fate of the emigrant, is also a figure for the strangeness of human life on a planet that Mahon apprehends in both metaphysical and ecological terms. The poet, especially, lives that displaced life: Ovid, for example, banished by Tiberius, walking by "greasy waters" in the "Scythian wind" ("Ovid in Tomis," Mahon 2011, 140–145). But exile also favors insight. Mahon's work, which includes animal poems, autobiographical reflection, meditations on art and literature, and disaffected but sometimes self-critical reckonings with Ulster politics, often strikes the note of dissidence: poetry cannot court worldly power if it is to tell the truth.

Lexically exact, formally conservative, manifestly well-made, illuminated by cosmopolitan literary and philosophical reference: this is the work of a poet who for all his ironic self-awareness revels in his writerly identity. It rises, when occasion warrants, to powerful direct address. Mahon established this distinctive voice in a substantial body of work published by his late forties. His later poetry takes some fresh directions. "Homage to Gaia" (Mahon 2011, 311–325) speaks in newly political terms about living "in the confused stink / of global warming." The verse-letter, a medium for public speech in some important earlier poems, takes on a more amply conversational tone in recent sequences addressed to Mahon's children and others. Mahon remains cosmopolitan, but now writes as one who has found a home. The last piece in *New Collected Poems*, "Dreams of a Summer Night" (Mahon 2011, 372–377), alludes to Ingmar Bergman in its title and Kafka, Mozart, and Brancusi in its text. But it situates itself in the known landscape of Kinsale in County Cork, bounded by the Bandon River, lit by "a single star" above the Inishannon woods. The collection includes a fine translation from Irish of "An Bonnán Buí" (The Yellow Bittern), by the eighteenth-century Ulster poet Mac Giolla Ghunna (Mahon 2011, 208).

Medbh McGuckian was the only Northern Irish woman poet to attract significant critical attention during the "Ulster Renaissance." In the Irish Republic, women establishing reputations in this period include Nuala Ní Dhomhnaill, Eavan Boland, Eiléan Ní Chuilleanáin, and Paula Meehan. Boland has written pointedly of the difficulties faced by women working in the Irish literary tradition, where male writers have figured the nation as a female presence or body and the representation of women's experience must reckon with such archetypes and fantasies. Her poem "Mise Éire" (Boland 2005, 128) is an oft-quoted reflection on this theme, which remains central in her recent collection *A Woman Without a Country* (Boland 2014). McGuckian's response to these challenges may seem paradoxical, for her poems echo dominant stereotypes. Many lyrics in *Selected Poems 1978–1994* (McGuckian 2013) present images of domestic space, the woman's erotic body, women's clothes, and of fruit and flowers as emblematic of feminine qualities and sensibilities. Their fragmentary narratives refer to topics and events—marriage, love-trysts, self-seclusion—traditionally associated with woman's fate. However, the fragments fail to cohere into a story, and the images compose no stable figure. "A Conversation Set to Flowers" (McGuckian 2013, 40) ends with a "hill-wind" that "blows at the book's edges / to open a page," casting an uncanny light on the earlier invocations of home, marriage, and children. In "Hotel" (McGuckian 2013, 36), the "heroine half-asleep" is to learn that "yes on its own can be a sign for silence, / even from that all-too-inviting mouth." Putting imagist techniques in the service of the Russian Formalists' ideal of "making it strange," McGuckian baffles the reader by refusing to render herself intelligible in the available language.

Paulin, Carson, and Muldoon

Most of the writers considered so far write poems susceptible of broad paraphrase: their work, however figurative, asks us to elicit its discursive meanings. McGuckian offers a contrast in her puzzling surfaces and her refusal of univocal sense, features that also characterize many poems by Tom Paulin, Ciaran Carson, and Paul Muldoon.

Paulin's early work does sometimes permit readings with a manifest political edge. "Desertmartin" and "Ballywaire" (reprinted in Paulin 2014, 44, 12) are places typifying the cultural stagnation of Ulster, as seen by a knowing and unfriendly eye. British imperial sentiment and fantasy are diagnosed in "A Rum Cove, A Stout Cove" (Paulin 2014, 49), whose mariner-hero Sol Grout embodies a loyalism "rusted, hard, like chains." But even in the early volumes, pieces referring to the condition of Ulster are accompanied by others, some of them translations, whose connotations are more elusive: their geography expands to include India, Russia, Latin America, and they reach back into a ghostly half-historical past. The title poem of *The Strange Museum* (1980, reprinted in Paulin 2014, 37) has the poet awaken in "an upstairs drawing-room," probably located in Belfast; but the equivocal note of happiness on which it concludes is private, invoking a "you" who has come from elsewhere. Since *Walking a Line* (1994), Paulin's work, including his versions of Rilke, Baudelaire, and others, favors an improvisatory style and informal syntax and shows an increasing preference for imagistic suggestiveness and indeterminacy.

Carson's second volume, *The Irish for No* (1987), inaugurated his highly distinctive contribution to Ulster poetry. His earlier work often depicted discrete scenes whose implications arise from carefully registered detail. *The Irish for No*, by contrast, is full of prolix life, crammed into long lines ungoverned by regular meter, as in "Belfast Confetti" (reprinted in Carson 2013, 93) where the hail of missiles—the "confetti"—includes not only "Nuts, bolts, nails, car-keys" thrown by a rioting crowd, but "A fount of broken type." Language seems to be drawn into the chaos it reflects. Carson used the poem's title again for his next volume (1989), where prose sections chronicling the city's history alternate with poems where its contemporary landscape is the setting for fragmentary narratives of rumor and misunderstanding, terror and pursuit. Carson's volumes of the 1980s and 1990s offer a uniquely sustained depiction of the Troubles, apprehending lethal threat in an idiom saturated and exhausted by the representation of violence; as the verse mimics that idiom, it passes an ironic, alienated judgment on it. Here, for example, in "58" (Carson 2013, 257), we witness the unintended killing of the bombers by a bomb aimed at the Dublin–Belfast railway:

> So it's mercury tilt and quicksilver flash as the Johnson slammed on its brakes
> And it's indecipherababble bits and bods, skuddicked and scrabbled like alphabet
>   bricks –
> A red hand. A rubber glove. The skewed grin of a clock. A clip of ammunition. A
>   breastpocketful of Bics.

Here, rather as in Muldoon's "The More a Man Has the More a Man Wants" (Muldoon 2001, 127–147), the war is a matter not of heroism but of petty criminality. The tone precludes the empathetic and tragic register in which Hewitt, Heaney, Montague, and Longley address the Troubles. In his later work, which includes a growing proportion of more personal and happier (but still enigmatic) poems, Carson continues to accommodate centrifugal linguistic energies in inventively capacious lines.

Muldoon's *Poems 1968–1998* (Muldoon 2001) brings together over 200 pieces from 8 volumes; and the work he has published since then continues to demonstrate great formal and thematic variousness. There are lyrics of place and memory, animal poems, reflections on sex, friendship, and intimacy—familiar topics often handled in disconcerting ways; riddling lapidary verses, such as the parable-like micro-poems of the sequence "Madoc" (Muldoon 2001, 202–321); and several long poems sustaining extraordinary momentum across their highly wrought stanzas. These include "Incantata," an elegy for the artist Mary Farl Powers, as well as the 20 pages of "The More a Man Has...," which combines myth, parody, documentary, and surrealism. Quite free of poetic diction, Muldoon's language is nonetheless resolutely literary. Ostentatiously learned, inhospitably demanding, it deploys colloquialisms and popular-cultural references in a cosmopolitan idiom that also embraces rare and archaic English words, fragments of Irish, and much intertextual allusiveness. While avoiding regular meter, Muldoon often adopts intricate rhyme-schemes: like many of his Ulster fellow poets, he persists with formal schemata that constrain the poem more tightly than is nowadays usual in English-language verse.

Negotiation with the constraints of form is offered as a display in which to take pleasure. An engaging example is "The Misfits" (Muldoon 2002, 8–11), all six stanzas of which use, in varying order, the same six syllables as line-endings: the poem's wit comes in part from the surprising aptness of the shifts and shapes to which it is thus forced. "Long Finish" (Muldoon 2001, 438–441), a love-poem celebrating 10 years of marriage, uses a similar formal device. In its theme, "The Misfits" goes against an established grain: rather than showing rural Ulster as the ground of poetic selfhood, Muldoon suggests that the youthful spirit may, with luck, escape that closed world of potatoes and heavy farmer-fathers—may "lift off, somehow, into the blue"—with the help of Bessie Smith's music and American cinema. Muldoon has lived in the United States since the late 1980s.

Even his admirers may ask whether the ludic difficulties of his *oeuvre* are compatible with full seriousness. "Sillyhow Stride," the long stanzaic poem that concludes *Horse Latitudes* (Muldoon 2006, 95–106), confronts that question directly, as had earlier poems setting private griefs and memories amid troubled public histories: notable among these is "At the Sign of the Black Horse, September 1999" (Muldoon 2001, 73–90), which invokes Yeats's apocalyptic fears in "A Prayer for My Daughter." Written in memory of the poet's friend Warren Zevon and his sister Maureen Muldoon, "Sillyhow Stride" makes structurally and semantically central use of references to John Donne. To foreground wit and allusion in a poem about death and loss involves tonal risk-taking very like Donne's: the echo is more than verbal when Muldoon writes:

> Go tell court huntsmen that the oxygen-masked King will ride
> ten thousand days and nights
> on a stride piano, yeah right.

The Future

Speaking at Seamus Heaney's funeral, Muldoon will have felt that his older contemporary's death marked a moment of transition as well as of loss. There has been strong critical agreement as to which Ulster poets merit discussion, and widespread acknowledgment of the exceptional contribution, quite out of proportion to the province's size, that they have made to English and Irish poetry since the 1960s. In public and international perception, Heaney was the leading figure, a Nobel Laureate and Oxford Professor of Poetry (1989–1994) (as was Muldoon from 1999 to 2004). While most of his fellow members of the "Ulster Renaissance" continue to bring out new work, Heaney's death invites us to consider which younger poets will join them in publishing poetry of lasting interest.

They are likely to include Sinéad Morrissey, made Belfast's inaugural Poet Laureate from July 2013 until the end of 2016, who in that role (as the web pages of the Seamus Heaney Centre for Poetry at Queen's University noted) was to be "engaged in several community-based writing projects" and to act as "an ambassador for poetry." Morrissey is both like and unlike her precursors in her embrace of a public identity and in the poetry she makes of private occasions. Several recent autobiographical pieces capture or refract angles of childish vision, as the growing-up of the two children to whom her latest volumes are dedicated recalls her own early memories. In "The Square Window," the title poem of her 2009 collection (Morrissey 2009, 32), there is a sense of threat, of something inimical pressing in. Yeats is echoed, as Muldoon echoes him, in the image of "my son" who "sleeps on unregarded in his cot." Landmarks near Belfast are named, in what seems an evocation of the distant Troubles. Then the poem takes a swerve—we may think of McGuckian or Paulin—away from what is shown in maps, into what readers of her work will be beginning to recognize as Morrissey's distinctive landscape, a place of concealments as well as revelations.

References

Boland, Eavan (2005). *New Collected Poems*. Manchester: Carcanet.

Boland, Eavan (2014). *A Woman Without a Country*. Manchester: Carcanet (e-book).

Brearton, Fran (2003). "Poetry of the 1960s: The 'Northern Ireland Renaissance'." In: *The Cambridge Companion to Irish Poetry* (ed. Matthew Campbell), 94–112. Cambridge: Cambridge University Press.

Carson, Ciaran (1987). *The Irish for No*. Oldcastle: Gallery Press.

Carson, Ciaran (1989). *Belfast Confetti*. Oldcastle: Gallery Press.

Carson, Ciaran (2013 (first publ. 2008)). *Collected Poems*. Oldcastle: Gallery Press.

Heaney, Seamus (1966). *Death of a Naturalist*. London: Faber.

Heaney, Seamus (1969). *Door into the Dark*. London: Faber.

Heaney, Seamus (1975). *North*. London: Faber.

Heaney, Seamus (1984). *Station Island*. London: Faber.

Heaney, Seamus (1987). *The Haw Lantern*. London: Faber.

Heaney, Seamus (1990). *New Selected Poems*. London: Faber.

Heaney, Seamus (1991). *Seeing Things*. London: Faber.

Hewitt, John (2007). *Selected Poems* (eds. Michael Longley and Frank Ormsby). Belfast: Blackstaff.

Lloyd, David (1993). "'Pap for the Dispossessed': Seamus Heaney and the Poetics of Identity." In: *Anomalous States: Irish Writing and the Postcolonial Moment*, 13–140. Dublin: Lilliput.

Longley, Edna (1996 (first publ. 1986)). "'Inner Emigré' or 'Artful Voyeur'? Seamus Heaney's *North*." In: *Poetry in the Wars*, 140–169. Newcastle: Bloodaxe.

Longley, Michael (2006). *Collected Poems*. London: Cape.

Longley, Michael (2017). *Angel Hill*. London: Cape.

MacNeice, Louis (1987). *Collected Poems*. London: Faber.

Mahon, Derek (2011). *New Collected Poems*. Oldcastle: Gallery Press.

McGuckian, Medbh (2013 (first publ. 1997)). *New Selected Poems*. Oldcastle: Gallery Press.

McKay, Susan (2008). *Bear in Mind these Dead*. London: Faber.

Montague, John (2012). *New Collected Poems*. Oldcastle: Gallery Press.

Morrissey, Sinéad (2009). *Through the Square Window*. Manchester: Carcanet.

Muldoon, Paul (2001). *Poems 1968–1988*. London: Faber.

Muldoon, Paul (2002). *Moy Sand and Gravel*. London: Faber.

Muldoon, Paul (2006). *Horse Latitudes*. London: Faber.

Paulin, Tom (1994). *Walking a Line*. London: Faber.

Paulin, Tom (2014). *New Selected Poems*. London: Faber.

Welch, Robert (2003). *The Concise Oxford Companion to Irish Literature*. Oxford: Oxford University Press (consulted in online edition).

Wills, Clair (1993). *Improprieties: Politics and Sexuality in Northern Irish Poetry*. Oxford: Clarendon Press.

2c.6
The Martian School: Toward a Poetics of Wonder

Małgorzata Grzegorzewska

The so-called Martian poets, despite the name given to the movement, did not explore outer space. Instead, their poetry aims at discovering the "unknownness" of the unexcitingly common, the everyday, the familiar. Trying to define the peculiar style of the Martian school, James Fenton claimed that these poems "insist[ed] on presenting the familiar at its most strange" (quoted in Jackaman 1989, 278). Christopher Reid's humorous poem "Two Dogs on a Pub Roof" (2001, 125), for instance, presents two dogs, instead of cats, walking on a roof: one minor change renders the image intensely amusing and slightly disturbing at the same time. Meanwhile, in Reid's *Katerina Brac*, which pretends to contain translations of texts originally written by a woman poet from some unspecified Central or East European country, we find the poem "Tin Lily" (1985, 23), which compares the loudspeaker on a military van to a threatening flower, "strafing the boulevards" (l. 21). This time, however, the astounding simile serves an entirely different purpose: it is designed to debunk a political system that is based on hate speech and aggressive propaganda: "This is not surrealism, / but an image of new reality, / a counterblast to Copernicus" (ll. 22–24). The phrase "new reality" refers to a surrealist absurdity enfleshed in a totalitarian dystopia where the lily flower, conventionally associated with innocence, is transformed into a means of infecting people's minds with fear and hostility. One may add in passing that Reid perfectly catches the atmosphere of the communist regimes in which people defined their everyday experience as genuinely "Orwellian" (no doubt Orwell's

---

A Companion to Contemporary British and Irish Poetry, 1960–2015, First Edition.
Edited by Wolfgang Görtschacher and David Malcolm.
© 2021 John Wiley & Sons Ltd. Published 2021 by John Wiley & Sons Ltd.

invention of Newspeak in *1984* foreshadowed the distorted use of language by state propaganda) or "Kafkaesque." In the Polish language we also have a saying, "Pure Mrożek," which mocks blind bureaucracy and refers to the fact that in the communist era, the "new reality" of the totalitarian state did not differ from the bizarre worlds represented in the plays of Sławomir Mrożek, the well-known Polish representative of the Theatre of the Absurd. At the same time, all the poems included in *Katerina Brac* explore one more effect of what Viktor Shklovsky called *ostranenye* by reminding the reader of the "inadvertently 'poetic' effects of translation – perhaps in homage to the Poles Zbigniew Herbert and Tadeusz Rosewicz [sic] or the Czech Miroslav Holoub [sic]" (McKendrick 2010, 990).

This strategy of *ostranenye*, of making the word deliberately strange or foreign, was characterized by the Russian Formalists as the very essence of poetic language, but the unsettling of formulaic usages does more than merely prevent the dull routine of communication; it endows poetic speech with a sense of wonder. By and large, Martian poetry aims at offering the reader an opportunity to feel the pleasing excitement that accompanies the solving of a clever riddle. This is not to say that the puzzle solved abolishes the sense of wonder, or that ingenious analogy can prevail over the ubiquitous sense of amazement that is so persistent in the poetry of the so-called Martian school. Quite the reverse, Martian simile aims at discovering reality which is inherently astonishing, always brimming with epiphanic novelty, splendor, and otherness, always ready to surprise us with its new, transfigured aspect. This can be seen, for instance, in the crisp, sharp images of a more recent poem by Craig Raine, entitled "How Snow Falls" (Raine 2011, 1). Every year, after fresh snowfall, we unavoidably end up surprised by "this new coldness in the air, / the pang / of something intangible," (ll. 3–5) "this transfiguration / we never quite get over" (l. 11–12). The experience of sudden illumination described here resembles falling in love (both in the sense of amorous frenzy: "love's vertigo" [l. 9]—and loving attention: "love's exactitude" [l. 10]). Not only does the fresh, dazzling whiteness fill the eyes, but the phenomenon is simultaneously perceived by other senses, such as touch ("Like the unshaven prickle of a sharpened razor" [l. 2]) and smell ("the sinusitis of perfume without the perfume" [l. 7]). The entire image is painfully pointed, sharp, cutting to the quick. Finally, the word "transfiguration," which may refer to the event reported in the Synoptic Gospels when Jesus revealed his divine nature to three chosen disciples, is, at the same time, a perfect instance of the "spectacular foretaste of glory divine" (Westphal 2003, 29). In the case of the biblical event, this means that at the moment of transfiguration the faith of the disciples is chastened not by the impenetrable night of the cross, but by the excess of light which emanates from Christ's shining face and his dazzling clothes. Although the event goes beyond anything they could possibly have anticipated, Peter, John, and James clearly wish to prolong it as long as possible, "to keep this presence present" (Westphal 2003, 29), as one commentator says, even despite the fact that the beatific vision on Mount Tabor is not just a glorious sight, but a powerful blast of reality that "overwhelms, overflows, swallows up, engulfs and envelops" (Westphal 2003, 29) the observers' selves. In Raine's poem, the same desire to arrest the moment of transfiguration is expressed in a phrase which points to the lasting effect of the bedazzling whiteness of a snowy landscape: "this transfiguration / *we never quite get over*" (ll. 11–12). The poet's account is lucid, expressive, and communicative, while at the same time, it points to the inherent ineffability of the experience, which overflows the senses and surpasses understanding, bringing poetry to the threshold of religious apophasis. The sensation is so powerful that one cannot "get over" it, that is recover from the shock of it; neither can it be fully comprehended, mastered, grasped, or successfully communicated, since no words appear sufficient to give it due significance. At the same time, this phrase alerts us to the fact that it is not only the landscape that changes when snow falls, but the observer who is also "transfigured" and who begins to see things in a new, more perceptive way, full of unforeseen discoveries. We, as readers, undergo a similar metamorphosis that prevents us from "getting over" the experience of reading the poem.

Viewed from this perspective, Martian "outrageous simile[s]" (Morrison and Motion 1982, 18) are not unlike witty metaphysical conceits, surprising the reader with a flash of light which erupts from the unexpected connection of ideas that at first glance seem to have nothing in common. Metaphysical wit is frequently praised as a unique form of grasping reality by expressing in a concise, even if entirely unexpected way the hidden affinity of things, as the most accomplished form of "speaking to the point." But there may be good reason to perceive in metaphysical conceits a liberating force of "speaking nonsense," if we agree that metaphysical poetry reveals the difficulty of naming things and forces the reader to engage in the arduous task of pursuing an elusive sense (Sławek 2012, 114–115, translated M.G.). Indeed, this is suggested by the famous definition of metaphysical style popularized by the defenders of poetic decorum, with its requirement of effortless elegance; as Dr. Johnson asserted, metaphysical poets were guilty of a most indecorous, violent "yoking" of "the most heterogeneous ideas" (2006, 23). Paraphrasing George Herbert's poetic parable about God's gifts bestowed on mankind in "The Pulley" (1991, 150), we may say that metaphysical poetry allows one to use all the resources of language, except the comfort of repose after accomplishment. In other words, this poetry takes advantage of the fact that all the language we have is both a reminder of experience and a remainder of reality, its residual "rest," which is always available for use "with repining restlessness" (Herbert, "The Pulley," l. 17). In this context, we may invoke Neil Corcoran's statement that "[i]t is certainly central to the Martian method that the terms of simile always summon unlikeness even as they propose likeness, *holding all experience in a kind of permanently ambivalent pun*" (Corcoran 2013, 240, emphasis added).

Both metaphysical conceit and Martian simile transform the perception of ordinary objects into what contemporary philosophy calls "saturated phenomena" (Marion 2002a, 225). This concept, introduced by Jean-Luc Marion, refers to the "bedazzlement" we experience in the face of the excess of intuition over intention: the saturated phenomenon opens our perception beyond the horizon of intentionality and forces the poetic image to grasp more than the ordinary appearance of things; in other words, this poetry alerts us to the silent call, the "mute interpellation" of beings (Marion 1998, 191). In perceiving ordinary objects, the observer can rely on a finite repertoire of "aspects" or profiles available while "intending" the entire object. (For example, in facing three-dimensional figures we always see only one side of the figure. When we are looking at the best-known west façade of the Cathedral of Notre Dame, we cannot at the same time admire the flying buttress of the chevet, which overlooks the east; while walking along the south side of the cathedral, we inevitably miss the view of its other, north side.) By contrast, when we encounter a saturated phenomenon, our horizons are overwhelmed by this object. On account of the fact that in these phenomena givenness modifies manifestation, Marion calls these phenomena "paradoxes" (Marion 2002a, 225). The concept of saturated phenomena can thus serve as a helpful means to understanding poetry as a form of epiphany or revelation, whereby all human faculties are suddenly "contract[ed]" into a span (as Herbert wrote in "The Pulley" l. 5), and the entire universe is "squeezed [...] into a ball" (as in Andrew Marvell's poem "To His Coy Mistress" [1984] 23, l. 41). This is also how surprise operates in Martian poems, which estrange the familiar in order to disclose the surprising, astonishing, and, therefore, miraculous, hidden under the surface of everyday experience. John Strachan and Richard Terry stress this aspect of Martian rhetoric as a key to successful poetic metaphors: "As we encounter these comparisons, we feel a sudden jolt of recognition at their aptness, but also a sense of their being hard won, or won in the face of an overriding implausibility and unlikelihood" (2000, 133).

The riddle which appears to be the constitutive feature of Martian poetry waits to be solved, but does not let us explain the enigma of the world away; "the most heterogeneous ideas yoked together" in a Martian simile never merge into a seamless whole, but always remain tremulously hostile to one another. The analogies established in these poems do not render the world more comprehensible, but on the contrary alert us to the inherent incomprehensibility and uninterpretability of existence. Some readers may see here a fundamental difference between metaphysical conceit and Martian simile, but, in fact, the baroque conceit is not so far from our contemporary existential anxiety. The difference, more subtle but no less significant, seems to lie elsewhere: in the transition from early modern metaphysics and its attending concern with how we come to know the world, to the Martian poets' exercise in contemporary phenomenology, allowing the phenomena of the world to show themselves and, thus, appear in our consciousness, and in post-phenomenology, which throws open the question of a genuinely revelatory givenness, divested of any prior antecedents. It may prove worthwhile to recall, in this connection, Fenton's succinct in 1978 analysis of what he called Raine's "phenomenological style": "During the contemplation of his subject [he] deliberately rejects certain modes of consciousness ... The only activity is that of a free contemplation, *without ulterior motive, eager if anything for the most improbable discoveries*" (quoted in Colby 1985, 616, emphasis added). Using the terms introduced by Marion, we could add in this context that this kind of eager attention frees the observer from "the ordinariness of the visible" (2002b, 55) and paves the way for visibility so dense that it opens infinite prospects of epiphanic disclosures which begin and end with surprise, astonishment, and wonder.

In order to illustrate this point, we may take a closer look at the poem to which the Martian movement owes its name, Craig Raine's "A Martian Sends a Postcard Home" (1979, 1). What deserves to be called "outlandish" in this report, purporting to come from alien visitors, is the point of view, which unsettles well-known images of people traveling, resting, working, eating, or making love; what is uncommon is the manner of perceiving, which does not exclude a sense of surprise or amazement. The reader is forced to imagine how our existence might be seen by a visitor from another planet. At the same time, the title itself sets the Martian in the role of a typical tourist who observes local habits with interest, but without engagement, and who puts down his observations in a message sent to his friends at home. For a reader in the twenty-first century, the effect of estrangement is enhanced by the distance in time: the Martian's habit of writing postcards may now seem eccentric because by our times it has become so old-fashioned. Time has thus supplied an element of defamiliarization beyond what the author could have foreseen, and this may be true of all Martian poetry, in its attempt to describe the everyday of its own times.[1] This could also be the reason why Raine's well-known riddles about wrist watches, telephones, and Model T are now enjoyed mainly for their out-of-date, partly oneiric and partly psychedelic imagery, very much in the same way as we watch the futurist technology of sci-fi films produced in the 1950s or 1960s, as represented for instance by the crudely formed, good-natured robot Roby in *Forbidden Planet* (dir. Fred M. Wilcox, 1956).

The unexpected ordinariness of the Martian's behavior in this poem (even if it is slightly old-fashioned) is, however, only the beginning of the wonder experienced by the reader of the poem. When we hear that "Caxtons are mechanical birds" (l. 1), we are reminded of a word used mainly for old prints (the word "Caxton" itself invokes a distant, unfamiliar realm of early modern printing), and we see books transfigured into man-made birds, which, instead of trying to fly, perch on a human hand, with their "many wings" (l. 1) outstretched. What is, thus, stressed is the emotional appeal of poetry and prose—"They cause eyes to melt / or the body to shriek without pain" (ll. 3–4)—and also the visual appeal of a beautiful book—"some are treasured for their markings" (l. 2). When fog or mist envelops the earth, the Martian guesses that this happens because "the sky is tired of flight / and rests its soft machine on the ground" (ll. 7–8). Yet even more intriguing than this modern kenning,[2] referring to the cloud as a "soft machine" of the sky, is the Martian's next observation, which compares the misty landscape to illustrations in old books protected by half-transparent leaves of tissue-paper: "Then the world is dim and bookish / like engraving under tissue paper" (ll. 9–10). Here we not only catch a glimpse of a splendid volume full of old-fashioned, finely etched pictures, but we are also reminded of the fact that the haze of mist or cloud, just like the excess of light, enhances a sense of the wondrous. One more analogy with reading books is evoked at the end of the poem to illustrate the jerking eye movement which occurs in some stages of sleep: "At night, when all colours die / they hide in pairs / and read about themselves / in colour, with their eyelids shut" (ll. 31–32). The fact that this sentence is framed by references to absence of "colour" and "in colour" emphasizes the poet's concern with visual perception, but, at the same time, the reference to dreams allows the reader to move beyond sheer visibility, and pass on from images to imagination as an alternative mode of seeing and comprehending reality.

The speaker's consistent interest in books as material seems closely connected with the pursuit of a sacramental formula of poetry that would allow the poet to transfigure ordinary objects into signs of intangible reality and enable the reader to touch, smell, and taste the mystery of existence. It has been noted in this context that "the tropes of the world as book and the world as sacrament evoke ideals of order which Martian poetry may ironize but to which they owe a ghostly or elegiac allegiance" (Corcoran 2013, 240). The longing for sacrament (if not the belief in the sacraments of the Church), so indubitably present in the previously discussed poem "How Snow Falls," is certainly also present in "A Martian Sends a Postcard Home." It informs the poem's concern with the world made flesh, that is, the world perceived by the sensible human body. This preoccupation with enfleshed experience becomes most apparent, paradoxically, in the Martian's shamelessly scatological account of the secret human ritual of defecation.

Opening the doors of wonder, Martian poetry could not be indifferent to the flesh, which belongs to the category of saturated phenomena: the flesh, says Marion, "allows one to feel; in short, before making itself be seen and appearing, it makes me feel (myself) and appear." Later he adds that "the essential property" of the flesh "has to do with its suffering, its passivity" (2002b, 87). In the light of this observation, Raine's humorous venture into carnal reality, together with the previous references to melting eyes or the body's shrieking "without pain" (l. 4), can be seen as a means of inviting the reader to see himself or herself "appear" in the process of reading, mediated by the sensible flesh, in which alone we can experience pleasure or pain.

Another characteristic trait of Martian poems which anchors them in human corporeality is their tacit preoccupation with death. In Christopher Reid's "Three Sacred Places in Japan" (2001, 11), for instance, the speaker evokes the images of "sea-weed wreaths" and "a beer-can, drunk" both "tugged by tide" ("Itsukushima," l. 16), and then addresses these trivial objects with an astonishing prayer, stressing in this way the unbearable lightness of human existence: "You Nothings / bless me in my next-to-nothingness" (ll. 17–18). This astounding apostrophe combines the previously mentioned acuteness of observation with an equally acute awareness of inevitable death. While pursuing the inexhaustible resources of the world's wonders and engendering in the reader the sense of joyful excess of being, the poem, at the same time, reveals the vanity of the created world.

Another poignant evocation of the memento mori topos borrowed from seventeenth-century English metaphysical poetry informs the imagery of Raine's "Dandelions" (1979, 21). Time has already turned these flowers into specters of their own glory: "bald as drumsticks / swaying by the roadside / like Hare Krishna pilgrims / bowing to the Juggernaut" (ll. 1–4). Death has deprived them of all beauty, joy, and longing for joy or beauty: "They have given up everything. / Gold gone and their silver gone / humbled with dust, hollow..." (ll. 5–7). Tossed and bewildered by the gust of indifferent wind, dead flowers "wither into mystery, / waiting to find out why they are / patiently, before nirvana" (ll. 15–17). The concept of nirvana chimes with two previous references to Eastern religions, the mention of Hare Krishna pilgrims and the Hindu allegory of fate, envisioned in the form of the mercilessly unstoppable car, the Juggernaut or *jagannath*—one of Krishna's titles—which crushes everything in its way. This touch of Indian culture is both "exotic" and, at the same time, perfectly familiar in the mouth of an English poet. Last but not least, when the dandelion's morbid vigil ends with a vision of rain which will fall on them "like vitriol" (l. 18), we are encouraged to solve one more puzzle, this time based on the secret arcana of alchemy, as the archaic name of any sulfate (in particular the strongly corrosive sulfuric acid) is also an acronym for the Latin maxim of the alchemists: "*V.isita I.nteriora T.errae R.ectificandoque, I.nvenies O.ccultum L.apidem*" ("Visit the interior of the earth and rectifying (purifying) you will find the hidden stone").

Yet even in a poem so full of cryptic references and set on the threshold of non-being, it is the vertigo of material reality which offers itself as if "in excess," amazing the reader, arresting sight, overflowing perception. Several aptly chosen ekphrastic references enhance the visual appeal of the poem. Dead dandelions resemble: the heroic burghers of Calais immortalized in Rodin's sculpture; miserable convicts in New South Wales; or Alberto Giacometti's surrealist sculptures and prints of human figures reduced to thin lines. Death, as yet another "saturated phenomenon," proves firmly rooted in the phenomenal world, always close at hand, waiting to surprise us somewhere "by the roadside" (l. 2), among the dying and dead dandelions. No anticipation can allow us to see it coming; it is always already here, always ahead of us.

The flesh, death, and countless daily transfigurations of everyday objects are the focus of the Martian poets' memento mori snapshots. Devoid of the chastising tones of moralistic vanity painting, but no less disturbing than those old-fashioned painted sermons on human mortality, the snapshots give a distinctly human touch to a school of poetry, the name of which points to visitors from outer space. Martian poetry begins in the wonder of existence and ends with the wonder of mortality. Its visual appeal may surpass even the intensity of gaze which the reader is likely to encounter in imagist poems; the visual riddles of Martian poets take the reader by surprise, pointing beyond the purely visible, toward the recognition of what Martin Heidegger deemed the most fundamental and constitutively human experience of wonder: "Among all beings, only man, called by the voice of Being, experiences the wonder of all wonders: that being is" (quoted in Marion 1998, 163).

NOTES

1 I owe this observation to Professor Jean Ward of the University of Gdańsk.

2 A typical device in Anglo-Saxon poetry based on the use of a compound that employs figurative language.

REFERENCES

Colby, Vineta (1985). *World Authors 1975–1980*. New York: H.H. Wilson.

Corcoran, Neil (2013). *English Poetry Since 1940*. New York: Routledge.

Fenton, James (1978). "Of the Martian School." *New Statesman* (20 October).

Herbert, George (1991). *The Complete English Poems* (ed. John Tobin). Harmondsworth: Penguin Books.

Jackaman, Rob (1989). *The Course of English Surrealist Poetry Since the 1930s*. Queenston, ON: Edwin Mellen Press.

Johnson, Samuel. 1787 (2006). *The Works of Samuel Johnson, The Lives of the Most Eminent English Poets*, vol. 4. Oxford: Oxford University Press.

Marion, Jean-Luc (1998). *Reduction and Givenness. Investigations of Husserl, Heidegger and Phenomenology* (trans. Thomas Carlson). Evanston, IL: Northwestern University Press.

Marion, Jean-Luc (2002a). *Being Given. Toward a Phenomenology of Givenness* (trans. Jeffrey L. Kosky). Stanford: Stanford University Press.

Marion, Jean-Luc (2002b). *In Excess. Studies of Saturated Phenomena* (trans. Robyn Horner and

Vincent Berraud). Fordham: Fordham University Press.

Marvell, Andrew (1984). *The Complete Poems* (ed. George deF. Lord). London: Everyman's Library.

McKendrick, Jamie (2010). "Contemporary Poetries in English, c. 1980 to the Present 2." In: *The Cambridge History of English Poetry* (ed. Michael O'Neill), 988–1004. Cambridge: Cambridge University Press.

Morrison, Blake and Motion, Andrew (1982). "Introduction." In: *Penguin Book of Contemporary British Poetry*, 11–20. Harmondsworth: Penguin Books.

Raine, Craig (1979). *A Martian Sends a Postcard Home*. Oxford: Oxford University Press.

Raine, Craig (2011). *How Snow Falls*. London: Atlantic Books.

Reid, Christopher (1985). *Katerina Brac*. London: Faber and Faber.

Reid, Christopher (2001). *Mermaids Explained*. Edited and selected with a Foreword by Charles Simic. New York: Harcourt.

Sławek, Tadeusz (2012). *Szekspir. Nicowanie świata*. Katowice: Wydawnictwo Uniwersytetu Śląskiego.

Strachan, John and Terry, Richard (2000). *Poetry*. Edinburgh: Edinburgh University Press.

Westphal, Merold (2003). "Transfiguration as saturated phenomenon." *Journal of Philosophy and Scripture* 1 (1, Fall): 26–35. http://www.philosophyandscripture.org/MeroldWestphal.pdf. (access 15 March 2015).

2c.7
Linguistically Innovative Poetry in the 1980s and 1990s

Scott Thurston

Linguistically Innovative Poetry (LIP) has been known under a plethora of terms: avant-garde, experimental, formally innovative, neomodernist, non-mainstream, post-avant, postmodernist, and the parallel tradition. It was first used by the poet Gilbert Adair in *Pages* magazine in reference to Robert Sheppard's assertion that a new poetry had emerged which was distinct from the period which poet and critic Eric Mottram had celebrated in his essay "The British Poetry Revival 1960–1975." Adair argued that "Linguistically innovative poetry (for which we have not yet a satisfactory name) has been operating since 1977" (Adair 1988, 68). Sheppard uses the term in his *The Poetry of Saying: British Poetry and its Discontents 1950–2000*, where he offers 1978–2000 as the period for LIP. *Linguistically innovative* is problematic in terms of its descriptive quality, but Sheppard argues that the meaning of the term resides more in its use to "constellate overlapping practices in the British alternative poetries from the 1980s onwards" (Sheppard 2005, 142).

Sheppard characterizes the approach of LIP as a going beyond of, if not a total break with, the experimentation of the British Poetry Revival, with "a poetics of increased indeterminacy and discontinuity, the use of techniques of disruption and of creative linkage," and he also notes an increased engagement with post-structuralist theory (Sheppard 2005, 142). The anthology *The New British Poetry: 1968–1988* (1988) contains a section edited by Ken Edwards entitled "Some Younger Poets," which was the first attempt to group together poets whose shared practices reflect the concerns of LIP. Edwards

---

A Companion to Contemporary British and Irish Poetry, 1960–2015, First Edition.
Edited by Wolfgang Görtschacher and David Malcolm.
© 2021 John Wiley & Sons Ltd. Published 2021 by John Wiley & Sons Ltd.

argues that these poets share a "ceaseless urge to create meaning and value in the forms and modalities of the language itself" (Allnutt et al. 1988, 270), and this emphasis on language starts to prepare the ground for the use of a term like *linguistically innovative*.

The first anthology to use LIP as a critical term was *Floating Capital: New Poets from London* (1991) edited by Adrian Clarke and Sheppard and published in the USA. In their afterword, the editors set out what they see as the shared "operational axioms" of the work:

> That poetry must extend the inherited paradigms of "poetry"; that this can be accomplished by delaying [...] a reader's process of naturalisation; that new forms of poetic artifice and formalist techniques should be used to defamiliarise the dominant reality principle [...]; and that poetry can use indeterminacy and discontinuity to fragment and reconstitute text to make new connections so as to inaugurate fresh perceptions, not merely mime the disruption of capitalist production.
>
> (Clarke and Sheppard 1991, 124)

These axioms, in effect, are saying the same thing—that this poetry uses language in such a way as to disrupt a reader's habitual way of reading, and, in so doing, enacts a critique of conventional styles of representation in literature, and by extension, the capitalist culture that produces it. The editors use the terms of Sheppard's own developing poetics to declare that such a poetry makes the reader an "active co-producer" of the poems and thus makes reading a process of an "education of activated desire" by which the reader comes to interpret the world anew (Clarke and Sheppard 1991, 124).

Another important LIP anthology was *Out of Everywhere: Linguistically Innovative Poetry by Women in North America and the UK* (1996) edited by Maggie O'Sullivan. Her editorial argues that "much of the most challenging, formally progressive and significant work over recent years, particularly in the US ..., is being made by women" (O'Sullivan 1996, 9). The predominance of the US poets in the collection, who number 21 to the 9 British poets included, bears this view out although the anthology was an important intervention in making women's contribution to the field in the United Kingdom more visible. The anthology is celebrated by a sequel entitled *Out of Everywhere 2* published in 2015, reflecting the much greater numbers of women experimenters in the United Kingdom today. O'Sullivan's editorial, like Edwards' and Clarke's/Sheppard's, also makes a claim for the language-oriented approach of the anthology's contributors who have "committed themselves to excavating *language* in all its multiple voices and tongues, known and unknown" (O'Sullivan 1996, 10: emphasis in original), while Wendy Mulford's "After.Word," as with Clarke/Sheppard, argues for an active and politicized reader: "the reader will need actively to enter into the procedures, and become a participant in discovering the new meaning being generated. It follows that there is no final authority of the text, in the text" (O'Sullivan 1996, 241).

While much of the creative activity gathered in these selections focused on London, another important center for alternative poetic practices was located in Cambridge and linked to the key influence of the poet J. H. Prynne. In the introduction to the Cambridge-oriented anthology *A Various Art* (1987), editors Tim Longville and Andrew Crozier make a claim for the poetics of the work in terms which are echoed almost exactly by Edwards and

O'Sullivan: "the most important common characteristic of these poets [is a] commitment to the discovery of meaning and form in language itself" (Crozier and Longville 1987, 14). To properly understand what it is to write in a "language-oriented" way, it is of course necessary to examine the poetry itself, and the following selections represent work from both the London and Cambridge groups.

Sheppard has argued that the poet Allen Fisher's long essay "Necessary Business" constitutes "the first developed poetics of linguistically innovative poetry" (Sheppard 2011, 36). Fisher began writing in the context of the British Poetry Revival, but his work underwent significant development in the 1980s in a way which reflected and influenced the advent of LIP. Clarke and Sheppard placed Fisher in a separate opening section of *Floating Capital* (alongside the great Sound and Concrete poet Bob Cobbing) in order to indicate the importance of the large-scale poetic project Fisher began in the 1980s called *Gravity as a consequence of shape*. *Brixton Fractals* (1985) was one of the first substantial showings of work from the *Gravity* project and contains the poem "African Boog" which opens:

> Went dicing on my bike
> Disappearance
> Meaning given by timbre
> Relational invariants from a flux
> She lives in advance of her days
> Speed
> Rooks carry aubergines over Tulse Hill Station
> He hung an 18 foot blackboard in the garden
> In all the beautiful continuity of hope
> The innocent
> (Fisher 2016, 42)

This passage, as elsewhere in *Brixton Fractals*, combines observations of the urban environment of South London where Fisher was then living, with phrases and sentences that conspicuously carry traces of belonging to other discourses in their use of technical language, for example, "Relational invariants from a flux" or other kinds of literary text "In all the beautiful continuity of hope." Fisher's habit throughout his work of appending lists of resources to his poems allows the reader in some cases to establish the sources of certain statements, so that, for example, the reference to the "foot blackboard in the garden" in fact derives from Constance Reid's 1970 biography of the mathematician David Hilbert. This source is also referenced at the end of the poem with the lines "Jump on bike, figure of eight around rose beds, to the blackboard" (Fisher, 46), thus tying together the opening image of the narrator-poet who dices with death as he cycles through Brixton and Hilbert's own passion for cycling. The printed version of the poem also uses different fonts for certain phrases—in the extract mentioned earlier in the text, placing the words "Disappearance," "Speed," and "The innocent" in a sans-serif face encourages the reader to speculate that these phrases belong together, and indeed, some kind of continuity emerges between these phrases as the poem develops, as if creating another text within the poem, an effect enhanced further by the use of multiple margins.

Fisher's approach here is therefore a kind of collage which emphasizes discontinuity in its juxtaposition, line by line, of material drawn from various sources. Thus, one could say this is a language-oriented poetics that is focused on treating the poem as a space to bring various fragments of text together in order to create something new. In a short essay entitled "Linking the Unlinkable," Robert Sheppard articulates a poetics of "creative linkage" (Sheppard 1999, 55), which might be usefully compared to Fisher's approach. Sheppard is responding to Jean-François Lyotard's lecture "Discussions, or Phrasing 'After Auschwitz'" and Jacques Derrida's reply to it, in which the latter argues: "if there is somewhere a *One must* it must link up with a *one must make links with Auschwitz*" (Lyotard 1989; Sheppard 1999, 54). The ethical imperative here—*contra* Theodor Adorno's famous statement that poetry after Auschwitz is barbaric—envisages a poetry which, as in Fisher's work, brings disparate materials together in order to propose new connections between them.

Sheppard is the author of *Twentieth Century Blues*, published in several volumes throughout the 1980s and 1990s and now collected as *Complete Twentieth Century Blues* (2008), which stands alongside Fisher's *Gravity* as one of the most substantial and significant achievements of LIP. The poem "Small Voice 2" (1997) demonstrates the technique of creative linkage:

> do not interrogate the taillamps's irradicated drone
> voice within vision musicates, released ears entune
> its captive turn, the others no longer
> fixed in the totality of permanent waste
>
> this pleasure animates a knot of rapturous
> ruptures mass graces *follow me* dirt from
> itself: erotic or aesthetic it prises each
> permission without distinction tinkles in shivered delight
>
> (Sheppard 2008, 250)

Here a sequence of phrases are offered without resolving into a fully recuperable narrative or argument while also negotiating a series of subtle continuities. The image of "taillamps's irradicated drone," which one is exhorted not to interrogate, sets off a chain of ideas about voice, vision, music, and listening, which are entangled with and perhaps escape the negativity of captive, fixed, permanent waste (perhaps, there is also a pun on mass graves in "mass graces"). The phrase "rapturous / ruptures" is readable as a version of creative linkage itself and reveals a pleasure "erotic or aesthetic." Creative linkage here achieves further ambiguities via syntax which might resolve the phrase "erotic or aesthetic it prises each"—with a pun on prizes—as a complete notion in itself, or one which modifies "permission without distinction," which in turn may link to "tinkles in shivered delight." "Permission without distinction" might also suggest a poetics of combining diverse materials, but what is crucial here is how this approach generates a distinctive movement of thought in the poem.

While Fisher's and Sheppard's work is central to the poetics of LIP, J. H. Prynne's poetry has decisively set the tone for the body of innovative writing emerging from the Cambridge context. A look at two stanzas from one of his distinctive pamphlet-length poems from the 1990s, *Not-You* (1993), may serve to establish some of the characteristic features of his style.

> If he cuts by hand he'll make it last
> in the strips of best-butter light, out to view
> speedy turns in the spoke, shave drawn fine
> & thin on the dish. Receive the planet
>
> As a flat offer, we are bid for the gilt
> rim on a supper tray; not half by choice
> the flush deepens to ingot words under
> killed steel, still curved at a glance.
> (Prynne 1993, 397)

One of the uncanny features of Prynne's writing is its capacity to simulate a powerful authority while remaining radically open to interpretation. The earlier stanzas seem to result from a kind of micro-attentiveness to a humble domestic act of buttering bread and placing it on a tray. The opening line suggests a kind of economy of cutting bread thinly by hand to make it last longer, while strips of "best-butter" light, albeit as metaphor, also suggest something of the way these humble items are implicated in the larger economy of consumerism—that this butter is better than a rival product. The next phrase "out to view / speedy turns in the spoke" feels like the kind of collage leap of Fisher's or Sheppard's work, where the "speedy turns" might describe the movement of a bicycle or the poem's turns at the line break—where "spoke" puns on both the part of a bicycle wheel and the verb to speak—before returning to a phrase which seems to reconnect to the act of laying food out "fine / & thin on the dish." The next sentence seems to re-establish a possible critique of consumerism in which the whole planet (or flat earth) is offered to us, while we are also, at another abrupt switch of scale, bid for the "gilt / rim" on the supper tray. There seems to be a resonant pun on "guilt" here, which suggests an ethical judgment accompanying the analysis of consumerist behavior which takes place almost against our will: "not half by choice." In the following lines, the multivalent word "flush" might be recruited to suggest the slang meaning of being in possession of money, and this flush deepens to "ingot words" as if turning language itself into a commodity. That this happens under the sign of "killed steel," evoking the image of the knife used to spread the butter but also a kind of attendant violence where "glance" might suggest a glancing blow or even a lance. If the movement of Prynne's argument feels somewhat more radical in its potential for ironic, critical statement than Sheppard's or Fisher's writing, it nevertheless uses language with deep attentiveness to its multiple meanings as encoded in its sonic structure in order to generate a complex but suggestive discourse which invites a critically engaged reader.

John Wilkinson is a poet associated with the Cambridge grouping who studied under Prynne. Wilkinson has written of his "metastatic" poetics in which he sees that what gives his own poems their coherence is "not a metaphorical development, but a set of linked and transforming entities, which can be syntactical gestures, vowel and consonant patterning, imagistic or discursive modes" (Wilkinson 1996, 54). This emphasis on the textual dynamics of linking materials, as well as what is being linked, seems characteristic of the approach of LIP in evoking both continuity and discontinuity in the texture of the poem. This approach may be observed in "Dicing with Death," the final poem of *The Interior Planets* (1994). The poem opens:

> Declension is the iniquity, rigid metre
> digging stony earth; his suitable dying
> lest it picks up where he'll leave off,
> must be cadenced like a good voice always.
> (Wilkinson 1994, 176)

This poem is an elegy, linked to the preceding "Stages Along the Lichway" and "Envoy," which are dedicated to and address the poet Mark Hyatt (1940–1972). What suggests something of the "linked and transforming entities" of Wilkinson's poetics is the way in which the terminology of poetry, language, and writing is integrated with that of death. Thus, the poem's opening phrase "Declension is the iniquity" both makes the judgment that decline and death are unjust while also punning on the grammatical sense of declension. The next phrase imagines "rigid metre / digging stony earth," as if the kind of formal poetic practice eschewed by Hyatt is also in some way linked to his destruction, as if digging his grave. A possible conceit continues from this notion to suggest that the poet's "suitable" dying might be ironically "cadenced like a good voice always," as if in accordance with an implied poetic decorum. The poem's argument seems most clearly articulated in the later phrase: "Death's / not death without this scansion," as if, again, the means by which poetry's rhythm is analyzed is somehow equivalent to a kind of death.

As reflected upon earlier in the case of the *Out of Everywhere* anthology, women's writing was under-represented in publications of the LIP period, while making as important a contribution. Geraldine Monk's remarkable book-length poem *Interregnum* (1994) is a key work of the 1990s, and its original publication by Creation Press signified a moment when LIP was poised to reach a larger audience. *Interregnum* explores the histories, stories, and myths around the so-called Pendle witches: 12 men and women from the village of Pendle in Lancashire who were accused of witchcraft and underwent trials resulting in 10 of them being hanged in Lancaster Castle in 1612. The third and longest section, "Interregnum," evokes the voices of the dead accused in passages like this extract in the voice of Elizabeth Southern:

> Unification creates power.   Creates remains.
> Unification creates exclusion.   Persecution.
> Random cells need violence
> to club and hang together –
>   hang together! Ha!
> Bloody comics in
> great bonds of fear –
> hate-baiting coagulated fear
> (Monk 2003, 154)

Here Monk, far from exploiting the eerie appeal of fantasies about supernatural powers, constructs her voices as aware of the forces of social and gendered power that are arrayed against them and which lead to their destruction: "we hadn't the learning / to read us right" (Monk 2003, 154). Language itself is ultimately found guilty as Anne Whittle accuses: "thi med it up [...] / they knotted uz proper / in tittle-tattle / & / chains" (Monk 2003, 153).

Like Monk, Maggie O'Sullivan has been a long-term resident in the north of England, although both are linked to London LIP through their early publication with Bob Cobbing's Writers Forum press. Monk and O'Sullivan produced a co-authored statement published in *City Limits* magazine in 1984 in which they argued that "the most effective chance any woman has of dismantling the fallacy of male creative supremacy is simply by writing poetry of a kind which is liberating by the breadth of its range and innovation [...] to exploit and realize the full potential and importance of language" (Monk and O'Sullivan 1984). Once again language itself is invoked to articulate the poetics of LIP, and its potential is radically realized in O'Sullivan's poetry. In her 1993 book *In the House of the Shaman*, the second section, "Kinship with Animals," borrows an epigraph from the artist Joseph Beuys—whose work also furnished the title for the collection—which focuses on the shamanic notion of transformation and substance. In the poems that follow, language appears as a charged, almost magical substance which is able to enact change in the world by the very act of writing, as in the poem "Starlings":

>   Lived Daily
>   or Both
>
>   Daily
>   the Living
>   structuring
>   Bone-Seed,
>
>   Pelage,
>   Aqueous
>   (O'Sullivan 1993, 41)

O'Sullivan's multimargin handling of the page space is one of the most distinctive features of her technique along with her focus on the sonic properties of words and working at the level of the single word or phrase rather than the sentence. The recombination and repetition of the opening phrases here foreground the act of writing as one of selection, a process which, in being shown in this way, makes us more aware of writing as an act rather than a product. As the poem progresses, the vocabulary of "Bone-Seed, / Pelage, / Aqueous" draws in natural objects as a possible evoking of the daily life of the starling, but, unlike Ted Hughes's poems about birds, O'Sullivan does not represent the starling in any obvious way, preferring instead to construct a linguistic texture which evokes the movement and energy of the bird:

>   *YONDERLY*—
>   Lazybed of need —
>   *CLOUD-SANG*
>   Tipsy Bobbles, Dowdy
>   wander.
>   (O'Sullivan 1993, 41)

If this poetry is a more intensified version of creative linkage, it is almost paradoxically concerned both with the materiality of language and the limits of its representational capacity; with what escapes, even transcends language, in its attempt to make acts of meaning in the world.

Anna Mendelssohn (aka Grace Lake or Anna Mendleson) (1948–2009) became associated with the Cambridge scene through studying at the University as a mature student. A prolific writer, only a small amount of her output was published during her lifetime, although her *Collected Poems* was published by the UK press Shearsman Books in 2020. The title poem of *Bernache Nonnette* (1995) uses long lines and a paratactic movement of placing unsubordinated clauses side by side:

> Before too much was known could he have been a trucker this was not known
> Wooden individuality, individuality could not bear the one off chance
> A quick word reflection, self-indicative, & chose philosophical witness instead
> (Lake 1995, 3)

Many ideas are set running in these opening lines—about knowledge, identity, language, witness—and yet the poem gathers this material in a kind of head-long momentum that does not allow for any more direct explication. A Bernache Nonnette is a barnacle goose—so-called because the mystery of its reproductive habits led Europeans to conclude that it must reproduce underwater, whereas the birds actually fly to the arctic to mate and rear their young. Andrew Duncan has seen Mendelssohn's use of the goose as "an attempt to challenge organized knowledge with personal experience" (Duncan 1997). The sonically dense and playfully energetic lines

> Testing another female's response mechanisms, it's cooked bernache nonnette
> He tells his tonth his ifth and fith, que que que que combresome, the heaving dearth
> & sunson shone projects, portends & finds a way to do the same in change of format
> (Lake 1995, 4)

include a pun on the idiom of having one's goose cooked which might allude to the fact that, due to their uncertain provenance, the geese were considered acceptable food during fasting until banned by Pope Innocent III in 1215. The cross-linguistic punning (with Spanish) on "combresome" might critically gesture toward a possible symbol of authority in the Spanish *cumber* "top, peak, summit," while the phrase "dearth / & sunson shone" might allude to the crucifixion. The more straightforward "finds a way to do the same in change of format" could suggest how interpretations of the natural world are made to fit human agendas. This analysis however feels highly provisional, reflecting the quite extreme discontinuity of this passage. Thus, Mendleson's writing enacts a critique of normative language use while also being vividly expressive, asking the reader to actively attend to every detail of her rich verbal textures.

In conclusion, it is hoped that this gallery of close readings has illustrated the key tenets of LIP: the use of collage techniques to link materials together in dis / continuous ways; the attentiveness to the material properties (sonic, visual) of words as much as to their capacity for multiple-meanings; and the desire to engage the reader through challenging established reading habits and cultural consensus. The demands of this disruptive and energetic approach to writing poetry have meant that the critical literature on the field has taken time to develop. Nevertheless, this critical attention is now maturing and generating new ways of reading the ongoing production of many of these remarkable poets who seek to find meaning and value in the "forms and modalities of the language itself."

References

Adair, Gilbert (1988). "Letter to Robert Sheppard." pp. 65–72. [This little magazine does not provide volume or edition numbers]

Allnutt, Gillian, D'Aguiar, F., Edwards, K., and Mottram, E. (eds.) (1988). *The New British Poetry 1968–88*. London: Paladin.

Clarke, Adrian and Sheppard, Robert (eds.) (1991). *Floating Capital: New Poets from London*. Elmwood Connecticut: Potes & Poets Press Inc.

Crozier, Andrew and Longville, Tim (eds.) (1987). *A Various Art*. London: Paladin.

Duncan, Andrew (1997). "Nine fine flyaway goose truths: *Bernache Nonnette* by Grace Lake." *Angel Exhaust*, p. 15. www.poetrymagazines.org.uk/magazine/record.asp?id=13920 (accessed 22 December 2014).

Fisher, Allen (1985). *Necessary Business*. London: Spanner.

Fisher, Allen (2016). *Gravity As a Consequence of Shape*. Hastings: Reality Street Editions.

Lake, Grace (1995). *Bernache Nonnette*. Cambridge: Equipage.

Lyotard, Jean-François (1989). "Discussions, or Phrasing 'After Auschwitz'." In: *The Lyotard Reader* (ed. Andrew Benjamin), 360–392. Oxford: Blackwell.

Monk, Geraldine (2003). *Selected Poems*. Great Wilbraham: Salt Publishing.

Monk, Geraldine and O'Sullivan, Maggie (1984). untitled statement in *City Limits* (13–19 July). reprinted on Galloping Dog Press flier, Spring 1986.

O'Sullivan, Maggie (1993). *In the House of the Shaman*. London: Reality Street Editions.

O'Sullivan, Maggie (ed.) (1996). *Out of Everywhere: Linguistically Innovative Poetry by Women in North America and the UK*. London: Reality Street Editions.

Prynne, J. H. (1993). *Not-You*. Cambridge: Equipage.

Reid, Constance (1970). *Hilbert*. London and Berlin: George Allen & Unwin and Springer-Verlag.

Sheppard, Robert (1999). "Linking the Unlinkable." In: *Far Language: Poetics and Linguistically Innovative Poetry 1978–1997*. Exeter: Stride Publications.

Sheppard, Robert (2005). *The Poetry of Saying: British Poetry and Its Discontents, 1950–2000*. Liverpool: Liverpool University Press.

Sheppard, Robert (2008). *Complete Twentieth-Century Blues*. Great Wilbraham: Salt Publishing.

Sheppard, Robert (2011). *When Bad Times Made for Good Poetry: Episodes in the History of the Poetics of Innovation*. Exeter: Shearsman Books.

Wilkinson, John (1994). *Flung Clear: Poems in Six Books*. Cambridge: Parataxis Editions.

Wilkinson, John (1996). "The metastases of poetry." *Parataxis* 8/9: 49–55.

2c.8
Concrete and Performance Poetry

Jerzy Jarniewicz

Jacques Prévert's "Picasso's Promenade" (1970, 124 – 127) is an anecdotal poem about a young painter who tries to paint an apple, but finds it impossible. Whenever he looks at the apple, the fruit seems to escape him: he sees the Garden of Eden, or the story of William Tell, or Isaac Newton sitting under the tree, but he cannot see the apple. Exhausted by these unsuccessful attempts, the painter falls asleep. It happens, however, that Picasso is walking by. He stops by the young artist's studio, looks through the open window, sees the apple, takes it, and eats it. This parabolic anecdote can be seen as an illustration of what concrete poetry is. Picasso becomes here an emblematic "concrete poet," who approaches the apple not for what it *means*, but for what it *is*, and makes proper use of it. The young artist in the studio, by contrast, unable to see the apple, sees various symbolic meanings that have accrued to the apple, and, as an artist, fails.

"A poem should not mean / But be," wrote Archibald MacLeish in a conclusion to his "Ars Poetica" (2000, 331), defining, thus, ambitions of the many generations of poets who have tried to close the gap between the word and the thing, between meaning and being. The word, in both its oral and written forms, is a material phenomenon, composed of sounds or letters. Yet, as used in everyday contexts, it has lost its physical qualities. Reduced to its informative function, it has become a transparent medium, leading readers or listeners directly to its meaning beyond language. Everyday use makes us ignore the material aspect of language and assume its utter transparency. The visuality of language, even in poetry, is considered a feature which is marginal and contingent. Its phonic quality, its "music," has enjoyed greater prestige and been used in literature with a considerable

A Companion to Contemporary British and Irish Poetry, 1960–2015, First Edition.
Edited by Wolfgang Görtschacher and David Malcolm.
© 2021 John Wiley & Sons Ltd. Published 2021 by John Wiley & Sons Ltd.

degree of autonomy, but almost always as a secondary aspect assisting or supporting the semantics of the utterance. Both, the graphic shape of language and its sound may <u>mean</u>, but, to quote MacLeish again, before they <u>mean</u>, before they turn into signs, they <u>are</u>.

"There are now so many kinds of experimental poetry being labeled 'concrete' that it is difficult to say what the word means," writes Mary Solt (1970, 7) in the introduction to her anthology *Concrete Poetry: A World View* (1970). The term can be understood historically, in its narrow sense, as the name of the movement initiated in German-speaking countries in the 1950s by poets such as Eugen Gomringer and Ernst Jandl. But it also has a wider definition, as a term for a more general and universal tendency, which reaching its peak in the decades after World War II can nevertheless be traced back to antiquity. The definition adopted here is the latter. Concrete poetry is a poetry that foregrounds its materiality. Since language is material because of its sounds and letters, to what can be heard or seen, concrete poetry falls into two subcategories: phonic, or sound poetry, and visual poetry.

At the roots of concrete poetry there are at least two long-running ambitions. One is the attempt to overcome the semiotic aspect of language, to make words physical, opaque, and self-referential. Poets who share this ambition try to suppress the signifying element, so that the poem can be looked at or listened to, but not understood or interpreted (as if such a thing was possible). Visual poetry in this tradition approaches the condition of abstract painting. Poets may use individual letters or larger portions of texts as purely visual forms, creating abstract patterns—the smaller the linguistic unit, the easier it is to cleanse it of its meaning and make it abstract. Sometimes such poets imitate handwriting and the art of calligraphy, producing esthetically interesting compositions, which though consisting of letters have minimal lexical meaning—or none at all. Typewriters have often been used not to write, but to "draw," or "paint" with, utilizing the space of the page. Belgian poet and painter Christian Dotremont produced a series of *logogrammes*, which imitate handwriting, but do not lend themselves to reading (Dotremont 2004). The shapes vaguely remind us of characters, but it is impossible to read them. The title of Dotremont's artworks is significant: "I write in order to see." To see, not to read. Reading would involve interpretation and understanding, seeing is an end in itself, when it satisfies the eye. It is no surprise that many poets who worked in this tradition had been trained as painters.

The other ambition underlying the development of concrete poetry is not to eliminate the semantics, but to deprive linguistic signs of their arbitrariness. Arbitrariness of signs, their conventional character, has been treated as a burden of literature, especially when seen against the supposedly natural signs of painting. Painters of figurative art use signs which are closer to the things they denote—by virtue of their similarity to these things. Of course, painting also depends on convention and to believe that it communicates the same thing to viewers raised in different cultures and in different epochs would be a mistake. Yet the degree of arbitrariness is much lower. Many concrete poets try to follow figurative painters, using language in such a way as to make its form less arbitrary, to discover in its form (in its "being") its meaning. The word "more" printed several times, each time in a larger print, representing voices of excited children watching a show and shouting louder and louder, as in Roger McGough's "Pantomime Poem," may be an example of this kind of concreteness (*Penguin Modern Poets 10*, 1974, 63).

Concrete poetry in one form or another has existed since the beginnings of literature. In antiquity, poets used to write *carmina figurata*, poems the shape of which resembled the object referred to. This tradition to shape the poem according to its meaning was famously adopted by George Herbert in such poems as "The Altar" or "The Dove," written respectively in the shape of an altar and of a dove. In the twentieth century, Dylan Thomas, continuing some strains of the metaphysical tradition, imitated Herbert's *carmina figurata* in his "Vision and Prayer," the shapes of which resemble diamonds and wings (or hourglasses). Victorian literature can boast one of the most widely known figurative poems, "The Mouse's Tale," which Lewis Carroll introduced into his *Alice in Wonderland*. The most famous examples of the modernist period were *Calligrammes* by Guillaume Apollinaire, which assumed the shapes of the things they referred to: streams of rain, an umbrella, or a heart (cf. Bohn 1993, 46–68).

There are more complex examples of poets' use of visuality of language. Poets, who look up to painters, follow Lessing's idea of the visual arts as spatial (as opposed to the temporal art of language). Space becomes an important factor in many concrete poems. By departing from the standardized way of printing (or writing) poems, they draw attention to the graphic composition of their poems, as in Mallarmé's "*Un coup de dés jamais n'abolira le hasard*" (1994, 124–145).

Though, as argued in the earlier text, concreteness in literature has always occurred, concrete poetry reemerged most spectacularly in the 1950s and 1960s. The movement quickly became an international phenomenon, with its representatives working worldwide in diverse places such as Germany, Brazil, France, Czechoslovakia, Switzerland, or Sweden. Initially, the movement showed strong ties with the political left, its impulse coming from the realization of a crisis of language, which had so often been manipulated and abused by twentieth-century ideologies. Concrete poetry promised the kind of language which, foregrounding its own materiality, would be immune to such manipulations. It also promised to offer a language that would transcend borders and cultural differences; a kind of utopian Esperanto, it would communicate directly, by its visual or phonic forms, without requiring the knowledge of national languages.

Concrete poetry flourished most in Germany or France, but in Britain, as in other English-speaking countries, it has been a marginal affair. It found its most interesting practitioners primarily in Scotland (though there were also important authors working in England, such as Bob Cobbing and Dom Sylvester Houédard). Edwin Morgan and Ian Hamilton Finlay are the two leading Scottish poets of international reputation who have contributed significantly to the development of the genre. Morgan's most interesting concrete poems come, predictably, from the 1960s, some of them appeared originally in *Starryveldt*, a pamphlet published by the Eugen Gomringer Press (1965), testifying to the international links of concrete poets. Morgan shared the concretists' hopes "for the transcultural communicative possibilities of concrete writing, even to the extent of forming 'the nucleus of the future universal common language'" (Nicholson 2002, 92). In some of his concrete poems, Morgan joins the visual with the phonic, as for example in "Siesta of a Hungarian Snake" (1996, 174), which consists of one line with a sequence of two alternating consonants *s* and *z*, both in capital letters and in lowercase. The line with its slimness and length visually resembles the reptile, but apart from being looked at it can also be read aloud. The sibilants are onomatopoeic, reproducing the hissing sound of the reptile. This natural reference is, however, supplemented with a cultural allusion hinted at in the title: the consonants are not only imitative of a natural sound, but they also recall the Hungarian language, characterized by the high frequency of the *zs* and *sz* clusters. By contrast, Morgan's "The Loch Ness Monster's Song" (1996, 248) is an example of a phonic poem— an attempt to invent an abstract language, reminiscent of the Dadaists' practices in this field (Hugo Ball, Richard Huelsenbeck). Morgan however tries to anchor his poem in the audial world by making his invented language onomatopoeic, for example, when the monster goes under water: *blm plm, blm plm, blm plm, blp*.

Morgan's permutation poems are more interesting in their relationships with concrete poetry. "Opening the Cage" is a series of variations on John Cage's dictum: "I have nothing to say and I am saying it and that is poetry" from his 1949 *Lecture on Nothing* (1973, 109, 109–127). In the 14 lines of the poem, Morgan rearranges the 14 words, adding or deleting nothing, but in such a way that each variation constitutes a sentence, grammatically correct, though not always clear or logical. For example: "Saying poetry is nothing and to that I say I am and have it" (Morgan 1996, 178). There is humor here, since the poem with its 14 lines pretends to be a sonnet, one of the most traditional poetic genres. If this permutation poem can be seen as concrete, it is because Morgan uses words as changeable elements, and rather than being guided by any meaning to be expressed develops the poem purely formally, reshuffling the words. Though nowhere does Morgan violate English grammar, the words of his poem function as abstract objects. There is no meaning to be expressed, the poet "has nothing to say," and he says it and that is poetry. Morgan's "Opening the Cage" is a good example of the way in which concrete poetry of the 1960s comes close to another art movement of that decade: conceptualism.

In Ian Hamilton Finlay's "Acrobats" from 1964 (2012, 140), first an outdoor poem made on the wall of the poet's farmhouse, later a poem published in a book, the poet realizes one of the dreams of literature: to overcome the linearity of language. In concrete poetry, the reader looks at the poem as at a drawing and perceives it simultaneously, encompassing it in one act of nonlinear perception. Before we enter into words, we perceive the shape of the poem, its spatial arrangement on the page (or on the wall), which in a concrete poem is always meaningful. Though Herbert's "The Altar" or Apollinaire's *Calligrammes* can be quoted here as examples, Finlay's poem moves one step further.

What Finlay tries to do is to maintain reading as the primary type of contact with the poem and yet to change the way we read. The poem is composed of one word from its title, which is repeated several times, forming 15 regular lines within each of which there is only one identical letter repeated by turns five and four times. If we were to read the poem traditionally from left to right, line after line, we would meet only meaningless letters. The text however imposes on the readers a different way of reading: a diagonal one. It can be read in four ways: down from top left, down from top right, up from bottom left, and up from bottom right. This is still linear reading, but one that does not have any clear order; which of the diagonals should we start with remains a matter of our choice. It is also a reading which questions the traditional way words are printed. This supposed anarchy of typography is functional—the rearrangement of letters corresponds to the activity of the acrobats. Their work is mimetically reproduced as typographical rearrangements. More than this, the reader's eye is forced to do the same: it performs acrobatic movements while reading. Readers turn into acrobats, mimicking what they read about: the poem becomes a performative act.

Poets' dreams of creating poems which would be like things, that is, not linear, but spatial, not abstract, but material, resembling the things they refer to, made many concrete poems leave the book altogether. The poem does not have to be confined to a page. Its immediate context does not have to be constituted by other poems, other pages, or the book itself. Though Finlay, after an initial period of liaison with international authors of concrete poetry, dissociated himself from the movement, his work exemplifies a very consistent development toward the concretist ideal. His poems first depart from linearity and get free from the confines of syntax (such is the sense of his one-word poems). Then they leave the book and turn into three-dimensional artifacts. And finally they melt into the landscape, becoming almost indistinguishable from its natural elements. Among Finlay's works there is a poem "wave / rock" from 1968 (2012, 28) sandblasted on a glass plate. This poem-object consists of two words "wave" and "rock." The way they are written—the words "wave" moving toward the words "rock," some of them overwritten on them, cumulating on the right side of the poem—suggests the beating of sea waves against a rocky coast. As Finlay wrote in his letter to Emmett Williams, "The poem is 'about' 2 imposing forces, but being a poem presents them in equipoise, resolved" (Finlay 2012, 29). The visual side of the poem shows its meaning—the poem is to be seen, rather than read. In fact, one could deduce the poem's meaning from the very form of the poem, without knowing the two English words. But the poem's originality lies in its material substrate, which is a transparent glass pane rather than a page from a book. The transparency of the pane makes it possible for the poem to include within itself everything that is beyond it. The poem on the glass pane, taken out into natural scenery, melts into its surroundings, or absorbs them. What is natural becomes integrated with the cultural artifact.

But Finlay made one more—giant—step further along the concretist line: the poet created a park called Little Sparta, 50 miles from Edinburgh. The park, which includes forests, streams, ponds, meadows, etc., includes also the poet's works, mostly stones with inscriptions, sculptures, pillars, sundials. These objects are Finlay's poems, material texts which have left the book behind and function within the natural environment of the park. This observation can be reformulated: Finlay's park is a "natural" book which gathers poems and non-poems, words and objects. Little Sparta seems to be the ultimate in the tradition of concrete poetry: the difference between words and things has been successfully annulled.

On the bank of a pond there is a small wooden boat with two words painted on the bow: "Never Enough." To ask what makes this poem would be to miss the point of the work, because any answer would only limit the work. The words on the bow of the boat may be read in a variety of ways, but they also mean that the poem is never completed or closed. It absorbs further and further contexts. We can agree that the poem is just the boat on which the two words have been painted. But why not include in this poem also the pond and its bank, where the boat rests? Or even, what is beyond the pond: fields, the emerging hill at the horizon? With each new element absorbed by our "poem," the words "Never Enough" become concretized and gain meaning. Never enough of traveling, never enough of sailing, never enough of reading.

Finlay's fondness for the sea manifests itself in many other works, including a simple poem made of a series of stone slabs, each with a word meaning a different type of boat: brig, schooner, keel, corvette, boomie, cog, muletta, trimaran, caravel (Hunt 2008, 18). The slabs are half buried in the ground, as if they were gravestones in the park's green lawn. The names of the boats on the stones affect the environment in which they are exhibited, and which, of course, is not a book, but grass. The power of the words is such that the grass turns in this process of metonymic and symbolic transformation into the green sea. If the slabs are boats in an underwater cemetery, then the green grass must be the sea. The change of the grass into the sea is a metonymic change, because of the contiguity between them, but it is also metaphoric, since the transformation is based on similarity: what they share is greenness and expanse.

In a different part of Finlay's Little Sparta, we can find a different way of absorbing cultural artifacts into what is natural, making the distinction between the two problematic. On the branch of one of the trees the poet hangs a wooden plate with two letters: A and D (Sheeler 2003, 108). A is bigger and includes in its lower part the other letter: these initials are Albrecht Dürer's. By hanging a plate with the artist's signature, Finlay changes the "natural" visual context against which the plate is perceived into Dürer's work, or more generally, he changes nature into an artwork. Other trees, bushes, reeds, and grass, all become cultural artifacts to the extent that we can look for visual analogs in Dürer's art. In this simple work, Finlay's concrete poetry, by merging with natural objects, questions the seemingly obvious difference between word and thing, between meaning and being. Finlay's poems can not only be read and perceived, they can also be touched, smelled, and tasted, as Picasso's apple that he found in the young artist's studio.

Performance poetry, though appearing under different names, is arguably the oldest form of literature. It is the kind of poetry which is improvised or composed specifically to be performed before a live audience and in public spaces. In modern Britain, it came to prominence as "oral poetry," in the 1960s. In contrast to concrete poetry, performance poetry has rapidly developed since then, becoming one of the most popular forms of literature of today. More and more poets think of their poems as essentially designed for voice. Giving live performances, reciting, singing, acting, involving the audience—this is how the American Beatniks propagated their work. The City Lights black-and-white pocketbooks have become legendary, but more important to the spirit of their verse were public readings, including the most famous one, at the Six Gallery in October 1955, when Ginsberg recited *Howl*. A few years earlier Dylan Thomas toured America, giving poetic performances to mass audiences. The stress put on the poet's voice was only a starting point for the development which we now call performance poetry. Poets soon enriched their readings by multimedia activities, using all kinds of props and costumes, introducing quasi-theatrical acting, merging their poems with music. In many cases what was at stake was the personality of the poet—the ideal of impersonal poetry, identified (too hastily) with Eliot and propagated by New Criticism and the academy, was contradicted by the poet standing in front of the audience, adding to poetry his or her personal traits: his emotions and temperament, his energy, wit, and charm.

Among the pioneers who propagated performance poetry in Britain was Michael Horovitz, the leading figure of the Underground, poet and editor of two anthologies, *Children of Albion* (1969) and *Grandchildren of Albion* (1992). He was one of the main organizers of the famous poetry reading in the Royal Albert Hall in 1965, which, with an audience of 7000 people and international poets such as Adrian Mitchell, Allen Ginsberg, Gregory Corso, and Lawrence Ferlinghetti, is considered to be the groundbreaking moment in the development of the movement. Since the mid-1960s, poetry readings have been organized almost everywhere. To quote Mitchell, they have been held "in studios, cellars, town halls, pubs, folk clubs, pop and jazz clubs, street corners, parks, Trafalgar Square, private houses, bookshops, churches" (Mitchell 1970).

Performance poetry emerged as an attempt to escape from the limitations of the linearity of language, expanding the concept of the poem so as to include random and unpredictable factors. During an act of performance, communication occurs through different sensory channels simultaneously. Marshall McLuhan (1967), who had launched a critique of print, opposed it to living speech, which involves auditory, visual, tactile, and olfactory sensations. In a development that shows an analogy with concrete poetry, performance poetry exhibited a deep distrust of the book, seeing it as a strongly commercialized medium of communication in the hands of profit-oriented publishing companies, a medium which fostered cultural alienation, separated writers from their audiences, confined literature to a sanctuary, and detached it from everyday life. Horovitz postulated that poetry should "jump the book," because "books—however beautiful—are more and more distant branches, and not the roots of culture communication" (Horovitz 1969, 323).

One can see performance poetry in the wider context of the developments in contemporary arts, especially that of an important shift from the artifact to creative activity, from work to process, which Lucy Lippard called the "dematerialization of art" (1997). Happenings (and poetic performances often turned into happenings) are just one example of this shift. In happenings, the actual shape of the event cannot be predicted, as there are many variables which contribute to the final effect. The tendency to see art as a process, not as an artifact, appears also in music. Jazz is a good example of art in which performance gains greater importance than composition. Jazz, because of the role of improvisation, is a collective, spontaneous, and largely unpredictable activity. The same can be said of other forms of music. It is not by chance that performance poetry has often appeared in alliance with jazz, but also with rock, punk, and rap. It adapted many ideas which had been fostered by the avant-garde, taking over, for example, the concept of Total Art, the *Gesamtkunstwerk*, which questions the separation of different arts. As one poet recalled, poetic events "involved spoken poetry with jazz, plays, mime, new music, electronics, speeches, film, light–sound projections, sculpture, dance," constructing "a *Gesamtweltbild* for all art media to inhabit" (Horovitz 1969, 322).

All kinds of poetry may be performed. But poetry which is composed with the intention of being performed exhibits characteristic formal features. During a performance, the poet has to interact with the audience, who may want the poet to stop delivering a particular poem or, on the contrary, to continue it. The form that lends itself best to such circumstances is a catalog. Based on enumeration, it can be extended at will by improvisation, or finished at any point. The effect has to be instantaneous; what matters is the audience's immediate reaction. Hence, it is almost a rule that performance poetry, often highly improvisational, makes generous use of humor and colloquial diction, depends much on the song-like qualities of poetry (repetitions, refrains, call-and-response), and, by inviting the audience to participate, creates a sense of community. Poetry has become an event, which, as Jonathan Raban remarks, "implicates all its participants, one cannot separate out the work itself from either the author who performs it or from the audience whose participatory response has become an essential ingredient of the total experience" (Raban 1971, 86).

Performance poetry, the rise of which coincided in Britain with the processes of devolution and the emergence of multicultural society, made extensive use of regional dialects, slang, and other "substandard" varieties of English, the characteristic features of which it would be impossible to record in writing. Among the various movements within performance poetry in the United Kingdom one can mention the Liverpool Poets (Adrian Henri, Roger McGough, and Brian Patten), the Ranters associated with the punk explosion of the mid-1970s (John Cooper Clarke, Joolz, Attila the Stockbroker), the new cabaret and music hall scene, with one of its centers in the Apples and Snakes venue in London (John Hegley, Liz Lochhead), or black rappers, such as Benjamin Zephaniah and Linton Kwesi Johnson (see: Hamilton 1994, 414). More recent poets include Patience Agbabi, who has produced a rap version of *The Canterbury Tales* (Agbabi 2015).

One of the movements that emerged from performance poetry was slam. Marc Smith, who organized the first slam event in Chicago in 1984, is considered to be the originator of the movement. Slam is more an entertainment, as performers are engaged in a competition, struggling to get the highest score from the audience or the judges. As in all contests, poets taking part in slam have to stick to rules, keeping within a strict time limit of 3 minutes. In effect, slam offers a homogenized variety of poetry that should have immediate appeal, being a product of an age of instant gratification. It offers no opportunity to re-experience the poem, relate its parts to the whole, go back to previous parts, or make it reverberate with other texts. The competitive side of slam locates it closer to a boxing match, where the other poet is not a partner in a dialogue, but an opponent to be eliminated in the nearest round. Nevertheless, slam has developed dynamically, gaining huge popularity worldwide, creating its stars and its audiences (cf. Woods 2008).

References

Agbabi, Patience (2015). *Telling Tales*. London: Canongate.

Bohn, Willard (1993). *The Aesthetics of Visual Poetry*. Chicago: The University of Chicago Press.

Cage, John (1973). *Silence. Lectures and Writings*. Hanover: Wesleyan University Press.

Dotremont, Christian (2004). *J'ecris pour voir*. Paris: Buches-Chastel.

Finlay, Ian Hamilton (2012). *Selections*. Berkeley: University of California Press.

Hamilton, Ian (ed.) (1994). *The Oxford Companion to Twentieth-Century Poetry*. Oxford: Oxford University Press.

Horovitz, Michael (ed.) (1969). "Afterword." In: *Children of Albion: Poetry of the 'Underground' in Britain*, 316–377. Harmondsworth: Penguin Books.

Hunt, John Dixon (2008). *Nature Over Again: The Garden Art of Ian Hamilton Finlay*. London: Reaktion Books.

Lippard, Lucy (1997). *Six Years: The Dematerialization of the Art Object from 1966 to 1972*. Berkeley: University of California Press.

MacLeish, Archibald (2000). "Ars Poetica." In: *Anthology of Modern American Poetry* (ed. Cary Nelson), 331. Oxford: Oxford University Press.

Mallarmé, Stéphane (1994). *Collected Poems*. Translated and with a Commentary by H. Weinfield. Berkeley: University of California Press.

McLuhan, Marshall (1967). *Understanding Media. The Extensions of Man*. London: Sphere Books.

Mitchell, Adrian (1970). "Poetry Explodes." *The Listener* (14 May).

Morgan, Edwin (1965). *Starryveldt*. Frauenfeld: Eugen Gomringer Press.

Morgan, Edwin (1996). *Collected Poems 1949–1987*. Manchester: Carcanet.

Nicholson, Colin (2002). *Edwin Morgan: Inventions of Modernity*. Manchester: Manchester University Press.

Penguin Modern Poets 10: Adrian Henri, Roger McGough, Brian Patten. rev. and enl. ed. 1974. Harmondsworth: Penguin Books.

Prévert, Jacques (1970). *Selections from 'Paroles'*. Translated and Introduced by Lawrence Ferlinghetti. Harmondsworth: Penguin Books.

Raban, Jonathan (1971). *The Society of the Poem*. London: Harrap.

Sheeler, Jessie (2003). *Little Sparta: The Garden of Ian Hamilton Finlay*. London: Frances Lincoln.

Solt, Mary Ellen (ed.) (1970). "A World Look at Concrete Poetry." In: *Concrete Poetry: A World View*, 7–66. Bloomington, London: Indiana University Press.

Woods, Scott (2008). "Poetry slams: the ultimate democracy in art." *World Literature Today* 82 (1): 16–19.

2c.9
Performances of Technology as Compositional Practice in British and Irish Contemporary Poetry

John Sparrow

Introduction

In this essay, I will introduce work by a selection of British poets whose practices engage with material processes as an integral part of their work. For these poets, there are multiple distinct performance approaches to the methodologies of composition they employ—methods tied to the interrogation of systems of language and the cultural systems these linguistic economies articulate and perpetuate.

I approach these poets and their works against a background of experimental writing that foregrounds the materiality of both word and medium, where poets utilize their writing machines and procedures as constitutive agents of meaning rather than as incidental elements. The poets I address here *perform* compositional acts, procedural and critical methods as rhetorical tools. By applying procedure as a compositional strategy, new perspectives on language and meaning can take place. As Jena Osman states:

> Procedure poems allow for that "multiple" functioning of language that is so often controlled and hidden away by its daily functioning[, the] smooth communication that relies on controlled semantic limits—is constantly threatened by language's expansive capabilities.
> (Osman 2002, 261)

The procedural poet engages with the complex multiplicities of physical and abstract systems of the environment, and uses these systems in alternative ways that produce a reframing of expressive agency.

The poets I discuss in the following text subject their works to external influence, to the chance elements of working with modular source contexts and processes. Their works, to varying degrees, incorporate multiple revision processes by placing both the writer and reader as performance participants. In doing so, each participant is placed into feedback loops with the medium or media being used, and the poets place themselves into a dialectical relationship with their own compositional processes. Under such conditions, authorial intention becomes deliberately and pointedly shifted from a sense of closed outcome to one of investigative process, the execution of a procedure, a score, or an algorithm; a responsive and reflexive poetic praxis.

These works cannot be distilled or abstracted into constrained genre terms that conform to established canons, and they convey an understanding of how language's "expansive capabilities" (see Osman's comment quoted in the earlier text) are released not only through a movement away from traditionally restrictive semiotic systems but also through the utilization of materials and influences usually considered extraneous to meaning. They create tensions with expressive protocols (a term I will briefly expand upon later), be they the mechanical protocols of printing presses, the protocols of the city and its myriad cultural processes and geographical evolutions, or the protocols of semiotics and syntax. They generate frictions between the internal and the external, the personal and the arbitrary, to construct new reading, performance, and meaning-making strategies.

Janet Cardiff

I will begin by looking at the "Walks" series, by performance artist and poet Janet Cardiff, which are part score, part recorded poem, part immersive performance. Cardiff's walks involve a participant immersing herself in immersive audio via a portable playback device and headphones. The audio is multiple in nature: part instructional guide, part poet, part story-teller, and part reactive voice, a shadow of a previous participant, and as texts, Cardiff's walks replace the reader with a participant, for whom the boundaries of instruction, poem, fiction, noise, and information become obfuscated. Discussing *The Missing Voice*, a London walk, Carolyn Christov-Bakargiev explains this complex layering of voices in the playback.

> There are two "Janets" in this walk: one "Janet" walks through the streets holding a recorder (just as you do, as walker/listener), while the other 'Janet'[sic] is a played-back recorded voice to which the first "Janet" is listening. You flip back and forth between two different periods in time. [...] Personal, scary memories of childhood blend with descriptions and narrative fragments.
>
> (Christov-Bakargiev 2003, 21)

The live and the recorded become complicated in this layered sensory approach. The recordings alone make unclear the certainty of what is live and what is not, when immersed in the city. The walks thus enact a seemingly paradoxical relationship between adaptation/ improvisation and rigidity of external processes.

> You slip in and out of "being her" as the sounds swirl around you [...]—so that the artificial environment [...] blends with the real environment [...T]he sounds seem to come from the actual surrounding [sic!]. Subconsciously, participants begin to breathe and walk in synch with the virtual body on the tape or CD, blurring the distinction between self and other.
> (Christov-Bakargiev 2003, 22)

In both her compositional approach and in the performance of her work, improvisation is crafted into a partnership with the constraints of the city's protocols. As Christov-Bakargiev discusses:

> Improvisation is an important part of Cardiff's process. She writes minimal scripts [...], records, and begins editing. Here, things change and shift, and she will often rewrite her script and record more. [...] Yet, for all the openness and improvisation that the Walks may go through, it is only due to very precise editing that this art can "work," since participants must be able to walk in comfortable synch with the [...] tour.
> (Christov-Bakargiev 2003, 23)

Cardiff's process of composition demonstrates how improvisation can be used in an editorial role, but also that the act of composition can *itself* be reflexive, shifting the author between active and passive roles; a process outside of traditional authorial control.

The "Walks" respond and prompt user reactions to the sites of her work, as her recordings "[shape] space acoustically [...] much as a sound technician would for a movie" (Christov-Bakargiev 2003, 21). But these works also produce an artifice of response *to* their surroundings, placing the user within a set sequence that synchronizes with the outside world, following the process of a conventional format while at the same time subverting the conventions of that format through vocal digressions, multiple recorded sound layers, and instructive comments that vary between directional and contextually responsive. For example, when Cardiff suddenly asks "did you hear that shot," the listener is forced into a sonic space that immediately creates tensions between the live environment and the recorded audio, as well as between what is real and factual, and what might be hyperbolic or deceptive.

The "Walks" create tensions between internal and external, and the combinatory sensory inputs fuse together the emotions, memories (first- and second-hand), and meanings to form an alternative context for personalizing the city space, and for the experience of navigating that space. Indeed, perceptions of personal/inside and other/outside are complicated through this process. The listener's internal voice is simultaneously complementary to and destabilized by Cardiff's recorded voice as well as the binaural enveloping sounds of a city recorded at a previous point in time. External sources are also internalized physically through the headphones, setting up a recombinant poetic situation that in turn interacts with the external stimuli of the live, present city. Unachievable inside the restrictive confines of the gallery space, these palimpsest sound texts form a praxis in, of, and in spite of the world.

In *Protocol: How Control Exists After Decentralization*, Alexander Galloway extends the common definition of protocol to specify its implications in computer-networked and networked-culture contexts. He explains how protocol facilitates the functioning of a distributed network, described as "[part of] a movement away from central bureaucracies and vertical hierarchies toward a broad network of autonomous social actors" (Galloway 2004, 32–33). This definition represents a way of thinking about modular structures in general, and is especially applicable to modular systems with their own rules. For these systems, protocol allows for mutual exchange between heterogeneous agents. Cardiff's "Walks" can be usefully framed within these modular qualities, in that discrete microprocesses work together to form cohesive wholes. Although these local systems in the surrounding city may themselves adhere to hierarchical structures, they are reframed against her recordings as variable agents in one cohesive, distributed performance that renders all modular parts either irreducibly constitutive to the experience or else lost in the excess of stimuli. The otherwise incidental aspects of the city thus become always-in-process catalysts to meaning within complex structures of interweaving live processes and histories.

The "Walks" take advantage of environmental cultural protocol through their immersion in the interrelated geographies, physicalities, dialects, histories, and live situations in and of the city. The strict *process* of recorded playback is itself a protocol, removed from subjective application, subject to the indeterminacies generated by the listener and her unique walking performance. The indifference of the recorded voice to these surrounding indeterminacies is what enables the complex mesh of influences that create assemblages of meaning. The reader, in contrast to the blind execution of playback, *is* encouraged subjectively to process the immersive whole as a live combinatory poetics.

Galloway notes how protocol

> *is a language that regulates flow, directs netspace, codes relationships, and connects life forms.* Protocol does not produce or causally effect objects, but rather is a structuring agent that appears as the result of a set of object dispositions. [...] It is etiquette for autonomous agents.
>
> (Galloway 2004, 74–75)

The environment of the city can be seen as an interaction of "autonomous agents" whose architecture is facilitated by protocols, and Cardiff's work forms an ongoing investigation of composite signification through overlapping memory and traces of experiences alongside immediate, first-hand experience. Her walks exploit both the transparency of protocol (a walk's ability to achieve a state of absorption in the work and the combinatory sensory inputs, for example) and the opposite—the jarring effect of the indifference of protocol to meaning, manifested in disconnections, shifting voices, inconsistencies between the documented and the live. Thus, the walker-listener is drawn in and out of absorptive states, encouraging fluctuating levels of reflexive attention to language, cultural protocol, and the relationship between the two. The fixed recordings of the digital recording, simultaneously in sync yet in contrast to the fluid actions and evolutions of the city, set in motion the cross-pollination of influences and *rendezvous* as creative catalysts, open to chance.

In *Mythologies*, Roland Barthes explains that a guidebook (in his case the *Blue Guide*) summarizes locations by common attributes such as monuments and restaurants, and thus reduces the potentials for experiencing those locations to those modes only. Barthes notes that:

[The] *Blue Guide* testifies to the futility of all analytical descriptions, those which reject both explanations and phenomenology: it answers in fact none of the questions which a modern traveller can ask himself while crossing a countryside which is real *and which exists in time*. To select only monuments suppresses at one stroke the reality of the land and that of its people, it accounts for nothing of the present, that is, nothing historical[.]

(Barthes 1972, 75–76)

By intersecting multiple source contexts in a carefully crafted fashion, the Walks not only allow for the moments of absorption described earlier, but also for potential moments of heightened awareness of place and cultural protocol that would otherwise go unnoticed. As Craig Saper notes in *Artificial Mythologies*:

What is traveling? Intersections. The rendezvous becomes that momentary intense intersection, like a train station, an empty value, which sets in motion a perpetual combination of lines.

(Saper 1997, 16)

What is increasingly interesting is how the "Walks" recordings—now over a decade old—risk an increasing departure from the historical context in which they were recorded. As the city transforms, it is likely that the recording, in its timelessness, would become more detached from the city in which the Walk would take place. I do not consider such a possibility a failure of the work, but on the contrary, a typification of the fragility of composite sources and media as contributing toward a stable narrative that this piece highlights. Furthermore, as the discrepancies through transformations increasingly separate the recording from the live, the potential for consistent, repeated intersections becomes rarer. However, one might consider how the subsequent increase in potential unintended, new interactions between the recordings and the live walking might yield even more expressive "intense intersections."

cris cheek

The work of cris cheek, though in many ways different to that of Cardiff, continues in investigating this sense of play with control and with the moment and moments of performance in live versus recorded settings.

In *The Church, The School, The Beer*, cheek's book comprises texts made up of numerous revision processes and overlapping materials. Colloquial speech, caught conversation snippets, commands, inner thoughts, and responses, all combine in the text to build a sense of an implied yet never actualized stable narrative. Like Cardiff, these texts seem always to be in the middle, always in process between productive and produced states, but unlike Cardiff's texts, it is the author himself who becomes the active-passive walker-as-responsive-agent in the compositional process.

The Church, The School, The Beer is an assemblage of cheek's processes of composition, which are themselves acts of performance. He imposes physical and geographical limits on his delineated environment as chosen from thematic context, within which he immerses himself and allows for the external to interact with his actions.

cheek's work presents a complex interplay of media processes and location, and the relationships between cognitive dissonance, transparency, and intermedial embodiment. The book is comprised of a series of edited transcriptions from recordings, presented as largely uniform blocks of fully justified text. These are interspersed with photography of cheek conducting the walks, and hand-written texts drawn out in the shape of maps, composed during walks during the research phase of the project. During the recording, there was a setup in an overlooking room that both received and recorded cheek's input.

> The writing made use of Citizens Band technology, CB radiocast live to a second floor gallery window of Cavendish House, at Norwich School of Art and Design. An extension speaker placed on the sill of the window with the most direct view onto this street intersection provided a listening post from which the writer could be viewed and the writing witnessed at a distance of approximately fifty meters.
>
> (cheek 2007, 188)

The resulting transcriptions are collected as a book that, as a bound physical object, represents a final version of a text (problematized by cheek's processes, as I discuss in the following text) that pays similar minute attention to details of space and visual layout, margins and interjection as does the compositional practice that forms them. The mix of media elements in the book itself (text, maps, on-location photography) foregrounds the live nature of each walk while collapsing time differentials via the textual space. The source materials of the poems are *specific events taking place in time*, and draw attention to the extensive use of mixed media cheek employs during each iterative act of composition.

During transcription, the texts are not edited to mask their liveness, and the sense that these are compositions performed at very specific moments and locations is reaffirmed by each walk's timestamped title. Indeed, the interruptions, shifts in vocal sources and dialects, and the transcription of breaks in transmissions all add to the sense that this is a composite text, a heterogeneity in which transcribing and editing are a "politics of inclusion" and "a politics of representation beyond simply the choices that an author can often make to take away the clouds and leave the headiness of a carefully framed blue sky" (cheek 2007, 193).

The Church, The School, The Beer foregrounds itself as a series of rhetorical detours intentional in process, but in which those applied processes are comprised of chance interventions, interruptions, and responses, all of which are incorporated into the text as equally valid expressional elements. These elements are refit into a new set of self-established presentational protocols on the page, and this allows the disparate sources to coexist outside of their conventional modes of reception, hence cheek's decision to omit quote marks "to create mere interplay between what might and what might not constitute such material" (cheek 2007, 193). As Allen Fisher observes about cheek's work:

> Predictability is thankfully lost at the thresholds between what is conserved and invented; stable and unstable; just as their aesthetic functions become elaborated by the social and marketing functions their book presentations interact with as part of production.
>
> (Fisher 2016, 41)

Thus, although *The Church, The School, The Beer* shifts between prolonged passages of syntactic flow and moments of disjunction, the consistent form and visual structure imply and facilitate a compatibility between fragments. The "conserved" and the "invented" have equal esthetic representation; a quality that similarly allows even breaks in transmission to become viable informational elements in the text. This is reinforced by paragraph breaks often occurring mid-sentence, reversing the intraparagraph shifts of voice and syntax so that interruptions happen within supposed stable spaces, whereas blocks and physical breaks split apart otherwise syntactic continuity. This blurs the lines between what constitutes information and what constitutes noise, and by extension questions established systems of communication and the use values conventionally tied to those systems.

Interference is used as a legitimate contribution to compositional strategy, integral as a material and experiential factor of communication. Self-descriptive performance notes—an oral equivalent of marginalia—are given equal status as the rest of the transcribed text. So too are breaks in transmission causing disruptions to apparent syntactic/semantic flow but nonetheless included in the texts.

An example of these kinds of inclusive transcriptions can be found in "Apprehension":

> ...I was going to come in to say that. Fast eggs, break in transmission and. Yes it was I know, did you see her catalogue? The hope is that I can encourage interference from the open channels that are also listening to this recording.
>
> (cheek 2007, 58)

Later, in "Push Bar," the flow of monological dictation is interrupted by direct address and a sudden jolt into the technological and geographical setup of the live process, always at risk of error:

> buggy, a strip with four stripes. If anybody is upstairs in the window, could they possibly press Play on the video recorder, behind the TV monitor?
>
> (cheek 2007, 65)

Again, the discrete, visually uniform rectangles of text imply points at which continuations and breaks *ought* to occur syntactically and semantically—points that the text itself subverts by often continuing seamlessly across paragraph blocks, and often shifting voice mid-paragraph.

Cheek, in placing himself physically in location and subjecting himself to the dictates of the surroundings, enacts what might be considered a variation of the Situationist *dérive*, a tactic that subverts the standardized navigation of the city. In a *dérive*, the wanderer can experience hitherto untapped creative potential by applying new navigational methodologies in lieu of conventional modes. In doing so, new creative potentials and observations might occur. *The Church, The School, The Beer*, though restricted to specific locales, is an experiment in creatively generative potential in walking, seeing, and listening to the city, as "texts driven by engagement and reflection on engagement with location" (cheek 2007, 188). In location, cheek applies a series of creative constraints: "ideas of: scale, perspective, contradiction, deliberate misunderstanding, anecdote, vernacular obsession, fictive quoting, imposed character, cartoon depiction, carnivalesque interpretation, […] and so on were mobilised" (cheek 2007, 190–191). Using any number of these constraints, cheek informs his dictations by stimulating new interactions and reconfigured observations with his surroundings. cheek then compounds this process by pushing it into a feedback loop, turning his own productions into new modular units that are repurposed to serve as source materials, as input used in subsequent walks. Mirroring the sense of enforced uniformity presented through the textual blocks, cheek's compositional processes also bring these internal and external, live and recorded materials into the composition process by treating them as expressively equal modular units. Anthony Curtis Adler, in talking about the performance of an analog medium during the reproduction of a work of art, notes:

> Each instance of reproduction is a handing down, not of work itself in its singularity, but of the aura as recorded trace of the singularity of the event. The aura is handed down only by being submitted to further distortion, which, however, again inscribes the moment of handing down as a singular event.
>
> (Adler 2012, 55)

cheek's recycling of his own material in iterations sets composition up as new cultural output, as processes of distortion that become new mediated starting points for further production, and in turn, further distortion through inscription.

These incorporations produce archeological layers of textual material in the work, complicating the sense of "live" and "history," as well as "internal" and "external," by switching them around. His previous recordings become new source materials, but, through that process, they also act as creative *interruptions* to cheek's dictation, further complicating the already-disrupted sense of product, information, and noise in the work. His performances become externalized starting points, outside voices interjecting into the current performance, the past interjecting into the present.

Bob Cobbing

Bob Cobbing was a highly influential figure in several schools of experimental writing, including British concrete poetry, and one of the major proponents for experimental performance, visual and sound poetry, and Writers Forum. As versatile as he was prolific, his influential reach was extensive, playing no small part in informing the theoretical and practical approaches of several poets mentioned in this essay, and well beyond. His style of work was as diverse as his influence, as he considered any text he produced, no matter how abstract, as a potential score that could be performed.

It would not be beneficial to attempt to limit Cobbing's works to one genre, such is the breadth of its scope. However, much of Cobbing's compositions can be framed within the classification of concrete poetry, itself a broad-ranging category. For the purposes of this essay, I will consider a selection of Cobbing's works within the general classes of "clean" and "dirty" concrete works. Cobbing's work occupies both of these areas, as well as exploratory spaces between the two.

The terms "clean" and "dirty" concrete have come to describe two discrete approaches to composition in concrete poetry over its decades of evolution, and Lori Emerson offers a useful summary of the distinction between the two terms. She explains the term *dirty concrete* as:

> a messy, typed-over aesthetic of concrete poems [... and] a deliberate attempt to move away from the clean lines and graphically neutral appearance of the concrete poetry from the 1950s and 60s [...].
>
> (Emerson 2011)

Emerson continues that the dirty concrete techniques

> draw attention to the literary artifact as both a created and mediated object – techniques which essentially turn the artifact inside-out. It is a philosophy of making [...], that erodes the division between surface and depth, inside and outside.
>
> (Emerson 2011)

Cobbing's works arguably touch on both sides of this concrete distinction, but within each form performance plays a pivotal role in the construction of expression, perhaps uniquely contextualized by his consideration of his texts, no matter how apparently abstract, as potential scores for performing verbally/sonically.

In what could be termed *clean* concrete works, Cobbing's words play games with semiotic arbitrariness and the processes of language. The materials here are the words themselves, the units of language, signifiers functioning as signs formulated by rules of use and, in turn, use *value*. *A B C / Wan Do Tree* (1978a), a collection of Cobbing's poems, comprises a vast range of formal approaches, including radical engagement with linguistic systems and their rules through wordplay, the treatment of words and letters as physical and visual materials, and the use of mechanical procedures in composition.

In *Sound Poems* (including *ABC in Sound* for the first time, 1965), for example, Cobbing uses a variety of language games suggestive of Oulipo techniques, treating linguistic rules as fundamental constraints for writing. The results are poems that visually foreground process, enacting and visualizing the systemic nature of language construction, and making opaque conventionally transparent meaning-making practices and literary techniques. A section of *ABC in Sound* (shown in the following text) uses alliterative palindromes to disrupt conventions of straightforward semantic closure, instead making use of constraints to form texts that function as visually representative of linguistic process. These appear as if the output of a compositional logic problem, and, as Robert Sheppard notes of *ABC in Sound*, "its use of puns, foreign languages, palindromes and technical jargon suggests elaborate craftsmanship" (Sheppard 2002).

At their more materially experimental level, Cobbing's poems challenge the transparency of semiotic systems by treating text literally as physical material, or as cris cheek notes: "Letters among letters threaten to form intra-words" (cheek 1999). Poems such as "Worm" (Cobbing 1978a) and "Whisper Piece" (Cobbing 2014, 33) use innovative spatial arrangement on the page, accompanied by methods of duplication and superimposition. Both convey effects of kinesis, introducing additional conceptual and interpretative potentials through formal methods that transcend traditional limitations.

```
wordrow    worn row
wombat tab mow
womb mow    wort row
weser re-sew
wolf flow
wolf-dog god flow
won't now
wonder red now
wordrow

drown word    drawn ward
ward draw    prawn warp
beware era web
ebor draw wardrobe
yawn way    yaws sway
yawl way    trawl wart
west india aid nit sew
wollaston not sallow
drownword

wordrow    wad daw
walhalla allah law
waler re law    waster fret saw
war raw    warsaw was raw
wayward draw yaw    warder red raw
wordrow

drownword    wordrow
wasp saw    way yaw
walnut tun law    walton not law
west sew    wend new    wed dew
weft few    won now    wen new
wordrow    drownword
```

In "Worm," this effect produces semi-solidity in the collected letters, chaining them together vertically down the page, visually representing "worms" as implied in the title. Clearly, there are full words in use here, but their slightly displaced duplicated overlapping renders them difficult, if not impossible to decipher. Language becomes visually expressive, implicitly significant but un-decodable, all the while remaining clearly linguistic material.

"Whisper Piece" takes this approach further, breaking language into letters that are then similarly duplicated and repositioned. At the top of the page, a broken-apart word, "movies," is easily readable in several parts of the page where left-to-right superimposed text does not turn the original text practically into blocks of text. At this upper portion of the page, there is almost a sense of overexpression, an abundance of material that renders conventional reading practices futile. Moving down the page, the words become increasingly pulled apart, breaking letters out into areas of larger white space, but now their resistance to regular interpretation is obscured by their sparsity and, again, their proximal duplication. Viewing the work as a whole from a distance shows how this transformation down the page enacts a visual kinetic metaphor, appearing as if some agent (wind?) is physically unsettling the material on the page and foregrounding the material process as an important expressive facet of composition.

In these examples, Cobbing presents texts as physical objects in space, always *in process*, both in terms of their reception and interpretation by a reader but also in terms of their folding outward materially, their overtly manifest material and mechanical manipulation suggesting an implicit openness to further manipulation.

In this regard, Cobbing's works can be retroactively contextualized by glitch concepts and practices. In glitch work, artists critique strict processes of software systems, either by documenting errors in systems (crashes, errors) or by manufacturing error through misusing the software or forcing unintended processes to interact with each other. These practices, though widely varying, nonetheless aim to critique cultural systems as extensions of the signification process enacted during the execution of code to produce artifacts whose expressive purpose necessitates transparency of the medium, format, and codec. This is an association aided by Lori Emerson's discussion of ubiquitous restrictive media. Emerson notes:

> [The] shift to the ideology of the user-friendly via the GUI is expressed in contemporary multitouch, gestural, and ubiquitous computing devices, […] whose interfaces are touted as utterly invisible and whose inner workings are therefore de facto inaccessible.
>
> (Emerson 2014, 49)

She then continues:

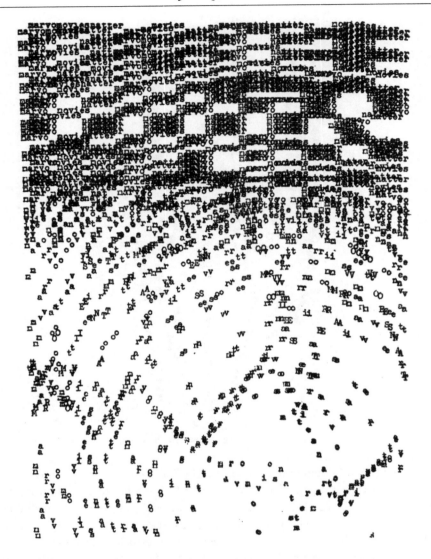

Arguably, one reason for the heightened engagement in hacking type(writing) in the mid-1960s to the mid-1970s was that the typewriter had become so ubiquitous in homes and offices that it had also become invisible to its users. The point at which a technology saturates a culture is the point at which writers and artists, whose craft is utterly informed by a sensitivity to their tools, begin to break apart that same technology to once again draw attention to the way in which it offers certain limits and possibilities to thought and expression.

(Emerson 2014, 50)

Emerson makes the association between restrictive material processes and how these shape and limit the expressive potentials of what these material constraints are able to produce. In both his texts-as-material and the actual performing of text compositions through the alternative use of its production media, Cobbing's works use both mechanical and semiotic systems against themselves, opening up their expressive capabilities while at the same time foregrounding their inner, concealed workings through their destabilization.

Cobbing's use of a technology, whether sonic or visual, cannot be extracted from its content, nor abstracted from its physical moment of use (a level of abstraction that *would* be arguable with certain digital processes, for example). His uses of writing machines extend standard modes of expression and the physical limits of the human body, but they also reinforce the sense that expression through the body is always contextualized by media *as extensions of* the body, and as active and validated agents in the process of expression. The limits of the medium are reversed, no longer failing to achieve the most efficient reproduction possible, but instead furthering the imperfections and decaying processes of machinery as constitutive to meaning.

In engaging with typewriters and copiers in an experimental way, Cobbing exploits technological protocol and hardware limitations as creative constraints in his work. The arbitrariness of the medium's process—its inability to recognize a phenomenological context for its actions—is used by Cobbing to execute processes that place semiotics into the same critical state, and suggest an analogous arbitrary system in a semiotic context. Likewise, in performance, no reading is technically incorrect, and aspects of the physicality of performance hitherto considered extraneous at best, but more likely antithetical to "clean" performance, become valid, and indeed preferred as unconstrained, expressive agents.

Cobbing notes of sound poetry:

> PARTLY [sound poetry] is a recapturing of a more primitive form of language, before communication by expressive sounds became stereotyped into words, when the voice was richer in vibrations, more mightily physical. The tape-recorder, by its ability to amplify and superimpose, and to slow down the vibrations, has enabled us to rediscover the possibilities of the human voice, until it becomes again something we can almost see and touch.
>
> (Cobbing 1978b, 39)

Cobbing's statement demonstrates an insight into how technology can be an expressive tool, an instrument performed reflexively by, with, and back onto the body. This is a praxis that seeks expression beyond the capabilities of standardized articulative modes, and which, as Cobbing intimates, moves away from restricted linguistic economy and recognizes the complex interdependency of language and medium. Adler notes when talking about the relationship of speech to writing in the context of technological reproduction:

> The "analog" moment, as it were, involves neither the preservation of sound, in its transience, through writing, nor the institution of a "perfect" writing, capable of representing the natural language of speech, but instead the replication and rewriting of a sonic event which is always already writing, but a writing which is inherently and irreducibly materially embodied.

It is fitting, then, that Cobbing nonetheless regards such texts as primarily performable, preferring instead that the visual and the sonic have no hierarchical privilege over each other.

In the notes at the end of *A B C / Wan Do Tree*, Cobbing states that the poems "are sound poems so much of the creative work must be done by the reader. The rhythms and patterns of sound may be discovered from the poems themselves but a few indications may help" (Cobbing 1978a). That these performances are only directed by the poet in the form of suggestions compounds this openness and newly facilitated interrelation of sensuous modes. In short, readers are encouraged to engage with these texts as they see fit, the instability of the implicit signs in these works functioning as a positive, even empowering status, rather than an insurmountable confrontation, and the separation of the visual and the sonic overridden. By transcending the restrictive patterns of conventional writing practices, these works do not become inexpressible. Instead, associated conventional patterns of speech are rendered no longer necessary, and indeed become inadequate in performance. Furthermore, they function visually as fluidly relatable to sonic representation, open to varied performance interpretations.

As Katalin Sándor notes regarding visual poetry:

> [V]isual print poetry rhetorically works through configurative writing functions and through a nonlinear or multilinear textual body that has no predefined pattern for readability and sequence, and is also open to remaking and reconfiguration.
>
> (Sándor 2012, 145–146)

Cobbing's processes often incorporated revisionary processes—a propensity that bled over to his collaborations, and it is worth briefly considering a collaborative work with Lawrence Upton, *Domestic Ambient Noise/Moise*. In these collaborations, compositional acts would form the basis for the materials of subsequent compositional acts, with each poet executing further compositional processes onto their counterpart's works. The process is described by Alaric Sumner as follows:

> This project consists of one poet presenting the other with a theme from which the second makes six variations. This is published as a booklet. The first poet will then choose a theme from this booklet from which to make another six variations – a second booklet – and so on. The project will be completed in 2000 with the 300th booklet – a total of more than 1800 pages of visual (visually emphatic) poetry.
>
> (Sumner, quoted in cheek 1999)

The result is a congruity in what might be considered a theme, but in which what cheek describes as a "consensual 'slippage'" (cheek 1999) creates ongoing contexts for further remixing and refraction, opening up the spaces for creative interventions through the lack of "predefined pattern" Sándor mentions in the earlier text. This openness leads to complex, material constructions that, as cheek goes on to note,

> present mimesis of excess. Forms of information storage, inscribing value to information that other writers might rightly or wrongly discard, thereby challenging conventions of usage and retrieval in the pool of meaning making. [...] Typically, it interrogates conventional boundaries of consensual meaning formation and in the process of so doing it establishes a construction site for potentially unassimilable proliferations of meaning.
>
> (cheek 1999)

These exchanges function as gift economies, the act of gift-giving that Craig Saper notes is a "viable alternative to market systems" (Saper 2001, 100). Their exchange of assemblages functions as intimate bureaucracies, a term used by Saper to define works of art that exploit the processes of mainstream culture.

> Using all the trappings of bureaucracies for poetic ends, these poets and artists shift the use and tone of the bureaucratic images from signaling authority to participation in ironic satire, parody, and inside jokes. The new tone also suggests a more serious endeavor: to create intense dynamic relationships among those who participate in the joke and move beyond the fascination with bureaucratic trappings as objects of ridicule into sociopoetic invention. [... They] appropriate the trappings of the systems now common in big business.
>
> (Saper 2001, 100)

cheek also notes how these exchanges, in their employment of material and technological "error," make them "integrated into the 'performance' of the writing" (cheek 1999). This is constituted by the irreversible nature of material processes being enacted in composition. Referencing Robert Smithson's consideration of entropy (using a sandbox as an example), cheek notes how entropy might be transposed onto writing and reading:

> [The] sand box becomes a sheet or sheaf of papers. The black sand is the 'writing' or the mark makings, the white sand conventionally, although not necessarily in *d a n / m* those negative spaces between them. The boy running becomes an eye scanning, a silent tongue sounding, and all necessary engagements of the human body–mind that constitute ontological production of meanings. The "greyness" which results is not a uniform grey, but composed of degrees, particularities, differentials of event. [...] Accretions of "greyness" throughout *d a n / m* can be read as metaphors of informational entropy.
>
> (cheek 1999)

Similarly to how a glitch process can perform irreversible edits to a file, process for these exchanged works is an ongoing aspect of the work that is inseparable from the material itself. One performance of a work becomes a permanent mark of a physical process at a specific point in time, becoming a new starting point for a new process; entropic moments that form new potentials.

Maggie O'Sullivan

The final works I wish to present in this essay are a selection by Maggie O'Sullivan. O'Sullivan is an artist, a poet, a performer, and an editor. In addition to her influential practice, she has edited the anthologies *Out of Everywhere* and *Out of Everywhere 2*, two important volumes of experimental writing by women. O'Sullivan's poetry confronts compositional and interpretational conventions, challenging, as Scott Thurston notes, the "normative language use [...,] engaging in a poetics which seeks to articulate areas of experience that are not normally recognized in mainstream culture" (Thurston 2004a, 16–17). This normative use is the product of a patriarchally dominated culture, and O'Sullivan's radical engagement with its language can be seen to demarginalize alternative expression through striking use of text/image, text placement on the page, and creative use of semantic disjuncture. Her texts persistently resist the supposed stability of form and sign synonymous with self-assured and self-perpetuating socially dominant codes.

In an interview, also with Scott Thurston, O'Sullivan talks about her compositional processes. Of particular interest to me is her explanation of her editing process, which she explains as a "building away from, a going out from the initial material/s" (Thurston 2004b, 7). This statement arguably typifies her works' movements away from dominant modes of closure around a unified subject and toward a more fluid dialectic between text and meaning that aims "always to move with the language, to move in a course that the language might present" (Thurston 2004b, 7).

A work such as *Murmur* (O'Sullivan 2004) interweaves such devices as syntactically disjointed phrases, word groups that are phonetically linked, large white spaces and generally innovative use of page space and layout, and visual form, including content boxed by pen inscription and sections of textual erasure. These assemblages are carefully constructed both visually and syntactically, in order to allow a willing reader the opportunity to engage in an alternative set of rules with a text.

Far from the conventional methods of reading a poem, one is encouraged to see words, phrases, and textual sections as shaped, literally crafted. Apparently disjointed syntax at once resists conventional semantic resolution while at the same time resisting being impenetrable or dismissible as merely nonsensical, instead becoming a process of discovery that explores the spaces between visual and textual contexts. *Murmur*, as with many of O'Sullivan's texts, occupies an expressively animating space between the subversion of conventional readings on the one hand, and the exploitation of those conventions to facilitate those subversions on the other. The text's visual components elicit meaning and direction through one's conventional use of, for example, boxed content, which imply hierarchical importance over the rest of the text, and form tensions between the standard top-to-bottom parsing of a page and the multiple zones of focus *within* each page, such as areas of almost-legible erasure.

O'Sullivan's work tends to create a drive of opposing forces in loaded fragments or phrases. By exploiting the expectations of conventional reading, her texts foreground those conventional expectations as almost an error, with each element on the page so full of potential associations that one certain resolution cannot be asserted. O'Sullivan facilitates this by creating momentary formations of patterns that switch between syntactic continuity and alternative continuative threads, such as alliterative, phonetic, or thematic (animals and animal anatomy or scientific taxonomy, for example), or though visual elements such as textual shaping or color.

Peter Middleton notes that O'Sullivan's work

> accommodates familiar lexical items, short bursts of regular syntax, and intimates both lexical and syntactic placement for many of the non-lexical sounds. It is both phonemic and non-phonemic, both purely sensuous sound and semantically active lexis.
>
> (Middleton 2011, 98)

These simultaneous modes create complex constructions of text as material—what Middleton describes as O'Sullivan's "textual density."

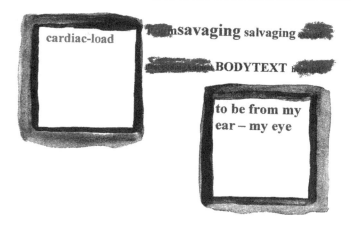

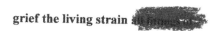

Typographical and visual use of the space of the page, as well as painterly marks in some books, stretch and slow elapsed time, and the changing intensities of expression create wide differences in the scale of the poem's instants. The poetry can feel very small or terrifying [sic] large, imminently integrable or a rubble dump where horrors lurk [...].

(Middleton 2011, 98)

Examples of this can be found in *A Natural History in 3 Incomplete Parts* (O'Sullivan 1985a), which intersperses extended sections of single-word sentences with moments of equally dense-but syntactically and grammatically resembling more familiar-structures, lists, and imagery. There are frequent sections of semantic units made discrete by their separations by full stops, which establish an interruptive pattern that soon becomes a rhythm, albeit remaining visually and often syntactically disjointed.

Certain parts of passages make individual associations deceptively straightforward: "Daily.nightly" offers an easy-to-parse and familiar dichotomy. This is immediately followed by "fetch.anthem.device.fetch," which, though not straightforwardly reconcilable in a semantic sense, nonetheless allows for a syntactic or conversational interpretation based on convention to exist, the repeated "fetch" implying the reassertion of a command. However, this is immediately followed by "mali.dip.dissolve.disarm.decoy.spatter.Blockade.shanty.shine-hush.prow.roused.instep.PROW." Again, the repeated use of "prow" implies some kind of imperative, though without a target or subject to reconcile or close it.

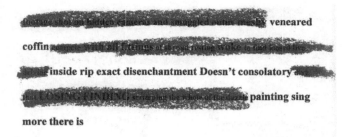

more there is

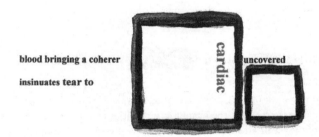

O'Sullivan's resistance to closure is both compounded and complicated by such continuities and interruptions throughout the text. There are repeated themes—references to "blood," "carnage," "prowl," to name just a few repeated motifs—but they are not explained in any way. Indeed, there is a persistent push–pull between competing tones—a context best described by O'Sullivan's words themselves—as is the shift between hyphenated compound terms such as "honey-carnage" or "gentle-violence."

These dichotomies themselves begin to become thematic. Syntactic harmony, though brief, starts to become an interruption, a new discomfort, a jarring departure from a newly established form. Furthermore, it is often followed by a resumption of the previous form, which foregrounds just how easily an apparently harmonious syntax quickly resumes its position of normative dominance.

O'Sullivan's careful use of visual elements in terms of placement, text shape, and imagery lends itself to a close visual reading, an almost analytical approach to meaning in microsections. The juxtaposition of elements triggers "semantically active" (Middleton 2011, 98) tensions that again lead to a more analytical approach to reading. However, as in the previous examples,

O'Sullivan's attention to the sounds of words in their mutual contexts simultaneously provokes a more "sensuous" reading. Similarly to the apparently thematic aspects of her work, there thus is a fluctuating shift between absorptive states throughout the work.

Though resistant on the surface to conventional reading strategies, the properties of O'Sullivan's text that I have outlined in the earlier text nonetheless allow for those sonic and visual cohabitation, leading to that "sensuous" reading that Middleton describes. The unfamiliar forms and constructions therefore invite interpretative processes that do not settle on the typical semantic closures through syntactic agreement, but instead exploit semiotic processes, opening up texts into exploded potentials of meaning. Sounds and structures fuse the otherwise disparate, even within the unit of the word itself.

States of Emergency (O'Sullivan 1985b), a less visually dense work than *A Natural History in 3 Incomplete Parts* (O'Sullivan 1985a), again combines and repeats taxonomies including those of natural environment, animals, medical terms, body parts, and organs. The focused juxtapositions are semantically generative and often feel violent, a receptive feeling that is compounded by the literal carving and reworking of words into neologisms. Words with usually positive connotations become tainted by their surroundings, as "Suckled" is followed immediately by "Monstrous." The page continues the violent image generation, though "fuck & tear / hawk & hammer / ," and "savage contraventions" (O'Sullivan 1985b, 17) and ending with "LONGEN / O / Sour Crucifisted / HELLS." Here, "Crucifisted" conjures images of suffering, pain, violence (and sexual violence). "Hell" is then pluralized and capitalized into "HELLS" in an assertion of eternal suffering made more violent by subtle syntactic adjustments.

O'Sullivan punctuates her work with these juxtapositions even down to the level of the words, as in her use of neologisms. These neologisms interact with the syntactically and visually unconventional forms in O'Sullivan's work to direct a reading that is open and yet establishes new, localized habits. The backdrop of unusual syntactic and visual constructions in her work lays down the foundation through which these neologisms excite complexities in meaning.

O'Sullivan's works thus subject themselves to *their own* unique conventions, expressive on *their own* terms. As Middleton explains:

> [Neologisms are not] just a new productivity of speech capable of replacing two or more words with one. Much of their force lies in the mixture of creativity on show and the slight fuzziness of meaning. Linguistic creativity is also a sign of power or agency, of being able to exercise some control in situations (men, everyday life) which often render us somewhat helpless. [...] Residual imprecision is important too, because it allows, as Derrida knew, room for imagination and new ideas to develop. Listeners are left to fill in their own interpretation as a contribution to the shared working out of what a discursive situation might mean to them, and this, like a mutual conversational game, is intersubjectively satisfying.
>
> (Middleton 2011, 101)

Although referring to her use of neologisms specifically in the context of *Palace of Reptiles*, I would argue that Middleton's assessment is applicable to the majority of O'Sullivan's published works. This and her subversions of stable language and form overall form systems of Artificial Myth, a term coined by Craig Saper which is based on Barthes' *punctum practice*. Artificial Myth functions as a collection of recessive ideas, detours [...] intersect[ing] even though they do not yet fit. [... This] practice has *less* to do with definitive meanings than with potential combinations and with changing the settings or frames for understanding. [...] The practice finds the intersections among different symbolic systems instead of working toward progress in any single system or epistemological frame.

(Saper 1997, 24)

O'Sullivan's competing modes and juxtaposed semantically loaded words contribute to the progressive establishment of personalized strategies of reading, "recessive" as a way or remaining always in process, always productive, and unassimilable into mainstream reading practices.

In finishing with this crucial aspect of O'Sullivan's work, I would apply this same overall concept to all of the poets and works discussed in this essay. O'Sullivan, Cardiff, cheek, and Cobbing each create modular systems in their works, which, through their performances of multimodal composition (incorporating chance, interruption, and intervention), utilize the myth of conventional reading as a frame through which to reconfigure and create new open systems of reading. These systems re-evaluate the status of what would conventionally be considered antithetical to expressive agency, and in unique ways offer critiques of the cultural systems which perpetuate those myths.

References

Adler, Anthony Curtis (2012). "Analog in the Age of Digital Reproduction: Audiophilia, Semi-Aura, and the Cultural Memory of the Phonograph." In: *Between Page and Screen: Remaking Literature Through Cinema and Cyberspace* (ed. Kiene Brillenburg Wurth), 48–61. New York: Fordham University Press.

Barthes, Roland (1972). *Mythologies*. New York: Noonday Press.

cheek, cris. (1999). "Domestic Ambient Noise / Moise." *Riding the Meridian*. http://www.heelstone.com/meridian/cheek/damntheory.html (accessed 10 January 2017).

cheek, cris (2007). *The Church, The School, The Beer*. Rhode Island: Plantarchy/Critical Documents.

Christov-Bakargiev, Carolyn (2003). *Janet Cardiff: A Survey of Works Including Collaborations with George Bures Miller*. New York: P.S.1 Contemporary Art Center.

Cobbing, Bob (1978a). *A B C / W A N D O T R E E. Collected Poems 2*. London: El Uel Uel U Publications.

Cobbing, Bob (1978b). "Some Statements on Sound Poetry." In: *Sound Poetry: A Catalog* (eds. Steve McCaffery and bp Nichol), 39–41. Toronto: Underwhich Editions.

Cobbing, Bob (2014). "Whisper Piece." In: *Typewriter Art: A Modern Anthology* (ed. Barrie Tullett), 33. London: Laurence King Publishing Ltd.

Emerson, Lori (2011). Talonbooks. "the origin of the term 'dirty concrete poetry' (en route to digital D.I.Y.).". http://talonbooks.com/meta-talon/the-origin-of-the-term-dirty-concrete-poetry-en-route-to-digital-diy (accessed 10 January 2017).

Emerson, Lori (2014). *Reading Writing Interfaces: From the Digital to the Bookbound*. Minnesota: University of Minnesota Press.

Fisher, Allen (2016). *Imperfect Fit: Aesthetic Function, Facture & Perception in Art and Writing Since 1950*. Alabama: University of Alabama Press.

Galloway, Alexander R. (2004). *Protocol: How Control Exists after Decentralization*. Massachusetts: MIT Press.

Middleton, Peter (2011). "'Ear Loads': Neologisms and Sound Poetry in Maggie O'Sullivan's *Palace of Reptiles*." In: *The Salt Companion to Maggie O'Sullivan* (ed. Ken Edwards), 97–122. Cambridge: Salt.

Osman, Jena (2002). "'Multiple' Functioning: Procedural Actions in the Poetry of Tina Darragh." In: *Telling It Slant* (eds. Mark Wallace and Steven Marks), 255–279. Alabama: University of Alabama Press.

O'Sullivan, Maggie (1985a). *A Natural History in 3 Incomplete Parts*. London: Magenta.

O'Sullivan, Maggie (1985b). *States of Emergency*. Oxford: International Concrete Poetry Archive.

O'Sullivan, Maggie (2011). *murmur*. Guildford: Veer Books.

Sándor, Katalin (2012). "Moving (the) Text: From Print to Digital." In: *Between Page and Screen: Remaking Literature Through Cinema and Cyberspace* (ed. Kiene Brillenburg Wurth), 144–156. New York: Fordham University Press.

Saper, Craig (1997). *Artificial Mythologies: A Guide to Cultural Invention*. Minnesota: University of Minnesota Press.

Saper, Craig (2001). *Networked Art*. Minnesota: University of Minnesota Press.

Sheppard, Robert (2002). "Bob Cobbing." https://www.theguardian.com/news/2002/oct/07/guardianobituaries.booksobituaries (accessed 10 January 2017).

Thurston, Scott (2004a). "Maggie O'Sullivan: Transformation and Substance." *Poetry Salzburg Review* 6: 15–20.

Thurston, Scott (2004b). "Maggie O'Sullivan/Scott Thurston: Emerging States." *Poetry Salzburg Review* 6: 6–14.

2c.10
"Here to Stay": Black British Poetry and the Post-WWII United Kingdom

Bartosz Wójcik

Caribbean Voices

A product of a convoluted imperial history, "Black British poetry," on its own a highly ambiguous, complex, and contested term (Evaristo and Daljit 2010, Lawson Welsh 2016), constitutes an example of "transnational"[1] practice (Ramazani 2009). In the words of Bernardine Evaristo (2010b), "[t]he terms 'black poet' or 'Asian poet' are, of course, problematic and controversial. Few writers want to be labelled, pigeon-holed, or solely-defined by race or skin colour" (11). Apart from being "a convenient shorthand for easy identification [at present]" (11), in the 1970s and 1980s, when the "Black British poetry" was typified by the most combative and direct style in the history of its evolution, the adjective "black" was "a label adopted by settlers of African and Asian descent in order to articulate an alliance, a collective stand against racism in Britain" (Procter 2003, 6). Examples of such use include Linton Kwesi Johnson's anthemic poem "It Dread Inna Inglan (For George Lindo)" (Johnson 1980, 19). Although established literary scholarship has embraced the term "Black British" to encompass writing by authors of *both* African and Asian descents (Walder 1999, 119), "born or based in Britain" (Lawson Welsh 2016, 194), because of considerations of length, this chapter focuses primarily on the creative output of British poets influenced by their Afro-Caribbean roots.

A Companion to Contemporary British and Irish Poetry, 1960–2015, First Edition.
Edited by Wolfgang Görtschacher and David Malcolm.
© 2021 John Wiley & Sons Ltd. Published 2021 by John Wiley & Sons Ltd.

In short, as a hybrid form, the poetry in question "gives expression and shape to a cross-geographic experience enjambed between the (post)colonies and the Western metropole" (Ramazani 2009, 163–164), providing evidence of, to borrow the Derek Walcott biographer Bruce King's term, the "internationalization of English literature" (2005), a complex process that came to prominence after the end of the Second World War, gaining significant momentum in the late 1950s and early 1960s with the pronounced rise of the decolonization movement in the colonies and the subsequent dismantling of the Empire.[2]

In fact, the war effort—given the West Indians' involvement in military assistance to "the mother country"—was a decisive factor in the creation of *Calling the West Indies*, the BBC radio program that provided Caribbean soldiers in the British army with a chance to have their messages broadcast to family members back home. This led to the birth of *Caribbean Voices*, the first West Indian literary radio show. Broadcast from London, it was created in 1943 by Jamaican-born poet Una Marson, a literary figure stalwart and educationist in her own right, and later edited and curated by, among others, the Irishman Henry Swanzy.[3] The program, whose guests included representatives of the then budding generation of island writers (and now universally acknowledged major figures within Caribbean literature), such as George Lamming, Samuel Selvon, V. S. Naipaul, Derek Walcott, and Edward Brathwaite, lasted till 1958; during its lifetime, it "enabled regular cultural exchanges between Britain and the Caribbean, as well as forging a sense of common black literary endeavour in Britain" (Lawson Welsh 2016, 178). *Caribbean Voices*, deemed by Brathwaite "the single most important literary catalyst for Caribbean imaginative and critical writing in English" (Hoyles and Hoyles 2002, 47), not only literally introduced the West Indian cadences and the orality of the region's Anglophone writing to European listeners, but, most importantly, reaffirmed the importance of local literature,[4] as the weekly broadcast "coincided with a peak of nationalist sentiment and activity [in the Antilles]" (Nanton 2000, 61). Furthermore, the program provided up-and-coming authors with financial rewards and with an unprecedented "platform of criticism for their work" (Nanton 2014, 585).

The Windrush Generation

Another formative event, whose nationwide resonance was to be wider than the domain of what would eventually be labeled "Black British poetry" (Lawson Welsh 2016, 178), was the arrival in 1948 of the first group of postwar West Indian immigrants to the United Kingdom, onboard the SS *Empire Windrush*,[5] historically referred to as "the Windrush Generation" and artistically immortalized in *Small Island* (2004), a bestselling novel by Andrea Levy, herself a child of Jamaican parents who crossed the Atlantic on the Windrush that year. Among the passengers on the now famous ship was also the celebrated Trinidadian calypsonian Lord Kitchener (b. Aldwyn Roberts), whose coming to the heart of the then Empire may be perhaps construed as the symbolic manifestation on British soil of the embodiment of the Caribbean oral traditions that would influence UK poetry in the years to come:

a heritage of song, speech and performance visible in such folk forms as the litanic work songs, chants, battle songs, Queh Queh songs, hymns, thousands of calypsos, mentos and reggae songs, sermons of both the grass-roots and establishment churches, riddles, jokes and word-games. (Rohlehr 1992, 166)

Though not a passenger on the *Windrush* itself,[6] Jamaican James Berry, who came to Britain in 1948 (Berry 2011a, 2), captured the collective life of the Afro-Caribbean diaspora in London, their toil and joy, as well as their interactions with the white majority in a series of poetic portraits written in Standard English and in Caribbean Creole, most notably in "White Child Meets Black Man" (Berry 2011a, 23), "Migrant in London" (Berry 2011a, 17), and in "On an Afternoon Train from Purley to Victoria, 1955" (Berry 2011a, 65). A noted poetry anthologist, whose landmark *Bluefoot Traveller* (1976) and *News for Babylon*[7] (1984) set out the literary achievements of Britain-domiciled "[d]escendants of the silent labour force of old empire" (Berry 1984, xii), gained literary prominence later in life with the publication of *Lucy's Letters and Loving* (1982). Using the voice of the title persona of Lucy, a Caribbean woman residing in England and writing letters to her longtime friend still living "back at Yard" (Berry 2011a, 35), in a Jamaican village of their youth, the poems grant readers a series of versified epistolary portraits of economic migrants "gone a foreign." Episodic, with each poem revolving round a core theme, such as Lucy's first experience of London, or her reflections upon Elizabeth II, the verse cycle records the passage of time—"Cousin John fine-shin boy / stretch up to sixfoot man (…) / Puppa is bones in the groun'" (Berry 2011a, 38, ll. 31–33)—and its impact on the speaker and her fluid relationship with Jamaica. While a beneficiary of modernity (affordable electricity, contraceptives, feminism, surplus food), she is concerned about her cultural deracination and retains a nostalgic yearning for "labrish" (gossip) from home. Upon returning to England from a holiday trip to the Caribbean, she simultaneously acknowledges that she has undergone a profound change while in England, becoming a British West Indian in the process (King 2005, 105–106). Unsurprisingly, Lucy arranges for Cousin Man-Man to purchase a plot of land on her behalf—"(…) I glad / it near the sea an 'not mount'n / lan'. It planted well I hear" (Berry 2011a, 39, ll. 3–5), and, not unlike the title Guyanese character of *Desmond's* (1989–1994), a Peckham-set TV series starring Norman Beaton, intends to retire in the Caribbean. By obvious contrast, as depicted in "From Lucy: New Generation," her children—"Westindies is jus' a place parents / born: Bob Marley's their only thought / in it (…)" (Berry 2011a, 40, ll. 19–21)—do not share her concerns. Black and British by birthright, though their right will be frequently challenged in the twentieth century—especially in the wake of Enoch Powell's "Rivers of Blood" speech (1968)—they seem to have more in common with "a brand new breed of blacks" (Johnson 1975, 21, l. 1), epitomized by the title "Yout Rebels" of Linton Kwesi Johnson's poem (Johnson 1975, 21), and with subjects of "intersecting public debates about race and immigration, education, unemployment and crime, nationalism, citizenship and the multicultural policies" (Lawson Welsh 2016, 178) that echoed throughout the late 1960s and well into the 1990s.[8]

The Caribbean Artists' Movement

If "[t]he Windrush history gave the British West Indians a usable past, a mythology of arrival [and] struggle" (King 2005, 225), as recounted by its first-hand witnesses and participants in *Windrush: The Irresistible Rise of Multi-Racial Britain* (Phillips and Phillips 1999), then thanks to Barbadian Edward Brathwaite, Jamaican Andrew Salkey, and Trinidadian John La Rose, who founded the Caribbean Artists' Movement (1966–1972), West Indian intellectual life in Britain started to gain wider currency. Characterized by grassroots activism, left-wing politics, and Afro-Caribbean retention,[9] the initiative yielded the first Black publishing house in the United Kingdom, New Beacon Books, and *Savacou*, a literary journal; other presses, such as Bogle-L'Ouverture Publications, were to follow suit shortly. A critically acclaimed poet, author of a seminal verse trilogy—*Rights of Passage* (1967), *Masks* (1968), *Islands* (1969), published together as *The Arrivants* (1973)—Brathwaite not only successfully "blended the techniques of modernism with West Indian speech" (King 2005, 103), but also infectiously argued in *History of the Voice* in favor of "nation language," asserting that "[t]he hurricane," a typical Caribbean occurrence and a byword for the pneuma of Antillean poetry, "does not roar in pentameters" (Brathwaite 1995, 10). This "Poundian redux" (Falci 2015, 56)—Brathwaite's performative practice of linguistic pluralism coupled with his sustained exploration of the Creole continuum, jazz rhythmicity, and Africanisms—redefined Anglophone literature (Breiner 1998), blazing the trail for the reggae-propelled and Rastafari-infused dub poetry[10] of the nascent generation, eloquently portrayed on the silver screen by Trinidadian-born filmmaker Horace Ové in *Pressure* (1976).

"Here to Stay"

Inspired by fellow Jamaican vernacular poet, master storyteller, and folklorist Louise Bennett, by the pan-Africanist decolonizing thought of West Indian pioneers, such as C. L. R. James and Aimé Césaire, as well as by the Black Power movement in the USA, London-based Linton Kwesi Johnson made his debut as a négritude surrealist with *Voices of the Living and the Dead* (1974). A keen admirer of the emancipatory agenda of roots reggae and a shrewd observer of world politics, he moved on to chronicle *de tings an' times* in a series of hard-hitting collections of poems written in Brixton Creole, including *Dread Beat An' Blood* (1975) and *Inglan is a Bitch* (1980). The very titles of these books manifest the "bellicose binarism of 'us' and 'them'" (Wójcik 2015, 149) intrinsic to his poetics. Brimming with Rastafarian lore,[11] "dread"

> is a reminder of the systemic oppression that instills chronic fear in the Black British subaltern; "beat" evokes both physical assault ("beat" as a police-patrolled area) and the musical heritage of the Black Atlantic ("beat" as rhythm); "blood" conjures up the image of violent confrontation, yet it is also a sign of one's genealogy, of one's bloodlines. (Wójcik 2015, 136–137)

Like Brathwaite, Johnson "places colonial history within a context which aims to empower the black population" (Walder 1999, 130), but he does so by the unique employment of the rhythms first utilized by Jamaican *toasters*, sound system deejays, and reggae lyricists, such as Big Youth and I-Roy. In his classic dub poems—identity-forming "Bass Culture," "Street 66" (a story of a confrontation between police officers and participants in a Caribbean "blues dance"), "Sonny's Lettah" (an epistolary account of the drama ensuing racial profiling), and historiographic "Reggae Sounds"—Johnson's social commitment to exposing inequalities endemic to the British system goes hand in hand with "making the music a form of protest as opposed to simply an expression of protest" (D'Aguiar 1995, 56). Seen, read, and heard in this light, "Reggae Sounds" seems both a form of ekphrasis and a record of lived experience:

> Shock-black bubble-doun-beat bouncing
> rock-wise tumble-doun sound music
> foot-drop find drum, blood story,
> bass history is a moving
> is a hurting black story.
> (Johnson 1975, 56, ll. 1–5)

Poems such as "New Craas Massahkah" and "Sonny's Lettah" (subtitled "Anti-Sus poem"[12]), which reads today like a 1970s predecessor of the global #BlackLivesMatter campaign, made Johnson "one of the country's most informed and forceful commentators on the state of Black Britain" (Anon. 1984, 6). His later work is characterized by critical and introspective responses to political and social developments after the fall of the Iron Curtain ("Mi Revalueshanary Fren"), including personal re-assessments of the life of his relatives and companions ("Reggae fi Dada," "Reggae fi Bernard," "Hurricane Blues"), and a metapoetic critique of his craft and status ("If I Woz a Tap Natch Poet"). His is a literary practice that found its dedicated acolytes in the 1980s, some of whom passionately—if only too rigidly—have followed his footsteps (Benjamin Zephaniah), while others (Jean Binta Breeze) have since masterfully "triangulated dub with other models of performance or spoken-word poetry" (Falci 2015, 163).

With Margaret Thatcher as the embodiment of reactionary politics and a culturally monolithic Britain, the 1980s, however, "saw a shift toward the more inclusive, if rather flawed, ideology of multiculturalism, and the encouragement of ethnic minority arts" (Lawson Welsh 2016, 187). The decade gave rise to new publishing opportunities,[13] especially to the rise in both the presence of Black female authors and, to quote the subtitle of *Watchers & Seekers* (1987)—a landmark poetry anthology published by Women's Press—in "creative writing by Black women in Britain." Representing a diversity of geographic and ethnic backgrounds, 26 contributors—among them Valerie Bloom, Merle Collins, Amryl Johnson, Grace Nichols, and Maud Sulter—are proof that the heavily masculinized literary scene was undergoing considerable reconstruction in the mid-1980s. The Guyanese Nichols made a name for herself with the publication of *I Is a Long Memoried Woman* (1983), a cycle of poems united by the narrative of "the spirit of the African women taken to the New World as slaves" (King 2005, 203). Shunning the language of mythologizing exceptionalism, these are complex texts of shifting female agency, and meditations upon ways of commemorating the Middle Passage, populated with historical Afro-Caribbean figures and figments of imagination. Compared to Brathwaite's Afro-Caribbean trilogies (Donnell and Lawson Welsh 1996, 369), the collection, like David Dabydeen's Indo-Caribbean *Coolie Odyssey* (1988) and *Turner*

(1994), sheds light on the practice of slavery and the experience of colonization in the face of their "obliteration in the sea and in the hegemonic discourses and institutions of empire" (Falci 2015, 164).

In *The Fat Black Woman's Poems* (1984), her second volume of verse, Nichols, voicing a stance parallel to Jean Binta Breeze's womanist/feminist perspective,[14] defies the patriarchal gaze and inscribes corporeality onto the body of the work.[15] The female figure, whether in "The Fat Black Woman's Instructions to a Suitor," or in "Invitation," "exemplifies the use of the erotic as power in her [daily] confrontation" (Lawson Welsh 2007, 35) with retrograde, Eurocentric British society, as well as with male normative expectations. In "The Fat Black Woman Goes Shopping," the persona battles with body shaming in the era before size zero:

> The fat black woman could only conclude
> That when it come to fashion
> The choice is lean.
> (Nichols 2010, 65, ll. 18–20)

Though dominated by the "Fat Black Woman's Cycle," the collection also zooms in on the pangs of homesickness gripping diasporic West Indians, the experience of which is a recurrent topos creatively embraced by writers throughout the history of Caribbean literature.[16] In "Like a Beacon," Nichols's London-based persona "leave[s] art galleries / in search of plantains / saltfish / sweet potatoes" (Nichols 2010, 55, ll. 5–7), while the protagonist of "Island Man" each morning

> (…) wakes up
> to the sound of blue surf
> in his head
> (Nichols 2010, 56, ll. 2–4).

If Johnson invited Jamaican bass culture to reverberate across British poetics, then Nichols's fellow Guyanese John Agard introduces elements of the Eastern Caribbean culture, such as calypso rhythms, the Carnival, and steelpan symbolism, into the literature of his new adopted country. Characterized by satire, allusion, wordplay, innuendo, and sensuality ("English Girl Eats Her First Mango"), his work is indebted more to the scathing "picong tongue" (Agard 2006, 40, l. 2) of calypsonians and griots, whom he vividly evokes in his poem "Feeling the Whirlwind (for Abdul Malik)," than to the brimstone and fire of roots reggae prophets. Even if he engages in historical revisionism, that is, in critique of the commodification of the Afro-Caribbean tradition and its demotion to the status of a tourist attraction, as in *Limbo Dancer in Dark Glasses* (1983), he does so with humor. His limbo dancer may be an avid reader of revolutionary intellectuals—Frantz Fanon, Walter Rodney, Che Guevara, Angela Davis, whose books were disseminated at the International Book Fairs of Radical Black and Third World Books (1982–1995)—yet, as in "Limbo Dancer's Reading Habits," he manages to advocate other pleasures as well:

> But limbo dancer also reads the Kama Sutra
> bending over backwards
> as well as The Joys of Natural Childbirth
> (Agard 1990, 32, ll. 12–14).

"Listen Mr. Oxford Don," one of Agard's best-known poems, is a text that marries two staple poetic modes—boasting and insulting (Fenton 2003)—as a form of resistance to monologic discourses. Addressing the title enforcer of prescriptive knowledge, Agard casts his self-avowed "simple immigrant / from Clapham Common" (Agard 1990, 44, ll. 2–3) as an outlaw, as "(…) a man on de run / (…) a dangerous one" (44, ll. 8–9), who is not equipped with any form of physical weapon, but "(…) only armed wit mih human breath" (44, l. 30):

> I don't need no axe
> to split/ up yu syntax
> I don't need no hammer
> to mash/ up yu grammar
> (44, ll. 14–17).

No fancy accoutrements are needed for the continuation, to evoke Louise Bennett, of the "colonizin' in reverse" (Markham 2001, 63) of the idiom of the erstwhile masters, as Agard's persona—ironically, only in a mildly creolized language—is "making de Queen's English accessory / to {his} offence" (Agard 1990, 44, l. 38). Indeed, "Listen Mr. Oxford Don" is an expression of Caribbean creativity, where the function of the newcomer "as experimentalist is to disturb the peace where peace means stasis and stagnancy" (D'Aguiar 1995, 62), but this is a thoroughly political act, a gesture of conspicuous rebellion, not far removed from the resistance practiced in Northern Irish poetry,[17] as attested to by Paul Muldoon's speaker in "Profumo," who "(…) would affix a stamp / with the Queen's head upside down (…)" (Muldoon 1987, 8, ll. 6–7).

Stage Meets Page

The 1990s was "a heady time for poetry in Britain" (Falci 2015, 181). Apart from the establishment of the Forward Prize for Poetry (1992) and the T. S. Eliot Prize for Poetry (1993), several initiatives aimed at popularizing verse were launched. National Poetry Day and the New Generation Poets promotion were inaugurated in 1994. The latter included David Dabydeen and Moniza Alvi, whose *The Country at My Shoulder* (1993) explores her hyphenated Pakistani-British belonging through a narrative in which the personal meets the historical. Thanks to Arts Council grants, the decade also experienced a professional surge on the British performance poetry circuit, which has been growing in strength since the inception of the Apples and Snakes performance poetry agency in 1982, as documented by *The Popular Front of Contemporary Poetry* (1992), an anniversary anthology. Catering to children, adolescents, and adults alike,[18] and steadily publishing his brand of "overtly inclusive and unashamedly democratic poetry" (Wójcik 2015, 244) throughout the 1990s,

Benjamin Zephaniah rose to national celebrity status: "As the black poetry scene became less militant and its rhetoric conventionalized, oral poetry became even more popular with competitive poetry slams attracting racially mixed audiences" (King 2005, 292).

This "large-scale renaissance of poetry in Britain" (Padel 2004, 1), which the critic dates back to the 1970s, would not be complete without a simultaneous return to the page and to formal experimentation. New arrivals to the poetry scene, such as Lemn Sissay and Patience Agbabi, "insisted on the textuality of their verse" (King 2005, 292), concurrently availing themselves of the hip hop idiom. A participant in the Afrostyle seminars held by Kwame Dawes, Agbabi debuted with *R.A.W.* (1995), garnering the praise of Merle Collins and Zephaniah, "riff[ing] on tradition, rap[ping] without apology, and refus[ing] to be a 'black' or 'white' poet" (Murphy 2010, 67). Her braggadocio is evident in "Rappin It Up": here, in a boisterously hip hop fashion, she disses a quartet of dead white males (Shakespeare, Milton, Wordsworth, Eliot), thereby symbolically erasing the validity of Elizabethan, Stuart/Puritan, Romantic, and Modernist literature to her experience as a modern British author. Still, cognizant of the fact that "Black culture goes deeper / than X and Nike" (Agbabi 1995, 50), she produces formally ambitious, deeply intertextual sonnets and sestinas in *Transformatrix* (2000) and in *Bloodshot Monochrome* (2008), while *Telling Tales* (2014) dazzles with her reworking of *The Canterbury Tales*.

A penchant, perhaps inspired by Brathwaite's "Sycorax video style," for typeface experiments—at work both in *R.A.W.* and in *Telling Tales*, as well as Agbabi's literary investigation of her Nigerian (biological) and British/Welsh (adoptive) roots—is what her creative output has in common with that of Jackie Kay, particularly with *The Adoption Papers* (1991). Tracing and blurring the entangled routes of identity, this cycle of poems is orchestrated as an interplay of three voices (daughter, adoptive mother, birth mother), each "distinguished typographically" (Kay 2005, 8), each contributing a distinct strand to the narrative fabric of "the competing claims of biology, family, society, and self-determination" (Tolan 2010, 194). Divided into 10 chapters, this major crossover work challenges the genre of autobiography, putting to the test preconceived notions of parentage, personality, and poetry.

Internationalization

In the 2000s, Black British poets are undoubtedly, to evoke Jamaican Poet Laureate Mervyn Morris, "writing in English*es*" (Akbar 2017), their work illustrating the fact that their "affiliations to the nation are mainly British but, importantly, they *work* internationally, borrowing from other cultures and literary traditions, not just British ones" (Lawson Welsh 2016, 191). This is true of millennial poets as diverse as Jay Bernard, Inua Ellams, Daljit Nagra, and Warsan Shire.

Still, according to *Free Verse* (2005), a report on publishing opportunities for Black and Asian poets in the United Kingdom (Kean 2005), fewer than 1% of poetry collections published domestically are authored by BME [Black and minority ethnic] writers (Kean 2005, Evaristo 2010, 11). Mentorship programs, such as "The Complete Works" or writers' workshops offered by London-based collective Malika's Kitchen (run by Malika Booker, Chair for the 2016 Forward Prizes for Poetry), are attempts to reverse the established trend.

Not unlike contemporary poetry itself, "the term Black British is an evolving one" (Dawes 2010, 19). Although old masters, as Walcott self-deprecatingly confesses in *The Prodigal*—"(…) When I got off / I found that I had missed the Twentieth Century" (Walcott 2005, 5, ll. 71–72)—may be detached from the experience of Kayo Chingonyi's vinyl digger persona in "The Room," not to mention from his preoccupation with "(…) telling a-side, from remix, / from test press that never saw the light of day" (McCarthy Woolf 2014, 119, ll. 9–10), recurring concerns like personal agency, cultural ownership, or language itself are still relevant to older and younger writers. A case in point is Jamaican-born UK-based writer Kei Miller, whose *There Is an Anger That Moves* (2007) opens with "How we became the pirates"—an internal monolog spurred on by an incident involving an English woman sneering at the speaker's Caribbean accent:

> So English poetry is no longer from England.
> You swear – *Lady, if I start a poem*
> *in this country*
> *it will not be yours.*
> (Miller 2007, 9, ll. 14–17)

After all, "in a contemporary culture where fixity of any sort, whether of form or identity, can seem a type of nostalgia" (Herbert 2010, 79), language remains a high-precision tool opening and closing doors, as in Roger Robinson's "Tobago Fruits":

> She offered me some water and asked *Where you from?*
> *From right here.* She shook her head *You're not from here, lately.*
> (Robinson 2013, 45, ll. 9–10)

For Adam Lowe, a poet of "Caribbean-Irish-English heritage" (McCarthy Woolf 2014, 55), language is an instrument for vocalizing British queer club culture. This he does through Polari, a gay slang, and neologisms of his own concoction with which he peppers his verse, such as "Vada That":

> Aunt nell the patter flash and gardy loo!
> Bijou, she trolls, bold, on lallies
> Slick as stripes down the Dilly
> (McCarthy Woolf 2014, 61, ll. 1–3).

His representation of the LGBTQ community is a twenty-first-century update on the already linguistically effervescent depiction of the affective on the part of Patience Agbabi, Jackie Kay, and Dorothea Smartt. To the uninitiated, this sociolect—admittedly, on literary steroids—may seem potentially as intimidating and incomprehensible as the Jamaican Creole of Louise Bennett's poems must have appeared to audiences weaned on Standard English in the late 1940s. Yet, this is what British poetry *also* sounds like in the 2010s.

At present, more than ever before, Black British poets skillfully resist the "pressure to write in a Black idiom adhering to stereotypically 'Black' content" (Ramey 2004, 133). Reflective of the times, they "registe[r] the power and continu[e] historic relevance of everyday speech forms" (Walder 1999, 149), mobilizing the language as a means of asserting the self and establishing dynamic relations with and within society at large. Fed by recognizably African, Asian, and Caribbean tributaries, their poetries encapsulate a meeting of continents, being constant expressions of and contributors to hybrid modalities. If, as Berry claims in his "Thinking About Poetry," poetry is indeed "human experience in discovery" (Berry 2011b, 14), then this chapter, to borrow the image from Agard's "Chilling Out Beside the Thames," constitutes an invitation to the recognition of "Trickster Nansi spinning from Shakespeare sky" (Agard 2006, 45, l. 8), its Black *and* British incarnation.

Notes

1 I rely here on Ramazani's notion of "the transnational" to refer to "poems and other cultural works that cross national borders, whether stylistically, topographically, intellectually, or otherwise" (2009, 181).

2 For the sake of the present chapter, I have decided to follow the concise (and convincing) typology of the twentieth-century Black British literary presence, as proposed by Lawson Welsh (2016), that is, "three main 'generations': Windrush, second generation, millennial" (181).

3 The importance of the contribution of Swanzy (1915–2004) to the validation and dissemination of Caribbean literature is reflected in the annual Bocas Henry Swanzy Award for Distinguished Service to Caribbean Letters, an accolade established in 2013 by the founders of the Bocas Literary Festival in Trinidad. Its recipients include John La Rose (posthumously) and Sarah White of New Beacon Books, as well as Jeremy Poynting of Peepal Tree Press; both publishing houses have been crucial to the development of, inter alia, Black British poetry. In comparison, the legacy of Una Marson, who was the first producer, from 1943 till 1945, of *Caribbean Voices* (Nanton 2014, 585), as a literary figure has only been recently reassessed (De Caires Narain 2002, Marson 2011).

4 The fact that the London-aired program upheld the hegemonic practice of the metropolis as the arbiter of taste was not overlooked by Swanzy's contemporaries (Nanton 2014, 587).

5 The significant African and Asian presence in the United Kingdom before the Second World War, not to mention before the docking of the SS *Empire Windrush* at Tilbury in 1948, is well documented (Fryer 1991; Gilroy 2007; Falci 2015), if only recently reaching wider circulation as well as—thanks to the BBC documentary series *Black and British: A Forgotten History*—wider audiences and readership (Olusoga 2016). In this way, too, it is poetically chronicled and imaginatively reworked. For instance, in her second collection *Ship Shape* (2008), Dorothea Smartt, "a Brit-born Bajan international" (Smartt 2014, 28), weaves a commemorative tale of "an unknown African who died shortly after his arrival at Sunderland Point on the Lune River estuary of Morecambe Bay" (Smartt 2008, 15). Evoking an early eighteenth-century social reality—the times "when Lancaster was becoming the fourth largest slave port in Britain" (16)—throughout her book Smartt strives to counter the history-induced anonymity of the slave who, in the words of Patience Agbabi, "[was] robbed of his family names" (91), who survived the Middle Passage, and met his bitter end on the English shore, "disposable as an animal past its use" (41). *The Emperor's Babe* (2001), Bernardine Evaristo's novel in verse, offers another imaginative take on the African presence in the British Isles.

Written in diversely rhythmical distichs, the narrative of Zuleika, a descendant of Sudanese migrants, explores the far-reaching issues of identity and belonging; this is a speculative-fiction-like panorama of life under Roman rule whose thematic scope is not limited by its Londinium 211 CE setting and includes negotiations of history, cultural exchange, migration, race, gender, and language. Interestingly, Fred D'Aguiar (1995, 51) dates back Black literary presence in Britain to the publication of Phillis Wheatley's poems in 1773.

6 Published almost half a century after the historic docking of the SS *Windrush* at Tilbury, Berry's *Windrush Songs* (2007) is a collection of verses that both pays homage to the title generation and critiques their hopes and aspirations.

7 "Babylon" is one of the key biblical concepts appropriated by Rastafarianism; its usage by Berry points to the scope of influence of this alter/native ideology on Black British poetry of the time.

8 The unapologetic militancy of numerous Black British poems of the era was forged in response to the relentlessly stoked cauldron of fiery xenophobic rhetoric, racist attacks, and exclusionary legislation, such as the 1958 Notting Hill riots, the 1981 New Cross Massacre, the 1971 Immigration Act, and the 1981 British Nationality Act.

9 Perhaps one of the most straightforward instances is evidenced by the adoption of "African cultural names" (Berry 1984, xxv). "The change of one's name is an act of regenerative rebellion of rebirth. Fictionalized characters, such as Alex Haley's Kunta Kinte, strive to retain their African denominations, not to be insultingly called names by their masters, which meant being symbolically enslaved anew. Similarly, many Black Atlantic (Gilroy 1993) writers intended to rename themselves or augment their ethnic origin by the addition of an Afrocentric and/or non-Western middle name" (Wójcik 2015, 31). Examples include: Edward "Kamau" Brathwaite, Linton "Kwesi" Johnson, or Jean "Binta" Breeze.

10 To Jamaican dub poet Oku Onuora, dub poetry is typified by its prosody, by "a built-in reggae rhythm – hence when the poem is read without any reggae rhythm, so to speak, backing, one can distinctly hear the reggae rhythm coming out of the poem" (Doumerc 2004, 129).

11 "One Love," the last section of Johnson's *Dread Beat An' Blood*, features his imaginative employment of Rastafarian "dread talk" (Angrosino 1993; Pollard 2000; Wójcik 2015).

12 The informal name "sus" refers to a stop-and-search law that dated back to the Vagrancy Act of 1824 and was notoriously employed in the late 1970s to police the black population of Britain (Procter 2003, 78).

13 Founded in 1978 by Neil Astley, Bloodaxe Books quickly grew into a major poetry publisher specializing in, among others, British Commonwealth writers. *The Bloodaxe Book of Contemporary Women Poets* (ed. Jeni Couzyn) was published in 1985, while *Hinterland: Caribbean Poetry from the West Indies and Britain* (ed. E. A. Markham) came out in 1989. Founded in 1986, the Leeds-based Peepal Tree Press is a publishing house specializing in Black British, Caribbean, and South-Asian writing.

14 A nuanced and multifaceted writer, Jean Binta Breeze consciously privileges the female in her poetry: "I'm always writing women's voices – women's voices from the Caribbean and from Black Britain" (Hoyles 2002, 214).

15 *Lazy Thoughts of a Lazy Woman* (1989), her subsequent collection, continues the feminist/womanist trajectory, offering memorable poems about sexuality, self-image, gender politics, and domestic responsibilities, such as "Dust" (Nichols 2010, 75) and "My Black Triangle" (Nichols 2010, 81).

16 Outstanding examples include Roger Robinson's "The Immigrant's Lament" (2013,

26), and Jamaican Kei Miller's "In This New Country" (2007, 9–17).

17 For more research on the relations between Caribbean and Irish poetry, see Alison Donnell, Maria McGarrity, Evelyn O'Callaghan, eds., *Caribbean Irish Connections* (University of the West Indies Press, 2015).

18 A similar strategy was adopted by Grace Nichols and John Agard, who have since produced a considerable body of children's poetry.

References

Agard, John (1990). *Mangoes and Bullets: Selected and New Poems 1972–84*. London: Serpent's Tail.

Agard, John (2006). *We Brits*. Tarset: Bloodaxe.

Agbabi, Patience (1995). *R.A.W.* London: Gecko Press.

Agbabi, Patience (2000). *Transformatrix*. Edinburgh: Payback Press.

Agbabi, Patience (2008). *Bloodshot Monochrome*. Edinburgh: Canongate.

Agbabi, Patience (2014). *Telling Tales*. Edinburgh and London: Canongate.

Akbar, Arifa (2017). "An Interview with Mervyn Morris." *Wasafiri Extra*. http://www.wasafiri.org/article/interview-mervyn-morris.

Alvi, Moniza (1993). *The Country at my Shoulder*. Oxford: OUP.

Angrosino, Michael V. (1993). "Dub Poetry and West Indian Identity." In: *Anthropology and Literature* (ed. Paul Benson), 73–88. Urbana and Chicago: University of Illinois Press.

Anon (1984). "Linton Kwesi Johnson" [Interview with LKJ]. *Echoes* (17 March), p. 6.

Berry, James (ed.) (1976). *Bluefoot Traveller: An Anthology of Westindian Poets in Britain*. London: Limestone Publications.

Berry, James (1982). *Lucy's Letters and Loving*. London and Port of Spain: New Beacon Books.

Berry, James (ed.) (1984). *News for Babylon: The Chatto Book of Westindian-British Poetry*. London: Chatto & Windus.

Berry, James (2011a). *A Story I Am In: Selected Poems*. Tarset: Bloodaxe.

Berry, James (2011b). "Thinking About Poetry." In: *A Story I Am In: Selected Poems*, 13–14. Tarset: Bloodaxe.

Brathwaite, Edward Kamau (1973). *The Arrivants: A New World Trilogy*. Oxford: OUP.

Brathwaite, Edward Kamau (1995). *History of the Voice: The Development of Nation Language in Anglophone Caribbean Poetry*. London: New Beacon.

Breiner, Laurence A. (1998). *An Introduction to West Indian Poetry*. Cambridge: CUP.

Dabydeen, David (1988). *Coolie Odyssey*. London: Hansib.

Dabydeen, David (1994). *Turner*. London: Jonathan Cape.

D'Aguiar, Fred (1995). "Have You Been Here Long? Black Poetry in Britain." In: *New British Poetries. The Scope of the Possible* (eds. Robert Hampson and Peter Barry), 51–71. Manchester: MUP.

Dawes, Kwame (2010). "Preface." In: *Red: An Anthology of Contemporary Black British Poetry* (ed. Kwame Dawes), 17–20. Leeds: Peepal Tree Press.

De Caires Narain, Denise (2002). *Contemporary Caribbean Women's Poetry: Making Style*. London and New York: Routledge.

Donnell, Alison and Lawson Welsh, Sarah (eds.) (1996). *The Routledge Reader in Caribbean Literature*. London and New York: Routledge.

Donnell, Alison, McGarrity, Maria, and O'Callaghan, Evelyn (eds.) (2015). *Caribbean Irish Connections: Interdisciplinary Perspectives*. Kingston: University of the West Indies Press.

Doumerc, Eric (2004). "Jamaica's First Dub Poets: Early Jamaican Deejaying as a Form of Oral Poetry." *Kunapipi* 26: 129–135.

Evaristo, Bernardine (2001). *The Emperor's Babe*. London: Penguin.

Evaristo, Bernardine (2010). "Why It Matters." In: *Ten New Poets* (eds. Bernardine Evaristo and Daljit Nagra), 11–16. London and Tarset: Spread the Word/Bloodaxe.

Evaristo, Bernardine and Nagra, Daljit (eds.) (2010). *Ten: New Poets*. London and Tarset: Spread the Word/Bloodaxe.

Falci, Eric (2015). *The Cambridge Introduction to British Poetry 1945–2000*. Cambridge: CUP.

Fenton, James (2003). *An Introduction to English Poetry*. London: Penguin.

Fryer, Peter (1991). *Staying Power: The History of Black People in Britain*. London: Pluto Press.

Gilroy, Paul (1993). *The Black Atlantic: Modernity and Double Consciousness*. Cambridge: Harvard University Press.

Gilroy, Paul (2007). *Black Britain. A Photographic History*. London: SAQI.

Herbert, W. N. (2010). "Malika Booker." In: *Ten New Poets* (eds. Bernardine Evaristo and Daljit Nagra), 79–80. London and Tarset: Spread the Word/Bloodaxe.

Hoyles, Asher and Hoyles, Martin (2002). *Moving Voices: Black Performance Poetry*. London: Hansib.

Johnson, Linton Kwesi (1974). *Voices of the Living and the Dead*. London: Race Today.

Johnson, Linton Kwesi (1975). *Dread Beat An' Blood*. London: Bogle L'Ouverture.

Johnson, Linton Kwesi (1980). *Inglan Is a Bitch*. London: Race Today Publications.

Kay, Jackie (2005). *The Adoption Papers*. Highgreen: Bloodaxe.

Kean, Danuta (ed.) (2005). *Free Verse: Publishing Opportunities for Black and Asian Poets*. London: Spread the Word www.spreadtheword.org.uk/wp-content/uploads/2016/11/Free-Verse-Report.pdf.

King, Bruce (2005). *The Internationalization of English Literature*. Oxford: OUP.

Lawson Welsh, Sarah (2007). *Grace Nichols. Writers and Their Work*. Tavistock: Northcote Publishers.

Lawson Welsh, Sarah (2016). "Black British Poetry." In: *The Cambridge Companion to British Poetry 1945–2010* (ed. Edward Larrissy), 178–196. Cambridge: CUP.

Levy, Andrea (2004). *Small Island*. London: Review.

Markham, E. A. (ed.) (2001). *Hinterland: Caribbean Poetry from the West Indies and Britain*. London: Bloodaxe.

Marson, Una (2011). *Selected Poems*. Leeds: Peepal Tree Press.

McCarthy Woolf, Karen (ed.) (2014). *Ten: The New Wave*. London and Hexham: Spread the Word/Bloodaxe.

Miller, Kei (2007). *There Is an Anger That Moves*. Manchester: Carcanet.

Muldoon, Paul (1987). *Meeting the British*. London: Faber and Faber.

Murphy, Catherine (2010). "Performing, Transforming, and Changing the Question: Patience Agbabi – Poet Enough." In: *Intimate Exposure: Essays on the Public-Private Divide in British Poetry since 1950* (eds. Emily Taylor Merriman and Adrian Grafe), 67–84. Jefferson, NC and London: McFarland.

Nanton, Philip (2000). "What Does Mr. Swanzy Want – Shaping or Reflecting? An Assessment of Henry Swanzy's Contribution to the Development of Caribbean Literature." *Caribbean Quarterly* 46 (1): 61–72.

Nanton, Philip (2014). "Political Tensions and *Caribbean Voices*: The Swanzy Years 1946–1954." In: *The Routledge Companion to Anglophone Caribbean Literature* (eds. Michael A. Bucknor and Alison Donnell), 585–590. New York and London: Routledge.

Nichols, Grace (1983). *I Is a Long Memoried Woman*. London: Karnak House.

Nichols, Grace (1984). *The Fat Black Woman's Poems*. London: Virago Press.

Nichols, Grace (2010). *I Have Crossed an Ocean: Selected Poems*. Tarset: Bloodaxe.

Olusoga, David (2016). *Black and British: A Forgotten History*. London: MacMillan.

Padel, Ruth (2004). *52 Ways of Looking at a Poem*. London: Vintage.

Phillips, Mike and Phillips, Trevor (1999). *Windrush: The Irresistible Rise of Multi-Racial Britain*. London: Harper Collins.

Pollard, Velma (2000). *Dread Talk: The Language of Rastafari*. Kingston: Canoe Press.

Procter, James (2003). *Dwelling Places. Postwar Black British Writing*. Manchester and New York: Manchester University Press.

Ramazani, Jahan (2009). *A Transnational Poetics*. Chicago and London: University of Chicago Press.

Ramey, Lauri (2004). "Contemporary Black British Poetry." In: *Black British Writing* (ed. R. Victoria Arana), 109–136. New York: Palgrave MacMillan.

Robinson, Roger (2013). *The Butterfly Hotel*. Leeds: Peepal Tree Press.

Rohlehr, Gordon (1992). "The Shape of That Hurt: An Introduction to Voiceprint." In: *The Shape of That Hurt and Other Essays* (ed. Gordon Rohlehr), 164–190. Port of Spain: Longman Trinidad Ltd.

Smartt, Dorothea (2008). *Ship Shape*. Leeds: Peepal Tree Press.

Smartt, Dorothea (2014). *Reader, I Married Him & Other Queer Goings-On*. Leeds: Peepal Tree Press.

Tolan, Fiona (2010). *New Directions: Writing Post 1990*. London: York Press.

Walcott, Derek (2005). *The Prodigal*. London: Faber and Faber.

Walder, Dennis (1999). *Post-Colonial Literatures in English: History, Language, Theory*. Oxford: Blackwell Publishers.

Wójcik, Bartosz (2015). *Afro-Caribbean Poetry in English: Cultural Traditions (1970s–2000s)*. Frankfurt: Peter Lang.

2c.11
Anglo-Jewish Poetry

David Malcolm

There is a critical consensus that it is hard to define Anglo-Jewish poetry and Anglo-Jewish literature in general.[1] For example, in *Writing Jewish: Contemporary British-Jewish Literature,* Ruth Gilbert writes at length of the ambiguities and complexities of the identities of British-Jewish writers, an interweaving of strands of assertion of that identity, of denial of it, of dealing with multiple and varying definitions, of impulses toward assimilation and insistence on distinctness, and of a varying sense of contextual and contingent anti-Semitism (2013, 1–18). In 1985, Efraim Sicher asked: "Is there such a thing as Jewish poetry, or the Jewish novel, or a Jewish drama?" (x). (He went on to write a whole book on the subject; presumably the answer to his question is a qualified yes.) Bryan Cheyette points to the problematic nature of the relevant categories by quoting Hannah Wirth's judgment that to attempt to define Jewish literature, in general, is an attempt to define the indefinable; according to Cheyette, all definitions based on nation, race, ethnicity, religion, motif, and theme break down (2007, 35). In an earlier essay, Cheyette admires the "fluid and unstable" features and "the heterodox and uncategorizable nature of British-Jewish writing" (2003, 52–53), arguing that an awareness of this fluidity offers, in fact, a much more accurate account of the realities of diasporic communities and their identities, than do hypostasized and ahistorical versions of them (46–52).

In his introduction to the important anthology *Passionate Renewal: Jewish Poetry in Britain since 1945* (2001), Peter Lawson also stresses the "conflicting, multiple answers" to the question of what is Jewish poetry and Jewish poetry in English and in Britain (2001a, 1). This position is confirmed by a discussion of specific poets. When Sicher writes of Jon

Silkin's poetry, he claims that "To categorize him as a Jewish voice would, I am convinced, be a grievous misunderstanding of his work and his views" (1985, 143). He makes a similar point about the complexities of dealing with the work of Dannie Abse, Ruth Fainlight, Elaine Feinstein, "and other Jewish poets": "It is perhaps an [sic] historical paradox that Jews born in Christendom, after centuries of Christian psalmists, should write in the same uncircumcised tongue as they, yet with the timelessness of the Hebrew prophets" (150). Anglo-Jewish poetry can, indeed, be seen to be a multifarious field when Claire M. Tylee argues that Mina Loy and Denise Levertov might legitimately be included within it (2006, 15). Complexities of definition also arise when one considers the presence of Yiddish poetry in Britain in the twentieth century, for example, that of Anna Margolin, A. N. Stencl, and Joseph Leftwich. Even the great Itzak Manger lived and worked in London for some years (Lawson 2001a,b, 3).

But there is also an insistence (explicit or implicit) among commentators that some variation of the term Anglo-Jewish poetry is cognitively viable. Lawson argues that "Historical, social and cultural experiences locate British Jews [and, by extension, British-Jewish writers] in specific contexts" (2001a, 3). There is inevitably variability and universality (that is, features shared with other groups of writers), but also specifics, he suggests. He quotes Anthony Rudolf's observation from 1980 concerning Jewish writing in Britain: "There are structures of shared feeling and common perception bequeathed by a dynamic heritage: there are psychic tensions created and psychic energies released (blocked too in certain quarters) by the dialectical components of that heritage" (2001a, 6; Rudolf and Schwartz 1980, 395). In a more recent essay, Lawson concludes that "Despite received critical opinion, there does appear to be a Jewish poetry in England" (2007, 132).

Indeed, commentators point to certain recurrent features that, despite historical and social specifics, do mark Anglo-Jewish poetry. These are predominantly thematic. They are: the motif and theme of rootlessness and exile; opposition to and appropriation of elements in British literature seemingly and in fact at odds with a broadly conceived Jewishness; and a concern with the dead and the Holocaust.

Rootlessness and exile: Cheyette celebrates the "cosmopolitan impurity" of Jewish writing (2007, 48) and the "self-consciously extraterritorial realm" of Anglo-Jewish literature (including verse) (2003, 77). In the Introduction to her collection *Jewish Women Writers in Britain* (2014), Nadia Valman writes of Elaine Feinstein's interest in the early Anglo-Jewish poet Amy Levy and Levy's "experience of alienation, of living between worlds" (1), a feature of both Feinstein's own writing and that of Ruth Fainlight that Lawson stresses in an essay in the same collection when he writes of their interest in "otherness" and "in-betweenness" (2014, 145–152). Sicher writes of Jon Silkin's and Dannie Abse's "rootlessness," of Silkin's interest in the "extraterritorial" quality of Isaac Rosenberg's poetry, and of the theme of loss and exile in Silkin's work (1985, 139, 144, 146). Some eminent Jewish poets in Britain can certainly be classed as refugee poets, for example, Michael Hamburger and Karen Gershon (Sicher 1985, 157). Phyllis Lassner points to Gershon's rejection of German (her first language) to write poetry in English, an adoption of another language that Gershon herself describes as simultaneously alienating and exciting (Lassner 2008, 48–49). "We learnt language [English] from scratch," Hamburger declared in 1966 of his experience of flight and exile (quoted Sicher 1985, 157). With regard to rootlessness, Sicher claims that the state of Israel has rarely been an answer for the sense of extraterritoriality that permeates Anglo-Jewish writing (1985, 165; see also Lawson 2001a, 12–13).

Opposition and appropriation: Sicher describes Dannie Abse's editing (with Howard Sergeant) of the *Mavericks* anthology in 1957 as being "in direct opposition" to a perceived little-middle-England insularity of Robert Conquest's *New Lines* anthology of the previous year (1985, 140). Lawson argues the same (the selection of nine poets in *Mavericks* includes work by Hamburger and Silkin, as well as by Abse himself), and he discusses in the same context Elaine Feinstein's rejection of the Movement's "Englishness" and her interest in more cosmopolitan and experimental poets (2007, 130–131). Cheyette, too, sees Silkin, Abse, and Feinstein writing against "received discourses of the nation state" (presumably Britain here), although also against those "of religion, race and ethnicity" (2003, 53). Appropriation may also be seen as a kind of qualified resistance, and I have already noted in the earlier text Sicher's argument that Abse, Fainlight, and Feinstein re-appropriate the language of the English translations of the Hebrew psalms for their own purposes as Anglo-Jewish writers (1985, 150). Lawson, too, notes an appropriation and a rendering Jewish of the local and English in Silkin's, Abse's, and Feinstein's work (6–8).

Death and the Holocaust: Inevitably, critics argue, these loom very large in modern Anglo-Jewish poetry. Sicher points to the importance of *kaddish* in Silkin's poetry, especially in his York poems ("The Coldness," "Resting Place," and "The Malabestia"). Directly concerned with an anti-Semitism embedded and occluded in England's past, these poems enunciate "an accusing absence which touches directly on the Holocaust" (1985, 147). In 1966, Hamburger declared that he is writing "for the horror-stricken. For those abandoned to butchery. For survivors" (quoted Sicher 1985, 157). All Anglo-Jewish writers, Sicher argues, "have been moved by the Holocaust into re-examining Jewish identity" (1985, 163). The title of Lassner's chapter on Feinstein in her 2008 study of Anglo-Jewish women writers is "Elaine Feinstein's Holocaust Imagination" (129–155), in which the genocide perpetrated against the Jews of Europe is seen to permeate Feinstein's verse and prose.

Despite the specificity of reference of the above to Jewish experience, commentators also note a transcendence and a universality within Anglo-Jewish poetry. For example, with regard to Fainlight's work, Lawson argues that "From her earliest writings, Fainlight has pronounced her faith in art as a place of transcendent calm that offers the consolations of a (non-Judaic) religion" (2014, 142; see also 145). In *Passionate Renewal*, Lawson writes both of specifically Jewish concerns but also of the presence of universal ones in Anglo-Jewish poetry (2001a, 3, 6). Sicher notes that Silkin attempts to be both specifically Jewish and yet also universal in his work (1985, 148–149).

In what follows, I offer an analysis of six poems by six Anglo-Jewish poets, Gerda Mayer, Karen Gershon, Ruth Fainlight, Dannie Abse, Michael Hamburger, and Jon Silkin. The poems of the first four address Jewish concerns head on, however universal these may ultimately be. Hamburger and Silkin are more overtly universal, although the Jewish references in their texts are strongly present and link them closely with the first group. Other poets and other poems might have been included in my discussion, but I believe the overall picture of Anglo-Jewish poetry would not be substantially different were that so.

Gerda Mayer's "Make Believe" appears in the collection *A Heartache of Grass* (1988, 48). It concludes the volume, thus taking a semantically privileged place in it. The title and the poem's endnote clearly announce its subject. It is an act of imagination relating to the speaker's (the author's) father, a victim of Nazi persecution, and, likely, Soviet persecution too. It is in part an attempt to bring him back to some kind of life. The text is neatly and precisely composed: two stanzas of six lines are followed by a two-line stanza, and then another six-line stanza is followed by a two-line unit. The poem breaks down in terms of focus into two larger units. The opening stanza, with its repeated "Say," merges into a second and a third stanza that develop the conditionality of the opening and realize it ("Quite dapper you stand" [l. 13]). The second larger unit explains why the speaker/author insists on her name, date, and place of birth: she imagines her father's not being dead and his reading her poems, knowing them to be hers. This section ends with an emotional appeal, "write to me father" (l. 23), an appeal that the poem informs us is fruitless (the father would be nearly a hundred, and he is almost certainly dead).

The poem is without rhymes, with little phonological orchestration (except recurrent /s/ sounds in stanza one), and line length is variable (from five through eleven syllables). However, variable line length is semantically loaded: the longer lines do stand out—"and say you were idly turning the pages" (l. 6), the biographical note and appeal at the poem's end (ll. 21–22), and even lines 10–12, which complete the act of denial of the father's death. Further, one of the strong organizing principles of the poem is syntactic parallelism. Stanza 1 is shaped by a repeated "Say" structure; stanza two by three parallel structures—"The blood ... the tears ... the earth," "neither ... nor," and "a friend of a friend of a friend." In stanzas three and four, parallelism is limited, but it is limited to the crucial "the year of my birth, / the name of my hometown" (ll. 19–20). A further element of organization lies in the number of main stresses per line. Most lines have two or three main stresses. The clear exceptions are again crucial: the culminating conditional of line 6 ("and say you were idly turning the pages") and the culmination of the whole poem that is biographical note and appeal rolled into one.

"Make Believe" is a powerful poem in which considerable craft is used (*nota bene* in a language that Mayer learned as a teenager—can we see this as an act of appropriation?) to build a complex utterance. Syntactic parallelism organizes the imaginary reviving of the father, only to shift to the unaccommodated drabness of the hopeless repeating of biographical information, and an equally hopeless appeal to the dead, crushed by the prose of an endnote.

The motifs of exile and absence, and a technical subtlety similar to Mayer's poem, mark Karen Gershon's "Home" (Lawson 2001a, b, 102). The title is initially reassuring, but becomes fraught with ambiguity and danger in the course of the poem. Home (Britain most likely, although it is not specified) is not the subject's home, not really. Her parents' home became a place of death. Had the speaker stayed there, she would have died too. Disruptions of the seemingly safe and orderly organize the poem. On one level, it appears an ordered and regular piece. It consists of two symmetrical eight-line stanzas. The thematic composition is logical: stanza 1 sets out the subject's present situation, her fears as "a German Jew" (l. 7); stanza 2 explains why she has such fears—past betrayal, indifference, and violence. Line length and number of main stresses per line are homogeneous. Eleven out of 16 lines have eight syllables each; the remaining five lines have seven syllables each. Lines either have three or four main stresses. Most lines could be scanned as predominantly iambic, and several must be so counted: for example, line 5, "that every time she leaves her home," and line 10, "she cannot think their future safe," fall naturally into iambic tetrameters.

However, there is much in this poem that is eerily disruptive. Home is not home, and is not safe. Neighbors turn out to be murderous. On a technical level, a purely iambic scansion of some lines is not possible. For example, line 3 begins with an anapest ("and behave"), line 4 ("one of them") begins with an amphimacer (/x/), and lines 6–8 each begins with a stressed syllable. Several lines look like iambic lines, but such a scansion would be metronomic and artificial, involving placing stresses on syllables that cannot legitimately be so accented. For example, to scan line 1 as an iambic tetrameter involves accenting the function word "have"; to maintain iambic consistency in lines 6 and 8, one would have to accent unstressed syllables in "terrified" and "enemies"; and should one really stress "who" in line 10, and omit the natural stress on "cared" and shift it to "what" in line 13 (as metronomic reading requires)?

Further, the poem, while certainly having an orderly and consistent rhyme scheme, operates with what are predominantly weak rhymes. In fact, there are only two full rhymes in the poem, the strategically placed lines 2 and 4 ("grow / know") and lines 14 and 16 ("played / stayed"). Other rhymes are of the order of "her / were," the anisobaric "sees / enemies," and "safe / life." At times, rhyming becomes opaque: does line 10 "own" rhyme with line 12 "home," and does that "home" also rhyme with line 13 "them"? Certainly, technically the poem is deeply destabilized. Fear, rootlessness, and otherness are enacted in the interplay of order and disorder, regularity and irregularity. Death, menace, and the Holocaust are present in the poem's disturbed rhythms and rhymes.

Memory and loss also permeate Ruth Fainlight's "Keeper" (Lawson 2001a,b, 71). The speaker lists objects that have belonged to members of her family, which are now in her possession. This suggests that these relatives, close ones, mother, father, aunt, perhaps a brother (Harry), a cousin, a grandfather, are now dead. From line 14, the speaker gives her response to the objects: an awareness of circumstance that changes how one sees a photograph (l. 14), recognition of self and non-recognition of self in a mirror (l. 16, 19), and a mixture of "joy / and anger" and an uncertainty whether to "cherish or destroy" the objects (ll. 22–24). There is a worn quality about them: "broken earrings," "faded suitcase," and "speckled mirror" (l. 3, 10, 18). For the reader (but not for the speaker), the objects have a mystery about them. They seem random, arbitrary, incoherent survivals (a lamp, a bookcase, books, plus fours, and so on). The fate of those to whom they belonged is unknown (to the reader), except inasmuch as all are most likely dead.

Dissociation, disjunction, and uncertainty are enacted technically in the poem. Despite regular stanza divisions, this text is best seen as a piece of relatively free verse. The number of syllables per line, and hence line length, seems unconstrained by any metrical pattern. There is no traditional guiding model. Further, lines vary substantially in length, having between four and nine syllables. Lines mostly contain three or four main stresses, but there is variation from two to five stresses. There are also several lines in which the number of accents is unresolved: for example, line 4, "Aunt Ann's crackle-glass lamp" (four or five stresses?); line 9, "those plaid plus-fours" (two or three?), line 17, "break through the surface" (two or three?); line 21, "claims me as its keeper" (two or three?); and line 23, "and anger I'm not sure whether" (three or four?). Enjambment is present between lines 2 and 3, lines 20 and 21, and lines 23 and 24. Even where it is uncertain whether there is strict enjambment, there is a mismatch of syntax and line: for example, the break between stanzas 4 and 5, in which an item from the list moves to the response section of the poem, knocking its 12–12 line symmetry askew. Other examples are: the syntactical straddling of stanzas 6 and 7; the syntactical movement in lines 16–19, in which subject is kept from verb, noun from qualifying phrase, and first clause from second in a compound sentence. This dissociation is evident in the key lines 22–23: "joy / and anger." The odd disjunctions of the text are made evident, too, in its drift toward rhyme at the end, rhyming that, in part, is disrupted by a stanza break. Thus, suddenly after an absence of rhyme, lines 21 and 23 almost rhyme in their homoioteleuton "keeper / whether," and lines 22 and 24 rise to a full rhyme in "joy / destroy."

Is "Keeper" a Jewish poem? The experience told of and enacted is surely a general one. But the author's identification and self-identification as Jewish is of importance, as, too, is the sinister irresolution of the circumstances and history of the objects. What might have happened to Cousin Fanny, why does the speaker feel "joy / and anger," and why does it seem that she is the sole keeper of these random and often damaged objects?

Anti-Semitism and gentile collusion or indifference, which are the circumstances of the three poems discussed in the earlier text, form the central subject matter of Dannie Abse's "After the Release of Ezra Pound" (Lawson 2001a,b, 23–24). But while Mayer's, Gershon's, and Fainlight's texts are private and reflective pieces, Abse's is a ferociously public poem, nominally addressed to a friend, but surely public rhetoric directed to a wider audience. (An equivalent and earlier text is Emanuel Litvinoff's "To T. S. Eliot" from 1952.) The occasion of the text is Ezra Pound's release from St. Elizabeths Hospital in 1958, despite his unrepentant anti-Semitic and Fascist affiliations. The poem is inspired by a gentile friend's invoking poets' and a thinker's forgiveness for Pound. The speaker of "After the Release of Ezra Pound" is having none of this exoneration. The poem is organized around the gentile world's ignoring or taking lightly Pound's release, and attempting to exculpate the old Fascist (stanzas 1, 2, half of 4, and 5). This is interwoven with the speaker's address to his (gentle) gentile friend (stanzas 3, 4, 6, and 8). A Jewish response to the matter—"But the circumcised did not laugh" (stanza 4, l. 17), "the raw Jewish cry" (stanza 5, l. 20)—and the speaker's own answer—the writers invoked would not have minced words (stanza 8, ll. 32–36)—set up an unambiguous contrast. Indeed, contrast runs throughout the whole text: sordid Soho, "immaculate" Zwemmer's (l. 16), fashionable coffee-bar philosophy, beautiful poetry, on the one hand, and blood, rage, and the camps, on the other.

The text is shaped as a piece of powerful public rhetoric—free verse (for which Pound was a tireless advocate) with stanzas of varying lengths (two to six lines), lines of varying lengths (eight to thirteen syllables) and varying numbers of main stresses (three to five)—a poem that simulates the flexibility of the spoken voice. But part of its rhetorical force comes from an intense sound orchestration, both general and local. One example must suffice. Note the sound patterning of the first stanza (ll. 1–5).

In Soho's square mile of unoriginal sin	/s/ /l/
where the fraudulent neon lights haunt,	/l/ /ɒ/ /h/
but cannot hide, the dinginess of vice,	/h/ /s/
the jeans and sweater boys spoke of Pound,	/s/ and /z/ /p/ /n/
and you, Paul, repeated your question.	/p/ /s/ /n/

The assonantal pattern of "mile/lights/hide/vice" is also worth pointing out here. The bardic dimension of this text, a fusion of Hebrew prophets, Welsh bards, Anglo-Saxon poetry, and Dylan Thomas, is inescapable. Abse answers the question from the heart of poetic tradition, not just from the indifferent heart of Soho and the raw heart of Jewry.

Mayer's, Gershon's, Fainlight's, and Abse's poems can be seen overtly to address Jewish matters, no matter how general the subjects of their poems may also be (loss, memory, historical cruelty, ignorant indifference). Michael Hamburger's "The Road" (published among "Dream Poems, 1961–1994" and dated 1961 in his *Collected Poems, 1941–1994* [1995, 437]) aims at a generality, which ultimately does touch on the concerns of many Anglo-Jewish writers. The road itself is a widespread symbol for movement through life and into the future, for escape and adventure. Indeed, Hamburger draws on this connotation. The road begins in a visionary landscape and leads "without end" (l. 5) into a more vivid and intense space. But the speaker is "detained" (l. 14); it is "the question" (l. 6) whether he can go further, for there are "frontiers" (l. 8) and he will be "detained" by an unspecified "new nation / Of displaced persons" (ll. 15–16). This nation will engage him in fruitless projects. "If only I could move on" (l. 24) he sadly says, as opposed to the repeated "Always" (l. 6, 14) of his doubt and prevention.

The free verse of the text is organized by that repeated "Always" and its sad answering "If only," but also by a syntactic parallelism of its two mirroring parts: the more intense landscape of possibility and that of detention. Lines 8–13 present this visionary escape, the syntax made even more intense by a clustering of alliteration (/m/ and /d/) in lines 10–13. Beyond the frontiers and limits are, indeed, "wilder, more alien countries" (l. 25). Lines 17–23 are also organized round the parallelisms of contrasting limitation: the parallel relative clauses "Who ..." and "Whose ..." (ll. 17–18) and the parallel clauses of "needed," "appealed," "involved," and "charged" (ll. 19–23). The speaker is torn between the intense freedom of lines 8–13 and the sterile but, it seems, unavoidable detention of lines 16–23. The poem's end is a very negative second conditional.

Such an existential situation is quite universal and Hamburger draws on this to produce a powerful poem of general resonance. But the Jewish markers in the text are also clear: there is the Holy Land south and east of Venice, as well as the Central European and Balkan world of the Jewish diaspora; a "new nation / Of displaced persons" surely suggests European Jewry, especially after 1945; "missions / To friends whom I never reached" (ll. 22–23) calls up the dead and lost of the Holocaust.

Some of Jon Silkin's poetry directly addresses Jewish subjects ("Resting Place," for example); other poems do not at all ("A Hand," for example). His "Flower Poems" (published in *Nature with Man* [1965]—see Silkin 1993, 66–67), however, present examples of fine poems that seem to be on a subject that is not particularly Jewish, but which under the surface take on a particular coloration. The poem "Moss" from this sequence is a case in point. Silkin's typical free verse, with its peculiar mixture of the colloquial and the vatic—"Patents will burn it out" (l. 1) and "With what does it propagate?" (l. 16)—sets out a strikingly paradoxical vision of moss. In stanza 1, it "shelters on the soil," yet "quilts it" (l. 2). It is animal-like, fungoid, not quite vegetable, mushroom and kidney at once. In stanza 2, the reader learns that one kind of moss has tiny flowers, so "minute" that they can seem "wide" (l. 14). In stanza 3, the speaker talks of moss spreading in quiet, in damp, in dark, in hidden and unattractive places. It does not produce "Defined creatures"—"It hovers tentatively between one life and another" (ll. 26–27). It "spreads only its kind – / A soft stone" (ll. 29–30). This last description is as paradoxical as earlier ones, and the contrary nature of moss is emphasized further when one learns that it "is passive," but that it "spreads wildly" (l. 33). It is "immune to nothing," although it seems resilient. It is beyond "misery" (ll. 34–35).

The final designation ("You cannot speak of misery to it" [l. 35]) pushes one to an anthropomorphic reading of the moss. On one level, the poem is an insightful attempt to capture the appearance and nature of a natural phenomenon, but, as in the other "Flower Poems,"[2] the plants discussed become metaphors for certain aspects of humanity. Here the moss's in-between status, its survival in unconsidered environments, its vulnerability, its resistance, its being beyond misery must suggest various discourses that have been attached to Jews over many centuries.

Despite difficulties in defining Anglo-Jewish poetry, it does seem possible to see recurrent concerns that are enacted varyingly in powerful poems by writers who can be designated Anglo-Jewish. The themes of rootlessness, death, absence, and resistance run throughout the poems discussed in the earlier text. There is a constant reference to Jewish matters, even when the poems (as in the case of Hamburger's and Silkin's) are most universal or furthest from those matters.

Notes

1 In this essay, I am disinclined to become tied up in the complexities of varying qualifiers such as Anglo-Jewish or British-Jewish, or, indeed, British and English, although in some contexts such discussion might be relevant and useful.

2 Moss is, of course, not a flower.

References

Cheyette, Bryan (2003). "Diasporas of the Mind: British Jewish Writing Beyond Multiculturalism." In: *Diaspora and Multiculturalism: Common Traditions and New Development* (ed. Monika Fludernik), 45–82. Amsterdam and New York: Rodopi.

Cheyette, Brian (2007). "On Being a Jewish Critic." In: *Anglophone Jewish Literature* (ed. Axel Stähler), 31–48. London and New York: Routledge.

Gilbert, Ruth (2013). *Writing Jewish: Contemporary British-Jewish Literature*. Basingstoke: Palgrave Macmillan.

Hamburger, Michael (1995). *Collected Poems, 1941–1994*. London: Anvil Press Poetry.

Lassner, Phyllis (2008). *Anglo-Jewish Women Writing the Holocaust: Displaced Witnesses*. Basingstoke: Palgrave Macmillan.

Lawson, Peter (2001a). "Introduction." In: *Passionate Renewal: Jewish Poetry in Britain since 1945—An Anthology* (ed. Peter Lawson), 1–20. Nottingham: Five Leaves/European Jewish Publication Society.

Lawson, Peter (ed.) (2001b). *Passionate Renewal: Jewish Poetry in Britain since 1945—An Anthology*. Nottingham: Five Leaves/European Jewish Publication Society.

Lawson, Peter (2007). "Otherness and Affiliation in Anglo-Jewish Poetry." In: *Anglophone Jewish Literature* (ed. Axel Stähler), 123–132. London and New York: Routledge.

Lawson, Peter (2014). "Otherness and Transcendence: The Poetry of Ruth Fainlight and Elaine Feinstein." In: *Jewish Women Writers in Britain* (ed. Nadia Valman), 135–155. Detroit: Wayne State University Press.

Mayer, Gerda (1988). *A Heartache of Grass*. Calstock, Cornwall: Peterloo Poets.

Rudolf, Anthony and Schwartz, Howard (eds.) (1980). *Voices within the Ark: The Modern Jewish Poets*. New York: Avon.

Sicher, Efraim (1985). *Beyond Marginality: Anglo-Jewish Literature after the Holocaust*. Albany: SUNY Press.

Silkin, Jon (1993). *Selected Poems*. London: Sinclair-Stevenson.

Tylee, Clare M. (2006). "Introduction." In: *"In the Open": Jewish Women Writers and British Culture* (ed. Clare M. Tylee), 11–25. Newark: University of Delaware Press.

Valman, Nadia (2014). "Feeling at Home: Jewish Women Writers in Britain, 1830–2010." In: *Jewish Women Writers in Britain* (ed. Nadia Valman), 1–9. Detroit: Wayne State University Press.

2c.12
Gay and Lesbian Poetry

Prudence Chamberlain

Introduction

More so than other identity categories within the United Kingdom, lesbians and gays have witnessed significant social and political change between 1960 and 2015. In fact, the 55-year period has not only included the decriminalization of homosexual sex acts, but also the introduction of civil partnerships, and equal marriage. Unfortunately, in spite of this legislative progress, discrimination and anti-gay violence is still rife. It is unsurprising then that wider social and cultural change is reflected in the body of poetry emerging from the identity category. Lesbian and gay poetry not only reflects identity, but implicitly and explicitly comments on the context from which it emerges.

Addressing lesbian and gay poetry as a whole, one must recognize that the two identities are not interchangeable. The intersections of gender and sexuality have ensured that the social and cultural aspects of gays and lesbians have developed in significantly different ways. Men, historically, have occupied a more privileged and public social position, while women are still fighting for equality. That said, it is male homosexuality, as opposed to lesbianism, that has been historically targeted in repressive legislation. Consequently, while gays and lesbians share similarly marginalized statuses, there are marked differences between their experiences of the last 55 years. That said, the two identities have shared one experience; their marginalization has resulted in their absence or lack of documentation. As David and Christine Kennedy write in their introduction to *Women's Experimental Poetry in Britain 1970–2010: Body, Time and Locale*, "it's all too easy to see literary criticism, like history, as a great forgetting" (2013, 5). It is therefore necessary to track lineages of LGBT poetry in an aim to remedy the "great forgetting" of literary criticism.

The question arises, then, of how best to define lesbian and gay poetry in order to write a comprehensive survey of its development. Labeling poetry as lesbian and gay could be read as an anti-universal gesture; the poems are positioned as purely representative of a subculture. While this chapter hopes to contest this understanding of the "universal," it will look exclusively to poets who are lesbian and gay-identified, and make reference to this identification throughout their work. This is not to suggest that the poems are autobiographical, but that the poets in question have an investment in the public recognition of homosexuality. There is no single "gay" or "lesbian" poetics to reflect the identities' developing social presence, but the works selected here do express same-sex desire, establish community, and engage with contemporary issues.

No Smoke Without You My Fire: Cruising Culture and Decriminalization

In 1967, England decriminalized homosexuality, a ruling which took longer to achieve in Northern Ireland, Ireland, and Scotland, where the same law was not passed until 1982, 1993, and 1980, respectively. The years that preceded legalization had cultivated a culture of cruising that thrived on anonymity and brief encounters. In fact, in *Radical Records: Thirty Years of Lesbian and Gay History, 1957–1987* (1988), Allan Horsfall writes that a gay man had to learn to "never reveal his name or address, never to discuss how he earned his living or where he worked, never to take anybody to his home" (17).

In 1968, Edwin Morgan (1920–2010), a Scottish poet, published *The Second Life* (1968), in which he documents the frustration and danger of street encounters. Indeed, Horsfall states that "there could hardly have been a less satisfactory basis for a social or sexual existence, but it was soundly rooted by a practiced awareness of the risks" (Horsfall, 1988, 18), all of which are made clear in Morgan's poem "Glasgow Green" (1968, 37–38). In the poem, Morgan evokes the danger of illicit nights in the city, exploring a specific encounter in Scottish dialect:

> Christ but I'm gaun have you Mac
> if it takes all night, turn over you bastard
> turn over, I'll –
>
> (ll. 16–18)

Despite the evident violence, Morgan writes "there's no crying for help" (l. 19), which speaks to the necessity of covert meetings and silent encounters.

In *Beyond the Last Dragon* (2010), Morgan's friend and biographer James McGonigal writes that Morgan "came to see 'Glasgow Green' as a plea for some kind of acceptance, a gay liberation poem written before that term had been invented" (95). Certainly, Morgan's poem asks the reader "And how shall these men live?" (l. 31), if they are confined to street encounters and loveless marriages. *The Second Life*, however, also offers some room for hope, with the inclusion of a number of romantic poems such as "One Cigarette," in which the smoke is "a signal / of so much love" (ll. 5–6), contrasting starkly with the cigarette that "glows and fades on a cough" (l. 2) in "Glasgow Green." Unlike the darkness of "Glasgow Green," which is the cover for cruising and violence, in "One Cigarette" (1968, 63) the speaker extinguishes the light, and, lying in the dark, breathes "long past midnight, your last kiss" (l. 17). The genderless "you" and "I" in the poem ensure that Morgan's work is not coded as heterosexual or homosexual, but offers instead an insight into intimacy and love.

The Love That Dares to Speak Its Name: The Gay Liberation Front

In England, the Gay Liberation Front was founded in 1970 but split in 1972, when the majority of lesbians established a splinter group that acknowledged gender oppression. The women involved felt that gay men were not addressing their male privilege in the shared struggle for equal rights. In spite of the divisions within the gay and lesbian movement, the 1970s was generally a decade of progress, with the first Gay Pride hosted in 1972, and Gay's the Word, the United Kingdom's only dedicated gay and lesbian bookshop, opening in 1979. Furthermore, The Gay and Lesbian Switchboard was established in 1979, to respond to telephone calls from people in the process of coming out, or looking to participate more fully in the community.

It is no surprise, then, that gay and lesbian poets were expressing their identities more openly. In 1976, *Gay News* published James Kirkup's poem "The Love That Dares to Speak Its Name," in which a centurion has sex with Christ's body following his crucifixion. Gesturing to Oscar Wilde, the title of the poem makes it evident that homosexuality will no longer be silent or shameful. Written in regular stanzas of six lines, the narrative explores a soldier making love to the recently dead Jesus, with references to the licking of wounds and penetration with spears. The poem is simultaneously blasphemous and erotic, with continual allusions to ejaculation.

> his dear, broken body all open wounds,
> and in each wound his side, his back,
> his mouth—I came and came and came
> (ll. 40–42)

In addition to its invocation of gay sex acts, Kirkup's poem makes an appeal to a wider audience, likening the suffering of homosexuals to that of Christ:

> - This is the passionate and blissful crucifixion
> same-sex lovers suffer, patiently and gladly.
> (ll. 49–50)

The poem's publication resulted in much controversy, and the editor of the *Gay Times*, Denis Lemon, was found guilty of blasphemy and sentenced to 9 months' suspended imprisonment and fined £500, publisher Gay News Limited was fined £1,000. Both the gay and lesbian communities, united by a shared investment in anti-censorship, responded supportively, with lesbian poet Maureen Duffy writing "The Ballad of the Blasphemy Trial," first published in *The Freethinker* in August 1977 and included in *Memorials of the Quick and the Dead* (1979). In her poem, Duffy defends the rights of poets to use historical and mythical symbols, writing "at the call of a poet / each must rise and come / and only one law is god here / they must be true to their name" (ll. 13–16). In regular quartets and a rhyme scheme ABCB, Duffy places Jesus and Socrates in dialogue with one another to condemn the short-sightedness of persecutors. Duffy, herself, had been out of the closet before legalization. Her work had always expressed same-sex desire, addressing the female body of a lover explicitly, evident in collections such as *Venus Touch* (1971) and *Evesong* (1975).

During this time, there were a number of gay and lesbian poets writing who were less explicit about their sexual preferences. U. A. Fanthorpe, who published her first collection *Side Effects* in 1978, addressed both sexuality and love in subversive and understated poems. Focusing on domestic settings, and moments of quietly shared intimacy, Fanthorpe created a body of writing that celebrated long-term partnership. In her book, *Acts of Resistance: The Poetry of U. A. Fanthorpe* (2009), Elizabeth Sandie writes that "it is hard to imagine what growing up in the repressive age of the early to mid-twentieth century would have felt like for Fanthorpe who was born in the year of the trial of Marguerite Radclyffe Hall's *The Well of Loneliness*" (106). This sentiment is best exemplified by "7301" and "Elegy for a Cat." The first documents "learning to hide / The sudden shining naked looks of love" (ll. 5–6), as well as thinking, "The rest of our lives, the rest of our lives / Doing perfectly ordinary things together" (ll. 7–8). The poem acknowledges the necessity of hiding the looks of love, while also celebrating the beauty of engaging in the ordinary, performing the actions of a typical couple, despite being invisible to a larger world. Similarly, the final stanza of "Elegy for a Cat" explores the simplicity of being a cohabiting couple.

> You who saw love, where innocent others
> Saw only convenience.
> (ll. 46–47)

Despite the advances in legislation during the 1970s, and what appeared to be a will toward public organization and visibility, a number of lesbian and gay-identified poets were continuing with life as usual, enjoying long-term relationships that did not garner the same celebration or recognition as their heterosexual counterparts.

I Stare at Death in the Mirror: Regressive 1980s and the AIDS Crisis

The 1980s could be described as the era of backlash, in which the organization and seeming progress of the 1970s was undone. On April 10, 1984, Gay's The Word, London's LGBT bookstore established in 1979, had allegedly "pornographic" stock—all imported titles—confiscated by Customs and Excise officers ("Operation Tiger") (Bryant 2009). The office of *Capital Gay* (1981–1995), London's free gay newspaper, was firebombed in December 1987. The Thatcher period also saw the passing of Section 28 in 1988, which prohibited the promotion of homosexuality by local authorities. In spite of this, there were a number of important developments in consolidating lesbian and gay communities. Between 1984 and 1985, eleven LGSM groups raised £11,000 to support the striking miners, while in 1987 and 1988, Thatcher's new legislation inspired a protest movement, Stop the Clause. In 1989, Stonewall, a charitable organization still running today, was established with the aim of reversing Section 28.

A number of feminist presses had been established in the 1970s, including Onlywomen Press (1974), The Women's Press (1978), and Sheba Feminist Press (1980). During the 1980s, these presses published a number of anthologies, such as *Hard Words and Why Lesbians Have to Say Them* (Onlywomen Press, 1979), *Dancing the Tightrope: New Love Poems by Women* (The Women's Press, 1987), *Naming The Waves: Contemporary Lesbian Poetry* (Virago Press, 1988), among others. These works collected lesbian feminist writing in one place, consolidating a sense of community through and within the body of poetry itself. In *Beautiful Barbarians* (1986), editor Lilian Mohin writes that "lesbians work toward significant change, develop skills and politics in what feels like isolation. With this book, I hope to make more public (some of) the continuing growth of lesbian strengths and perceptions" (Mohin 1986, 7–8). For Mohin, collecting lesbian poetry is intrinsically linked to politics and creating wider communities. The work is considered, particularly in *Beautiful Barbarians*, to be politically engaged by virtue of the doubly marginalized identity of woman and lesbian. Furthermore, the "making public" of such experience is considered a necessary form of activism, giving legitimate voice and a platform to otherwise overlooked members of society.

The AIDS crisis had a great impact on the lesbian and gay community, arguably uniting the two against increasing homophobia. While some contend that this moment in history led to the rise of homonormativity, with an emphasis on becoming "acceptable" within straight culture, it also marked a historical moment of unity. Throughout this period, there were several individual male poets considering the illness, as well as AIDS/HIV-themed anthologies being published by gay presses. However, gay poetry as a whole was limited by the epidemic. As poet and critic Gregory Woods claims, "some of our most promising writers have been lost to AIDS" (Woods 2003, 26).

The greatest loss Woods identifies is that of Adam Johnson, whose *Collected Poems* (2003) was published posthumously by Carcanet. In the afterword, Neil Powell writes that after his diagnosis, Johnson wrote about his illness with great urgency: "by then he had learnt the power of reticence and decorum, so that the poems simultaneously address the universal theme of man confronting his own mortality" (Powell 2003, 85). The poet always addresses his sexuality openly, with poems such as "It Is What We Wanted, Isn't It?" and "Leather Guise," both celebrating same-sex encounters and culture, where "being gay is a serious business / when you're a leather man" (ll. 26–27). "The Playground Bell" and "Poem on St. Patrick's Day" are the most reflective on impending death. In the former, Johnson writes: "I went out every night / Picked and up stayed wherever there was drink / With men whose names were last thing on my mind" (ll. 2–4). He also describes his first trip to Heaven, a famous gay bar under Charing Cross, and S&M experimentation in Amsterdam. These incidents and experiences lapse into a more reflective engagement with death, with the final stanza stating, "I stare at death in a mirror behind the bar / And wonder when I sacrificed my blood" (ll. 68–69). "Poem on St. Patrick's Day" is even more reflective, using the space of the familiar bed to demonstrate how the ill body no longer has a natural place among the living. The poem ends with the stanza:

> So, while I can get out,
> I'll go down in the light
> Of a new season,
> To where you are dancing.
> (ll. 19–24)

Giving a Fuck: AIDS Anthologies and Mainstream Success

In 1994, after "more than a dozen years into the epidemic, with no cure in sight," (Anthony and Daniels 1994, 7), the Oscars Press published *Jugular Defences: An AIDS Anthology*. The Oscars Press was a London-based small publisher of exclusively gay and lesbian poetry, operating with financial support from the London Arts Board. The introduction raises a number of useful questions with regard to the place of poetry within communities, suggesting it responds to "the need for solace in the nightmare, for ritual and elegy" (Anthony and Daniels 1994, 8). Ultimately, for the two editors, "what matters is that a poem needs to be written. Here are poets cutting through the niceties of contemporary verse with its schools and theories because they have something to do" (Anthony and Daniels 1994, 8). The poems, thus, are positioned as an absolute necessity, in which a community is no longer divided into theoretical or location-based subgroups, but converges to produce a collection that stands in solidarity. The poems range from the explicit and visceral, preoccupied with the infected body, to the highly medical and technical, and to simple love poems. The multiplicity of texts demonstrates the ways in which members of a diverse community respond to tragedy, while still creating links with each other.

The gay and lesbian poetry scene of the 1990s was not exclusively defined by the AIDS crisis. At that time, Jackie Kay, a half-Nigerian, half-Scottish lesbian poet who became the current Scottish makar, or national poet, in 2016, and Carol Ann Duffy, a bisexual Northern poet, were both writing prolifically and winning awards. The women were also, incidentally, a couple, whose split led to the production of Kay's *Life Mask* (2005) and Duffy's T. S. Eliot Prize winning *Rapture* (2005). In her debut collection, *The Adoption Papers* (1991), the Scottish First Book of the Year Award, Kay uses three voices to explore the roles of child, adoptive mother, and biological mother in the process of adoption. *Other Lovers* (1993) and *Off Colour* (1998) were similarly concerned with aspects of identity, with Kay addressing the themes of race and Scottish identity, lesbianism and relationships, and drawing on the categories in which she is placed to create nuanced and universally emotional work. By 1990, Duffy had won a Somerset Maugham Award (1988) and a Scottish

Arts Council Book Award (1990) for *Selling Manhattan* (1987) and *The Other Country* (1990), respectively. Her real success, however, was with her fourth collection *Mean Time* (1993), which received the Forward Prize for Best Collection, the Whitbread Prize for Poetry, and an award from the Scottish Arts Council.

I've Dignified a House of Ill-Repute: The Twenty-First Century and Social Acceptance

Despite political progress, and a number of lesbian and gay writers represented within the poetry world, inequality has continued into the twenty-first century. Carol Ann Duffy was appointed as Britain's first bisexual poet laureate in 2009, having previously lost out on the role to Andrew Motion, in part on account of her sexuality (Flood 2009). Certainly, a ruling in 2000 that allowed gays and lesbians to serve in the military, in addition to the 2004 Civil Partnership Bill, means that the inequality once associated with gay and lesbian identities has been less evident socially and politically. In fact, legislation has changed, so that every normative social institution welcomes homosexuals, necessitating less of an investment in counter culture.

However, in the Autumn 2003 edition of *Magma*, dedicated entirely to poetry on same-sex relationships, Gregory Woods offered a different view on homosexuality and poetry in his essay "Other Avenues." Responding to a review of one of his anthologies, Woods writes, "[t]he suggestion is that a poet like me writes pornography, and that the only kind of reader who could possibly like my poetry is one who masturbates to it—necessarily, therefore, a gay man" (2003, 23). Addressing another critic, who reviewed his 2002 published *The District Commissioner's Dreams*, Woods writes that "the idea that gay experience might have something to teach us all [...] does not even remotely occur to him. It is not his experience, so he is not interested" (2003, 23). Woods's essay, which is appropriately outraged, gives a cynical insight into the operations of the poetry world with regard to sexuality. Homosexuality, when expressed explicitly or made evident within poems, immediately demarcates the work as "niche," solely intended for perusal by a specific minority group. The fact that heterosexual experience is still so strongly considered as the "universal," while gay love poems can have no relevance to non-gays, resonates with Wood's claim that "in literary criticism, gay deaths can be identified with by straight men, but gay love cannot" (2003, 25).

Liz Yorke poses yet more problematic questions in her essay "British Lesbian Poetics: A Brief Exploration" (1999). She asks, "In a post-feminist, post-lesbian feminist, postmodern or queer world, should lesbian work remain clearly identifiable, even when it refuses to claim lesbian 'identity' as such?" (Yorke 1999, 80). As such, it might be more fruitful to consider the idea of "queerness" in relation to poetry. While it still creates a relationship between sexuality and poetic practice, the queer relates to resistance to normative practices and mainstream assimilation. *Chroma: A Queer Literary Journal* (2004–2010), and events such as Polari, an LGBT literary salon hosted by Paul Burston, engage with and embrace this widening of the lesbian and gay category to include more divergent identities. Queerness, while acknowledging that sexuality is a spectrum intrinsically linked to social order and political contexts, also enacts a refusal to be co-opted in the expression of identity. In her essay "Queer Poetry by Definition" (2012), Cherry Smyth defines queer as a term that "eschewed the positive imagery campaigns that attempted to make gay and lesbian 'lifestyles' more acceptable to the hetero mainstream, and developed a strategy that was unapologetic, sexual and raging" (Smyth 2012, 10).

Outside the mainstream, queer poetics thrive within the avant-garde, partly on account of their (queer poetics') openness and fluidity. Indeed, as Smyth states, queer poetry itself is resistant to definition. She asks: "[i]s it defined by same-sex object choice, by self-appellation, by its reader, its LGBT themes, its confrontational erotics and / or its language and aesthetics?" (Smyth 2012, 1). Sophie Mayer, poet and film scholar, also addresses the difficulties of queer poetry in her essay "Hanging out Beneath Orlando's Oak Tree, or Towards a Queer British Poetry," in which she laments the ghettoization of LGBT writers and the fact that poetry is not successfully intertwined with life in Britain. Most rousingly, she calls for queer poetry that "needs to be recognised—like queer lives—as part of the stream of human existence, and more specifically for this article as part of the heritage and ongoing formation of British literary culture" (Mayer 2009, 4).

Both Mayer's and Smyth's calls for a queer poetics are answered by a number of contemporary writers, including Nat Raha, Jay Bernard, Sophie Robinson, Timothy Thornton, Caroline Bergvall, and John McCullough. In *Women's Experimental Poetry in Britain 1970–2010: Body, Time and Locale*, authors Kennedy and Kennedy suggest that the politics of experimental writers can often be misunderstood. They write that aligning these poets "with radical political moments might lead one to imagine that their poetry expresses an assertive identity politics" (2013, 13). Similarly, contemporary queer poets could be understood as articulating stable identities as a means by which to communicate a radical politics of otherness. However, the queer poets are far more engaged with the process of "voicing" and "unvoicing" as outlined by Kennedy and Kennedy (2013, 13), in which the subject can be both made and unmade by formally innovative work. This enables a fragmentation and multiplicity that is both formally experimental and politically engaged, as opposed to reducible to simplistic identity politics. Bernard's work, including *your sign is cuckoo, girl* (2008), *English Breakfast* (Math Paper Press, 2014), and *The Read and Yellow Nothing* (2016), is concerned with race and shifting subjectivities among familial and urban contexts. Raha's works, such as *mute exterior intimate* (Oystercatcher Press, 2013) and *of sirens, body & faultlines* (2018), are a poetics of fragments, with gender, sexuality, race, and politics colliding. By contrast, Robinson is a lyric inflected inheritor of a New York School style, with influences from the visual, such as Francesca Woodman, to modernists, such as Gertrude Stein. The intertextual work enacts what "has to happen to representation if queer desire and queer loss are to be registered" (Kennedy and Kennedy 2013, 155). In a feature of the poet in *The Independent*, Robinson stated that "I usually gravitate towards work that is both vulnerable and violent" (Robinson 2013), which perhaps speaks to the political strength, as well as tenderness, of contemporary queer poetics. McCullough has received particular critical acclaim for his works *The Frost Fairs* (Salt, 2011), which is considered transatlantic gay and intersex identity, and *Spacecraft* (Penned in the Margins, 2016), a book that addressed the AIDS-related death of McCullough's first partner. The former won the Polari First Book Prize, and was named Book of the Year for *The Independent* and The Poetry School. The latter was book of the year for *Sabotage Reviews* and the London Review Bookshop.

Conclusion

As this chapter has demonstrated, it is impossible to analyze lesbian and gay poetry without a consideration of the contexts within which it has been produced and disseminated. The political progress of the category has ensured that poetry itself remains dynamic and changeable, reflecting its unique times and developments in terms of legislative improvements. As Andrew McMillan, multi-award winning author of *Physical* (Jonathan Cape, 2015), wrote in a 2015 piece for *The Independent* "[p]oetry, if it's anything at all, is surely the recording of a history by which our society will be judged ... That's why it's important to bear witness, honestly and directly." However, there are evidently three problems at work for lesbian and gay poetry, which are yet to be resolved, irrespective of social change. Woods's article argues that there is still a ghettoization of lesbian and gay writers. Certainly, this chapter itself contributes to the separate consideration of LGBTQ poets, as distinct from their heterosexual peers. This will continue to be problematic as long as heterosexuality is positioned as the universal. Second, in spite of social and political progress, there is still some discrimination at work. Again, Woods's article states that gay and lesbian poems are continually read against the identity politics of the poet, as opposed to being read as stand-alone texts. Finally, as is suggested by the emergence of queer poetics in the United Kingdom, there has been a total sanitization of lesbian and gay identity, and by extension, gay and lesbian poetry. However, there is evident a desire to resist this new found "acceptability," by producing work that continues to contest and resist heteronormative hegemony and a staid social order.

References

Anthony, Steve and Daniels, Peter (eds.) (1994). *Jugular Defences: An AIDS Anthology*. London: The Oscars Press.

Bernard, Jay (2014). *English Breakfast*. Singapore: Math Paper Press.

Bernard, Jay (2016). *The Red and Yellow Nothing*. London: Ink Sweat & Tears.

Bryant, Christopher (2009). "The 1980s Backlash: the 25th Anniversary of the Raid on Gay's the Word Bookshop." *Polari Magazine*. http://www.polarimagazine.com/features/25th-anniversary-raid-gay's-the-word-bookshop/ (accessed 6 May 2020).

Duffy, Maureen (1979). *Memorials of the Quick and the Dead*. London: H. Hamilton.

Duffy, Carol Ann (1987). *Mean Time*. London: Anvil Press Poetry.

Duffy, Carol Ann (1990). *The Other Country*. London: Picador.

Duffy, Carol Ann (1993). *Selling Manhattan*. London: Anvil Press Poetry.

Duffy, Carol Ann (2005). *Rapture*. London: Picador.

Fanthorpe, U. A. (2005). *Collected Poems 1978–2003*. Calstock: Peterloo Poets.

Flood, Alison (2009). "Carol Ann Duffy Becomes First Female Laureate." *The Guardian*. https://www.theguardian.com/books/2009/may/01/carol-ann-duffy-poet-laureate (accessed 6 May 2020).

Horsfall, Allan (1988). "Battling for Wolfenden. Prejudice and Harassment in the Fifties and Sixties' Pressure for Parliamentary Reform; Role of the Press; Early Gay Organizations in the North-West of England, Critiques of Labour Politicians." In: *Radical Records: Thirty Years of*

Lesbian and Gay History, 1957–1987 (eds. Bob Cant and Susan Hemmings), 15–33. London: Routledge.

Johnson, Adam (2003). *Collected Poems*. Manchester: Carcanet.

Kay, Jackie (1991). *The Adoption Papers*. Newcastle-upon-Tyne: Bloodaxe Books.

Kay, Jackie (1993). *Other Lovers*. Newcastle-upon-Tyne: Bloodaxe Books.

Kay, Jackie (1998). *Off Colour*. Newcastle-upon-Tyne: Bloodaxe Books.

Kay, Jackie (2005). *Life Mask*. Tarset: Bloodaxe Books.

Kennedy, David and Kennedy, Christine (2013). *Women's Experimental Poetry in Britain 1970–2010: Body, Time and Locale*. Liverpool: Liverpool University Press.

Kirkup, James (1976). "The Love That Dares to Speak Its Name." *Gay News* (June), 96: 26.

Mayer, Sophie (2009). "Hanging Out Beneath Orlando's Oak Tree, or Towards a Queer British Poetics." *Horizon Review* https://www.academia.edu/369337/Hanging_Out_Beneath_Orlandos_Oak_Tree_or_Towards_a_Queer_British_Poetry (accessed 6 May 2020).

McCullough, John (2011). *The Frost Fairs*. London: Salt Publishing.

McCullough, John (2016). *Spacecraft*. London: Penned in the Margins.

McGonigal, James (2010). *Beyond the Last Dragon: A Life of Edwin Morgan*. Dingwall: Sandstone.

McMillan, Andrew (2015). *Physical*. London: Jonathan Cape.

Mohin, Lilian (ed.) (1986). *Beautiful Barbarians: Lesbian Feminist Poetry*. London: Onlywomen Press.

Morgan, Edwin (1968). *The Second Life*. Edinburgh: Edinburgh University Press.

Powell, Neil (2003). "Afterword." In: *Adam Johnson: Collected Poems* (ed. Neil Powell), 83–87. Carcanet: Manchester.

Raha, Nat (2013). *mute exterior intimate*. Norfolk: Oystercatcher Press.

Raha, Nat (2018). *of sirens/body & faultlines*. Guildford: Veer Books.

Robinson, Sophie (2009). *a*. Los Angeles: Les Figues Press.

Robinson, Sophie (2010). *Lotion*. Norfolk: Oystercatcher Press.

Robinson, Sophie (2012). *The Institute of Our Love in Disrepair*. S.I.: Bad Press.

Robinson, Sophie (2013). "One to watch: Sophie Robinson, Poet, 27." *The Independent*. www.independent.co.uk/arts-entertainment/art/reviews/one-to-watch-sophie-robinson-poet-27-8647852.html (accessed 6 May 2020).

Sandie, Elizabeth (2009). *Acts of Resistance: The Poetry of U. A. Fanthorpe*. Calstock: Peterloo Poets.

Smyth, Cherry (2012). "Queer Poetry by Definition." *Poetry Review* (Offending Frequencies special issue) 102: 10–14.

Thornton, Timothy (2011). *Jocund Day*. Cambridge: Mountain Press.

Thornton, Timothy (2015). *Water and Burning Effects On—Off*. Cambridge: Shit Valley.

Woods, Gregory (2003). "Other Avenues: Gregory Woods on the State of Gay and Lesbian Poetry in Britain." *Magma* 27: 22–26.

Yorke, Liz (1999). "British Lesbian Poetics: A Brief Exploration." *Feminist Review* 62: 78–90.

2c.13
Women Poets in the British Isles

Marc Porée

Viewed from abroad, from Continental Europe in particular, the strength, diversity, and popularity of the poetry currently being written and published, but also performed and sung, by women poets living in the British Isles are quite spectacular. The strength in question concerns mainstream and experimental poetry alike. In the latter field, the presence of Denise Riley, Veronica Forrest-Thomson, but also Geraldine Monk, Marianne Morris, Caroline Bergvall, and others, has made itself increasingly felt (Kennedy 2013, 6). Riley, in particular, comes as close as can be to the New York School poets, whose combination of art theory and philosophy with everyday speech and pop culture has been a dominant pattern in the last half-century. The younger generation of poets experimenting with language is not to be outdone: Redell Olsen, Jennifer Cooke, Andrea Brady, Sophie Robinson, Francesca Lisette, while not bent on occupying post-national, "Post-Marginal Positions" of eminence (quoted Kennedy 2013, 6) for the sake of occupying them, elaborate highly idiosyncratic strategies of assertion, which simultaneously voice and "unvoice" the self (Kennedy 2013, 11–12).

Even more remarkable is the nature of the change undergone in the course of the last four to five decades: a sea change, by all standards and accounts, which has seen women poets go, from the 1960s onward, from virtual invisibility, or say, almost complete absence (from anthologies) to almost total exposure.[1] As they emerge in ever greater numbers, the contemporaries of Eavan Boland (1944–2020), Carol Ann Duffy, Ruth Padel, Jo Shapcott, Selima Hill, Alice Oswald, and Julia Copus are clearly behaving as the self-appointed agents of a substantial shift in the balance of poetic or literary power. Under the lasting impact of feminism, power is being

---

A Companion to Contemporary British and Irish Poetry, 1960–2015, First Edition.
Edited by Wolfgang Görtschacher and David Malcolm.
© 2021 John Wiley & Sons Ltd. Published 2021 by John Wiley & Sons Ltd.

transferred away from its traditional strongholds toward new constituencies that are at once poetical and political. Women are now making history, by taking it in their own hands as well as by writing it: when Mary Robinson took office as first woman President of Ireland in 1990, she read a poem by Eavan Boland during her inaugural speech. After being turned down for the position by Tony Blair, allegedly on the grounds of her being a lesbian, Carol Ann Duffy was finally elected Poet Laureate in 2009. Throughout her tenure, Duffy stood by her word neither to water down her irreverent wit nor to lower her poetic guard in the accomplishment of her official literary obligations, while continuing to have her finger "on the national pulse." Some time after her appointment (a major breakthrough in 400 years of male occupancy of the position), she issued a mini-anthology of her favorite poets, including a strong selection of bicultural, Black, or Asian-British writers, such as Moniza Alvi, Sujata Bhatt, Jackie Kay, Imtiaz Dharker, and Grace Nichols, thereby indicating the quite extraordinary variety of poetic voices in the field: Duffy never was the tree that hides the forest (Duffy 2012). Her gesture also took the form of an apposite reminder: over the decades, women poets can count themselves fortunate to have been able to rely on talented female editors of women-only anthologies—Fleur Adcock (1987), Carole Rumens (1985, 1990), Linda France (1993), Barbara Burford (1999), Deryn Rees-Jones (2005b)—to make their work known to increasingly large audiences.

In the words of Shelley's "A Defence of Poetry," the uninhibited freedom of women has "invented" a "revolution in opinions" (Shelley 2003, 679)—feminism, in short—as well as having "produced" a poetry of both vindication of and emancipation from sex and gender. Initiated in the 1970s, when it first proceeded from a rage explicitly directed at centuries of masculine domination, the movement lost some of its initial bitterness over the decades. As, in turn, the feminist, post-feminist, post-post-feminist agendas ran their full courses, undergoing major inflections while never exhausting themselves, an exhilarating sense of confidence in women's abilities emerged, so much so that their coming into their own has come to resemble the striking of a fine balance. Now, *strike* is definitely the right verb in view of the uncompromising nature of this newly gained poise. But it took more than a few sensational, neogothic poems about female murderers ("Judith" by Vicki Feaver, "The Fish Daughter" by Pascale Petit, "Dreaming Frankenstein," by Liz Lochhead, and "Delicious Babies" by Penelope Shuttle) for the need to be revenged on masculinity and patriarchy to more or less consume itself. And there is no doubt that Angela Carter, with her powerful blend of magic realism, dark fantasy, and sophisticated reappropriation of the stuff of fairy tales, acted as a supremely ironic midwife, urging many a woman poet to come out of the closet—"So I Climbed Out of the Hatch" (Davis 1991, 24). Formerly eruptive, now simmering beneath the surface, violence remains part and parcel of the poetry written by women, and understandably so. Having said that, newer and fairer power-sharing transactions were indeed negotiated, figuratively speaking, in the 1990s, thus paving the way for a presently far less confrontational mood.

Retracing the different phases and "temporalities" of that history of progressive empowerment would take more time and space than are allotted to this chapter. Suffice it to say that the road to emancipation or self-reliance has been a bumpy one, with its ups and downs, its painful setbacks, and lasting breakthroughs, in the face of lasting prejudices and rearguard battles still fought in certain quarters. Divided loyalties inevitably stood in the way too: female identity in writing has long (re)presented itself, for better or for worse, in the guise of low-key discretion, verging on silence. To depart from that line has been a necessity, but, at the same time, it feels like a betrayal of sorts, leading poets such as Angela Hamblin and Anna Wilson to capitalize, as it were, on the use of the lower-case first person "i," so as to immure themselves from the perils of hectoring. More so than male poets, for whom the concept of masculine poetry does not exist, women poets feel torn apart between their loyalty to a collective body of sister poets and the urge to perfect their singularity as poets on their own individual terms. In the words of Jackie Kay, it is more difficult to come together on the basis of "our differences" than on that of "our similarities" (quoted Dowson and Entwistle 2005, 3). In that respect, Fleur Adcock has repeatedly expressed her fear lest women's poetry be "shunted into a ghetto, occupying the 'Women's section' of the bookshops rather than the poetry section, and taught in 'Women's Studies' courses at universities" (Adcock 1987, 2). To which she adds: "Part of this could be blamed on women themselves, or on certain women writers, who take a radically separatist attitude, rejecting 'patriarchal standards' and 'the language of the oppressors,' claiming that men do not understand the tones of voice in which women express themselves, and addressing their work exclusively to other women" (Adcock 1987, 2). Lastly, acknowledging the catholicity, the universality of their writerly commitments is bound to clash with more "particular" preoccupations, say with the female body, menstrual bleeding, the menopause, etc. This is not an easy dilemma to solve, and it takes the cool authority of a Denise Riley to categorically brush aside the seductions of *écriture féminine*: "Don't read this as white ink flow, pressed out / Of retractable nipples. No, / Black as his is mine" ("Milk Ink," 1–3, *SP,* 104).

The ride, what is more, is far from over. A plateau has been climbed, not quite the "Mountain" mentioned in the title of Lilian Mohin's anthology (Mohin 1979), which seemed out of reach some 30 years ago. If anything, though, the present vastly improved situation should not be taken for granted. Complacency is the last thing to be expected from women poets, far too lucid as to the persistence of a continual "double bind," "which mocks them for writing poetry as themselves, but castigates them for challenging their male counterparts on their own terms" (Dowson and Entwistle 2005, 2). After all, if one is to agree that political devolution (as argued in Porée 2008a) may have constituted an unconscious model for their empowerment, coinciding as it effectively did with the (partial) devolution of legislative and executive powers to Scotland, Wales, and Northern Ireland from 1997, the implication has to be that poetic devolution still has a long way to go to be effective. In the same way as London-based governing bodies still have retained the upper hand in the running of the country, male literary strongholds remain largely uneroded. However, a large body of women poets is currently resisting Englishness, and refuting colonial representations that cast the nation as a female body. As Deryn Rees-Jones strongly puts it, "none of the women suggest in their writing that there is something intrinsic or essential about their gender or their nationality; rather they question both gender and nation as fixed entities to explore the tensions which arise between them" (Rees-Jones 2005a, 175). Liz Lochhead's "Bagpipe Muzak, Glasgow 1990" came about at a time when Scottish devolution was indeed becoming a real possibility; with hindsight, its radicality strikes one as prophetic.

> So – watch out Margaret Thatcher, and tak'tent Neil Kinnock
> Or we'll tak'the United Kingdom and brekk it like a bannock.
> (*Bagpipe Muzak* 1991, 52–53)

Are the subsequent referendums, on Scottish independence and on the EU, likely to have further altered the picture, in yet more dramatic ways? It is still a little too early to tell. But one thing is certain. Women poets have grown into acknowledged "legislators" (Shelley's term, it will be remembered), at least of the British Isles. In 2014, the five Poet Laureates were women, and Celts, into the bargain: Gillian Clarke (Wales), Liz Lochhead (Scotland), Carol Ann Duffy (England), Sinéad Morrissey (Northern Ireland), and, as Ireland Professor of Poetry, Paula Meehan (Republic of Ireland) (cf. "The Female Poets Who Have Earned Their Laurels," *The Guardian* 2014). They performed together for the first time at the Women of the World Festival at London's Southbank Centre in March 2014.

This chapter can no more hope to contain the manifold productions of five decades than "The cool black skin of the Bible" and the "atlas green" can hold Kathleen Jamie's "The Queen of Sheba" (Jamie 1994) within their remit. Nor can they be regulated, in the broader context of a historical juncture marked by the all-pervasive impact of deregulation on so many economic, social, political, and even *literary* aspects of life in the United Kingdom. Indeed, in his controversial *The Deregulated Muse* (1998), Sean O'Brien sees contemporary poetry profoundly affected by the proliferation of centrifugal forces (region, class, genre, ethnic origin, race, religion) leading to multiple divisions, and preventing "the emergence of a dominant line" (O'Brien 1998, 9). Incidentally, it is not in the least surprising that women poets, be they devolved or deregulated, should recoil from the very idea of a "domination," perceived as fundamentally alien to their democratic and egalitarian aspirations. Instead, and quite characteristically, women poets have preferred to devote their energies to the elaboration, mostly in common, though not quite as a syndicated pool, of a variety of writing strategies, the very efficiency of which qualifies them as fit representatives of a Deleuzian "*agent collectif d'énonciation*" (collective agent of enunciation), bent on improving the art of "becoming-minor" in the face of the domineering Doxa.

Dowson has taken stock of such "enlivening strategies," and their name is Legion: "antifeminine language and regenerating metaphors; 'ex / centricity' – empowering parody and satire that deflate gender stereotypes; disruptive forms and syntax; dramatic monologues that mask and dialogues that fracture a fixed lyrical 'I'; and exuberant performative strategies from the theatrical to the purely vocal or digital" (Dowson and Entwistle 2015, 39). To this rattlebag of poetic tricks should be added the corrosive force of laughter, humor, and irony, which works miracles when it comes to subverting the arrogance, and the *gravitas*, of patriarchy. Wendy Cope, Liz Lochhead, U. A. Fanthorpe ("Women Laughing"), Selima Hill, and many others thrive on *vis comica,* construing its impropriety as proper to women. But they may well have been outlaughed by Duffy's "The Laughter of Stafford Girls' High": thanks to the exponential growth of laughter, a repressive educational process aimed at churning out girls like a factory line is sarcastically brought down in flames. In flames and in style, indeed, and the proposition is made here that this constitutes a defining characteristic of the category, women poets are prone to "*Etre un style*" (Be a style)

(Macé 2010, 43). Being a style rather than being women (versus not being men, for that matter) saves one from some of the most debilitating strictures pertaining to gendered beings. That one of the most represented facets of the "stylistic operation" in question should be *anger* goes without saying, given the circumstances, but it will be admitted that the "privilege" the latter "hath" (*King Lear*, Act II, scene 2) is no more, but also no less womanly than manly.

As a matter of fact, fewer and fewer women poets are angry nowadays. The man-hating days are over and they know better than to fight battles that have already been fought and won. They are conscious, too, that such a role model, of raw anger, as provided by American poets like Sylvia Plath ("Lady Lazarus") or Anne Sexton ("After Auschwitz"), but homegrown Edith Sitwell's detestations dating back to a much earlier era, as in *Façade, And Other Poems, 1920–1935* (1950), could also qualify, is a more than ambivalent one, for it has done as much harm as it has done good. The paradigm of the flayed-alive poet, consumed by the white heat of her burning passion, however attractive and inspiring, is clearly not a sustainable one, and women poets have been wise to steer clear from that burning bush, having set their sights on endurance and stability. The comforts of a balanced mind and a poised pen are surely not something to turn away from, at least not on principle. Another tutelary figure that women poets have been in two minds about is idiosyncratically English. Stevie Smith's *Selected Poems* came out in 1962, the year of Alvarez's famous anthology, *The New Poetry*, which did not have a single word for women poets. "[M]arginalized as an oddity[, now] celebrated as a major English poet of the twentieth century" (Lee 2016), Smith crystallizes a great deal of the condescending criticisms traditionally voiced about the poetry written by women: eccentric, quirky, childish, imbalanced, insecure, her voice and poetic technique "not adequate to the sombre recognitions" (Heaney 1980, 201); hence, the need to distance oneself as lastingly as possible from that image, however grossly reductive it may be. Conversely, the hazards of falling into the trap of, and being "recuperated" (Guy Debord's term) by mainstream poetry, cannot be underestimated. "[A]llegiance to a poetry espousing a moderate rationality, similar perhaps to the temperate reasonableness demanded by [the] Movement" (Buck 1996, 92), subservience to an intrinsically conservative model of literary quality, for which the advocation of humanism demands that sexual differences be "transcended" (Buck 1996, 92), can be lethal to one's craft or sullen art, and has very little to recommend them. By way of consequence, women poets cannot afford to be anything but alert and vigilant. And yet, it is an uninhibited poem, "The Queen of Sheba" by Jamie, which captures best the disenfranchised genius of the period. Defiantly aroused and arousing, the eastern Queen queens it, holding the powers-that-be in awe and in check. Her "arrival" from "heathenish Arabia" to Scotland is not without autobiographical undertones. A sensuous embodiment of dissidence, delinquency, and desire, she laughs the laugh of Hélène Cixous's "Medusa" (Cixous 2010), a triumph of jubilant, rather than militant, poetry.

Reinstating contradictions and paradoxes as the true engine of history, women poets plead poetic briefs which were formerly off-limits, in view of their proximity to ancillary and time-worn "Themes for Women." Domesticity is one of them, with "Ironing" by Vicki Feaver brilliantly negotiating the transition from feminist rejection to post-post-feminist endorsement of domestic chores. Animality and "Extimacy" are two other such briefs. Unabashed about electing an "Animal Muse of their Own" (Porée 2008a, b), be it a mad cow (Shapcott), a pig (Penelope Shuttle), starlings (Maggie O'Sullivan), a hare (Pauline Stainer), they practice a poetry of "Open Diagnosis" (Susan Wicks 1994), of the "intime" turned inside out, displayed in Rimbaud-like fashion on the page: "And sent my long gold clitoris to sea / Between my legs, streamlined and sweet / Like a barge" ("Monkeys," 13–17, Duffy, *NWP* 86). They have also felt drawn to scienticity (thought to be a masculine prerogative), affirming their intention to explore the new frontiers ahead, where "Things happen / simultaneously / and in very direction / at once" ("Quanta," 15–18, Stainer 1994, 70). But unfixity is certainly the brief of briefs. Women poets tend to write as if they were "*Passe-muraille(s)*" (named after a 1943 tale by Marcel Aymé), as if they could walk through walls with perfect ease. Conversely, they dread nothing more than being imprisoned in stone, immobilized inside the wall (Dutilleul's fate at the end of Aymé's story). They focus on moments of being, when ready-made categories (race, country of origin, gender, all kinds of affiliation or allegiance) crack or burst at the seams. Their poems are keen to explore lilting, tilting, slanting, sliding, sinking moments—"veering" moments, as argued by Nicholas Royle in his investigation into images of swerving, loss of control, digressing, and deviating, present in all major literary genres, including poetry (Royle 2011). Indeed, what with his emphasis on the kinetic, and his fine understanding of "inclination" as a basis "for thinking about the strangeness of life, the singularity of being in the world" (Royle 2011, iix), Royle's general theory of literature as veering happens to address itself most particularly to the "signature-effect" (Royle 2011, viii) of so many contemporary women poets—and to what draws them to the tantalizingly new possibilities involved in veering within one's environment. Last but not least, besides empowering women poets in ways that differ markedly from the mastery commanded by their male counterparts, veering, together with the ability to step across lines, gives them an edge, it would seem, when it comes to coping with the difficult and dangerous times we are experiencing. In an age when walls of the past are seen returning on the international scene with a vengeance, "*passe-murailles*" are indeed a blessing.

Such a considerable asset need not be ascribed to any presumably feminine disposition; it simply but powerfully proceeds from such poetic achievements as are already produced in the here and now. *Meddle English* (2011) by Caroline Bergvall is one of them, provided one takes language, and the inherent question of identity, to be a crucial index of the predicaments of today and tomorrow. Born to a Norwegian father and a French mother, Bergvall grew up in Switzerland, Norway, and France, spending longer periods in the USA and England where she lives and works. Nomadic and disfluent, with a keen interest in experimenting with blockages, verbal and grammatical slips, traffickings and mashups of all kinds, hers is an accent-conscious poetry that dwells in the space between languages with a view to cross-grafting them almost beyond recognition. It does not "accept English as a standard but as a site for meddling: a meddling that allows for the kind of transformation that is the foundation of exchange" (Bernstein). Her desire is to "irritate English at its epiderm" and to combat the uniformizing and flattening effects of "Middling English." Her *Shorter Chaucer Tales* (Bergvall 2006) hyperglotic and spiked, are a case in point. "To meddle with English," she writes, "is to be in the flux that abounds, the large surf of one's clouded contemporaneity." (Bergvall 2011, 14). A staunch believer in the merits of creolization and polylingualism, Bergvall shares her sustained investigation into the combined perils and seductions of being "else-here" (Bergvall 2002), "Out of Everywhere" (O'Sullivan 1996), with growing numbers of writers, Gwyneth Lewis in particular, with a mixed linguistic background (Broqua 2007). Bergvall journeys, too, in text and their translations, Dante's *Divine Comedy* for instance. VIA (2005) is a title that bespeaks her desire to create by way of transit, transportation, and transition; by means of variation and (Derridian) "*différance*," in brief. Meddling, as Bergvall conceives it, is not just linguistic: 60 years after Bellmer, her «Les jets de la poupee» (2001) displayed her keen interest in such forward-looking issues as the prosthetic body and genetic engineering, showing her collection, in the words of Keith Tuma, to be situated exactly "at the centre of questions destined to be crucial in the twenty-first century and involving sexuality, technology, agency, ethics, and identity" (Tuma 2001, 912). Typically, her experimental writing crosses many borders and boundaries, "national, regional, urban borders, unknown streets, spaces, places, bodies, names, faces" (Bergvall 2011, 19): "Something crosses over comes."

One of the most liberating effects of feminism was the realization that such notions as womanhood, femininity, feminism remain purely totemic words as long as they are not conceived of in terms of temporalities. This is an insight superbly formulated by the philosopher and feminist Denise Riley, in a ground-breaking paper, "Does a Sex Have a History? 'Women' and Feminism" (1987, 35–45), the relevance of which has not aged in the least.

> For there are differing temporalities of "women which act to replace the alternatives of eternity or undifferentiation with at times a woman. So they escape that unappetizing choice between the monotony of women" who are always solidly women, and the evanescence of no-longer-women, post-women, who have seen it all and are tired of it.
>
> (Riley 1987, 38)

This is definitely a writer's insight, half intuitive half analytical, illuminating no doubt, in that it removes the burden—the curse—of unchanging identities. Identities, and that would extend to gendered identities, change in time—a truism, one would object to, but one that generations of women poets have proved quick to respond to, each in her own time-bound and time-changed ways. In Vicki Feaver's "Hemingway's Hat" (Feaver 2006), sexual roles begin to change hands, emotional moorings shift, as imprisoning gender roles are left on the threshold of the bedroom. Gradually, but irresistibly, the boundaries separating male from female space dissolve, heralding the birth of a new dispensation. Kate Tempest's debut collection *Hold Your Own* (2014), centered around the figure of Tiresias, the blind prophet who was born a man but spent years as a woman, dwells at length on the almost ad lib shifting and sliding from male to female.

It is the same Denise Riley, in a different temporality however, who was awarded the 2012 Forward Prize for Best Single Poem for "A Part Song." Aligned with her long-standing commitment to song, the universality of her "soundings" implemented in "Listening for lost people" exceeds the circumstantial nature of a poem inspired by the death of her adult son, and confers upon it a fully anthropological dimension, attuned to the plight of the endless others whose adult children have also died in far worse circumstances:

> Each child gets cannibalised by its years.
> It was a man who died, and in him died
> The large-eyed boy, then the teen peacock
> In the unremarked placid self-devouring
> That makes up being alive. But all at once
> Those natural overlaps got cut, then shuffled
> Tight in a block, their layers patted square.
> ("A Part Song," part IV, Riley 2016, 2–14; 3)

The solidarity of mothers, and of parents more globally, need not diminish the strength of such verse (of which Lucy Anne Watt's "The Tree Position" [*Forward* 2016, 173–174], spoken by the grieving mother of a son who never returned from war "in a country the colour of sand," is another example). For one, Riley's attentive listening foregrounds sustained interaction between the living and the dead in ways that have always been the hallmark of English literature, in which the furthest-reaching literary ventures are so often "restorations of the furthest past" (Conrad 1985, vii). What is more, her non-elegiac threnody stirs all the more deeply as one's formal expectations find themselves thought-provokingly renewed and retuned in the process.

Likewise, in a compelling state-of-the-nation poem (*Let Them Eat Chaos*, 2016), released both as a collection and as an album, the poet-cum-rapper Kate Tempest listens for, rather than to, seven lonely Londoners, wide awake at 4.18 in the morning, adrift in a Europe that is itself "lost"—admittedly in more ways than one, given the outcome of the EU referendum of June 2016. Now, the urgency of Tempest's timely radical empathy for the living or the profoundly timeless deliberation of Riley's negotiation with the dead entails far more than the pursuit of "lostness" for its own sake. Not uncuriously, along with most of their fellow poets, they are driven by curiosity, which includes a scrupulous concern with the form, rhythm, and layout of the poem on (and off) the page, a need to bring searing care and prying inquisitiveness to bear on their idiosyncratic material, whether public or private, animate or inanimate, vocal or unvocal.

It is this relentless determination to interfere, trespass, but also foster, shed (skins, identities, tongues, countries), so as the better to molt, jump borders, never get cold feet despite one's underlying insecurity, that will continue to make women poets of the British Isles memorable in the decades ahead, and meddlesome and "disreputable" too (Holland 1997). For the "Force of poetry" is so hyperbolic, and so overwhelming, too, *la force du féminin* construed as "a gesture, a style, a figure that dismisses fixities" (Regard 2002, 6), that neither the latter nor the former is ever likely to give up the fight, let alone retreat from "the flagrancy of lyric operations" (Culler 2015, 351).

Note

1 In the recent *100 Prized Poems: Twenty-five Years of the Forward Books* (Forward 2016), edited by William Sieghart, 46 poems, out of a total of 100, are by women poets: a pretty favorable ratio – though still not covering a full half of the volume.

References

Adcock, Fleur (ed.) (1987). "Introduction." In: *The Faber Book of Twentieth-Century Women's Poetry*, 1–15. London: Faber and Faber.

Aymé, M. (1943). "Le passe-murailles." In: *The Man Who Could Walk Through Walls*. (trans. Karen Reshkin). 2006. http://stresscafe.com/translations/pm/index.htm.

Bergvall, Caroline (2001). "Les jets de la poupee." In: *Anthology of Twentieth-Century British and Irish Poetry* (ed. Keith Tuma), 912–919. Oxford et al.: Oxford University Press.

Bergvall, Caroline (2002). "Writing at the Crossroads of Languages." In: *Telling It Slant: Avant-Grade Poetics of the 1990s* (eds. Mark Wallace and Steven Marks), 207–223. Tuscaloosa and London: The University of Alabama Press.

Bergvall, Caroline (2005). "Via." In: *In Fig*, 67–71. London: Salt.

Bergvall, Caroline (2006). *Shorter Chaucer Tales* http://writing.upenn.edu/pennsound/x/Bergvall.html (accessed 6 May 2020).

Bergvall, Caroline (2011). *Meddle English: New and Selected Texts*. Callicoon, NY: Nightboat.

Bernstein, Charles (n.d.). "Caroline Bergvall's *Meddle English*." *Jacket2* http://jacket2.org/commentary/caroline-bergvalls-meddle-english (accessed 6 May 2020).

Broqua, Vincent (2007). "Pressures of Never-at-Home." *Jacket* (April), p. 32 http://jacketmagazine.com/32/p-broqua.shtml (accessed 6 May 2020).

Buck, Claire (1996). "Poetry and the Women's Movement in Postwar Britain." In: *Contemporary British Poetry: Essays in Theory and Culture* (eds. James Acheson and Romana Huk), 81–111. Albany: State University of New York Press.

Burford, Barbara (1999). *A Dangerous Knowing: Four Black Women Poets*. London: Sheba Press.

Cixous, Hélène (2010, 2010). *Le rire de la Méduse et autres ironies*, préface de Frédéric Regard. Paris: Galilée.

Conrad, Peter (1985). *The Everyman History of English Literature*. London: Dent.

Culler, Jonathan (2015). *Theory of the Lyric*. Cambridge, MA: Harvard University Press.

Davies, Hilary (1991). *The Shanghai Owner of the Bonsai Shop*. London: Enitharmon Press.

Dowson, Jane and Entwistle, Alice (eds.) (2005). "Introduction." In: *A History of Twentieth-Century British Women's Poetry*, 1–6. Cambridge: Cambridge University Press.

Dowson, Jane and Entwistle, Alice (2015). "Poetry on Page and Stage." In: *The History of British Women's Writing, 1970 – Present*, vol. 10 (eds. Mary Eagleton and Emma Parker), 36–50. London: Palgrave Macmillan.

Duffy, Carol Ann (2002). *Feminine Gospels*. London: Picador.

Duffy, Carol Ann (2012). *Jubilee Lines: 60 Poets for 60 Years*. London: Faber and Faber.

Duffy, Carol Ann (2014). "Carol Ann Duffy on Five Years as Poet Laureate: 'It Has Been a Joy'". Nicholas Wroe. *The Observer* (September), p. 27. https://www.theguardian.com/books/2014/sep/27/carol-ann-duffy-poet-laureate-interview (accessed 6 May 2020).

Feaver, Vicki. 1996 (2006). *The Book of Blood*. London: Jonathan Cape.

France, Linda (ed.) (1993). *Sixty Women Poets*. Newcastle: Bloodaxe.

Heaney, Seamus (1980). "A Memorable Voice: Stevie Smith" {1976}. In: *Preoccupations: Selected Prose 1968–1978*, 199, 199–201, 201. New York: Farrar, Straus and Giroux.

Holland, Jane (1997). *Disreputable*. Newcastle: Bloodaxe.

Jamie, Kathleen (1994). *The Queen of Sheba*. Newcastle: Bloodaxe.

Kennedy, David (2013). *Women's Experimental Poetry in Britain 1970–2010: Body, Time & Locale* (ed. Christine Kennedy). Liverpool: Liverpool University Press.

Lee, Hermione (2016). "A Poet Unlike Any Other." *The New York Review of Books* (9 June) http://www.nybooks.com/articles/2016/06/09/stevie-smith-poet-unlike-any-other (accessed 6 May 2020).

Lochhead, Liz (1991). *Bagpipe Muzak*. Toronto: Penguin.

Macé, Marielle (2010). "Du Style." *Critique* 2010/1–2 (n° 752–753). Paris: Minuit.

Mohin, Lilian (1979). *One Foot on the Mountain: An Anthology of British Feminist Poetry 1969 – 1979*. London: Onlywomen Press.

O'Brien, Sean (1998, 1998). *The Deregulated Muse*. Newcastle: Bloodaxe Books.

O'Sullivan, Maggie (1996). *Out of Everywhere: Linguistically Innovative Poetry by Women in North America & the UK*. London: Reality Street.

Porée, Marc (2008a). "Contemporary British Women Poets (1985–2005): A New Legislature." Introduction to *Contemporary British Women Poets (1985–2005), E-rea* [Online], 6.1.

Porée, Marc (2008b). "An Animal Muse of Their Own. *Contemporary British Women Poets (1985–2005), E-rea* [Online], 6.1.

Rees-Jones, Deryn (2005a). *Consorting with Angels. Essays on Modern Women Poets*. Newcastle: Bloodaxe Books.

Rees-Jones, Deryn (ed.) (2005b). *Modern Women Poets*. Newcastle: Bloodaxe Books.(*MWP*).

Regard, Frédéric (2002). *La force du féminin. Sur trois essais de Virginia Woolf*. Paris: La Fabrique éditions.

Riley, Denise (1987). "Does Sex Have a History: 'Women' and Feminism." *New Formations 1*. London: Methuen. http://banmarchive.org.uk/collections/newformations/01_35.pdf (accessed 6 May 2020).

Royle, Nicholas (2011). "Advertisement." In: *Veering: A Theory of Literature*, viii–ix. Edinburgh: Edinburgh University Press.

Rumens, Carol (ed.) (1985). *Making for the Open: The Chatto Book of Post-Feminist Poetry 1964–1984*. London: Chatto & Windus.

Rumens, Carol (ed.) (1990). *New Women Poets*. Newcastle: Bloodaxe. *(NWP)*.

Shelley, Percy Bysshe (2003). *The Major Works* (eds. Zachary Leader and Michael O'Neill). Oxford: Oxford University Press.

Sitwell, Edith (1950). *Façade and Other Poems 1920–1935*. London: Duckworth.

Stainer, Pauline (1994). *The Ice-Pilot Speaks*. Newcastle: Bloodaxe.

Tempest, Kate (2014). *Hold Your Own*. London et al.

Tempest, Kate (2016). *Let Them Eat Chaos*. London: Picador.

The Female Poets Who Have Earned Their Laurels (2014) *The Guardian* (3 March) https://www.theguardian.com/lifeandstyle/2014/mar/03/female-poets-have-earned-laurels (accessed 6 May 2020).

Tuma, Keith (ed.) (2001). *Anthology of Twentieth-Century British and Irish Poetry*. Oxford et al: Oxford University Press.

Watt, Lucy Ann (2016). "The Tree Position." (2013). In: *100 Prized Poems: Twenty-Five Years of the Forward Books* (ed. William Sieghart), 173–174. London: Forward Worldwide.

Wicks, Susan (1994). *Open Diagnosis*. London: Faber and Faber.

2c.14
Irish Women Poets

Monika Szuba

Introduction

As Nuala Ní Dhomhnaill argues, "Irish poetry in the second half of the twentieth century has been forcefully changed by women's writing" (2005, 43), further adding that its emergence was neither smooth nor easy, but "often obstructed, hysterically fought against, condescended to and patronised" (2005, 43). Similarly, Eavan Boland has famously stated that she "began writing in a country where the word woman and the word poet were almost magnetically opposed. One word was used to invoke collective nurture, the other to sketch out self-reflexive individualism [...] they were oil and water and could not be mixed" (1996, xi). Several decades later, Irish poetry sees itself much transformed thanks to the work of women poets.

Critics argue that Medbh McGuckian and Eiléan Ní Chuilleanáin "insist upon the feminine dimension of the world" (Grennan 1999, 293), a statement that may be extended to all the poets in question here. They are "celebrated for their collective contribution as female writers to what had been a male-dominated tradition and for their individual visions and styles" (Michener 2014, 154), which demonstrates that these poets have become an important part of the cultural fabric of contemporary poetry in Ireland. Irish women poetry is now represented by many and various authors such as Eavan Boland, Nuala Ní Dhomhnaill, Medbh McGuckian, Paula Meehan, Colette Bryce, Rita Ann Higgins, Moya Cannon, Leontia Flynn, Mary O'Malley, Kerry Hardie, Vona Groarke, Sinéad Morrissey, Caitriona O'Reilly, to mention just a few. The ever-expanding bibliographies demonstrate a keen interest in their work.

A Companion to Contemporary British and Irish Poetry, 1960–2015, First Edition.
Edited by Wolfgang Görtschacher and David Malcolm.
© 2021 John Wiley & Sons Ltd. Published 2021 by John Wiley & Sons Ltd.

For the purposes of this chapter, I have selected Eavan Boland, Eiléan Ní Chuilleanàin, Nuala Ní Dhomhnaill, Medbh McGuckian, and Paula Meehan. Thanks to new, challenging angles, these poets create complex visions, blending myth and folklore, recovering the lost and the forgotten voices of Irish women, and exploring domestic life. Strongly emphasizing female subjectivity, their work speaks of the intersections of the private and the political. They demonstrate a deep awareness of tradition, a knowledge that they employ in order to contest established rules and challenge literary conventions in poetic forms and themes.

Eavan Boland

Born in Dublin in 1944, Eavan Boland published her first collection of poems in 1962 (*23 Poems*). Her fifth collection, *In Her Own Image* (1980), brought her wider recognition. Her extensive bibliography includes books of poetry as well as essays, for example, *In a Time of Violence* (1994), *Outside History* (1990), *Domestic Violence* (2007), *Collected Poems* (2008), *New Selected Poems* (2013), and *A Poet's Dublin* (2014).

In the preface to her essay collection, *Object Lessons*, Boland writes, "I began to write in an enclosed, self-confident literary culture. The poet's life stood in a burnished light in the Ireland of that time. Poets were still poor, had little sponsored work, and could not depend on a sympathetic reaction to their poetry. But the idea of the poet was honored" (1996, ix). Yet a concept of a poet who was a woman seemed irreconcilable. Boland describes this fraught situation, remembering the need to find her own place. Boland has attempted to reconcile these two concepts, and she continually does this with success decades later. As she admits, "I found my poetic voice by shouting across that distance" (1996, xi) to achieve a bold, empowering poetic voice.

Admired for her deftness with which she navigates poetic traditions, Boland focuses on "the mystery of being a poet in the puzzle of time and sexuality and nationhood" (1996, xiii). She delves into Irish history and mythology, offering a renewed vision. She also employs classical myths, for instance the story of Demeter (e.g., "What Language Did") to discuss problems of female identity (cf. House 2006). Her poetry challenges conventional constructions of femininity and subverts them. Since her first collection, Boland has been writing against fixed female images reproduced in literature, obfuscating women and silencing them. In the place of these inadequate representations, Boland offers portrayals of womanhood in an attempt to capture female experience, frequently concentrating on the unspeakable and the unspoken, and celebrating the commonplace and the ordinary, emphasizing the role of domestic experience in poetry.

She is concerned with the body politics, in particular with reference to fixed gender roles. In the poem "Anorexic" from the collection *In Her Own Image*, the opening line "Flesh is heretic" (l. 1), suggesting religious concerns of the poem, is impersonal, a statement whose source can be divined from the word "heretic," which comes from Greek *hairetikos*, "able to choose." Deprived of choice in her ascetic "self-denials" (l. 6), the speaker's voice is revealed in the second line as the poem moves from the impersonal construction to a confession: "My body is a witch / I am burning it" (ll. 2–3) only to change in the second line of the next stanza into the third person singular ("her curves and paps and wiles" [l. 5]). Shifting pronouns—from *I* to *she*—foreground the speaker's growing distance to herself, her diminishing, or perhaps nonexistent agency. She is in the process of disassociating from the self, losing her body to the social and cultural practices which regulate the body. Thus, the speaker disassociates herself from herself. The poem travels between the first- and the third-person pronouns until the final line of the fifth stanza "She has learned her lesson" (l. 18), words which emphasize punitive disciplinary methods. The body is presented as a battleground of conflicting forces. Religious references are further stressed by the word "sinless" (l. 30), as well as suggestions of the Fall, the serpent, and Eden. The poem demonstrates a female struggle to gain power over her own body, the perpetual debate between the personal and the political. Technically the poem is composed of strong, short lines, with an irregular rhyme scheme, occasional enjambments, and anaphoras.

Boland's rootedness in Ireland is a place underlined in *A Poet's Dublin*, a collection which combines her poems and prose with her photographs, edited by Paula Meehan and Jody Allen Randolph. Gathering many of Boland's best known verses and the images captured by her, the book demonstrates the inextricable connection of the poet's self and the city. The volume concludes with a conversation between Boland and Meehan, titled "Two Poets and a City," in which Meehan suggests that "each poem is also a time capsule" (Boland 2014, 97), as these poems were written over five decades, "opening emotional channels in memory" (2014, 97). For Boland, even though she did not grow up there, Dublin was "a place of origin ... [t]hat nameless city" in her poems (2014, 97). Both her and Meehan are "Dublin poets," Boland argues (2014, 97), each inventing it in her own manner. Eavan Boland died in Dublin in 2020.

Eiléan Ní Chuilleanáin

Born in Cork in 1942, Eiléan Ní Chuilleanáin is a Fellow of Trinity College Dublin and an emeritus professor of the School of English. From 2016 to 2018, she was Ireland's Professor of Poetry. She specializes in Renaissance literature and translation, themes also present in her poetry. She translates from Irish, Italian, and Romanian. Founder member of the literary journal *Cyphers* in 1975, Ní Chuilleanáin is still one of its main editors. She has published many poetry collections, including *Acts and Monuments* (1966), *The Magdalene Sermon* (1989), *Selected Poems* (2009), and *The Sun-Fish* (2010). She has translated Ileana Malancioiu's *After the Raising of Lazarus* (2005) and Nuala Ní Dhomhnaill's *The Water Horse* (2001, with Medbh McGuckian). Her poetry has been described as "oblique," but "concrete" (Holdridge 2007, 115).

In her poetry, Ní Chuilleanáin emphasizes the feminine and the body, introducing multiple points of view as she focuses on women figures in Irish history and culture. She attempts to redefine femininity, exploring domestic life in poetic ways. Similarly to Boland, Ní Chuilleanáin translates female experience into poetry, concerned with the overlooked and the unrepresented. As Clutterbuck argues, "Irish women's poetry not only suggests that a causal link exists between the silencing of women's lived reality and the trauma of national history, but that the silenced woman can speak most clearly for that trauma exactly in her own voice as woman" (2011, 114).

Ní Chuilleanáin revisits and revises various myths, including that of Odysseus (e.g., "The Second Voyage" and "Odysseus Meets the Ghosts of the Women," both poems from the volume *The Second Voyage*—Ní Chuilleanáin 1977), employing the journey motif as "an analogue to the woman writer's process" (Conboy 1990, 71). The revision is part of "the primary project shared by these two Irish poets [to] demythologize and re-historicize" (Sarbin 1993, 86), and thus the poet imagines female journeys toward empowerment. These journeys begin with memory. For instance, in "The Absent Girl" (1977, 13), the woman, "conspicuous by her silence" (l. 1), is akin to a ghost. Mute, she is unnoticed, passed by, and looked through: "they pass her without a sound / And when they look for her face / Can only see the clock behind her skull" (ll. 5–7). She "searches for a memory lost" and "misses" her ligaments and the marrow of her bones." The enjambment in the first line—"The absent girl is" (l. 1)—creates a powerful ambiguity, a space which indicates that the girl's identity remains open. Her separation from others is foregrounded by the glass (lines 4 and 10) and windowpanes (l. 9). Unseen, she is also unseeing as "Grey hair blinds her eyes" (l. 8). Even though the clock reminds us of time (lines 7 and 14), the girl is beyond it (lines 11 and 15): "with no beating heart / Lung or breast how can she tell the time?" (ll. 14–15). Bodiless and mute, the absent girl remains a shadow presence of erasure of women from history and culture.

Nuala Ní Dhomhnaill

Born in Lancashire, England, in 1952, Nuala Ní Dhomhnaill was brought up speaking Irish. She made a deliberate decision to write in Irish Gaelic. She has published collections in Irish, for example, *An Dealg Droighin* (1981), as well as bilingual editions, *Pharaoh's Daughter* (1990) and *The Astrakhan Cloak* (1992) among others. Her poetry has been translated into English by Paul Muldoon, Medbh McGuckian, and Seamus Heaney. A discussion of Ní Dhomhnaill's poems poses problems for a non-Gaelic speaker, who has to rely on English translations, accepting the inevitable loss. Ní Dhomhnaill has explained her choice both in poetry (e.g. "The Language Issue," "Oscailt an Tuama," "The Exhumation") and in prose, where she has called Gaelic "the corpse that sits up and talks back" (Ní Dhomhnaill 1995, 27). Together with other poets, she has contributed to a literary movement INNTI, committed to revitalizing Irish language.

Haberstroh calls her work "revolutionary" in terms of creating a female image in contemporary Irish poetry (1996, 162). Ní Dhomhnaill's poetry engages with language and women's issues, often in political ways, presenting women figures who defiantly refuse to play the assigned roles. Her poetry frequently demonstrates a powerful refusal to subscribe to stereotypical gender roles. She is concerned with the underrepresented female voices and neglected Irish language spanning from ancient myths to contemporary culture.

Ní Dhomhnaill frequently focuses on retelling folk tales, including Gaelic myths, stories of queens and goddesses. Recurrent figures include a mermaid, which underlines an ability to create and regenerate. Shapeshifting too belongs in the landscape of mythology and the world of fairy tales, pointing to the power of reinvention. The title of the collection *The Fifty Minute Mermaid* (2007) offers a contrasting image of the mermaid of folklore, a timeless being, brought together with a short span of time. Juxtaposing original Irish versions with parallel English translations by Paul Muldoon inevitably provokes meditations on the co-existence of two languages, the precedence of Irish, and temporality. Poems such as "The Merfolk and Literature," "Founding Myth," and "Another Founding Myth" depict people who are out of their element and thus forced to live in self-denial. Having come out of the sea, *murúcha*, or the merfolk, presented in "The Merfolk and Literature" (2007, 39), despite being able to read and write, choose not to produce their own literature but they have a founding myth, not unlike the biblical story from *Exodus*. The narrator keeps her distance but also expresses deep sympathy for the *murúcha*, emphasizing a sense of ambiguity, which dominates the whole collection. In terms of poetic technique, there are long lines, which lack regular metric patterns, and occasional, equally irregular rhymes.

Paula Meehan

Ireland's Professor of Poetry from 2013 to 2015, Paula Meehan was born in 1955 in Dublin. Her volumes of poetry include: *Return and No Blame* (1984), *Reading the Sky* (19865), *The Man Who Was Marked by Winter* (1991), *Pillow Talk* (1994), *Dharmakaya* (2000), *Painting Rain* (2009). As is frequently stressed, her poetry is performative and communal, an examination of various aspects of dwelling in culture (e.g., "The Garden of the Sleeping Poet," first published in 1983 and "Hunger Strike"—Meehan 1986). Some of Meehan's poems explore traumatic childhood experiences (e.g., "Fist"—Meehan 2000, 13). Critics highlight the importance of memory in her work, demonstrating "the incorporation of the stranger within the self" (Collins 2009, 138). Her poetry is at times sensual, even erotic, exploring the body politics and the tension between personal and political, individual, and social. Her poetic visions offer "a form of discourse that is anarchic, dispersive, groundless" (Auge 2009, 62), and the poet herself has expressed an attempt "to write something that was both visionary and quotidian" (Hobbs 1997, 66).

The eco-feminist concerns of her poetry are frequently discussed (cf. Kirkpatrick 2005; Holdridge 2007, 2009). Particularly in *Dharmakaya* (2000) and *Painting Rain* (2009), Meehan offers a vision of the world where all creatures compose an interdependent whole, where everything is interconnected and trees are our kin. Striving for a holistic vision of the world, Meehan employs numerous Buddhist references (e.g., in the form of epigraphs to both collections). She admits to having been influenced by Gary Snyder, who drew on Buddhist sources (cf. Randolph 2009, 246–250). *Painting Rain* is said "to contain nature on canvas, is a wolf tree, a nexus of culture and nature, a landscape etched with the palimpsests of the primeval as well as the historical traces of human history" (Holdridge 2009, 166). *Dharmakaya*, the title signifying the reality body, "the Primary Clear Light of Pure Reality," as Stanislav Grof writes in *The Tibetan Book of the Dead* (quoted in Meehan 2000, 6), one of the three bodies of the Buddha, is a meditation on being and non-being. Meehan employs meditation techniques, such as mindfulness, breath, and a flowing rhythm, stressing full awareness. For instance, "Take a breath. Hold it. Let it go" (Meehan 2000, 15) refers to breath as "the structuring device of the poem marking its stanzaic structure" (Kirkpatrick 2005 quoted in Collins 2015, 103).

Meehan uses startling interstanzaic enjambments for other purposes, as for instance in the poem "Not Your Muse" (1994, 24), where the run-on lines reflect the speaker's daring voice, breaking boundaries. In line with counter-narratives prevalent in her poetry, a bold female voice directly expresses her dissatisfaction with the given role, posing straightforward questions and urgently demanding explanations. The word "battledressed" (l. 22) reminds us of the battleground that is the female image. The first line presents a self-confident speaker in her rejection of a prescribed function emphasized by the two negations: "I'm not your muse, not that creature." Neither "that creature" nor the "painted doll" (l. 23) capture her essence. The frankness in which the speaker addresses the artist—"Look at you" (l. 17)—stands in stark contrast with the idealized image offered by him. As the speaker points out, it is lacking in truth: "Not a gesture that's true // on that canvas, not a droopy breast, / wrinkle or stretchmark in sight" (ll. 18–20). Her informal, even colloquial language ("droopy" (l. 19), "kinks" (l. 10)) clashes with the words "rapt, besotted" (l. 18), ironically depicting the artist, whose formal register does not match the speaker's. These words are equally false as his paintings. What is more, the painting makes the woman "whole and shining," (l. 9) which proves to be another falsity. In the last stanza, however, the question "who am I" (l. 21), deprived of a question mark, becomes merely a bitter statement. With this sad constatation in the last stanza, the female agency seems to vanish completed with the contrasting image: the lines "your painted doll against the harsh light / I live by, against a brutal merciless sky" (ll. 23–24), ending the poem, challenge false constructs of femininity imposed by patriarchal culture.

Medbh McGuckian

Born in 1950 in Belfast, Northern Ireland, Medbh McGuckian was raised in a Catholic family. In 1985, she became the first woman poet to be writer-in-residence at Queen's University in Belfast. Her volumes of poetry include *Selected Poems 1978–1994* (1997), *The Currach Requires No Harbours* (2007), and *The High Caul Cap* (2013) among others. In a book-length study, *The Poetry of Medbh McGuckian*, Shane Alcobia-Murphy and Richard Kirkland argue that even though she is "one of Northern Ireland's foremost poets," she "has not won the critical acclaim accorded to her peers" (Alcobia-Murphy and Kirkland 2010, 1).

Her decision to change the English name "Maeve" into the Irish form "Medbh" demonstrates a strong statement of belonging. Her poems contain oblique references to politics, which thus become coded messages of political resistance. They are an attempt to retrieve a long-lost language and culture, and establish a dialogue between them in the present-day Northern Ireland. Anglo-Irish binary is acutely expressed in her poems, and an inescapable sense of division is felt. Considered "extravagant" (Schwerter 2013, 130) or "avant-garde" (Brazeau 2004, 127), McGuckian uses various formal methods, introducing obfuscation. As the poet herself admits, "I began to write poetry so that nobody would read it. Nobody. Even the ones who read it would not understand it" (Medbh McGuckian (1995), quoted Summers-Bremner 2006, 40). Citing other critics, Schwerter argues that McGuckian's poetry has "a destabilising and confusing effect on the audience," and is "often seen as cryptic and impenetrable" (Schwerter 2013, 130).

McGuckian creates "with a connection to pre- and post-revolutionary Russia," finding parallels and correlations with its authors (Alcobia-Murphy 2010, 1). She demonstrates an interest in Russian poetry—including the work of Boris Pasternak, Anna Akhmatova, Marina Tsvetaeva, and Osip Mandelstam—an influence that can be detected in her technique. As their work informs her poetry, some critics have attempted an analysis in the context of Russian poets (cf. Schwerter, Alcobia-Murphy).

McGuckian focuses on a female perspective, foregrounding the validity of gender relations. Analyzing her oeuvre in the context of Julia Kristeva's work (cf. Brigley-Thompson, Brazeau), critics explore various kinds of "maternal thinking," including images (and metaphors) of motherhood (cf. Beer 1992). Focusing on the nature of gender, she stresses its social aspects and a lack of a stable identity (cf. Wills 1993, 158; Brigley-Thompson 2009, 400). This fluidity is present in her poems, whose general principle includes shifting perspectives. For instance, in the title poem from her 2002 collection, *The Face of the Earth* (2002, 12–13), McGuckian explores the ebb and flow of desire, emphasized in the second stanza by end-line consonance, breath bracketing the poem. Ambiguity is the predominant feature of the text, governing irregular stanzas, repetitions, and hints of rhyme.

Conclusion

Writing across the margins, Eavan Boland, Eiléan Ní Chuilleanàin, Nuala Ní Dhomhnaill, Medbh McGuckian, and Paula Meehan revise the roles of women in Irish history and culture. They have thoroughly modernized the Irish tradition, exploding long-established myths, and introducing new readings. Their poetry concerns social and political issues, emphasizing female agency and reclaiming women's place. They are concerned with the production of gender roles, frequently concerned with the portrayal of women in domestic spaces and female bodies, stressing tensions between the individual and the tribal. They do not romanticize the Irish past, but propose a demythologization, demystifying stereotypes and stories by submitting culture to profound revisions, overtly challenging literary tradition.

References

Alcobia-Murphy, Shane (2010). "Introduction." In: *The Poetry of Medbh McGuckian* (eds. Shane Alcobia-Murphy and Richard Kirkland), 1–21. Cork: Cork UP.

Alcobia-Murphy, Shane and Kirkland, Richard (eds.) (2010). *The Poetry of Medbh McGuckian*. Cork: Cork UP.

Allen Randolph, Jody (2009). "The Body Politic: A Conversation with Paula Meehan." *An Sionnach: A Journal of Literature, Culture, and the Arts* 5 (1 and 2): 239–271. http://muse.jhu.edu/journals/an_sionnach/v005/5.1.randolph01.html.

Auge, Andrew J. (2009). "The Apparitions of 'Our lady of the Facts of Life': Paula Meehan and the Visionary Quotidian." *An Sionnach: A Journal of Literature, Culture, and the Arts* 5 (1–2): 50–64. http://muse.jhu.edu/journals/an_sionnach/v005/5.1.auge.html.

Beer, Ann (1992). "Medbh McGuckian's Poetry: Maternal Thinking and a Politics of Peace." *The Canadian Journal of Irish Studies* 18 (1) Women and Irish Politics: 192–203. http://www.jstor.org/stable/25512909.

Boland, Eavan (1962). *23 Poems*. Dublin: Gallagher.

Boland, Eavan (1980). *In Her Own Image*. Dublin: Arlen House.

Boland, Eavan (1990). *Outside History*. Manchester: Carcanet.

Boland, Eavan (1994). *In a Time of Violence*. Manchester: Carcanet.

Boland, Eavan (1996). *Object Lessons: The Life of the Woman and the Poet in Our Time*. London: Vintage.

Boland, Eavan (2007). *Domestic Violence*. Manchester: Carcanet.

Boland, Eavan (2014). *A Poet's Dublin* (eds. Paula Meehan and Jody Allen Randolph). Manchester: Carcanet.

Brazeau, Robert (2004). "Troubling Language: Avant-Garde Strategies in the Poetry of Medbh McGuckian." *Mosaic: A Journal for the Interdisciplinary Study of Literature* 37 (2): 127–144. http://search.proquest.com.ezproxy.is.ed.ac.uk/docview/205341088?accountid=10673.

Brigley-Thompson, Zoë (2009). "The Life and Death of Language: A Kristevan Reading of the Poets Gwyneth Lewis and Medbh McGuckian." *Orbis Litterarum* 64 (5): 385–412. https://doi.org/10.1111/j.1600-0730.2009.00969.x.

Chuilleanáin, Eiléan Ní (1966). *Acts and Monuments*. Dublin: The Gallery Press.

Chuilleanáin, Eiléan Ní (1977). *The Second Voyage*. Winston-Salem: Wake Forrest UP.

Chuilleanáin, Eiléan Ní (1989). *The Magdalene Sermon*. Oldcastle: The Gallery Press.

Chuilleanáin, Eiléan Ní (2010). *The Sun-Fish*. Oldcastle: The Gallery Press.

Clutterbuck, Catriona (2011). "The Irish History Wars and Irish Women's Poetry: Eiléan Ní Chuilleanáin and Eavan Boland." In: *The Cambridge Companion to Twentieth-Century British and Irish Women's Poetry* (ed. Jane Dowson), 97–118. Cambridge: Cambridge UP.

Collins, Lucy (2009). "A Way of Going Back: Memory and Estrangement in the Poetry of Paula Meehan." *An Sionnach: A Journal of Literature, Culture, and the Arts* 5 (1–2): 127–139. http://muse.jhu.edu/journals/an_sionnach/v005/5.1.collins.html.

Collins, Lucy (2015). *Contemporary Irish Women Poets: Memory and Estrangement*. Oxford: Oxford University Press.

Conboy, Sheila C. (1990). ""What You Have Seen is Beyond Speech": Female Journeys in the Poetry of Eavan Boland and Eiléan Ní Chuilleanáin." *The Canadian Journal of Irish Studies* 16 (1): 65–72. http://www.jstor.org/stable/25512810.

Dhomhnaill, Nuala Ní (1981, 1981). *An Dealg Droighin*. Dublin: Clo Mercier.

Dhomhnaill, Nuala Ní (1990). *Pharaoh's Daughter*. Oldcastle: Gallery Books.

Dhomhnaill, Nuala Ní (1992). *The Astrakhan Cloak* (trans. P. Muldoon). Oldcastle: Gallery Press.

Dhomhnaill, Nuala Ní (1995). "Why I Chose to Write in Irish: The Corpse that Sits Up and Talks Back." *The New York Times Book Review* (8 January) 8: 27–28.

Dhomhnaill, Nuala Ní (2000). *The Water Horse: Poems in Irish* (trans. M. McGuckian and E.N. Chuilleanáin). Winston-Salem: Wake Forest UP.

Dhomhnaill, Nuala Ní (2005). *Selected Essays* (ed. Ooona Frawley). Dublin: New Island.

Dhomhnaill, Nuala Ní and Muldoon, Paul (2007). *The Fifty Minute Mermaid*. Oldcastle: Gallery Books.

Grennan, Eamon (1999). *Facing the Music: Irish Poetry in the Twentieth Century*. Omaha: Creighton UP.

Haberstroh, Patricia Boyle (1996). *Women Creating Women: Contemporary Irish Women Poets*. Syracuse, NY: Syracuse UP.

Hobbs, John (1997). "An Interview with Paula Meehan." *Nua: Studies in Contemporary Irish Writing* 1 (1): 53–68.

Holdridge, Jefferson (2007). "A Snake Pouring Over the Ground: Nature and the Sacred in Eiléan Ní Chuilleanáin." *Irish University Review* 37, 1, Spring-Summer, Special Issue Eiléan Ní Chuilleanáin: 115–130. https://doi.org/10.2307/25517341.

Holdridge, Jefferson (2009). "The Wolf Tree: Culture and Nature in Paula Meehan's *Dharmakaya* and *Painting Rain*." *An Sionnach: A Journal of Literature, Culture, and the Arts* 5 (1–2): 156–168. http://muse.jhu.edu/journals/an_sionnach/v005/5.1.holdridge.html.

House, Veronica (2006). "'Words We Can Grow Old and Die In': Earth Mother and Ageing Mother in Eavan Boland's Poetry." In: *The Body and Desire in Contemporary Irish Poetry* (ed. Irene Gilsenan Nordin), 103–123. Dublin, Portland: Irish Academic Press.

Kirkpatrick, Kathryn (2005). "'Between Breath and No Breath': Witnessing Class Trauma in Paula Meehan's *Dharmakaya*." *An Sionnach: A Journal of Literature, Culture, and the Arts* 1 (2): 47–64. http://connection.ebscohost.com/c/essays/20846166/between-breath-no-breath-witnessing-class-trauma-paula-meehans-dharmakaya.

McGuckian, Medbh (1997). *Selected Poems. 1978–1994*. Oldcastle: Gallery Books.

McGuckian, Medbh (2002). *The Face of the Earth*. Oldcastle: Gallery Books.

McGuckian, Medbh, Dhomhnaill, Nuala Ni, and O'Connor, Laura (1995). "Comhra." *Southern Review* 13 (3): 581–614.

McMullen, Kim (2001). "'That the Science of Cartography is Limited': Historiography, Gender, and Nationality in Eavan Boland's Writing in a Time of Violence." *Women's Studies* 29: 495–517. https://doi.org/10.1080/00497878.2000.9979328.

Meehan, Paula (1984). *Return and No Blame*. Dublin: Beaver Row Press.

Meehan, Paula (1986). *Reading the Sky*. Dublin: Beaver Row Press.

Meehan, Paula (1991). *The Man Who Was Marked by Winter*. Oldcastle: The Gallery Press.

Meehan, Paula (1994). *Pillow Talk*. Oldcastle: The Gallery Press.

Meehan, Paula (2000). *Dharmakaya*. Manchester: Carcanet.

Meehan, Paula (2009). *Painting Rain*. Manchester: Carcanet.

Michener, Christian (2014). "The Female Figure in Eiléan Ní Chuilleanáin's Poetry by Patricia Boyle Haberstroh." Review. *New Hibernia Review*. 18 (1): 154–156. Spring/Earrach https://doi.org/10.1353/nhr.2014.0013.

Sarbin, Deborah (1993). "'Out of Myth into History': The Poetry of Eavan Boland and Eiléan Ní Chuilleanáin." *The Canadian Journal of Irish Studies* 19 (1): 86–96. http://www.jstor.org/stable/25512952.

Schwerter, Stephanie (2013). *Northern Irish Poetry and the Russian Turn Intertextuality in the Work of Seamus Heaney, Tom Paulin and Medbh McGuckian*. London/New York: Palgrave Macmillan.

Summers-Bremner, Eluned (2006). "History's Impasse: Journey, Haunt and Trace in the Poetry of Medbh McGuckian." In: *The Body and Desire in Contemporary Irish Poetry* (ed. Irene Gilsenan Nordin), 40–54. Dublin, Portland: Irish Academic Press.

Wills, C. (1993). *Improprieties: Politics and Sexuality in Northern Irish Poetry*. Oxford: Clarendon Press.

2c.15
Religious Poetry, 1960–2015

Hugh Dunkerley

Introduction

The period 1960–2015 has been one of decline of traditional Christian belief in Britain and Ireland. In a 2014 survey, only 14% of British people described themselves as practicing Christians (*The Telegraph*, April 26, 2014). In the same issue, Rowan Williams, the former Archbishop of Canterbury, declared that Britain is now a "post-Christian" country ("Rowan Williams: I didn't really want to be Archbishop"). In Ireland, the long grip of the Catholic Church has loosened, a process speeded up by the appalling revelations of sexual abuse by priests. At the same time, interest in "spirituality" has gained ground. Some of this finds expression in alternative religions such as Buddhism, while elsewhere a vague longing can be detected in the pick-and-mix offerings of the New Age movement. In addition to these changes, immigration has meant that new believers are more likely to be Muslim or Hindu than Christian. So although traditional Christian belief has waned, religion itself has not, as some militant atheists hoped, disappeared. Instead we live in a pluralistic society where religious belief has mutated in all sorts of ways, some of them decidedly woolly, others dangerously fundamentalist.

The aim of this chapter is to explore how poets in Britain and Ireland have responded to these changes. I do not intend to offer a single definition of religious poetry, as I believe this to be impossible in the current situation, except to state that the poets I will examine are all concerned in one way or another with the "religious dimension" as the Australian poet Les Murray describes it: "Some might want to call it a dimension of wonder, of quest, of value, of

A Companion to Contemporary British and Irish Poetry, 1960–2015, First Edition.
Edited by Wolfgang Görtschacher and David Malcolm.
© 2021 John Wiley & Sons Ltd. Published 2021 by John Wiley & Sons Ltd.

ultimate significance or the like" (Murray 1992, 142 "Some Religious Stuff I Know About Australia"). In a poem entitled "Poetry and Religion," Murray states, "God is the poetry caught in any religion" (Murray 1998, 267, l. 17). There are literary problems for the religious poet writing today, especially if he or she is drawing on the imagery of orthodox belief. Back in 1949, the critic Helen Gardner identified such a difficulty, one which is now even more relevant. "The religious poet today cannot rely upon a common fund of religious imagery and religious symbolism, upon liturgical phrases, and great sayings from the Scriptures, to which each of his readers can bring his own private wisdom and experience" (Gardner 1949, 61).

Poetry has long been associated with religious belief. The first poems to be written down, *The Epic of Gilgamesh*, *Inanna*, *The Iliad and the Odyssey*, all deal with the relationships between the gods and humans. The Bible itself, in the King James translation, contains passages that could, in a variety of ways, be classed as poetry. In the sixteenth and seventeenth centuries, there was a remarkable flowering of religious poetry in England. John Donne, George Herbert, and John Milton were all poets of faith, though much of their poetry is about the struggles with that faith. These poets were writing from within a Christian world view. Their readers would have understood the references and the stories they drew upon. With the Romantic period, a new way of engaging with the sacred comes to the fore. Influenced by the new fascination for untamed nature and by the theories of Rousseau, Wordsworth, and Coleridge saw the sacred in nature around them. In Wordsworth's early poetry, we see the Christian God replaced by a pantheistic attitude.

> In nature and the language of the sense,
> The anchor of my purest thoughts, the nurse,
> The guide, the guardian of my heart, and soul
> Of all my moral being.
> ("Lines Written a Few Miles above
> Tintern Abbey," Wordsworth 1974, 165)

Wordsworth may later have revised his earlier notions of pantheism, but the genie was out of the bottle. The sacred in English poetry was no longer tied to conventional religion. For Coleridge, it was the imagination which represented the sacred faculty of mankind as "a repetition in the finite mind of the eternal act of creation in the infinite" (*Biographia Literaria*, ed. Watson, 1975, 167). For Blake, organized religion was a corrupt institution which prevented humans from experiencing their true, divine nature, as in his poem "The Garden of Love." For T. S. Eliot in the early to mid-twentieth century, the search for faith can be traced through "The Waste Land" to the mysticism of "Four Quartets." Although Eliot converted to Anglicanism, his poetry is rich with references to a range of religious beliefs, including Hinduism and Buddhism.

I have structured this chapter in three sections: "Faith and Doubt," "Mysticism and Feminism," and "New Voices." As with any structure it is to some extent arbitrary, but it will hopefully illuminate certain movements and tendencies in poetry about religious experience in the last 65 years through a selection of a number of representative poets. On the whole, I have stuck to poets who are either writing in, or come out of, a Christian tradition. However, this is not to denigrate in any way the work of poets from other religious traditions, rather it is to acknowledge that the majority of poetry written around religious themes in Britain and Ireland in the period tends to draw on Christianity in one way or another.

Faith and Doubt: Elizabeth Jennings, Geoffrey Hill, and R. S. Thomas

In *Every Changing Shape*, her study of religious poetry, Elizabeth Jennings describes all art as "a participation in the eternal act of creation" ("Images in Abeyance," Jennings 1961, 30). She also draws parallels between the priest and the poet, as Barry Sloan points out in his article "Poetry and Faith: The Example of Elizabeth Jennings."

> From this perspective, the poet, like the priest, is a mediator, a wo/man metaphorically set aside and ordained to utter words that are transformative and repeatedly point to the reconciliation and acceptance that Christians also believe are the very essence of the mystery of the Eucharist.
> (Sloan 2006, 393)

In a poem entitled "A Metaphysical Point about Poetry," quoted by Sloan, Jennings states, "I wish to say that God / Is present in all poetry that's made / With form and purpose" (Jennings 2002, 322). However, this is not to suggest that Jennings's poetry is free from suffering and conflict. While she is a poet who is, as Sloan suggests, "a pre-eminent example of a writer whose Christian faith and denominational allegiance to Catholicism are repeatedly explored in her poetry over almost fifty years" (Sloan 2006, 393), she also clearly acknowledges the role of poetry as a way of exploring conflict. In *Every Changing Shape*, she suggests that "Poetry is not a rationalisation but a revelation and what is healing in it, both for the poet and his readers, is the ability to depict conflict at its most vulnerable point…" (Jennings, "The Unity of Incarnation," 1961, 108). This attitude is clear in a poem entitled "To a Friend with a Religious Vocation." The poem opens with the lines "Thinking of your vocation, I am filled / With thoughts of my own lack of one" (ll. 1–2). Jennings then goes on to state how she has "a sense, / vague and inchoate, with no symmetry, / Of purpose" (ll. 5–7). Unlike the mystic's liberating experience of silence, for the poet silence is the enemy. The poem ends with the final verse alluding perhaps to Jennings's struggle with depression.

> Yet with the same convictions that you have
> (It is but your vocation that I lack),
> I must, like you, believe in perfect love.
> In the dark, the dark that draws me back
> Into a chaos where
> Vocations, visions fail, the will grows slack
> And I am stunned by silence everywhere.
> (Jennings 1967, 114, ll. 22–28)

Jennings is a poet who was initially seen as part of The Movement, a group whose members eschewed what they saw as the excesses of poets such as Dylan Thomas. Her formal intelligence and the apparent accessibility of her language are keystones of her work. As Barry Sloan states, "[h]er phrasing implies a notable confidence in the capacity of language—in its stability and potential to communicate shared meanings—far removed from the shifting ironies of post-modernity" (Sloan 2006, 393).

Geoffrey Hill is a very different poet to Jennings. He has stated that "the grasp of true religious experience is a privilege reserved for the few" and that the poet's task is "to make lyrical poetry out of a much more common situation—the sense of *not* being able to grasp true religious experience" (quoted in Hart 1986, 54). Henry Hart, discussing Hill's attitude to religion, states that "[a]s with most modern 'religious poets,' Hill's attitudes towards orthodox beliefs are perplexed" (Hart 1986, 53). Hart goes on to quote Hill. "If poetry has any value, that value must presuppose the absolute freedom of poetry to encompass the maximum range of belief or disbelief" (Hart 1986, 53). Hill's poetry is densely allusive and is often about history and the role language. But he uses the imagery of Christianity in many of his poems. In "Lachrimae," a series of sonnets from *Tenebrae*, which echo Donne's "Holy Sonnets," the image of Christ on the cross recurs again and again. The poems move between a desire to imitate Christ and a realization of how impossible this is. "Lachrimae Coactae" begins:

> Crucified Lord, however much I burn
> to be enamoured of your paradise,
> knowing what ceases and what will not cease,
> frightened of hell, not knowing where to turn,
>
> I fall between harsh grace and hurtful scorn.
> (Hill 1985, 148, ll. 1–5)

The final poem, "Lachrimae Amantis," refuses to bring closure or affirmation; rather it ends with an image of being "half-faithful."

> So many nights the angel of my house
> has fed such urgent comfort through a dream,
> whispered "your lord is coming, he is close"
> that I have drowsed half-faithful for a time
> bathed in pure tones of promise and remorse:
> tomorrow I shall wake to welcome him.
> (Hill 1985, 151, ll. 9–14)

If Hill is a poet who is an outsider hoping for the consolations of belief, then R. S. Thomas is an insider. A priest by profession, Thomas saw religion and poetry as compatible. In an article written for the Times Literary Supplement in 1960, Thomas argues that "it is within the scope of poetry to express or convey religious truth, and to do so in a more intense and memorable way than any other form is able to" (quoted in Morgan 2003, 151). He goes on to suggest a "symbiosis" between the two professions of priest and poet. In his introduction to *The Penguin Book of Religious Verse* (1963), Thomas defines religious poetry as "the imaginative representation of an experience of ultimate reality" (quoted in Morgan 2003, 152). This is certainly a very different view of the relationship between religion and poetry to the one expressed by Hill. But readers expecting Thomas's poetry to be a straightforward confirmation of Christian orthodoxy will be disappointed, as Elaine Shepherd suggests in *R.S. Thomas: Conceding an Absence*:

> If we come to R.S. Thomas looking for reassurance and comfort, we shall certainly be disappointed. But if we come willing to explore with him what it means to be human, if we are willing to accept all the disorder of life and not insist on imposing order, if we are prepared to "sit loosely with orthodoxy," then the unorthodoxy of his work, arising as it does from a fearsome integrity, will at least force us to think for ourselves, and at best liberate us for that doubt which makes faith continually creative.
>
> (Shepherd 1996, 9)

Thomas's poems deal with a number of themes, chief among them religious belief, nature, and the experience of being a parish priest in rural Wales. The language of Thomas's poems is apparently simple in contrast to Hill's, but his images, clear as they are, often concern themselves with notions of the unutterable. His approach can differ at times, but a key approach of his poetry is the *via negativa*, best illustrated in the poem of that name in which "God is that great absence / in our lives" (Thomas 1993, 220, ll. 2–3).

The *via negativa* has a long history in Christian thought, and can usefully be linked to poetry through Keats's notion of negative capability, the need for the poet to be "in uncertainties, mysteries and doubts without any irritable reaching after fact and reason..." (Keats, 1958, 193–194). Sometimes the waiting is a waiting on what seems to be nothing, as in "In Church" which culminates in the following lines:

> There is no other sound
> In the darkness but the sound of a man
> Breathing, testing his faith
> On emptiness, nailing his questions
> One by one to an untenanted cross.
> (Thomas 1993, 180, ll. 16–20)

The key to how one reads this poem is surely in the interpretation of the final image. On the one hand it could suggest the absence of Christ as something lacking, a failure of faith. On the other hand, it could suggest that the cross is untenanted because Christ has risen.

A more positive image of the emptying of self-required by the *via negativa* can be seen in "The Moor." Thomas states that "What God was there made himself felt / Not listened to, in clean colours..." (Thomas, 1993, 166, ll. 5–6). Thomas uses the imagery of nature to express the presence of God. The language of the poem is of course metaphorical, for the very nature of the *via negativa* requires an acknowledgment of the provisional nature of any description of the divine. The poem fuses the natural and the religious, so the moor is "like a church" and the nature and religious imagery again come together at the end of the poem in the imagery of bread breaking as in the act of communion. But finally the experience is none of these things, but something ineffable that is gestured toward by the words. It is in the "cession" of the mind's "kingdom" that revelation comes, in the giving up of the dominion of the self to something greater and that cession surely includes the giving up of concepts too, an ability to enter in the state of negative capability.

Mysticism and Feminism: Kathleen Raine and Gillian Allnutt

That mystical vision has correspondences with poetry is clear from Thomas's poems. But that vision has been elaborated by a number of important female poets in the late twentieth and early twenty-first centuries. In this section, I will look at the work of Kathleen Raine and that of Gillian Allnutt, who have pursued a writing which explores issues of faith from a post-feminist viewpoint.

Kathleen Raine wrote extensively about William Blake. As Brian Keeble suggests, like Blake she believed that "one power alone makes a poet—imagination, the divine vision" (Keeble 2016, 118). In a time when such ideas were unfashionable, Raine's work was often uncompromising in its direct address of religious themes. In a series of memories and essays collected in *Faces of Day and Night* (Raine 1972), Raine refers to mystical experiences she had as both a child and an adult. Although Raine converted to Catholicism in the 1940s, a decision she later regretted, she was in fact more influenced by Eastern traditions, neo-Platonism, and Jungian psychology than Christianity. Her early poetry does try to marry her Christian upbringing to her poetic imagination, and there is a middle period when she tries, rather unsuccessfully, to yoke her poetry to her Catholic conversion. But in the later work, there is little or no sense of a denominational religious framework of any kind. Rather, the vision here is of the "One."

> Each is the presence of the all,
> And all things bear the signature
> Of one unfathomable thought,
> Lucid as universal light…
> ("In My Seventieth Year,"
> Raine 1981, 232, ll. 14–16)

Later in the same poem, she asks "Is this perhaps what men called God / before the word lost meaning?" (ll. 52–53) The problem with this kind of poetry is that it can sound more like a statement of belief that an evocation of an actual religious experience.

Gillian Allnutt's work draws on Christianity for its imagery, particularly Celtic Christianity. But it is always alive to history and to female experience. Allnutt is a writer who is not afraid to make the reader do some work in the poem. Consequently, her poems are devoid of the kind of bald statements of belief which can let down Raine's work. Rather, hers is a poetry of holes, as Karyn Costa describes in a review of Allnut's 2004 collection *Sojourner*.

What is most striking is how difficult it is to express aloud what is often too painful to even think about. The poems are hesitant, words are repeated, many are monologues as no one listens to what is trying to be said. These poems are full of holes. Holes left by people who have come and gone; others on the page—as many pauses as the speaker searches for the right words or simply the strength to utter them: "What was hard to understand—the holes / in everything, the held wings broken." (Costa 2004)

Rather than spell out a meaning, Allnutt's poems hint at states of mind, at spiritual experiences. In "Epiphany," the "holes" in the poem are represented physically in the layout of the poem as well as in the minimal imagery.

>   Epiphany (Yorkshire Dales)
>   *(for John)*
>
>   Solitude   your death   a drover's
>   road   two dry stone walls   the borders
>   of the earth   each stone a hand's width and the berth of God
>
>   Where blackthorn lays the wind bare to the bone
>   you herded stars.
>
>   (Allnutt 2007, 27)

Allnutt's poems often trace or recreate imaginatively the experience of women in Christianity. In "Magdalene," Jesus's words are mixed with a range of registers which suggest not only the biblical story of Magdalene, but also historical and social contexts. Mary Magdalene is described as "Muddled of lore" (Allnutt 2007, 168, l. 1), then later as "as the moon / attendant" (Allnutt 2007, 168, ll. 5–6), and finally as "Common, prostitute" (Allnutt 2007, 168, l. 9).

In Allnutt's poems, the spiritual quest is often represented as a paring away, and the poems reflect this in their forms as well as their contents. In "Anchorage," which takes Julian of Norwich as its subject, "love takes the hard ground" (Allnutt 2007, 106, l. 2). The poem ends with an image of fecundity as "bone / flowers like blackthorn" (Allnutt 2007, 106, ll. 6–7). In "The Road Home," "It is the road to God / that matters now, the ragged road, the wood" (Allnutt 2007, 107, ll. 1–2). Comparing the spiritual journey to the exile of Hansel and Gretel in the wood, Allnutt declares "You won't be going back to the hut" (Allnutt 2007, 107, l. 7). The hut represents the human world with all its social concerns.

>   the *cul de sac* of the world
>   in a field
>
>   that's permanently full
>   of people
>
>   looking for a festival
>   of literature, a fairy tale,
>
>   a feathered
>   nest of brothers and sisters…
>   (Allnutt 2007, 108,
>   ll. 10–16)

The poem ends on the suggestion of a journey, a spirituality path grounded in a "first world" and "bared now to the word *God*" (Allnutt 2007, 108, ll. 17–18).

New Voices

Michael Symmons Roberts is a contemporary poet who is also a practicing Catholic. In an interview with Sue Gaisford in *The Tablet*, he talks about the relationship between faith and doubt in his work. "One of the things that is there in my work, whether I want it to be or not, is the constant dialogue between faith and doubt. I had it as an atheist, and now I've switched sides, as it were, it's still going on. But now I'm on the other side of the argument" (Gaisford 2014, 6). For Symmons Roberts, it is the making of a poetry out of the conditions of the contemporary world that is vital. His work engages with science, contemporary urban landscapes, and war. He is aware of the decline of shared religious imagery, declaring in the same interview that "the stories of Christianity are no longer common ground." However, he does not see this as only a loss, as Gaisford goes on to suggest. "Yet, quoting Dietrich Bonhoeffer, he believes that we have to forge new metaphors; that the religion of the future will be framed around new language, new ways of talking about these things. It is a loss, but it is also liberating" (Gaisford 2014, 6).

Much of this new language involves images of the contemporary, physical world. Symmons Roberts's 2004 collection *Corpus* uses the body as a locus for concerns which are often metaphysical. "Food for Risen Bodies," a sequence of six poems which are dotted through the collection, emphasizes the physicality of resurrection. In "Food for Risen Bodies II," he writes of Christ:

> Now on Tiberias' shores he grills
> a carp and catfish breakfast on a charcoal fire.
> This is not hunger, this is resurrection:
>
> he eats because he can, and wants to
> taste the scales, the moist flakes of the sea,
> to rub the salt into his wounds.
> (Symmons Roberts 2004, 1, ll. 4–9)

Symmons Roberts's poems are often set in a contemporary world torn apart by war. So in "Gifts," he presents us with a contemporary account of the three wise men, but one where the gifts are rejected as too dangerous, where Caspar's gold ends up "beaten into leaf // to line the windows of stretch limos" (Symmons Roberts 2004, 55, ll. 15–16) and Balthazar's frankincense is "ground into a fragrance / to mask the stench of battlefields, / to calm the nerves / on death row, / to steady trigger-fingers"(Symmons Roberts 2004, 56, ll. 30–35).

"Night Drive" from the collection *The Half Healed* shows us God cruising the streets:

> Skipping the lights with no place
> to get to, driving for the sake
>
> past ranks of shop-front mannequins
> held hostage by fluorescent hum,
>
> past betting shops and taxi ranks,
> past fights and lovers, holy drunks.
> (Symmons Roberts 2008,
> 34, ll. 5–10)

Later in the poem, this appearance has become legendary. "Years later, some will say his face / was wet, or that he closed his eyes // and drove into the river. Others, / war vets, homeless, desperate poor // will say he came to eat there, / found friends at their bonfires" (Symmons Roberts 2008, 35, ll. 32–36). The poem ends with an image of snow "unseasonal, unprecedented." And yet "Everyone and no one knows who sent it" (Symmons Roberts 2008, 35, ll. 41–42).

Colette Bryce's poems deal with contemporary concerns too, particularly the effects of growing up in Northern Ireland. In her first collection, *The Heel of Bernadette*, the influences of Catholicism are clear, though mixed with love and family relationships. In "Itch," a poem which Bryce describes as "a playful take on 'who we are' as versus who we're supposed to be in our parents' eyes (ears?)" (Bryce 2013, 4), a mother's inability to listen is the result of preconceived religious ideas. In the final couplet of the poem, it is the word "wishes" that suggests the ways in which our own fears and desires can be clothed as belief.

> Things I begin to tell her,
> I believe she cannot hear
>
> for the whispering like wishes
> of Jesus softly breathing there.
> (Bryce 2000, 13, ll. 8–11)

The poem "The Heel of Bernadette" explores human love through the image of touching the heel of a statue of St. Bernadette, the "one touch of imagined skin" (Bryce 2000, 37, l. 9) which is worn by "losses, wishes, mute petitions" (Bryce 2000, 37, l. 12). The final verse mixes the sacred and the human with an image of a very real body in an incantation.

> forehead, sternum, yoke of shoulders,
> Holy Spirit, Son and Father
> help us, now we're farther, older,
> find in ourselves the child believer
> (Bryce 2000, 37, ll. 13–16)

"Early Version" from her second collection *The Full Indian Rope Trick* reimagines the story of Jesus walking on the water, describing how "he'd crouched upon the shore, alone, engaged / in silent prayer, when, looking down, he started— / seeing his own image crouching there" (Bryce 2005, 23, ll. 5–7). Jesus walks across the lake "on the soles / of his liquid self" (Bryce 2005, 23, ll. 13–14). When he reaches the boat, he asks the disciples to open "what he always / called our 'fettered minds'" (Bryce 2005, 23, ll. 19–20). By injecting the story with the physical details of the actual miracle itself, Bryce succeeds in reanimating the mystery of the original. "The Word" brilliantly presents us with an image of Christ returning to the contemporary world, not as one person, but as many, suggesting the words of Matthew 25: "And the King shall answer and say unto them, Verily I say unto you, Inasmuch as ye have done it unto one of the least of these my brethren, ye have done it unto me."

> He arrived, confused, in groups at the harbours,
> walking unsteadily over the gangways;
> turned up at airports, lost in the corridors,
> shunted and shoved from Control to Security.
> (Bryce 2005, 24, ll. 1–4)

The account is narrated from the point of view of those for whom the refugees, homeless, and asylum seekers are a nuisance and a threat. They even disturb those attending church, "milking / the faithful, blocking the porch" (Bryce 2005, 24, l. 17–18). The speakers turn to "the Word."

> We turned to the Word; called to our journalists, they heard
> and hammered a word through the palms of His hands: SCAM.
> They battered a word through the bones of His feet: CHEAT.
> (Bryce 2005, 24–25, ll. 22–24)

In the end "He" is killed and buried. The poem closes with a reference to the stone and the tomb. "We are safer now, for much has changed, / now the Word is the law is a huge, immovable stone, // should He rise again" (Bryce 2005, 25, ll. 32–34). While taking a similarly contemporary take on the second coming Symmons Roberts's "Night Drive," Bryce's poem is more up-front about its politics.

Having surveyed religious poetry from 1960 to 2010, what conclusions can we draw about the nature of such poetry? Doubt is certainly a major issue for a number of poets, whose subject matter is often religious belief and its relationship to the countervailing pressures of modern science-based views of reality. But perhaps this is part of a larger tendency in poetry itself. As Gaisford comments in her interview with Michael Symmons Roberts, "Roberts has been called a religious poet for a secular age. But he feels that his work is not essentially different from that of his contemporaries, that poetry is a large room, containing many shades of belief and unbelief" (Gaisford 2014, 6). However, the mystical tradition as exemplified by the work of Gillian Allnutt continues to provide a rich seam for poetry, gesturing, as it does, to an experience of the divine ground which is beyond both denomination as well as nomination. What is clear is that the attenuated nature of much modern belief is often reflected in the form and language of poems. It is certainly harder in the twenty-first century to imagine a poet writing as Elizabeth Jennings did with "confidence in the capacity of language—

in its stability and potential to communicate shared meanings" (Sloan 2006, 393). Rather, language itself is having to be remade to fit the demands of religious experience in the modern world. As Michael Symmons Roberts suggests in his interview with Sue Gaisford, perhaps "the religion of the future will be framed around new language, new ways of talking about these things. It is a loss, but it is also liberating" (Gaisford 2014, 6).

References

Allnutt, Gillian (2007). *How the Bicycle Shone: New and Selected Poems*. Tarset: Bloodaxe Books.

Blake, William (1988). *Selected Poetry and Prose* (ed. David Punter). London: Routledge.

Bryce, Colette (2000). *The Heel of Bernadette*. London: Picador.

Bryce, Colette (2005). *The Full Indian Rope Rope Trick*. London: Picador.

Bryce, Colette (2013). "Interview." In: *The Wake Forest Series of Irish Poetry*, vol. iii (ed. Conor O'Callaghan), 3–14. Winston-Salem, NC: Wake Forest University Press.

Coleridge, Samuel Taylor (1975). *Biographia Literaria* (ed. George Watson). London: Dent.

Costa, Karyn. (2004). E-rea, 2.2. http://erea.revues.org/458 (accessed 6 May 2020).

Gaisford, Sue (2014). Master of Metaphor: Interview with Michael Symmons Roberts. *The Tablet* http://archive.thetablet.co.uk/article/15th-february-2014/6/the-tablet- (accessed 15 May 2015).

Gardner, Helen (1949). *The Art of T. S. Eliot*. London: Cresset Press.

Hart, Henry (1986). *The Poetry of Geoffrey Hill*. Carbondale: Southern Illinois University Press.

Hill, Geoffrey (1985). *Collected Poems*. London: Penguin.

Jennings, Elizabeth (1961). *Every Changing Shape*. London: André Deutsch, London.

Jennings, Elizabeth (1967). *Collected Poems*. London: Macmillan.

Jennings, Elizabeth (2002). *New Collected Poems*. Manchester: Carcanet.

Keats, John (1958). *The Letters of John Keats*, vol. 2 (ed. H.E. Rollins). Cambridge: Cambridge University Press.

Keeble, Brian (2016). "Who Speaks for the Dust?: Kathleen Raine and the Vocation of Poetry." *Sewanee Review* 124 (1): 117.

Morgan, Christopher (2003). *R. S. Thomas: Identity, Environment and Deity*. Manchester: Manchester University Press.

Murray, Les (1992). *The Paperbark Tree*. Manchester: Carcanet.

Murray, Les (1998). *Collected Poems*. Manchester: Carcanet Press.

Raine, Kathleen (1972). *Faces of Day and Night*. London: Enitharmon Press.

Raine, Kathleen (1981). *Collected Poems*. London: George Allen and Unwin.

Shepherd, Elaine (1996). *R. S. Thomas: Conceding an Absence*. London: Macmillan.

Sloan, Barry (2006). "Poetry and Faith: The Example of Elizabeth Jennings." *Christianity and Literature* 55 (3, Spring): 393–414.

Symmons Roberts, Michael (2004). *Corpus*. London: Jonathan Cape.

Symmons Roberts, Michael (2008). *The Half Healed*. London: Jonathan Cape.

Thomas, R. S. (1993). *Collected Poems 1945–1990*. London: Phoenix.

Williams, Rowan, and Cole Morton (2014). "I Didn't Really Want to Be Archbishop." *The Telegraph* (6 April) www.telegraph.co.uk/news/features/10789740/Rowan-Williams-I-didnt-really-want-to-be-Archbishop.html (accessed 26 November 2017)

Wordsworth, William (1974). *Poetical Works* (ed. Thomas Hutchinson). Oxford: Oxford University Press.

2c.16
Love Poetry

Eleanor Spencer

On the day before Valentine's Day in 1999, journalist Emma Brockes suggested in *The Guardian* that the British public might have rather fallen out of love with love poetry. "In our cynical, postmodern age," she asked, "has love poetry become as trite as the doggerel in a valentine [sic] card?" (Brockes 1999). A quick perusal of the poetry section in your local Waterstones bookshop today, though, would seem to refute Brockes's suggestion that the public appetite for love poetry is on the wane. You will most likely find any number of accessible and attractive anthologies of "love poetry," among them: *The Nation's Favourite Love Poems*, edited by Daisy Goodwin (1997); *The Bloomsbury Book of Love Poems*, edited by Benjamin Zephaniah (1999); *Hand in Hand: An Anthology of Love Poems*, edited by Carol Ann Duffy (2001); *The New Penguin Book of Love Poetry*, edited by Jon Stallworthy (2003); *The New Faber Book of Love Poems*, edited by James Fenton (2008); and *Penguin's Poems for Love*, edited by Laura Barber (2010). That several of these anthologies are now in their second or third editions suggests that *somebody* must be buying them. It would seem, then, that "love poetry," far from having been unceremoniously dumped by the reading public, still has a place in the hearts of Waterstones customers, at least.

Many of the more contemporary poems included in recent anthologies of love poetry ostensibly bear little resemblance to canonical stalwarts such as Elizabeth Barrett Browning's "Sonnet 43" from *Sonnets from the Portuguese* or Shakespeare's "Sonnet 116," and even revel in their seeming anti-romantic sentiments. In its narrowest definition, we might think of a love poem as one in which a speaker passionately expresses his or her love (or lust) for an individual, often the internal addressee. The poet might pledge undying devotion, or praise the beloved's

---

A Companion to Contemporary British and Irish Poetry, 1960–2015, First Edition.
Edited by Wolfgang Görtschacher and David Malcolm.
© 2021 John Wiley & Sons Ltd. Published 2021 by John Wiley & Sons Ltd.

peerless good looks. In the aftermath of the New Critical purge, and the Confessional splurge, though, we would do better to widen our poetic parameters somewhat. Jon Stallworthy suggests that any new definition must be "one, like a seine net, large enough to take in all" (Stallworthy 1976, 20). He goes on, "So I consider a love poem to be not only the lover's 'ballad / Made to his mistress's eyebrow,' but any poem about any aspect of one human being's desire for another" (1976, 20). So, a love poem is, quite simply, a poem about love: about falling in love; falling out of love; unrequited love; the agonies and the ecstasies; the dreams and the disappointments; the declarations and the disavowals; the good, the bad, and the ugly.

In the first half of the twentieth century, the rise of a poetics of impersonality, steered by W. B. Yeats, T. S. Eliot, and Ezra Pound, led to a critical disdain for any poetry which wore—or appeared to wear—its heart on its sleeve. In addition to this New Critical distaste for the poem as medium of genuine (rather than performative) self-expression, the subject of "love" was effectively blacklisted by the Modernists. As Tim Hancock notes, "in their pioneering *A Survey of Modernist Poetry* published in 1927, Laura Riding and Robert Graves dismissed the Georgian poets by cataloging the 'uncontroversial subjects' that were seen as their stock in trade, subjects including 'nature and love and leisure and old age and childhood and animals and sleep'" (Hancock 2003, 3). Five years later, "F.R. Leavis offered another damning list of hackneyed themes, suggesting that the public had 'become accustomed to the idea that certain things are poetical e.g. flowers, dawn, dew, birds, love, archaisms, and country place-names'" (Hancock 2003, 3). It seemed that "love" was a permissible subject for "serious" poetry only when derided, degraded, or savagely deconstructed. The opening lines of Mina Loy's sequence "Songs to Joannes" (originally titled "Love Songs") unceremoniously overthrow any naïve generic expectations that the reader might have.

> Spawn of Fantasies
> Silting the appraisable
> Pig Cupid
> His rosy snout
> Rooting erotic garbage.
> (Loy, 1996, 53)

If, as Eliot's *The Waste Land* suggests, in the aftermath of World War I we were left with only "stony rubbish" and a "heap of broken images," then "love" is no exception, and its familiar images are worn, corrupted, and cheapened through overuse (Eliot 1971, 38).

The fierce aversion to Georgian sentimentality that we see in the work of the Modernists had subdued by the 1960s into the kind of studied skepticism and wry world-weariness that we recognize in the poetry of Philip Larkin. As you might expect from a poet who famously declared "deprivation is for me what daffodils were for Wordsworth" (Larkin 1983, 47), the course of true love does not always run smooth, and many of Larkin's poems are pervaded by a sense of romantic relegation; of being sidelined or left behind as luckier (or lustier) others *"all go down the long slide / Like free bloody birds"* ("High Windows." Larkin 2012, 80, ll. 15–16). If the rose is the traditional emblem of romance, then the speaker of "Wild Oats" is able to admire and aspire to this ideal only from a tongue-tied distance.

> About twenty years ago
> Two girls came in where I worked –
> A bosomy English rose
> And her friend in specs I could talk to.
> (Larkin 2012, 68, ll. 1–4)

The voluptuous vowels and seductive sibilance of the phrase "bosomy English rose" contrasts almost comically with the stilted monosyllables of "friend in specs." Donald Davie famously referred to Larkin's poetry as "one of lowered sights and patiently diminished expectations" (Davie 1973, 71). Even with such "lowered sights," though, Larkin's pessimists still find themselves disappointed. If the "two snaps, / Of bosomy rose with fur gloves on" (ll. 22–23) that the speaker confesses to keeping in his wallet, 20 years on, are painful reminders of his romantic inadequacy—"Unlucky charms" (l. 24)—then they also perhaps attest to something more affirmatory: the resilience of hope.

In "An Arundel Tomb," the tourists who flock to the effigy-topped tomb of the Earl and Countess see "with a sharp tender shock, / His hand withdrawn, holding her hand," (ll. 11–12) and eagerly interpret this small sculpted detail as proof of the platitude that true love conquers all, even death (Larkin 2012, 71). However, all is not as it seems. The double meaning of the repeated word "lie" throws into doubt this touching pose, and our growing realization that "Such faithfulness in effigy" (l. 14) is but "A sculptor's sweet commissioned grace" (l. 16) is confirmed in the famous (and oft misquoted) final stanza.

> Time has transfigured them into
> Untruth. The stone fidelity
> They hardly meant has come to be
> Their final blazon, and to prove
> Our almost-instinct almost true:
> What will survive of us is love.
> (ll. 37–42)

Though Larkin himself described "An Arundel Tomb" as "rather a romantic poem," these closing lines are only "almost" affirmatory, and say far more about our own need to believe in the death-defying lastingness of love than about the historical reality of these figures' lives (Larkin 2012, 436). What has survived here is not love, but an impulse to believe in love, and to credit love with the power to transcend death. Significant here, but almost always overlooked, is Larkin's use of the first-person plural "our." In other poems including "The Large Cool Store" and "Faith Healing," the speaker refers aloofly to "their sort" and to "the women," distancing himself from the tawdry desires or undignified neediness of the "cut price crowd." The desire—even the need—to believe that "What will survive of us is love," though, is not only theirs, but also *ours*; it is something innately human, a shared desire that transcends class and education.

In Larkin's verse, mordant, often savagely self-deprecating humor functions as a dubious defense against disappointment in matters of the heart. A Venn diagram of the contents of *The Nation's Favourite Comic Poems* (1998) and *The Nation's Favourite Love Poems* would reveal a not insignificant overlap between the two volumes. Humor—often of the bluest variety—and mischievous wit are the surest ways of jettisoning outmoded soppiness or self-indulgence, as poems such as Hugo Williams's "Toilet" and John Fuller's "Valentine" aptly demonstrate. Ostensibly an *apologia* for the speaker's "indelicate" desires, Fuller's poem revels in its startling juxtapositions of the madcap melodramatic and the quotidian:

> I'd like to cross two hemispheres
> And have you chase me.
> I'd like to smuggle you across frontiers
> Or sail with you at night into Tangiers.
> I'd like you to embrace me.
> (Fuller 1996, 301, ll. 52–56)

The speaker casts himself in a variety of stock romantic roles; he is alternately the dastardly seducer ("Sometimes I feel it is my fate / To chase you screaming up a tower" ll. 9–10) and the willing victim of a deadly femme fatale ("I'd let you put insecticide / Into my wine" ll. 65–66). The often precarious polysyllabic rhymes deftly countermand any potential mawkishness and lend the poem an incantatory quality; this is virtuosic verbal seduction—or even ravishment by rhyme:

> I'd even like you if you were the Bride
> Of Frankenstein
> Or something ghoulish out of Mamoulian's
> *Jekyll and Hyde*.
> I'd even like you as my Julian
> Of Norwich or Cathleen ni Houlihan.
> (ll. 67–72)

The poem offers its playful take on the Petrarchan convention of the blazon as the speaker approvingly itemizes his beloved's many physical charms: "I like your eyes, I like their fringes. / The way they focus on me gives me twinges. / Your upper arms drive me berserk. / I like the way your elbows work, / on hinges ..." (ll. 28–32). Such a burlesque of the surgical male gaze is nothing new; even in the early seventeenth century, poets such as Shakespeare (in "Sonnet 130") and Andrew Marvell (in "To His Coy Mistress") were parodying the hyperbolic litanies that even then were associated with subpar Petrarchan verse.

In the closing lines of this poem that deliberately eschew the word "love" in favor of the cooler, more insouciant "like," we observe something of a change in tone. Gone is the comical cataloging of carnal (even semi-criminal) desires to be replaced by something more exposed and infinitely more vulnerable: "I'd like to be your only audience, / The final name in your appointment book, / Your future tense" (ll. 93–95).

If Fuller uses surreal imagery and contortions of rhyme to avoid becoming mired in sentimentality, then Wendy Cope uses the defiantly untranscendent ordinariness of modern (sub) urban life in much the same way. In *The Nation's Favourite Love Poems*, only Shakespeare and John Donne appear more frequently than Cope, and the popular appeal of her mischievous musings lies in precisely her foregrounded rejections of the traditionally "romantic." Writing about her fondness for the poetry of George Herbert, Cope says, "At the beginning of a new poetry notebook I write 'Dare to be true' from one of Herbert's stanzas on honesty" (Cope 2003). Cope's verse unapologetically privileges what is "true" over what is poetic or romantic, and several of her most popular poems impishly undermine the conventions of the long English amatory tradition. Of "Giving Up Smoking," Cope comments, "people who have never been addicted to nicotine don't understand what an intense love poem it is"; while "Shakespeare sonnet[s]" and "Beethoven quartet[s]" may be the traditional currency of the wooing lover, a sly cigarette is the true yardstick of yearning for any former smoker (Cope 1986, 32). "Strugnell's Bargain" is a comically literal re-reading of Philip Sidney's "Song from Arcadia: My True Love Hath My Heart," and concludes that while sweet nothings are easily exchanged, vital organs are best kept to oneself: "But now, whenever one of us refers / To 'my heart,' things get rather complicated" (Baker 1990, 325, ll. 3–4). The speaker, a would-be wooer misplaced in this "unarmorial age," is frustrated by the unforeseen repercussions of his grand romantic gesture: "I ask you, do you think that Sir Philip Sidney / Got spoken to like that?" (ll. 9–10). Whereas grand gestures and orotund declarations tend to fall flat in Cope's verse, she deftly captures the way in which even the most everyday experiences take on a vivid hue when one is in love. In "The Orange," the speaker muses, "[…] that orange, it made me so happy, / As ordinary things often do / Just lately" (Cope 2009, 28, ll. 5–7). Cope's "huge orange" (l. 1) is not a "red, red rose" nor even Edwin Morgan's more obviously sensual "Strawberries," yet this absurd, "oversized" fruit is transfigured into an unlikely emblem of "peace and contentment" (l. 8). The unvarnished closing line—"I love you. I'm glad I exist" (l. 12)—is hardly Shakespearean, nor does it need to be. Again, Cope "dare[s] to be true" rather than striving for highfalutin effect.

Perhaps as a result of this principled commitment to "truth," many of Cope's poems are brief, even to the point of terseness (the acerbic four-liner "Loss," for example). If, as Dorothy Parker wrote, "brevity is the soul of lingerie" (quoted in Woollcott 1934, 146) then it is also the hallmark of many contemporary love poems. Adrian Mitchell's epigrammatic "Celia, Celia" (Mitchell 2012) is a case in point. Written to Mitchell's wife, the poem is a knowing nod to Ben Jonson's "To Celia" (1616), known to many as "Drink to Me Only with Thine Eyes." Whereas Jonson's speaker's gift of a "rosy wreath" (l. 9) is summarily returned by his intended, we may assume that Mitchell's flippant flâneur fares rather better. Extravagant praise of the distant beloved is replaced here by unashamed sexual desire for a fond and familiar partner. The Petrarchan predicament of unrequited love was a mainstay of Renaissance love poetry, and many courtly love lyrics dramatize the thrill of the chase with little or no concern as to what becomes of that infatuation once the chase is over and the prize is won. While there are notable examples of Renaissance love lyrics extolling the virtues of security in marriage (Donne's "A Valediction: Forbidding Mourning," for example), they are vastly outnumbered by those poems of unanswered, forbidden, or ill-fated love. Denis de Rougemont suggests that

> Romance only comes into existence where love is fatal, frowned upon and doomed by life itself. What stirs lyrical poets to their finest flights is neither the delight of the senses nor the fruitful contentment of the settled couple; not the satisfaction of love but its *passion*. And passion means suffering.
>
> (de Rougemont 1983, 15)

Are "passion" and "contentment" mutually exclusive, then? Must love hurt? Carol Ann Duffy's "Valentine," while rejecting the clichéd trappings of Valentine's Day ("Not a red rose or a satin heart" (l. 1); "Not a cute card or a kissogram" (l. 12)), juxtaposes the lexical field of romance with that of violence and pain (Duffy 2006, 115). The speaker promises (or perhaps threatens) the beloved that the love token of an onion "will blind you with tears / like a lover," (ll. 7–8) and that its "fierce kiss will stay on your lips, / possessive and faithful" (ll. 14–15). The tentative proposal of commitment and security in the image of the onion's "platinum loops [which] shrink to a wedding ring" (l. 19) is immediately undercut by the calculated indifference of the throwaway "if you like" (l. 20). The first word of the next verse paragraph ("Lethal," l. 21) does not refer to the clinging scent of the onion but to that constricting loop; the symbol of possession and power. The isolated line "I am trying to be truthful" is simultaneously a commitment to truth and an admission of the difficulty of finding "Words at once true and kind, / Or not untrue and not unkind" (Larkin 2012, 61).

Both axiom and neuroscience teach us that whereas the early stages of courtship are a raging torrent of phenethylamine-triggered emotional intensity (the highs *and* the lows) and testosterone-driven carnal urgency, the "settled couple" is sustained by a steady drip-feed of endorphins, the hormone responsible for feelings of security, fondness, and attachment. Tim Hancock suggests that "since the mid-nineteenth century there has been an increasing tendency, at least in the West, to write about this bond of attachment" (Hancock 2007, 199), leading to what Patricia Ball has termed "the poetry of relationships" (Ball 1976, 1). A poetics of relationships—of constancy and commitment rather than carnality and conflict—does not warm every reader's (or critic's) heart though. In his 1980 review of Seamus Heaney's *Field Work*, Al Alvarez was not intending to be complimentary when he described the tone of the volume as "in a word, married."

Marriage and domesticity, however, are not necessarily the death knells of excitement and desire, as Heaney's poems of marriage reveal. Here, we have not the fraught, passionless proximity of the silent couple in Larkin's "Talking in Bed," but what Blake Morrison calls "a blend of sexual passion and domestic affection unique in modern British poetry" (Morrison 1982, 83). In "The Skunk" (admittedly, not the most promising title for a love poem), the poet recalls a series of late night trysts many years before when he lived separately from his wife while lecturing at the University of California: "Night after night / I expected her like a visitor" (Heaney 1979, 48, ll. 3–4). Heaney creates a ripe sense of erotic anticipation here; the end stopped lines mimic hitched breaths and expectant pauses. Though Margaret Drabble claims that "the best love poems are written by the most faithless lovers" (*The Guardian* 2012), it is no "other woman" that the poet tensely awaits, but an "intent and glamourous" (l. 17) skunk. His separation from his wife has heightened the poet's senses almost painfully; in her physical absence she pervades the very "night earth and air // Of California" (ll. 12–13) "[C]omposing / Love-letters again" (ll. 9–10) is the poet's attempt to bridge this distance between them, and the word "wife" (l. 10) is transfigured into something simultaneously familiar and unknown; with "its slender vowel" (l. 11) it acquires a sensuous, almost tangible body of its own. In the final two stanzas, recollection and reality meet and merge as we discover what elicited this heady reminiscence:

> It all came back to me last night, stirred
> By the sootfall of your things at bedtime,
> Your head-down, tail-up hunt in a bottom drawer
> For the black plunge-line nightdress.
> (ll. 21–24)

Like the skunk, the poet's wife in her natural habitat is both "Ordinary" and "mysterious" (l. 18), "Mythologized" and "demythologized" (l. 19). She is transfigured in the poet's transfixed gaze; he is a rapt voyeur once again. If there is a juxtaposition here of the erotically charged ("stirred" (l. 21); "plunge-line" (l. 24)) with the cozily domestic ("bedtime" (l. 22); an impatient "hunt in a bottom drawer" (l. 23)), then it is not a disagreeable one; this is what desire in marriage (and, moreover, middle-age) looks like. Moreover, such an audacious poem could only be written within the context of a long and fond relationship; as Christopher Ricks sagely counsels "you have to love your wife most trustingly, and trust in the reciprocity, before you would trust yourself to a comparison of her to a skunk" (Ricks 1979, 100).

In stark contrast to the familiarity, fondness, and reciprocity celebrated in Heaney's poems of conjugal love is the clandestine craving expressed in Duffy's "Warming Her Pearls." Petrarchan love lyrics lend themselves to, or even invite, a homosexual reading as there is a tendency to use not the gender-specific third-person "he" and "she" but the gender-neutral "you" and "I." Similarly, more contemporary poets like Edwin Morgan quietly take advantage of the same grammatical imprecisions and gender-neutral terms of endearment ("my honey"; "my love") when exploring same-sex desires. Given that homosexuality was not decriminalized in Scotland until 1980, discretion was a practical necessity for Morgan rather than an artistic principle. In "Strawberries" (1968), though the lovers slowly savor their sugar-dipped strawberries, "not hurrying the feast / for one to come" (ll. 13–14), it is implicit that their blissful repast is dependent on a temporary "forgetfulness" of reality.

> let the sun beat
> on our forgetfulness
> one hour of all
> the heat intense
> and summer lightening
> on the Kilpatrick hills
>
> let the storm wash the plates
> (Morgan 2000, 39, ll. 27–33)

James McGonigal suggests that Morgan's necessary obfuscation of his sexuality within his verse "makes this a love poetry for the whole of humanity. It's inclusive: men and women can read themselves into it" (Crown 2008). Duffy's "Warming Her Pearls" (1987), on the other hand, is a poem of unequivocal feminine and lesbian desire. Duffy suggests that some of the poems in the selected volume *Love Poems* "are wearing a mask [...] as though at the Venice Carnival" (Duffy 2013). The "mask" of the nineteenth-century lady's maid in this dramatic monologue affords Duffy the freedom to explore the complexities of a lesbian, cross-class infatuation in a voice not entirely her own. If the pearls are a means of physical connection between the maid and her mistress, then they are also a powerful symbol of the distance and difference—certainly of class and possibly of sexuality—between them. As in her "Valentine," passion is here, too, associated with violence; the line "Slack on my neck, her rope" (l. 8) is suggestive of enslavement or brings to mind the disquieting image of a noose (Duffy 2006, 60). While the mistress is the Petrarchan ideal of serene femininity ("her cool, white throat" (l. 4); "watch the soft blush seep through her skin" (l. 14) and "her slim hand" (l. 19)), the maid is increasingly consumed by her illicit yearning: from "slow heat" (l. 7) to "red lips" (l. 16) to "I burn" (l. 24). The maid relishes the thought that her desire possessively, powerfully inscribes itself on her mistress's body, too.

> She's beautiful. I dream about her
> in my attic bed; picture her dancing
> with tall men, puzzled by my faint, persistent scent
> beneath her French perfume, her milky stones.
> (ll. 9–12)

Is it the mistress who is "puzzled" by this curious scent, or the anonymous "tall men" with whom she dances? Does being the (oblivious?) object of burning lesbian desire destabilize the mistress's footing within these heteronormative spaces? Duffy writes that "Poets, when they write a love poem, cannot be unaware of the long tradition of poets standing behind them—their stores of images and metaphors and forms" (Duffy 2013). Certainly, this poem reprises the familiar Petrarchan trope of forbidden or unrequited love, but that the desirous speaker is female subverts the traditional dynamic of male active subject and female passive object.

It seems, then, that despite a perennial cynicism as to the motives and merits of "love poetry," we cannot, nor do we have any desire to, end this particular love affair. As Edwin Morgan's "Love" joyously proclaims

> Love is the food of music, art, poetry. It
>   fills us and fuels us and fires us to create.
> Love is terror. Love is sweat. Love is bashed
>   pillow, crumpled sheet, unenviable fate.
> (Morgan 2007, 90, ll. 3–6)

References

"Love Poems: Writers Choose Their Favourites for Valentine's Day" (2012). *The Guardian* (10 February). http://www.theguardian.com/books/2012/feb/10/love-poems-writers-favourites-valentines-day (accessed 29 June).

Alvarez, Al (1980). "A Fine Way with the Language." *The New York Review of Books* (6 March): 16–17.

Baker, Kenneth (1990). *Unauthorized Versions: Poems and Their Parodies*. London: Faber and Faber.

Ball, Patricia (1976). *The Heart's Events: The Victorian Poetry of Relationships*. London: Athlone.

Barber, Laura (2010). *Penguin's Poems for Love*. London: Penguin Classics.

Brockes, Emma (1999). "How do I love thee?" *The Guardian* (13 February). http://www.theguardian.com/books/1999/feb/13/poetry (accessed 29 June 2015).

Cope, Wendy (1986). *Making Cocoa for Kingsley Amis*. London: Faber and Faber.

Cope, Wendy (2003). "A Poet True to Himself." *The Guardian* (6 December). http://www.theguardian.com/books/2003/dec/06/featuresreviews.guardianreview31 (accessed 29 June 2015).

Cope, Wendy (2009). *Two Cures for Love: Selected Poems 1979–2006*. London: Faber and Faber.

Crown, Sarah (2008). "Zest and Grit: Interview with Edwin Morgan." *The Guardian* (26 January). http://www.theguardian.com/books/2008/jan/26/poetry (accessed 29 June 2015).

Davie, Donald (1973). *Thomas Hardy and British Poetry*. London: Routledge and Kegan Paul.

De Rougemont, Denis (1983). *Love in the Western World*. New Haven: Princeton.

Duffy, Carol Ann (2001). *Hand in Hand: An Anthology of Love Poems*. London: Picador.

Duffy, Carol Ann (2006). *Selected Poems*. London: Penguin.

Duffy, Carol Ann (2013). "Carol Ann Duffy on Her Collection *Love Poems*—*Guardian* Book Club." *The Guardian* (8 February). http://www.theguardian.com/books/2013/feb/08/carol-ann-duffy-book-club (accessed 29 June 2015).

Morgan, Edwin (2007). *A Book of Lives*. Manchester: Carcanet.

Eliot, T. S. (1971). *The Complete Poems and Plays: 1909–1950*. New York: Harcourt Brace Jovanovich.

Fenton, James (2008). *The New Faber Book of Love Poems*. London: Faber and Faber.

Fuller, John (1996). *Collected Poems*. London: Chatto and Windus.

Goodwin, Daisy (1997). *The Nation's Favourite Love Poems*. London: BBC Books.

Hancock, Tim (2003). ""Unworthy of a Serious Song"? Modern Love Poetry and its Critics." *The Cambridge Quarterly*, 32 (1): 1–25.

Hancock, Tim (2007). "The Chemistry of Love Poetry." *The Cambridge Quarterly*, 36 (3): 197–228.

Heaney, Seamus (1979). *Field Work*. London: Faber and Faber.

Larkin, Philip (1983). "An Interview with the *Observer*." In: *Required Writing: Miscellaneous Pieces 1955–1982*, 47–56. London: Faber and Faber.

Larkin, Philip (2012). *The Complete Poems* (ed. Archie Burnett). London: Faber and Faber.

Loy, Mina (1996). *The Lost Lunar Baedeker: Poems of Mina Loy* (ed. Roger L. Conover). New York: Farrar, Straus & Giroux.

Mitchell, Adrian (2012). *Come on Everybody: Poems 1953–2008*. Tarset, Northumberland: Bloodaxe.

Morgan, Edwin (2000). *New Selected Poems*. Manchester: Carcanet Press.

Morrison, Blake (1982). *Seamus Heaney. Contemporary Writers*. London: Routledge.

Ricks, Christopher (1979). "The Mouth, the Meal and the Book" (Review of *Field Work*). *London Review of Books* 1 (2). www.lrb.co.uk.ezphost.dur.ac.uk/v01/n02/christopher-ricks/the-mouth-the-meal-and-the-book (accessed 29 June 2015).

Stallworthy, Jon (ed.) (1976). "Introduction." In: *The Penguin Book of Love Poetry*, 19–28. London: Penguin.

Woollcott, Alexander (1934). *While Rome Burns*. New York: The Viking Press.

Zephaniah, Benjamin (1999). *The Bloomsbury Book of Love Poems*. London: Bloomsbury.

2c.17
Political Poetry

Ian C. Davidson and Jo Lindsay Walton

Ever since Plato barred the poets from his ideal republic, for their distorting abstractions of the materiality of civic life (Plato 1994 [c. 380 BCE] 607b5–6), poets have been trying to prove their worth as "the unacknowledged legislators of the world" (Shelley 2002 [1821], 535) who produce "news that STAYS news" (Pound 2011 [1934], 13). For one modern reinterpreter of Plato, the philosopher Alain Badiou, poetry is one of the four "conditions of philosophy"—along with love, science, and politics – that are also "truth procedures" (Badiou 2008 [1992], 42). Badiou constructs a notion of truth as a type of being, which is produced by an exceptional event, such as the avant-garde poem, and embodied within a collective subjectivity faithful to that event. So in Badiou's formulation, poetry may do *more* than express or participate in politics. In its most fully realized incarnation, the poetic may be *equal* to the political. Yet Badiou also declares "the age of poets" to have ended with Celan (Badiou 1999, 70). It is difficult to think of any contemporary equivalent that could answer to Badiou's description of poetry. If such a thing exists at all, would it really look like those objects we normally call "poems"?

In postwar Britain and Ireland, many poets have assumed that politics and truth are related most decisively not only in the *exceptional* event, but also in daily, current events. For poetry to be news that stays news, it must contain some kind of news in the first place. The poet Tony Harrison asks, "Why shouldn't poetry address what happened yesterday, and be published in the newspaper?" (Harrison 2007 n.p.). In one occasional piece written in 2003—and published in a newspaper—Harrison uses alliteration-studded iambic heptameter to engineer a collision of everyday speech with high artifice. The poem is vigorous, sardonic, relatively unadorned, and unabashedly slipshod in its construction. It registers disgust at a remark made by Geoff Hoon, the Minister of Defence at the time, that Iraqi mothers would one day thank him for using cluster bombs:

> Baghdad Lullaby
>
> Ssshhh! Ssshhhh! though now shrapnel makes you shriek
> and deformities in future may brand you as a freak,
> you'll see, one day, disablement's a blessing and a boon
> sent in baby-seeking bomblets by benefactor Hoon.
> (Harrison 2003 n.p.)

To write political poems, Harrison suggests that you need "the objective eye, but also a feeling of engagement" (Harrison 2007 n.p.), and that it is better "to write for the whole of society than for the poetry-reading public" (Harrison 2015 n.p.). Rhyme and rhythm are, for Harrison, "like plugging myself into a life-support system, especially when I'm looking at subjects that seem too terrible to talk about. The heart beats iambically; the form keeps the connection to the heartbeat" (ibid.). If, according to Badiou, the truth of any situation comes from elements within that situation that cannot be made consistent with it (despite the best efforts of "the state" of that situation to harmonize it), then perhaps Harrison's work aspires to just the opposite: rooting itself in the commonality of English speech patterns, and even into a continuous score of systoles and diastoles that reaches back to the first human hearts.

Yet poetry of this type—poetry which reaches for clarity, directness, demotic sensibility, and topics of general importance—always confronts problems of address. To look objectively, then to speak truthfully to everybody on behalf of everybody, is at best a regulative ideal. That is, it is an occasionally useful *focus imaginarius*, but not something really attainable in practice. The politics of any poem might instead be approached by asking: who is speaking to whom, in what language, and with what permissions? Harrison's "Baghdad Lullaby" sarcastically purports to address the Iraqi people on behalf of Geoff Hoon. Perhaps on another level, Hoon himself is Harrison's addressee. "[D]eformities in future may brand you as a freak" (q.v.) could be heard as the long-shot plea for Hoon to consider his own place in history.

The many identities within poetry—identities of poets, readers, speakers, addressees, and others, including non-humans—mean that all poems are inescapably political. In postwar Britain and Ireland, growing awareness of this *necessarily* political status of poetry has influenced poets who set out to write poetry that is in some sense *distinctively* political. R. S. Thomas's 1952 "Welsh Landscape" laments and lambasts a legacy of English colonial damage, but struggles to register how the poem's own voice has been conditioned by the oppressive history it describes. It would prefer to reject the rhetoric of presence—the first-person pronoun is only ever implicit—and to reject any possibility of rapprochement between poetry and current affairs. The poem's claim is that there is "no present in Wales, / And no future; / There is only the past" (Thomas 1986, 16). By stark contrast, Gillian Clarke's 1982 poem "Letter from a Far Country" inserts its speaker into a long history of family, community, and the Welsh nation. Here the speaking voice is often plural, a feminine "we" that has been "counting, | folding" and whose "airing cupboards | are full of our satisfactions" (Clarke 1982, 48–49). In the poetry of the 1970s and 1980s, implausible aloofness like Thomas's becomes rarer, and techniques like Clarke's more familiar. Poetry explores how a poet's singular everyday experiences relate to the larger histories of identity groups—gender, sexuality, race, ethnicity, nationality, language group—to which they "belong," often in complex and ambivalent ways. Class tends to enter this picture primarily as sociological class, or what Max Weber called "status groups" (Weber [1922] 1978): that is, cultural distinctions tend to be emphasized over economic exploitation and inequality.

If poets have a political obligation to speak truth to power, perhaps it is their own truths they must begin with. For instance, in Grace Nichols's 1984 collection *The Fat Black Woman's Poems*, Nichols mingles the histories and geographies of Guyana and the United Kingdom in explorations of race, femininity, motherhood, and migration. While "Shopping in London Winter" "[t]he fat black woman curses in Swahili / Yoruba / and nation language." She is frustrated by the cold, by "de pretty face salesgals / exchanging slimming glances," and by the lack of choice above a size fourteen (Nichols 2003 [1984], 11). The third-person perspective is used, and while "the fat black woman" is the speaking subject of this poem, not its object, her subjectivity is pervaded by her objectification, and by bleak humor doing the work of self-care: slimy, belittling glances become "slimming," the paltry choice of clothes is described as "lean."

By the 1990s, identity politics was firmly established in mainstream public discourse about poetry. But the framing of complex questions about complex identities was often shaped by an Arts Council hoping to justify arts spending as a plank of social cohesion and civic flourishing, and by the appropriative and fetishistic marketing and editorial practices of publishers. Such attitudes can threaten "to recreate *ad infinitum* the existing paradigm of voices speaking from 'the daily marginalization of the darker voice'" (Parmar 2015, n.p.). The wider background was a progressive narrative of multiculturalism, diversity, and inclusivity. Post-Cold War, pronouncements were heard that the traditional "left versus right" landscape had been superseded, usurped by more individual-centered "life politics" (Giddens 1991, 215) or "subpolitics" (Beck 1997, 52). On one hand, much opposition to this hopeful narrative was ridden with racism, xenophobia, and/or hardline nationalist or privatist belligerence. On the other, it was a narrative which deserved serious opposition, since it usually stopped short of confronting the economic conditions which enable and empower such prejudices. Serious opposition was marginalized, however, as key institutions of the social-democratic left instead capitulated to neoliberal macroeconomic ideas and to the power of global finance: in Ireland, corporatist "social partnership" agreements saw trade unions accepting low tax as a substitute for wage increases; in the United Kingdom, the Labour Party was busy developing its own distinctive brand of Thatcherism.

The modest shift in the sociology of prominent poets was nonetheless important in presenting voices and subjectivities previously excluded, marginalized, exoticized, or even, in the case of queer sexualities, forbidden by law. Furthermore, it is important not to caricature this identity-centric strand of political poetry as narrowly confessional and mimetic. Such poetry is often pervaded with the kind of seductive artifice of which Plato would presumably disapprove. Harrison's remarks about prosody resemble William Wordsworth's in the "Preface" to *Lyrical Ballads* that meter helps to limit the "undue proportion of pain" connected with certain words, images, and feelings (Wordsworth and Coleridge 2013 [1802], 110). But whereas Harrison seems to invoke a kind of *authenticity* as the mechanism—the indisputable biological materiality of the heartbeat—for Wordsworth, as for many modern poets, the way that metrical composition copes with subjects almost too terrible to talk about is by mixing them with *unreality*. Clarke, for instance, describes "Letter from a Far Country" as "a letter from a fictitious woman to all men," and calls the Far Country itself "childhood, womanhood, Wales, the beautiful country where the warriors, kings and presidents don't live, the private place where we all grow up" (Clarke 1992, 1). Such poetry can be just as invested in *complicating* the problems around who should address whom, and how, as it is in resolving them. It can present personal experience not only to claim it, but also to estrange, defamiliarize, or disavow it.

A less identity-centric strand of political poetry, which moves away from the notion of a "speaker" or "lyric I," has nevertheless often preserved the aspiration to situate itself truthfully, and honor its own conditions of address. J. H. Prynne remarks, "If writers and poets think that language can somehow resist [...] involvement with the worst, while claiming natural affinity with the best, then they are guilty of a naive idealism" (Prynne 2000, 24). Barry MacSweeney's account of the miners' strikes of the 1840s and 1970s, *Black Torch* fluently plays dominant and marginalized Englishes against each other: overleaf from "his cough eeh the doctor says / he'll always be bad / ut never gets loose," the reader finds the improbable and imperious assertion, "yes / there is a certain percentage / of bronchitis [...] / coal is vegetable in origin / therefore it is organic / therefore unharmful" (MacSweeney 1978, 31–32). Toward the close of *Black Torch*, a fragment of journalistic ethics—"I must protect my sources" (ibid. 74)—sounds like a bitter pun, hinting at the poet's fruitless solidarity with the miners, people he cannot "protect."

Lee Harwood's work may contain a subject-position, but it is one that is mobile and evasive. Its politics usually appears as a series of asides, moments when this voice slips into another voice, or a sudden shift of attention forces the reader to question the stability of perspective. This aporia enables Harwood to imagine alternate worlds, not through transcending the world which actually exists, but through the opening up of alternative possibilities nested within it. In "Notes of a Post Office Clerk" (Harwood 2004 [1975], 244), he complains: "I'm sick of living in one room / I'm sick of being poor / I'm sick of the rich taking from the poor / (and them pretending to not even know it!) // I'm sick of the rich." This outburst does not lead to confrontation, but to a series of associations and the realization that "maybe where the sky meets the sea there is a lone freighter" (ibid. 248), another world which is out to sea. While it is true that there are things to be done, "simple, practical, and just acts, / moves toward a real 'socialism'" (ibid. 253), for now political unease seems to let the speaker in this poem skip incremental progress, bringing him unaccountably closer to those unknown figures on the unknown freighters who are out to sea.

A poem like Denise Riley's "Lure 1963" goes further into deliberate instability. The poem takes its title from an abstract painting by Gillian Ayres, and combines descriptions of that painting with lines from pop songs: "I roam around around around around acidic yellows, globe" (Riley 2000a, 50). When the subjects who speak in poems are in an elaborate state of flux, it may suggest a rejection of certain kinds or uses of authority: the authoritative aspect of interpellation, as well as the authoritative address of the reader by the poem. Riley's poem brings together the liberating colors of the abstract paintings and the lines of the songs to produce a situation that is never still. Its revolutionary nature is in the permanently destabilized figure, still aware that "you are not listening to a word I say" (ibid.).

Sustaining such instability can take some ingeniousness. In Sophie Robinson's "a mirror made of flesh" (Robinson 2015), a mirrored subject must negotiate the everyday politics of work and love. From the two gloved hands of the opening line, a series of dualities construct a self that is never still but always moving between reflections. A hammer becomes "a hammer hammering a hammer!" and "ice buckets made of ice!" eventually tip out "a chicken eating KFC!" This is neither quite a love that collapses back on itself nor one that projects upon the body of the beloved. It shifts and oscillates till it becomes "rust" and "steel"—the mirror's endless capacity to generate imagery corrupted to a single industrial image, suggestive of the drudgery of work and of eventual ruin—before resuming a mercurial rave into an affirmative ending, where singular and plural combine: "i like you – all of you –|& even though everything|is disappointing & gross|you are all ok|the way you are."

To try grasp the flux of Robinson's poem as a kind of mimetic truth is not necessarily to depoliticize it: perhaps the poem invokes the way the boundaries of the self may dissolve or behave aberrantly in sex, love, friendship, or in moments of epiphanic togetherness, and points to the poverty of existing forms of both individualism and collectivism. But the same flux might also be left without overt justification, insofar as it exemplifies a strand of political poetry that prefers possibilities over fixed truths, undecidability over taxonomy, exception over totality, dialectic over domination, process over product, openness over closure, and indeed a strand which likes multiplicity, provisionality, fluidity, and hybridity, and rejects hierarchical binaries. As a heckler of Shelley once proclaimed, "[w]hatever is possible to our imaginations, or in our dreams [...] is possible, probable, and of common occurrence in this new system of poetry. Things may exchange their nature, they may all have a new nature, or have no nature" ("Seraphina" in Barcus, ed., 2003 [1821], 291).

This speculative strand has been nourished, from the postwar years to the present, by diverse theoretical contexts: post-Marxism, poststructuralism, continental feminist philosophy, US Language poetry, ecological studies, posthumanist philosophy. Most recently, it has drawn on the shared theory and culture emerging from participatory democratic and social justice activism movements such as Occupy and Black Lives Matter. With its typically ambiguous and shifting syntax and semantics, its discursive and perspectival plenitude, and its many *sui generis* principles of expressive and affective organization, this poetry recruits readers who are "capable of being in uncertainties, mysteries, doubts" (Keats 2009 [1817], 41), while also soliciting those readers' speculative faculties into a collective project to imagine radically different modes of social being.

On the other hand, the aspiration to truthfully disclose the poem's conditions of production has often been braided with the aspiration to demystify, to critique ideology, or in Shelley's words, to mark "the before unapprehended relations of things" (Shelley 2002, 512). Andrea Brady's 2010 *Wildfire: A Verse Essay on Obscurity and Illumination* is a thickly citational genealogy of incendiary weapons from Greek fire to white phosphorous. Its online incarnation hyperlinks to source material, the metatext acting simultaneously as a scholarly apparatus, and as an allegory of the poem's reluctant complicity with the violent energies it tracks. In this context, poetry's political obligation can become pedagogic, the obligation to bear witness and deliver expert advice, whether or not it is heeded. Why should anyone listen? J. H. Prynne asks: "Why should the accuracy in diagnosis of poets [...] ever be trusted?" (quoted in Sutherland 2012, 217).

One possible answer is that poets have at least one special interest about which they may be able to speak knowledgably, which is language itself. The poet Tom Leonard's essay "On The Mass Bombing Of Iraq And Kuwait, Commonly Known As 'The Gulf War'" (Leonard 2013 [1991], 106) could be an example of violence being made a little clearer, not obfuscated, through close attention to its linguistic dimension. Leonard writes, "It has been an essential part of the military bombing campaign: the largest bombardment of anti-language to which the British public has ever been exposed" (Leonard 2013 [1991], 106).

Poets' dilettantism may also itself be a source of expertise, letting poets flout received divisions of intellectual labor. There is a strand of postwar poetry—much of it associated with Cambridge—whose poets seek to be philologists, polymaths, and dialecticians. For this strand, political truth means confronting *totality*, in a sense that can be traced to Hegel via the Frankfurt School and Marx, or understood more loosely as the big yet detailed picture of human existence. If such poetry can keep alive the free and true movement of intellect and feeling within "everything existing" (Marx 1978 [1843], 12), despite the ideology which tries to imprison it, then perhaps it performs a tacit critique of that ideology. One danger of such an approach is that it may promote a kind of self-deceiving inwardness. Adjacent political projects may be rejected as mere fragments of totality, and the legitimacy of those rejections may become the true lodestar which guides the supposedly dialectical examination of totality.

Furthermore, as Badiou points out, truth is a type of being. To put this another way, ideology is material, impervious to critique. It is not enough to discover and to tell the truth, if our entire way of being is false. In the long poem "Filth Screed," Sean Bonney writes that "[n]o-one has yet spoken a language which is not the language of those who establish, enforce, and benefit from the facts" (Bonney 2005, 87). In "Letter on Poetics (After Rimbaud)," Bonney succinctly lies: "in the enemy language it is necessary to lie" (Bonney 2011a, n.p.). His "Letter on Silence" ends with the reminiscence: "Like that time we marched on Parliament, burned it to the ground. Remember that? It was fantastic" (Bonney 2011b, n.p.). These are fantastic lies. Yet they also try to reveal something true. The idea that poetry is built out of materials that are inherently false crops up repeatedly in modern British and Irish political poetry, as do the notions that poetry is necessarily "wrong" (Sutherland 2010, 765), "unfree" (Jarvis 2010, 280 [cf., e.g., Jarvis 2006, 5]), stupid, failed, broken, wounded, or injurious—although such words do occasionally take on hopeful or constructive connotations.

Judith Butler writes how "[a]n aesthetic enactment of an injurious word may both use a word and mention it" (Butler 1997, 99), and for some political poetry, this doubled quality can be a way of confronting its own fallen nature. It is a type of irony which is "always poised to wrench a phrase out of its context" and "commits this linguistic violence of dismembering, not gratuitously but as it exposes the contingent formation of that very context—and so, ultimately, restores its history to it" (Riley 2000b, 183). However, it is also perhaps ironic, in a sense closer to Morissette's than Riley's (cf. Morissette and Ballard 1995), that Cambridge has played such a key role in curating the poetic contribution to "the ruthless criticism of everything existing" (Marx 1978 [1843], 12), insofar as totalizing critique is by definition curiously dispossessed and free-floating—you could do it from anywhere—whereas the Oxbridge citadels form a singular, dense nexus of privilege, which cries out for sophisticated ruthless criticism of more limited and focused scope.

As Riley also points out, probably punningly, "[i]t is boring to be always wounded" (Riley 2000b, 125). Amid continuous catastrophe, political poetry also sets out to recover a spark which is not quite extinguished by humanity's domination of itself (cf. Bloch 1986). William Blake wrote that "[t]here is a Moment in each Day that Satan cannot find / Nor can his Watch Fiends find it, but the Industrious find / This Moment & it multiply" (Blake 1998, 193). Blake's conviction is reminiscent of Badiou's, in that the political is sought not so much within the everyday, but within its briefly flickering exemptions. Bonney writes in "Working Notes on Political Poetry // I Don't Talk to Cops"—that "[t]he problem I have is [...] how to make whatever it is that is trapped in aesthetics, idealism and in history learn to speak" (Folkebiblioteket 2011, n.p.).

More cynically though, it might be said that poetry can cope with subjects "that seem too terrible to talk about" (Harrison q.v.) because what is said in poetry does not actually matter. In "So Few Richards, So Many Dicks" Marianne Morris writes: "I got my pen / I got my pen I got my pen / my pen my pen my fucking pen [...]" (Morris 2010, 4); in a later article Morris points out how "[a] lot of people, if you say the phrase 'political poetry' to them, will respond with something like, 'poetry doesn't change anything'" (Morris 2012, 152). In "Letter on Poetics (after Rimbaud)," Bonney writes: "I started thinking the reason the student movement failed was down to the fucking slogans. They were awful. As feeble as poems" (Bonney 2011b, n.p.). In "Letter on Silence," Bonney breaks with both Wordsworth's and Harrison's notions of the relationship between prosody and suffering, by suggesting that poetry can only translate "the endless whacks of police clubs" (Bonney 2011a, n.p.). Questions about efficacy of poetry are not always posed in such good faith. Self-styled "tough questions" about audience threaten to silence or marginalize dissent, unless an impeccable audience for that dissent can somehow be produced.

However questions about audience—or better yet, questions about a community of language users—*do* become important whenever a poem's politics are championed for doing something dramatic to language, or for discovering or inventing a new kind of language. Poets seldom specify the precise relations between what is enacted in their poems, in language generally, and in the world at large. Perhaps the closest any modern British or Irish poetry has come to quite literally creating new language is by vitalizing existing vernacular expression: for instance, in the dub poetry of Linton Kwesi Johnson, or in Tom Leonard's *Six Glasgow Poems* (1969), which suggest more phonetic transcription than Hugh MacDiarmid's synthetic Scots. Badiou describes poets as "those who seek to create in language new names to name that which, before the poem, has no name" (Badiou 2014 n.p.). But for the most part, large historical processes confiscate the new names poetry dreams up, relentlessly recuperating, repurposing, neutralizing, and/or neglecting the "achievements" of political poets.

One response to this threat of appropriation is a kind of tactical inwardness. In the strand of political poetry which is about poetry itself, in-jokes and coterie rivalries intermingle with more intriguing and unpredictable kinds of reflexivity. Tom Raworth offers a coda to poet laureate Carol Ann Duffy's occasional verse: "If I could take my tongue out of your arse / (Through drag me as a train down aisles you tread) / The tiny Royal turd upon my tongue / Would quiver as my heart that you are wed" (Raworth 2007, 47; cf. Duffy 2011). Verity Spott's advice on the performance of "Marxy" poetry warns you, the poet, that "you may experience laughter. It is, after all, funny to juxtapose suffering and pop culture. If your audience do laugh scowl at them as if they have done something wrong. You understand the brutality of culture and its intricate relations. Katy Perry is not funny. Katy Perry is pure death" (Spott 2015 n.p.). One recent collaborative project, "The Book of the City of Ladies" (2014–), which borrows its title from Christine de Pizan's 1405 work, has the astute vigor of civic evidence, a dossier with ramifications. Begun and largely assembled by Andrea Brady, it is a bricolage whose fragments are all unnamed female figures appearing in contemporary work by male poets, it has some of the power of a disturbing statistic or data visualization. But it simultaneously works as a series of specific, concrete critiques: discreetly challenging each original contributor to confront his heightened complicity with rape culture (Brady 2015).

Another version of this provisional inwardness focuses not on poets, but on participants of radical political movements. Linton Kwesi Johnson constructs an incisively equivocal persona in "Di Great Insohreckshan," his poem about the Brixton Rising of April 1981. The UK Government commissioned the Scarman Report to investigate the events. In "Di Great Insohreckshan," Johnson, who was outside of the United Kingdom during the Brixton Rising, dislodges the illegitimate detective figure of Lord Scarman, and pieces together his own report on events which both intensively celebrates them ("it woz a truly an historical okayjan // it woz event af di year / an I wish I ad been dere / wen wi run riot all ovah Brixtan") while simultaneously taking care to preserve the meticulous, collaborative, arduous character of the uprising now past ("wi buil wi barricade [...] wi sen out wi scout"), and to set sights firmly on the future ("ow dem run gaan / goh plan countah-hackshan / but di plastic bullit / an di waatah canon / will bring a blam-blam").

The spaces of radical politics are produced in distinction to recuperative mechanisms, such as those of state, capital, and patriarchy. In this sense, radical politics can be seen as a kind of avant-garde in itself. Political poetry has the potential, or at least the obligation, to be the avant-garde of the avant-garde: that is, to critique, nourish, inform, disrupt, and otherwise reflect upon the practice of radical politics from a place of partial independence. For instance, recent debates across a variety of contexts—including NGOs and informal charitable initiatives, grassroots campaigns, protests, direct action groups, and groups organized around mutual aid—raise questions about how to strengthen the norms around consensus decision making, around allyship, and around the cultivation of safer spaces (cf., e.g., Anonymous Refused 2014). In light of poetry's particular concern with problems of address, it is plausible that poets could make significant nudges to the way participants in radical political movements talk to and about one another. Seeking "new manners to / smash fascists" (Raha 2015, 3) certainly incurs the risk of reinventing the exhausted models of liberal progressives ("*sorry we are so nice to / you* do not / understand / liberalism as global blood // tsunami" [ibid., 12]), or those of the traditional left.

But it is unclear whether any contemporary political poetry really can claim to be the avant-garde to the avant-garde in this sense. Perhaps the task is not really achievable.

Perhaps no independent place is sustainable through poetry's own energies; and/or perhaps the various projects of radical politics are too precarious to benefit from anything other than relatively unambiguous solidarity. However, it is also worth returning to a question we started with: when poems realize their political potential, do they still look like those things that we conventionally call "poems"? Chris Goode is known primarily as a theater-maker, but has a background and sideline in poetry, and his plays are filled with things that look like they might be poems. At the climax of Goode's 2014 solo show *Men in the Cities*, a monstrous surge of language, both pathological and enthralling, swirls around the never quite realized possibility of solidarity with Michael Adebolajo and Michael Adebowale, the politically motivated murderers of the British Army soldier, Fusilier Lee Rigby. Goode's plays *Hippo World Guest Book* (2007), *Monkey Bars* (2012), and *Stand* (2015) use a variety of verbatim-theatrical techniques to conduct a sustained enquiry into utopian theory and praxis. Like Brady et al.'s *The Book of the City of Ladies* (2014–), or the found poetry of Nick-e Melville's *Alert State is Heightened* (2014) and *Notes* (2014–), these performances reject the notion (influential in some contemporary US conceptual writing) that the idea of a work should take priority over its minute execution (cf. LeWitt 1967). Instead, they examine the ways in which acts of resistance are rooted in privilege, while taking pains not to dampen the momentum of such acts.

Maybe, like Badiou's events, genuinely political poems not only challenge definitions of the poem, but break out of poetry itself—constructing a "way of being" (q.v.) that can be true in more than one context. Political poets have diligently explored the ways in which people "dissect nature along lines laid down by our native languages" (Whorf 1956, 214) and the extralinguistic ramifications of projects of linguistic reform. For instance, they have frequently obsessed, often brilliantly, over pronouns (cf., e.g., Edwards in Riley 1992; Milne 1993). Pronouns are particularly curious and potent linguistic condensations of social normativity, and the sites where "the relations where our genders fall / as the simplest of words" (Raha 2015, 19). However, poets—at least, in the ordinary sense of "poets"—have never come close to the bold yet levelheaded experiments-in-solidarity currently being undertaken by trans people and their allies: the political, the linguistically innovative, and the everyday are united in an effort to produce a social reality unprecedently responsive to individual self-determinations, in particular as regards gender and sexuality (cf., e.g., Nicholas 2014). Whether or not this activity counts as political poetry, it surely counts as both *polis* and *poiesis*.

References

Anonymous Refused 2014. "For Your Safety and Security." http://anonymousrefused.tumblr.com/post/99047385737/for-your-safety-and-security. (accessed 24 August 2015).

Badiou, Alain (1999). *Manifesto for Philosophy* (trans. Norman Madarasz). Albany: State University of New York Press.

Badiou, Alain (2008 [1992]). *Conditions* (trans. Steven Corcoran). London: Continuum.

Badiou, Alain (2014). *The Age of the Poets and Other Writings on Twentieth-Century Poetry and Prose*, edited and translated by Bruno Bosteels, with an introduction by Emily Apter and Bruno Bosteels. London and New York: Verso.

Beck, Ulrich (1997). "Subpolitics: Ecology and the Disintegration of Institutional Power." *Organization & Environment* 10: 52–65.

Blake, William (1998 [1811]). *Milton a Poem* (eds. Robert N. Essick and Joseph Viscomi). New Jersey: Princeton University Press.

Bloch, Ernst (1986 [1954 / 1955 / 1959]). *The Principle of Hope*, vol. 1-3 (trans. N.eville Plaice, Stephen Plaice and Paul Knight). Cambridge: MIT Press.

Bonney, Sean (2005). *Blade Pitch Control Unit*. Cambridge: Salt.

Bonney, Sean (2011a). "Letter on Poetics (after Rimbaud)." http://abandonedbuildings.blogspot.co.uk/2011/06/letter-on-poetics.html (accessed 5 November 2015).

Bonney, Sean (2011b). "Letter on Silence." http://abandonedbuildings.blogspot.co.uk/2011/08/letter-on-silence.html (accessed 15 August 2015).

Brady, Andrea (2010). *Wildfire: A Verse Essay on Obscurity and Illumination*. San Francisco: Krupskaya.

Brady, Andrea (2015). "Book of the City of Ladies." *Chicago Review* 59 (1–2): 180–186.

Butler, Judith (1997). *Excitable Speech: A Politics of the Performative*. New York and London: Routledge.

Clarke, Gillian (1982). *Letter from a Far Country*. Manchester: Carcanet.

Clarke, Gillian (1992). "The Poet's Introduction." In: *Six Women Poets*, vol. 1 (ed. Judith Kinsman). Oxford: Oxford University Press.

Duffy, Carol Ann (2011). "Rings." *The Guardian* (23 April). https://www.theguardian.com/books/2011/apr/23/wedding-carol-ann-duffy-poetry (Accessed 23 August 2019).

Edwards, Ken (1992). "Grasping the Plural." In: *Poets on Writing: Britain 1970-1991* (ed. Denise Riley), 21–29. London: Palgrave MacMillan.

Folkebiblioteket (2011). Sean Bonney. "Working Notes on Political Poetry // I Don't Talk to Cops." http://blogg.deichman.no/folkebiblioteket/folkebiblioteket-4 (accessed 15 August 2015).

Giddens, Anthony (1991). *Modernity and Self-Identity: Self and Society in the Late Modern Age*. Cambridge: Polity Press.

Harrison, Tony (2003). "Baghdad Lullaby" by Tony Harrison in "Writers on Iraq". *The Guardian* online http://www.theguardian.com/world/2003/apr/09/iraq.writersoniraq (accessed 15 August 2015).

Harrison, Tony (2007). Beats of the Heart. Interview with Tony Harrison by M. Jaggi. *The Guardian* online http://www.theguardian.com/books/2007/mar/31/poetry.tonyharrison (accessed 15 August 2015).

Harrison, Tony (2015). "Tony Harrison: Still Open for Business." Interview with Tony Harrison by S. Moss. *The Guardian* online http://www.theguardian.com/books/2015/feb/26/tony-harrison-celebration-winner-2015-david-cohen-prize (accessed 15 August 2015).

Harwood, Lee (2004). *Collected Poems: 1964–2004*. Exeter: Shearsman Books.

Jarvis, Simon (2006). *Wordsworth's Philosophic Song*. Cambridge: Cambridge University Press.

Jarvis, Simon (2010). "Unfree Verse: John Wilkinson's *The Speaking Twins*." *Paragraph* 33 (2): 280–295.

Keats, John (2009). *Selected Letters* (eds. John Mee and Robert Gittings). New York: Oxford University Press (World's Classics).

Leonard, Tom. (1969). *"Six Glasgow Poems."* Insert in Glasgow University Magazine (May).

Leonard, Tom (2013). *Definite Articles: Prose 1973-2012*. Edinburgh: Word Power Books.

LeWitt, Sol (1967). "Paragraphs on Conceptual Art." *Artforum* (10 June), pp. 79–83.

MacSweeney, Barry (1978). *Black Torch*. London: New London Pride.

Marx, Karl (1978). "For a Ruthless Criticism of Everything Existing." In: *The Marx-Engels Reader* (ed. Robert C. Tucker), 12–15. New York: Norton.

melville, nick-e (2014). *Alert State Is Heightened: An Imperative Imprimatura*. Edinburgh: Sad Press.

Milne, Drew (1993). "Agoraphobia, and the Embarrassment of Manifestos: Notes Toward a Community of Risk." *Parataxis* 3: 25–39.

Morissette, Alanis and Ballard, Glen. (1995). "Ironic." *Jagged Little Pill*. Maverick Records. CD.

Morris, Marianne (2010). *So Few Richards, So Many Dicks*. Buffalo: Punch Press.

Morris, Marianne (2012). "Introduction to "Lyric & Polis: A Symposium of Poetry & Poetics."." In: *Crisis Inquiry* (ed. Rich Owens), 152–155. Scarborough: Punch Press.

Nicholas, Lucy (2014). *Queer Post-Gender Ethics: The Shape of Selves to Come*. London: Palgrave Macmillan.

Nichols, Grace (2003 [1984]). *The Fat Black Woman Poems*. London: Virago.

Parmar, Sandeep (2015). "Not a British Subject: Race and Poetry in the UK." *Los Angeles Review of Books* (6 December) https://lareviewofbooks.org/article/not-a-british-subject-race-and-poetry-in-the-uk/ (accessed 6 March 2020).

Plato (1994 [c.380 BCE]). *The Republic* (trans. Robin Waterfield). Oxford: Oxford University Press.

Pound, Ezra (2011 [1934]). *The ABC of Reading* (ed. Michael Dirda). New York: New Directions.

Prynne, J. H. (2000). "A Quick Riposte to Handke's Dictum About War and Language." *Quid* 6 (November): 23–26.

Raha, Nat (2015). *Of Sirens – Body and Faultlines*. London: Sociopathic Distribution.

Raworth, Tom (2007). *Caller and Other Pieces*. Washington DC: Edge Books.

Riley, Denise (2000a). *Selected Poems*. Hastings: Reality Street.

Riley, Denise (2000b). *The Words of Selves: Identification, Solidarity, Irony*. Stanford: Stanford University Press.

Robinson, Sophie (2015). "Two by Sophie Robinson." *The Brooklyn Rail*. http://www.brooklynrail.org/2015/02/poetry/two-sophie-robinson (accessed 21 August 2015).

Seraphina (2003 [1821]). "Seraphina and Her Sister Clementina's Review of *Epipsychidion*." In: *Percy Bysshe Shelley: The Critical Heritage* (ed. James E. Barcus), 289–295. London and New York: Routledge.

Shelley, Percy Bysshe (2002 [1821]). "In Defence of Poetry." In: *Shelley's Poetry and Prose*, 2e (eds. Donald Reiman and Reil Fraistat), 510–535. New York: Norton.

Spott, Verity (2015). "A Short Essay on How to Make Your Poetry More Marxy." http://twotornhalves.blogspot.co.uk/2015/02/a-short-essay-on-how-to-make-your.html. (accessed 24 October 2015).

Sutherland, Keston (2010). "Wrong Poetry." *Textual Practice* 24 (4): 765–782.

Sutherland, Keston (2012). "Statement for the Helsinki Poetics Conference 2010." In: *Crisis Inquiry* (ed. Rich Owens), 217–222. Scarborough: Punch Press. The quoted text is from a letter from Prynne to Ed Dorn, 24 October 1978.

Thomas, R. S. (1986). *Selected Poems: 1946–1968*. Newcastle upon Tyne: Bloodaxe Books.

Weber, Max (1978). *Economy and Society*, vol. 2 (eds. Guenther Roth and Claus Wittich). Berkeley: University of California Press.

Whorf, Benjamin Lee (1956). *Language Thought and Reality*. Cambridge Mass: MIT Press.

Wordsworth, William and Coleridge, Samuel Taylor (2013 [1800/1802]). *Lyrical Ballads 1798 and 1802* (ed. Fiona Stafford). Oxford: Oxford University Press.

2c.18
Radical Landscape Poetry in Scotland

Alan Riach

Landscape poetry enters the English-language tradition most radically with James Thomson's *The Seasons* (1726), and most centrally with Wordsworth, whose fearfulness and wonder were domesticated by William Gilpin's notion of "the picturesque." The first poem to prioritize the depiction of a place, "Cooper's Hill" (1642) by John Denham, is an Anglo-royalist Irishman's representation of the English location of his adopted home in Surrey, with London and Windsor in sight, reflecting on the radical politics of the Civil War. This essay argues that the radicalism intrinsic to the matter of these "*landscape*" poets was reconfigured in the work of Scottish poets who began publishing after the Second World War, most emphatically since the 1960s.

"Radical landscape poetry" means more than one thing, of course. "Landscape poetry" we might describe as: poetry which engages with (i) a scene, the scenic, that is, topography, terrain; (ii) an ecology of presence, which engages the human in this scene, in relation to its geography and other living species; (iii) a political, historical, or social landscape, a site-specific point of departure into enquiries of contemporary, historical, or projected political and social ways of living, relations of position, power, stability, and movement. Other extrapolations relate more or less to these three meanings. Latterly, the term "radical landscape poetry" has often referred to formal radicalism in poetic technique, rather than explicit political enquiry or the specifics of topography, but these are never completely separable. Where a place is, where you stand to see it, how you move through it, how you see it, how you say what you say about it, how you are placed, or place yourself, in relation to

---

A Companion to Contemporary British and Irish Poetry, 1960–2015, First Edition.
Edited by Wolfgang Görtschacher and David Malcolm.
© 2021 John Wiley & Sons Ltd. Published 2021 by John Wiley & Sons Ltd.

it, and the language in which you write, are never innocent questions, and this is nowhere more evident than in the radical landscape poetry of Scotland in the 50 years under review.

The modern Scots drew not only from mainstream English-language tradition but from Gaelic and vernacular Scots poetry—from the eighteenth century, not only Thomson, but also Duncan Ban MacIntyre and Robert Burns. Their immediate provocateur in the 1920s was Hugh MacDiarmid (1892–1978), whose poetry from the 1920s to the 1950s generated a new vision of Scotland's landscapes, providing coordinate points and new confidence in attachment to specific localities that might be deemed peripheral by metropolitan centers, cosmopolitan sophistications, or imperial authority. The pluralities here are essential. MacDiarmid's originality was to create a vision of Scotland characterized by diversity, therefore opposed to the centralizing ethos of imperialism, in politics, economics, language, cultural value, and social practice. His priority was politically national in a way quite distinct from any of his contemporaries in British poetry. The generation that followed him did not imitate this national vision but characteristically began from their native or favored locations within this multiple, multivocal nation. As Norman MacCaig put it: "Landscape is my religion" (MacCaig 2005, xxxi). This is much more than devotional. It is a sense of possession and responsibility most fully explored by MacCaig in "A Man in Assynt" (1967/1968) that returns us to the radicalism of pre-revolutionary Europe.

> Who owns this landscape? –
> The millionaire who bought it or
> the poacher staggering downhill in the early morning
> with a deer on his back?
>
> Who possesses this landscape? –
> The man who bought it or
> I who am possessed by it?
> (MacCaig 2005, 221–228 [222], ll. 32–38)

The intensity of MacCaig's question, "Who owns this landscape?," could be easily swollen to deformity by the mad possessiveness of absentee landowners (it is a familiar story in Scotland); yet Scotland's radical landscape poetry of 1960–2010 is a necessary corrective and builds on the various foundations of national cultural identity MacDiarmid secured.

The actuality of landscape is not only visualized, depicted, to be seen, but is also to be experienced as an inhabitant, so that its presence is not only given as an acquired property of visual knowledge, even less as a financial or military property in international calculation, but rather as a haunting, recurring, tidal presence. The waters of oceans and rivers tell us of the changing world as surely as mountains and stones speak of perpetuity and continuity across geological time (Riach 2011, 58–71). The radical nature of landscape poetry is to enact the necessity of change along with that of constant resistance. This ethos of landscape as lived-in continues to Norman Nicholson (1914–1987), with the Lakes providing a sense of deep stability, generational presence. George Mackay Brown (1921–1996), closer to Nicholson than any other modern Scottish poet, delivers a similar sense of the quotidian, yet is much more given to poems of violence, whether in Christian martyrdom, the self-sacrifice of people for the good of others, or the stories of international seafarers, whose lives counterpoint those who stay at home. A poet of the Orkney archipelago off the north coast of Scotland, Brown evoked the islands and seascapes, their history and legends, particularly commemorating the generations of his parents and grandparents, as in "Hamnavoe." (Brown 2006) His central themes are aligned with the essential rhythms of the everyday, the rites and rituals that help keep things sacred. Yet he returned to the figure of St. Magnus repeatedly, and his poems follow liturgical patterns of repetition with patience and bright imagery. In "Uranium," history itself becomes a landscape humanity passes through, from stone to bronze ages, farming and fishing, to the modern militarized era, poised tremblingly, after millennia, in the nuclear world, before "the magnificent door of fire" (Brown 1981, 58, 30). The more radical tradition of landscape poetry in which Brown takes part evokes an ecology of landscape in various terrains, in terms most closely described by John Berger, Fiona Stafford, and Edward Dorn.

In an essay entitled "A Story for Aesop," Berger talks about "the *address* of the landscape" (67) signifying the meaning of place as it is experienced not only in its daily visualization but also in its economic, physical, and social relations with the people who live in it, upon it, and through it across generations, how the landscape addresses you (Berger 1991, 3–81, l. 68).

Fiona Stafford, in her book *Local Attachments*, says this: "the vital significance of local attachments for art arises from truth's need for strong foundations." Poetry needs "local attachments" because truth needs real foundations to build on, fly from, and return to (Stafford 2010, 21).

Asked whether he would consider himself a "landscape poet," the American poet Edward Dorn replied: "If you are on earth, you are on a landscape, and there's nothing much you can do about that." When pressed further about the idea of "landscape as a character," he replied:

> You're talking more about "haunt" actually. That gets to involve the "human in place." [...] Both Lawrence and Pound took their intellectual cues from Thomas Hardy, who was the literary giant of their youth. If you follow Lawrence, to have a true local, you have to have gods of the local. You can't have monotheism. It does not tolerate the local. Monotheism is centrality of power and total control.
>
> (Dorn 2007, 92–116 [98–101])

Dorn refers to religion and politics, but crucially for the Scots, the same principle applies to language and nationality. MacDiarmid's understanding of Scotland as a diversity of landscapes arose from his experience in the 1930s of the archipelagos of Shetland, then Orkney and the Western Isles. This became clear with the publication of *Collected Poems* (1962) and his last book, *Direadh* (1974), in which he locates himself at the summit of one of the Cuillins, the mountain range on the Isle of Skye, looking over, imagining, all Scotland, and considering the human and natural terrain in the moment of his presence and the history, both human and geological, that precedes and will follow it. The title of the book is a Gaelic word meaning the act of surmounting, or getting higher. Louisa Gairn, in her book *Ecology and Modern Scottish Literature*, notes: "MacDiarmid anticipates the idea of 'ecopoetics' developed by Jonathan Bate, who suggests that *poiesis* 'is language's most direct path or return to the *oikos*, the place of dwelling'" (Gairn 2008, 130).

The foundation for the major Scottish poets' publishing "radical landscape poetry" from 1960 is, therefore, a complex national provenance that has reference far beyond Scotland. T. S. Eliot experienced this in 1933, traveling through Scotland, and the result was "Rannoch, by Glencoe," the only one of his five landscape poems to record otherness beyond their author's qualifying presence (Gish 2014). MacDiarmid, in his political commitment to national political independence for Scotland, was not a "local" poet, even though the Borders, and later, Shetland, were geographical localities which informed his writing deeply. Nothing is more accurately described as a "radical landscape poem" than MacDiarmid's "On a Raised Beach" (1935) (Riach 2000, 613–629). Yet he was in that generation of poets who were pre-eminently publishing after 1960, who could be described more correctly as poets of "local attachment," and in the generation that followed them, in Scotland, that the most conspicuous reconfiguration has been in terms of gendered identity, the poetic articulation of the experiences, perspectives, and understanding of women. Still, the idea of "radical landscape" applies to all three generations.

The first major book by Somhairle MacGill-Eain/Sorley MacLean (1911–1996) was *Dàin do Eimhir* (1943), and the lyric sequence "An Cuilithionn" / "The Cuillin" was mainly written in 1939, but continued to be revised and was only published in English in the late 1980s. Here, the mountain range on the island of Skye stands as a living symbol of heroic opposition to those forces that would foreclose life's potential, from the Clearances of the eighteenth and nineteenth centuries, to twentieth-century fascism. This is how it ends:

> Beyond the lochs of the blood of the children of men,
> beyond the frailty of plain and the labour of the mountain,
> beyond poverty, consumption, fever, agony,
> beyond hardship, wrong, tyranny, distress,
> beyond misery, despair, hatred, treachery,
> beyond guilt and defilement: watchful,
> heroic, the Cuillin is seen
> rising on the other side of sorrow.
> (MacLean 2011, 414 [ll. 184–191])

The central poem of MacLean's career is "Hallaig" (1954), a haunting elegy for a cleared township on his native island of Raasay, where the ruined homes of his ancestors can still be seen in a beautiful location redolent with its own tragedy. In resonant symbolism, MacLean likens his poem to the bullet that will kill the deer of time and preserve the memory of his people and his place forever: "chunnacas na mairbh beò" / "the dead have been seen alive" (230–235 [232/233], l. 29). His later elegy for his brother Calum and his passionate denunciation of the authority of nuclear weaponry in "Screapadal" (c.1972–1982) evoke specific landscapes with particular meaning, either as capable of sustaining tragic loss or as occupied by forces inimical to human well-being.

Iain Crichton Smith (1928–1998) is most closely associated with Lewis in the Outer Hebrides, where austere religion permeates social convention and forms a hard stratum of judgment, which ultimately he turned to his own advantage. In "Poem of Lewis" the "fine graces / of poetry" (ll. 1–2) are seen as irrelevant to his people, unless they come naturally, like water from the deepest well (Smith 2011, 3). His major collections appeared regularly from the 1960s till his death, beginning with *The Long River* (1955), inhabiting a Highland terrain alongside non-human species in *Deer on the High Hills* (1962), anatomizing archipelagic identity in *The Permanent Island* (1975) and political history in *The Exiles* (1984), then applying all these concerns autobiographically in *A Life* (1986).

Archipelagic poetics are equally the methods of urban poets. In this sense, "landscape" includes "cityscape." In "Heart of Stone" (1965), Alexander Scott (1920–1989) ambiguously praises and disdains his native Aberdeen. In "Edinburgh Sonnets" (1960s), Robert Garioch (1909–1981) depicts characters, daily encounters, and events. Vivid evocations of old Edinburgh and its raucous, sensitive, loving, and drinking inhabitants fill the poems of Sydney Goodsir Smith (1915–1975). If Garioch's urban Edinburgh Scots is reductively vernacular, Goodsir Smith's Scots is rhetorically charged: there is elation, but there is also the pox (Goodsir Smith 1975, 171). Norman MacCaig (1910–1996) also depicts Edinburgh. In "City Fog" (1980), it is dull:

> Even the Tollcross clock
> looks glum, as if it knew
> five past ten might as well be
> ten past five.
> (MacCaig 2005, 385,
> ll. 16–19)

When he writes of Lochinver in the north-west, though, the landscape is measured not by Greenwich Mean Time but geological deep time. This gives profundity and weight to his sequence of elegies, "Poems for Angus" (1976–1978) (MacCaig 2005, 332–338). The significance of landscape poetry is clear from the titles of some of his collections: *Surroundings* (1967), *A Man in My Position* (1969), *Old Maps and New* (1978), *The Equal Skies* (1980), and *A World of Difference* (1983).

The title of Edwin Morgan's first book, *The Vision of Cathkin Braes* (1952), announces two key coordinates: a specific local reference to a hillside overlooking Glasgow, and an idea that a "vision" is required to arise from that locality, to see it new but move out from it, to go further. "Trio," from his first major volume, *The Second Life* (1968), begins with three figures: "Coming up Buchanan Street, quickly, on a sharp winter evening / a young man and two girls / under the Christmas lights." The Glasgow street-name, the celebration of human contact, and the prospect of giving at a time of festivity (Christian or otherwise) are centered in the cityscape (Morgan 1996, 172–173 [173]). This was crucial in Morgan's work, most evident in *Glasgow Sonnets* (1972), *From Glasgow to Saturn* (1973), and returned to most gloriously in *Cathures* (2002). Central to his *oeuvre*, in *Sonnets from Scotland* (1984), national identity became prioritized: how might the past be read anew, the future made differently, what do present urgencies provoke? Like other major works of its time, in literary and cultural criticism and history as well as poetry, it appeared in the context of Scottish national self-reappraisal in the aftermath of the disallowed devolution referendum and the election of the Conservative government in 1979. Morgan's initiative was not to take an explicitly politicized stance but to reimagine Scotland from prehistory ("There is no beginning") to unknown futurity.

Through and since the work of these poets, radical landscape poetry has become an elemental component of Scottish poetry generally. Many poems are prompted not simply by a scenic apprehension of landscape but by a specific locality that triggers a process of understanding that includes personal, political, national and international, ecological ideas and enquiries. At its best this vitalizes self-apprehension and physical context, as in "Loch Thom" (1977) by W. S. Graham (1918–1986), a magnificent epiphany describing the "lonely freshwater loch" (l. 17) in the hollow of hills above his native town, industrial Greenock, south-west of Glasgow, to which he would walk as a child. As an adult, his return visit is chilly, restrained, heart-wrenching (Graham 2005, 220–221).

Site-specific locations are key elements here in meditations and interrogations of personal, social, and political components of national and universal identities. Since the 1970s, the geographical "landscape" aspect of this was radically altered by an assertion of gender. Liz Lochhead (born 1947) broke new ground in this respect, with her first, best-selling book, *Memo for Spring* (1972), in which her lyrical, autobiographical poems depicted a young woman in the context of industrial or rural Lanarkshire. Her second book, though, took her to the Hebrides, *Islands* (1978). Here, the two sections, "Inner" and "Outer," related both to her own reflections and outward expressions but also to the geographical terms for the two archipelagos off Scotland's west coast. Characteristic of the change Lochhead heralded in the 1970s and 1980s are her poems "What the Pool Said, on Midsummer's Day" and "Mirror's Song." The latter begins with the command "Smash me looking-glass glass [...]" (l. 1) and ends with the line "a woman giving birth to herself" (Lochhead 2011, 70–71, l. 40). It is as if this act of self-generation and regeneration, both geographical and individual, exemplifies the struggle in the poem in the process of a nation giving birth to itself. Around 1992, Lochhead said: "[...] until recently I've felt that my country was woman. I feel that my country is Scotland as well. At the moment I know that I don't like this macho Scottish culture, but I also know that I want to stay here and negotiate it" (Lochhead 1992, 203–223 [204]).

Poets whose work could be more thoroughly explored in terms of radical landscape in the period include Kenneth White (born 1936), whose theories of *"geopoetics"* have acquired a significant vogue, from *The Cold Wind of Dawn* (1966) to *The Bird Path* (1989) and *Handbook for the Diamond Country* (1990). Stewart Conn (born 1936), in *Stolen Light: Selected Poems*, demonstrates repeatedly a countryman's understanding of the hard realities of the farming world, as does Jim Carruth (born 1963), appointed poet laureate of Glasgow in 2014. Douglas Dunn (born 1942), in *Northlight* (1988), affirms the value of his return to Scotland from previous residence in England. Gaelic poets contemporary with Sorley MacLean warrant full recognition in themselves: George Campbell Hay (1915–1984), fluent in Gaelic, Scots, and English, a songwriter and intellectual whose extended sequence *Mochtàr is Dùghall* (written during and after the Second World War but not published till 1982) explores an encounter between a Highlander and a North African soldier during that war; and Derick Thomson (1921–2012), like Iain Crichton Smith, a Lewis man whose evocations of that place are central to his work, as they are with the poetry of Ian Stephen (born 1955).

Island poems engage similar priorities. In Skye, John Purser (born 1942) writes with incomparable immediacy of life as a crofter; Angus Peter Campbell (born 1954) and Rody Gorman (born 1960) carry forward Gaelic priorities; Meg Bateman (born 1957), writing in Gaelic and translating her poems into English, published *Aotromachd agus dàin eile/Lightness and Other Poems* (1997) and *Soirbheas/Fair Wind* (2007). As editor and translator of anthologies of early Gaelic poetry, Bateman also provided both new versions of ancient texts and new ways of contextualizing new writing. Aonghas MacNeacail (born 1942), born on Skye but long resident in the Scottish Borders, was from the start committed to free verse, influenced by the American Black Mountain poets, therefore distinct from more traditional Gaelic forms. His politics come through most forcefully in personal application: "when i was young / it wasn't history but memory" (MacNeacail 1997, 13). In Shetland, Christine De Luca (born 1947), Robert Alan Jamieson (born 1958), and Jen Hadfield (born 1978) have written in vastly different forms and styles of address, but are frequently focused on the Shetland locations, or express themselves distinctively in ways that arise from them. In Orkney, Andrew Greig (born 1951), who established his reputation as an iconoclastic yet highly sensitized poet with *Men On Ice* (1977), consolidated it in *This Life, This Life: Selected Poems 1970–2006* (2006). Landscape here is both literal and metaphorical, climbing mountains, living on islands, traveling, and in residence. Site-specific island landscapes are explored in *Slate Voices: Cwmorthin and the Islands of Netherlorn* (2014) by Mavis Gulliver, centered on the islands of Seil, Easdale, Luin, and Belnahua, where slate-quarrying was the major, and now entirely redundant, human industry. These are only a sampling of poets working in radical landscape poetry in the early twenty-first century.

Urban Scotland continues to be depicted, with Glasgow memorable in Donny O'Rourke's "Great Western Road" (O'Rourke 2002, 131–132); and Paisley is a regular context for the poems of Graham Fulton, while Edinburgh is much more than merely a backdrop in the poems of Ron Butlin and Tessa Ransford. But Glasgow and Edinburgh are complemented by poetry from other cities and a growing awareness of the psychogeography and interconnectedness of city and rural life, in the national context. W. N. Herbert (born 1961), coediting the anthology *Whaleback City: The Poetry of Dundee and Its Hinterland* (Herbert and Jackson 2013), linked a rich modern scene back to both the most radical Scottish poet between Burns and MacDiarmid, the neglected James Young Geddes (1850–1913), and further to *The Wallace* (c. 1477) of Blind Harry (c. 1440–1492). This gives a deep historical context for the poetry of Dundee from 1960 to 2010, particularly, and memorable works by Herbert himself, Douglas Dunn, Lydia Robb, John Glenday, Don Paterson, Bashabi Fraser, Valerie Gillies, John Burnside, Matthew Fitt, Ellie MacDonald, and Pippa Little.

In the extracts Herbert and Jackson give from Geddes's "Glendale & Co. (After Walt Whitman)," the ecstatic, rhapsodic long line of the great American poet is applied with sustained irony and bitterly suppressed fury to the description of "A Firm of undoubted respectability" where the buildings are "palatial and mammoth" and the clock towers are lit up at night: "their discs flare like angry eyes in watchful supervision" as the workers, "thousands strong" hurry "in obedience to summons." Glendale himself dwells in the quiet suburbs, with a view of "the glamour of distance"—not "the dingy alleys, the filthy closes" but "Extensive landscape, sea-scape: – / A serenity as of Heaven." Meanwhile, the workers live in the slums, "Stairs unclean, the sinks in the passages sending forth unpleasant effluvia, / Plaster broken streaming with moisture" (Herbert and Jackson 2013, 199–205).

Lewis Spence (1874–1955), in "Great Tay of the Waves," imagines the river sinking into his unconscious dreams:

> O that yon river micht nae mair
>   Rin through the channels o' my sleep;
> My bluid has felt its tides owre sair,
>   Its waves hae drooned my dreams owre deep.
>   (Herbert and Jackson 2013, 17, ll. 1–4)

Bashabi Fraser (born 1954) connects the two jute cities, Dundee and Calcutta/Kolkata by linking their rivers, in "From the Ganga to the Tay," imagining 400-pound jute bales compressed by hydraulic power processed into "golden slivers" on the shores of one river, then the other:

> Toned finer and finer
> With fastidious combs
> Then twisted into roves
> Which, just like our
> Distributaries, roam
> Into diverse streams
> (Herbert and Jackson 2013, 123–125, ll. 71–76)

The anthology as a whole takes the landscapes, cityscapes, and seascapes of a specific geographical location and its hinterland as its primary focus but then reaches back through history for depth of reference, and out, internationally, inhabiting its primary territory with the ghosts of other people and their stories. Imperial political history, the economics of industrialization, and the occupation of subconscious dreamworlds reach from historical poems to modernity. This demonstrates how the poets of the late twentieth and early twenty-first centuries who predominate in the book can best be read in that historical context. The landscape itself is occupied by time and past presences.

Arguably the most radical of all landscape poetry is that created by Ian Hamilton Finlay (1925–2006), realized in the garden of Little Sparta at Stonypath, his home in the Lanarkshire hills. The poems take place, actually, in a specific landscape that remains to be visited and explored every summer. They are related to the poems of Thomas A. Clark, emphasizing the values of taking your time, walking and living in landscapes experienced not as possessions but visceral, continual experiences. Clark's poems are sampled in *The Ground Aslant: An Anthology of Radical Landscape Poetry*, with others by poets writing in the early twenty-first century, for whom the national provenance is hardly noticeable. However, the matter of nationality is not irrelevant, as can be seen in the phrases that precede, and follow, the word itself in this extract from "Carcajou" by Colin Simms (born 1939):

>   Not just opening minds:
> like a thaw lifting blinds for chords and cords to saw opening the minds
> your way is just leading timber away education is more than that.
>   needing naturally, nationality has nothing to do with it
> it is the place we are, whether we find it neither near nor far whether we mind it
>   imagination
>
>   (Tarlo 2011, 26)

Nationality here is needed, "naturally," but also has nothing to do with presence, "the place we are," or in the words of Charles Olson (1910–1970): "I have this sense, / that I am one / with my skin / Plus this – plus this: / that forever the geography / [...] leans in / on me" (Olson 1983, 184–185 [p.185], 41–47).

In "Crossing the Loch" (Jamie 1999, 1–2), Kathleen Jamie (born 1962) recounts "how we rowed toward the cottage" across a bay, in a cold breeze, after a night drinking in a pub. The crossing is scary, hills "hunched" around the loch and the water itself seem to conceal nuclear submarines, nightmares lurking below. Yet the travelers arrive safely at their destination, from which they will enter their futures. As the poem ends, the boat may be safe, the pilgrims ashore, but the radical landscape is still there, recognized, occupied, and still promising, in the most vital ways.

REFERENCES

Berger, John (1991). "A Story for Aesop." In: *Keeping a Rendezvous*, 53–81. New York: Vintage.

Brown, George Mackay (1981). "Uranium." In: *Seven Poets* (ed. Christopher Carrell), 58. Glasgow: Third Eye Centre.

Brown, George Mackay (2006). "Hamnavoe." In: *The Collected Poems of George Mackay Brown* (eds. Archie Bevan and Brian Murray), 24. London: John Murray.

Dorn, Edward (2007). "Waying the West: The Cooperman Interviews." In: *Ed Dorn Live: Lectures, Interviews, and Outtakes* (ed. Joseph Riley), 92–116. Ann Arbor: University of Michigan Press.

Gairn, Louisa (2008). *Ecology and Modern Scottish Literature*. Edinburgh: Edinburgh University Press.

Gish, Nancy K. (2014). "Satellite Culture and Eliot's Glencoe." *Complutense Journal of English Studies* 22: 35–40. Accessed online 12 March 2014: http://revistas.ucm.es/index.php/CJES/article/view/46958/44062. (accessed 05/04/2018).

Graham, W. S. (2005). "Loch Thom." In: *New Collected Poems* (ed. Matthew Francis), 220–221. London: Faber and Faber.

Herbert, W.N. and Jackson, Andy (eds.) (2013). *Whaleback City: The Poetry of Dundee and Its Hinterland*. Dundee: Dundee University Press.

Jamie, Kathleen (1999). "Crossing the Loch." In: *Jizzen*, 1–2. London: Picador.

Lochhead, Liz (1992). "Knucklebones of Irony." In: *Poem, Purpose and Place: Shaping Identity in Contemporary Scottish Verse* (ed. Colin Nicholson), 203–223. Edinburgh: Polygon.

Lochhead, Liz (2011). *A Choosing: Selected Poems*. Edinburgh: Polygon.

MacCaig, Norman (2005). *The Poems of Norman MacCaig* (ed. Ewen McCaig). Edinburgh: Polygon.

MacGill-Eain, Somhairle / Sorley MacLean (2011). "The Cuillin." In: *Gheal Leumraich / White Leaping Flame: Collected Poems* (eds. Christopher Whyte and Emma Dymock), 343–415. Edinburgh: Polygon.

MacNeacail, Aonghas (1997). *A Proper Schooling*. Edinburgh: Polygon.

Morgan, Edwin (1996). "Trio." In: *Collected Poems*, 172–173. Manchester: Carcanet.

Olson, Charles (1983). "Maximus to Gloucester, Letter 27 [withheld]." In: *The Maximus Poems*, 41–47. Berkeley: University of California Press.

O'Rourke, Donny (2002). "Great Western Road." In: *Dream State: The New Scottish Poets* (ed. Donny O'Rourke), 131–132. Edinburgh: Polygon, second edition.

Riach, Alan (2000). "The Idea of Order in 'On a Raised Beach': The Language of Location and the Politics of Music." In: *Terranglian Territories: Proceedings of the Seventh International Conference on the Literature of Region and Nation* (ed. Susanne Hagemann), 613–629. Frankfurt: Peter Lang.

Riach, Alan (2011). "Returning to Assynt." *Archipelago* 6: 58–71.

Smith, Sydney Goodsir (1975). *Collected Poems 1941–1975*. London: John Calder.

Smith, Iain Crichton (2011). *New Collected Poems* (ed. Matthew McGuire). Manchester: Carcanet.

Stafford, Fiona (2010). *Local Attachments: The Province of Poetry*. Oxford: Oxford University Press.

Tarlo, Harriet (ed.) (2011). *The Ground Aslant: An Anthology of Radical Landscape Poetry*. Exeter: Shearsman Books.

2c.19
Coincidentia Oppositorum: Myth in Contemporary Poetry

Erik Martiny

In his scholarly mythographic work, *The White Goddess* (1948), Robert Graves claimed that poetry and myth originally enjoyed something of a special relationship. As he put it, "all the totem societies in ancient Europe were under the dominion of the Great Goddess, the Lady of the Wild Things; dances were seasonal and fitted into an annual pattern from which gradually emerges the single grand theme of poetry: the life, death and resurrection of the Spirit of the Year, the Goddess's son and lover" (Graves 1975, 422). By stressing this primordial connection, Graves's work also helped to strengthen the bond between myth and poetry in the second half of the twentieth century by inspiring poets that began composing their work in the wake of his seminal study and the rise of anthropological studies in general. Just as James George Frazer's *The Golden Bough* (1890) had a determining influence on such myth-infused poems as T. S. Eliot's *The Waste Land* or William Carlos Williams's *Paterson*, Graves's monumental book had an electrifying effect on the later generation of poets who launched their careers in the late 1950s and early 1960s.

In what follows, I refer to myth in the broad sense of any story that contains supernaturally enhanced human beings and/or stories that involve paranormal events or objects. For reasons of space, I have left out fairytales but have included Biblical myths and some legends because of their prominence and for the simple fact that the boundary between legend and myth is often tenuous.

The most convenient starting point for a discussion of myth in poetry is in the realm of Classical mythology simply because it is still so prevalently referenced, even among English language poets possessing a strong recorded bulk of national myths, as is the case with Celtic Irish folklore. Poets like W. B. Yeats and Seamus Heaney were keen to promote ancient Gaelic mythology but in practice often resorted to Hellenistic references in their poems partially for the imaginative allure of these myths but perhaps more because they are widely known and therefore readily understandable by anyone having had sufficient exposure to Western culture. Just as many Irish poets published and still publish in English imprints, these same poets employ the international lingua franca of Greek mythology in order to reach a wider audience.

The one most predominant Greek mythographic intertext in twentieth-century poetry is, also unsurprisingly, Homer's *Odyssey* (Graziosi and Greenwood 2007). The fact that James Joyce (also influenced by Frazer's *The Golden Bough*) began the century with his monumental poetic prose work *Ulysses* was undoubtedly also instrumental in stimulating this trend among both Irish and British poets alike. If any were needed, Paul Durcan's poem "Ulysses" (*Daddy, Daddy*, 1990) is demonstrative bibliogenetic hard evidence of this. For readers interested in delving into this, I have written an extended analysis of how Durcan's poem relates to both Homer and Joyce in the context of Freud's theory of family romance in an article entitled "Modern Versions of *Nostos* and *Katabasis*: A Survey of Homeric Hypertexts in Recent Anglophone Poetry" (Martiny 2009). Durcan's "Ulysses" is characteristic of much contemporary postconfessional Homeric poetry in that it focuses on family relationships.

Odysseus has been a popular figure among contemporary Irish poets: perhaps because of Ireland's small-island geographical features, it has had the same appeal as in the Caribbean with Derek Walcott, Lorna Goodison, and others. Eiléan Ní Chuilleanáin reworked Homer's tale in a number of poems in *The Second Voyage* (1977), a collection the title poem of which chronicles Odysseus's return to Ithaca. In comparison with Lorna Goodison's revisionist appropriation of the *nostos* (homecoming) motif, Ní Chuilleanáin's apparently depoliticized use of the male persona of Odysseus might seem a little surprising, especially for a book published in the middle of the 1970s, a period of intense feminist activism in America and parts of Europe. One might suggest that this measures the gap that existed between literary feminism in Ireland and the rest of the Anglophone world at the time; it might equally well be said merely to reflect the poet's estheticist appreciation of myth. Whatever the case may be, the poem does not seem to question either the cult of the male hero or his patriarchal leanings. On the contrary, the poet unquestioningly adheres to Odysseus and his thirst for adventure. At most, it appropriates the male precursor's story and explores the poet's longing for exotic enterprise in a way that is non-confrontational and untypical of mainstream feminist reworkings of myth and fairytale. Ultimately, the poem seems more interested in offering a paean to the working of water and the exotic allure of the sea than in refashioning Penelope or engaging in feminist discourse.

Homer's familial trio has mainly been employed to discuss father and son relationships. The Northern Irish poet Michael Longley draws repeatedly on the Homeric epic to scrutinize topics such as violence between men, and affection between father and son. His "Laertes" (*Gorse Fires*, 1991, 33) is an interesting case in point which masterfully illustrates that the use of mythological personae does not in any way exclude the expression of powerful emotion. It recounts a moving encounter between father and son after Odysseus' 20-year absence and stands as an elegy for Longley's own father, a paean to time past and a breaking of the taboo surrounding physical contact between Irish males, especially between father and son. In a letter to me, Longley has remarked that his "father and Laertes overlap – the poem is partly a belated lamentation for my father."(Longley 2005)

John Montague, also a poet born in Northern Ireland, has strikingly rendered the story in one of his most notable father poems, "The Cage" (1995, 43–44). The autobiographical speaker of this poem depicts his father in a tragic light, as alienated from his son as he is from others, an Odysseus figure trapped in the underworld of his unhappiness, working in the Brooklyn underground, "listening to a subway / shudder the earth" (1995, 43, ll. 6–7). In the final stanza, the speaker (who identifies himself as Telemachus) reenacts a descent into hell, a disempowered Odysseus figure himself, attempting to make elegiac contact with the haunting but irretrievable dead.

> Often as I descend
> into subway or underground
> I see his bald head behind
> the bars of the small booth;
> the mark of an old car
> accident beating on his
> ghostly forehead.
> (1995, 44, ll. 36–42)

The beating scar on his face acts as an eloquent metonymic sign of the father's repetition compulsion. Montague swerves away from Homer's story to illustrate the forces that separate father and son. The poem ends pessimistically, highlighting the impossibility of connection and communication between the two family members.

By contrast, Paul Durcan's exploration of the Ulysses story is a far more upbeat affair. His quest narrative is employed as a search for intellectual and emotional lineage and a means of placing himself within the canon of Irish literature (claiming filial descent from Joyce) and within the canon of world literature (by having indirect recourse to Homer as literary guarantor). Durcan's "Ulysses" (2009, 238–240) is also an elegy that attempts to come to terms with the conflictive loss of the paterfamilias. The poem stands as a posthumous confrontation between a son and his late father. As the first lyric dedicated to Durcan's father after his death, it constitutes the first step in the poet's reassessment of his deceased father. As a connecting narrative, it is therefore not the most radical of Durcan's portrayals of his father, who is elsewhere depicted as a brutal, fascistic figure. The poem is ultimately to be seen as a rather lenitive text designed to reaffirm the bond between a son and his deceased father, recently separated by death. The Ulysses myth is ideal as an initiatory gesture of reaffiliation. The ultimately affirmative teleology of Homer's story is perfectly suited to the will for reconnection as the epic is structured by the diametrically opposed poles of distance and proximity, alienation, and reconciliation. Its underworld chapter also adapts itself to narratives that seek to explore the world of the departed.

Homer's epic has fared well as a hypotext for recent British poets also in comparison with other Greek myths, most strikingly in the work of Peter Redgrove, the poet who, after Robert Graves and Edwin Muir, became the main purveyor of Greek myths in Britain (Kirk 1974), resisting Philip Larkin's wholesale rejection of myth. Like Louis MacNeice, Norman MacCaig, and Michael Longley before him, Redgrove tends to focus on a part of Homer's homecoming story that runs contrary to the nostalgia implied in the *nostos* motif in that he centers on Odysseus' 1-year stay in Circe's island paradise. Redgrove's magnificent collection, *Assembling a Ghost* (1996), contains a number of memorable rewritings or what Gérard Genette calls palimpsestic extensions of mythical narratives. Redgrove's two poems recounting Odysseus's encounter with Circe, "To Circe" (33–34) and "Better Than Before" (45–46), also seem to engage with previous hypertexts of Homer's source text. It is, however, difficult to determine to what extent Redgrove's renewals were prompted by other precursors such as Plutarch or La Fontaine who have modified the meaning of Circe's swinish transformations before him. These previous rewritings of the Circe passage all strove to suggest that the swines' disinclination to become men again was motivated by misanthropic disgust of mankind. Redgrove also overturns the standard view of Circe's enchantment, making the metamorphosis appear in a highly positive light as a eugenic improvement of human nature. The aim of Redgrove's poems is not to allegorize man's vileness in comparison with the idealized pigs: they explore man's repressed animal drives as well as the sensual and even spiritual potential of what he calls "piggery-paradise" ("To Circe", 34, I.1). In this poem, Redgrove imagines that Odysseus is transformed along with his companions, thus discreetly editing out the protective herb provided by Hermes in Homer's original version. When Circe's spell begins to wane, Redgrove's Odysseus remains spiritually and physically enthralled by the experience.

The reasons for Odysseus' popularity among contemporary poets are no doubt manifold. The facts of literary history (Joyce and Confessionalism, respectively) can be adduced. The incremental importance of family ties in the twentieth century undoubtedly also accounts for much of the interest in this particular myth, as does the concomitant longing to escape the entrapments of family life. The myth is so expansive that it can accommodate virtually anything, but its central dynamic of departure and return provide the contradictory allure of adventure and homecoming, the spice of Circe and the patience of Penelope. As I will show in the following section on Celtic myth, the prominence of the Sweeney legend springs from the same *coincidentia oppositorum*, the unification of the contraries of departure and repose.

One might say that successive waves of fascination with the Arthurian legend up to the start of the twentieth century momentarily used up creative interest in reworking this particular Celtic story in poetry, allowing room for other Celtic heroes to take the center of the page. Arthur and his knights have not been replaced entirely by those mythical figures that might have been deemed the most obvious successors by popular appeal, at least within Ireland: the demi-god Cù Chulainn whose stories appear in the Ulster Cycle and the hunter-warrior Fionn mac Cumhaill whose magical exploits are recounted by his equally illustrious son Oisin in the Fenian Cycle.

As suggested previously, the Irish Celtic magical tale that has had the most impact on modern poetry is the less widely known story of the mad king Sweeney, who under Saint Ronan's curse was condemned to roam the Earth naked and crazed and levitating like a bird for having thrown a spear at Ronan's bell, thus symbolically blaspheming against Christianity. The myth provides an interesting reflection of the tense transition between paganism and Christianity in Ireland. Although it seems to recapitulate the legend of the Wandering Jew in a more elaborate context, the legend of Sweeney predates the dissemination of the Wandering Jew story by several centuries. The plights of the two damned anti-heroes were probably inspired by the Biblical myth of Cain, a figure who was also left to wander and scavenge without being able to settle.

It is likely that T. S. Eliot's verse drama *Sweeney Agonistes* (1932) played its part in showcasing this particular tale outside of Ireland, making the story available to other American writers. Joseph Heller refers to it in *Catch 22* and the poet W. D. Snodgrass alludes to the madness of Suibhne in the opening of *Heart's Needle* (1959). In the context of contemporary Irish poetry in English, accounts of Sweeney the legendary poet-king have mostly survived in personalized translations by Seamus Heaney (*Sweeney Astray*, 1983) and Trevor Joyce. In his sixth collection, *Station Island* (1984), Heaney returned to the figure of Sweeney in poems he prefers to call "glosses" (a kind of intermediary category between translation and invention). In the introduction to this collection, Heaney observes that he identified with the Sweeney myth as "an aspect of the quarrel between free creative imagination and the constraints of religious, political, and domestic obligation," thus making Sweeney a kind of double for Odysseus. His Sweeney poems provide fantastic opportunities for exploring the hardships of solitude in the *poète maudit* tradition but also offer a bird's-eye view of the Irish countryside and Irish ways. Here is a sample from "The First Kingdom" in the "Sweeney Redivivus" section of *Station Island* that fuses culture and nature by evoking a biocentric version of one of Ireland's most iconic emblems.

> The royal roads were cow paths.
> The queen mother hunkered on a stool
> and played the harpstrings of milk
> into a wooden pail.
> (1990, 195, ll. 1–4)

A major contribution to the dissemination of Irish myths to a much broader English-speaking readership was Thomas Kinsella's translation of *The Táin* in 1969 during the height of the Troubles in Northern Ireland. In 2007, another Northern Irish writer, the poet Ciaran Carson, published a second translation of the battle-inspired text of ancient mythical heroes such as Cú Chulainn, allowing the demi-god some coverage outside of the Irish schoolroom. *The Táin* deals with Cú Chulainn's almost single-handed defense of Ulster against Queen Méabh's invasion from Connacht. Although the epic is about Celts fighting off other Celts, one can easily see what attractions the figure of a Hibernian superman holds for militantly anti-imperialist poets such as Kinsella and Carson.

The fusion of Norse mythology with Celtic culture is outstandingly achieved in some of Seamus Heaney's early poems. In "Funeral Rites" (1990, 52–55), Heaney seamlessly merges Celtic, Christian, and Nordic culture, drawing on Ireland's Viking heritage. Heaney's poem assumes a transformative function in that it focuses on the cultural legacy of the invader, rather than associating the Viking invasion of Ireland merely with violence and despoliation. Myth is used in this poem not just to make sense of history but to heal the conflicts that it causes. "Funeral Rites" begins by evoking the workaday realities of life in Northern Ireland during the Troubles, describing successive funerals. By dint of subtly handled metaphors, Heaney introduces prehistoric parallels, giving us temporal and geographical overlapping by creatively alluding to the oxymoronic Norwegian glaciers known as *svartisen* (literally "the black ice"): "before the nails were sunk / and the black glacier / of each funeral pushed away." It also brings to mind the passage of glaciers that smoothed the rocks on which Vikings made their mythological petroglyphs referenced later in the "cupmarked stones." Having noted the therapeutic value of funeral processions, the speaker of this poem expresses his yearning to deepen these appeasing ceremonies by imagining the resurgence of ancient rituals as a way of putting an end to violence in Northern Ireland: "I would restore // the great chambers of Boyne, / prepare a sepulchre / under the cupmarked stones" (1990, 53, II.8–11).

The magical thinking of mythopoeic wish-fulfillment is, however, complicated in subsequent verses when the speaker compares the funerary procession entering a megalithic mound "[q]uiet as a serpent" (1990, 54, II.23). The immediate association for the reader is the Biblical serpent, the suggestion being potentially that the procession is in itself malign but that it is burying that evil of untimely violent death in the mound just as one buries the hatchet as a symbolic proclamation of peace in Iroquois rituals. In the last section of the poem, the snake is recontextualized implicitly by the reference to Gunnar, a figure from Old Norse mythology. The closing remarks of the poem are full of wish-fulfilling, performative language as the speaker imagines that the funeral he has just been to will be the last one ever caused by violence in Northern Ireland and pictures Gunnar chanting joyfully at the moon.

Heaney's choice of the Gunnar myth is particularly interesting. The etymology of Gunnar's name is deeply martial as it means "attacker, warrior" and of course in modern English puns on the word "gunner." The ending of the poem succeeds in stripping Gunnar's name of any violent association by foregrounding musicality and the plenitude of the moon. Heaney does not so much reverse as sift the original Nordic myth of its violence, making Gunnar into a story that culminates in peace. In Heaney's poem, Gunnar becomes a kind of Orpheus before the loss of Eurydice, at a time when he lulled all nature to sleep, the very epitome of the pathetic fallacy which the speaker longs for in this poem, a figure that will radiate peace and transform his surroundings. Heaney's use of Norse myth is partially revisionary in that he edits out the central image of Gunnar thrown into a pit of snakes with his hands bound, forcing him to play the harp with his toes to put the snakes to sleep, but still being given the death bite by one of them. The modifications Heaney gives to the myth are obviously motivated by the desire to retain the tone of lofty solemnity and de-emphasize the comic horror of Gunnar's death. This kind of selectivity in the treatment of myth is of course a feature that goes back to the origins of literature's interaction with ancient folk myths. Even a neoclassicist such as Alexander Pope was, on occasion, wont to carve out the semantic kernel of time-honored classical myths. In the apocalyptic closing moments of *The Dunciad*, for instance, Pope goes against the grain of the classical imagery he borrows, making the beloved messenger of the gods and helper of mankind into a figure of the benightedness of Hanoverian rule, and the 100-eyed monster that he slays into a symbol of the demise of Queen Anne's enlightened reign: "The sickening stars fade off the ethereal plain; / As Argus' eyes by Hermes' wand oppressed / Closed one by one to everlasting rest." (Pope 2008)

Heaney's reworking of the Gunnar story is in keeping with Bronisław Malinowski's functionalist analysis of myth: Malinowski held that the main purpose of myth was to validate and reinforce cultural values and cohesion. In this line of thinking, one might argue that Heaney's poem is socially functional. It provides a modified myth (stripped to what the poet perceives as its essential mytheme) and presents it as a proactive, personally and socially therapeutic story.

In other poems, such as "North," Heaney does mention illustrious Scandinavian god-heroes like Thor to suggest the outdatedness of the belligerence associated with this figure, but his most cogent use of Norse culture is profoundly mythopoeic in that he usually bypasses standard Nordic myths to generate myths around the offshoots of these myths. Instead of focusing centrally on Scandinavian mythology, he mythologizes the victims of superstition. In poems such as "The Grauballe Man," "Bog Queen," "Punishment," and "The Tollund Man," all published in the first half of the 1970s, Heaney uses the resurrectionary art of Robert Browning to give life to the ritually executed people preserved in the bogs of northern Europe. One of the most captivating is "Bog Queen," a dramatic monologue in which a putrefying crone figure chronicles what the passage of history does to her body in terms that are both belittling and aggrandizing in turn. Heaney's densely packed, hypersensual word-hoarding succeeds in gemifying the victims of violent myth, offering counter-mythification, a kind of postburial word-wrapping of the deceased that transforms indignity into elevated verbal dignity.

Much of the energy in these poems derives from the poet's instinctive fascination for the earth and the secret treasures it encapsulates. This poetry is more than archaeological, possessing distinctly geomantic properties. Although Heaney's early collections are clearly geared politically at promoting peace, they are ambivalently positioned because of their insistently sensual response to the subterranean victims of violence. There is such an overwhelming philotellurian relish at work in these poems that they inevitably partake in the chthonic cults of yore, despite Heaney's condemnation of them.

This obsessive anthropomorphic response to a kind of earth mother is present also, though less famously, in the poetry of Peter Redgrove. A few years before Heaney's bog body poems, Redgrove started mythologizing his attraction for Gaia in a series of mud-bath poems that made the properties of mud represent the poet's fascination with hidden mysteries as well as the potential allure of original slime, menstrual sex, excrement, physical and mental penetralia. Although Heaney's work may be indirectly related to the chthonic practices of The Golden Dawn via W. B. Yeats's association with this hermetic order, Redgrove's philotellurianism was directly inspired by the secret society and the "sex magick" explored by Aleister Crowley. Like Heaney, Redgrove was inspired by ancient chthonic deities but he eschews any mention of them, offering personalized latter-day versions. The most well-known of Redgrove's mud poems is "The Idea of Entropy at Maenporth Beach" (*Dr. Faust's Sea-Spiral Spirit*, 1972), a poem in which he mythologizes a naked mud-bather, making her into a paradoxically blended intellectual ingénue-cum-chthonic goddess arguing in favor of the merits of darkness and dirt in connection with their opposites.

In other texts, Redgrove interacts freely with mythologies of every ilk, often in a syncretic manner that fuses Christian mythology with all manner of myths from Hinduism and European paganism to modern myths such as Frankenstein and Dracula to Egyptian myths. His texts inspired by ancient Egyptian mythology mostly appear in *The Apple-Broadcast*. A poem such as "The Eye of Dr. Horus" (1981, 36) is characteristic of twentieth-century reappraisals of myth in that it both mythologizes contemporary matter and demythologizes it within the same text. In mythology-inspired poems by poets such as Ted Hughes, Carol Ann Duffy, and Peter Redgrove, myths often occur alongside an element of deflationary humor which allows these poets to indulge in the pleasures of aggrandizement without foregoing the pleasures of iconoclasm and bathos. This can be interpreted as a dialectic tension between magical thinking and rationalism but one might, from another perspective, also suggest that the humor is not always intended to ironically deflate and deride but to accompany the myth-making impulse in a spirit of Bacchic revelry.

In a more univocally serious vein, let us compare two poems that mention Isis, the ancient Egyptian patroness of magic and nature and mother of Horus, conceived with her brother Osiris. Both Hughes and Redgrove wrote poems centering on Isis, an impulse that can be viewed as the combined influence of Robert Graves's *The White Goddess* and the second-wave feminist Goddess Movement of the 1970s. Redgrove's "Pagan Poem" (1981, 10) is characteristic of the poet's penchant for hybridizing mythology since he starts the poem by evoking (and thus invoking) the Greek moon goddess Selene and ends it with a shower of miniaturized meteors likened to "the dress of Isis, / Her dress of stone and light all pleated" (ll. 13–14). This might at first seem incoherent but as the title of the poem indicates, it is meant to be a poem that melds all kinds of pagan myths. Moreover, this kind of mythological melding is something that has always occurred from time immemorial. Roman mythology did not only fuse with Greek mythology but with Egyptian myths too. Although the cult of Isis still exists intact even today, as the international, multifaith 21 000 members of the Fellowship of Isis attest, Isis also fused with the cult of Venus and later the Christian Marianist cult, another example of the harmonious conjunction of complementary opposites.

One of Hughes's better later poems is "Isis" (1998, 111–112) in *Birthday Letters*, the collection he wrote for Sylvia Plath. In the poem, Isis is presented in terms that coincide with the tenets of the feminist Goddess Movement in that she is praised as a counterpart to Death who is characterized as male in the poem by association with Plath's prematurely deceased father. Hughes calls her "Magnae Deorum Matris" (1998, 112, l. 36), the Great Mother Goddess, also associating her like Redgrove with the moon (rather than with her usual attribute, the cow-horned sun). Hughes imagines Plath being possessed by Isis as she gives birth, denying the sway of Death. The poem is both chilling and moving at the same time, showing how myth can be used not just to indulge in poetic magic but to transcend the horror of depression and suicide. While T. S. Eliot argued for the use of myth as a way of making sense of history, post-confessional mythographers such as Hughes often employ it to make sense of and appease the traumas of personal history. Hughes's use of Isis to symbolize rebirth and regeneration (she is a fertility goddess and brings Osiris back to life) makes this poem a textbook example of the psychotherapeutic value of myth as theorized respectively by Freud and Jung.

I have included several anthologies of Christian poetry in the works listed in the following text to compensate for the fact that in this section I will only be considering poems that undermine Biblical mythology. In the poems retained here, Biblical myths are generally treated in a somewhat deflationary, but highly imaginative manner. Looking back at religious poets of the past in *The White Goddess*, Graves wonders if Christianity is "a suitable religion for a poet" (1975, 422), suggesting that poetry and orthodox Christian values make for uneasy bedfellows. I wish to argue here that in poetry since the 1960s, Judeo-Christian mythology (what C. S. Lewis somewhat paradoxically called "true myth") has nevertheless been a fertile source of inspiration in a frequently, but far from exclusively, iconoclastic spirit, allowing spiritually inclined poets to work through the contradiction between pagan revelry and Christian sanctity.

Both Hughes and Redgrove poke fun at the narrow-mindedness of Christian doctrines. While Redgrove's interaction with Biblical imagery is simultaneously both playful and in earnest, Hughes produced a series of more one-sidedly burlesque poems that tend toward the cartoonish in their depiction of God and other prestigious Biblical figures especially in two consecutive collections, *Wodwo* (1967) and *Crow* (1970). What makes these two poets so arresting is the dialectic interaction in their work between a neoromantic faith in the power of poetry to recreate what the mythographer Mircea Eliade called "sacred time," an idea he gleaned from the aboriginal Australian notion of Dreamtime. Eliade's belief was that the performance of religious rituals not only commemorated mythical stories but reenacted them directly. The musical magic at work in Hughes's work and even more so in Redgrove's poetry is arguably a form of religious incantation that ratifies Eliade's idea of the eternal return but it is at times undercut by bathos, signaling the eternal return of rational skepticism or pessimism. In simple Latin terms, these texts become a kind of battling ground between *homo religiosus* and *homo rationalis*, creating a sort of embattled unity of opposites, what the ancient natural philosophers called *coincidentia oppositorum* (Eliade 1971).

Let us turn to the equally riveting poems produced by two women in a slightly different spirit. In the works of Carol Ann Duffy and Eavan Boland, Biblical narrative appears almost entirely stripped of hierophanic connotations. That is not to say that their verbal music is less powerful; it is simply that one remains focused on the idea that the main thrust of their poems is anti-Biblical in that it is geared toward undermining patriarchal oppression. Carol Ann Duffy's collection *The World's Wife* (1999) contains some Christian myths viewed through the perspective of the nameless women hidden behind the iconic husband. Along with revisionism, this filling-in of the narrative gaps in mythological stories is a recurrent feature of feminist reworkings in prose and poetry. Duffy's "Mrs. Lazarus" (1999, 49–50) is a later, less belligerent version of Sylvia Plath's "Lady Lazarus," but it voices with great harshness the grief of a widow's bereavement and then the trauma of having to face a husband come back from the dead, having had his return foisted upon her.

> He lived. I saw the horror on his face.
> I heard his mother's crazy song. I breathed
> his stench; my bridegroom in his rotting shroud,
> moist and disheveled from the grave's slack chew,
> croaking his cuckold name, disinherited, out of his time.
> (1999, 50, ll. 36–40)

Another of Sylvia Plath's inheritors, the Irish poet Eavan Boland produced some scathing revisionist renderings of Biblical motifs in a collection entitled *In Her Own Image* (1980). The title poem possesses a highly subtle and teasing mastery of irony in that it can be perceived both ironically and unironically simultaneously. The poem opens with an image that can be read as both negative and positive: "It is her eyes: / the irises are gold / and round they go / like the ring on my wedding finger, / round and round" (1989, 33, ll. 1–5). On one level, the line evokes an aggrandized godly alter ego, the spinning gold eyes evoking a mesmerizing capacity for magic and symbolizing eternity. In a different perspective, they suggest a potentially strong element of dehumanization, the figure's eyes spinning like those of a mechanical toy. Other images in the poem are equally ambivalent: "Let her wear amethyst thumbprints, / a family heirloom, / a sort of burial necklace" (ll. 18–20). The line foregrounds preciousness and value again through the use of the semi-precious amethyst stone but these purple thumbprints also remind one of the marks left on the throat of victims who have been strangled.

The companion poem that follows this poem in the collection is on the contrary mordantly and unequivocally ironic. "In His Own Image" uses the Biblical phrase in a recontextualized manner to describe in expressionistic Plathian terms the violence done to women by brutal god-like men.

> He splits my lip with his fist,
> shadows my eye with a blow,
> knuckles my neck to its proper angle.
> What a perfectionist!
> (1989, 34, ll. 28–31)

This bitingly ironic engagement with Biblical mythology is characteristic of its time: Catholic Ireland in the 1970s was still very much in the sway of the Church and its condoning of, or ineffectual opposition to, wife-battering and crimes against children. Nevertheless, it is likely that in years to come, poets will still resort to Biblical motifs to sort out the legacy of Catholicism and the iron grip it had on Ireland into the 1980s. The future of mythological poetry seems assured even within our rationalist, agnostic times. Anthologies of contemporary religious poetry by eminent figures such as Harold Bloom (2006) and Les Murray (1986) attest to its vivacity.

An area that remains relatively untouched by the finer poets is futuristic mythology. Although poetry and science fiction are conventionally perceived as two mutually exclusive areas of literature, at least two upstanding recently deceased poets have delved into this potentially fruitful conjunction: Peter Redgrove and the Scottish poet Edwin Morgan. Redgrove was a tireless explorer of areas that are not traditionally viewed as belonging within the remit of poetry so it comes as no surprise that he broached the perceptual gap between these two literary realms, if only punningly, in poems such as "Silence Fiction" (1981, 119–120). His poem on proto-science fiction "Frankenstein in the Forest" (*Dr. Faust's Sea-Spiral Spirit*) is one of his most captivating. The difference between this and Redgrove's other mythological poems is slight, however, and his interest in the future or faraway galaxies remains relatively limited unless one considers that his esthetic is essentially about defamiliarizing the ordinary in a way that anticipated the so-called Martian poets of the 1970s and 1980s. Morgan's poetry is a more full-hearted exploration of what is generally known as speculative poetry.

References

Bloom, Harold (ed.) (2006). *American Religious Poems: An Anthology*. New York: Library of America.

Boland, Eavan (1980). *In Her Own Image*. Dublin: Arlen House.

Boland Eavan (1989). *Selected Poems*. Manchester: Carcanet.

Duffy, Carol Ann (1999). *The World's Wife*. London: Picador.

Durcan, Paul (2009). *Life Is a Dream. 40 Years Reading Poems 1967–2007*. London: Harvill Secker.

Eliade, Mircea (1971). *The Myth of the Eternal Return: Cosmos and History*. Princeton: Princeton University Press.

Eliot, T. S. (1963). *Collected Poems: 1909–1962*. London: Faber and Faber.

Frazer, James (2009). *The Golden Bough: A Study in Magic and Religion*. Oxford: Oxford Paperbacks.

Graves, Robert (1975 [1948]). *The White Goddess: A Historical Grammar of Poetic Myth*. New York: Farrar, Straus and Giroux.

Graziosi, Barbara and Greenwood, Emily (eds.) (2007). *Homer in the Twentieth Century*. Oxford: Oxford University Press.

Heaney, Seamus (1983). *Sweeney Astray: A Version from the Irish*. New York: Farrar, Straus and Giroux.

Heaney, Seamus (1990). *New Selected Poems: 1966–1987*. London: Faber and Faber.

Hughes, Ted (1998). *Birthday Letters*. London: Faber and Faber.

Kinsella, Thomas (2002 [1969]). *The Tain*. Oxford: Oxford Paperbacks.

Kirk, G. S. (1974). *The Nature of Greek Myths*. London: Penguin.

Longley, Michael (1998). *Selected Poems*. London: Cape.

Longley, Michael (2005). letter to the author (24 January).

Martiny, Erik (2009). "Modern Versions of *Nostos* and *Katabasis*: A Survey of Homeric Hypertexts in Recent Anglophone Poetry." *Anglia* 127 (3): 469–479.

Murray, Les (1986). *Anthology of Australian Religious Poetry*. Melbourne: Collins Dove.

Ní Chuilleanáin, Eiléan (1977). *The Second Voyage*. Winston-Salem: Wake Forest University Press.

Pope, Alexander (2008). *Selected Poetry*. Oxford: Oxford Paperbacks.

Redgrove, Peter (1972). *Dr. Faust's Sea-Spiral Spirit*. London: Routledge and Kegan Paul.

Redgrove, Peter (1981). *The Apple-Broadcast and Other New Poems*. London: Routledge and Kegan Paul.

Redgrove, Peter (1987). *The Black Goddess and the Sixth Sense*. London: Bloomsbury www.fellowshipofisis.com.

Redgrove, Peter (1996). *Assembling a Ghost*. London: Jonathan Cape.

Redgrove, Peter (2006). *A Speaker for the Silver Goddess*. Exeter: Stride.

Section 2d. The Past and Other Countries

2d.1
History and Poetry

Jerzy Jarniewicz

The 1960s in British poetry started, arguably, with a heated debate kindled by an introduction to a poetry anthology, one that called for a radical rethinking of the condition of British poetry and for a departure from its allegedly constricting principles. The anthology in question was *The New Poetry* published in 1962 and edited by Alfred Alvarez. The critic found British poetry parochial, suffering from what he diagnosed as the gentility principle, and defined the latter as "a belief that life is always more or less orderly, people always more or less polite, their emotions and habits more or less decent and more or less controllable; that God, in short, is more or less good" (Alvarez 1962, 25). His indictment of contemporary poetry was based on the assumption that this kind of writing works "to preserve the idea that life in England goes on much as it always has, give or take a few minor changes in the class system" (Alvarez 1962, 25).

If Alvarez is right, postwar poets remained persistently blind to the destructive forces which showed themselves at work in the history of the twentieth century. The horrors without—of the two world wars, the Holocaust, Nazi extermination camps, the nuclear threat—have their equivalent in the equally destructive forces within, which psychoanalysis helped to define. That modern history has radically reshaped the world, annulling much of the language with which this world is described, and has been largely ignored by poets who go on writing as if they lived in the pre-1914 world. To show how the new awareness has marked the poetry elsewhere, Alvarez turned to Eastern European poets writing "under pressure" of history, facing the horrors of two totalitarianisms. His appreciation of the Polish poet, Zbigniew Herbert, and particularly of his responsiveness to history, seems as important in his argument as the critique of British verse in the "Gentility Principle." In furthering his point, Alvarez does not refrain from contrasting Western and East European poets in a sweeping statement: "where [Western poets] create worlds which are autonomous, internalized, complete in their own heads, Herbert's is continually exposed to the impersonal, external pressures of politics and history" (Alvarez 1968, 143).

It is impossible to estimate to what extent later interest in recent history as shown in British poetry was sparked off by Alvarez's thesis, but it certainly had its impact. Sylvia Plath's change of poetic style offers an example of Alvarez's direct influence in this matter. Particularly telling here is Plath's use of historical references in her poem "Lady Lazarus," in which she uses the Holocaust as metaphor for her inner destructiveness. "my skin / Bright as a Nazi lampshade" (ll. 4–5), writes Plath merging the narrative of the speaker's suicidal drives with a detail from the world of extermination camps: an instance of the Nazis' efficacious economy that made them use the skin of dead prisoners as material for producing functional objects, such as lampshades. Plath's poems, criticized by some as a morally dubious practice of instrumentalizing the Holocaust, which she herself had not experienced, showed nevertheless the new possibilities of the use of history in poetry. "I think that personal experience shouldn't be a kind of shut box and a mirror-looking narcissistic experience. I believe it should be generally relevant, to such things as Hiroshima and Dachau, and so on" (Lucie-Smith 1982, 391). Though accused of appropriating someone else's suffering, her poems can be defended as an interesting implementation of prosopopoeia, a device of giving voice to those who perished and cannot speak in their own words. Prosopopoeia would soon become one of the forms which history has assumed in British poetry.

What is characteristic of the way British and Irish poets use history is that in most cases the history they are interested in is a recent one, the events of the twentieth century, though there are of course examples of looking back much further: to the Anglo-Saxon world in Geoffrey Hill's *Mercian Hymns* (1985), or to the Vikings' rule in Basil Bunting's *Briggflatts* (two important poets whom I will not discuss here due to the focus of this chapter). It is often a past that, though the poets have not experienced it, has exerted marked impact on their lives. It exists in personal and public memories, and it can be traced in the immediate environment: in photographs, books, newspapers, and everyday trivia.

That history, as a phantom reality that has passed and hence does not exist anymore, cannot be approached directly and does not lend itself to one fixed interpretation, seems to be a belief shared by most of the poets. Consequently, poets do not recreate the past, but rather focus on the way in which history, as narratives of the past, is produced and how it acquires legitimacy. Their concern with history is thus more an epistemological, "metahistorical," or textual, than an attempt at a metaphysical approach to history that would make poets construct their Yeatsian gyres (though there is a trace of this in, for example, Heaney's poetry, which I will discuss later). History is rarely hypostasized or personified, as it was, for example, in Auden's "Spain," where it "may say Alas" to the defeated but cannot "help nor pardon" (2001, 309–311, 311, 104), or in Eliot's "Gerontion" where it is said to have "many cunning passages, contrived corridors" (1983, 39–41, 40, 35). In effect, the history that appears in modern poetry is often what can be called "history incarnate"—the past as it is preserved in material everyday objects. In Craig Raine's poem "The Train Set," a wooden German toy train which the poet plays with brings to mind "different trains" (to quote Steve Reich's famous composition), these other trains that carried Jews to extermination camps. History here is no longer a philosophical concept, metaphysical entity, or an impersonal mechanism, but becomes something physical and tangible (Raine 1979, 45–46).

Seamus Heaney, five years senior to Raine, exemplified a similar attitude to history when in one of his uncollected essays, "Place, Pastness, Poems," he wrote that objects provide points of "entry into a common emotional ground of memory and belonging" (1986, 31). Objects in Heaney's verse included, at first, the ones burdened with public history, such as Viking trial pieces and quern stones (in *North*), but later became more private and quotidian: a smoothing iron, a snowshoe, an iron spike, or an old piece of pewter (*Station Island*). To Daniel Tobin, Heaney's objects, as the ones just mentioned, "are sources through which our lives are attuned with our own pasts" (Tobin 1999, 203). "A Sofa in the Forties" (Heaney 1984, 7–9) puts together individual and collective experience, drawing on the poet's memory and indirectly evoking the Holocaust by alluding, as in Raine's poem, to "distant trains" (l. 35). The children are said to have "entered history and ignorance" (l. 25), when, playing on a sofa turned into a train, they hear, but cannot truly understand the voice from the wireless with the news from the war in the outer world (Heaney 1996, 8).

Denis Donoghue observed that "precisely, because he does not present history in linear terms, Heaney offers the reader not a teleology implicit in historical representation, but a present moment still in touch with its depth" (Donoghue 1986, 173). This presentness of history is what characterizes most modern poems that tackle the theme of history. Heaney's early poems made use of the metaphor of digging, as in farming or archeology, the process of unearthing the successive layers of the past to bring to light what lies at the bottom, the origin, the starting point. Later on, he dropped the metaphor replacing it with stitching, changing the spade for the needle, to the effect that the concept of the past which, hidden, has to be uncovered disappears. History is now more like a process of conceiving the past, producing tentative versions of it, tearing them apart, and starting the process anew. A vertical concept of history, the one visualized as depth and going down for roots, gave way to a horizontal one: the past becoming more like a map than an archeological excavation. In a conversation we had in 2000 in Kraków, Heaney said:

> I guess my own situation now is more scattered or diverse. I said to you the other night that if I were to choose a pseudonym now I would choose the name *sartor*, and I do think more and more of the great grandfather tailor. The poems began with digging with the spade, digging into the centre, but I think now I would use the image of the needle, perhaps, unpicking the stitches and restitching it into a different shape, and moving around like a tailor, the tailor moving around with the needle, rather than the guy with the spade. That's just the symptom of some kind of change, loosening of the roots.
>
> (Jarniewicz 2002, 173)

Depth and roots as metaphors of the past give way to the concept of a territory, or surface. Susan Sontag observed that "reality has always been interpreted through the reports given by images" (Sontag 1982, 349). Since photography has long been the most popular visual medium, it is no wonder that many poets approach reality, including history, through photographs. Ted Hughes's poem "Six Young Men" opens the way to the days of the First World War through the description of a photograph of six soldiers: "Six months after this picture they were all dead" (Hughes 1979, 54–55, 54, 9). Douglas Dunn used an old photograph to set off on a journey in time, to recreate the history of an old Scottish institution in "St Kilda's Parliament, 1879–1979," adopting the persona of the Victorian photographer: "You need only to look at the faces of these men / Standing there like everybody's ancestors, / This flick of time I shuttered in a face" (Dunn 1981, 13–15, 14, 55–57). Michael Longley used photos he saw in a Holocaust exhibition in Montreal in 1986 and during his visits to Łódź and Lublin in 1988, as points of entrance to history in his poem sequence "Ghetto" (Longley 1991, 40–43).

In all these cases the photograph is not a transparent windowpane making it possible to see the (nonexisting) past. As a medium it is physically here, reminding the readers of its mediatory character, connecting with the past not only mimetically by what it visually represents, but also by its physical contact (via light) with its object: Roland Barthes calls it "the perfect analogon of reality" (Barthes 1983, 194). Photography, as it is used by poets, serves as a reminder that history is never a reflection of the past, but always an artful creation. One of the consequences of such knowledge is that any account of the past, any historical narrative, is always provisional, liable to changes and refutations; it is always to a certain degree arbitrary, created by the poet, who not only passively *reconstructs*, but also actively *completes* "the lacunae in definition, areas of indeterminateness" (as Roman Ingarden would call it [1979, 40]), or, in Roland Barthes's words, fills "the vacuum of pure, meaningless series" (Barthes 1981, 7). In this way, writing about history comes close to creative writing, and history to literary artifacts—a lesson which many poets took from Hayden White's *Metahistory* (1973). "Viewed simply as verbal artifacts histories and novels are indistinguishable from one another," wrote White (White 1978, 122), claiming that history is primarily a textual construct, built, or, as White has it, "emplotted" according to the rules of rhetoric and linguistic protocols, to satisfy the human need for meaning and order.

Kurosawa's masterpiece *Rashomon* (1950), in which what happened—a murder during a journey—changes depending on who recounts the events, can be treated as an illustration of the literary nature of history, which always depends on the point of view, or, in other words, on who tells the story. No wonder that Raine half a century later found Kurosawa's film still pertinent and wrote his own *Rashomon* (2001), also offering different versions of the same story depending on the perspective taken by the narrators: the bandit, the murdered husband talking through a medium, his wife, the woodcutter, and, finally, all four. In his early Martian poems, Raine demonstrated how an unusual point of view—of an alien, a child, or a mentally deranged person—can alter reality, or, in Viktor Shklovsky's sense of the term, "make it strange"; now he adopts the same strategy to history, to narrative reality, defamiliarizing and subjectivizing the past. His most ambitious work in this genre is *History: The Home Movie*, a long epic poem, recounting the history of his and his wife's families. Based on thorough research, checked by fact checkers at the publishing house, and set in recognizable historical reality, with many historical personalities (for example, Lenin), the poem is nevertheless an artifact, something that the poet does not forget to remind us about already in the subtitle: it is "a home *movie*" (Raine 1994).

This new awareness of history as an arbitrary, artificial, and textual construct required from the poets new ways of legitimizing it. Stephen Romer, 14 years younger than Raine, spent a year between 1989 and 1990 in Łódź, Poland, where he visited the area of the former Jewish ghetto. He wrote a sequence of poems inspired by this experience. In "All Souls," he contrasts the busy Roman Catholic cemetery on All Souls Day, when Poles visit the graves of their dead, and the empty, desolate Jewish cemetery, which the poet goes to with a friend: "Someone knew of a hole in the wire. / We wriggled through, / into the pitted acres / and walked by feeble torchlight" (Romer 1997, 72–73, 72, 17–20). In the third and final section of the poem, Romer introduces Chaim Rumkowski, the tragic, controversial Eldest of the Łódź ghetto, and quotes verbatim from *The Ghetto Chronicle*. We witness the poet's journey into history, his transfer from 1990 to 1941, which is well motivated: the poem starts with an account of his private experience of visiting the Jewish cemetery as if in defiance of the silence and oblivion which surround the place on a day of widespread grave-visiting. This establishes the setting for history, for the Rumkowski story, which the poet recounts by referring to documents from the period. The poet never leaves the contemporary world; it is history which seems to visit him: "In Poland you are constantly coming into contact with history in the rawest sense – it's grittier, not least because the air is grittier and you're having to breathe it in [...]. I felt all the time in Łódź a sense of being dragged under by its history, never getting free of it" (Romer 1993, 37).

A whole range of poems on history and inspired by history emerged in Northern Ireland. With the upsurge of the Troubles in the late 1960s, Irish poets, always engaged in history, in this Joycean nightmare from which they were trying to awaken, became more concerned with identifying historical processes, confronting them with personal experience, and examining various, often competing historical narratives. The renewed interest in history, usually of the twentieth century, was motivated by a belief that by examining the past the poet will find an analog for the troubled realities of the day, the characteristic features of which were chaos, confusion, and noise. The Irish Troubles, marked by sectarian violence and state repression, made poets look for precedences and patterns that would reintroduce a semblance of order, that would give meaning to what looked absurd. For a while, a metaphysics of history entered the scene. In his early poems, Seamus Heaney introduced the concept of the omphalos, the navel, represented by a tree, a tower, or a pump in the farmyard. This unchanging center of the changing world—"the still point of the turning world," to quote the famous line from Eliot's *Four Quartets*—referred to ancient Greek mythology and the semi-circular stone in Apollo's Temple in Delphi, in which time can be transcended and all space accumulated. Through this concept, the contingent and chaotic world of contemporary history was expected to find its place, and proper meaning, in an unchanging pattern defined by the omphalos.

Heaney's most daring and controversial use of history as an explanatory analogy to the horrors of today can be found in his "bog poems," first published in *Wintering Out* and, more significantly, in *North*. When reading P. V. Glob's book, *The Bog People* (1971), he came across photographs of the Iron-Age corpses reclaimed from the bog, which were perfectly preserved due to its chemical qualities. In their faces, which looked as if the victims were asleep rather than dead, Heaney found similarities with his Irish relatives and neighbors, thus linking Iron-Age northern Europe with present-day Ireland. Since most of the corpses were victims of religious rituals or tribal lynchings, Heaney drew an analogy between them and the casualties of contemporary sectarian violence. In "Punishment" (Heaney 1975, 30–33), the photograph of a shaved and tarred girl, possibly lynched for adultery, makes the poet think of Irish women who were also punished for fraternizing with the British. In the tripartite structure of "The Tollund Man" (Heaney 1972, 47–48), the poet moves from the description of a photograph of one of the Iron-Age corpses to his memories of another photograph, the one from the times of the Irish Civil War in the 1920s ("Stockinged corpses / Laid out in the farmyards" [Heaney 1972, 48, II, ll. 7–8]), and finally leaves the mediated world of pictures and imagines a journey into the "real" world of the Iron-Age bog man: a land which is both foreign and familiar.

This cycle of poems, by drawing parallels between "man-killing parishes" ("The Tollund Man," Heaney 1972, 48, III, l. 10) of the past and of today's Ireland, between pre-Christian violence and contemporary terror, suggests, perhaps inadvertently, some kind of cosmic, universal law at work. The criticism which Heaney's bog poems provoked was leveled at the poet's attempt to isolate contemporary events in Northern Ireland from their social and political determinants and to present them as characteristic of human beings in general. The violence, defined by a concrete political situation, was thus turned into a myth, the effect of which was, according to a number of critics, the justification of violence. In effect the poet could assume the quietist attitude of someone who understands, forgives, and remains uninvolved: "I who have stood dumb / when your betraying sisters, / cauled in tar, / wept by the railings / [...] understand the exact / and tribal, intimate revenge"—wrote Heaney in his conclusion of "Punishment" (Heaney 1975, 30–31; 31, ll. 37–40, ll. 43–44). Most characteristic of these critical voices, disoriented by Heaney's position, was Ciaran Carson's review, in which he called Heaney "a laureate of violence – a mythmaker, an anthropologist of ritual killing, an apologist for 'the situation,' in the last resort, a mystifier," or David Lloyd's accusation of the poet for his attempt "to reduce history to myth, furnishing an aesthetic resolution to conflicts constituted in quite specific historical junctures by rendering disparate events as symbolic moments expressive of an underlying continuity of identity" (quoted in Andrews 1998, 84–87).

Concern with history in modern poetry may fulfill also another function when it leads to rewriting the past in the name of underprivileged or silenced groups, such as women. Feminist poets question the absolute character of patriarchal narratives and try to reclaim from history marginalized events and personalities. History is thus corrected, or complemented, to become more inclusive, responding to the needs and expectations of modern readers. Carol Ann Duffy's *The World's Wife* (1999) exemplifies the tendency in contemporary literature to rewrite history in order to redress the balance of the past. Hitherto silenced voices can now be heard; characters, which in dominant narratives had not been given any attention, become now central characters. Among Duffy's protagonists one finds wives of mythical and legendary figures, such as Mrs. Midas or Mrs. Sisyphus, but also historical personages: Mrs. Darwin, Anne Hathaway, Frau Freud, or, more contemporary celebrities, Elvis's Twin Sister, and the Kray Sisters. This mixture of historical and mythological material has the effect of questioning the distinction between the two kinds of writing about the past, both of which may be regarded as literary artifacts (cf. Hayden White) and may serve to legitimize social norms and institutions. Duffy's collection may be entertaining, but it makes a serious point: those who write about the past are the ones who wield political and economic power; history is the language of the privileged. Published in 1999, at a "historical" moment of transition, on the threshold of the millennium, these poems defined new territories of the past still to be explored.

Alice Oswald's *Memorial* (2011) offers a different approach to history. She does not look for emblems of the past, for objects in which history is preserved and lets itself be seen, neither does she rewrite dominant accounts of the past: her approach is to reduce. A classicist, she has taken Homer's *The Iliad* and wiped out 80% of the text, leaving only two types of passages: similes and biographies of soldiers. She claims that the former derived from pastoral lyric, the latter from lament poetry. Oswald has also made a list of Greek and Trojan soldiers killed during the war, which opens the poem and runs for nine pages. Over 200 names, written in capital letters, foreign-sounding and unfamiliar to most of the readers, stand for the lives which had not drawn Homer's attention, mentioned only briefly in the epic. These names bring to mind the roll of the dead, or, indeed, modern memorials, such as the one in Washington, dedicated to American soldiers killed in Vietnam, with its wall covered with thousands of names, as well as the similarly designed monument in Srebrenica dedicated to the victims of the massacre of 1995. Oswald's poem, deprived of the narrative of Homer's original, turns into a verbal monument to all victims of ancient and modern wars, but it also asks questions about the role of poetry in shaping the narratives of events which brought about the death of so many and in commemorating those who perished in these events (echoing perhaps the Yeatsian "our part [is] to murmur name upon name" ["Easter 1916"] 204, ll. 60–61). It is history as text that becomes Oswald's concern, or the textual nature of history, the way in which it can be "translated" or appropriated: modeled, shaped, curtailed, expanded, made to acquire new meanings, in a manner not dissimilar from the practice of *détournement* as described by Guy Debord (Knabb 2006, 14–20). On the one hand, she deconstructs one of the founding texts of the Western world; on the other, she uses it as a means of intervening in the events of modern history. Homer's poem is both her goal and her medium.

It is not what she saves is most crucial in this project, but what she decides to eliminate: the poem's narrativity. *Memorial* is an antinarrative gesture, surprisingly so in times when history has been declared to be primarily a *narrative* construct. Oswald's poem is an attempt to forestall narrativization of history, in a belief that to turn an event into a narrative would be to impose order on what is a violation of order. If I am right that in *Memorial* Oswald, apart from the many other things that she is doing, also commemorates victims of the wars in Vietnam and Bosnia, she may be also trying to prevent turning those victims' tragic lives into heroic narratives, subservient to some ideology, creed, or political interest. Her poetry aspires, not to supply an objective, "true" account of what happened, as that would be impossible, but to coin a language which will not abuse the memory of those who perished. The language pruned and minimalized, deprived of the order of syntax and of the attractiveness of a narrative—a mere catalog of the lost world.

References

Alvarez, Alfred. (ed.) (1962). *The New Poetry*. Harmondsworth: Penguin Books.

Alvarez, Alfred. (1968). *Beyond All This Fiddle*. London: Allen Lane.

Andrews, Elmer (1998). *The Poetry of Seamus Heaney*. Cambridge: Icon Books.

Auden, W. H. (2001). "Spain." In: *Anthology of Twentieth-Century British and Irish Poetry* (ed. Keith Tuma), 309–311. Oxford: Oxford University Press.

Barthes, Roland (1981). "The Discourse of History" (trans. S. Bann). *Comparative Criticism*, 3, pp. 7–20.

Barthes, Roland (1983). *Selected Writings* (ed. Susan Sontag). London: Fontana.

Bunting, Basil (1987). "Briggflatts." In: *Collected Poems*, 37–62. Oxford: Oxford University Press.

Donoghue, Denis (1986). *We Irish*. Berkeley: University of California.

Duffy, Carol Ann (1999). *The World's Wife*. London: Picador.

Dunn, Douglas (1981). *St. Kilda's Parliament*. London: Faber and Faber.

Eliot, T.S. (1983). "Gerontion." In: *Collected Poems 1909–1962*, 39–41. London: Faber and Faber.

Glob, P. V. (1971). *"The Bog People: Iron-Age Man Preserved"* (trans R. Bruce-Mitford). London: Paladin.

Heaney, Seamus (1972). *Wintering Out*. London: Faber and Faber.

Heaney, Seamus (1975). *North*. London: Faber and Faber.

Heaney, Seamus (1984). *Station Island*. London: Faber and Faber.

Heaney, Seamus (1986). "Place, Pastness, Poems: A Triptych." *Salmagundi* 69: 31.

Heaney, Seamus (1996). *The Spirit Level*. London: Faber and Faber.

Hill, Geoffrey (1985). "Mercian Hymns." In: *Collected Poems*, 105–136. Harmondsworth: Penguin Books.

Hughes, Ted (1979). *The Hawk in the Rain*. London: Faber and Faber.

Ingarden, Roman (1979). "Artistic and Aesthetic Values." In: *Aesthetics* (ed. Harold Osborne), 39–54. Oxford: Oxford University Press.

Jarniewicz, Jerzy (2002). *The Bottomless Centre: The Uses of History in the Poetry of Seamus Heaney*. Lodz: Wydawnictwo Uniwersytetu Lodzkiego.

Knabb, Ken (ed.) (2006). *Situationist International: Anthology*. Revised and Expanded Edition. Berkeley: Bureau of Public Secrets.

Longley, Michael (1991). *Gorse Fires*. London: Secker and Warburg.

Lucie-Smith, Edward (ed.) (1982). *British Poetry since 1945*. Harmondsworth: Penguin Books.

Oswald, Alice (2011). *Memorial: An Excavation of the Iliad*. London: Faber and Faber.

Raine, Craig (1979). *A Martian Sends a Postcard Home*. Oxford: Oxford University Press.

Raine, Craig (1994). *History: The Home Movie*. London: Penguin.

Raine, Craig (2001). *Rashomon*. Dordrecht: Wagner & Van Santen.

Romer, Stephen (1993). "Honouring the Vertical Man. An Interview with Stephen Romer." *Oxford Poetry* 1: 37–39.

Romer, Stephen (1997). *Plato's Ladder*. Oxford: Oxford University Press.

Sontag, Susan (1982). *A Susan Sontag Reader.* Harmondsworth: Penguin Books.

Tobin, Daniel (1999). *Passage to the Centre: Imagination and the Sacred in the Poetry of Seamus Heaney.* Lexington: The University Press of Kentucky.

White, Hayden (1978). *Tropics of Discourse: Essays in Cultural Criticism.* Baltimore: John Hopkins University Press.

Yeats, William Butler (1984). *Collected Poems.* London: Macmillan.

2d.2
British and Irish Poets Abroad/in Exile

Glyn Pursglove

Introduction

No modern British Government has regarded (or is ever likely to regard) poetry as a matter of sufficient seriousness to think it worth sending poets into exile by means of judicial or governmental order. The term "exile" cannot, therefore, be applied to British or Irish poets of this period in the same sense that it applies to earlier poets such as Ovid and Dante or, in the twentieth century, Joseph Brodsky or Pablo Neruda, all exiled by the emperor or government of their homelands.

Even if none of them was exiled in the same sense as those listed in the earlier text, it remains true that a number of significant British and Irish poets spent most of their lives as poets abroad. Some distinctions can be made among these poets, though such distinctions are not hard and fast. Some, like Peter Russell and James Kirkup, very much willed their departures from, and their lives outside, Britain in a process we might very reasonably describe as self-imposed exile. Others, like Leslie Norris and Dick Davis, though they may, to varying degrees, have shared some of the antipathies that drove Russell and Kirkup from Britain, were also taken abroad by their working lives outside poetry (as teachers and academics). It is surely no coincidence that all of these named (with the partial exception of Norris) were of a decidedly international cast of mind, drawing on—and often translating—poetry from many languages. In what follows I shall attempt a necessarily brief and partial discussion of three of these poets, seeking to explore

---

A Companion to Contemporary British and Irish Poetry, 1960–2015, First Edition.
Edited by Wolfgang Görtschacher and David Malcolm.
© 2021 John Wiley & Sons Ltd. Published 2021 by John Wiley & Sons Ltd.

what kind of significance(s) life abroad/exile has had for their poetic work and its shaping. I shall treat Peter Russell at greatest length, believing, with Dana Gioia, that his is an exemplary case in this context: "The second half of Russell's career has become a long exile reminiscent of the first generation of Modernists, like Pound, Eliot, Joyce, H.D., and Lawrence, all aesthetic and spiritual refugees from their homelands" (Gioia 2005, 31).

Peter Russell

Peter Russell (1921–2003) was born into an affluent family. His father died when he was very young, and his mother was an invalid.

> I was left mainly to the care of a governess and four or five domestic servants. The governess read me endless fairy and folk tales, and later, Greek and Roman mythology, before I could read or write. My destiny was settled then.
>
> (Russell 1993a, 80)

At the age of six he was sent, as a boarder, to a preparatory school, where he was taught Latin and Greek. "By nine years old I was reading Homer and Plato, and Virgil and Horace in the original languages. That wasn't quite as exceptional as it may sound [...] today" (ibid). From 1935 to 1939 he studied at Malvern College, a public school of considerable distinction. Looking back at his school years, Russell has written that his

> schooling [...] consisted primarily of [...] Latin and Greek, with a good measure of British history. We learned basic French, and I had studied Spanish and Italian by myself sufficiently to read the Oxford Books of Italian, Spanish and French poetry by myself [...] In 1936 I switched to the study of the sciences, which led me to learn German.
>
> (Russell 1993b, 11)

In 1939, Russell won a place to read Natural Sciences at King's College, Cambridge. However, he chose not to take up his place. Instead, with remarkably bad timing he chose to spend the summer of 1939 in Heidelberg, where he "became deeply absorbed with German romantic poetry" (ibid.).

For obvious reasons Russell returned to Britain and, later in 1939, volunteered for the Royal Artillery. His military service was to continue until 1946, period during which he was several times promoted, finally achieving the rank of Major in 1945, as an intelligence officer. According to Russell, his "time in India, Burma and Malaya was mainly spent in learning the various languages and studying the various religions and philosophy" (Russell 1981, 23). However, a brief flirtation with communism led to a court martial toward the end of his military service.

He was, then, a man with certain social advantages—including his public school education and his rank as a Major—and with some disadvantages too, socially speaking, including his court martial and his fascination with kinds of knowledge for which the establishment had little time. What he chose to do on leaving the army was to become a student, not, now, of the sciences in Cambridge, but of English at Queen Mary College, London. He was a student from 1946 to 1949. He did not, however, take a degree; many years later, in conversation with me, he explained his failure to graduate by telling me that he feared that, if he had a degree, he might become an academic! He undertook some teaching while a student, giving lectures for the City Literary Institute, the Linguists Club, and the Workers Educational Association. In 1947, he made his first visit to Italy, armed with letters of introduction from the then imprisoned Ezra Pound, with whom he had been in correspondence. In 1949, he founded, and until 1956 edited, the remarkable periodical *Nine: A Magazine of Literature and the Arts*, a journal essentially Poundian in its concern with the literature of many languages and many times (see Görtschacher 1996)—(for a full index of the contents of *Nine*, see Pursglove 2000a). Russell's own contributions to *Nine* included verse translations from Cavalcanti, Petrarch, Camões, Garcilaso de la Vega, and Gutierre de Cetina, as well as essays, notes, and reviews on Pound, Yeats, Monteverdi, Adrian Stokes, and Gavin Douglas's translation of the *Aeneid*.

In an English literary world in which Philip Larkin and the Movement poets were coming to be regarded as central figures, Russell's poetic preoccupations and attitudes were strikingly out of step. Larkin effectively became, in the words of Donald Davie, "the unofficial laureate of post-1945 England" (Davie 1973, 64); Larkin dismissed most of the elements of precisely the tradition which Russell held in such high regard. He spoke derisively of what he called the "myth-kitty," asserting that "the whole of the ancient world, the whole of classical and biblical mythology means very little" (Larkin 1983, 69) and dismissed Orpheus, Faust, and Judas as "stale old Wardour Street lay figures" (ibid., 70). He similarly dismissed the multilingual, internationalist approach of Eliot, Pound, or Russell, declaring "deep down I think foreign languages are irrelevant" (ibid., 69). For Russell (in whose work mythology is of prime importance and for whom the epithet "philomythes" which Patrick Boyde applied to Dante (see Boyde 1983) would be wholly appropriate), such views, and their seeming acceptance in and endorsement by the English literary world, could only be abhorrent; a poet like Russell who translated poetry from at least 13 languages (including Arabic, French, German, Italian, Serbo-Croat, Swedish, Greek, Latin, Russian, and Persian) (see Pursglove 1995a) could not feel comfortable in a poetic world whose central figure deemed foreign languages irrelevant.

Disillusionment with the prevailing attitude to poetry in literary London was fundamental to Russell's eventual choice of what I have called self-imposed exile. For a poet whose aspirations were to write a poetry which was historically comprehensive, the times were altogether unpropitious.

> Men have been writing poetry for at least five millennia. Many of the most effective elements in this poetry must, in the nature of things, go back to sources in the Palaeolithic. Much of the poetry being published by the Establishment publishers of today draws on memories that go back no further than Darwin, Freud and Nietzsche, if indeed it goes back that far.
>
> (Russell 1997a, vii)

Of the poetic atmosphere of the late 1950s Russell later wrote that for him "the then dominant 'Movement' poets, Larkin above all, seemed intolerably provincial and irrelevant" (Russell 1993c, 11). The atmosphere was creatively inhibiting: "The English mob of so-called literati never gave me anything but a sense of being cramped, of having to conform with petty socio-literary codes which were beneath contempt" (ibid. 15). When he came to collect the poems he wrote in those years, he gave the two volumes titles which were essentially self-deprecating: *The Duller Olive* (Russell 1993b) and *A False Start* (Russell 1993c). This was work which, for the most part, Russell wanted to leave behind (in more than one sense).

Other reasons for Russell's self-exile were more purely personal. Between 1951 and 1963, he set up and ran two bookshops, first in Tunbridge Wells and then, on the closure of that shop in 1959, in Soho in London. Russell's financial failure was such that in 1963 he was declared bankrupt. His emotional life was also in considerable turmoil—as detailed in the autobiographical introductions to *The Duller Olive* and *A False Start*. In November of 1963, Russell left for Berlin and was never (save for brief visits) to live in England again.

> I arrived at the railway station in Berlin on about 20th November 1963 [...]. I had nothing with me but an English five pound note, a hand-grip with a change of underwear, and a suitcase full of paperbacks and typescripts [...]. I left behind me a lot of troubles and difficulties arising out of the bankruptcy back in the spring of my bookshop, eight months of living very precariously by occasional broadcasts for the B.B.C., and book reviewing and lecturing. More troubling still was the thought that I had left my Nigerian girl-friend in a rather shabby manner [...] Thus it was in a state of intense conflict that I descended on to the platform in Berlin, but at least there was one thing above all about which I had no doubts whatever. I wanted to go on writing poetry, and most of all, my very long "epic" poem *Ephemeron*. That ultimately was the deciding factor.
>
> (Russell 1994, 11–12)

Russell spent a year in Berlin—and later wrote that "during that year of intense work [...] I felt I had at last become a real poet" (Russell 1993a, 93). In November of 1964 he moved to Venice.

> I arrived with my suitcase of clothes and another larger one of books and manuscripts, and some $10 in my pocket. *Incipit vita nova*! My bags were heavy but my heart was light. After the always heavy atmosphere of Berlin, not to say London, I felt a wonderful sense of release.
>
> (ibid., 93–94)

Italy was to be home for Russell until his death, though for many years he traveled widely, living and working in Canada, Yugoslavia, and the USA between 1973 and 1977. From September 1977 until the Iranian Revolution, he taught (and studied) at the Imperial Academy of Philosophy in Teheran. He returned to Venice in the spring of 1979 before moving to Pian di Scò in Tuscany in the mountain range known as the Pratomagno, between Florence and Arezzo. He lived in, or near, this small town until the last few years of his life, when ill health forced a move to a sanatorium in the nearby hill town of Castelfranco di Sopra.

The beginning of Russell's years of exile marked a turning point in his work. He judged, as we have seen, that he only became "a real poet" during his time in Berlin. During his years in London there had been long spells when he wrote little or no poetry. With his "exile" he suddenly wrote poetry abundantly. So, for example, the poems he wrote in one year in Venice occupy over 330 pages (see Russell, 1995). Of course, an increase in mere quantity matters little. What *does* matter is that Russell's exile years saw the writing of most of his best work. He had written some successful poems during his years in London, notably *The Elegies of Quintilius* and the better parts of the very uneven long poem *Visions and Ruins* (for publication details of both of these, see Pursglove 1995a), but much of his work was sadly inferior, often uncreatively bookish, rather clotted, and unmusical. While it would be wrong to speak of a wholesale transformation in Russell's work being occasioned by his exile, it was clear from the first collection published after his departure from England—*The Golden Chain: Lyrical Poems 1964–1969* (Russell 1970)—that his work had developed greatly. This privately published collection contains, in poems such as "Delphi," "Blind Homer," "Mnemosyne," "Late Winter Spring," and, above all, "The Golden Chain" itself (see Pursglove 2000b), a new maturity of thought and music. Poems with debts to Blake, Yeats, Pound, Celtic myth, Sufic thought and poetry, Greek philosophy, and modern thinkers such as Jung, Eliade, and Coomaraswamy, seem fully assimilated and transmuted within a newly assured individual poetic voice, the poet's trust placed in the traditional languages of symbol and myth so as to produce a poem on the powers of love and poetry.

Elsewhere in the collection Russell achieves a similar weight of resonance, with even greater brevity, as in "Blind Homer" (Russell 1970, 17):

> Blind Homer, sniggered at by the ignorant soldiery
> Invented Olympus, propped among the mules;
> And Greece exploded into golden flames, and Europe
> Slowly grew out of his long hexameters.
>
> *Berlin*
> *9th August 1964*

But it was not only in short lyrics that Russell, removed from the cramping weight of life in London, found himself able to write with a new freedom and intensity. He produced an extensive series of longer poems, densely packed with metaphysical and philosophical thought, explorations of the life and nature of the human spirit. When he gathered many of these in *Elemental Discourses* (Russell 1981), he included just two pre-exile poems, "The Spirit and the Body" (written in 1956) and "A Celebration" (1962), the remaining 39 poems all belonging to his later post-exile years. They include a number of what are undoubtedly Russell's major poems, such as "Missing A Bus," "Remembering Geography," and, most notably, "The Holy Virgin of Mileševa" (see Pursglove 1995b), in which he explores themes such as the "artificial paradise / The world of art" (Russell 1981, 167) and the origins and nature of language itself.

> The first Adam did not name the things.
> He knew the evident spirit
> Of everything that breathes,
> Knowing the life in stones and lakes and caves,

> The hidden power of mountains, rivers, trees —
> The definite voice of wind and waterfall..
>
> (ibid., 166)

In these texts, we can also see what is perhaps his most important theme, one expressed in the title of one of Russell's most brilliant and learned prose works, *The Image of Woman as a Figure of the Spirit* (Russell 1992a):

> *I long to grasp the ikon's magic power,*
> *To gaze intent upon the beauteous face,*
> *The curve of cheek and nose and hand,*
> *The long fingers' twig-like innocence;*
> *To know the life behind the thing,*
> *To see the thing in all its glory*
> *And then to be myself*
> *A part of that hid life.*
>
> (Russell 1981, 167)

In the Introduction to *Elemental Discourses*, Russell describes these longer poems as "contemplations."

> The root of the word is connected with *templum*, a temple, that is, a sacred space *cut out* (Greek *temnein* = to cut) by an augur for taking observations [...] I intend the poems as sacred spaces cut out of the chaos of the profane consciousness, spaces in which to consider and observe, to concentrate the mind and to come nearer to an understanding of the realities of existence.
>
> (ibid., 45)

Russell continued to write poems of this kind after the publication of *Elemental Discourses*. One of the finest was "Albae Meditatio," written in 1991 and first published in *A Progress of the Soul* in 1992 (Russell 1992b). Though soaked in the language and idioms of Persian poetry and Sufism (see Loloi 2000), the poem is just as open to a reading in terms of Platonic and neo-Platonic writings on love, Medieval or (particularly) Renaissance theories of love, or in terms of what Dante has to say of love and the Spirit or, indeed of the traditions of Jewish prophecy or Biblical symbolism—the late Russell is nothing if not syncretic. Indeed, there is a sense in which a poem such as "Albae Meditatio" might be described (though not altogether adequately) as a poetic study in comparative religion and poetry. Without being merely derivative, the poem is equally indebted to Cecco d'Ascoli and to Ibn Daoud. Yet for all its religious and philosophical themes, what is equally striking is the vivacious fidelity to appearances of the poem's opening lines:

> Already it's getting light and the first birds
> Are twittering in the walnut tree, and you
> Are hidden everywhere from my fallacious eye.

> Some of the pale green leaves at this hour
> Appear bright yellow, smooth grey of the walnut bark
> Jet like the young girl's cable braids swinging like bell ropes.
> (Russell 2000, 54)

At much the same time that Russell was writing such long poetic "contemplations," he was also producing great many more directly autobiographical poems, often in the form of sonnets, explorations of the experience of old age. As Dana Gioia observes in the last 10 years of Russell's life (Gioia 1994/1995, 32):

> In poems like "Anziano," "Smoke," or "My Last Birthday," [Russell] has emerged as a memorable poet of old age. Wrestling with tradition, especially the ghost of Yeats, Russell has found in mortality his most impassioned subject.

Many of Russell's poetic themes and concerns come together in the body of work which perhaps constitutes his most distinctive and remarkable work, what can be referred too briefly as his Quintilius poems. Quintilius—or, to give him his full name, Cittinus Aurelianus Quintilius Stultus first entered Russell's poetic life late in the 1940s. A poet called Quintilius was referred to by Horace (*Ars poetica*, ll. 438–444; Horace 1989, 73) as a friend, poet, and critic. But none of the poems by *that* Quintilius have survived. Russell's Quintilius is his *invention* (perhaps in both the modern and older senses of that word). Russell's *The Elegies of Quintilius* was initially presented as translations of Latin originals, complete with a pseudo-scholarly apparatus (see Russell 1954, 1975). The best of these elegies (such as "The Dispossessed" and "The Golden Age") are highly accomplished pastiches of precisely the kind of poems a late Roman poet might have written in imitative admiration of earlier masters of the elegy (he was perhaps a reader of Tibullus in particular). For *Russell's* Quintilius does not belong to the Augustan era; he is rather a kind of vagabond poet of the fifth century. He "lived," thus, in one of the most remarkable periods in European history. Peter Brown (Brown 1971/1995) provides a brief but brilliant and suggestive introduction to this time, a book which unintentionally serves as an illuminating context for a reading of Quintilius. The Quintilian elegies were essentially acts of poetic ventriloquism, Russell speaking through a consistently adopted mask. In his post-exile Quintilius poems, Russell attempts something much more ambitious and brings it off successfully with remarkable frequency. In Russell's own words, "Instead of the Poundian technique of a modern consciousness penetrating into the past I use the device of a consciousness from the distant past penetrating 'unconsciously' into the future!" (Russell 1997b, 221).

The result is poetry often dizzyingly cross-historical and trans-historical. Writing ostensibly about one confused and confusing period at the end of an era of relative cultural stability, Quintilius/Russell seems often to be writing also of another such time (our own). What might have been thought to be a simple reference often turns out, given the poet's deployment of wit and irony, to be multifaceted. Take, for example, Quintilius's use of the word *neoteros* and its cognates (see Russell 1997b, 69–78). In both text and notes, the "translator" teases the reader as to whether the word should be understood purely in its classical sense and/or as an allusion to the contentious anthology *The New Poetry* edited by Michael Hulse, David Kennedy, and David Morley (Hulse et al. 1993). Given that the anthology was published in 1993 and that the relevant poems by Quintilius were "translated" between 1993 and 1996, the allusion is surely intended; Russell can be assumed to have in mind a fashionable contemporary term representative of what he sees as the depressingly common conflation (in our own times) of the languages of marketing/business and poetry (see Russell 1997c, *passim*).

The Quintilius of Russell's apocalypse is simultaneously a comic and heroic figure—comic in the frequency of his intellectual pratfalls, heroic in his refusal to give up his commitment to a search for two related ideals—the knowledge of God and the ideal woman. It may be true to say that Quintilius "is" Russell. Perhaps it is truer to say that he is also all poets in the centuries *between* Quintilius and Russell. Quintilius has evidently read (impossibly enough) the work of Dante, Shakespeare, Milton, Voltaire, Goethe, Hölderlin, Novalis, T. S. Eliot, Ezra Pound, and many others, and his use of their work has about it a startling kind of innocence and freshness, as if he was unaware of what he was doing, rather than being consciously allusive. It is a central tenet of Russell's poetics that

> The world we live in is not merely the sum of our immediate direct perceptions and of our reactions to the material conditions we live in [...] It is the sum of the perceptions and interpretations of fifty or a hundred generations of our forebears [...] It is [the] neglect of human culture as a whole, in spite of all the admirable specialist scholarship on it, that distresses me in our contemporary poets and so-called creative writers [...] If there is one received view of the world in any one moment of history it is bound to be limited and circumscribed, since it has omitted so much of the great thought of the past.
>
> (Russell 1995, 27–28)

The creation of Quintilius and his work can be seen as the culmination of Russell's willed self-exile from the times in which he lived, analogous to his willed self-exile from the place and society into which he happened to be born. Like that of one of his great masters, Ezra Pound, Russell's work is the record of an exilic flight from the parochialism of both geography and history.

James Kirkup

Like Russell, James Kirkup (1918–2009) chose to spend most of his working life as a poet (from 1959 until his death) in self-elected exile from England. Like Russell, Kirkup too was very much an internationalist in his literary interests and tastes. Both were prolific and accomplished translators from a sizeable range of languages. But there were also important differences between the two. While he remained in England, Kirkup was much better able than Russell to accommodate his work to the prevailing tastes of the literary establishment. 1951 saw the publication by Oxford University Press (OUP) of Kirkup's first substantial collection,

The Submerged Village. Further collections followed from OUP in 1952, 1954, 1957, 1959, and 1963. His work in this period stripped away much of the extravagance of his earlier writing and was characterized by a new precision of language. The title poem of *A Correct Compassion* (1952)—an account of a heart operation—has been widely anthologized and much admired for the exactness of its observation and its language. But the poem is far more than reportage; as a meditation on art and its "correct compassion," it is sophisticated and deft. As a kind of defense of poetry, it is persuasive and moving. Compared to the case of Russell, Kirkup's exile effected a less radical transformation in the manner and quality of the poetry he wrote, perhaps because Kirkup's reasons for abandoning England were less literary than those of Russell and had more to do with his own personality and way of life.

A clue is offered by a reading (and indeed, by the titles) of two of Kirkup's volumes of autobiography: *A Poet Could Not But Be Gay* (Kirkup 1991) and *Me All Over: Memoirs of a Misfit* (Kirkup 1993). The earlier of these two books, with its impudent appropriation of a line from one of Wordsworth's most famous poems, "I Wandered Lonely as a Cloud" (Wordsworth 1969, 149) makes pretty clear one of the ways in which Kirkup felt himself "a misfit"—his sexuality. Although he has frequently been identified as a homosexual and though his work appeared in *Gay News* and has been published in more than one anthology of Gay Verse, Kirkup himself, in a piece written late in his life, rejected this identification.

> I was not, as popularly supposed, a homosexual but, strictly speaking, a bisexual – someone in an even more precarious position than an outright homo or het, because I was constantly living on a knife-edge between two worlds, two impulses, two attractions, of which the male was the stronger in purely sexual terms, the female in spiritual and idealistic terms of pure love and intellectual fellowship to which sex occasionally added something extra but not all that important.
> (Kirkup 1998a, 62)

In the same piece, Kirkup wrote of his "curious ambivalent sexuality" (ibid., 63). Elsewhere Kirkup defined himself as "a pacifist-anarchist bisexual poet" (Kirkup 1998b, 66).

Neither politically nor sexually was Kirkup at all suited to life in the social and moral atmosphere of 1950s England. It was, one suspects, his sense of himself as a misfit, rather than any purely literary considerations that prompted him to leave England. Having said that, it is also clear that he saw English society, both in his own time and earlier, as particularly inimical to poets and poetry. In an essay published in 1998, he writes that "Great Britain has destroyed many of its poets" (Kirkup 1998c, 305), citing Marlowe, Cowper, Smart, Chatterton, Byron, Clare, Swinburne, Wilde, and Lionel Johnson as examples, and observes that "In England today, true poetry is dead [...] Great Britain has its own secret methods for suppressing thought and repressing freedom of expression" (ibid., 306). One might, of course, think that there is a kind of special pleading going on in this essay when one reads Kirkup's assertion that "[l]ike most great poets, Shelley was passionately bisexual" (ibid., 313).

Whether or not Kirkup was really repressed (poetically, rather than personally) by life in England is debatable, but it is, at any rate, undeniable that the work he wrote during his long, self-chosen exile is characterized by its openness to an enormous range of possibilities, by its extraordinary variety of subject and form. His time in Japan saw him develop a striking fluency in anglicized versions of some Japanese verse forms. *Tanka Tales* (Kirkup 1997a), for example, employs the traditional poetic form of 31 syllables disposed in five lines (5,7,5,7,7) to discuss subjects ranging from the Brothers Grimm to the pottery of Bernard Leach, while *A Certain State of Mind* (Kirkup 1995) is a central text in the modern English reception and understanding of the haiku. His *Modern Japanese Poetry* of 1978, published in an enlarged edition as *Burning Giraffes* (Kirkup 1996), is a standard work, and he published other very significant translations of both classical and contemporary Japanese poetry, such as *We of Zipangu* (Takahashi 2006), a fascinating collection of accomplished versions from the contemporary Japanese poet Mutsuo Takahashi, made in collaboration with Tamaki Makoto.

Naturally he wrote extensively on Japanese subjects, strikingly so in *Pikadon* (Kirkup 1997b), an epic on the bombing of Hiroshima and Nagasaki, the full title of which describes it as a "dramatic documentary poem for speakers, singers and dancers" (ibid., i), that combines detailed focus on individuals with larger historical analysis, its lyrical passages often very moving, its anger intelligent and exact. But he was just as likely to write lyrics on jazz or football, on Olympic athletes or mythology, on the sea or science fiction, on sex or Paganini.

As a translator he worked on poetry, drama, and fiction by, among others, Valéry, Camara Laye, Jerzy Andrzejewski, Theodor Storm, Simone de Beauvoir, Heinrich von Kleist, Schiller, Dürrenmatt, and Ibsen.

Like Russell, Kirkup was an extraordinarily prolific poet. Indeed, of both it might be said that they might have served their reputations better by writing less. Neither was especially well-endowed with the gift of self-criticism, and, in both cases, exile cut them off from a wider circle of competent English readers, the friendliest of whom could have offered constructive criticism that the poet(s) might have found useful and productive.

Desmond O'Grady

Although Desmond O'Grady (1935–2014) wrote all of his mature poetry while living outside the land of his birth, and though he displayed the same kind of internationalist outlook on poetry and the same commitment to translation that characterize both Peter Russell and James Kirkup, he cannot sensibly be described as an exile in the same way that that those two can. O'Grady initially left Ireland while still in his teens, but unlike Russell and Kirkup he never adopted another country as a lasting home. He was, rather, an inveterate traveler. Indeed, the title of one of his most significant collections of poetry, *The Wandering Celt* (O'Grady 2001), might very reasonably be applied to O'Grady himself.

O'Grady was born in Limerick and spent his childhood in West Clare and County Kenny. He was educated as a boarder at the Cistercian College near Roscrea in County Offaly. On leaving that College he immediately made his way to Paris, against the wishes of his parents, who wanted him to study for a profession. "When I went to Paris all I knew was that I wanted to get out of Ireland" (O'Grady 2003, 10). He spent some time working at the famous bookshop of Shakespeare and Company, and while in Paris became acquainted with Samuel Beckett. Late in the 1950s he moved to Italy, "because Italy was cheaper. Rome was more liveable than Paris, and the climate was more salubrious. The Italians were more congenial people than the French" (ibid., 15). In Rome, he was Deputy Head of an English school from 1957 to 1962. While in Italy he began what was to be an enduring friendship with Ezra Pound, spending some years as his secretary. Earlier he had met the film director Federico Fellini in Rome and, indeed, appeared briefly (as an Irish poet!) in his 1960 film *La Dolce Vita*. He cofounded and organized the Spoleto Poetry Festival in 1966. Further travels took him to Greece and to the USA, where he became a postgraduate student (and a teaching fellow) at Harvard, in Celtic Languages and Comparative Studies. He went on to teach at the American University in Cairo and the University of Alexandria. He returned to Ireland only in the late 1980s and lived in Kinsale until his death from a heart attack.

Though he himself was perhaps an "expat" rather than an exile, the theme of exile is prominent in O'Grady's work. One of the poems in his first collection, *Chords and Orchestrations*, published by The Echo Press, Limerick 1956, is entitled "Self-Exile" and contrasts the young poet with "These small men, belted and buttoned up astern" who "Bend to their sailing business deliberately as priests":

> At my back the madness of the town,
> In my face a remote sanity of my own.
> (O'Grady 1996, 6)

One of the most interesting of O'Grady's late poems, included in *The Wandering Celt* (O'Grady 2001) is "Ovid from Exile," full of the kind of solitary sadness which O'Grady rarely seems to have felt in his years away from Ireland. O'Grady's Ovid finds his place of exile defined by linguistic isolation. He has learned the prevailing languages of the place: "To communicate I've learned the rudiments / of both their languages, Getic and Sarmatian / ... / But nobody here can language me Latin" (ibid., 459). For O'Grady exile was, as Thomas McCarthy puts it, "not victimhood in the conventional Irish poetic narrative sense – rather, it is a deeper encounter, a dialogue between cultures" (McCarthy 2003, 67). O'Grady's wide-ranging linguistic facility and his gift for friendship ensured that his exiles / travels were constantly nourishing, poetically speaking:

> My history – racial, continental, insular –
> occupies me most. My each migration
> from and to my island maps me that.
> Each depart, return's a search for origin.
> ("Exile from Exile," O'Grady 1996, 390)

Along with his enduring consciousness of belonging to a community of poets, this meant that wherever he was his true home was in poetry, past and present. In another sense his home was the very idea of Europe; in O'Grady's own words, *his* Europe "is old Europe – in a pincers that embraces Old Petersburg and old Alexandria" (O'Grady 1994, xi). Indeed, the large volume of O'Grady's collected translations (O'Grady 1994) provides an effective guide to the poetry of that "old Europe" and makes a very coherent collection, being one man's experience and vision. It ranges from the Ancient World to the Modern (from Sappho and Simonides to Lorca and Montale, via Abu Nuwas and Sedulius Scottus). The whole might be viewed as the home O'Grady built before he came home, in the literal sense, to Ireland.

Conclusion

In her brilliant—and endlessly stimulating—book *Shards of Love*, María Rosa Menocal argues that "the medieval – and thus what we call the modern and postmodern – lyric is invented in bitter exile" (Menocal 1994, 91). Accepting this as a truth about the larger history of poetry, one may see in it a pattern often repeated in the life and work of individual poets. Certainly, for Russell, Kirkup, and O'Grady, "exile" (even if not especially "bitter") proved poetically empowering. At a time when the poetry of their home country was finding in Larkin, "the stay-at-home provincial Englishman" (Gioia 1994/1995, 80), a new model for poetry, Russell and Kirkup, who both rejected that model, chose exile, and their work flourished thereafter. O'Grady chose to leave behind him "the Ireland of the 1950s where provincial conservatism, isolation and Catholic political hegemony forced a kind of schizophrenic catharsis in the mind of every individualistic and creative being" (McCarthy 2003, 67) and to forge for himself a new "European" identity, through which, and out of which, his poetry grew.

References

Boyde, Patrick (1983). *Dante, Philomythes and Philosopher: Man in the Cosmos*. Cambridge: Cambridge University Press.

Brown, Peter (1971/1995). *The World of Late Antiquity*. London: Thames and Hudson (revised ed. 1995).

Davie, Donald (1973). *Thomas Hardy and British Poetry*. London: Routledge & Kegan Paul.

Gioia, Dana (1994/1995). "The Image Russellian." *Agenda* 32: 3–4: 79–80.

Gioia, Dana (2005). "A Note on Peter Russell." *The Tennessee Quarterly* 2 (1): 31–32.

Görtschacher, Wolfgang (1996). "'Continuing the Dances of the Ages': Peter Russell's Literary Magazine *Nine*." In: *The Road to Parnassus* (ed. James Hogg), 269–280. Salzburg: University of Salzburg.

Horace (1989). *Horace: Epistles Book II and Epistle to the Pisones (Ars Poetica)* (ed. Niall Rudd). Cambridge: Cambridge University Press.

Hulse, Michael, Kennedy, David, and Morley, David (eds.) (1993). *The New Poetry*. Bloodaxe: Newcastle upon Tyne.

Kirkup, James (1991). *A Poet Could Not but Be Gay*. London: Peter Owen.

Kirkup, James (1993). *Me all over: Memoirs of a Misfit*. London: Peter Owen.

Kirkup, James (1995). *A Certain State of Mind: An Anthology of Classic, Modern and Contemporary*

Japanese Haiku in Translation with Essays and Reviews. Salzburg: University of Salzburg.

Kirkup, James (1996). *Burning Giraffes*. Salzburg: University of Salzburg.

Kirkup, James (1997a). *Tanka Tales and Various Works in Traditional Tanka Form*. Salzburg: University of Salzburg.

Kirkup, James (1997b). *Pikadon: An Epic Poem*. Salzburg: University of Salzburg.

Kirkup, James (1998a). "Stepping Eastwards." In: *Diversions: A Celebration for James Kirkup on his Eightieth Birthday* (ed. James Hogg), 54–64. Salzburg: University of Salzburg.

Kirkup, James (1998b). "Lives of Quiet Inspiration." In: *Diversions: A Celebration for James Kirkup on his Eightieth Birthday* (ed. James Hogg), 65–79. Salzburg: University of Salzburg.

Kirkup, James (1998c). "Shelley: The Romantic Rebel—A Poet for Our Times." In: *Diversions: A Celebration for James Kirkup on His Eightieth Birthday* (ed. James Hogg), 302–324. Salzburg: University of Salzburg.

Larkin, Philip (1983). *Required Writing*. London: Faber and Faber.

Loloi, Parvin (2000). "Sufi Elements in Peter Russell's *Albae Meditatio*." *The Swansea Review* 19: 58–78.

McCarthy, Thomas (2003). "Translation and Exile in the Poetry of Desmond O'Grady." In: *A Desmond O'Grady Casebook* (eds. Wolfgang Görtschacher and Andreas Schachermayr), 67–73. Salzburg: Poetry Salzburg.

Menocal, María Rosa (1994). *Shards of Love: Exile and the Origins of the Lyric*. Durham, NC: Duke University Press.

O'Grady, Desmond (1994). *Trawling Tradition: Translations 1954–1994*. Salzburg: University of Salzburg.

O'Grady, Desmond (1996). *The Road Taken: Poems 1956–1996*. Salzburg: University of Salzburg.

O'Grady, Desmond (2001). *The Wandering Celt*. Dublin: The Dedalus Press.

O'Grady, Desmond (2003). "Some Record: An Interview with Desmond O'Grady." In: *A Desmond O'Grady Casebook* (eds. Wolfgang Görtschacher and Andreas Schachermayr), 3–55. Salzburg: Poetry Salzburg.

Pursglove, Glyn (1995a). *A Bibliography of Peter Russell*. Salzburg: Universität Salzburg, Institut für Anglistik und Amerikanistik.

Pursglove, Glyn (1995b). "The Life Behind the Thing: Peter Russell's 'The Holy Virgin of Mileševa.'." *Agenda* 32 (3–4): 84–96.

Pursglove, Glyn (2000a). "*NINE*: An Index." *The Swansea Review* 19: 136–152.

Pursglove, Glyn (2000b). "Links in *The Golden Chain*: Contexts for a Lyric by Peter Russell." *The Swansea Review* 19: 95–111.

Russell, Peter (1954). *Three Elegies of Quintilius*. Tunbridge Wells: The Pound Press.

Russell, Peter (1970). *The Golden Chain: Lyrical Poems 1964–1969*. Venice: Author.

Russell, Peter (1975). *The Elegies of Quintilius*. London: Anvil Press.

Russell, Peter (1981). *Elemental Discourses*. Salzburg: Universität Salzburg, Institut für Anglistik und Amerikanistik.

Russell, Peter (1992a). *The Image of Woman as a Figure of the Spirit*. Salzburg: University of Salzburg.

Russell, Peter (1992b). *A Progress of the Soul: Five Poems*. Pian di Scò, Privately printed.

Russell, Peter (1993a). *Poetic Asides II*. Salzburg: University of Salzburg.

Russell, Peter (1993b). *The Duller Olive*. Salzburg: University of Salzburg.

Russell, Peter (1993c). *A False Start: London Poems 1959–63*. Salzburg: University of Salzburg.

Russell, Peter (1994). "Introduction." In: *Berlin-Tegel 1964: Poems and Translations*, 11–59. Salzburg: University of Salzburg.

Russell, Peter (1995). *Venice Poems 1965*. Salzburg: University of Salzburg.

Russell, Peter (1997a). *Omens and Elegies—Descent—Visions and Ruins—Agamemnon in Hades*. Salzburg: University of Salzburg.

Russell, Peter (1997b). *From the Apocalypse of Quintilius*, sel. and introd. Glyn Pursglove. Salzburg: University of Salzburg.

Russell, Peter (1997c). *Language & Spirit in the Age of Antichrist*. London: Temenos Academy.

Russell, Peter (2000). "Albae Meditatio." *Swansea Review* 19: 54–57.

Takahashi, Mutsuo (2006). *We of Zipangu* (trans. James Kirkup and Takari Makoto). Nanholme Mill: Arc Publications.

Wordsworth, William (1969). *Poetical Works* (ed. Thomas Hutchinson), revised Ernest de Selincourt. London, Oxford: Oxford University Press.

SECTION 3
Poets and Poems: Canon, Off-Canon, Non-Canon

3.1
John Agard

Ralf Hertel

Born in British Guiana (today Guyana) and having moved to Britain in 1977, John Agard (born 1949) is one of the most prominent poets giving voice to the experiences of the West Indian immigrants of his generation. Generally speaking, his poetry is often marked by an attempt to negotiate between his Afro-Guyanese roots and his experiences as an immigrant in Britain. This negotiation of different cultural influences shows in his poetry not least on the level of form, for instance in his oscillation between Standard English and Caribbean Creole. It also becomes visible in his mixture of traditional English genres such as the sonnet ("Shakespeare Addresses Tabloids after Dark Lady Rumour" in *We Brits* 2006, 39) and the anthem ("Alternative Anthem" in the same collection, 35), on the one hand, and, on the other, the rhythms of the calypso or the limbo dance, as we encounter it in *Man to Pan* (1982), a cycle of poems to be performed with drums and steelpans, and in *Limbo Dancer in Dark Glasses* (1983).

Some poems play with representatives, symbols, and icons of Englishness such as Shakespeare, Dr. Johnson, the Union Jack, the stiff upper lip, the weather, or the kettle: "Put the kettle on / Put the kettle on / It is the British answer / to Armageddon. // Never mind taxes rise / Never mind trains are late / One thing you can be sure of / and that's the kettle, mate" ("Alternative Anthem," in *We Brits* 2006, 39). These are paired with others exploring Caribbean mythology and folklore (for instance, in the figure of Anansi, the trickster spider, in *Come Down Nansi* {2000a]). Other poems attempt to rewrite British history by drawing attention to the presence of Caribbean and South-American figures neglected in official English history, such as John Edmonstone, "the freed black slave who

---

A Companion to Contemporary British and Irish Poetry, 1960–2015, First Edition.
Edited by Wolfgang Görtschacher and David Malcolm.
© 2021 John Wiley & Sons Ltd. Published 2021 by John Wiley & Sons Ltd.

taught Darwin taxidermy at Edinburgh," according to Agard's explanatory note to his poem "The Ascent of John Edmonstone," or Francis Barber, "Jamaican-born companion" who, in "Dr Johnson, a Jamaican and a Dictionary (1755)" (both in *We Brits* 2006, 23 and 43), unwittingly makes the English writer reflect on his dictionary entry on the term "slave." It should be noted, though, that Agard's poetry is by no means reduced to the negotiation of Caribbean and British influences but is highly varied in topic and style, ranging from the erotic (*Lovelines for a Goat-Born Lady* 1990) to the openly political ("Memo to Professor Enoch Powell," in *We Brits* 2006, 27) and to children's verse. Often, it teasingly occupies a middle ground between the political and the playful, foregrounding the ideological dimension of language itself.

The negotiation of English and Caribbean traditions shows perhaps most prominently in the form Agard chooses for the presentation of his poems. On the one hand, he seeks recognition through the publication of his poetic texts in anthologies; on the other, he lays great stress on the oral delivery of his poetry. Tellingly, his collection *Alternative Anthem: Selected Poems* (2009) comes with a DVD of the author reciting his own poetry, "a live album of poems from books published over three decades" (back cover), and Agard is a frequent performer at festivals worldwide, demonstrating that his poetry derives as much from the oral traditions of Caribbean cultures as it does from English literary influences. Consequently, Agard has refused the label "poet" and invented the term "poetsonian," a term that enables him to free himself from conventional expectations vis-à-vis poetry and links his work to the oral tradition of what he terms the "calypsonian." He explains this in an introductory text to his early collection *Mangoes and Bullets: Selected and New Poems, 1972–1984* (1985) entitled "Himself Interviews Himself" in a language that itself ("Is just…") betrays traces of the oral.

> The whole resurgence of the oral art in poetry has caused black poets to come up with words of their own making. You can think of jazzoetry/Gil Scott-Heron calling himself bluesician or bluesologist/you also got dub poetry, using reggae beat/rapso poetry/ & a number of white poets call themselves ranters. Not that anything is wrong with the word poet. Is just that most people have come to see "poet" & "poetry reading," in very distant cerebral terms. So using these other terms I just mentioned is like subverting the expectations of audiences. Is a way of reclaiming other art forms into poetry like theatre & not treating poetry as isolated.
>
> ("Himself Interviews Himself," in Agard 1985, 6)

Both as poet and performer, Agard, who self-published his early poetry in Guyana, has found wide recognition. He has been awarded several prestigious prizes (among them the Casa de las Américas Prize, the Guyana Prize, the Paul Hamlyn Award for Poetry, and the Queen's Gold Medal for Poetry). He has been writer-in-residence for the BBC, the National Maritime Museum at Greenwich, and at London's Southbank Centre, and his poems have been used as set texts for GSCE examination syllabuses. The Commonwealth Institute has employed him as a touring speaker in order to promote understanding of Caribbean poetry and culture in hundreds of schools nationwide.

"Listen Mr Oxford Don" from *Mangoes and Bullets* (44), his best-known and most frequently discussed poem, provides an excellent example of Agard's playful, yet strongly political poetry self-consciously and ironically exploring the ideological power of language.

Listen Mr Oxford don

Me not no Oxford don 1
me a simple immigrant
from Clapham Common
I didn't graduate
I immigrate 5

But listen Mr Oxford don
I'm a man on de run
and a man on de run
is a dangerous one

I ent have no gun 10
I ent have no knife
but mugging de Queen's English
is the story of my life

I dont need no axe
to split/ up yu syntax 15
I dont need no hammer
to mash/ up yu grammar

I warning you Mr Oxford don
I'm a wanted man
and a wanted man 20
is a dangerous one

Dem accuse me of assault
on de Oxford dictionary/
imagine a concise
peaceful man like me/
dem want me serve time 25
for inciting rhyme to riot
but I tekking it quiet
down here in Clapham Common

I'm not a violent man Mr Oxford don
I only armed wit mih human breath 30
but human breath
is a dangerous weapon

So mek dem send one big word after me
I ent serving no jail sentence

> I slashing suffix in self-defence 35
> I bashing future wit present tense
> and if necessary
>
> I making de Queen's English accessory/to my offence
> (Agard 2009, 16)¹

"Listen Mr Oxford Don" demonstrates how Agard's poetry reflects on the experience of first-generation immigrants to Britain, and on their struggle to define their identity between the cultures they have grown up with and the English culture they often wish to belong to. It also foregrounds the specific role language plays in this process. Here, the experience of straddling two cultures is reflected on various levels. It shows, for instance, in the language employed, which in itself straddles English culture and Caribbean influences (for a brief discussion of Agard's use of Creole language, see Hadfield and Hadfield 2005). The way the poem is presented to the reader in Agard's anthology *Alternative Anthem* is revealing, too. Printed on the page it fulfills traditional expectations of volumes of poetry; yet the DVD of Agard's poetic recitals accompanying this anthology demonstrates impressively how much is gained by placing this poem in the context of an oral culture that has often been linked to Caribbean modes of poetry (such as dub poetry). Once one has witnessed how Agard sings, breathes, chants, and spits out the verses, it is difficult to dissociate the written poem from this performance. The poem gains in immediacy and urgency, and "Listen Mr Oxford Don" turns from being a poem about immigrant experience into a script for the voice of the immigrant himself.

Agard's method of juxtaposing English and non-English elements shows on the formal level of the poem, too. By choosing poetry in order to express the speaker's struggle with words, Agard stands in a venerable poetic tradition reaching back as far as Shakespeare's "Sonnet 130" ("My mistress' eyes are nothing like the sun"). Yet, how venerable, or respectable, is the poetic form in Agard's hands? Quite obviously, he sets out to break various conventions here, and indeed, it is this frustration of expectations that creates the dominant effect of the poem. "Listen Mr Oxford Don" defies traditional meter and violates the rhythmic flow of words through the harsh clash of spondaic elements—the opening line, for instance, contains in its harsh monosyllabic rhythm only one unstressed syllable ("Mé nót nó Óxford dón," l. 1). We find wrenched rhyme in this poem (Óxford dón–Clápham Commón, ll. 1 and 3, no áxe–syntáx, ll. 14–15; Óxford dón–weapón, ll. 29 and 32), half rhyme (Oxford don–Clapham Common–on the run, ll. 1, 3, and 7), awkward mosaic rhyme (dictionary–man like me, ll. 23–24), and autorhyme (breath–breath, ll. 30–31, run–run, ll. 7–8, man–man, ll. 19–20)—all forms of rhyme considered clumsy in traditional poetics. In addition, Agard employs a bewildering mishmash of end rhymes, initial rhymes (I slashing–I bashing) and middle rhymes (time–rhyme, ll. 25–26, necessary–accessory, ll. 38–38), of cross rhymes (gun–knife–English–life, ll. 10–14), embracing rhymes (don–man–man–one, ll. 18–21), and rhyming couplets (no axe–syntax, ll. 14–15, hammer–grammar, ll. 16–17), to the effect that the reader is never quite sure when to expect the next rhyme.

Rhetorical and syntactical devices underline the impression of deliberate clumsiness. Pleonasms ("I ent no," l. 10; "dont need no," l. 16) and ellipses create an artless, hard impression, and catachresis yokes together disparate elements in jumbled images—how can one "mug" the Queen's English (l. 12), "assault" a dictionary (ll. 22–23), or "incite" rhyme to riot (l. 26)? Grammar does not accord with that of Standard English ("I warning you," l. 18, "I only armed," l. 30); punctuation is entirely absent, causing a lack of syntactical order, which is heightened by the prominent use of caesurae. These caesurae, at times, amount to the verbal equivalent of a rude one-finger gesture, breaking up sentences so that parts such as "up yu grammar" (l. 17) and "up yu syntax" (l. 15) stand out, playfully evoking the rude language of an "up yours" invective.

In short: Agard's "Listen Mr Oxford Don" violates all traditional expectations of a "good" poem. Yet, I would argue, it is precisely this frustration of expectations that renders it so powerful; this "bad" poem is the perfect lyrical form to express the reality of a "bad" life. The sound of the poem is harsh? So is the life of the immigrant, Agard suggests. Its rhythm is irregular and unpredictable? So, perhaps, is immigrant life. The rhyme is second-rate? If rhyme creates harmony and cohesion, perhaps Agard's use, or rather abuse, of rhyme is the appropriate way to suggest that the lives of immigrants often are not harmonious and do not always appear to be meaningful. If the verses rhyme, it is often only because Agard breaks with the conventions of grammar and accepted style (e.g., "graduate" rhymes with "immigrate," ll. 4–5, when the verb should—to be grammatically correct—be "immigrated"; "riot" rhymes with "quiet," ll. 26–27, when grammar demands "quietly"), or asks the reader to enunciate the words in Caribbean pronunciation (only then might "don" rhyme with "run," ll. 6–8). Implicitly, this technique indicates that if there is meaning and harmony in the immigrant's life, it is provided—and not destroyed—by hybrid language and Creole influences. If the poem lacks all punctuation and traditional sentence structure, this is also appropriate as it reflects an immigrant's experience in a foreign country, an experience which also sometimes lacks order and structure. In other words: If so much appears to be "wrong" in this poem, perhaps this makes it appropriate. The violence Agard does to meter, rhyme, and syntax—in a word, to language—can be interpreted as an attempt to mirror the violence done to immigrants of his generation. In order to depict a life often outside law and social acceptance, Agard cleverly employs a language that violates accepted literary forms and rules. Thus, the poem in its verbal violence makes the reader *hear* the violence that forms part of the immigrant experience. Here, as elsewhere, Agard's poem draws attention to its own language as a site of struggle.

This situation of struggle in language becomes particularly obvious in Agard's recorded performance of the poem. Here, as in some of his other performances, the tension between the written and the spoken word is foregrounded, with Agard's trickster's voice pitted against authorities of written English such as "de Oxford Dictionary" (l. 23). Indeed, here and elsewhere, dictionaries figure prominently in Agard's poetry (see for instance "Reporting from the Frontline of the Great Dictionary Disaster" or "Dr Johnson, a Jamaican and a Dictionary," both in *We Brits* 2006, 32 and 43). In "Listen Mr Oxford Don," the speaker finds himself accused of an "assault" (l. 22) on the dictionary, and the suggested physicality is significant, since Agard's attack on the dictionary, indeed, possesses a physical dimension, a dimension which becomes palpable only in his performance. Agard challenges the dictionary not only by employing a non-standard, Creole form of English at odds with the "Queen's English" (l. 38) preserved in the dictionary; Agard's decision to present "Listen Mr Oxford Don" as an oral performance, as well as a written poem, imbues his attack with the physical violence the speaker finds himself accused of.

Dictionaries, of course, stand for an attempt to define the meaning, functions, and forms of words. In its list of historical usages of specific words, the Oxford English Dictionary also historicizes the meaning of terms; it pins down the specific meaning of a specific word at a specific moment in time. Agard's use of vocabulary can be seen as an act of rejecting such an authority and as an attempt at reclaiming language, at redefining language as one's own, and at making words reflect one's experiences, rather than subjecting one's experiences to the logic of dictionary entries. Rachael Gilmour shows how in this particular poem Agard even goes a step further, beyond merely questioning such an authority, and indeed makes the dictionary "accessory" to his "offence." She quotes a study from the 1970s which shows how the expression "mugging" encodes "associations of blackness with disorder and criminality," suggesting that the terms "mugging" and "black criminality" had become "virtually synonymous" by the late 1970s (Gilmour 2014, 349). Yet by defining the speaker's crime as "mugging de Queen's English" (l. 12), Agard re-signifies the term in what can be understood as a political gesture. If the poem's speaker is a "mugger," who "has seized that which does not rightly belong to him—the English language—for his own ends" (Gilmour 2014, 349), this act of appropriation includes the very term "mugging" itself. For as Gilmour shows, the meaning of this term is not reduced to ethnically connoted violence, but comprises, among the definitions offered by the Oxford English Dictionary, also the sense of "learning by hard and concentrated study" and "grimacing performative excess." Agard's speaker is a "mugger" in these senses of the word, too; a speaker learning the lessons of immigrant experience the hard way and—at least in Agard's own oral rendering of the poem—an excessive performer. Hence, Agard turns the very instrument often employed in a prescriptive, and restrictive, deployment of the English language—the Oxford English Dictionary—against such a reductive employment of language that would turn English into "jail sentences" taking away the speaker's freedom of self-expression.

> Thus a poem that takes as one of its central objects "de Oxford dictionary" exploits the etymological complexities of English which are that dictionary's central concern. It is precisely "de Oxford dictionary," apparent guarantor of linguistic standardization as well as ethnolinguistic Englishness, that reveals the multivalency of the English sign – as multiple, in fact, as the creole forms against which the poem seemingly sets it [...]. (Gilmour 2014, 349–350)

Agard's strategy of creating ambivalence can be observed elsewhere, too. In particular, his stress on performance runs counter to attaching fixed meanings to words. As "Listen Mr Oxford Don" demonstrates, words become flexible in shape and reference; they deviate from accepted grammatical and orthographic forms (e.g., "tekking," l. 27, "ent," l. 10, "I warning," l. 18), and become ambiguous in their meaning (as for instance in the ambiguously rude verse "I dont need no axe / to split / up yu syntax," ll. 14–15). In the process of enunciation, meaning often materializes onomatopoetically; in "Listen Mr Oxford Don" this is the case for instance in Agard's drawn-out pronunciation of "breath" (ll. 30–31), his pulsating, rhythmic lines "I'm a man on de run / and a man on de run / is a dangerous one" (ll. 7–9), aptly rendered in breathless run-on-lines, or the harsh, spat-out caesura of the verses "I dont need no axe / to split / up yu syntax" (ll. 14–15), in which Agard's sharp voice quite audibly cuts the verse in two. Agard's oral performance, thus, shifts the focus away from meaning that is seemingly transfixed in dictionary entries toward a meaning that is sensuously accessible and comes to life when filled with the speaker's "human breath"—not coincidently this poem's "epicenter" in performance (Gilmour 2014, 348), its inspiration quite literally. Agard's oral renditions appear as acts of resistance, countering the petrification of meaning, as an attempt to escape the strictures of definitions. Here, perhaps, lies a clue to Agard's obsession with language and his playful usage of it: his struggle to free language from clear-cut definitions and to make it ambiguous can be understood as a political act, verbally mirroring immigrants' attempts to escape clear-cut, black-and-white definitions that do not apply to their experiences. Questioning the seemingly authoritative system of language, Agard attempts to provide the sort of in-between space in language which he claims for the immigrant in his poem "Half-Caste."

> explain yuself
> wha yu mean
> when yu say half-caste
> yu mean when tchaikovsky
> sit down at dah piano
> an mix black key
> wid a white key
> is a half-caste symphony [...]
> (Agard 2009, 123, ll. 23–30)

Here, again, Agard's obsession with words encoding prejudices, such as the "half-caste" of the title, and his striving to empty words of such connotations become visible. Through witty conceits, this poem destabilizes notions of the purity of culture generally and of Englishness specifically, and frees the term "half-caste" of its narrowly racist usage. In this regard, "Half-Caste" is typical for much of Agard's poetry, which often works to destabilize fixed meanings by ascribing alternative connotations to words, and which creates a level of meaning in the interstices of enunciation and the written text. It seems that, for Agard, poems employing such elements of ambiguity present the fitting form of literature to express the experiences of immigrants, themselves often situated in-between cultures.

In the larger context of immigrant writing, Agard's poetry has sometimes been understood as being representative, in particular, of the experiences of immigrants who, like

Agard himself, had arrived from the West Indies in the 1970s and 1980s. If the first wave of immigration in the 1950s and 1960 might be characterized by a sense of disillusionment, triggered by the cultural shock of realizing that Great Britain was not the country many immigrants had imagined, Agard's poetry bears witness to the second wave of immigrants' struggle to integrate themselves. In his volume of *The Oxford English Literary History*, Bruce King describes the development of British ethnic writing as a movement "from immigrant lives and memories, to claims of being British and protest against discrimination, to nuanced stories telling of Black and Asian lives which show that areas of England have a rich and diverse history, society, and culture made by immigrants and their children" (King 2004, 8–9). King regards Agard as being representative of the second phase described here, counting him among the "rebel black performing poet[s]" (King 2004, 202). Indeed, Agard's insistence on orality as well as his struggle with the authorities of language might be understood as a crucial contribution to the Black British protest culture of the period.

In comparison, Agard's more recent poetry has met with more reserved reactions. King adds that "like other protest poets of the 1980s Agard ha[s] become accepted and tamed," calling collections of poetry such as *From the Devil's Pulpit* (1997) "tame stuff" (King 2004, 201–202). He is not alone in his disappointment, and referring to *We Brits*, Ben Wilkinson "begins to crave the grammatical mash-ups and genuine excitement of Agard's early poems over this comparatively watered-down work," (Wilkinson 2009) while a reviewer for *The Guardian* remarks of the same collection that "Agard's new couplets are about as revolutionary as Betjeman's" and amount to little more than a "safe mix of the cosy and the postcolonial" (Noel-Tod 2007). Some seem to regret the loss of "a core of lyrical anger" that had given his earlier work such as *Mangoes and Bullets* "its distinctive bite" (Brown 1994, 26).

However, the change of tone in Agard's poetry might also reflect the changed nature of his immigrant experience. If some of his more recent poetry appears to struggle less, perhaps this is so because it partakes in a more general development within Black British writing, which, after the phase of struggle and protest, finds expression in more optimistic voices. In the field of prose writing, Zadie Smith's *White Teeth* (2001), with its—albeit ambivalent—depiction of England in the 1990s as a "Happy Multicultural Land" (Smith 2001, 465), might serve as an example for such a tentatively optimistic stance. In this context, perhaps, Agard's dedication to children's verse (e.g., *I Din Do Nuttin* [1983], *We Animals Should Like a Word with You* [1996], or *Under the Moon and Over the Sea* [2002], co-edited with his wife, the poet Grace Nichols) betrays a similar optimism, as it does not so much address racial injustices but aims to speak to the generation of the future in ways in which questions of ethnicity become obsolete, and other issues—attitudes toward parents, humor, experiences at school, relations to animals and the environment—become more important than skin color in shaping the identity of children. Limiting Agard, and other Black British immigrant poets of his generation, to being protest writers would, again, be reductive and would run counter to Agard's poetic struggle for the liberation of the immigrants' language and poetry.

NOTE

1 Agard's poems are reprinted with kind permission by Bloodaxe Books.

REFERENCES

Agard, John (1982). *Man to Pan*. Ciudad de la Habana: Ediciones Casa de las Américas.

Agard, John (1983). *I Din Do Nuttin*. London: Bodley Head.

Agard, John (1985). *Mangoes and Bullets: Selected and New Poems 1972–1984*. London, Sydney: Pluto Press.

Agard, John (1990). *Lovelines for a Goat-Born Lady*. London: Serpent's Tail.

Agard, John (1996). *We Animals Would Like a Word with You*. London: Bodley Head.

Agard, John (1997). *From the Devil's Pulpit*. Tarset: Bloodaxe.

Agard, John (2000a). *Come Down Nansi*. Reprinted in *Weblines*. Tarset: Bloodaxe.

Agard, John (2000b). *Limbo Dancer in Dark Glasses*. Reprinted with *Come Down Nansi* in *Weblines*. Tarset: Bloodaxe.

Agard, John (2005). *Half-Caste*. London: Hodder and Stoughton.

Agard, John (2006). *We Brits*. Tarset: Bloodaxe.

Agard, John (2009). *Alternative Anthem: Selected Poems with Live DVD*. Tarset: Bloodaxe.

Agard, John and Nichols, Grace (eds.) (2002). *Under the Moon and Over the Sea*. London: Walker.

Brown, Stewart (1994). "John Agard." In: *Enyclopedia of Postcolonial Literatures in English* (eds. Eugene Benson and L.W. Conolly), 25–26. London/New York: Routledge.

Gilmour, Rachael (2014). "Doing Voices: Reading Language as Craft in Black British Poetry." *The Journal of Commonwealth Literature* 49 (3): 343–357. https://doi.org/10.1177/0021989414529121.

Hadfield, Jill and Charles (2005). "What is English?" *ELT Journal* 59.3: 250–254.

King, Bruce (2004). *The Oxford English Literary History: The Internationalization of English Literature, 1948–2000*, vol. 13. Oxford: Oxford University Press.

Smith, Zadie (2001). *White Teeth*. London: Penguin.

Noel-Tod, Jeremy (2007). "Rioting Rhymes?" Review of John Agard, *We Brits*. *The Guardian*, www.theguardian.com/books/2007/jan/20/featuresreviews.guardianreview25 (accessed 23 November 2017).

Wilkinson, Ben (2009). "John Agard: Critical Perspective." British Council. http://literature.britishcouncil.org/writer/john-agard. (accessed 30 June 2015).

3.2
Eavan Boland

Peter Hühn

Eavan Boland was born on September 24, 1944, in Dublin. Her father was a career diplomat, her mother a painter. The family moved to London in 1950, when her father was appointed Irish Ambassador to the United Kingdom and, later to New York, when he became Ireland's permanent representative at the United Nations. In 1958, she returned to Dublin to attend Holy Child School in Killiney. From 1962 to 1966, she studied English and Latin at Trinity College Dublin. In 1969, she married the novelist Kevin Casey. The family settled in the Dublin suburb of Dundrum; they had two daughters. Eavan Boland held teaching positions at Trinity College (Dublin), Bowdoin College (Brunswick, Maine), The University of Iowa (International Writing Program), the School of Irish Studies (Dublin), and she was writer in residence at Trinity College and the National Maternity Hospital (Dublin). Since 1995, she had been a professor of English at Stanford University, where she directed the Creative Writing Program in the Genre Poetry. She died on April 27, 2020.

Boland published 13 volumes of poetry, *New Territory* (1967), *The War Horse* (1975), *In Her Own Image* (1980), *Night Feed* (1982), *The Journey and Other Poems* (1987), *Outside History: Selected Poems, 1980–1990* (1990), *In a Time of Violence* (1994), *An Origin Like Water: Collected Poems 1967–1987* (1996), *The Lost Land* (1998), *Code* (US title: *Against Love Poetry*, 2001), *New Collected Poems* (2005), *Domestic Violence* (2007), *A Woman Without a Country* (2014), and *A Poet's Dublin* (2014). A fourteenth posthumous volume, *The Historians*, was published by Carcanet Press in October 2020. In addition to numerous essays and reviews (collected in Allen Randolph, ed. 2007), she also wrote two volumes of autobiographical and theoretical prose, *Object Lessons: The Life of the Woman and the Poet in Our Time* (1995)

A Companion to Contemporary British and Irish Poetry, 1960–2015, First Edition.
Edited by Wolfgang Görtschacher and David Malcolm.
© 2021 John Wiley & Sons Ltd. Published 2021 by John Wiley & Sons Ltd.

and *A Journey with Two Maps: Becoming a Woman Poet* (2011), the former narrating and reflecting on her experiences mainly within the Irish context, the latter from a wider, international perspective.

Boland was one of Ireland's foremost poets,[1] in the South as well as in the North. Since the beginning of her career in the late 1960s, the Irish poetic scene has changed considerably in several respects. The male-oriented literary tradition and the Irish Revival have decreased in influence and, following Boland, a number of other women poets have come to the fore, such as Eithne Strong, Medbh McGuckian, Nuala Ní Dhomhnaill, Paula Meehan, and Eiléan Ní Chuilleanáin (see Haberstroh 1996 and Schrage-Früh 2004), widening the range of themes, attitudes, and perspectives. When Boland began to write, the Irish poetic tradition offered her no models, neither for her themes nor for her stance as a woman poet. So she had to establish her role and develop her topics on her own in a long process of reflection and practice.

In both respects, she drew on two sources, her experience of being a woman in relation to two contexts. One pervasive impetus came out of her realization of the marginalized, passive role and the objectified, merely emblematic function of women in Irish myth, history, and national, patriotic ideology, the Irish self-concept of a long-suppressed and heroically liberated culture and society. This extreme marginalization of woman in the cultural discourse of Ireland Boland saw specifically reflected in the fact that there was no place and no model for a woman poet within the male-dominated Irish poetic tradition. So both as a woman and as a poet, she lacked vital points of reference for orientation inside her own culture for her identity and her writing. The other strong impetus for her poetry, closely related to this general—public—context, grew out of her own private experiences as an ordinary woman, housewife, and mother, living in a suburb, on the outskirts of Dublin. For this topic of ordinary, daily life, notably of women, precedents were also lacking in the Irish literary tradition.[2] And through her private experience of ordinary, daily life Boland established an imaginative link to the unrecorded, suppressed lives of ordinary Irish women of the lower classes in the past, especially in times of distress and suffering such as the Great Famine, thereby defining herself in her Irish identity.

It is indicative of Boland's characteristic highly self-reflective approach to writing poetry that, in *Object Lessons*, she narrated and analyzed in detail the long process of experience, reflection, and poetic practice through which she found her individual position and perspective and was able to write meaningfully addressing relevant issues of the collective Irish self-concept. In the chapter "Subject Matters," she summed up her aim in its various thematic aspects as follows:

> I wanted to see the powerful public history of my own country joined by the private lives and solitary perspectives, including my own, which the Irish poetic tradition had not yet admitted to authorship. I wanted to see the effect of an unrecorded life – a woman in a suburban twilight under a hissing streetlight – on the prescribed themes of public importance.
> (Boland 1996 [¹1995], 187)

She discovered a connection between her womanhood and her nationhood, "an emblematic relation between the defeats of womanhood and the suffering of a nation" (Boland 1996, 148), leading to an emphasis on "the sense of powerlessness, loss, and defeat which characterizes her nation's history" (Schrage-Früh 2004, 89). A prerequisite for this achievement is the need to avoid what poetry traditionally—especially, as Boland contends, in the Romantic lyric mode—tends to do: fixing men and women in certain relations and exempting them from change and ultimately from mortality (Boland 1996, 210–211). Against this tendency, she posits her paradoxical intention to combine poetic preservation and continuity with fluidity and change: "I want a poem I can grow old in. I want a poem I can die in. It is a human wish, meeting language and precedent at the point of crisis" (Boland 1996, 209).

Boland started, in *New Territory* (1967), by writing from within the male-dominated traditional context of Irish history, literature, and myth, for the most part adopting male perspectives and positions, orienting herself frequently to the powerful model of W. B. Yeats. In her two subsequent collections, however, especially in *In Her Own Image* (1980), she increasingly developed critical feminist and ethical social-political attitudes toward the national past as well as to the present condition of Irish society, proceeding to subvert the fixed, objectified, and subordinated images of woman, her silence and passivity, which pervade the Irish poetic tradition. One important part of Boland's project of exploring and representing images of women in Irish culture and tradition is the desire to recover and resurrect the suppressed or marginalized lives of ordinary women from past periods and establish links between herself and woman in history. This recovery of past lives derives from an ethical imperative, and it is moreover motivated by Boland's desire to relate her self-image to the Irish nation in its historical depth. These subversive alternative concepts were indicative of a strong feminist attitude, insisting on essential differences between the sexes, their separate views, and realities, ultimately based on a biological category, the female body as a source of resistance. But that attempt to supplant the traditional male images of woman ran the risk of assuming a similarly essentialist quality as manifested in the incriminated concepts. Becoming aware of this "separatist" tendency (Boland 1996, 243–245), Boland proceeded to employ various techniques to avoid essentializing effects and dissolve one-sided fixities in her subsequent collections.[3] This development is particularly apparent in the changes which Boland's use of classical and Irish myths underwent in the course of her poetic career.[4] The objectifying and fixating tendencies in the recourse to myth characteristic of her earlier volumes were modified or overcome in *Outside History* (1990) and *In a Time of Violence* (1994). She first rejected mythic images altogether emphatically moving from myth into history and later used the opposing concepts of myth and history specifically to highlight the changeable and mortal human condition. As a result, Boland's concepts both of Irishness and womanhood came ultimately to be presented as fluid and unstable categories.

In the following, the thematic range of Boland's poetry and her characteristic approach to her topics will be exemplified by the analyses of three poems representing central concerns of hers: the everyday experience of women and mothers, the place of woman in Irish mythology and national self-concept, and the plight of ordinary women in Irish history.

The theme of the daily, specifically the everyday experience of a woman and mother in a contemporary suburban environment, is the topic the "Ode to Suburbia," first published in 1975 in *The War Horse* (Boland 2005: 66–67).

This poem, addressed in the form of an ode to the personification of the suburb, thematizes the typical life of an ordinary housewife and mother on the outskirts of a big city, as conditioned by the uniformity of this environment and its impact notably on women, who stay there all day. The poem traces the daily life of housewives from morning (1) to midnight (31), stressing their alienating entanglement: spying on each other (1–5), disciplining their noisy children, preparing meals (9–13), and longing for a profound change (31–36). The secret longing for a different life underlies the realistic description in the allusions to the fairy tale of Cinderella, in Charles Perrault's version ("ugly sister," 5; "mirrors," 8; "silver slipper," 15; "coach," 21; "metamorphosis," 31), envisaging a magical transformation of a dreary everyday existence into female self-fulfillment (19–20). However, the allusions serve only to subvert this expectation. Rather than being Cinderella herself, the protagonist's role is that of her ugly sister (5), who looks at herself in the mirror (8–9). The slipper does not fit her (14–16), no carriage magically takes her to the ball (19–24), and there is no magic fairy (20) to liberate her from her unfortunate condition. Instead of winning a prince with her beauty, suburbia's "plainness" seduces and corrupts the countryside (26–27). Yet, despite the failure to follow the fairy-tale schema, the protagonist continues to see herself as a Cinderella (39–40), whose potential status is to become a reality in the future. This latent vitality is described by the metaphor of the untamable savageness of a lion, associated with Cinderella (both sleep on the hearth). However, this expectation of a future vital self-realization (31) is sarcastically revealed as an illusion: the lion, unable to catch anything more than a mouse, is in fact only a tame cat. The irony of the last two stanzas corroborates the critical perspective on the secret hopes of suburban existence for a miraculous change.

The lack of changes in the woman's suburban existence is said to relate to her femininity, intensified and spread by her mentality. Initially, her position as a victim is foregrounded by references to her confinement ("claustrophobia," 3), her unappealing appearance ("varicose," "ugly," 4, 5), and her subjection to the duties of cooking and caring for her child (10–13). Her status as a victim is further highlighted by the suburban mentality in which she becomes an aging spinster (32–33) and is thereby deprived of her feminine attractiveness. Yet her behavior implies that she herself strengthens the hold of suburban life on her. She is prepared to adapt and compromise, and this readiness then fools others (28–30).

More generally, the discrepancy between the passive and active aspects of the protagonist's role, indicated by the ambivalence of "the mind / Which spinstered you" (32–33), determines the mode of speech in the poem. The speaker is identified as a suburban housewife who seeks to capture the conditions of her life and understands herself by means of the poem's narrative. A paradoxical ambiguity marks the distinctive connection of the two schemata (the routine course of daily life, the eventful course of the fairy tale) and the bitter irony to which her counterfactual insistence on the survival of her vitality is subject. On the one hand, the belief that she is different is shown to be an illusion; on the other, this self-ironizing attitude toward her secret longings is, because it demonstrates the faculty of self-criticism, evidence that she is indeed different, that she has not been completely corrupted by the suburban world after all.

The ironic and distancing narrative of a routine day in her life and of the changes that fail to occur in it allows the speaker to engage critically with (her own) suburban existence. She seeks to understand the mechanisms that govern the structure of her daily existence and her life in general, the mechanisms behind the existential conditions and constraints imposed on her innate vitality by her environment and its mentality. She seeks to expose her secret dreams of "metamorphosis" as the illusions they are. And finally, she seeks to use this critical attitude to go beyond illusions and assure herself of the identity and vitality she would like to have and the necessity of the change she would have to undergo.

The thematic development is closely reflected in the prosodic form, which in the regularity of the stanzas adheres to conventional poetic principles, though not based on any particular traditional pattern. The stanzas are all of equal length (six lines), the ending always marked by a shorter line. The elaborate rhyme scheme—three (pure or impure) rhymes in each stanza in changing constellations—stresses repetition of the same with variation but without any true progressive development.[5]

"Mise Éire" (Irish for "I am Ireland"), first published in 1987 in *The Journey*, addresses the presentation of woman within the Irish national tradition. It does so by defiantly alluding to "I am Ireland" (1914) by Patrick Pearse, the later leader of the Easter Rising of 1916 against British occupation, executed after its suppression. In his poem Ireland is personified as an old woman, the mythic figure of Mother Ireland, who has been forsaken by her children and who is implicitly meant to instigate violent heroic action for the nation.

By alluding to Pearse's heroic patriotic poem in the Irish translation of his English title, Boland calls up the traditional female personification of the nation with a vengeance—but only to reject it outright: "I won't go back to it" (1, 16). This national stereotype is characterized by its geographical features ("the Gulf Stream," "the small farm," 7–8) and especially by its effect and function: encouraging heroic action in men ("oaths" in secret places, 4) and alleviating memories of defeat, injustice, or inaction in the past ("bandage up the history," 11; "crime," 13; "palsy of regrets," 15) through poetry ("songs," 10; "the words / that make the rhythm of the crime," 12–13). Against the traditional idealized stereotype of the Mother Ireland figure—or, more generally, the simplified, objectified image of woman in the Irish poetic tradition—the speaker then posits two unheroic realistic images of woman from Irish history with which she does personally identify in their unadorned rawness. She declares, "My roots are brutal" (17) and "I am the woman" (18, 28), offering images exemplifying the extremes of moral degradation and economic suffering to which women were subjected through hardship (under British occupation, especially during the Famine): the garrison whore prostituting herself to British soldiers for fine clothes (18–27), and the poor mother with her emaciated baby forced to emigrate in the hope of finding better living conditions overseas (28–35). As against the mythic mother figure of Ireland, these are real ordinary women living in a specific historical period and "bearing witness to the real defeats of Irish history, the real sufferings of Irish women" (Hagen and Zelman 2004: 25), suppressed and forgotten in Ireland's male-dominated national narrative.

In two respects Boland's attempt to present the reality of Irish women in her poetry is marked by self-consciousness and a paradoxical quality. On one hand, she employs a new unpoetical harsh—"modern"—style ("a new language," 40), which combines foreignness with familiarity ("mingling the immigrant [i.e. English] / guttural with the vowels / of homesickness," 36–38). The new harsh language, underpinning the subversive move of the utterance, manifests itself also in the prosody of the poem, the short, emphatic lines and the jarring stanza and line breaks (cf. Falci 2009: *passim*). But this language clearly is not the speech of the women portrayed ("who neither / knows nor cares," 38–39). On the other hand, Boland is aware that her alternative female figures, though presented in a new poetic style, ultimately also become stereotypes and are in danger of themselves turning into objects and clichés, really no different from the old mythic type which they are meant to supplant ("a passable imitation / of what went before," 43–44). The brutal reality of past suffering ("scar," 41) will thereby lose its rousing critical potential after a while ("heals," 42). But it is characteristic of Boland's approach that she is acutely aware of this danger and that, by explicitly naming it at the end of her poem, she avoids the hypostasizing effect of her women figures. She thus makes the reader conscious of the inescapably paradoxical process of portraying "real" women in poetry as alternatives to the stereotypes and that no female figure alone can represent the state of the nation.[6]

"The Making of an Irish Goddess," the third poem in the twelve-part sequence "Outside History," first published in the collection of the same name in 1990, deals with the relation between history and myth and the position of self and personal experience in that constellation, that is, with respect to time and human changeableness and mortality. The poem refers to the classical (Roman and Greek) myth of Ceres (in Greek, Demeter), the goddess of vegetation and agricultural fertility, a favorite mythological reference in Boland's poetry. Ceres's daughter Proserpina (in Greek, Persephone) had been abducted by Pluto (in Greek, Hades), the god of the underworld, leaving her mother in deep grief, which caused the desolation of nature. Finally, an agreement was reached about Proserpina's periodic return to her mother, which ensured the regular alternation of the seasons on earth.

Boland's interest in the Roman goddess and her personal affinity with her has to do with two motifs inherent in the myth: on one hand, Ceres's association with the fruitfulness of the earth and, on the other, her mother's love for her daughter Proserpina and the intense pain caused by her loss. Both aspects of this affinity are thematized by the speaker at the end of the poem: her "sickle-shaped" hand (38) alludes to Ceres's association with agriculture and harvest, her anxiously searching look at her own daughter "in the distance" (41) calls up Ceres's love for Proserpina.

Against this emotional affinity, however, the speaker uses the Roman goddess as an oppositional figure of reference in order to define her own human existence and Irish identity. The central dimension of this opposition is the relation to time. While Ceres has "no sense of time" (2), the speaker is subject to time and therefore in need of it: "I need time – / my flesh and that history" (11–12). Ceres's timelessness shows in the phenomenon that she experiences the earth in its permanent ideal state—inherent wealth (5), unchanging fruitfulness and fertility (6–9), without deterioration, decline, and suffering ("seasonless," "unscarred," 10). This is what she perceives on her mythic descent "to hell" (1), that is, on her way to Hades in search of her daughter. By contrast, the speaker's time-bounded condition manifests itself individually in her "flesh" and collectively in "history" (12). Both aspects are subsequently described in more detail and directly linked with each other. As for herself, her body ages and loses its fertility as well as its beauty ("blemish"), and—partly as a consequence of childbirth—it bears lasting marks of injury and pain, "a scar" (14–20). This injured body is then declared "an accurate inscription / of that agony" (22–23)—thus directing the look back in the history of Ireland to the great Famine of the 1840s, the devastation of the fields and the subsequent starvation of a large part of the population—a devastation similar to the one caused by the absence of mourning Ceres from the earth in the myth, but in its consequences for the people much more infernal and devastating than Ceres's descent to "hell," involving cannibalism (26) and spiritual annihilation on account of the prevalent religious doctrines ("whose souls, they would have said, / went straight to hell, / followed by their own," 27–29).[7]

After thus contrasting mythic timelessness and human mortality, the speaker proceeds to formulate the function of myth for her and mankind, a kind of aphoristic formula emphatically foregrounded and marked off from the other lines of the poem by alliteration, assonance, and parallelism: "myth is the wound we leave / in the time we have" (31–32). Myth is hereby placed into the context of human temporality and suffering as its paradoxical expression, referring to its timeless opposite. The title of the poem describes the process by which the ancient myth of Ceres is being redefined by the speaker as representing the Irish historical experience in the role of a mortal woman, replacing the traditional images of "Mise Éire," Mother Ireland, and Cathleen Ni Houlihan. But the title is also partly ironic: Boland, as the author, is guarding herself against repeating the incriminated error of creating just another falsifying objectified image of woman. The attempt to "make a Goddess" paradoxically undoes itself—if one "*makes*" a Goddess, she cannot really "*be*" a Goddess. But on account of the self-conscious and ironic awareness of the paradoxical nature of such a postulate, this emblematic figure as which the speaker establishes herself can be taken to present indeed a realistic image of Ireland in her female experience of pain and loss, in the end exemplified—as in the ancient myth—by the imminent painful loss of her daughter as the inevitable natural consequence of being human, alive and subject to temporal change (42).

Notes

1 For a general overview of Boland's poetry and its development, see, for example, Allen Randolph (2014); Haberstroh (1996), 59–90; Schrage-Früh (2004), 27–90; and Villar-Argáiz (2007).

2 For a general overview, cf. Hagen and Zelman (2004).

3 This development is traced in great detail in Villar-Argáiz (2007). See also the analysis of Boland's paradoxical strategies in Huck (2003), 271–311.

4 See the detailed analysis of Boland's use of mythic motifs and concept in Müller (2007).

5 See Hühn (2005). Schrage-Früh (2004, 31–32) briefly comments on the poem, but misses the irony, when she interprets "mystery" as a reference

to "domestic happiness." Otherwise, "Ode to Suburbia" has almost completely been neglected in criticism.

6 Cf. the discussion of "Mise Éire" in Clutterbuck (2009).

7 Cf. the interpretation in Villar-Argáiz (2007), 243–249.

REFERENCES

Allen Randolph, Jody (ed.) (2007). *Eavan Boland: A Sourcebook: Poetry, Prose, Interviews, Reviews, and Criticism*. Manchester: Carcanet.

Allen Randolph, Jody (2014). *Eavan Boland*. Lanham, MD: Bucknell University Press.

Boland, Eavan (1996 [¹1995]). *Object Lessons: The Life of the Woman and the Poet in Our Time*. London: Vintage.

Boland, Eavan (2005). *New Collected Poems*. Manchester: Carcanet.

Clutterbuck, Catriona (2009). "'Mise Eire', Eavan Boland." *Irish University Review: A Journal of Irish Studies* 39: 289–300.

Falci, Eric (2009). "Meehan's Stanzas and the Irish Lyric After Yeats." *An Sionnach* 5: 226–238.

Haberstroh, Patricia Boyle (1996). *Women Creating Women: Contemporary Irish Women Poets*. Syracuse, NY: Syracuse University Press.

Hagen, Patricia L. and Zelman, Thomas W. (2004). *Eavan Boland and the History of the Ordinary*. Dublin: Maunsel and Company.

Huck, Christian (2003). *Das Paradox der Mythopoetik: Dichtung und Gemeinschaft in der irischen Literatur: Yeats, Heaney, Boland*. Heidelberg: Winter.

Hühn, Peter (2005). "Eavan Boland: 'Ode to Suburbia.'." In: *Peter Hühn and Jens Kiefer. The Narratological Analysis of Lyric Poetry: Studies in English Poetry from the 16th to the 20th Century*, 213–221. Berlin and New York: de Gruyter.

Müller, Sabina J. (2007). *Through the Mythographer's Eye: Myth and Legend in the Work of Seamus Heaney and Eavan Boland*. Tübingen: Francke Verlag.

Schrage-Früh, Michaela (2004). *Emerging Identities: Myth, Nation and Gender in the Poetry of Eavan Boland, Nuala Ní Dhomhnaill, and Medbh McGuckian*. Trier: Wissenschaftlicher Verlag.

Villar-Argáiz, Pilar (2007). *Eavan Boland's Evolution as a Irish Woman Poet: An Outsider within an Outsider's Culture*. Edwin Mellen: Lewiston/Queenston/Lampeter.

3.3
Paul Durcan

Jessika Köhler

The poet Paul Durcan (1944) was born and raised in Dublin. He also spent some time with his extended family in Turlough, County Mayo, which may account for his perceptive portrayal of the peculiar idiosyncrasies of Ireland's rural and urban communities. Since *Endsville* (1976), his first collection of poetry, he has published over 20 books of poetry. All of them are informed by a distinctive poetic voice, which John Goodby has characterized as a "suspiciously deadpan discursive narrativ[e]" presented by a "radically naïve but self-questioning narrator [...] who mixed literal and phantasmagoric event" (Goodby 2000, 180).

Often classed alongside Brendan Kennelly, Durcan is particularly renowned as a poet of the public sphere for his powerful performances and his outspoken political engagement and active participation in the national discourse. His poetic oeuvre, however, resists easy categorization in that it traces a wide arc between two radically different modes; that of political satire, on the one hand, and an unflinchingly open, frank and exhaustive exploration of his personal life, like his failed marriage, his fraught relationship to his father, and his own psychological issues, on the other.

The journey, both physical and metaphorical, is central to a poetry that is informed by constant movement and breaching of borders, both geographically—within the island and beyond—and mentally in terms of a psychological journey of self-discovery, as well as through imaginative experimentation. Fintan O'Toole has quite fittingly called Durcan "the national bard of the Republic of Elsewhere" (O'Toole 1996, 40). Durcan's Ireland is unremittingly entrenched in the global world, and his poetry shows a disdain for any

---

A Companion to Contemporary British and Irish Poetry, 1960–2015, First Edition.
Edited by Wolfgang Görtschacher and David Malcolm.
© 2021 John Wiley & Sons Ltd. Published 2021 by John Wiley & Sons Ltd.

national concept of insularity, as the title of some of Durcan's collections already make abundantly clear, that is, *O Westport in the Light of Asia Minor* (1975), *Going Home to Russia* (1987), and *Greetings to Our Friends in Brazil* (1999).

In the boom years of Celtic Tiger Ireland, which radically and suddenly changed the realities of Irish life, Durcan's poetry became a mouthpiece for the modernizing trend in Irish society by unmercifully holding a mirror up to its rigid and outmoded institutions, such as the Catholic Church or the Gaelic Athletic Association (GAA). In his early poetry such an engagement often coincided with a resort to stereotypical representations of the targets of politically liberal Ireland. It is Durcan's keen power of observation that allows him to perfectly—and comically—capture the paradox situation of contemporary Ireland: "He writes out of a society that has become post-modern without ever really becoming modern, a place in which the global village is still a one-horse town" (O'Toole 1996, 32).

Varied transformative impulses are the driving force behind Durcan's in-depth creative engagement with contemporary Irish life. These impulses acknowledge the instability of the current moment, an instability caused by the simultaneity of all everyday experience. Durcan translates this simultaneity by conflating apparently antagonistic modes, focuses, and techniques, that is, humor and melancholy, private and public, familiarity and estrangement. Despite his degree in history and archaeology, Durcan's poetry is a relentless probing of the present in all its diverse chaotic detail. It is also an ongoing effort of turning the banal everyday into poetry. Durcan is a storyteller with a keen eye for the absurdities that abound in the proceedings of everyday life.

The long rambling narrative poem "The Beckett at the Gate" (Durcan 2009, 168–174) from *Going Home to Russia* is a masterpiece of transforming Beckettian absurdity into a poem. "That spring in Dublin" (Durcan 2009, 168, l. 1) the narrator finds himself constantly accosted by people enquiring "Have you not seen Barry McGovern's Beckett?" (Durcan 2009, 168, ll.6, 10) and even worse "Have you not been to the Beckett at the Gate?" (Durcan 2009, 168, ll. 6, 11). Cultural hype seems inescapable and is portrayed as an intrusive and overwhelming force. In the first stanza, the term "barking" (Durcan 2009, 168, ll. 3–5, 9) is used repeatedly to describe the way these questions are addressed to the narrator. And by depicting Dublin's cultural elite, disparagingly called "cultural groupies" (Durcan 2009, 168, l. 103) at one point, in animalistic terms, behaving like dogs, Durcan mockingly questions their apparent civilized and cultured status. His "limp tail of ejection" (Durcan 2009, 168, l. 18) also involves the imagery of the canine, and the pun, with its connotation of impotence and male failure, mockingly highlights the severity of the narrator's outsider position. The isolated citydweller is a recurrent character in Durcan's poetry. Both poet and narrator exist in a liminal realm, as marginalized figures. They are observers rather than participants in the action.

The constant repetition of the phrases "Have you not seen Barry McGovern's Beckett?" (Durcan 2009, 168, ll. 6, 10) and "Have you not been to the Beckett at the Gate?" (Durcan 2009, 168, ll. 8, 11) can also be viewed as a ritualized performative act in that it functions as a literary representation of social re-enactment. Jeffrey C. Alexander defines rituals as:

episodes of repeated and simplified cultural communication in which the direct partners to a social interaction, and those observing it, share a mutual belief in the descriptive and prescriptive validity of the communication's symbolic contents and accept the authenticity of one another's intentions. (Alexander 2006, 29)

The performativity of social interaction is here both related to the theatrical experience of Beckett's play—a ritualized social interaction detached from religion is after all highly reminiscent of Beckett's work—and to the poem, which is a dramatic piece in its own right. Durcan's poetry is defined by the idea of performance, always highly aware of the oral tradition it stems from and its intended listening audience.

At the same time, the title of the poem and its intrinsic ambivalence caused by the play on words, which relates both to the theater the play is staged at and the phrase "the enemy at the gate," create an atmosphere of apprehension. The allusion to Samuel Beckett as the fearsome other presents the literary forefather as a stifling, even monstrous, presence. It illustrates an anxiety of influence, which is heightened by the constant repetition of the phrase throughout the poem, like an eerie echo haunting the poet. The thought that being able to enjoy the play in solitude, "Would make the next hour and a half / If not less of a cauchemar /At least a bearable *cauchemar*" (Durcan 2009, 170, ll. 94–96), again subtly evokes Beckett as a nightmarish figure through the epiphora. The foreign word constitutes an allusion to Beckett's affinity for French, while the term itself, which translates as "nightmare," reinforces the sense of unease associated with the literary precursor. Although the tone, here, is rather playful, the notion of the Irish literary tradition as a source of intimidation permeates this poem, also refiguring the narrator's impotence in terms of the poet's own insecurities. As all father figures in Durcan's work, Beckett is treated with apprehensive suspicion.

The Beckett play portraying "things that were not happening" (O'Toole 1996, 27) is realized in a poem about a play that is "not happening". While the narrator is painstakingly precise in detailing the journey to and from the theater, as well as the seating arrangements within the theater ("C9 was the number of my ticket, / Centre, third row from the front" (Durcan 2009, 168, ll. 31–32)), the play itself marks a notable absence in the poem. None of the particulars of the play itself are mentioned, not even the title. The only performance the reader gets to experience is not the performance on stage but the performance of the woman sitting next to the narrator, who "gave herself over to her own laughter" (Durcan 2009, 171, l. 130), kicked him in the legs, nudged his kneecaps, leaned her head on his shoulder, grabbed his arm, and howled. Here, the shift in focus toward the "young woman to boot" (Durcan 2009, 169, l. 69) foregrounds the narrator's state of isolation and speaks of loneliness and a real need for human companionship, but also an inability to connect with others, particularly women. Michelle, whose name he discovers accidentally, is ironically reading *One Hundred Years of Solitude*. The narrator's sudden obsession with Michelle is underlined by the synesthesia in the line "And howl – luminously howl" (Durcan 2009, 171, l. 151), which makes her the focus of his entire sensory experience and also stresses his idealization of her by noting her radiance.

In trying to describe Michelle, the poet resorts to listing female figures from the New and the Old Testament (Susannah, Judith, Sarah, Rachel, Eve, Martha, Mary, and Magdalen) before ending in "Michelle was – well Michelle." (Durcan 2009, 171, l. 124) By offering a whole variety of feminine qualities and actions that are associated with these biblical characters – from the extraordinary beauty of Sarah to Judith's seducing and killing of Holofernes, whom Durcan mentions explicitly – the poet underscores the perceived sacredness of women and celebrates feminine diversity. For the narrator, the woman next to him is both elusively close and unattainable. It is precisely the act of idealization that leads to her unattainability. Like a fleeting vision his romantic attachment to Michelle ends when the play ends. The potential of transcendence associated with the feminine remains ultimately unachieved.

Another chance meeting with Michelle at a bus stop, which the narrator passes on his solitary journey home, equally fails to lead to anything else, when "She scrutinized [him] serenely / As if she had never seen [him] before –" (Durcan 2009, 173, ll. 225–226) and he walks on. But the encounter leads to a change of heart, a decision to engage more actively in social pastimes, jestingly portrayed by the (upper) middle class leisure activity of playing tennis and the accompanying tennis metaphors and puns. The silent unanswered prayer to Michelle to join him, however, places this resolution firmly in the realm of fantasy.

The middle sequence of the poem features a poetic walk through nighttime Dublin, an adaptation of the aimless wanderings in Beckett's work. The narrator appears introspective and yet mischievously self-deprecating as individual and environment are conglomerated. By conflating romantic pastoral imagery and the sights of the city ("At Ringsend there was a full moon over / The Sugar Loaf and the Wicklow Hills" [Durcan 2009, 173, ll. 202–203]) the poet playfully undermines the traditional concepts of poetic esthetics grounded in landscape poetry. The leisurely pace of the poem reflects the pace of the walker, but although Durcan executes the act of the *flâneur* and reads the familiar landmarks of the city, he soon finds the familiar transformed into something else. The transformative qualities of the city let him experience his home city in a trance. The image of "the river," symbolic for the continuous movement that defines both the city and Durcan's poetry, is the pivotal image of this change. It is, also, a place that connects the city to the wider world. Like the bridge the narrator finds himself on, it is a place in-between, which then ironically functions as a "fulcrum of poignancy" as the narrator faces his own estrangement in the supposedly familiar place: "As I balanced in a trance on the humpbacked bridge, / On a fulcrum of poignancy, / And I felt like a stranger in a new city" (Durcan 2009, 173, ll. 211–213). Paradoxically, the constant process of transformation lends Durcan's "vision of reality" (Durcan 2009, 173, l. 216) its authenticity.

Key phrases re-occur in the mutterings of the narrator to himself on his walk home. Durcan's sharp wit and mocking critique are highlighted by the constant repetition of phrases, particularly those that carry multiple meanings, in a continual process of echoing and transforming the core issues of his social critique. The same processes shape his poetic construction of place, which cannot be detached from the surreal social constitutions that inform it. O'Toole argues that what makes Durcan so successful as a poet is his ability to adequately reflect the reality of modern Irish life by using surrealism (O'Toole 1996, 27).

The term *surrealist*, however, is not applicable to Durcan in the conventional sense. As Derek Mahon, to whom this poem is dedicated, notes "Durcan is not a Surrealist but a Cubist, one transfixed by the simultaneousness of disparate experience, all sides of the question" (Mahon 1996, 166). Durcan's particular brand of surrealism is deeply committed to an accurate representation of reality. He possesses an uncanny ability to perceive and portray the obscurity of contemporary existence and elevate the seemingly mundane in the process.

Ultimately, the poet returns to the notion of theatrical performance. The lines that have functioned as a chorus throughout the poem are repeated and reach a crescendo, in an echo of the cacophony of contemporary noise, culminating in the final frenzied repetitions:

> *There's a beckett at the gate, there is a beckett*
> *at the gate, Michelle;*
> *There's a Beckett at the gate, there is a Beckett*
> *at the gate, Michelle.*
> (Durcan 2009, 174, ll. 245–246)

In "Meeting the President (31 August 1995)" (Durcan 2009, 448–452) from *Greetings to Our Friends in Brazil* (1999) Durcan's father "eight years dead" (Durcan 2009, 448, I. l. 2) returns forcefully: "Driving up to the Phoenix Park" (Durcan 2009, 448, I. l. 1) he "Shoulders me aside; / Playfully crudely" (Durcan 2009, 448, I. ll. 6–7) and takes over the narrator's/son's body. The John Durcan persona features heavily in his son's poetry, most vividly in *Daddy, Daddy* (1990), the collection Durcan put together immediately after his father's death, and this persona is representative of an intense conflict between inherently male, constrictive, traditional values ascertained—often brutally—by patriarchal dominance and an inability to adhere to this repressive value system. Durcan's elegies for his father are, therefore, trapped between the sustained sting of parental disapproval and mourning the loss of a primordial connection. The possession of the son's body by the father then relates to an ongoing psychological struggle with the memory of the deceased. However, the process of aging also turns the poet into his father in a very physical way, as a look in the mirror reveals: "As I get older, my dead father gets younger. / My hands on the driving wheel are my father's hands. / My shoulders in the driving seat are my father's shoulders." (Durcan 2009, 448, I. ll.11–13) The chiasm immediately followed by the parallelism underlines Durcan's experience, the aging process, on the stylistic level, as he finds himself becoming more and more similar to a man with whom he had very little in common.

The poem also addresses Durcan's own role as a father, when he depicts his daughter: "She – cross-legged on the couch with the Koran – / She is a week back from Marrakesh –" (Durcan 2009, 449, II. ll. 6–7). The liberal-minded cosmopolitan young woman serves as an almost exaggerated anti-thesis of everything that Durcan's father stood for when he was alive, and she may represent a hopeful outlook for a more liberated future. If the father figure represents Ireland's restrictive traditionalism, the daughter functions as a mediating presence representing the new face of the island uninhibited by former conventional codes.

Familiarity and strangeness pervade all spheres of Durcan's poetry and feature even in his frequent portrayal of his family members. Here, particularly, the characters that by their very nature should be deeply familiar are distorted until they appear almost impersonal to the detached narrator.

Being possessed by his father, the poet/narrator experiences his home city anew.

> Riding upriver across the city of Dublin
> Is for my father the most sensual of rides.
> Every streetname an enigma of consolation
> (Durcan 2009, 449, III. ll. 1–3)

Durcan's poetic urban terrain is determined by the psychological topography of loss and at the same time provides the wonderfully strange concept of an "enigma of consolation." (Durcan 2009, 449, III. l.3) And yet, other places remain tangibly close: "This all appears to be happening in the middle of Dublin city; / Musically it is all happening to the tune of County Mayo" (Durcan 2009, 450, III. ll. 31–32). The permeability of place in postmodern, globalized Ireland is also evoked by more far-flung places such as "Marrakesh," (Durcan 2009, 449, II. l. 7) "Zambia," (Durcan 2009, 450, IV. l. 11) and "Bosnia-Herzegovina." (Durcan 2009, 450, V. l. 2) "Foreign names in Irish poetry are always a potential form of escape" (Redmond 2012, 409) and, despite being anything but escapist, Durcan uses these "forms of escape" with relish. In addition, I would contest, Durcan is the poet who uses Irish place names most frequently, usually in long litanies that connect one place to the next, also employed in "The Beckett at Gate." The perpetual quality of movement reverberates through a poetry, which also repeatedly takes place on transport in a heterotopian transitional space between two places, for example, "El Flight 106: New York–Dublin," (Durcan 2009, 158–159) "The Dublin–Belfast Railway Line," (Durcan 1990, 60) and "The Dublin–Paris–Moscow Line" (Durcan 1993, 237–239).

Stairs are another transitional place. Writing on the importance of "the Journey" in *Paul Durcan's Diary*, his collection of prose pieces which were broadcast on RTÉ Radio 1, the poet states: "Are we not all of us Travellers, in our deepest, buried innermost human feelings? When we are children and adolescents, every hour and every day is a journey." The journey is a concept that encompasses the most mundane aspects of human life: "I am seven years of age and the staircase is a journey in which I can spend all day travelling up and down the stairs, up and down the banisters" (Durcan 2003, 23). Here, we experience another form of journey as the ascent and descent of the stairs also symbolize personal achievements in the public sphere, connoting the social ladder.

In typical Durcan fashion, the title of the poem ("Meeting the President, 31 August 1995") is slightly misleading. The meeting with the president herself, who remains unnamed, is a brief encounter making up a mere four lines of the 128-line long poem. Durcan has dedicated a number of poems to Mary Robinson's election as the first Irish woman president, which he optimistically viewed as a symbol of the pervasive changes in contemporary Irish society and a chance for the Irish to shed what was previously a monolithic culture. In this poem, however, the focus is on the resurgence of the poet's/narrator's father, while the president serves as a symbol of what the poet has accomplished.

Transformation and surrealism remain constant presences in Durcan's poetry, as the narrator bizarrely turns into an animal, or possibly a combination of animals, clicking his "hooves on the floor" (Durcan 2009, 451, VI. 7) and trying "not to bleat or bellow" (Durcan 2009, 451, VI. l. 9). The trope of animal transformation is common in Durcan's poetry and Erik Martiny has observed that it seems

> to be employed to express a feeling of estrangement, a melancholic sense of dehumanising abjection. Despite the comedy implicit in these images, Durcan's personae do not really seem to choose to be transformed into animals; rather, they submit to their metamorphoses as a release from the pressures of the human condition, and paradoxically also as a way of signaling a very human sense of self-debasement. (Martiny 2010, 414)

The narrator's sense of estrangement is both directed toward the self, an expression of his inner turmoil, and his environment, the city's transformative qualities and the disconcerting political environment, but the metamorphosis seems to be primarily a more extreme excess of the poet's/narrator's inability to escape the grip of his father. The anxiety of influence the poet exhibits in regard to his literary forefathers, like Beckett, seems to be an extension of the Durcanian narrator's anxiety—even paralysis—evoked by his father's influence over him.

For a moment, the poet creates the allusion that he has succeeded in shaking off his father's overbearing presence: "I look around and stare at my father – / A red deer standing sideways to the car." (Durcan 2009, 451, V. ll. 19–20). It is as if the meeting with the president was enough of an achievement to retroactively validate the poet's life choices in the eye of the strict, traditionally-minded father. However, as the poem continues it becomes clear that the poet/narrator has not shaken off his father's ghost, but has transformed into the animal himself. He now enters a bar where the barman takes care of him: "Rubbing the back of my neck, stroking my nose, / Feeding my thick, wet, steaming, dribbling lips / With crisps and peanuts." (Durcan 2009, 451, VI. ll. 4–64). "Nijinsky when I'm alive," the barman confides when asked his name, elucidating the strange rapport between poet/animal and the stranger. The Russian ballet dancer and choreographer Vaslav Nijinsky lived from 1889 to 1950 and can be considered as one of the greatest artistic minds of the twentieth century. In 1919, however, while living in exile in Switzerland his mental instability slowly began to make itself noticeable. A diary written at the time chronicles his descent into madness. In March of the same year he had to be institutionalized for the first time and was later diagnosed with schizophrenia. The dancer spent the last 30 years of his life in different mental hospitals and asylums. "Death came unexpectedly, for I wanted it. [...] I have not lived long" (Nijinsky 2000, 151) and "I am not a dying man. I'm alive, and therefore suffer," (Nijinsky 2000, 172) reads Nijinsky's diary, which is divided in two parts, "On Life" and "On Death". An echo of this peculiar dichotomy is found in the line "when I'm alive," (Durcan 2009, 451, VI. ll. 12, 14) which

Durcan has the barman repeat twice. Apart from the autobiographical details, Nijinsky's diary is also deeply concerned with animal rights and vegetarianism. It also addresses bestiality, however, which lends some troubling overtones to the depiction of the barman's caresses.

By mentioning Nijinsky, Durcan subtly evokes his own autobiography. His family had him committed to a psychiatric hospital in Dublin and later to a Harley Street Clinic in London, where he was given electric convulsion therapy (Tallant 2007). The connection between both men, Nijinsky and Durcan, then, is founded in their shared experience of forced hospitalization and in their artistry, Nijinsky's diary also features poetry, highlighting the thin line between delusion and creativity. Durcan has openly addressed his forced hospitalization in a number of poems (i.e. "1966" [Durcan 1990, 124–127], "Philadelphia, Here I Come" [Durcan 2009, 558–559], "Apartheid" [Durcan 2009, 242–243]), particularly those depicting his dysfunctional relationship with his father, and the subliminal reminder in this poem may express that an ultimate reconciliation between the son and the memory of his father may never be achieved.

The last stanza moves seamlessly from the personal plane to a more universal one. The narrator returns home to his mother roaring at him—a continuation of the animal terminology—and finds himself hoping she would "stop roaring," (Durcan 2009, 452, VII. l. 4) a thought then paralleled twice, "If only John, Bill, Gerry, Ian, David would stop roaring. / If only everybody in the world would stop roaring." (Durcan 2009, 452, VII. ll. 5–6) Here, the poet returns to the political arena by casually listing the major political actors of the peace process in Northern Ireland on a first name basis, making it seem like they are also part of his family. The poet's/narrator's personal demons transform into public ones, and he suddenly finds himself haunted by the general level of noise in the public arena. His ideal image of peacefulness comes from the natural world: gales petering out into snowdrops. Ending in the last feverish wish "If only the world would be quiet and watch it" (Durcan 2009, 452, VII. l. 9). The concluding "watch it" could refer either to the snowdrops, symbolizing a return to a more natural state of being in the world, or a colloquial demand to be more careful. The poet stays deliberately ambiguous.

The specific note of the date in the poem's title is significant and not uncommon in Durcan's poetry, reinforcing an illusory sense of reality and fostering the realism of the poetic event. Thus, the poet creates an impression of himself as a chronicler of events, particularly those in his own life. Durcan's obsession with the calendar is also found in his prose writing *Paul Durcan's Diary*. "Treasure Island" (Durcan 2009, 556–558) from *The Laughter of Mothers* (2007) also begins with an explicit recourse to the calendar: "October 16th, 1950" (Durcan 2009, 556, l. 1). The poem depicts the narrator's sixth birthday when his "mother took him to see his first film" (Durcan 2009, 556, l. 2) and the specificity of the date marks the mundane occasion as extraordinary and worthy of poetry. The poetic mode of transition in Durcan's poetry extends beyond the idea of life and death, which is particularly noticeable in his poetic reanimation of his dead relatives as literary personae, revisiting of past experiences, and creation of fictionalized memories. While his poetry shows little interest in Heaneyesque excavatory practices of engaging with the national past, the journey of self-exploration constantly leads him into the recesses of his own past.

Durcan's poetry displays a keen awareness of the "multiplication of cultural forms" (Goodby 2000, 180) stemming from technological advancements in the Republic since the 1960s. In his work, the presence of other media constantly infringes on the sphere of the poem, thus serving both as a realistic reflection of the saturation of the public sphere by mass culture (i.e., radio, TV, press, cinema) and an unprejudiced exploration of the impact of other media on its own art form. The common conception of Durcan's poetry as popular rather than avant-garde is neither something the poet shies away from, nor is he critical toward the achievements of popular culture. "Treasure Island" is one of a number of poems in a collection that pays tribute to the poet's deceased mother, which recount the shared experience of novel, play, or film, and which celebrate the freedom of imagination provided by them. Some of them take place within the context of the son's forced hospitalization and wrongly diagnosed schizophrenia. The simple enjoyment of a day out at the cinema offers a place of refuge to both mother and son, a shared space of intimate closeness that exhibits a healing capacity. From "the swing-doors within swing-doors, / Veil upon veil of a temple / Proceeding to an inner sanctum" (Durcan 2009, 557, ll. 17–19) to the "girl acolyte strapped to her tray" (Durcan 2009, 557, l. 21) the whole imagery of the cinematic experience carries strong overtones of a religious moment and, indeed, possesses a certain sanctity. The poet finds something undeniably spiritual and uplifting in this first encounter with mass media.

Sheila MacBride, the poet's mother, features as a diametrically opposed character to the darkly intimidating father figure in Durcan's work. She is described as a nurturing presence that provides a safe haven ("Safe in the abyss" [Durcan 2009, 557, l. 26]). By depicting his mother's attire ("plum-red lipstick," "pearl necklace," and "pearl earrings" [Durcan 2009, 557, ll. 28–29]) in awed terms and referring to the cinema as a "second extension of [her] bedroom" (Durcan 2009, 557, l. 14), the narrator exhibits more of an affinity with feminine than masculine spheres. The shared moment between mother and son is depicted in intimate terms as the poet proceeds to blur the line between public and personal, imagination and reality. The narrator speaks of "his young mother, his first sweetheart" (Durcan 2009, 557, l. 32) and the romantic overtones here profusely express his tender feelings toward his mother. The poem reverberates an unambiguous fondness that the poet finds much harder to express for the judgmental father figure.

In the cinema, reality and fiction start to blend for the small child, but the experience is not merely magical as he comes to the profound realization "That the price of knowledge is death." (Durcan 2009, 558, l. 55) When mother and son emerge from the cinema, "As out of a book of the Old Testament," (Durcan 2009, 558, l. 57) the city has also transformed: "All of Dublin was black water and icy lights / And his mother queued for a Number 11 bus. / They sailed home aboard the *Hispaniola*" (Durcan 2009, 558, ll. 59–61). This transformative moment where the ordinary is suddenly changed, that slight shift lends Durcan's poems their surreal quality. The child-like mindset of the narrator offers a simpler view of the world where the imagination is much more readily engaged. However, there is also always a troubling aspect to this transformative moment.

> Thenceforth, aged six years, his life,
> In all its people and in all its places,
> Would be a *Treasure Island*
> A tropic idyll forever under threat,
> (Durcan 2009, 558, ll. 65–68)

The recognition of the instability of reality poses its own threat. Taken in combination with the next few poems about shared cinematic or theatrical experiences between mother and son, the threat here may well lie in the rejection of traditional maleness, which Durcan has identified as the major factor in his hospitalization (cf. Tallant 2007). However, it is not just the son who has been fundamentally changed by the cinematic experience, for the image of the mother has also undergone a process of transformation, as she is once again juxtaposed to, and at the same time defined by, her intimidating husband: "Sweet Sheila MacBride, who had married John Durcan, / One of the black, red-roaring fighting Durcans of Mayo." (Durcan 2009, 558, ll. 70–71)

"I was three years of age in the full of my days," (Durcan 2015, 3, l. 1) reads the first line of Durcan's latest collection *The Days of Surprise*. And while the notion certainly seems implausible the statement itself carries conviction. "Never again to be so fully myself" (Durcan 2015, 3, l. 2), the speaker continues introducing a note of wistful recollection. In this recollection the self is "not a who or a what / But a where." (Durcan 2015, 3, ll. 9–10). The eponymous "57 Dartmouth Square", the poet's childhood home, becomes the narrator's identity. "I was a place." (Durcan 2015, 3, l. 11) the speaker ascertains, but what reads like the natural culmination of the first stanza is turned into the first line of the second stanza instead and the blank line in between has an unsettling effect, underlining the finite nature of this state of being.

The experience of the self as a place is described as an "apotheosis" (Durcan 2015, 3, l. 14), which the speaker would never know again, thus, raising the significance of both the memory of the childhood home and the child's way of experiencing the world onto a spiritual level. The line "Heaven was a place – not a placeless heaven –" (Durcan 2015, 3, l. 22) seems to function in much the same way, even if a little whimsically exaggerated. Moreover, the line recalls "The Placeless Heaven: Another Look at Kavanagh," an essay by Seamus Heaney. Here Heaney discusses the difference between Kavanagh's early and late poetry and traces Kavanagh's poetic influence on his own work in terms of Kavanagh's portrayal of place. He views Kavanagh's early poetry as one firmly rooted in a real topographical place and its community, whereas his later poetry features place predominantly as a detached luminous entity of the mind. In Heaney's own words: "It was and remains an imagined realm, even if it can be situated at an earthly spot, a placeless heaven rather than a heavenly place." (Heaney 1989, 182) Durcan clearly echoes this line in his poem, thus, casually inserting his poetry within a poetic tradition and lineage. Durcan places his own roots not in the parochial rural locals of Kavanagh's and Heaney's poetry, but in the urban Dublin environment of his childhood. His poetic identity is formed by the physical experience of his immediate environment, and he elevates the authenticity of this ordinary physical experience. As a poet Durcan has come into his own and *The Days of Surprise* displays a self-assured poetic voice where reading "poetry to one another" (Durcan 2015, 92, l. 50) becomes the only way "to stay sane" (Durcan 2015, 92, l. 49). In fact, it is Heaney, who features as a poetic voice from beyond in the moving elegy "Breaking News" (Durcan 2015, 125), that bestows the title of "Poet Durcan" (Durcan 2015, 125, l. 20).

Placed in the beginning of the collection, along with a number of poems that sees the narrator through childhood, puberty, and early adulthood before reaching his late sixties, "57 Dartmouth Square" may well represent a sort of earliest childhood memory, and as such the moment of being fully oneself is inherently temporary. The comprehensive conflation of the self with the home, including the wonderfully tongue-in-cheek metaphor of coming "in and out of" (Durcan 2015, 4, ll. 44) the self, is unavoidably transitory and a moment of transformation is inevitable: "One day I'd cease to be 57 Darthmouth Square, / Becoming instead the *Barge Man at the Tiller / In a Cloth Cap*" (Durcan 2015, 5–6, ll. 68–70). The barge man is one of many characters populating the poem, but in this instance the italicized description is more reminiscent of a work of art than an actual person. The transformative impulse layers the personal with the abstract so that the self becomes as permanently susceptible to change as the whole of contemporary experience.

Place remains the only stable constant of the poem. Time, on the other hand, is less clearly defined. From the specific period "1947–48" (Durcan 2015, 3, l. 15; 4, ll. 31, 37) and later "6 May 1954" (Durcan 2015, 6, l. 76), we move on to less specific temporal events "in winter" (Durcan 2015, 6, l. 86), "In the summertime" (Durcan 2015, 7, l. 95) to "Christmas Day" which was not even "really Christmas Day" (Durcan 2015, 7, l. 101). Thus, the poet captures the peculiar nature of memory perfectly. Instances stick out clearly but memory as a whole is frustratingly vague and deceptive. As the speaker grows older the reality of his surroundings becomes more pronounced: "A shocking epiphany of my child's accumulating horror / At the cracks – no, the chasms – in the social fabric of Dublin." (Durcan 2015, 7, ll. 99–100). And yet, the poet seems much more accepting of the inconsistencies of both contemporary Irish and his personal life finding his own niche as a "happy neurotic" (Durcan 2015, 8, l. 118).

In Durcan's poetry, the "elsewhere" or "otherness" experienced in every moment manifests itself in images of transformation. The arbitrariness of contemporary experience is, thus, expressed in an unpretentious and yet consistently inventive poetic style. The use of free verse, eschewing ornate or experimentally deconstructivist modes of literary expression, seems deceptively simple but upon closer inspection reveals a multiply layered examination of the contemporary world. In addition, the natural conversational style of Durcan's poetry, with its many repetitions, polyptotons, and puns, emphasizes the transformative qualities of language. However, the potential for reinvention inherent in the idea of transformation never truly takes form because the poet remains faithful to portraying exactly what he perceives.

References

Alexander, Jeffrey C. (2006). "Cultural Pragmatics: Social Performance Between Ritual and Strategy." In: *Social Performance: Symbolic Action, Cultural Pragmatics and Ritual* (eds. Jeffrey C. Alexander, Bernhard Giesen and Jason L. Mast), 29–90. Cambridge: Cambridge University Press.

Durcan, Paul (1987). *Going Home to Russia*. Belfast: The Blackstaff Press.

Durcan, Paul (1990). *Daddy, Daddy*. Belfast: The Blackstaff Press.

Durcan, Paul (1999). *Greetings to Our Friends in Brazil*. London: The Harvill Press.

Durcan, Paul (2003). *Paul Durcan's Diary*. Dublin: New Island Books.

Durcan, Paul (2007). *The Laughter of Mothers*. London: Harvill Secker.

Durcan, Paul (2009). *Life Is a Dream. 40 Years Reading Poems 1967–2007*. London: Harvill Secker.

Durcan, Paul (2015). *The Days of Surprise*. London: Harvill Secker.

Goodby, John (2000). *Irish Poetry since 1950: From Stillness into History*. Manchester: Manchester University Press.

Heaney, Seamus (1989). "The Placeless Heaven: Another Look at Kavanagh." In: *Tradition and Influence in Anglo-Irish Poetry* (eds. Terence Brown and Nicholas Grene), 181–193. London: The Macmillan Press.

Mahon, Derek (1996). "Orpheus Ascending." In: *The Kilfenora Teaboy: A Study of Paul Durcan* (ed. Colm Tóibín), 163–170. Dublin: New Island Books.

Martiny, Erik (2010). "Comic Abjection in the Poetry of Paul Durcan." *English Studies*: 91–94, 412–424. https://doi.org/10.1080/00138381003647616.

Nijinsky, Vaslav F. (2000). *The Diary of Vaslav Nijinsky* (trans. K. Fitzlyon) (ed. Joan Acocella). London: Penguin Books.

O'Toole, Fintan (1996). "In the Light of Things as They Are: Paul Durcan's Ireland." In: *The Kilfenora Teaboy: A Study of Paul Durcan* (ed. Colm Tóibín), 26–41. Dublin: New Island Books.

Redmond, John (2012). "Engagement with the Public Sphere: Durcan and Kennelly." In: *The Oxford Handbook of Modern Irish Poetry* (eds. Fran Brearton and Alan Gillis), 403–418. Oxford: Oxford University Press.

Tallant, Nicola (2007). "Kidnapped by His Family and Put in a Mental Home." Interview. *Sunday Independent*. https://www.independent.ie/unsorted/migration/kidnapped-by-his-family-and-put-in-a-mental-home-668173.html (accessed 9 December 2018).

3.4
James Fenton

David Malcolm

Introduction

James Fenton[1] is a successful, highly regarded (although his status is not without controversy), contemporary poet. His output includes a wide range of different kinds of poetry—love lyrics, songs, found poems, poems with a clear political-historical subject matter, literary social satire, and ballads (Prestwich 2012, 102; Wilmer 1994, 54). He is certainly taken seriously, and has continually been so taken, by commentators (see, for example: Schmidt 1989, 25; Levi 1991, 27–28, 35–37). The enthusiasm that Michael Schmidt and Peter Levi feel for his work is reflected by other critics. Dana Gioia calls him "the major poet of his generation" (2003, 20). Edmund Prestwich calls him "a towering figure" (2012, 102). Clive Wilmer's review of *Out of Danger* (1993) praises his technical skill and range of subject, and the appropriateness of the one to the other (1994, 54–55). Reviewing *Yellow Tulips: Poems 1968–2011* (2012), Patrick McGuinness admires the same features, and argues that Fenton establishes an important place for poetry in the modern world (2012, 14).

Fenton's standing and importance are, however, questioned by some commentators. In a review of *Yellow Tulips* published in *Stand*, Owen Lowery calls some poems "archaic or artificial," Fenton's "ballad metres" in anything but his comic verse "excruciating," and, if he does find some aspects of Fenton's work interesting, damns it with faint praise (2013, 92–94). Stephen Burt is severe in his comments on Fenton. Writing in 1995, he accuses the war poems and political poems in *Out of Danger* as having "parasitized their occasions rather than evading or transforming them through art" (46). "It is the aesthetic of the guilt

---

A Companion to Contemporary British and Irish Poetry, 1960–2015, First Edition.
Edited by Wolfgang Görtschacher and David Malcolm.
© 2021 John Wiley & Sons Ltd. Published 2021 by John Wiley & Sons Ltd.

trip," he writes (47). Fenton's poems "eschew both the interest we seek in modern poetry – changes in diction, polysemy, mixed emotions, new metaphors – and the interest of a good short story" (50). He "versifies reportage" without a "world view" (50).

However valued, Fenton is consistently placed in the same tradition and context. He is constantly, and rightly, compared to Auden (for example, Corcoran 2001, 358; Gioia 2003, 14; Lowery 2013, 91). He is also connected with the Martian poets, such as Craig Raine and Christopher Reid; indeed, he is credited with inventing the name (O'Brien 2003, 574; Pollard 2016, 100–101). Other commentators find echoes of Kipling and T. S. Eliot in his work (Prestwich 2012, 102; Corcoran 2001, 358). Most critics point to a distinctive working with historical and political subjects, with personal experiences, and with traditional genres and forms (Schmidt 1989, 25; Wilmer 1994, 54). Indeed, Gioia sees Fenton as a successful reviver of "moribund" forms (2003, 21).

In the following essay, I will analyze four very different poems—different in terms of genre, metrics, use of rhyme, language, and subject matter—which are themselves substantial texts worthy of attention, and also ones which indicate certain common features of Fenton's poetry. I think my analyses call into question the negative verdicts passed on his verse.

"A German Requiem"

"A German Requiem" (1981) is a poem composed of nine short poems revolving round figures and experiences from post-Second World War German history and society (Fenton 1983, 9–19). I would like to focus on the first of these nine poems, which clearly sounds a dominant note in the group as a whole, both in terms of motif (forgetting and remembering) and of language (the pattern established here—"It is not what ..."—is repeated in the last section of the sequence as a conclusion to the whole text).

The title of the sequence—"A German Requiem"—is immediately striking. It promises a certain breadth of scope (an English poem on German matters!), and also carries with it the suggestion that it may be about some of the darker aspects of European history. A requiem itself is a text of prayer for the repose of the dead, and, thus, automatically marks the poem as being of some seriousness, containing an element of mourning. It also indicates a rootedness in traditional forms and genres (to which the requiem belongs), and this is borne out in the statements and counterstatements, the antiphonal parallelisms of the text itself, recalling as they do the statements and responses of a religious ritual.

This first poem of the sequence is (like the rest of the group) written in unrhymed verse. It contains 11 lines, with a wide variety of main stresses per line (from three to six). Again, this flexibility in line length is common throughout the whole sequence, and allows for a variety of effects, from the ritualistic to the conversational. This opening poem is further marked by the way in which each line is end-stopped, and, indeed, ends in a period. The majority of lines consist of one completed, graphical sentence, although some lines contain two sentences. Not all these sentences are strictly grammatical sentences, line 7—"What you must go on forgetting all your life"—being an elliptical version of the previous line with "It is" omitted. The effect of this type of end-stopping is peculiar and difficult to analyze, but it is as if the separate sentences gain a force and discrete prominence through it, a sense of austere clarity.

But it is the prominence of repetitions and parallelisms beyond the arrangement of the lines which strikes the reader forcibly. The first seven lines are organized around an array of devices of repetition and parallelism. Anaphora gives shape to lines 1 and 2—"It is not what…" / "It is what…"; "It is not…" / "It is…." In addition, line 2 concludes with the epistrophe "the houses" / "the houses." Line 3 is an example of symploce, that is, both initial and final repetitions, while lines 4 and 5 begin with anaphora. The same device is apparent in the next two lines through the repeated "what" and the elliptical presence of the implied "It is." These two lines are further shaped by yet another paralleling device, that of polyptoton, the repetition of a word with varying grammatical inflections—thus: "forgotten," "forget," "forgetting." The presence of these devices obviously carries substantial meaning within the text. They serve to emphasize very strongly the motifs of memory and forgetting which they contain, but they also embody a kind of ritual repetitiveness, and one which, further, builds up to a climax. The "It is" / "It is" pattern is repeated over six lines, only to vary in lines 6 and 7 to an elliptical, hidden repetition, which also builds to a climax by the modifications of "forget" in those lines. The antiphonies of the requiem culminate in line 7.

The compositional division of the introductory poem is emphasized through this climax, as it is through the absence of the same density of parallel phrases in the concluding four lines of the text. Here only the last two lines—"Yesterday…," "Today…"—provide a relatively weak syntactic parallelism. In addition, the language of the two sections of the poem (lines 1–7 and lines 8–11) also shifts in terms of formality, the first section being markedly informal and the second substantially more formal. The unspecified deixis of the "It is," which shapes the first seven lines, belongs to very informal speech and writing (it really means something like "what is important is" or "it's all a matter of"), while a phrase such as "oblivion should discover a ritual" or words such as "enterprise" and "reproach" are clearly much more formal. The direct, forceful simplicity of the first seven lines modulates into a more elaborate, a more evasive language, just as one might seek to cover guilt in fine phrases.

If the deixis of the "It" that runs through the first seven lines is in a strict sense obscure, this is true of other pronouns too throughout the whole poem. Who are the "they" of line 1? And who is the "you" of the remainder of the text? Why does one modulate into the other? Further, is the "you" a concrete person, an addressee of the poem, or is it the equivalent of the general "one," or does it, indeed, shift from the latter to the former in the course of the poem, perhaps around line 7? The very ambiguity is central, appropriate to the deceptive forgetting that runs throughout the poem, but also perhaps broadening out the poem's focus. "They" and "you" are involved, but perhaps also "one" and "us."

Although the addressee is ambiguous, the speaker is quite precisely configured. The voice is marked by the kind of traditional linguistic virtuosity noted in the earlier text—rhetorical vigor in the parallelisms and climax of the first seven lines, the informal force of the language in those lines, and then the sophistication of lexis in the last four. The speaker is also a knowing one. He knows what has vanished; he knows what is to be forgotten. He also knows what will happen: you will probably not be the only one trying to forget; you will overcome your guilt and join the others. He knows what is in your mind—that in the past "the very furniture seemed to reproach you." He also possesses an amount of rather obscure information about the world: he knows what "the Widow's Shuttle" (line 11) is. (This is usually glossed as one of the buses which at one time took German war-widows to visit graveyards, but the actual denotation of the metaphor is not necessarily the most important issue, but rather the shaping of the speaker as a possessor of specialized knowledge.) This configuration of the speaker lasts throughout the entire "Requiem." He shows himself consistently knowledgeable, in command of details of family histories as well as of national catastrophes, of collective as well as of individual dishonesties. However, in the last section of the "Requiem," the speaker is revealed as also willing to forget, as, indeed, wishing to forget. Although he speaks of "the enquirer" here, this figure may be close to himself, and, thus, he too becomes implicated in the conspiracy of forgetting that is the poem's subject. "He forgets to pursue the point. / It is not what he wants to know. / It is what he wants not to know."

The world that the speaker has such easy knowledge of is both private and public. It is the world of people's hidden feelings, "memories," (line 4) the reproaches of the furniture, but it is also a world of history and politics, the houses that have been knocked down, the streets that no longer exist. In the context of the poem's title, this presumably refers to a mid-twentieth German history of the seizure of Jewish property, the massive bombing of cities by the Allies, and the changing street names that reflect the different political regimes between the 1930s and the 1950s. The "memories" which haunt, which must be forgotten are presumably, too, those of complicity with a murderous regime. Indeed, even the private "furniture" (line 10) which reproaches the addressee could be readily construed as the furniture of murdered victims or opponents of the regimes. The "Widow's Shuttle" (line 11) is carrying war-widows, not those whose husbands have died of natural causes. And this world has apocalyptic elements. Houses have vanished; whole streets no longer exist. Later in the "Requiem" we learn of squares and parks "filled with the eloquence of young cemeteries" (line 46) "when so many had died, so many and at such speed" (line 41). One of the agents or victims of this history certainly perceives it as apocalypse. The cataclysm of mid-century German history is seen as a time "When the world was at its darkest, / When the black wings passed over the rooftops" (lines 63–64)—with echoes of Exodus 12 and Revelation 6.12 and 8.

"I Saw a Child"

The title of the poem "I Saw a Child" (from Fenton's collection *Out of Danger* published in 1993) suggests precisely the opposite of what the text is (Fenton 1993, 39–40). It promises, perhaps, a Romantic poem on childhood innocence, on a child's freedom from civilized corruption, and its consequent perceptiveness like Wordsworth's "The Idiot Boy" or "We Are Seven." It might also indicate a Christian hymn, again drawing on the symbol of the child as innocent and yet, by virtue of that innocence, wise (one thinks of Blake's "Songs of Innocence" here). But one is rapidly disabused. The second line of the poem begins with the cynical and knowing "Stick with me," and the poem goes on to tell us that the "fields are mined" (line 5), thus scarcely places for a child to sport and play, or even walk.

But despite its reversal of expectations as one reads beyond the title, "I Saw a Child" is a highly traditional piece of lyric verse. It is, above all, very regular in terms of rhythm and stanza form. It is fundamentally iambic, with an admixture of anapests, lines 1, 2, 5, and 6 of each stanza being tetrameters and the middle (shorter) two lines in each being dimeters. Several lines do not, in fact, start with a complete iambic foot; they are acephalous or headless lines (or catalectic ones), lacking the opening unstressed syllable that would make the initial foot fully iambic. This is not surprising, given the frequency of directive and imperative forms in the poem—"Stick with me," "Clutch my hand," "Don't let go," and so on. The repeated "Far from..." lines that open stanzas 3, 4, and 5 are also inevitably acephalous, in that the first word "far" has to be stressed. Here, as with the directives noted in the earlier text, metrical deviation is a consequence of phonological word stress and also of the semantic stress that is laid on these words and (in the case of the directives) on their grammatical form. The deviation is, however, well within the norms of traditional English versification. Indeed, the poem carries vague echoes of the rondeau, of the wide variety of six-line stanzas in English verse, or of the playful richness of line length and rhyme schemes that one finds in Donne's *Songs and Sonnets* ("Goe, and catch a falling starre... ," or "The Message," for example).

Stanza layout carries meaning with it too. The two shorter lines (lines 3 and 4 of each stanza) are inevitably highlighted, the instructions they give and the questions they ask being foregrounded by the graphical arrangement of lines. The relationship of line to syntax also strikes the reader. As in the opening poem of "A German Requiem," verse line and grammatical sentence usually overlap in "I Saw a Child." In the first two stanzas each line is a sentence; in the remaining three, this is true apart from the first two lines of each stanza, although in each case these two lines form a complete sentence. In "I Saw a Child" (as in "A German Requiem"), this technique gives a sense of directness, accessibility, a kind of simple austerity to the text. These are observations pulled from experience which must be given in a clear form; these are instructions which you must follow if you are to survive; they are simple questions ("Is this you? / Is this me?"), which demand that the addressee place himself/herself vis-à-vis the created world of the poem.

The rhyme scheme is predominantly quite regular in "I Saw a Child." In all stanzas, lines 1, 2, and 6 rhyme, although in stanza 3 "again" is really an eye-rhyme with "brain" and "pain" rather than a phonological one. In stanzas 1, 3, and 4, lines 4 and 5 rhyme, although in stanza 1 "go" and "cold" are examples of assonance, rather than full rhymes. In stanza 2, "path" and "bright," although graphically very different, almost chime in consonance. However, not even this is true of stanza 5, where lines 3, 4, and 5 stand out by their complete lack of any rhyme. Here foregrounding of the questions these lines contain, and of the dismal summation of "The fields are mined and the night is long" (line 29) may be the purpose of this marked lack of rhyme.

In "A German Requiem," I noted the prominent use of repetition and parallelism. The same can be observed in "I Saw a Child." Syntactically, the poem is composed of a few repeated patterns. These are:

1. "I saw"-type sentences which record the mental experiences of the speaker;
2. directives or imperatives giving advice or instructions to the addressee—"Stick with me," for example;
3. quasi-factual statements about the world, often (although not always) relational in form—for example, "The fields are mined and the moon is bright" (line 11);
4. questions—of which there are only two toward the poem's end, and which are highlighted by their deviance from the text's syntactic norms (and rhyme scheme).

If syntax is insistently parallel, so too is lexis. It is largely informal to neutral (perhaps only "the wisdom of the brain / blood / heart" [lines 13, 19, 25] shifts the formality level a little higher), again—as in "A German Requiem"—achieving a high degree of accessibility for the addressee. Lexis is, however, above all, strikingly repetitive and certain phrases echo throughout the text—"I saw a child," "Stick with / to," "The wind blows," "Clutch my hand / heart," "The fields are mined," "Far from the wisdom," "The Blue Vein River." Syntactic parallelism clearly emphasizes certain features of the poem: the speaker has observed specific phenomena; he knows specific things about the world; he has certain instructions to give you, and two very serious questions to put to you. The central features of the world he talks about are made clear through the repeated lexis—the child, the danger of the "fields," the river (which must be crossed?), the necessity of staying close to one's guide ("Stick with me," "Clutch my hand"), the unwisdom, the insanity of the world he talks of. As in "A German Requiem," lexis and syntax here seem to aim at a maximum ease of understanding, a maximum directness and clarity.

Another aspect of the speaker of "I Saw a Child" seems similar to that of the speaker in "A German Requiem." On one level, he, too, seems to be possessed of unusual and privileged knowledge (like the narrator of a Kipling ballad, for example, "The Ballad of East and West"). The parallel syntax of so much of the poem embodies this. The speaker has seen certain things ("I saw a child with silver hair," line 1); he knows about the state of the world ("The fields are mined and the wind blows cold," line 5); and he gives you advice about what to do ("Stick with me and I'll take you there," line 2). He is at least passing himself off as a guide to the dangerous fields that surround the Blue Vein River (itself an item of rather abstruse knowledge—is it a river in Cambodia, say, or a river from an invented landscape?). "Clutch my hand," "Stick to the path," "Stay with me," he urges, especially "when the shooting starts" (line 30). The knowledge he possesses is specialized and exotic; most British readers of the poem would not, one imagines, know what to do under those circumstances.

But do we trust him? The speaker in "I Saw a Child" is markedly more ambiguous than that in "A German Requiem." On one level, he sometimes fails to rhyme. The deviations from full rhyme noted in the earlier text—"go / cold" (lines 4 and 5), "brain / again" (lines 13 and 18)—and the failure to rhyme in stanza 5 might suggest something is not quite right with this speaker. In addition, the rather strange line in stanza 3, "Tell me we may be friends again" (line 18), might give the reader pause. Why did we stop being friends? Did he lead us astray once before? Indeed, on another level, we must be in some doubt as to who is speaking at certain points in the text, and to whom. Is there one speaker throughout? There is certainly no punctuation to suggest otherwise, but neither is there in Keats's "La Belle Dame Sans Merci" (where there are two speakers). Who says "Clutch my hand," and gives all the other instructions to stay close? Could it be the child? And if there is one speaker, whom is he addressing—the child, an unspecified addressee ("Is this you? / Is this me?" [lines 27 and 28]), or sometimes one, sometimes the other? And if it is the child, we come back to the disturbing "Tell me we may be friends again" (line 18) with its suggestions of past betrayal and failure. The ambiguities intrigue the reader, and enrich the poem.

The world of which the speaker, however ambiguous he may be, has knowledge in "I Saw a Child" shares certain features with that of "A German Requiem." It is a world of politics and recent history made material, a deeply hostile and dangerous world. "The fields are mined" (line 5), the speaker declares. "The Blue Vein River" (line 7) which we have to cross (one presumes) conjures up for the reader the conflicts of Southeast Asia between the 1950s and the present. Sooner or later "the shooting" (line 30) will start. The whole world that is evoked by the poem is one of danger and hostility—"the wind blows cold" (line 5), the river is "broad and deep" (line 7) (and therefore hard to cross), "branches creak," "shadows leap" (line 8), "the moon is bright" (line 11) (presumably not good if you wish to cross enemy territory by night), a child reaches "from the mud" (line 20) and is "torn apart" (line 26), the "night is long" (line 29) (a night of waiting, a night spent crossing dangerous terrain?). And the danger and hostility are, one assumes, connected with the politics that surround the poem's world. Only for the refugee in flight in a place of war do all these elements become menacing. Is this world an apocalyptic one like that of "A German Requiem"? Perhaps in part it is. The child of the opening line has "silver hair," and we learn in stanza 2 that it "will never sleep" (line 12). These features certainly make the child rather sinister and emblematic, a haunting spirit rather than a real child, although its sufferings are real enough. A strange Christ-child come to judge? Is the Blue Vein River a river of death? Certainly, the landscape of the poem is a damned and unforgiving one. The "shooting" is inevitable.

"Cut-Throat Christ: or the New Ballad of the Dosi Pares"

"Cut-Throat Christ: or the New Ballad of the Dosi Pares" (like "I Saw a Child" from the *Out of Danger* collection) possesses many similar features to the two poems discussed in the earlier text (Fenton 1993, 50–54). The subtitle aligns itself firmly with a traditional genre by declaring itself to be a "New Ballad," while the "Dosi Pares" of the remainder of the subtitle is the embodiment of a kind of specialized and exotic knowledge that the speaker of the poem possesses. In fact, this phrase, like several others, has to be explained in a note at the volume's end. (There we are told that the *dosi pares* are the Twelve Peers of Charlemagne, who form the subject of Tagalog ballads in the Philippines.)

The text of "Cut-Throat Christ" itself is at once very traditional and at the same time standing at an oblique angle to that tradition. It does not follow traditional English ballad form, either in rhyme scheme, rhythmic pattern, or stanza form. And yet it echoes the ballad so clearly. (In fact, many ballads, both traditional and literary, deviate substantially from the paradigmatic tetrameter–trimeter–tetrameter–trimeter / abcb pattern.) "Cut-Throat Christ" is composed of four-line stanzas, rhyming aabb, with a refrain inserted intermittently. There are usually four main stresses in each line, and the lines are frequently anapestic although there is a great deal of irregularity. For example, in line 7 the rhythm changes from anapestic to iambic, and in line 8 it is rather unclear how one is meant to read the line, as one can make it have four, five, or even six main stresses. There are numerous lines where the number of weak stresses attached to a strong stress make it difficult to talk about traditional accentual-syllabic categories of iambs and anapests, and make one want rather to refer to the even more traditional accentual meters of Anglo-Saxon verse and folk and nursery rhymes. Examples of such lines are: "And when I brought my *beinte-nuebe* for the boss to see" (stanza 7, line 27); "So I go barefoot down to Quiapo and the streets are packed" (stanza 23, line 89); and, "And General Ching, the EPD, the senatorial bets" (stanza 25, line 99). To maintain the four-main-stress pattern of the poem here, one must place the first main stress in the first example on "brought," in the second on "foot," and in the third on "Ching." This clearly involves having a large number of weak stresses preceding the main stress, in a way that barely fits in with normal scansion, but in a way that is quite acceptable in folk or nursery rhyme. This kind of irregularity gives the poem an authentically rough feel, the sort of effect Coleridge aims at by using fourth line dimeters rather than trimeters at various points in "The Rime of the Ancient Mariner." This sense of genuine roughness (one associates folk-tradition products like ballads with an unpolished quality) is augmented by shifting word stress in order to rhyme fully. Thus, in stanza 3, "fraternity" must be pronounced with the stress on the final syllable, as opposed to the second syllable, in order to rhyme fully (and to avoid being an anisobaric rhyme). The same is true in stanza 12 with the rhymes "flee" and "military" (lines 47 and 48). Thus, although "Cut-Throat Christ" does not follow a classic ballad pattern in rhythm and rhyme, it clearly echoes traditional balladic forms, albeit in oblique ways. It is, after all, a "New Ballad" and one—at least professedly—from a non-English and non-European cultural context.

The speaker of the ballad, his world, and his language all allow one to identify "Cut-Throat Christ" further with a ballad tradition. Ballads often depict the violent deeds of outlaw figures, their depredations and betrayals. "Cut-Throat Christ" follows this model closely. The speaker and protagonist is a minor Manila gangster (a "punk"); the story material of the ballad involves his betrayal of his gang leader and his own betrayal by the authorities. The action is clearly set in a world of crime and violent deeds. In addition, the narrative has some of the ellipses, the sudden jumps in action that are associated with traditional ballads. For example, the speaker's career as a gangster is almost entirely omitted, as is his agreement to betray his boss to the police. The language, too, is a highly informal one, as one might expect from a quasi-folk-product. Lexis such as "kids" (for children), "momma," "rich bitch," "there aint" [sic], "this guy says," "squeal" (for inform), "ran like fuck," "Cos," and much more is obviously very informal, indeed colloquial with elements of criminal argot to boot. In addition, there are a few items of lexis which are clearly rooted in the world of Filipino crime, some of which are explained in notes—"*beinte-nuebe*" (a kind of knife), "plenty stainless" (gin), "long necks" (bottles of spirits), the "EPD" (not explained in notes, but presumably a department of the Manila police), and the "Black Nazarene" (a statue of Christ favored by the Manila criminal fraternity). Once again, the effect aimed at is one of an authentic product of a demotic tradition, although one should note here also that the speaker is, like those in "A German Requiem" and "I Saw a Child," a knowledgeable figure, and behind him stands the figure of the text's implied author, who is able to explain what he will not. The knowledgeability of the poem's speaker is not just access to an arcane argot, but is also expressed in his generic statements about the world, as in the text's refrain.

> *There's a Christ for a whore and a Christ for a punk*
> *A Christ for a pickpocket and a drunk*
> *There's a Christ for every sinner but one thing there aint –*
> *There aint no Christ for any cutprice saint.*
> (lines 13–16, 33–36, 53–56, 81–84)

Mutatis mutandis, a neoclassical poet could scarcely be more apodictic, more sure of his knowledge of the world.

The world of which the gangster of "Cut-Throat Christ" has knowledge compares closely with those of "A German Requiem" and "I Saw a Child." Here, too, it is a world of politics, things, violence, and danger—of knives, murder, rich ladies, bottles of gin, the Manila Superhighway, political candidates ("the senatorial bets"), Armalite rifles, and the EPD. The poem's speaker and protagonist has to negotiate a world as dangerous as the mined fields of "I Saw a Child" or the dreadful mid-century history of Germany in "A German Requiem." You have to choose between General Ching or Jesus, who in this poem is not Christ, but a Manila gangster boss. However, in the last line of the stanza, the speaker turns to the Black Nazarene, a statue of Christ which, according to Fenton's notes, is an object of a cult, particularly among criminals, in Manila. In the poem's last six stanzas, its protagonist seeks refuge in Quiapo, the statue's home. Here all the figures, and some more, of the poem are gathered together in a procession to honor the statue.

> And there's the man who killed the Carmelites, the Tad-tad gang,
> The man who sells the Armalites in Alabang
> And General Ching, the EPD, the senatorial bets,
> The twelve disciples and the drum majorettes. ...(lines 93–96)

I do not think it overinterpretation to see an apocalyptic element here. All Manila seems to be on the street, all the speaker's world at least, walking in a procession to honor a dark god, who is able to "crush them to eternity" at any moment (line 88). It is at least a *danse macabre*, or even a parade of souls at the Last Judgment. The speaker's last words reinforce this. "Cut-Throat Christ," he calls, "don't turn your back on me" (line 104).

"Rain"

"Rain" is the last poem in Fenton's most recent collection, *Yellow Tulips* (2012, 164), and thus assumes a privileged position in the *œuvre* to date. It differs from the poems discussed in the earlier text in its lack of overt political and historical focus. It is short and modest, yet it demonstrates great craftsmanship and the ability that Fenton possesses to tease powerful resonances out of modest moments and means. Only seven lines long, it a short and enigmatic piece, representative of a recurring tendency in Fenton's work. (See, for example, the discussion of "I Saw a Child" in the earlier text.) Rain falls on the sea and on some seafarers. How many seafarers are there? Where is the boat? It is distant from land, but how distant? When is this happening—now, or long in the past? Where are the voyagers going? They have "torn" hands and "channelled" faces. Their sail is "torn" and they collect water in a pail. Are they shipwrecked? Are they lost? Are they fleeing something? The situation, whatever it is, seems bad. The rain that falls on them is "sweet." This is repeated twice. It brings some kind of relief, some hope of survival; it means the voyage can continue. The mariners' faces are channeled, and so is the sea. Is it torn by the wind? Is it full of dangerous currents? Is a heavy swell beginning?

Technically, the poem strikes a fine balance between order and disorder, and, thus, perhaps between danger and hope. Lines are irregular in length, varying from 4 to 10 syllables. But lines 3 and 5 are 10 syllables long each and symmetrically enclose a central fourth line (the shortest) of four syllables, which itself consists of two iambs. However, rhythm and meter are irregular too, and, indeed, some lines—lines 1, 3, and 5—are difficult to scan satisfactorily. Nevertheless, there is an iambic skeleton to the poem. Six clear iambs occur, and the phrase "their channelled faces" is close to being iambic—an iamb and amphibrach linked in one semantic unit—but just misses it. The last line contains three iambs, which are quite difficult to separate. Again, one wants to ask questions. Is this the triumphant swell of the waves? Will they take the travelers to safety or overwhelm them?

Phonological orchestration is strong, but local: /s/ in line 1; /f/ in line 2; /t/ in line 3; /l/ in line 4; /s/ and /r/ in line 6. There is no strongly consistent sound pattern except a repetition of /s/, perhaps appropriate for a benign rainfall, but a sweet sound balanced by the harsher /r/ and /t/ sounds that also weave through the text. Rhyme, too, is unsettling and odd. Lines 2 and 3—"land/hands"—almost rhyme, but not quite, as do lines 5 and 6—"sky/eyes." Lines 1 and 7 do not properly rhyme, as "sea" is simply repeated, and, in any case, at some distance. Line 4 has internal consonance—"fill/pail"—not rhyme as such. Everything is just a little off.

The poem is modest, but very powerful in its enigmatic purview. The sea voyage has long carried a strong resonance in European literatures. Coleridge's Ancient Mariner knew the saving power of the rain (see part V), but that voyage certainly did not end well. Will this one?

Conclusion

The four poems discussed show considerable differences, but also substantial similarities. The first three take up exotic, non-British subjects—German history, the landscape of flight and war, Manila's underworld—and all have a knowledgeable guide to those worlds. Although the poems' speakers are not without ambiguous qualities (and in "Cut-Throat Christ" he is, of course, a murderer and traitor), they do possess a lot of recondite knowledge which they pass on to the poems' readers. They do so in a language which is relatively accessible, and when its informality shifts into argot, the implied author is ready with a glossary. Poetic forms are traditional—the requiem, the rhyming lyric, the ballad—as is what one might call the poems' rhetoric, patterns of parallelism and repetition, which emphasize features of the texts' worlds and, indeed, the speakers' view of that world. These worlds are worlds of a particular and consistent configuration—of "things" in a broad sense (houses, streets, bombs, mines, rifles, knives, bottles of gin, the realia of life in Manila), of politics and history. And it is a deeply dangerous world; the fields are mined, the bombs fall, the gangsters and the EPD seek you out. Deeply specific worlds, they carry nevertheless a resonance beyond themselves. Forgetting a dark history might not only be a necessity and temptation for mid-twentieth-century Germans; refugees cross minefields not only in Southeast Asia; gang bosses and the EPD make life miserable in places beyond Manila. These worlds, too, have apocalyptic notes to them—in the cataclysm of mid-century German history, in the "child with silver hair," and in a quasi-Last Judgment in a district of Manila.

The poems offer little comfort in all this; one's guides are somewhat compromised themselves. "Stick with me when the shooting starts," one of them says. But would you trust him?

In "Rain," the speaker offers little information, although he presumably does know who the voyagers are, where they are going, and what chances they have. But their trip, in a poem published in 2012, has to strike echoes of the situation of refugees fleeing on small boats from cataclysm and brutality. The reader can decide whom to refer these seafarers to. Cubans? Vietnamese? Syrians? Somalis? Here, there is no guide, and not much promise of success, only the "sweet rain" that can keep you going a little longer over a dangerous sea. Perhaps Burt (1995, 46, 50) would call this poem parasitic and lacking in world view. Others might call it humane. Others—like myself—might also lack a redemptive *Weltanschauung* in the face of the idiocies, brutalities, and lies of the twentieth and twenty-first centuries, of which Fenton seems such a potent and sophisticated recorder and judge.

Note

1 Earlier and different versions of this essay appeared in Polish in Malcolm (2002) and in English in Malcolm (2003).

References

Burt, Stephen (1995). "Rap for People Who Don't Listen to Rap, or, James Fenton: Poet into Pop Star." *Thumbscrew* 2 (Spring): 44–51.

Corcoran, Neil (2001). "James Fenton." In: *Contemporary Poets*, 7e (ed. Thomas Riggs), 357–359. Detroit etc.: St. James Press.

Fenton, James (1983). *The Memory of War and Children in Exile: Poems 1968–1983*. Harmondsworth: Penguin.

Fenton, James (1993). *Out of Danger: Poems*. Harmondsworth: Penguin.

Fenton, James (2012). *Yellow Tulips: Poems 1968–2011*. London: Faber and Faber.

Gioia, Dana (2003). *Barrier of a Common Language: An American Looks at Contemporary British Poetry*. Ann Arbor: University of Michigan Press.

Levi, Peter (1991). *The Art of Poetry: The Oxford Lecture, 1984–1989*. New Haven and London: Yale University Press.

Lowery, Owen (2013). Review of *Yellow Tulips*. *Stand* 12.2: 91–94.

Malcolm, David (2002). "'Trzymaj się mnie, gdy zacznie się strzelanina': Przewodnicy, tradycje, rzeczy i apokalipsy w poezji Jamesa Fentona." In: *Eseje o współczesnej poezji brytyjskiej i irlandzkiej, volume 3* (ed. David Malcolm), 126–141. Gdańsk: Gdańsk University Press.

Malcolm, David (2003). "'Stick with Me and I'll Take You There': The Speaker and History in the Poetry of James Fenton." *Acta Neophilogica* 5: 175–185.

McGuiness, Patrick (2012). "Where Poetry Belongs." Review of *Yellow Tulips*. *Guardian Review* (8 September): 14.

O'Brien, Sean (2003). "Contemporary British Poetry." In: *A Companion to Twentieth-Century Poetry* (ed. Neil Roberts), 571–584. Malden, MA, and Oxford: Blackwell.

Pollard, Natalie (2016). "Stretching the Lyric: The Anthology Wars, Martianism and After." In: *The Cambridge Companion to British Poetry, 1945–2010* (ed. Edward Larrissy), 99–115. Cambridge: Cambridge University Press.

Prestwich, Edmund (2012). "Review of *Yellow Tulips*." *The North* 50: 102–105.

Schmidt, Michael (1989). *Reading Modern Poetry*. London/New York: Routledge.

Wilmer, Clive (1994). "Dismay in Love and War." Review of *Out of Danger*. *Poetry Review* 83.4: 54–55.

3.5
Bill Griffiths

Ian C. Davidson

Bill Griffiths's work and life are characterized by diversity and mobility. He was always on the move, whether geographically from London to Seaham, in a poetic practice between forms and topics, or in the broader ranges of a working life that included being an archivist, dialectician, publisher, musician, translator, storyteller, and local historian. This characteristic of movement is matched by his deployment of poetic forms that often use the space of the page or the variability of live performance to position themselves between indeterminate readings, and between languages and registers, creating poems that challenge notions of authorship and of an authoritative reader. These shifting textual variations are typical of a writer who sustained a mobile relationship vis-à-vis mainstream society, living in squats in London, as a guest worker in Germany, and in a houseboat, before settling in Seaham in County Durham in North East England.

Griffiths was born in 1948 and brought up in London, the son of a schoolteacher father and a mother who was a civil servant and an orchestral musician. He died in Seaham, County Durham in 2007. As a poet he was most readily identified with the British Poetry Revival and the London experimental poetry scene through his association with, among others, Bob Cobbing and Eric Mottram. His immediate peers in the 1970s and 1980s included those involved with the Writers Forum Workshops such as cris cheek, Paula Claire, Clive Fencott, Allen Fisher, John Muckle, Lawrence Upton, Geraldine Monk, and many others. A combined interest in the material text and its performance was to form an important part of his work, although his deep historical interests, particularly in Anglo-Saxon culture, also marked his work.

A Companion to Contemporary British and Irish Poetry, 1960–2015, First Edition.
Edited by Wolfgang Görtschacher and David Malcolm.
© 2021 John Wiley & Sons Ltd. Published 2021 by John Wiley & Sons Ltd.

He was identified as an ex-Hells Angel and a former member of the Uxbridge Nomads motorcycle group (he wore "colours" long after he sold his motorcycle), before he studied to take an undergraduate degree and then a PhD in Anglo-Saxon, completed in 1987, at King's College London. Although he was never to speak positively of his experience at university (see Lancaster 2014, 17), his writing often portrays a Saxon world over which the Norman conquest is only a superficial veneer.[1] He also published extensively within Anglo-Saxon studies, and extended that interest to producing versions of early medieval Welsh poetry, including the *Gododdin* (1974) and *Llywarch Hen* (1978). Griffiths's work is firmly located within a British context, and sits outside many of the transatlantic interests of those (most notably Eric Mottram) who were also part of the British Poetry Revival.

For Griffiths, there are formal relations between life and work that transcend normal biographical analysis. The relationships between his life, the poetry, and its methods of publication and distribution are structural as well as coincidental, and the result of a combination of economic necessity and esthetic choice. He was fundamentally anti-establishment, an anarchist, deeply critical of the Labour party in Durham and a strong supporter of the miners' cause during the Miners' Strike of 1984–1985. The forms of the poetry and the circulation of multiple versions of the same poem similarly undermine and challenge any notion of authority, whether that provided by the publisher, author, critic, or expert. His publications, often from his own press, draw on the materiality of manuscript culture, of single varying versions, as well as an idea of print that relates as much to the political pamphlet as it does to the mass circulation printed text.

His publications are extensive. Much of his poetry from 1966 to 1996 is now collected in three significant volumes, *Collected Earlier Poems (1966–1980)* (2010), *Collected Poems and Sequences (1981–1991)* (2014), and *Collected Poems Volume 3 (1992–1996)* (2016). There remains a large quantity of uncollected work in poetry, essay form, and prose fiction, as well as additional major scholarly publications such as his dialect dictionaries. Griffiths also ran two small presses, Pirate Press from 1971 to 1980, and Amra Imprint from 1989 (the year he moved to the North East of England) until his death in 2007. These presses mainly published Griffiths's own work, and—to give some indication of scale—there are 11 separate publications of Griffiths's work by the Pirate Press in 1973, and 14 separate publications by his Amra Imprint in 1993 alone. These range from poetic texts (*Joanne's Book*) to local history (*Seaham: A Provisional Bibliography*) and essays on prison reform. Through Pirate and Amra, Griffiths occasionally published work by others, either alone or in collaboration, including Jeremy Adler, Steve Clewes, Ian Davidson, John Muckle, Geraldine Monk, and Tom Pickard. Printed in small editions, often with additions such as hand-colored covers, and often in a number of editions that had differences between them, Pirate and Amra publications were distributed through his own mailing list of readers, through readings and small press events, and later through websites. Griffiths claimed, with some pride, to know nothing of marketing, and was certainly more comfortable within a radical counterculture of contempt for the market than in following more mainstream patterns of textual production and distribution. However, he was also very effective in building websites for himself and others.

The recycling and repetition that we find in his poems, where lines from poems or entire short poems are used again to generate new texts, carry over into the process of publication. Some of the work from Pirate Press and Amra Imprint were later published in more substantial collections with larger scale publishers, although these were still often those which were marginal to mainstream literary activity and specialized in experimental or innovative poetries. Major selections of his work appeared in his lifetime with Coach House (1984), Etruscan (1999), Talus (1998 and 2001), West House Books (2002), and Salt (2002), as well as one excursion into more mainstream publishing with Paladin (1992). The challenge of editing Griffiths's poetry, and producing "authoritative" collected poems from the small publications, and selecting one text from the many variations of some of his best known poems and sequences such as "Cycles," is documented by Alan Halsey, the foremost bibliographic scholar on Griffiths (Halsey 2007, 2010, 2014). Griffiths also wrote short stories, often ghost stories based in Seaham. These were principally published through Amra, alongside pamphlets presenting histories of the region made up of information gathered from Durham archives. His dialect dictionaries, the result of his work with the Centre for Northern Studies at Northumbria University, gained considerable recognition and led to appearances on national television. In this chapter, I provide bibliographical information for his major publications, but I would urge readers to seek out his pamphlets and broadsheets, in which his work was often first published. The attention given by Griffiths to the material and esthetic qualities of these publications offers different contexts within which to read them.

Critical work on Griffiths's poetry is mainly gathered in two publications, *The Salt Companion to Bill Griffiths* edited by William Rowe (2007) and a special issue of *The Journal of British and Irish Innovative Poetry* edited by Ian Davidson (2014). Both contain a range of historical accounts, scholarly essays, and personal reminiscence, but there is little overlap between them. There are also important studies of Griffiths's work by Clive Bush in *Out of Dissent* and by Robert Sheppard in *The Poetry of Saying* (2005). Griffiths's work also features extensively in Ian Davidson's *Ideas of Space in Contemporary Poetry* (2007) and in Andrew Duncan's *The Failure of Conservatism in Modern British Poetry* (2003). Rowe's *Companion* contains an important bibliography by Doug Jones, based to some extent on Griffiths's own bibliographic records which he kept on disk, and although Halsey's editing has amended some aspects of that bibliography, it remains a very useful starting point for understanding the range of Griffiths's work.

Griffiths's earliest published poems, mostly through Writers Forum but also in *Poetry Review* during the editorship of Eric Mottram between 1971 and 1977, and then by his own Pirate Press, frequently refer to his experiences in motorcycle gangs. These poems form a major part of the first half of the *Collected Earlier Poems*. The longest group of texts, at just under 40 pages, is the "Cycle" poems, a title that combines reference to a motorbike, to a song cycle, and to the story cycle of a saga. The themes of the "Cycle," motorcycling, the law, and structures of power, first appear in "Black Mass" (Griffiths 2010, 26–27), while those of mobility and domesticity are seen in the short sequence "1–7" (48–49). The 16 poems of the "Cycle" (64–103), some with subtitles, use a jagged trochaic rhythm that combines some of the qualities of the orality of the saga with an experimental modernist free-verse page, an esthetic that echoes the interests of Writers Forum in the relationship between the materialism of the text, its graphic qualities, and its performance. The poems frequently link motorcycling, the law, and prison. They are all located in a Britain that is characterized not by traditional "Englishness," but by a diversity of modern and archaic languages. In the poems, language, syntax, and form combine past and present. It is a Britain in which history is always present, and in which the sources of cultural and economic power are always actively engaged in the subject of the poetry. The "Cycle" of poems is given a form of completion in a later return of the term, in "Paracycle" (170–177), a poem that is based in domesticity and family life. It is a place where subjectivity becomes more realized than in the moving bodies and landscapes of the "Cycle" poems, and where it is "Years since I'm thinking about / Vanishing, that is / Absolute vanishing" (Griffiths 2010, 171). It is still, however, a temporary place where the speaker is "[...] waiting for all things to sort themselves out." All he can do by the end is engage in a routine of masculine domesticity and "explain the fan-heater to Graham" (177). The law is also constantly present, and "Paracycle" is informed by a Foucauldian notion of a disciplinary power that uses historical precedent and modern surveillance to invade all aspects of contemporary life, both private and public. Griffiths might appear to live outside commodification, with the exception of the occasional motorcycle brand, but cannot live outside processes of law.

Two other important sequences draw on experiences of motorcycling. "Sixteen Poems for Vic the Gypsy, Bob and Others" (Griffiths 2010, 107–110) is a first-person narrative that begins with a reference to the abbey of Rievaulx in Yorkshire and ends with an "Angel" who "woz run into the cells / to fight hisself" (110). In between, the poem captures the romance of the "run" as seen from the back of a motorcycle in a Britain in which the law is never far behind, whether the law of poetry in the strict form of the rondeau, or the confines of a cell (see Hampson 2007). "War W. Windsor" (Griffiths 2010, 113–128) appears as the most specifically autobiographical of the poems in the volume. It begins with a text for "4 Voices," which operates as a visual and oral cut-up, splicing in and collaging phrases from other poems and creating new combinations of the texts through their spatial arrangement on the page. The four columns create a visual text that implies four voices, but, at times, these blur into each other, and the multiple margins slide across to create a further irregularity. Two first-person sections of the sequence are arranged into prose paragraphs, with the first, "Into Prison" (117–118), providing a powerful narrative of incarceration and its dehumanizing qualities, and the second, "War W. Windsor Text 5" (124–127), giving an extended narrative of the battles between motorcycle gangs, supported by references to newspaper articles as a kind of evidence. Other poems cut in Romany words, and sometimes a translation is provided. The sequence is extremely powerful, and deeply emotional, expressing an articulate rage at the misuse of power. Any arrival of the "Angels" was, as Griffiths says, frequently catastrophic, and they were most comfortable when they were between places. The place of arrival was also, frequently, prison.

These poems remain a unique record in British culture and counterculture, simultaneously celebrating and providing a critique of a search for liberation that often led to incarceration, while refusing to romanticize those involved. The poetics, that is the language and its organization into lines, stanzas, poems, and sequences, has no parallels. Although extended critical debate is still developing with regard to Griffiths's work, these early poems are frequently used as an example of his method and his poetics (see Rowe (2007), Bush (1997), Halsey (2007), and Davidson (2007, 2014) as examples). The startling rhythms and unexpected syntax produce a poetry that is not only about the experience of motorcycling, but also reflects its unpredictability. Griffiths kept returning to this material, revisiting it in *Bikers* (written with John Muckle 1990), in which his poem "Speedway" is probably the most celebratory of his motorcycling poems, albeit describing a journey that is going nowhere, and finally in *Tyne Txts* (written with Tom Pickard 2003).

The breadth of Griffiths's historical interests is found in the form, subject matter, and the rhetoric of some early poems. "The Gesta Alfredi: Rex Anglie" (Griffiths 2010, 145–152) begins in prose paragraphs, before turning to verse for "Alfred's Songs," although this is a verse which lacks punctuation and in which gaps appear within the lines. Further sections use a number of visual techniques including varied typefaces and unconventional capitalization. A number of "praise poems" echo those of medieval court poetry as well as religious poetry, and provide an opportunity to reassess the work of Justice Melford Stevenson, a judge who was either eccentric or vicious, according to perspective, and who sentenced a member of the Angry Brigade to 15 years in prison (Carr 2010, 120). Other poems, such as "Six Walks Around Tenby" (158–159), explore the British landscape, although never in a romantic or reductive sense, but rather in ways that combine a broad spatial awareness with a deep historical sensibility. A poem in six sections, each one representing a "walk," it contains a description of a picture of a mermaid, a numbered series of observations about hitchhiking, a section in French about neighboring Manorbier, and a pastoral description of a walk that spins out to Tyre and Sidon. This is no picture postcard, or view from above, however, but rather a fragmented form that allows the speaker (Griffiths) to combine varieties of information he has gathered. His approach to another place, Colchester, is similar ("Encomium Urbis: Colchester," 160). Written in increasingly disjointed phrases, the poem is made up of a series of direct observations, which take in varying uses and histories, military and marine histories, and the speaker's own experiences as a motorcyclist passing through the landscape. Place is important to Griffiths, but he has more the tortured view of John Clare and the social conscience of Blake than any measured or apparently neutral contemplation that can control facts. The perspective is multiple, the flow of information is unchecked, and apparently unfiltered.

Griffiths's second volume of collected poems, *Collected Poems and Sequences 1981–1991* (Griffiths 2014), follows a similar structure and is made up of a number of sections, corresponding to individual publications. The range of material is also similarly broad, as is the variety of poetic forms. The opening "Further Songs & Dances of Death" (Griffiths 2014, 11–16) takes its cue from Calvocoressi's biography of Mussorgsky to write four "numbers" on four different themes. Written in two sets, the first is made up of four prose paragraphs, each one consisting of short phrases that are either numbered to indicate speakers or are separated with a "-." The second set is in more familiar free verse, although with words broken across the end of the line, non-standard capitalization, and archaic spellings. The opening lines are every bit as powerful as those of "Cycle":

> chal-ked cave
> [...]
> the stunt viaduct en
> a loop iz the stomach. (14)

The corresponding sequences not only establish connections between their elements but also between the two sets, in meditations on death and the body that take in the Russian fairy tale of Anika and also construct an underworld. Mythologies are further drawn on throughout this second volume, but perhaps more explicitly in "A Book of Legends *incorporating* Quire Book" (193–225). First published by Writers Forum and Amra Imprint in 1991, it includes references to the Zoroastrian Mazda, to Zakar-Baal, the king of Byblos, to the Sun God Ra, to Jason and the Argonauts, and to the Tjeker, one of the "sea-peoples" expelled from Egypt. Some poems appear to be reworkings of historical material, although no sources are given. Others, such as "Sherds" (204–206), appear to comment on the process of constructing a world from the fragments of information that have survived, fragments that become bricks for constructing houses.

These mythologies continue another significant theme of this second volume of his poems, that of seafaring. Unable to afford a house in London, Griffiths bought a houseboat made from an ex-lifeboat, a vessel he described as "notoriously thin-hulled" (Rowe 2007, 186), and which was subsequently set on fire and destroyed when being repaired in Uxbridge. Some papers were burnt, and while among the poetry community there was a common understanding that significant material was lost, Griffiths himself was to remark later, in a note on an unpublished list of performances provided by Paula Claire, that "not much of value was lost ... ended up with books, music and mss singed neatly all round the edge." It appears that Griffiths lived on the houseboat, which he named the *Cimmerian*, for about 2 years, and then, after spending a further 2 years visiting Brightlingsea in Essex, he moved to North East England and bought a "Tyneside flat" in Seaham. It is fitting that the name of the boat should refer to the lost peoples called the Cimmerians, as well as the historical antecedents of the Welsh or the "Cymry." In many ways, the boat comes to replace the motorcycle of the first volume of the collected poems as a metaphor for a way of living and experiencing society, culture, and the landscape, and one that challenged more usual and controlled patterns of human movement and engagement. A long sequence, entitled "The Book of the Boat: Inland- and Blue-water Texts" (Griffiths 2014, 73–102), gives details of a number of boat trips and boat-related excursions. The poetics, as usual, challenge the process of reading, and "Moving the Boat" (78) is marked out in staves and as a text for three voices, while "The Rabbit Hunt" (79–83) is a long narrative that sits somewhere between a dramatic text, a prose narrative, and a poem. In this sequence, Griffiths refers specifically to the burning of his boat at Uxbridge Boat Centre (84), and includes a number of "logs" of journeys both in prose paragraphs and in short numbered and fragmented "sea shanties." The coast and the sea, normally that of South East England, also appear in *Morning Lands* (1990) and in his work located on the North East English coast after his move to Seaham.

Collected Poems and Sequences (1981–1991) not only represents a shift from the motorcycle to the boat, but it also provides evidence of a growing interest in philosophy as a subject for poetry, with extended treatments of the ideas of Plotinus and Darwin. The Plotinus sequence (137–149) contains four extended meditations on particular themes in the writer's philosophy, while the Darwin sequence (151–191) contains a much broader range of material, and is made up either implicitly or explicitly of "dialogues," in which the implications of Darwin's ideas are explored. Darwin is variously in conversation with Josiah Wedgwood, his wife, a finch, and a sea captain, among others. These are deeply scholarly works that demonstrate a facility with complex philosophical notions, which Griffiths relentlessly interrogates. While these texts might struggle to find a wide readership, they are brilliant examples of the ways that poetry, and writing more generally, might seek out appropriate forms for reworking complex and familiar ideas. Although sometimes characterized as obscure, and using a range of references that bewilder the reader, Griffiths is also always keen to connect with an audience. "Darwin's Dialogues," in particular, can be seen as a way of popularizing the ideas of Darwin and making them accessible to a broader readership. That its methods of publication and distribution make this unlikely is an irony that does not eradicate the intention.

Collected Poems Volume 3 (1992–1996) was again edited by Halsey and published in 2016. That this 500-page book collects work from just 5 years demonstrates the intense stimulation and inspiration Griffiths derived from his time in the North East of England. While some themes are familiar, such as prison and prisoners, they receive different kinds of treatment.[2] In poems and poem sequences such as "Delvan's Book" (149–166), "Star Fish Jail" (190–210), and "Liam's Song" (211–220), the voice of the prisoner, which is explicitly not the voice of the poet, often tells the story. On the title page of the second edition of the pamphlet version of *Star Fish Jail* (1993a), the name of the pamphlet is preceded by "Bill Griffiths Presents," a suggestion that his role is more facilitator of production and distribution rather than author. In a (mainly) prose pamphlet not included in the *Collected Poems Volume 3*, *Seventy-Six Day Wanno, Mississippi and Highpoint Journal*, the text is described as "from the work of D. R. MacIntosh and Bill Griffiths" (n.d. but material inside is dated 1993). It is made up of journal entries, copies of handwritten letters, and lineated text with no specified origin and more poetic expression. In email correspondence, Halsey refers to it as a "documentary" work, that he did not feel able to include in a *Collected Poems*, a decision made easier by Griffiths' recycling the more poetic elements of the work in other sequences. (See Roberts 2018 for a more detailed description and consideration of the different editions of this work). In these works, Griffiths has moved from those earlier descriptions of prison in "Cycles," where, as Halsey says in the introduction, "the speaker or persona is unidentified and thus easily mistaken for the poet himself" (Griffiths 2016, 5). Halsey later goes on to say in email correspondence that although "'Cycles' is usually read as if autobiography, which it certainly isn't" (07/07/2018), in these later works Griffiths is explicitly drawing on the voices of others.

Incarceration, for Griffiths, is a method of social control enacted through the architecture of prisons and the imposed behaviors of a prison system that is deeply dehumanizing. He befriended a number of prisoners, and became involved in campaigning to correct miscarriages of justice. The records of this work and his correspondence with prisoners form a significant part of his published output in the

1990s, and the poems set his concern with notions of liberation in a much wider contemporary context through the use of individual accounts and broader historical analyses. Poems about prison in *Volume 3* begin with "Review of Brian Greenaway and Notes from Delvan MacIntosh" (Griffiths 2016, 85–104; Griffiths 1993b). Brian Greenaway was a Hell's Angel who converted to Christianity while in prison, and published a memoir of his experiences. This is the book Griffiths reviews, and in which Greenaway describes a form of rebirth:

> All the frustration and anger that held me as a prisoner began to drain away through my feet. At the same time it was just as though a hole opened up in my head and God's love began pouring in. For the first time I was experiencing real love and it was God's pure love.
>
> (Greenaway 1982, 92)

The first part of the review poem is written in the voice of Greenaway. Reminiscent of "Cycles" in parts, it presents the excitement and romance of the nomadic motorcycling life of the Hell's Angel:

> Rap-pa-pa-pa.
> The bike talking to me.
> I too was born with a full language (have never known anything else).
> With foot and wrist I match the best of the bike.
> It supposes one mind between us.
>
> (Griffiths 2016, 89)

This fusion between bike and rider provides the means of escape from inclusion in a society that seemed to always mean betrayal and where "half my wages" are paid "as rent" (87). The link between rider and machine is forcibly broken when "the chromed fare messenger of my muscles lammed straight into a / road block" (89). The process of sentencing and incarceration is one in which the sound of the bike recedes and Greenaway's outlaw identity is removed, preparing him for his Christian rebirth, as "I was stripped of my lid and boots" (90) and "bits (badges) [were] torn off the leather," and his possessions were "turned into lists" (90–91). Nameless, he is given the role of leader by the prison guards ("if I didn't keep the guys in line / ... / it was me for punishment" (94)), one that he subverted through a switch from enforcer to spiritual leader. Greenaway's book, the one under review, spends considerable time describing the social and family conditions that produced the violent Hell's Angel who became Christian, and a process of rebirth that was also a process of renaming, a christening and a baptism:

> He
> Called us a new name
> which the mouth of the lord shall name. (95)

As a review, it is a strange text that takes Greenaway's memoir, a co-written conventional narrative that draws on the pulp fiction genre of biker novels and the rhetoric of conversion, to construct a poem that transcends the memoir in profundity if not in emotional range. Greenaway's book might be easy to dismiss, but it is strangely moving and, finally, convincing. It is, however, a review in which Griffiths quite clearly uses the eyes of someone else to see the world. The story and its subject is Greenaway. The text is made even more strange by its juxtaposition to "Notes from Delvan MacIntosh," who features in a number of other publications, and was "a friend of a friend" of Griffiths (Griffiths 2016, 86). While some of the material might clearly be records of events related by MacIntosh in his own voice, other sections of the poem are more complex and poetic and less straightforward first-person narrative. "Notes" begins with a section addressed to "STEVE AND PAUL" that relates in first person the robbery of the one-armed bandit at "BURGERKING." MacIntosh is arrested during the robbery and dragged out by the police, suffering injuries. The suggestion from both the title and text is that these "notes" are a text that Griffiths has transcribed. Toward the end of the first page, the narrative concludes with:

>   ALL KNEE MINE GASHED
>   HOW THE FUCK CAN I WALK?
>   TAKE YOU TO THE TOMBS. (98)

The homogeneity of the presentation in capital letters, and a layout that does not use the left-hand margin as its starting point but draws the poem together as a single visual image, conceals sudden shifts in tone, perspective, and vocabulary. From a first-person narrative of an actual event in the distinctive voice of another that we assume to be MacIntosh, the poem shifts on that last line above. Another question mark might bind the lines together, as if referring to a planned trip with "STEVE AND PAUL" that must now wait until injuries are healed, but its absence means that the "YOU" becomes indeterminate. Is it MacIntosh, being spoken to by the poet? Are the "TOMBS" police cells, and is this the next part of the story?

After a one-line stanza break, the poem combines narrative interjections, observations and cries for help, but they are now set within the context of a world, sometimes mythical, of the poem, not the narrator. As Halsey says, Griffiths might be writing through the voices of others, whether in the case of Greenaway or MacIntosh, but he sets them within the broader context of the poem. This is not an act of appropriation or a limitation, but broadens and deepens the implications of the voices of the speaker. His generalizations do not explain the speaker, or form a moderating voice that "others" them, but construct a poem that lives with them. It gives them a framework within which they can exist and that critiques dichotomies of guilty and innocent, legal and illegal, and right and wrong. The poem works thoroughly through the meanings and implications of inside and outside, and all the permutations of that in the context of a prisoner, who is inside, and a poet who is not, ideas of internal and external, and what happens to the body of the prisoner and what might go on inside their head. Griffiths, however, neither abstracts or theorizes beyond the immediate event, but rather gives that event other possibilities. The final line returns to a conversation between two people about a specific anecdote, and ends on the words "SHALL I SHOW YOU THAT?" The materiality of the proposition, of evidence in front of the eyes of the speaker and the listener, proves the situation beyond doubt.

Griffiths returns to some of this material in the collection "Delvan's Book" (Griffiths 2016, 149–165). Dedicated to MacIntosh, the first poem, "Account," is a retelling of the arrest told from the point of view of MacIntosh in more conventional, although unpunctuated, lineation and (mainly) in a number of quatrains. Griffiths imagines how it might feel to carry out a robbery:

> But you work headless
> In the cave behind the waterfall
> In the island at lake-centre
> In the silent snake-snow (151)

The poem ends with the speaker, caught in the act of the crime, responding to the beating by police by a "roll in the glass, more and more. / Just one more bit of life" (152). The rolling in the glass is an act of self-harm that might allow a potential claim for damages, but also reduces MacIntosh to nameless flesh, a precursor for the loss of individuality that characterizes the life of the prisoner, and the process that prepares Greenaway for rebirth as a Christian. Another poem in the collection, "Wandsworth," deals more directly with the controlled space of the prison, and the first five stanzas of the poem intertwine information on "speleology" (the study of caves), with a narrative by MacIntosh that presumably originates from written correspondence as it includes the request "visit me maybe" (156–157). Through bringing together the text on underground caves, presumably a found text and reproduced in italics, and the description of prison life, Griffiths suggests physical restriction, lack of light, and danger. It is however a lack of light that also gives a means of escape from the panopticon of the Victorian prison, that promises to keep all prisoners under surveillance at all times. The juxtaposition of caves and prisons suggests endless possibilities, where prison life is like a cave system that can go off into multiple directions and has *"porcupines," "frozen waterfalls," "more than eight-thousand bats,"* and *"a series of vast sloping chambers."* It contains estheticized representations of itself in the "mural engravings" and "clay statues" of "horses, bison, deer, lion, and rhinoceros." This internal architecture provides both a place of incarceration and an internal world that can construct means of escape from the present condition. While MacIntosh can only swear to "get back at those bastards" in the penultimate stanza, the end of the poem moves from present time and space into a set of mythic possibilities. Merlin becomes a "fool locked in stone," a possible reference to a representation of Merlin in a cliff face near Tintagel, and the shepherded flock becomes "luminous peached slugs" that telescope back to a more distant view of the "earth with blazing towers." The poem ends with an image of the "shocked tort'ed figure" of the accused, that combines the legal sense of tort as an imposed wrong that causes injury, with the medical sense of torted as marked by tension and the middle English use of torted as twisted. Griffiths, therefore, not only gives voice to others in order that they may speak to contemporary concerns but also locates them within historical perspectives that include the real time of history with the mythical, and often make no distinction. In this case, he does this through a final stanza that might move out into the mythical with Merlin and a "gravid people-loser dragon," but returns to a real figure in a real court, albeit one that is also capable of taking on mythic and almost Christ-like qualities.[3]

Griffiths does not adopt the voice of the prisoners, but rather gives them voice in a context that does not deny his own presence. In doing so, he expands and develops his own cosmology and includes the voices in different historical and cultural contexts, often combining dialect-inflected narrative with work by an assumed narrator, and "Liam's Song" (211–220) is a good example. But it is to the use of dialect in the poems that I now want to turn as the other major feature of the third volume of his collected poems. While Griffiths always drew on varieties of language usage in his poetry, with a particular interest in ways of speaking and dialects outside official or mainstream language and culture, this became a more marked feature of his work on moving to North East England. In a personal email, Bill Lancaster, who ran the Centre for Northern Studies at Northumbria University where Griffiths worked through the 1990s and until his death, describes him as "immersed in his dialect work." He testifies not only to Griffiths's deep commitment to his locality but also to the way he included varieties of local residents in his work either through giving readings and setting up events or through getting young people involved in performances (personal email 13.07/18). In *Collected Poems Volume 3*, Halsey includes a 28-page section written in North East dialect called "Dialect Poems" including "The Cuddy Anthem" described as a "mini dialect anthology" (121–149). As with the prison poems Griffiths denies sole authorship, and the anthology claims in a humorous preface that these poems are the result of an unsuccessful competition to celebrate the appointment of a new Bishop of Durham, and the individual poets are not named. The poems are therefore located in a ballad tradition of communal ownership, rather than the notion of the poem as the expression of an individual sentiment or feeling from a particular perspective. The first poem however has none of the formal qualities of the ballad. It combines the typographical processes of modernist experimentation and the appearance of a manuscript text, where a gap is left in the middle of each line to provide a caesura that is both seen and heard. The untitled poem also glosses certain words by including them in an open squared bracket on the right-hand side of the page. As is common with other (mainly) nineteenth-century versions of Old English or medieval manuscripts, the word being glossed is not identified, providing Griffiths with another potential space in which to introduce ambivalence and play. Located in their own column these words not only reflect back on the previous lines, sometimes with a variety of possibilities, but also construct their own commentary. The poem describes the banners of the mining lodges in Durham Cathedral, a practice at the annual Durham Miners' Gala where a service at the Cathedral remains an important part of the celebrations and includes the blessing of any new banners. Bill Griffiths regularly attended the Gala (see Lancaster, 21) and this poem, more old English in its form than folk song, celebrates the work of the miners and the importance of coal.

The poems that follow have, in various ways, more elements of the traditional ballad. With regular rhyme and rhythm, and broadly following ballad meter, they are written in a consistent dialect voice and have a clear narrative or purpose. Along with the poetic elements, there are choruses in rhyming couplets such as

His maumy beak is yuck wi' reek	[rotten
Divn't unsteek, divn't even keek	[unlatch (the door) ... peek

(125)

that suggest song as well as poem, and also use the written page and a second right-hand margin to introduce spatial elements where words sit alongside each as they develop possibilities for varieties of meaning. The narratives are generally located in a post-industrial working-class landscape and express a radical working-class politics, and often seem to refer to specific people, places, and incidents. The third poem, for example, is an untitled work that seems to refer to one individual and names the village of Murton in County Durham, an ex-mining town close to where Griffiths lived in Seaham. The first titled poem in the collection, "The Emergency," is a dialogue on the storing of ammonium nitrate and apparently relates a specific local event. It is written in ballad meter with regular quatrains and an a,b,c,b rhyme scheme. While some accenting is irregular or difficult to sound without a more in-depth understanding of North East dialect than this reader, the work generally follows the ballad practice of four accented syllables in line 1 and three of the quatrain and three accented syllables for lines 2 and 4. Similarly, in the tradition of the folk ballad, they often construct a narrative through dialogue.

Anyone becomes fair game for Griffiths in this dialect work, and in his hands the ballad becomes a form of attack and defense. "Pumpkin heed" (124–125) seems to refer to a corrupt councilor in the village of Murton, an attack on councils continued in the poem beginning "We are upaheet ..." (127–128) that combines prose paragraphs and irregular dialect poetry. The poem entitled "HOW THEY NEARLY CAUGHT ALFRED WESTOE AN' HIS GANG" takes as its focus the grave robbing actions of Elfrid Westow, who removed the remains of Bede from Jarrow and took them, with many others, to Durham.[4] The poem is narrated by an anonymous individual phoning the 0800 Crimestoppers number that can be used to report a crime. Widely advertised in the 1990s in the United Kingdom, it promised a reward and anonymity in that you did not have to give your name. The poem gives one side of the conversation in modern dialect, while leaving no doubt that the reported crime is that of grave robbing some thousand years ago. Griffiths incorporates historical events, often revised, into a dialect that is thoroughly contemporary. Other poems include the highly regular, such as "The Parlous Chase" (137–138) which rhymes a,b,a,b and follows ballad meter more consistently, and "Jetty Song" again a.b,a,b, but with the second and fourth lines in parentheses to give the effect of a sung chorus. The final entry in "Dialect Poems" is a return to the collision of free verse with dialect to reflect on the impact on the community of the closure of Vane Tempest Colliery in 1992. The deep irony of the text reflects the naming of the pit after the Londonderry family, who owned estates in County Durham that included Seaham. On being deemed unprofitable, the now redundant miners (there had been over a 1000 regularly employed there) now have a chance to use their redundancy pay to "hev yor ain share ov / emptiness and exile" (146).

It is too easy to link the prison poems and the dialect work by saying that Griffiths's concern was, finally, with language. It is more precise than that, and more dispersed. His interest lies in the spoken language of particular nomadic and located social groups and cultures; the gypsies, biker gangs, prisoners, and those whose language keeps them far from the metropolitan centers. It is their voices that sound in his work, and their voices that he is committed to publishing, not in the sense of self-expression, or individual liberation and the heroic, but in order that the voices of those least likely to be heard are placed within broader cultural contexts and given deeper historical associations in order to examine what they might mean and the ways they might change and influence history, not just live outside of it. In the way that he not only gives voice to those marginalized and often unheard groups, but also develops their voices in different contexts, Griffiths is unique among poets in late twentieth-century Britain.

The highly performative nature of Griffiths's textual output, and particularly the very many pamphlets, broadsheets, and visual texts, found another form of expression in performed "sound" poetry. During his time in London, when such performance work was characteristic of the experimental London poetry scene, and through his connections with Writers Forum, he performed with Bob Cobbing and Paula Claire, as part of the group Konkrete Canticle. They achieved some international recognition, performing in Europe, Canada, and the United Kingdom. The trip to Canada was particularly productive, and it led to Griffiths's only major non-UK publication (*A Tract against the Giants*, Toronto: Coach House Press, 1984). Some of this work is described by Paula Claire in her contribution to *The Salt Companion* (Rowe 2007), in which she gives details of performances between 1978 and 1992. They were characterized by improvisation, the use of non-verbal sound, the notion of the poem (and a poem might include non-verbal marks on a page) as a score for performance, the incorporation of everyday objects, and the use of the body as a vehicle for expression (Claire 2007). Griffiths was also an occasional performer with the group JGJGJGJG made up of cris cheek, Clive Fencott, and Lawrence Upton. His move to North East England brought an end to group-based performances, but his more conventional readings remained a genuine delight as they explored the more complex music of his work.

In addition to the three volumes of collected poems, he wrote across an astonishing range on language, ecology, culture, and landscape. Much of it resulted from his role as a researcher in the Centre for Northern Studies in Northumbria University, Newcastle, where he worked with Bill Lancaster from 1996 to the time of his death. Following his work archiving the papers of Eric Mottram for King's College London, a long period of paid work began for Griffiths, which, although it had the insecurity that came with project funding, was to sustain him in the North East. The Centre was awarded a number of grants through the Heritage Lottery Fund to work on dialect dictionaries, and produced four volumes, including those on the specialized vocabularies of "Pitmatic," the language of the coalfields, on cooking, and on the coast and fishing, this last published posthumously (see Griffiths 2005a,b, 2007, 2008). He was also assistant editor of *Northern Review: A Journal of Regional and Cultural Affairs*, and completed a book-length history of the Northern Sinfonia Orchestra (Griffiths 2004). Alongside the dialect dictionaries, he wrote other studies of the region, often appearing to work out his ideas in a number of small pamphlets published through Amra before developing his ideas for larger publications. In 1991, for example, he published six Seaham "readers" on various local topics through Amra, and he went on to publish 28 Seaham-related items through Amra, alongside an increasing number of articles for *Northern Review*. This work has received no critical attention, and Griffiths's relation to the North East of England and its impact on his work is only beginning to be assessed. Much of the work is difficult to obtain, although partial collections are in copyright libraries and in Griffiths's archive at Brunel University London, as well as in Bob Cobbing's archive in the British Library. Griffiths's work is resistant to collection, presenting challenges that go beyond even those described by Halsey in his accounts of editing the poet's work.

Although he died at an early age, Griffiths's output was characterized not only by volume, but also by diversity. This essay has focused on Griffiths's poetic output. I have little doubt, however, that a more comprehensive examination of his work from these later years that takes account of the range of his interests and publications would support readings of the poetry not only of the later period but also from his earlier work, making evident concerns that have not yet received attention. There may be an emerging critical consensus around his earlier poems, and the three volumes of collected poems have provided historical and conceptual contexts within which the poetry might be read, but the totality of his output remains critically unexamined. His work on local history has started to bring new contexts for examining his work on myth, while his extended treatments of philosophers such as Boethius and Plotinus provide further approaches to the verse. Griffiths's life was spent challenging, or simply ignoring, the boundaries between different art forms and between art and other things. His response would often be through poetry that drew on historical precedent to construct new kinds of music. His continual shifts of emphasis might make him difficult to keep up with, and diversity of his work and range of reference make it easy to become impatient, but Griffiths would be amused at the way his work challenges conventional critical approaches. If the subjects of his early poems are characterized by movement across space, often only keeping one step ahead of the law, his later work is marked by movement between forms of writing, types of knowledge, modes of expression, and ways of thinking.

Notes

1 See his long-term interest in Boethius, for example, as both an Anglo-Saxon scholar in *Alfred's Metres of Boethius* (Pinner: Anglo-Saxon Books, 1991) and as a poet in *Materia Boethiana* (Newcastle: Galloping Dog, 1984).

2 Critical accounts of Griffiths's work on prisons can be found in Davidson (2007, 2014), Rowe (2014), Seed (2007), and Roberts (2018).

3 I have written of other "prison" poems, most notably *Star Fish Jail* in Davidson 2014 and will not repeat my arguments here, but they similarly combine the voice of a prisoner within the overall context of the poem.

4 https://www.lindisfarne.org.uk/canon-tristram/kate15.htm

References

Bush, Clive (1997). *Out of Dissent: A Study of Five Contemporary British Poets*. London: Talus.

Carr, Gordon (2010). *The Angry Brigade*. Oakland: PM Press.

Claire, Paula (2007). "Bill Griffiths: A Severe Case of Hypergraphia." In: *The Salt Companion to Bill Griffiths* (ed. William Rowe), 37–50. Cambridge: Salt.

Davidson, Ian (2007). *Ideas of Space in Contemporary Poetry*. Basingstoke: Palgrave Macmillan.

Davidson, Ian (2014). "Introduction to "Special Issue on the Poetry of Bill Griffiths."." *Journal of British and Irish Innovative Poetry* 6 (1): 5–11.

Duncan, Andrew (2003). *The Failure of Conservatism in Modern British Poetry*. Cambridge: Salt.

Greenaway, Brian (with Brian Kellock) (1982). *Hell's Angel*. Oxford: Lion.

Griffiths, Bill (1974). *The Gododdin*. London: Pirate Press/Writers Forum.

Griffiths, Bill (1978). *Llywarch Hen in Welsh/English*. London: Writers Forum.

Griffiths, Bill (1984). *A Tract against the Giants*. Toronto: Coach House Press.

Griffiths, Bill (1990). *Morning Lands*. Seaham: Amra.

Griffiths, Bill (1992). *Future Exiles: 3 London Poets*. Paladin Re/Active Anthology 1. London: Paladin.

Griffiths, Bill (1993a). *Starfish Jail*. Seaham: Amra.

Griffiths, Bill (1993b). *Review of Brian Greenaway/Notes from Delvan MacIntosh*. Seaham: Amra.

Griffiths, Bill (1998). *Nomad Sense*. London: Talus.

Griffiths, Bill (1999). *A Book of Spilt Cities*. Burkfastleigh: Etruscan Books.

Griffiths, Bill (2001). *The Ushabtis*. London: Talus.

Griffiths, Bill (2002). *Durham and Other Sequences*. Sheffield: West House Books.

Griffiths, Bill (2004). *Northern Sinfonia: "A Magic of its Own"*. Newcastle: Northumbria University Press.

Griffiths, Bill (2005a). *A Dictionary of North East Dialect*. Newcastle: Northumbria University Press.

Griffiths, Bill (2005b). *Stotty 'n' Spice Cake: The Story of North East Cooking*. Newcastle: Northumbria University Press.

Griffiths, Bill (2007). *Pitmatic: The Talk of the North East Coalfield*. Newcastle: Northumbria University Press.

Griffiths, Bill (2008). *Fishing and Folk: Life and Dialect on the North Sea Coast*. Newcastle: Northumbria University Press.

Griffiths, Bill (2010). *Collected Earlier Poems (1966–80)* (eds. Alan Halsey and Ken Edwards). Hastings: Reality Street.

Griffiths, Bill (2014). *Collected Poems and Sequences (1981–91)* (ed. Alan Halsey). Hastings: Reality Street.

Griffiths, Bill (2016). *Collected Poems Volume 3 (1992–96)* (ed. Alan Halsey). Hastings: Reality Street.

Griffiths, Bill and Muckle, John (1990). *Bikers*. Middlesex: Amra.

Griffiths, Bill and Pickard, Tom (2003). *Tyne Txts*. Seaham: Amra.

Halsey, Alan (2007). "Pirate Press: A Bibliographical Excursion." In: *The Salt Companion to Bill Griffiths* (ed. William Rowe), 55–71. Cambridge: Salt.

Halsey, A. (2010). "Abysses & Quick Vicissitudes: Some Notes on the Mimeo Editions of Bill Griffiths." *Mimeo Mimeo* 4: 41–50.

Halsey, Alan (2014). "Abysses and Quick Vicissitudes: Some Notes on the Mimeo Editions of Bill Griffiths." In "Special Issue on Bill Griffiths. *The Journal of British and Irish Innovative Poetry*, (ed. I. Davidson) 6 (1): 41–54.

Hampson, Robert (2007). "Bill Griffiths and the Old English Lyric." In: *The Salt Companion to Bill Griffiths* (ed. William Rowe), 72–87. Cambridge: Salt.

Lancaster, Bill (2014). "Bill Griffiths's Northern Days." In "Special Issue on Bill Griffiths." *The Journal of British and Irish Innovative Poetry* (ed. I. Davidson) 6 (1): 13–26.

Roberts, Luke (2018). "Grave Police Music: On Bill Griffiths." *Journal of British and Irish Innovative Poetry* 10 (1) https://doi.org/10.16995/biip.48.

Rowe, Will (ed.) (2007). *The Salt Companion to Bill Griffiths*. Cambridge: Salt.

Rowe, Will (2014). "Violence and Form in Bill Griffiths's Cycles." In "Special Issue on Bill Griffiths." *The Journal of British and Irish Innovative Poetry*, (ed. I. Davidson) 6 (1): 100–112.

Seed, John (2007). "'In Music Fair Sweet': Bill Griffiths in Durham." In: *The Salt Companion to Bill Griffiths* (ed. William Rowe), 108–121. Cambridge: Salt.

Sheppard, Robert (2005). *The Poetry of Saying*. Liverpool: Liverpool University Press.

3.6
Excluding Visions of Life in Poems by Thom Gunn

Tomasz Wiśniewski

1.

The poetic language of Thom Gunn is nothing like a consistent exploration of a single poetic manifesto. On the contrary, the poet makes use of a host of traditions, assumes multifarious strategies, and interweaves them with the peculiarities and idiosyncrasies of his style. In practical terms, this means that when approaching his poems, one is puzzled by the frequency of esthetic inconsistencies and semantic contradictions. His is certainly not an *oeuvre* that aims to establish a coherent vision of the world. Rather than that, Gunn's objective is to interweave the singularity of his poetic signature with a broad spectrum of more or less canonical artistic techniques and poetic conventions. As Roman Jakobson has it, diachrony is projected here into synchrony, with the full awareness of the necessity of acquiring autonomous and idiosyncratic solutions in individual poems (Jakobson 1987, 64–65).

Such a strategy leads to particularly interesting solutions whenever we analyze collections of poems published by Gunn. They tend to reveal considerable internal coherence, endow the structure of a sequence of poems with semantic force, and, additionally, attentively respond to the solutions dominating in earlier—or later—volumes. In *The Man with Night Sweats*, for example, compositional segmentation of the sequence into four unequal parts lays stress on the esthetic and semantic shifts in the ongoing poetic account of the "AIDS plague" that demolished those around Gunn in the 1980s in California. But when we look closer at individual poems, we may observe that the elegiac dominant of the collection does

---

A Companion to Contemporary British and Irish Poetry, 1960–2015, First Edition.
Edited by Wolfgang Görtschacher and David Malcolm.
© 2021 John Wiley & Sons Ltd. Published 2021 by John Wiley & Sons Ltd.

not prevent particular texts from establishing highly autonomous entities and exploring singular esthetic solutions. This is striking when we compare, for example, "The Hug" with "A Sketch of the Great Dejection," or "Odysseus on Hermes" with "To the Dead Owner of a Gym." In short, the construction of the collection proves that in Gunn individual poems realize their artistic and esthetic potential simultaneously on several communicative levels. The meanings that are created in one of these levels do not have to fully conform to the ones appearing on others (I discuss this feature of *The Man with Night Sweats* in more detail in Wiśniewski (2011)).

A similar observation—though from a completely different angle—is made by Robert Pinsky:

> Inside and outside, prudent and crazy – this doubleness is more than a matter of personality, and beyond gossip, more than simply psychological or social: because as an artist, too, Thom Gunn is all-of-the-above. To see only the meticulous prosody or only the flamboyant sexuality, only the scholarship or only the hedonism, only England or San Francisco, only literature or only gay life – or to see only stereotypes of these categories – is to misperceive Gunn's genius.
> (Pinsky 2009, 287)

Indeed, Gunn's poetry makes extensive use of the abovementioned contradictions and ambiguities. For him, they become intrinsic features of his artistic signature, since they allow for a creation of a particularly multifarious world vision. This is reflected in composition, just as it is in the sonic arrangement of poems.

2.

A comparative analysis of an early poem "Jesus and His Mother" (from *The Sense of Movement*), "Street Song" (from *Moly*), and "Jack Straw's Castle" (from *Jack Straw's Castle*) reveals some consequences of the abovementioned observations for the singular experience of reading Gunn's poems. When read together, the poems abound in surprising twists, unexpected solutions, and unresolved *aporia*. Their differed semantics mutually enrich one another.

By definition, the title of "Jesus and His Mother" enlivens the whole tradition of Christian imagery.[1] The first line reveals that Mary, who is the speaker, is shaped less as an iconographic deity than as a mother, a representative of humankind. She is discomforted by the thought that her only son belongs more to his father/God than to her. The second line shifts from an emotive/descriptive/concrete to a more conative/metaphorical dimension. As it turns out, she addresses her words to her son/Jesus so as to urge him to stay in "this garden ripe with pears." Biblical connotations of such a request reveal the metaphorical status of the presented situation: the mother's complaint is balanced with the religious connotations of "this garden." Whereas in line 1, Mary lays emphasis on her human experience (symbolic → human), in line 2 her complaint is set beyond earthly time and earthly space (human → symbolic). This is not necessarily a Christian allegory ("ripe with pears"), but the Biblical imaginary is at the roots of the opening lines and it is not treated with easy mockery, or witty irony.

Although the image abounds in juxtapositions (e.g.: human experience vs. Biblical imagery, mother vs. son/father/God, concrete situation vs. universal connotations), the opening sentence establishes a rigid structural arrangement for the poem. The regular iambic pace of these eight-syllable end-stopped lines is broken only by the trochaic opening of the second line. Such an inversion helps to stress the moment when Mary's request— "Stay in this garden"—sets the communicative situation for the entire poem (a mother making a request to her son/Jesus). The sonic arrangement accentuates the opening diphthong [my/mine/ripe] and puts it in contrast with a different one [stay]. As it soon turns out, this is furthered by the rhyme patterning of the seven-line stanza: ABBAABC (where A: mine/shine/brine; B: pears/wears/tears; and C: own). The associations set by the rhyming words are important for the opening metaphor in at least one case: it is accurate to hear "tears" in the phrase "this garden ripe with pears" in order to explore the whole potential of the metaphor set in the opening sentence.

In principle, the remaining lines of the poem conform to the eight-syllable line pattern. Similarly, the remaining five stanzas are consistently composed as septets, and they make use of the rhyme pattern which is set in the first one. The C rhyme is always exact, as line 7 in each stanza finishes with the phrase "not my own." Its interstanzaic prominence is obvious (i.e., it links together all of the stanzas), especially because the quotation marks used in stanzas I, III, V, and VI make it clear that at this point the son responds to his mother.

But at the same time, each stanza proposes—within the repeated structural arrangement—a slightly different approach to the overall theme. The second stanza is less explicit with its apostrophic character: the "you" of the poem is temporarily suspended. The recollection of a physical encounter with God—"[t]hat silent foreigner," (l. 9) who "seemed much like another man" (l. 8)—replaces the Biblical image of the Annunciation and leads to the expression of the question of how she could know what she began, "Meeting the eyes more furious than / The eyes of Joseph, those of God?" (ll. 12–13). Her concluding echo of her son's words "I was my own and not my own" (l. 14) sanctions the sensual dimension of this recollection.

The third stanza is again more self-aware of the communicative plane. The motif of the Apostles is introduced ("these twelve labouring men" (l. 15)), as is the theme of the mother's detachment from her son ("I do not understand your words" (l. 16)). As recollections from his childhood prove, for her, even at present—that is, in the pseudo-Biblical "now"— Jesus is perceived by Mary primarily as a child. For sure she is worried, though, that they are not as close in their relation as they used to be.

The fourth stanza depicts a future granted by the profession acquired by Jesus ("Here are your tools" (l. 23)) and the fifth one refers to the Biblical scene of his early visit at the temple (Luke 2, 41–52). The degree of departure from the Biblical story might be well illustrated by describing the teachers with the phrase "scholars in furred gown" (l. 32). In the sixth stanza, the conflict between Mary's human nature and the divine role imposed on her concludes when she pleads Jesus to treat her as the mother as she "cannot reach to call

[him] Lord" (l. 40). His refrain-like response furthers her misery: "I am my own and not my own" (l. 42). As it turns out, the human and the divine will not necessarily meet.

Even such a provisional analysis of "Jesus and his Mother" reveals some features of Gunn's poetic language. These are:

1. a stability of the communicative situation that is supported by a consistently structured composition;
2. employment of conventional devices for setting elementary phonosemantic relations between the sonic tissue (e.g., rhyme, an iambic/trochaic arrangement) with the overall semantics (pears/tears) and compositional matters (e.g., the refrain-like line);
3. grounding the central metaphor in a juxtaposition of two contrasting types of imagery (religious and secular), so as to explore the paradoxical facets of Mary's motherly love.

3.

Even though similar features can be observed in "Street Song," they lead to other semantic consequences. The whole text is dominated by a single voice—that of Midday Mick, a drug trafficker, advertising his wares on the streets of San Francisco. There are not many features that would personify the speaker, except for some stereotypical detail: Midday Mick is "too young to grow a beard" (l. 1), wears "dirty denim" (l. 3) and "dark glasses" (l. 3), and boasts to sell the best stuff around. Suitable as it is for his profession, such a schematic description makes the speaker a generalized type of a character rather than a substantially depicted individual. It is vital for his listeners ("everyone who passes" (l. 4)) to learn what he is offering rather than who he is. The message provided within this specific song is succinctly presented in line 24: "Join me and see the world I sell." These are purely hedonistic pleasures which are on offer.

But the poem as an artistic text is not restricted to its message. The overall esthetic potential of "Street Song" shifts from more immediate referential implications toward sheer pleasure indicated by its sonic tissue. This aims to underscore the specific orality of advertising drugs. Bearing in mind the origins of the song convention, one is not surprised by the fact that the poem accommodates sonic idiosyncrasies of a street song within the structures of a poetic language. For Gunn, the sonic complexity of dialects emerging from the shady here and now turns out to be as inspiring as the grand issues emerging from Biblical stories.

"Street Song" consists of five six-line stanzas, in which eight-syllable lines dominate. As the syntactic and semantic arrangements suggest, each stanza is internally integrated, which increases their functional autonomy. Stanzas are promoted as elementary compositional units. Regular rhyme pattern (AABBCC) strengthens the importance of the sonic tissue but does not bear more elaborate consequences for the semantics. Rhyming couplets strengthen the improvised-like style of this song. Frequent employment of alliteration—its role is stressed already in the title—lays emphasis on the internal arrangement of certain lines. This means that compositional autonomy of these concrete lines increases when compared to phonetically less organized lines.

Alliteration is particularly prominent in the following cases:

"But yes **m**an it was **m**e you heard"
(line 2),
"In **d**irty **d**enim and **d**ark glasses",
(line 3)
"<u>My</u> <u>m</u>ethedrine, <u>my</u> double-sun",
(line 13)
"— They burn **s**o **s**weet, they **s**moke **s**o smooth",
(line 17)
"Call it <u>h</u>eaven, call it <u>h</u>ell"
(line 23),
"With **M**idday **M**ick **m**an you can't lose".
(line 28)

Even if it is non-intentional that in the majority of these examples (lines 3, 13, 17, and 23) the rules of the Anglo-Saxon alliterative line apply, the echo of this rudimentary oral convention in the street song of a San Francisco drug dealer seems to sanction the genius of the English language. When grasping structures around him, Gunn the poet is attentive to poetic conventions that seemed sanctioned and petrified over a 1000 years earlier. The alliterative quality of these lines suggests their reference to Elizabethan songs; thus, readers may interpret them as "monuments" in the collective memory of English poetry.[2]

Still, the structuring of most lines is bound immediately to the drug trafficking context. The final lines of the first and the fifth stanzas, for example, constitute the compositional framework for the entire text, which means that they stress its beginning and ending. Being the shortest—six-syllable—lines, they are graphically italicized. As a list of drugs, they form an exact repetition: "***Keys lids acid and speed***" (lines 6 and 30). The lines are interesting on the rhythmical plane since their opening disturbs the otherwise strongly iambic structuring of the poem. Such a dropping of the two unstressed syllables is functional, since it draws our attention to the very names of the double stress on "Keys" and "lids." A similar disturbance of the iambic rhythm occurs on the occasion of another such list of drugs, where the unstressed syllable is shifted from the opening to the second half-line: "**Cla**ra Green, Aca**pul**co Gold" (line 10). These two examples illustrate certain phonosemantic qualities of "Street Song": (i) the importance of lists of drugs within the lines, and (ii) the rhythmic exceptionality of their names. Midday Mick is well aware of how to make his drugs sound attractive.

But there is one more important conclusion resulting from the abovementioned discussion. Lines 6, 10, and 30 reflect the structure of the entire "Street Song": both compositional levels (the lines and the text) are determined by the principle of enumeration. Rudimentary as it is, the "message" of Midday Mick's song is rhetorically extended by the simple fact that each stanza advertises different qualities of the drugs on offer, and their numerous effects. Stanza I, which introduces the speaker and his profession, concludes in a sharp enumeration of "Keys," "lids," "acid," and "speed." Stanza II stresses the genuine quality of his "grass," which is "not oregano" (l. 7) and names various kinds of marijuana: "Clara Green," "Acapulco Gold" (l. 10), and "Panama Red" (l. 11). Whereas stanza III introduces "methedrine"—"my double-sun" (l. 13), and "lumps of hash" (l. 16) that "burn so sweet" and "smoke so smooth" (l. 17), stanza IV focuses on "pure acid" (l. 21). The final stanza V goes full circle and returns to what we already know from the opening one: "Keys," "lids," "acid," and "speed" (l. 30). As is so frequently the case with enumeration, in "Street Song," the pure joy of the sonic tissue—the sounds of words and the rhythms of their arrangement—constitutes the core of the text's semantics.

When reading "Jesus and His Mother" and "Street Song" in a comparative way, one is struck by Gunn's skillful employment of analogous poetic strategies for the creation of two different visions of the world. The poems are linked by structural precision, regular compositional arrangement, well-crafted sonic tissue, and stable communicative situations. But whereas "Jesus and His Mother" attempts to deautomatize the culturally and religiously sanctioned dilemma as to whether Mary is of divine or human nature, the artistic ambition of "Street Song" is far more concentrated on earthly pleasures. The latter poem aims to grasp the language of the twentieth-century street and to "record" a kind of experience which might be stereotypically perceived as coming from the margins of the "civilized" world. It is crucial that for Gunn neither of the poetic attempts is perceived as more, or less, accurate and appropriate. The quality of the language of Mary and Midday Mick is equally, if differently, rooted in the diachronic dimension of poetry: on the one hand, we come across an unorthodox treatment of the Biblical tradition, and, on the other, we are surprised by the hint at an unexpected recurrence of structures associated with the Anglo-Saxon alliterative line and Elizabethan song. All in all, Gunn's poetic language seems to encompass remote aspects of the cultural heritage.

4.

As a note after the poem in the collection *Jack Straw's Castle* announces, the poem "Jack Straw's Castle" was written between 1973 and 1974.[3] Even a provisional reading of this 11-section poem makes us aware that its analysis requires a completely different approach to the one proposed for the two previous poems. The 11 sections vary in length, organization of lines, and structural qualities. Their overall metrical and syllabic arrangements are fluctuating, which in itself might be the subject of an interesting analysis. Although most of these parts are unrhymed, at least two of them are structured in accordance with this elementary poetic device: part 3 makes use of an inexact rhyme pattern (ABACCB) and part 11 contains rhyming couplets. It is explicit that each part is ruled by independent principles and, thus, sanctions its compositional autonomy.

In short, "Jack Straw's Castle" makes use of a completely different poetic tradition than "Jesus and His Mother" and "Street Song"—that of free verse (in an interview with Jim Powell, Gunn mentions he is aware of a stereotypical classification of his work, in which the rhyme and the meter would testify to his being an English poet, whereas his free verse poems inscribe him into American traditions. Gunn prefers to think of himself as an Anglo-American poet (Gunn 1993, 218)).[4] When reading "Jack Straw's Castle," I find it necessary to be attentive to a broad range of poetic solutions that are part of Gunn's craftsmanship in the other two texts. Some echoes of their more regular patterning are functional here. In a sense, my objective for the remaining part of this article is to explore the poet's following statement: "I always hoped that my experiences with free verse would enrich my metrical verse as well. And vice versa, of course. At one time I hoped that I could combine the virtues of free verse with those of metric – which is a little like the alchemists' search for the philosophers' stone" (Gunn 1993, 220).

Numerous compositional, thematic, and logical inconsistencies that are conspicuous in "Jack Straw's Castle" suggest the principle of extension as decisive for the poem's overall semantics. When reading the poem, we are struck not only by contrasts between subsequent compositional units, but also by rapid shifts in introduced points of view and types of employed imagery.

The opening two lines establish the core metaphor of Jack Straw sitting in his castle and watching the rain. The description is done in the third-person singular, which establishes the frame for the ongoing poetic communication. Although the phrase "he says" that appears in line 4 seems to strengthen the external perspective, the rest of the poem is shaped as a kind of internal monologue (soliloquy) of Jack Straw and is delivered in direct speech. The opening metaphor hints at certain features of the presented image: when it is raining outdoors, Jack Straw is engrossed in his castle and we get access to his thoughts ("the castle of his psyche"). In addition to this, however, Jack Straw's speech has been framed by the two lines uttered by someone who is "watching" him. Marginal as it may seem, the contrast between the external and the internal perspectives reoccurs as a theme throughout the poem. In part 9, for example, we come across a passage in which Jack Straw is explicit about relations between the subjective world of his "castle" and external reality: "Outside the castle, somewhere, there must be / A real Charles Manson, a real woman crying, / And laws I had no hand in, like gravity" (ll. 24–26). The internal world of the castle and the non-semiotic reality of the world outside are ontologically divergent spheres, and Jack Straw's monologue is preoccupied mainly with the former and treats the latter as a point of possible reference. Yet, the meanings ascribed to contrast are transformed in the final line of the poem: "With dreams like this, Jack's ready for the world" (XI. 36). The compositional framework re-evaluates Jack Straw's account of exploring dark cellars and nightmare-like visions into a specific rite of passage. In the eyes of an external observer ("frame" speaker? reader?), the visions ("dreams") presented in the poem prepare Jack for "the world."

Such shifts of perspectives are well illustrated by part 7, where three quite similar lines extend the definition of the speaker simply by adding short clauses:

> I am the man on the rack.
> I am the man *who puts the man* on the rack.
> I am the man who watches the man *who puts the man* on the rack.
> (edited by T.W.)

The rapid shifts between the perspectives of a victim, an oppressor, and an observer are interesting because they tell us a lot about the semantics of the poem. It is to be read in a rather dynamic way and with full awareness that what is stated may change completely when looked upon from a different perspective.

On the metaphorical plane, similar shifts of perspective are marked whenever Jack Straw moves in his castle from one room to another (part 5), enters the cellars (part 6) and attempts to climb back from "the bottom" (part 9), is woken up in his cold kitchen (part 10), or has the impression he is accompanied by another human being (e.g., Charles Manson, or someone in his bed). The vital prominence of such dynamic shifts for the poem is further reflected on the compositional plane, wherever the rules organizing particular units are rapidly transformed. In this view, the apparently inconsequential description presented in part 2 acquires important meanings: the cries from next door extend the disturbance of Jack Straw's internal world.

5.

In his introduction to the collection of essays entitled *At the Barriers: On the Poetry of Thom Gunn*, Joshua Weiner lays emphasis on the fact that in Gunn's poetry "the voice is humane, direct, candid, unselfconscious, personal, *and*, apparently, objective" (2009, 3). This is certainly true in the three poems I have just discussed in as far as a reading of them is attentive to the shifting perspective characterizing the poetic language of this poet. Anyone who deals with Gunn's texts should remember that the voices of Mary, Midday Mick, and Jack Straw are not the only voices present in these poems. When treating these speakers—as well as traditions and experiences that stand behind them—Gunn seems to be as genuine and serious as he is playful and eluding. These are poems that explore excluding, if mutually enriching, visions of life.

Notes

1 Stefania Michelucci suggests that "Jesus and his Mother" alludes to William Butler Yeats's poem "The Mother of God" (2009, 67).

2 In his interview with James Campbell, Gunn argues that: "[…] I was put in mind of Elizabethan street songs – you know: open markets, people carrying their wares on trays round their necks. […] 'Street Song' was about the street cries of San Francisco. *Keys*, incidentally, were kilos of marijuana, *lids* were ounces. The other two speak for themselves" (Campbell 2000, 40).

3 In the endnote which is meant to help the reader of *Collected Poems* understand the meaning of the title, Gunn writes: "'Jack Straw's Castle': the Oxford dictionary defines Jack Straw as 'a ′straw man′; a man of no substance, worth, or consideration.' A pub in Hampstead is called Jack Straw's Castle, but I just took the name and intended no allusions to Hampstead in the poem. Little Ease was a cell in which you could not stand, sit, or lie" (Gunn 1994, 491). This note was not included when it was first published in the volume *Jack Straw's Castle* (1976).

4 See also James Campbell (1999). "Thom Gunn, Anglo-American Poet." *Agenda* 37: 2–3. 70–74.

References

Campbell, James (1999). "Thom Gunn, Anglo-American Poet." *Agenda* 37: 2–3. (Thom Gunn at Seventy): 70–74.

Campbell, James (2000). *Thom Gunn in Conversation with James Campbell*. London: Between the Lines.

Gunn, Thom (1957). "Jesus and His Mother." In: *The Sense of Movement*, 39–40. London: Faber and Faber.

Gunn, Thom (1971). "Street Song." In: *Moly*, 37–38. London: Faber and Faber.

Gunn, Thom (1976). "Jack Straw's Castle." In: *Jack Straw's Castle*, 48–56. New York: Farrar, Straus and Giroux.

Gunn, Thom (1993). *Shelf Life: Essays, Memoirs and an Interview*. London/Boston: Faber and Faber.

Gunn, Thom (1994). *Collected Poems*. London/Boston: Faber and Faber.

Jakobson, Roman (1987). *Language in Literature*. Cambridge/Massachusetts/London: Harvard University Press.

Michelucci, Stefania (2009). *The Poetry of Thom Gunn: A Critical Study* trans. Jill Franks. Jefferson, NC/London: McFarland and Company.

Pinsky, Robert (2009). "Coda: Thom Gunn, Inside and Outside." In: *At the Barriers: On the Poetry of Thom Gunn* (ed. Joshua Weiner), 287–292. Chicago: Chicago University Press.

Weiner, Joshua (ed.) (2009). *At the Barriers: On the Poetry of Thom Gunn*. Chicago: Chicago University Press.

Wiśniewski, Tomasz (2011). "Compositional Tensions within a Collection of Poems: *The Man with Night Sweats* by Thom Gunn." In: *Here/Now-Then/There: Traditions, Memory, Innovation in Modern British and Irish Poetry* (eds. Ludmiła Gruszewska Blaim and David Malcolm), 125–153. Gdańsk: University of Gdańsk Press.

3.7
"Now Put It Together": Lee Harwood and the Gentle Art of Collage

Robert Sheppard

When Lee Harwood died in 2015, leaving behind *Collected Poems*, which was published in 2004, and a further volume, *The Orchid Boat*, which appeared 10 years later, it was clear that he had been writing a poetry of wonder and amazement, often with a naïve, wide-eyed, and even camp gaze upon the world, for over 40 years. Combined with collagic sensibility, this creates a paradoxical complexity that nudges (rather than forces) the reader into co-creation with its fragments. Harwood's writing is a mode of slow accretion, of building blocks of poetry (and prose), and presenting them in relationship with others, to allow them to resonate with one another. One thinks of collage as a technique of rip and tear, shuffle and paste, fix and finish, but for Harwood it is often a slow game, a question of listening and of paying attention to the world rather than producing a determined and determining discourse about it. This can still have alarming results; in William Rowe's words, "Instead of using simple location, in one time and one place, Harwood's poems shift without warning between different times and places. In any one poem, there can be a variety of different frames" (Rowe 2009, 15).

"As your eyes are blue" from the early 1960s is his first achieved poem in this mode. It is located (or rather dislocated) within and between Rowe's "frames." Hesitancy and textual discontinuity are evident in broken utterance, syntactic dislocation, and rupture, from the start.

> As your eyes are blue
> you move me – and the thought of you –
> I imitate you.
> (Harwood 2004, 28, ll. 1–3)

A Companion to Contemporary British and Irish Poetry, 1960–2015, First Edition.
Edited by Wolfgang Görtschacher and David Malcolm.
© 2021 John Wiley & Sons Ltd. Published 2021 by John Wiley & Sons Ltd.

Rowe also notes that "Harwood's poems avoid giving us completed persons or completed feelings," though the obsessive address from a shadowy "I" to "you" and the feeling of loss are unmistakable here; the parenthetical "and the thought of you" indicates that this is not a poetry of definitive statement, except where one isolates a single line or passage (Rowe 2009, 25). Harwood found a structural homology in French *nouvelle vague* cinema, "this continual cross-cut collage effect – no plot, no beginning-middle-end routine," as he called it (Harwood and Mottram 1975/1976, 12). But "I imitate you" could equally refer to *literary* imitation and the figure addressed is John Ashbery, with whom Harwood had a literary and erotic liaison in the early 1960s, culminating in the American volume that first collected this poem, *The Man with Blue Eyes* (1966), which won the Frank O'Hara Prize and, as Tony Lopez says, of the British volume that later contained that book: "I would propose Lee Harwood's *The White Room* [1968] as a second-generation New York School book because it arises from his relationship with John Ashbery and through that establishes a poetics that lasts in Harwood's work through the next two books, *Landscapes* [1969] and *The Sinking Colony* [1970]" (Lopez 2007, 77). In less formal terms, Jeremy Reed has described the poem as "a love poem as important to its time as Shakespeare's androgynously sexed sonnets were to his" (Reed 2005, 124). The poem immediately but indifferently cuts to another scene:

> yet a roof grey with slates
> or lead. The difference is little
> and even you could say as much
> through a foxtail of pain   even you
> (Harwood 2004, 28, ll. 4–7)

This "foxtail" is a surrealist image that teases with possible semantic resolution amid its dream-like indetermination (and may owe to Harwood's occupation simultaneously to the writing of the poem, as translator of the Dadaist and Surrealist poet Tristan Tzara). It quivers out of sight the moment it is seen, and yet its indefinable pain remains, the "even you" repeating. Spatial lineation aids the cross-cut effect in providing a non-stanzaic, non-metrical means of delineating conflicting discourses, selves, and voices, so that the text is both polyphonic and heteroglossic, in Bakhtinian terms. The aspects of conventional realist enumeration that occurs ("a roof grey") seem curiously inessential; in the presence (or absence) of the lover "the difference is little" (Harwood 2004, 28, ll. 4–5). However, as J. H. Prynne wrote of *The White Room* as a whole, the poem displays "an intensely affective life floated out onto language through an almost indefinitely transferable allegory of 'feeling'" (Prynne 1969, 7). Loss is married to an unspecified threat:

> "cancel the tickets" – a sleep talk
> whose horrors razor a truth that can
> walk with equal calm through palace rooms
> chandeliers tinkling in the silence as winds batter the gardens
> outside formal lakes shuddering at the sight
> of two lone walkers
> (Harwood 2004, 28, ll. 14–19)

The sense of unease underlies every section like a dream, the razored truth that could haunt the idyllic scene. There is also "gleeful excitement in luxury, like a child let loose in a sweet shop," as Lopez notes of some of the palatial and exotic impedimenta of *The Man with Blue Eyes*, vistas that were "very grand indeed" for a twenty something Briton of his time, even one like Harwood at the center of the British Poetry Revival, a participant in "underground" poetry, a magazine editor, book seller, and translator (Lopez 2007, 72).

The central tension that Harwood calls his *"puritan-cavalier routine,"* between lyric self-disclosure and "cavalier" fiction-making, is a distinguishing feature of all his writing, an oscillation between "being a tap-dancer and try[ing] to talk straight," between plainness and the baroque, notational realism and elaborate fictiveness, a conflict between the influences of Robert Creeley and Charles Olson, on the one hand, and Ashbery and Borges, on the other (Harwood and Mottram 1975/1976, 13). When the two tendencies co-exist in a poem, as here, they assist polyphony, produce complexity. The fiction self-corrects, "of course this exaggerates," as if aware of its incredibility, relocating the absorbed walkers, who threaten to become romanticized against their sympathetic background, in a more human, though cultivated, landscape (Harwood 2004, 28, l. 20).

> you know even in the stillness of my kiss
> that doors are opening in another apartment
> on the other side of town
> (Harwood 2004, 28, ll. 23–25)

Harwood seems to have the details of this poem in mind, when he says that his poetics is to create poetry where there is "some sort of perspective where the man was outside himself as well as inside himself ... [It] makes the moment seem the more valid because it's in perspective. It's not just suspended in some egocentric vision, and it becomes like a world" (Harwood and Bockris 1971, 9–10). For example:

> a newly designed red bus drives quietly down Gower Street
> a brilliant red   "how could I tell you..."
> with such confusion
> (Harwood 2004, 28, ll. 30–32)

As Rowe says, "When Harwood explores intimacies of feeling almost too delicate for the voice to sustain, he deploys the hesitancies and gaps of everyday speech, the places where meaning breaks down into the sheer lapse of lived time" (Rowe 2009, 7). Despite "meetings disintegrating / and a general lack of purpose only too obvious in the affairs of state," several optimistic attempts at narrative evade obsession, but fade into resignation: "why bother one thing equal to another" (Harwood 2004, 29, ll. 33–35, 39). Throughout the poem, this growing feeling of hopelessness and longing suggests that events are self-defeating; "dinner parties whose grandeur stops all conversation" (Harwood 2004, 29, 40). The way this poem mediates its empirical and imaginary experiences is more important than what is said about them. There exists the constant pull toward the fictive or the memorized, while erotic obsession still draws the "I" toward "you" and its personal and private domestic interior. As Geoff Ward says, we find "an importation into experience of a tonal innocence which is recognized as true to life, but which in the new setting of the page must henceforth wear invisible quotation marks" (Ward 2007, 37). The poem's movement is circular and not all the quotation marks are invisible, however innocent and "wide-eyed" the longing (Ward 2007, 37).

> but
> the afternoon sunlight which shone in
> your eyes as you lay beside me watching for ... –
> we can neither remember – still shines as you
> wait nervously by the window for the ordered taxi
> to arrive   if only I could touch your naked shoulder
> now   "but then...."
>   (Harwood 2004, 29, ll. 41–47)

"Now" is irrevocably cut off from "then," memory is imperfect, but desire is irrepressible in its anxious repetitiveness and unfinish:

> – and still you move me
> and the distance is nothing
> "even you –
>   (Harwood 2004, 29,
>   ll.50–52)

So many Harwood tropes are explored here that it is a surprise to find other poems in *The White Room* adopting more obvious narrative, even allegorical, strategies, though often with a camp edge to deflate seriousness, replete with the mysterious menace that haunts so many of Harwood's poems. F. T. Prince, a neglected British poet admired by Ashbery, issued the warning that Harwood was "pattering on" (Harwood and Mottram 1975/1976, 13). Harwood realized the danger: "You get a tone of voice going, and it's very elegant and witty ... and then it comes out as yards of material which you just reel off" (Harwood and Mottram 1975/1976, 13). The best poems extend their range beyond this New York mode into fictions about colonial vanity, Orientalism, military and naval disasters, outback life, the Wild West—modern mythologies—and about the nature of poetry itself. Poets, characteristically for Harwood, "only ever fail, miserably – / some more gracefully than others," but that grace is—like "innocence"—held in suspicion (Harwood 2004, 96, ll. 142–143).

"Pattering on" was sharply dealt with in *Landscapes* (1969). The section "Landscapes" is a sequence of eight poems that meditates dreamily upon the doubleness of its title, the name of a fine art genre as well as a geographical term. The role of artifice is obvious in this interplay of nature and culture, erotic encounter and representation. "When the Geography was Fixed" plays on the conceit that "one woman in the gallery ... liked the picture and somehow the delicate / hues of her complexion were reflected in it" (Harwood 2004, 100, ll. 37, 41–42). This creates an ontological uncertainty, a sort of palimpsest world, in which the appearance and disappearance of imagery on a canvas is an analog for the mechanisms of consciousness and memory. "Question of Geography" concludes:

>   – you paint over the picture and start on
> the new one but all the same it's still there
> beneath the fresh plains of colour
>   (Harwood 2004, 108, ll. 26–28)

Yet this fictionalizing is eroticized by the destabilizing presence of the woman throughout the sequence: "'When the geography was fixed' comes to ironize its own title," comments Alice Entwistle. It "evenhandedly insists on recognizing, or perhaps more accurately, *realizing* woman [...] as equal participant in the creative act, a knowing collaborator in an esthetics [...] of 'process', of relationship" (Entwistle 2007, 118). However, in "The Coast," half lines and caesurae attempt semantic simplicity, while representations of a woman as atomized body parts and the specifics of coastal geography merge: "the town dissolves   sex   thighs   legs" (Harwood 2004, 125, l. 20). As Andy Brown points out, "Harwood moves from the matter of fact placement of landscape detail to the transformative sublimation of self *into landscape*, turning this into a metaphor of love," a move which can be seen as prefiguring the "mountain poems" of the 1980s onward (Brown 2007, 191).

The Sinking Colony experiments more radically with fragmentation, resulting in one of Harwood's great (but admittedly atypical) poems, "Animal Days," a narrative of colonialism and erotic obsession. It is pared down, a variety of cut up, but rather than to Burroughs or Tzara, the debt is to Ashbery's fragmented "Europe" (in his 1962 volume *The Tennis Court Oath*), but Harwood's poem seems located anywhere but Europe: "the indian chiefs / what are the wounds, anyway, and their cost?" (Harwood 2004, 150, ll. 28–29). A more general influence for the poems of the late 1960s was the practice of New York poet Joe Ceravolo. "He used that punctuation with lots of spaces and [...] I thought that really works" (Harwood and Corcoran 2008, 42). Fragmentation and collage suit the evocation of what a later postcolonial poem, "One, Two, Three," calls "confused longing" with its numbed calendars of pain (Harwood 2004, 201, l. 60). But in "Linen," such intensely isolated shards of truncated utterance invite readerly intervention, as if the reader could literally step into the silence and complete the text, although the poem emphatically ends with its own excessive paired similes that borrow from "cavalier" New York baroque (however odd they are as analogies for the sensation of touching skin). We are invited to *help* the poem reach its figurative climax, not to provide it.

>   touching you   like the
>   and soft as
>   like the scent of flowers and
>   like an approaching festival
>   whose promise is failed through carelessness
>   (Harwood 2004, 144, ll. 20–24)

This gesture of openness destabilizes our usual procedures of reading poetry; as Rowe says: "To give oneself to reading a Harwood poem means to loosen the hold of interpretation which, by always having something to say, clutters the apprehension of the silences, the empty spaces and times the poem acknowledges" (Rowe 2009, 44–45). One empirical study, by Vesna Klein, has shown that, despite my apprehension of these lines as a "gesture," some readers *do* feel impelled to fill the gaps when presented with this poem (see Rowe 2009, 28).

Apprehending "One, Two, Three," first published in *HMS Little Fox* (1975), Rowe's lacunary reader is oriented toward textual completion of the poem by the insistent final line, "Now put it together," clearly an invitation to construct a new entity from its three separate parts (Harwood 2004, 201, l. 62). Its fragments are less gestures of openness, motivated by their delicate contexts which enact a theme of resistance to separation. Parables of Mughal and colonial power are juxtaposed with notations of the personal in quite new (and lasting) ways. "One" begins with "An emperor gives a gift, stylishly, / and a Mughal miniature records it" (Harwood 2004, 199, ll.1–2). There is an immediate admission that, to be affected by this art, the viewer has to engage with its otherness, that it too is a gift that may not be reduced to "colour and gold on paper":

> we're dazzled   – all this art
> and surprises   "Keeping the doors open"
> Right?
> (Harwood 2004, 199, ll. 3–6)

"Keep your doors open," Harwood explains in interview, acknowledging the phrase as from a Hopi rite of passage, "is what real learning is doing" (Harwood and Bockris 1971, 11). As the text itself is open, then the reader's faculties should remain open in the face of the "delight" of being "fascinated by the delicacy" of art objects, and open to human experience (Harwood 2004, 199, ll. 7, 20). The narrator "enters" the artwork (a rhetorical feature of many of Harwood's poems); the division between art and life-world is transgressed to emphasize their interdependence. When this happens, appropriately enough, the emperor is involved in an act of "exchange," an image of the reciprocation evoked throughout the section. Yet even this perspective is not totally satisfying; the "distance," the "private separations," still remain (Harwood 2004, 199; ll. 29, 16).

Whereas the first section deals with esthetics, the third deals largely with historical knowledge (both public and private) and the lack of "recognition" of, exchange with, history (Harwood 2004, 201, l. 56). Against the inert posturing that attempts to halt this exchange, the reader is asked to imagine the children of "the survivors" of the "disaster ... living in a calm beyond this knowledge" without reciprocity, without "some form of recognition" of the knowledge of the otherness of people throughout history (Harwood 2004, 201, ll. 51–56). These delicate fragmentary parts sandwich the irritated "straight-talking" of "Two": "away the hills / (Fuck 'the hills')" with its absorption by, and obsession with, "my mouth on your throat / my body smells of your body" (Harwood 2004, 200, ll. 38–41). This balanced poise both pleads for, and suggests, sexual exchange and mutual responsibility.

Harwood called "The Long Black Veil: a notebook 1970–1972" "the end product, the 'flower' of my work to date" (Harwood 1975, dust jacket). Harwood's poetics speculates upon the poem as the "presentation of informations and the art as mover, catalyst – to somehow work together, be one" (Harwood 1975, dust jacket). Harwood benefited from "an American permission" to write this sequence under the sign of Olson's *The Maximus Poems*, with its juxtaposition of materials (Olson 1960; Ward 1976, 14). Eventually, the techniques of notational bare utterance upon the open, map-like, page-space, and the invasion of lyric concision by prose quotation—those plural "informations" foregrounded by Harwood—became stylized, even mannered, and largely abandoned by Harwood after *Boston–Brighton* (1977). But "The Long Black Veil" opens the texture of the "notebook" to lyric progression. This suits the continual restlessness that is both geographical (the frames switch from Brighton to California, Canada to an imagined ancient Egypt) and autobiographical. Paul Selby is particularly sensitive to the transatlantic poetics and the transcontinental focus:

> [W]hereas Olson's 'Projective Verse' essay emphasizes restless poetic energy and an immediacy of perception as the keys to open-form composition [...] Harwood's poetics of scattering leads here to a poetics of the open-form that consists of hesitations, gaps, of apparently torn textual leaves, fraught with 'leaving' and emotional 'drift'. His poetics, that is, seems troubled by a sort of inherent pastoralism of the open-form that effectively veils the politics of colonial power and cultural appropriation that is – historically at least – central to transatlantic relationships. (Selby 2007, 101)

Nevertheless, the poem steals its title from a US country song about the dead narrator's fatal love for his best friend's wife. An adulterous relationship is the center and the central absence of the poem too, with its complex interplay of obsessive focus and informational dispersion. In Book Six—midway—"questions of complexity" are dealt with most fully (Harwood 2004, 177, Book 6, l. 1). Harwood quotes E. M. Forster's obituary for André Gide which praises Gide for transmitting much of "life's complexity, and the delight, the duty of registering that complexity and of conveying it" (Harwood 2004, 177, Book 6, 5–7). Harwood revises Jung's essay, "Marriage as a Psychological Relationship," to develop both a theory of a constantly decentering process in his work and as a model for human relationships.

> The distinctions
> "Oh, Jung" (1875–1961) on "Marriage..." (1925)
>
> The container *and* the contained
> not *or*
>
> one within the other
> a continual shifting   and that both ways
> – more a flow – from the simplicity to the complexity,
> "unconscious" to conscious,
>   and then back again?
> and the move always with difficulty, and pain   a pleasure
>   (Harwood 2004, 177, Book 6, ll. 8–17)

In Jung's theory of marriage, the container is a complex character, the contained simple and psychologically dependent upon the other. There are pleasurable but also painful resolutions between them as the container looks in vain for his or her level of complexity in the partner, whose simplicity is also disrupted by the search. Harwood subverts the underlying dominant-submissive polarity of Jung's essay, with his emphatic "*and*" which suggests that the roles in his own *extra*-marital relationship are interchangeable, dynamic, and discontinuous.

Amid such mutability, process is both a mode of consciousness and a mode of catalytic communication:

> not so much a repetition
> but a moving around a point, a line
> – like a backbone – and that too moving
> (on)
> (Harwood 2004, 177, Book 6, ll. 18–21)

Part of the function of the "backbone" moving around a (moving) point is that there should be no single point of view, that it should remain "complex." The "straight-talking" parts do not contradict the elaborate artifice of others, for they are complementarities, mutually exclusive positions that support one another, an attitude confirmed toward the end of the poem: "Yes and No" (Harwood 2004, 188, Book 11, l. 3).

In the concluding "Book Twelve: California Journal," the continual shifting of place and movement, of change and exchange, and of dream and the here and now, comes to poetic fulfillment in an extraordinarily powerful piece of prose, which is nevertheless not a resolution. "Making love, the final blocks clear. My body taken into her body completely, and then her body into my body… She anoints my wrists" (Harwood 2004, 193, Book 12, ll. 5–6). As in "One, Two, Three," there is ritual exchange: "She accepts the objects – the stone, the orange blossom. / She gives the objects – the whittled twig, the dried seed pod" (Harwood 2004, 194, Book 12, ll. 4–5). Lovemaking is complete in the sense that it has reached a certain stage of intensity, and in the sense of it constituting a final act (with the funereal equation of bodies "before burial" and the lovers "before our parting") (Harwood 2004, 193, Book 12, ll. 10–11). The "she" is associated with the Egyptian goddess Hathor. Entwistle, identifying the woman as the artist Bobbie Louise Hawkins (then married to Robert Creeley), concludes: "*The Long Black Veil* leaves little doubt of Hawkins' Hathor-like centrality to Harwood's evolving poetics. [… T]he poem both confirms and complicates Bobbie's implicitly Muse-like function: her catalyzing impact on Harwood's sense of creative purpose and selfhood" (Entwistle 2007, 115).

Far from being an "end-product," *The Long Black Veil* was an "evolving poetics" for the rest of Harwood's career. As Rowe says, "Some of the possibilities opened up by the exploratory writing of *The Long Black Veil* can only fully be appreciated by reading the later books […] [Its] compositional features […] are now to be found spread throughout the various poems that make up a book" (Rowe 2009, 42). Harwood's development, mixing modes as he sees fit, but often juxtaposing longer passages, seems a gentler form of collage, exemplified in a poem from *All the Wrong Notes* (1981), "Faded ribbons around the lost bundle now being devoured by moths," which binds together discrete "bundles" of lyric, prose, fiction, and fact. Cavalier fictionalizing raises "the question of where vanity and obsession meet or divide or…" (Harwood 2004, 312, l. 77), while the natural world offers the seductions of puritan enumeration: "blackbird's song / skylark's trill" (Harwood 2004, 313, ll. 94–95). But the will to creative linkage, *deliberate* juxtaposition, is represented as a series of "meetings" between incongruities: "A 13th century ceiling meets Schubert meets / a glass of chilled white wine and a ripe peach," in this case an interinanimation of cultural artifacts and personal tastes (Harwood 2004, 313, ll. 91–92). Yet the instability this restlessness conjures also has the effect of problematizing the readerly will to totality. As Rowe notes: "If Harwood uses spatial frames to distinguish outside and inside, distance and closeness, and time frames to separate abstraction from immediacy, represented time from real time, there is also […] a way in which his poems dissolve the frames" (Rowe 2009, 19).

There is also a personal dimension to this imaginative restlessness, in which "meeting" can degenerate into slippage and evasion, as suggested by Harwood's remark of 1993: "I know I can be trusted when navigating in cloud on a mountainside but certainly not when trying to navigate sexual and some emotional 'clouds'" (Harwood 1994, 151). Indeed, *In the Mists* (1993), "mountain poems" written between 1988 and that year, signals that preference for another "meeting," this time of man and nature, culture and environment. One poem's deliberate clumsy title, "If you think this is just descriptions, it isn't," reminds the reader that attention and detail, in writing about the environment, may approach evocation and vision, and *can* be "trusted" (Harwood 2004, 404). Harwood calls this poem "a rebuke to those who dismiss poetry that has what they call a pastoral rather than an urban setting" (Harwood and Corcoran 2008, 89), yet he often switches and dissolves frames quite abruptly, as in "Cwm Uchaf," which, despite indicating a rural Welsh location, opens far away ("In Brighton someone yells from a window") but progresses even farther off, "On the moon in a vast barren crater / a rock very slowly crumbles into fine dust," before drawing back to "a sighing wind the noise of distant waves" (Harwood 2004, 408, ll. 1–4), a mode of contextualization of spatial process that Ian Davidson considers. "The way Harwood stands back and looks at himself, both at the landscape he is in and his reaction to the landscape and the self in it, means that he can keep the poem moving between the general and the specific, between action and observation and between different perspectives which combine those of place and space" (Davidson 2007, 203).

Such delights were overshadowed by the death of Harwood's poet friend, Paul Evans, whom he had known since 1965, which occurred while climbing with Harwood on Crib-y-ddysgl, Wales, in 1991. *In the Mists* contains a number of elegies, including the starkly notational "On the Ledge," which narrates the incidents of the fatal accident, even to "a final thudding stillness," although even here there exists an attempt at redemptive imaginative recovery as Harwood keeps "the poem moving."

> and you gone silently down
> through grey winter air
> the mountains we loved
> (Harwood 2004,
> 406, ll. 7, 14–16)

As Mari Hughes-Edwards comments, "Union and alienation are rendered synonymously visible in Harwood's fusion of the absent dead, the grieving survivor and the landscape that once united them, but now marks their permanent separation." (Hughes-Edwards 2007, 149)

Two extraordinary sequences in *Morning Light* (1998) suggest the formal means Harwood employs against "permanent separation." "Dreams of Armenia" presents the history of a near-forgotten genocide, and, in relationship to this, a love story, and features the most tender, resonant but chilling, lines in the whole of his *oeuvre*: "They would do this to you, my love, / and to our son," which compounds horror across the slight pause of the line-break (Harwood 2004, 444, ll. 15–16). Harwood has commented that the poem "is more a praise of Armenia and the Armenia I imagine" (Harwood and Corcoran 2008, 94), but—as ever—history keeps breaking in with dates and bald facts that one associates with the objectivism of Charles Reznikoff, enumerations of "Massacres, shootings, bayoneting, hacking" (Harwood 2004, 444, l. 12). The "Armenian song that tears your heart" (Harwood 2004, 441, l. 1) or lovemaking "in the hot night lying together" cannot obviate the terror, but then that is the unsettling point of these collagic juxtapositions (Harwood 2004, 443, l. 3). "'Who remembers the Armenians?' said Hitler years later as he set on the Jews" (Harwood 2004, 444, l. 10–11). The fact is, this poem *remembers*, despite (or because) it is a love poem, contextualized by fact and "informations," and in its way is more effective than "The Long Black Veil."

The 50 short sections of "Days and Nights" (some of them single lines) reflect Harwood's brief employment as a museum attendant (they were "written" in Harwood's head, as "accidental sightings," the text's subtitle). They range from single word entries, such as the parenthetical "(space)" (Harwood 2004, 421, l. 3), which attempts to look outward, and "sullen" (Harwood 2004, 422, l. 19), which looks inward, to meditations on their own development. One explains Harwood's preference for gerund forms throughout his work: they leave the utterance "always in the present ing ing" (Harwood 2004, 421, l. 6). There is nothing quite as minimal as this in Harwood's work, although he refers to Tom Raworth's serial composition "Stag Skull Mounted" (1970), from which it quotes, commenting on its own failure of method, or failure *as* method. "As Tom once wrote 'this trick doesn't work'" (Harwood 2004, 422, l. 4). "The line that says nothing. A chair creaks," in fact says quite a deal about how one thought fills immensity (Harwood 2004, 419, l. 4). Structurally, "Days and Nights" testifies to the continuing influence of Ashbery's "Europe," and to the miniature box-sculptures of Joseph Cornell, to whom the piece is dedicated, the constructor of his own "poetic enactments," as Dore Ashton calls his famous boxes (Ashton 1974, 1). In the final "sighting," the reader is left peering into the miniature but expansive interiors of those assemblages: "The white box contains a landscape" (Harwood 2004, 423, l. 14). Cornell himself was first excited by collage when he saw Max Ernst's work, but it was later with his friend Duchamp that he "shared … a love for sudden juxtapositions, of perfectly ordinary and even vulgar objects. But seashells, pressed flowers, and butterflies were in the final analysis closer to Cornell's vision," as Ashton explains (Ashton 1974, 77). Harwood's gentle attitude to literary collage is similar to this cabinet of curiosities approach, closer to the juxtapositions of the Victorian commonplace book than to those of Burroughs or Dada-period Tzara, but by now recognizably Harwoodian.

The Orchid Boat was published in 2014, the year after Harwood received one of his few public accolades, a Cholmondeley Award, whose citation mentions that "his active internationalism has had an influence on decades of British Poetry" (Harvey 2014). The book contains some of Harwood's most carefully written poems, including "The Books" which remembers "a dense history" of torched books and people at the library in Alexandria, "its destruction by Christian fanatics / and the savage murder of the mathematician Hypatia," an indictment as factual as the earlier pleas for Armenia (Harwood 2014, 16, 25, 21–22). "But that shrinks into the shadows, / when faced with our daily history," Harwood remarks, switching the frame closer to home, pointed and poignant (Harwood 2014, 16, 26–27).

> The young officer, my father, 1940,
> having to shoot one of his own men,
> his stomach ripped open beyond saving,
> begging to be put out of his agony.
> (Harwood 2014, 17, 31)

This reprises the lack of intergenerational "recognition" explored in "One, Two, Three": "How did my father / live with that moment for years and years?" (Harwood 2014, 17, 33–34). The effect of the technique of collage, as ever, offsets such horrific "moments" against returns to the opening "cavalier" motif of the poem, "She climbed down from the tree the next day a queen," a fairytale moment (even if lifted from a 1952 pre-Coronation news report) which a catalyzed "we" share: "As we all do, and then set out / across golden stubble to the river" (Harwood 2014, 16–17, ll. 1, 38–39). This meeting, as often, introduces a touch of deflationary camp:

> I don't intend to sit here waiting in my coffin,
> gathering dust until the final slammer,
> adjusting my tiara.
> (Harwood 2014, 17, ll. 40–42)

Indeed, it is time to "head for the frontier," a characteristic Harwood frame-shift of transit *and* transitional catalysis (Harwood 2014, 17, l. 45). The poetics developed in *The Long Black Veil* is still collagic and mobile.

References

Ashbery, John (1962). *The Tennis Court Oath*. Middleton: Wesleyan University Press.

Ashton, Dore (1974). *A Joseph Cornell Album*. New York: The Viking Press.

Brown, Andy (2007). "Echoes of the *Oikos*: an Ecocritical Reading." In: *The Salt Companion to Lee Harwood* (ed. Robert Sheppard), 171–194. Cambridge: Salt Publications.

Davidson, Ian (2007). "Nowhere Else—The Later Poems." In: *The Salt Companion to Lee Harwood* (ed. Robert Sheppard), 195–206. Cambridge: Salt Publications.

Entwistle, Alice (2007). *"and .../ not or:* Gender and Relationship in Lee Harwood's Poetics." In: *The Salt Companion to Lee Harwood* (ed. Robert Sheppard), 104–126. Cambridge: Salt Publications.

Harvey, John (2014). Harvey's blog *Mellowtone 70Up* at http://mellotone70up.wordpress.com/2013/06/14/lee-harwood-award-winner (accessed 9 December 2014).

Harwood, Lee (1966). *The Man with Blue Eyes.* New York: Angel Hair Books.

Harwood, Lee (1969). *Landscapes.* London: Fulcrum Press.

Harwood, Lee (1970). *The Sinking Colony.* London: Fulcrum Press.

Harwood, Lee (1975). *H.M.S. Little Fox.* London: Oasis Books.

Harwood, Lee (1977). *Boston-Brighton.* London: Oasis Books.

Harwood, Lee (1993). *In the Mists: Mountain Poems.* Nottingham: Slow Dancer Press.

Harwood, Lee (1994). *Contemporary Authors Autobiography Series*, vol. 19, 135–153. Detroit: Gale Research.

Harwood, Lee (1998). *Morning Light.* London: Slow Dancer Press.

Harwood, Lee (2004). *Collected Poems.* Exeter: Shearsman.

Harwood, Lee (2014). *The Orchid Boat.* London: Enitharmon.

Harwood, Lee and Bockris, Victor (1971). "Extracts from a Conversation with Lee Harwood." *Pennsylvania Review*: 7–14.

Harwood, Lee and Corcoran, Kelvin (2008). *Lee Harwood: Not the Full Story – Six Interviews by Kelvin Corcoran.* Exeter: Shearsman.

Harwood, Lee and Mottram, Eric (1975/1976). "A Conversation." *Poetry Information* (9 October) 14: 4–18.

Hughes-Edwards, Mari (2007). "'Love and Other Obsessions': The Poetry of Desire." In: *The Salt Companion to Lee Harwood* (ed. Robert Sheppard), 127–152. Cambridge: Salt Publications.

Lopez, Tony (2007). *"The White Room* in the New York Schoolhouse." In: *The Salt Companion to Lee Harwood* (ed. Robert Sheppard), 69–84. Cambridge: Salt Publications.

Olson, Charles (1960). *The Maximus Poems.* New York: Jargon/Corinth.

Prynne, J. H. (1969). "In Love and Something, or Other." Varsity (24 May), p. 7.

Reed, Jeremy (2005). "As Your Eyes Are Blue: Lee Harwood's Collected Poems." *Tears in the Fence* 40: 123–130.

Rowe, William Walton (2009). *Three Lyric Poets: Harwood, Torrance, MacSweeney.* Tavistock: Northcote House.

Selby, Paul (2007). "Transatlantic Poetics in *H.M.S. Little Fox* and *Boston-Brighton.*" In: *The Salt Companion to Lee Harwood* (ed. Robert Sheppard), 85–103. Cambridge: Salt Publications.

Ward, Geoffrey (1976). "On Tom Raworth." *Perfect Bound* (first issue), pp. 114–119.

Ward, Geoffrey (2007). "Lee Harwood's Guaranteed Fine Weather Suitcase." In: *The Salt Companion to Lee Harwood* (ed. Robert Sheppard), 35–53. Cambridge: Salt Publications.

3.8
Listening to Words and Silence: The Poetry of Elizabeth Jennings

Jean Ward

In a review of Elizabeth Jennings's *New Collected Poems*, edited by the poet's long-time friend Michael Schmidt and published posthumously in 2002, Anthony Haynes asks the question: "If with the passage of time only such anthology pieces as 'Absence,' 'The Young Ones' or 'One Flesh' were to be remembered, how much would that matter?" (Haynes 2002, 19).

Haynes suggests that on one level, it would not matter much at all, since these poems function as microcosms of Jennings's whole poetic cosmos. Among the typical qualities that they exhibit Haynes includes their "plain style" and "unabashed use of monosyllables"; and he also praises the "psychological perceptiveness, the painterly eye, the craftsman-like versification" that characterize them, claiming that these, like "the provincial outlook with its focus on the personal and the local," are features of Jennings's whole oeuvre. The connotations of the word "provincial" might imply criticism; but evidently this is not Haynes's intention, as is clear from the implied second answer to his question: that it would matter very much indeed if we remembered only these few poems and lost a sense of the scope of the whole corpus of poetry. He goes on to say: "Her tributes to other writers and artists (from Augustine to Auden, from Mantegna to Klee) and to ancient cultures establish a broad and eclectic background for her work. Those close-up concerns with the personal and the local come to seem like prisms through which larger themes (in particular, love and grace) can be delineated, rather than tokens of any narrowness or lack of ambition" (Haynes 2002, 19).

A Companion to Contemporary British and Irish Poetry, 1960–2015, First Edition.
Edited by Wolfgang Görtschacher and David Malcolm.
© 2021 John Wiley & Sons Ltd. Published 2021 by John Wiley & Sons Ltd.

In fact, the wider canvas of Jennings's *oeuvre*, not only in thematic terms but also in terms of the writers to whom her sympathies are drawn, is already implicit in those characteristics that Haynes identifies in the three poems he selects. Plain style and unabashed use of monosyllables: "You loved the monosyllable and it / Runs through your music" (ll. 19–29), writes Jennings in "For George Herbert" (Jennings 2012, 549), adding a phrase in which the echo of Herbert's "Antiphon (I)" (Herbert 1967, 19) is subtly audible: "I / Can hear between its graces music yet / More deep and much more high" (ll. 20–22). Herbert, it is worth noting, only narrowly missed being Jennings's choice, when she was interviewed for *Desert Island Discs* in 1993, as the one book besides the Bible and Shakespeare that she would wish to accompany her days as a castaway. "Painterly eye"? In *The Collected Poems*, only one poem separates one of her many ekphrases of well-known paintings, "*Mantegna's Agony in the Garden*" (99–100), from the following description, in a poem dedicated to David Jones, of … the artist's studio? A painting in the artist's studio? "Window upon the wall, a balcony / With a light chair" (ll. 1–2): the levels of reality seem to coalesce like the "air and water so / Mingled you could not say which was the sun / And which the adamant yet tranquil spray" ("Visit to an Artist," 101, ll. 2–4). And the "provincial outlook," the "focus on the personal and local," through which "larger themes" are filtered? Again, the kinship of outlook with Jones is not far to seek: "the works of man, unless they are of 'now' and of 'this place', can have no 'for ever'" (Preface to *The Anathemata*, 1972, 24).

By the time that Haynes wrote his review, Jennings's work had appeared not only in successive individual collections, beginning with the unassumingly titled *Poems* (1953), but also in *Selected Poems* (1979), *Collected Poems* (1986), and in *New Collected Poems* (2002), the book which is the subject of the review. Ten years later, in 2012, Carcanet published a new collection, under the outstanding editorship of Emma Mason: *The Collected Poems*. It is from this edition that all quotations in this essay are taken. Jennings was a popular and well-loved poet during her lifetime, but the commissioning of this collection indicates the way that interest in her work has continued to grow since her death. From the touching anecdote recounted in the first paragraph of a short preface about the "small ceramic sheep" (Mason 2012b, xli) that Jennings once inexplicably gave to the editor, then a student, through nearly 1000 pages of carefully edited poems, to the last, moving sentence of a finely written Afterword, identifying in Jennings's poetry "a tenderness that evades sentiment by finding its bearings in discernment and kindness" (Mason 2012a, 982), Mason has done a wonderful service to both the common reader and the scholar. By recalling poems not reprinted since their first publication in the original collections and providing access to a huge number of previously unpublished poems, she has made it possible to look again at Jennings's achievement, to test once more the claims previously made for her and to ensure that it will *not* be only a handful of (deservedly) anthologized poems for which she is remembered. Importantly, the previously unpublished poetry of 1992–2000 presented in Mason's collection includes a series of sonnets of "homage" to some of the poets who meant most to Jennings: Wallace Stevens, Yeats, Herbert, Chaucer, Vaughan, Browning, Auden, and Coleridge. The order is the one in which the poems appear in *New Collected Poems*, suggesting the way in which writers of diverse provenance mingle in what James Aitchison (2013, 192) might call a "fellowship" of poets dear to Jennings's heart.

In addition to all this, by giving serious and respectful attention to Jennings's profound Roman Catholic faith, Mason has ensured that it will never again be considered a marginal aspect of her work or regarded as a disqualification for according her the status of a major poet. The very first sentence of Mason's Afterword, designed, as the publisher's blurb puts it, to "illuminate the faith at the heart of [Jennings's] poetry," describes the poet as "a devout Roman Catholic" and declares the intention of "establishing her as one of the most significant modern Christian poets to emerge from post-war Britain" (2012a, 961). I have discussed elsewhere (2007, 2009) the way in which over many decades the vital part played in Jennings's poetry by what Mason calls "her intense and moving commitment to Roman Catholicism" (2012b, xli) was consistently ignored or downplayed in anthologies, literary encyclopedias, and critical writing. At best, the matter was treated with a reserve that bordered on disdain. True, Haynes concludes his review of *New Collected Poems* by stating that "Jennings's claims to major achievement derive ultimately from her role as a Catholic poet. By this I mean not so much her articulation of specifically Catholic concerns (her poems on Mass, for example) but something almost the opposite: it is in the relation between Catholicism and catholicity that much of the richness of her writing lies" (Haynes 2002). But Haynes was writing for a Catholic newspaper; in the wider community of critics, this conclusion was neither obvious nor unambiguous. Even in Michael Schmidt's sympathetic Preface, the accent of dubiety remains: "Her self-effacement cannot conceal the anachronistic nature of her quest, the presumption that in 1961 or 2001 her concerns retain *direct* meaning for poet and reader" (Schmidt 2002, xxiii). In the final sentences of Mason's Afterword, these ghosts are at last conclusively laid to rest: "Her achievement [...] is her ability to translate the intensity and happiness of her Christian faith into a canon of accessible poems that *reach out to a community of readers even as they do not assume their welcome* [emphasis added]" (2012a, 982).

Now, perhaps, there might even seem to be a possible danger of going too far the other way; the vital relationship between Jennings's Catholicism and her poetry is consistently underlined in the criticism of those who have written on her work most recently: Cathy Parc, Stephen McInerney, Barry Sloan, Anna Walczuk, and Jeremy Stevens. However, the fact that the focus of Jennings's faith and art is incarnational, as I have argued especially in discussing her essay on David Jones in *Seven Men of Vision* ("Visiting an Artist: Elizabeth Jennings Contemplates the 'Assiduous Craft' of David Jones," 2013) and in an article on her poetics for the volume *Sound Is / As Sense* ("'Be quiet and listen, listen': Sound, Rhythm and the Paradoxes of History and Faith in Elizabeth Jennings's Poetry"), mitigates this danger, providing for a vision that is utterly earthly and everyday, yet shot through with intimations of divine presence. The tensions between the natural and supernatural, the ordinary and the extraordinary, the human and the divine—in other words, those tensions summed up in the Christian doctrine of the Incarnation—are increasingly recognized as being at the heart of her poetics. Mason, and after her Walczuk, recalls Sloan (2006, 394) with approval: "she thought and wrote in the intersection of 'the divine and the human [...] the material and the spiritual, the mundane and the mysterious'" (Mason 2012a, 964; see also Walczuk 2017, 72). Furthermore, Jennings's poetry never escapes into trite religiosity; it emerges from too much personal turmoil and pain for that. As Parc points out, quoting the poet's own words from *Christianity and Poetry* (107): being a "Catholic" poet means "being willing to go to the edge of Hell itself in search of God and of Truth" (Parc 2013, 307). In a review of *The Faber Book of Religious Verse* edited by Helen Gardner, Jennings herself wrote that "absolute certainty of belief, however exquisitely versified, so easily smacks of smugness" (*The Tablet*, 11 October, 1986, 16).

Among the many poems that Mason's new edition of Jennings's work has rescued from oblivion is "Agony in any Garden" (Jennings 2012, 82), a poem not reprinted since its original publication in *A Sense of the World* (1958). There is nothing smug about a poem which begins, as if breaking out from the midst of painful contemplation: "And anybody's agony might be / This garden and this time" (82, ll. 1–2). (It is worth noting here that the withholding of the capital letter from the "any" of the title, which goes against convention, corresponds perfectly with the poem's subject: the scene of *this* agony does not merit capitalization. It is "anybody's agony," which might take place in "any" garden.) A few pages later in *The Collected Poems* we find another working-over of the same theme, "*Mantegna's Agony in the Garden*" (99–100). This, though it is a poetic ekphrasis, a contemplation of an artist's contemplation, at a further remove from Gethsemane, conscious that here "The agony is formal" (99, l. 1), seems still to carry a similar message that is anything but smug: no artistry of arrangement or composition can get away from the fact that, as the telling short sentence has it, "Pain is particular" (100, l. 19). In this context, where attention is drawn to the "careful placing" (l. 16) in the painting "Of mountain, men and agony" (l. 17), the "particular" quality of pain might even have a secondary meaning (fussy, pedantic) that relates it to the commonplace, unexalted, petty experience and way of experiencing of that "anyone" who in "Agony in any Garden," in turn, "might reach / His pitch of hopelessness" (l. 4–5). It is significant that "*Mantegna's Agony in the Garden*" names neither Jesus nor the disciples, apart from Judas. By such unobtrusive means as these, Jennings's poetry constantly draws together the ordinary and the extraordinary; suffering that is mundane, often borne without dignity or "greatness" ("Agony in any Garden," l. 7), is taken up into the mystery of the Passion. This is not done by reference to any of the formal symbolism that informs Mantegna's painting, in which, as John Drury tells us, the Passion is associated with the Mass by the group of cherubs holding the instruments of Christ's Passion and by Christ's kneeling at a stone which looks like an altar (1999, 93–94). These symbols are not even mentioned in Jennings's ekphrasis; it is the human element in the drama (the "three / Bodies" (ll. 1–2) that are "stretched in pure repose" (l. 2), Judas approaching with his procession, "the praying figure" [l. 11]), and the ordinary natural world ("Three playful rabbits" [l. 8]) which interests her; and indeed the poem may be said to reject symbolism altogether: "a barren tree" (l. 2) and the vulture (if it *is* a vulture) "crouching there" (l. 21) are interpreted not as "symbol" but as "prophecy" (l. 22), implying *real*, not symbolic fulfillment. "Pain is particular" (l. 19); the drama of the Passion is real, not symbolic, continually re-enacted in human affairs.

It is of cardinal significance that in "*Mantegna's Agony in the Garden*" it is the human *body* that is foregrounded: the "fingers" (l. 4), "arms" (l. 5), "sandalled feet" (l. 6) of the sleeping disciples; and yet at the same time the intersection of this bodily humanity with the divine is implied by the reference to the "halo" (l. 3) of the first of them, which "leans against a tree" (l. 3). Everywhere in Jennings we find the same incarnational interpenetration of the human and the divine. Stephen McInerney, discussing the use of the word "seeing" (l. 14) in the final sentence of "Grapes" (Jennings 2012, 311), one of many sonnets originally published in *Growing-Points* (1975), makes the perceptive comment that this gerund "does two things simultaneously, shifting the poem in two apparently opposite directions: toward a mystical 'seeing' on the one hand, and on the other a natural 'seeing'. The supernatural by definition transcends the natural, and yet the implication is that Christ's Passion is somehow already inscribed into the processes of the natural world" (2010, 214).

"Grapes" is a poem about visual contemplation, calling on the addressee to "look now" (l. 10), to "see" (l. 4), but it would do as well as any other to illustrate what Mason calls Jennings's "philosophy of poetry," whose aim is to make us "contemplative and attentive listeners of the world" (2012a, 964–965). It is in such contemplation that Mason detects the poet's attraction to Simone Weil (2012a, 966), though she does not omit to point out Jennings's reservations concerning the latter. Michael Schmidt, similarly, declares on the back cover of *New Collected Poems*: "Elizabeth Jennings listens carefully," thinking particularly of listening to history and the surprising question asked in one of Jennings's late poems, "Concerning History" (Jennings 2012, 786–791), "Does history tell love stories?" (l. I. 16). The poem quoted by Mason, "Love Needs an Elegy" (981), is one of many that strive to "listen" to the world, to "winds' parley with trees," (l. 14) for instance ("Forgiveness," Jennings 2012, 431–442), or that adjure the addressee to "Be quiet and listen, listen" (l. III. 26), as in the urgent injunction in the last part of "Concerning History." As Mason perceives, in her Preface to *The Collected Poems*, "The sense of words falling through a reflective silence defines much of Jennings's poetry" (Mason 2012b, xli). In *"Mantegna's Agony in the Garden,"* for instance, in spite or even because of the fact that its contemplation is entirely visual, the silence is, as the popular saying goes, almost audible. Drury has remarked that in the painting we cannot hear Christ's prayer or his surrender; instead "the body, by means of which it is all done, must tell it all" (1999, 90). Jennings's reflection on this painting creates an intensely listening space in which, as Mason so well expresses it, "meaning breathes through the page rather than being stated or declared" (xli); not for nothing, after all, does the sonnet "Grapes" resort to the image of ripe grapes on the vine "Swinging upon a pendulum of breath" (311, l. 11). Mason finds this "breathing" of meaning especially in "the countless 'O's that appear throughout her volumes of published work" (xli–xlii); she might have extended the comment to the previously unpublished work that her research has now made available. The passionate poem "Being" (Jennings 2012, 905), for example, contains as many as four of these ejaculative, prayerful "O"s, breathed from a kind of border between language and silence. They recall the poetry of both Herbert and Hopkins, two of the most prominent among Jennings's poetic "fellows," and even perhaps, in the plea "O let me not / Be nothing, nowhere, punished" (ll. 19–20), Louis MacNeice's well-known "Prayer before Birth," itself a reminiscence of Herbert.

Anna Walczuk has discussed the way in which in Jennings's poetry silence is thematized as a way toward communion with God (2017, 227–236), for example, in "Making a Silence" (Jennings 2012, 288; Walczuk 2017, 232). But it is typical of Jennings, poet of the intersections of the mundane and the mysterious, as Sloan aptly divines, that silence is seen, in this poem and elsewhere, as a means also of communion between persons. The silence that is "the greatest one of them all" (l. 9), the one that brings the gift of God's "infinite gracious peace" (l. 12), is an extension of those other silences: the one to lull a child to sleep or "help someone sick" (l. 4), the quiet of a night in which "you can feel the stars / And mercy over the world" (ll. 7–8). These silences, too, are gracious and merciful, images of that greater silence of God's felt presence. Silence as a motif in one of Jennings's most frequently anthologized poems, "One Flesh" (Jennings 2012, 210–211), singled out in Haynes's review, also implies the good silence that can be the means of communion between persons, respecting their differentness and separation, yet allowing them to be in fellowship with each other, "Strangely apart" (l. 13) and at the same time also "strangely close together" (l. 13): "Silence between them like a thread to hold / And not wind in" (ll. 14–15).

Strange, indeed: and this is another key word in Jennings, oxymoronically linking the familiar with the incomprehensible, as when Mary speaks in "The Annunciation" of "a strange child that is my own" (Jennings 2012, 81, l. 18). "One Flesh," with its commonplace, almost hackneyed details of the book that the man is holding but not reading, the light kept on late, the woman "dreaming of childhood" (l. 3), watching the shadows on the ceiling, recalls the early association of Jennings with the Movement poets, and is particularly reminiscent of Philip Larkin's "Talking in Bed" (1964, 29); but significantly, the two people in Jennings's poem are *not* talking, and the poem's movement is in a quite different direction, toward the mystical meaning of the phrase alluded to in the poem's title: "Therefore shall a man leave his father and his mother, and shall cleave unto his wife: and they shall be one flesh" (Gen. 2: 24). With the perspective defined in the penultimate line, "These two who are *my* father and *my* mother [emphasis added]" (l. 17), the everyday, particular situation of one couple becomes an emblem of far more than the (unachieved and unachievable) ideal set up in Larkin's poem. More than the talking that ought to be "an emblem of two people being honest" (Larkin 29, l. 3), the silence between "my father and my mother" points toward the true, paradisal communion of human beings who are God's delighted gift to each other in a world where they can still meet God "walking in the garden in the cool of the day" (Gen. 3: 8). In this context, perhaps even the phrase "How cool they lie" (l. 8), so far from endorsing the idea of the death of passion implied in the poem's last line, is a reminiscence of the prelapsarian "holy communion" where human beings are at one with one another and with God.

Silence, however, in Jennings's poetry is far from inevitably implying happy communion. Cathy Parc's reading of "Whitsun Sacrament" (Jennings 2012, 320), for example, which she describes as "a truly apophatic text" because it causes "possession and dispossession, fulfillment and frustration, to paradoxically coalesce" (Parc 2013, 317), makes Jennings, like R. S. Thomas, a poet of the hidden God, the God whose silence is that of absence rather than of presence. The shade of one of Hopkins's "terrible sonnets" of abandonment hovers in the phrase "Spirit, Spirit, where / Are you to be caught now" (ll. 6–7) ("Comforter, where, where is your comforting?" writes Hopkins in "No worst, there is none," 1970, 100, l. 3). In "Whitsun Sacrament," it is the negative, the absent, or soon to be absent, that is emphasized: "childhood just about to leave" (l. 2); "not sure we believe" (l. 4); questions whose answers do not satisfy; the Spirit, the dove, peace that are sought for and not found; and finally, in the face of our "most need" (l. 14), only "Christ at his silentest" (l. 15). Mason has noted Jennings's predilection for the negative prefix "un-" (961); in one of the poems singled out by Haynes, for instance, "The Young Ones," we find three examples: "unread" (l. 4), "Unfinished" (l. 12), "unsure" (l. 16) (Jennings 2012, 180–181). The titles of as many as 12 poems from Mason's collection begin with the words "No," "Not," or "Nothing." One of these poems, furthermore, is a quotation from the very same sonnet as the one alluded to in "Whitsun Sacrament": Hopkins's "No worst, there is none." This sonnet, incidentally, also supplied the title for Jennings's disturbing collection *The Mind Has Mountains* (1966), which focuses on the experiences associated with depression and mental breakdown.

"Nothing" is the opening word of a poem whose subject is, surprisingly, the first Joyful Mystery of the Rosary: "Nothing will ease the pain to come" ("The Annunciation," Jennings 2012, 80–81). Certainties of joyful experience are repeatedly undercut in the poem by the warning reservations of the word "though": "Though now she sits in ecstasy" (l. 2); "Though in her heart new loving burns" (l. 10); "Though a god stirs beneath her breast" (l. 23). Of the 15 lines of one of the frequently anthologized poems mentioned in Haynes's review, "Absence" (Jennings 2012, 67), five contain the words "nothing," "no," or "not." True, their implication on the surface of it is positive: "Nothing was changed" (l. 2); "there was no sign that anything had ended" (l. 4). But in "the gardens" (l. 2) where lovers once met and do so no more, the lack of change, the continuing "ecstasy" (l. 7) of "thoughtless birds" (l. 6) becomes a terrible mockery, much as in John Donne's "Twicknam Garden" (Gardner 1976, 66), of which Jennings's poem is subtly reminiscent. The negative implications of the title word, which is repeated in the poem itself, dominate the poem; "absence" (l. 12) comes to seem a "savage force" (l. 12), capable of destroying the garden.

These apophatic notes in Jennings's poetry, however, are counterpointed by an equally powerful cataphatic strain, a joyous "sense of the world." In an article significantly entitled "Saved by Poetry," Jennings writes of an experience that she had as a child of about ten: "I remember going out one night into our front garden in Oxford which was full of small trees and shrubs. The sky was crowded with stars and I felt an exaltation such as I had never known before and have never known since so fully and richly" (*The Tablet* 15 May 1993). In the same article, she says that at a certain point in her life, "reading poetry became a kind of secular sacrament, a true grace"; it was poetry and painting that were finally to restore her sense of the wonder of the world and at the same time bring her Roman Catholic faith "to a radiant life." Both of these things come together in the experience of the Eucharist, so frequently the overt ("At Mass (I)," "At Mass (II)," Jennings 2012, 741, 743) or covert ("Grapes," 311) subject of Jennings's poetry; and here, again, Hopkins is Jennings's poetic companion. This time, however, it is the Hopkins of "Felix Randal" (Hopkins 86), filled with joy in his priestly vocation, in his ability to bring the help of the sacraments to those entrusted to his care.

"This seeing the sick endears them to us, us too it endears" is the reflection that begins the sestet in Hopkins's poem; Jennings's response also has the form of a sonnet, significantly entitled "Homage to Gerard Manley Hopkins: After Receiving Communion in

Hospital" (Jennings 2012, 801–802). The poem begins with conversational directness, in a manner that suggests that the experience referred to in the title has made it possible to appreciate the words of the priest-poet, not merely as poetic expression but as "proved upon the pulses," as it were: "Hopkins, I understand exactly now / What you meant when you told us that the sick / Endear us to them" (ll. 1–3). In her essay on Hopkins in *Every Changing Shape*, Jennings suggests that David Jones's saying, "There is no escape from incarnation" might form the "epigraph" to all of Hopkins's work (Jennings 1961, 97). Pointing in the conclusion to her discussion (Jennings 1961, 110) to Hopkins's sense of the dignity of the *body*, she quotes some lines from his sonnet "The Caged Skylark": "Man's spirit will be fleshbound when found at best" (Hopkins 71, l. 12). The title of her direct poetic tribute to Hopkins sets it in a context in which the spirit is pre-eminently "fleshbound," in which indeed the body itself is confined, within the walls of a hospital. It is here, in the heart of the world's in*carn*ational suffering, where attention is inevitably focused on the body, that the sick person comes to "know what Hopkins meant." In the peace that comes "after receiving communion in hospital," the human oneness of body and soul is restored. It matters not that "I know my flesh behaves // Oddly" (ll. 8–9), for in the Eucharist "I know also I am / Within Heaven's confines" (ll. 9–10). The wonder in "A tiny piece of bread unleavened" (l. 6) is the mystery of *Deus absconditus*, the hidden, incarnate God who is silent but present, who comes, as one might say, "fleshbound," to meet and be one with fleshbound creatures. This is the *latens Deitas*, the God of St. Thomas Aquinas's Eucharistic hymn and of Jennings's joyous contemplation, in the sonnet addressed to Hopkins and in countless other places: in the previously unpublished "A Hidden King" (Jennings 2012, 877), for example; or in the incomprehensible "hiding God-made-Man" of "Consecration (II)" (l. 16), the Christ "so quietly lent // To all," (ll. 12–13) the God who "Hides in this frail Host" (l. 6) (Jennings 2012, 745–746).

Cathy Parc has argued recently that in some of Jennings's poetry, the experiences of her adolescence are relived "without any real poeticizing" in such a way that "the page finally turned into a confessional" (312). Given the phrases quoted, it appears that it is mainly the poems originally published in *Times and Seasons* (1992) that are the subject of this criticism; but it is not entirely clear in what the lack of "real poeticizing" consists. More than 20 years earlier, Samuel Maio had concluded, quite to the contrary, that the distancing effects of structures of meter and rhyme in Jennings's work tend to produce a poetry that universalizes individual, personal experience; and indeed that her Catholicism was "a force regulating excessive 'confessionals' in her poetry" (1991, 23). "Consecration (II)" certainly supports this claim: its gaze is focused on the actions of the priest, seen with the bodily eye, and the actions of God, seen with the eye of faith, and this, combined with the use of plural pronouns, allows the expression of personal feeling to be powerfully implied and yet not directly stated. With the enjambment poised over the stanza break and the negative formulation, "So that *no ecstasy* [emphasis added] // Should too excite us, God / Hides in this frail Host" (ll. 4–6), intimate feeling is both expressed and held in check. Against the background of the poem's exquisitely simple, almost entirely monosyllabic vocabulary, the word "ecstasy" stands out, an attempt to "Find words" (l. 15) for the astonishing mystery of the Mass and the collective and individual experience of it.

"Consecration (II)" does not emerge directly out of Jennings's childhood or adolescent experience, like those that Parc holds up for criticism; but similar things could surely also be said of one of the poems that Parc does quote: "First Confession" (Jennings 2012, 660). While its very subject, a child's first experience of sacramental confession within the framework of the Roman Catholic church, evidently arises from Jennings's own experience, the poem's carefully rhymed stanzaic structure allows the experience to be contained and ordered, reflected on from an adult perspective (the sacrament is "healing" (l. 13), after all), its significance taken in, a conclusion drawn from it that is not merely personal: "the child's right element / Of joy should not be risked so early" (ll. 15–16). The poem concludes with three powerful monosyllables of which, appropriately, the last is "shut"; and while there is regret in this final phrase ("childhood's door slams shut" [l. 18]), there is also perhaps an implied exorcizing of the feeling expressed in the poem's opening line ("So long ago and yet it taunts me still"): the memory can taunt no longer. Thus the poem moves from the painful account of a particular experience to acceptance and a kind of understanding. It is difficult to see how a poem of such finesse can be described either as straightforwardly confessional or as lacking in "real poeticizing." Mason shows much more acuity than Parc, first in sketching out a distinct contrast between the "confident [...] mode of expression" of Jennings's poetry and the "persistently anxious and depressed personality" of the writer (975), and secondly in a claim she makes in her discussion of the poets who are important to Jennings: her "veneration of [Robert] Frost's ability to achieve a muted and held-back affective power that refused to divulge personal detail is central to her own identification as a Christian poet, and not a quiet confessional one" (976).

I have been critical of some aspects of Parc's approach to Jennings; but I fully agree with her when she writes that Jennings's poetry "aims at unveiling the ins and outs of an experience which was lived through, without in any way unravelling its deeper mystery" (Parc 2013, 305). There certainly seems to be something about Jennings's art that suggests being content to live with mystery in an attitude of contemplative listening, without trying to master or understand it. The same applies to her approach to art, especially the art of poetry, including her own. When asked to compile an anthology of some of the poems that had "helped to shape [her] judgment and [her] art," Jennings recalled the "transfiguring" experience of reading G. K. Chesterton's "Lepanto" at the age of 13 (Introduction to *A Poet's Choice*, Jennings 1996, xiii–xiv). Quite evidently it was not merely the excitement of the poem's action, but the vigor of its rhythms and the orchestration of its sounds that stirred her. As she wrote early in her career, in *Christianity and Poetry*, "Most poets [...] experience this feeling of the form working through them at its own pace and rhythm" (Jennings 1965, 43); she is speaking of Spenser, but she could equally be speaking of herself. Despite the high value that she placed on craft and her virtuoso handling of traditional poetic forms, many poems in Jennings's *oeuvre* that take art as their subject express a conviction that the poem emerges somehow independently of its author: "On Making," for instance (Jennings 2012, 46), or "The Way of Words and Language" (Jennings 2012, 538–539). It is worth pondering the last lines of a sonnet entitled "Steps towards Poems" which Jennings herself quotes in "Saved by Poetry": speaking of the way that a poem always "rides free" (l. 10) and "will not come / To easy bidding" (ll. 10–11), she concludes, "Revere it but do not think of it too much. / It never will add up into a sum" (Jennings 2012, 705, l. 14).

The opening line of one poem, "Pieta," unpublished before Mason's collection appeared, suggests the vital importance of the mysterious to human flourishing: "We thrive, it seems, on mystery" (Jennings 2012, 917, l. 1). The simplicity of the ekphrasis carried out in this poem, in which "A girl, scarcely grown up / Supports a dead man on her yielding lap," (ll. 2–3) restores, by defamiliarization, the extraordinariness of an image to which custom has inured us. Similarly, Jennings's poetry strives not to lose the sense of the mystery in everyday life and the ordinary experience of human love. This is a mystery that, to judge from the sonnet "The Way They Live Now" (Jennings 2012, 669), she might have feared was disappearing. Alluding in the title to the corrupt and greedy world depicted in Trollope's satirical novel of 1875, the poem sadly accuses the contemporary world of reducing love to a mere commodity to be grasped in one instant appropriating gesture: "You take the whole of love" (l. 11). By contrast, the simple, perfect rhyme "chance / glance" in the final lines leaves an image of the lovely mystery that there can and should be in the experience of other human beings, as in every aspect of life: "We lived by touch / And doubt and by the purposes of chance / And yet I think our slow ways carried much / That you have missed – the guess, the wish, the glance" (ll. 11–14). It is the "slow way," the way of listening, which is the guiding principle of Jennings's art.

References

Aitchison, James (2013). *New Guide to Poetry and Poetics*. Amsterdam/New York: Rodopi.

Drury, John (1999). *Painting the Word*. New Haven/London: Yale University Press.

Gardner, Helen (ed.) (1972). *The Metaphysical Poets*. Harmondsworth: Penguin Books.

Haynes, Anthony (2002). "Most Catholic Poet." Review of *New Collected Poems* by E. Jennings. *The Tablet* (13 April): 19–20.

Herbert, George (1967). *A Choice of George Herbert's Verse*, selected with an introduction by R. S. Thomas. London: Faber and Faber.

Hopkins, Gerard Manley (1970). *Poems*. Oxford: Oxford University Press.

Jennings, Elizabeth (1953). *Poems*. Eynsham: Fantasy Press.

Jennings, Elizabeth (1958). *A Sense of the World*. London: Andre Deutsch.

Jennings, Elizabeth (1961). *Every Changing Shape*. London: Andre Deutsch.

Jennings, Elizabeth (1965). *Christianity and Poetry*. London: Burns and Oates.

Jennings, Elizabeth (1966). *The Mind Has Mountains*. London: Macmillan.

Jennings, Elizabeth (1976). *Seven Men of Vision: An Appreciation*. London: Vision Press.

Jennings, Elizabeth (1979). *Selected Poems*. Manchester: Carcanet.

Jennings, Elizabeth (1986). Review. *The Faber Book of Religious Verse* (ed. H. Gardner) *The Tablet* (11 October), p. 16.

Jennings, Elizabeth (1986). *Collected Poems*. Manchester: Carcanet.

Jennings, Elizabeth (1992). *Times and Seasons*. Manchester: Carcanet.

Jennings, Elizabeth (1993). *Desert Island Discs*. Interviewed by S. Lawley (8 January), BBC Radio 4 podcast.

Jennings, Elizabeth (1993). "Saved by Poetry." *The Tablet* (15 May): 13.

Jennings, Elizabeth (1996). *A Poet's Choice*. Anthology selected by Elizabeth Jennings. Manchester: Carcanet.

Jennings, Elizabeth (2002). *New Collected Poems* (ed. Michael Schmidt). Manchester: Carcanet.

Jennings, Elizabeth (2012). *The Collected Poems* (ed. Emma Mason). Manchester: Carcanet.

Jones, David (1972. Preface). *The Anathemata*. London: Faber and Faber.

Larkin, Philip (1964). *The Whitsun Weddings*. London: Faber and Faber.

Lawley, Sue (1993). Interview with Elizabeth Jennings. *Desert Island Discs* (8 January), BBC Radio 4 podcast.

Maio, Samuel (1991). "A Sound and Fruitful Attitude: The Poetry of Robert Conquest, Elizabeth Jennings, and Charles Causley." *The Formalist* 2 (2): 22–23.

Mason, Emma (2012a. Afterword. Elizabeth Jennings). *The Collected Poems*. Manchester: Carcanet.

Mason, Emma (2012b. Preface. Elizabeth Jennings). *The Collected Poems*. Manchester: Carcanet.

McInerney, Stephen (2010). "'Art with Its Largesse and Its Own Restraint': The Sacramental Poetics of Elizabeth Jennings and Les Murray." In: *Between Human and Divine: The Catholic Vision in Contemporary Literature* (ed. Mary R. Reichardt), 207–225. Washington, D.C.: The Catholic University of America Press.

Parc, Cathy (2013). "'Tongue(s) of Fire': Echoes of the Sacred in Elizabeth Jennings's Poetry." In: *Poetry and Religion: Figures of the Sacred* (eds. Ineke Bockting, Jennifer Kilgore-Caradec and Cathy Parc), 305–327. Bern: Peter Lang.

Schmidt, Michael (2002. Preface. Elizabeth Jennings). *New Collected Poems*. Manchester: Carcanet.

Sloan, Barry (2006). "Poetry and Faith: The Example of Elizabeth Jennings." *Christianity and Literature* 55 (3): 393–414.

Walczuk, Anna (2017). *Elizabeth Jennings and the Sacramental Nature of Poetry*. Kraków: Jagiellonian University Press.

Ward, Jean (2007). "Elizabeth Jennings: An Exile in her Own Country?" *Literature and Theology* 21 (2): 198–213.

Ward, Jean (2009). *Christian Poetry in the Post-Christian Day: Geoffrey Hill, R. S. Thomas, Elizabeth Jennings*. Frankfurt am Main: Peter Lang.

Ward, Jean (2013). "Visiting an Artist: Elizabeth Jennings Contemplates the 'Assiduous Craft' of David Jones." In: *Poets of the Past, Poets of the Present* (eds. Monika Szuba and Tomasz Wiśniewski), 93–113. Wydawnictwo Uniwersytetu Gdańskiego: Gdańsk/Sopot.

Ward, Jean (2016). "'Be Quiet and Listen, Listen'. Sound, Rhythm and the Paradoxes of History and Faith in Elizabeth Jennings's Poetry." In: *Sound Is/As Sense* (eds. David Malcolm and Wolfgang Görtschacher), 181–200. Gdańsk: Wydawnictwo Uniwersytetu Gdańskiego.

3.9
"Forever in Excess": Barry MacSweeney, Consumerism, and Popular Culture

Paul Batchelor

Barry MacSweeney was a poet of excess. His finest moments occur when his writing is almost overwhelmed by musical effects, emotion, allusion, or influence. A prolific, protean writer, as soon as he became aware of a new voice, style, or subject, he would appropriate and modify it to suit his purposes. MacSweeney's speedy responsiveness may be understood in terms of his lifelong career as a journalist, producing copy to a deadline and keeping ahead of the competition—as S. J. Litherland has noted, "the romance and drama of the newsroom entered his poetics" (Litherland 2013, 170–181; 171)—but it also relates to his abiding interest in popular culture and consumerism. As these aspects of his poetry have received relatively little attention, this essay will keep them in mind while giving an overview of some of MacSweeney's most significant work.

MacSweeney's first book, *The Boy from the Green Cabaret Tells of His Mother* (hereafter *Cabaret*), appeared in 1968 from a leading commercial press, Hutchinson. At this time poetry was being read, or heard, by an unusually large audience, and MacSweeney's formative experiences as a poet were bound up with issues of fame, celebrity, notoriety, and exploitation. Eric Homberger describes the changing literary scene.

> The gap between academic verse and its opposite – call it "naked" or whatever – became a permanent feature of the landscape, to the consequent impoverishment of both. There was no end to the cant, posturing, self-promotion, cabals and logrolling. It was, one supposes, the way things had always been, only more so. […] Culture came to be Balkanized, with new "scenes" emerging in Liverpool, Newcastle, New York, the Pacific North-West, and the Heartland of the Midwest. […] There was a lot of protest poetry, poems which sounded like song lyrics (and vice versa) […].
> (Homberger 1977, 179)

A Companion to Contemporary British and Irish Poetry, 1960–2015, First Edition.
Edited by Wolfgang Görtschacher and David Malcolm.
© 2021 John Wiley & Sons Ltd. Published 2021 by John Wiley & Sons Ltd.

Cabaret contained its share of posturing and protest poetry, but its principal failing is the clumsiness of its attempt to consume and regurgitate the "Balkanized" literary scene: it consists of imitations of the styles of its day, from Prynne's dense lyricism to audience-pleasing Liverpool pop poetry. There are also numerous references to popular music, for example, "Sealine" (dated June 20, 1967; *Desire Lines* 2018, 27) begins with the word "woman," a reference to the folk song Nina Simone popularized as "See-Line Woman" (first released as a B-side to "Mississippi Goddam" in 1964). The most pervasive influence is that of Bob Dylan. Terry Kelly has written of MacSweeney's lifelong devotion to Dylan's music (Kelly 2013, 157–169), and the Dylanesque trope of the wise, wandering youth informs both the early poetry—for example, "we are young dont [sic] touch us / we make love & we are refreshed" ("Touching," MacSweeney 1968, 53, ll. 1–2)—and the way that it was marketed (*Cabaret*'s blurb describes MacSweeney as a troubadour, and says that the poems are for the young). When his publisher arranged for him to be nominated for the Professorship of Poetry at Oxford, the 20-year-old MacSweeney (who had three "O" Levels, and had never been to university) became, for a few months anyway, a celebrity. Many newspapers and magazines ran features on the story and interviewed the poet. *Penthouse* gave him the most sympathetic hearing (Anon. *Penthouse* 1968, 12).

> MacSweeney accepts all the publicity that comes his way philosophically. He wonders whether he is quite big enough to warrant it and knows that publicity alone can't keep him alive … But it seems certain that he has enough talent to ensure that he doesn't become the nine days' wonder that people predict for him.

Commentators usually portray MacSweeney as the unwitting victim of Hutchinson's publicity stunt, as when Gordon Burn writes that "it was a less celebrity-fixated culture then, and MacSweeney wasn't wise to the ways of the world, and didn't see the train until it hit him" (Burn 2000). MacSweeney himself endorsed this view when he was interviewed by Eric Mottram: "What do you expect me to do? I'm 16, 17, from a working class background, that has no literary connections […]. I didn't know what the hell was going on" (Mottram 1977, 25). But he was a little disingenuous. In a *Daily Telegraph* article on October 30, 1968, Anne Steele writes that she interviewed MacSweeney "in a café in Great Portland Street […] he pushed the tomato ketchup bottle away before the photographer arrived murmuring 'I don't want a working class image'" (Steele 1968). In other articles collected in the Barry MacSweeney Papers, he complains that all of his television interviews have been staged in slum settings. In other words, MacSweeney realized that he was being packaged as a working-class wonder boy, but could not withdraw from the process altogether: the prospect of fame was too tempting. On October 13, 1968, Murray Sayle wrote an article for the *Sunday Times* that included fabricated quotes from MacSweeney,[1] leading to Kingsley Amis calling him "a trendy hippie of no achievements" in the *New Statesman* (Amis 1968). MacSweeney subsequently defended himself in a *Guardian* interview, but lost the Oxford Chair vote to John Fuller by three votes to 350. After this he was treated as a figure of fun, dropped by his publisher, and forgotten about.

This brutal schooling in how he could be packaged, consumed, and discarded left MacSweeney with a deep and enduring suspicion of academic or otherwise official literary culture. He embraced the emerging small-press poetic communities that then called themselves the British Poetry Revival.[2] Nevertheless, he had benefitted from the brief bubble of popularity that poetry had enjoyed, and would occasionally express nostalgia for it: "4,000 turn up at Newcastle City Hall to hear intermingling joy-sounds from local poets & rock groups (a cut of the door takings – those were the days!)" (MacSweeney 1979, 38). Having misrepresented himself in *Cabaret*, and having been more damagingly misrepresented by the media, MacSweeney was disinclined to present the kind of single, unified persona that might have appealed to a popular audience; but a buried wish for such an audience may be inferred by his continuing identification with pop culture heroes. The paradox of engaging with popular culture while writing increasingly difficult poetry defines much of the poetry MacSweeney wrote in the 1970s. In his introduction to *Desire Lines: Unselected Poems 1966–2000*, editor Luke Roberts writes that his selection "emphasize[s] MacSweeney's sequence-length experimentation" during the 1970s, and he includes two long, challenging poems that were abandoned prior to publication. The many references to popular culture in these works, which were not written to court a wider audience, show how central they were to MacSweeney's process. The 1972 poem "Toad Church" (DL 83–96) features shout-outs to "the divine / Bing Crosby" (91, ll. 124–125) and T-Rex (94, l. 208), while "Pelt Feather Log" (DL 107–129), from 1974, includes a reference to "Protocol harm" (111, l. 80), a play on the name of the 1960s rock band Procol Harum, and "watch the river flow" (117, l. 346), a reference to Bob Dylan's 1971 single "Watching the River Flow."

MacSweeney's most thoroughgoing engagement with rock-star mythology in this period is found in *Just 22 and I Don't Mind Dyin': The Official Poetical Biography of Jim Morrison, Rock Idol* (WT 2003, 20–22; hereafter *Just 22*), which was first published in 1971. Instead of a biography, the poem consists of a collage of lines ranging in tone from the faux naïf "If finesse is crinkly you're a / Dairy Box wrapper" (21, ll. 39–40), which sounds like a parody of the gauche moments in *Cabaret*, to the bracing exhortation "Wake up cunt you're living your life in bed" (20, l. 8). The poem reflects the priorities of late 1960s culture in the relish it takes in its own novelty, and in its impatience for pleasure: why build context, can't we just have the best lines right now? A compendium of gestures, attitudes, and one-liners, the poem attempts to bottle Morrison's lightning spirit. It begins:

> Rock litmus. Titration from Springfield, she
> wore no colour besides, unfashionable & mean, held
> such chemistry in high frond.
> Nothing else to commend her before she died.
> (20, ll. 1–4)

In its paratactic mix of registers, referents, and tones, *Just 22* enacts the freak out: the 1960s notion of the sudden insight that obliterates and reintegrates the ego. Such experiences could be facilitated by guru figures such as Dylan or Morrison, and *Just 22* is offered as a performance of MacSweeney's shamanic powers. A footnote states: "Written on 25 September 1971, High

Barnet, Hertfordshire" (22). This was a one-off performance, an album recorded in a single take, and in an interview with Eric Mottram, MacSweeney claimed to have produced it having taken "about 45 Benzedrine [...], with headphones on listening to Doors records on the turntable, about 4 hours non-stop. [...] That was the ritual" (Mottram 1977, 36).[3] Mottram does not share MacSweeney's enthusiasm for Dylan and the Doors, and is dismissive of what he calls the "rather corny Freudian Oedipalism" in "The End" (Mottram 1977, 35).

MacSweeney's engagement with rock-star-guru self-mythologizing deepens in the 35 poems collected in *Odes* (WT 1978, 35–81), which were written between 1971 and 1978. Strictly speaking, none of these poems is an ode, nor are they especially musical, and, as MacSweeney conceded, they are too complex to work well in performance (Mottram 1977, 37); they are, however, concerned with the figure of the singer, whether poet or rock star, in contemporary culture. Several poems are named after hero/heroine figures (Jim Morrison, Thomas Chatterton, Mia Farrow, and Emanuel Swedenborg), but titles that promise identification usually bear a teasingly oblique relation to their poems: although Morrison is referred to in several *Odes*, he does not appear in "Jim Morrison Ode." Likewise, the two poems called "Chatterton Ode" make only indirect references to Chatterton, who is given a more straightforward consideration in "Ode:Resolution." A further five poems actually depict hero figures in a relatively straightforward manner. Most of the remaining poems concern the poet's own relationships with women. In *Cabaret*, MacSweeney had engaged in slavish imitation of his literary influences, but in *Odes* he holds such figures up to criticism. Consider, for example, "Viper Suck Ode" (62), in which we read "You cannot petition / the Lord / with prayer" (ll. 11–13). This is a quotation from "The Soft Parade," the title track of The Doors album from 1969, but whereas Jim Morrison delivers this line with the near-hysterical rage of a hellfire preacher, MacSweeney lets the words lie inert on the page, and adds the condescending "That's right / Jim" (ll. 14–15). The poem begins by invoking vipers and tigers—Morrison's song lyrics and poetry include many references to such creatures—but ends with the domestic bath and shower, deflating Morrison's visionary posturing, and implicitly admonishing his self-destructive tendencies.

While some of the poems in *Odes* are critical of the solipsism and self-indulgence of rock stars, in others MacSweeney writes about himself as though he were such a figure. In this he is following Michael McClure, a Beat poet who became a prominent figure in 1960s counterculture, and who helped Morrison publish his book of poems, *The Lords*. McClure's poetry also contains addresses to dead rock stars, cryptic leaps of association, and a rejection of sustained syntax, but the most obvious shared characteristic is the use of center-justified lines, which appeared exotic and prestigious in the 1960s and 1970s because of the relative difficulty and expense of typesetting them. However, where McClure's lines explode joyously from a reactive center, MacSweeney's often seem hemmed-in by the white space around them, as in "Real Ode" (63–65; 63, ll. 4–8):

(We
met for lunch
in secret
Soho
squares.)

A rock star might arrange a secret lunch in order to avoid swarms of fans, but MacSweeney's reasons are more banal: the quoted lines are a private reference to the early days of his relationship with Elaine Randell, when he already had a girlfriend. Note the way the layout of the quoted lines masks a perfectly regular line of iambic pentameter, something that would be anathema to McClure: combining antithetical styles and antecedents is characteristic of MacSweeney's work. Another poem, "Snake Paint Sky" (45), appears to conflate Morrison-as-Lizard-King with Jeremy Prynne. Only MacSweeney would do this:

> beaming Anaconda of parthian monumentalism your
> votes gloss acidly these white stone derivations
> I'm forever in excess to... (ll. 1–3)

Later in this poem, MacSweeney refers more specifically to his debt to Prynne's poetic technique in *The White Stones* (1969):

> confluence
> of equally mad
> sources
> electrically
> bridled (ll. 11–15)

These lines refer to Prynne's engagement with an eclectic range of scientific and other theoretical discourses. By drawing on such various source material, Prynne was not hoping to reach an ideally informed readership that could assimilate every reference; rather, he sought to draw attention to the political exclusions of any single, unified point of view. When academic readers follow Mottram's lead and denigrate or overlook MacSweeney's many references to popular culture they unwittingly downplay the confluence of sources, which is the most Prynnean aspect of these poems. Although the compacted language in *Odes* is reminiscent of Prynne—in "Ode," for example, we read "But / clank another / point to / the maquis, altar / in the offside, together / by the feminine / time" (43, ll. 19–25)—the differences are telling, and as Robert Sheppard has noted, *Odes* "lacks the sophisticated smoothness of tone associated with much Cambridge poetry" (Sheppard 1999, 14). This lack is not necessarily a negative, as MacSweeney's work was increasingly characterized by its sudden shifts of register, and by the cracks that open between discourses; this would reach its delirious climax in the sometimes obscene and violent poetry MacSweeney wrote between 1979 and 1982, especially in "Liz Hard" (WT 2003, 95–100) and "Jury Vet" (WT 2003, 101–131).

"Jury Vet" is an intensification of the sexual focus of *Odes*. In the earlier volume, some of the sexually explicit references sound bawdy rather than offensive: "lavender torpedo" ("Torpedo," 58, l. 11), "naked pencil" ("Torpedo," 58, l. 1), "Gristle piston" ("Panther Freckles," 49, l. 11), "moons / of fat" ("Ode Peace Frog," 50, ll. 8–9), and "the vulva / clam" ("Snake Paint Sky," 45, ll. 23–24). But a new note is heard in some of *Odes'* compounds of obscenity and fashion-industry language, such as "frig tits when they / lubricate / the starlet's feathered // twat" ("Ode Stem Hair" 48, ll. 12–15), or these lines from "Fox Brain Apple Ode" (52, ll. 9–12):

> Moths flame inside her
> crimson yoni,
> as if she were a Zodiac
> in pink July

These lines are reworked in "Jury Vet" (101, ll. 10–18):

> Thrill box arias in the lust of tampon grandeur.
> Frill tease stockingtop flames.
> Sue cancels each Deneuving rivulet of horn.
> Swelling lapus cuffchunks,
> yoni triggered like a frigidaire
> in a
> Zodiac
> of
> magenta Aprils.

Throughout *Jury Vet*, sartorial details dazzle and cascade, giving the poem a lush, thick texture like an expensive fabric. The references to music and fashion lead Clive Bush to see the poem as an attack on consumer culture: "the young vainly attempt to turn the fact that they have been targeted by a cynical mass production machine, known curiously by the name of 'popular' culture, into some kind of self-authored gesture" (Bush 1997, 413). The poem unquestionably portrays consumerism as a code for compulsive overindulgence, resulting in fetishistic obsession and self-loathing, but the poem is far from being a straightforward attack. MacSweeney's enthusiastic acceptance of the star myth, and his love of the objects he lists, amounts to a quintessentially punk position in which the speaker revels in his abject, defeated state, and wishes above all to offend the reader. Punk's paradoxical position (antisocial, anticapitalist, antisystem, and yet also forming a community, a fashion, and an ethos) made perfect sense to MacSweeney, since, as Marianne Morris has observed in an insightful essay on MacSweeney's work of this period, punk's requirement was "not exactly that it should oppose what it loathed, but that it should become something equally loathsome as a mode of opposition" (Morris 2004, 13).

The assaults on female celebrities such as Catherine Deneuve in "Jury Vet" are more complicated than the poem's self-destructive tendencies. The spectacle of sexualized violence becomes a means by which the damaged self-projects itself onto the object of its desire/disgust, but the question of whether the misogyny is a critique of consumerism or simply symptomatic of internalized prejudice is left deliberately unresolved. John Wilkinson has offered a provocative and persuasive reading of the poem's volatility and excess as an example of "male panic" at the advent of Margaret Thatcher (Wilkinson 2013, 87–106) and a robust defense of the poem's centrality to MacSweeney's oeuvre (Wilkinson 2007, 77–96).

Despite its punk-derived ethos, references in "Jury Vet" to music are respectful and without irony: MacSweeney sets quotations apart by printing them in capital letters, or using them as section titles, as in "BE A NICE GIRL KISS THE WARDERS" (a phrase from Elvis Costello's 1978 song "Pump It Up"). By doing so, MacSweeney does not subvert the authority of the lyrics he quotes, unlike his treatment of classical music references in "Liz Hard II" (WT 2003, 99–100) in which Liz informs us "Beethoven's a bang, / but Schubert / is a thigh-suck" (ll. 29–31) and that "I haven't got TCHAIKOVSKY TITS OR A DELIUS DANGLING TWAT" (l. 26). In other words, MacSweeney believed in a canon: punk was in, classical was out. Although MacSweeney's juxtaposition of, say, Pink Military and Thomas Wyatt might initially seem postmodern, these figures are cited for their authority: he still believes in the individual artist and the possibility of finding meaning and value in the creation and appreciation of artworks. This belief in the endurance of the individual, despite the assaults of consumerism, leads to a sudden and not entirely convincing change of tone in the final section of the poem, in which fetishism and brutality suddenly give way to rhapsodic tenderness.

"Wild Knitting" (WT 2003, 132–138), MacSweeney's next major poem, written in 1983, carries an epigraph from a contemporaneous song by Elvis Costello: "Everyday, everyday, everyday, I write the book." Despite this, the poem is highly critical of those who listen to "Rockstar posies, rubbishers / of text." The poem is a howl of protest at Thatcherism's assault on English industries and communities, and is unforgiving of the "Securicor / I'm only glad to be off the dole blokes" (132, ll. 3–4) who have allowed the "Albion Mills" (132, l. 6) to fall redundant. In a remarkable volte-face, mindless capitulation to Thatcher's vision is equated with punk attitudinizing:

> ...all
> the broken dollpeople say: Meat meat give me
> meat, boss: Boss me
> Up
> or I go Bostik nostril
> & totally Sickrude, need to be
> ordered, regular fishcakes & spam
> every day I write the book
> the bad book. (132, ll. 6–14)

As in "Jury Vet," the tone changes in the final section when an affecting image of the beloved is rescued from the flames: "So close to death / & the cover of September Vogue. / Always a September girl" (138, ll. 253–254). This is also the first positive reference to consumerism in the poem. From this point, the poem forms an elegiac lament that is more compelling because less sentimental than the equivalent moment in "Jury Vet." "Wild Knitting" ends with the image of a couple still threatened by the pernicious prefabrications of the cosmetics industry, journalism, and popular culture. Nevertheless, they go on, wearing the war-paint of the enemy, "fantastically / liprouged" (ll. 265–266), and willing to risk "the penalties / of speech / & blood" (ll. 267–269). "Wild Knitting" relocates the area where hope may be fostered from the public to the private sphere, and any hope in its conclusion is qualified and provisional.

After "Wild Knitting," references to rock music and popular culture disappear from MacSweeney's poetry for 8 years. Their absence coincides with a crisis in confidence

MacSweeney suffered. Between 1984 and 1985 he wrote *Ranter*, a book-length poem that engaged with revolutionary movements during the English Civil Wars. *Ranter* was an unusually controlled performance from a poet who is always at his best when driving his creative energies to excess. MacSweeney edited out references to Dylan lyrics from early drafts of the poem[4] and planted numerous references to Basil Bunting and Ken Smith in order to attract a new publisher, Bloodaxe Books (Batchelor 2013, 107–130). When *Ranter* failed to attract Bloodaxe, or any other large publisher (he had sent the manuscript to Faber and even to his old enemy Hutchinson), MacSweeney fell into depression and writer's block for several years, and his longstanding drink problem intensified into alcoholism.[5]

The poems MacSweeney wrote as he began to emerge from his depression were published as a pamphlet titled *Hellhound Memos* in 1993. These poems return repeatedly to the blues figure of the lost man at the crossroads, though the setting is contemporary Newcastle:

> Chapped fingers play the bottleneck
> at Gallowgate crossroads
> where we have lost Robert Johnson to some deep connection
> down the hellhound trail… ("19," WT 2003, 192, ll. 11–14)

The bottleneck refers to a blues guitar slide, the bottleneck of traffic at Gallowgate (an area in Newcastle City Centre), and to drinking in public. The vignette displays two characteristics of the blues that attracted MacSweeney. First, the blues are a working-class form: there are no blues sung from the point-of-view of judges, tax inspectors, or dentists, only from the point-of-view of the victims of these figures. The singer is one of the exploited, even when celebrating a minor victory such as duping someone out of money or cheating on a partner. Second, the blues are always self-orientated. Almost all objects and natural phenomena fulfill a dual role, asking to be read on a descriptive, realist plane and on a symbolic plane relating to the singer's state of mind: for example, a sunset might lead to the line "I hate to see the evening sun go down, / it makes me feel I'm on my last go round,"[6] and references to fishing (one of the few free pleasures available to any African-American in the 1930s) invariably refer figuratively to infidelity (as when Robert Johnson, in "Dead Shrimp Blues," worries that "someone been fishin' in my pond"). Likewise, in *Hellhound Memos*, the Gallowgate crossroads or the B&Q store ask to be read both as specific urban-realist locations and as portals to a surreal, purgatorial realm.[7]

The reader, from a safe distance, might appreciate MacSweeney's use of crystal coupon goblets and B&Q as witty signifiers of the compulsory, repetitive overconsumption that characterizes late capitalist society; but this perspective does not appear available to the speaker himself, to whom the amassed objects of his synthetic desires are sources of horror: "Hellhound, thee with vast purchase, off, off!" ("6," DL 2018, 219, l. 3). Here, "purchase" refers both to the hellhound's grip on the speaker, and to the annual rent or return from land. The hellhounds are depicted "carping and crapping" over what had once been common ground ("13," WT 2003, 190–191; 190, l. 4). A few lines later, the speaker asserts his connection to John Clare—"I miss my stew-bearing Mary" (l. 13)—and to Clare's poems of protest at enclosure: he is "taxed" (191, l. 21). MacSweeney connects the enclosure of common ground in the seventeenth century with the owner-occupier ethos that B&Q uses to market itself (B&Q

thrived during the 1980s house-price boom). MacSweeney's historicizing is acute: he is contrasting common land with Thatcher-era municipal ground: the former was owned by all and tended by all; the latter, officially owned by the local council, is territory fought over by gangs of bored youths. The fallen society is not described so much as dramatized through a multiplicity of voices and registers that include blues motifs, advertising shtick, cookery instructions, tabloid sloganeering, and the officialese of police reports.

Throughout *Hellhound Memos*, MacSweeney invokes his musical and literary heroes: "Anne Sexton, Robert Johnson, Barry MacSweeney at the crossroads / Swapping riffs on an Olympia portable…" ("Hellhound Rapefield Memo," DL 2018, 220, ll. 6–7). It is the act of *naming* these antecedents that is important here. Detail is not built up: instead, the roll call is compulsively repeated in order to sustain an aggrandizing self-myth that, like equivalent gestures in blues lyrics, is a reaction to society's negative perception of the individual: as Robert Johnson sang in "Crossroads Blues": "Me and the devil were walking side by side…."

Some of MacSweeney's most beautiful and affecting writing can be found in his next volume, *Pearl* (WT 2003, 193–216), first published in 1995, with additional poems appearing in the 1999 pamphlet *Pearl in the Silver Morning* (WT 2003, 319–325). These poems tell of the poet's childhood friendship with a mute girl, Pearl, whom he taught to write. Some of the poems are "spoken" by Pearl, but the repeated assertion "I am Pearl" should also be understood as MacSweeney's declaring that he, too, is a silenced, damaged child. Consumerism is now once more an evil to be rejected. He is careful not to commodify Sparty Lea's rural environs, and is withering in his dismissal of "the turbo-mob, weird souls dreaming of car-reg // numbers and mobile phone codes" ("Cushy Number," 320, ll. 9–10), for whom cottages in beautiful landscapes mean simply "bijou conversion possibilities" (l. 8). MacSweeney avoids sentimentalizing Pearl and her suffering, and sounds a nostalgic note only in the sequence's numerous images of now-defunct industry, as in Pearl's "Woolworth butterfly blue plastic clip, still made in Britain / then…" ("Fever," 203, ll. 19–20).

Completing the process of self-examination that began in *Hellhound Memos* and continued in *Pearl*, the 1997 collection *The Book of Demons* (WT 2003, 217–290) tells of MacSweeney's experience of alcoholism and detox in 1990s Newcastle. Rather than simply expressing hero-worship for other doomed singers, he projects the blues anti-hero aspect of himself and invites the reader to identify with it. The hellhounds were merely paranoid projections, and could be warded off by invoking the holy names of Anne Sexton, Robert Johnson, and Barry MacSweeney; by contrast, the demons are more richly symbolic, for in a sense they *are* Anne Sexton, Robert Johnson, and Barry MacSweeney—they are embodiments of the self-destructive tendencies that he once found attractive, and which he believed helped make him a poet. To take just one example of the poet espousing this view, consider these lines from 1974's "Pelt Feather Log" (DL 2018, 107–129):

> I stare into the many-faceted base
>   of my cider glass
> & feel the power of poetry
> extending its plumed arm through my mouth!
>   (112, ll. 88–91)

Later in the poem, MacSweeney writes "open yr throat / and swallow the world" (118, ll. 368–369), lines that could stand as an *ars poetica* for his work at this time, but in *The Book of Demons* the time has come for the poet to take account of his lifelong consumption, and the act of vomiting acquires a symbolic as well as a literal dimension. For example, "Strap Down in Snowville" (266–268) finds the poet "drunken to the last, flung / to the lost in the final Labour council-run / public toilet on earth" (266, ll. 8–10), boasting that "This is *my* toilet cubicle now! I can vomit as I like" (267, l. 55). In an essay that considers the various ways in which MacSweeney "casts out" his demons, influences, old selves, and alcohol addiction, W. N. Herbert has noted that "Whether MacSweeney is systematically assigning roles or, as so often, adopting and absorbing personae and voices, is less important here than the sense of his career-long psychodrama of influences reaching a point of resolution in tandem with the recovery from addiction" (Herbert 2013, 156).

Along with blues references, and name-checks for Muddy Waters and Huddie Ledbetter, there are quotations from Bob Dylan (including one quotation from "Isis" and three from "I and I"), Maurice Chevalier in the line "And the leaves in the trees seem to whisper Louise because they're nuts" ("John Bunyan To Johnny Rotten," 288, l. 175), and Bonnie Raitt in the line "Get out the shotgun put it in the gunrack" ("Free Pet With Every Cage," 220, l. 1). The line "I am leader of the beguiled and fear of straps across my chest" ("Buying Christmas Wrapping Paper On January 12," 222, l. 23) alludes to Steve Earle's song "Ellis Unit One," which is the "Dead man walking theme tune" ("Angel Showing Lead Shot Damage," 230, l. 19) that will later provide MacSweeney with the title of "When The Lights Went Out A Cheer Rose In The Air" (301–303). Johnny Cash is referenced in several poems: "Number 13 tattooed on his neck. / Beast caged behind frail and fragile bars" ("Angel Showing Lead Shot Damage," 230, ll. 20–21), "Stripes on your shoulders, stripes on your back & on your hands" ("Strap Down In Snowville," 268, l. 82), "Cry, cry, cry" ("Lost Pearl," 213, l. 3), and "walk the line" ("Sweeno, Sweeno," 272, l. 116). Punk returns in the collection's closing poem, "John Bunyan To Johnny Rotten," which ends with a sudden declaration of allegiance: "!God Save the / Queen!" (290, ll. 247–248). Given Johnny Rotten's presence in the title, this asks to be read as a quote from a Sex Pistols song, linking it to MacSweeney's punk-influenced lineage of dissent; but the line also refers to the nightly playing of the national anthem at the end of BBC broadcasting (MacSweeney was now living alone and often drank through the night), and is a tribute to Jackie Litherland, the "warrior queen" who had supported him through detox and to whom the collection is dedicated (217).

These references to music may appear extraneous to the real work of *The Book of Demons*, which takes us on a tour of the postindustrial North of England during the dying days of John Major's government, but they contribute to the collection's apocalyptic outlook: this is the end of days, when the dead—including dead rock stars—will walk the earth. Although it was published only a few months after Labour's landslide victory in the UK general election on 1 May 1997, it is undeluded by that false dawn, and scathing in its assessment of Tony Blair's centrist party: "At least I'm not a replicant Labour party goon"

("Demons In My Pocket," 238, l. 7). Luke Roberts draws out many of the ways these poems situate themselves with regard to the history of radical socialist politics and the Blairite neoliberalism (Roberts 2017, 203–205), but cannot see, or affects not to see, the role that fashion plays. After referring to MacSweeney's homage to Kazimir Malevich— "I wear a cap in honour of you" ("Shreds of Mercy / The Merest Shame," 231–232; 231, l. 25)—and to his appearance in "Demons Swarm Upon Our Man And Tell The World He's Lost" "wearing only an orange Cuba baseball cap" (244–245; 245, l. 61), Roberts's interpretation is telling: "Clothed in the fashion accessories of revolutionary history, perhaps MacSweeney, the self-declared 'fantasticalist', testifies to the debasement of 'actual politics'. But we should be careful not to mistake this for a slide into reaction. In the previous three decades, MacSweeney's politics *were* real [...]" (Roberts 2017, 207). MacSweeney's politics are *still* real in these poems, and have *always* been "[c]lothed in the fashion accessories of revolutionary history." Roberts may see a dichotomy between fashion and politics, but MacSweeney did not.[8]

Between completing *The Book of Demons* and his death in May 2000, MacSweeney wrote hundreds of poems, only some of which appear in *Wolf Tongue* and *Desire Lines*. Among these is at least one major achievement, a book-length series of Apollinaire versions, *Horses in Boiling Blood*. Subtitled "a Collaboration, a Celebration," this collection would be MacSweeney's final work of self-mythology and self-reinvention. Once more, MacSweeney's primary identification with a precursor is augmented by references to movie stars and musical heroes, often country singers such as Emmylou Harris, Willie Nelson, or Jimmie Rodgers. The selection of Apollinaire versions that appears in *Desire Lines* omits many of these poems: "The Heartbroken Starre" (MacSweeney 2004, 31) features a cameo appearance by Burt Lancaster; "I'm Waiting Forever" (MacSweeney 2004, 37) is dedicated to Willie Nelson and praises "Elvis The Killer Buddy & Cash" (l.12); "Please Can Anyone Tell Me Where I Find Love?" (MacSweeney 2004, 47–48) is an homage to Elvis Presley, but also name-checks Eddie Cochran, Buddy Holly, Otis Redding, Ricky Nelson, Lynyrd Skynyrd, and Frank Sinatra, and so on. The pleasures of consumerism are extolled in "Horses Boiling In Blood or The Fenwick's Third Floor Hair-do" (MacSweeney 2004, 38–39), one of several poems in the collection that unironically sings the praises of the department store in Newcastle. In "Miss the Mississippi and Thee" (MacSweeney 2004, 15–16), translator and subject appear to have produced, either by a process of overidentification or consumption, a hybrid figure, "Gwillam Mad MacSweeney" (15, l. 33), who moves freely between the trenches of the First World War and Newcastle in the late 1990s, haunted by foreknowledge of his impending death. Apollinaire's poetry combines conventional lyricism with modernist fragmentation, and De Chirico celebrates this in his *Ritratto premonitore di Guillaume Apollinaire*, depicting the poet as a marble bust wearing sunglasses. Like Apollinaire's, MacSweeney's poetry draws strength from its contradictions. Popular culture references work in a variety of ways, and indicate that the poet was fully engaged in his work, bringing his entire personality to bear on the poetry. To MacSweeney, writing well-meant writing with fluency and speed, greedily appropriating styles, voices, forms and tropes, surfing on associations, digressions, overstatement, and flights of fancy.

Notes

1 MacSweeney is reported as saying that Shakespeare was "a waste of time" and that "I tried hash, pot and grass. The result is I have the Newcastle police watching my house right now. But you don't need that stuff to write poetry—poetry has nothing to do with the mind" (Sayle 1968).

2 See Mottram 1993. Mottram's consideration of the British Poetry Revival excludes some of the poetic communities centered on Cambridge, and Peter Barry favors the more comprehensive term "radical" poetries in his account of the struggles between the Poetry Society and the Arts Council in this period (Barry 2006). For a sense of the intellectual debates taking place in some of the radical poetry communities at this time, see Pattison, Pattison, and Roberts, 2012, which republishes a selection of pieces that originally appeared in *The English Intelligencer*, a privately circulated magazine that ran between 1966 and 1968 (See Pattison et al. 2012).

3 Mottram's interview with MacSweeney was recorded on December 14, 1974.

4 See Barry MacSweeney Papers (GB 186 BM), Special Collections, Robinson Library, Newcastle University: BM 1/13/4.

5 See Whetstone 1997, in which MacSweeney says that his alcoholism followed the ending of his second marriage: "It started with solitary drinking but really the alcoholism came in the last eight or nine years when I was alone. I've been twice married and twice divorced."

6 See W. C. Handy, "The St Louis Blues." The line was used in many other songs.

7 For more on MacSweeney as an urban poet, see Barry 2000, 61–101.

8 For more on the importance of fashion to MacSweeney, see Litherland 2013, 173–174.

References

Amis, Kingsley (1968). *The New Statesman* (15 November). Barry MacSweeney Papers, (GB 186 BM), Special Collections, Robinson Library. Newcastle University: BM 6/1/1.

Anon (1968). "A Hit in Verse." *Penthouse* 4 (5): 12. [unsigned article].

Barry, Peter (2000). *Contemporary British Poetry and the City*. Manchester: Manchester University Press.

Barry, Peter (2006). *Poetry Wars: British Poetry of the 1970s and the Battle of Earls Court*. Cambridge: Salt Publishing.

Batchelor, Paul (2013). "False Fathers, Desperate Readers, and the Prince of Sparty Lea." In: *Reading Barry MacSweeney* (ed. Paul Batchelor), 107–130. Tarset: Bloodaxe.

Burn, Gordon (2000). "Message in a Bottle." *Guardian* 1 (6) https://www.theguardian.com/books/2000/jun/01/poetry.features (accessed 20 February 2020).

Bush, Clive (1997). "Parts in the Weal of Kynde: Barry MacSweeney." In: *Out of Dissent: a study of Five Contemporary British Poets*. London: Talus.

Herbert, W.N. (2013). "Barry MacSweeney and the Demons of Influence: *Pearl* and *The Book of Demons*." In: *Reading Barry MacSweeney* (ed. Paul Batchelor), 141–156. Tarset: Bloodaxe.

Homberger, Eric (1977). *The Art of the Real: Poetry in England and America since 1939*. London: J. M. Dent & Sons Ltd.

Kelly, Terry (2013). "Not Dark Yet: Barry MacSweeney, Bob Dylan and the Jesus Christ Almighty." In: *Reading Barry MacSweeney* (ed. Paul Batchelor), 157–169. Tarset: Bloodaxe.

Litherland, S. J. (2013). "Barry MacSweeney: A Life in Headlines." In: *Reading Barry MacSweeney* (ed. Paul Batchelor), 170–181. Tarset: Bloodaxe.

MacSweeney, Barry (1968). *The Boy from the Green Cabaret Tells of His Mother*. London: Hutchinson.

MacSweeney, Barry (1971). *Just 22 and I Don't Mind Dyin': The Official Poetical Biography of Jim Morrison, Rock Idol*. London: Curiously Strong [collected as "Just Twenty Two—And I Don't Mind Dying" in *Wolf Tongue*, 20–23].

MacSweeney, Barry (1978). *Odes 1971–1978*. London: Trigram Press [collected in *Wolf Tongue*, 35–81].

MacSweeney, Barry (1979). "The British Poetry Revival, 1965–1979." In: *South East Arts Review*, 9: 33–46.

MacSweeney, Barry (1985). *Ranter*. Nottingham: Slow Dancer Press [collected in *Wolf Tongue*, 139–177].

MacSweeney, Barry (1993). *Hellhound Memos*. London: The Many Press [poems 1, 2, 3, 4, 8, 9, 10, 11, 13, 18, and 19 are collected in *Wolf Tongue*, 185–192; poems 5, 6, 7, 12, 14, 15, 16 and 17 are collected in *Desire Lines*, 217–225].

MacSweeney, Barry (1995). *Pearl*. Cambridge: Equipage [collected in *Wolf Tongue*, 193–216].

MacSweeney, Barry (1997). *The Book of Demons*. Tarset: Bloodaxe Books [collected in *Wolf Tongue*, 217–290].

MacSweeney, Barry (1999). *Pearl in the Silver Morning*. Cambridge: Poetical Histories [collected in *Wolf Tongue*, 319–325].

MacSweeney, Barry (2003). *Wolf Tongue: Selected Poems 1965–2000*. Tarset: Bloodaxe.

MacSweeney, Barry (2004). *Horses in Boiling Blood: a Collaboration, a Celebration*. Cambridge: Equipage [a selection of these poems appears in *Desire Lines*, 245–303].

MacSweeney, Barry (2018). *Desire Lines: Unselected Poems 1966–2000* (ed. Luke Roberts). Bristol: Shearsman.

Morris, Marianne (2004). "The Abused Become the Abusers: The Poetry of Barry MacSweeney." In: *Quid*, 14: 4–21.

Mottram, Eric (1977). "MacSweeney/Pickard/Smith: Poets from North East England Interviewed by Eric Mottram." In: *Poetry Information*, 18: 21–39.

Mottram, Eric (1993). "The British Poetry Revival, 1960–1975." In: *New British Poetries: The Scope of the Possible* (eds. Hampson Robert and Barry Peter), 15–50. Manchester: Manchester University Press.

Pattison, Neil, Pattison, Reitha, and Roberts, Luke (eds.) (2012). *Certain Prose of the English Intelligencer*. London: Mountain Press.

Prynne, J.H. (1969). *The White Stones*. Lincoln: Grosseteste Press.

Roberts, Luke (2017). *Barry MacSweeney and the Politics of Post-War British Poetry: Seditious Things*. London: Palgrave MacMillan.

Sheppard, Robert (1999). *Far Language: Poetics and Linguistically Innovative Poetry 1978–1997*. Exeter: Stride.

Sayle, Murray (1968). "The Making of a Professor." *Sunday Times* (13 October). Barry MacSweeney Papers, BM 6/1/1.

Steele, Anne (1968). "Never Mind Who's Going to be Professor—What IS poetry?." *Daily Telegraph* (30 October). Barry MacSweeney Papers, BM 6/1/1.

Whetstone, David (1997). "A Thirst to Survive That Helped Beat the Demons." *The Journal* 11.

Wilkinson, John (2007). *The Lyric Touch: Essays on the Poetry of Excess*, 77–96. Cambridge: Salt Publishing.

Wilkinson, John (2013). "The Iron Lady and The Pearl: Male Panic in Barry MacSweeney's 'Jury Vet'." In: *Reading Barry MacSweeney* (ed. Paul Batchelor), 87–106. Tarset: Bloodaxe.

3.10
When Understanding Breaks in Waves: Voices and Messages in Edwin Morgan's Poetry

Monika Kocot

Introduction

It does seem that the number of possibilities of entering the poetic world of Edwin Morgan is infinite, just as infinitely variegated as is Scotland's first national poet's creative imagination (Kocot 2016, 204). In one of the chapters of *Beyond the Last Dragon*, Morgan's literary biography, James McGonigal writes: "In the multiplicity of his work are signs of who and what he was and is. Even fragments can speak" (2012, 438). Indeed, at times (especially when seen from a distance), these fragments seem to create a sort of pattern. Obviously, this pattern has nothing to do with regularity or repetition. Far from it. Throughout his life, Morgan's main artistic preoccupation was to go beyond expectations, to explore the unknown, to affirm the new. We may speak here of a pattern of irregularity, of joyful jaggedness and transgressive border-crossing, of mercurial reinventions. In his article "Edwin Morgan: A Sunburst of Possibility Amid the Grey" published on August 22, 2010, a few days after Morgan's death, Alan Spence sums up his master's importance: "In grey postwar Glasgow, his work was a sunburst of hope and possibility. He wrote about the world we inhabited, but placed it in a global, even a universal, context – *From Glasgow to Saturn*" (Spence 2010). Spence emphasizes Morgan's honesty, humor, humanity, and compassion which in his view enabled Morgan to reach across any age gap. "His dazzling technique, the verbal pyrotechnics, were always in the service of something more, something deeper," Spence adds. In this article I will try to stress the importance of Spence's argument; in my opinion, the links between Morgan's humanity, compassion, his mercurial playfulness, and the thought-provoking nature of his poems' messages are of crucial significance.

In 2008, 2 years before Morgan's death, Robyn Marsack and Hamish Whyte edited a collection *From Saturn to Glasgow: Fifty Favourite Poems by Edwin Morgan* in which they asked writers and critics to select their favorite Morgan poetic piece and, if possible, justify their choice. When giving his reasons for choosing "The First Men on Mercury" (selected tellingly by one more Poet Laureate—Liz Lochhead), Andrew Motion notes: "It's hard to choose a single poem to celebrate Edwin's poetry, since its power depends in important ways on its abundance" (2008, 28). The book offers an inspiring perspective of looking at Morgan's output, and as the editors point out it sends us back to re-read his poems "with wonder at his seemingly endless inventiveness, the persistent curiosity and openness with which he views this world and imagined worlds, and his undimmed faith in the human" (2008, 8). All of the poems I discuss here are included in *From Saturn to Glasgow*, and I will be referring to the poets' comments on their favorite poetic pieces.

In Iain Crichton Smith's opinion, Edwin Morgan's poetry has always been large, zestful, and imaginative, composed of straight narrative, concrete poetry, science fiction, satire. "It has been life enhancing, technology-welcoming, adventurous, protean [...]. Its range of languages is gargantuan, using Latin, French, demotic Glasgow, grave Academe, the language of the computer and of geology" (Smith 1989, 13). As Marsack puts it, Morgan sought a tension between his subject matter and the chosen disciplines of form (Kocot 2016, 10); he wanted "a kind of Whitmanesque inclusiveness without Whitman's gorgeous egotism" (1990, 27). Indeed, Morgan's impact on other (Scottish) poets could also be compared to that of Whitman. In one of the chapters of *Beyond the Last Dragon* (2012), Morgan's literary biographer, James McGonigal refers to the group of young poets who gathered around Morgan. He mentions Peter McCarey, Alan Riach, Robert Crawford, David Kinloch, W. N. Herbert, and Richard Price. The group was known as the Informationists, and their shared focus was the poetic exploration of the contemporary impact of information on the working of the mind, human relationships, and culture at local as well as global levels. McGonigal notes that Basil Bunting once compared Ezra Pound to Edmund Spenser, in that "both writers left an 'encyclopaedia of possibilities' for other poets to develop" (2012, 298) and asserts that Morgan's poetry was a "similar treasure-house of strategies and themes" (2012, 298–299).

Since, to paraphrase Whitman, Morgan is "large and contains multitudes," each critic will find his/her own key to his poetic world (Kocot 2016, 10), for as Colin Nicholson aptly puts it, "nothing else would do for a poetry recurrently involving freedom from coercion and restraint, and where only structure of perception and hypothesis at hand is operative" (2002, 10). Some researchers study his dialogue with the space of the city of Glasgow, and by extension the space of Scottishness(es), with the emphasis put on Scottish literary tradition or sometimes playful and sometimes quite solemn convergence of languages (English, Scots, Glaswegian); some explore Morgan's science-fiction poems and his visions of the past, the present, and imagined futures; some investigate the vast collection of his sonnets; others still analyze his *avant-garde* experiments with form (for instance his concrete poetry, or cut-outs). The 1990 book *About Edwin Morgan*, edited by Robert Crawford and

Hamish Whyte, Rodney Stenning Edgecombe's *Aspects of Form and Genre in the Poetry of Edwin Morgan* (2003), Colin Nicholson's *Inventions of Modernity* (2002), and McGonigal's *Beyond the Last Dragon: A Life of Edwin Morgan* (2012) attempt to sketch a map of Morgan's astonishing output in poetry, poetic drama, and literary translation. In addition, there are hundreds of academic and nonacademic articles and essays on Morgan's work.

In my book *Playing Games of Sense in Edwin Morgan's Writing* (2016), I explore various manifestations of Morgan's dialogical thinking, his "verbal pyrotechnics," mythopoetic "writing-through," games of (linguistic) *anamorphosis*, but I also focus on the multidimensional process of deciphering his messages, and I try to show that the game of reading Morgan's poetry (and drama) is about being "in receipt." The way I see it, one of the key features of Morgan's writing is his dialogical thinking which makes us think about the Bakhtinian study of Dostoevsky's prose. "To be means to communicate dialogically. When dialogue ends, everything ends. Thus dialogue, by its very essence, cannot and must not come to an end" (Bakhtin 1984, 252). This is how Bakhtin describes the importance of dialogue in Dostoevsky's poetics. For Bakhtin, Dostoevsky "could hear dialogic relationships everywhere, in all manifestations of conscious and intelligent human life" (Bakhtin 1984, 40). Bakhtin sees this dialogism in the structure of the novel, between its elements, but also at the microlevel of the passages of dialogue involving characters, in their words and gestures (Kocot 2016, 15). My claim is that Morgan's case is similar in the sense that various kinds of dialogism are visible in his imagery building, in the structures of the poems, but also in the philosophies of his poetic and dramatic pieces (Kocot 2016, 15), and each of the poems I have chosen focuses on a given type of dialogism employed in sense creation. As I argue elsewhere, it is worth noting that "games of (cultural) transgression are integral to Morgan's forms of attention" (Kocot 2016, 12): Ezra Pound's modernist dictum "MAKE IT NEW" changes into Morgan's "CHANGE RULES" and Jasper Johns's "Take an Object. Do something to it. Do something else to it" (Kocot 2016, 13).

"The First Men on Mercury" (Morgan 1996, 267–268)

Nicholson observes that Morgan's interest in "social, personal, linguistic and cultural othernesses comes to us in the poetics of communicative rationality, which often operates through mind-bending syntax" (2002, 5). This interest is closely related to his practice of translation. Morgan was attracted to a number of poets, and he translated into English or Scots from Anglo-Saxon, Russian, Portuguese, German, Spanish, Italian, French, ancient Greek, Dutch, Khmer, Armenian, and Hungarian. One of his most cherished authors was Velimir Khlebnikov, the master of Russian *zaum* (beyond sense) poetry. We may notice many Khlebnikov-like games with word-roots, or games of pure sound in Morgan's poems, but "The First Men on Mercury" is special. Not only does it foreground the theme of broken communication, but it also explores the convergence of languages (English, Scots, nonsense, and pure sound). Motion calls it "a kind of poetic cornucopia" and adds that it is "adventurous, transgressive, fun (but serious too), and stamped with a mark of imaginative boldness which is vintage Morgan" (2008, 28). It is as if Morgan tried to "resurrect the creative imagination through a development of the linguistic *ostranenie* ('alienation,' 'making strange')" (Kocot 2016, 16, 101). By making this gesture, Morgan follows in the footsteps of one of his poetic masters, Khlebnikov, for whom (as well as for the Russian formalist critics of the 1920s) *ostranenie* was (one of) the most essential part of poetry-making.

This frequently anthologized poem, which combines an interesting example of lateral thinking, the realm of science-fiction poetry, colonization, and last but not least translation, creates a unique opportunity to give voice to the voiceless (Kocot 2016, 119). In an interview with Russell Jones, Morgan says that "Mercury is much too hot for any kind of tongue we'd recognise," and he adds that in order "to get away from the ubiquitous Mars background" (Jones 2009), he chooses Mercury as a setting for a puzzling dialogue.

> One of my long-standing interests has been science fiction. I enjoy writing science-fiction poems, and try to give them some "point," so that they are not merely fantastic. In "The First Men on Mercury," I imagine the first successful Earth expedition to the planet Mercury, and an attempt at conversation between the leader of the expedition and the first Mercurian who comes up to see what has happened. Again, to get the full effect of this poem, you ought to try reading it aloud [...].
> (Morgan 1990c, "The Loch Ness Monster's Song," 255)

This is how the poem begins:

> ——We come in peace from the third planet.
> Would you take us to your leader?
>
> ——Bawr stretter! Bawr. Bawr. Stretterhawl?
>
> ——This is a little plastic model
> of the solar system, with working parts.
> You are here and we are there and we
> are now here with you, is this clear?
>
> Gawl horrop. Bawr Abawrhannahanna!
> (Morgan 1996, 267, ll. 1–8)

For W. N. Herbert, the poem "satisfies a Scottish fantasy; the Earthmen are condescending and imperialist dolts, outwitted by some power of the enigmatic, anti-authoritarian Mercurians that they cannot even comprehend" (1990, 67). We can see the message of linguistic authority in the first line, and in the following lines it is made explicitly clear that if the Mercurians want to make conversation, they have to use English. But the request is denied. "Bawr stretter! Bawr. Bawr. Stretterhawl?" shows that the Mercurians are not willing to compromise their linguistic position. For a reader with a good command of Scots, the language of the Mercurians is not a piece of mere sound instrumentation. As Russell Jones notes, "Bawr" translates into standard English as "practical joke," "stretter" is remarkably similar to "strett" which means "straight," and "hawl" resembles "haw" which translates as "livid" or "pale." This leads us to an intriguing translation of the Mercurian sentence: "you must be joking, pale faces" (Kocot 2016, 120). Morgan's semi-Scottish aliens are not barbarians, as one might have assumed; they represent more than they first appear to do (Kocot 2016, 120). The poem indirectly mocks and deconstructs humans' patronizing colonial approach and their projections of English as the language of authority and dominance. The idea of superiority is even more vividly ridiculed in the humans' inability to learn the language of the other. Believing that they are the supreme beings of the universe, they do not notice that the Mercurians have learnt their language and are willing to use it. The process of convergence of languages is slow but unstoppable (Kocot 2016, 120).

While the humans and aliens slowly engage in a conversation, we notice, and this observation is both shocking and amusing (this is where the mastery of Morgan's linguistic design can be observed), that the humans are speaking "alienish" and the aliens are speaking English. "Go back to your planet," the aliens say, "Go back in peace, take what you have gained / but quickly" (268, ll. 36–38), to which the humans respond: "Stretterworra gawl, gawl ..." (268, l. 39). The Mercurian conclusion is meaningful and ironic: "Of course, but nothing is ever the same, / now is it? You'll remember Mercury" (Morgan 1996, 268, ll. 40–41). Morgan succeeds in showing "a peculiar processual transformation from apparent gibberish" (Kocot 2016, 121) to a fully rendered language of power—English. The political message underlying his argument is simple: if you want to challenge your oppressor, you have to use his/her language; given the Scots elements in the poem's Mercurian lexemes, it also "sends the message to the English, and quite obviously the message is not clear to them" (Kocot 2016, 121).

"Message Clear" (Morgan 1996, 159)

> I like poetry that comes not out of "poetry" but out of a story in today's newspaper, or a chance personal encounter in a street, or the death of a famous person: I am very strongly moved by the absolute force of what actually happens, because after all, that is it, there is really nothing else that has its poignance, its razor edge. It is not an easy poetry to write, and I think it requires a peculiar kind of imagination that is willing to bend itself to meet a world which is lying there in the rain like an old shoe.
>
> (Morgan 1990a, "A Poetry Before Poetry" 192)

This quote signals Morgan's strong emphasis on drawing his inspiration from the here and now, and the importance of emotional (even if not expressed openly) response to "what actually happens," in other words, the importance of conscious being-in-the-world. Rodney Edgecombe calls it Morgan's "urgent humanism" (Edgecombe 2003, 3), and adds that "even the most austere and constructivist of his concrete lyrics disclose a breathing human presence through the interstices of their designs" (Edgecombe 2003, 3). This is evident particularly in the emergent "Message Clear."

The whole poem emerged as it were from only one line "i am the resurrection and life" which literally speaking "forced itself" on Morgan. Quite unexpectedly it came to his mind at a moment when he was on a bus, coming home from the hospital where his father was dying of cancer. Morgan recalls that "about half of it was in my head going home on the bus and I had to come in and write down as much of it as I could right away before it disappeared" (quoted in Herbert 1990, 73). There is an interesting reference to this story in Alan Spence's play *No Nothing*, an homage to two great Glaswegians: Edwin Morgan and Jimmy Reid. Near the end of the play, Reid and Morgan discuss Morgan's "Message Clear." Morgan describes his experiment as "[p]laying with form. But more than that. Unscrambling. Breaking the code. The code being language" (Spence 2015, 47, ll. 6–7):

> EDDIE   Took the line *I am the resurrection and the life* … Saw what other words and phrases were in there, hidden. Like, *I am here … I act … I run* … And they flow down the page and come together in the original line, the starting point.
> JIMMY   Rearrange the following into a well-known phrase or saying …
> EDDIE   It's easy to be reductive.
> JIMMY   It just all sounds a bit technical, you know. Clinical. Analytical. And just, ever so slightly up itself.
> EDDIE   I know all that. But when I wrote it, it felt *given* … I was on the bus, on the way home from Robroyston Hospital where my father was dying … And the words just came. I saw them, emerging, flowing together into that one line, that mantra. I am the resurrection and the life.
>
> (Spence 2015 47, ll. 9–26)

As I argue elsewhere, "even if a given text, be it a concrete or science-fiction poem, seems a bit technical, or analytical, we must never forget that at the core of Morgan's writing there is a vibrant radiance that speaks directly to the heart, but the message is clear only when our hearts are ready to welcome the beams" (Kocot 2018, 197). In "Message Clear," those beams are less metaphorical and more "concrete" due to the poem's typography and Morgan's application of the technique of textual latency, which can be defined "as that paradoxical depth of the surface of the text that reveals that it is hiding something and indicates how that something can be found" (Walker 1999, 158).

At first glance, the poem seems to be having no structure, no cohesive or lexical unity. The poem's framework (can we call it a script?) is not continuous; it seems broken. Each line consists of separate letters, fragments of words or phrases. Morgan is playing a game with his readers, by "hiding," to use Spence's word, a 55-line-long, multistrand narrative in Christ's *I am the resurrection and the life*. One could argue that what is present/hidden, visible/invisible, audible/inaudible depends on the eyes and ears of the reader. When we read the poem aloud—and as we know this aspect of poetry has always been very dear to Morgan—we can easily notice that seemingly meaningless graphs do make sense, and the scenes seem less and less effaced, wiped out. In order to hear what Spence calls the mantra, and, obviously, the long and winding road leading to the mantra, we need to enter a processual re-reading of the subsequent lines, scenes as it were, where the meanings of overt and hidden text are constantly questioned, deconstructed.

Despite its title (which can read "message received," "message checked," "message confirmed," or obviously "simple message"), the poem is not that easy to grasp, and it provokes various, apparently divergent readings. For Nicholson, the poem, "supposedly a monologue spoken by Christ on the cross, reconstructs a gospel triangulation of word, beginning and godhead (John 1.1) by going forth and multiplying spatialised forms for one of Jesus's utterances" (2002, 95). "Message Clear" as a concrete poem might also function as a kind of language generator which, to refer to Manuel Portela's insightful analysis, "provides a microcosm both of the linguistic processes of word and sentence creation and of the more basic and fundamental structuring processes of the phonetic, syntactical, semantic, and pragmatic elements that produce language" (Portela 2006). Roderick Watson suggests that "[i]t is as if we are witnessing some interrupted [...] communication, only gradually patching itself together. Perhaps the sender is having difficulty; perhaps the receiver is faulty; perhaps the atmospheric conditions are unpropitious" (1997, 175). Is it possible that these critics are talking about one and the same poem? What is it that makes them focus on completely different aspects of the poem, and is there a common ground in these three perspectives? The methodology of reading is the key issue here. In his "Morgan's Words," partly devoted to the analysis of "Message Clear," W. N. Herbert emphasizes that Morgan's work as a whole "exhibits a concern to find those messages in things which have been overlooked because of the status of those things," and he sees Morgan's poetic insight as something Scottish, but also having "something of the kabbalist" (1990, 73). If we follow Herbert's intuition, then in order to make the "message clear," we must actively decipher and reconstruct the poem, and then, to come back to Nicholson's observations, we may see that the poem "seems to assemble itself as it goes along" (2002, 95).

We cannot forget that "Message Clear" is a "verbivocovisual" concrete experiment, and the process of sense creation is here threefold: the constructivist scheme produces its own meanings; the technique of repetition and difference as a strategy of composition initiates an incessant game of re/deconstruction of meaning; and verbal performance introduces and strengthens the text's morphodynamics. We are dealing with fragments of sentences, short phrases, at times only with single words, with no punctuation whatsoever. The reader must "gather" single graphs into words, words into phrases, and the final outcome depends greatly on how the reader reads, or re-reads, subsequent enjambments, which in turn activates (or does not activate) the processes of sense creation (Kocot 2016, 62–63).

Despite its fragmented nature, "Message Clear" remains a continuous, spherical poem; The poem's construction is convincing: the places occupied by the graphs are not incidental, that is to say, a given line is composed of graphs which have been methodically arranged according to "a stable and fully-organised set of graphs given in the poem's last line" (Kocot 2016, 64). It seems that the horizontal disorder of graphs in each line is compensated for by the rigid vertical stability of "script-graphs" in the last line (Kocot 2016, 64). More than that, the text's fragmentation and nonlinearity of meanings may be associated with the poem's philosophy, based on textual latency (Kocot 2016, 62–63). The deeply existential phrase "am i" of the first line, which can be read as referring to the name of God—I AM (Gen. 3. 14)—when seen in relation to the last line, takes us back to the Gospel of John 1. 1–2 ("In the beginning was the Word, and the Word was with God, and the Word was God. He was with God in the beginning"). The anaphorical reference of "i am" to Jesus's "i am the resurrection and the life" creates a peculiar framework of meditation on the essence of human nature in relation to the divine. I agree with Marsack, who chooses the poem for *From Saturn to Glasgow*, and notes that "the form of the poem in its gaps and hesitations, its uncertainties and repetitive certainties, mimics the whole stuttering process of coming to the great recognition of the closing line: 'i am the resurrection and the life'. The message emerges, and it is clear" (2008, 53).

Let us see how it works. For instance, in one "scene," the fragmented images reflect the story of Jesus coming to Zion, to be hailed as hero, the Messiah, and destroyer of the status quo and later to be crucified as a sectarian, as an outcast, as a common human being: "i am rife / in / ion [zion] and / i die / a mere sect / a mere section / of / the life / of / men." The crucifixion itself is also metaphorically represented by the graphs which make a small cross, graphically pointing to the life of Christ—and all people's within him—crucified on the cross (Kocot 2016, 65).

```
                              o              f
           the                               life
                              o              f
      m    e              n
```

This cross is actually the second cross in the poem, as the initial scene ("am i / if / i am he / hero / hurt / there and / here and / here / and / there") takes the shape of the Saint Andrew's saltire cross.

Another graphic game is the line "i am here," with the geometrical center of the poem precisely at its center. Surprisingly, the center points to nothing; it is situated in a graphic void, but it seems "central" to the poem's message. It is the first of 17 subsequent lines beginning with "i," linked with identity building (the process of individuation?). While the poem's framework is not continuous, with the emergence of "i" graphs, the poem's downward left-hand side edges are no longer jagged and uneven. Also, toward the end of the poem, the scenes seem less and less effaced, wiped out, and the plot thickens: we enter an Egyptian mythic timespace, and with each line we explore the fascinating conflation of the Egyptian and Christian mythologies, parallels between the functions and attributes of Ra and Thoth, as well as I AM (JHVH) and Logos/Jesus Christ (Kocot 2016, 66–68).

If we recall Herbert's observation concerning the kabbalist element in Morgan's text, we discover additional levels of sense creation. Both the Kabbalah and "Message Clear" explore the issue of God's manifestation. As Marc-Alain Ouaknin puts it, in Judaism, the first question is: "How did God manifest himself / how does God still manifest himself to people?" (2000, 371). This question, in so many different forms, permeates Morgan's poem as well. Another parallel would be the idea of the textual world as not given, but rather in the process of becoming/creation, and the indeterminacy of texts because their structure is "visible-invisible" (Kocot 2016, 73). The symbolic meaning of the most frequently used graphs/phonemes would reveal the very same motifs that have been identified in our reading: identity quest, identity in motion, and a dialogue of unity and plurality of voices (Kocot 2016, 74). Last, the Kabbalistic attitude toward the text is expressed both in reading and interpretation. To interpret means to discover meaning, and not truth. Interpretation is not discovering mystery, but rather a discovery that mystery exists (Ouaknin 2000, 376).

"Testament" (Morgan 1985, 118–119)

"Through the storm he walked before he gave his sermon"—the poem begins. Readers immediately find themselves in the times of Jesus. The imagery and the participants in the scene suggest that we are witnessing the moment when Jesus walked on the water to save his disciples from drowning in the stormy Sea of Galilee (the miracle is recorded in three of the Gospels: Matthew 14:22–36; Mark 6:45–56; John 6:16–21). We learn that the disciples were terrified with the sudden and extremely violent storm, and that they were even more terrified when they saw Jesus: "they choked as they half saw him out there / going or coming, who knows, through the sea-lumps" (Morgan 1985, 118, ll. 4–5). The Gospels say the disciples thought he was a ghost. In Morgan's poem we read:

> His face was like a sheet of lightning. "Beside him,
> his injured arm in a sling, was Red Nelson,
> his sou-wester gone and his fair hair plastered in wet,
> wind-blown ringlets about his face. His whole attitude
> breathed indomitability, courage, strength.
> It seemed almost as though the divine
> were blazing forth from him."
> (Morgan 1985, 118, ll. 6–12)

Let us focus on the moment when the story about Jesus begins to twist and turn in a truly Morganian way. The puzzling quotation is not related to our story whatsoever; it looks as if it was taken out of context and simply pasted into the poem; who is that Red Nelson with injured arm in a sling? Yet the last two sentences seem to be part of the narrative of Jesus walking on the water. The central character is an embodiment of indomitability, courage, and strength; he seems divine, or it seems like the divine element is "blazing forth from him." This poem is one of the best examples of Morgan's dialogue with other literary texts (in this case, The New Testament) and the way he initiates games with his readers. In *From Saturn to Glasgow*, there is a short but telling response to the poem's poetic challenge. McGonigal, the author of Morgan's literary biography *Beyond the Last Dragon*, and one of Morgan's closest friends, writes: "I like the poem's mystery, and its guarded then unguarded witness statement about mystery. It speaks to EM's lifelong argument with Christianity, threaded through his work. I like the way the quote is unexplained" (2008, 78). The quotation is surely unexplained. More than that, it is rewritten, without quotation marks, in the latter part of the poem which in a whirlwind-like movement comes back to the story of the Messiah. It should be noted here that in the biblical version of the story, it was the miracle of Jesus's walking on the water that, more than any other, convinced the disciples that Jesus was, indeed, the Son of God. He proved himself to be in command of the elements, something only the divine is capable of. One of the Gospels has it that the disciples in the boat recognized his divinity and worshiped him, saying: "Truly you are the Son of God" (Matthew 14:32–33). Is this mentioned in our poem? No, we only learn that the disciples bale water until "things blew themselves out" (Morgan 1985, 118, l. 14). They do not even notice that He is on board and is helping them in their struggle. When they reach the shore, we learn that:

> There was no sermon.
> They dried their rags on stones, he kept his on,
> sitting a little apart, his sou'wester gone
> and his fair hair plastered in wet, wind-blown
> ringlets about his face. His whole attitude breathed
> indomitability, courage, strength. It seemed
> almost as though the divine were blazing forth from him.
> (Morgan 1985, 118, ll. 16–20)

The first line in the quotation stands in contrast to the promise of a sermon in the first line of the poem, or so it seems. The word "seems" plays a crucial role in this passage, and in the poem as a whole. By applying the rule of repetition and difference, Morgan rewrites the Red Nelson quotation in such a way that the original, mysterious passage refers now to Jesus. Strangely, however, while the original quotation emphasized Red Nelson's divine nature, its rewritten, appropriated version openly questions Jesus's divinity. This is achieved by placing enjambments in different moments of the sentence structure. On the one hand, the "indomitability, courage, strength" that characterize Jesus are weakened by the phrase "It seemed"; on the other, the last line begins with "almost as though" which puts the whole issue of divinity in metaphorical quotation marks.

In the latter part of the poem, we are facing what seems like the testimony of the writer of the Gospel:

> They asked me to write this faithfully.
> I do, and yet I am not sure that I do.
> Sometimes I frown at what the pen has said.
> (Morgan 1985, 119, ll. 4–5)

Morgan refers here to the problematic issue of authenticity, of the so-called (historical) "truth" and its faithful representation or retelling. But at the same time, the speaker shares his feelings concerning faith in one of the most important lines in the poem: "My understanding breaks in waves, dissolves" (Morgan 1985, 119, l. 26). When commenting on the poem, McGonigal notes that "[t]he washed-out rags and patches on the shore of belief also appeal, and its manifestation of power and powerlessness" (2008, 78). This line, more than any other, opens the possibility of meeting the divine. The last three lines put the matter explicitly, in an exclamatory mode, which changes the perspective of viewing the scene on the Sea of Galilee, and the message(s) of the poem as a whole, especially if we find the source of the mysterious quotation. The passage on Red Nelson comes from *The Cruise of the Dazzler* (chapter "Perilous Hours") by Jack London (1960), one of Morgan's favorite authors. If we link the story from the novel (together with its imagery and message) with the story of Jesus walking on the water, and Morgan's emotional meditation on the nature of faith in the poem's final stanza, then the title will open even more perspectives of interpretation. The mastery with which Morgan succeeds in capturing the meanderings of the shimmering mystery of faith is remarkable.

The struggle for meaning in Morgan's poetry is intense and often processual. It is certainly determined by various games of sense creation: "verbivocovisual" sense constellations, latent textuality, and the rhetoric of re/misreading as well as a de/reconstructivist rule of repetition and difference in his mythopoetic "written-through" pieces (Kocot 2016, 13). In an interview, Morgan remarks: "I think of poetry as partly an instrument of exploration, like a spaceship, into new fields of feeling or experience (or old fields which become new in new contexts and environments), and partly a special way of recording moments and events (taking the "prose" out of them, the grit of the facts of the case, as being in our age extremely important)" (1990a, "A Poetry Before Poetry," 192). Whoever bravely enters the spaceship of his poetry will surely discover the unknown beauty of the distant places in the universe, but, more importantly, the mystery of the commonplace, the here and now.

References

Bakhtin, Mikhail (1984). *Problems of Dostoevsky's Poetics*.(trans. C. Emerson). Minneapolis: Minnesota UP.

Edgecombe, Rodney Stenning (2003). *Aspects of Form and Genre in the Poetry of Edwin Morgan*. Amersham: Cambridge Scholars Press.

Herbert, W. N. (1990). "Morgan's Words." In: *About Edwin Morgan* (eds. Robert Crawford and Hamish White), 65–74. Edinburgh: Edinburgh UP.

Jones, Russell (2009). "Computer Error: Voices and Translations in Edwin Morgan's Science Fiction Poetry." *FORUM: University of Edinburgh Postgraduate Journal of Culture and the Arts* (9 Autumn) http://www.forumjournal.org/article/view/629/914 (accessed 20 August 2009).

Kocot, Monika (2016). *Playing Games of Sense in Edwin Morgan's Writing*. Frankfurt am Main: Peter Lang.

Kocot, Monika (2018). "The Whittrick Play of *No Nothing*: Alan Spence, Edwin Morgan, and Indra's Net." In: *Text Matters*, 8: 189–211.

London, Jack (1960). *The Call of the Wild, The Cruise of the Dazzler, and Other Stories of Adventure with the Author's Special Report, Gold Hunters of the North*, 223–228. New York: Platt & Munk.

Marsack, Robyn (1990). "A Declaration of Independence: Edwin Morgan and Contemporary Poetry." In: *About Edwin Morgan* (eds. Robert Crawford and Hamish White), 25–38. Edinburgh: Edinburgh UP.

Marsack, Robyn and Whyte, Hamish (eds.) (2008). *From Saturn to Glasgow. Fifty Favourite Poems by Edwin Morgan*. Edinburgh, Manchester: Scottish Poetry Library and Carcanet.

McGonigal, James (2012). *Beyond the Last Dragon: A Life of Edwin Morgan*. Dingwall: Sandstone Press Ltd.

Morgan, Edwin (1985). *Selected Poems*. Manchester: Carcanet.

Morgan, Edwin (1990a). "A Poetry Before Poetry." In: *Nothing Not Giving Messages: Reflections on Work and Life* (ed. Hamish White), 191–193. Edinburgh: Polygon.

Morgan, Edwin (1990b). *Nothing Not Giving Messages: Reflections on Work and Life* (ed. Hamish White). Edinburgh: Polygon.

Morgan, Edwin (1990c). "The Loch Ness Monster's Song', 'The First Men on Mercury', 'Off Course', and 'Flakes'." In: *Nothing Not Giving Messages: Reflections on Work and Life* (ed. Hamish White), 254–255. Edinburgh: Polygon.

Morgan, Edwin (1996) [1990]. *Collected Poems*. Manchester: Carcanet.

Nicholson, Colin (2002). *Inventions of Modernity*. Manchester: Manchester UP.

Ouaknin, Marc-Alain (2000). *Mysteries of the Kabbalah*. (trans. Josephine Bacon). New York, London: Abbeville.

Portela, Manuel (2006). "Concrete and Digital Poetics." *Leonardo Electronic Almanac* 14: 5/6. http://leoalmanac.org/journal/vol_14/lea_v14_n05-06/mportela.asp (accessed 20 August 2016).

Smith, Iain Crichton (1989). "Vintage Morgan." *Cencrastus* 32: 13.

Spence, Alan (2010). "Edwin Morgan: A Sunburst of Possibility Amid the Grey." http://Theguardian.com. The Observer (22 August) https://www.theguardian.com/books/2010/aug/22/edwin-morgan-scottish-poet-dies (accessed 1 August 2015).

Spence, Alan (2015). *No Nothing*. Aberdeen: Aberdeen UP.

The Holy Bible: English Standard Version (2001). Wheaton, Illinois: Crossways Bibles.

Walker, Keith Louise (1999). *Countermodernism and Francophone Literary Culture: The Game of Slipknot*. Durham: Duke University Press.

Watson, Roderick (1997). "Edwin Morgan: Messages and Transformations." In: *British Poetry from the 1950s to the 1990s: Politics and Art* (eds. Gary Day and Brian Doherty), 170–192. London: Macmillan.

3.11
Grace Nichols

Pilar Sánchez Calle

Introduction

Grace Nichols was born in Georgetown, Guyana, in 1950, and grew up in a small country village on the Guyanese coast. She moved to the city with her family when she was eight. She worked as a teacher and journalist and, as part of a Diploma in Communications at the University of Guyana, spent time in some of the most remote areas of Guyana, a period that influenced her writings and initiated a strong interest in Guyanese folk tales, Amerindian myths, and the South American civilizations of the Aztec and Inca. In 1977, she moved to London and has lived in the United Kingdom since 1977. Her first poetry collection, *i is a long memoried woman*, was published in 1983 and won the Commonwealth Poetry Prize. Subsequent poetry collections include *The Fat Black Woman's Poems* (1984), *Lazy Thoughts of a Lazy Woman* (1989), *Sunris* (1996), and *Picasso, I Want My Face Back* (2009). She also writes books for children, inspired predominantly by Guyanese folklore and Amerindian legends, including *Come on into My Tropical Garden* (1988) and *Give Yourself a Hug* (1994). *Everybody Got A Gift* (2005) includes new and selected poems, and her collection, *Startling the Flying Fish* (2006), contains poems which tell the story of the Caribbean. Her latest books are *I Have Crossed an Ocean: Selected Poems* (2010), *Cosmic Disco* (2013), and *The Insomnia Poems* (2017) (British Council 2018).

According to Sarah Lawson Welsh, the Nichols's work remains relatively unknown to general readers, despite her having written one novel, six major poetry collections, and over 14 books for children, as well as having been frequently included in anthologies since

---

A Companion to Contemporary British and Irish Poetry, 1960–2015, First Edition.
Edited by Wolfgang Görtschacher and David Malcolm.
© 2021 John Wiley & Sons Ltd. Published 2021 by John Wiley & Sons Ltd.

her arrival in Britain in 1977. British universities and colleges of higher education teach her work, although frequently only on courses of women's writing, postcolonial or "new" literatures in English. Critical comment on Nichols's work is scarce and has been published in collections of critical essays on Caribbean women's writing, on black women's writing, in specialist postcolonial literature journals, or in contemporary poetry journals. There are few interviews and commentaries on her work given by the author herself (Lawson Welsh 2007, 1). The first anthology to include Nichols's work was *News for Babylon: The Chatto Book of Westindian-British Poetry* (1984), edited by James Berry. By the early 1990s, Nichols's work was, however, appearing in a wide range of anthologies (*So Very English*, 1991; *Six Women Poets*, 1992; *Sixty Women Poets*, 1993), as well as in journals and magazines (Lawson Welsh 2007, 10).

A revision of the current scholarship on Grace Nichols's work shows that several critical approaches to her poetry focus on her subversive use of language, Caribbean myths, the oral tradition, and slave songs to question negative stereotypes about black women's identities. For these scholars, Nichols's poems suggest new ways of creating historiography and narratives of resistance against victimization. Magali Cornier Michael emphasizes Nichols's attempt to write an alternative history of slavery that represents the lives of slaves and particularly of slave women. In her first collection, *i is a long memoried woman* (1983), Nichols writes a poetic sequence made up of serialized poems with a variety of speakers. This technique allows for the presence of multiple personal stories about slavery, which creates a memory of slavery that is both an individual and a collective experience (Cornier Michael 2009, 226).

Özlem Türe Abaci shares some of Cornier Michael's views about Nichols's poetry. Türe Abaci describes *i is a long memoried woman* as a journey that starts with the slave woman's linguistic displacement, and leads to her appropriation of the colonizer's language and her display of a hybrid language that includes her memories of her lost homeland in Africa and her experiences in the New World. This new language is a sign of her communal and individual identity. The protagonist now has the future in her hands (Türe Abaci 2009, 69).

Other approaches to *i is a long memoried woman* consider the oppressed black body as Nichols's source of inspiration for her poems. For Gina Wisker, the poems are written from the body, which marks their rhythms and inflections. Stanza and line breaks are created not by punctuation but by the need to breathe and by the body's movements (1993, 26). The speaker of these poems resists victimization through the bonds she establishes with other women and projects a fundamentally optimistic attitude (Wisker 1993, 32).

Sarah Broom shares Gina Wisker's approach concerning the importance of the female body in three books by Grace Nichols. In *i is a long memoried woman*, Broom points out the exploration of repressed dimensions of female sexuality and eroticism, as well as the beauty and sexual energy associated with the black female body (2006, 99). Nichols's collection *The Fat Black Woman's Poems* (1984) celebrates the body of a contemporary fat woman as beautiful, powerful, sensual, and erotic. The poems are written in a humorous and cheerful tone, moving freely between first-person and third-person accounts of being a fat black woman in present-day Britain (Broom 2006, 100–101). In *Lazy Thoughts of a Lazy Woman and Other Poems* (1989), the author links femininity with the specificity of the experience of the female body. The speaker of the poems finds herself connected with eternal natural cycles. Nichols seems to suggest that her different voice comes from her body (Broom 2006, 102). Broom avoids the word "essentialist" to define some of Nichols's poems because she considers that Nichols may defend the existence of something stable and universal about woman based on her bodily experiences, but she is also interested in achieving change and in the hybridization of cultures and experiences as a reality (Broom 2006, 106).

Ana Bringas López reads *The Fat Black Woman's Poems* and *Lazy Thoughts of a Lazy Woman* as a challenge to black women's objectification and denigration in the Western British society to which Nichols has emigrated (2003, 13). Humor and irony are Nichols's main deconstructive strategies to question the myths that have oppressed black women, such as the image of beauty supported by the fashion and slimming industries (2003, 12). For Bringas López, Nichols's poems in these books reject the stereotype of the black woman as a victim, and represent the variety of experiences and identities that build black womanhood. These cannot be contained in any single poem (Bringas López 2003, 16).

Jahan Ramazani and Aleide Fokkema discuss Grace Nichols's poems as well as other postcolonial poets focusing on issues such as home, belonging, exile, identity, and cultural displacement. Ramazani uses the term "translocal" to refer to a diasporic sensibility in poems that reimagine disparate geocultural spaces and histories, particularly metropolitan Britain as seen by migrants from its former colonies. He finds it a relevant term to help describe those poems by Nichols which evoke her former life in the Caribbean and convey the sensory present of London (2007). From a linguistic point of view, Nichols's speaker uses both Creole ("me home") and standard English ("my home"), and feels at home both in the West Indies and England, showing that she is a "vernacular cosmopolitan" (Bhabha 2000, 141), who exists between cultures without nostalgia or a sense of victimization (Ramazani 2007).

In his approach to Nichols's poetry, Aleide Fokkema questions one of the basic tenets of postcolonial criticism: writers who have left their native surroundings for a new country lose their sense of identity, and are unable to recover it again. Their works embody this quest for their lost identity or for the establishment of a new one, which are both linked to a sense of place (Fokkema 1998, 101). Fokkema shows how Nichols explores the relation between home and identity in her collections *The Fat Black Woman's Poems* and *Lazy Thoughts of a Lazy Woman*, as well as the clash of two cultures, two homes, London and Guyana, without indulging in nostalgia (1998, 103). Nichols celebrates her divided identity with relief and optimism and gets rid of the eternal quest for identity and belonging associated with immigrants (Fokkema 1998, 105).

Paraskevi Papaleonida considers that a critical method focusing on synthesis is a useful one in the reading and analyzing Nichols's poetry because it allows readers to appreciate the cross-cultural elements and multiple voices present in her poems, for example, those of the colonizer, the slave woman, the Caribbean woman, or the English migrant, enhancing their distinct but not necessarily oppositional nature (Papaleonida 1997, 126–129). Thus, dialogic synthesis avoids polarization between the center and the margin, the colonizer's and the colonized's languages, which suits Nichols's poetic practice. "I like working in both standard English and Creole," she declares (Nichols 1990, 284). "Difference, diversity and unpredictability make me tick" (Nichols 1990, 284).

Lawson Welsh holds that the concept of cultural hybridity is very important when discussing and analyzing the creative work of diaspora writers such as Nichols. In her book *Grace Nichols* (2007), she emphasizes the hybrid nature of Nichols's poetry and her use of many different registers, styles, and genres. This critic also admires the presence of Creole and Standard English and the varied cultural resources of Caribbean, African, and European origins that we find in her books. For Lawson Welsh, Nichols is a writer across two worlds, and her affiliation to Britain and the Caribbean should not be considered in opposition; on the contrary, she is constantly crossing the borders between both cultures and ways of life.

Reading Grace Nichols

My approach to the reading of four poems by Grace Nichols is based on her own words about her concept of poetry and how she develops her poetic work. For Nichols, poetry is a synthesizing force (Nichols 1988, 103). She articulates her different identities in her poems: a black woman of Caribbean origin who has been living in Britain since 1977 and feels at ease within several cultural and linguistic traditions. Nichols dismantles traditional stereotypes about black women and rejects victimization. "I cannot subscribe to the 'victim mentality'," she insists (Nichols 1990, 284). "I reject the stereotype of the 'long-suffering black woman'" (Nichols 1990, 284). In her poems, Nichols merges two cultures, two homes, London and Guyana (Fokkema 1998, 103), and her relationship with her homeland is always ambivalent. "In one way it's like coming back [...] but on another level, you can never go back. [...] It gives you that kind of special feeling but it doesn't mean you want to come back" (quoted in Lawson Welsh 2007, 106). The homeland becomes idealized which makes any return a journey into disillusionment (Lawson Welsh 2007, 104).

The first poem I wish to discuss is "In My Name," from *i is a long memoried woman* (1983), which mainly focuses on black female slaves' experiences after having been taken from Africa to work on sugarcane plantations on a Caribbean island. This poem is marked by an optimism, which contrasts with other gloomy or violent poems in this volume. "In My Name" shares a fundamentally optimistic undercurrent that is apparent in Nichols's subsequent collections. The poem's persona is a slave woman pregnant with her overseer's child. She is about to give birth to her baby, and instead of rejecting it or expressing rage against her master, she shows her love for the child and an absence of guilt for its conception. The whole poem can be read as a prayer or as part of a Christian baptism liturgy (Bringas López 2003, 10). We can distinguish two parts in it, the first seven stanzas, where the poetic voice emphasizes her loving disposition to receive the baby, and then the last five stanzas, where the speaker expresses her hopes and longings for the baby's life.

The speaker of the poem uses the capital "I" to emphasize her individual subjectivity and not the "i" in lower case which suggests a communal identity, as we see in other poems in this volume. She is telling her own individual story, about her feelings in the face of this special motherhood. The multiple repetition of the first person possessive pronoun throughout the poem asserts the speaker's willingness to envision a positive future for her baby by claiming her link to it (Cornier Michael 2009, 220).

The woman describes her pregnant belly as "an arc / of black moon" (ll. 3–4). The word "arc" evokes light and stars, and its positive connotations transform the ill omen associated to a "black moon." The presence of natural elements increases the actuality of the poem by emphasizing the physical conditions in which this birth is going to take place, "I squat over / dry plantain leaves" (ll. 5–6).

The lines "in my name / in my blood" (ll. 9–10) reveal the mother's wish to assume her affiliation to her baby by showing her blood ties to it and giving it her name, a personal and a social recognition. Also, the phrases "my tainted // perfect child" (ll. 13–14), "my bastard fruit" (l. 15), "my strange mulatto" (l. 18) point out the speaker's determination to free her child from the negative circumstances of its conception. The baby is not tainted, but perfect, because it is her child. The maternal look of love turns a bastard son into "my bastard fruit" (l. 15) and "my sea grape" (l. 17). The baby is a part of the woman and she is not rejecting it, but loving it.

The following two stanzas resemble prayers where the speaker, by using anaphora, calls on dangerous animals to stay away from her baby, for example, "Let the snake slipping in deep grass / be dumb before you" (ll. 20–21). The lines "Let the evil one strangle on his own tongue / even as he sets his eyes upon you" (ll. 24–25) anticipate worse dangers than those lurking among the sugarcanes or in the forests: the voices that insist on the baby's not being either a slave or free, but the product of an unwelcome sexual relationship. The words "on his own tongue" oppose the previous ones "in my name," suggesting the use of words as weapons against the protective shield erected by the mother's name.

The female speaker rejects self-victimization and the stigma of shame and guilt that the baby could have meant for her (Bringas López 2003, 11). She reappropriates her own body and proceeds to baptize her son with her blood and her tears, which acquire a positive and liberating potential. The final line suggests an upward movement; the baby will not drown in an abyss of sorrow but will swim to the surface, to life—"and with my tears / I've pooled the river Niger // now my sweet one it is for you to swim" (ll. 28–30).

In "Two Old Black Men on a Leicester Square Park Bench," from the volume *The Fat Black Woman's Poems* (1984), Nichols questions easy oppositions between Britain and "back home" (Lawson Welsh 2007, 89). The speaker of the poem is an external observer who wonders about the dreams and thoughts of two old black men killing time in a British park. Thus, Nichols acquires a more distanced standpoint that allows her to reflect on the complexities of "home" without becoming too personal or essentialist.

The first stanza opens with a direct inquiry about the contents of the two old black men's dreams, "What do you dream of you / old black men sitting" (ll. 1–2). The color gray predominates in a physical and psychological way: it is cold, there is a gray pigeon around, and their fingers are defined as "ashy" (l. 9). It is winter, and also the winter of their lives. The lines "wrapped up in scarves / and coats of silence" (4–5), and "ashy fingers trembling" (9), prefigure the final dissolution of the old men's bodies and also the definitive silence of death. No matter the content of their dreams, the speaker of the poem seems to suggest that reality imposes itself upon those dreams. This first stanza reflects a migrant present for the two old black men, where the imagined sun of a faraway country cannot heat them.

The second stanza focuses on the possible content of the two old men's dreams: revolutions, women, exotic landscapes, probably their Caribbean homeland. The speaker transmits the sense of unreliability, fragmentation, and fragility associated with memory (Lawson Welsh 2007, 100): "do you dream revolutions / you could have forged" (ll. 12–13) and "ghost memories of desire" (l. 18). The migrant fantasizes about participation in revolutions the nature of which remains dubious (the word "forge" means "create," but also "imitate with a deceptive purpose"). The sorrow of a lost love is also questioned because nostalgia and pain can become addictive feelings. The last line in the second stanza suggests the persistence of memories that time has made unreliable and connected to an imaginary land or a mythic place of desire (Lawson Welsh 2007, 90).

The last stanza of the poem offers the observing persona's final comment on black migrants' idealizations of home, which intensify when the news from their far away countries reveal difficult living conditions.

> after all the letters from
> home spoke of hardships
> and the sun was traded long ago (ll. 21–23)

These migrants' past is a foreign country that has disappeared long ago, diluted by distance and time (Lawson Welsh 2007, 90). Even one of the most recognizable features traditionally associated with Caribbean countries, the Sun, is now sold as a part of the tourist attractions of their homeland. The one-line final stanza emphasizes this gap between the migrants' memories of a static country and the transformations that country has undergone after their departure. Their alienation is linked to their permanent nostalgia for a place that does not exist the way they knew it. This provokes a sense of emptiness that their lives in the countries they have emigrated to cannot fill.

"Wherever I Hang," from the book *Lazy Thoughts of a Lazy Woman* (1989), also deals with the subject of what home means for the Caribbean migrant in Britain. Nichols gives a playful turn to this dramatic and important question of belonging. The author uses some expressions in Creole in this poem, a use which is less marked in poems of regret and resignation such as the previous one analyzed. According to Lawson Welsh, this poem can be considered a Creole monologue or voice-portrait, which belongs to a rich tradition within Caribbean poetry, with early practitioners including Claude McKay, Una Marson, and Louise Bennett. It is a tradition that has been adapted by poets such as Valerie Bloom and David Dabydeen (Lawson Welsh 2007, 90–92).

The poem is characterized by a sense of humor, which is evident in the syntactically and semantically unfinished title, "Wherever I Hang." Readers are invited to complete this saying, the original phrasing of which is "home is where you lay / hang your hat." Other sayings related to home come to mind, such as "home is where the heart is." Nichols offers a personal and irreverent approach to the serious concepts of home, belonging, and identity, questioning stereotypes associated with immigrants and their (it is claimed) permanent sense of loss produced by their painfully divided identities. Jahan Ramazani refers to Nichols's diasporic sensibility in this poem (2007), and her split affinities between an exotic Caribbean birthplace with "de hummingbird splendor" (l. 4) and London's "misty greyness" (l. 9). From a linguistic point of view, Nichols's progressive acculturation is also marked by her initial use of Creole English, "I leave me people, me land, me home" (l. 1) and her gradual shift to Standard English throughout the poem. The words "my home" (l. 31) in the last line confirm that the speaker is able to feel at home almost anywhere (Ramazani 2007).

The poem possesses a colloquial tone marked by the double anaphora "And de ..." and "And is so...," which orchestrate a crescendo of feelings and perceptions in both stanzas. These anaphoric expressions also transmit a sense of immediacy and urgency as if the poem were being written as the images, emotions, and feelings develop in the speaker's mind. The first line announces the speaker's decision to abandon her country: "I leave me people, me land, me home" (l. 1). There is no idealization of the home country. The protagonist leaves behind the exoticism associated with her Caribbean home; the Sun and the magnificent birds do not prevent her from experiencing the less glamorous aspects of her land—"And de hummingbird splendour / Had big rats in de floorboard" (ll. 4–5). This future trip to the old metropolis does not involve loss of personal identity; on the contrary, it is an opportunity for the speaker to reinforce her multiple identities—"So I pick up me new-world-self" (l. 6). We perceive a sense of relief at the possibility of escaping from the burden of unchanging sameness (Fokkema 1998, 105), as well as the drive to explore new perspectives of the self.

The persona's first contacts with England suggest a dream-like atmosphere: "At first I feeling like I in dream – / de misty greyness" (ll. 8–9). These words refer to what Nichols has defined as the "sense of unreality" (Dawes 2001, 137) felt by the migrant in Britain. These impressions dissipate particularly after looking at Lord Nelson's statue, which is as solid as the big rats in the floorboard in line 5, but it points upward at the sky. So far, the speaker has not found rats coming up from the underground, only people. Also, Nelson's statue may anticipate the possibility of having a different life in England, where some of her dreams can become as solid as the walls she has touched and as true as Nelson's statue.

In the next stanza, the poetic voice describes her gradual adaptation to life in England without victimization. After mentioning the traditional stereotypes about the cold English weather, she alludes to a different kind of adaptation to English life, the one that has to do with behavior and ways of life. "I begin to change my calypso ways," she declares (l. 20). She is changing something that is intimately associated with her Caribbean identity. The speaker has relegated improvisation and impulse, traditional features of the music that she identifies with, as models of behavior in England. She must warn people before visiting them, and she has to wait for her turn in a queue. She feels nostalgic about home, but she is now used to English life. The speaker admits her confusion about home and belonging at the end of this stanza, when she says, "I don't know really where I belaang" (l. 28). The colloquial expression "belaang" involves boredom and suggests that the speaker of the poem does not wish to become too serious about place and belonging.

Self-division and displacement are positive and liberating aspects of identity in the three final lines of the poem: "Yes, divided to de ocean / Divided to de bone" (ll. 29–30), as well as a humorous and frivolous turn to this dramatic and important question of belonging, "Wherever I hang me knickers – that's my home" (l. 31).

In this poem, Nichols questions some basic tenets in postcolonial theory, such as that which establishes that place defines cultural affiliation (Fokkema 1998, 101). Indeed, when migrants become displaced this leads to exile, a phenomenon traditionally associated with lost identity. Either they root themselves in their new countries, or go back to their homelands because if they do not belong; thus, they become marginalized. The emphasis on the connection between home and identity places the migrant writer for ever on the margins of culture (Fokkema 1998, 102). Nichols talks about home, identity, and the contrast between cultures, but in a positive and celebratory way: her identity may be divided, but this is no tragedy, and what is more, it makes life easier (Fokkema 1998, 105). She is a "vernacular cosmopolitan," according to Homi Bhabha (2000, 141), who feels at home both in the Caribbean and in England, celebrating all the richness involved in cultural hybridity.

> the tension is very much there. I don't think it could be reconciled. You try to reconcile it. But the tension is always there and maybe it's a good thing [...] it's not only the tension of physical difference between Guyana (or the Caribbean) and England, it's also in terms of language, culture – Creole versus Standard English, for example ...
>
> (Dawes 2001, 137)

The last poem I would like to discuss in this essay is "Wings," included in Nichols's collection *Sunris* (1996). This poem is dedicated to the Jamaican poet John Figueroa, whose comments about Caribbean people's interests in roots instead of wings inspired Nichols. She reflects about the migrants' drive to hold on tight to their origins, their "roots," and how this permanent downward look may limit their individual development and their chances to be influenced by and to influence the life, culture, and society of the country to where they have migrated. Nichols considers that roots and origins should not constitute a burden that pulls people down, otherwise they run the risk of being choked and buried alive. Roots should push people up and make them fly. Only when in flight can people have a perspective of their past and present life. Only then can they envision their future with optimism and freedom. The poem is built through a contrast between images associated with the ground ("roots," "compelling earth," "love-tugging land," "root-lovers," "root-grounders," and "root-worshippers") and images linked to flight and upward movement ("wings," "airy staircase," "migratory pull").

The first stanza deals with roots and rootedness, an essential drive in human beings who need to experience "the sustenance of our roots" (l. 4) to have a balanced life. Nichols suggests that this constant search for what lies underneath and behind becomes dangerous when a situation of uprootment occurs.

> we moved around like
> bereaving trees, constantly touching
> our sawn-off places. (ll. 7–9)

The "many guises" (l. 6) mentioned by the speaker may represent the political, economic, or personal reasons why people have to emigrate or leave their country. The poetic voice compares emigrants to trees, the branches of which have been cut off. Like the tree, the person has suffered an amputation, and this loss, this gap, seems to absorb the person's energies like a black hole.

Caribbean migrants do not resemble "bright migrant birds" (l. 11) because, unlike birds, which never look back when they fly toward a warmer land, the migrants are pulled down by their roots toward the earth. This attraction for what lies beneath and behind can seriously limit future flights (ll. 17–18).

Migrants tend to indulge themselves in what they think they have lost, basically their land, their country. This loss is described in materialistic terms, "old hoarding mourners, / constantly counting / our sea-chest of losses" (ll. 23–25). This attachment to the physical land prevents them from discovering within themselves the most precious gifts they have absorbed from those roots, "the imperishable gift of our wings" (l. 28).

The next stanza explains that "the imperishable gift of our wings" (l. 28) led their ancestors to dream of a better life, not by looking back or downward, but by climbing "the airy staircase / whenever they contemplated / rock and a hard place" (ll. 31–33).

The speaker of the poem continues to explore the metaphorical possibilities of wings and the idea of flight in the remaining stanzas, emphasizing transcendence from fixity and the past (Lawson Welsh 2007, 118). Both impulses, the "migratory-pull" (l. 35) and the "homing-instinct" (l. 36) become real because of wings, and lead migrants to find their "havens" (l. 38). This diasporic image of the West Indian crossing the Atlantic toward Europe or back home suggests cultural hybridity. Only the roots that become wings can enrich the European haven, and European ways may as well influence their Caribbean homeland.

Even without the "migratory-pull" or "homing instinct," the poem's persona considers that wings are essential and oppose the paralyzing worship of roots. One can fly only with wings, and this initial flight can lead to higher ones: "it's still wings taking us back / to the bigger presence of wings" (ll. 42–43).

The idea of a hybrid identity is not linked to physical mobility, but to a willingness to use personal roots and the past as impulses to transcend victimization and nostalgia. Thus, cultural hybridity may appear as a space of boundless possibilities (Lawson Welsh 2007, 119). Wings become a tool to heal and relieve the consequences of an oppressive history, the suffering and the scars on the backs of Caribbean people.

Conclusion

The realities of contemporary social life in Britain as well as in many other international cities of the world reflect what Nichols discusses in her poetry: persons with fluid identities who have several places that can be called home, who fight for their personal freedom and happiness, but who also allow into themselves features of a communal identity. They can look back without anger and with faith in the future.

Nichols's poems reveal her ability to be at ease with herself in many locations: in her birthplace, but also in England. Her poetry does not insist on victimization, because Nichols does not feel like a victim. She does not represent all the sufferings of black women throughout history; on the contrary, Nichols shows confidence in the process of reverse colonization, and many of her poems describe how the growing presence of people of former British colonies, of different racial origins, has contributed to enrich British cultural life, despite conflicts having to do with social, racial, and economic discrimination. Humor and optimism are essential motifs in her poetry, which she uses to escape the burden of old stereotypes associated with black women and immigrants. Nichols's poems are attractive and enriching because of their linguistic and thematic diversity. Her lines offer provocative, intimate, comic, and thoughtful representations of the challenges of living in multicultural societies and in a globalized world.

References

Bhabha, Homi (2000). "The Vernacular Cosmopolitan." In: *Voices of the Crossing: The Impact of Britain on Writers from Asia, the Caribbean, and Africa* (eds. Ferdinand Denis and Naseem Khan), 133–142. London: Serpent's Tail.

Bringas López, Ana (2003). "Representations of Black Omen in Grace Nichols's Poetry: From Otherness to Empowerment." *Revista Alicantina de Estudios Ingleses* 16: 3–19. https://doi.org/10.14198/raei.2003.16.03.

British Council (2018). "Writers. Grace Nichols." https://literature.britishcouncil.org/writer/grace-nichols (accessed 10 September 2018).

Broom, Sarah (2006). *Contemporary British and Irish Poetry: An Introduction*. Basingstoke: Palgrave Macmillan.

Cornier Michael, Magali (2009). "Telling History Other-Wise: Grace Nichols' *I Is a Long Memoried Woman*." In: *Reclaiming Home, Remembering Motherhood, Rewriting History: African American and Afro-Caribbean Women's Literature in the Twentieth Century* (eds. Verena Thelle and Marie Drews), 210–232. Newcastle upon Tyne: Cambridge Scholars Publishing.

Dawes, Kwame (2001). "Grace Nichols." In: *Talk Yuh Talk: Interviews with Anglophone Caribbean Poets* (ed. Kwame Dawes), 135–147. Charlottesville: The University Press of Virginia.

Fokkema, Aleid (1998). "On the (False) Idea of Exile: Derek Walcott and Grace Nichols." In: *(Un)Writing Empire* (ed. Theo D'haen), 99–113. Amsterdam: Rodopi.

Lawson Welsh, Sarah (2007). *Grace Nichols*. Tavistock: Northcote House and British Council.

Nichols, Grace (1988). "Grace Nichols." In: *Let It Be Told: Essays by Black Women in Britain* (ed. Lauretta Ngcobo), 95–105. London: Virago.

Nichols, Grace (1990). "The Battle with Language." In: *Caribbean Women Writers: Essays from the First International Conference* (ed. Selwyn R. Cudjoe), 283–289. Wellesley: Calaloux Publications.

Nichols, Grace (2010). *I Have Crossed an Ocean: Selected Poems*. Newcastle upon Tyne: Bloodaxe Books.

Papaleonida, Paraskevi (1997). "'holding my beads in my hand': Dialogue, Synthesis and Power in the Poetry of Jackie Kay and Grace Nichols." In: *Kicking Daffodils: Twentieth-Century Women Poets* (ed. Vicki Bertram), 125–139. Edinburgh: Edinburgh University Press.

Ramazani, Jahan (2007). "Black British Poetry and the Translocal." In: *The Cambridge Companion to Twentieth-Century English Poetry* (ed. Neil Corcoran), 200–214. New York: Cambridge University Press https://doi.org/10.1017/CCOL052187081X.015 (accessed 10 September 2018).

Türe Abaci, Özlem (2009). "I am "holding my beads in my hands": Strategies of Subversion and Resistance in Grace Nichols's Poetry." In: *Identidad, migración y cuerpo femenino* (eds. Silvia del Pilar Castro Borrego and M. Isabel Romero Ruiz), 61–70. Oviedo: KRK Ediciones.

Wisker, Gina (1993). "'Writing the Body': Reading Joan Riley, Grace Nichols and Ntozake Shange." In: *Black Women's Writing* (ed. Gina Wisker), 19–42. Basingstoke: Macmillan.

3.12
F. T. Prince

Will May

Introduction

In 1958, F. T. Prince copied out Philip Larkin's poem "Arrival" from *The Sunday Times* in his journal. The title might have given him a warning that this new poet would come to dominate postwar poetry, and his lugubrious style would shape a generation of modern verse. He might have heard a hint of a rival in the title, too. Prince goes on to lambast the poem for its unachieved conclusion, and its turn to an imagined sublimity. He ponders how he might have finished the same poem, reasonably confident he might have made something better from it. The anecdote tells us much about the world of a poet who spent much of life at the margins of things. A late poem, "Finis Coronat Opus," finds Prince cozily looking forward to his posthumous legacy: "in databanks one snoozes / Safe in the bosom of the Muses / With Larkins, Harrisons and Hugheses" (Prince 2012, 301). Yet he must have known that his place in a lineage that included Larkin, Harrison, and Hughes was far from assured. Very few of the many generations of students taught by Prince while he was professor in the English Department at the University of Southampton knew he was a poet. Poetic tributes to him praise his obscurity: "I don't know anyone who's met F.T. Prince," notes Lee Harwood, whimsically, in "The Late Poem" (Harwood 2004, 58). Critics attempting to rescue his reputation call him "unjustly neglected" without giving readers a sense of what they should be attending to (Davie 1955, 93).

The work of the British South African-born poet Prince brings together a number of postwar schools of poetry, yet his writing career, which runs from the 1930s to 1995,

A Companion to Contemporary British and Irish Poetry, 1960–2015, First Edition.
Edited by Wolfgang Görtschacher and David Malcolm.
© 2021 John Wiley & Sons Ltd. Published 2021 by John Wiley & Sons Ltd.

unsettles any neat periodization. At various points in his career, both Siegfried Sassoon and John Ashbery considered themselves his contemporaries. While "An Epistle to a Patron" was included in *The Oxford Book of English Verse* (1999), and "Soldiers Bathing" has been much anthologized since its first appearance in 1942, his poetry is not often included in literary histories of the century. The diversity of his voices and forms might give us one reason for this omission, but another is his refusal to adopt a poetic persona: he gave few interviews throughout his career, was often cajoled into print, and his understanding of a poetic vocation found little space for being fashionable. In the 1930s, when his Oxford contemporaries were insisting that poetry should be political, partisan, and demotic, he worked on a series of dramatic monologues and metaphysical lyrics that would become his first collection. *Poems* was published late in 1938, under the shadow of the Munich Crisis. Thirty years later, when Britain was discovering performance poetry, he completed *Memoirs in Oxford*, a long autobiographical poem published by the Fulcrum Press in 1970. The one moment when his poetic journey and the historical climate aligned was with the publication of "Soldiers Bathing." His Christian reading of men swimming after combat found an audience eager for World War Two poetry. Prince worked in the Intelligence Corps and was made a Captain in 1943, making him a more feasible war poet than the likes of Auden, who had emigrated to the USA.

Part of the story of Prince's postwar writing is the importance of small presses in supporting new work, although he would move to Carcanet for his *Collected Poems* in 1993. While Prince began his career in Faber, T. S. Eliot's early support for his work soon faded. Although his marginality has proved part of his appeal for a series of poets, from Susan Howe to Geoffrey Hill, he was known primarily during his lifetime as a Milton scholar. His 1954 study *The Italian Element in Milton's Verse* was followed by an edition of Shakespeare's poetry. When he was asked to give the Clark Lectures in Cambridge in 1972, it was his reputation as a scholar rather than a poet which prompted the invitation.

His poetry does not make the colloquial appeals to its readers of Louis MacNeice or W. H. Auden; its most obvious reference points are Shelley, Pound, and Yeats. Yet the variety of his forms, the particularity of his syntax, and the range of his intellectual interests can challenge the reader. His study of Milton takes particular delight in the Italian tradition of *asprezza*, a difficulty or obduracy in a poem that the reader must face down, and we find this throughout his own work, whether in the scholarly reading that underpins *Drypoints of the Hasidim*, a long poem from the 1970s, or the obscure rhetorical questions which continually shift the relationship between the subject and object of his poems. His dramatic monologues inhabit the world of Zulu kings ("Chaka"); in a selection of love poems from *The Doors of Stone* (1962), he resurrects a dormant Italian verse form, the strambotti. While many of the moves he made in his lifetime suggest a poet indifferent to his posthumous reception, it is telling how many of his poems return to the subject of reputation—from the long poem *Afterword on Rupert Brooke* (1977), which considers how postwar biographies have reshaped our sense of Brooke's life and work, to the account of Laurence Sterne's belated literary career in "A Last Attachment." Many of his speakers are troubled by the possibility they might be forgotten: "Michelangelo in Old Age" bids us not to "forget the poor old man" (Prince 2012, 79), while a poem attending to Strafford, the Lord Deputy of Ireland who was hanged for treason, suggests he can be spared a worse death by posterity. Prince's arrival into the story of postwar poetry, unlike Larkin's, has proved to be posthumous.

"Grimness and Uncertainty"

Prince was born in Kimberley, South Africa in 1912 to a Jewish diamond merchant from the East End of London, and a Scottish teacher. His difficult relationship with his Presbyterian mother—"choked with faults of every kind" (Prince 2012, 138)—was recalled in *Memoirs in Oxford*. Despite his religious background, he was educated at the Catholic Christian Brothers' College in Kimberley, writing his first Keatsian verses at the age of 14. Early emotional difficulties meant that he was removed from all games or social activities when at school; he was to suffer from depression for much of his life. An unpublished memoir suggests that what amounted to solitary confinement for much of his early years was both a blessing and curse: "within this fortress and powerhouse of privilege I was granted a privilege of my own" (Prince, "Personal Notes and Queries" n.d.). He thought the low ridges and veldt of Kimberley "monotonous" (Prince, 'Personal Notes and Queries' n.d.), but spent long summers in the Cape bathing with friends, and reading Shelley, Whitman, and Baudelaire. If he found South Africa's literary climate stultifying, he also called the country "the source of my appetite and feeling for *light*" (Prince, "Personal Notes and Queries" n.d.).

After a chance meeting with the South African philosopher John Findlay on a cruise ship, he abandoned an architecture course at the University of Witwatersrand and applied to read English at Balliol College, Oxford in 1931. He arrived in England at "a portentous turning point in world affairs" (Prince, "Personal Notes and Queries" n.d.), but found the political and religious debates of his contemporaries baffling, as he notes in a rare interview (Devereux 1988). Lacking the specific English experiences of class and school which underpinned so much Oxford poetry from the 1930s, he found himself adrift. His diary from the period records a number of botched meetings with Wittgenstein and Spender. However, letters from Roy Campbell helped introduce him to Winifred Holtby and T. S. Eliot, who would publish "An Epistle to a Patron" in the *Criterion*.

After finishing his degree, he undertook some work on Chatterton's poetry at Princeton. By the time of his father's death in 1938, he was working as a research assistant at Chatham House, the Royal Institute for International Affairs. He was called up in 1940, and soon became an Army Intelligence officer, spending much of the war working as a cryptanalyst at Bletchley Park. From there, he went to teach at Southampton in 1946, accepting a Chair in English in 1957.

In 1937, Prince converted to Catholicism, following writers such as Evelyn Waugh, who joined the Roman Catholic Church in 1930. He suggests his conversion was prompted by "those few pre-war years of increasing grimness and uncertainty" (Prince, "Personal Notes and Queries" n.d.); it was as much political as religious. In a decade that continually asked writers to take sides and stances, Prince turned to a higher form of authority. Prince was unconvinced by communism, and similarly with the idea that poetry should communicate with a wide audience. Although his first collection *Poems* (1938) was published by Faber, subsequent poems Prince sent to Eliot were rejected for being too abstract, or emotionally obscure.

After the war, Prince elected to publish his works with smaller presses. Although more out of stubbornness than deliberate design, this decision helped to introduce him to a younger, more experimental group of Anglo-American poets, who celebrated the intellectual challenges of this marginal voice. Geoffrey Hill praised him as an intellectual ally; Susan Howe called his work a beacon; John Ashbery began a correspondence with him that would have a profound influence on the direction of his verse (see Hazzard 2015).

"What may I offer?"

A number of poets and critics have noted the apparent shift between Prince's first collection, with its syntactical games, dramatic monologues, and its occasionally dandyish locutions, and his postwar work which Geoffrey Hill has claimed is "hag-ridden by sincerity" (Hill 2002, 30). Yet, despite Prince's Catholic approach to form and his intellectual breadth, his poetry often returns to a set of binaries: power and submission, freedom and bondage, gifting and losing, experience and recollection, the lyric and the dramatic.

The poem which begins Prince's collected works is "An Epistle to a Patron." It is a poem of rococo diction and wonderfully metaphysical excess: an architect promises his patron both the total glory of creation, the flattering obsequy of subservience, and the fawning threat of discretion. Like a scissor-arch, the poem's syntactical architecture holds aloft the impossible, "hanging together / Like an argument, with beams, ties and sistering pilasters" (Prince 2012, 13). It is a servitude which reaches incredible heights. The speaker has learnt how to use both words and people, the "now advancing, now withdrawing faces, whose use I know" (Prince 2012, 14). Yet this is not a work of groveling verbosity: the architect's gift for flattery suggests other, untold, rhetorical skills. Though he trumpets the "extravagant gist of this communication" (Prince 2012, 15), the reader is left to wonder if the gist of his epistle is as it appears. The poem's elaborations combine the psychological depth of Browning, the playful courtly politics of Pope, and the preposterous splendor of Renaissance masters, but its focus on the engine of power is not as far from the 1930s as it appears.

The hyperbolic promises of "An Epistle to a Patron" are echoed throughout Prince's first collection, which is full of gifts ambivalently given or unwisely received. As Prince himself noted of his first collection years later, "it projected a threatened world order and culture" (Prince, "Personal Notes and Queries" n.d.), where no nation, or worldview could go unchallenged, and all hierarchies were unsettled. More recently, Sean Pryor (2012) has noted how the collection's vermiculate syntax is suggestive of a political dance; even the natural landscape is held in check with a language of political control, as Prince's monologue for Edmund Burke suggests:

> my instruments must intricately
> Simulate an involuntary ascension, melt in flight.
> And that austere insolence of tune was (nowhere near
> The loud grudge of levellers) a manner of grovelling
> To some tyranny of snow at morning.
> (Prince 2012, 27)

Here, the Burkean vision of sublimity is precarious, Icarian, and old certainties are unsettled: the story of flying too close to the Sun is remade as a submissive gesture to the snow. The collocation of "austere" and "insolence" is typical of Prince, his verse's apparent submission to the dry and the scholastic revisioned as kind of heroism. Burke's desire to "simulate" the "involuntary" tells us something about the Romantic legacy in Prince's work too: Shelley and Keats are gifts his poetry receives with the full knowledge that their immediacy must be somehow refashioned to be taken for new.

The gifts of his first collection are often unsure what they might be or to whom they might be given: tellingly, for a poet imagining his audience, the titles are full of datives, the dominant mode of the book: "To My Sister," "To A Man on his Horse," "For the Deserted." The poem "For Fugitives," like many of Prince's imagined monologues, finds its speaker in exile, wondering how the relationship between him and his lover might be transformed by distance, by martial conquest, and being "on this the other shore" (Prince 2012, 39). With any kind of exchange comes the possibility of guilt, and the speaker is haunted by the proximity of giving and forgiving, and the knowledge that even something freely offered may have the appearance of being stolen: "And for you whose it was / Who can forgive me? what may I offer?" (Prince 2012, 39). The poem which follows, "For Thieves and Beggars," hears a particular mixture of bondage and liberation in the sounds of parting lovers, whose voices are "captured, caressed, and freed" (Prince 2012, 40). The most intimate of exchanges are infected with power, and the question of giving becomes one of owning. Even in a more conventional love poem, "The Dice," consummation and reconciliation seem a kind of fiction: "we make up all between us" (Prince 2012, 59).

This tension animates Prince's poetry throughout his career, returning to the central demand of "An Epistle to a Patron": "I wish for liberty, let me then be tied" (Prince 2012, 15). Even the apparently straightforward biographical narrative of *Memoirs in Oxford* is overshadowed by a treasured photo of the poet's father which had inexplicably gone missing from the family home: "He has given it – but to whom?" (Prince 2012, 129). Prince's most famous poem "Soldiers Bathing" has usually been read as an attempt to find Christian consolation in the century's deadliest conflict, but it is also, as Adam Piette has pointed out, a laying bare of power relations (Piette 2004, 45). The speaker watches the "freedom" of the soldiers who "belong to me" (Prince 2012, 55). War finds each soldier "being a slave and making slaves of others" (Prince 2012, 55). The soldiers bathing are transformed into the suffering body of Christ, but the poem is forced to acknowledge that the speaker takes pleasure in looking on at that suffering. It also gestures to the frailty of its conclusion, mindful that "who nowadays is conscious of our sins?" (Prince 2012, 56). Meaningless suffering generates aesthetic pleasure; the sin becomes the unspoken delight in surveying the soldiers, both warriors and servile.

The homoerotic qualities of the poem, clearly part of its appeal for E. M. Forster, point to other kinds of enslavement faced by the male lovers in Prince's poems. A dramatic monologue from *The Doors of Stone* (1963) which traces "The Old Age of Michelangelo" finds no liberation in worshipping the male body: in its place is only "The world's desert and death, the dusty prison / Where we have shut ourselves, or the sky shuts us" (Prince 2012, 79). "To a Man on his Horse" from *Poems* expresses erotic desire not for the poem's radiant addressee, but instead wishes to become the horse's groom, combing his body in "simple and indecorous sweetness" (Prince 2012, 17). The urge is far from simple, suggesting a desire that both must defer and debase itself. The impulse returns as late "His Dog and Pilgrim," from 1983, where Prince reimagines the pilgrimage of St. Rocco through the eyes of his faithful dog, who brought him scraps of leftover food when he lay infected with the plague. The dog's purpose is to serve his new master, yet even for a dog, the need to express the relationship in the language of hierarchy gets him into some rhetorical riddles: "where he is what is / which I am but for" (Prince 2012, 213). The dog's purpose, like the poem's, is always contingent on another body. Whether Prince's poems are reimagining the anxieties of a Zulu king (as in the early poem "Chaka"), or promising architectural splendor for an unnamed patron, they explore the frail truces and evasions of power throughout his career.

"This or That Well-known Story"

Although John Ashbery's favorite Prince poem is "The Moonflower," an early lyric first published in the 1950s, one of Prince's most substantial gifts to British postwar poetry has been the dramatic monologue: "Strafford" from *The Doors of Stone* (1963) is echoed in Hill's poem "Funeral Music" in *King Log* (1968); Prince's 1962 poetic tribute to Tommaso Campanella, the Renaissance poet and philosopher, who spent 27 years imprisoned in Naples after being accused of conspiracy, prompts Hill's 1968 poem "Men are a Mockery of Angels." While the figures Prince alights on for his dramatic monologues span centuries and cultures—the fourth-century saint Gregory Nazianzen, Richard Lionheart, the thirteenth-century French poet Jean Bodel—common to many of these voices is their sense of being marginal, out of time, or revolutionary. "Moult sont Prud'hommes les Templiers" takes its title from the French poet Guiot de Provins, who spoke out about the excesses of the Catholic Church in the twelfth century. His role as poet pits him against clerics and monarchs—"Kings and Bishops murder law"—and the philosophers of his day—"Scholars wind a rope of straw, / Call it a golden chain" (Prince 2012, 88). The poet's vocation becomes truth-telling; they remain the only figures of authority resistant to corruption. Yet they are also outcasts: the poet Jean Bodel, whose voice is ventriloquized in "Les Congés du Lépreux," is dogged with leprosy, and pierced with "plague and sores beyond relief" (Prince 2012, 89). The poem is based on a longer one by Bodel himself, which takes leave of his friends as disease sends him into exile. It is telling that this work which balances poetic craft with social ostracism so appealed to Prince; to write is to devise worlds for "friends whom I shall never see" (Prince 2012, 89). When poets are not the victims of these dramatic monologues, they are offered as the saviors: Gregory of Nazianzen takes in a world of factions and conflict, dreaming of "new tongues for the expression of new things!" (Prince 2012, 103). The monologues catch their subjects in moments of abject crisis: a type of bondage, whether it be physical infirmity, incarceration, or political suppression, always threatens to silence them.

If these figures are gifted with truth, but denied the means to expound it, another strand of Prince's poetry explores the problems when lyric truth is subject to narrative ambiguity. *Afterword on Rupert Brooke* (1977) explores the legacy of Brooke's life and poetry in light of the 1964 biography by Christopher Hassall, and the posthumously published letters between Brooke and his lover, Ka Cox. The long syllabic poem, as Attridge (2015) has noted, follows the meter of Robert Bridges's *The Testament of Beauty* (1930), but is written intuitively; it suggests the difficulty of making "God's vulgar lyric *Rupert Brooke*" into a legend (Prince 2012, 171). As the poem implies, an Englishman with better taste might have left us less of a legend, but nothing nearer to the truth:

> For it is also true,
> The legend, and not to be discarded even
> If one should now re-model and re-write so much.
> (Prince 2012, 171)

The poem has much to tell us about the way literary history might inflate, resurrect, or dismantle a lyric voice. The apparent inevitability to Brooke's beauty and his premature death cannot have made his own decisions any easier, or his attempt to answer "the young live piercing question of *What is it for?* / *What to do and why do it?*" (Prince 2012, 172). Death defines the urgency of his endeavor, and guards against the fear of "Feeling nothing" and being "afraid / Of meaning nothing" (Prince 2012, 174). The poem frames itself around his relationship with Ka Cox as a way of directing us to the contingencies of his life, returning us to a moment when "everything stood still but meant another thing" (Prince 2012, 183).

Although Prince would likely deny it, there are a number of affinities with Brooke's story and his own: war "might look like a way out" for Brooke (Prince 2012, 183), as it was for the frustrated and lonely young man who heard World War II being announced in the Balliol College common room. In *The Stranger's Child* (2011), Alan Hollinghurst creates a fictional poet half way between Brooke and Prince, famous for a poem about soldiers. The comparison is borne out by Prince's extended autobiographical poem, *Memoirs in Oxford* (1970). Like Brooke, Prince's poetic past must be excavated to make sense of his vocation: Prince's poem is halfway between a *Prelude* and a projected biography written by another hand. The poem was prompted by Prince's return to Oxford for an All Souls Fellowship in 1968–1969, a period when the évènements in Paris were making themselves felt even in Oxford, with graffiti and picketing throughout the city. It is written in the stanzaic rhymed verse of Shelley's *Peter Bell*, in tribute to the poet whose work Prince received at school for a poetry prize, but its portrait of a disappointed poet is less sure-footed than its meter, finding Prince "*incontentabile*," never satisfied but always "cutting, cancelling, rubbing, fingering" and "sometimes changing bad for worse" (Prince 2012, 143). An older Prince would look back on this poem with some misgivings, troubled by its claims he had "somehow escaped" his psychological burdens (Prince, "Personal Notes and Queries" n.d.). It tells of Prince's arrival in Oxford in the 1930s, and his difficult relationship with his mother and his homeland: as the poem suggests, home might be nothing more than a preparation, but it is never clear what for. Prince's Oxford has more than a nod to Wordsworth, with its "discoloured tower and domes" (Prince 2012, 132) but brings no more salvation than Wordsworth's Cambridge in the *Prelude*; the speaker's indifference to the "melancholy public labours" of the English people (Prince 2012, 144) suggests poetry as a vocation, but the poem is full of the sense of a life missed, or misspent. As Pollard

(2015) has suggested, Prince's is a creativity driven by self-interrogation. Echoing the voice of *Afterword on Rupert Brooke*, the speaker takes on the expansive voice of posterity, but "the old biography," that "damp-stained book" lying at the center of *Memoirs in Oxford* (Prince 2012, 144) is Prince's own story, and many of the pages remain unopened.

Prince's long poems often return to the tensions between poetic endeavor and the notion of a good life, drawing on literary and historical figures presumably well-known to his readers. Yet in Prince's 1975 poem *Drypoints of the Hasidism*, which pieces together the history of Hasidism, a liberal spiritual movement led by the mystic Baal Shem Tov (1700–1760), we find characters sitting together and telling "this or that well-known story" to an audience unsure of their referents (Prince 2012, 158). The poem was published by Anthony Rudolf's Menard Press, and an expository essay by Prince was given free to anyone buying the poem. While Prince's essay lays out some of the religious context for the 400-line work, and notes it was inspired by Martin Buber's *The Early Masters* (1959), it also offers some unexpected reference points for the poem:

> I hoped it was "worth a new notebook," didn't begin to see "how to do it," but thought it should "allude" to "the Church and poetry nowadays – confusion, frenzies of liberation – and divine sparks" [...] but I see how odd an approach this may seem to what went on in eighteenth-century Polish and Ukranian Jewry. What could it have to do with the Catholic Church or "the poetry revival" of the 1960s? [...] the ferment in the Church since Vatican II might be seen as only one manifestation of the more general unsettlement of moral and social values in Western countries in the 1960s. And in England and American the "poetry scene" must certainly be regarded as part of that.
>
> (Prince 1974, 29–30)

Prince returns to Hasidism as a movement radical for its ideas about dissemination; mystics were encouraged to share their experiences with people of all kinds. In this way, the poem also becomes a means of thinking about the much more recent discussion about audience, authority, and reception. A poet apparently at the margins of postwar British poetry writers a long, allusive, obscure poem whose subject is exactly the newly democratic world his poetry appears to reject. The story of Prince's poetry, like the analogical subjects of the poems themselves, is not the one we think we know.

"Late and yet Late"

In 2012, the Special Collections of the Hartley Library at the University of Southampton announced that a previously embargoed literary archive had come to light. F. T. Prince had left a vast collection of his diaries, correspondence, drafts, lectures, and notebooks. The archive, made public on the centenary of Prince's birth, revealed the extent of John Ashbery's interest in his work, the key role Prince played in mentoring poets such as Lee Harwood and Tom Raworth, and the high esteem he was held in by writers from Siegfried Sassoon and C. S. Lewis to Susan Howe. It is hard to think of a comparable postwar British or Irish poet whose reach and influence is so eclectic, and so transatlantic.

The archive also included a number of unpublished works, including the poem *Memoirs of Caravaggio*, which was one of two collections of poems from the archive published by

Perdika Press in 2015. This poem, written in 1957, is in some ways the companion piece of "The Old Age of Michelangelo." The speaker can only "see the thing in fragments" (Prince 2015, 12), as he imagines Caravaggio lying in wait for a pardon, seeing what his fate might be. Prince returns throughout his career to the artist whose final destiny is undecided. In "A Last Attachment," he recounts Laurence Sterne's affair with Eliza Draper, and compares this late passion with his own writing career, which could not come about until "youth had gone with all its nonsense" (Prince 2012, 193). Prince's career might at first seem to offer the opposite version of Sterne's belatedness: his own unpublished memoir sets up his writing as one of the

> products of the British Empire, including the "old" Commonwealth in its last phase: over-extended, and aware that is must find ways to revise and limit its abilities.
> (Prince, "Personal Notes and Queries" n.d.)

This reading of Prince's work makes T. S. Eliot's rejection of his postwar writing understandable: prince is a poet who belongs to the past. Yet the significance of Prince's work both for British and American avant-garde poets belies Prince's own belittling of his career. The recent collection of critical essays on his work, *Reading F. T. Prince*, may yet help us rethink a poet who is "honest about the perils of patronage or prestige" (May 2017, 2). Our appreciation for his poetry—its richness, its variety, its intellectual breadth, its unique exploration of the relationship between power and the powerless—comes "Late and yet late, the better" (Prince 2012, 194).

References

Attridge, Derek (2015). "F.T. Prince's Syllabics." (ed. W. May, 2017), 11–26.

Davie, Donald (1955). *Articulate Energy: An Enquiry into Syntax in English Diction*. London: Routledge.

Devereux, Stephen (1988). *F.T. Prince*. Grahamstown: National English Literary Museum.

Harwood, Lee (2004). *Collected Poems*. Exeter: Shearsman.

Hazzard, Oli (2015). "'We See All Things As They Might Be': F. T. Prince and John Ashbery." (ed. W. May, 2017), 106–128.

Hill, Geoffrey (2002). "Il Cortegiano: F.T. Prince's *Poems* (1938)." *PN Review* 29 (1): 28–32.

May, Will (ed.) (2017). *Reading F. T. Prince*. Liverpool: Liverpool University Press.

Piette, Adam (2004). "World War Two: Contested Europe." In: *The Cambridge History of Twentieth-Century English Literature* (eds. Laura Marcus and Peter Nicholls), 417–435. Cambridge: Cambridge University Press.

Pollard, Natalie (2015). "Fugitive Pieces: F.T Prince and Sculpture" (ed. W. May, 2017), 181–210.

Prince, F. T. (1974). "Discovering the Hasidim." *European Judaism*: 29–33: July.

Prince, F. T. (2012). *Collected Poems*. Manchester: Carcanet.

Prince, F. T. (2015). *Memoirs of Caravaggio* (ed. Peter Robinson). Enfield: Perdika Press.

Prince, F. T. Archive (n.d.). "Personal Notes and Queries." Special Collections, Hartley Library. University of Southampton.

Pryor, Sean (2012). "Poetry and Decision: F. T. Prince in September 1938." *Review of English Studies* 63 (262): 818–840. https://doi.org/10.1093/res/hgs001.

3.13
Kathleen Raine

Glyn Pursglove

Given her poetic achievement and the substantial body of her published verse, it is initially surprising that Kathleen Raine should so often be absent from "representative" anthologies of the English poetry of the twentieth century and from histories of that poetry. So, for example, one looks in vain for her work in widely circulated anthologies such as *The Bloodaxe Book of 20th Century Poetry* (Longley 2000) and *British Poetry since 1945* (Lucie-Smith 1970); she gets only a perfunctory mention in Deryn Rees Jones's *Consorting with Angels: Essays on Modern Women Poets* (Rees-Jones 2005); she is entirely absent from works such as *Contemporary British Poetry* by James Acheson and Romana Huk (1996) and Nerys Williams's *Contemporary Poetry* (Williams 2011). She merits a single brief mention in *The Cambridge History of Twentieth-Century English Literature* (Marcus and Nicholls 2004). Although she has written learnedly, powerfully, and extensively on poetry and the tradition of poetics within which she herself has worked, she is also wholly unrepresented in well-known collections of writings on poetics by twentieth-century poets such as James Scully's *Modern Poets on Modern Poetry* (Scully 1966) or *Strong Words: Modern Poets on Modern Poetry* (Herbert and Hollis 2000). Many more such omissions are detailed in Sabine Coelsch-Foisner's *Revolution in Poetic Consciousness* (Coelsch-Foisner 2002, I. 30–37).

These absences reflect the very nature, though certainly not the quality, of Raine's work. In a review written in 1956, Edwin Muir observed that "Her poetry is outside all the modern categories" (quoted on the back cover of the paperback edition of Raine's *Collected Poems* of 2000 [Raine 2008]). Raine's work since then has forcefully demonstrated the truth of Muir's observation. Indeed, so inimical did Raine find the prevailing thought-world of the poetry of her own time that she probably regarded many omissions as a kind of indirect compliment (and there were certainly occasions on which she refused permission for her poems to be included in specific anthologies, when she believed that it would present her work in an unsuitable context).

Raine's critical prose, though much of it concerns her great master William Blake and other Romantic poets such as Coleridge and Shelley, as well as later figures such as Yeats, Muir, Vernon Watkins, and David Gascoyne, also provides a kind of prolegomenon to her own poetic work. In what follows I shall attempt to provide a guide to what I might call Raine's "intellectual milieu," using the phrase in the sense deployed by Louis I. Bredvold in his 1934 book *The Intellectual Milieu of John Dryden*. Where a poet so far outside the poetic mainstream as Raine is concerned, such a study (though necessarily far briefer than Bredvold's treatment of *his* author!) is essential for any intelligent approach to the poetry itself. A central text here is Raine's *Defending Ancient Springs*, a collection of essays first published in 1967. A quotation from her essay on Edwin Muir will make a good starting point:

> At the present time much that is called poetry is little more than the autobiography of the artist; it is the critical fashion to discount the imagination and to make "sincere" feeling or "realistic" description the test of merit.
>
> (Raine 1985, 3)

For Raine, on the other hand, the proper concern of the poet is *not* "to describe natural appearances, or to compare one natural appearance with another" (Raine 2007, 23). Both phrases are taken from Raine's lecture *Poetry in Relation to Traditional Wisdom* given to The Guild of Pastoral Psychology in 1957 (Raine 1958). What Raine views as the poet's task, a task undertaken by all the poets she admires most, is expressed clearly in a comment on Yeats, a comment which characteristically leads her back to Blake: "Yeats saw the poet's task as being not to reflect the age but to inspire, to illuminate every age with a vision of higher realities, these being timeless and always accessible to those who 'raise their thought to heaven' as Blake so simply puts it" (Raine 1999, 22).

Given Raine's antipathy to the predominantly positivist and materialist climate of her times, it is hardly surprising that she should be at odds with so much in the poetic and critical world. Indeed, such is the depth of her discomfort with that world that some of its key terms take on profoundly different, or even antonymic, meanings in her discourses on poetry. A key example is the word *original* and its cognates. In an essay on Thomas Taylor and English Romantic poetry, she writes:

> I belong to a generation which grew up in the unquestioned belief that every new development in human thought and in the arts comes about through breaking with the rules and restraints of the past, a revolutionary iconoclasm which "frees" the mind of the artists for the production or reception of "new ideas." This assumption originated perhaps in a false analogy with science and the experimental method. [...] But even the little history I had learned at school should have taught me better: had not the Italian Renaissance arisen out of "a revival of learning" dormant for a thousand years? [...] I have come to believe that every flowering of

poetry and the other arts originates in a "revival of learning"; not in "originality" in the modern sense, but in a return to the origins, to first principles.

(Raine 1968a, 230)

It is in this second sense that Raine's own work as a poet is profoundly "original." It follows that any intelligent reading of Raine's poetry must be based on some understanding of those "first principles," those "origins" to which she believed the poetry of her own times should return. Raine has often referred to these principles as "the learning of the Imagination" (see Raine 1999) and it is to the tradition of that "learning" that she seeks to "return" in her own work as a poet.

> [B]y their reiteration of faith in the imagination the English poets, from Spenser to Milton, from Blake and Coleridge to Keats and Shelley, from Yeats to Edwin Muir and Vernon Watkins, have preserved in English culture a knowledge obscured by her philosophers (Locke, Blake's enemy, was the type of all later positivists who believe man to possess no knowledge except through the senses) and indeed by her religion, which has taken the bias of a temperamental pragmatism. Without knowledge of the mind and access to its fountains no true poetry can be written.
>
> (Raine 1985, 19–20)

But, of course, such English poets were in no way novel in their poetic faith, the tradition of the imagination which they drew on having its origins long before any of them were born. She would have said of all these poets, as she wrote of Blake that he "was not an originator of those ideas to which his genius gave such dynamic energy [...]. Rather he gathered the diverse strands of an excluded and rejected tradition into a new and powerful unity and coherence" (Raine 1981, 37).

A similar synthesis of traditions largely excluded by the contemporary mindset underpins Raine's work. At its core is a kind of innate Platonism. In using this last phrase, I have in mind a famous dictum by Samuel Taylor Coleridge:

> Every man is born an Aristotelian, or a Platonist. I do not think it possible that any one born an Aristotelian can become a Platonist; and I am sure no born Platonist can change into an Aristotelian, they are the two classes of men, besides which it is next to impossible to conceive a third.
>
> (Coleridge 1851, 100–101)

It is salutary to put these words by Coleridge next to a response to them made by the Victorian theologian Frederick Denison Maurice. In conversation with Sir Edward Strachey (1812–1901) (probably in 1836, when the young Strachey was studying with Maurice), Maurice responded to his pupil's quotation of Coleridge's words with the observation that "All little children are Platonists, and it is their education which makes men Aristotelians" (Maurice 1884, I. 206–207).

The central thrust of Raine's life and work has been to fight against what she sees as the destructive forces of (in a broad sense) the "Aristotelian" nature of her education and times. Much of that battle is the subject of the first three volumes of her outstanding autobiography, *Farewell Happy Fields* (Raine 1973), *The Land Unknown* (Raine 1975), and *The Lion's*

Mouth (Raine 1977), collected as *Autobiographies* (Raine 1991). Often echoic of Blake and Traherne, the pages of *Farewell Happy Fields*—with its title taken from Milton's *Paradise Lost* (I. 249)—are beautifully eloquent in their evocation and analysis of the adult Raine's understanding of the Platonism of her childhood. The youthful and instinctive Platonism which this volume of autobiography evidences—her intuition of the existence of "an ideal world of Forms or Universals, beyond the visible world in which we actually live" (Newsome 1974, 5), and her sense that "these Forms were the original ideas of all created things—is divine and immutable within the eternal order, but finite and changing within the temporal, visible world" (ibid.); her partly formed sense that the state of the actual world "may be [...] a pointer to the degree to which finite minds can forget or depart from the divine original" (ibid). These early apprehensions were to be sustained and developed in her later years, to be formulated more thoroughly, by a course of study—study for which the philosophical underpinning was provided by familiarity with the works of Plato and of followers of, and commentators upon, that work, including early Neoplatonists such as Plotinus (c. 204/5–c. 270), Porphyry (c. 234–c. 305), Iamblichus (c. 245–c.325), Proclus (412–485), and John Philoponus (c. 490–c.570), as well as later translators and interpreters of the tradition, such as Ficino, Pico della Mirandola, Cambridge Platonists like Henry More and Ralph Cudworth, Thomas Taylor (the great Neoplatonic philosopher of English Romanticism), and Stephen McKenna, whose work on Plotinus informs so much in the poetry of Yeats.

For Raine, the encounter with the writings of Jung marked an important stage in her understanding of the "learning of the Imagination." In Jung she found "a key to the great symbolic tradition of myth and poetry—to the significance of Neoplatonic myths, of the traditions of magic and alchemy, of religious symbolism" (Raine 1958, 11). Raine's growing attraction to Indian religion and metaphysics (see Raine 1990) also encouraged her study of, and contact with, a number of scholars and metaphysicians of the *religio perennis*, such as Frithjof Schuon, Titus Burckhardt, René Guénon, and Henry Corbin. Of these scholar-philosophers, all influenced by the religious thought of the Islamic world and of India, the most important for Raine was Corbin. His importance to her is evidenced by the prominence given to the first English translation of an important piece by Corbin in the initial issue of *Temenos*, of which Raine was a founding co-editor (Corbin 1981). Raine valued him particularly for his elaboration of the concept of the "Imaginal" or *mundus imaginalis*. A profound and learned scholar of Iranian thought, both Islamic and pre-Islamic, Corbin developed this concept through his reading of the works of thinkers such as Shihābuddin Yahyà Suhrawardī (d. 1191), Dā'ūd Qaysarī (d. 1350), Abd al-Karīm Jīlī (d. 1403), Muhsin Fayz Kâshānī (d. 1680), and Sheikh Ahmad Ahsā'ī (d. 1826). Corbin's seminal work *Spiritual Body and Celestial Earth* (Corbin 1977) contains both a collection of key texts and brilliant essays by Corbin. Only a brief and partial account of the concept of *mundus imaginalis* can be offered here, but it will, I hope, be enough to show how it chimes with Raine's worldview, as it has already been discussed. Corbin writes of the tradition of Iranian thought which predicates "a threefold universe: an intelligible universe, a sensory universe, and between the two a universe for which it is difficult to find a satisfactory term" (Corbin 1977, 78). Corbin chooses finally to designate this intermediate universe by the term *mundus imaginalis:* "the *imaginative* world is the world of the soul, which is made Image by the organ of the soul, thereby revealing to it its own Image" (ibid.). It is:

> A universe which symbolises both *with* corporeal substance, because it possesses shape, dimensions, and extent – and *with* separated or intelligible substance, because it is essentially made of light (*nūrānī*). It is both immaterial matter and the incorporeal corporealized. It is the limit which separates them and at the same time unites them.
>
> (ibid, 78–79)

Corbin argues that knowledge of this *mundus imaginalis* is accessible by a "particular mode of perception of beings and things" (ibid., 10), which he calls "the active Imagination" (ibid., 11), insisting that:

> the active Imagination [...] will not produce some arbitrary, even lyrical, construction standing between us and "reality," but will, on the contrary, function directly as a faculty and organ of knowledge just as *real* as – if not more real than – the sense organs.
>
> (ibid., 11)

(For more valuable insights on this subject, see also Corbin 1969.)

It is clear why such ideas should appeal so strongly to Raine and how they complement the kind of Platonic and Neoplatonic ideas outlined earlier. It is perhaps relevant to note that it is now widely recognized that the writings of Plato and the Neoplatonists were formative influences on the thought of many Islamic theologians and philosophers.

Raine finds much of the poetry written by her contemporaries to be characterized by

> [A] rejection of metaphor [...] only direct description or at most simile is tolerated. This rejection of the characteristic poetic figures of metaphor, symbol, personification, and, at the apex, myth, is not arbitrary, it is logical and honest, for it represents a rejection of affirmations implicit in these linguistic figures. [...] Those poets who allow themselves to describe only sensible appearances, or to compare these one with another (simile) have understood that this is demanded by the materialistic view of reality.
>
> (Raine 1985, 109)

For Raine, on the other hand, for whom "not matter but mind is the primary reality" (Raine 1999, 22), symbol and myth are central to the very nature, to the "first principles," of poetry. They are so, she believes, in historical terms (the historical origins of poetry, insofar as they can be identified, being everywhere bound up with myth and symbol) and because to attempt to write a poetry which eschews their presence is to cut oneself off from "the mainstream of human civilisation" (Raine 1999, 30).

The greatest poets are heirs to this (now) "excluded" (ibid.) mainstream and it follows that

> The symbols of the poets are not decorative, nor do they reflect an out-of-date science. They are, in the strictest sense, a language whose terms were, and still are, the understood currency

of a certain kind of discourse: discourse not about the landscape of nature, but the landscape of the imagination, or in Plato's terms the world of the archetypes.

(Raine 2007, 26)

"True" poets can thus be seen to speak an essentially common language: for while "the symbolic vocabulary of every poet is a little different, or larger or smaller" (ibid., 12), "we find that Spenser, Milton, Shelley, Blake, Yeats, all speak the same language, employ the same terms, describe the same world – with infinite variation and life; but their symbols, far from being private and personal, are traditional, and used deliberately and knowingly" (ibid.).

In her Warton Lecture on English Poetry, "Waste Land, Holy Land," read before the British Academy in December 1976, Raine closes with a summative statement of her concept of poetry, of her belief:

that poetry is the proper language of the soul; a speech that never ceases to tell those who are in the time-world of a timeless region that lies beyond the reach of intellectual judgements and evaluations. When the frontier of our consciousness is closed we inhabit a waste land to which neither wealth nor culture can impart life, which no social reform can restore. Thus understood poetry is no mere adornment of the everyday scene but a necessary knowledge of our immortal selves.

(Raine 1976, 397)

Raine's poetic ambitions, as the foregoing exploration of her poetics will, I hope, have made clear, are high and it would be wrong to claim that she always fulfills those ambitions. The nature of her aims has allowed her to produce some remarkable and powerful poems, but it has also meant that she has left more or less untouched many of the themes and subjects which most modern readers of poetry expect to encounter in a poet's work. One misses, for example, the radical political engagement present in the work of poets she admires, such as Blake and Yeats.

Some striking sentences by G. K. Chesterton (another whose thinking lay outside the mainstream of his times) will serve to lead us into Raine's poetry itself.

All poems might be bound in one book under the title of *Paradise Lost*. And the only object of writing *Paradise Lost* is to turn it, if only by a magic and momentary illusion, into *Paradise Regained*.

(Chesterton 1923, p. 6)

Raine would, I feel sure, have agreed with this statement, though she would have phrased it somewhat differently (if only because her prose never possesses the kind of playful seriousness of which Chesterton was such a master); she would have begun by referring to "all true poems" not just "all poems" and she would have avoided any mention of "illusion" (one reason why Corbin settled on the word "imaginal"—and why Raine endorsed that word—is that it avoids the associations of the word "imaginary").

Raine is pre-eminently a poet of "lost Paradise." Such a theme is already implicit—and sometimes explicit—in her poems of the 1940s, such as "Leaving Martindale" (Raine 2008, 16–17), "The Speech of Birds" (ibid. 21), "The Tree of Heaven" (ibid. 32–33),

"The Spring" (ibid. 35–36), and "The Rose" (ibid. 38). The inversion of Milton's title and of Chesterton's jocoserious suggestion for the title of the book in which "all poems" might be included gives Raine a favorite phrase to which she returns on several occasions. Thus, her final individual collection, *Living with Mystery: Poems 1987–1991*, contains a superb sequence of four poems under the collective title "Lost Paradise" (Raine 1992, 27–30). The "loss" of [a] Paradise—whether Paradise has been apprehended as a particular relationship with nature, as the experience of a "special" place, of childhood, or of love—is one symbol of the exiled soul, and as Raine's friend and fellow-poet Peter Russell has rightly observed, "The myth of the soul in *exile* is exquisitely presented [...] in very many (perhaps in *all*) of Katherine Raine's poems" (Russell 1994, 119). The expulsion from Eden is, of course, only one of many "myths" of the "soul in exile." Others such as the stories of Eros and Psyche and of Demeter and Persephone are, as Russell also observes, "omnipresent in [Raine's] poetry" (ibid., 116). The Edenic myth is explored in, for example, "Lament" (Raine 2008, 82), "Childhood" (ibid., 157–158), "The locked gates" (ibid., 99), "Message from Home" (ibid., 99–101), "Ninfa Revisited" (ibid., 154–156), "This" (Raine 1992, 25), and many other poems. Some lines from "Ninfa Revisited" show Raine at her most powerfully lucid, writing in language of great simplicity, yet evoking a complex tradition:

> In Paradise each man is born:
> The orient wheatfields of Traherne
> Fired by Blake's angel-peopled sun,
> Wordsworth's tree, of many one:
> Eden is for each alone
> To cultivate, like old Voltaire,
> Form in similitude of Heaven,
> Or sell for money, or lay waste.
>
> [...]
>
> The nightingale is but a word
> In the lost speech of Paradise.
> (ibid., 155–156, ll. 62–69, 83–84)

The myth of Demeter and Persephone/Kore is treated in, for example, "Kore in Hades" (Raine 2008, 107–108) and in the first poem of "Lost Paradise," "Persephone Remembers" (Raine 1992, 27). Again, many more examples might be cited. Eros and Psyche are the "subject" (in a special sense) of major poems such as "The Marriage of Psyche" (Raine 2008, 92–93), "Eros Remembered" (Raine 1992, 72–75), and "Metaphors of Eros" (ibid., 77–79). But the mere listing of individual poems does not do justice to the absoluteness with which Raine's poetry is unified by its concern with this central myth of the exile of the soul, in a manner very like her scholarly and critical writings. Her poetry, in its acts of anamnesis, bears witness to a personal experience and affirms its universal value, its potential to reawaken others to their "Lost Paradise." One of Raine's last poems, while not one of her finest, still says something important about how she saw herself and her work.

> What I do, think, feel, see
> Here and now, will be nothing to me
> When, soon, I am gone, but may be
> For you, somewhere, sometimes, a way
> Of knowledge, or glimpse of an elsewhere
> That was, and is, therefore
> A parcel of your treasury,
> Not I who was, but you who are,
>
> (Raine 1992, 84)

A powerful culmination of that work can be found in her remarkable sequence of 132 short poems, *On A Deserted Shore* (Raine 2008, 178–215), first published in 1973. At a "personal" level the poems constitute an extended elegy for Gavin Maxwell (1914–1969) with whom Raine had an intense, but finally disastrous relationship (for another account of this relationship, see *The Lion's Mouth* (Raine 1977)). Read in terms of the kind of "learning of the Imagination" which Raine believes to be the true language of poetry, it is revealed as another poem of the soul's exile. This is everywhere implicit in the sequence's symbolic language of "empty seas" and the "harmony of the spheres," "the bird's undying voice," "the pure stream," and the "buried seed." It is made explicit in some of the poems, such as nos. 13 (Raine 2008, 183), 28 (ibid., 187), 33 (ibid., 188), 43 (ibid., 191) ("Lost Paradise / With all its trees adrift / In the great flood of night," ll. 1–3), 58 (ibid., 196), and 87 (ibid., 203). Quotation (and discussion) of one section in its entirety offers some indication of how Raine's work, even when it seems most personal, resonates with an archetypal power.

> 83
> Two wanderers in a single dream
> By paths of gold on silver seas
> We to lost paradise came home,
> Together stood beneath those blossoming trees,
> But went our ways
> Uncomforted, and each alone.
>
> (Raine 2008, 202)

If we read this at the "personal" level—as being about the relationship between Maxwell and Raine, it is easy to find things in these six lines to sustain such a reading. Some of the most important episodes in the narrative arc of that relationship took place at and around Maxwell's coastal home in the Scottish Highlands. In *The Lion's Mouth*, Raine writes of the waters by which that house stood as "those silver seas" (Raine 1977, 34). Central to the narrative is a rowan tree (Raine 1977, *passim*) and refers to her experience there as her "last return to the earthly paradise" (ibid., 33). The painful separation chronicled in *The Lion's Mouth* echoes throughout *On a Deserted Shore*.

But there is, of course, more to the language of these six lines than mere autobiography, however powerful. The "paths of gold" and the "silver seas" are the stuff of folk tales and fairy stories. The phrase "paths of gold," though not a direct quotation, also resonates with an important passage in the writings of William Blake (whose work has always meant so much to Raine and of whom she has been one of the great elucidators). Chapter 4 of Blake's great poem *Jerusalem* begins with a prose address, "To the Christians," which is prefaced by this quatrain:

> I give you the end of a golden string,
> Only wind it into a ball,
> It will lead you in at Heaven's gate
> Built in Jerusalem's wall.
> (Blake 1969, 716)

A golden string that leads back to "lost Paradise" is surely a kind of "path of gold." Indeed Raine uses the same phrase (without explicitly acknowledging Blake) in *The Lion's Mouth*: "That golden string which had once (or so I imagined) united me with Gavin had become a severed cord from whose living substance my life bled away continually" (Raine 1977, 95). But as well as the "paths of gold" in line 2 here, the "seas" have a traditional and Blakean significance too. Raine, writing of Blake elsewhere, provides a brief elucidation which throws further light on the lines under discussion:

Odysseus, for the Neoplatonists, symbolized man, whose progress from birth to death, through material existence, is likened to the hero's perilous adventures. The sea was universally taken in the ancient world as a symbol of the material world, on account of its mutable flux. Blake's phrase "the sea of time & space" is therefore a traditional piece of Neoplatonic symbolism.
(Raine 1968b, I. 79)

Raine's quotation from Blake is taken from a letter to Thomas Butts, dated January 10, 1802 (Blake 1969, 812).

Raine's comments quoted in the earlier text allow (or perhaps require) us to see the word "wanderers" in line 1 of the poem under discussion as an allusion to the tale of Odysseus, as interpreted in the neoplatonic tradition.

What the casual modern reader might have taken to be merely a poem of human (even sexual) love emerges, when seen in contexts such as these, as rather—or perhaps one should say "also"?—a poem of the soul's pilgrimage on earth, a pilgrimage here a brief "coming home" to "lost paradise," before a an ensuing renewed expulsion therefrom:

> But went our ways
> Uncomforted, and each alone.

In an earlier section (51) of *On a Deserted Shore*, Raine presents her narrative in terms which contain an unmistakable allusion to Milton:

> Time was
> When each to other was a glass,
> And I in you and you in me beheld
> Lost Paradise,

> With every tree and bird so clear
> Regained it seemed.
> We did not guess how far
> From the heart's mirror the reflected star.
> (Raine 2008, 194)

The whole of this section throws light on the section (83) under discussion, but I quote it here primarily as evidence of how far Milton's *Paradise Lost* (and, indeed, *Paradise Regained*) condition the idiom of *On a Deserted Shore*. It is, therefore, relevant and necessary to consider the closing lines of section 83 of Raine's sequence: "But went our ways / Uncomforted, and each alone," in the light of the closing lines of *Paradise Lost*:

> They hand in hand with wandering steps and slow,
> Through Eden took their solitary way.
> (Milton 1971, 642)

The lines bring us back, again, to the word "wandering" (which in Milton carries the sense of "erring"), but the powerful poignancy of the lines in large part resides in the juxtaposition of "hand in hand" with "solitary." The joining of hands seems a gesture of unity and mutual faith, yet each remains "solitary." Raine's rewriting of the lines gives us a couple "uncomforted"—even to the extent of being "hand in hand," following not a shared "way"—"their solitary way," but going "our ways" (the plural being crucial), "each alone."

Much more might be said of the six lines which make up section 83 of *On a Deserted Shore*, but this relatively brief account of them shows, I believe, how—as so often in the best of Raine's poetry, the "meaning" exists in the creative interplay between words from the personal life and the outer life, on the one hand and, on the other hand, that realm and language which belong to what Raine has variously called "the learning of the imagination" and "traditional wisdom."

References

Acheson, James and Huk, Romana (eds.) (1996). *Contemporary British Poetry*. Albany: State University of New York Press.

Blake, William (1969). *Complete Writings* (ed. Geoffrey Keynes). London: Oxford University Press.

Bredvold, Louis I. (1934). *The Intellectual Milieu of John Dryden: Studies in Some Aspects of Seventeenth-Century Thought*. Ann Arbor: University of Michigan Press.

Chesterton, Gilbert Keith (1923). "The Romance of Rhyme." In: *Fancies Versus Fads*, 1–19. London: Methuen & Co.

Coelsch-Foisner, Sabine (2002). *Revolution in Poetic Consciousness: An Existential Reading of Mid-Twentieth-Century British Women's Poetry*. Tübingen: Stauffenberg.

Coleridge, Samuel Taylor (1851). *Specimens of the Table Talk*, 3e (ed. H.N. Coleridge). London: John Murray.

Corbin, Henry (1969). *Creative Imagination in the Sufism of Ibn 'Arabi*. Translated from the French by Ralph Manheim. Princeton: Princeton University Press.

Corbin, Henry (1977). *Spiritual Body and Celestial Earth*. Translated from the French by Nancy Pearson. Princeton: Princeton University Press.

Corbin, Henry (1981). "Towards a Chart of the Imaginal," (trans. Peter Russell), vol. I, 23–36. Temenos.

Herbert, W.N. and Hollis, Matthew (eds.) (2000). *Strong Words: Modern Poets on Modern Poetry*. Tarset: Bloodaxe Books.

Longley, Edna (ed.) (2000). *The Bloodaxe Book of 20th Century Poetry*. Tarset: Bloodaxe Books.

Lucie-Smith, Edward (ed.) (1970). *British Poetry since 1945*. Harmondsworth: Penguin Books.

Marcus, Laura and Nicholls, Peter (eds.) (2004). *The Cambridge History of Twentieth-Century English Literature*. Cambridge: Cambridge University Press.

Maurice, Frederick (1884). *The Life of Frederick Denison Maurice: Chiefly Told in His Letters*, vol. 2 (ed. Frederick Maurice). London: Macmillan & Co.

Milton, John (1971). *Paradise Lost* (ed. Alastair Fowler). London: Longman.

Newsome, David (1974). *Two Classes of Men: Platonism and English Romantic Thought*. London: John Murray.

Raine, Kathleen (1958). *Poetry in Relation to Traditional Wisdom* (Guild Lecture No. 97). London: Guild of Pastoral Psychology.

Raine, Kathleen (1968a). "Thomas Taylor, Plato, and the English Romantic Movement." *The Sewanee Review* 76 (2): 230–257.

Raine, Kathleen (1968b). *Blake and Tradition*. Princeton: Princeton University Press (Bollingen Series).

Raine, Kathleen (1973). *Farewell Happy Fields*. London: Hamish Hamilton.

Raine, Kathleen (1975). *The Land Unknown*. London: Hamish Hamilton.

Raine, Kathleen (1976). "Waste Land, Holy Land." *Proceedings of the British Academy* 62: 379–397.

Raine, Kathleen (1977). *The Lion's Mouth*. London: Hamish Hamilton.

Raine, Kathleen (1981). *Science and Imagination in William Blake*, vol. 1, 37–58. Temenos.

Raine, Kathleen (1985 [1967]). *Defending Ancient Springs*. Ipswich: Golgonooza Press.

Raine, Kathleen (1990). *India Seen Afar*. Bideford: Green Books.

Raine, Kathleen (1991). *Autobiographies*. London: Skoob.

Raine, Kathleen (1992). *Living with Mystery: Poems 1987–91*. Ipswich: Golgonooza Press.

Raine, Kathleen (1999). *W. B. Yeats and the Learning of the Imagination*. Ipswich: Golgonooza Press.

Raine, Kathleen (2007). "Poetry in Relation to Traditional Wisdom." *Temenos Academy Review* 10: 21–35.

Raine, Kathleen (2008 [2000]). *Collected Poems*. Ipswich: Golgonooza Press.

Rees-Jones, Deryn (2005). *Consorting with Angels: Essays on Modern Women Poets*. Tarset: Bloodaxe Books.

Russell, Peter (1994). "A Note on Kathleen Raine." *Agenda* 31:4–32:1, 102–121.

Scully, James (1966). *Modern Poets on Modern Poetry*.

Williams, Nerys (2011). *Contemporary Poetry*. Edinburgh: Edinburgh University Press.

3.14
"Everything Except Justice Is An Impertinence": The Poetry of Peter Riley

Peter Hughes

"I was born in Stockport, in July 1940, during an air-raid. From the hospital window you could see Manchester burning in the distance." So begins the autobiographical section on Peter Riley's website. He goes on to describe the urban environment of his childhood and then adds "the western slopes of the Pennines are visible in the distance from Stockport, with an arm of them coming round to the south in Cheshire." Those hills have remained a dominant presence in Riley's poetry and provide a site for investigative meditations on what it means to inhabit the world. Location is foregrounded in Riley's writing. Some texts are situated in France, Greece, Italy, and Romania. But it is the English Peak District which draws Riley's poetry back most often.

This is not to say that Riley's poetry is "nature poetry." His curt aside in *Alstonefield* quickly slaps away that notion:

> It would be specious to pretend
> that any bit of British countryside is anything
> but an agricultural factory marked Piss Off.
> (Riley 2003a, 23, ll. 18–20)

What does interest Riley is the interrelationships between people and their physical, social, cultural, and linguistic environments. He worries away at the question: how can these dynamic relationships become or remain benign? How can they be steered ethically in a period of history when government shows distain for the social good, and rewards the selfish individual at the expense of the community? So the geographical locations of his

---

A Companion to Contemporary British and Irish Poetry, 1960–2015, First Edition.
Edited by Wolfgang Görtschacher and David Malcolm.
© 2021 John Wiley & Sons Ltd. Published 2021 by John Wiley & Sons Ltd.

poems are not scenes glimpsed through a window, but the dynamic sites of real people living and thinking in the world. The work explores and generates a poetics of habitation. Not much of the landscape would be clearly visible in Riley's poems anyway because they often have a nocturnal setting. Stars are more common than flowers and provoke reflections on time, distance, and loss as well as issues of cultural and environmental inheritance.

One of Riley's most recent poetry publications is *Due North* (2015). The cover features a sharply focused monochrome photograph of Heights Road, Hebden Bridge, taken by Richard Gascoigne. The dark road leads into a central zone of small fields and sparse habitation. Immediately behind is the moor, an unpunctuated horizon, then a sky full of snow, impending darkness, or both. The image looks at first glance to show a place both bleak and uninviting. But the detailed clarity enables us to make out interesting patterns in the terrain, in the forms of the fields, the few buildings, and the relationships between the signs of human activity and the underlying landscape. It is a highly appropriate image for the poetry.

The publication of *Due North* comes 2 years after Riley moved back north, to Hebden Bridge, after a stay of over 20 years in Cambridge. Before that he lived for a decade in the Peak District. The title *Due North* is an interesting choice. The apparent simplicity of the word "due" as an adverb qualifying "north," and meaning "exactly" or "precisely," hides a welter of almost submerged suggestions. These include an adjectival sense of "due" as "expected or planned for at a certain time" and "of the proper quality or extent." There is also a hovering or latent sense of "due" as substantive, meaning "one's right, what is owed one" and "obligatory payment or fee." The presence of a dance of possibilities underneath apparent simplicity is a feature of Riley's work that the reader soon comes to recognize.

Specific locations and contexts are important in Riley's writing and he is suspicious of poetry which drifts through the ether dealing in generalities, language about language. The Pennine landscape has functioned as heartland in his poetry for decades. His writings from the late 1970s and early 1980s, which went to form *Lines on the Liver* and *Tracks and Mineshafts*, were dominated by that landscape. Other examples of work which reference that location include the very long poem *Alstonefield*, and the much shorter *XIV Pieces*.

Riley's first publication, *Love-Strife Machine*, came out from Ferry Press in 1969. One of his *Poems written on 11th May 1968* urges:

> work—to make it as feasible
> that the lines should intersect the way they do
> on the map
> of it all.
>   (Riley 1969, 9, ll. 14–17)

Here is a demand for scrupulous accountability yoked to soaring ambition. Ambition for change was in the air in May 1968, the Paris spring, as it should be now. But the energies in Riley's first book also come out of the excitement of American poetry, which offered a series of stimulating alternatives to the Movement orthodoxies dominating much of the

British poetry scene. Donald Allen's groundbreaking 1960 anthology *The New American Poetry* had made available a startling range of modern options. This important book showcased poets associated with Black Mountain (such as Creeley, Blackburn, Duncan, Levertov, Olson, Dorn, and Wieners), New York poetry (including Ashbery, Koch, O'Hara, Schuyler, and Guest), and West Coast poets (including Spicer, Ginsberg, Whalen, Snyder, and Lamantia). This work had an exhilarating effect on several British poets, including Riley. He found himself in a loose alliance of poets which included Andrew Crozier, Jeremy Prynne, John James, Barry MacSweeney, and Douglas Oliver. *The English Intelligencer*, which Riley was to edit for part of 1967, was a mimeographed worksheet distributed to a group of like-minded readers. Some of its contents have been usefully republished in *Certain Prose of The English Intelligencer* (Cambridge: Mountain Press, 2012), edited by Neil Pattison, Reitha Pattison, and Luke Roberts. *The English Intelligencer* sought to transplant to a British setting Stan Persky's San Francisco journal *Open Space*. In terms of Riley's writing in *Love-Strife Machine*, the American influence can be felt in such moments as:

> to blaze through language as if blazing through
> life got all burnt-out
> a built-in
> defense structure is too expensive
> (Riley 1969, 12, ll. 1–4)

But there is an exciting modernity about all aspects of this striking production from Andrew Crozier's Ferry Press. The geometric design of the cover (by Michael Craig-Martin), the Courier font, the unconventional and inconsistent use of punctuation, the non-standard size of the book, and the rapid shifts throughout the text all seem to herald a new departure. Yet a good deal of the second half of the book carries reminders of Riley's rootedness in British poetry of the 1940s and earlier. There are two aspects of 1940s British poetry which visibly resurface in his work. One is an emphasis on a regional locality; the other is Romanticism. Consider these lines from *Love-Strife Machine*:

> the wind across the chimney top
> vibrates a column of air & a low iron
> fills the room. I think the waves
> are tearing at my chest
> I think the storm wind has my mind
> petrified with its monotonous message from the sky…
> …the stars are little sucking mouths
> all over the sky
> they draw my soul out of the house
> into the weather, set to their
> awful tune, the air
> rushes over, they pulse
> with pain at the extremes of cold and heat…
> (Riley 1969, 54, ll. 1–17)

If the new American poetry and the crafted Romanticism of British 1940s poetry were two of the crucial contexts of Peter Riley's own work, then music soon became a third. Perhaps music could be considered an aspect of 1940s Romanticism too. But in Riley's work music tends to have a social dimension; not so much an Aeolian harp in a depopulated nocturnal location, as a group improvisation requiring attentive listening and sensitive interaction. *Love-Strife Machine* contains many references to music including the names of Mahler, Mozart, Berlioz, Wagner, and Adam de la Halle. There is also a sequence called "four rondeaux," a poem called "song," two poems called "2 Machaut songs," and two more pieces called "2 serious songs." Music is also invoked in a more general sense, most memorably in a poem entitled "visiting the university." Riley writes:

> we ... no longer know how to sustain the music beyond
> the first bright hope
> (Riley 1969, 66, ll. 7–8)

These lines strike a distinctly Wordsworthian note. Music is used as a term for creative and harmonious continuation into the future. As Riley's work develops, the presence of music becomes increasingly important as a shared experience, a form of benign bonding, also a symbol of generous social interaction, and of poetry itself.

Charles Olson, self-styled "archaeologist of morning" (the title of one of Olson's books), was one of Riley's key influences from the new American poetry. Olson attached great importance to investigating the local. This did not mean commenting drily on street scenes or writing "nature poetry." It involved delving into the deep history of where one lived to earn a sense of its geological foundations and ongoing processes: looking at the history of flora, fauna, and human settlement, tracing the emergence of hunting habits, agricultural and trading practices, and the evolution of culture in every sense. Such a vision of poetry and place was to occupy Riley for decades. In the late 1970s, he amassed a considerable amount of writing "originally thought of as a work in the open-field mode concerning lead mining in the carboniferous limestone zone of Derbyshire and North Staffordshire," as he writes in the Preface to *The Derbyshire Poems*. This material was the basis for *Tracks and Mineshafts* (1983a) and *Lines on the Liver* (Ferry Press 1981). Despite those publication dates, *Tracks and Mineshafts* does come first compositionally. These texts were republished by Shearsman in 2010 as *The Derbyshire Poems*, which also included the associated texts *Following the Vein* (1975) and *Two Essays* (1983b).

The Derbyshire Poems are among Peter Riley's most challenging and rewarding works. They are challenging for two reasons. The first is that *Tracks and Mineshafts* is excerpted and refigured from a longer draft work and feels compressed, nuggety, as though some of its connectors had been removed. The second reason is the nature of the project which uses the imagery of mining in the underground darkness to communicate a vision of the experience of living. Riley suggests that the only place we can ever inhabit is the present moment and that we are unable to stand outside it in order to reflect, evaluate, or plan. But the mind's moment is so cluttered with doubt, inaccurate data from the past, and unhelpful fears and urges regarding the future that it is unable to engage entirely with the present.

> If we could inhabit the moment we would be able to contemplate and dispose its factors in such a way as to understand completely our motivations and accidentals, and at least properly set them on their better courses.
>
> (Riley 2010, 194, ll. 19–22)

In the absence of such a comfortable engagement, we are obliged to scratch away in the darkness making our way from one alienated site to the next. We follow apparently gleaming routes through the earth, though anything of value we unearth goes to replenish the coffers of the canny, not ourselves. One of the interesting threads we can follow through the texts of *The Derbyshire Poems* is the word "thread" itself, together with its associates such as "string" or "line." These words are sometimes used to fuse aspects of geology, history, human feeling, and writing. Riley writes about the veins of minerals and metal ores through limestone evocatively and at length. He recalls and extends the traditional anthropomorphic language of lead mining according to which "Veins are 'quick' (with ore) or 'dead' (without ore)" (Riley 2010, 175, ll. 20–21). He describes a quick vein thus:

> The metal trends westwards and upwards, final outcast of an oceanic pulse rising towards the atmosphere. This bright thread worms its way towards the sky along borderlines and faults in the tables of sleepy limestone ... A line, then, compounded of metal, oil, and heat, traces the edges of sedimental stasis and sets up a challenge on the edge of contentment.
>
> (Riley 2010, 38, ll. 6–14)

That final word may take us by surprise if we are not familiar with Riley's writing. He uses the hidden gleam of ore to suggest an impulse toward richer thought and making, and a rejection of complacency.

> It glows in the subterranean night, calling us, persuading us to faster and sharper acts – a tight, iridescent vein packed with sleeping princesses and red thorns...
>
> (Riley 2010, 38, ll. 15–18)

The "princesses" let us know that the call described in this passage is a call to the imagination. And if the gleaming line or thread finds itself in a cavity between the surrounding rock strata then it is able to realize itself in extraordinary ways.

> Gaining cavities, cracks and entire vacant layers of the stratification, it opens out into efflorescences: crystals and cave-pearls, colours of sky and flesh held in translucent stone, breaking into the spaces in formal excrescences.
>
> (Riley 2010, 38, ll. 20–24)

It is hard not to see these "formal excrescences" as standing for poetry, or artworks in general, as well as meaning exactly what they say. That sense of correspondence between geological processes and the imagined or written is compounded in a subsequent passage.

> It is as if a whole warehouse of books lies under the sea, the books stacked on their sides; the pages congeal together, the languages forgotten, cubic masses of documentation totally inert. But the

gilt letters one by one float off the bindings and assemble on the surface in a matrix of red and blue inks, a dazzling unreadable scum, a potentiality. And waits there, as if expecting us … the nascent language is there, and ready, as soon as our organs of perception are tuned to meet it.
(Riley 2010, 38, ll. 25–33)

I have quoted at length from *Tracks and Mineshafts* because of its intrinsic merit, but also because its matter informs so much of Peter Riley's subsequent work over the years. Those texts were written over 30 years ago but even in *Due North* (2005), Riley returns to those same landscapes, most notably in section XI, "The Ascent of Kinder Scout." It would be inaccurate to suggest, however, that there is some simplistic parallel in Riley's work between the processes of geology and geomorphology on the one hand, and thought or writing on the other. His work abounds in instances of the complexities of the traces of human activity on and within the earth. Here is one example:

…a wind-swept table-land littered with old furniture, crumbling headgear, forgotten shafts, tumuli, TV masts, telegraph poles, engine houses now barns, neglected greystone walling, broken ground with mounds, hollows, and crumbling banks.
(Riley 2010, 43, ll. 12–15)

For all his emphasis on precisely delineating physical phenomena, and forging a linked poetic language of the imagination, there is always a strong social and political dimension to Riley's writing. This is linked to an ethics of care, of avoiding harm to others. Unsurprisingly this appears frequently with reference to one other significant individual, in the context of love. "Night outside is the theatre of our patience / as you lie beside me in the dark loft" (Riley 2010, 18, ll. 1–2), to cite a characteristic example. But language is for communication, not just meditative reflection: "language … unwinds a thread of perception out of one body into another" (Riley 2010, 71, ll. 8–10). It is what may enable a group, or community, or the whole of humanity, to cohere and survive. "The flesh is willing but the structure aches," writes Riley (Riley 2010, 68, l. 16), and that structure is a product of economic and political forces.

Tracks and Mineshafts leads into *Lines on the Liver*, and the latter book exhibits a dramatic contrast between the long, dense prose sections at the beginning and the very short three-line pieces at the end, entitled "The Replies." The book seems to enact a process by which the welter of thoughts, cargoes of received wisdom, philosophies, and senses of being that surge through the Derbyshire poems begin to be controlled. The massive project from which the Derbyshire poems were eventually distilled has given way to groups of shorter, more highly structured pieces and sequences. Some of Riley's 1980s productions, such as "Ospita" and "Noon Province," exemplify this new sense of form and patterning. *Lines on the Liver* ends with one of Riley's most memorable images. He describes a bleak area of the Pennines in North Staffordshire where there was a phone box, in the middle of nowhere, which did not work. It was sometimes used as a shelter by a tramp called John Dooley who, according to Riley, spent all his days walking the local roads. This section of the book ends thus:

[...] one night in thin driving snow and some hill mist my headlights caught him in that
telephone box, staring straight out, not at me, as I veered onto the top of the climb. [...] And
I was past in a flash, but he had the receiver to his mouth and ear.

(Riley 1981 62, ll. 36–42)

"Ospita" first appeared as the fourth in the Poetical Histories series, which Peter Riley himself edited. He had moved from the Peak District to Cambridge in the mid-1980s and had brought with him a supply of good-quality paper from the workshop of a printer who had died. Between 1985 and 2004, there were 60 numbered issues of Poetical Histories and the series ended only because Riley ran out of that stock of paper.

"Ospita," a title derived from the word "hospital" shorn of its first and last letters, stands for an institution of care, a kind of ministry of goodness. It is clearly an important sequence for Riley as its ten 14-line stanzas are reproduced in the Carcanet volume *Passing Measures*. "Ospita" is a sonnet sequence of sorts, with hints of rhyme schemes sometimes surfacing then disappearing. It suggests a desire to engage more fully with formal constraints in order to establish an evident relationship with older traditions in English poetry. Yet it retains the challenging surfaces of Riley's earlier work and has more in common with the work of Jeremy Prynne than does Riley's later work. Its rapid shifts and distinctive choices of vocabulary are such that Riley felt it useful to write a substantial commentary on the sequence. The commentary is on his website (www.aprileye.co.uk/ospitanotes.html).

Another notable sequence of the 1980s is "Noon Province," first published as one of the Poetical Histories series in 1989. This group of poems moves away from the familiar Peak District and its environs and is cast in a Mediterranean setting. It starts by celebrating "Valuable small acts" in "Arriving at Dawn" (Riley 2000, 67, l. 1), and foregrounding simple, shared necessities such as food stuffs ("olives," "cheeses," "honey") in "Market Day" (Riley 2000, 67, ll. 2–3) against elemental backdrops ("day," "light," "town," "night," "sky," "stars," "ground") in "Roofwatch" (Riley 2000, 68). Such simplicities, however, blend with rhetorical flourishes such as "O fine in their farming the stars / Rally and exit all night" (Riley 2000, 68, "Roofwatch," ll. 10–11), which serve to locate this poetry of immediate attention with the musics and conventions of longer-standing traditions in British poetry. There are significant continuities with Riley's earlier work too—more white paths over high ground, renewed insistence on ethical choice, and the same emphasis on reflective meditation and loving action at this instant as the only site of human and artistic authenticity. "Everything except justice is an impertinence" (l. 10), the most resonant line in the whole of his work, rings out in "Lacoste" (Riley 2000, 72, "Lacoste," l. 10). But there is also a new directness which will characterize much of Riley's later work as well. This is best demonstrated with a more substantial extract, this time from "Just a Song."

> The path leads clearly down to the edge
> Of the slope and rejoins the road where
> It hangs over the wide valley scattered
> With house lights and a steady glow

> From behind the far hills. Someone has left
> An old white horse in a field with food
> Water and shelter, standing through the night.
> (Riley 2000, 76, ll. 21–27)

But this is not quite as simple as it looks. The surface meaning has a kind of counterpoint. The first line ends on the "edge" (l. 21) that is not just the edge of the slope but the edge of the world, the edge of a life. Similarly, the end of line 25 tells us that "Someone has left," as well as "Someone has left / An old white horse in a field" (ll. 25–26). So these nuances chime with each other, and with the growing darkness. The sun has set. It is perhaps worth mentioning that this white horse in the darkness also chimes with, and takes its place alongside, a host of pale presences throughout Riley's work. They are often, but not always, associated with limestone glimpsed in the distance, or at night. One of the earliest instances is in *Tracks and Mineshafts*: "Nightscape cast in space, patches of / white rock glowing in fuzzy darkness" (Riley 2010, 46, "Pure Dread," ll. 7–8). Day is over and this is "Just a Song," the title calling to mind the old sentimental classic "Just a Song at Twilight." The entire "Noon Province" sequence is constantly aligning itself with music of one kind or another.

Music has always been important to Riley (he is an accomplished pianist) and the earlier project *The Musicians, The Instruments* (1978) celebrated contemporary improvised jazz with appropriate wit and verve. But in "Noon Province" the music tends to be of an earlier vintage. Johannes Ockeghem and Orlande de Lassus, Franco-Flemish composers of the fifteenth and sixteenth centuries, respectively, are introduced into the landscape of the setting and the texture of the poem by means of the Walkman that the poet listens to on his travels. Those great composers of soaring choral music become part of the local and the present. So does Dante. Riley refers more than once to a pocket edition of the Italian author which accompanies him on this journey. These three leading exponents of religious art are plaited into Riley's sequence, and their work physically carried into these contemporary settings by the author, for secular purposes. These works of art model a response to life which is substantial, ambitious, beautiful, and highly structured. They represent a refutation of pettiness, and an urge to create with a certain resonance and magnificence.

This brings us to one of the central characteristics of Riley's poetry, a quality which separates him from many of his peers. Riley is a socialist and an atheist, yet he sometimes adopts vocabulary associated with monarchy or religion and applies such terms in ways which are affirmative. This is not because he is a closet-Royalist, or a secret believer in a God. It is because he insists on retaining the glow and resonance—the awe and wonder—that made much religious art luminous. But he insists that such effects and feelings are the proper consequences of human artistry at work in the contexts of the real world. The first example in Riley's published work comes as early as the second poem in the first book, *Love-Strife Machine*. He refers to walking up to Jacob's Ladder, a visionary pathway between heaven and earth in Genesis, and a steep path in the Peak District. And he calls it "the kingly remedy" (Riley 1969, 10, "Poems Written on 11th May 1968," l. 11). However, what is most important about this experience, with all its high-sounding descriptors, is that it is in the local hills, available to all. Here is another example, this time from *Lines on the Liver*.

> ...in front of me, in front of everything I say or see, always, is that pastoral dome stuffed with regal immanence tier on tier.
>
> (Riley 1981r, 3, ll. 22–23)

This refers to extraordinary fissures, hidden waterways, and underground chambers rich with the luster of lead ore, but the physical is also transformed into a visionary gleam that could have escaped through a crack in Dante's *Paradiso*.

Riley's website is enlightening on the subject of religious structures of speech and thought (as it is on most aspects of his work). Remembering his childhood, he writes:

> It was also important to fill the lungs and shout out the hymns. It was a powerful insight into how the lyrical text works, that it is not necessarily either small-scale or "personal." We didn't believe a word of it [...] carols, anthems, Biblical readings [...]. These things weren't belief structures, they were magnificent participatory architecture. The great slow Victorian hymns arched over us and confirmed the vast extent of our breath, with all the doors open.
>
> The terms (God, Lord, faith etc.) were linguistic abstracts of great power [...] like magnificent frescoes, magnificent narratives. [...] "Angels" were not involved in this commerce that surrounded us, they were in "realms of glory" singing creation; they were winged words. It wasn't just that we were momentarily enclosed in a mythology, it was also that the arena which lay open to the imagination stood revealed.
>
> (www.aprileye.co.uk/biography.html)

Much of Peter Riley's poetry concerns itself with questions about how to live meaningfully and ethically. So it was slightly startling to find him writing a prose book which actually offered answers, albeit not unproblematically. *The Dance at Mociu* came out from Shearsman in 2003. It gathered together 31 short pieces relating to Riley's visits to Transylvania, in northern Romania. Riley considered the peasant culture he found there "advanced, or at least exemplary" (Riley 2003b, 13, ll. 23). The book presents a moving and closely observed constellation of images and episodes from communities where individuals are not alienated from their neighbors or surroundings, where local music accompanies all communal rituals such as christenings, weddings, and funerals, and where civility seems endemic. This luminous and persuasive little book will become a classic in its own right, but it also indispensable for a fuller understanding of Riley's poetic vision.

Romania is not the only foreign setting for Riley's writing. In 2009, Shearsman published *Greek Passages*, a book which brings together the fruits of several stays in Greece made by Riley between 2002 and 2005. These prose poems engage with similar themes and preoccupations to those in the Transylvanian work. But in the Greek pieces there is a greater historical and political dimension in which current wars and crises are juxtaposed with telling local detail.

Peter Riley has returned to the north both literally and imaginatively in recent years. He now lives in Hebden Bridge, between the Peak District and the Yorkshire Dales. *XIV Pieces* and *Due North* both focus on this zone.

The beautifully produced pamphlet and CD which together make up *XIV Pieces* came out from Longbarrow Press in 2012. The first poem, "Alstonefield 1995," revisits several of Riley's long-standing concerns. These include Alstonefield itself, ideas about economics and civility, music, the physical world as a constant and significant factor in life and art, and the imaginative leap which fuses them all together. After witnessing an act of generosity in a local pub, Riley rounds off his poem with the line "I walk back to my lodgings through virtuoso bell-ringing" (Riley 2012, "Alstonefield 1995," 1, l. 7). The music seems to celebrate the generosity and broadcast its benign effects. These poems are riddled with song from Britain, France, Romania, and as far away as southern Africa, the last represented by the San Bush people who "close one eye / and sing about the food supply. / It is incredibly beautiful" (Riley 2012, "*!KUNG MUSIC*," 13, ll. 1–3). Alongside the music there are the pale white forms we have come to expect from Riley, hovering against the darkness. They are white stones, unwritten pages, a house at the end of the road, the faces of workers queuing for the bus at dusk, or grave markers.

It is appropriate to end this brief survey of Peter Riley's poetry with *Due North*. The book opens with a vast geographical and historical sweep as tribes slowly migrate northward with their herds over the plains of Africa. This is made to chime with the movements and struggles of later economic migrants internationally, and within Europe, and in local population shifts toward the northern towns from the countryside. Throughout the book there is a desire for explicitly stated and shared values which would enable the tribe or group to function as a community. There is a yearning for ambition and work to be yoked to a sense of the common good, here and now. And for philosophy, politics and poetics to be "working down to the local where it opens out" (14, l. 20), "free to all, stuff of life/free of ideological baggage" (Riley 2015, "Housman's Question,"7, ll. 2–3). The epicenter of this work, and one of Riley's most impressive achievements, is section XI, "The Ascent of Kinder Scout," first published in 2014 as a pamphlet by Longbarrow Press. It celebrates the famous mass trespass of 1932, protesting against the status of the hills, which were a privatized grouse-shoot for the rich. Riley puts the action into the present tense, thrillingly: "Stamping the ground, stamping mystery and privilege into the soil, we walk up into our work, hauled on our breath. The foundation of the state is not violence but education" (Riley 2015, 75). To stamp is also to print, and the power of the breath is to be used for the people, and this is a ringing statement of Riley's poetics. Language, poetry, and song are social, says Riley. They evolved as safeguards and constructive bonds. "The original calls were reciprocal, to, a purpose, keep away from the edge, maintain contact in the mist" (Riley 2015, 75). His work is a secular hymn of praise to justice and equity, to locality and community.

> It could all be wiped out at any moment by a falling aeroplane or a Tory axe, this town and all its chat.
>
> (Riley 2015, "The Ascent of Kinder Scout," 83, ll. 6–7)

> On the horizon Kinder Scout is a shadow lost in the black sky, an enormous gravestone in memory of the welfare state.
>
> (Riley 2015, "The Ascent of Kinder Scout," 84, ll. 3–5)

Riley has been known to say that as a writer he is not concerned with politics, but his poetry knows better.

REFERENCES

Riley, Peter (1969). *Love Strife Machine*. London: Ferry Press.

Riley, Peter (1975). *Following the Vein*. London: Albion Village Press.

Riley, Peter (1978). *The Musicians The Instruments*. London: Many Press.

Riley, Peter (1981). *Lines on the Liver*. London: Ferry Press.

Riley, Peter (1983a). *Tracks and Mineshafts*. Matlock: Grossest Press.

Riley, Peter (1983b). *Two Essays*. Matlock: Grossest Press.

Riley, Peter (2000). *Passing Measures*. Manchester: Carcanet.

Riley, Peter (2003a). *Alstonefield: A Poem*. Manchester: Carcanet.

Riley, Peter (2003b). *The Dance at Mociu*. Bristol: Shearsman.

Riley, Peter (2009). *Greek Passages*. Bristol: Shearsman.

Riley, Peter (2010). *The Derbyshire Poems*. Bristol: Shearsman.

Riley, Peter (2012). *XIV Pieces*. Swindon: Longbarrow Press.

Riley, Peter (2015). *Due North*. Bristol: Shearsman.

Peter Riley's website www.aprileye.co.uk

3.15
Anne Stevenson

Eleanor Spencer

Introduction

Questions of influence, inheritance, and affiliation are inevitably asked of any poet, but for a poet of dual nationality, such as the British-American Anne Stevenson, such questions are particularly loaded. Stevenson's pitch on Parnassus is contested or uncertain territory, as she suggests in "Temporarily in Oxford" (1977), written during her Fellowship at Lady Margaret Hall at Oxford University.

> Where they will bury me
> I don't know.
> Many places might not be
> sorry to store me.
> (Stevenson 2004, 61, ll. 1–4)

That the speaker imagines her earthly remains "stored" like left luggage, coupled with the word "temporarily," suggests a life characterized by travel and transience, of temporary abodes and impermanent attachments. Stevenson's speaker seems to favor the prospect of an afterlife of dispersal in air, rather than a permanent committal—and commitment—to solid ground, musing:

> But if they are kind,
> they'll burn me and
> send me to Vermont.
> I'd be an education for the trees
> and would relish, really,
> flaring into maple each October –
> my scarlet letter to you. (ll. 14–20)

Though the speaker's imagination is clearly drawn to Hawthorne's New England here, and though she later suggests that the American Midwest has "right of origin," it was actually the English Fens that "bore" the poet. In this poem and others, Stevenson reveals an ambivalent attitude toward her birthplace ("It seems I can't get away from dampness and learning"), the word "bore" functioning in both senses of the word.

Stevenson was born in Cambridge, England, in January 1933, while her father, the American philosopher, Charles L. Stevenson, studied under Ludwig Wittgenstein and G. E. Moore at Cambridge University. In 1934, the family returned to America, and Stevenson spent her early years in and around the university towns of Cambridge, Massachusetts, and New Haven. The peripatetic family also lived variously in Berkeley and Chicago before settling in Ann Arbor when Charles L. Stevenson took up a position at the University of Michigan in 1946. After graduating from the University of Michigan with a Humanities degree and the Major Hopwood Prize for Poetry in 1954, Stevenson married an English childhood friend, Robin Hitchcock, in Cambridge, England, in 1955. With her first husband, she lived variously in Belfast, New York, and Mississippi. Following the disintegration of this first marriage in 1961, Stevenson returned to the University of Michigan where she embarked on a Master's Degree in English Literature under the tutelage of Donald Hall. In 1965, now married to the English sinologist Mark Elvin, she published her first volume of poetry, *Living in America*, with Generation Press. In 1971, following a Fellowship at the Radcliffe Institute at Harvard, she made yet another transatlantic crossing, moving with Elvin to Glasgow. Following a second divorce, and stints in Oxford, Reading, and Hay-on-Wye, in 1981 Stevenson was appointed Northern Arts Fellow at the Universities of Durham and Newcastle, and made what became a permanent home in the North-East of England, first in Langley Park, a former mining village in County Durham, and then in Durham city. She died on September 14, 2020.

During a poetic career that spanned some 50 years, Stevenson published 16 collections of poetry. *Poems 1955–2005* incorporates the majority of this published work, in addition to new and uncollected earlier poems. Unusually, this volume presents Stevenson's work in what the poet calls "small thematic galleries" rather than in "a long chronological corridor" (Kelley 2008). While this will perhaps frustrate those "sycophant PhDs" intent on tracing the development of Stevenson's mature poetic, it does reveal a number of persistent preoccupations in Stevenson's work (Stevenson 2006). Early poems anticipate later ones both in tone and theme, and late poems reprise—and even revise—the philosophical labors of their early precursors.

Stevenson's work was published by both British and American presses over the course of her 50-year-long career, and she received prizes and awards on both sides of the Atlantic, most notably: the inaugural Northern Rock Foundation Writer's Award (2002); the Neglected Masters Award by the Poetry Foundation of America (2007); and the Lannan Foundation's Lifetime Achievement Award (2007). Despite this critical recognition, though, Neil Astley, Stevenson's editor at Bloodaxe, suggests that "she never quite receives her due because the American establishment regards her as a British poet, while the British think she's American" (Hickling 2004). Stevenson seems to fall between two stools, then: still too American to be wholly embraced as a British poet, and now too British to be regarded as an American poet, simultaneously belonging to both nations and to neither.

Between two stools, though, is a position that Stevenson seems very fond of, even a position that is necessary to her art. She says, "Ever since I can remember I have been aware of living at what E. M. Forster called 'a slight angle' to the universe [...] I have always had to create my own angular environment or perish" (Hickling 2004). The title of her 2003 collection, *A Report from the Border*, affirms the poet's commitment to the borderlands between nations and cultures. "[T]hat's the whole point about borders," she says. "It's the best place from which to be able to see both sides" (Hickling 2004). Marginal or liminal places and spaces exerted an irresistible pull on the émigré poet throughout her career, and her poems often seek out and celebrate interstitial ground: "the marram-scarred, sandbitten margins" of the beach at Carnoustie (Stevenson 2004, 22, l. 5), the "line between land and water" in "A River" (1969), or land that is abandoned, deserted, or condemned, as in "Demolition" (1985) and "Salter's Gate" (1993) (Stevenson 2004, 47, 88, 97).

Even in those poems which explicitly locate themselves in time and space, we recognize a characteristic detachment, a refusal to "belong" completely or too comfortably. Stevenson's status as "outsider" is not only a biographical fact, but a deliberate stance within her poetry, from her earliest collections to her most recent. Many poems register intense feelings of dislocation and otherness, of being simultaneously a part of, but apart from, the world around us. Often this disconnection is represented in the visual metaphor of a pane of glass, as in "Travelling Behind Glass" (1974), "If I Could Paint Essences" (1982), "From My Study" (1993), and "The Wrekin" (2000) (Stevenson 2004).

Whether writing about American or British landscapes, the poet retains an outsider's detachment, never allowing the permanent resident's veil of familiarity to obscure what is really there. In a relatively early poem, "England" (1969), her incisive gaze makes it clear that she is neither a wistful tourist, "mesmerized by the sun," nor a permanent resident, dully accustomed to "the endless / Identical pavements" (Stevenson 2004, ll. 8, 30–31). It is her willingness to acknowledge the "stinginess of England" (l. 26) that marks her out as not wholly American, and her ability to see the rare moments of beauty in a post-industrial or urban landscape that marks her out as not wholly British. Similarly, "Ann Arbor" (1965), subtitled "A Profile," is no wistful *billet-doux* to Stevenson's childhood environs but a sociologist's dispassionate study of this self-consciously urbane "microcosm." Observed from a safe distance, the inhabitants are reduced to the stock characters of the American campus novel: "driven from their garrets, / thin graduate students gripe in the beer joints," and "The women who do not run for alderman / paint pictures, write poetry or give expensive parties" (Stevenson 2004, 32–33, ll. 17–18, 32–33).

Stevenson acknowledges the complex relationship between her milieu and her work in a 1983 interview with *Oxford Poetry*: "Had I stayed in America, undoubtedly I would have been a different poet. How different I can't say. It's impossible to speculate on one's alternative selves" (*Oxford Poetry* 1983, 43–49). She writes that, "like Elizabeth Bishop [...] I mostly think of poems as 'being true to life'" (Stevenson, personal communication). Unsurprisingly, Stevenson's first collection, *Living in America* (1965), written largely during her time as an MA student at the University of Michigan, is firmly and explicitly set in the diverse landscapes and locales of America. Titles include "Living in America," "Harvard," "Still Life in Utah," "Nightmare in North Carolina," "Ann Arbor," "The Dear Ladies of Cincinnati," and "Sierra Nevada" (Stevenson 2004). Similarly, her 1977 collection, *Enough of Green*, written during her tenure as Fellow in Writing at Dundee University, gives us the monochromatic landscapes and seascapes of the Scottish east coast, and her 1984 illustrated volume, *Black Grate Poems*, is a poetic portrait of the former mining community of Langley Park in County Durham. More recently, following her removal for part of the year to a cottage in Ardudwy, the precipitous landscape of North Wales provided the setting and subject for a large number of poems (mainly those in the "Poems from Cwm Nantcol" section of *Poems 1955–2005*). Though the itinerant poet rejects the notion of her *own* rootedness in any one particular landscape, her poems clearly emerge from specific locales.

One of the most characteristic features of her poetry is her ability to hold in fine balance an engagement with both the here and now and the dizzying sweep of deep time. Deep time—a comprehension of our human dramas played out against an indifferent geological landscape, billions of years in the making—is an unwieldy concept, but one that proves to be curiously empowering for Stevenson. This seemingly ethically motivated insistence on a long geological perspective is, she ventures, a peculiarly American inheritance, one that is shared with Charles Olson and Gary Snyder.

> Poets in America[,] men and women, feel they have a special relationship with Nature which is geographical, geological, even astronomical, and only secondarily social or historical.
> (CUL MS Add. 9451 n.d. (Prose))

Landscapes are geological first and last: human experience is ultimately as inconsequential as "a tissue dropped on Everest" (Stevenson 2007, 44, l. 27). Human habitations become unstable, flickering, almost unreal in this long view. In "Pennine" (1982), the speaker notes how, "Randomly, fells erupt in armoured cliffs / That might be houses – might, in this cloud, be / Slack, grit, slag, moss, a memory of mills" (Stevenson 2004, 83, ll. 4–6).

Aside from this "American" fascination with deep time, Stevenson has her own characteristically firm views on what characterizes the American and the British poetic temperament. "The danger for English poets lies in a kind of Edwardian wistfulness – or in cleverness," she ventures. "Shy of emotion, the English back away into description or wit. The hazard for Americans, of course, is over emotion. And excessive, boring egotism" (*Oxford Poetry* 1983, 43–49). Stevenson conceives of herself as an heir to both British and American traditions, concluding, "I suppose I work in both traditions and inherit the weaknesses (and I hope some of the strengths) of each. I try to keep an open mind and write like myself" (*Oxford Poetry* 1983). It is this determination to "write like myself" that is perhaps her most American trait. What is at the heart of American poetry, she suggests, is not a rigidly Adamic self-estrangement from the burden of anteriority, but a principled insistence on self-determination. "What's important is not whether you're formal or 'free,' but whether you succeed in doing what you set out to do. Authenticity and energy are what matter" (*Oxford Poetry* 1983). Stevenson has written at length about her early literary education, steeped in the "old" European tradition:

> Like many poets, I began to write verse when I was introduced to Shakespeare and the English Romantics as a child... I especially remember my father, an amateur musician, reading with fervor Scott's *Marmion* and *The Lady of the Lake*, Coleridge's Ancient Mariner, Arnold's "The Forsaken Merman" and "Sohrab and Rustum," Browning's "My Last Duchess," [and] Lord Macaulay's "Horatius at the Bridge."
>
> (Stevenson 1998, 121)

The young poet had no sense then, as now, that these dead, white, male, European writers should not speak as suggestively to her—a young girl growing up in the American Midwest—as to another European, male author. As such, she was often critical of that American poetry which infers that "there is no need any longer to wrestle with meter, rhyme, form or anything 'dead' like that which might suggest that American poetry has anything to do with the English tradition" (CUL MS Add. 9451 n.d.).

If she refuses to consider herself excluded from a European poetic tradition, then she also refuses to cast herself, or be cast by others, as the dispossessed victim of an exclusive patriarchal tradition. In a 1992 essay, "Inside and Outside History" (originally published as a response to Eavan Boland's 1990 collection *Outside History*), Stevenson criticizes the tendency of contemporary female poets to denigrate a tradition from which they assume they are excluded. That Stevenson never felt herself to be "outside" the dominant poetic tradition means that she never felt the need to align and ally herself with a separate women's counter-tradition. Indeed, while Stevenson's poetry often concerned itself with uniquely female experience and struggle—for example, "The Victory" (1969), *Correspondences* (1974), "The Myth of Medea" (2007)—she is one of a number of contemporary female poets who vigorously resist being either pigeonholed or promoted on account of their gender. In a 1979 essay, "Writing as a Woman," the poet insists that "A good writer's imagination should be bisexual or transsexual" (Stevenson 1998, 20). For a female poet to accept the label of "woman poet" is, she suggests, to be "complicitous" in the wholesale consignment of female poets "to the ghetto" (Stevenson 1998, 88).

Against Romantics

From her earliest volumes onward, Stevenson's poems reveal the poet's richly ambivalent relationship to both the work and to the enduring mythos of the English Romantic poets. An unpublished early poem, "Against Romantics," delivers a scathing assessment of a "Romantic" figure who cannot dare—or cannot *bear*—to believe in the "neutrality" and indifference of the natural world to human fate.

> His real cowardice was
> he would not see
> beyond the inspiring words
> to the real sea
> where he might have done something
> almost heroically had
> he dared believe
> in its neutrality.
>   (CUL MS Add. 9451 n.d. (Poems))

This unpublished poem is an early incarnation of the published poem "He and It" (1982). Unable to face up to the reality that no divine truth or affirmation can be divined from natural phenomena, and that man is just another living organism in an ecological chain, "He" uses his vivid imagination to create for himself a responsive natural world in which "sky burns, wind bites, / swans hound him with meaning" (Stevenson 2004, 269, ll. 18–19). As far as "He" is concerned, even a natural world that seems unkindly disposed toward him is more consoling than a natural world that is ignorant of and indifferent to his existence.

We find a similarly pejorative characterization of the "Romantic" in Stevenson's prose and correspondence. In a heated 1989 exchange of letters with Olwen Hughes and Al Alvarez in the *New York Review of Books*, the poet suggests that "Romanticism, for societies as well as for individuals, represents a stage of adolescence in which, like Sylvia Plath in her last poems, the 'self' cries out in despair when confronted with its individual impotence" (Stevenson et al. 1989). Similarly, in the essay "Stations: Seamus Heaney and the Sacred Sense of the Sensitive Self," Stevenson associates Romanticism with a strategy of psychological "retreat": a "withdrawal from the world into a sacred area of personal sensitivity" (Stevenson 1998, 98).

Despite this Bloomian "misreading" of Romantic ideology and praxis within her prose, she develops within her later work a renovated and pragmatic "Romanticism" that will, to use Wallace Stevens's word, "suffice" in these late philosophical days. Her poetry resurrects key Romantic concerns and uncertainties, as it explores the complex, protean relationship between the perceiving mind and the perceived world, and questions the potentiality of the creative imagination to serve as an illuminating and coalescing force in what seems to be an increasingly arbitrary universe. If the short poem "On Going Deaf" (2000) is ostensibly a candid rumination upon the poet's progressive hearing loss, then it is also a statement of the importance of the imagination within her work.

> I've lost a sense. Why should I care?
> Searching myself, I find a spare.
> I keep that sixth sense in repair
> And set it deftly, like a snare.
>   (Stevenson 2004, 351)

The simile with which "On Going Deaf" ends introduces a characteristic ambivalence, implying that the imagination (or at least, Stevenson's imagination) is perhaps not wholly benevolent: that it can deceive and entrap. Indeed, the poem itself, with its taut syntax and tightly wound AAAA rhyme scheme, begins to seem like a "snare," deftly set to ambush the unsuspecting reader. Reviews of Stevenson's work have tended to overlook the authority of the imagination within her poetry, praising instead her supposedly "classical" virtues; the almost camera-like clarity of her vision and the tautness of her wit. In Stevenson's poetry, we see occasional, darting flashes of Romantic idealism. In "Coming Back to Cambridge" (1974), the speaker asserts that "Nothing that really matters really exists" (l. 49), the audacity of the statement emphasized by its being suspended, as if in mid-air, between verse paragraphs (Stevenson 2004, 59). It is "Burnished" (1982), though, in which we find Stevenson's most sustained flirtation with Blakean idealism, but here, as elsewhere, such unbridled idealism cannot be sustained for long. Holding a horse chestnut in her hand, the speaker is commanded by an imagined incarnation of Blake:

> Now close your eyes. I felt the whole world warmed.
> It was breathing its native heat in my blind skin.
> When I looked again, it was a leather ocean
> lapping a small sandy island. No one
> appeared to live there. Now where its gleam had been
> is a breast with a shrivelled nipple, like a dry wound.
> (Stevenson 2004, 65, ll. 13–18)

Having closed her eyes upon the "real" world, the speaker is "blind." The visceral image of the "shrivelled nipple" is a metaphor for the speaker's experience of the Blakean creative imagination: what at first seemed nourishing and plentiful is revealed to have run dry, leaving only hunger and disenchantment. In Stevenson's work, such giddy imaginative flights inevitably end in a disillusioned plummet back to earth. On the whole, then, Stevenson's imagination is evident not so much in the soaring architecture of "stately pleasure dome[s]" as in the subtle heightening or attuning of the poet's already highly attuned five senses; it is more a mode of "seeing" than a means of make-believe.

Beyond the Confessional

For Stevenson, the Confessional movement (or moment) of the late 1950s and 1960s represents a resurgence, even an apogee, of the Romantic impulse of self-sanctification. Stevenson's uneasy relationship with the Confessionals is much in evidence in her poetry of the late 1960s and 1970s. For those poets who outlived the Confessionals, the question of how to explore personal experience without "confessing" was both an esthetic and an ethical one. It is possible to trace Stevenson's efforts to "depersonalize" her verse from the mid-1950s onward. "The Women," written in 1955, radically reimagines the poet's experience of domestic dissatisfaction as a surreal mythopoeic dreamscape. Crucially, there are no personal pronouns here: the speaker is a remote observer, if not absent, then at least far distant. The women, the young Stevenson among them, are depicted as strangely inhuman as they passively "Sit among dahlias all the afternoons, / While quiet processional seasons / Drift and subside at their doors like dunes" (Stevenson 2004, 46, ll. 2–4). These "waiting"

(l. 1) wives are in the thrall of their Triton-like husbands, yet it is Stevenson-as-poet who wields the ultimate power over her imaginative constructs. By the late 1960s, though, Stevenson had eschewed Plath's exhausted "myth kitty" for a polylogic poetic. The short poem "Generations" (1969) situates the poet's own anguish firmly in a lineage of feminine discontent, and posits her own traumatic experience as but a part and product of a wider context of feminine suffering. Again, there is no confessional lyric "I" here, and in this poem, the poet newly alights upon the poetic mode that would come to maturation in what has come to be her best-known volume, *Correspondences* (1974). Indeed, the poem is described by Stevenson as "probably [...] the seed from which *Correspondences* grew" (Stevenson 1998, 12).

Subtitled "A Family History in Letters," *Correspondences* is an ambitious and formally innovative book-length polylogic epistolary poem, comprising letters, journal entries, obituaries, and the miscellaneous writings of six generations of a fictional New England family, the Chandlers. *Correspondences* is by far Stevenson's most ambitious project, and has been reproduced in its entirety in both her *Selected Poems* (1987) and *Poems 1955–2005*. Despite the poet's suggestion that "from *Correspondences* I think a biographer might learn a fair amount about my mistakes," the poem is by no means a thinly veiled confession or *cri du coeur*, and can be most usefully understood as a response to, and a reaction against, "Confessional" poetry (Nelson 2000, 55). Indeed, Neil Roberts suggests that "the multiple perspective and historical reach of the text ... supply the alternative, or challenge, to confessionalism" (Roberts 1999, 63). *Correspondences* draws significantly on two separate bodies of nineteenth- and early twentieth-century correspondence; the first, "a trunk full of nineteenth-century family letters," discovered in 1962; and the second, the papers of the Beecher-Stowe family, housed in the Arthur and Elizabeth Schlesinger Library at Harvard University, where Stevenson held a fellowship in 1970 (Stevenson 1998, 14). Stevenson explains that her guiding poetic principle was "to get feelings right but to invent 'facts'" (Stevenson 1998, 18). We might at first think this poetic strategy somewhat similar to Lowell's "fiction coloured with first-hand evidence" in *The Dolphin*, yet whereas Lowell "markets" his personal experience—real-life "letter and talk"—as fiction, Stevenson presents these poems as real-life historical documents (Lowell 2003, 689). Through the letters and journal entries of these characters, the poet not only explores her own complex experiences and emotions, but also allows herself to be spoken through as she quotes verbatim, borrows from, and reworks, the various source texts. She is both a ventriloquist, animating a cast of fictional characters with her own modulated voice, and a conduit through which the long-buried voices of silenced women might be heard: Abigail, whose "hand's gone numb" as she writes in the dark; Marianne, whose journal is destroyed by fire; Maura, whose "desire for a share of the world's knowledge" is denounced as "unfeminine" by her overbearing father; and Ruth, who sacrifices her own literary ambitions for her husband and children (Stevenson 2004).

Sylvia Plath, in particular, came to embody what Stevenson saw as the excesses and indulgences of the Confessional poets. In a very Plathian way, Stevenson clearly conceives of the dead poet as a kind of malevolent dark double. In an undated typescript titled "The Making of Bitter Fame," Stevenson explains:

Plath and I were born within months of each other in the autumn and winter of 1932 and 1933. We had in common American parents of German descent, though her background, unlike mine, was undilutedly Teutonic. Our fathers were both university professors. As children, we attended similar public (state) elementary schools, and as teenagers, we graduated in the same year (1950) from middle-class, "college oriented" American high schools [...]. What Sylvia Plath and I had unequivocally in common in the 1950s was, of course, marriage to an Englishman and transplantation, as naïve young women, from open-minded, prosperous America to class-ridden, war-depleted England.

(CUL MS Add. 9451 n.d. (Prose))

Their respective transatlantic trajectories in fact came within mere feet of crossing. Helen Hitchcock, the mother of Stevenson's first husband, ran St. Botolph's Rectory, the "spiritual home" of that group of poets including Plath and Ted Hughes. Stevenson recollects that on many occasions she would hear the "roistering" poets singing uproariously in the kitchen, but that she never joined them. "I was too shy, and Robin would have been very disapproving" (Gatti 2007).

In 1986, Stevenson, at the request of Olwyn Hughes, undertook the writing of a critical biography of Plath. *Bitter Fame: A Life of Sylvia Plath* was published in 1989 to a mixed critical response. While Blake Morrison praises the biography as "the coolest, most intelligent and most authoritative account of the life to date" (Stevenson 1989, cover matter), Al Alvarez dismisses it as "a minor poet's envy of a major poet" (Stevenson et al. 1989). The difficulties experienced by Stevenson during the writing of *Bitter Fame* have been well documented in Janet Malcolm's biography of Plath's biographers, *The Silent Woman* (1994). During the writing of *Bitter Fame*, Stevenson wrote three poems about Plath, all of which are included in the "In Memoriam" section of *Poems 1955–2005*, under the sub-heading "Three Poems for Sylvia Plath." Although intimacy or even acquaintance has historically not been a prerequisite for the writing of elegy, it perhaps seems strange that the life and death of Plath should weigh so heavily on Stevenson's mind. Stevenson herself acknowledges the strangeness of this one-sided relationship in "A Lament for the Makers" (2006), as she describes a meeting with the shades of Hughes and Plath in the "underworld of words" (Part one, III, l. 10). It is curious that although it is Stevenson who is the living, breathing poet and Plath the diaphanous "shade," it is Stevenson who is "invisible," "insubstantial," and "unknown" (ll. 87–91). Stevenson admitted in interviews that it is to her chagrin that in the aftermath of the *Bitter Fame* furor she became better known as Plath's biographer than as a long-established poet in her own right. The trauma which those three "elegies" must set about healing, then, is not so much the death of Plath, but Stevenson's painful experience of writing *Bitter Fame*.

Male elegists traditionally figure themselves as the sons of dead fathers from whom they inherit—or usurp—poetic power. In "Letter to Sylvia Plath," however, Stevenson boldly inverts the elegist's traditional posture of childlike deference to the dead, and casts herself as the mother who alternately soothes and scolds a childlike Plath. By casting Plath as "poor Sylvia," "a frantic Alice," and a "famous girl," Stevenson (55 years of age when this poem was written) affects a separation between them and draws attention to her own surviving powers (Stevenson 2004, 384, ll. 49, 53). In keeping with the inversion of the traditional parent–child casting, Stevenson seems largely unconcerned with wresting an inheritance from the dead poet, and instead attempts to emphasize the distance and difference between Plath's poetry and her own. Plath is portrayed (or perhaps caricatured) in this poem as "lady of pallors and foetal jars /and surgical interiors," whose poems are full of her "crippled dreams / and ineradicable screams" (ll. 5–6, 51–52). The poem implies that whereas Plath was imprisoned in the windowless cell of her own damaged psyche, Stevenson is alert and responsive to the material world around her.

The Treachery of Words

Whatever Stevenson's poems are ostensibly "about," they are always, on one level, "about" language. Even as her poems delight in the potential of words to express, enact, excite, and enliven, they are acutely aware of the limitations of language. If Stevenson's poetry gravitates toward unsettling liminal spaces, it is partly because it is at these frontiers, both geographical and psychological, at which words fail us, or are found wanting. It is tempting to see Stevenson's ambiguous relationship with words as a bequest from her philosopher father, whose controversial *Ethics and Language* (1944) posits that our perception of certain events or ethical quandaries is conditioned by the language used by ourselves and by others. Though subsequently acknowledged as a seminal work in the field of emotivism, the book resulted in his dismissal from Yale University because of its insistence on the linguistic construction rather than the absolute nature of moral concepts such as "good" and "evil." Stevenson's poem "Saying the World" reprises her father's wariness of words as it warns the reader that "The way you say the world is what you get" (Stevenson 2004, 18, l. 1). We are "trapped" in a Wittgensteinian cycle of language-conditioned experience and experience-conditioned language. Language is figured as a "net," one that we have made in order to capture and fix the material word around us. This net, though, can easily turn on, and hopelessly entangle, its creators. "The words swim out to pin you in their net" (l. 3), the poem warns.

This metaphor of the net owes something to Robert Graves's "cool web" from the poem of the same name (Graves 2003, 283, l. 9). Graves's poem suggests that language "winds us in" to protect us from the horrors of the non-human, non-linguistic world. Many of Stevenson's poems, too, posit language as a psychological barrier that affords us a measure of control (or the illusion thereof) over speechless nature: "O see and say them, make yourself forget / The world is vaster than the alphabet" (Stevenson 2004, 18, ll. 12–13). The tight ABA rhyme scheme with its emphatic masculine rhymes creates a sense of almost mechanical precision and predictability: is this "the mind's machine" at work, imposing order on the "profligate" world? (ll. 6, 14). The enveloping of the B rhyme within the A rhyme, coupled with the insistent internal alliteration and assonance ("way," "world," and "what"; "whose eyes accuse"), suggests the insidious tightening of the "net" of language. The forceful statement in the final line, "The absolute's irrelevant" (l. 19), followed by an emphatic full-stop, seems to close this poem down; the speaker has apparently rejected language on the grounds that it assumes and imposes absolutes on the irreducible complexity of life. However, this is not the final word. One of the poet's characteristic second thoughts ("And yet [...]," l. 19) counters this conclusion, opening the whole poem out again. At the end of "Saying the World," then, we have a dilemma akin to the one articulated in the short poem "Vertigo" (2000). The poet can either reject "the treachery of words" (Stevenson 1998, 170, l. 6) and "take that step into silence," or she can "turn and exist" with a full knowledge of both the delights and the dangers of language (Stevenson 2004, 28, l. 8). "Saying the World" is, therefore, a disclaimer of sorts, where Stevenson makes plain that she is fully aware of the compromises necessitated by every utterance.

It is perhaps the blessing *and* the burden of poets that they are never free from this desire to engage with the world through language, even when that world seems powerfully to resist their efforts. Many of Stevenson's poems take as their inspiration or occasion a failure, as the poet makes poetic capital out of the seeming falling-short of her own linguistic or poetic abilities. In one of the "Poems from Cwn Nantcol," "Binoculars in Ardudwy" (1993), we find a speaker attempting to capture a rural scene in North Wales through both the lens of her binoculars and through language. In the second stanza, the speaker uses words in the most straightforward way, as a Saussurean pointing finger: "There's a farmer, Land Rover, black dog / trotting, now rolling on his back" (Stevenson 2004, 71, ll. 5–6). In the third stanza, though, the language takes a seemingly inevitable figurative turn, as she urges, "Look now, the sun's reached out / painting turf over ice-smoothed stone" (l. 10). She figures her binoculars as "a noose / I hold to my focusing eyes" (ll. 13–14), the word "noose" recalling the tightening "net" of language in "The Way You Say the World" (Graves 2003, 283, l. 9). The magnifying lens of the binoculars hauls the view "across // a mile of diluvian marsh" (l. 17), the word "hauling" together with the image of the noose suggestive of a kind of violence committed on the landscape. However, the scene ultimately proves resistant, even actively so, to this attempted seizure:

> Then, just as I frame it, the farm
> wraps its windows in lichenous weather
> and buries itself in its tongue. (ll. 20–22)

The speaker assumes that "Not my eyes but my language is wrong, / And the cloud is between us forever" (ll. 23–24). She suggests that a speaker of the English "language" cannot truly belong in this Welsh landscape, where the very fields whisper in impenetrable Welsh "language."

> Under cover of mist and myth
> the pieced fields whisper together,
> 'Find invisible *Maes-y-garnedd...*,
> *Y Llethr... Foel Ddu... Foel Wen.*' (ll. 25–28)

This poem, however, is about a far more fundamental foreignness than that of an English speaker in Welsh-speaking North Wales. It is not only English that is "wrong" in this landscape, but any language, all languages: the farm does not have a "tongue" and fields do not whisper in either Welsh or English. It is this that ultimately separates the speaker from her surroundings, a linguistic creature in a nonlinguistic environment. The most profound displacement in Stevenson's work, then, is not the transposition felt by the poet as an immigrant in England, or as an emigrant in America, but the inveterate sense of peripatesis humans experience as transitory occupants of an apathetic natural world. Perhaps perversely, Stevenson's verse derives a kind of comfort from this very indifference. As the speaker in "Stone Milk" (2007) concludes, "Not the milk of kindness, but the milk of stones / is food I'm learning to long for" (Stevenson 2007, 35, ll. 26–27).

References

"An Interview with Anne Stevenson" (1983). *Oxford Poetry* 1 (2): 43–49. http://www.oxford poetry.co.uk/interviews.php?int=i2_anne stevenson (accessed 27 August 2018).

CUL MS Add. 9451 (n.d.). Cambridge University Library, Department of Manuscripts and University Archives, Literary Papers and Correspondence of Anne Stevenson.

Gatti, Tom (2007). "Anne Stevenson: The Secret Life of a Poet." *The Times* (Books) (14 December). http://www.arlindo-correia.org/anne_stevenson. html (accessed 29 May 2015).

Graves, Robert (2003). *The Complete Poems*. London: Penguin Classics.

Hickling, Alfred (2004). "Border Crossings." *The Guardian* (4 October). http://www.theguardian. com/books/2004/oct/02/featuresreviews. guardianreview14 (accessed 28 May 2015).

Kelley, Rich (2008). "Interview with Anne Stevenson." *Library of America e-Newsletter*. http://www.anne-stevenson.co.uk/downloads/ Stevenson_interview.pdf (accessed 29 May 2015).

Lowell, Robert (2003). *Collected Poems* (eds. Frank Bidart and David Gewanter). London: Faber and Faber.

Malcolm, Janet (1994). *The Silent Woman: Sylvia Plath and Ted Hughes*. New York: Alfred Knopf.

Nelson, Helena (2000). "Anne Stevenson in Conversation." *The Dark Horse* (Summer). http:// www.thedarkhorsemagazine.com/Resources/ AnneStevensonInterview.pdf (accessed 29 May 2015).

Roberts, Neil (1999). *Narrative and Voice in Postwar Poetry*. London: Longman.

Stevenson, Anne, Alvarez, Al, and Hughes, Olwyn (1989). Sylvia Plath: An Exchange. *New York Review of Books* (26 October). http://www. nybooks.com/articles/archives/1989/oct/26/ sylvia-plath-an-exchange/?pagination=false (accessed 29 May 2015).

Stevenson, Anne (1965). *Living in America*. Ann Arbor: Generation Press.

Stevenson, Anne (1989). *Bitter Fame: A Life of Sylvia Plath*. London: Viking.

Stevenson, Anne (1998). *Between the Iceberg and the Ship: Selected Essays. Poets on Poetry*. Ann Arbor: The University of Michigan Press.

Stevenson, Anne (2004). *Poems 1955–2005*. Tarset, Northumberland: Bloodaxe.

Stevenson, Anne (2006). *A Lament for the Makers*. Thame: Clutag Press.

Stevenson, Anne (2007). *Stone Milk*. Tarset, Northumberland: Bloodaxe.

Stevenson, Charles L. (1944). *Ethics and Language*. Repr. 1960. Yale University Press.

3.16
Paula Meehan—Vocal Cartographies: Public and Private

Wolfgang Görtschacher

In August 1995, I conducted an interview with Theo Dorgan, then Director of Poetry Ireland. In it he foresaw a re-emergence of the ancient tradition of *dinnseanchas*, the lore of naming the place, as a trope, which entailed that poets were "find[ing] personal and poetic sustenance in an examination of origins" and "the hidden histories of individual poets' domains [were] beginning to come true" (Dorgan 2000, 750). As examples in support of his thesis, he offered the work of two emerging poets he held in high esteem: "a certain vision of the history of Belfast is beginning to emerge in the poetry of Ciaran Carson, of Dublin in the poems of Paula Meehan" (Dorgan 2000, 750). Carson, who at the time had already published five collections, among them *The Irish for No* (1987) and *Belfast Confetti* (1989), was an obvious example. Terry Eagleton had drawn attention to "a cartographer's or archaeologist's erudition" in Carson's work (Eagleton 1991, 20), while Frank Ormsby had noted "the extensive use of map imagery [in the same poet's] Belfast poems," which, he believed, was employed "to convey the labyrinthine nature of the city and the way it changes daily to create a nightmarish atmosphere of dislocation in a familiar place" (Ormsby 2001, 72). Mentioning Paula Meehan in this context was perhaps more anticipatory than evident at the time, although her *oeuvre* also comprised four volumes of poetry in 1995, *The Man Who Was Marked by Winter* (1991) and *Pillow Talk* (1994) being the most important. A year later Eavan Boland confirmed Dorgan's outlook when she called Meehan "one of the strongest, most music[al] and assured presences in this generation" (Boland 1996, 142). Nuala Ní Dhomhnaill shared this evaluation when she chose Meehan's poem "The Pattern" for the section "1990–1999 Tidal Surge" which she edited for the volume

---

A Companion to Contemporary British and Irish Poetry, 1960–2015, First Edition.
Edited by Wolfgang Görtschacher and David Malcolm.
© 2021 John Wiley & Sons Ltd. Published 2021 by John Wiley & Sons Ltd.

Watching the River Flow: A Century in Irish Poetry (1999). She described Meehan as a "major female voice from the 90s" and the poem as "a classic" offering "[a] richly textured evocation of a childhood growing up in Dublin's inner city" as well as of a "deeply ambiguous relationship between mother and daughter" (Ní Dhomhnaill 1999, 222).

Twenty years and many publications and awards later, it is interesting to offer a critical *résumé* that readers may want to compare with—and consider in the context of—early pronouncements. On March 21, 2019, Dublin City University paid tribute to "one of Ireland's foremost poets" (Dublin City University 2019) by conferring on her the title of honorary Doctor of Philosophy. On this occasion, Mary Shine Thompson described Meehan's verse as "elegantly wrought, often magically incantatory, and always accessible, but, like Seamus Heaney's, charged with a challenging undercurrent." DCU President Brian MacCraith offered, as reasons for bestowing this honor, Meehan's "body of exceptional work, allied with, and inextricable from, [her] compassion, clarity, and courage" (Dublin City University 2019). Five and a half years earlier, in September 2013, DCU had also been the setting of President Michael D. Higgins's announcement that Meehan had been awarded the position of Ireland Professor of Poetry, the sixth poet and second woman, following in the footsteps of John Montague (1998), Nuala Ní Dhomhnaill (2001), Paul Durcan (2004), Michael Longley (2007), and Harry Clifton (2010). Following the award of the Nobel Prize in Literature to Seamus Heaney in 1995, the Ireland Chair of Poetry was set up in 1998 by the An Chomhairle Ealaíon (the Arts Council of the Republic of Ireland), the Arts Council of Northern Ireland, Trinity College Dublin, Queen's University Belfast, and University College Dublin. Gerard Smyth, poetry editor of *The Irish Times*, called Meehan "a poet of solidarity – solidarity with the dispossessed, with mother earth, with her sisters and brothers in the craft." He particularly stressed her "radical and independent [...] ways of seeing" that have enabled her to achieve "a recalibration of the Irish poem, drawing it into a different state of mind; her poems are often a skillful blending of a shared and personal history" (Smyth 2013).

During the prescribed 3-year term, the Ireland Chair of Poetry spends a semester in residence in each of the three universities and gives an annual formal public lecture. Meehan's three lectures were published under the title of *Imaginary Bonnets with Real Bees in Them* in 2016. In a review of the volume, Thomas McCarthy stressed the innovative potential of Meehan's book and called it "both a sourcebook and a catechism for new kinds of poetries." Her lectures offer "a poetry beyond rhetoric, [...] outmoded nationalisms and loyalisms," a poetry that is based on a "person-centred aesthetic [...] derive[d] from the direct treatment of all things." McCarthy is the only critic among the many who have reviewed *Imaginary Bonnets* who hints at a personally significant characteristic of Meehan's poetry when he says that "Meehan eats words, reprocessing words like wild honey" (McCarthy 2016). Especially in her first lecture, which gave the volume its title, Meehan asks basic but crucial questions that should concern every poet, questions which are derived from her distrust of the phrase "show me, don't tell me": "why [...] should an abstract noun be an abomination? What about the music? The tune of the poem? The dance of the poem?" (Meehan 2016, 7). Toward the end of her lecture, Meehan defines what I regard as the core of her poetics:

Much of the truth force of a poem inheres in the rhythmic patterns, or lack of them, the breath patternings, the poem's designs on taking our breath away, the organizing of the words into rhetorical patterns, periodic phrases, anaphoric utterance that carries us up, up, up and out of the earthbound stricture of the poem, the craft free of gravity, true agent of flight.

(Meehan 2016, 20)

The scholarly journal *An Sionnach* published a Paula Meehan double issue in autumn 2009 to accompany the launch of her poetry collection *Painting Rain*. It celebrates and critiques, as guest-editor Jody Allen Randolph points out, Meehan's "poetic choices, her playwriting, and the social and ethical commitments that underlie both" (Allen Randolph 2009a, 5). However, neither in the 18 essays nor in the one interview is any serious regard paid to the one aspect which, as the quoted words show, Meehan herself clearly sees as central. Eric Falci, in his essay "Meehan's Stanzas and the Irish Lyric after Yeats," does have a certain interest in sound and rhythmic organization in Meehan's poetry, but feels impelled to restrain it. The final section of his paper is apologetic. He finds it necessary to defend his approach against potential objections of being "deeply, damagingly formalist" and having "failed to think about the broader themes and stakes of her work" (Falci 2009, 236).

Although Meehan frankly admits that "I am not a theorist but a craftswoman" (Meehan 2010) and "would not have written those lectures if I hadn't been given the chance, because it's not a milieu I'm drawn to" (Wallace 2015), she has over the years made very interesting comments, mostly in interviews, on the relation of sound to meaning. In "Slitting the Songbird's Throat to See What Makes It Sing," her short essay for the Laois Education Centre, Meehan makes it quite clear that, for her, "[t]he transmission of poetry across generations remains [...] an oral transmission" (Meehan 2009b, 176). This belief and her technique of writing poetry are thoroughly grounded in childhood experiences:

When I was a child I had to learn off by heart a verse of poetry in English and Irish every school day. Mostly I had no idea what the words meant but it did give me a source of power later when I came to make poems myself, a store of line lengths and rhythmical patterns I have drawn on ever since. The hearing of poetry is a crucial part of the oral transmission, and a great source of comfort. I remember my body rocking to the stress patterns in a poem and reconnecting to a very old pulse (my mother's heartbeat?).

(Meehan 2009b, 176)

The biological–mystical note of the final query does not surprise; it affirms, confirms the poet's view of poetry as a primitive, primal, and fundamental way of experiencing the world, more fundamental—and prior to—the mode of understanding. In her *résumé* again she expresses her belief that "[w]e are in danger of elevating meaning to a fetishistic level at the expense of the real experience of poetry, a very physical experience." Bearing auditory witness—as well as visual—her close friend Ciaran Carson confirms the thesis that for Meehan "poetry [is] a very physical experience": "I hear you read your poems aloud and your feet keeping counterpoint to their music untwining the lines widdershins" (Carson 2009, 140). In the interview with Luz Mar González-Arias, Meehan elaborates further on this aspect:

> All the elements of poetry are very much rooted in physical experience, like the rhythm of the poem, its music, it is indeed a physical experience. In fact, that's the only way I like working with poetry, as something that is made to work on other people's bodies out of my own body. Not that the mind isn't important. You are looking for a complementary balance. But ultimately, I think you can bypass the ego and the mind with a poem in a way that is difficult to do with any other kind of expression, apart from music.
>
> (González-Arias 2000, 195)[1]

Painting Rain (2009a), Paula Meehan's seventh collection, contains the sequence "Six Sycamores," first published as a pamphlet by Crowquill in 2004, with sculpture and drawings by Marie Foley. Originally from Dublin's north inner city, Meehan has always been aware that her native town "was incredibly well-mapped in literary terms. But, yet, *my* city wasn't. [...] So, although there were all these maps I still felt rudderless in terms of my own life" (González-Arias 2000, 296). In his poem "It Takes Trees in Summer," Brendan Kennelly defines Meehan's stance in poetic terms when his persona refers to the early sound maps of Meehan's childhood while she was growing up in the city off Gardiner Street and later, when, as an older child, she moved to Finglas (Kennelly 2009). Asked by Jody Allen Randolph about sonic elements of her childhood that particularly contributed to her development as a poet, Meehan said:

> I grew up in an oral tradition: the stories, the singers, the old people, the lore, the sometimes very empowering lore. I soon developed, I believe, a hunger for ritualized sound, in and of itself. [...] It was a vivid, interesting, and textured world for me with a lot of song, a lot of music, not least the music of the city itself, the steel hoop rims on cobbles, the horses' hooves. There was an abattoir near us. I remember the squealing of pigs and cries of sheep waiting to be slaughtered. The music of the Latin, of the bells of the church, all of that – a fantastically rich childhood in sonic terms.
>
> (Allen Randolph 2009b, 239)

In the central sequence of *Painting Rain*, "Six Sycamores"[2] (Meehan 2009a, 28–33), Meehan takes her readers to such a site and thus achieves the aim, defined in her interview with Allen Randolph, of "integrat[ing] [her] work as a private memorialist with an impulse to express collective memory" (Allen Randolph 2009b, 260). The sequence was commissioned by the Office of Public Works on the occasion of the opening of the Link Building between number 51 and number 52, on the east side of St. Stephen's Green, Dublin, in 2001. In order to mirror "the architectural complexity and the ornamentation of the houses themselves" and "what they stand for, the ascendancy class, the class privilege of the whole colonial adventure," Meehan decided to experiment with the sonnet, as both "house and poem are received forms that can be re-inhabited and are re-inhabited" (Allen Randolph 2009b, 261). For Meehan the sonnet structure mirrors "something of the architectural complexity and the ornamentation of the houses themselves." On the other hand, in the history of the genre of the sonnet, Meehan sees represented "how they had been shells for many different kinds of lives, for office workers now, for tenement families, for the rich, for the original owners of the houses, for the merchant and professional classes" (Allen Randolph 2009b, 261). "The karma of the form," as Meehan defines it, is, for her, grounded in Ireland's history as a colony, in that some of the Elizabethan courtier and soldier poets, with whom the sonnet came into English, "were also the agents of colony here in a policy of ethnic cleansing in Munster" (Allen Randolph 2009b, 261).

The first sonnet of this sequence, "The Sycamore's Contract with the Citizens" (Meehan 2009a, 28), seems to offer a formal correlative to exactly that colonial connection, with its rhyme scheme—abab/cdcd/efef/gg—modeled on that of the Shakespearean or English sonnet. Through the rhyming lexemes however, the persona infiltrates and undermines this colonial ideology. The semantic connection of the a-rhymes "crown" (l. 1) and "down" (l. 3) suggests, I would argue, the persona's revolutionary ethos in the colonial context. The *in-medias-res* beginning of the poem ("To look up in autumn"), expressed as an invitation or suggestion to the unnamed addressee or the reader, is best understood in opposition to the lexeme "crown" at the line break. The dash, as medial caesura, enhances the opposition on both a rhythmic and a visual level, while the syllabic division of the two half-lines—six syllables versus four syllables—clearly favors the Irish speaker's stance. This opposition is further enhanced by the phonological quality of the diphthong /aʊ/ in connection with the nasal /n/, which has a certain synesthetic quality that strengthens the vertical direction. The rhythmic quality of lines 1 and 3 is also characterized by enjambment, which contributes to the downward movement sparked off by the semantic correspondence of "crown" and "down." This oppositional dynamic is also expressed in the meter of lines 1 and 3.

> To lóok úp in áutumn – the fíery crówn
> lóosing and nétting the ský by túrns; the séeds
> stópping tíme, hélicóptering lázily dówn
> to cráshland on páths ór on a pád of wéeds (ll. 1–4)

The first half-line of line 1 contains one iamb and two trochees, while the second half-line consists of two iambs. If we regard the iambic pentameter line as one of the typical characteristics of the English sonnet, and the iamb as the typical foot of such a sonnet, this metrical structure, bringing in the trochees, evokes oppositional forces. Furthermore, it is interesting to note the assonance of /aɪ/ in "fiery," "sky," "by," and "time," which musically underlines the operation of power, semantically expressed in the activity of the crown and, by implication, the nature of English colonial policy toward the Irish population. On the other hand, the noun "sky" seems to work as a semantic pole, as it is alliteratively connected with "seeds" and "stopping." If we consider the b-rhymes of "seeds" and "weeds," in the same context as we have done before, they seem to contribute further to the negative atmosphere that emanates from the spatial setting. Even if we were to remain within the extended imagery, it is interesting to note the self-effacing persona; the only agents in the first quatrain are the personified "crown"—with demonstrative arbitrariness—"loosing and netting the sky by turns" and the personified "seeds" ("helicoptering lazily") which have the power of "stopping time." The ing-forms of "loosing / netting" (l. 2) and "stopping / helicoptering" (l. 3) denote contrasting forms of activity and movement. The ambiguity of these elliptical phrases is only dissolved with the temporal subordinate clause "when you were a child" in line 5.

Another semantic opposition, that between "crown" and "seeds," seems to be suggested by the parallelism of ll. 1–2 and ll. 2–4. The "crown" exercises power over the sky ("loosing and netting"), which is expressed by the coordinating conjunction "and," thus connecting the contrasting non-finite verbs. The syntax of S-V-and-V-O semantically suggests a subject ("crown") with absolute power, as it were, of divine ordinance. The activities of the "seeds," on the other hand, are represented, in terms of syntax, paratactically in ll. 2–3, and in l. 4 with an infinitive-plus-object construction. From the infinitive "to crashland," which has onomatopoeic qualities, two parallel constructions are dependent: "on paths" as well as "on a pad of weeds" (l. 4) are phonetically connected by the alliteration of /p/. The latter phrase is again connected with the infinitive by the triple assonance of /æ/ and the consonance of /d/ in "pad" and "crashland."

The temporal subordinate clause, which contains the appeal to the unidentified addressee, is delayed until the very end of the first sentence. In ll. 1–4, the persona has been self-effacing, and no personal reference has been offered to the reader. Structurally, the addressee is completely separated from the first four lines, since the subordinate clause belongs to the second quatrain. This effect is further strengthened by the syntactic caesura, though unmarked, as we could imagine a period at the end of line 4. Metrically, the interstanzaic enjambment achieves a connection between the first and the second stanza, which is further enhanced on the phonological level by the alliteration of /w/ in "weeds" (l. 4), "when," and "were" (both l. 5) and the consonance of /d/ in "pad" (l. 4) and "child" (l. 5).

The rhyming words of the second quatrain again seem to create an opposition: the c-rhymes "birds / words" (ll. 5, 7) imply the addressee's sympathy if not identification with nature. On the other hand, the d-rhymes "shades / fades" (ll. 6, 8) suggest the persona's wish to get rid of the colonial "shades" that are associated with these buildings. The second sentence (ll. 5–8) is connected with the first by the conjunction "And" (l. 5); the elliptical syntax—the personal pronoun "you" is missing—has an indirect anaphoric effect, as we can infer from the first half-line of line 5 and the function of the coordinating conjunction "And." As in the first quatrain, Meehan's structure is characterized by enjambment (ll. 5–7) and parallelism (ll. 6–8). The simile of ll. 5–6 ("the birds / as the souls of the builders") is disconnected by the line break and the second part of the construction is carried on to l. 6. The phonemic devices of the alliteration of /b/ in "birds" and "builders" together with the consonance of /l/ and /ld/ in "child," "souls," and "builders" work to achieve a cohesive effect. Moreover, it is interesting to note the semantically suggestive connection between "child" and "builders." The connection is also stressed by the architecture of the neighboring lines—both lexemes are followed by a medial caesura—and the visual effect on the page, in that "child" and "builders" share the letters "ild," which we could call an internal eye-rhyme.

The first line of the third quatrain takes up the syntactic structure of the introductory line of the poem and varies it. This time, however, the persona leaves the reader in no doubt that what s/he suggests is "To remember the planters" (l. 9). The atmosphere, which is much more affirmative than in the first two quatrains, is syntactically characterized by enumeration in ll. 10–11—of the nouns "spade, rake, hoe" (l. 10); and adverb-plus-adjective in "so crafty, so good, / so sharp, so meet" (ll. 10–11). The rhythm has changed completely after l. 9 which consists of two anapaests and three iambs and, quite exceptionally for Meehan's poem, has no medial caesura but is end-stopped. The carefully crafted pattern of l. 10 seems to rotate around the noun "forms" (l. 10), with "spade" at the initial and "good" (l. 10) at the terminal positions functioning as opposite poles. These lexemes are also connected phonetically with the consonance of /d/. A similar phonetic pattern can be witnessed in line 12, the corresponding line as far as the end-rhyme scheme is concerned, with the assonance of /ʌ/ between "enough" and "bud." But let me return to ll. 10–11: the enumeration of monosyllabic lexemes creates a lively metrical pattern of a staccato character that turns line 10 into a nominally iambic pentameter combining a spondee and three trochees with the iamb. The only disyllabic lexeme ("crafty") in l. 10, after which a comma marks a caesura, initiates a change of rhythm from trochee to iamb, which is sustained in the first two feet ("so sharp, so meet") of line 11. This metrical-syntactic pattern corresponds with the activity of the planters around St. Stephen's Green. Furthermore, assonance of /uː/ between "tools" (l. 9), "fool" (l. 11), and "improve" (l. 12) enhances the meaning of ll. 11–12. A similar effect is achieved by the assonantal pattern of the long vowel /ɑː/ that connects the noun "planters" with the adjectives "crafty" and "sharp" and supports the characterization of the planters' activities. Another assonance, this time of /iː/, connects the adjective "meet" (l. 11) and the verb/noun "Dream" (l. 12). Finally, the phonetic quality of the end-rhymes seems to stress a certain stylistic/semantic development. In ll. 1–8, the rhyme scheme consists of very traditional end-rhymes ("crown / down," "seeds / weeds," "birds / words," "shades / fades"). In ll. 9–12, this changes: the e-rhymes "tools / fool" do not have the voiced fricative /z/ in common, which could still be regarded as a minimal change. For the f-rhymes "good / bud" the only phonetic link is the consonance of /d/, which connects them with six of the previous eight end-rhymes. The invitation to the addressee of "Dream of bud" (l. 12), which completes the third quatrain and at the same time provides a semantic link with the final couplet, functions as a premature climax. This effect is further enhanced by the consonantal echo—again significantly of the voiced plosive /d/. The semicolon marking the line break of l. 12 contributes to a further increase of the climactic effect in that it maximizes the reader's attention.

The final couplet is linked with the previous quatrain in that Meehan once again uses the coordinating conjunction "and" (l. 13). The assonantal echo of /əʊ/ between "opening" (l. 13), "probes," and "below" (both l. 14), and of /ɔː/ in "sycamore" (l. 13), "for," "source," and the final noun "metaphor" (all l. 14), evokes and enacts, musically, the semantic link between them. The phonetic quality of the two assonances underlines the meaning of ll. 13–14. Meehan once again uses personification in "earth's opening gesture" (l. 13) and "the sycamore / as it probes below ground" (ll. 13–14). The sycamore's exploratory action "below ground" (l. 14) and the metapoetical reference to "this metaphor" (l. 14) give the impression to the readers that we have come full circle, directing them back to the title. The alliteration of /s/ gives prominence to the semantic link between "sycamore" (l. 13) and "source" (l. 14); it also connects the final couplet with the title "The Sycamore's Contract with the Citizens" and, thus, foregrounds the personification of "sycamore" and the relationship with Dublin's citizens, which is legally sealed with a contract.

In a technique that Meehan shares with Rae Armantrout (Görtschacher 2010), she juxtaposes these sonnets with short monologues by ordinary people who are not stakeholders, "unornamented in plain speech with its own little dramatic vignette out of a life" (Allen Randolph 2009b, 262). In the titles of these monologues, which are based on naval time, the poet is keeping a log. For example, in "09.20 First Sycamore" (Meehan 2009a, 28), the persona is self-effacing, which makes the juxtaposition of a young outsider's voice with the sonnet of "The Sycamore's Contract with the Citizens" all the more striking, urgent, and dramatic. Meehan enables her readers to eavesdrop on what she calls "a conversation between the casual throw-away vernacular of the little pieces and the more tightly wrapped language and ritualized energy of the sonnets" (Allen Randolph 2009b, 262). The first of these "little pieces," as Meehan unassumingly calls the complementary free-verse poems, introduces her readers to a girl who is *"late for school"* (l. 5). If we were to regard the institution of the school as being representative of the claims of the establishment and her being late as indicative of a natural lack of enthusiasm or even of an antagonistic and oppositional attitude, we have established a pragmatic connection with the similar attitude represented subliminally in the sonnet that precedes it. I would argue that the girl's attitude is also expressed by her *"smok{ing of} a last fag"* (l. 6) and the song by Bob Dylan that she listens to on her Walkman. The intertextual line, "he that's not busy being born is busy dying" (l. 4), is taken, in a slightly revised form, from Dylan's song "It's Alright, Ma (I'm Only Bleeding)." Its presence invokes the tradition of protest which the tardy schoolgirl symptomatically exemplifies, while the bitter understatement of the title of the song it calls to mind, as well as the line itself with its quality of high-serious moral statement, intensifies the suggestion of the problematic issues of the larger, colonial context. If we read l. 2 (*"a stone in her boot"*) in the context of Yeats's "Easter, 1916" ("The stone's in the midst of all. // Too long a sacrifice / Can make a stone of the heart," ll. 56–58), this would further confirm our assumption about the anonymous girl.

Five of these six lines—the Dylan line sticks out from the rest—are very short, have between two and three stresses, and the syntactic caesurae at the line breaks are not marked. The parallelism of ll. 1–2 *"a girl stops for a moment / a stone in her boot"* (indefinite article plus noun) and of ll. 5–6 *"she's late for school / she smokes a last fag"* (personal pronoun plus verb) affects a structural connection between these descriptive lines. Musically speaking, Meehan seems to attach a central status to the two lines involving Bob Dylan (ll. 3–4). In line 4, characteristic of many of Dylan's anti-establishment lyrics, the alliteration of the voiced plosive /b/ is prominent and connects four of the nine lexemes making up the line. The phonetic quality of the plosive /b/ and the word-length (monosyllabic and disyllabic lexemes) enhance the meaning of the line. We are reminded of Dylan's performance when words pour out quickly and he barely takes a breath between lines, so that the intricate rhyme scheme is often missed by his audience. This atmosphere is in sharp contrast to the girl's situation, who *"stops for a moment,"* probably because *"a stone {is} in her boot."* Stylistically, one might affirm, the first two lines and the last two lines are very similar to Dylan's. Nineteen out of the 20 lexemes are monosyllabic. Alliteration of the voiceless fricative /s/ in *stops, stone, school*, and *smokes* connects ll. 1–2 and ll. 3–4 and foregrounds the sound-meaning proximity. The prominence of the nasal sounds /n/ and /ŋ/ (*moment, stone in, on, Walkman, Dylan, not, being born, dying*) has a cohesive function. The girl's situation is expressed by short and abrupt sentences with a very basic syntax (S-V-O). The phonemic structure, the sound quality, and the basic declarative sentences seem to be indicative of the girl's forlorn situation. In the twenty-first century her anti-establishment gestures appear to be meaningless.[3]

In the sequence "Six Sycamores," Meehan once again manifests her "strong sense of landscape, community, and selfhood as the triangulation" in her work. "[T]he concerns," she claims in the interview with Allen Randolph, "are global and always have been" (Allen Randolph 2009b, 264). Meehan's persona, I would argue, becomes the "professional memory of the tribe" (Allen Randolph 2009b, 268). She relates to what she calls "one of poetry's oldest functions" which for her "is to not just memorialize place, but to translate a place into language so that it can be an archive in itself but also a measuring stick for future change" (Allen Randolph 2009b, 267).[4]

NOTES

1 Elsewhere Meehan notes: "Sound has a profound effect on the body and through the body on consciousness. I have always believed that my purpose is shamanic – the manipulation of energy for the purpose of gaining power. My poems are like medicine bundles – I make them as power objects to send into the world to effect change. Hopefully for the good, though I am aware that there is a strong cursing tradition available to me. I consider that the nuclear option!" (Meehan 2010).

2 A version of this analysis appeared in Wolfgang Görtschacher 2016, 99–107.

3 In this context I would like to refer to Lance Daly's 2008 film *Kisses*, which features two eleven-year-olds who are sent down some streets of Dublin and whose poetic guide is Bob Dylan. Mark Jenkins offers the following *résumé* in his review: "If *Kisses* makes Dublin look as ominously deep-shadowed as Gotham City, that's appropriate to the child's-eye view. The movie is keyed to its expressive young actors, with special attention to the threats that loom for O'Neill's Kylie. The almost-pubescent girl escapes her uncle only to find herself in a city populated by hookers, strippers and an apparent pederast so scary he might as well be the local bogeyman the kids have feared all their lives. Dublin is no city of refuge, then. When Dylan and Kylie return to the 'burbs and the color drains from their lives again, they could even conclude, however sadly, that there's no place like home." (Jenkins 2010)

4 In this context, see also Eavan Boland 2014.

REFERENCES

Allen Randolph, Jody (2009a). "Text and Context: Paula Meehan." *An Sionnach* 5 (1–2): 5–16.

Allen Randolph, Jody (2009b). "The Body Politic: A Conversation with Paula Meehan." *An Sionnach* 5 (1–2): 239–271.

Boland, Eavan (1996). "New Wave 2: Born in the 50s; Irish Poets of the Global Village." In: *Irish Poetry since Kavanagh* (ed. Theo Dorgan), 136–146. Blackrock, Portland, OR: Four Courts Press.

Boland, Eavan (2014). *A Poet's Dublin* (eds. Paula Meehan and Jody Allen Randolph). Manchester: Carcanet.

Carson, Ciaran (2009). "Painting Rain for Paula Meehan." *An Sionnach* 5 (1–2): 140–141.

Dorgan, Theo (2000). "Poetry Ireland and *Poetry Ireland Review*. Interview with Wolfgang Görtschacher." In: *Contemporary Views on the Little Magazine Scene* (ed. Wolfgang

Görtschacher), 731–767. Salzburg et al.: Poetry Salzburg.

Dublin City University (2019). "DCU Confers Honorary Doctorate on Renowned Irish Poet, Paula Meehan" (21 March). https://www.dcu.ie/news/news/2019/Mar/DCU-confers-honorary-doctorate-renowned-Irish-poet-Paula-Meehan.shtml (accessed 9 August 2019).

Eagleton, Terry (1991). "Capacious Arcs." Review of Ciaran Carson: *Belfast Confetti*. *Poetry Review* 81 (2): 20–21.

Falci, Eric (2009). "Meehan's Stanzas and the Irish Lyric after Yeats." *An Sionnach* 5 (1–2): 226–238.

González-Arias, Luz Mar (2000). "'Playing with the Ghost of Words': An Interview with Paula Meehan." *Atlantis* 22 (1): 187–204.

Görtschacher, Wolfgang (2010). "Vocal Cartographies: Public and Private." *Poetry Salzburg Review* 17: 175–183.

Görtschacher, Wolfgang (2016). "Slitting the Poem's Throat to See What Makes It Sing: Sound / Sense Maps in Paula Meehan's Poetry." In: *Sound Is / As Sense: Essays on Modern British and Irish Poetry*, vol. 6 (eds. Wolfgang Görtschacher and David Malcolm), 95–107. Gdańsk: University of Gdańsk.

Jenkins, Mark (2010). "*Kisses*: Kids at Large in a Dylan-Haunted Dublin." *National Public Radio* (15 July) https://www.npr.org/templates/story/story.php?storyId=128465377&t=1565345123096 (accessed 9 August 2019).

Kennelly, Brendan (2009). "It Takes Trees in Summer." *An Sionnach* 5 (1–2): 25–26.

McCarthy, Thomas (2016). "The Bears and the Bees." Review of Paula Meehan: *Imaginary Bonnets with Real Bees in Them*. *Dublin Review of Books* (1 October) http://www.drb.ie/essays/the-bears-and-the-bees (accessed 9 August 2019).

Meehan, Paula (2009a). *Painting Rain*. Manchester: Carcanet.

Meehan, Paula (2009b). "Slitting the Songbird's Throat to See What Makes It Sing." In: *Resource Materials for Teaching Language. Leaving Certificate English Syllabus* (ed. Tom Mullins), 175–176. Dublin: NCCA.

Meehan, Paula (2010). E-mail to the author (30 July).

Meehan, Paula (2016). *Imaginary Bonnets with Real Bees in Them*. Dublin: University College Dublin Press.

Ní Dhomhnaill, Nuala (1999). "Tidal Surge 1990–1999." In: *Watching the River Flow: A Century in Irish Poetry* (eds. Noel Duffy and Theo Dorgan), 219–225. Dublin: Poetry Ireland.

Ormsby, Frank (2001). "Poetry." In: *Stepping Stones: The Arts in Ulster 1971–2001* (eds. Mark Carruthers and Stephen Douds), 52–78. Belfast: Blackstaff.

Smyth, Gerald (2013). "A Poet of Solidarity." *The Irish Times* (14 September) https://www.irishtimes.com/culture/books/a-poet-of-solidarity-1.1526904 (accessed 8 August 2019)

Wallace, Arminta (2015) "What Is Poetry? Three Masters Look for Answers." *The Irish Times* (22 June). https://www.irishtimes.com/culture/books/what-is-poetry-three-masters-look-for-answers-1.2255718 (accessed 9 August 2019).

Index

Abse, Dannie, 113, 320–21, 324–25
Acumen, 33, 37, 40
Adcock, Fleur, 15, 68, 82, 340, 341
Agard, John, 310, 311, 314, 316, 443–51
Agbabi, Patience, 280, 312–14
Agenda, 6, 34, 37–38
Albert Hall (reading – 1965), 160–61, 238, 279
Allnutt, Gillian, 69, 111–12, 264, 364–66, 368
Alvarez, Al, 3, 64, 66, 111, 160–61, 204, 206, 214–18, 343, 376, 417–18, 612, 615
Alvi, Moniza, 311, 340
American Poetry, 3, 64–5, 68, 71–86, 101–02, 133, 139, 141, 145, 179, 181–82, 184, 186, 191, 204, 208–10, 223, 235–39, 278–79, 343, 389, 395, 506–07, 512–13, 515, 517, 520, 538, 581, 596–98, 608–11, 613
Amis, Kingsley, 76, 82, 160, 203, 214, 216, 218, 536
Anglo-Jewish Poetry, 319–27

anthologies, 33–34, 40, 45, 63–70, 83, 89, 92, 110–11, 179, 186, 203–11, 225, 278, 297, 333–35, 339, 358, 371, 399, 411–12, 444, 525, 561–62, 583–84
Arc Publications (publishers), 40, 44, 46
Armitage, Simon, 84, 103, 112, 146, 177, 191, 195, 197, 202
Antrobus, Raymond, 178
Arts Council England, 38, 39, 41, 43–45, 50
Ashbery, John, 35, 81, 182, 210, 512–15, 520, 574, 576, 578, 580, 597
Attridge, Derek, 6, 7, 144
Auden, W. H., 72, 99, 132–34, 141, 146, 160, 195, 197, 202–03, 211, 418, 474, 523–24, 574

Bateman, Meg, 399
Beckett, Samuel, 184, 437, 462–67
Bennett, Louise, 309, 311, 313
Bergvall, Caroline, 107–08, 115, 336, 339, 344–45

A Companion to Contemporary British and Irish Poetry, 1960–2015, First Edition.
Edited by Wolfgang Görtschacher and David Malcolm.
© 2021 John Wiley & Sons Ltd. Published 2021 by John Wiley & Sons Ltd.

Bernard, Jay, 65–6, 178, 312, 336
Berry, Emily, 66, 177, 205
Berry, James, 307, 314–16, 562
Berryman, John, 120, 133, 204
Black British Poetry, 3, 16–17, 21, 25, 207, 224, 305–18, 443–51
Black Mountain School, 72, 101–2, 182, 399, 597
Blake, William, 170, 208, 235, 360, 364, 387, 431, 477, 489, 584–86, 588–89, 591, 613
Bloodaxe (publishers), 40, 44–5, 54–6, 64, 68, 82, 206, 315, 542
Bloom, Valerie, 309, 566
Boland, Eavan, 66, 72, 79–80, 103, 146, 195, 250, 339, 340, 349, 350–51, 355, 411–12, 453–59, 611, 619, 627
Bonney, Sean, 52, 187–88, 386–87, 390
Booker, Malika, 178
Brady, Andrea, 111–13, 186–87, 339, 385–86, 388, 389
Brathwaite, Edward Kamau, 186, 306, 308–9, 312
Breeze, Jean Binta, 309–10, 315
Bridges, Robert, 579
British Poetry Revival, 3, 101, 184–85, 209, 235–43, 263, 265, 485–86, 513, 537, 546
Brooke, Rupert, 574, 578–80
Brown, George Mackay, 395–95
Bryce, Collette, 367–68
Bunting, Basil, 35, 101–3, 121, 146, 192–95, 197, 209–11, 237, 418, 542, 550
Burnside, John, 6, 42, 48–50, 52–53, 55–56, 84, 177, 399

Cambridge School, 181–84, 264–66, 270
Campbell, Roy, 574
Cape (publishers), 44–5, 54–6, 206
Capildeo, Vahni, 54, 178
Carcanet (publishers), 34, 40, 44–5, 54–6, 206
Cardiff, Janet, 284–87
Carson, Ciaran, 113, 140, 177, 246, 250–51, 407, 422, 619, 621
Causley, Charles, 32, 58, 82, 533
Chatto & Windus (publishers), 44–5, 51, 54, 56
cheek, cris, 287–91, 296–97, 302, 485, 497

Chingyoni, Kayo, 178
Clare, John, 435, 489, 542
Clark, Kevin, 71–2, 76, 81, 83–5
Clarke, Gillian, 342, 382–84
Cobbing, Bob, 32, 184, 210–11, 235, 239–41, 265, 269, 275, 290–97, 485, 497–98
Coleridge, S. T., 99, 193, 360, 480, 524, 584–85
Collins, Merle, 309, 312
concrete poetry, 273–78
Conquest, Robert, 63, 110, 181, 203–4, 214–15, 217–19, 221
Constantine, David, 19–20, 34, 41, 100, 139
Cookson, William, 34, 38, 40, 59
Cope, Wendy, 139, 342, 374–75
Crawford, Robert, 177, 206, 550, 559
creative writing programs (UK), 205–6
Crichton Smith, Iain, 42, 204, 396–98, 402, 550, 560
Croft, Andy, 47–48, 59
Crozier, Andrew, 181–82, 208–10, 236, 238–39, 241, 597

Dabydeen, David, 309, 311, 566
D'Aguiar, Fred, 111, 309, 311, 315
Davie, Donald, 76, 82, 203–4, 214, 217–19, 373, 429
Davies, Hilary, 17–18, 38, 340
Donne, John, 139, 176–77, 252, 360, 362, 374–75, 477, 529
Duffy, Carol Ann, 3, 5, 21–22, 42, 81, 84, 112–13, 165, 177, 334–35, 339–40, 342, 344, 371, 376–78, 388, 410–11, 422–23
Duffy, Maureen, 332
Dunn, Douglas, 52, 56, 64, 103, 123–24, 204, 225, 398–99
Durcan, Paul, 82, 404–5, 461–72, 620
Dylan, Bob, 536–38, 542, 544, 626–27

elegy, 119–27
Eliot, T. S., 38, 88, 98–9, 103, 140, 145, 151, 159–60, 164–65, 186, 193–95, 197, 206, 229, 278, 312, 324, 360, 372, 396, 403, 407, 410, 418, 421, 428–29, 434, 474, 574–75, 581
T. S. Eliot Prize, 49, 51–57, 311, 334

Ellams, Inua, 312
Emerson, Lori, 291, 293–94
Empson, William, 203–4
English Intelligencer, The (journal), 181, 238–39, 597
Enright, D. J., 160, 203–4, 215–120

Faber & Faber (publishers), 40, 44–5, 52–6, 202, 206
Fainlight, Ruth, 320–21, 323–25
Fanthorpe, U. A., 332
Farley, Paul, 55–6, 123, 177, 206
Feaver, Vicki, 177, 340, 343, 345
Feinstein, Elaine, 83, 113, 181, 320–21
Fenton, James, 23, 64, 97, 202, 255, 258, 311, 371, 473–84
Ferlinghetti, Lawrence, 35, 279, 281
Finlay, Ian Hamilton, 35, 102, 237, 275–78, 400
Fisher, Allen, 90–1, 206, 210, 235, 237, 240–41, 265–67, 288, 485
Fisher, Roy, 146, 162–63, 208, 210, 238
Forbes, Peter, 35, 44, 59, 202, 207, 212
Forrest-Thomson, Veronica, 183, 208, 241, 339
Forward Prize, 48–9, 51–7, 87
Fraser, Bashabi, 400
Frazer, James George, 403–4
free verse, 143–58
Fuller, John, 113, 374, 537
Fuller, Roy, 4, 139

Garioch, Robert, 397
Gascoyne, David, 66, 237–38, 584
gay and lesbian poetry, 3, 329–38
Gershon, Karen, 320–25
Ginsberg, Allen, 223–24, 238–40, 278–79, 597
Gioia, Dana, 215, 221, 428, 433, 438, 473–74
Goode, Chris, 89, 93, 389
Goodison, Lorna, 404
Graham, W. S., 66, 237, 398
Graves, Robert, 171, 372, 403, 406, 410–11, 616–17
Greenlaw, Lavinia, 112, 176
Griffiths, Bill, 235, 241, 485–99
Grosseteste Review/Grosseteste Press (journal/publishers), 67, 181, 208, 241
Gunn, Thom, 4, 76, 82, 143–45, 176, 177, 204, 214, 217–18, 501–9

Hamburger, Michael, 40, 42–43, 60, 82, 204, 320–21, 325–27
Hardy, Thomas, 20, 123, 395
Harrison, Tony, 3, 14–15, 52, 64, 82, 103, 121–22, 135–36, 191, 195–96, 381–84, 387, 573
Harsent, David, 56, 177
Harwood, Lee, 8–9, 10, 32, 149, 182, 208, 210, 235, 237–39, 241, 384, 511–22, 573, 580
Hay, George Campbell, 398
Heaney, Seamus, 3, 9–10, 42, 50, 56, 64, 72–76, 99–100, 103–4, 125–26, 129, 133, 136–37, 141, 146, 151–53, 169, 173, 176, 245–49, 252, 343, 352, 376–77, 404, 407–9, 419, 421–22, 469–71, 612, 620
Heath-Stubbs, John, 82
Henri, Adrian, 208, 212, 224–31, 233–35, 280–81
Herbert, George, 257, 275–76, 360, 524–25, 527
Herbert, W. N., 84, 399, 550, 552, 554–55
Herbert, Zbigniew, 256, 417–18
Hewitt, John, 245–46, 248–49, 251, 253
Hill, Geoffrey, 3, 1011, 38, 56, 82, 120, 134–35, 146, 155–57, 159–60, 164–65, 177, 194–95, 204, 361–63, 418, 574, 576, 578
Hobsbaum, Philip, 6, 125, 216, 247
Hogg, James, 33
Holloway, John, 217–19
Holocaust, 320–21, 323, 325, 417–20
Homer, 140–41, 162, 404–6, 423, 428, 431
Hopkins, Gerard Manley, 23–24, 170, 527–30
Horovitz, Michael, 160, 205, 208, 223, 238, 278–79
Howe, Sarah, 177–78, 207
Howe, Susan, 574, 576, 580
Hughes, Ted, 3, 10, 40, 42, 72, 76, 78–79, 100, 125, 147–49, 157, 171–72, 176, 204, 269, 410–11, 573, 615
Hulse, Michael, 64, 204–5, 208, 434

James, C. L. R., 308
James, John, 179–80
Jamie, Kathleen, 146, 175, 342–43, 400
Jennings, Elizabeth, 82, 111, 176, 214, 217–20, 361–62, 368, 523–33

Johnson, Adam, 333–34
Johnson, Linton Kwesi, 16–17, 66, 280, 305, 307–10, 315, 387–88
Jones, David, 66, 101, 191, 193–95, 197, 206, 209, 237, 524–25, 530
Joseph, Anthony, 186
Joseph, Jenny, 12–13, 82

Kavanagh, Patrick, 57–58, 61, 82, 139, 142, 246, 470–72, 627
Kay, Jackie, 21, 84, 146, 312–13, 334–35, 340–41
Keats, John, 98, 150, 169–71, 219, 363, 385, 479, 575, 577
Kennedy, David, 5, 63–70, 204, 329, 336, 434
Kennelly, Brendan, 139, 142, 191, 461, 472, 622, 628
Khalvati, Mimi, 22–25, 49, 113
Kirkup, James, 40, 331, 338, 427, 434–36, 438–40

Langley, R. F., 154–55, 181
Larkin, Philip, 3, 7–8, 10, 35, 72, 76–78, 88, 100, 102–3, 111, 126, 146, 160, 172–73, 176, 181, 203–4, 211, 214–15, 218, 372–74, 376, 406, 429–30, 438, 528, 573, 575
La Rose, John, 308, 314
Lawrence, D. H., 137, 145, 214, 395, 428
Lawson, Peter, 319–24
Leonard, Tom, 103, 146, 181, 386–87
Levertov, Denise, 72, 83, 102–3, 105, 210, 320, 597
Lewis, Gwyneth, 175–176
Linguistically Innovative Poetry, 3, 68, 263–71
little magazines, 32–38
Liverpool Poets, 3, 280, 340–42, 348, 398, 401, 550
Lochhead, Liz, 280, 340–42, 348, 398, 401, 550
Logue, Christopher, 161–62, 167, 213
Longley, Michael, 42, 52, 82, 126, 139, 176, 204, 245–49, 404–6, 620
love poetry, 371–79
Lowe, Adam, 313
Lowell, Robert, 72, 83, 86, 120, 133, 138–39, 141–42, 170, 204, 209, 614, 618
Loy, Mina, 206, 370, 372
lyric poetry, 169–78, 179–89

MacCaig, Norman, 35, 204, 394, 397, 406
MacDiarmid, Hugh, 101, 181, 209, 387, 394–96, 399
MacIntyre, Duncan Ban, 394
MacLean, Sorley (SomhairleMacGill-Eain), 396, 398
MacNeice, Louis, 82, 103, 246, 406, 527, 574
MacSweeney, Barry, 146, 209, 236–37, 239, 384, 535–47, 597
Mahon, Derek, 82, 204, 246–50
Manger, Itzak, 320
Manson, Peter, 186, 188
Margolin, Anna, 320
Markham, E. A., 69, 311, 315
Marriott, D. S., 23–25, 185–86
Marson, Una, 306, 314
Martian Poets, 3, 64, 204, 255–62, 474
Maxwell, Glyn, 102, 144, 174–75, 202
Mayer, Gerda, 321–22, 324–25
McCarthy, Patricia, 37, 40
McCullough, John, 336
McGough, Roger, 208, 224, 226–27, 230–33, 274, 280
McGuckian, Medbh, 80–82, 172–73, 204, 246–47, 250, 349–52, 354–55, 454
McMillan, Andrew, 48, 56, 177–78, 337–38
Meehan, Paula, 250, 342, 349–51, 353–55, 619–28
Mendelssohn, Anna (Anna Mendelson, Grace Lake), 183, 270
Mengham, Rod, 185
Merrill, James, 195
Mersey Sound (anthology), 225–28, 233
Miller, Kei, 178, 206, 313
Milton, John, 134, 164, 170, 312, 360, 434, 574, 585–86, 588–89, 591–92
Mitchell, Adrian, 88, 160–61, 164, 224, 279, 375
Modern Poetry in Translation (journal), 34, 40
Monk, Geraldine, 146, 268–69, 339, 485–86
Montague, John, 11–2, 37, 42, 82, 246, 248, 405, 620
Moore, Marianne, 209
Moore, Nicholas, 66, 237
Morgan, Edwin, 139, 146, 208, 275–76, 330–31, 375, 377–78, 397, 412, 549–60

Morley, David, 64, 70, 204, 208, 212, 434, 438
Morris, Marianne, 115–17, 339, 387, 391, 540, 547
Morrison, Blake, 64, 111, 203–5, 208, 213–15, 376, 615
Morrissey, Sinéad, 55–56, 177, 247, 253–54, 342, 349
Motion, Andrew, 51, 64, 84, 97, 111, 113, 124, 203–5, 208, 215, 335, 550–51
Mottram, Eric, 35, 66, 88, 101, 111, 162, 184–85, 209–10, 216, 236, 240–42, 265, 485, 486–87, 497, 512–14, 536, 538–39, 546
Movement, The, 3, 64, 67–68, 76, 88, 99, 111–13, 161, 181–82, 203, 206, 209–10, 213–21, 321, 343, 362, 429–30, 596–97
Muir, Edwin, 406, 583–85
Muldoon, Paul, 3, 20–21, 56, 72, 79, 82, 126, 133, 137–39, 146, 176, 202, 246–47, 249–52, 311, 352–53
Murray, Les, 359–60, 412
mythology/myth, 15, 17, 20, 25, 69, 78, 81, 133, 140, 170, 183, 193, 197, 205, 220, 237, 251, 268, 308, 332, 350, 352–53, 355, 377, 403–13, 421–23, 428–34, 443, 454–55, 457–59, 490, 493–95, 498, 514, 537, 551, 556, 559, 561–62, 586–87, 603, 611, 613–14, 617

Nagra, Daljit, 56, 206–7, 212, 317
Nichols, Grace, 82, 146, 309–10, 315–16, 340, 383, 450, 561–71
Nicholson, Norman, 394
Ní Chuilleanáin, Eiléan, 36, 250, 349–52, 355, 404, 454
Ní Dhomhnaill, Nuala, 250, 349–53, 355, 454, 619–20
Nine (journal), 429, 438–39

O'Grady, Desmond, 436–38
O'Hara, Frank, 179–80, 210
Olson, Charles, 101–2, 141, 145, 181–82, 210, 224, 235, 239–41, 401, 513, 517, 597–98, 610
O'Sullivan, Maggie, 68, 143–45, 149, 154, 184, 191, 264–65, 269, 297–302, 344–45
Oswald, Alice, 42, 54, 56, 59, 140–42, 339, 423–24

Padel, Ruth, 56, 84, 165, 167, 176, 178, 312, 318, 339
Paterson, Don, 35, 71, 84, 111–14, 122–23, 129–32, 140, 173–74, 399
Patten, Brian, 208, 224–28, 230, 232–33, 280
Paulin, Tom, 35, 82, 163, 245–47, 250–51
Performance Poetry, 278–81, 283–303, 497
Pitter, Ruth, 176
Plath, Sylvia, 82, 120, 125, 147–49, 161, 170–72, 176, 343, 410–12, 418, 612, 614–16
PN Review (journal), 34, 37–38, 45–46, 49, 59–61, 188, 581
poetry presses, 42–48
poetry prizes, 31–61, 48–58, 205
Poetry Review (journal), 35, 37, 51, 88, 101, 202–3, 240, 487
Poetry Salzburg Review/Poetry Salzburg (journal/publishers), 37, 40, 51, 57
Poetry Society, 35–36, 51, 67, 202, 240
Poetry Wales (journal), 34, 37
Pollard, Clare, 64–66
Porter, Peter, 160–62, 176–77
Pound, Ezra, 65, 88, 99, 102–3, 132, 179, 186, 191–95, 206, 209–10, 241, 324, 372, 395, 428–29, 431, 433–34, 437, 550–51, 574
Prince, F. T., 514, 573–81
Prynne, J. H., 67, 88, 146, 153, 157, 181–83, 185–86, 206, 208, 210, 235, 237, 239–40, 264, 266–67, 384, 386, 512, 536, 539, 597, 601

Raha, Nat, 388–89
Raine, Craig, 64, 82, 202, 204, 256, 258–61, 419–21, 473
Raine, Kathleen, 364, 583–93
Raworth, Tom, 139, 147, 149–50, 166, 182, 208, 210, 236, 241, 388, 520, 580
Reading, Peter, 161, 163–64
Reality Street (publishers), 91–2, 114, 139
Redgrove, Peter, 125, 204, 406, 409–13
Rees-Jones, Deryn, 68–69, 177, 340–41, 583
Reid, Christopher, 158, 201–2, 204, 255, 260, 462, 474
religious poetry, 359–69, 523–33
Riley, Denise, 154, 157, 184, 206, 209, 236, 240, 339, 341, 345–46, 384–87, 389

Riley, Peter, 5, 139, 181, 208, 239, 595–605
Rilke, Rainer Maria, 40, 65, 81, 129–31, 174, 251
Riviere, Sam, 165–66
Roberts, Michèle, 68
Robertson, Robin, 42, 84, 177
Robinson, Roger, 313, 315
Robinson, Sophie, 336, 339, 385
Rogers, W. R., 246
Romer, Stephen, 42–43, 61, 421, 424
Rumens, Carol, 56, 68, 70, 139, 142, 340, 348
Russell, Peter, 142, 427–36, 438-40, 589, 593

Salkey, Andrew, 308
Salt (publishers), 46–47, 186, 206
Sampson, Fiona, 4–6, 35, 109, 111, 113–14, 117
satire, 159–67
Schmidt, Michael, 4, 34, 38, 473–74, 523, 525, 527
Scots (language), 21, 25, 181, 387, 397, 550–53
Scupham, Peter, 139
Selvon, Sam, 306
Sexton, Anne, 79, 343, 543
Shapcott, Jo, 339, 344
Shearsman (publishers), 91, 114, 186
Shelley, Percy Bysshe, 169–70, 385, 435, 574–75, 577, 579, 584–85, 588
Sheppard, Robert, 18, 84, 87, 89, 91, 111–14, 184, 210, 263–67, 291, 487, 539
Shire, Warsan, 312
Shuttle, Penelope, 340, 344
Silkin, Jon, 82, 85, 320–21, 325–27
Simic, Charles, 71, 84, 113
Simmons, James, 246–48
Sinclair, Iain, 66–67, 88–89, 108, 111, 114, 208, 236–37, 241
Sissay, Lemn, 312
Smith, Stevie, 23, 82, 146, 162, 211, 343
Smith, Sydney Goodsir, 397
Smartt, Dorothea, 313–14, 318
Smokestack Books (publishers), 47–48
sonnet, 9–10, 129–42
Spence, Alan, 549, 554

Spott, Verity, 187, 388, 391
Stevenson, Anne, 13–14, 81–82, 103, 124–25, 131–32, 140, 607–18
Sutherland, Keston, 146, 186–87, 386, 391
Swanzy, Henry, 306, 314
Symmons Roberts, Michael, 52–53, 177, 366–69
Szirtes, George, 54, 139, 142

technology (and performance), 283–303
Tempest, Kate, 191, 195, 197, 206, 345–46
Thomas, Dylan, 99, 203, 237, 275, 278, 362–64
Thomas, R. S., 146, 361, 382–83, 528
Thurston, Scott, 297–98
Tomlinson, Charles, 82, 177, 214
Tonks, Rosemary, 162
Tuma, Keith, 5, 83–84, 111, 211, 345
Turnbull, Gael, 237–39

Upton, Lawrence, 239, 296, 485, 497

Wain, John, 216, 218
Walcott, Derek, 35, 38, 42, 50, 55, 97, 105, 306, 313, 318, 404, 570
Warner, Val, 18–19
Weissbort, Daniel, 40–41, 62
White, Kenneth, 398
Whitman, Walt, 145, 399–400, 550, 575
Wilkinson, John, 267–68
Williams, William Carlos, 76, 82, 101, 132, 141, 145, 181, 186, 209–10, 224, 403
women's poetry, 3, 25, 68–69, 82, 339–48, 349–57, 453–59, 611
Wordsworth, William, 23, 98–99, 102, 150, 170, 227, 312, 360, 384, 387, 393, 435, 476, 579, 598

Yeats, W. B., 99, 160, 173, 202, 219, 372, 404, 409, 418, 423, 431, 433, 455, 524, 574, 584–86, 588, 621, 626

Zephaniah, Benjamin, 280, 309, 312, 371, 379